Paperback Russian Dictionary

Russian–English
English–Russian

Русско–английский
Англо–русский

Della Thompson

Oxford   New York

OXFORD UNIVERSITY PRESS

1996

Oxford University Press, Walton Street, Oxford OX2 6DP

Oxford New York
Athens Auckland Bangkok Bombay
Calcutta Cape Town Dar es Salaam Delhi
Florence Hong Kong Istanbul Karachi
Kuala Lumpur Madras Madrid Melbourne
Mexico City Nairobi Paris Singapore
Taipei Tokyo Toronto
and associated companies in
Berlin Ibadan

Oxford is a trade mark of Oxford University Press

British Library Cataloguing in Publication Data
Data available

Library of Congress Cataloging in Publication Data
The Oxford paperback Russian dictionary: Russian–English, English–Russian:
[russko-angliĭskiĭ, anglo-russkiĭ / Della Thompson [editor].
p. cm.
"First published 1995 as 'The Oxford Russian Minidictionary' " — CIP t.p. verso.
1. Russian language—Dictionaries—English.   2. English language—Dictionaires—Russian.
I. Thompson, Della
491.73'21—dc20   PG2640.094   1996   95–35725
ISBN 0–19–864341–1

10 9 8 7 6 5 4 3 2 1

Typeset by Azbuka
Printed in Great Britain by
Mackays of Chatham PLC

Contents

Preface

This latest addition to the Oxford Russian dictionary range is designed primarily for English-speaking users. It provides a handy yet extremely comprehensive reference work for students of Russian, tourists, and business people.

Particular attention has been given to the provision of inflected forms where these cause difficulty, and to showing the stressed syllable of every Russian word as well as changes in stress where they occur. Perfective and imperfective aspects are distinguished and both are given wherever appropriate.

Thanks are due to Alexander and Nina Levtov for their editorial help and valuable advice on contemporary Russian usage, and to Helen McCurdy for help with proof-reading.

D.J.T.

March 1995

Introduction

In order to save space, related words are often grouped together in paragraphs, as are cross-references and compound entries.

The swung dash (~) and the hyphen are also used to save space. The swung dash represents the headword preceding it in bold, or the preceding Russian word, e.g. **Georgian** *n* грузи́н, ~ка. The hyphen is mainly used, in giving grammatical forms, to stand for part of the preceding, or (less often) following, Russian word, e.g. **приходи́ть** (-ожу́, -о́дишь).

Russian headwords are followed by inflexional information where considered necessary. So-called regular inflexions for the purpose of this dictionary are listed in the Appendices.

Where a noun ending is given but not labelled in the singular, it is the genitive ending; other cases are named; in the plural, where cases are identifiable by their endings, they are not labelled, e.g. **сестра́** (*pl* сёстры, сестёр, сёстрам). The gender of Russian nouns can usually be deduced from their endings and it is indicated only in exceptional cases (e.g. for masculine nouns in **-а, -я,** and **-ь,** neuter nouns in **-мя,** and all indeclinable nouns).

Verbs are labelled *impf* or *pf* to show their aspect. Where a perfective verb is formed by the addition of a prefix to the imperfective, this is shown at the headword by a light vertical stroke, e.g. **про|лепета́ть.** When a verb requires the use of a case other than the accusative, this is indicated, e.g. **маха́ть** *impf*, **махну́ть** *pf* + *instr* wave, brandish.

Both the comma and the ampersand (&) are used to show alternatives, e.g. **хоте́ть** + *gen, acc* means that the Russian verb may govern either the genitive or accusative; **сирота́** *m* & *f* orphan means that the Russian noun is treated as masculine or feminine according to the sex of the person denoted; **Cossack** *n* каза́к, -а́чка represents the masculine and feminine translations of Cossack; **dilate** *vt* & *i* расширя́ть(ся) means that the Russian verb forms cover both the transitive and intransitive English verbs.

Stress

The stress of Russian words is shown by an acute accent over the vowel of the stressed syllable. The vowel **ё** has no stress-mark since it is almost always stressed. The presence of two stress-marks indicates that either of the marked syllables may be stressed.

Changes of stress in inflexion are shown, e.g.

i) **предложи́ть** (-жу́, -жишь)

The absence of a stress-mark on the second person singular indicates that the stress is on the preceding syllable and that the rest of the conjugation is stressed in this way.

ii) **нача́ть** (...............; на́чал, -а́, -о)

The final form, на́чало, takes the stress of the first of the two preceding forms when these differ from each other. Forms that are not shown, here на́чали, are stressed like the last form given.

iii) **дождь** (-дя́)

The single form given in brackets is the genitive singular and all other forms have the same stressed syllable.

iv) **душа́** (*acc* -у; *pl* -и)

If only one case-labelled form is given in the singular, it is an exception to the regular paradigm. If only one plural form is given (the nominative), the rest follow this. In other words, in this example, the accusative singular and all the plural forms have initial stress.

v) **скоба́** (*pl* -ы, -а́м)

In the plural, forms that are not shown (here instrumental and prepositional) are stressed like the last form given.

Proprietary terms

This dictionary includes some words which are, or are asserted to be, proprietary names or trade marks. Their inclusion does not imply that they have acquired for legal purposes a non-proprietary or general significance, nor is any other judgement implied concerning their legal status. In cases where the editor has some evidence that a word is used as a proprietary name or trade mark this is indicated by the label *propr*, but no judgement concerning the legal status of such words is made or implied thereby.

Abbreviations used in the Dictionary

abbr	abbreviation	loc	locative
abs	absolute		
acc	accusative	m	masculine
adj, adjs	adjective(s)	math	mathematics
adv, advs	adverb(s)	med	medicine
aeron	aeronautics	meteorol	meteorology
agric	agriculture	mil	military
anat	anatomy	mus	music
approx	approximate(ly)	n	noun
archaeol	archaeology		
archit	architecture	naut	nautical
astron	astronomy	neg	negative
attrib	attributive	neut	neuter
aux	auxiliary	nn	nouns
		nom	nominative
bibl	biblical		
biol	biology	o.s.	oneself
bot	botany		
		parl	parliamentary
chem	chemistry	part	participle
cin	cinema(tography)	partl	particle
coll	colloquial	pers	person
collect	collective(ly)	pf	perfective
comb	combination	philos	philosophy
comm	commerce	phon	phonetics
comp	comparative	p'ot	photography
comput	computing	pnys	physics
conj, conjs	conjunction(s)	pl	plural
cul	culinary	polit	political
		poss	possessive
dat	dative	predic	predicate; predicative
def	definite	pref	prefix
derog	derogatory	prep	preposition; prepositional
det	determinate	pres	present (tense)
dim	diminutive	pron, prons	pronoun(s)
		propr	proprietary term
eccl	ecclesiastical	psych	psychology
econ	economics		
electr	electricity	refl	reflexive
electron	electronics	rel	relative
emph	emphatic	relig	religion; religious
esp	especially	rly	railway
etc.	etcetera		
		sb	substantive
f	feminine	sg	singular
fig	figurative	sl	slang
fut	future (tense)	s.o.	someone
		sth	something
gen	genitive	superl	superlative
geog	geography		
geol	geology	tech	technical
geom	geometry	tel	telephony
gram	grammar	theat	theatre
		theol	theology
hist	historical		
imper	imperative	univ	university
impers	impersonal	usu	usually
impf	imperfective		
indecl	indeclinable	v	verb
indef	indefinite	v aux	auxiliary verb
indet	indeterminate	vbl	verbal
inf	infinitive	vi	intransitive verb
instr	instrumental	voc	vocative
int	interjection	vt	transitive verb
interrog	interrogative	vulg	vulgar
		vv	verbs
ling	linguistics	zool	zoology

A

a[1] *conj* and, but; **a (не) то** or else, otherwise.

a[2] *int* oh, ah.

абажу́р lampshade.

абба́тство abbey.

аббревиату́ра abbreviation.

абза́ц indention; paragraph.

абонеме́нт subscription, season ticket. **абоне́нт** subscriber.

абориге́н aborigine.

або́рт abortion; **де́лать** *impf*, **с~** *pf* ~ have an abortion.

абрико́с apricot.

абсолю́тно *adv* absolutely. **абсолю́тный** absolute.

абстра́ктный abstract.

абсу́рд absurdity; the absurd. **абсу́рдный** absurd.

абсце́сс abscess.

аванга́рд advanced guard; vanguard; avant-garde. **аванга́рдный** avant-garde. **аванпо́ст** outpost; forward position.

ава́нс advance (*of money*); *pl* advances, overtures. **ава́нсом** *adv* in advance, on account.

авансце́на proscenium.

авантю́ра (*derog*) adventure; venture; escapade; shady enterprise. **авантюри́ст** (*derog*) adventurer. **авантюри́стка** (*derog*) adventuress. **авантю́рный** adventurous; adventure.

авари́йный breakdown; emergency. **ава́рия** accident, crash; breakdown.

а́вгуст August. **а́вгустовский** August.

а́виа *abbr* (*of* **авиапо́чтой**) by airmail.

авиа- *abbr in comb* (*of* **авиацио́нный**) air-, aero-; aircraft; aviation. **авиали́ния** air-route, airway. **~но́сец** (**-сца**) aircraft carrier. **~по́чта** airmail.

авиацио́нный aviation; flying; aircraft. **авиа́ция** aviation; aircraft; airforce.

авока́до *neut indecl* avocado (pear).

аво́сь *adv* perhaps; **на ~** at random, on the off-chance.

австрали́ец (**-и́йца**), **австрали́йка** Australian. **австрали́йский** Australian. **Австра́лия** Australia.

австри́ец (**-и́йца**), **австри́йка** Austrian. **австри́йский** Austrian. **А́встрия** Austria.

авто- *in comb* self-; auto-; automatic; motor-. **автоба́за** motor-transport depot. **~биографи́ческий** autobiographical. **~биогра́фия** autobiography; curriculum vitae. **автобус** bus. **~вокза́л** bus-station. **авто́граф** autograph. **~запра́вочная ста́нция** petrol station. **~кра́т** autocrat. **~крати́ческий** autocratic. **~кра́тия** autocracy. **~магистра́ль** motorway. **~маши́на** motor vehicle. **~моби́ль** *m* car. **~но́мия** autonomy. **~но́мный** autonomous; self-contained. **~пило́т** automatic pilot. **~портре́т** self-portrait. **~ру́чка** fountain-pen. **~ста́нция** bus-station. **~стра́да** motorway.

автома́т slot-machine; automatic device, weapon, etc.; sub-machine gun; robot; (**телефо́н-**)~ public call-box. **автоматиза́ция** automation. **автоматизи́ровать** *impf & pf* automate; make automatic. **автомати́ческий** automatic.

а́втор author; composer; inventor; (*fig*) architect.

авторизо́ванный authorized.

авторите́т authority. **авторите́тный** authoritative.

а́вторск|ий author's; **~ий гонора́р** royalty; **~ое пра́во** copyright. **а́вторство** authorship.

ага́ *int* aha; yes.

аге́нт agent. **аге́нтство** agency. **агенту́ра** (network of) agents.

агита́тор agitator, propagandist; canvasser. **агитацио́нный** propaganda. **агита́ция** propaganda, agitation;

campaign. **агити́ровать** *impf* (*pf* **с~**) agitate, campaign; (try to) persuade, win over. **агитпу́нкт** *abbr* agitation centre.

аго́ния agony.

агра́рный agrarian.

агрега́т aggregate; unit.

агресси́вный aggressive. **агре́ссия** aggression. **агре́ссор** aggressor.

агроно́м agronomist. **агроно́мия** agriculture.

ад (*loc* -ý) hell.

ада́птер adapter; (*mus*) pick-up.

адвока́т lawyer. **адвокату́ра** legal profession; lawyers.

администрати́вный administrative. **администра́тор** administrator; manager. **администра́ция** administration; management.

адмира́л admiral.

а́дрес (*pl* -á) address. **адреса́т** addressee. **а́дрес|ный** address; ~**ая кни́га** directory. **адресова́ть** *impf* & *pf* address, send.

а́дский infernal, hellish.

адъюта́нт aide-de-camp; **ста́рший ~** adjutant.

ажу́р|ный delicate, lacy; ~**ая рабо́та** openwork; tracery.

аза́рт heat; excitement; fervour, ardour, passion. **аза́ртн|ый** venturesome; heated; ~**ая игра́** game of chance.

а́збука alphabet; ABC.

Азербайджа́н Azerbaijan. **азербайджа́нец** (-нца), **азербайджа́нка** Azerbaijani. **азербайджа́нский** Azerbaijani.

азиа́т, ~**ка** Asian. **азиа́тский** Asian, Asiatic. **А́зия** Asia.

азо́т nitrogen.

а́ист stork.

ай *int* oh; oo.

а́йсберг iceberg.

акаде́мик academician. **академи́ческий** academic. **акаде́мия** academy.

аквала́нг aqualung.

акваре́ль water-colour.

аква́риум aquarium.

акведу́к aqueduct.

акклиматизи́ровать *impf* & *pf* acclimatize; ~**ся** become acclimatized.

аккомпанеме́нт accompaniment; **под ~** +*gen* to the accompaniment

of. **аккомпаниа́тор** accompanist. **аккомпани́ровать** *impf* +*dat* accompany.

акко́рд chord.

аккордео́н accordion.

акко́рдн|ый by agreement; ~**ая рабо́та** piece-work.

аккредити́в letter of credit. **аккредитова́ть** *impf* & *pf* accredit.

аккумуля́тор accumulator.

аккура́тный neat, careful; punctual; exact, thorough.

акри́л acrylic. **акри́ловый** acrylic.

акроба́т acrobat.

аксессуа́р accessory; (stage) props.

аксио́ма axiom.

акт act; deed, document; **обвини́тельный ~** indictment.

актёр actor.

акти́в (*comm*) asset(s).

активиза́ция stirring up, making (more) active. **активизи́ровать** *impf* & *pf* make (more) active, stir up. **акти́вный** active.

акти́ровать *impf* & *pf* (*pf also* **с~**) register, record, presence or absence of; (*sl*) write off.

а́ктовый зал assembly hall.

актри́са actress.

актуа́льный topical, urgent.

аку́ла shark.

аку́стика acoustics. **акусти́ческий** acoustic.

акуше́р obstetrician. **акуше́рка** midwife.

акце́нт accent, stress. **акценти́ровать** *impf* & *pf* accent; accentuate.

акционе́р shareholder. **акционе́рный** joint-stock. **а́кция**[1] share; *pl* stock. **а́кция**[2] action.

а́лгебра algebra.

а́либи *neut indecl* alibi.

алиме́нты (*pl*; *gen* -ов) (*law*) maintenance.

алкоголи́зм alcoholism. **алкого́лик** alcoholic. **алкого́ль** *m* alcohol. **алкого́льный** alcoholic.

аллего́рия allegory.

аллерги́я allergy.

алле́я avenue; path, walk.

аллига́тор alligator.

алло́ hello! (*on telephone*).

алма́з diamond.

алта́рь (-я́) *m* altar; chancel, sanctuary.

алфави́т alphabet. **алфави́тный** alphabetical.

а́лчный greedy, grasping.

а́лый scarlet.

альбо́м album; sketch-book.

альмана́х literary miscellany; almanac.

альпи́йский Alpine. **альпини́зм** mountaineering. **альпини́ст, альпини́стка** (mountain-)climber.

альт (-á; *pl* -ы́) alto; viola.

альтернати́ва alternative. **альтернати́вный** alternative.

альтруисти́ческий altruistic.

алюми́ний aluminium.

амазо́нка Amazon; horsewoman; riding-habit.

амба́р barn; storehouse, warehouse.

амби́ция pride; arrogance.

амбулато́рия out-patients' department; surgery. **амбулато́рный больно́й** *sb* outpatient.

Аме́рика America. **америка́нец** (-нца), **америка́нка** American. **америка́нский** American; US.

аминокислота́ amino acid.

ами́нь *m* amen.

аммиа́к ammonia.

амни́стия amnesty.

амора́льный amoral; immoral.

амортиза́тор shock-absorber. **амортиза́ция** depreciation; shock-absorption.

ампе́р (*gen pl* ампе́р) ampere.

ампута́ция amputation. **ампути́ровать** *impf & pf* amputate.

амфетами́н amphetamine.

амфи́бия amphibian.

амфитеа́тр amphitheatre; circle.

ана́лиз analysis; ~ кро́ви blood test. **анализи́ровать** *impf & pf* analyse. **анали́тик** analyst. **аналити́ческий** analytic(al).

ана́лог analogue. **аналоги́чный** analogous. **анало́гия** analogy.

анана́с pineapple.

анархи́ст, ~ка anarchist. **анархи́ческий** anarchic. **ана́рхия** anarchy.

анатоми́ческий anatomical. **анато́мия** anatomy.

анахрони́зм anachronism. **анахрони́ческий** anachronistic.

анга́р hangar.

а́нгел angel. **а́нгельский** angelic.

анги́на sore throat.

англи́йск|ий English; ~ая була́вка safety-pin. **англича́нин** (*pl* -ча́не, -ча́н) Englishman. **англича́нка** Englishwoman. **А́нглия** England, Britain.

анекдо́т anecdote, story; funny thing.

анеми́я anaemia.

анестезио́лог anaesthetist. **анестези́ровать** *impf & pf* anaesthetize. **анестези́рующее сре́дство** anaesthetic. **анестези́я** anaesthesia.

анке́та questionnaire, form.

аннекси́ровать *impf & pf* annex. **анне́ксия** annexation.

аннули́ровать *impf & pf* annul; cancel, abolish.

анома́лия anomaly. **анома́льный** anomalous.

ано́нимка anonymous letter. **ано́нимный** anonymous.

анонси́ровать *impf & pf* announce.

аноре́ксия anorexia.

анса́мбль *m* ensemble; company, troupe.

антагони́зм antagonism.

Анта́рктика the Antarctic.

анте́нна antenna; aerial.

антибио́тик antibiotic(s).

антидепресса́нт antidepressant.

антиква́р antiquary; antique-dealer. **антиквариа́т** antique-shop. **антиква́рный** antiquarian; antique.

антило́па antelope.

антипа́тия antipathy.

антисемити́зм anti-Semitism. **антисеми́тский** anti-Semitic.

антисе́птик antiseptic. **антисепти́ческий** antiseptic.

антите́зис (*philos*) antithesis.

антите́ло (*pl* -á) antibody.

антифри́з antifreeze.

анти́чность antiquity. **анти́чный** ancient, classical.

антоло́гия anthology.

антра́кт interval.

антраци́т anthracite.

антреко́т entrecôte, steak.

антрепренёр impresario.

антресо́ли (*pl; gen* -ей) mezzanine; shelf.

антропо́лог anthropologist. **антрополо́гический** anthropological. **антрополо́гия** anthropology.

анфила́да suite (of rooms).

анчо́ус anchovy.

аншла́г 'house full' notice.

апарте́йд apartheid.

апати́чный apathetic. **апа́тия** apathy.

апелли́ровать *impf & pf* appeal. **апелляцио́нный суд** Court of Appeal. **апелля́ция** appeal.

апельси́н orange; orange-tree. **апельси́нный, апельси́новый** orange.

аплоди́ровать *impf* +*dat* applaud. **аплодисме́нты** *m pl* applause.

апло́мб aplomb.

Апока́липсис Revelation. **апокалипти́ческий** apocalyptic.

апо́стол apostle.

апостро́ф apostrophe.

аппара́т apparatus; machinery, organs. **аппарату́ра** apparatus, gear; (*comput*) hardware. **аппара́тчик** operator; apparatchik.

аппе́ндикс appendix. **аппендици́т** appendicitis.

аппети́т appetite; **прия́тного ~а!** bon appétit! **аппети́тный** appetizing.

апре́ль *m* April. **апре́льский** April.

апте́ка chemist's. **апте́карь** *m* chemist. **апте́чка** medicine chest; first-aid kit.

ара́б, ара́бка Arab. **ара́бский** Arab, Arabic.

арави́йский Arabian.

аранжи́ровать *impf & pf* (*mus*) arrange. **аранжиро́вка** (*mus*) arrangement.

ара́хис peanut.

арби́тр arbitrator. **арбитра́ж** arbitration.

арбу́з water-melon.

аргуме́нт argument. **аргумента́ция** reasoning; arguments. **аргументи́ровать** *impf & pf* argue, (try to) prove.

аре́на arena, ring.

аре́нда lease. **аренда́тор** tenant. **аре́ндная пла́та** rent. **арендова́ть** *impf & pf* rent.

аре́ст arrest. **арестова́ть** *pf*, **аре́стовывать** *impf* arrest; seize, sequestrate.

аристокра́т, ~ка aristocrat. **аристократи́ческий** aristocratic. **аристокра́тия** aristocracy.

арифме́тика arithmetic. **арифмети́ческий** arithmetical.

а́рия aria.

а́рка arch.

А́рктика the Arctic. **аркти́ческий** arctic.

армату́ра fittings; reinforcement; armature. **армату́рщик** fitter.

арме́йский army.

Арме́ния Armenia.

а́рмия army.

армяни́н (*pl* -я́не, -я́н), **армя́нка** Armenian. **армя́нский** Armenian.

арома́т scent, aroma. **арома́тный** aromatic, fragrant.

арсена́л arsenal.

арте́ль artel.

арте́рия artery.

арти́куль *m* (*gram*) article.

артилле́рия artillery.

арти́ст, ~ка artiste, artist; expert. **артисти́ческий** artistic.

артри́т arthritis.

а́рфа harp.

архаи́ческий archaic.

арха́нгел archangel.

архео́лог archaeologist. **археологи́ческий** archaeological. **археоло́гия** archaeology.

архи́в archives. **архиви́ст** archivist. **архи́вный** archive, archival.

архиепи́скоп archbishop. **архиере́й** bishop.

архипела́г archipelago.

архите́ктор architect. **архитекту́ра** architecture. **архитекту́рный** architectural.

арши́н arshin (*71 cm.*).

асбе́ст asbestos.

асимметри́чный asymmetrical. **асимметри́я** asymmetry.

аске́т ascetic. **аскети́зм** asceticism. **аскети́ческий** ascetic.

асоциа́льный antisocial.

аспира́нт, ~ка post-graduate student. **аспиранту́ра** post-graduate course.

аспири́н aspirin.

ассамбле́я assembly.

ассигна́ция banknote.

ассимиля́ция assimilation.

ассисте́нт assistant; junior lecturer, research assistant.

ассортиме́нт assortment.

ассоциа́ция association. **ассоции́ровать** *impf & pf* associate.

а́стма asthma. **астмати́ческий** asthmatic.

астро́лог astrologer. **астроло́гия** astrology.

астрона́вт astronaut. **астроно́м** astronomer. **астрономи́ческий** astronomical. **астроно́мия** astronomy.

асфа́льт asphalt.

ата́ка attack. **атакова́ть** *impf & pf* attack.

атама́н ataman (*Cossack chieftain*); (gang-)leader.

атеи́зм atheism. **атеи́ст** atheist.

ателье́ *neut indecl* studio; atelier.

а́тлас[1] atlas.

атла́с[2] satin. **атла́сный** satin.

атле́т athlete; strong man. **атле́тика** athletics. **атлети́ческий** athletic.

атмосфе́ра atmosphere. **атмосфе́рный** atmospheric.

а́том atom. **а́томный** atomic.

атташе́ *m indecl* attaché.

аттеста́т testimonial; certificate; pedigree. **аттестова́ть** *impf & pf* attest; recommend.

аттракцио́н attraction; sideshow; star turn.

ау́ *int* hi, cooee.

аудито́рия auditorium, lecture-room.

аукцио́н auction.

ау́л aul (*Caucasian or Central Asian village*).

ауто́псия autopsy.

афе́ра speculation, trickery. **афери́ст** speculator, trickster.

афи́ша placard, poster.

афори́зм aphorism.

А́фрика Africa. **африка́нец** (-нца), **африка́нка** African. **африка́нский** African.

аффе́кт fit of passion; temporary insanity.

ах *int* ah, oh. **а́хать** *impf* (*pf* **а́хнуть**) sigh; exclaim; gasp.

аэро|вокза́л air terminal. **~дина́мика** aerodynamics. **~дро́м** aerodrome, air-field. **~зо́ль** *m* aerosol. **~по́рт** airport.

Б

б *partl*: *see* **бы**

ба́ба (*coll*) (old) woman; **сне́жная ~** snowman.

ба́бочка butterfly.

ба́бушка grandmother; grandma.

бага́ж (-а́) luggage. **бага́жник** carrier; luggage-rack; boot. **бага́жный ваго́н** luggage-van.

баго́р (-гра́) boat-hook.

багро́вый crimson, purple.

бадья́ (*gen pl* -де́й) tub.

ба́за base; depot; basis; **~ да́нных** database.

база́р market; din.

ба́зис base; basis.

байда́рка canoe.

ба́йка flannelette.

бак[1] tank, cistern.

бак[2] forecastle.

бакала́вр (*univ*) bachelor.

бакале́йный grocery. **бакале́я** groceries.

ба́кен buoy.

бакенба́рды (*pl*; *gen* -ба́рд) side-whiskers.

баклажа́н (*gen pl* -ов *or* -жа́н) aubergine.

бакте́рия bacterium.

бал (*loc* -у́; *pl* -ы́) dance, ball.

балага́н farce.

балала́йка balalaika.

бала́нс (*econ*) balance.

баланси́ровать *impf* (*pf* **c~**) balance; keep one's balance.

балбе́с booby.

балдахи́н canopy.

балери́на ballerina. **бале́т** ballet.

ба́лка[1] beam, girder.

ба́лка[2] gully.

балко́н balcony.

балл mark (*in school*); degree; force; **ве́тер в пять ~ов** wind force 5.

балла́да ballad.

балла́ст ballast.

балло́н container, carboy, cylinder; balloon tyre.

баллоти́ровать *impf* vote; put to the vote; **~ся** stand, be a candidate (**в** *or* **на**+*acc* for).

балова́ть *impf* (*pf* **из~**) spoil, pamper; **~ся** play about, get up to tricks; amuse o.s. **баловство́** spoiling; mischief.

Балти́йское мо́ре Baltic (Sea).

бальза́м balsam; balm.

балюстра́да balustrade.

бамбу́к bamboo.

ба́мпер bumper.

бана́льность banality; platitude. **бана́льный** banal.

бана́н banana.

ба́нда band, gang.

банда́ж (-á) truss; belt, band.

бандеро́ль wrapper; printed matter, book-post.

ба́нджо *neut indecl* banjo.

банди́т bandit; gangster.

банк bank.

ба́нка jar; tin.

банке́т banquet.

банки́р banker. **банкно́та** banknote. **банкро́т** bankrupt. **банкро́тство** bankruptcy.

бант bow.

ба́ня bath; bath-house.

бар bar; snack-bar.

бараба́н drum. **бараба́нить** *impf* drum, thump. **бараба́нная перепо́нка** ear-drum. **бараба́нщик** drummer.

бара́к wooden barrack, hut.

бара́н ram; sheep. **бара́нина** mutton.

бара́нка ring-shaped roll; (steering-) wheel.

барахло́ old clothes, jumble; odds and ends. **барахо́лка** flea market.

бара́шек (-шка) young ram; lamb; wing nut; catkin. **бара́шковый** lambskin.

ба́ржа (*gen pl* барж(е́й)) barge.

ба́рин (*pl* -ре *or* -ры, бар) landowner; sir.

барито́н baritone.

ба́рка barge.

ба́рмен barman.

баро́кко *neut indecl* baroque.

баро́метр barometer.

баро́н baron. **бароне́сса** baroness.

баро́чный baroque.

баррика́да barricade.

барс snow-leopard.

ба́рский lordly; grand.

барсу́к (-á) badger.

барха́н dune.

ба́рхат (-у) velvet. **ба́рхатный** velvet.

ба́рыня landowner's wife; madam.

ба́рыш (-á) profit. **бары́шник** dealer; (ticket) speculator.

ба́рышня (*gen pl* -шень) young lady; miss.

барье́р barrier; hurdle.

бас (*pl* -ы́) bass.

баскетбо́л basket-ball.

басносло́вный mythical, legendary; fabulous. **ба́сня** (*gen pl* -сен) fable; fabrication.

басо́вый bass.

бассе́йн (*geog*) basin; pool; reservoir.

бастова́ть *impf* be on strike.

батальо́н battalion.

батаре́йка, батаре́я battery; radiator.

бато́н long loaf; stick, bar.

ба́тька *m*, **ба́тюшка** *m* father; priest. **ба́тюшки** *int* good gracious!

бах *int* bang!

бахва́льство bragging.

бахрома́ fringe.

бац *int* bang! crack!

баци́лла bacillus. **бациллоноси́тель** *m* carrier.

бачо́к (-чка́) cistern.

ба́шка head.

башлы́к (-á) hood.

башма́к (-á) shoe; **под ~о́м у**+*gen* under the thumb of.

ба́шня (*gen pl* -шен) tower, turret.

баю́кать *impf* (*pf* y~) sing lullabies (to). **ба́юшки-баю́** *int* hushabye!

бая́н accordion.

бде́ние vigil. **бди́тельность** vigilance. **бди́тельный** vigilant.

бег (*loc* -ý; *pl* -á) run, running; race. **бе́гать** *indet* (*det* бежа́ть) *impf* run.

бегемо́т hippopotamus.

бегле́ц (-á), **бегля́нка** fugitive. **бе́глость** speed, fluency, dexterity. **бе́глый** rapid, fluent; fleeting, cursory; *sb* fugitive, runaway. **беговой** running; race. **бего́м** *adv* running, at the double. **беготня́** running about; bustle. **бе́гство** flight; escape. **бегу́н** (-á), **бегу́нья** (*gen pl* -ний) runner.

беда́ (*pl* -ы) misfortune; disaster; trouble; ~ **в том, что** the trouble is (that). **бедне́ть** *impf* (*pf* o~) grow poor. **бе́дность** poverty; the poor. **бе́дный** (-ден, -дна́, -дно) poor. **бедня́га** *m*, **бедня́жка** *m & f* poor thing. **бедня́к** (-á), **бедня́чка** poor peasant; poor man, poor woman.

бедро́ (*pl* бёдра, -дер) thigh; hip.

бе́дственный disastrous. **бе́дствие** disaster. **бе́дствовать** *impf* live in poverty.

бежа́ть (бегу́ *det*; *indet* бе́гать) *impf*

(*pf* по~) run; flow; fly; boil over; *impf* & *pf* escape. **бе́женец** (-нца), **бе́женка** refugee.

без *prep*+*gen* without; ~ **пяти́ (мину́т) три** five (minutes) to three; ~ **че́тверти** a quarter to.

без-, безъ-, бес- *in comb* in-, un-; non-; -less. **без|алкого́льный** non-alcoholic. ~**апелляцио́нный** peremptory, categorical. ~**бо́жие** atheism. ~**бо́жный** godless; shameless; outrageous. ~**боле́зненный** painless. ~**бра́чный** celibate. ~**бре́жный** boundless. ~**ве́стный** unknown; obscure. ~**вку́сие** lack of taste, bad taste. ~**вку́сный** tasteless. ~**вла́стие** anarchy. ~**во́дный** arid. ~**возвра́тный** irrevocable; irrecoverable. ~**возме́здный** free, gratis. ~**во́лие** lack of will. ~**во́льный** weak-willed. ~**вре́дный** harmless. ~**вре́менный** untimely. ~**вы́ходный** hopeless, desperate; uninterrupted. ~**гла́зый** one-eyed; eyeless. ~**гра́мотный** illiterate. ~**грани́чный** boundless, infinite. ~**да́рный** untalented. ~**де́йственный** inactive. ~**де́йствие** inertia, idleness; negligence. ~**де́йствовать** *impf* be idle, be inactive; stand idle.

безде́лица trifle. **безделу́шка** knick-knack. **безде́льник** idler; ne'er-do-well. **безде́льничать** *impf* idle, loaf.

бе́здна abyss, chasm; a huge number, a multitude.

без-. бездоказа́тельный unsubstantiated. ~**до́мный** homeless. ~**до́нный** bottomless; fathomless. ~**доро́жье** lack of (good) roads; season when roads are impassable. ~**ду́мный** unthinking. ~**ду́шный** heartless; inanimate; lifeless. ~**жа́лостный** pitiless, ruthless. ~**жи́зненный** lifeless. ~**забо́тный** carefree; careless. ~**заве́тный** selfless, wholehearted. ~**зако́ние** lawlessness; unlawful act. ~**зако́нный** illegal; lawless. ~**засте́нчивый** shameless, barefaced. ~**защи́тный** defenceless. ~**зву́чный** silent. ~**зло́бный** good-natured. ~**ли́чный** characterless; impersonal. ~**лю́дный** uninhabited; sparsely populated; lonely.

безме́н steelyard.

без-. безме́рный immense; excessive. ~**мо́лвие** silence; silent, mute. ~**мяте́жный** serene; placid. ~**надёжный** hopeless. ~**надзо́рный** neglected. ~**наказанно** *adv* with impunity. ~**нака́занный** unpunished. ~**но́гий** legless; one-legged. ~**нра́вственный** immoral.

безо *prep*+*gen* = **без** (*used before* **весь** *and* **вся́кий**).

безобра́зие ugliness; disgrace, scandal. **безобра́зничать** *impf* make a nuisance of o.s. **безобра́зный** ugly; disgraceful.

без-. безогово́рочный unconditional. ~**опа́сность** safety; security. ~**опа́сный** safe; secure. ~**ору́жный** unarmed. ~**основа́тельный** groundless. ~**остано́вочный** unceasing; non-stop. ~**отве́тный** meek, unanswering; dumb. ~**отве́тственный** irresponsible. ~**отка́зно** *adv* without a hitch. ~**отка́зный** trouble-free, smooth-(running). ~**отлага́тельный** urgent. ~**относи́тельно** *adv*+к+*dat* irrespective of. ~**отчётный** unaccountable. ~**оши́бочный** unerring; correct. ~**рабо́тица** unemployment. ~**рабо́тный** unemployed. ~**разли́чие** indifference. ~**разли́чно** *adv* indifferently; it is all the same. ~**разли́чный** indifferent. ~**рассу́дный** reckless, imprudent. ~**ро́дный** alone in the world; without relatives. ~**ро́потный** uncomplaining; meek. ~**ру́кавка** sleeveless pullover. ~**ру́кий** armless; one-armed. ~**уда́рный** unstressed. ~**уде́ржный** unrestrained; impetuous. ~**укори́зненный** irreproachable.

безу́мец (-мца) madman. **безу́мие** madness. **безу́мный** mad. **безу́мство** madness.

без-. безупре́чный irreproachable, faultless. ~**усло́вно** *adv* unconditionally; of course, undoubtedly. ~**усло́вный** unconditional, absolute; indisputable. ~**успе́шный** unsuccessful. ~**уста́нный** tireless. ~**уте́шный** inconsolable. ~**уча́стие** indifference, apathy. ~**уча́стный** indifferent, apathetic. ~**ымя́нный**

nameless, anonymous; ~**ымя́нный**
па́лец ring-finger. ~**ыску́сный** artless, ingenuous. ~**ысхо́дный** irreparable; interminable.
бейсбо́л baseball.
бека́р (*mus*) natural.
бека́с snipe.
беко́н bacon.
Белару́сь Belarus.
беле́ть *impf* (*pf* по~) turn white;
show white.
белизна́ whiteness. **бели́ла** (*pl; gen*
-и́л) whitewash; Tippex (*propr*).
бели́ть (**бе́лишь**) *impf* (*pf* вы́~,
на~, по~) whitewash; whiten;
bleach.
бе́лка squirrel.
беллетри́ст writer of fiction.
беллетри́стика fiction.
бело- *in comb* white-, leuco-.
белогварде́ец (-е́йца) White
Guard. ~**кро́вие** leukaemia.
~**ку́рый** fair, blonde. ~**ру́с**,
~**ру́ска**, ~**ру́сский** Belorussian.
~**сне́жный** snow-white.
белови́к (-а́) fair copy. **беловой**
clean, fair.
бело́к (-лка́) white (*of egg, eye*); protein.
белошве́йка seamstress. **бело-
шве́йный** linen.
белу́га white sturgeon. **белу́ха** white
whale.
бе́л|ый (бел, -а́, бе́ло) white; clean,
blank; *sb* white person; ~**ая берёза**
silver birch; ~**ое кале́ние** white heat;
~**ый медве́дь** polar bear; ~**ые но́чи**
white nights, midnight sun.
бельги́ец, **-ги́йка** Belgian.
бельги́йский Belgian. **Бе́льгия**
Belgium.
бельё linen; bedclothes; underclothes; washing.
бельмо́ (*pl* -а) cataract.
бельэта́ж first floor; dress circle.
бемо́ль *m* (*mus*) flat.
бенефи́с benefit (performance).
бензи́н petrol.
бензо- *in comb* petrol. **бензоба́к**
petrol-tank. ~**во́з** petrol tanker.
~**запра́вочная** *sb* filling-station.
~**коло́нка** petrol pump. ~**прово́д**
petrol pipe, fuel line.
берёг *etc.*: *see* **бере́чь**
бе́рег (*loc* -у́; *pl* -а́) bank, shore;

coast; **на** ~**у́ мо́ря** at the seaside.
берегово́й coast; coastal.
бережёшь *etc.*: *see* **бере́чь.**
бережли́вый thrifty. **бе́режный**
careful.
берёза birch. **Берёзка** hard-cur-
rency shop.
бере́менеть *impf* (*pf* за~) be(come)
pregnant. **бере́менная** pregnant
(+*instr* with). **бере́менность** pregnancy; gestation.
берёт beret.
бере́чь (-регу́, -режёшь; -рёг, -ла́)
impf take care of; keep; cherish; husband; be sparing of; ~**ся** take care;
beware (+*gen* of).
берло́га den, lair.
беру́ *etc.*: *see* **брать**
бес devil, demon.
бес-: *see* **без-**
бесе́да talk, conversation. **бесе́дка**
summer-house. **бесе́довать** *impf*
talk, converse.
беси́ть (бешу́, бе́сишь) *impf* (*pf* вз~)
enrage; ~**ся** go mad; be furious.
бес-. **бесконе́чность** infinity; end-
lessness. ~**коне́чный** endless.
~**коры́стие** disinterestedness. ~**ко-
ры́стный** disinterested. ~**кра́йний**
boundless.
бесо́вский devilish.
бес-. **беспа́мятство** unconsciousness. ~**парти́йный** non-party
~**перспекти́вный** without pros-
pects; hopeless. ~**пе́чность** careless-
ness, unconcern. ~**пла́тно** *adv* free.
~**пла́тный** free. ~**пло́дие** sterility,
barrenness. ~**пло́дность** futility.
~**пло́дный** sterile, barren; futile.
~**поворо́тный** irrevocable. ~**по-
до́бный** incomparable. ~**позво-
но́чный** invertebrate.
беспоко́ить *impf* (*pf* о~, по~) disturb, bother; trouble; ~**ся** worry;
trouble. **беспоко́йный** anxious;
troubled; fidgety. **беспоко́йство**
anxiety.
бес-. **бесполе́зный** useless.
~**по́мощный** helpless; feeble.
~**поро́дный** mongrel, not thoroughbred. ~**поря́док** (-дка) disorder;
untidy state. ~**поря́дочный** disorderly; untidy. ~**поса́дочный** non-
stop. ~**по́чвенный** groundless.
~**по́шлинный** duty-free. ~**поща́д-**

ный merciless. **~прáвный** without rights. **~предéльный** boundless. **~предмéтный** aimless; abstract. **~препя́тственный** unhindered; unimpeded. **~прерЫ́вный** continuous. **~престáнный** continual.

беспризóрник, -ница waif, homeless child. **беспризóрный** neglected; homeless; *sb* waif, homeless child.

бес-. беспримéрный unparalleled. **~принци́пный** unscrupulous. **~пристрáстие** impartiality. **~пристрáстный** impartial. **~просвéтный** pitch-dark; hopeless; unrelieved. **~пýтный** dissolute. **~свя́зный** incoherent. **~сердéчный** heartless. **~си́лие** impotence; feebleness. **~си́льный** impotent, powerless. **~слáвный** inglorious. **~слéдно** *adv* without trace. **~словéсный** dumb; silent, meek; (*theat*) walk-on. **~смéнный** permanent, continuous. **~смéртие** immortality. **~смéртный** immortal. **~смы́сленный** senseless; foolish; meaningless. **~смы́слица** nonsense. **~сóвестный** unscrupulous; shameless. **~сознáтельный** unconscious; involuntary. **~сóнница** insomnia. **~спóрный** indisputable. **~срóчный** indefinite; without a time limit. **~стрáстный** impassive. **~стрáшный** fearless. **~сты́дный** shameless. **~тáктный** tactless.

бестолкóвщина confusion, disorder. **бестолкóвый** muddle-headed, stupid; incoherent.

бес-. бесфóрменный shapeless. **~харáктерный** weak, spineless. **~хи́тростный** artless; unsophisticated. **~хозя́йственный** improvident. **~цвéтный** colourless. **~цéльный** aimless; pointless. **~цéнный** priceless. **~цéнок: за ~цéнок** very cheap, for a song. **~церемóнный** unceremonious. **~человéчный** inhuman. **~чéстить (-éщу)** *impf* (*pf* **о~чéстить**) dishonour. **~чéстный** dishonourable. **~чи́сленный** innumerable, countless.

бесчýвственный insensible; insensitive. **бесчýвствие** insensibility; insensitivity.

бес-. бесшýмный noiseless.

бетóн concrete. **бетóнный** concrete.

бетономешáлка concrete-mixer. **бетóнщик** concrete-worker.

бечевá tow-rope; rope. **бечёвка** cord, string.

бéшенство rabies; rage. **бéшеный** rabid; furious.

бешý *etc.: see* **бесúть**

библéйский biblical. **библиографи́ческий** bibliographical. **библиогрáфия** bibliography. **библиотéка** library. **библиотéкарь** *m*, **-тéкарша** librarian. **би́блия** bible.

бивáк bivouac, camp.

би́вень (-вня) *m* tusk.

бигуди́ *pl indecl* curlers.

бидóн can; churn.

биéние beating; beat.

бижутéрия costume jewellery.

би́знес business. **бизнесмéн** businessman.

билéт ticket; card; pass. **билéтный** ticket.

биллиóн billion.

билья́рд billiards.

бинóкль *m* binoculars.

бинт (-á) bandage. **бинтовáть** *impf* (*pf* **за~**) bandage. **бинтóвка** bandaging.

биóграф biographer. **биографи́ческий** biographical. **биогрáфия** biography. **биóлог** biologist. **биологи́ческий** biological. **биолóгия** biology. **биохи́мия** biochemistry.

би́ржа exchange.

би́рка name-plate; label.

бирюзá turquoise

бис *int* encore.

би́сер (*no pl*) beads.

бискви́т sponge cake.

битá bat.

би́тва battle.

биткóм *adv*: **~ наби́т** packed.

биту́м bitumen.

бить (бью, бьёшь) *impf* (*pf* **за~, по~, про~, удáрить**) beat; hit; defeat; sound; thump, bang; smash; **~ в цель** hit the target; **~ на+**acc strive for; **~ отбóй** beat a retreat; **~ по+**dat damage, wound; **~ся** fight; beat; struggle; break; +instr knock, hit, strike; +instr struggle with, rack one's brains over.

бифштéкс beefsteak.

бич (-á) whip, lash; scourge; homeless person. **бичевáть (-чýю)** *impf*

flog; castigate.
бла́го good; blessing.
бла́го- *in comb* well-, good-.
Благове́щение Annunciation.
~ви́дный plausible, specious. **~во-**
ле́ние goodwill; favour. **~воспи́-**
танный well-brought-up.
благодари́ть (-рю́) *impf* (*pf* по~)
thank. **благода́рность** gratitude; **не**
сто́ит благода́рности don't mention
it. **благода́рный** grateful. **бла-**
года́ря́ *prep+dat* thanks to, owing
to.
благо-. благоде́тель *m* benefactor.
~де́тельница benefactress. **~де́-**
тельный beneficial. **~ду́шный**
placid; good-humoured. **~жела́тель**
m well-wisher. **~жела́тельный**
well-disposed; benevolent. **~зву́ч-**
ный melodious, harmonious. **~на-**
дёжный reliable. **~наме́ренный**
well-intentioned. **~получие** well-
being; happiness. **~получно** *adv* all
right, well; happily; safely. **~по-**
лучный happy, successful; safe.
~прия́тный favourable. **~при-**
я́тствовать *impf* +*dat* favour.
~разу́мие sense; prudence. **~раз-**
у́мный sensible. **~ро́дие:** ва́ше
~ро́дие Your Honour. **~ро́дный**
noble. **~ро́дство** nobility. **~скло́н-**
ность favour, good graces.
~скло́нный favourable; gracious.
~слови́ть *pf*, **благословля́ть** *impf*
bless. **~состоя́ние** prosperity.
~твори́тель *m*, **-ница** philanthropist. **~твори́тельный** charitable,
charity. **~тво́рный** salutary; beneficial; wholesome. **~устро́енный**
well-equipped, well-planned; with all
amenities.
блаже́нный blissful; simple-minded.
блаже́нство bliss.
бланк form.
блат (*sl*) string-pulling; pull, influence. **блатно́й** criminal; soft, cushy.
бледне́ть (-е́ю) *impf* (*pf* по~)
(grow) pale. **бле́дность** paleness,
pallor. **бле́дный** (-ден, -дна́, -о)
pale.
блеск brightness, brilliance, lustre;
magnificence.
блесну́ть (-ну́, -нёшь) *pf* flash, gleam;
shine. **блесте́ть** (-ещу́, -сти́шь *or*
бле́щешь) *impf* shine; glitter.

блёстка sparkle; sequin.
блестя́щий shining, bright; brilliant.
бле́ять (-е́ет) *impf* bleat.
ближа́йший nearest, closest; next.
бли́же *comp of* **бли́зкий, бли́зко.**
бли́жний near, close; neighbouring;
sb neighbour. **близ** *prep+gen* near,
by. **бли́з|кий** (-зок, -изка́, -о) near;
close; imminent; **~кие** *sb pl* one's
nearest and dearest, close relatives.
бли́зко *adv* near (от+*gen* to). **близ-**
не́ц (-а́) twin; *pl* Gemini. **бли-**
зору́кий short-sighted. **бли́зость**
closeness, proximity.
блик patch of light; highlight.
блин (-а́) pancake.
блинда́ж (-а́) dug-out.
блиста́ть *impf* shine; sparkle.
блок block, pulley, sheave.
блока́да blockade. **блоки́ровать**
impf & *pf* blockade; **~ся** form a bloc.
блокно́т writing-pad, note-book.
блонди́н, блонди́нка blond(e).
блоха́ (*pl* -и, -а́м) flea.
блуд lechery. **блудни́ца** whore.
блужда́ть *impf* roam, wander.
блу́за, блу́зка blouse.
блю́дечко saucer; small dish. **блю́до**
dish; course. **блю́дце** saucer.
боб (-а́) bean. **бобо́вый** bean.
бобр (-а́) beaver.
Бог (*voc* Бо́же) God; **дай ~** God
grant; **~ его́ зна́ет** who knows? **не**
дай ~ God forbid; **Бо́же (мой)!** my
God! good God!; **ра́ди ~а** for God's
sake; **сла́ва ~у** thank God.
богате́ть *impf* (*pf* раз~) grow rich.
бога́тство wealth. **бога́тый** rich,
wealthy; *sb* rich man. **бога́ч** (-а́) rich
man.
богаты́рь (-я́) *m* hero; strong man.
боги́ня goddess. **Богома́терь**
Mother of God. **богомо́лец** (-льца),
богомо́лка devout person; pilgrim.
богомо́лье pilgrimage. **богомо́ль-**
ный religious, devout. **Богоро́дица**
the Virgin Mary. **богосло́в** theologian. **богосло́вие** theology. **бого-**
служе́ние divine service. **боготво-**
ри́ть *impf* idolize; deify. **бого-**
ху́льство blasphemy.
бодри́ть *impf*. stimulate, invigorate;
~ся try to keep up one's spirits.
бо́дрость cheerfulness, courage.
бо́дрствовать be awake; stay

awake; keep vigil. **бо́дрый** (бодр, -á, -о) cheerful, bright.

боеви́к (-á) smash hit. **боево́й** fighting, battle. **боеголо́вка** warhead. **боеприпа́сы** (pl; gen -ов) ammunition. **боеспосо́бный** battle-worthy. **бое́ц** (бойца́) soldier; fighter, warrior.

Бо́же: see **Бог. бо́жеский** divine; just. **боже́ственный** divine; **божество́** deity; divinity. **бо́ж|ий** God's; ~ья коро́вка ladybird. **божо́к** (-жка́) idol.

бой (-ю; loc -ю́; pl -и́, -ёв) battle, action, fight; fighting; slaughtering; striking; breakage(s).

бо́йкий (бо́ек, бойка́, -о) smart, sharp; glib; lively.

бойко́т boycott.

бо́йня (gen pl бо́ен) slaughter-house; butchery.

бок (loc -у́; pl -á) side; flank; ~ о́ ~ side by side; на́ ~ to the side; на ~у́ on one side; по́д ~ом near by; с ~у from the side, from the flank; с ~у на́ бок from side to side.

бока́л glass; goblet.

боково́й side; lateral. **бо́ком** adv sideways.

бокс boxing. **боксёр** boxer.

болва́н blockhead. **болва́нка** pig (of iron etc.).

болга́рин (pl -га́ры), **болга́рка** Bulgarian. **болга́рский** Bulgarian. **Болга́рия** Bulgaria.

бо́лее adv more; ~ всего́ most of all; тем ~, что especially as.

боле́зненный sickly; unhealthy; painful. **боле́знь** illness, disease; abnormality.

боле́льщик, -щица fan, supporter. **боле́ть**[1] (-ею) impf be ill, suffer. **боле́ть**[2] (-ли́т) impf ache, hurt.

боло́тистый marshy. **боло́то** marsh, bog.

болта́ть[1] impf stir; shake; dangle; ~ся dangle, swing; hang about.

болта́ть[2] impf chat, natter. **болтли́вый** talkative; indiscreet. **болтовня́** talk; chatter; gossip. **болту́н** (-á), **болту́нья** chatterbox.

боль pain; ache. **больни́ца** hospital. **больни́чный** hospital; ~ листо́к medical certificate. **бо́льно**[1] adv painfully, badly; predic+dat it hurts.

бо́льно[2] adv very, terribly. **больно́й** (-лен, -льна́) ill, sick; diseased; sore; sb patient, invalid.

бо́льше comp of **большо́й, мно́го**; bigger, larger; greater; more; ~ не not any more, no longer; ~ того́ and what is more; adv for the most part.

большеви́к Bolshevik. **бо́льш|ий** greater, larger; ~ей ча́стью for the most part. **большинство́** majority. **больш|о́й** big, large; great; grown-up; ~а́я бу́ква capital letter; ~о́й па́лец thumb; big toe; ~и́е sb pl grown-ups.

бо́мба bomb. **бомбардирова́ть** impf bombard; bomb. **бомбарди́ровка** bombardment, bombing. **бомбарди́ровщик** bomber. **бомбёжка** bombing. **бомби́ть** (-блю́) bomb. **бомбоубе́жище** bomb shelter.

бор (loc -у́; pl -ы́) coniferous forest. **бордо́вый** wine-red. **бордю́р** border. **боре́ц** (-рца́) fighter; wrestler. **борзы́й** swift. **борма́шина** (dentist's) drill. **бормота́ть** (-очу́, -о́чешь) impf (pf про~) mutter, mumble. **борода́** (acc бо́роду; pl бо́роды, -ро́д, -áм) beard. **борода́вка** wart. **борода́тый** bearded. **борозда́** (pl бо́розды, -о́зд, -áм) furrow; fissure. **борозди́ть** (-зжу́) impf (pf вз~) furrow; plough. **борона́** (acc бо́рону; pl бо́роны, -ро́н, -áм) harrow. **борони́ть** impf (pf вз~) harrow. **боро́ться** (-рю́сь, бо́решься) impf wrestle; struggle, fight. **борт** (loc -у́; pl -á, -о́в) side, ship's side; front; за ~, за ~ом overboard; на ~, на ~у́ on board. **бортпроводни́к** (-á) air steward. **бортпроводни́ца** air hostess. **борщ** (-á) borshch (beetroot soup). **борьба́** wrestling; struggle, fight. **босико́м** adv barefoot. **босни́ец** (-и́йца), **босни́йка** Bosnian. **босни́йский** Bosnian. **Бо́сния** Bosnia. **босо́й** (бос, -á, -о) barefooted. **босоно́жка** sandal. **бот, бо́тик** small boat. **бота́ник** botanist. **бота́ника** botany.

ботани́ческий botanical.

боти́нок (-нка) (*ankle-high*) boot.

бо́цман boatswain

бо́чка barrel. **бочо́нок** (-нка) keg, small barrel.

боязли́вый timid, timorous. **боя́знь** fear, dread.

боя́рин (*pl* -я́ре, -я́р) boyar.

боя́рышник hawthorn.

боя́ться (бою́сь) *impf* +*gen* be afraid of, fear; dislike.

брак¹ marriage.

брак² defective goods; waste. **бракова́ть** *impf* (*pf* за~) reject.

браконьёр poacher.

бракоразво́дный divorce. **бракосочета́ние** wedding.

брани́ть *impf* (*pf* вы́~) scold; abuse; curse; ~ся (*pf* по~) swear, curse; quarrel. **бра́нн|ый** abusive; ~ое сло́во swear-word.

брань bad language; abuse.

брасле́т bracelet.

брасс breast stroke.

брат (*pl* -тья, -тьев) brother; comrade; mate; lay brother; monk. **брата́ться** *impf* (*pf* по~) fraternize. **братоуби́йство** fratricide. **бра́тский** brotherly, fraternal. **бра́тство** brotherhood, fraternity.

брать (беру́, -рёшь; брал, -а́, -о) *impf* (*pf* взять) take; obtain; hire; seize; demand, require; surmount, clear; work; +*instr* succeed by means of; ~ся +за+*acc* touch; seize; get down to; +за+*acc* or *inf* undertake; appear, come.

бра́чный marriage; mating.

бреве́нчатый log. **бревно́** (*pl* брёвна, -вен) log, beam.

бред (*loc* -у́) delirium; raving(s).

бре́дить (-е́жу) *impf* be delirious, rave; +*instr* rave about, be infatuated with. **бредо́вый** delirious; fantastic, nonsensical.

бреду́ *etc.*: *see* **брести́**. **бре́жу** *etc.*: *see* **бре́дить**

бре́згать *impf* (*pf* по~) +*inf or instr* be squeamish about. **брезгли́вый** squeamish.

брезе́нт tarpaulin.

бре́зжить(ся *impf* dawn; gleam faintly, glimmer.

брёл *etc.*: *see* **брести́**

брело́к charm, pendant.

бремени́ть *impf* (*pf* о~) burden. **бре́мя** (-мени) *neut* burden; load.

бренча́ть (-чу́) *impf* strum; jingle.

брести́ (-еду́, -едёшь; брёл, -а́) *impf* stroll; drag o.s. along.

брете́ль, брете́лька shoulder strap.

брешь breach; gap.

бре́ю *etc.*: *see* **брить**

брига́да brigade; crew, team. **бригади́р** brigadier; team-leader; foreman.

бриллиа́нт, брилья́нт diamond.

брита́нец (-нца), **брита́нка** Briton. **брита́нск|ий** British; Б~ие острова́ the British Isles.

бри́тва razor. **бри́твенный** shaving. **бри́тый** shaved; clean-shaven. **брить** (бре́ю) *impf* (*pf* по~) shave; ~ся shave (o.s.).

бровь (*pl* -и, -е́й) eyebrow; brow.

брод ford.

броди́ть (-ожу́, -о́дишь) *impf* wander, roam, stroll; ferment. **бродя́га** *m & f* tramp, vagrant. **бродя́жничество** vagrancy. **бродя́чий** vagrant; wandering. **броже́ние** ferment, fermentation.

броне- *in comb* armoured, armour. **броневи́к** (-а́) armoured car. ~во́й armoured. ~но́сец (-сца) battleship; armadillo.

бро́нза bronze; bronzes. **бро́нзовый** bronze; tanned.

брониро́ванный armoured.

брони́ровать *impf & pf* (*pf also* за~) reserve, book.

бронхи́т bronchitis.

бро́ня¹ reservation; commandeering. **броня́**² armour.

броса́ть *impf*, **бро́сить** (-о́шу) *pf* throw (down); leave, desert; give up, leave off; ~ся throw o.s., rush; +*inf* begin; +*instr* squander; pelt one another with; ~ся в глаза́ be striking. **бро́ский** striking; garish, glaring. **бросо́к** (-ска́) throw; bound, spurt.

бро́шка, брошь brooch.

брошю́ра pamphlet, brochure.

брус (*pl* -сья, -сьев) squared beam, joist; (паралле́льные) ~ья parallel bars.

брусни́ка red whortleberry; red whortleberries.

брусо́к (-ска́) bar; ingot.

бру́тто *indecl adj* gross.

бры́згать (-зжу *or* -гаю) *impf*, **бры́знуть** (-ну) *pf* splash; sprinkle. **бры́зги** (брызг) *pl* spray, splashes; fragments.

брыка́ть *impf*, **брыкну́ть** (-ну́, -нёшь) *pf* kick.

брюзга́ *m & f* grumbler. **брюзгли́-вый** grumbling, peevish. **брюзжа́ть** (-жу́) *impf* grumble.

брю́ква swede.

брю́ки (*pl*; *gen* брюк) trousers.

брюне́т dark-haired man. **брюне́тка** brunette.

брю́хо (*pl* -и) belly; stomach. **брюшно́й** abdominal; ~ тиф typhoid.

бряца́ть *impf* rattle; clank, clang.

бу́бен (-бна) tambourine. **бубене́ц** (-нца́) small bell.

бу́бны (*pl*; *gen* -бён, *dat* -бна́м) (*cards*) diamonds. **бубно́вый** diamond.

буго́р (-гра́) mound, hillock; bump, lump.

будди́зм Buddhism. **будди́йский** Buddhist. **будди́ст** Buddhist.

бу́дет that will do; +*inf* it's time to stop.

буди́льник alarm-clock. **буди́ть** (бужу́, бу́дишь) *impf* (*pf* про~, раз~) wake; arouse.

бу́дка box, booth; hut; stall.

бу́дни (*pl*; *gen* -ней) *pl* weekdays; working days; humdrum existence. **бу́дний**, **бу́дничный** weekday; everyday; humdrum.

бу́дто *conj* as if, as though; ~ (бы), (как) ~ apparently, ostensibly.

бу́ду *etc.: see* быть. **бу́дучи** being. **бу́дущ|ий** future; next; ~ее *sb* future. **бу́дущность** future. **бу́дь(те)**: *see* быть

бужу́: *see* буди́ть

бузина́ (*bot*) elder.

буй (*pl* -и́, -ёв) buoy.

бу́йвол buffalo.

бу́йный (бу́ен, буйна́, -о) violent, turbulent; luxuriant, lush. **бу́йство** unruly behaviour. **бу́йствовать** *impf* create an uproar, behave violently.

бук beech.

бука́шка small insect.

бу́ква (*gen pl* букв) letter; ~ в бу́кву literally. **буква́льно** *adv* literally. **буква́льный** literal. **буква́рь** (-я́) *m* ABC. **буквое́д** pedant.

буке́т bouquet; aroma.

букини́ст second-hand bookseller.

бу́кля curl, ringlet.

бу́ковый beech.

букси́р tug-boat; tow-rope. **букси́-ровать** *impf* tow.

буксова́ть *impf* spin, slip.

була́вка pin.

бу́лка roll. **бу́лочная** *sb* baker's. **бу́лочник** baker.

булы́жник cobble-stone, cobbles.

бульва́р avenue; boulevard.

бульдо́г bulldog.

бульдо́зер bulldozer.

бу́лькать *impf* gurgle.

бульо́н broth.

бум (*sport*) beam.

бума́га cotton; paper; document. **бума́жка** piece of paper; note. **бума́жник** wallet; paper-maker. **бума́жн|ый** cotton; paper; ~ змей kite.

бу́нкер bunker.

бунт (*pl* -ы́) rebellion; riot; mutiny. **бунта́рь** (-я́) *m* rebel; insurgent. **бунтова́ть(ся** *impf* (*pf* вз~) rebel; riot. **бунтовщи́к** (-á), **-щи́ца** rebel, insurgent.

бур auger.

бура́в (-á; *pl* -á) auger; gimlet. **бура́вить** (-влю) *impf* (*pf* про~) bore, drill.

бура́н snowstorm.

буреве́стник stormy petrel.

буре́ние boring, drilling.

буржуа́ *m indecl* bourgeois. **буржуази́я** bourgeoisie. **буржуа́зный** bourgeois.

бури́льщик borer, driller. **бури́ть** *impf* (*pf* про~) bore, drill.

бурли́ть *impf* seethe.

бу́рный (-рен, -рна́, -о) stormy; rapid; energetic.

буров|о́й boring; ~а́я вы́шка derrick; ~а́я (сква́жина) borehole; ~о́й стано́к drilling rig.

бу́рый (бур, -á, -о) brown.

бурья́н tall weeds.

бу́ря storm.

бу́сина bead. **бу́сы** (*pl*; *gen* бус) beads.

бутафо́рия (*theat*) props.

бутербро́д open sandwich.

буто́н bud.

бу́тсы (*pl*; *gen* -ов) *pl* football boots.

буты́лка bottle. **буты́ль** large bottle; carboy.

буфе́т snack bar; sideboard; counter. **буфе́тчик** barman. **буфе́тчица** barmaid.

бух int bang, plonk. **бу́хать** impf (pf **бу́хнуть**) thump, bang; bang down; thunder, thud; blurt out.

буха́нка loaf.

бухга́лтер accountant. **бухгалте́рия** accountancy; accounts department.

бу́хнуть (-ну) impf swell.

бу́хта bay.

бушева́ть (-шу́ю) impf rage, storm.

буя́н rowdy. **буя́нить** impf create an uproar.

бы, б partl I. +past tense or inf indicates the conditional or subjunctive. **II.** (+ни) forms indef prons and conjs.

быва́лый experienced; former; habitual, familiar. **быва́ть** impf be; happen; be inclined to be; **как ни в чём не быва́ло** as if nothing had happened; **быва́ло** partl used to, would; **мать быва́ло ча́сто пе́ла э́ту пе́сню** my mother would often sing this song. **бы́вший** former, ex-.

бык (-а́) bull, ox; pier.

были́на ancient Russian epic.

бы́ло partl nearly, on the point of; (only) just. **был|о́й** past, bygone; ~**о́е** sb the past. **быль** true story; fact.

быстрота́ speed. **бы́стрый** (быстр, -а́, -о) fast, quick.

быт (loc -ý) way of life. **бытие́** being, existence; objective reality; **кни́га Бытия́** Genesis. **бытово́й** everyday; social.

быть (pres 3rd sg есть, pl суть; fut бу́ду; past был, -а́, -о; imper бу́дь(те)) impf be; be situated; happen. **бытьё** way of life.

бычо́к (-чка́) steer.

бью etc.: see **бить**

бюдже́т budget.

бюллете́нь m bulletin; ballot-paper; doctor's certificate.

бюро́ neut indecl bureau; office; writing-desk. **бюрокра́т** bureaucrat. **бюрократи́зм** bureaucracy. **бюрократи́ческий** bureaucratic. **бюрокра́тия** bureaucracy; bureaucrats.

бюст bust. **бюстга́льтер** bra.

В

в, во prep I. +acc into, to; on; at; within; through; **быть в** take after; **в два ра́за бо́льше** twice as big; **в на́ши дни** in our day; **войти́ в дом** go into the house; **в понеде́льник** on Monday; **в тече́ние**+gen during; **в четы́ре часа́** at four o'clock; **высото́й в три ме́тра** three metres high; **игра́ть в ша́хматы** play chess; **пое́хать в Москву́** go to Moscow; **сесть в ваго́н** get into the carriage; **смотре́ть в окно́** look out of the window. **II.** +prep in; at; **в двадца́том ве́ке** in the twentieth century; **в теа́тре** at the theatre; **в трёх киломе́трах от го́рода** three kilometres from the town; **в э́том году́** this year; **в январе́** in January.

ваго́н carriage, coach; ~**-рестора́н** restaurant car. **вагоне́тка** truck, trolley. **вагоновожа́тый** sb tram-driver.

ва́жничать impf give o.s. airs; +instr plume o.s., pride o.s., on. **ва́жность** importance; pomposity. **ва́жный** (-жен, -жна́, -о) important; weighty; pompous.

ва́за vase, bowl.

вазели́н Vaseline (propr).

вака́нсия vacancy. **вака́нтный** vacant.

ва́кса (shoe-)polish.

ва́куум vacuum.

вакци́на vaccine.

вал[1] (loc -ý; pl -ы́) bank; rampart; billow, roller; barrage.

вал[2] (loc -ý; pl -ы́) shaft.

ва́ленок (-нка; gen pl -нок) felt boot.

вале́т knave, Jack.

ва́лик roller, cylinder.

вали́ть[1] impf flock, throng; **вали́(те)!** have a go!

вали́ть[2] (-лю́, -лишь) impf (pf по~, с~) throw down, bring down; pile up; ~**ся** fall, collapse.

валово́й gross; wholesale.

валто́рна French horn.

валу́н (-á) boulder.

вальс waltz. **вальси́ровать** impf waltz.

валю́та currency; foreign currency.
валя́ть *impf* (*pf* на~, с~) drag; roll; shape; bungle; ~ дурака́ play the fool; валя́й(те)! go ahead!; ~ся lie, lie about; roll, wallow.
вам, ва́ми: *see* вы
вампи́р vampire.
ванда́л vandal. вандали́зм vandalism.
вани́ль vanilla.
ва́нна bath. ва́нная *sb* bathroom.
ва́рвар barbarian. ва́рварский barbaric. ва́рварство barbarity; vandalism.
ва́режка mitten.
варёный boiled. варе́нье jam. вари́ть (-рю́, -ришь) *impf* (*pf* с~) boil; cook; ~ся boil; cook.
вариа́нт version; option; scenario.
вас: *see* вы
василёк (-лька́) cornflower.
ва́та cotton wool; wadding.
ватерли́ния water-line. ватерпа́с (spirit-)level.
вати́н (sheet) wadding. ва́тник quilted jacket. ва́тный quilted, wadded.
ватру́шка cheese-cake.
ватт (*gen pl* ватт) watt.
ва́учер coupon (*exchangeable for government-issued share*).
ва́фля (*gen pl* -фель) wafer; waffle.
ва́хта (*naut*) watch. вахтёр janitor, porter.
ваш (-его) *m*, ва́ша (-ей) *f*, ва́ше (-его) *neut*, ва́ши (-их) *pl*, *pron* your, yours.
вбега́ть *impf*, вбежа́ть (вбегу́) *pf* run in.
вберу́ *etc.*: *see* вобра́ть
вбива́ть *impf of* вбить
вбира́ть *impf of* вобра́ть
вбить (вобью́, -бьёшь) *pf* (*impf* вбива́ть) drive in, hammer in.
вблизи́ *adv* (+от+*gen*) close (to), near by.
вбок *adv* sideways, to one side.
вброд *adv*: переходи́ть ~ ford, wade.
вва́ливать *impf*, ввали́ть (-лю́, -лишь) *pf* throw heavily, heave, bundle; ~ся fall heavily; sink, become sunken; burst in.
введе́ние introduction. введу́ *etc.*: *see* ввести́

ввезти́ (-зу́, -зёшь; ввёз, -ла́) *pf* (*impf* ввози́ть) import; bring in.
вве́рить *pf* (*impf* вверя́ть) entrust, confide; ~ся +*dat* trust in, put one's faith in.
вверну́ть (-ну́, -нёшь) *pf*, ввёртывать *impf* screw in; insert.
вверх *adv* up, upward(s); ~дном upside down; ~ (по ле́стнице) upstairs. вверху́ *adv* above, overhead.
вверя́ть(ся) *impf of* вве́рить(ся)
ввести́ (-еду́, -едёшь; ввёл, -а́) *pf* (*impf* вводи́ть) bring in; introduce.
вви́ду *prep*+*gen* in view of.
ввинти́ть (-нчу́) *pf*, вви́нчивать *impf* screw in.
ввод lead-in. вводи́ть (-ожу́, -о́дишь) *impf of* ввести́. вво́дный introductory; parenthetic.
ввожу́ *see* вводи́ть, ввози́ть
вво́з importation; import(s). ввози́ть (-ожу́, -о́зишь) *impf of* ввезти́
вво́лю *adv* to one's heart's content.
ввысь *adv* up, upward(s).
ввяза́ть (-яжу́, -я́жешь) *pf*, ввя́зывать *impf* knit in; involve; ~ся meddle, get or be mixed up (in).
вглубь *adv* & *prep*+*gen* deep (into), into the depths.
вгляде́ться (-яжу́сь) *pf*, вгля́дываться *impf* peer, look closely (в+*acc* at).
вгоня́ть *impf of* вогна́ть. вдава́ться (вдаю́сь, -ёшься) *impf of* вда́ться
вдави́ть (-авлю́, -а́вишь) *pf*, вда́вливать *impf* press in.
вдалеке́, вдали́ *adv* in the distance, far away. вдаль *adv* into the distance.
вда́ться (-а́мся, -а́шься, -а́стся, -ади́мся; -а́лся, -ла́сь) *pf* (*impf* вдава́ться) jut out; penetrate, go in.
вдво́е *adv* twice; double; ~ бо́льше twice as big, as much, as many. вдвоём *adv* (the) two together, both. вдвойне́ *adv* twice as much, double; doubly.
вдева́ть *impf of* вде́ть
вде́лать *pf*, вде́лывать *impf* set in, fit in.
вдёргивать *impf*, вдёрнуть (-ну) *pf* в+*acc* thread through, pull through.
вде́ть (-е́ну) *pf* (*impf* вдева́ть) put in, thread.

вдобавок *adv* in addition; besides.

вдова widow. **вдовец** (-вца) widower.

вдоволь *adv* enough; in abundance.

вдогонку *adv* (за+*instr*) after, in pursuit (of).

вдоль *adv* lengthwise; ~ и поперёк far and wide; in detail; *prep+gen or* по+*dat* along.

вдох breath. **вдохновение** inspiration, **вдохновённый** inspired. **вдохновить** (-влю) *pf*, **вдохновлять** *impf* inspire. **вдохнуть** (-ну, -нёшь) *pf* (*impf* **вдыхать**) breathe in.

вдребезги *adv* to smithereens.

вдруг *adv* suddenly.

вдуматься *pf*, **вдумываться** *impf* ponder, meditate; +в+*acc* think over. **вдумчивый** thoughtful.

вдыхание inhalation. **вдыхать** *impf of* вдохнуть

вегетарианец (-нца), **-нка** vegetarian. **вегетарианский** vegetarian.

ведать *impf* know; +*instr* manage, handle. **ведение**[1] authority, jurisdiction.

ведение[2] conducting, conduct; ~ книг book-keeping.

ведомость (*gen pl* -ей) list, register. **ведомственный** departmental. **ведомство** department.

ведро (*pl* вёдра, -дер) bucket; vedro (*approx* 12 *litres*)

веду *etc.*: *see* **вести. ведущий** leading.

ведь *partl & conj* you see, you know; isn't it? is it?

ведьма witch.

веер (*pl* -á) fan.

вежливость politeness. **вежливый** polite.

везде *adv* everywhere.

везение luck. **везучий** lucky. **везти** (-зу, -зёшь; вёз, -ла) *impf* (*pf* по~) convey; bring, take; *impers+dat* be lucky; **ему не везло** he had no luck.

век (*loc* -у; *pl* -á) century; age; life, lifetime. **век** *adv* for ages.

веко (*pl* -и, век) eyelid.

вековой ancient, age-old.

вексель (*pl* -я, -ей) *m* promissory note, bill (of exchange).

вёл *etc.*: *see* **вести**

велеть (-лю) *impf & pf* order; не ~ forbid.

великан giant. **великий** (велик, -а *or* -á) great; big, large; too big; ~ пост Lent.

велико- *in comb* great. **Великобритания** Great Britain. **великодушие** magnanimity. **~душный** magnanimous. **~лепие** splendour. **~лепный** splendid.

величавый stately, majestic. **величайший** greatest, supreme. **величественный** majestic, grand. **величество** Majesty. **величие** greatness, grandeur. **величина** (*pl* -ины, -ам) size; quantity; magnitude; value; great figure.

велосипед bicycle. **велосипедист** cyclist.

вельвет velveteen; ~ в рубчик corduroy.

вельможа *m* grandee.

вена vein.

венгерец (-рца), **венгерка** Hungarian. **венгерский** Hungarian. **венгр** Hungarian. **Венгрия** Hungary.

вендетта vendetta.

венерический venereal.

венец (-нца) crown; wreath.

веник besom; birch twigs.

венок (-нка) wreath, garland.

вентиль *m* valve.

вентилятор ventilator; extractor (fan). **вентиляция** ventilation.

венчание wedding; coronation. **венчать** *impf* (*pf* об~, по~, у~) crown; marry; ~ся be married, marry. **венчик** halo; corolla; rim; ring, bolt.

вера faith, belief.

веранда veranda.

верба willow; willow branch. **вербн|ый**; ~ое воскресенье Palm Sunday.

верблюд camel.

вербовать *impf* (*pf* за~) recruit; win over. **вербовка** recruitment.

верёвка rope; string; cord. **верёвочный** rope.

вереница row, file, line, string.

вереск heather.

веретено (*pl* -тёна) spindle.

верещать (-щу) *impf* squeal; chirp.

верить *impf* (*pf* по~) believe, have faith; +*dat or* в+*acc* trust (in), believe in.

вермишель vermicelli.

вернее *adv* rather. **верно** *partl* probably, I suppose. **верность** faithfulness, loyalty.

вернуть (-ну, -нёшь) *pf* (*impf* возвращать) give back, return; ~ся return.

верный (-рен, -рна, -о) faithful, loyal; true; correct; reliable.

верование belief. **веровать** *impf* believe. **вероисповедание** religion; denomination. **вероломный** treacherous, perfidious. **вероотступник** apostate. **веротерпимость** (religious) toleration. **вероятно** *adv* probably. **вероятность** probability. **вероятный** probable.

версия version.

верста (*pl* вёрсты) verst (*1.06 km.*).

верстак (-а) work-bench.

вертел (*pl* -а) spit, skewer. **вертеть** (-чу, -тишь) *impf* turn (round); twirl; ~ся turn (round), spin. **вертлявый** fidgety; flighty.

вертикаль vertical line. **вертикальный** vertical. **вертолёт** helicopter. **вертушка** flirt.

верующий *sb* believer.

верфь shipyard.

верх (*loc* -ý; *pl* -й) top; summit; height; *pl* upper crust, top brass; high notes. **верхний** upper; top. **верховный** supreme. **верховой** riding; *sb* rider. **верховье** (*gen pl* -ьев) upper reaches. **верхолаз** steeplejack. **верхом** *adv* on horseback; astride. **верхушка** top, summit; apex; top brass.

верчу *etc.*: *see* **вертеть**

вершина top, summit; peak; apex. **вершить** *impf* +*instr* manage, control.

вершок vershok (*4.4 cm.*); smattering.

вес (*loc* -ý; *pl* -á) weight.

веселить *impf* (*pf* раз~) cheer, gladden; ~ся enjoy o.s.; amuse o.s. **весело** *adv* merrily. **весёлый** (весел, -á, -о) merry; cheerful. **веселье** merriment.

весенний spring.

весить (вешу) *impf* weigh. **веский** weighty, solid.

весло (*pl* вёсла, -сел) oar.

весна (*pl* вёсны, -сен) spring.

весной *adv* in (the) spring.

веснушка freckle.

вест (*naut*) west; west wind.

вести (веду, -дёшь; вёл, -á) *impf* (*pf* по~) lead, take; conduct; drive; run; keep; ~ себя behave, conduct o.s.; ~сь be the custom.

вестибюль *m* (entrance) hall, lobby.

вестник herald; bulletin. **весть**[1] (*gen pl* -ей) news; **без вести** without trace. **весть**[2]: Бог ~ God knows.

весы (*pl*; *gen* -ов) scales, balance; Libra.

весь (всего *m*, вся, всей *f*, всё, всего *neut*, все, всех *pl*) *pron* all, the whole of; **всего хорошего!** all the best!; **всё** everything; **без всего** without anything; **все** everybody.

весьма *adv* very, highly.

ветвь (*gen pl* -ей) branch; bough.

ветер (-тра, *loc* -ý) wind. **ветерок** (-рка) breeze.

ветеран veteran.

ветеринар vet.

ветка branch; twig.

вето *neut indecl* veto.

ветошь old clothes, rags.

ветреный windy; frivolous. **ветров|ой** wind; ~ое стекло windscreen. **ветряк** (-á) wind turbine; windmill.

ветхий (ветх, -á, -о) old; dilapidated; В~ завет Old Testament.

ветчина ham.

ветшать *impf* (*pf* об~) decay; become dilapidated.

веха landmark.

вечер (*pl* -á) evening; party. **вечеринка** party. **вечерний** evening. **вечерня** (*gen pl* -рен) vespers. **вечером** *adv* in the evening.

вечно *adv* for ever, eternally. **вечнозелёный** evergreen. **вечность** eternity; ages. **вечный** eternal.

вешалка peg, rack; tab, hanger. **вешать** *impf* (*pf* взвесить, повесить, свешать) hang; weigh (out); ~ся hang o.s.; weigh o.s.

вешу *etc.*: *see* **весить**

вещание broadcasting. **вещать** *impf* broadcast.

вещевой clothing; ~ мешок hold-all, kit-bag. **вещественный** substantial, material, real. **вещество** substance; matter. **вещь** (*gen pl* -ей) thing.

ве́ялка winnowing-machine. **ве́яние** winnowing; blowing; trend. **ве́ять** (ве́ю) *impf* (*pf* про~) winnow; blow; flutter.

взад *adv* backwards; ~ и вперёд back and forth.

взаи́мность reciprocity. **взаи́мный** mutual, reciprocal.

взаимо- *in comb* inter-. **взаимоде́йствие** interaction; co-operation. **~де́йствовать** *impf* interact; cooperate. **~отноше́ние** interrelation; *pl* relations. **~по́мощь** mutual aid. **~понима́ние** mutual understanding. **~связь** interdependence, correlation.

взаймы́ *adv*: взять ~ borrow; дать ~ lend.

взаме́н *prep+gen* instead of; in return for.

взаперти́ *adv* under lock and key; in seclusion.

взба́лмошный unbalanced, eccentric.

взбега́ть *impf*, **взбежа́ть** (-егу́) *pf* run up.

взберу́сь *etc.*: *see* **взобра́ться**. **вз|беси́ть(ся** (-ешу́(сь, -е́сишь(ся) *pf*. **взбива́ть** *impf of* **взбить**. **взбива́ться** *impf of* **взобра́ться**

взби́тый whipped, beaten. **взбить** (взобью́, -бьёшь) *pf* (*impf* **взбива́ть**) beat (up), whip; shake up.

вз|борозди́ть (-зжу́) *pf*.

вз|бунтова́ться *pf*.

взбуха́ть *impf*, **взбу́хнуть** (-нет; -ух) *pf* swell (out).

взва́ливать *impf*, **взвали́ть** (-лю́, -лишь) *pf* load; +на+*acc* saddle with.

взве́сить (-е́шу) *pf* (*impf* **ве́шать**, **взве́шивать**) weigh.

взвести́ (-еду́, -едёшь; -ёл, -á) *pf* (*impf* **взводи́ть**) lead up; raise; cock; +на+*acc* impute to.

взве́шивать *impf of* **взве́сить**

взвива́ть(ся *impf of* **взви́ть(ся**

взви́зг scream; yelp. **взви́згивать** *impf*, **взви́згнуть** (-ну) *pf* scream; yelp.

взвинти́ть (-нчу́) *pf*, **взви́нчивать** *impf* excite, work up; inflate. **взви́нченный** worked up; nervy; inflated.

взвить (взовью́, -ёшь; -ил, -á, -о) *pf* (*impf* **взвива́ть**) raise; ~ся rise, be hoisted; soar.

взвод[1] platoon, troop.

взвод[2] notch. **взводи́ть** (-ожу́, -о́дишь) *impf of* **взвести́**

взволно́ванный agitated; worried. **вз|волнова́ть(ся** (-ну́ю(сь) *pf*.

взгляд look; glance; opinion. **взгля́дывать** *impf*, **взгляну́ть** (-яну́, -я́нешь) *pf* look, glance.

взго́рье hillock.

вздёргивать *impf*, **вздёрнуть** (-ну) *pf* hitch up; jerk up; turn up.

вздор nonsense. **вздо́рный** cantankerous; foolish.

вздорожа́ние rise in price. **вз|дорожа́ть** *pf*.

вздох sigh. **вздохну́ть** (-ну́, -нёшь) *pf* (*impf* **вздыха́ть**) sigh.

вздра́гивать *impf* (*pf* **вздро́гнуть**) shudder, quiver.

вздремну́ть *pf* have a nap, doze.

вздро́гнуть (-ну) *pf* (*impf* **вздра́гивать**) start; wince.

вздува́ть(ся *impf of* **вздуть**[1]**(ся**

взду́мать *pf* take it into one's head; **не взду́май(те)!** don't you dare!

взду́тие swelling. **взду́тый** swollen. **вздуть**[1] *pf* (*impf* **вздува́ть**) inflate; **~ся** swell.

вздуть[2] *pf* thrash.

вздыха́ть *impf* (*pf* **вздохну́ть**) breathe; sigh.

взима́ть *impf* levy, collect.

взла́мывать *impf of* **взлома́ть**. **вз|леле́ять** *pf*.

взлёт flight; take-off. **взлета́ть** *impf*, **взлете́ть** (-лечу́) *pf* fly (up); take off. **взлётный** take-off; **взлётно-поса́дочная полоса́** runway.

взлом breaking open, breaking in. **взлома́ть** *pf* (*impf* **взла́мывать**) break open; break up. **взло́мщик** burglar.

взлохма́ченный dishevelled.

взмах stroke, wave, flap. **взма́хивать** *impf*, **взмахну́ть** (-ну́, -нёшь) *pf* +*instr* wave, flap.

взмо́рье seaside; coastal waters.

вз|мути́ть (-учу́, -у́ти́шь) *pf*.

взнос payment; fee, dues.

взнузда́ть *pf*, **взну́здывать** *impf* bridle.

взобра́ться (взберу́сь, -ёшься; -а́лся, -ла́сь, -а́ло́сь) *pf* (*impf* **взбира́ться**) climb (up).

взобью́ *etc.*: *see* **взбить. взовью́** *etc.*:

see **взвить**

взойти (-йду́, -йдёшь; -ошёл, -шла́) *pf* (*impf* вос-, всходи́ть) rise, go up; на+*acc* mount.

взор look, glance.

взорва́ть (-ву́, -вёшь; -а́л, -а́, -о) *pf* (*impf* взрыва́ть) blow up; exasperate; ~ся burst, explode.

взро́слый *adj & sb* adult.

взрыв explosion; outburst. **взрыва́тель** *m* fuse. **взрыва́ть** *impf*, **взрыть** (-ро́ю) *pf* (*pf also* взорва́ть) blow up; ~ся explode. **взрывно́й** explosive; blasting. **взрывча́тка** explosive. **взры́вчатый** explosive.

взъеро́шенный tousled, dishevelled. **взъеро́шивать** *impf*, **взъеро́шить** (-шу) *pf* tousle, rumple.

взыва́ть *impf of* **воззва́ть**

взыска́ние penalty; exaction. **взыска́тельный** exacting. **взыска́ть** (-ыщу́, -ы́щешь) *pf*, **взы́скивать** *impf* exact, recover; call to account.

взя́тие taking, capture. **взя́тка** bribe. **взя́точничество** bribery. **взя́ть(ся** (возьму́(сь, -мёшь(ся; -я́л(ся, -а́(сь, -о(сь) *pf of* **брать(ся**

вибра́ция vibration. **вибри́ровать** *impf* vibrate.

вивисе́кция vivisection.

вид[1] (*loc* -у́) look; appearance; shape, form; condition; view; prospect; sight; **де́лать вид** pretend; **име́ть в ~у́** intend; mean; bear in mind.

вид[2] kind; species.

вида́ться *impf* (*pf* по~) meet. **виде́ние**[1] sight, vision. **виде́ние**[2] vision, apparition.

ви́део *neut indecl* video (cassette) recorder; video film; video cassette. **видеоигра́** video game. **видеока́мера** video camera. **видеокассе́та** video cassette. **видеомагнитофо́н** video (cassette) recorder.

ви́деть (ви́жу) *impf* (*pf* у~) see; ~ **во сне** dream (of); ~ся see one another; appear. **ви́димо** *adv* evidently. **ви́димость** visibility; appearance. **ви́димый** visible; apparent, evident. **ви́дный** (-ден, -дна́, -о) visible; distinguished.

видоизмене́ние modification. **видоизмени́ть** *pf*, **видоизменя́ть** *impf* modify.

видоиска́тель *m* view-finder.

ви́жу *see* **ви́деть**

ви́за visa.

визг squeal; yelp. **визжа́ть** (-жу́) *impf* squeal, yelp, squeak.

визи́т visit. **визи́тка** business card.

викторина quiz.

ви́лка fork; plug. **ви́лы** (*pl*; *gen* вил) pitchfork.

вильну́ть (-ну́, -нёшь) *pf*, **виля́ть** *impf* twist and turn; prevaricate; +*instr* wag.

вина́ (*pl* ви́ны) fault, guilt; blame.

винегре́т Russian salad; medley.

вини́тельный accusative. **вини́ть** *impf* accuse; ~ся (*pf* по~) confess.

ви́нный wine; winy. **вино́** (*pl* -а) wine.

винова́тый guilty. **вино́вник** initiator; culprit. **вино́вный** guilty.

виногра́д vine; grapes. **виногра́дник** vineyard. **виногра́дный** grape; wine. **винокуре́нный заво́д** distillery.

винт (-а́) screw. **винти́ть** (-нчу́) *impf* screw up. **винто́вка** rifle. **винтово́й** screw; spiral.

виолонче́ль cello.

вира́ж (-а́) turn; bend.

виртуо́з virtuoso. **виртуо́зный** masterly.

ви́рус virus. **ви́русный** virus.

ви́селица gallows. **висе́ть** (вишу́) *impf* hang. **ви́снуть** (-ну; вис(нул)) *impf* hang; droop.

ви́ски *neut indecl* whisky.

висо́к (-ска́) temple.

високо́сный год leap-year.

вист whist.

вися́чий hanging; ~ **замо́к** padlock; ~ **мост** suspension bridge.

витами́н vitamin.

витиева́тый flowery, ornate. **вито́й** twisted, spiral. **вито́к** (-тка́) turn, coil.

витра́ж (-а́) stained-glass window. **витри́на** shop-window; showcase.

вить (вью, вьёшь; вил, -а́, -о) *impf* (*pf* с~) twist, wind, weave; ~ся wind, twine; curl; twist; whirl.

вихо́р (-хра́) tuft. **вихра́стый** shaggy.

вихрь *m* whirlwind; vortex; **сне́жный** ~ blizzard.

ви́це- *pref* vice-. **вице-адмира́л** vice-admiral. **~президе́нт** vice-president.

вицмунди́р (dress) uniform.
ВИЧ (*abbr of* **ви́рус иммуно-дефици́та челове́ка**) HIV.
вишнёвый cherry. **ви́шня** (*gen pl* -шен) cherry, cherries; cherry-tree.
вишу́: *see* **висе́ть**
вишь *partl* look, just look!
вка́лывать *impf* (*sl*) work hard; *impf of* **вколо́ть**
вка́пывать *impf of* **вкопа́ть**
вкати́ть (-ачу́, -а́тишь) *pf*, **вка́тывать** *impf* roll in; administer.
вклад deposit; contribution. **вкла́дка** supplementary sheet. **вкладно́й лист** loose leaf, insert. **вкла́дчик** depositor.
вкла́дывать *impf of* **вложи́ть**
вкле́ивать *impf*, **вкле́ить** *pf* stick in.
вкли́ниваться *impf*, **вклини́ться** *pf* edge one's way in.
включа́тель *m* switch. **включа́ть** *impf*, **включи́ть** (-чу́) *pf* include; switch on; plug in; ~**ся в**+*acc* join in, enter into. **включа́я** including. **включе́ние** inclusion, insertion; switching on. **включи́тельно** *adv* inclusive.
вкола́чивать *impf*, **вколоти́ть** (-очу́, -о́тишь) *pf* hammer in, knock in.
вколо́ть (-олю́, -о́лешь) *pf* (*impf* **вка́лывать**) stick (in).
вкопа́ть *pf* (*impf* **вка́пывать**) dig in.
вкось *adv* obliquely.
вкра́дчивый ingratiating. **вкра́дываться** *impf*, **вкра́сться** (-аду́сь, -аде́шься) *pf* creep in; insinuate o.s.
вкра́тце *adv* briefly, succinctly.
вкривь *adv* aslant; wrongly, perversely.
вкруг = **вокру́г**
вкруту́ю *adv* hard(-boiled).
вкус taste. **вкуси́ть** (-ушу́, -у́сишь) *pf*, **вкуша́ть** *impf* taste; partake of. **вку́сный** (-сен, -сна́, -о) tasty, nice.
вла́га moisture.
влага́лище vagina.
владе́лец (-льца), **-лица** owner. **владе́ние** ownership; possession; property. **владе́тель** *m*, **-ница** possessor; sovereign. **владе́ть** (-е́ю) *impf* +*instr* own, possess; control.
влады́ка *m* master, sovereign.
влады́чество dominion, sway.
вла́жность humidity; moisture.

вла́жный (-жен, -жна́, -о) damp, moist, humid.
вла́мываться *impf of* **вломи́ться**
вла́ствовать *impf* +(**над**+) *instr* rule, hold sway over. **властели́н** ruler; master. **вла́стный** imperious, commanding; empowered, competent. **власть** (*gen pl* -е́й) power; authority.
вле́во *adv* to the left (**от**+*gen* of).
влеза́ть *impf*, **влезть** (-зу; влез) *pf* climb in; get in; fit in.
влёк *etc.*: *see* **влечь**
влета́ть *impf*, **влете́ть** (-ечу́) *pf* fly in; rush in.
влече́ние attraction; inclination. **влечь** (-еку́, -ечёшь; влёк, -ла́) *impf* draw; attract; ~ **за собо́й** involve, entail.
влива́ть *impf*, **влить** (волью́, -ёшь; влил, -а́, -о) *pf* pour in; instil.
влия́ние influence. **влия́тельный** influential. **влия́ть** *impf* (*pf* **по**~) **на**+*acc* influence, affect.
вложе́ние enclosure; investment. **вложи́ть** (-ожу́, -о́жишь) *pf* (*impf* **вкла́дывать**) put in, insert; enclose; invest.
вломи́ться (-млю́сь, -мишься) *pf* (*impf* **вла́мываться**) break in.
влюби́ть (-блю́, -бишь) *pf*, **влюбля́ть** *impf* make fall in love (**в**+*acc* with); ~**ся** fall in love. **влюблённый** (-лён, -а́) in love; *sb* lover.
вма́зать (-а́жу) *pf*, **вма́зывать** *impf* cement, putty in.
вмени́ть *pf*, **вменя́ть** *impf* impute; impose. **вменя́емый** (*law*) responsible; sane.
вме́сте *adv* together; ~ **с тем** at the same time, also.
вмести́лище receptacle. **вмести́мость** capacity; tonnage. **вмести́тельный** capacious. **вмести́ть** (-ещу́) *pf* (*impf* **вмеща́ть**) hold, accommodate; put; ~**ся** go in.
вме́сто *prep*+*gen* instead of.
вмеша́тельство interference; intervention. **вмеша́ть** *pf*, **вме́шивать** *impf* mix in; implicate; ~**ся** interfere, intervene.
вмеща́ть(ся *impf of* **вмести́ть(ся**
вмиг *adv* in an instant.
вмина́ть *impf*, **вмять** (вомну́, -нёшь) *pf* press in, dent. **вмя́тина** dent.

внаём, внаймы *adv* to let; for hire.

вначáле *adv* at first.

вне *prep+gen* outside; ~ **себя** beside o.s.

вне- *pref* extra-; outside; -less. **внебрáчный** extra-marital; illegitimate. **~врéменный** timeless. **~клáссный** extracurricular. **~очереднóй** out of turn; extraordinary. **~штáтный** freelance, casual.

внедрéние introduction; inculcation. **внедрúть** *pf*, **внедрять** *impf* inculcate; introduce; **~ся** take root.

внезáпно *adv* suddenly. **внезáпный** sudden.

внéмлю *etc.: see* **внимáть**

внесéние bringing in; deposit. **внестú** (-сý, -сёшь; внёс, -лá) *pf* (*impf* **вносúть**) bring in; introduce; deposit; insert.

внéшне *adv* outwardly. **внéшний** outer; external; outside; foreign. **внéшность** exterior; appearance.

вниз *adv* down(wards); ~ **по+**dat down. **внизý** *adv* below; downstairs.

вникáть *impf*, **вникнуть** (-ну; вник) *pf* +в+acc go carefully into, investigate thoroughly.

внимáние attention. **внимáтельный** attentive. **внимáть** *impf* (*pf* **внять**) listen to; heed.

вничью *adv*: **окóнчиться** ~ end in a draw; **сыгрáть** ~ draw.

вновь *adv* anew, again.

вносúть (-ошý, -óсишь) *impf of* **внестú**

внук grandson; *pl* grandchildren, descendants.

внýтренний inner; internal. **внýтренность** interior; *pl* entrails; internal organs. **внутрú** *adv* & *prep+gen* inside. **внутрь** *adv* & *prep+gen* inside, in; inwards.

внучáта (*pl; gen* -чáт) grandchildren. **внучáтый** second, great-; ~ **брат** second cousin; ~ **племянник** greatnephew. **внýчка** grand-daughter.

внушáть *impf*, **внушúть** (-шý) *pf* instil; +dat inspire with. **внушéние** suggestion; reproof. **внушúтельный** inspiring; imposing.

внятный distinct. **внять** (*no fut*, -ял, -á, -о) *pf of* **внимáть**

во: *see* **в**

вобрáть (вберý, -рёшь; -áл, -á, -о)

pf (*impf* **вбирáть**) absorb; inhale.

вобью *etc.: see* **вбить**

вовлекáть *impf*, **вовлéчь** (-екý, -ечёшь; -ёк, -еклá) *pf* draw in, involve.

вóвремя *adv* in time; on time.

вóвсе *adv* quite; ~ **не** not at all.

во-вторы́х *adv* secondly.

вогнáть (вгоню́, -óнишь; -гнáл, -á, -о) *pf* (*impf* **вгонять**) drive in.

вóгнутый concave. **вогнýть** (-нý, -нёшь) *pf* (*impf* **вгибáть**) bend or curve inwards.

водá (*acc* вóду, *gen* -ы́; *pl* -ы) water; *pl* the waters; spa.

водворúть *pf*, **водворять** *impf* settle, install; establish.

водúтель *m* driver. **водúть** (вожý, вóдишь) *impf* lead; conduct; take; drive; **~ся** be found; associate (with); be the custom.

вóдка vodka. **вóдн|ый** water; **~ые лы́жи** water-skiing; water-skis.

водо- *in comb* water, water-; hydraulic; hydro-. **водобоязнь** hydrophobia. **~ворóт** whirlpool; maelstrom. **~ём** reservoir. **~измещéние** displacement. **~кáчка** water-tower, pumping station. **~лáз** diver. **~лéй** Aquarius. **~непроницáемый** waterproof. **~отвóдный** drainage. **~пáд** waterfall. **~пóй** watering-place. **~провóд** water-pipe, water-main; water supply. **~провóдчик** plumber. **~раздéл** watershed. **~рóд** hydrogen. **вóдоросль** water-plant; seaweed. **~снабжéние** water supply. **~стóк** drain, gutter. **~хранúлище** reservoir.

водружáть *impf*, **водрузúть** (-ужý) *pf* hoist; erect.

водянúстый watery. **водянóй** water.

воевáть (вою́ю) *impf* wage war.

воевóда *m* voivode; commander.

воединó *adv* together.

военкóм military commissar.

военно- *in comb* military; war-. **воéнно-воздýшный** air-, air-force. **воéнно-морскóй** naval. **~плéнный** *sb* prisoner of war. **воéннополевóй суд** court-martial. **~слýжащий** *sb* serviceman.

воéнн|ый military; war; *sb* serviceman; **~ое положéние** martial law;

~ый суд court-martial.

вожа́к (-á) guide; leader. **вожа́тый** *sb* guide; tram-driver.

вожделе́ние desire, lust.

вождь (-я́) *m* leader, chief.

вожжа́ (*pl* -и, -е́й) rein.

вожу́ etc.: see **води́ть**, **вози́ть**

воз (*loc* -ý, *pl* -ы́) cart; cart-load.

возбуди́мый excitable. **возбуди́тель** *m* agent; instigator. **возбуди́ть** (-ужу́) *pf*, **возбужда́ть** *impf* excite, arouse; incite. **возбужда́ющ|ий:** **~ее сре́дство** stimulant. **возбужде́ние** excitement. **возбуждённый** excited.

возвести́ (-еду́, -дёшь; -вёл, -ла́) *pf* (*impf* **возводи́ть**) elevate; erect; level; +к+*dat* trace to.

возвести́ть (-ещу́) *pf*, **возвеща́ть** *impf* proclaim.

возводи́ть (-ожу́, -о́дишь) *impf of* **возвести́**

возвра́т return; repayment. **возврати́ть** (-ащу́) *pf*, **возвраща́ть** *impf* (*pf also* **верну́ть**) return, give back; **~ся** return; go back, come back. **возвра́тный** return; reflexive. **возвраще́ние** return.

возвы́сить *pf*, **возвыша́ть** *impf* raise; ennoble; **~ся** rise. **возвыше́ние** rise; raised place. **возвы́шенность** height; loftiness. **возвы́шенный** high; elevated.

возгла́вить (-влю) *pf*, **возглавля́ть** *impf* head.

во́зглас exclamation. **возгласи́ть** (-ашу́) *pf*, **возглаша́ть** *impf* proclaim.

возгора́емый inflammable. **возгора́ться** *impf*, **возгоре́ться** (-рю́сь) *pf* flare up; be seized (with).

воздава́ть (-даю́, -даёшь) *impf*, **возда́ть** (-а́м, -а́шь, -а́ст, -ади́м; -а́л, -а́, -о) *pf* render.

воздвига́ть *impf*, **воздви́гнуть** (-ну; -дви́г) *pf* raise.

возде́йствие influence. **возде́йствовать** *impf & pf* +на+*acc* influence.

возде́лать *pf*, **возде́лывать** *impf* cultivate, till.

воздержа́ние abstinence; abstention. **возде́ржанный** abstemious. **воздержа́ться** (-жу́сь, -жишься) *pf*, **возде́рживаться** *impf* refrain; ab-

stain.

во́здух air. **воздухонепроница́емый** air-tight. **возду́шн|ый** air, aerial; airy; flimsy; **~ый змей** kite; **~ый шар** balloon.

воззва́ние appeal. **воззва́ть** (-зову́, -вёшь) *pf* (*impf* **взыва́ть**) appeal (о+*prep* for).

воззре́ние opinion, outlook.

вози́ть (вожу́, во́зишь) *impf* convey; carry; bring, take; **~ся** romp, play noisily; busy o.s.; potter about.

возлага́ть *impf of* **возложи́ть**

во́зле *adv & prep*+*gen* by, near; near by; past.

возложи́ть (-жу́, -жишь) *pf* (*impf* **возлага́ть**) lay; place.

возлю́бленный beloved; *sb* sweetheart.

возме́здие retribution.

возмести́ть (-ещу́) *pf*, **возмеща́ть** *impf* compensate for; refund. **возмеще́ние** compensation; refund.

возмо́жно *adv* possibly; +*comp* as ... as possible. **возмо́жность** possibility; opportunity. **возмо́жный** possible.

возмужа́лый mature; grown up. **возмужа́ть** *pf* grow up; gain strength.

возмути́тельный disgraceful. **возмути́ть** (-ущу́) *pf*, **возмуща́ть** *impf* disturb; stir up; rouse to indignation; **~ся** be indignant. **возмуще́ние** indignation. **возмущённый** (-щён, -щена́) indignant.

вознагради́ть (-ажу́) *pf*, **вознагражда́ть** *impf* reward. **вознагражде́ние** reward; fee.

возненави́деть (-и́жу) *pf* conceive a hatred for.

вознесе́ние Ascension. **вознести́** (-несу́, -несёшь; -нёс, -ла́) *pf* (*impf* **возноси́ть**) raise, lift up; **~сь** rise; ascend.

возника́ть *impf*, **возни́кнуть** (-нет; -ник) *pf* arise, spring up. **возникнове́ние** rise, beginning, origin.

возни́ца *m* coachman.

возноси́ть(ся (-ошу́(сь, -о́сишь(ся) *impf of* **вознести́(сь. возноше́ние** raising, elevation.

возня́ row, noise; bother.

возобнови́ть (-влю) *pf*, **возобновля́ть** *impf* renew; restore; **~ся**

begin again. **возобновле́ние** renewal; revival.

возража́ть *impf*, **возрази́ть** (-ажу́) *pf* object. **возраже́ние** objection.

во́зраст age. **возраста́ние** growth, increase. **возраста́ть** *impf*, **возрасти́** (-тёт; -ро́с, -ла́) *pf* grow, increase.

возроди́ть (-ожу́) *pf*, **возрожда́ть** *impf* revive; **∼ся** revive. **возрожде́ние** revival; Renaissance.

возро́с *etc.*: *see* **возрасти́**. **возро́сший** increased.

во́зчик carter, carrier.

возьму́ *etc.*: *see* **взять**

во́ин warrior; soldier. **во́инск|ий** military; **∼ая пови́нность** conscription. **во́инственный** warlike. **вои́нствующий** militant.

вой howl(ing); wail(ing).

войду́ *etc.*: *see* **войти́**

во́йлок felt. **во́йлочный** felt.

война́ (*pl* -ы) war.

во́йско (*pl* -а́) army; *pl* troops, forces. **войсково́й** military.

войти́ (-йду́, -йдёшь; вошёл, -шла́) *pf* (*impf* **входи́ть**) go in, come in, enter; get in(to).

вокза́л (railway) station.

во́кмен Walkman (*propr*), personal stereo.

вокру́г *adv & prep+gen* round, around.

вол (-а́) ox, bullock.

вола́н flounce; shuttlecock.

волды́рь (-я́) *m* blister; bump.

волево́й strong-willed.

волейбо́л volleyball.

во́лей-нево́лей *adv* willy-nilly.

волк (*pl* -и, -о́в) wolf. **волкода́в** wolf-hound.

волна́ (*pl* -ы, во́лна́м) wave. **волне́ние** choppiness; agitation; emotion. **волни́стый** wavy. **волнова́ть** *impf* (*pf* вз∼) disturb; agitate; excite; **∼ся** be disturbed; worry, be nervous. **волноло́м, волноре́з** breakwater. **волну́ющий** disturbing; exciting.

волоки́та red tape; rigmarole.

волокни́стый fibrous, stringy. **воло́кно́** (*pl* -а) fibre, filament.

волоку́ *etc.*: *see* **воло́чь**

во́лос (*pl* -ы, -о́с, -а́м); *pl* hair. **волоса́тый** hairy. **волосно́й** capillary.

во́лость (*pl* -и, -е́й) volost (*administrative division*).

волочи́ть (-очу́, -о́чишь) *impf* drag; **∼ся** drag, trail; **+за**+*instr* run after, court. **воло́чь** (-оку́, -очёшь; -о́к, -ла́) *impf* drag.

во́лчий wolf's; wolfish. **волчи́ха**, **волчи́ца** she-wolf.

волчо́к (-чка́) top; gyroscope.

волчо́нок (-нка; *pl* -ча́та, -ча́т) wolf cub.

волше́бник magician; wizard. **волше́бница** enchantress. **волше́бный** magic, magical; enchanting. **волшебство́** magic, enchantment.

вольнонаёмный civilian. **во́льность** liberty; license. **во́льный** (-лен, -льна́, -о, во́льны́) free; free-style.

вольт[1] (*gen pl* вольт) volt.

вольт[2] (*loc* -у́) vault.

вольфра́м tungsten.

во́ля will; liberty.

вомну́ *etc.*: *see* **вмять**

вон *adv* out; off, away.

вон *partl* there, over there.

вонза́ть *impf*, **вонзи́ть** (-нжу́) *pf* plunge, thrust.

вонь stench. **воню́чий** stinking. **воня́ть** stink.

вообража́емый imaginary. **воображи́ть** *impf*, **вообрази́ть** (-ажу́) *pf* imagine. **воображе́ние** imagination. **вообрази́мый** imaginable.

вообще́ *adv* in general; generally.

воодушеви́ть (-влю́) *pf*, **воодушевля́ть** *impf* inspire. **воодушевле́ние** inspiration; fervour.

вооружа́ть *impf*, **вооружи́ть** (-жу́) *pf* arm, equip; **∼ся** arm o.s.; take up arms. **вооруже́ние** arming; arms; equipment. **вооружённый** (-жён, -а́) armed; equipped.

воо́чию *adv* with one's own eyes.

во-пе́рвых *adv* first, first of all.

вопи́ть (-плю́) *impf* yell, howl. **вопию́щий** crying; scandalous.

воплоти́ть (-ощу́) *pf*, **воплоща́ть** *impf* embody. **воплоще́ние** embodiment.

вопль *m* cry, wail; howling.

вопреки́ *prep+dat* in spite of.

вопро́с question; problem. **вопроси́тельный** interrogative; questioning; **∼ знак** question-mark.

вор (pl -ы, -óв) thief; criminal.

ворва́ться (-ву́сь, -вёшься; -а́лся, -ла́сь, -ало́сь) pf (impf **врыва́ться**) burst in.

воркотня́ grumbling.

воробе́й sparrow.

орова́тый thievish; furtive. **ворова́ть** impf (pf с~) steal. **воро́вка** woman thief. **воро́вски** adv furtively. **воровско́й** thieves'. **воровство́** stealing; theft.

во́рон raven. **воро́на** crow.

воро́нка funnel; crater.

вороно́й black.

во́рот[1] collar; neckband.

во́рот[2] winch; windlass.

воро́та (pl; gen -ро́т) gate(s); gateway; goal.

вороти́ть (-очу́, -о́тишь) pf bring back, get back; turn back; ~**ся** return.

воротни́к (-а́) collar.

во́рох (pl -а́) heap, pile; heaps.

воро́чать impf turn; move; +instr have control of; ~**ся** move, turn.

ворочу́(сь etc.: see **вороти́ть(ся**

вороши́ть (-шу́) impf stir up; turn (over).

ворс nap, pile.

ворча́ть (-чу́) impf grumble; growl. **ворчли́вый** peevish; grumpy.

восвоя́си adv home.

восемна́дцатый eighteenth. **восемна́дцать** eighteen. **во́семь** (-сьми́, instr -семью or -семью́) eight. **во́семьдесят** eighty. **восемьсо́т** (-сьмисо́т, -стами́) eight hundred. **во́семью** adv eight times.

воск wax, beeswax.

воскли́кнуть (-ну) pf, **восклица́ть** impf exclaim. **восклица́ние** exclamation. **восклица́тельный** exclamatory; ~ **знак** exclamation mark.

восково́й wax; waxy; waxed.

воскреса́ть impf, **воскре́снуть** (-ну; -éc) pf rise from the dead; revive. **воскресе́ние** resurrection. **воскресе́нье** Sunday. **воскреси́ть** (-ешу́) pf, **воскреша́ть** impf resurrect; revive. **воскреше́ние** resurrection; revival.

воспале́ние inflammation. **воспалённый** (-лён, -а́) inflamed. **воспали́ть** pf, **воспаля́ть** impf inflame; ~**ся** become inflamed.

воспита́ние upbringing, education. **воспи́танник, -ница** pupil. **воспи́танный** well-brought-up. **воспита́тель** m tutor; educator. **воспита́тельный** educational. **воспита́ть** pf, **воспи́тывать** impf bring up; foster; educate.

воспламени́ть pf, **воспламеня́ть** impf ignite; fire; ~**ся** ignite; flare up. **воспламеня́емый** inflammable.

вос|по́льзоваться pf.

воспомина́ние recollection, memory; pl memoirs; reminiscences.

вос|препя́тствовать pf.

воспрети́ть (-ещу́) pf, **воспреща́ть** impf forbid. **воспреще́ние** prohibition. **воспрещённый** (-щён, -а́) prohibited.

восприи́мчивый impressionable; susceptible. **воспринима́ть** impf, **восприня́ть** (-иму́, -и́мешь; -йнял, -á, -о) pf perceive; grasp. **восприя́тие** perception.

воспроизведе́ние reproduction. **воспроизвести́** (-еду́, -едёшь; -вёл, -á) pf, **воспроизводи́ть** (-ожу́, -о́дишь) impf reproduce. **воспроизводи́тельный** reproductive. **воспроизво́дство** reproduction.

вос|проти́виться (-влюсь) pf.

воссоедине́ние reunification. **воссоедини́ть** pf, **воссоединя́ть** impf reunite.

восстава́ть (-таю́, -таёшь) impf of **восста́ть**.

восста́ние insurrection.

восстанови́ть (-влю́, -вишь) pf (impf **восстана́вливать**) restore; reinstate; recall; ~ **про́тив**+gen set against. **восстановле́ние** restoration.

восста́ть (-а́ну) pf (impf **восстава́ть**) rise (up).

восто́к east.

восто́рг delight, rapture. **восторга́ться**+instr be delighted with, go into raptures over. **восто́рженный** enthusiastic.

восто́чный east, eastern; easterly; oriental.

востре́бование: до востре́бования to be called for, poste restante.

восхвали́ть (-лю́, -лишь) pf, **восхваля́ть** impf praise, extol.

восхити́тельный entrancing; de-

lightful. **восхити́ть** (-хищу́) *pf*,
восхища́ть *impf* enrapture; ~ся
+*instr* be enraptured by. **восхи-
ще́ние** delight; admiration.
восхо́д rising. **восходи́ть** (-ожу́,
-о́дишь) *impf of* **взойти́**; ~ к+*dat* go
back to, date from. **восхожде́ние**
ascent. **восходя́щий** rising.
восше́ствие accession.
восьма́я *sb* eighth; octave. **вось-
ме́рка** eight; figure eight; No. 8; figure of eight.
восьми- *in comb* eight-; octo-. **восьм-
мигра́нник** octahedron. ~**деся́тый**
eightieth. ~**ле́тний** eight-year; eight-
year-old. ~**со́тый** eight-hundredth.
~**уго́льник** octagon. ~**уго́льный**
octagonal.
восьмо́й eighth.
вот *partl* here (is), there (is); this (is);
~ и всё and that's all; ~ как! no!
really? ~ так! that's right!; ~ что!
no! not really? **вот-во́т** *adv* just, on
the point of; *partl* that's right!
воткну́ть (-ну́, -нёшь) *pf* (*impf* **вты-
ка́ть**) stick in, drive in.
вотру́ *etc.*: *see* **втере́ть**
воцари́ться *pf*, **воцаря́ться** *impf*
come to the throne; set in.
вошёл *etc.*: *see* **войти́**
вошь (вши; *gen pl* вшей) louse.
вошью́ *etc.*: *see* **вшить**
вою́ *etc.*: *see* **выть**
вою́ю *etc.*: *see* **воева́ть**
впада́ть *impf*, **впасть** (-аду́) *pf* flow;
lapse; fall in; +в+*acc* verge on, approximate to. **впаде́ние** confluence,
(river-)mouth. **впа́дина** cavity, hollow; socket. **впа́лый** sunken.
впервы́е *adv* for the first time.
вперёд *adv* forward(s), ahead; in future; in advance; **идти́** ~ (*of clock*)
be fast. **впереди́** *adv* in front, ahead;
in (the) future; *prep*+*gen* in front of,
before.
впечатле́ние impression. **впечат-
ли́тельный** impressionable.
вписа́ть (-ишу́, -и́шешь) *pf*, **впи́сы-
вать** *impf* enter, insert; ~ся be en-
rolled, join.
впита́ть *pf*, **впи́тывать** *impf* absorb,
take in; ~ся soak.
впи́хивать *impf*, **впихну́ть** (-ну́,
-нёшь) *pf* cram in; shove.
вплавь *adv* (by) swimming.

вплести́ (-ету́, -етёшь; -ёл, -а́) *pf*,
вплета́ть *impf* plait in, intertwine;
involve.
вплотну́ю *adv* close; in earnest.
вплоть *adv*; ~ до+*gen* (right) up to.
вполго́лоса *adv* under one's breath.
вполне́ *adv* fully, entirely; quite.
впопыха́х *adv* hastily; in one's haste.
впо́ру *adv* at the right time; just right,
exactly.
впосле́дствии *adv* subsequently.
впотьма́х *adv* in the dark.
впра́ве *adv*: **быть** ~ have a right.
впра́во *adv* to the right (**от**+*gen* of).
впредь *adv* in (the) future; ~ до+*gen*
until.
впро́голодь *adv* half starving.
впро́чем *conj* however, but; though.
впры́скивание injection. **впры́ски-
вать** *impf*, **впры́снуть** (-ну) *pf* inject.
впряга́ть *impf* **впрячь** (-ягу́, -яжёшь;
-яг, -ла́) *pf* harness.
впуск admittance. **впуска́ть** *impf*,
впусти́ть (-ущу́, -у́стишь) *pf* admit,
let in.
впусту́ю *adv* to no purpose, in vain.
впущу́ *etc.*: *see* **впусти́ть**
враг (-а́) enemy. **вражда́** enmity.
вражде́бный hostile. **враждова́ть**
be at enmity. **вра́жеский** enemy.
вразбро́д *adv* separately, disunitedly.
вразре́з *adv*: **идти́** ~ с+*instr* go
against.
вразуми́тельный intelligible, clear;
persuasive.
враспло́х *adv* unawares.
враста́ть *impf*, **врасти́** (-тёт; врос,
-ла́) *pf* grow in; take root.
врата́рь (-я́) *m* goalkeeper.
врать (вру, врёшь; -ал, -а́, -о) *impf*
(*pf* **на**~, **со**~) lie, tell lies; talk nonsense.
врач (-а́) doctor. **враче́бный** medical.
враща́ть *impf* rotate, revolve; ~ся
revolve, rotate. **враще́ние** rotation,
revolution.
вред (-а́) harm; damage. **вреди́тель**
m pest; wrecker; *pl* vermin. **вре-
ди́тельство** wrecking, (act of) sabotage. **вреди́ть** (-ежу́) *impf* (*pf* **по**~)
+*dat* harm; damage. **вре́дный** (-ден,
-дна́, -о) harmful.
вре́зать (-е́жу) *pf*, **вре́за́ть** *impf* cut

in; set in; (*sl*) +*dat* hit; ~**ся** cut (into); run (into); be engraved; fall in love.

временами *adv* at times. **временно** *adv* temporarily. **временной** temporal. **временный** temporary; provisional. **время** (-мени; *pl* -мена, -мён, -ам) *neut* time; tense; ~ **года** season; ~ **от времени** at times, from time to time; **на** ~ for a time; **сколько времени?** what is the time?; **тем временем** meanwhile.

вровень *adv* level, on a level.

вроде *prep*+*gen* like; *partl* such as, like; apparently.

врождённый (-дён, -á) innate.

врознь, врозь *adv* separately, apart.

врос etc.: *see* **врасти́. вру** etc.: *see* **врать**

врун (-á), **врунья** liar.

вручать *impf*, **вручи́ть** (-чý) *pf* hand, deliver; entrust.

вручную *adv* by hand.

врыва́ть(ся *impf of* **ворва́ться**

вряд (ли) *adv* it's not likely; hardly, scarcely.

вса́ди́ть (-ажý, -а́дишь) *pf*, **вса́живать** *impf* thrust in; sink in. **вса́дник** rider, horseman. **вса́дница** rider, horsewoman. **вса́сывать** *impf of* **всоса́ть**

всё, все *pron*: *see* **весь**. **всё** *adv* always, all the time; ~ **(ещё)** still; *conj* however, nevertheless; ~ **же** all the same.

все- *in comb* all-, omni-. **всевозмо́жный** of every kind; all possible. ~**дозво́ленность** permissiveness. ~**ме́рный** of every kind. ~**ми́рный** world, world-wide. ~**могу́щий** omnipotent. ~**наро́дно** *adv* publicly. ~**наро́дный** national; nation-wide. ~**объе́млющий** comprehensive, all-embracing. ~**росси́йский** All-Russian. ~**си́льный** omnipotent. ~**сторо́нний** all-round; comprehensive.

всегда́ always.

всего́ *adv* in all, all told; only.

вселе́нная *sb* universe.

всели́ть *pf*, **вселя́ть** *impf* install, lodge; inspire; ~**ся** move in, install o.s.; be implanted.

всено́щная *sb* night service.

всео́бщий general, universal.

всерьёз *adv* seriously, in earnest.

всё-таки *conj & partl* all the same, still. **всецело** *adv* completely.

вска́кивать *impf of* **вскочи́ть**

вскачь *adv* at a gallop.

вскипа́ть *impf*, **вс|кипе́ть** (-плю) *pf* boil up; flare up.

вс|кипяти́ть(ся (-ячý(сь) *pf*.

всколыхну́ть (-нý, -нёшь) *pf* stir; stir up.

вско́льзь *adv* slightly; in passing.

вско́ре *adv* soon, shortly after.

вскочи́ть (-очý, -о́чишь) *pf* (*impf* **вска́кивать**) jump up.

вскри́кивать *impf*, **вскри́кнуть** (-ну) *pf* shriek, scream. **вскрича́ть** (-чý) *pf* exclaim.

вскрыва́ть *impf*, **вскрыть** (-ро́ю) *pf* open; reveal; dissect. **вскры́тие** opening; revelation; post-mortem.

вслед *adv & prep*+*dat* after; ~ **за**+*instr* after, following. **всле́дствие** *prep*+*gen* in consequence of.

вслепу́ю *adv* blindly; blindfold.

вслух *adv* aloud.

вслу́шаться *pf*, **вслу́шиваться** *impf* listen attentively.

всма́триваться *impf*, **всмотре́ться** (-рю́сь, -ри́шься) *pf* look closely.

всмя́тку *adv* soft(-boiled).

всо́вывать *impf of* **всу́нуть**

всоса́ть (-сý, -сёшь) *pf* (*impf* **вса́сывать**) suck in; absorb; imbibe.

вс|паха́ть (-ашý, -а́шешь) *pf*, **вспа́хивать** *impf* plough up. **вспа́шка** ploughing.

вс|пе́ниться *pf*.

всплеск splash. **всплёскивать** *impf*, **всплесну́ть** (-нý, -нёшь) *pf* splash; ~ **рука́ми** throw up one's hands.

всплыва́ть *impf*, **всплыть** (-ывý, -ывёшь; -ыл, -á, -о) *pf* rise to the surface; come to light.

вспомина́ть *impf*, **вспо́мнить** *pf* remember; ~**ся** *impers*+*dat*: **мне вспо́мнилось** I remembered.

вспомога́тельный auxiliary.

вс|поте́ть *pf*.

вспры́гивать *impf*, **вспры́гнуть** (-ну) *pf* jump up.

вспуха́ть *impf*, **вс|пу́хнуть** (-нет; -ух) *pf* swell up.

вспыли́ть *pf* flare up. **вспы́льчивый** hot-tempered.

вспы́хивать *impf*, **вспы́хнуть** (-ну)

pf blaze up; flare up. **вспышка** flash; outburst; outbreak.

вставать (-таю́, -таёшь) *impf of* **встать**

вста́вить (-влю) *pf*, **вставля́ть** *impf* put in, insert. **вста́вка** insertion; framing, mounting; inset. **вставн|о́й** inserted; set in; ~ые зу́бы false teeth.

встать (-а́ну) *pf (impf* **встава́ть**) get up; stand up.

встрево́женный *adj* anxious. **вс|трево́жить** (-жу) *pf*.

встрепену́ться (-ну́сь, -нёшься) *pf* rouse o.s.; start (up); beat faster.

встре́тить (-е́чу) *pf*, **встреча́ть** *impf* meet (with); ~ся meet; be found. **встре́ча** meeting. **встре́чный** coming to meet; contrary, head; counter; *sb* person met with; пе́рвый ~ the first person you meet, anybody.

встря́ска shaking; shock. **встря́хивать** *impf*, **встряхну́ть** (-ну́, -нёшь) *pf* shake (up); rouse; ~ся shake o.s.; rouse o.s.

вступа́ть *impf*, **вступи́ть** (-плю́, -пишь) *pf* +в+*acc* enter (into); join (in); +на+*acc* go up, mount; ~ся intervene; +за+*acc* stand up for. **вступи́тельный** introductory; entrance. **вступле́ние** entry, joining; introduction.

всу́нуть (-ну) *pf (impf* **всо́вывать**) put in, stick in.

всхли́пнуть (-ну) *pf*, **всхли́пывать** *impf* sob.

всходи́ть (-ожу́, -о́дишь) *impf of* **взойти́**. **всхо́ды** (*pl; gen* -ов) (corn-) shoots.

всю: *see* **весь**

всю́ду *adv* everywhere.

вся: *see* **весь**

вся́к|ий any; every, all kinds of; ~ом слу́чае in any case; на ~ий слу́чай just in case; *pron* anyone. **вся́чески** *adv* in every possible way.

вта́йне *adv* secretly.

вта́лкивать *impf of* **втолкну́ть**. **вта́птывать** *impf of* **втопта́ть**. **вта́скивать** *impf*, **втащи́ть** (-щу́, -щишь) *pf* drag in.

втере́ть (вотру́, вотрёшь; втёр) *pf (impf* **втира́ть**) rub in; ~ся insinuate o.s., worm o.s.

втира́ть(ся *impf of* **втере́ть(ся**

вти́скивать *impf*, **вти́снуть** (-ну) *pf* squeeze in; ~ся squeeze (o.s.) in.

втихомо́лку *adv* surreptitiously.

втолкну́ть (-ну́, -нёшь) *pf (impf* **вта́лкивать**) push in.

втопта́ть (-пчу́, -пчешь) *pf (impf* **вта́птывать**) trample (in).

вторга́ться *impf*, **вто́ргнуться** (-нусь; вто́ргся, -лась) *pf* invade; intrude. **вторже́ние** invasion; intrusion.

вто́рить *impf* play or sing second part; +*dat* repeat, echo. **втори́чный** second, secondary. **вто́рник** Tuesday. **втор|о́й** second; ~о́е *sb* second course. **второстепе́нный** secondary, minor.

второпя́х *adv* in haste.

в-тре́тьих *adv* thirdly. **втро́е** *adv* three times. **втроём** *adv* three (together). **втройне́** *adv* three times as much.

вту́лка plug.

втыка́ть *impf of* **воткну́ть**

втя́гивать *impf*, **втяну́ть** (-ну́, -нешь) *pf* draw in; ~ся +в+*acc* enter; get used to.

вуа́ль veil.

вуз *abbr (of* **вы́сшее уче́бное заведе́ние**) higher educational establishment; college.

вулка́н volcano.

вульга́рный vulgar.

вундерки́нд infant prodigy.

вход entrance; entry. **входи́ть** (-ожу́, -о́дишь) *impf of* **войти́**. **входно́й** entrance.

вхолосту́ю *adv* idle, free.

вцепи́ться (-плю́сь, -пишься) *pf*, **вцепля́ться** *impf* +в+*acc* clutch, catch hold of.

вчера́ *adv* yesterday. **вчера́шний** yesterday's.

вчерне́ in rough.

вче́тверо *adv* four times. **вчетверо́м** *adv* four (together).

вши *etc.: see* **вошь**

вшива́ть *impf of* **вшить**

вши́вый lousy.

вширь *adv* in breadth; widely.

вшить (вошью́, -ьёшь) *pf (impf* **вшива́ть**) sew in.

въе́дливый corrosive; caustic.

въезд entry; entrance. **въезжа́ть** *impf*, **въе́хать** (-е́ду, -е́дешь) *pf*

(+в+*acc*) ride in(to); drive in(to); crash into.

вы (вас, вам, ва́ми, вас) *pron* you.

выбега́ть *impf*, **вы́бежать** (-егу, -ежишь) *pf* run out.

вы́|белить *pf*.

вы́беру *etc.*: *see* **вы́брать**. **выбива́ть(ся** *impf of* **вы́бить(ся**. **выбира́ть(ся** *impf of* **вы́брать(ся**

вы́бить (-бью) *pf* (*impf* **выбива́ть**) knock out; dislodge; ~ся get out; break loose; come out; ~ся из сил exhaust o.s.

вы́бор choice; selection; *pl* election(s). **вы́борный** elective; electoral. **вы́борочный** selective.

вы́|бранить *pf*. **выбра́сывать(ся** *impf of* **вы́бросить(ся**

вы́брать (-беру) *pf* (*impf* **выбира́ть**) choose; elect; take out; ~ся get out.

выбрива́ть *impf*, **вы́брить** (-рею) *pf* shave.

вы́бросить (-ошу) *pf* (*impf* **выбра́сывать**) throw out; throw away; ~ся throw o.s. out, leap out.

выбыва́ть *impf*, **вы́быть** (-буду) *pf* из+*gen* leave, quit.

выва́ливать *impf*, **вы́валить** *pf* throw out; pour out; ~ся tumble out.

вы́везти (-зу; -ез) *pf* (*impf* **вывози́ть**) take, bring, out; export; rescue.

вы́верить *pf* (*impf* **выверя́ть**) adjust, regulate.

вы́вернуть (-ну) *pf*, **вывёртывать** *impf* turn inside out; unscrew; wrench.

выверя́ть *impf of* **вы́верить**

вы́весить (-ешу) *pf* (*impf* **выве́шивать**) weigh; hang out. **вы́веска** sign; pretext.

вы́вести (-еду; -ел) *pf* (*impf* **выводи́ть**) lead, bring, take, out; drive out; remove; exterminate; deduce; hatch; grow, breed; erect; depict; draw; ~сь go out of use; become extinct; come out; hatch out.

выве́тривание airing; weathering.

выве́шивать *impf of* **вы́весить**

вы́вих dislocation. **выви́хивать** *impf*, **вы́вихнуть** (-ну) *pf* dislocate.

вы́вод conclusion; withdrawal. **выводи́ть(ся** (-ожу(сь, -о́дишь(ся) *impf of* **вы́вести(сь. вы́водок** (-дка) brood; litter.

вывожу́ *see* **выводи́ть**, **вывози́ть**

вы́воз export; removal. **вывози́ть** (-ожу́, -о́зишь) *impf of* **вы́везти**. **вывозно́й** export.

вы́гадать *pf*, **выга́дывать** *impf* gain, save.

вы́гиб curve. **выгиба́ть** *impf of* **вы́гнуть**

вы́глядеть (-яжу) *impf* look, look like. **выгля́дывать** *impf*, **вы́глянуть** (-ну) *pf* look out; peep out.

вы́гнать (-гоню) *pf* (*impf* **выгоня́ть**) drive out; distil.

вы́гнутый curved, convex. **вы́гнуть** (-ну) *pf* (*impf* **выгиба́ть**) bend, arch.

выгова́ривать *impf*, **вы́говорить** *pf* pronounce, speak; +*dat* reprimand; ~ся speak out. **вы́говор** pronunciation; reprimand.

вы́года advantage; gain. **вы́годный** advantageous; profitable.

вы́гон pasture; common. **выгоня́ть** *impf of* **вы́гнать**

выгора́ть *impf*, **вы́гореть** (-рит) *pf* burn down; fade.

вы́|гравировать *pf*.

выгружа́ть *impf*, **вы́грузить** (-ужу) *pf* unload; disembark. **вы́грузка** unloading; disembarkation.

выдава́ть (-даю́, -даёшь) *impf*, **вы́дать** (-ам, -ашь, -аст, -адим) *pf* give (out); issue; betray; extradite; +за+*acc* pass off as; ~ся protrude; stand out; present itself. **вы́дача** issue; payment; extradition. **выдаю́щийся** prominent.

выдвига́ть *impf*, **вы́двинуть** (-ну) *pf* move out; pull out; put forward, nominate; ~ся move forward, move out; come out; get on (in the world). **выдвиже́ние** nomination; promotion.

выделе́ние secretion; excretion; isolation; apportionment. **вы́делить** *pf*, **выделя́ть** *impf* pick out; detach; allot; secrete; excrete; isolate; ~ ку́рсивом italicize; ~ся stand out, be noted (+*instr* for).

выдёргивать *impf of* **вы́дернуть**

вы́держанный consistent; self-possessed; firm; matured, seasoned. **вы́держать** (-жу) *pf*, **выдёрживать** *impf* bear; endure; contain o.s.; pass (*exam*); sustain. **вы́держка**[1] endurance; self-possession; exposure.

вы́держка² excerpt.

вы́дернуть (-ну) *pf* (*impf* **выдёргивать**) pull out.

вы́дохнуть (-ну) *pf* (*impf* **выдыха́ть**) breathe out; **~ся** have lost fragrance or smell; be past one's best.

вы́дра otter.

вы́|драть (-деру) *pf*. **вы́|дрессировать** *pf*.

выдува́ть *impf of* **вы́дуть**

вы́думанный made-up, fabricated.

вы́думать *pf*, **выду́мывать** *impf* invent; fabricate. **вы́думка** invention; device; inventiveness.

вы́|дуть *pf* (*impf also* **выдува́ть**) blow; blow out.

выдыха́ние exhalation. **выдыха́ть(ся** *impf of* **вы́дохнуть(ся**

вы́езд departure; exit. **выездн|о́й** exit; **~а́я се́ссия суда́** assizes.

выезжа́ть *impf of* **вы́ехать**

вы́емка taking out; excavation; hollow.

вы́ехать (-еду) *pf* (*impf* **выезжа́ть**) go out, depart; drive out, ride out; move (house).

вы́жать (-жму, -жмешь) *pf* (*impf* **выжима́ть**) squeeze out; wring out.

вы́жечь (-жгу) *pf* (*impf* **выжига́ть**) burn out; cauterize.

выжива́ние survival. **выжива́ть** *impf of* **вы́жить**

выжига́ть *impf of* **вы́жечь**

выжида́тельный waiting; temporizing.

выжима́ть *impf of* **вы́жать**

вы́жить (-иву) *pf* (*impf* **выжива́ть**) survive; hound out; **~ из ума́** become senile.

вы́звать (-зову) *pf* (*impf* **вызыва́ть**) call (out); send for; challenge; provoke; **~ся** volunteer.

выздора́вливать *impf*, **вы́здороветь** (-ею) *pf* recover. **вы́здоровле́ние** recovery; convalescence.

вы́зов call; summons; challenge.

вы́золоченный gilt.

вызу́бривать *impf*, **вы́|зубрить** *pf* learn by heart.

вызыва́ть(ся *impf of* **вы́звать(ся.** **вызыва́ющий** defiant; provocative.

вы́играть *pf*, **вы́и́грывать** *impf* win; gain. **вы́игрыш** win; gain; prize. **вы́игрышный** winning; lottery; advantageous.

вы́йти (-йду; -шел, -шла) *pf* (*impf* **выходи́ть**) go out; come out; get out; appear; turn out; be used up; have expired; **~ в свет** appear; **~ за́муж** (за+*acc*) marry; **~ из себя́** lose one's temper.

выка́лывать *impf of* **вы́колоть.**

выка́пывать *impf of* **вы́копать**

выка́рмливать *impf of* **вы́кормить**

вы́качать *pf*, **выка́чивать** *impf* pump out.

выки́дывать *impf*, **вы́кинуть** *pf* throw out, reject; put out; miscarry, abort; **~ флаг** hoist a flag. **вы́кидыш** miscarriage, abortion.

вы́кладка laying out; lay-out; facing; kit; computation, calculation. **вы́кла́дывать** *impf of* **вы́ложить**

выключа́тель *m* switch. **выключа́ть** *impf*, **вы́ключить** (-чу) *pf* turn off, switch off; remove, exclude.

выкола́чивать *impf*, **вы́колотить** (-лочу) *pf* knock out, beat out; beat; extort, wring out.

вы́колоть (-лю) *pf* (*impf* **выка́лывать**) put out; gouge out; tattoo.

вы́|копать *pf* (*impf also* **выка́пывать**) dig; dig up, dig out; exhume; unearth.

вы́кормить (-млю) *pf* (*impf* **выка́рмливать**) rear, bring up.

вы́корчевать (-чую) *pf*, **выкорчёвывать** *impf* uproot, root out; eradicate.

выкра́ивать *impf of* **вы́кроить**

вы́|красить (-ашу) *pf*, **выкра́шивать** *impf* paint; dye.

выкри́кивать *impf*, **вы́крикнуть** (-ну) *pf* cry out; yell.

вы́кроить *pf* (*impf* **выкра́ивать**) cut out; find (*time etc.*). **вы́кройка** pattern.

вы́крутить (-учу) *pf*, **выкру́чивать** *impf* unscrew; twist; **~ся** extricate o.s.

вы́куп ransom; redemption.

вы́|купать¹(ся *pf*.

выкупа́ть² *impf*, **вы́купить** (-плю) *pf* ransom, redeem.

вы́лазка sally, sortie; excursion.

выла́мывать *impf of* **вы́ломать**

вылеза́ть *impf*, **вы́лезти** (-зу; -лез) *pf* climb out; come out.

вы́|лепить (-плю) *pf*.

вы́лет flight; take-off. **вылета́ть**

impf, **вы́лететь** (-ечу) *pf* fly out; take off.

вылéчивать *impf*, **вы́лечить** (-чу) *pf* cure; ~ся recover, be cured.

вылива́ть(ся *pf of* **вы́лить(ся**

вы́|линять *pf*.

вы́лить (-лью) *pf* (*impf* **вылива́ть**) pour out; cast, found; ~ся flow (out); be expressed.

вы́ложить (-жу) *pf* (*impf* **выкла́дывать**) lay out.

вы́ломать *pf*, **вы́ломить** (-млю) *pf* (*impf* **выла́мывать**) break open.

вы́лупиться (-плюсь) *pf*, **вылупля́ться** *impf* hatch (out).

вы́лью *etc.*: *see* **вы́лить**

вы́|мазать (-мажу) *pf*, **вома́зывать** *impf* smear, dirty.

выма́нивать *impf*, **вы́манить** *pf* entice, lure.

вы́мереть (-мрет; -мер) *pf* (*impf* **вымира́ть**) die out; become extinct. **вы́мерший** extinct.

вы́мести (-ету) *pf*, **вы́метать** *impf* sweep (out).

вымога́тельство blackmail, extortion. **вымога́ть** *impf* extort.

вымока́ть *impf*, **вы́мокнуть** (-ну; -ок) *pf* be drenched; soak; rot.

вы́молвить (-влю) *pf* say, utter.

вы́|мостить (-ощу) *pf*. **вы́мою** *etc.*: *see* **вы́мыть**

вы́мпел pennant.

вы́мрет *see* **вы́мереть. вымыва́ть(ся** *impf of* **вы́мыть(ся**

вы́мысел (-сла) invention, fabrication; fantasy.

вы́|мыть (-мою) *pf* (*impf also* **вымыва́ть**) wash; wash out, off; wash away; ~ся wash o.s.

вы́мышленный fictitious.

вы́мя (-мени) *neut* udder.

вына́шивать *impf of* **вы́носить²**

вы́нести (-су; -нес) *pf* (*impf* **выноси́ть¹**) carry out, take out; carry away; endure.

вынима́ть(ся *impf of* **вы́нуть(ся**

вы́нос carrying out. **выноси́ть¹** (-ошу, -óсишь) *impf of* **вы́нести. выноси́ть²** *pf* (*impf* **вына́шивать**) bear; nurture. **вы́носка** carrying out; removal; footnote. **вы́носливость** endurance; hardiness.

вы́нудить (-ужу) *pf*, **вынужда́ть** *impf* force, compel. **вы́нужденный** forced.

вы́нуть (-ну) *pf* (*impf* **вынима́ть**) take out.

выпада́ть *impf of* **вы́пасть**

выпа́ливать *impf of* **вы́полоть**

выпа́ривать *impf*, **вы́парить** evaporate; steam.

выпа́рывать *impf of* **вы́пороть²**

вы́пасть (-аду; -ал) *pf* (*impf* **выпада́ть**) fall out; fall; occur, turn out; lunge.

выпека́ть *impf*, **вы́печь** (-еку; -ек) *pf* bake.

выпива́ть *impf of* **вы́пить**; enjoy a drink. **вы́пивка** drinking bout; drinks.

выпи́ливать *impf*, **вы́пилить** *pf* saw, cut out.

вы́писать (-ишу) *pf*, **выпи́сывать** *impf* copy out; write out; order; subscribe to; send for; ~ из больни́цы discharge from hospital; ~ся be discharged. **вы́писка** writing out; extract; ordering, subscription; discharge.

вы́|пить (-пью) *pf* (*impf also* **выпива́ть**) drink; drink up.

вы́плавить (-влю) *pf*, **выплавля́ть** *impf* smelt. **вы́плавка** smelting; smelted metal.

вы́плата payment. **вы́платить** (-ачу) *pf*, **выпла́чивать** *impf* pay (out); pay off.

выплёвывать *impf of* **вы́плюнуть**

выплыва́ть *impf*, **вы́плыть** (-ыву) *pf* swim out, sail out; emerge; crop up.

вы́плюнуть (-ну) *pf* (*impf* **выплёвывать**) spit out.

выполза́ть *impf*, **вы́ползти** (-зу; -олз) *pf* crawl out.

выполнéние execution, carrying out; fulfilment. **вы́полнить** *pf*, **выполня́ть** *impf* execute, carry out; fulfil.

вы́|полоскать (-ощу) *pf*.

вы́|полоть (-лю) *pf* (*impf also* **выпа́ливать**) weed out; weed.

вы́|пороть¹ (-рю) *pf*.

вы́пороть² (-рю) *pf* (*impf* **выпа́рывать**) rip out, rip up.

вы́|потрошить (-шу) *pf*.

вы́правка bearing; correction.

выпра́шивать *impf of* **вы́просить**; solicit.

выпровáживать *impf*, **вы́прово-**

дить (-ожу) *pf* send packing.

вы́просить (-ошу) *pf* (*impf* вы-**пра́шивать**) (ask for and) get.

выпряга́ть *impf of* вы́прячь

вы́прямить (-млю) *pf*, **выпрямля́ть** *impf* straighten (out); rectify; ~ся become straight; draw o.s. up.

вы́прячь (-ягу) -яг) *pf* (*impf* выпряга́ть) unharness.

вы́пуклый protuberant; bulging; convex.

вы́пуск output; issue; discharge; part, instalment; final-year students; omission. **выпуска́ть** *impf*, **вы́пустить** (-ущу) *pf* let out; issue; produce; omit. **выпускни́к** (-á), -и́ца final-year student. **выпускн|о́й** discharge; exhaust; ~о́й экза́мен finals, final examination.

вы́путать *pf*, **вы́путывать** *impf* disentangle; ~ся extricate o.s.

вы́пью *etc.: see* вы́пить

выраба́тывать *impf*, **вы́работать** *pf* work out; work up; draw up; produce, make; earn. **вы́работка** manufacture; production; working out; drawing up; output; make.

выра́внивать(ся *impf of* вы́ров-нять(ся

выража́ть *impf*, **вы́разить** (-ажу) *pf* express; ~ся express o.s. **выраже́ние** expression. **вырази́тельный** expressive.

выраста́ть *impf*, **вы́расти** (-ту; -рос) *pf* grow, grow up. **вы́растить** (-ащу) *pf*, **выра́щивать** *impf* bring up; breed; cultivate.

вы́рвать[1] (-ву) *pf* (*impf* вырыва́ть[2]) pull out, tear out; extort; ~ся break loose, break free; escape; shoot.

вы́|рвать[2] (-ву) *pf*.

вы́рез cut; décolletage. **вы́резать** (-ежу) *pf*, **выреза́ть**, **вырезы-вать** *impf* cut (out); engrave. **вы́-резка** cutting out, excision; cutting; fillet.

вы́ровнять *pf* (*impf* выра́внивать) level; straighten (out); draw up; ~ся become level; equalize; catch up.

вы́родиться *pf*, **вырожда́ться** *impf* degenerate. **вы́родок** (-дка) degenerate; black sheep. **выро-жде́ние** degeneration.

вы́ронить *pf* drop.

вы́рос *etc.: see* вы́расти

вы́рою *etc.: see* вы́рыть

выруба́ть *impf*, **вы́рубить** (-блю) *pf* cut down; cut (out); carve (out). **вы́рубка** cutting down; hewing out.

вы́|ругать(ся *pf.*

выру́ливать *impf*, **вы́|рулить** *pf* taxi.

выруча́ть *impf*, **вы́ручить** (-чу) *pf* rescue; help out; gain; make. **вы́руч-ка** rescue; gain; proceeds; earnings.

вырыва́ть[1] *impf*, **вы́рыть** (-рою) *pf* dig up, unearth.

вырыва́ть[2](ся *impf of* вы́рвать(ся

выса́дить (-ажу) *pf*, **выса́живать** *impf* set down; put ashore; transplant; smash; ~ся alight; disembark. **вы́-садка** disembarkation; landing; transplanting.

выса́сывать *impf of* вы́сосать

вы́свободить (-божу) *pf*, **высво-божда́ть** *impf* free; release.

высека́ть *impf of* вы́сечь[2]

выселе́ние eviction. **вы́селить** *pf*, **выселя́ть** *impf* evict; evacuate; move; ~ся move, remove.

вы́|сечь[1] (-еку; -сек) *pf.* **вы́сечь**[2] (-еку; -сек) *pf* (*impf* высека́ть) cut (out); carve.

вы́сидеть (-ижу) *pf*, **выси́живать** *impf* sit out; stay; hatch.

вы́ситься *impf* rise, tower.

выска́бливать *impf of* вы́скоблить

вы́сказать (-кажу) *pf*, **выска́зы-вать** *impf* express; state; ~ся speak out. **выска́зывание** utterance; pronouncement.

выска́кивать *impf of* вы́скочить

вы́скоблить *pf* (*impf* выска́бли-вать) scrape out; erase; remove.

вы́скочить (-чу) *pf* (*impf* выска́ки-вать) jump out; spring out; ~ c+*instr* come out with. **вы́скочка** upstart.

вы́слать (вы́шлю) *pf* (*impf* высыла́ть) send (out); exile; deport.

вы́следить (-ежу) *pf*, **высле́жи-вать** *impf* trace; shadow.

выслу́живать *impf*, **вы́служить** (-жу) *pf* qualify for; serve (out); ~ся gain promotion; curry favour.

вы́слушать *pf*, **выслу́шивать** *impf* hear out; sound; listen to.

высме́ивать *impf*, **вы́смеять** (-ею) *pf* ridicule.

вы́|сморкать(ся *pf.* **высо́вывать-(ся** *impf of* вы́сунуть(ся

высо́кий (-о́к, -а́, -о́ко́) high; tall; lofty; elevated.

высоко- *in comb* high-, highly. **высокоблагоро́дие** (your) Honour, Worship. **~во́льтный** high-tension. **~го́рный** mountain. **~ка́чественный** high-quality. **~квалифици́рованный** highly qualified. **~ме́рие** haughtiness. **~ме́рный** haughty. **~па́рный** high-flown; bombastic. **~часто́тный** high-frequency.

вы́сосать (-осу) *pf* (*impf* **выса́сывать**) suck out.

высота́ (*pl* -ы) height, altitude. **высо́тный** high-altitude; high-rise.

вы́|сохнуть (-ну; -ох) *pf* (*impf also* **высыха́ть**) dry (out); dry up; wither (away).

вы́спаться (-плюсь, -пишься) *pf* (*impf* **высыпа́ться²**) have a good sleep.

вы́ставить (-влю) *pf*, **выставля́ть** *impf* display, exhibit; post; put forward; set down; take out; +*instr* represent as; **~ся** show off. **вы́ставка** exhibition.

выста́ивать *impf of* **вы́стоять**

вы́|стегать *pf*. **вы́|стирать** *pf*.

вы́стоять (-ою) *pf* (*impf* **выста́ивать**) stand; stand one's ground.

вы́страдать *pf* suffer; gain through suffering.

выстра́ивать(ся *impf of* **вы́строить(ся**

вы́стрел shot; report. **вы́стрелить** *pf* shoot, fire.

вы́|строгать *pf*.

вы́строить *pf* (*impf* **выстра́ивать**) build; draw up, order, arrange; form up. **~ся** form up.

вы́ступ protuberance, projection. **выступа́ть** *impf*, **вы́ступить** (-плю) come forward; come out; perform; speak; +*из+gen* go beyond. **выступле́ние** appearance, performance; speech; setting out.

вы́сунуть (-ну) *pf* (*impf* **высо́вывать**) put out, thrust out; **~ся** show o.s., thrust o.s. forward.

вы́|сушить(ся (-шу(сь) *pf*.

вы́сший highest; high; higher.

высыла́ть *impf of* **вы́слать**. **вы́сылка** sending, dispatch; expulsion, exile.

вы́сыпать (-плю) *pf*, **высыпа́ть**

impf pour out; spill; **~ся¹** pour out; spill.

высыпа́ться² *impf of* **вы́спаться**

высыха́ть *impf of* **вы́сохнуть**

высь height; summit.

выта́лкивать *impf of* **вы́толкать**, **вы́толкнуть**. **выта́скивать** *impf of* **вы́тащить**. **выта́чивать** *impf of* **вы́точить**

вы́|тащить (-щу) *pf* (*impf also* **выта́скивать**) drag out; pull out.

вы́|твердить (-ржу) *pf*.

вытека́ть *impf* (*pf* **вы́течь**); **~ из+gen** flow from, out of; result from.

вы́тереть (-тру; -тер) *pf* (*impf* **вытира́ть**) wipe (up); dry; wear out.

вы́терпеть (-плю) *pf* endure.

вы́тертый threadbare.

вы́теснить *pf*, **вытесня́ть** *impf* force out; oust; displace.

вы́течь (-чет; -ек) *pf* (*impf* **вытека́ть**) flow out, run out.

вытира́ть *impf of* **вы́тереть**

вы́толкать *pf*, **вы́толкнуть** (-ну) *pf* (*impf* **выта́лкивать**) throw out; push out.

вы́точенный turned. **вы́|точить** (-чу) *pf* (*impf also* **выта́чивать**) turn; sharpen; gnaw through.

вы́|травить (-влю) *pf*, **вытра́вливать** *impf*, **вытравля́ть** *impf* exterminate, destroy; remove; etch; trample down, damage.

вытрезви́тель *m* detoxification centre. **вы́трезвить(ся** (-влю(сь) *pf*, **вытрезвля́ть(ся** *impf* sober up.

вы́тру *etc.: see* **вы́тереть**

вы́|трясти (-су; -яс) *pf* shake out.

вытря́хивать *impf*, **вытряхнуть** (-ну) *pf* shake out.

выть (во́ю) *impf* howl; wail.

вытя́гивать *impf*, **вы́тянуть** (-ну) *pf* stretch (out); extend; extract; endure; **~ся** stretch, stretch out, stretch o.s.; shoot up; draw o.s. up. **вытя́жка** drawing out, extraction; extract.

вы́|утюжить (-жу) *pf*.

вы́учивать *impf*, **вы́учить** (-чу) *pf* learn; teach; **~ся** +*dat or inf* learn.

выха́живать *impf of* **вы́ходить²**

вы́хватить (-ачу) *pf*, **выхва́тывать** *impf* snatch out, up, away; pull out.

вы́хлоп exhaust. **выхлопно́й** exhaust, discharge.

вы́ход going out; departure; way out,

exit; vent; appearance; yield; ~ **за́муж** marriage. **вы́ходец** (-дца) emigrant; immigrant. **выходи́ть**[1] (-ожу́, -о́дишь) *impf of* вы́йти; +**на**+*acc* look out on.

выходи́ть[2] (-ожу) *pf* (*impf* вы́-ха́живать) nurse; rear, bring up. **вы́ходка** trick; prank.

выходн|о́й exit; going-out, outgoing; discharge; ~**о́й день** day off; ~**о́й** *sb* person off duty; day off. **выхожу́** *etc.*: *see* **выходи́ть**[1]. **вы́хожу** *etc.*: *see* **вы́ходить**[2]

вы́цвести (-ветет) *pf* (*impf* выцвета́ть *impf* fade. **вы́цветший** faded.

вычёркивать *impf*, **вы́черкнуть** (-ну) *pf* cross out.

вы́черпать *pf*, **вычёрпывать** *impf* bale out.

вы́честь (-чту; -чел, -чла) *pf* (*impf* вычита́ть) subtract. **вы́чет** deduction. **вычисле́ние** calculation. **вычисли́-тель** *m* calculator. **вычисли́тель-н|ый** calculating, computing; ~**ая маши́на** computer. **вы́числить** *pf*, **вычисля́ть** *impf* calculate, compute. **вы́|чистить** (-ищу) *pf* (*impf also* вычища́ть) clean, clean up. **вычита́ние** subtraction. **вычита́ть** *impf of* **вы́честь** **вычища́ть** *impf of* **вы́чистить**. **вы́чту** *etc.*: *see* **вы́честь**

вы́швырнуть (-ну) *pf*, **вышвы́ри-вать** *impf* chuck out.

вы́ше higher, taller; *prep*+*gen* be-yond; over; *adv* above.

вы́ше- *in comb* above-, afore-. **вы́-шеизло́женный** foregoing. ~**на́-званный** afore-named. ~**ска́занный**, ~**ука́занный** aforesaid. ~**упомя́-нутый** afore-mentioned.

вы́шел *etc.*: *see* **вы́йти**

вышиба́ла *m* chucker-out. **вышиба́ть** *impf*, **вы́шибить** (-бу; -иб) *pf* knock out; chuck out.

вышива́ние embroidery, needle-work. **вышива́ть** *impf of* **вы́шить**. **вы́шивка** embroidery.

вышина́ height.

вы́шить (-шью) *pf* (*impf* вышива́ть) embroider. **вы́шитый** embroidered. **вы́шка** tower; (**бурова́я**) ~ derrick. **вы́шлю** *etc.*: *see* **вы́слать**. **вы́шью** *etc.*: *see* **вы́шить**

вы́явить (-влю) *pf*, **выявля́ть** *impf*

reveal; make known; expose; ~**ся** be revealed.

выясне́ние elucidation; explanation. **вы́яснить** *pf*, **выясня́ть** *impf* elu-cidate; explain; ~**ся** become clear; turn out.

Вьетна́м Vietnam. **вьетна́мец**, **-мка** Vietnamese. **вьетна́мский** Viet-namese.

вью *etc.*: *see* **вить**

вью́га snow-storm, blizzard.

вьюно́к (-нка́) bindweed.

вьючн|ый pack; ~**ое живо́тное** beast of burden.

вью́щийся climbing; curly.

вяжу́ *etc.*: *see* **вяза́ть**. **вя́жущий** bind-ing; astringent.

вяз elm.

вяза́ние knitting, crocheting; binding, tying. **вяза́нка**[1] knitted garment. **вяза́нка**[2] bundle. **вя́заный** knitted, crocheted. **вяза́нье** knitting, cro-chet(-work). **вяза́ть** (вяжу́, вя́жешь) *impf* (*pf* с~) tie, bind; knit, crochet; be astringent; ~**ся** accord; tally. **вя́з-ка** tying; knitting, crocheting; bunch. **вя́зкий** (-зок, -зка́, -о) viscous; sticky; boggy. **вя́знуть** (-ну; вяз(нул), -зла) *impf* (*pf* за~, у~) stick, get stuck. **вя́зовый** elm.

вязь ligature; arabesque.

вя́леный dried; sun-cured.

вя́лый limp; sluggish; slack. **вя́нуть** (-ну; вял) *impf* (*pf* за~, у~) fade, wither; flag.

Г

г. *abbr* (*of* год) year; (*of* го́род) city; (*of* господи́н) Mr.

г *abbr* (*of* грамм) gram.

га *abbr* (*of* гекта́р) hectare.

га́вань harbour.

гага́чий пух eiderdown.

гад reptile; repulsive person; *pl.* vermin. **гада́лка** fortune-teller. **гада́ние** for-tune-telling; guess-work. **гада́ть** *impf* (*pf* по~) tell fortunes; guess.

га́дина reptile; repulsive person; *pl.* vermin. **га́дить** (га́жу) *impf* (*pf* на~) +**в**+*prep*, **на**+*acc*, *prep* foul, dirty, de-file. **га́дкий** (-док, -дка́, -о) nasty, vile, repulsive. **га́дость** filth, muck; dirty trick; *pl* filthy expressions.

гадю́ка adder, viper; repulsive person.

га́ечный ключ spanner, wrench.

газ¹ gauze.

газ² gas; wind; дать ∼ step on the gas; сба́вить ∼ reduce speed.

газе́та newspaper. газе́тчик journalist; newspaper-seller.

газиро́ванный aerated. га́зовый gas.

газо́н lawn. газонокоси́лка lawn-mower.

газопрово́д gas pipeline; gas-main.

га́йка nut; female screw.

гала́ктика galaxy.

галантере́йный магази́н haberdasher's. галантере́я haberdashery.

гала́нтный gallant.

галере́я gallery. галёрка gallery, gods.

галифе́ indecl pl riding-breeches.

га́лка jackdaw.

галлюцина́ция hallucination.

гало́п gallop.

га́лочка tick.

га́лстук tie; neckerchief.

галу́шка dumpling.

га́лька pebble; pebbles, shingle.

гам din, uproar.

гама́к (-а́) hammock.

га́мма scale; gamut; range.

гангре́на gangrene.

га́нгстер gangster.

ганте́ль f dumb-bell.

гара́ж (-а́) garage.

гаранти́ровать impf & pf guarantee. гара́нтия guarantee.

гардеро́б wardrobe; cloakroom. гардеро́бщик, -щица cloakroom attendant.

гарди́на curtain.

гармонизи́ровать impf & pf harmonize.

гармо́ника accordion, concertina. гармони́ческий, гармони́чный harmonious. гармо́ния harmony; concord. гармо́нь accordion, concertina.

гарнизо́н garrison.

гарни́р garnish; vegetables.

гарниту́р set; suite.

гарь burning; cinders.

гаси́тель m extinguisher; suppressor. гаси́ть (гашу́, га́сишь) impf (pf за∼, по∼) extinguish; suppress. га́снуть (-ну; гас) impf (pf за∼, по∼, у∼) be extinguished, go out; grow feeble.

гастро́ли f pl tour; guest-appearance, performance. гастроли́ровать impf (be on) tour.

гастроно́м gourmet; provision shop. гастрономи́ческий gastronomic; provision. гастроно́мия gastronomy; provisions; delicatessen.

гауптва́хта guardroom.

гаши́ш hashish.

гварде́ец (-е́йца) guardsman. гварде́йский guards'. гва́рдия Guards.

гво́здик tack. гвозди́ка pink(s), carnation(s); cloves. гво́здики (-ов) pl stilettos. гвоздь (-я́; pl -и, -е́й) m nail; tack; crux; highlight, hit.

гг. abbr (of го́ды) years.

где adv where; ∼ бы ни wherever. где́-либо adv anywhere. где́-нибудь adv somewhere; anywhere. где́-то adv somewhere.

гекта́р hectare.

ге́лий helium.

гемоглоби́н haemoglobin.

геморро́й haemorrhoids. гемофили́я haemophilia.

ген gene.

ге́незис origin, genesis.

генера́л general. генера́льн|ый general; ∼ая репети́ция dress rehearsal.

генера́тор generator.

генера́ция generation; oscillation.

гене́тика genetics. генети́ческий genetic.

гениа́льный brilliant. ге́ний genius.

гео- in comb geo-. гео́граф geographer. ∼графи́ческий geographical. ∼гра́фия geography. гео́лог geologist. ∼логи́ческий geological. ∼ло́гия geology. ∼метри́ческий geometric. ∼ме́трия geometry.

георги́н dahlia.

геофи́зика geophysics.

гепа́рд cheetah.

гепати́т hepatitis.

гера́нь geranium.

герб arms, coat of arms. ге́рбов|ый heraldic; ∼ая печа́ть official stamp.

геркуле́с Hercules; rolled oats.

герма́нец (-нца) ancient German. Герма́ния Germany. герма́нский Germanic.

гермафроди́т hermaphrodite.

R герметичный hermetic; hermetically sealed; air-tight.

геройзм heroism. **геройня** heroine. **геройческий** heroic. **герой** hero. **геройский** heroic.

герц (*gen pl* герц) hertz.

ге́рцог duke. **герцоги́ня** duchess.

г-жа *abbr* (*of* госпожа́) Mrs.; Miss.

гиаци́нт hyacinth.

ги́бель death; destruction, ruin; loss; wreck; downfall. **ги́бельный** disastrous, fatal.

ги́бкий (-бок, -бка́, -бко) flexible, adaptable, versatile; supple. **ги́бкость** flexibility; suppleness.

ги́бнуть (-ну; гиб(нул)) *impf* (*pf* по~) perish.

гибри́д hybrid.

гига́нт giant. **гига́нтский** gigantic.

гигие́на hygiene. **гигиени́ческий, -и́чный** hygienic, sanitary.

гид guide.

гидравли́ческий hydraulic.

гидро- *pref* hydro-. **~электроста́нция** hydro-electric power-station.

гие́на hyena.

ги́льза cartridge-case; sleeve; (cigarette-)wrapper.

гимн hymn.

гимна́зия grammar school, high school.

гимна́ст gymnast. **гимна́стика** gymnastics. **гимнасти́ческий** gymnastic.

гинеко́лог gynaecologist. **гинеколо́гия** gynaecology.

гипе́рбола hyperbole.

гипно́з hypnosis. **гипнотизёр** hypnotist. **гипнотизи́ровать** *impf* (*pf* за~) hypnotize. **гипноти́ческий** hypnotic.

гипо́теза hypothesis. **гипотети́ческий** hypothetical.

гиппопота́м hippopotamus.

гипс gypsum, plaster (of Paris); plaster cast. **ги́псовый** plaster.

гирля́нда garland.

ги́ря weight.

гистерэктоми́я hysterectomy.

гита́ра guitar.

гл. *abbr* (*of* глава́) chapter.

глав- *abbr in comb* head, chief, main.

глава́ (*pl* -ы) head; chief; chapter; cupola. **глава́рь** (-я́) *m* leader, ringleader. **главк** central directorate. **главнокома́ндующий** *sb* commander-in-chief. **гла́вн|ый** chief, main; ~ым о́бразом chiefly, mainly,

for the most part; ~ое *sb* the main thing; the essentials.

глаго́л verb.

гла́дить (-а́жу) *impf* (*pf* вы́~, по~) stroke; iron. **гла́дкий** smooth; plain. **гла́дко** *adv* smoothly. **гладь** smooth surface.

глаз (*loc* -у́; *pl* -а́, глаз) eye; в ~а́ to one's face; за ~а́+*gen* behind the back of; смотре́ть во все ~а́ be all eyes.

глазиро́ванный glazed; glossy; iced; glacé.

глазни́ца eye-socket. **глазно́й** eye; optic; ~ врач oculist. **глазо́к** (-зка́) peephole.

глазу́нья fried eggs.

глазу́рь glaze; syrup; icing.

гла́нды (гланд) *pl* tonsils.

гла́сность publicity; glasnost, openness. **гла́сный** public; vowel; *sb* vowel.

гли́на clay. **гли́нистый** clayey. **гли́няный** clay; earthenware; clayey.

гли́ссер speed-boat.

глист (*intestinal*) worm.

глицери́н glycerine.

гло́бус globe.

глота́ть *impf* swallow. **гло́тка** gullet; throat. **глото́к** (-тка́) gulp; mouthful.

гло́хнуть (-ну; глох) *impf* (*pf* за~, о~) become deaf; die away, subside; grow wild.

глубина́ (*pl* -ы) depth; heart, interior. **глубо́кий** (-о́к, -а́, -о́кó) deep; profound; late, advanced; extreme. **глубокомы́слие** profundity. **глубокоуважа́емый** (*in formal letters*) dear.

глуми́ться (-млю́сь) *impf* mock, jeer (над+*instr* at). **глумле́ние** mockery.

глупе́ть (-е́ю) *impf* (*pf* по~) grow stupid. **глупе́ц** (-пца́) fool. **глу́пость** stupidity. **глу́пый** (глуп, -а́, -о) stupid.

глуха́рь (-я́) *m* capercaillie. **глух|о́й** (глух, -а́, -о) deaf; muffled; obscure; vague; dense; wild; remote; deserted; sealed; blank; ~о́й, ~а́я *sb* deaf man, woman. **глухонемо́й** deaf and dumb; *sb* deaf mute. **глухота́** deafness. **глуши́тель** *m* silencer. **глуши́ть** (-шу́) *impf* (*pf* за~, о~) stun; muffle; dull; jam; extinguish; stifle;

suppress. **глушь** backwoods.

глы́ба clod; lump, block.

глюко́за glucose.

гляде́ть (-яжу́) *impf* (*pf* по~, гля́нуть) look, gaze, peer; ~ в о́ба be on one's guard; (того́ и) гляди́ it looks as if; I'm afraid; **гля́дя** по+*dat* depending on.

гля́нец (-нца) gloss, lustre; polish.

гля́нуть (-ну) *pf* (*impf* **гляде́ть**) glance.

гм *int* hm!

г-н *abbr* (*of* **господи́н**) Mr.

гнать (гоню́, го́нишь; гнал, -á, -o) *impf* drive; urge (on); hunt, chase; persecute; distil; ~ся за+*instr* pursue.

гнев anger, rage. **гне́ваться** *impf* (*pf* раз~) be angry. **гне́вный** angry.

гнедо́й bay.

гнездо́ (*pl* гнёзда) nest.

гнёт weight; oppression. **гнету́щий** oppressive.

гни́да nit.

гние́ние decay, putrefaction, rot. **гнило́й** (-и́л, -á, -o) rotten; muggy. **гнить** (-ию́, -иёшь; -и́л, -á, -o) *impf* (*pf* с~) rot. **гное́ние** suppuration. **гно́иться** *impf* (*pf* с~) suppurate, discharge matter. **гной** pus. **гно́йник** abscess; ulcer. **гно́йный** purulent.

гну́сный (-сен, -сна́, -o) vile, foul.

гнуть (гну, гнёшь) *impf* (*pf* со~) bend; aim at; ~ся bend; stoop.

гнуша́ться *impf* (*pf* по~) disdain; +*gen or instr* shun; abhor.

гобеле́н tapestry.

гобо́й oboe.

гове́ть (-е́ю) *impf* fast.

говно́ (*vulg*) shit.

говори́ть *impf* (*pf* по~, сказа́ть) speak, talk; say; tell; ~ся: как говори́тся as they say.

говя́дина beef. **говя́жий** beef.

го́гот cackle; loud laughter. **гогота́ть** (-очу́, -о́чешь) *impf* cackle; roar with laughter.

год (*loc* -у́; *pl* -ы or -á, *gen* -о́в or лет) year. **года́ми** *adv* for years (on end).

годи́ться, (-жу́сь) *impf* be fit, suitable; serve.

годи́чный a year's; annual.

го́дный (-ден, -дна́, -o, -ы or -ы́) fit, suitable; valid.

годова́лый one-year-old. **годово́й** annual. **годовщи́на** anniversary.

гожу́сь *etc.*: *see* **годи́ться**

гол goal.

голени́ще (boot-)top. **го́лень** shin.

голла́ндец (-дца) Dutchman. **Голла́ндия** Holland. **голла́ндка** Dutchwoman; tiled stove. **голла́ндский** Dutch.

голова́ (*acc* го́лову; *pl* го́ловы, -о́в -áм) head. **голова́стик** tadpole. **голо́вка** head; cap, nose, tip. **головн|о́й** head; leading; ~а́я боль headache; ~о́й мозг brain, cerebrum; ~о́й убо́р headgear, headdress. **головокруже́ние** giddiness, dizziness. **головоло́мка** puzzle. **головоре́з** cut-throat; rascal.

го́лод hunger; famine; acute shortage. **голода́ние** starvation; fasting. **голода́ть** *impf* go hungry, starve; fast. **голо́дный** (го́лоден, -дна́, -o, -ы or -ы́) hungry. **голодо́вка** hunger-strike.

гололёд, гололе́дица (period of) black ice.

го́лос (*pl* -á) voice; part; vote. **голоси́ть** (-ошу́) *impf* sing loudly; cry; wail. **голосло́вный** unsubstantiated, unfounded.

голосова́ние voting; poll. **голосова́ть** *impf* (*pf* про~) vote; vote on.

голу́бка pigeon; (my) dear, darling. **голубо́й** light blue. **голу́бчик** my dear (fellow); darling. **го́лубь** *m* pigeon, dove. **голубя́тня** (*gen pl* -тен) dovecot, pigeon-loft.

го́лый (гол, -лá, -ло) naked, bare.

гомоге́нный homogeneous.

го́мон hubbub.

гомосексуали́ст homosexual. **гомосексуа́льный** homosexual.

гондо́ла gondola.

гоне́ние persecution. **го́нка** race; dashing; haste.

гонора́р fee.

го́ночный racing.

гонча́р (-á) potter.

го́нщик racer. **гоню́** *etc.*: *see* **гнать**.

гоня́ть *impf* drive; send on errands; ~ся +за+*instr* chase, hunt.

гора́ (*acc* го́ру; *pl* го́ры, -áм) mountain; hill; в го́ру uphill; под го́ру downhill.

гора́здо *adv* much, far, by far.

горб (-á, *loc* -ý) hump; bulge. **гор-ба́тый** hunchbacked. **го́рбить** (-блю) *impf* (*pf* с~) arch, hunch; ~ся stoop. **горбу́н** (-á) *m*, **горбу́нья** (*gen pl* -ний) hunchback. **горбу́шка** (*gen pl* -шек) crust (*of loaf*).

горди́ться (-ржу́сь) *impf* put on airs; +*instr* be proud of. **го́рдость** pride. **го́рдый** (горд, -á, -о, го́рды) proud. **горды́ня** arrogance.

го́ре grief, sorrow; trouble. **горева́ть** (-рю́ю) *impf* grieve.

горе́лка burner. **горе́лый** burnt. **горе́ние** burning, combustion; enthusiasm.

го́рестный sad; mournful. **го́ресть** sorrow; *pl* misfortunes.

горе́ть (-рю́) *impf* (*pf* с~) burn.

го́рец (-рца) mountain-dweller.

го́речь bitterness; bitter taste.

горизо́нт horizon. **горизонта́ль** horizontal. **горизонта́льный** horizontal.

гори́стый mountainous, hilly. **го́рка** hill; hillock; steep climb.

го́рло throat; neck. **горлово́й** throat; guttural; raucous. **го́рлышко** neck.

гормо́н hormone.

горн[1] furnace, forge.

горн[2] bugle.

го́рничная *sb* maid, chambermaid.

горнорабо́чий *sb* miner.

горноста́й ermine.

го́рный mountain; mountainous; mineral; mining. **горня́к** (-á) miner.

го́род (*pl* -á) town; city. **городо́к** (-дка́) small town. **городско́й** urban; city; municipal. **горожа́нин** (*pl* -áне, -áн) *m*, **-жа́нка** town-dweller.

гороско́п horoscope.

горо́х pea, peas. **горо́шек** (-шка) spots, spotted pattern; души́стый ~ sweet peas; зелёный ~ green peas. **горо́шина** pea.

горсове́т *abbr* (*of* городско́й сове́т) city soviet, town soviet.

горсть (*gen pl* -éй) handful.

горта́нный guttural. **горта́нь** larynx.

горчи́ца mustard. **горчи́чник** mustard plaster.

горшо́к (-шка́) flowerpot; pot; potty; chamber-pot.

го́рький (-рек, -рька́, -о) bitter.

горю́ч|ий combustible; ~ee *sb* fuel. **горя́чий** (-ря́ч, -á) hot; passionate;

ardent.

горячи́ться (-чу́сь) *impf* (*pf* раз~) get excited. **горя́чка** fever; feverish haste. **горя́чность** zeal.

гос- *abbr in comb* (*of* госуда́рственный) state.

го́спиталь *m* (military) hospital.

го́споди *int* good heavens! **господи́н** (*pl* -ода́, -о́д, -áм) master; gentleman; Mr; *pl* ladies and gentlemen.

госпо́дство supremacy. **госпо́дствовать** *impf* hold sway; prevail. **Госпо́дь** (Го́спода, *voc* Го́споди) *m* God, the Lord. **госпожа́** lady; Mrs.

гостеприи́мный hospitable. **гостеприи́мство** hospitality. **гости́ная** *sb* drawing-room, sitting-room. **гости́ница** hotel. **гости́ть** (гощу́) *impf* stay, be on a visit. **гость** (*gen pl* -éй) *m*, **го́стья** (*gen pl* -ий) guest, visitor.

госуда́рственный State, public. **госуда́рство** State. **госуда́рыня**, **госуда́рь** *m* sovereign; Your Majesty.

готи́ческий Gothic.

гото́вить (-влю) *impf* (*pf* с~) prepare; ~ся prepare (o.s.); be at hand. **гото́вность** readiness, willingness. **гото́вый** ready.

гофриро́ванный corrugated; waved; pleated.

грабёж robbery; pillage. **граби́тель** *m* robber. **граби́тельский** predatory; exorbitant. **гра́бить** (-блю) *impf* (*pf* о~) rob, pillage.

гра́бли (-бель *or* -блей) *pl* rake.

гравёр, **гравиро́вщик** engraver. **гра́вий** gravel. **гравирова́ть** *impf* (*pf* вы~) engrave; etch. **гравиро́вка** engraving.

гравитацио́нный gravitational.

гравю́ра engraving, print; etching.

град[1] city, town.

град[2] hail; volley. **гра́дина** hailstone. **гра́дус** degree. **гра́дусник** thermometer.

граждани́н (*pl* гра́ждане, -дан) *m*, **гражда́нка** citizen. **гражда́нский** civil; civic; civilian. **гражда́нство** citizenship.

грамза́пись (gramophone) recording.

грамм gram.

грамма́тика grammar. **граммати́ческий** grammatical.

гра́мота reading and writing; official document; deed. **гра́мотность**

literacy. **грамотный** literate; competent.

граммпластинка (gramophone) record.

гранат pomegranate; garnet. **граната** shell, grenade.

грандиозный grandiose.

гранёный cut, faceted; cut-glass.

гранит granite.

граница border; boundary, limit; **за границей, за границу** abroad. **граничить** *impf* border.

грань border, verge; side, facet.

граф count; earl.

графа column. **график** graph; chart; schedule; graphic artist. **графика** drawing; graphics; script.

графин carafe; decanter.

графиня countess.

графит graphite.

графический graphic.

графлёный ruled.

графство county.

грациозный graceful. **грация** grace.

грач (-á) rook.

гребёнка comb. **гребень** (-бня) *m* comb; crest. **гребец** (-бца) rower, oarsman. **гребной** rowing. **гребу** *etc.*: *see* грести

грёза day-dream, dream. **грезить** (-éжу) *impf* dream.

грек Greek.

грелка hot-water bottle.

греметь *impf* (*pf* про~) thunder, roar; rattle; resound. **гремучая змея** rattlesnake.

грести (-ебу, -ебёшь; грёб, -бла) *impf* row; rake.

греть (-éю) *impf* warm, heat; ~ся warm o.s., bask.

грех (-á) sin. **греховный** sinful. **грехопадение** the Fall; fall.

Греция Greece. **грецкий орех** walnut. **гречанка** Greek. **греческий** Greek, Grecian.

гречиха buckwheat. **гречневый** buckwheat.

грешить (-шу) *impf* (*pf* по~, со~) sin. **грешник, -ница** sinner. **грешный** (-шен, -шна, -о) sinful.

гриб (-á) mushroom. **грибной** mushroom.

грива mane.

гривенник ten-copeck piece.

грим make-up; grease-paint.

гримировать *impf* (*pf* за~) make up; +*instr* make up as.

грипп flu.

гриф neck (*of violin etc.*).

грифель *m* pencil lead.

гроб (*loc* -ý; *pl* -ы *or* -á) coffin; grave. **гробница** tomb. **гробовой** coffin; deathly. **гробовщик** (-á) coffin-maker; undertaker.

гроза (*pl* -ы) (thunder-)storm.

гроздь (*pl* -ди *or* -дья, -дéй *or* -дьев) cluster, bunch.

грозить(ся (-ожý(сь) *impf* (*pf* по~, при~) threaten. **грозный** (-зен, -знá, -о) menacing; terrible; severe.

гром (*pl* -ы, -óв) thunder.

громада mass; bulk, pile. **громадный** huge, colossal.

громить (-млю) *impf* destroy; smash, rout.

громкий (-мок, -мкá, -о) loud; famous; notorious; fine-sounding. **громко** *adv* loud(ly); out loud. **громкоговоритель** *m* loud-speaker. **громовой** thunder; thunderous; crushing. **громогласный** loud; public.

громоздить (-зжý) *impf* (*pf* на~) pile up; ~ся tower; clamber up. **громоздкий** cumbersome.

громче *comp of* громкий, громко

гроссмейстер grand master.

гротескный grotesque.

грохот crash, din.

грохотать (-очý, -óчешь) *impf* (*pf* про~) crash; rumble; roar.

грош (-á) half-copeck piece; farthing. **грошовый** cheap; trifling.

грубеть (-éю) *impf* (*pf* за~, о~, по~) grow coarse. **грубить** (-блю) *impf* (*pf* на~) be rude. **грубиян** boor. **грубость** rudeness; coarseness; rude remark. **грубый** (груб, -á, -о) coarse; rude.

груда heap, pile.

грудина breastbone. **грудинка** brisket; breast. **грудной** breast, chest; pectoral. **грудь** (-й *or* -и, *instr* -ю, *loc* -й; *pl* -и, -éй) breast; chest.

груз load; burden.

грузин (*gen pl* -ин), **грузинка** Georgian. **грузинский** Georgian.

грузить (-ужý, -ýзишь) *impf* (*pf* за~, на~, по~) load, lade, freight; ~ся load, take on cargo.

Грузия Georgia.

грузный (-зен, -знá, -о) weighty;

bulky. **грузови́к** lorry, truck. **грузово́й** goods, cargo. **гру́зчик** stevedore; loader.

грунт ground, soil; priming. **грунтова́ть** *impf* (*pf* за~) prime. **грунтово́й** soil, earth; priming.

гру́ппа group. **группирова́ть** *impf* (*pf* с~) group; ~ся group, form groups. **группиро́вка** grouping. **группово́й** group; team.

грусти́ть (-ущу́) *impf* grieve, mourn; +по+*dat* pine for. **гру́стный** (-тен, -тна́, -о) sad. **грусть** sadness.

гру́ша pear.

гры́жа hernia, rupture.

грызть (-зу́, -зёшь; грыз) *impf* (*pf* раз~) gnaw; nag; ~ся fight; squabble. **грызу́н** (-á) rodent.

гряда́ (*pl* -ы, -áм) ridge; bed; row, series; bank. **гря́дка** (flower-)bed.

гряду́щий approaching; future.

гря́зный (-зен, -зна́, -о) muddy; dirty. **грязь** (*loc* -и́) mud; dirt, filth; *pl* mud-cure.

гря́нуть (-ну) *pf* ring out, crash out; strike up.

губа́ (*pl* -ы, -áм) lip; *pl* pincers.

губерна́тор governor. **губе́рния** province. **губе́рнский** provincial.

губи́тельный ruinous; pernicious. **губи́ть** (-блю́, -бишь) *impf* (*pf* по~) ruin; spoil.

гу́бка sponge.

губна́я пома́да lipstick.

гу́бчатый porous, spongy.

гуверна́нтка governess. **гуверне́р** tutor.

гуде́ть (гужу́) *impf* (*pf* про~) hum; drone; buzz; hoot. **гудо́к** (-дка́) hooter, siren, horn, whistle; hoot.

гудро́н tar. **гудро́нный** tar, tarred.

гул rumble. **гу́лкий** (-лок, -лка́, -о) resonant; booming.

гуля́нье (*gen pl* -ний) walk; fête; outdoor party. **гуля́ть** *impf* (*pf* по~) stroll; go for a walk; have a good time.

гуманита́рный of the humanities; humane. **гума́нный** humane.

гумно́ (*pl* -а, -мен *or* -мён, -ам) threshing-floor; barn.

гурт (-á) herd; flock. **гуртовщи́к** (-á) herdsman. **гурто́м** *adv* wholesale; en masse.

гуса́к (-á) gander.

гу́сеница caterpillar; (caterpillar) track. **гу́сеничный** caterpillar.

гусёнок (-нка; *pl* -ся́та, -ся́т) gosling. **гуси́н|ый** goose; ~ая ко́жа gooseflesh.

густе́ть (-éет) *impf* (*pf* за~) thicken. **густо́й** (густ, -á, -о) thick, dense; rich. **густота́** thickness, density; richness.

гусы́ня goose. **гусь** (*pl* -и, -éй) *m* goose. **гусько́м** *adv* in single file.

гутали́н shoe-polish.

гу́ща grounds, sediment; thicket; thick. **гу́ще** *comp of* **густо́й.**

ГЭС *abbr* (*of* гидроэлектроста́нция) hydro-electric power station.

Д

д. *abbr* (*of* дере́вня) village; (*of* дом) house.

да *conj* and; but.

да *partl* yes; really? well; +*3rd pers of v*, may, let; **да здра́вствует...!** long live ..!

дава́ть (даю́, -ёшь) *impf of* дать; **дава́й(те)** let us, let's; come on; ~ся yield; come easy.

дави́ть (-влю́, -вишь) *impf* (*pf* за~, по~, раз~, у~) press; squeeze; crush; oppress; ~ся choke; hang o.s.

да́вка crushing; crush. **давле́ние** pressure.

да́вний ancient; of long standing. **давно́** *adv* long ago; for a long time. **да́вность** antiquity; remoteness; long standing. **давны́м-давно́** *adv* long long ago.

дади́м etc.: *see* дать. **даю́** etc.: *see* дава́ть

да́же *adv* even.

да́лее *adv* further; **и так ~** and so on, etc. **далёкий** (-ёк, -á, -ёко) distant, remote; far (away). **далеко́** *adv* far; far off; by a long way; ~ **за** long after; ~ **не** far from. **даль** (*loc* -и́) distance. **дальне́йший** further. **да́льний** distant, remote; long; ~ **Восто́к** the Far East. **дально-зо́ркий** long-sighted. **да́льность** distance; range. **да́льше** *adv* further; then, next; longer.

дам etc.: *see* дать

да́ма lady; partner; queen.

да́мба dike; dam.

да́мский ladies'.

Да́ния Denmark.

да́нные *sb pl* data; facts. **да́нный** given, present. **дань** tribute; debt.

данти́ст dentist.

дар (*pl* -ы́) gift. **дари́ть** (-рю́, -ришь) *impf* (*pf* по~) +*dat* give, make a present.

дарова́ние talent. **дарова́ть** *impf & pf* grant, confer. **дарови́тый** gifted. **дарово́й** free (of charge). **да́ром** *adv* free, gratis; in vain.

да́та date.

да́тельный dative.

дати́ровать *impf & pf* date.

да́тский Danish. **датча́нин** (*pl* -а́не, -а́н), **датча́нка** Dane.

дать (дам, дашь, даст, дади́м; дал, -а́, да́ло́) *pf* (*impf* дава́ть) give; grant; let; ~ взаймы́ lend; ~ся *pf of* дава́ться

да́ча dacha; **на да́че** in the country. **да́чник** (holiday) visitor.

два *m & neut*, **две** *f* (двух, -ум, -умя́, -ух) two. **двадцатиле́тний** twenty-year; twenty-year-old. **двадца́тый** twentieth; ~ые го́ды the twenties. **два́дцать** (-и́, *instr* -ью́) twenty. **два́жды** *adv* twice; double. **двена́дцатый** twelfth. **двена́дцать** twelve.

дверь (*loc* -и́; *pl* -и, -е́й, *instr* -я́ми *or* -ьми́) door.

две́сти (двухсо́т, -умста́м, -умяста́ми, -ухста́х) two hundred.

дви́гатель *m* engine, motor; motive force. **дви́гать** (-аю *or* -и́жу) *impf*, **дви́нуть** (-ну) *pf* move; set in motion; advance; ~ся move; advance; get started. **движе́ние** movement; motion; exercise; traffic. **дви́жимость** chattels; personal property. **дви́жимый** movable; moved. **дви́жущий** motive.

дво́е (-и́х) two; two pairs.

двое- *in comb* two-; double(-). **двоебо́рье** biathlon. ~**же́нец** (-нца) bigamist. ~**же́нство** bigamy. ~**то́чие** colon.

двои́ться *impf* divide in two; appear double; **у него́ двои́лось в глаза́х** he saw double. **дво́йка** two; figure 2; No. 2. **дво́йник** (-а́) double. **двойно́й** double,

twofold; binary. **дво́йня** (*gen pl* -о́ен) twins. **дво́йственный** two-faced; dual.

двор (-а́) yard; courtyard; homestead; court. **дворе́ц** (-рца́) palace. **дво́рник** yard caretaker; windscreen-wiper. **дво́рня** servants. **дворо́вый** yard, courtyard; *sb* house-serf. **дворяни́н** (*pl* -я́не, -я́н), **дворя́нка** member of the nobility or gentry. **дворя́нство** nobility, gentry.

двою́родн|ый; ~**ый брат**, ~**ая сестра́** (first) cousin; ~**ый дя́дя**, ~**ая тётка** first cousin once removed. **двоя́кий** double; two-fold.

дву-, двух- *in comb* two-; bi-; double. **двубо́ртный** double-breasted. ~**ли́чный** two-faced. ~**но́гий** two-legged. ~**ру́чный** two-handed; two-handled. ~**ру́шник** double-dealer. ~**смы́сленный** ambiguous. ~(**х**)**спа́льный** double. ~**сторо́нний** double-sided; two-way; bilateral. ~**х-годи́чный** two-year; two-year-old; biennial. ~**хле́тний** two-year; two-year-old; biennial. ~**хме́стный** two-seater; two-berth. ~**хмото́рный** twin-engined. ~**хсот-ле́тие** bicentenary. ~**хсо́тый** two-hundredth. ~**хта́ктный** two-stroke. ~**хэта́жный** two-storey. ~**язы́ч-ный** bilingual.

деба́ты (-ов) *pl* debate.

де́бет debit. **дебетова́ть** *impf & pf* debit.

деби́т yield, output.

де́бри (-ей) *pl* jungle; thickets; the wilds.

дебю́т début.

де́ва maid, maiden; Virgo.

девальва́ция devaluation.

дева́ться *impf of* де́ться

деви́з motto; device.

деви́ца spinster; girl. **де́ви́ч|ий** girl-ish, maidenly; ~**ья фами́лия** maiden name. **де́вка** wench, lass; tart.

де́вочка (little) girl. **де́вственник**, **-ица** virgin. **де́вственный** virgin; innocent. **де́вушка** girl. **девчо́нка** girl.

девяно́сто ninety. **девяно́стый** ninetieth. **девя́тка** nine; figure 9; No. 9. **девятна́дцатый** nineteenth. **девятна́дцать** nineteen. **девя́тый** ninth. **де́вять** (-и́, *instr* -ью́) nine. **девятьсо́т** (-тисо́т, -тиста́м, -тьюста́ми, -тиста́х) nine hundred.

дегенери́ровать *impf & pf* degenerate.

дёготь (-гтя) tar.

дегуста́ция tasting.

дед grandfather; grandad. **де́душка** grandfather; grandad.

дееприча́стие adverbial participle.

дежу́рить *impf* be on duty. **дежу́рный** on duty; *sb* person on duty. **дежу́рство** (being on) duty.

дезерти́р deserter. **дезерти́ровать** *impf & pf* desert.

дезинфе́кция disinfection. **дезинфици́ровать** *impf & pf* disinfect.

дезодора́нт deodorant; air-freshener.

дезориента́ция disorientation. **дезориенти́ровать** *impf & pf* disorient; ~ся lose one's bearings.

де́йственный efficacious; effective. **де́йствие** action; operation; effect; act. **действи́тельно** *adv* really; indeed. **действи́тельность** reality; validity; efficacy. **действи́тельный** actual; valid; efficacious; active. **де́йствовать** *impf* (*pf* по~) affect, have an effect; act; work. **де́йствую|щий** active; in force; working; ~ее лицо́ character; ~ие ли́ца cast.

декабри́ст Decembrist. **дека́брь** (-я́) *m* December. **дека́брьский** December.

дека́да ten-day period *or* festival.

дека́н dean. **декана́т** office of dean.

деклама́ция recitation, declamation. **деклами́ровать** *impf* (*pf* про~) recite, declaim.

деклара́ция declaration.

декорати́вный decorative. **декора́тор** scene-painter. **декора́ция** scenery.

декре́т decree; maternity leave. **декре́тный о́тпуск** maternity leave.

де́ланный artificial, affected. **де́лать** *impf* (*pf* с~) make; do; ~ вид pretend; ~ся become; happen.

делега́т delegate. **делега́ция** delegation; group.

делёж (-а́), **делёжка** sharing; partition. **деле́ние** division; point (*on a scale*).

деле́ц (-льца́) smart operator.

делика́тный delicate.

дели́мое *sb* dividend. **дели́мость** divisibility. **дели́тель** *m* divisor.

дели́ть (-лю́, -лишь) *impf* (*pf* по~, раз~) divide; share; ~ шесть на́ три divide six by three; ~ся divide; be divisible; +*instr* share.

де́ло (*pl* -а́) business; affair; matter; deed; thing; case; ~ в са́мом де́ле really, indeed; ~ в том the point is; как (ва́ши) дела́? how are things?; на са́мом де́ле in actual fact; по де́лу, по дела́м on business. **делови́тый** business-like, efficient. **делово́й** business; business-like. **де́льный** efficient; sensible.

де́льта delta.

дельфи́н dolphin.

демаго́г demagogue.

демобилиза́ция demobilization. **демобилизова́ть** *impf & pf* demobilize.

демокра́т democrat. **демократиза́ция** democratization. **демократизи́ровать** *impf & pf* democratize. **демократи́ческий** democratic. **демокра́тия** democracy.

де́мон demon.

демонстра́ция demonstration. **демонстри́ровать** *impf & pf* demonstrate.

де́нежный monetary; money; ~ перево́д money order.

де́нусь *etc.: see* де́ться

день (дня) *m* day; afternoon; днём in the afternoon; на днях the other day; one of these days; че́рез ~ every other day.

де́ньги (-нег, -ньга́м) *pl* money.

департа́мент department.

депо́ *neut indecl* depot.

депорта́ция deportation. **депорти́ровать** *impf & pf* deport.

депута́т deputy; delegate.

дёргать *impf* (*pf* дёрнуть) pull, tug; pester; ~ся twitch; jerk.

дереве́нский village; rural. **дере́вня** (*pl* -и, -ве́нь, -вня́м) village; the country. **де́рево** (*pl* -е́вья, -ьев) tree; wood. **деревя́нный** wood, wooden.

держа́ва power. **держа́ть** (-жу́, -жишь) *impf* hold; support; keep; ~ пари́ bet; ~ себя́ behave; ~ся hold; be held up; hold o.s.; hold out; +*gen* keep to.

дерза́ние daring. **дерза́ть** *impf*, **дерзну́ть** (-ну́, -нёшь) *pf* dare.

дёрзкий impudent; daring.
дёрзость impertinence; daring.
дёрн turf.
дёрнуть(ся (-ну(сь) *pf of* **дёргать(ся**
деру́ *etc.: see* **драть**
деса́нт landing; landing force.
де́скать *partl indicating reported speech.*
десна́ (*pl* дёсны, -сен) gum.
де́спот despot.
десятиле́тие decade; tenth anniversary. **десятиле́тка** ten-year (*secondary*) school. **десятиле́тний** tenyear; ten-year-old. **десяти́чный** decimal. **деся́тка** ten; figure 10; No. 10; tenner (*10-rouble note*). **деся́ток** (-тка) ten; decade. **деся́тый** tenth. **де́сять** (-и, *instr* -ью) ten.
детдо́м children's home. **детса́д** kindergarten.
дета́ль detail; part, component. **дета́льный** detailed; minute.
детекти́в detective story.
детёныш young animal; *pl* young. **де́ти** (-те́й, -тям, -тьми, -тях) *pl* children.
де́тская *sb* nursery. **де́тский** children's; childish. **де́тство** childhood.
де́ться (де́нусь) *pf* (*impf* **дева́ться**) get to, disappear to.
дефе́кт defect.
дефи́с hyphen.
дефици́т deficit; shortage. **дефици́тный** scarce.
дешеве́ть (-е́ет) *impf* (*pf* по~) fall in price. **деше́вле** *comp of* **дёшево**, **дешёвый**. **дёшево** *adv* cheap, cheaply. **дешёвый** (дёшев, -á, -o) cheap; empty, worthless.
де́ятель *m*: **госуда́рственный** ~ statesman; **обще́ственный** ~ public figure. **де́ятельность** activity; work. **де́ятельный** active, energetic.
джаз jazz.
дже́мпер pullover.
джентельме́н gentleman.
джинсо́вый denim. **джи́нсы** (-ов) *pl* jeans.
джо́йстик joystick.
джу́нгли (-ей) *pl* jungle.
диабе́т diabetes.
диа́гноз diagnosis.
диагона́ль diagonal
диагра́мма diagram.
диале́кт dialect. **диале́ктика** dialectics.

диало́г dialogue.
диа́метр diameter.
диапазо́н range; band.
диапозити́в slide, transparency.
диафра́гма diaphragm.
дива́н sofa; divan.
диверса́нт saboteur. **диве́рсия** sabotage.
диви́зия division.
диви́ться (-влю́сь) *impf* (*pf* по~) marvel (at + *dat*).
ди́вный marvellous. **ди́во** wonder, marvel.
дида́ктика didactics.
дие́з (*mus*) sharp.
дие́та diet. **диети́ческий** dietetic.
ди́зель *m* diesel; diesel engine. **ди́зельный** diesel.
дизентери́я dysentery.
дика́рь (-я́) *m*, **дика́рка** savage. **ди́кий** wild; savage; queer; preposterous. **дикобра́з** porcupine. **дикорасту́щий** wild. **ди́кость** wildness, savagery; absurdity.
дикта́нт dictation. **дикта́тор** dictator. **диктату́ра** dictatorship.
диктова́ть *impf* (*pf* про~) dictate. **ди́ктор** announcer. **ди́кция** diction.
диле́мма dilemma.
дилета́нт dilettante.
дина́мика dynamics.
динами́т dynamite.
динами́ческий dynamic.
дина́стия dynasty.
диноза́вр dinosaur.
дипло́м diploma; degree; degree work. **диплома́т** diplomat. **диплома́тический** diplomatic.
директи́ва instructions; directives. **дире́ктор** (*pl* ~á) director; principal. **дире́кция** management.
дирижа́бль *m* airship, dirigible.
дирижёр conductor. **дирижи́ровать** *impf* +*instr* conduct.
диск disc, disk; dial; discus.
ди́скант treble.
дискре́тный discrete; digital.
дискримина́ция discrimination.
диску́ссия discussion, debate.
диспансе́р clinic.
диспе́тчер controller, dispatcher.
ди́спут public debate.
диссерта́ция dissertation, thesis.
дистанцио́нный distance, distant,

remote; remote-control. **диста́нция** distance; range; region.

дисципли́на discipline.

дитя́ (-я́ти; *pl* де́ти, -е́й) *neut* child; baby.

дифтери́т diptheria.

дифто́нг diphthong.

диффама́ция libel.

дичь game.

длина́ length. **дли́нный** (-нен, -нна́, -о) long. **дли́тельность** duration. **дли́тельный** long, protracted. **дли́ться** *impf* (*pf* про~) last.

для *prep+gen* for; for the sake of; ~ того́, что́бы... in order to.

дневáльный *sb* orderly, man on duty. **дневни́к** (-á) diary, journal. **дневно́й** day; daily. **днём** *adv* in the day time; in the afternoon. **дни** *etc.*: *see* **день**

дни́ще bottom.

ДНК *abbr* (*of* дезоксирибонукле́и́новая кислота́) DNA.

дно (дна; *pl* до́нья, -ьев) bottom.

до *prep+gen* (up) to; as far as; until; before; to the point of; **до на́шей э́ры** BC; **до сих пор** till now; **до тех пор** till then, before; **до того́, как** before; **до того́, что** to such an extent that; to the point where; **мне не до** I'm not in the mood for.

доба́вить (-влю) *pf*, **добавля́ть** *impf* (+*acc or gen*) add. **доба́вка** addition; second helping. **добавле́ние** addition; supplement; extra. **доба́вочный** additional.

добега́ть *impf*, **добежа́ть** (-егу́) *pf* +до+*gen* run to, as far as; reach.

добива́ть *impf*, **доби́ть** (-бью, -бьёшь) *pf* finish (off); ~ся+*gen* get, obtain; ~ся своего́ get one's way.

добира́ться *impf of* **добра́ться**

до́блесть valour.

добра́ться (-беру́сь, -ёшься; -а́лся, -ла́сь, -а́ло́сь) *pf* (*impf* **добира́ться**) +до+*gen* get to, reach.

добро́ good; **э́то не к добру́** it is a bad sign.

добро- *in comb* good-, well-. **добро-во́лец** (-льца) volunteer. **~во́льно** *adv* voluntarily. **~во́льный** voluntary. **~де́тель** virtue. **~де́тельный** virtuous. **~ду́шие** good nature. **~ду́шный** good-natured. **~жела́-тельный** benevolent. **~ка́чест-**

венный of good quality; benign. **~со́вестный** conscientious.

доброта́ goodness, kindness. **доб-ро́тный** of good quality. **до́брый** (добр, -á, -о, до́бры) good; kind; **бу́дьте добры́**+*imper.* please; would you be kind enough to.

добыва́ть *impf*, **добы́ть** (-бу́ду; до́бы́л, -á , -о) *pf* get, obtain, procure; mine. **добы́ча** output; mining; booty.

добью *etc.*: *see* **доби́ть. доведу́** *etc.*: *see* **довести́**

довезти́ (-езу́, -езёшь; -вёз, -ла́) *pf* (*impf* **довози́ть**) take (to), carry (to), drive (to).

дове́ренность warrant; power of attorney. **дове́ренный** trusted; *sb* agent, proxy. **дове́рие** trust, confidence. **дове́рить** *pf* (*impf* **доверя́ть**) entrust; ~ся +*dat* trust in; confide in.

до́верху *adv* to the top.

дове́рчивый trustful, credulous.

доверя́ть *impf of* **дове́рить**

довесо́к (-ска) makeweight.

довести́ (-еду́, -едёшь; -вёл, -á) **доводи́ть** (-ожу́, -о́дишь) *impf* lead, take (to); bring, drive (to). **до́вод** argument, reason.

довое́нный pre-war.

довози́ть (-ожу́, -о́зишь) *impf of* **довезти́**

дово́льно *adv* enough; quite, fairly. **дово́льный** satisfied; pleased. **до-во́льство** contentment. **дово́ль-ствоваться** *impf* (*pf* у~) be content.

догада́ться *pf*, **дога́дываться** *impf* guess; suspect. **дога́дка** surmise, conjecture. **дога́дливый** quick-witted.

до́гма dogma.

догна́ть (-гоню́, -го́нишь; -гна́л, -á, -о) *pf* (*impf* **догоня́ть**) catch up (with).

догова́риваться *impf*, **догово-ри́ться** *pf* come to an agreement; arrange. **до́гово́р** (*pl* -ы *or* -á, -о́в) agreement; contract; treaty. **догово́рный** contractual; agreed.

догоня́ть *impf of* **догна́ть**

догора́ть *impf*, **догоре́ть** (-ри́т) *pf* burn out, burn down.

дое́ду *etc.*: *see* **дое́хать. доезжа́ть** *impf of* **дое́хать**

дое́хать (-е́ду) *pf* (*impf* **доезжа́ть**)

+до+*gen* reach, arrive at.

дождáться (-дýсь, -дёшься; -áлся, -нáсь, -áлóсь) *pf* +*gen* wait for, wait until.

дождевúк (-á) raincoat. **дождевóй** rain(y). **дождлúвый** rainy. **дождь** (-я́) *m* rain; ~ идёт it is raining.

дожива́ть *impf*, **дожи́ть** (-иву́, -ивёшь; дóжил, -á, -о) *pf* live out; spend.

дожида́ться *impf* +*gen* wait for.

дóза dose.

дозвóлить *pf*, **дозволя́ть** *impf* permit.

дозвони́ться *pf* get through, reach by telephone.

дозóр patrol.

дозрева́ть *impf*, **дозре́ть** (-éет) *pf* ripen.

доистори́ческий prehistoric.

дои́ть *impf* (*pf* по~) milk.

дойти́ (дойду́, -дёшь; дошёл, -шла́) *pf* (*impf* **доходи́ть**) +до+*gen* reach; get through to.

док dock.

доказа́тельный conclusive. **доказа́тельство** proof, evidence. **доказа́ть** (-ажу́) *pf*, **дока́зывать** *impf* demonstrate, prove.

докати́ться (-ачу́сь, -а́тишься) *pf*, **дока́тываться** *impf* roll; boom; +до+*gen* sink into.

докла́д report; lecture. **докладна́я** (запи́ска) report; memo. **докла́дчик** speaker, lecturer. **докла́дывать** *impf of* **доложи́ть**

дóкрасна́ *adv* to red heat; to redness.

дóктор (*pl* -á) doctor. **дóкторский** doctoral. **дóкторша** woman doctor; doctor's wife.

доктри́на doctrine.

докуме́нт document; deed. **документа́льный** documentary. **документа́ция** documentation; documents.

долби́ть (-блю́) *impf* hollow; chisel; repeat; swot up.

долг (*loc* -ý; *pl* -и́) duty; debt; взять в ~ borrow; дать в ~ lend.

дóлгий (дóлог, -лга́, -о) long. **дóлго** *adv* long, (for) a long time. **долгове́чный** lasting; durable. **долгожда́нный** long-awaited. **долгоигра́ющая пласти́нка** LP.

долголе́тие longevity. **долго-**

ле́тний of many years; long-standing. **долгосро́чный** long-term.

долготá (*pl* -ы) length; longitude.

долево́й lengthwise. **дóлее** *adv* longer.

должа́ть *impf* (*pf* за~) borrow.

дóлжен (-жна́) *predic*+*dat* in debt to; +*inf* obliged, bound; likely; must, have to, ought to; должно́ бы́ть probably. **должни́к** (-á), **-ни́ца** debtor. **дóлжное** *sb* due. **должностно́й** official. **дóлжность** (*gen pl* -éй) post, office; duties. **дóлжный** due, fitting.

долина valley.

дóллар dollar.

доложи́ть[1] (-ожу́, -óжишь) *pf* (*impf* **докла́дывать**) add.

доложи́ть[2] (-ожу́, -óжишь) *pf* (*impf* **докла́дывать**) +*acc* or о+*prep* report; announce.

долóй *adv* away, off; +*acc* down with!

долотó (*pl* -а) chisel.

дóлька segment; clove.

дóльше *adv* longer.

дóля (*gen pl* -éй) portion; share; lot, fate.

дом (*loc* -ý; *pl* -á) house; home. **дóма** *adv* at home. **дома́шн|ий** house; home; domestic; home-made; ~яя хозя́йка housewife.

дóменн|ый blast-furnace; ~ая печь blast-furnace.

домини́ровать *impf* dominate, predominate.

домкра́т jack.

дóмна blast-furnace.

домовладе́лец (-льца), **-лица** houseowner; landlord. **домово́дство** housekeeping; domestic science. **домо́вый** house; household; housing.

домога́тельство solicitation; bid. **домога́ться** *impf* +*gen* solicit, bid for.

домо́й *adv* home, homewards. **домохозя́йка** housewife. **домрабо́тница** domestic servant, maid.

доне́льзя *adv* in the extreme.

донесе́ние dispatch, report. **донести́** (-сý, -сёшь; -нёс, -слá) *pf* (*impf* **доноси́ть**) report, announce; +*dat* inform; +на+*acc* inform against; ~сь be heard; +до+*gen* reach.

дóнизу *adv* to the bottom; све́рху ~ from top to bottom.

до́нор donor.

доно́с denunciation, information. **доноси́ть(ся** (-ношу́(сь, -но́сишь(ся) *impf of* **донести́(сь**

доно́счик informer.

донско́й Don.

доны́не *adv* hitherto.

до́нья *etc.: see* **дно**

до н.э. *abbr* (*of* **до на́шей э́ры**) BC.

допла́та additional payment, excess fare. **доплати́ть** (-ачу́, -а́тишь) *pf*, **допла́чивать** *impf* pay in addition; pay the rest.

допо́длинно *adv* for certain. **допо́длинный** authentic, genuine.

дополне́ние supplement, addition; (*gram*) object. **дополни́тельно** *adv* in addition. **дополни́тельный** supplementary, additional. **допо́лнить** *pf*, **дополня́ть** *impf* supplement.

допра́шивать *impf*, **допроси́ть** (-ошу́, -о́сишь) *pf* interrogate. **допро́с** interrogation.

до́пуск right of entry, admittance. **допуска́ть** *impf*, **допусти́ть** (-ущу́, -у́стишь) *pf* admit; permit; tolerate; suppose. **допусти́мый** permissible, acceptable. **допуще́ние** assumption.

дореволюцио́нный pre-revolutionary.

доро́га road; way; journey; route; **по доро́ге** on the way.

до́рого *adv* dear, dearly. **дорогови́зна** high prices. **дорого́й** (**до́рог**, -а́, -о) dear.

доро́дный portly.

дорожа́ть *impf* (*pf* **вз~**, **по~**) rise in price, go up. **доро́же** *comp of* **до́рого**, **дорого́й**. **дорожи́ть** (-жу́) *impf* +*instr* value.

доро́жка path; track; lane; runway; strip; runner, stair-carpet. **доро́жный** road; highway; travelling.

доса́да annoyance. **досади́ть** (-ажу́) *pf*, **досажда́ть** *impf* +*dat* annoy. **доса́дный** annoying. **доса́довать** be annoyed (**на**+*acc* with).

доска́ (*acc* **до́ску**, *pl* -и, -со́к, -ска́м) board; slab; plaque.

досло́вный literal; word-for-word.

досмо́тр inspection.

доспе́хи *pl* armour.

досро́чный ahead of time, early.

достава́ть(ся (-таю́(сь, -ёшь(ся) *impf of* **доста́ть(ся**

доста́вить (-влю) *pf*, **доставля́ть** *impf* deliver; supply; cause, give. **доста́вка** delivery.

доста́ну *etc.: see* **доста́ть**

доста́ток (-тка) sufficiency; prosperity. **доста́точно** *adv* enough, sufficiently. **доста́точный** sufficient; adequate.

доста́ть (-а́ну) *pf* (*impf* **достава́ть**) take (out); get, obtain; **до**+*gen* touch; reach; *impers* suffice; ~**ся** +*dat* be inherited by; fall to the lot of; **ему́ доста́нется** he'll catch it.

достига́ть *impf*, **дости́гнуть**, **дости́чь** (-и́гну -сти́г) *pf* +*gen* reach, achieve; +*gen or* **до**+*gen* reach. **достиже́ние** achievement.

достове́рный reliable, trustworthy; authentic.

досто́инство dignity; merit; value. **досто́йный** deserved; suitable; worthy; +*gen* worthy of.

достопримеча́тельность sight, notable place.

достоя́ние property.

до́ступ access. **досту́пный** accessible; approachable; reasonable; available.

досу́г leisure, (spare) time. **досу́жий** leisure; idle.

до́сыта *adv* to satiety.

досье́ *neut indecl* dossier.

досяга́емый attainable.

дота́ция grant, subsidy.

дотла́ utterly; to the ground.

дотра́гиваться *impf*, **дотро́нуться** (-нусь) *pf* +**до**+*gen* touch.

дотя́гивать *impf*, **дотяну́ть** (-яну́, -я́нешь) *pf* draw, drag, stretch out; hold out; live; put off; ~**ся** stretch; reach; drag on.

до́хлый dead; sickly. **до́хнуть**[1] (-нет, дох) (*pf* **из~**, **по~**, **с~**) die; kick the bucket.

дохну́ть[2] (-ну́, -нёшь) *pf* draw a breath.

дохо́д income; revenue. **доходи́ть** (-ожу́, -о́дишь) *impf of* **дойти́**. **дохо́дный** profitable. **дохо́дчивый** intelligible.

доце́нт reader, senior lecturer.

до́чиста *adv* clean; completely.

до́чка daughter. **дочь** (-чери, *instr* -черью; *pl* -чери, -чере́й, *instr* -черьми́) daughter.

дошёл *etc.*: *see* **дойти**

дошко́льник, -ница child under school age. **дошко́льный** pre-school.

доща́тый plank, board. **дощечка** small plank, board; plaque.

дойрка milkmaid.

драгоце́нность jewel; treasure; *pl* jewellery; valuables. **драгоце́нный** precious.

дразни́ть (-ню, -нишь) *impf* tease.

дра́ка fight.

драко́н dragon.

дра́ма drama. **драмати́ческий** dramatic. **драмату́рг** playwright. **драматурги́я** dramatic art; plays.

драп thick woollen cloth.

драпиро́вка draping; curtain; hangings. **драпиро́вщик** upholsterer.

драть (деру́, -рёшь; драл, -á, -о) *impf* (*pf* вы́~, за~, со~) tear (up); irritate; make off; flog; ~ся fight.

дре́безги *pl*; в ~ to smithereens. **дребезжа́ть** (-жи́т) *impf* jingle, tinkle.

древеси́на wood; timber. **древе́сный** wood; ~ у́голь charcoal.

дре́вко (*pl* -и, -ов) pole, staff; shaft.

древнегре́ческий ancient Greek. **древнееврейский** Hebrew. **древнеру́сский** Old Russian. **дре́вний** ancient; aged. **дре́вность** antiquity.

дрейф drift; leeway. **дрейфова́ть** *impf* drift.

дрема́ть (-млю, -млешь) *impf* doze; slumber. **дремо́та** drowsiness.

дрему́чий dense.

дрессиро́ванный trained; performing. **дрессирова́ть** *impf* (*pf* вы́~) train; school. **дрессиро́вка** training. **дрессиро́вщик** trainer.

дроби́ть (-блю́) *impf* (*pf* раз~) break up, smash; crush; ~ся break to pieces, smash. **дробови́к** (-á) shot-gun. **дробь** (small) shot; drumming; fraction. **дро́бный** fractional.

дрова́ (дров) *pl* firewood.

дро́гнуть (-ну) *pf*, **дрожа́ть** (-жу́) *impf* tremble; shiver; quiver.

дро́жжи (-éй) *pl* yeast.

дрожь shivering, trembling.

дрозд (-á) thrush.

дро́ссель *m* throttle, choke.

дро́тик javelin, dart.

друг¹ (*pl* -узья́, -зéй) friend. **друг²**:

~ дру́га (дру́гу) each other, one another. **друго́й** other, another; different; на ~ день (the) next day.

дру́жба friendship. **дружелю́бный, дру́жеский, дру́жественный** friendly. **дружи́ть** (-жу́, -у́жи́шь) *impf* be friends; ~ся (*pf* по~ся) make friends. **дру́жный** (-жен, -жна́, -о) amicable; harmonious; simultaneous, concerted.

дря́блый (дрябл, -á, -о) flabby.

дря́зги (-зг) *pl* squabbles.

дрянно́й worthless; good-for-nothing. **дрянь** rubbish.

дряхле́ть (-е́ю) *impf* (*pf* о~) become decrepit. **дря́хлый** (-хл, -лá, -о) decrepit, senile.

дуб (*pl* -ы́) oak; blockhead. **дуби́на** club, cudgel; blockhead. **дуби́нка** truncheon, baton.

дублёнка sheepskin coat.

дублёр understudy. **дублика́т** duplicate. **дубли́ровать** duplicate; understudy; dub.

дубо́вый oak; coarse; clumsy.

дуга́ (*pl* -и) arc; arch.

ду́дка pipe, fife.

ду́ло muzzle; barrel.

ду́ма thought; Duma; council. **ду́мать** *impf* (*pf* по~) think; +*inf* think of, intend. **ду́маться** *impf* (*impers* +*dat*) seem.

дунове́ние puff, breath. **ду́нуть** (-ну) *pf of* **дуть**

дупло́ (*pl* -а, -пел) hollow; hole; cavity.

ду́ра, дура́к (-á) fool. **дура́чить** (-чу) *impf* (*pf* о~) fool, dupe; ~ся play the fool.

дуре́ть (-е́ю) *impf* (*pf* о~) grow stupid.

дурма́н narcotic; intoxicant. **дурма́нить** *impf* (*pf* о~) stupefy.

дурно́й (-рен, -рнá, -о) bad, evil; ugly; мне ду́рно I feel faint, sick. **дурнота́** faintness; nausea.

ду́тый hollow; inflated. **дуть** (ду́ю) *impf* (*pf* вы́~, по~, ду́нуть) blow; ду́ет there is a draught. **дутьё** glass-blowing. **ду́ться** (ду́юсь) *impf* pout; sulk.

дух spirit; spirits; heart; mind; breath; ghost; smell; в ~e in a good mood; не в моём ~e not to my taste; ни слу́ху ни ~у no news, not a word.

духи́ (-о́в) *pl* scent, perfume. **Ду́хов день** Whit Monday. **духове́нство** clergy. **духови́дец** (-дца) clairvoyant; medium. **духо́вка** oven. **духо́вный** spiritual; ecclesiastical. **духово́й** wind. **духота́** stuffiness, closeness.

душ shower(-bath).

душа́ (*acc* -у; *pl* -и) soul; heart; feeling; spirit; inspiration; **в душе́** inwardly; at heart; **от всей души́** with all one's heart.

душева́я *sb* shower-room.

душевнобольно́й mentally ill, insane; *sb* mental patient; lunatic. **душе́вный** mental; sincere, cordial.

души́стый fragrant; ~ **горо́шек** sweet pea(s).

души́ть (-шу́, -шишь) *impf* (*pf* за~) strangle, stifle, smother.

души́ться (-шу́сь, -шишься) *impf* (*pf* на~) use, put on, perfume.

ду́шный (-шен, -шна́, -о) stuffy, close.

дуэ́ль duel.

дуэ́т duet.

ды́бом *adv* on end; **у меня́ во́лосы вста́ли** ~ my hair stood on end. **дыбы́**: **станови́ться на** ~ rear; resist.

дым (*loc* -у́; *pl* -ы́) smoke. **дыми́ть** (-млю́) *impf* (*pf* на~) smoke; ~**ся** smoke, steam; billow. **ды́мка** haze. **ды́мный** smoky. **дымов|о́й** smoke; ~**а́я труба́** flue, chimney. **дымо́к** (-мка́) puff of smoke. **дымохо́д** flue.

ды́ня melon.

дыра́ (*pl* -ы), **ды́рка** (*gen pl* -рок) hole; gap.

дыха́ние breathing; breath. **дыха́тельн|ый** respiratory; breathing; ~**ое го́рло** windpipe. **дыша́ть** (-шу́, -шишь) *impf* breathe.

дья́вол devil. **дья́вольский** devilish, diabolical.

дья́кон (*pl* -á) deacon.

дю́жина dozen.

дюйм inch.

дю́на dune.

дя́дя (*gen pl* -ей) *m* uncle.

дя́тел (-тла) woodpecker.

Е

ева́нгелие gospel; the Gospels. **евангели́ческий** evangelical.

евре́й, **евре́йка** Jew; Hebrew. **евре́йский** Jewish.

Евро́па Europe. **европе́ец** (-е́йца) European. **европе́йский** European.

Еги́пет Egypt. **еги́петский** Egyptian. **египтя́нин** (*pl* -я́не, -я́н), **египтя́нка** Egyptian.

его́ *see* он, оно́; *pron* his; its.

еда́ food; meal.

едва́ *adv & conj* hardly; just; scarcely; ~ **ли** hardly; ~ (**ли**) **не** almost, all but.

еди́м *etc.*: *see* есть¹

едине́ние unity. **едини́ца** (figure) one; unity; unit; individual. **еди́ничный** single; individual.

едино- *in comb* mono-, uni-; one; co-. **единобра́чие** monogamy. ~**вла́стие** autocracy. ~**вре́менно** *adv* only once; simultaneously. ~**гла́сие**, ~**ду́шие** unanimity. ~**гла́сный**, ~**ду́шный** unanimous. ~**кро́вный брат** half-brother. ~**мы́слие** likemindedness; agreement. ~**мы́шленник** like-minded person. ~**утро́бный брат** half-brother.

еди́нственно *adv* only, solely. **еди́нственный** only, sole. **еди́нство** unity. **еди́ный** one; single; united.

е́дкий (-док, едка́, -о) caustic; pungent.

едо́к (-á) mouth, head; eater.

е́ду *etc.*: *see* е́хать

её *see* она́; *pron* her, hers; its.

ёж (ежа́) hedgehog.

еже- *in comb* every; -ly. **ежего́дник** annual, year-book. ~**го́дный** annual. ~**дне́вный** daily. ~**ме́сячник**, ~**ме́сячный** monthly. ~**неде́льник**, ~**неде́льный** weekly.

ежеви́ка (*no pl*; *usu collect*) blackberry; blackberries; blackberry bush.

е́жели *conj* if.

ёжиться (ёжусь) *impf* (*pf* съ~) huddle up; shrink away.

езда́ ride, riding; drive, driving; journey. **е́здить** (е́зжу) *impf* go; ride, drive; ~ **верхо́м** ride. **ездо́к** (-á) rider.

ей *see* она́

ей-бо́гу *int* really! truly!

ел *etc.*: *see* есть¹

ёле *adv* scarcely; only just. **ёле-ёле** *emphatic variant of* **ёле**

ёлка fir-tree, spruce; Christmas tree.
ёлочка herring-bone pattern.
ёлочный Christmas-tree. ель fir-tree; spruce.
ем etc.: see есть¹
ёмкий capacious. ёмкость capacity.
ему́ see он, оно́
епи́скоп bishop.
е́ресь heresy. ерети́к (-á) heretic. ерети́ческий heretical.
ёрзать impf fidget.
еро́шить (-шу) impf (pf взъ~) ruffle, rumple.
ерунда́ nonsense.
е́сли if; ~ бы if only; ~ бы не but for, if it were not for; ~ не unless.
ест see есть¹
есте́ственно adv naturally. есте́ственный natural. естество́ nature; essence. естествозна́ние (natural) science.
есть¹ (ем, ешь, ест, еди́м; ел) impf (pf съ~) eat; corrode, eat away.
есть² see быть; is, are; there is, there are; у меня́ ~ I have.
ефре́йтор lance-corporal.
е́хать (е́ду) impf (pf по~) go; ride, drive; travel; ~ верхо́м ride.
ехи́дный malicious, spiteful.
ешь see есть¹
ещё adv still; yet; (some) more; any more; yet, further; again; +comp still, yet even; всё ~ still; ~ бы! of course! oh yes! can you ask?; ~ не, нет ~ not yet; ~ раз once more, again; пока́ ~ for the present, for the time being.
е́ю see она́

Ж

ж conj: see же
жа́ба toad.
жа́бра (gen pl -бр) gill.
жа́воронок (-нка) lark.
жа́дничать impf be greedy; be mean. жа́дность greed; meanness. жа́дный (-ден, -дна́, -о) greedy; avid; mean.
жа́жда thirst; +gen thirst, craving for. жа́ждать (-ду) impf thirst, yearn.
жаке́т, жаке́тка jacket.
жале́ть (-е́ю) impf (pf по~) pity, feel sorry for; regret; +acc or gen grudge.

жа́лить impf (pf у~) sting, bite.
жа́лкий (-лок, -лка́, -о) pitiful. жа́лко predic: see жаль
жа́ло sting.
жа́лоба complaint. жа́лобный plaintive.
жа́лованье salary. жа́ловать impf (pf по~) +acc or dat of person, instr or acc of thing grant, bestow on; ~ся complain (на+acc of, about).
жа́лостливый compassionate. жа́лостный piteous; compassionate. жа́лость pity. жаль, жа́лко predic, impers (it is) a pity; it grieves; +gen grudge; как ~ what a pity; мне ~ его́ I'm sorry for him.
жалюзи́ neut indecl Venetian blind.
жанр genre.
жар (loc -ý) heat; heat of the day; fever; (high) temperature; ardour.
жара́ heat; hot weather.
жарго́н slang.
жа́реный roast; grilled; fried. жа́рить impf (pf за~, из~) roast; grill; fry; scorch, burn; ~ся roast, fry.
жа́рк|ий (-рок, -рка́, -о) hot; passionate; -óе sb roast (meat).
жаро́вня (gen pl -вен) brazier. жар-пти́ца Firebird. жа́рче comp of жа́ркий
жа́тва harvest. жать¹ (жну, жнёшь) impf (pf с~) reap, cut.
жать² (жму, жмёшь) impf press, squeeze; pinch; oppress.
жва́чка chewing, rumination; cud; chewing-gum. жва́чн|ый ruminant; ~ое sb ruminant.
жгу etc.: see жечь
жгут (-á) plait; tourniquet.
жгу́чий burning. жёг etc.: see жечь
ждать (жду, ждёшь; -ал, -á, -о) impf +gen wait (for); expect.
же, ж conj but; and; however; also; partl giving emphasis or expressing identity; мне же ка́жется it seems to me, however; сего́дня же this very day; что же ты де́лаешь? what on earth are you doing?
жева́тельная рези́нка chewinggum. жева́ть (жую́, жуёшь) impf chew; ruminate.
жезл (-á) rod; staff.
жела́ние wish, desire. жела́нный longed-for; beloved. жела́тельный desirable; advisable. жела́ть impf

(*pf* по~) +*gen* wish for, desire; want. **желе́** *neut indecl* jelly.

железа́ (*pl* же́лезы, -лёз, -за́м) gland; *pl* tonsils.

железнодоро́жник railwayman. **железнодоро́жный** railway. **желе́зн|ый** iron; ~**ая доро́га** railway. **желе́зо** iron.

железобето́н reinforced concrete.

жёлоб (*pl* -á) gutter. **желобо́к** (-бка́) groove, channel, flute.

желте́ть (-е́ю) *impf* (*pf* по~) turn yellow; be yellow. **желто́к** (-тка́) yolk. **желту́ха** jaundice. **жёлтый** (жёлт, -á, жёлто) yellow.

желу́док (-дка) stomach. **желу́дочный** stomach; gastric.

жёлудь (*gen pl* -е́й) *m* acorn.

жёлчный bilious; gall; irritable. **жёлчь** bile, gall.

жема́ниться *impf* mince, put on airs. **жема́нный** mincing, affected. **жема́нство** affectedness.

же́мчуг (*pl* -á) pearl(s). **жемчу́жина** pearl. **жемчу́жный** pear(ly).

жена́ (*pl* жёны) wife. **жена́тый** married.

жени́ть (-ню́, -нишь) *impf & pf* (*pf also* по~) marry. **жени́тьба** marriage. **жени́ться** (-ню́сь, -нишься) *impf & pf* (+**на**+*prep*) marry, get married (to). **жени́х** (-á) fiancé; bridegroom. **же́нский** woman's; feminine; female. **же́нственный** womanly, feminine. **же́нщина** woman.

жердь (*gen pl* -е́й) pole; stake.

жеребёнок (-нка; *pl* -бя́та, -бя́т) foal. **жеребе́ц** (-бца́) stallion.

жеребьёвка casting of lots.

жерло́ (*pl* -a) muzzle; crater.

жёрнов (*pl* -á, -óв) millstone.

же́ртва sacrifice; victim. **же́ртвенный** sacrificial. **же́ртвовать** *impf* (*pf* по~) present, make a donation (of); +*instr* sacrifice.

жест gesture. **жестикули́ровать** *impf* gesticulate.

жёсткий (-ток, -тка́, -о) hard, tough; rigid, strict.

жесто́кий (-то́к, -á, -о) cruel; severe. **жесто́кость** cruelty.

жесть tin(-plate). **жестяно́й** tin.

жето́н medal; counter; token.

жечь (жгу, жжёшь; жёг, жгла) *impf*

(*pf* с~) burn; ~**ся** burn, sting; burn o.s.

живи́тельный invigorating. **жи́вность** poultry, fowl. **жив|о́й** (жив, -á, -о) living, alive; lively; vivid; brisk; animated; poignant; bright; **на ~ую ни́тку** hastily, anyhow; **шить на ~ую ни́тку** tack. **живопи́сец** (-сца) painter. **живопи́сный** picturesque. **жи́вопись** painting. **жи́вость** liveliness.

живо́т (-á) abdomen; stomach. **животново́дство** animal husbandry. **живо́тное** *sb* animal. **живо́тный** animal.

живу́ *etc.: see* **жить. живу́чий** hardy. **живьём** *adv* alive.

жи́дк|ий (-док, -дка́, -о) liquid; watery; weak; sparse; ~**ий криста́лл** liquid crystal. **жи́дкость** liquid, fluid; wateriness, weakness. **жи́жа** sludge; slush; liquid. **жи́же** *comp of* **жи́дкий**

жи́зненный life, of life; vital; living; ~ **у́ровень** standard of living. **жизнеописа́ние** biography. **жизнера́достный** cheerful. **жизнеспосо́бный** capable of living; viable. **жизнь** life.

жи́ла vein; tendon, sinew.

жиле́т, жиле́тка waistcoat.

жиле́ц (-льца́), **жили́ца** lodger; tenant; inhabitant.

жили́ще dwelling, abode. **жили́щный** housing; living.

жи́лка vein; fibre; streak.

жил|о́й dwelling; habitable; ~**о́й дом** dwelling house; block of flats; ~**áя пло́щадь, жилпло́щадь** floor-space; housing, accommodation. **жильё** habitation; dwelling.

жир (*loc* -ý; *pl* -ы́) fat; grease. **жире́ть** (-ре́ю) *impf* (*pf* о~, раз~) grow fat. **жи́рный** (-рен, -рна́, -о) fatty; greasy; rich. **жирово́й** fatty; fat.

жира́ф giraffe.

жите́йский worldly; everyday. **жи́тель** *m* inhabitant; dweller. **жи́тельство** residence. **жи́тница** granary. **жи́то** corn, cereal. **жить** (живу́, -вёшь; жил, -á, -о) *impf* live. **житьё** life; existence; habitation.

жму *etc.: see* **жать**[2]

жму́риться *impf* (*pf* за~) screw up one's eyes, frown.

жнивьё (*pl* -ья, -ьев) stubble (-field).

жну *etc.*: see **жать**[1]

жокей jockey.

жонглёр juggler.

жрать (жру, жрёшь; -ал, -á, -о) guzzle.

жрéбий lot; fate, destiny; ~ брóшен the die is cast.

жрец priest. **жрица** priestess.

жужжáть (-жжý) hum, buzz, drone; whiz(z).

жук (-á) beetle.

жýлик petty thief; cheat. **жýльничать** (*pf* с~) cheat.

журáвль (-я́) *m* crane.

журить *impf* reprove.

журнáл magazine, periodical. **журналист** journalist. **журналистика** journalism.

журчáние babble; murmur. **журчáть** (-чит) *impf* babble, murmur.

жýткий (-ток, -ткá, -о) uncanny; terrible, terrifying. **жýтко** *adv* terrifyingly; terribly, awfully.

жую *etc.*: see **жевáть**

жюри *neut indecl* judges.

З

за *prep* I. +*acc* (*indicating motion or action*) *or instr* (*indicating rest or state*) behind; beyond; across, the other side of; at; to; **за гóрод, зá гóродом** out of town; **за рубежóм** abroad; **сесть за роя́ль** sit down at the piano; **сидéть за роя́лем** be at the piano; **зá угол, за углóм** round the corner. II. +*acc* after; over; during, in the space of; by; for; to; **зá вáше здорóвье!** your health!; **вести зá руку** lead by the hand; **далекó зá пóлночь** long after midnight; **зá два дня до**+*gen* two days before; **зá три киломéтра от дерéвни** three kilometres from the village; **платить за билéт** pay for a ticket; **за послéднее врéмя** lately. III. +*instr* after; for; because of; at; during; **год за гóдом** year after year; **идти за молокóм** go for milk; **за обéдом** at dinner.

забáва amusement; game; fun.

забавля́ть *impf* amuse; ~ся amuse o.s. **забáвный** amusing, funny.

забастовáть *pf* strike; go on strike. **забастóвка** strike. **забастóвщик** striker.

забвéние oblivion.

забéг heat, race. **забегáть** *impf,* **забежáть** (-егý) *pf* run up; +к+*dat* drop in on; ~ вперёд run ahead; anticipate.

заберý *etc.*: see **забрáть**

забивáние jamming. **забивáть(ся** *impf of* **забить(ся**[1]

забинтовáть *pf,* **забинтóвывать** *impf* bandage.

забирáть(ся *impf of* **забрáть(ся**

забитый downtrodden. **забить**[1] (-бью, -бьёшь) *pf* (*impf* **забивáть**) drive in, hammer in; score; seal, block up; obstruct; choke; jam; cram; beat up; beat; ~ся hide, take refuge; become cluttered or clogged; +в+*acc* get into, penetrate. **за|бить(ся**[2] *pf* begin to beat. **забия́ка** *m & f* squabbler; bully.

заблаговрéменно *adv* in good time; well in advance. **заблаговрéменный** timely.

заблестéть (-ещý, -естишь *or* -éщешь) *pf* begin to shine, glitter, glow.

заблудиться (-ужýсь, -ýдишься) *pf* get lost. **заблýдший** lost, stray. **заблуждáться** *impf* be mistaken. **заблуждéние** error; delusion.

забóй (pit-)face.

заболевáемость sickness rate. **заболевáние** sickness, illness; falling ill. **заболевáть**[1] *impf,* **заболéть**[1](-éю) *pf* fall ill; +*instr* go down with. **заболевáть**[2] *impf,* **заболéть**[2] (-лит) *pf* (begin to) ache, hurt.

забóр[1] fence.

забóр[2] taking away; obtaining on credit.

забóта concern; care; trouble(s). **забóтить** (-óчу) *impf* (*pf* о~) trouble, worry; ~ся *impf* (*pf* по~) worry; take care (о+*prep* of); take trouble; care. **забóтливый** solicitous, thoughtful.

за|браковáть *pf.*

забрáсывать *impf of* **забросáть, забрóсить**

забрáть (-берý, -берёшь; -áл, -á, -о)

pf (*impf* забира́ть) take; take away; seize; appropriate; ~ся climb; get to, into.

забреда́ть *impf*, **забрести́** (-еду́, -едёшь; -ёл, -а́) *pf* stray, wander; drop in.

за|брони́ровать *pf*.

заброса́ть *pf* (*impf* забра́сывать) fill up; bespatter, deluge. **забро́сить** (-о́шу) *pf* (*impf* забра́сывать) throw; abandon; neglect. **забро́шенный** neglected; deserted.

забры́згать *pf*, **забры́згивать** *impf* splash, bespatter.

забыва́ть *impf*, **забы́ть** (-бу́ду) *pf* forget; ~ся doze off; lose consciousness; forget o.s. **забы́вчивый** forgetful. **забытьё** oblivion; drowsiness.

забью́ *etc.: see* **забить**

зава́ливать *impf*, **завали́ть** (-лю́, -лишь) *pf* block up; pile; cram; overload; knock down; make a mess of; ~ся fall; collapse; tip up.

зава́ривать *impf*, **завари́ть** (-арю́, -а́ришь) *pf* make; brew; weld. **зава́рка** brewing; brew; welding.

заведе́ние establishment. **заве́довать** *impf* +*instr* manage.

заве́домо *adv* wittingly. **заве́домый** notorious, undoubted.

заведу́ *etc.: see* **завести́**

заве́дующий *sb* (+*instr*) manager; head.

завезти́ (-зу́, -зёшь; -ёз, -ла́) *pf* (*impf* завози́ть) convey, deliver.

за|вербова́ть *pf*.

заве́ритель *m* witness. **заве́рить** *pf* (*impf* заверя́ть) assure; certify; witness.

заверну́ть (-ну́, -нёшь) *pf* (*impf* завёртывать, завора́чивать) wrap, wrap up; roll up; screw tight, screw up; turn (off); drop in, call in.

заверте́ться (-рчу́сь, -ртишься) *pf* begin to turn *or* spin; lose one's head.

завёртывать *impf of* **заверну́ть**

заверша́ть *impf*, **заверши́ть** (-шу́) *pf* complete, conclude. **заверше́ние** completion; end.

заверя́ть *impf of* **заве́рить**

заве́са veil, screen. **заве́сить** (-е́шу) *pf* (*impf* заве́шивать) curtain (off).

завести́ (-еду́, -ёшь; -вёл, -а́) *pf* (*impf* заводи́ть) take, bring; drop

off; start up; acquire; introduce; wind (up), crank; ~сь be; appear; be established; start.

заве́т behest, bidding, ordinance; Testament. **заве́тный** cherished; secret.

заве́шивать *impf of* **заве́сить**

завеща́ние will, testament. **завеща́ть** bequeath.

завзя́тый inveterate, out-and-out.

завива́ть(ся *impf of* **завить(ся**. **зави́вка** waving; curling; wave.

зави́дно *impers*+*dat*: мне ~ I feel envious. **зави́дный** enviable. **зави́довать** *impf* (*pf* по~) +*dat* envy.

завинти́ть (-нчу́) *pf*, **зави́нчивать** *impf* screw up.

зави́сеть (-и́шу) *impf* +**от**+*gen* depend on. **зави́симость** dependence; **в зави́симости от** depending on, subject to. **зави́симый** dependent.

зави́стливый envious. **за́висть** envy.

завито́й (за́вит, -а́, -о) curled, waved. **завито́к** (-тка́) curl, lock; flourish. **зави́ть** (-вью́, -вьёшь; -и́л, -а́, -о) *pf* (*impf* завива́ть) curl, wave; ~ся curl, wave, twine; have one's hair curled.

завладева́ть *impf*, **завладе́ть** (-е́ю) *pf* +*instr* take possession of; seize.

завлека́тельный alluring; fascinating. **завлека́ть** *impf*, **завле́чь** (-еку́, -ечёшь; -лёк, -ла́) *pf* lure; fascinate.

заво́д[1] factory; works; studfarm.

заво́д[2] winding mechanism. **заводи́ть(ся** (-ожу́(сь, -о́дишь(ся) *impf of* **завести́(сь. заводно́й** clockwork; winding, cranking.

заводско́й factory; *sb* factory worker. **заво́дчик** factory owner.

за́водь backwater.

завоева́ние winning; conquest; achievement. **завоева́тель** *m* conqueror. **завоева́ть** (-ою́ю) *pf*, **завоёвывать** *impf* conquer; win, gain; try to get.

завожу́ *etc.: see* **заводи́ть, завози́ть**

заво́з delivery; carriage. **завози́ть** (-ожу́, -о́зишь) *impf of* **завезти́**

завора́чивать *impf of* **заверну́ть**. **заворо́т** turn, turning; sharp bend.

завою́ *etc.: see* **завы́ть**

завсегда́ *adv* always. **завсегда́тай** habitué, frequenter.

за́втра tomorrow. **за́втрак** breakfast; lunch. **за́втракать** *impf* (*pf* **по~**) have breakfast; have lunch. **за́втрашний** tomorrow's; ~ **день** tomorrow.

завыва́ть *impf*, **завы́ть** (-во́ю) *pf* (begin to) howl.

завяза́ть (-яжу́, -я́жешь) *pf* (*impf* **завя́зывать**) tie, tie up; start; ~ся start; arise; (*of fruit*) set. **завя́зка** string, lace; start; opening.

за|вя́знуть (-ну; -я́з) *pf*. **за|вя́зывать(ся** *impf of* **завяза́ть(ся**

за|вя́нуть (-ну; -я́л) *pf*.

загада́ть *pf*, **зага́дывать** *impf* think of; plan ahead; guess at the future; ~ **зага́дку** ask a riddle. **зага́дка** riddle; enigma. **зага́дочный** enigmatic, mysterious.

зага́р sunburn, tan.

за|гаси́ть (-ашу́, -а́сишь) *pf*. **за|га́снуть** (-ну) *pf*.

загво́здка snag; difficulty.

заги́б fold; exaggeration. **загиба́ть** *impf of* **загну́ть**

за|гипнотизи́ровать *pf*.

загла́вие title; heading. **загла́вн|ый** title; ~**ая бу́ква** capital letter.

загла́дить (-а́жу) *pf*, **загла́живать** *impf* iron, iron out; make up for; expiate; ~ся iron out, become smooth; fade.

за|гло́хнуть (-ну; -гло́х) *pf*.

заглуша́ть *impf*, **за|глуши́ть** (-шу́) *pf* drown, muffle; jam; suppress, stifle; alleviate.

загляде́нье lovely sight. **загляде́ться** (-яжу́сь) *pf*, **загля́дываться** *impf* **на**+*acc* stare at; be lost in admiration of. **загля́дывать** *impf*, **загляну́ть** (-ну́, -нешь) *pf* peep; drop in.

загна́ть (-гоню́, -го́нишь; -а́л, -а́, -о) *pf* (*impf* **загоня́ть**) drive in, drive home; drive; exhaust.

загнива́ние decay; suppuration. **загнива́ть** *impf*, **загни́ть** (-ию́, -иёшь; -и́л, -а́, -о) *pf* rot; decay; fester.

загну́ть (-ну́, -нёшь) *pf* (*impf* **загиба́ть**) turn up, turn down; bend.

загова́ривать *impf*, **заговори́ть** *pf* begin to speak; tire out with talk; cast a spell over; protect with a charm (**от**+*gen* against). **за́говор** plot; spell. **загово́рщик** conspirator.

заголо́вок (-вка) title; heading; headline.

заго́н enclosure, pen; driving in. **загоня́ть**[1] *impf of* **загна́ть**. **загоня́ть**[2] *pf* tire out; work to death.

загора́живать *impf of* **загороди́ть**

загора́ть *impf*, **загоре́ть** (-рю́) *pf* become sunburnt; ~ся catch fire; blaze; *impers*+*dat* want very much. **загоре́лый** sunburnt.

загороди́ть (-рожу́, -ро́дишь) *pf* (*impf* **загора́живать**) enclose, fence in; obstruct. **загоро́дка** fence, enclosure.

за́городный suburban; country.

загота́вливать *impf*, **загота́влять** *impf*, **загото́вить** (-влю) *pf* lay in (a stock of); store; prepare. **загото́вка** (State) procurement, purchase; laying in.

загради́ть (-ажу́) *pf*, **загражда́ть** *impf* block, obstruct; bar. **загражде́ние** obstruction; barrier.

заграни́ца abroad, foreign parts. **заграни́чный** foreign.

загреба́ть *impf*, **загрести́** (-ебу́, -ебёшь; -ёб, -ла́) *pf* rake up, gather; rake in.

загри́вок (-вка) withers; nape (of the neck).

за|гримирова́ть *pf*.

загроможда́ть *impf*, **загромозди́ть** (-зжу́) *pf* block up, encumber; cram.

загружа́ть *impf*, **за|грузи́ть** (-ужу́, -у́зишь) *pf* load; feed; ~ся +*instr* load up with, take on. **загру́зка** loading, feeding; charge, load, capacity.

за|грунтова́ть *pf*.

загрусти́ть (-ущу́) *pf* grow sad.

загрязне́ние pollution. **за|грязни́ть** *pf*, **загрязня́ть** *impf* soil; pollute; ~ся become dirty.

загс *abbr* (*of* **отде́л за́писи а́ктов гражда́нского состоя́ния**) registry office.

загуби́ть (-блю́, -бишь) *pf* ruin; squander, waste.

загуля́ть *pf*, **загу́ливать** *impf* take to drink.

за|густе́ть *pf*.

зад (*loc* -у́; *pl* -ы́) back; hindquarters; buttocks; ~**ом наперёд** back to front.

задава́ть(ся (-даю́(сь) *impf of* **зада́ть(ся**

задави́ть (-влю́, -вишь) *pf* crush; run over.

зададим etc., **задам** etc.: see **задать**

задание (-тков) pl abilities, promise.

задаток (-тка) deposit, advance.

задать (-ам, -ашь, -аст, -адим; задал, -а, -о) pf (impf **задавать**) set; give; ~ **вопрос** ask a question; ~**ся** turn out well; succeed; ~**ся мыслью, целью** make up one's mind. **задача** problem; task.

задвигать impf, **задвинуть** (-ну) pf bolt; bar; push; ~**ся** shut; slide. **задвижка** bolt; catch.

задворки (-рок) pl back yard; backwoods.

задевать impf of **задеть**

заделать pf, **заделывать** impf do up; block up, close up.

задену etc.: see **задеть**. **задёргивать** impf of **задёрнуть**

задержание detention. **задержать** (-жу, -жишь) pf, **задерживать** impf delay; withhold; arrest; ~**ся** stay too long; be delayed. **задержка** delay.

задёрнуть (-ну) pf (impf **задёргивать**) pull; draw.

задеру etc.: see **задрать**

задеть (-ену) pf (impf **задевать**) brush (against), graze; offend; catch (against).

задира m & f bully; trouble-maker. **задирать** impf of **задрать**

задний back, rear; **дать** ~**ий ход** reverse; ~**яя мысль** ulterior motive; ~**ий план** background; ~**ий проход** anus. **задник** back; backdrop.

задолго adv +**до**+gen long before.

задолжать pf. **задолженность** debts.

задор fervour. **задорный** provocative; fervent.

задохнуться (-нусь, -нёшься; -охся or -улся) pf (impf **задыхаться**) suffocate; choke; pant.

задрать (-деру, -дерёшь; -ал, -а, -о) pf (impf also **задирать**) tear to pieces, kill; lift up; break; provoke; insult.

задремать (-млю, -млешь) pf doze off.

задрожать (-жу) pf begin to tremble.

задувать impf of **задуть**

задумать pf, **задумывать** impf plan; intend; think of; ~**ся** become thoughtful; meditate. **задумчивость** reverie. **задумчивый** pensive.

задуть (-ую) pf (impf **задувать**) blow out; begin to blow.

задушевный sincere; intimate.

за|душить (-ушу, -ушишь) pf.

задыхаться impf of **задохнуться**

заедать impf of **заесть**

заезд calling in; lap, heat. **заездить** (-зжу) pf override; wear out. **заезжать** impf of **заехать**. **заезженный** hackneyed; worn out. **заезжий** visiting.

заём (займа) loan.

заесть (-ем, -ешь, -ест, -едим) pf (impf **заедать**) torment; jam; entangle.

заехать (-еду) pf (impf **заезжать**) call in; enter, ride in, drive in; reach; +**за**+acc go past; +**за**+instr call for, fetch.

за|жарить(ся pf.

зажать (-жму, -жмёшь) pf (impf **зажимать**) squeeze; grip; suppress.

зажечь (-жгу, -жжёшь; -жёг, -жгла) pf (impf **зажигать**) set fire to; kindle; light; ~**ся** catch fire.

заживать impf of **зажить**. **заживить** (-влю) pf, **заживлять** impf heal. **заживо** adv alive.

зажигалка lighter. **зажигание** ignition. **зажигательный** inflammatory; incendiary. **зажигать(ся** impf of **зажечь(ся**

зажим clamp; terminal; suppression. **зажимать** impf of **зажать**. **зажимной** tight-fisted.

зажиточный prosperous. **зажить** (-иву, -ивёшь; -ил, -а, -о) pf (impf **заживать**) heal; begin to live.

зажму etc.: see **зажать**. **за|жмуриться** pf.

зазвенеть (-ит) pf begin to ring.

зазеленеть (-еет) pf turn green.

заземление earthing; earth. **заземлить** pf, **заземлять** impf earth.

зазнаваться (-наюсь, -наёшься) impf, **зазнаться** pf give o.s. airs.

зазубрина notch.

за|зубрить (-рю, -убришь) pf.

заигрывать impf flirt.

зайка m & f stammerer. **заикание** stammer. **заикаться** impf, **заикнуться** (-нусь, -нёшься) pf stammer, stutter; +**о**+prep mention.

займствование borrowing. **займствовать** impf & pf (pf also **по**~) borrow.

заинтересо́ванный interested. **заинтересова́ть** *pf*, **заинтересо́вывать** *impf* interest; **~ся** +*instr* become interested in.

за́искивать *impf* ingratiate o.s.

зайду́ etc.: see **зайти́**. **займу́** etc.: see **заня́ть**

зайти́ (-йду́, -йдёшь; зашёл, -шла́) *pf* (*impf* **заходи́ть**) call; drop in; set; +в+*acc* reach; +за+*acc* go behind, turn; +за+*instr* call for, fetch.

за́йчик little hare (*esp. as endearment*); reflection of sunlight. **за́йчиха** doe hare.

закабали́ть *pf*, **закабаля́ть** *impf* enslave.

закады́чный intimate, bosom.

зака́з order; на ~ to order. **заказа́ть** (-ажу́, -а́жешь) *pf*, **зака́зывать** *impf* order; book. **заказн|о́й** made to order; **~о́е (письмо́)** registered letter. **зака́зчик** customer, client.

зака́л temper; cast. **зака́ливать** *impf*, **закали́ть** (-лю́) *pf* (*impf* also **закаля́ть**) temper; harden. **зака́лка** tempering, hardening.

зака́лывать *impf of* **заколо́ть**. **закаля́ть** *impf of* **закали́ть**. **зака́нчивать(ся** *impf of* **зако́нчить(ся**

зака́пать *pf*, **зака́пывать**[1] *impf* begin to drip; rain; spot.

зака́пывать[2] *impf of* **закопа́ть**

зака́т sunset. **заката́ть** *pf*, **зака́тывать**[1] *impf* begin to roll; roll up; roll out. **закати́ть** (-ачу́, -а́тишь) *pf*, **зака́тывать**[2] *impf* roll; **~ся** roll; set.

заква́ска ferment; leaven.

закида́ть *pf*, **заки́дывать**[1] *impf* shower; bespatter.

заки́дывать[2] *impf*, **заки́нуть** (-ну) *pf* throw (out, away).

закипа́ть *impf*, **закипе́ть** (-пи́т) *pf* begin to boil.

закиса́ть *impf*, **заки́снуть** (-ну; -ис, -ла) *pf* turn sour; become apathetic. **за́кись** oxide.

закла́д pawn; pledge; bet; **би́ться об ~** bet; **в ~е** in pawn. **закла́дка** laying; bookmark. **закладно́й** pawn.

закла́дывать *impf of* **заложи́ть**

закле́ивать *impf*, **закле́ить** *pf* glue up.

за|клейми́ть (-млю́) *pf*.

заклепа́ть *pf*, **заклёпывать** *impf*

rivet. **заклёпка** rivet; riveting.

заклина́ние incantation; spell. **заклина́ть** *impf* invoke; entreat.

заключа́ть *impf*, **заключи́ть** (-чу́) *pf* conclude; enter into; contain; confine. **заключа́ться** consist; lie, be. **заключе́ние** conclusion; decision; confinement. **заключённый** *sb* prisoner. **заключи́тельный** final, concluding.

закля́тие pledge. **закля́тый** sworn.

закова́ть (-кую́, -куёшь) *pf*, **зако́вывать** *impf* chain; shackle.

зако́лачивать *impf of* **заколоти́ть**

заколдо́ванный bewitched; **~ круг** vicious circle. **заколдова́ть** *pf* bewitch; lay a spell on.

зако́лка hair-grip; hair-slide.

заколоти́ть (-лочу́, -ло́тишь) *pf* (*impf* **зако́лачивать**) board up; knock in; knock insensible.

за|коло́ть (-олю́, -о́лешь) *pf* (*impf also* **зака́лывать**) stab; pin up; (*impers*) **у меня́ заколо́ло в боку́** I have a stitch.

зако́н law. **законнорождённый** legitimate. **зако́нность** legality. **зако́нный** legal; legitimate. **законо-** in comb law, legal. **законове́дение** law, jurisprudence. **~да́тельный** legislative. **~да́тельство** legislation. **~ме́рность** regularity, normality. **~ме́рный** regular, natural. **~прое́кт** bill.

за|консерви́ровать *pf*. **за|конспекти́ровать** *pf*.

зако́нченность completeness. **зако́нченный** finished; accomplished. **зако́нчить** (-чу) *pf* (*impf* **зака́нчивать**) end, finish; **~ся** end, finish.

закопа́ть *pf* (*impf* **зака́пывать**[2]) begin to dig; bury.

закопте́лый sooty, smutty. **за|копте́ть** (-ти́т) *pf*. **за|копти́ть** (-пчу́) *pf*.

закорене́лый deep-rooted; inveterate.

закосне́лый incorrigible.

закоу́лок (-лка) alley; nook.

закочене́лый numb with cold. **за|коченеть** (-е́ю) *pf*.

закра́дываться *impf of* **закра́сться**

закра́сить (-а́шу) *pf* (*impf* **закра́шивать**) paint over.

закра́сться (-аду́сь, -адёшься) *pf* (*impf* **закра́дываться**) steal in, creep in.

закра́шивать *impf of* **закра́сить**

закрепи́тель *m* fixative. **закрепи́ть** (-плю́) *pf*, **закрепля́ть** *impf* fasten; fix; consolidate; +**за**+*instr* assign to; **~ за собо́й** secure.

закрепости́ть (-ощу́) *pf*, **закрепоща́ть** *impf* enslave. **закрепоще́ние** enslavement; slavery, serfdom.

закрича́ть (-чу́) *pf* cry out; begin to shout.

закро́йщик cutter.

закро́ю *etc.: see* **закры́ть**

закругле́ние rounding; curve. **закругли́ть** (-лю́) *pf*, **закругля́ть** *impf* make round; round off; **~ся** become round; round off.

закружи́ться (-ужу́сь, -у́жи́шься) *pf* begin to whirl *or* go round.

за|крути́ть (-учу́, -у́тишь) *pf*, **закру́чивать** *impf* twist, twirl; wind round; turn; screw in; turn the head of; **~ся** twist, twirl, whirl; wind round.

закрыва́ть *impf*, **закры́ть** (-ро́ю) *pf* close, shut; turn off; close down; cover; **~ся** close, shut; end; close down; cover o.s.; shelter. **закры́тие** closing; shutting; closing down; shelter. **закры́тый** closed, shut; private.

закули́сный behind the scenes; backstage.

закупа́ть *impf*, **закупи́ть** (-плю́, -пишь) *pf* buy up; stock up with. **заку́пка** purchase.

заку́поривать *impf*, **заку́порить** *pf* cork; stop up; coop up. **заку́порка** corking; thrombosis.

заку́почный purchase. **заку́пщик** buyer.

заку́ривать *impf*, **закури́ть** (-рю́, -ришь) *pf* light up; begin to smoke.

закуси́ть (-ушу́, -у́сишь) *pf*, **заку́сывать** *impf* have a snack; bite. **заку́ска** hors-d'oeuvre; snack. **заку́сочная** *sb* snack-bar.

за|ку́тать *pf*, **заку́тывать** *impf* wrap up; **~ся** wrap o.s. up.

зал hall; **~ ожида́ния** waiting-room.

залега́ть *impf of* **зале́чь**

за|ледене́ть (-е́ю) *pf*

залежа́лый stale, long unused. **залежа́ться** (-жу́сь) *pf*, **залёжи**-**ваться** *impf* lie too long; find no market; become stale. **за́лежь** de-

posit, seam; stale goods.

залеза́ть *impf*, **зале́зть** (-зу; -ез) *pf* climb, climb up; get in; creep in.

за|лепи́ть (-плю́, -пишь) *pf*, **залепля́ть** *impf* paste over; glue up.

залета́ть *impf*, **залете́ть** (-ечу́) *pf* fly; +**в**+*acc* fly into.

залечивать *impf*, **залечи́ть** (-чу́, -чишь) *pf* heal, cure; **~ся** heal (up).

зале́чь (-ля́гу, -ля́жешь; залёг, -ла́) *pf* (*impf* **залега́ть**) lie down; lie low; lie, be deposited.

зали́в bay; gulf. **залива́ть** *impf*, **зали́ть** (-лью́, -льёшь; за́ли́л, -а́, -о) *pf* flood, inundate; spill on; extinguish; spread; **~ся** be flooded; pour, spill; +*instr* break into.

зало́г deposit; pledge; security, mortgage; token; voice. **заложи́ть** (-жу́, -жишь) *pf* (*impf* **закла́дывать**) lay; put; mislay; pile up; pawn, mortgage; harness; lay in. **зало́жник** hostage.

залп volley, salvo; **~ом** without pausing for breath.

залью́ *etc.: see* **зали́ть**. **заля́гу** *etc.: see* **зале́чь**

зам *abbr* (*of* **замести́тель**) assistant, deputy. **зам-** *abbr in comb* (*of* **замести́тель**) assistant, deputy, vice-.

за|ма́зать (-а́жу) *pf*, **зама́зывать** *impf* paint over; putty; smear; soil; **~ся** get dirty. **зама́зка** putty; puttying.

зама́лчивать *impf of* **замолча́ть**

зама́нивать *impf*, **замани́ть** (-ню́, -нишь) *pf* entice; decoy. **зама́н-чивый** tempting.

за|маринова́ть *pf*.

за|маскирова́ть *pf*, **замаскиро́-вывать** *impf* mask; disguise; **~ся** disguise o.s.

зама́х threatening gesture. **зама́-хиваться** *impf*, **замахну́ться** (-ну́сь, -нёшься) *pf* +*instr* raise threateningly.

зама́чивать *impf of* **замочи́ть**

замедле́ние slowing down, deceleration; delay. **заме́длить** *pf*, **замедля́ть** *impf* slow down; slacken; delay; **~ся** slow down.

замёл *etc.: see* **замести́**

заме́на substitution; substitute. **заме-ни́мый** replaceable. **замени́тель** *m* (+*gen*) substitute (for). **замени́ть** (-ню́, -нишь) *pf*, **заменя́ть** *impf* replace; be a substitute for.

замере́ть (-мру́, -мрёшь; за́мер, -ла́, -о) *pf* (*impf* **замира́ть**) stand still; freeze; die away.

замерза́ние freezing. **замерза́ть** *impf*, **за|мёрзнуть** (-ну) *pf* freeze (up); freeze to death.

заме́рить *pf* (*impf* **замеря́ть**) measure, gauge.

замеси́ть (-ешу́, -е́сишь) *pf* (*impf* **заме́шивать²**) knead.

замести́ (-ету́, -етёшь; -мёл, -а́) *pf* (*impf* **замета́ть**) sweep up; cover.

замести́тель *m* substitute; assistant, deputy, vice-. **замести́ть** (-ещу́) *pf* (*impf* **замеща́ть**) replace; deputize for.

замета́ть *impf of* **замести́**

заме́тить (-е́чу) *pf* (*impf* **замеча́ть**) notice; note; remark. **заме́тка** mark; note. **заме́тный** noticeable; outstanding.

замеча́ние remark; reprimand. **замеча́тельный** remarkable; splendid.

замеча́ть *impf of* **заме́тить**

замеша́тельство confusion; embarrassment. **замеша́ть** *pf*, **заме́шивать¹** *impf* mix up, entangle. **заме́шивать²** *impf of* **замеси́ть**

замеща́ть *impf of* **замести́ть**. **замеще́ние** substitution; filling.

зами́нка hitch; hesitation.

замира́ть *impf of* **замере́ть**

за́мкнутый reserved; closed, exclusive. **замкну́ть** (-ну́, -нёшь) *pf* (*impf* **замыка́ть**) lock; close; **~ся** close; shut o.s. up; become reserved.

за́мок¹ (-мка) castle.

замо́к² (-мка́) lock; padlock; clasp.

замолка́ть *impf*, **замо́лкнуть** (-ну; -мо́лк) *pf* fall silent; stop.

замолча́ть (-чу́) *pf* (*impf* **зама́лчивать**) fall silent; cease corresponding; hush up.

замора́живать *impf*, **заморо́зить** (-ро́жу) *pf* freeze. **заморо́женный** frozen; iced. **за́морозки** (-ов) *pl* (slight) frosts.

замо́рский overseas.

за|мочи́ть (-чу́, -чишь) *pf* (*impf also* **зама́чивать**) wet; soak; ret.

замо́чная сква́жина keyhole.

замру́ *etc.*: *see* **замере́ть**

за́муж *adv*: **вы́йти ~** (за+*acc*) marry.

за́мужем *adv* married (за+*instr* to).

за|му́чить (-чу) *pf* torment; wear out; bore to tears. **за|му́читься** (-чусь) *pf*.

за́мша suede.

замыка́ние locking; short circuit.

замыка́ть(ся *impf of* **замкну́ть(ся**

за́мысел (-сла) project, plan. **замы́слить** *pf*, **замышля́ть** *impf* plan; contemplate.

за́навес, занаве́ска curtain.

занести́ (-су́, -сёшь; -ёс, -ла́) *pf* (*impf* **заноси́ть**) bring; note down; (*impers*) cover with snow etc.; (*impers*) skid.

занима́ть *impf* (*pf* **заня́ть**) occupy; interest; engage; borrow; **~ся** +*instr* be occupied with; work at; study.

зано́за splinter. **занози́ть** (-ожу́) *pf* get a splinter in.

зано́с snow-drift; skid. **заноси́ть** (-ошу́, -о́сишь) *impf of* **занести́**. **зано́счивый** arrogant.

заня́тие occupation; *pl* studies. **заня́той** busy. **за́нятый** (-нят, -а́, -о) occupied; taken; engaged. **заня́ть(ся** (займу́(сь, -мёшь(ся; за́нял(ся, -а́(сь, -о(сь) *pf of* **занима́ть(ся**

заодно́ *adv* in concert; at one; at the same time.

заостри́ть *pf*, **заостря́ть** *impf* sharpen; emphasize.

зао́чник, -ница student taking correspondence course; external student. **зао́чно** *adv* in one's absence; by correspondence course. **зао́чный курс** correspondence course.

за́пад west. **за́падный** west, western; westerly.

западня́ (*gen pl* -не́й) trap; pitfall, snare.

за|накова́ть *pf*, **запако́вывать** *impf* pack; wrap up.

запа́л ignition; fuse. **запа́ливать** *impf*, **запали́ть** *pf* light, kindle; set fire to. **запа́льная свеча́** (spark-)plug.

запа́с reserve; supply; hem. **запаса́ть** *impf*, **запасти́** (-су́, -сёшь; -а́с, -ла́) *pf* store, store; lay in a stock of; **~ся** +*instr* provide o.s. with; stock up with. **запасно́й** *sb* reservist. **запасно́й, запа́сный** spare; reserve; **~ вы́ход** emergency exit.

за́пах smell.

запа́хивать *impf*, **запахну́ть²** (-ну́, -нёшь) *pf* wrap up.

запа́хнуть¹ (-ну; -а́х) *pf* begin to smell.

запа́чкать *pf*.

запека́ть(ся *impf of* **запе́чь(ся. запеку́** *etc.*: *see* **запе́чь**

запелена́ть *pf*.

запере́ть (-пру́, -прёшь; за́пер, -ла́, -ло) *pf* (*impf* **запира́ть**) lock; lock in; bar; ~**ся** lock o.s. in.

запеча́тать *pf*, **запеча́тывать** *impf* seal. **запечатлева́ть** *impf*, **запечатле́ть** (-е́ю) *pf* imprint, engrave.

запе́чь (-еку́, -ечёшь; -пёк, -ла́) *pf* (*impf* **запека́ть**) bake; ~**ся** bake; become parched; clot, coagulate.

запива́ть *impf of* **запи́ть**

запина́ться *impf of* **запну́ться. запи́нка** hesitation.

запира́ть(ся *impf of* **запере́ть(ся**

записа́ть (-ишу́, -и́шешь) *pf*, **запи́сывать** *impf* note; take down; record; enter; ~**ся** register, enrol (в+*acc* at, in). **запи́ска** note. **записн|о́й** note; inveterate; ~**а́я кни́жка** notebook. **за́пись** recording; registration; record.

запи́ть (-пью́, -пьёшь; за́пил, -а́, -о) *pf* (*impf* **запива́ть**) begin drinking; wash down (with).

запиха́ть *pf*, **запи́хивать** *impf*, **запихну́ть** (-ну́, -нёшь) *pf* push in, cram in.

запишу́ *etc.*: *see* **записа́ть**

запла́кать (-а́чу) *pf* begin to cry.

заплани́ровать *pf*.

запла́та patch.

заплати́ть (-ачу́, -а́тишь) *pf* pay (за+*acc* for).

заплачу́ *etc.*: *see* **запла́кать. заплачу́** *see* **заплати́ть**

заплести́ (-ету́, -етёшь; -ёл, -а́) *pf*, **заплета́ть** *impf* plait.

запломбирова́ть *pf*.

заплы́|в heat, round. **заплыва́ть** *impf*, **заплы́ть** (-ыву́, -ывёшь; -ы́л, -а́, -о) *pf* swim in, sail in; swim out, sail out; be bloated.

запну́ться (-ну́сь, -нёшься) *pf* (*impf* **запина́ться**) hesitate; stumble.

запове́дник reserve; preserve; **госуда́рственный** ~ national park. **запове́дный** prohibited. **за́поведь** precept; commandment.

заподазривать *impf*, **заподо́зрить** *pf* suspect (в+*prep* of).

запозда́лый belated; delayed. **запозда́ть** *pf* (*impf* **запа́здывать**) be late.

запо́й hard drinking.

заполза́ть *impf*, **заползти́** (-зу́, -зёшь; -олз, -зла́) creep, crawl.

запо́лнить *pf*, **заполня́ть** *impf* fill (in, up).

запомина́ть *impf*, **запо́мнить** *pf* remember; memorize; ~**ся** stay in one's mind.

за́понка cuff-link; stud.

запо́р bolt; lock; constipation.

запоте́ть (-е́ет) *pf* mist over.

запою́ *etc.*: *see* **запе́ть**

запра́вить (-влю) *pf*, **заправля́ть** *impf* tuck in; prepare; refuel; season; dress; mix in; ~**ся** refuel. **запра́вка** refuelling; seasoning, dressing.

запра́шивать *impf of* **запроси́ть**

запре́т prohibition, ban. **запрети́ть** (-ещу́) *pf*, **запреща́ть** *impf* prohibit, ban. **запре́тный** forbidden. **запреще́ние** prohibition.

запрограмми́ровать *pf*.

запро́с inquiry; overcharging; *pl* needs. **запроси́ть** (-ошу́, -о́сишь) *pf* (*impf* **запра́шивать**) inquire.

за́просто *adv* without ceremony.

запрошу́ *etc.*: *see* **запроси́ть. запру́** *etc.*: *see* **запере́ть**

запру́да dam, weir; mill-pond.

запряга́ть *impf*, **запря́чь** (-ягу́, -яжёшь; -яг, -ла́) *pf* harness; yoke.

запуга́ть *pf*, **запу́гивать** *impf* cow, intimidate.

за́пуск launching. **запуска́ть** *impf*, **запусти́ть** (-ущу́, -у́стишь) *pf* thrust (in); start; launch; (+*acc or instr*) fling; neglect. **запусте́лый** neglected; desolate. **запусте́ние** neglect; desolation.

запу́тать *pf*, **запу́тывать** *impf* tangle; confuse; ~**ся** get tangled; get involved.

запущу́ *etc.*: *see* **запусти́ть**

запча́сть (*gen pl* -е́й) *abbr* (*of* **запасна́я часть**) spare part.

запыха́ться *pf* be out of breath.

запью́ *etc.*: *see* **запи́ть**

запя́стье wrist.

запята́я *sb* comma.

запятна́ть *pf*.

зараба́тывать *impf*, **зарабо́тать** *pf* earn; start (up). **за́работн|ый: ~ая пла́та** wages; pay. **за́работок** (-тка) earnings.

заража́ть *impf*, **зарази́ть** (-ажу́) *pf* infect; **~ся** +*instr* be infected with, catch. **зара́за** infection. **зарази́тельный** infectious. **зара́зный** infectious.

зара́нее *adv* in good time; in advance.

зараста́ть *impf*, **зарасти́** (-ту́, -тёшь; -ро́с, -ла́) *pf* be overgrown; heal.

за́рево glow.

за|регистри́ровать(ся *pf*.

за|ре́зать (-е́жу) *pf* kill, knife; slaughter.

зарека́ться *impf of* **заре́чься**

зарекомендова́ть *pf*: **~ себя́** +*instr* show o.s. to be.

заре́чься (-еку́сь, -ечёшься; -ёкся, -екла́сь) *pf* (*impf* **зарека́ться**) +*inf* renounce.

за|ржа́веть (-еет) *pf*.

зарисо́вка sketching; sketch.

зароди́ть (-ожу́) *pf*, **зарожда́ть** *impf* generate; **~ся** be born; arise. **заро́дыш** foetus; embryo. **зарожде́ние** conception; origin.

заро́к vow, pledge.

заро́с *etc*.: *see* **зарасти́**

заро́ю *etc*.: *see* **зары́ть**

зарпла́та *abbr* (*of* **за́работная пла́та**) wages; pay.

заруба́ть *impf of* **заруби́ть**

зарубе́жный foreign.

заруби́ть (-блю́, -бишь) *pf* (*impf* **заруба́ть**) kill, cut down; notch. **зару́бка** notch.

заруча́ться *impf*, **заручи́ться** (-учу́сь) *pf* +*instr* secure.

зарыва́ть *impf*, **зары́ть** (-ро́ю) *pf* bury.

заря́ (*pl* зо́ри, зорь) dawn; sunset.

заря́д charge; supply. **заряди́ть** (-яжу́, -я́дишь) *pf*, **заряжа́ть** *impf* load; charge; stoke; **~ся** be loaded; be charged. **заря́дка** loading; charging; exercises.

заса́да ambush. **засади́ть** (-ажу́, -а́дишь) *pf*, **заса́живать** *impf* plant; drive; set (**за**+*acc* to); **~ (в тюрьму́)** put in prison. **заса́живаться** *impf of* **засе́сть**

заса́ливать *impf of* **засоли́ть**

засвети́ть (-ечу́, -е́тишь) *pf* light; **~ся** light up.

за|свиде́тельствовать *pf*.

засе́в sowing; seed; sown area.

засева́ть *impf of* **засе́ять**

заседа́ние meeting; session. **заседа́ть** *impf* sit, be in session.

засе́ивать *impf of* **засе́ять**. **засе́к** *etc*.: *see* **засе́чь**. **засека́ть** *impf of* **засе́чь**

засекре́тить (-ре́чу) *pf*, **засекре́чивать** *impf* classify as secret; clear, give access to secret material.

засеку́ *etc*.: *see* **засе́чь**. **засе́л** *etc*.: *see* **засе́сть**

заселе́ние settlement. **засели́ть** *pf*, **заселя́ть** *impf* settle; colonize; populate.

засе́сть (-ся́ду; -се́л) *pf* (*impf* **заса́живаться**) sit down; sit tight; settle; lodge in.

засе́чь (-еку́, -ечёшь; -ёк, -ла́) *pf* (*impf* **засека́ть**) flog to death; notch.

засе́ять (-е́ю) *pf* (*impf* **засева́ть**, **засе́ивать**) sow.

заси́лье dominance, sway.

заслони́ть *pf*, **заслоня́ть** *impf* cover, screen; push into the background. **засло́нка** (*furnace*, *oven*) door.

заслу́га merit, desert; service. **заслу́женный** deserved, merited; Honoured; time-honoured. **заслу́живать** *impf*, **заслужи́ть** (-ужу́, -у́жишь) *pf* deserve; earn; +*gen* be worthy of.

засмея́ться (-ею́сь, -еёшься) begin to laugh.

заснима́ть *impf of* **засня́ть**

засну́ть (-ну́, -нёшь) *pf* (*impf* **засыпа́ть**) fall asleep.

засня́ть (-ниму́, -и́мешь; -я́л, -а́, -о) *pf* (*impf* **заснима́ть**) photograph.

засо́в bolt, bar.

засо́вывать *impf of* **засу́нуть**

засо́л salting, pickling. **засоли́ть** (-олю́, -о́лишь) *pf* (*impf* **заса́ливать**) salt, pickle.

засоре́ние littering; contamination; obstruction. **засори́ть** *pf*, **засоря́ть** *impf* litter; get dirt into; clog.

за|со́хнуть (-ну; -со́х) *pf* (*impf also* **засыха́ть**) dry (up); wither.

заста́ва gate; outpost.

заставáть (-таю́, -таёшь) *impf of* **заста́ть**

заста́вить (-влю) *pf*, **заставля́ть** *impf* make; compel.

заста́иваться *impf of* **застоя́ться**.

заста́ну etc.: see **заста́ть**

заста́ть (-а́ну) pf (impf **застава́ть**) find; catch.

застёгивать impf, **застегну́ть** (-ну́, -нёшь) pf fasten, do up. **застёжка** fastening; clasp, buckle; **~-мо́лния** zip.

застекли́ть pf, **застекля́ть** impf glaze.

засте́нок (-нка) torture chamber.

засте́нчивый shy.

застига́ть impf, **засти́гнуть**, **засти́чь** (-и́гну -сти́г) pf catch; take unawares.

засти́чь see **засти́гнуть**

засто́й stagnation. **засто́йный** stagnant.

за|сто́пориться pf.

застоя́ться (-и́тся) pf (impf **заста́иваться**) stagnate; stand too long.

застра́ивать impf of **застро́ить**

застрахо́ванный insured. **за|страхова́ть** pf, **застрахо́вывать** impf insure.

застрева́ть impf of **застря́ть**

застрели́ть (-елю́, -е́лишь) pf shoot (dead); **~ся** shoot o.s.

застро́ить (-о́ю) pf (impf **застра́ивать**) build over, on, up. **застро́йка** building.

застря́ть (-я́ну) pf (impf **застрева́ть**) stick; get stuck.

за́ступ spade.

заступа́ться impf, **заступи́ться** (-плю́сь, -пишься) pf +за+acc stand up for. **засту́пник** defender. **засту́пничество** protection; intercession.

застыва́ть impf, **засты́ть** (-ы́ну) pf harden, set; become stiff; freeze; be petrified.

засу́нуть (-ну) pf (impf **засо́вывать**) thrust in, push in.

за́суха drought.

засы́пать[1] (-плю) pf, **засыпа́ть** impf fill up; strew.

засыпа́ть[2] impf of **засну́ть**

засыха́ть impf of **засо́хнуть**.

зася́ду etc.: see **засе́сть**.

затаённый (-ён, -ена́) secret; repressed. **зата́ивать** impf, **затаи́ть** pf suppress; conceal; harbour; **~ дыха́ние** hold one's breath.

зата́пливать impf of **затопи́ть**.

зата́птывать impf of **затопта́ть**

зата́скивать impf, **затащи́ть** (-щу́, -щишь) pf drag in; drag off; drag away.

затвердева́ть impf, **за|тверде́ть** (-е́ет) pf become hard; set. **затверде́ние** hardening; callus.

затво́р bolt; lock; shutter; flood-gate.

затвори́ть (-рю́, -ришь) pf, **за|творя́ть** impf shut, close; **~ся** shut o.s. up, lock o.s. in. **затво́рник** hermit, recluse.

затева́ть impf of **зате́ять**

затёк etc.: see **зате́чь. затека́ть** impf of **зате́чь**

зате́м adv then, next; **~ что** because.

затемне́ние darkening, obscuring; blacking out; black-out. **затемни́ть** pf, **затемня́ть** impf darken, obscure; black out.

зате́ривать impf, **затеря́ть** pf lose, mislay; **~ся** be lost; be mislaid; be forgotten.

зате́чь (-ечёт, -еку́т; -тёк, -кла́) pf (impf **затека́ть**) pour, flow; swell up; become numb.

зате́я undertaking, venture; escapade; joke. **зате́ять** pf (impf **затева́ть**) undertake, venture.

затиха́ть impf, **зати́хнуть** (-ну; -ти́х) pf die down, abate; fade. **зати́шье** calm; lull.

заткну́ть (-ну́, -нёшь) pf (impf **затыка́ть**) stop up; stick, thrust.

затмева́ть impf, **затми́ть** (-ми́шь) pf darken; eclipse; overshadow. **затме́ние** eclipse.

зато́ conj but then, but on the other hand.

затону́ть (-о́нет) pf sink, be submerged.

затопи́ть[1] (-плю́, -пишь) pf (impf **зата́пливать**) light; turn on the heating.

затопи́ть[2] (-плю́, -пишь) pf, **затопля́ть** impf flood, submerge; sink.

затопта́ть (-пчу́, -пчешь) pf (impf **зата́птывать**) trample (down).

зато́р obstruction, jam; congestion.

за|тормози́ть (-ожу́) pf.

заточа́ть impf, **заточи́ть** (-чу́) pf incarcerate. **заточе́ние** incarceration.

затра́гивать impf of **затро́нуть**

затра́та expense; outlay. **затра́тить** (-а́чу) pf, **затра́чивать** impf spend.

затрéбовать pf request, require; ask for.

затрóнуть (-ну) pf (impf **затрáгивать**) affect; touch (on).

затруднéние difficulty. **затруднительный** difficult. **затруднить** pf, **затруднять** impf trouble; make difficult; hamper; ~ся +inf or instr find difficulty in.

за|тупиться (-пится) pf.

за|тушить (-шý, -шишь) pf extinguish; suppress.

затхлый musty, mouldy; stuffy.

затыкáть impf of **заткнýть**

затылок (-лка) back of the head; scrag-end.

затя́гивать impf, **затянýть** (-нý, -нешь) pf tighten; cover; close, heal; spin out; ~ся be covered; close; be delayed; drag on; inhale. **затя́жка** inhaling; prolongation; delaying, putting off; lagging. **затяжнóй** long-drawn-out.

заурядный ordinary; mediocre.

зáутреня morning service.

заýчивать impf, **заучить** (-чý, -чишь) pf learn by heart.

за|фаршировáть pf. **за|фиксировáть** pf. **за|фрахтовáть** pf.

захвáт seizure, capture. **захватить** (-ачý, -áтишь) pf, **захвáтывать** impf take; seize; thrill. **захвáтнический** aggressive. **захвáтчик** aggressor. **захвáтывающий** gripping.

захлебнýться (-нýсь, -нёшься) pf, **захлёбываться** impf choke (от+gen with).

захлестнýть (-нý, -нёшь) pf, **захлёстывать** impf flow over, swamp, overwhelm.

захлопнуть (-ну) pf, **захлóпывать** impf slam, bang; ~ся slam (to).

захóд sunset; calling in. **заходить** (-ожý, -óдишь) impf of **зайти**

захолýстный remote, provincial. **захолýстье** backwoods.

за|хоронить (-ню, -нишь) pf. **за|хотéть(ся** (-очý(сь, -óчешь(ся, -отúм(ся) pf.

зацвести (-етёт; -вёл, -á) pf, **зацветáть** impf come into bloom.

зацепить (-плю, -пишь) pf, **зацеплять** impf hook; engage; sting; catch (за+acc on); ~ся за+acc catch on; catch hold of.

зачастýю adv often.

зачáтие conception. **зачáток** (-тка) embryo; rudiment; germ. **зачáточный** rudimentary. **зачáть** (-чнý, -чнёшь; -чáл, -á, -о) pf (impf **зачинáть**) conceive.

зачёл etc.: see **зачéсть**

зачéм adv why; what for. **зачéм-то** adv for some reason.

зачёркивать impf, **зачеркнýть** (-нý, -нёшь) pf cross out.

зачерпнýть (-нý, -нёшь) pf, **зачéрпывать** impf scoop up; draw up.

за|черствéть (-éет) pf.

зачéсть (-чтý, -чтёшь; -чёл, -члá) pf (impf **зачитывать**) take into account, reckon as credit. **зачёт** test; **получить, сдать ~ по**+dat pass a test in; **постáвить ~ по**+dat pass in. **зачётная книжка** (student's) record book.

зачинáть impf of **зачáть**. **зачинщик** instigator.

зачислить pf, **зачислять** impf include; enter; enlist; ~ся join, enter.

зачитывать impf of **зачéсть**. **зачтý** etc.: see **зачéсть**. **зашёл** etc.: see **зайти**

зашивáть impf, **зашить** (-шью, -шьёшь) pf sew up.

за|шифровáть pf, **зашифрóвывать** impf encipher, encode.

за|шнуровáть pf, **зашнурóвывать** impf lace up.

за|шпаклевáть (-люю) pf. **за|штóпать** pf. **за|штриховáть** pf. **зашью** etc.: see **зашить**

защита defence; protection. **защитить** (-ищý) pf, **защищáть** impf defend, protect. **защитник** defender. **защитный** protective.

заявить (-влю, -вишь) pf, **заявля́ть** impf announce, declare; ~ся turn up. **зая́вка** claim; demand. **заявлéние** statement; application.

зáяц (зáйца) hare; stowaway; **éхать зáйцем** travel without a ticket.

звáние rank; title. **звáный** invited; ~ **обéд** banquet, dinner. **звáтельный** vocative. **звать** (зовý, -вёшь; звал, -á, -о) impf (pf **по~**) call; ask, invite; **как вас зовýт?** what is your name?; ~ся be called.

звездá (pl звёзды) star. **звёздный** star; starry; starlit; stellar. **звёз-**

дочка little star; asterisk.
звенеть (-ню) *impf* ring; +*instr* jingle, clink.
звено (*pl* звенья, -ьев) link; team, section; unit; component. **звеньевой** *sb* section leader.
зверинец (-нца) menagerie. **звероводство** fur farming. **зверский** brutal; terrific. **зверство** atrocity. **зверствовать** *impf* commit atrocities. **зверь** (*pl* -и, -ей) *m* wild animal.
звон ringing (sound); peal, chink, clink. **звонить** *impf* (*pf* по~) ring; ring up; ~ кому-нибудь (по телефону) ring s.o. up. **звонкий** (-нок, -нка, -о) ringing, clear. **звонок** (-нка) bell; (telephone) call.
звук sound.
звуко- *in comb* sound. **звукозапись** (sound) recording. ~**изоляция** sound-proofing. ~**непроницаемый** sound-proof. ~**сниматель** *m* pickup.
звуковой sound; audio; acoustic. **звучание** sound(ing); vibration. **звучать** (-чит) *impf* (*pf* про~) be heard; sound. **звучный** (-чен, -чна, -о) sonorous.
здание building.
здесь *adv* here. **здешний** local; не ~ a stranger here.
здороваться *impf* (*pf* по~) exchange greetings. **здорово** *adv* splendidly; very (much); well done!; great! **здоровый** healthy, strong; well; wholesome, sound. **здоровье** health; за ваше ~! your health! как ваше ~? how are you? **здравница** sanatorium.
здравомыслящий sensible, judicious. **здравоохранение** public health.
здравствовать *impf* be healthy; prosper. **здравствуй(те)** how do you do?; hello! **да здравствует!** long live! **здравый** sensible; ~ **смысл** common sense.
зебра zebra.
зевать *impf*, **зевнуть** (-ну, -нёшь) *pf* yawn; gape; (*pf* also про~) miss, let slip, lose. **зевок** (-вка), **зевота** yawn.
зеленеть (-еет) *impf* (*pf* по~) turn green; show green. **зелёный** (зелен,

-а, -о) green; ~ **лук** spring onions. **зелень** green; greenery; greens.
земельный land.
земле- *in comb* land; earth. **землевладелец** (-льца) landowner. ~**делец** (-льца) farmer. ~**делие** farming, agriculture. ~**дельческий** agricultural. ~**коп** navvy. ~**ройный** excavating. ~**трясение** earthquake.
земля (*acc* -ю; *pl* -и, земель, -ям) earth; land; soil. **земляк** (-á) fellow-countryman. **земляника** (*no pl*; *collect*) wild strawberry; wild strawberries. **землянка** dug-out; mud hut. **земляной** earthen; earth; earthy. **землячка** country-woman. **земной** earthly; terrestrial; ground; mundane; ~ **шар** the globe.
зенит zenith. **зенитный** zenith; anti-aircraft.
зеркало (*pl* -á) mirror. **зеркальный** mirror; smooth; plate-glass.
зернистый grainy. **зерно** (*pl* зёрна, зёрен) grain; seed; kernel; core; **кофе в зёрнах** coffee beans. **зерновой** grain. **зерновые** *sb pl* cereals. **зернохранилище** granary.
зигзаг zigzag.
зима (*acc* -у, *pl* -ы) winter. **зимний** winter, wintry. **зимовать** *impf* (*pf* пере~, про~) spend the winter; hibernate. **зимовка** wintering; hibernation. **зимовье** winter quarters. **зимой** *adv* in winter.
зиять *impf* gape, yawn.
злак grass; cereal.
злить (злю) *impf* (*pf* обо~, о~, разо~) anger; irritate; ~**ся** be angry, be in a bad temper; rage. **зло** (*gen pl* зол) evil; harm; misfortune; malice.
зло- *in comb* evil, harm, malice. **зловещий** ominous. ~**воние** stink. ~**вонный** stinking. ~**качественный** malignant; pernicious. ~**памятный** rancorous, unforgiving. ~**радный** malevolent, gloating. ~**словие** malicious gossip. ~**умышленник** malefactor; plotter. ~**язычный** slanderous.
злоба spite; anger; ~ **дня** topic of the day, latest news. **злобный** malicious. **злободневный** topical. **злодей** villain. **злодейский** villainous. **злодейство** villainy; crime, evil

deed. **злодея́ние** crime, evil deed.
злой (зол, зла) evil; wicked; malicious; vicious; bad-tempered; severe.
зло́стный malicious; intentional.
злость malice; fury.
злоупотреби́ть (-блю́) *pf*, **злоупотребля́ть** *impf* +*instr* abuse. **злоупотребле́ние**+*instr* abuse of.
змеи́ный snake; cunning. **змей** snake; dragon; kite. **змея́** (*pl* -и) snake.
знак sign; mark; symbol.
знако́мить (-млю) *impf* (*pf* о~, по~) acquaint; introduce; ~**ся** become acquainted; get to know; +**c**+*instr* meet, make the acquaintance of. **знако́мство** acquaintance; (circle of) acquaintances. **знако́м|ый** familiar; **быть** ~**ым c**+*instr* be acquainted with, know; ~**ый**, ~**ая** *sb* acquaintance.
знамена́тель *m* denominator. **знамена́тельный** significant. **зна́мение** sign. **знамени́тость** celebrity. **знамени́тый** celebrated, famous. **зна́мя** (-мени; *pl* -мёна) *neut* banner; flag.
зна́ние knowledge.
зна́тный (-тен, -тна́, -о) distinguished; aristocratic; splendid.
знато́к (-а́) expert; connoisseur. **знать** *impf* know; **дать** ~ inform, let know.
значе́ние meaning; significance; importance. **зна́чит** so then; that means. **значи́тельный** considerable; important; significant. **зна́чить** (-чу) *impf* mean; signify; be of importance; ~**ся** be; be mentioned, appear. **значо́к** (-чка́) badge; mark.
зна́ющий expert; learned.
зноби́ть *impf, impers*+*acc*: **меня́**, *etc.*, **зноби́т** I feel shivery.
зной intense heat. **зно́йный** hot; burning.
зов call, summons. **зову́** *etc.*: *see* **звать**
зо́дчество architecture. **зо́дчий** *sb* architect.
зол *see* **зло, злой**
зола́ ashes, cinders.
золо́вка sister-in-law (*husband's sister*).
золоти́стый golden. **зо́лото** gold. **золото́й** gold; golden.
золочёный gilt, gilded.

зо́на zone; region.
зонд probe. **зонди́ровать** *impf* sound, probe.
зонт (-а́), **зо́нтик** umbrella.
зоо́лог zoologist. **зоологи́ческий** zoological. **зооло́гия** zoology. **зоопа́рк** zoo. **зооте́хник** livestock specialist.
зо́ри *etc.*: *see* **заря́**
зо́ркий (-рок, -рка́, -о) sharp-sighted; perspicacious.
зрачо́к (-чка́) pupil (*of the eye*).
зре́лище sight; spectacle.
зре́лость ripeness; maturity; **аттеста́т зре́лости** school-leaving certificate. **зре́лый** (зрел, -а́, -о) ripe, mature.
зре́ние (eye)sight, vision; **то́чка зре́ния** point of view.
зреть (-е́ю) *impf* (*pf* со~) ripen; mature.
зри́мый visible.
зри́тель *m* spectator, observer; *pl* audience. **зри́тельный** visual; optic; ~ **зал** hall, auditorium.
зря *adv* in vain.
зуб (*pl* -ы *or* -бья, -о́в *or* -бьев) tooth; *cog.* **зуби́ло** chisel. **зубно́й** dental; tooth; ~ **врач** dentist. **зубовра́чебный** dentists', dental; ~ **кабине́т** dental surgery. **зубочи́стка** toothpick.
зубр (European) bison; die-hard.
зубри́ть (-рю́, зу́бри́шь) *impf* (*pf* вы́~, за~) cram.
зубча́тый toothed; serrated.
зуд itch. **зуде́ть** (-и́т) itch.
зы́бкий (-бок, -бка́, -о) unsteady, shaky; vacillating. **зыбь** (*gen pl* -е́й) ripple, rippling.
зюйд (*naut*) south; south wind.
зя́блик chaffinch.
зя́бнуть (-ну; зяб) *impf* suffer from cold, feel the cold.
зябь land ploughed in autumn for spring sowing.
зять (*pl* -тья́, -тьёв) son-in-law; brother-in-law (*sister's husband or husband's sister's husband*).

И, Й

и *conj* and; even; too; (*with neg*) either; **и... и** both ... and.

и́бо *conj* for.

и́ва willow.

игла́ (*pl* -ы) needle; thorn; spine; quill. **иглоука́лывание** acupuncture.

игнори́ровать *impf* & *pf* ignore.

и́го yoke.

иго́лка needle.

иго́рный gaming, gambling. **игра́** (*pl* -ы) play, playing; game; hand; turn; ~ **слов** pun. **игра́льн|ый** playing; ~**ые ко́сти** dice. **игра́ть** *impf* (*pf* **сыгра́ть**) play; act; ~ **в**+*acc* play (*game*); ~ **на**+*prep* play (*an instrument*). **игри́вый** playful. **игро́к** (-а́) player; gambler. **игру́шка** toy.

идеа́л ideal. **идеали́зм** idealism. **идеа́льный** ideal.

иде́йный high-principled; acting on principle; ideological.

идеологи́ческий ideological. **идеоло́гия** ideology.

идёт *etc.: see* **идти́**

иде́я idea; concept.

иди́ллия idyll.

идио́т idiot.

и́дол idol.

идти́ (иду́, идёшь; шёл, шла) *impf* (*pf* **пойти́**) go; come; run, work; pass; go on, be in progress; be on; fall; +(**к**+)*dat* suit.

иере́й priest.

иждиве́нец (-нца), -**ве́нка** dependant. **иждиве́ние** maintenance; **на иждиве́нии at** the expense of.

из, изо *prep*+*gen* from, out of, of.

изба́ (*pl* -ы) izba (hut).

изба́вить (-влю) *pf*, **избавля́ть** *impf* save, deliver; ~**ся** be saved, escape; ~**ся от** get rid of; get out of.

избало́ванный spoilt.

избега́ть *impf*, **избе́гнуть** (-ну; -бе́г-(нул)) *pf*, **избежа́ть** (-егу́) *pf* +*gen or inf* avoid; escape, evade.

изберу́ *etc.: see* **избра́ть**

избива́ть *impf of* **изби́ть. избие́ние** slaughter, massacre; beating, beating-up.

избира́тель *m*, ~**ница** elector, voter. **избира́тельный** electoral; election. **избира́ть** *impf of* **избра́ть**

изби́тый trite, hackneyed. **изби́ть** (изобью́, -бьёшь) *pf* (*impf* **избива́ть**) beat unmercifully, beat up; massacre.

и́збранн|ый selected; select; ~**ые** *sb*

pl the élite. **избра́ть** (-беру́, -берёшь; -а́л, -а́, -о) *pf* (*impf* **избира́ть**) elect; choose.

избы́ток (-тка) surplus; abundance. **избы́точный** surplus; abundant.

и́зверг monster. **изверже́ние** eruption; expulsion; excretion.

изверну́ться (-ну́сь, -нёшься) *pf* (*impf* **извора́чиваться**) dodge, be evasive.

изве́стие news; information; *pl* proceedings. **извести́ть** (-ещу́) *pf* (*impf* **извеща́ть**) inform, notify.

изве́стка lime.

изве́стно it is (well) known; of course, certainly. **изве́стность** fame, reputation. **изве́стный** known; well-known; famous; notorious; certain.

известня́к (-а́) limestone. **и́звесть** lime.

извеща́ть *impf of* **извести́ть. извеще́ние** notification; advice.

извива́ться *impf* coil; writhe; twist, wind; meander. **изви́лина** bend, twist. **изви́листый** winding; meandering.

извине́ние excuse; apology. **извини́ть** *pf*, **извиня́ть** *impf* excuse; **извини́те (меня́)** excuse me, (I'm) sorry; ~**ся** apologize; excuse o.s.

изви́ться (изовью́сь, -вьёшься; -и́лся, -а́сь, -ось) *pf* coil; writhe.

извлека́ть *impf*, **извле́чь** (-еку́, -ечёшь; -ёк, -ла́) *pf* extract; derive, elicit.

извне́ *adv* from outside.

изво́зчик cabman; carrier.

извора́чиваться *impf of* **изверну́ться. изворо́т** bend, twist; *pl* tricks, wiles. **изворо́тливый** resourceful; shrewd.

изврати́ть (-ащу́) *pf*, **извраща́ть** *impf* distort; pervert. **извраще́ние** perversion; distortion. **извращённый** perverted; unnatural.

изги́б bend, twist. **изгиба́ть(ся** *impf of* **изогну́ть(ся**

изгна́ние banishment; exile. **изгна́нник** exile. **изгна́ть** (-гоню́, -го́нишь; -а́л, -а́, -о) *pf* (*impf* **изгоня́ть**) banish; exile.

изголо́вье bed-head.

изголода́ться be famished, starve; +**по**+*dat* yearn for.

изгоню́ *etc.: see* **изгна́ть. изгоня́ть**

impf of изгна́ть

и́згородь fence, hedge.

изгота́вливать *impf*, изгото́вить (-влю) *pf*, изготовля́ть *impf* make, manufacture; ~ся get ready. изготовле́ние making, manufacture.

издава́ть (-даю́, -даёшь) *impf of* изда́ть

и́здавна *adv* from time immemorial; for a very long time.

издади́м *etc.: see* изда́ть

издалека́, и́здали *advs* from afar.

изда́ние publication; edition; promulgation. изда́тель *m* publisher. изда́тельство publishing house. изда́ть (-а́м, -а́шь, -а́ст, -ади́м, -а́л, -а́, -о) *pf* (*impf* издава́ть) publish; promulgate; produce; emit; ~ся be published.

издева́тельство mockery; taunt. издева́ться *impf* (+над+*instr*) mock (at).

изде́лие work; make; article; *pl* wares.

изде́ржки (-жек) *pl* expenses; costs; cost.

из|до́хнуть *pf*.

из|жа́рить(ся *pf*.

изжо́га heartburn.

из-за *prep*+*gen* from behind; because of.

излага́ть *impf of* изложи́ть

излече́ние treatment; recovery; cure. излечи́ть (-чу́, -чишь) cure; ~ся be cured; +от+*gen* rid o.s. of.

изли́шек (-шка) surplus; excess. изли́шество excess; over-indulgence. изли́шний (-шен, -шня) superfluous.

изложе́ние exposition; account. изложи́ть (-жу́, -жишь) *pf* (*impf* излага́ть) expound; set forth; word.

изло́м break, fracture; sharp bend. изло́ма́ть *pf* break; smash; wear out; warp.

излуча́ть *impf* radiate, emit. излуче́ние radiation; emanation.

из|ма́зать (-а́жу) *pf* dirty, smear all over; use up; ~ся get dirty, smear o.s. all over.

изме́на betrayal; treason; infidelity.

измене́ние change, alteration; inflection. измени́ть[1] (-ню́, -нишь) *pf* (*impf* изменя́ть[1]) change, alter; ~ся change.

измени́ть[2] (-ню́, -нишь) *pf* (*impf* изменя́ть[2]) +*dat* betray; be unfaithful to. изме́нник, -ица traitor. изменя́емый variable. изменя́ть[1,2](ся *impf of* измени́ть[1,2](ся

измере́ние measurement, measuring. изме́рить *pf*, измеря́ть *impf* measure, gauge.

измождённый (-ён, -а́) worn out.

из|му́чить (-чу) *pf* torment; tire out, exhaust; ~ся be exhausted. изму́ченный worn out.

измышле́ние fabrication, invention.

измя́тый crumpled, creased; haggard, jaded. из|мя́ть(ся (изомну́(сь, -нёшь-(ся) *pf*.

изна́нка wrong side; seamy side.

из|наси́ловать *pf* rape, assault.

изна́шивание wear (and tear). изна́шивать(ся *impf of* износи́ть(ся

изне́женный pampered; delicate; effeminate.

изнемога́ть *impf*, изнемо́чь (-огу́, -о́жешь; -о́г, -ла́) *pf* be exhausted. изнеможе́ние exhaustion.

изно́с wear; wear and tear; deterioration. износи́ть (-ошу́, -о́сишь) *pf* (*impf* изна́шивать) wear out; ~ся wear out; be used up. изно́шенный worn out; threadbare.

изнуре́ние exhaustion. изнурённый (-ён, -ена́) exhausted, worn out; jaded. изнури́тельный exhausting.

изнутри́ *adv* from inside, from within.

изо *see* из

изоби́лие abundance, plenty. изоби́ловать *impf* +*instr* abound in, be rich in. изоби́льный abundant.

изоблича́ть *impf*, изобличи́ть (-чу́) *pf* expose; show. изобличе́ние exposure; conviction.

изобража́ть *impf*, изобрази́ть (-ажу́) *pf* represent, depict, portray (+*instr* as); ~ из себя́+*acc* make o.s. out to be. изображе́ние image; representation; portrayal. изобрази́тельн|ый graphic; decorative; ~ые иску́сства fine arts.

изобрести́ (-ету́, -етёшь; -ёл, -а́) *pf*, изобрета́ть *impf* invent; devise. изобрета́тель *m* inventor. изобрета́тельный inventive. изобрете́ние invention.

изобью́ *etc.: see* изби́ть. изовью́сь *etc.: see* изви́ться

изо́гнутый bent, curved; winding.

изогну́ть(ся (-ну́(сь, -нёшь(ся) *pf* (*impf* **изгиба́ть(ся)** bend, curve.

изоли́ровать *impf & pf* isolate; insulate. **изоля́тор** insulator; isolation ward; solitary confinement cell. **изоля́ция** isolation; quarantine; insulation.

изомну́(сь *etc.: see* **измя́ть**

изо́рванный tattered, torn. **изорва́ть** (-ву́, -вёшь; -а́л, -а́, -о) *pf* tear, tear to pieces; **~ся** be in tatters.

изощрённый (-рён, -а́) refined; keen. **изощри́ться, изощря́ться** *impf* acquire refinement; excel.

из-под *prep+gen* from under.

Изра́иль *m* Israel. **изра́ильский** Israeli.

из|расхо́довать(ся *pf.*

и́зредка *adv* now and then.

изре́зать (-е́жу) *pf* cut up.

изрече́ние dictum, saying.

изры́ть (-ро́ю) *pf* dig up, plough up. **изры́тый** pitted.

изря́дно *adv* fairly, pretty. **изря́дный** fair, handsome; fairly large.

изуве́чить (-чу) *pf* maim, mutilate.

изуми́тельный amazing. **изуми́ть** (-млю́) *pf*, **изумля́ть** *impf* amaze; **~ся** be amazed. **изумле́ние** amazement.

изумру́д emerald.

изуро́дованный maimed; disfigured. **из|уро́довать** *pf.*

изуча́ть *impf*, **изучи́ть** (-чу́, -чишь) *pf* learn, study. **изуче́ние** study.

изъе́здить (-зжу) *pf* travel all over; wear out.

изъяви́ть (-влю́, -вишь) *pf*, **изъявля́ть** *impf* express.

изъя́н defect, flaw.

изъя́тие withdrawal; removal; exception. **изъя́ть** (изыму́, -мешь) *pf.* **изыма́ть** *impf* withdraw.

изыска́ние investigation, research; prospecting; survey. **изы́сканный** refined. **изыска́ть** (-ыщу́, -ы́щешь) *pf*, **изы́скивать** *impf* search out; (try to) find.

изю́м raisins.

изя́щество elegance, grace. **изя́щный** elegant, graceful.

ика́ть *impf*, **икну́ть** (-ну́, -нёшь) *pf* hiccup.

ико́на icon.

ико́та hiccup, hiccups.

икра́[1] (hard) roe; caviare.

икра́[2] (*pl* -ы) calf (*of leg*).

ил silt; sludge.

и́ли *conj* or; **~... ~** either ... or.

и́листый muddy, silty.

иллюзиони́ст illusionist. **иллю́зия** illusion.

иллюмина́тор porthole. **иллюмина́ция** illumination.

иллюстра́ция illustration. **иллюстри́ровать** *impf & pf* illustrate.

им *see* **он, они́, оно́**

им. *abbr* (*of* **и́мени**) named after.

и́мени *etc.: see* **и́мя**

име́ние estate.

имени́ны (-и́н) *pl* name-day (party).

имени́тельный nominative. **и́менно** *adv* namely; exactly, precisely; **вот ~!** exactly!

име́ть (-е́ю) *impf* have; **~ де́ло с**+*instr* have dealings with, have to do with; **~ ме́сто** take place; **~ся** be; be available.

и́ми *see* **они́**

имита́ция imitation. **имити́ровать** *impf* imitate.

иммигра́нт, ~ка immigrant.

импера́тор emperor. **импера́торский** imperial. **императри́ца** empress. **империали́зм** imperialism. **империали́ст** imperialist. **империалисти́ческий** imperialist(ic). **импе́рия** empire.

и́мпорт import. **импорти́ровать** *impf & pf* import. **и́мпортный** import(ed).

импровиза́ция improvisation. **импровизи́ровать** *impf & pf* improvise.

и́мпульс impulse.

иму́щество property.

и́мя (и́мени; *pl* имена́, -ён) *neut* name; first name; noun; **~ прилага́тельное** adjective; **~ существи́тельное** noun; **~ числи́тельное** numeral.

и́наче *adv* differently, otherwise; **так и́ли ~** in any event; *conj* otherwise, or else.

инвали́д disabled person; invalid. **инвали́дность** disablement, disability.

инвента́рь (-я́) *m* stock; equipment; inventory.

инде́ец (-е́йца) (American) Indian. **инде́йка** (*gen pl* -е́ек) turkey(-hen).

инде́йский (American) Indian.

и́ндекс index; code.

индиа́нка Indian; American Indian.

инди́ец (-и́йца) Indian.

индивидуали́зм individualism. **индивидуа́льность** individuality. **индивидуа́льный** individual. **индиви́дуум** individual.

инди́йский Indian. **И́ндия** India. **инду́с, инду́ска** Hindu. **инду́сский** Hindu.

индустриализа́ция industrialization. **индустриализи́ровать** *impf* & *pf* industrialize. **индустриа́льный** industrial. **инду́стрия** industry.

индю́к, индю́шка turkey.

и́ней hoar-frost.

ине́ртность inertia; sluggishness. **ине́рция** inertia.

инжене́р engineer; ~-меха́ник mechanical engineer; ~-строи́тель *m* civil engineer.

инжи́р fig.

инициа́л initial.

инициати́ва initiative. **инициа́тор** initiator.

инквизи́ция inquisition.

инкруста́ция inlaid work, inlay.

инкуба́тор incubator.

ино- *in comb* other, different; hetero-. **иногоро́дний** of, from, another town. ~ро́дец (-дца) non-Russian. ~ро́дный foreign. ~сказа́тельный allegorical. ~стра́нец (-нца), ~стра́нка (*gen pl* -нок) foreigner. ~стра́нный foreign. ~язы́чный speaking, of, another language; foreign.

иногда́ *adv* sometimes.

ино́й different; other; some; ~ раз sometimes.

и́нок monk. **и́нокиня** nun.

инотде́л foreign department.

инсектици́д insecticide.

инспе́ктор inspector. **инспе́кция** inspection; inspectorate.

инста́нция instance.

инсти́нкт instinct. **инстинкти́вный** instinctive.

институ́т institute.

инстру́ктор instructor. **инстру́кция** instructions.

инструме́нт instrument; tool.

инсули́н insulin.

инсцениро́вка dramatization, adap-

tation; pretence.

интегра́ция integration.

интелле́кт intellect. **интеллектуа́льный** intellectual.

интеллиге́нт intellectual. **интеллиге́нтный** cultured, educated. **интеллиге́нция** intelligentsia.

интенси́вность intensity. **интенси́вный** intensive.

интерва́л interval.

интерве́нция intervention.

интервью́ *neut indecl* interview.

интере́с interest. **интере́сный** interesting. **интересова́ть** *impf* interest; ~ся be interested (+*instr* in).

интерна́т boarding-school.

интернациона́льный international.

интерни́ровать *impf* & *pf* intern.

интерпрета́ция interpretation. **интерпрети́ровать** *impf* & *pf* interpret.

интерье́р interior.

инти́мный intimate.

интона́ция intonation.

интри́га intrigue; plot. **интригова́ть** *impf*, (*pf* за~) intrigue.

интуи́ция intuition.

инфа́ркт infarct; coronary (thrombosis), heart attack.

инфекцио́нный infectious. **инфе́кция** infection.

инфля́ция inflation.

информа́ция information.

инфракра́сный infra-red.

иод *etc.: see* **йод**

ио́н ion.

ипохо́ндрик hypochondriac. **ипохо́ндрия** hypochondria.

ипподро́м racecourse.

Ира́к Iraq. **ира́кец** (-кца) Iraqi. **ира́кский** Iraqi.

Ира́н Iran. **ира́нец** (-нца), **ира́нка** Iranian. **ира́нский** Iranian.

ирла́ндец (-дца) Irishman. **Ирла́ндия** Ireland. **ирла́ндка** Irishwoman. **ирла́ндский** Irish.

ирони́ческий ironic. **иро́ния** irony.

иррига́ция irrigation.

иск suit, action.

искажа́ть *impf*, **исказ́ить** (-ажу́) *pf* distort, pervert; misrepresent. **искаже́ние** distortion, perversion.

искале́ченный crippled, maimed. **искале́чить** (-чу) *pf* cripple, maim; break.

искáть (ищу́, и́щешь) *impf* (+*acc or gen*) seek, look for.

исключáть *impf*, **исключи́ть** (-чу́) *pf* exclude; eliminate; expel. **исключéние** *prep*+*gen* except. **исключéние** exception; exclusion; expulsion; elimination; **за исключéнием** +*gen* with the exception of. **исключи́тельно** *adv* exceptionally; exclusively. **исключи́тельный** exceptional; exclusive.

искóнный primordial.

ископáемое *sb* mineral; fossil. **ископáемый** fossilized, fossil.

искорени́ть *pf*, **искореня́ть** *impf* eradicate.

и́скоса *adv* askance; sidelong.

и́скра spark.

и́скренний sincere. **и́скренность** sincerity.

искривлéние bend; distortion, warping.

ис|купáть¹(ся *pf*.

искупáть² *impf*, **искупи́ть** (-плю́, -пишь) *pf* atone for; make up for. **искуплéние** redemption, atonement.

искуси́ть (-ушу́) *pf of* **искушáть**

искýсный skilful; expert. **искýсственный** artificial; feigned. **искýсство** art; skill. **искусствовéд** art historian.

искушáть *impf* (*pf* **искуси́ть**) tempt; seduce. **искушéние** temptation, seduction.

испáнец (-нца) Spaniard. **Испáния** Spain. **испáнка** Spanish woman. **испáнский** Spanish.

испарéние evaporation; *pl* fumes. **испари́ться** *pf*, **испаря́ться** *impf* evaporate.

ис|пáчкать *pf*. **ис|пéчь** (-еку́, -ечёшь) *pf*.

исповéдовать *impf* & *pf* confess; profess; **~ся** confess; make one's confession; +*в*+*prep* unburden o.s. of. **и́споведь** confession.

исподтишкá *adv* in an underhand way; on the quiet.

исполи́н giant. **исполи́нский** gigantic.

исполкóм *abbr* (*of* **исполни́тельный комитéт**) executive committee. **исполнéние** fulfilment, execution. **исполни́тель** *m*, **~ница** executor;

performer. **исполни́тельный** executive. **испóлнить** *pf*, **исполня́ть** *impf* carry out, execute; fulfil; perform; **~ся** be fulfilled.

испóльзование utilization. **испóльзовать** *impf* & *pf* make (good) use of, utilize.

ис|пóртить(ся (-рчу(сь) *pf*. **испóрченный** depraved; spoiled; rotten.

исправи́тельный correctional; corrective. **испрáвить** (-влю) *pf*, **исправля́ть** *impf* rectify, correct; mend; reform; **~ся** improve, reform. **исправлéние** repairing; improvement; correction. **исправленный** improved, corrected; revised; reformed. **испрáвный** in good order; punctual; meticulous.

ис|прóбовать *pf*.

испýг fright. **ис|пугáть(ся** *pf*.

испускáть *impf*, **испусти́ть** (-ущу́, -ýстиш) *pf* emit, let out.

испытáние test, trial; ordeal. **испытáть** *pf*, **испы́тывать** *impf* test; try; experience.

исслéдование investigation; research. **исслéдователь** *m* researcher; investigator. **исслéдовательский** research. **исслéдовать** *impf* & *pf* investigate, examine; research into.

истаскáться *pf*, **истáскиваться** *impf* wear out; be worn out.

истекáть *impf of* **истéчь**. **истéкший** past.

истéрика hysterics. **истери́ческий** hysterical. **истери́я** hysteria.

истечéние outflow; expiry. **истéчь** (-ечёт; -тёк, -лá) *pf* (*impf* **истекáть**) elapse; expire.

и́стина truth. **и́стинный** true.

истлевáть *impf*, **истлéть** (-éю) *pf* rot, decay; be reduced to ashes.

истóк source.

истолковáть *pf*, **истолкóвывать** *impf* interpret; comment on.

ис|толóчь (-лку́, -лчёшь; -лóк, -лклá) *pf*.

истóма languor.

исторгáть *impf*, **истóргнуть** (-ну; -óрг) *pf* throw out.

истóрик historian. **истори́ческий** historical; historic. **истóрия** history; story; incident.

истóчник spring; source.

истощáть *impf*, **истощи́ть** (-щу́) *pf*

exhaust; emaciate. **истоще́ние** emaciation; exhaustion.

ис|тра́тить (-а́чу) *pf.*

истреби́тель *m* destroyer; fighter. **истреби́ть** (-блю́) *pf*, **истребля́ть** *impf* destroy; exterminate.

ис|тупи́тся (-пится) *pf.*

истяза́ние torture. **истяза́ть** *impf* torture.

исхо́д outcome; end; Exodus. **исходи́ть** (-ожу́, -о́дишь) *impf* (+из or от+*gen*) issue (from), come (from); proceed (from). **исхо́дный** initial; departure.

исхуда́лый undernourished, emaciated.

исцеле́ние healing; recovery. **исцели́ть** *pf*, **исцеля́ть** *impf* heal, cure.

исчеза́ть *impf*, **исче́знуть** (-ну; -е́з) *pf* disappear, vanish. **исчезнове́ние** disappearance.

исче́рпать *pf*, **исче́рпывать** *impf* exhaust; conclude. **исче́рпывающий** exhaustive.

исчисле́ние calculation; calculus.

ита́к *conj* thus; so then.

Ита́лия Italy. **италья́нец** (-нца), **италья́нка** Italian. **италья́нский** Italian.

ИТАР-ТА́СС *abbr* (*of* Информацио́нное телегра́фное аге́нтство Росси́и; *see* ТАСС) ITAR-Tass.

и т.д. *abbr* (*of* и так да́лее) etc., and so on.

ито́г sum; total; result. **итого́** *adv* in all, altogether.

и т.п. *abbr* (*of* и тому́ подо́бное) etc., and so on.

иуде́й, иуде́йка Jew. **иуде́йский** Judaic.

их their, theirs; *see* **они́**.

иша́к (-а́) donkey.

ище́йка bloodhound; police dog.

ищу́ *etc.: see* **иска́ть**

ию́ль *m* July. **ию́льский** July.

ию́нь *m* June. **ию́ньский** June.

йо́га yoga.

йод iodine.

йо́та iota.

K

к, ко *prep*+*dat* to, towards; by; for;

on; on the occasion of; **к пе́рвому января́** by the first of January; **к тому́ вре́мени** by then; **к тому́ же** besides, moreover; **к чему́?** what for?

-ка *partl modifying force of imper or expressing decision or intention;* **да́йте-ка пройти́** let me pass, please; **скажи́-ка мне** do tell me.

каба́к (-а́) tavern.

кабала́ servitude.

каба́н (-а́) wild boar.

кабаре́ *neut indecl* cabaret.

кабачо́к (-чка́) marrow.

ка́бель *m* cable. **ка́бельтов** cable, hawser.

каби́на cabin; booth; cockpit; cubicle; cab. **кабине́т** study; surgery; room; office; Cabinet.

каблу́к (-а́) heel.

кабота́ж coastal shipping. **кабота́жный** coastal.

кабы́ if.

кавале́р knight; partner, gentleman. **кавалери́йский** cavalry. **кавалери́ст** cavalryman. **кавале́рия** cavalry.

ка́верзный tricky.

Кавка́з the Caucasus. **кавка́зец** (-зца), **кавка́зка** Caucasian. **кавка́зский** Caucasian.

кавы́чки (-чек) *pl* inverted commas, quotation marks.

каде́т cadet. **каде́тский ко́рпус** military school.

ка́дка tub, vat.

кадр frame, still; close-up; cadre; *pl* establishment; staff; personnel; specialists. **ка́дровый** (*mil*) regular; skilled, trained.

кады́к (-а́) Adam's apple.

каждодне́вный daily, everyday. **ка́ждый** each, every; *sb* everybody.

ка́жется *etc.: see* **каза́ться**

каза́к (-а́; *pl* -а́ки, -а́ков), **каза́чка** Cossack.

каза́рма barracks.

каза́ться (кажу́сь, ка́жешься) *impf* (*pf* по~) seem, appear; *impers* **ка́жется, каза́лось** apparently; **каза́лось бы** it would seem; +*dat*: **мне ка́жется** it seems to me; I think.

Казахста́н Kazakhstan. **каза́чий** Cossack.

каземе́т casemate.

казённый State; government; fiscal;

public; formal; banal, conventional. **казна́** Exchequer, Treasury; public purse; the State. **казначе́й** treasurer, bursar; paymaster.

казино́ *neut indecl* casino.

казни́ть *impf & pf* execute; punish; castigate. **казнь** execution.

кайма́ (*gen pl* **каём**) border, edging. **как** *adv* how; what; **вот** ~! you don't say!; ~ **вы ду́маете?** what do you think?; ~ **его́ зову́т?** what is his name?; ~ **же** naturally, of course; ~ **же так?** how is that?; ~ **ни** however. **как** *conj* as; like; when; since; +*neg* but, except, than; **в то вре́мя** ~ while, whereas; ~ **мо́жно, нельзя́**+*comp* as … as possible; ~ **мо́жно скоре́е** as soon as possible; ~ **нельзя́ лу́чше** as well as possible; ~ **то́лько** as soon as, when; **ме́жду тем,** ~ while, whereas. **как бу́дто** *conj* as if; *partl* apparently. **как бы** how; as if; **как бы… не** what if, supposing; **как бы… ни** however. **ка́к-либо** *adv* somehow. **ка́к-нибудь** *adv* somehow; anyhow. **как раз** *adv* just, exactly. **как-то** *adv* somehow; once.

кака́о *neut indecl* cocoa.

како́в (-á, -о́, -ы́) *pron* what, what sort (of); ~ **он?** what is he like?; ~ **он собо́й?** what does he look like?; **пого́да-то какова́!** what weather! **каково́** *adv* how. **како́й** *pron* what; (such) as; which; ~**… ни** whatever, whichever. **како́й-либо, како́й-нибудь** *prons* some; any; only. **како́й-то** *pron* some; a; a kind of.

как раз, ка́к-то *see* **как**

ка́ктус cactus.

кал faeces, excrement.

каламбу́р pun.

кале́ка *m & f* cripple.

календа́рь (-я́) *m* calendar.

кале́ние incandescence.

кале́чить (-чу) *impf* (*pf* **ис~, по~**) cripple, maim; ~**ся** become a cripple.

кали́бр calibre; bore; gauge.

ка́лий potassium.

кали́тка (wicket-)gate.

каллигра́фия calligraphy.

кало́рия calorie.

кало́ша galosh.

ка́лька tracing-paper; tracing.

калькуля́ция calculation.

кальсо́ны (-н) *pl* long johns.

ка́льций calcium.

ка́мбала flat-fish; plaice; flounder.

камени́стый stony, rocky. **каменно-у́гольный** coal; ~ **бассе́йн** coal-field. **ка́менный** stone; rock; stony; hard, immovable; ~ **век** Stone Age; ~ **у́голь** coal. **каменоло́мня** (*gen pl* -мен) quarry. **ка́менщик** (stone) mason; bricklayer. **ка́мень** (-мня; *pl* -мни, -мне́й) *m* stone.

ка́мера chamber; cell; camera; inner tube, (football) bladder; ~ **хране́ния** cloak-room, left-luggage office. **ка́мерный** chamber. **камерто́н** tuning-fork.

ками́н fireplace; fire.

камко́рдер camcorder.

камо́рка closet, very small room.

кампа́ния campaign; cruise.

камы́ш (-á) reed, rush; cane.

кана́ва ditch; gutter.

Кана́да Canada. **кана́дец** (-дца), **кана́дка** Canadian. **кана́дский** Canadian.

кана́л canal; channel. **канализа́ция** sewerage (system).

канаре́йка canary.

кана́т rope; cable.

канва́ canvas; groundwork; outline, design.

кандалы́ (-о́в) *pl* shackles.

кандида́т candidate; ~ **нау́к** person with higher degree. **кандидату́ра** candidature.

кани́кулы (-ул) *pl* vacation; holidays.

кани́стра can, canister.

канони́ческий canon(ical).

кано́э *neut indecl* canoe.

кант edging; mount. **кантова́ть** *impf*; «**не** ~» 'this way up'.

кану́н eve.

ка́нуть (-ну) *pf* drop, sink; **как в во́ду** ~ vanish into thin air.

канцеля́рия office. **канцеля́рский** office; clerical. **канцеля́рщина** red-tape.

ка́нцлер chancellor.

ка́пать (-аю *or* -плю) *impf* (*pf* **ка́пнуть, на~**) drip, drop; trickle; +*instr* spill.

капе́лла choir; chapel.

ка́пелька small drop; a little; ~ **росы́** dew-drop.

капельме́йстер conductor; bandmaster.

капилля́р capillary.

капита́л capital. **капитали́зм** capitalism. **капитали́ст** capitalist. **капиталисти́ческий** capitalist. **капита́льный** capital; main, fundamental; major.

капита́н captain; skipper.

капитули́ровать *impf & pf* capitulate. **капитуля́ция** capitulation.

капка́н trap.

ка́пля (*gen pl* -пель) drop; bit, scrap. **ка́пнуть** (-ну) *pf of* ка́пать

капо́т hood, cowl, cowling; bonnet; house-coat.

капри́з caprice. **капри́зничать** *impf* play up. **капри́зный** capricious.

капу́ста cabbage.

капюшо́н hood.

ка́ра punishment.

кара́бкаться *impf* (*pf* вс~) clamber.

карава́н caravan; convoy.

кара́кули *f pl* scribble.

караме́ль caramel; caramels.

каранда́ш (-á) pencil.

каранти́н quarantine.

кара́т carat.

кара́тельный punitive. **кара́ть** *impf* (*pf* по~) punish.

карау́л guard; watch; ~! help! **карау́лить** *impf* guard; lie in wait for. **карау́льный** guard; *sb* sentry, sentinel, guard.

карбюра́тор carburettor.

каре́та carriage, coach.

ка́рий brown; hazel.

карикату́ра caricature; cartoon.

карка́с frame; framework.

ка́ркать *impf*, **ка́ркнуть** (-ну) *pf* caw, croak.

ка́рлик, **ка́рлица** dwarf; pygmy. **ка́рликовый** dwarf; pygmy.

карма́н pocket. **карма́нник** pickpocket. **карма́нный** *adj* pocket.

карни́з cornice; ledge.

карп carp.

ка́рта map; (playing-)card.

карта́вить (-влю) *impf* burr.

картёжник gambler.

карте́чь case-shot, grape-shot.

карти́на picture; scene. **карти́нка** picture; illustration. **карти́нный** picturesque; picture.

карто́н cardboard. **карто́нка** cardboard box.

картоте́ка card-index.

карто́фель *m* potatoes; potato(-plant). **карто́фельн|ый** potato; ~ое пюре́ mashed potatoes.

ка́рточка card; season ticket; photo. **ка́рточный** card.

карто́шка potatoes; potato.

карусе́ль merry-go-round.

ка́рцер cell, lock-up.

карье́р[1] full gallop.

карье́р[2] quarry; sand-pit.

карье́ра career. **карьери́ст** careerist.

каса́ние contact. **каса́тельная** *sb* tangent. **каса́ться** *impf* (*pf* косну́ться) +*gen or* до+*gen* touch; touch on; concern; что каса́ется as regards.

ка́ска helmet.

каска́д cascade.

каспи́йский Caspian.

ка́сса till; cash-box; booking-office; box-office; cash-desk; cash.

кассе́та cassette. **кассе́тный магнитофо́н** cassette recorder.

касси́р, **касси́рша** cashier.

кастра́т eunuch. **кастра́ция** castration. **кастри́ровать** *impf & pf* castrate, geld.

кастрю́ля saucepan.

катало́г catalogue.

ката́ние rolling; driving; ~ верхо́м riding; ~ на конька́х skating.

катапу́льта catapult. **катапульти́ровать(ся** *impf & pf* catapult.

ката́р catarrh.

катара́кта cataract.

катастро́фа catastrophe. **катастрофи́ческий** catastrophic.

ката́ть *impf* (*pf* вы́~, с~) roll; (take for a) drive; ~ся, roll, roll about; go for a drive; ~ся верхо́м ride, go riding; ~ся на конька́х skate, go skating.

категори́ческий categorical. **катего́рия** category.

ка́тер (*pl* -á) cutter; launch.

кати́ть (-ачу́, -а́тишь) *impf* bowl along, rip, tear; ~ся rush, tear; flow, stream, roll; кати́сь, кати́тесь get out! clear off! **като́к** (-тка́) skating-rink; roller.

като́лик, **католи́чка** Catholic. **католи́ческий** Catholic.

ка́торга penal servitude, hard labour. **ка́торжник** convict. **ка́торжн|ый**

penal; ~ые **рабо́ты** hard labour; drudgery.

кату́шка reel, bobbin; spool; coil.

каучу́к rubber.

кафе́ *neut indecl* café.

ка́федра pulpit; rostrum; chair; department.

ка́фель *m* Dutch tile.

кача́лка rocking-chair. **кача́ние** rocking, swinging; pumping. **кача́ть** *impf* (*pf* **качну́ть**) +*acc or instr* rock, swing; shake; ~ся rock, swing; roll; reel. **каче́ли** (-ей) *pl* swing.

ка́чественный qualitative; highquality. **ка́чество** quality; в **ка́честве**+*gen* as, in the capacity of.

ка́чка rocking; tossing.

качну́ть(ся (-ну́(сь, -нёшь(ся) *pf of* **кача́ть(ся**. **качу́** *etc.*: *see* **кати́ть**

ка́ша gruel, porridge; **завари́ть ка́шу** stir up trouble.

ка́шель (-шля) cough. **ка́шлянуть** (-ну) *pf*, **ка́шлять** *impf* (have a) cough.

кашта́н chestnut. **кашта́новый** chestnut.

каю́та cabin, stateroom.

ка́ющийся penitent. **ка́яться** (ка́юсь) *impf* (*pf* **по~**, **рас~**) repent; confess; **ка́юсь** I (must) confess.

кв. *abbr* (*of* **квадра́тный**) square; (*of* **кварти́ра**) flat.

квадра́т square; quad; **в квадра́те** squared; **возвести́ в ~** square. **квадра́тный** square; quadratic.

ква́кать *impf*, **ква́кнуть** (-ну) *pf* croak.

квалифика́ция qualification. **квалифици́рованный** qualified, skilled.

квант, ква́нта quantum. **ква́нтовый** quantum.

кварта́л block; quarter. **кварта́льный** quarterly.

кварте́т quartet.

кварти́ра flat; apartment(s); quarters. **квартира́нт, -ра́нтка** lodger; tenant. **кварти́рная пла́та, квартпла́та** rent.

кварц quartz.

квас (*pl* -ы́) kvass. **ква́сить** (-а́шу) *impf* sour; pickle. **ква́шеная капу́ста** sauerkraut.

кве́рху *adv* up, upwards.

квит, кви́ты quits.

квита́нция receipt. **квито́к** (-тка́) ticket, check.

КГБ *abbr* (*of* **Комите́т госуда́рственной безопа́сности**) KGB.

ке́гля skittle.

кедр cedar.

ке́ды (-ов) *pl* trainers.

кекс (fruit-)cake.

ке́лья (*gen pl* -лий) cell.

кем *see* **кто**

ке́мпинг campsite.

кенгуру́ *m indecl* kangaroo.

ке́пка cloth cap.

кера́мика ceramics.

керога́з stove. **кероси́н** paraffin. **кероси́нка** paraffin stove.

ке́та Siberian salmon. **ке́тов|ый:** ~ая икра́ red caviare.

кефи́р kefir, yoghurt.

кибернетика cybernetics.

кива́ть *impf*, **кивну́ть** (-ну́, -нёшь) *pf* (голово́й) nod (one's head); (+на+*acc*) motion (to). **киво́к** (-вка́) nod.

кида́ть *impf* (*pf* **ки́нуть**) throw, fling; ~ся fling o.s.; rush; +*instr* throw.

кий (-я́; *pl* -и́, -ёв) (*billiard*) cue.

киле́в|о́й keel; ~а́я ка́чка pitching.

кило́ *neut indecl* kilo. **килова́тт** kilowatt. **килогра́мм** kilogram. **киломе́тр** kilometre.

киль *m* keel; fin. **кильва́тер** wake.

ки́лька sprat.

кинжа́л dagger.

кино́ *neut indecl* cinema.

кино- *in comb* film-, cine-. **киноаппара́т** cinecamera. ~**арти́ст**, ~**арти́стка** film actor, actress. ~**журна́л** news-reel. ~**за́л** cinema; auditorium. ~**звезда́** film-star. ~**зри́тель** *m* film-goer. ~**карти́на** film. ~**опера́тор** camera-man. ~**плёнка** film. ~**режиссёр** film director. ~**теа́тр** cinema. ~**хро́ника** news-reel.

ки́нуть(ся (-ну(сь) *pf of* **кида́ть(ся**

кио́ск kiosk, stall.

ки́па pile, stack; bale.

кипари́с cypress.

кипе́ние boiling. **кипе́ть** (-плю́) *impf* (*pf* **вс~**) boil, seethe.

кипу́чий boiling, seething; ebullient. **кипяти́льник** kettle, boiler. **кипяти́ть** (-ячу́) *impf* (*pf* **вс~**) boil; ~ся boil; get excited. **кипято́к** (-тка́) boiling water. **кипячёный** boiled.

Кирги́зия Kirghizia.

кирка́ pick(axe).

кирпи́ч (-á) brick; bricks. **кирпи́ч-ный** brick; brick-red.

кисе́ль *m* kissel, blancmange.

кисе́т tobacco-pouch.

кисея́ muslin.

кислоро́д oxygen. **кислота́** (*pl* -ы) acid; acidity. **кисло́тный** acid. **ки́с-лый** sour; acid. **ки́снуть** (-ну; кис) *impf* (*pf* про~) turn sour.

ки́сточка brush; tassel. **кисть** (*gen pl* -éй) cluster, bunch; brush; tassel; hand.

кит (-á) whale.

кита́ец (-áйца; *pl* -цы, -цев) Chinese. **Кита́й** China. **кита́йский** Chinese. **китая́нка** Chinese (woman).

китобо́й whaler. **кито́вый** whale.

кичи́ться (-чу́сь) *impf* plume o.s.; strut. **кичли́вость** conceit. **кичли́-вый** conceited.

кише́ть (-ши́т) *impf* swarm, teem. **кише́чник** bowels, intestines. **кише́ч-ный** intestinal. **кишка́** gut, intestine; hose.

клавеси́н harpsichord. **клавиату́ра** keyboard. **кла́виша** key. **кла́виш-ный**: ~ инструме́нт keyboard in-strument.

клад treasure.

кла́дбище cemetery, graveyard.

кла́дка laying; masonry. **кладова́я** *sb* pantry; store-room. **кладовщи́к** (-á) storeman. **кладу́** *etc.*: *see* **класть**

кла́няться *impf* (*pf* поклони́ться) +*dat* bow to; greet.

кла́пан valve; vent.

кларне́т clarinet.

класс class; class-room. **кла́ссик** clas-sic. **кла́ссика** the classics. **клас-сифици́ровать** *impf* & *pf* classify. **класси́ческий** classical. **кла́ссный** class; first-class. **кла́ссовый** class.

класть (-аду́, -адёшь; -ал) *impf* (*pf* положи́ть, сложи́ть) lay; put.

клева́ть (клюю́, клюёшь) *impf* (*pf* клю́нуть) peck; bite.

кле́вер (*pl* -á) clover.

клевета́ slander; libel. **клевета́ть** (-ещу́, -е́щешь) *impf* (*pf* на~) +на+*acc* slander; libel. **клеветни́к** (-á), -ни́ца slanderer. **клеветни́че-ский** slanderous; libellous.

клеёнка oilcloth. **кле́ить** *impf* (*pf* с~) glue; stick; ~ся stick; become sticky. **клей** (*loc* -ю́; *pl* -и́) glue, ad-hesive. **кле́йкий** sticky.

клейми́ть (-млю́) *impf* (*pf* за~) brand; stamp; stigmatize. **клеймо́** (*pl* -а) brand; stamp; mark.

кле́йстер paste.

клён maple.

клепа́ть *impf* rivet.

кле́тка cage; check; cell. **кле́точка** cellule. **кле́точный** cellular. **клетча́т-ка** cellulose. **кле́тчатый** checked.

клёш flare.

клешня́ (*gen pl* -éй) claw.

кле́щи (-éй) *pl* pincers, tongs.

клие́нт client. **клиенту́ра** clientèle.

кли́зма enema.

клик cry, call. **кли́кать** (-и́чу) *impf*, **кли́кнуть** (-ну) *pf* call.

кли́макс menopause.

кли́мат climate. **климати́ческий** climatic.

клин (*pl* -нья, -ньев) wedge. **клино́к** (-нка́) blade.

кли́ника clinic. **клини́ческий** clini-cal.

клипс clip-on ear-ring.

клич call. **кли́чка** name; nickname. **кли́чу** *etc.*: *see* **кли́кать**

клок (-á; *pl* -о́чья, -ьев *or* -и́, -о́в) rag, shred; tuft.

клёкот bubbling; gurgling. **клокота́ть** (-о́чет) *impf* bubble; gurgle; boil up.

клони́ть (-ню́, -нишь) *impf* bend; in-cline; +к+*dat* drive at; ~ся bow, bend; +к+*dat* near, approach.

клоп (-á) bug.

кло́ун clown.

клочо́к (-чка́) scrap, shred. **кло́чья** *etc.*: *see* **клок**

клуб[1] club.

клуб[2] (*pl* -ы́) puff; cloud.

клу́бень (-бня) *m* tuber.

клуби́ться *impf* swirl; curl.

клубни́ка (*no pl*; *usu collect*) straw-berry; strawberries.

клубо́к (-бка́) ball; tangle.

клу́мба (flower-)bed.

клык (-á) fang; tusk; canine (*tooth*).

клюв beak.

клю́ква cranberry; cranberries.

клю́нуть (-ну) *pf of* **клева́ть**

ключ[1] (-á) key; clue; keystone; clef;

wrench, spanner.

ключ² (-á) spring; source.

ключево́й key. **ключи́ца** collarbone.

клю́шка (hockey) stick; (golf-)club.

клюю́ etc.: see **клева́ть**

кля́кса blot, smudge.

кляну́ etc.: see **клясть**

кля́нчить (-чу) impf (pf вы́~) beg.

кляп gag.

клясть (-яну́, -яне́шь; -ял, -á, -о) impf curse; ~**ся** (pf по~**ся**) swear, vow.

кля́тва oath, vow. **кля́твенный** on oath.

кни́га book.

книго- in comb book, biblio-. **книгове́дение**[1] bibliography. ~**веде́ние**[2] book-keeping. ~**изда́тель** m publisher. ~**лю́б** bibliophile, book-lover. ~**храни́лище** library; book-stack.

кни́жечка booklet. **кни́жка** notebook; bank-book. **кни́жный** book; bookish.

кни́зу adv downwards.

кно́пка drawing-pin; press-stud; (push-)button, knob.

кнут (-á) whip.

княги́ня princess. **кня́жество** principality. **княжна́** (gen pl -жо́н) princess. **кня́зь** (pl -зья́, -зе́й) m prince.

ко see **к** prep.

коали́ция coalition.

кобура́ holster.

кобы́ла mare; (vaulting-)horse.

ко́ваный forged; wrought; terse.

кова́рный insidious, crafty; perfidious. **кова́рство** insidiousness, craftiness; perfidy.

кова́ть (кую́, -ёшь) impf (pf под~) forge; hammer; shoe.

ковёр (-вра́) carpet; rug; mat.

кове́ркать impf (pf ис~) distort, mangle, ruin.

ко́вка forging; shoeing.

коври́жка honeycake, gingerbread.

ко́врик rug; mat.

ковче́г ark.

ковш (-á) scoop, ladle.

ковы́ль m feather-grass.

ковыля́ть impf hobble.

ковырну́ть (-ну́, -нёшь) pf, **ковыря́ть** impf dig into; tinker; +в+prep pick (at); ~**ся** rummage; tinker.

когда́ adv when; ~ (**бы**) **ни** whenever; conj when; while; as; if. **когда́-**

либо, когда́-нибудь advs some time; ever. **когда́-то** adv once; formerly; some time.

кого́ see **кто**

ко́готь (-гтя; pl -гти, -гте́й) m claw; talon.

код code.

кодеи́н codeine.

ко́декс code.

ко́е-где́ adv here and there. **ко́е-ка́к** adv anyhow; somehow (or other). **ко́е-како́й** pron some. **ко́е-кто́** pron somebody; some people. **ко́е-что́** (-чего́) pron something; a little.

ко́жа skin; leather; peel. **ко́жанка** leather jacket. **ко́жаный** leather. **коже́венный** leather; tanning. **ко́жный** skin. **кожура́** rind, peel, skin.

коза́ (pl -ы) goat, nanny-goat. **козёл** (-зла́) billy-goat. **козеро́г** ibex; Capricorn. **ко́зий** goat; ~ **пух** angora. **козлёнок** (-нка; pl -ля́та, -ля́т) kid. **ко́злы** (-зел) pl coach driver's seat; trestle(s); saw-horse. **ко́зни** (-ей) pl machinations. **козырёк** (-рька́) peak. **козырно́й** trump. **козырну́ть** (-ну́, -нёшь) pf, **козыря́ть** impf lead trumps; trump; play one's trump card; salute. **ко́зырь** (pl -и, -е́й) m trump.

ко́йка (gen pl ко́ек) berth, bunk; bed.

кокаи́н cocaine.

ко́ка-ко́ла Coca-Cola (propr).

коке́тка coquette. **коке́тство** coquetry.

коклю́ш whooping-cough.

ко́кон cocoon.

ко́кос coconut.

кокс coke.

кокте́йль m cocktail.

кол (-á; pl -лья, -ьев) stake, picket.

ко́лба retort.

колбаса́ (pl -ы) sausage.

колго́тки (-ток) pl tights.

колдова́ть impf practise witchcraft. **колдовство́** sorcery. **колду́н** (-á) sorcerer, wizard. **колду́нья** (gen pl -ний) witch, sorceress.

колеба́ние oscillation; variation; hesitation. **колеба́ть** (-е́блю) impf (pf по~) shake; ~**ся** oscillate; fluctuate; hesitate.

коле́но (pl -и, -ей, -ям) knee; (in pl) lap. **коле́нчатый** crank, cranked; bent; ~ **вал** crankshaft.

колесни́ца chariot. **колесо́** (*pl* -ёса) wheel.

коле́я rut; track, gauge.

ко́лика (*usu pl*) colic; stitch.

коли́чественн|ый quantitative; ~ое **числи́тельное** cardinal number. **коли́чество** quantity; number.

колле́га *m* & *f* colleague. **колле́гия** board; college.

коллекти́в collective. **коллективиза́ция** collectivization. **коллекти́вный** collective. **коллекционе́р** collector. **колле́кция** collection.

колли́зия clash, conflict.

коло́да block; pack (*of cards*).

коло́дец (-дца) well.

ко́локол (*pl* -á, -óв) bell. **колоко́льный** bell. **колоко́льня** bell-tower. **колоко́льчик** small bell; bluebell.

колониали́зм colonialism. **колониа́льный** colonial. **колониза́тор** colonizer. **колониза́ция** colonization. **колонизова́ть** *impf* & *pf* colonize. **коло́ния** colony.

коло́нка geyser; (*street*) water fountain; stand-pipe; column; **бензи́новая** ~ petrol pump. **коло́нна** column.

колори́т colouring, colour. **колори́тный** colourful, graphic.

ко́лос (-óсья, -ьев) ear. **колоси́ться** *impf* form ears.

колосса́льный huge; terrific.

колоти́ть (-очу́, -о́тишь) *impf* (*pf* по~) beat; pound; thrash; smash; ~ся pound, thump; shake.

коло́ть[1] (-лю́, -лешь) *impf* (*pf* рас~) break, chop.

коло́ть[2] (-лю́, -лешь) *impf* (*pf* за~, кольну́ть) prick; stab; sting; slaughter; ~ся prick.

колпа́к (-á) cap; hood, cowl.

колхо́з *abbr* (*of* **коллекти́вное хозя́йство**) kolkhoz, collective farm. **колхо́зник**, ~ица kolkhoz member. **колхо́зный** kolkhoz.

колыбе́ль cradle.

колыха́ть (-ы́шу) *impf*, **колыхну́ть** (-ну́, -нёшь) *pf* sway, rock; ~ся sway; flutter.

кольну́ть (-ну́, -нёшь) *pf of* **коло́ть**

кольцо́ (*pl* -а, -ле́ц, -льцам) ring.

колю́ч|ий prickly; sharp; ~ая про́волока barbed wire. **колю́чка** prickle; thorn.

коля́ска carriage; pram; side-car.

ком (*pl* -мья, -мьев) lump; ball.

ком *see* **кто**

кома́нда command; order; detachment; crew; team. **команди́р** commander. **командирова́ть** *impf* & *pf* post, send on a mission. **командиро́вка** posting; mission, business trip. **командиро́вочные** *sb pl* travelling expenses. **кома́ндование** command. **кома́ндовать** *impf* (*pf* с~) give orders; be in command; +*instr* command. **кома́ндующий** *sb* commander.

кома́р (-á) mosquito.

комба́йн combine harvester.

комбина́т industrial complex. **комбина́ция** combination; manoeuvre; slip. **комбинезо́н** overalls, boiler suit; dungarees. **комбини́ровать** *impf* (*pf* с~) combine.

коме́дия comedy.

коменда́нт commandant; manager; warden. **комендату́ра** commandant's office.

коме́та comet.

ко́мик comic actor; comedian. **ко́микс** comic, comic strip.

комисса́р commissar.

комиссионе́р (commission-)agent, broker. **комиссио́нн|ый** commission; ~ый **магази́н** second-hand shop; ~ые *sb pl* commission. **коми́ссия** commission; committee.

комите́т committee.

коми́ческий comic; comical. **коми́чный** comical, funny.

ко́мкать *impf* (*pf* с~) crumple.

коммента́рий commentary; *pl* comment. **коммента́тор** commentator. **комменти́ровать** *impf* & *pf* comment (on).

коммерса́нт merchant; businessman **комме́рция** commerce. **комме́рческий** commercial.

коммивояжёр commercial traveller.

комму́на commune. **коммуна́льный** communal; municipal. **коммуни́зм** communism.

коммуника́ция communication.

коммуни́ст, ~ка communist. **коммунисти́ческий** communist.

коммута́тор switchboard.

коммюнике́ *neut indecl* communiqué.

ко́мната room. **ко́мнатный** room; indoor.

комо́д chest of drawers.

комо́к (-мка́) lump.

компа́кт-ди́ск compact disc. **компа́ктный** compact.

компа́ния company. **компаньо́н**, ~**ка** companion; partner.

компа́ртия Communist Party.

ко́мпас compass.

компенса́ция compensation. **компенси́ровать** *impf* & *pf* compensate.

ко́мплекс complex. **ко́мплексный** complex, compound, composite; combined. **комплéкт** (complete) set; complement; kit. **комплектова́ть** *impf* (*pf* **с~**, **у~**) complete; bring up to strength. **комплéкция** build; constitution.

комплимéнт compliment.

композитор composer. **композиция** composition.

компонéнт component.

компóст compost.

компóстер punch. **компости́ровать** *impf* (*pf* **про~**) punch.

компóт stewed fruit.

компрéссор compressor.

компромети́ровать *impf* (*pf* **с~**) compromise. **компроми́сс** compromise.

компью́тер computer.

комсомóл Komsomol. **комсомóлец** (-льца), -**лка** Komsomol member. **комсомóльский** Komsomol.

кому́ *see* **кто**

комфóрт comfort.

конвéйер conveyor.

конвéрт envelope; sleeve.

конвóйр escort. **конвойровать** *impf* escort. **конвóй** escort, convoy.

конгрéсс congress.

конденса́тор condenser.

конди́терская *sb* confectioner's, cake shop.

кондиционéр air-conditioner. **кондициóнный** air-conditioning.

конду́ктор (*pl* -á), -**торша** conductor; guard.

коневóдство horse-breeding. **конёк** (-нька́) *dim of* **конь**; hobby(-horse).

конéц (-нца́) end; **в конце́ концо́в** in the end, after all. **конéчно** *adv* of course. **конéчность** extremity. **ко-**

нéчный final, last; ultimate; finite.

кони́ческий conic, conical.

конкрéтный concrete.

конкурéнт competitor. **конкурéнция** competition. **конкури́ровать** *impf* compete. **ко́нкурс** competition; contest.

ко́нница cavalry. **ко́нный** horse; mounted; equestrian; ~ **заво́д** stud.

конопля́ hemp.

консервати́вный conservative. **консерва́тор** Conservative.

консервато́рия conservatoire.

консерви́ровать *impf* & *pf* (*pf also* **за~**) preserve; can, bottle. **консéрвн|ый** preserving; ~**ая ба́нка** tin; ~**ый нож** tin-opener. **консéрвооткрыва́тель** *m* tin-opener. **консéрвы** (-ов) *pl* tinned goods.

конси́лиум consultation.

конспéкт synopsis, summary. **конспекти́ровать** *impf* (*pf* **за~**, **про~**) make an abstract of.

конспирати́вный secret, clandestine. **конспира́ция** security.

конста́ция ascertaining; establishment. **констати́ровать** *impf* & *pf* ascertain; establish.

конституциóнный constitutional. **конститу́ция** constitution.

констру́ировать *impf* & *pf* (*pf also* **с~**) construct; design. **констру́кти́вный** structural; constructional; constructive. **констру́ктор** designer, constructor. **констру́кция** construction; design.

ко́нсул consul.

консульта́ция consultation; advice; clinic; tutorial. **консульти́ровать** *impf* (*pf* **про~**) advise; +**с**+*instr* consult; ~**ся** obtain advice; +**с**+*instr* consult.

конта́кт contact. **конта́ктные ли́нзы** *f pl* contact lenses.

контéйнер container.

контéкст context.

континéнт continent.

конто́ра office. **конто́рский** office.

контраба́нда contraband. **контрабанди́ст** smuggler.

контраба́с double-bass.

контрагéнт contractor. **контра́кт** contract.

контра́льто *neut/fem indecl* contralto (*voice/person*).

контрама́рка complimentary ticket.
контрапу́нкт counterpoint.
контра́ст contrast.
контрибу́ция indemnity.
контрнаступле́ние counter-offensive.
контролёр inspector; ticket-collector. **контроли́ровать** *impf* (*pf* **про~**) check; inspect. **контро́ль** *m* control; check; inspection. **контро́льн|ый** control; **~ая рабо́та** test.
контрразве́дка counter-intelligence; security service. **контрреволю́ция** counter-revolution.
конту́зия bruising; shell-shock.
ко́нтур contour, outline; circuit.
конура́ kennel.
ко́нус cone.
конфедера́ция confederation.
конфере́нция conference.
конфе́та sweet.
конфискова́ть *impf & pf* confiscate.
конфли́кт conflict.
конфо́рка ring (*on stove*).
конфу́з discomfort, embarrassment. **конфу́зить** (**~у́жу**) *impf* (*pf* **с~**) confuse, embarrass; **~ся** feel embarrassed.
концентра́т concentrate. **концентрацио́нный** concentration. **концентра́ция** concentration. **концентри́ровать(ся** *impf* (*pf* **с~**) concentrate.
конце́пция conception.
конце́рт concert; concerto. **концертме́йстер** leader; soloist. **конце́ртный** concert.
концла́герь *abbr* (*of* **концентрацио́нный ла́герь**) concentration camp.
конча́ть *impf*, **ко́нчить** *pf* finish; end; +*inf* stop; **~ся** end, finish; expire. **ко́нчик** tip. **кончи́на** decease.
конь (**-я́**; *pl* **-и, -е́й**) *m* horse; knight. **конькй** (**-о́в**) *pl* skates; **~ на ро́ликах** roller skates. **конькобе́жец** (**-жца**) skater.
конья́к (**-а́**) cognac.
ко́нюх groom, stable-boy. **коню́шня** (*gen pl* **-шен**) stable.
кооперати́в cooperative. **кооперати́вный** cooperative. **коопера́ция** cooperation.
координа́та coordinate. **координа́ция** coordination.

копа́ть *impf* (*pf* **копну́ть, вы́~**) dig; dig up, dig out; **~ся** rummage.
копе́йка copeck.
ко́пи (**-ей**) *pl* mines.
копи́лка money-box.
копи́рка carbon paper. **копирова́льный** copying. **копи́ровать** *impf* (*pf* **с~**) copy; imitate.
копи́ть (**-плю́, -пишь**) *impf* (*pf* **на~**) save (up); accumulate; **~ся** accumulate.
ко́пия copy.
копна́ (*pl* **-ы, -пён**) shock, stook.
копну́ть (**-ну́, -нёшь**) *pf of* **копа́ть**
ко́поть soot.
коптеть (**-пчу́**) *impf* swot; vegetate.
копти́ть (**-пчу́**) *impf* (*pf* **за~, на~**) smoke, cure; blacken with smoke.
копче́ние smoking; smoked foods. **копчёный** smoked.
копы́то hoof.
копьё (*pl* **-я, -пий**) spear, lance.
кора́ bark, rind; cortex; crust.
кора́бельный ship; naval. **кораблевожде́ние** navigation. **кораблекруше́ние** shipwreck. **кораблестрое́ние** shipbuilding. **кора́бль** (**-я́**) *m* ship, vessel; nave.
кора́лл coral.
коре́йский Korean. **Коре́я** Korea.
корена́стый thickset. **корени́ться** *impf* be rooted. **коренно́й** radical, fundamental; native. **ко́рень** (**-рня;** *pl* **-и, -е́й**) *m* root. **корешо́к** (**-шка́**) root(let); spine; counterfoil.
корзи́на, корзи́нка basket.
коридо́р corridor.
кори́ца cinnamon.
кори́чневый brown.
ко́рка crust; rind, peel.
корм (*loc* **-у́;** *pl* **-а́**) fodder.
корма́ stern.
корми́лец (**-льца**) bread-winner. **корми́ть** (**-млю́, -мишь**) *impf* (*pf* **на~, по~, про~**) feed; **~ся** feed; +*instr* live on, make a living by. **кормле́ние** feeding. **кормово́й¹** fodder.
кормово́й² stern.
корнево́й root; radical. **корнеплоды** (**-ов**) root-crops.
коро́бить (**-блю**) *impf* (*pf* **по~**) warp; jar upon; **~ся** (*pf also* **с~ся**) warp.
коро́бка box.

коро́ва cow.

короле́ва queen. короле́вский royal. короле́вство kingdom. коро́ль (-я́) *m* king.

коромы́сло yoke; beam; rocking shaft.

коро́на crown.

коронаротромбо́з coronary (thrombosis).

коро́нка crown. коронова́ть *impf* & *pf* crown.

коро́ткий (ко́роток, -тка́, ко́ротко, ко́ро́тки) short; intimate. ко́ротко *adv* briefly; intimately. коротково́лновый short-wave. коро́че *comp of* коро́ткий, ко́ротко

корпора́ция corporation.

ко́рпус (*pl* -ы, -ов *or* -á, -óв) corps; services; building; hull; housing; case; body.

корректи́ровать *impf* (*pf* про~, с~) correct, edit. корре́ктный correct, proper. корре́ктор (*pl* -á) proof-reader. корректу́ра proof-reading; proof.

корреспонде́нт correspondent. корреспонде́нция correspondence.

корро́зия corrosion.

корру́пция corruption.

корт (tennis-)court.

корте́ж cortège; motorcade.

ко́ртик dirk.

ко́рточки (-чек) *pl*; сиде́ть на ко́рточках squat.

корчева́ть (-чу́ю) *impf* root out.

ко́рчить (-чу) *impf* (*pf* с~) contort; *impers* convulse; ~ из себя́ pose as; ~ся writhe.

ко́ршун kite.

коры́стный mercenary. коры́сть avarice; profit.

коры́то trough; wash-tub.

корь measles.

коса́[1] (*acc* -у, *pl* -ы) plait, tress.

коса́[2] (*acc* ко́су; *pl* -ы) spit.

коса́[3] (*acc* ко́су; *pl* -ы) scythe.

ко́свенный indirect.

коси́лка mowing-machine, mower.

коси́ть[1] (кошу́, ко́сишь) *impf* (*pf* с~) cut; mow (down).

коси́ть[2] (кошу́) *impf* (*pf* по~, с~) squint; be crooked; ~ся slant; look sideways; look askance.

косме́тика cosmetics, make-up.

косми́ческий cosmic; space. космо-

дро́м spacecraft launching-site. космона́вт, -на́втка cosmonaut, astronaut. ко́смос cosmos; (outer) space.

косноязы́чный tongue-tied.

косну́ться (-ну́сь, -нёшься) *pf of* каса́ться

косогла́зие squint. косо́й (кос, -á, -о) slanting; oblique; sidelong; squinting, cross-eyed.

костёр (-тра́) bonfire; camp-fire.

костля́вый bony. ко́стный bone. ко́сточка (small) bone; stone.

косты́ль (-я́) *m* crutch.

кость (*loc* и́; *pl* -и, -éй) bone; die.

костю́м clothes; suit. костюми́рованный fancy-dress.

костяно́й bone; ivory.

косы́нка (*triangular*) head-scarf, shawl.

кот (-á) tom-cat.

котёл (-тла́) boiler; copper, cauldron.

котело́к (-лка́) pot; mess-tin; bowler (hat). коте́льная *sb* boiler-room, -house.

котёнок (-нка; *pl* -тя́та, -тя́т) kitten.

ко́тик fur-seal; sealskin.

котле́та rissole; burger; отбивна́я ~ chop.

котлова́н foundation pit, trench.

кото́мка knapsack.

кото́рый *pron* which, what; who; that; ~ час? what time is it?

котя́та *etc.: see* котёнок

ко́фе *m indecl* coffee. кофева́рка percolator. кофе́ин caffeine.

ко́фта, ко́фточка blouse, top.

коча́н (-á *or* -чна́) (cabbage-)head.

кочева́ть (-чу́ю) *impf* be a nomad; wander; migrate. кочёвник nomad. кочево́й nomadic.

кочега́р stoker, fireman. кочега́рка stokehold, stokehole.

кочене́ть *impf* (*pf* за~, о~) grow numb.

кочерга́ (*gen pl* -рёг) poker.

ко́чка hummock.

кошелёк (-лька́) purse.

ко́шка cat.

кошма́р nightmare. кошма́рный nightmarish.

кошу́ *etc.: see* коси́ть

кощу́нство blasphemy.

коэффицие́нт coefficient.

КП *abbr* (*of* Коммунисти́ческая па́ртия) Communist Party. КПСС *abbr* (*of* Коммунисти́ческая па́ртия

Советского Союза) Communist Party of the Soviet Union, CPSU.

краб crab.

крáденый stolen. **крадý** etc.: see **красть**

краевéдение regional studies.

крáжа theft; ~ со взлóмом burglary.

край (loc -ю́; pl -я́, -ёв) edge; brink; land; region. **крáйне** adv extremely. **крáйний** extreme; last; outside, wing. **крáйность** extreme; extremity.

крал etc.: see **красть**

кран tap; crane.

крапи́ва nettle.

красáвец (-вца) handsome man. **красáвица** beauty. **краси́вый** beautiful; handsome.

краси́тель m dye. **крáсить** (-áшу) impf (pf вы́~, о~, по~) paint; colour; dye; stain; ~ся (pf на~) make-up. **крáска** paint, dye; colour.

краснéть (-éю) impf (pf по~) blush; redden; show red.

красноармéец (-éйца) Red Army man. **красноармéйский** Red Army. **красноречи́вый** eloquent.

краснотá redness. **краснýха** German measles. **крáсн|ый** (-сен, -снá, -о) red; beautiful; fine; ~ое дéрево mahogany; ~ая сморóдина (no pl; usu collect) redcurrant; redcurrants; ~ая строкá (first line of) new paragraph.

красовáться impf impress by one's beauty; show off. **красотá** (pl -ы) beauty. **крáсочный** paint; ink; colourful.

красть (-адý, -адёшь; крал) impf (pf у~) steal; ~ся creep.

крáтер crater.

крáткий (-ток, -ткá, -о) short; brief. **кратковрéменный** brief; transitory. **краткосрóчный** short-term.

крáтное sb multiple.

кратчáйший superl of **крáткий**. **крáтче** comp of **крáткий**, **крáтко**

крах crash; failure.

крахмáл starch. **крахмáлить** impf (pf на~) starch.

крáше comp of **краси́вый**, **краси́во**

крáшеный painted; coloured; dyed; made up. **крáшу** etc.: see **крáсить**

кревéтка shrimp; prawn.

креди́т credit. **креди́тный** credit. **кредитоспосóбный** solvent.

крéйсер (pl -á, -óв) cruiser.

крем cream.

кремáтóрий crematorium.

кремéнь (-мня́) m flint.

кремль (-я́) m citadel; Kremlin.

крéмний silicon.

крéмовый cream.

крен list, heel; bank. **крени́ться** impf (pf на~) heel over, list; bank.

крепи́ть (-плю́) impf strengthen; support; make fast; constipate; ~ся hold out. **крéпк|ий** (-пок, -пкá, -о) strong; firm; ~ие напи́тки spirits. **креплéние** strengthening; fastening.

крéпнуть (-ну; -еп) impf (pf о~) get stronger.

крепостни́чество serfdom. **крепостн| óй** serf; ~óе прáво serfdom; ~óй sb serf.

крéпость fortress; strength. **крéпче** comp of **крéпкий**, **крéпко**

крéсло (gen pl -сел) arm-chair; stall.

крест (-á) cross. **крести́ны** (-и́н) pl christening. **крести́ть** (крещý, -éстишь) impf & pf (pf also о~, пере~) christen; make sign of the cross over; ~ся cross o.s.; be christened. **крест-нáкрест** adv crosswise. **крéстник**, **крéстница** godchild. **крéстн|ый**; ~ая (мать) godmother; ~ый отéц godfather. **крестóвый похóд** crusade. **крестонóсец** (-сца) crusader.

крестья́нин (pl -я́не, -я́н), **крестья́нка** peasant. **крестья́нский** peasant. **крестья́нство** peasantry.

крещéние christening; Epiphany. **крещён|ый** (-ён, -енá) baptized; sb Christian. **крещý** etc.: see **крести́ть**

крива́я sb curve. **кривизнá** crookedness; curvature. **криви́ть** (-влю́) impf (pf по~, с~) bend, distort; ~ душóй go against one's conscience; ~ся become crooked or bent; make a wry face. **кривля́ться** impf give o.s. airs.

кривóй (крив, -á, -о) crooked; curved; one-eyed.

кри́зис crisis.

крик cry, shout.

кри́кет cricket.

кри́кнуть (-ну) pf of **кричáть**

криминáльный criminal.

кристáлл crystal. **кристалли́ческий** crystal.

критерий criterion.
критик critic. **критика** criticism; critique. **критиковать** *impf* criticize. **критический** critical.
кричать (-чу) *impf* (*pf* **крикнуть**) cry, shout.
кров roof; shelter.
кровавый bloody.
кроватка, кровать bed.
кровеносный blood-; circulatory.
кровля (*gen pl* -вель) roof.
кровный blood; thoroughbred; vital, intimate.
крово- *in comb* blood. **кровожадный** bloodthirsty. **~излияние** haemorrhage. **~обращение** circulation. **~пролитие** bloodshed. **~пролитный** bloody. **~смешение** incest. **~течение** bleeding; haemorrhage. **~точить** (-чит) *impf* bleed.
кровь (*loc* -и) blood. **кровяной** blood.
кроить (крою) *impf* (*pf* с~) cut (out). **кройка** cutting out.
крокодил crocodile.
кролик rabbit.
кроль *m* crawl(-stroke).
крольчиха she-rabbit, doe.
кроме *prep+gen* except; besides; ~ того besides, moreover.
кромка edge.
крона crown; top.
кронштейн bracket; corbel.
кропотливый painstaking; laborious.
кросс cross-country race.
кроссворд crossword (puzzle).
крот (-á) mole.
кроткий (-ток, -ткá, -тко) meek, gentle. **кротость** gentleness; mildness.
крохотный, крошечный tiny.
крошка crumb; a bit.
круг (*loc* -ý; *pl* -и) circle; circuit; sphere. **круглосуточный** round-the-clock. **круглый** (кругл, -á, -о) round; complete; ~ год all the year round. **круговой** circular; all-round. **кругозор** prospect; outlook. **кругом** *adv* around; *prep+gen* round. **кругосветный** round-the-world.
кружевной lace; lacy. **кружево** (*pl* -á, -ев, -áм) lace.
кружить (-ужý, -ýжишь) *impf* whirl, spin round; ~ся whirl, spin round.
кружка mug.

кружок (-жкá) circle, group.
круиз cruise.
крупа (*pl* -ы) groats; sleet. **крупица** grain.
крупный large, big; coarse; ~ый план close-up.
крутизна steepness.
крутить (-учý, -ýтишь) *impf* (*pf* за~, с~) twist, twirl; roll; turn, wind; ~ся turn, spin; whirl.
крутой (крут, -á, -о) steep; sudden; sharp; severe; drastic. **круча** steep slope. **круче** *comp of* **крутой**, **круто** **кручу** *etc.*: *see* **крутить**
крушение crash; ruin; collapse.
крыжовник gooseberries; gooseberry bush.
крылатый winged. **крыло** (*pl* -лья, -льев) wing; vane; mudguard.
крыльцо (*pl* -а, -лéц, -цáм) porch; (front, back) steps.
Крым the Crimea. **крымский** Crimean.
крыса rat.
крыть (крою) *impf* cover; roof; trump; ~ся be, lie; be concealed. **крыша** roof. **крышка** lid.
крюк (-á; *pl* -ки, -ков *or* -ючья, -чьев) hook; detour. **крючок** (-чкá) hook.
кряду *adv* in succession.
кряж ridge.
крякать *impf*, **крякнуть** (-ну) *pf* quack.
кряхтеть (-хчý) *impf* groan.
кстати *adv* to the point; opportunely; at the same time; by the way.
кто (кого, кому, кем, ком) *pron* who; anyone; ~ (бы) ни whoever. **кто-либо, кто-нибудь** *prons* anyone; someone. **кто-то** *pron* someone.
куб (*pl* -ы) cube; boiler; в ~е cubed.
кубик brick, block.
кубинский Cuban.
кубический cubic; cube.
кубок (-бка) goblet; cup.
кубометр cubic metre.
кувшин jug; pitcher. **кувшинка** water-lily.
кувыркаться *impf*, **кувыркнуться** (-нусь) *pf* turn somersaults. **кувырком** *adv* head over heels; topsy-turvy.
куда *adv* where (to); what for; +*comp* much, far; ~ (бы) ни wherever. **куда-либо, куда-нибудь** *adv* any-

where, somewhere. **куда́-то** *adv* somewhere.

ку́дри (-е́й) *pl* curls. **кудря́вый** curly; florid.

кузне́ц (-á) blacksmith. **кузне́чик** grasshopper. **ку́зница** forge, smithy.

ку́зов (*pl* -á) basket; body.

ку́кла doll; puppet. **ку́колка** dolly; chrysalis. **ку́кольный** doll's; puppet.

кукуру́за maize.

куку́шка cuckoo.

кула́к (-á) fist; kulak. **кула́цкий** kulak. **кула́чный** fist.

кулёк (-лька́) bag.

кули́к (-á) sandpiper.

кулина́рия cookery. **кулина́рный** culinary.

кули́сы (-и́с) wings; **за кули́сами** behind the scenes.

кули́ч (-á) Easter cake.

кулуа́ры (-ов) *pl* lobby.

кульмина́ция culmination.

культ cult. **культиви́ровать** *impf* cultivate.

культу́ра culture; standard; cultivation. **культури́зм** body-building. **культу́рно** *adv* in a civilized manner. **культу́рный** cultured; cultivated; cultural.

куми́р idol.

кумы́с koumiss (*fermented mare's milk*).

куни́ца marten.

купа́льный bathing. **купа́льня** bathing-place. **купа́ть** *impf* (*pf* вы́-, ис~) bathe; bath; ~ся bathe; take a bath.

купе́ *neut indecl* compartment.

купе́ц (-пца́) merchant. **купе́ческий** merchant. **купи́ть** (-плю́, -пишь) *pf* (*impf* покупа́ть) buy.

ку́пол (*pl* -á) cupola, dome.

купо́н coupon.

купоро́с vitriol.

купчи́ха merchant's wife; female merchant.

кура́нты (-ов) *pl* chiming clock; chimes.

курга́н barrow; tumulus.

куре́ние smoking. **кури́льщик**, **-щица** smoker.

кури́ный hen's; chicken's.

кури́ть (-рю́, -ришь) *impf* (*pf* по~) smoke; ~ся burn; smoke.

ку́рица (*pl* ку́ры, кур) hen, chicken.

куро́к (-рка́) cocking-piece; **взвести́** ~ cock a gun; **спусти́ть** ~ pull the trigger.

куропа́тка partridge.

куро́рт health-resort; spa.

курс course; policy; year; exchange rate. **курса́нт** student.

курси́в italics.

курси́ровать *impf* ply.

ку́ртка jacket.

курча́вый curly(-headed).

ку́ры *etc.*: see **ку́рица**

курьёз a funny thing. **курьёзный** curious.

курье́р messenger; courier. **курье́р-ский** express.

куря́тник hen-house.

куря́щий *sb* smoker.

куса́ть *impf* bite; sting; ~ся bite.

кусо́к (-ска́) piece; lump. **кусо́чек** (-чка) piece.

куст (-á) bush, shrub. **куста́рник** bush(es), shrub(s).

куста́рн|ый hand-made; handicrafts; primitive; ~ая промы́шленность cottage industry. **куста́рь** (-я́) *m* craftsman.

ку́тать *impf* (*pf* за~) wrap up; ~ся muffle o.s. up.

кути́ть (кучу́, ку́тишь) *impf*, **кутну́ть** (-ну́, -нёшь) *pf* carouse; go on a binge.

куха́рка cook. **ку́хня** (*gen pl* -хонь) kitchen; cuisine. **ку́хонный** kitchen.

ку́ча heap; heaps.

ку́чер (*pl* -á) coachman.

ку́чка small heap *or* group.

кучу́ see **кути́ть**

куша́к (-á) sash; girdle.

ку́шанье food; dish. **ку́шать** *impf* (*pf* по~, с~) eat.

куше́тка couch.

кую́ *etc.*: see **кова́ть**

Л

лабора́нт, -а́нтка laboratory assistant. **лаборато́рия** laboratory.

ла́ва lava.

лави́на avalanche.

ла́вка bench; shop. **ла́вочка** small shop.

лавр bay tree, laurel.

ла́герный camp. **ла́герь** (*pl* -я́ *or* -и,

-éй *or* -ей) *m* camp; campsite.
лад (*loc* -ý; *pl* -ы́, -о́в) harmony; manner, way; stop, fret.
ла́дан incense.
ла́дить (ла́жу) *impf* get on, be on good terms. **ла́дно** *adv* all right; very well! **ла́дный** fine, excellent; harmonious.
ладо́нь palm.
ладья́ rook, castle; boat.
ла́жу *etc.: see* **ла́дить, ла́зить**
лазаре́т field hospital; sick-bay.
ла́зать *see* **ла́зить. лазе́йка** hole; loop-hole.
ла́зер laser.
ла́зить (ла́жу), **ла́зать** *impf* climb, clamber.
лазу́рный sky-blue, azure. **лазу́рь** azure.
лазу́тчик scout; spy.
лай bark, barking. **ла́йка¹** (Siberian) husky, laika.
ла́йка² kid. **ла́йковый** kid; kidskin.
ла́йнер liner; airliner.
лак varnish, lacquer.
лака́ть *impf* (*pf* **вы́~**) lap.
лаке́й footman, man-servant; lackey.
лакирова́ть *impf* (*pf* **от~**) varnish, lacquer.
ла́кмус litmus.
ла́ковый varnished, lacquered.
ла́комиться (-млюсь) *impf* (*pf* **по~**) +*instr* treat o.s. to. **ла́комка** *m* & *f* gourmand. **ла́комство** delicacy. **ла́комый** dainty, tasty; +**до** fond of.
лакони́чный laconic.
ла́мпа lamp; valve, tube. **лампа́да** icon-lamp. **ла́мпочка** lamp; bulb.
ландша́фт landscape.
ла́ндыш lily of the valley.
лань fallow deer; doe.
ла́па paw; tenon.
ла́поть (-птя; *pl* -и, -éй) *m* bast shoe.
ла́почка pet, sweetie.
лапша́ noodles; noodle soup.
ларёк (-рька́) stall. **ларь** (-я́) *m* chest; bin.
ла́ска¹ caress.
ла́ска² weasel.
ласка́ть *impf* caress, fondle; **~ся** +**к**+*dat* make up to; fawn upon. **ла́сковый** affectionate, tender.
ла́сточка swallow.
латви́ец (-и́йца), **-и́йка** Latvian. **латви́йский** Latvian. **Ла́твия**

Latvia.
лати́нский Latin.
лату́нь brass.
ла́ты (лат) *pl* armour.
латы́нь Latin.
латы́ш, латы́шка Latvian, Lett. **латы́шский** Latvian, Lettish.
лауреа́т prize-winner.
ла́цкан lapel.
лачу́га hovel, shack.
ла́ять (ла́ю) *impf* bark.
лба *etc.: see* **лоб**
лгать (лгу, лжёшь; лгал, -á, -о) *impf* (*pf* **на~, со~**) lie; tell lies; +**на**+*acc* slander. **лгун** (-á), **лгу́нья** liar.
лебеди́ный swan. **лебёдка** swan, pen; winch. **ле́бедь** (*pl* -и, -éй) *m* swan, cob.
лев (льва) lion.
левобере́жный left-bank. **левша́** (*gen pl* -éй) *m* & *f* left-hander. **ле́вый** *adj* left; left-hand; left-wing.
лёг *etc.: see* **лечь**
лега́льный legal.
леге́нда legend. **легенда́рный** legendary.
лёгк|ий (-гок, -гка́, лёгки) light; easy; slight, mild; **~ая атле́тика** field and track events. **легко́** *adv* easily, lightly, slightly.
легко- *in comb* light; easy, easily. **легкове́рный** credulous. **~вéс** light-weight. **~мы́сленный** thoughtless; flippant, frivolous, superficial. **~мы́слие** flippancy, frivolity.
легков|о́й: **~а́я маши́на** (private) car. **лёгкое** *sb* lung. **лёгкость** lightness; easiness. **ле́гче** *comp of* **лёгкий, легко́**
лёд (льда, *loc* -у) ice. **ледене́ть** (-е́ю) *impf* (*pf* **за~, о~**) freeze; grow numb with cold. **ледене́ц** (-нца́) fruit-drop. **леденя́щий** chilling, icy.
ле́ди *f indecl* lady.
ле́дник¹ ice-box; refrigerator van. **ледни́к²** (-á) glacier. **леднико́вый** glacial; **~ пери́од** Ice Age. **ледо́вый** ice. **ледоко́л** ice-breaker. **ледяно́й** ice; icy.
лежа́ть (-жу́) *impf* lie; be, be situated. **лежа́чий** lying (down).
ле́звие (cutting) edge; razor-blade.
лезть (-зу; лез) *impf* (*pf* **по~**) climb; clamber, crawl; get, go; fall out.
лейбори́ст Labourite.

лейка watering-can; funnel.

лейтенáнт lieutenant.

лекáрство medicine.

лéксика vocabulary. **лексикóн** lexicon; vocabulary.

лéктор lecturer. **лéкция** lecture.

лелéять (-éю) *impf* (*pf* вз~) cherish, foster.

лён (льна) flax.

ленúвый lazy.

ленингрáдский (of) Leningrad. **лéнинский** (of) Lenin; Leninist.

ленúться (-нюсь, -нишься) *impf* (*pf* по~) be lazy; +*inf* be too lazy to.

лéнта ribbon; band; tape.

лентя́й, -я́йка lazy-bones. **лень** laziness.

лепестóк (-ткá) petal.

лéпет babble; prattle. **лепетáть** (-ечý, -éчешь) *impf* (*pf* про~) babble, prattle.

лепёшка scone; tablet, pastille.

лепúть (-плю́, -пишь) *impf* (*pf* вы́~, за~, с~) model, fashion; mould; ~ся cling; crawl. **лéпка** modelling. **лепнóй** modelled, moulded.

лес (*loc* -ý; *pl* -á) forest, wood; *pl* scaffolding.

лесá (*pl* лéсы) fishing-line.

леснúк (-á) forester. **леснúчий** *sb* forestry officer; forest warden. **леснóй** forest.

лесо- *in comb* forest, forestry; timber wood. **лесовóдство** forestry. ~заготóвка logging. ~пúлка, ~пúльня (*gen pl* -лен) sawmill. ~рýб woodcutter.

лéстница stairs, staircase; ladder.

лéстный flattering. **лесть** flattery.

лёт (*loc* -ý) flight, flying.

летá (лет) *pl* years; age; скóлько вам лет? how old are you?

летáтельный flying. **летáть** *impf*, **летéть** (лечý) *impf* (*pf* полетéть) fly; rush; fall.

лéтний summer.

лётный flying, flight.

лéто (*pl* -á) summer; *pl* years. **лéтом** *adv* in summer.

лéтопись chronicle.

летосчислéние chronology.

летýч|ий flying; passing; brief; volatile; ~ая мышь bat. **лётчик, -чица** pilot.

лечéбница clinic. **лечéбный** medical; medicinal. **лечéние** (medical) treatment. **лечúть** (-чý, -чишь) *impf* treat (от for); ~ся be given, have treatment (от for).

лечý *etc.*: *see* летéть, лечúть

лечь (ля́гу, ля́жешь; лёг, -лá) *pf* (*impf* ложúться) lie, lie down; go to bed.

лещ (-á) bream.

лжесвидéтельство false witness.

лжец (-á) liar. **лжúвый** lying; deceitful.

ли, ль *interrog partl & conj* whether, if; **ли,... ли** whether ... or; рáно ли, пóздно ли sooner or later.

либерáл liberal. **либерáльный** liberal.

лúбо *conj* or; ~... ~ either ... or.

лúвень (-вня) *m* heavy shower, downpour.

ливрéя livery.

лúга league.

лúдер leader. **лидúровать** *impf & pf* be in the lead.

лизáть (лижý, -ешь) *impf*, **лизнýть** (-нý, -нёшь) *pf* lick.

ликвидáция liquidation; abolition. **ликвидúровать** *impf & pf* liquidate; abolish.

ликёр liqueur.

ликовáние rejoicing. **ликовáть** *impf* rejoice.

лúлия lily.

лилóвый lilac, violet.

лимáн estuary.

лимúт limit.

лимóн lemon. **лимонáд** lemonade; squash. **лимóнный** lemon.

лúмфа lymph.

лингвúст linguist. **лингвúстика** linguistics. **лингвистúческий** linguistic.

линéйка ruler; line. **линéйный** linear; ~ корáбль battleship.

лúнза lens.

лúния line.

линóлеум lino(leum).

линя́ть *impf* (*pf* вы́~, по~, с~) fade; moult.

лúпа lime tree.

лúпкий (-пок, -пкá, -о) sticky. **лúпнуть** (-ну; лип) *impf* stick.

лúповый lime.

лúра lyre. **лúрик** lyric poet. **лúрика** lyric poetry. **лирúческий** lyric; lyrical.

лиса́ (*pl* -ы), **-си́ца** fox.

лист (-а́; *pl* -ы́ *or* -ья, -о́в *or* -ьев) leaf; sheet; page; form; **игра́ть с ~а́** play at sight. **листа́ть** *impf* leaf through. **листва́** foliage. **ли́ственница** larch **ли́ственный** deciduous.

листо́вка leaflet. **листово́й** sheet, plate; leaf. **листо́к** (-тка́) *dim of* **лист**; leaflet; form, pro-forma.

Литва́ Lithuania.

лите́йный founding, casting.

литера́тор man of letters. **литерату́ра** literature. **литерату́рный** literary.

лито́вец (-вца), **лито́вка** Lithuanian. **лито́вский** Lithuanian.

лито́й cast.

литр litre.

лить (лью, льёшь; лил, -а́, -о) *impf* (*pf* **с~**) pour; shed; cast, mould. **литьё** founding, moulding; castings, mouldings. **ли́ться** (льётся; ли́лся, -а́сь, ли́ло́сь) *impf* flow; pour.

лиф bodice. **ли́фчик** bra.

лифт lift.

лихо́й[1] (лих, -а́, -о) dashing, spirited.

лихо́й[2] (лих, -а́, -о, ли́хи́) evil.

лихора́дка fever. **лихора́дочный** feverish.

лицево́й facial; exterior; front.

лицеме́р hypocrite. **лицеме́рие** hypocrisy. **лицеме́рный** hypocritical.

лицо́ (*pl* -a) face; exterior; right side; person; **быть к лицу́** +*dat* suit, become.

личи́нка larva, grub; maggot. **ли́чно** *adv* personally, in person. **ли́чность** personality; person. **ли́чный** personal; private; **~ соста́в** staff, personnel.

лиша́й lichen; herpes; shingles. **лиша́йник** lichen.

лиша́ть(ся *impf of* **лиши́ть(ся**

лише́ние deprivation; privation. **лишённый** (-ён, -ена́) +*gen* lacking in, devoid of. **лиши́ть** (-шу́) *pf* (*impf* **лиша́ть**) +*gen* deprive of; **~ся** +*gen* lose, be deprived of. **ли́шний** superfluous; unnecessary; spare; **~ раз** once more; **с ~им** odd, and more.

лишь *adv* only; *conj* as soon as; **~ бы** if only, provided that.

лоб (лба, *loc* лбу) forehead.

ло́бзик fret-saw.

лови́ть (-влю́, -вишь) *impf* (*pf* **пойма́ть**) catch, try to catch.

ло́вкий (-вок, -вка́, -о) adroit; cunning. **ло́вкость** adroitness; cunning.

ло́вля (*gen pl* -вель) catching, hunting; fishing-ground. **лову́шка** trap.

ло́вче *comp of* **ло́вкий**

логари́фм logarithm.

ло́гика logic. **логи́ческий**, **логи́чный** logical.

ло́говище, **ло́гово** den, lair.

ло́дка boat.

ло́дырничать *impf* loaf, idle about. **ло́дырь** *m* loafer, idler.

ло́жа box; (masonic) lodge.

ложби́на hollow.

ло́же couch; bed.

ложи́ться (-жу́сь) *impf of* **лечь**

ло́жка spoon.

ло́жный false. **ложь** (лжи) lie, falsehood.

лоза́ (*pl* -ы) vine.

ло́зунг slogan, catchword.

лока́тор radar *or* sonar apparatus.

локомоти́в locomotive.

ло́кон lock, curl.

ло́коть (-ктя; *pl* -и, -е́й) *m* elbow.

лом (*pl* -ы, -о́в) crowbar; scrap, waste. **ло́маный** broken. **лома́ть** *impf* (*pf* **по~**, **с~**) break; cause to ache; **~ся** break; crack; put on airs; be obstinate.

ломба́рд pawnshop.

ло́мберный стол card-table.

ломи́ть (ло́мит) *impf* break; break through, rush; *impers* cause to ache; **~ся** be (near to) breaking. **ло́мка** breaking; *pl* quarry. **ло́мкий** (-мок, -мка́, -о) fragile, brittle.

ломо́ть (-мтя́; *pl* -мти́) *m* large slice; hunk; chunk. **ло́мтик** slice.

ло́но bosom, lap.

ло́пасть (*pl* -и, -е́й) blade; fan, vane; paddle.

лопа́та spade; shovel. **лопа́тка** shoulder-blade; shovel; trowel.

ло́паться *impf*, **ло́пнуть** (-ну) *pf* burst; split; break; fail; crash.

лопу́х (-а́) burdock.

лорд lord.

лоси́на elk-skin, chamois leather; elk-meat.

лоск lustre, shine.

лоску́т (-а́; *pl* -ы́ *or* -ья, -о́в *or* -ьев) rag, shred, scrap.

лосни́ться *impf* be glossy, shine.

ло́со́сь *m* salmon.

лось (*pl* -и, -ей) *m* elk.
лосьо́н lotion; aftershave; cream.
лот lead, plummet.
лотере́я lottery; raffle.
лото́к (-тка́) hawker's stand *or* tray; chute; gutter; trough.
лохма́тый shaggy; dishevelled.
лохмо́тья (-ьев) *pl* rags.
ло́цман pilot.
лошади́ный horse; equine. **ло́шадь** (*pl* -и, -ей, *instr* -дьми́ *or* -дя́ми) horse.
лощёный glossy, polished.
лощи́на hollow, depression.
лоя́льный fair, honest; loyal.
лубо́к (-бка́) splint; popular print.
луг (*loc* -ý; *pl* -á) meadow.
лу́жа puddle.
лужа́йка lawn, glade.
лужёный tin-plated.
лук[1] onions.
лук[2] bow.
лука́вить (-влю) *impf* (*pf* с~) be cunning. **лука́вство** craftiness. **лука́вый** crafty, cunning.
лу́ковица onion; bulb.
луна́ (*pl* -ы) moon. **луна́тик** sleepwalker.
лу́нка hole; socket.
лу́нный moon; lunar.
лу́па magnifying-glass.
лупи́ть (-плю́, -пишь) *impf* (*pf* от~) flog.
луч (-á) ray; beam. **лучево́й** ray, beam; radial; radiation. **лучеза́рный** radiant.
лучи́на splinter.
лу́чше better; ~ всего́, ~ всех best of all. **лу́чш|ий** better; best; в ~ем слу́чае at best; всего́ ~его! all the best!
лы́жа ski. **лы́жник** skier. **лы́жный спорт** skiing. **лыжня́** ski-track.
лы́ко bast.
лысе́ть (-е́ю) *impf* (*pf* об~, по~) grow bald. **лы́сина** bald spot; blaze. **лы́сый** (лыс, -á, -о) bald.
ль *see* ли
льва *etc.*: *see* лев. **льви́ный** lion, lion's. **льви́ца** lioness.
льго́та privilege; advantage. **льго́тный** privileged; favourable.
льда *etc.*: *see* лёд. **льди́на** block of ice; ice-floe.
льна *etc.*: *see* лён. **льново́дство**

flax-growing.
льнуть (-ну, -нёшь) *impf* (*pf* при~) +к+*dat* cling to; have a weakness for; make up to.
льняно́й flax, flaxen; linen; linseed.
льстец (-á) flatterer. **льсти́вый** flattering; smooth-tongued. **льстить** (льщу) *impf* (*pf* по~) +*dat* flatter.
лью *etc.*: *see* лить
любе́зность courtesy; kindness; compliment. **любе́зн|ый** courteous; obliging; kind; бу́дьте ~ы be so kind (as to).
люби́мец (-мца), **-мица** pet, favourite. **люби́мый** beloved; favourite.
люби́тель *m*, **-ница** lover; amateur. **люби́тельский** amateur. **люби́ть** (-блю́, -бишь) *impf* love; like.
любова́ться *impf* (*pf* по~) +*instr or* на+*acc* admire.
любо́вник lover. **любо́вница** mistress. **любо́вный** love-; loving. **любо́вь** (-бви́, *instr* -бо́вью) love.
любозна́тельный inquisitive.
любо́й any; either; *sb* anyone.
любопы́тный curious; inquisitive. **любопы́тство** curiosity.
лю́бящий loving.
лю́ди (-е́й, -ям, -дьми́, -ях) *pl* people. **лю́дный** populous; crowded. **людое́д** cannibal; ogre. **людско́й** human.
люк hatch(way); trap; manhole.
лю́лька cradle.
люминесце́нтный luminescent. **люминесце́нция** luminescence.
лю́стра chandelier.
лю́тня (*gen pl* -тен) lute.
лю́тый (лют, -á, -о) ferocious.
ляга́ть *impf*, **лягну́ть** (-ну́, -нёшь) *pf* kick; ~ся kick.
ля́гу *etc.*: *see* лечь
лягу́шка frog.
ля́жка thigh, haunch.
ля́згать *impf* clank; +*instr* rattle.
ля́мка strap; тяну́ть ля́мку toil.

M

мавзоле́й mausoleum.
мавр, маврита́нка Moor. **маврита́нский** Moorish.
магази́н shop.
маги́стр (holder of) master's degree.

магистра́ль main; main line, main road.

маги́ческий magic(al). **ма́гия** magic.

магнети́зм magnetism.

ма́гний magnesium.

магни́т magnet. **магни́тный** magnetic. **магнитофо́н** tape-recorder.

мада́м *f indecl* madam, madame.

мажо́р major (key); cheerful mood. **мажо́рный** major; cheerful.

ма́зать (ма́жу) *impf* (*pf* вы~, за~, из~, на~, по~, про~) oil, grease; smear, spread; soil; ~ся get dirty; make up. **мазо́к** (-зка́) touch, dab; smear. **мазу́т** fuel oil. **мазь** ointment; grease.

майс maize.

май May. **ма́йский** May.

ма́йка T-shirt.

майо́р major.

мак poppy, poppy-seeds.

макаро́ны (-н) *pl* macaroni.

мака́ть *impf* (*pf* макну́ть) dip.

маке́т model; dummy.

макну́ть (-ну́, -нёшь) *pf of* мака́ть

макре́ль mackerel.

максима́льный maximum. **ма́ксимум** maximum; at most.

макулату́ра waste paper; pulp literature.

маку́шка top; crown.

мал *etc.*: *see* ма́лый

малахи́т malachite.

мале́йший least, slightest. **ма́ленький** little; small.

мали́на (*no pl*; *usu collect*) raspberry; raspberries; raspberry-bush. **мали́новый** raspberry.

ма́ло *adv* little, few; not enough; ~ того́ moreover; ~ того́ что... not only ....

мало- *in comb* (too) little. **малова́жный** of little importance. **~вероя́тный** unlikely. **~гра́мотный** semiliterate; crude. **~ду́шный** fainthearted. **~иму́щий** needy. **~кро́вие** anaemia. **~ле́тний** young; juvenile; minor. **~о́пытный** inexperienced. **~чи́сленный** small (in number), few.

мало-ма́льски *adv* in the slightest degree; at all. **ма́ло-пома́лу** *adv* little by little.

ма́л|ый (мал, -а́) little, (too) small; са́мое ~ое at the least; *sb* fellow;

lad. **малы́ш** (-а́) kiddy; little boy.

ма́льчик boy. **мальчи́шка** *m* urchin, boy. **мальчуга́н** little boy.

малю́тка *m & f* baby, little one.

маля́р (-а́) painter, decorator.

маляри́я malaria.

ма́ма mother, mummy. **мама́ша** mummy. **ма́мин** mother's.

ма́монт mammoth.

мандари́н mandarin, tangerine.

манда́т warrant; mandate.

манёвр manoeuvre; shunting. **маневри́ровать** *impf* (*pf* с~) manoeuvre; shunt; +*instr* make good use of.

мане́ж riding-school.

манеке́н dummy; mannequin. **манеке́нщик, -щица** model.

мане́ра manner; style. **мане́рный** affected.

манже́та cuff.

маникю́р manicure.

манипули́ровать *impf* manipulate. **манипуля́ция** manipulation; machination.

мани́ть (-ню́, -нишь) *impf* (*pf* по~) beckon; attract; lure.

манифе́ст manifesto. **манифеста́ция** demonstration.

мани́шка (false) shirt-front.

ма́ния mania; ~ вели́чия megalomania.

ма́нная ка́ша semolina.

мано́метр pressure-gauge.

ма́нтия cloak; robe, gown.

мануфакту́ра manufacture; textiles.

манья́к maniac.

марафо́нский бег marathon.

марга́нец (-нца) manganese.

маргари́н margarine.

маргари́тка daisy.

марино́ванный pickled. **маринова́ть** *impf* (*pf* за~) pickle; put off.

марионе́тка puppet.

ма́рка stamp; counter; brand; trademark; grade; reputation.

ма́ркий easily soiled.

маркси́зм Marxism. **маркси́ст** Marxist. **маркси́стский** Marxist.

ма́рлевый gauze. **ма́рля** gauze; cheesecloth.

мармела́д fruit jellies.

ма́рочный high-quality.

Марс Mars.

март March. **ма́ртовский** March.

марты́шка marmoset; monkey.

марш march.

ма́ршал marshal.

марширова́ть *impf* march.

маршру́т route, itinerary.

ма́ска mask. **маскара́д** masked ball; masquerade. **маскирова́ть** *impf (pf за~)* disguise; camouflage. **маски-ро́вка** disguise; camouflage.

Ма́сленица Shrovetide. **маслёнка** butter-dish; oil-can. **масли́на** olive. **ма́сло** *(pl* -а́, ма́сел, -сла́м) butter; oil; oil paints. **маслобо́йка** churn. **маслобо́йня** *(gen pl* -о́ен), **масло-заво́д** dairy. **масляни́стый** oily. **ма́сляный** oil.

ма́сса mass; a lot, lots.

масса́ж massage. **масси́ровать** *impf & pf* massage.

масси́в massif; expanse, tract. **масси́вный** massive.

ма́ссовый mass.

ма́стер *(pl* -а́), **мастери́ца** foreman, forewoman; (master) craftsman; expert. **мастери́ть** *impf (pf с~)* make, build. **мастерска́я** *sb* workshop. **мастерско́й** masterly. **мастерство́** craft; skill.

масти́ка mastic; putty; floor-polish.

масти́тый venerable.

масть *(pl* -и, -е́й) colour; suit.

масшта́б scale.

мат[1] checkmate.

мат[2] mat.

мат[3] foul language.

матема́тик mathematician. **матема́тика** mathematics. **математи́ческий** mathematical.

материа́л material. **материали́зм** materialism. **материалисти́ческий** materialist. **материа́льный** material.

матери́к *(-а́)* continent; mainland. **материко́вый** continental.

матери́нский maternal, motherly. **матери́нство** maternity.

мате́рия material; pus; topic.

ма́тка womb; female.

ма́товый matt; frosted.

матра́с, матра́ц mattress.

матрёшка Russian doll.

ма́трица matrix; die, mould.

матро́с sailor, seaman.

матч match.

мать (ма́тери, *instr* -рью; *pl* -тери, -ре́й) mother.

ма́фия Mafia.

мах swing, stroke. **маха́ть** (машу́, ма́шешь) *impf*, **махну́ть** (-ну́, -нёшь) *pf +instr* wave; brandish; wag; flap; go; rush.

махина́ция machinations.

махови́к *(-а́)* fly-wheel.

махро́вый dyed-in-the-wool; terry.

ма́чеха stepmother.

ма́чта mast.

маши́на machine; car. **машина́льный** mechanical. **машини́ст** operator; engine-driver; scene-shifter. **маши-ни́стка** typist; ~**стенографи́стка** shorthand-typist. **маши́нка** machine; typewriter; sewing-machine. **машинопи́сный** typewritten. **маши́нопись** typing; typescript. **маши-ностро́ение** mechanical engineering.

мая́к *(-а́)* lighthouse; beacon.

ма́ятник pendulum. **ма́яться** *impf* toil; suffer; languish.

мгла haze; gloom.

мгнове́ние instant, moment. **мгно-ве́нный** instantaneous, momentary.

ме́бель furniture. **меблиро́ванный** furnished. **меблиро́вка** furnishing; furniture.

мегава́тт *(gen pl* -а́тт) megawatt. **ме-го́м** megohm. **мегато́нна** megaton.

мёд *(loc* -у́; *pl* -ы́) honey.

меда́ль medal. **медальо́н** medallion.

медве́дица she-bear. **медве́дь** *m* bear. **медве́жий** bear('s). **медве-жо́нок** *(-нка; pl* -жа́та, -жа́т) bear cub.

ме́дик medical student; doctor. **медикаме́нты** *(-ов) pl* medicines.

медици́на medicine. **медици́нский** medical.

ме́дленный slow. **медли́тельный** sluggish; slow. **ме́длить** *impf* linger; be slow.

ме́дный copper; brass.

медо́вый honey; ~ **ме́сяц** honey-moon.

медосмо́тр medical examination, check-up. **медпу́нкт** first aid post. **медсестра́** *(pl* -сёстры, -сестёр, -сёстрам) nurse.

меду́за jellyfish.

медь copper.

меж *prep+instr* between.

меж- *in comb* inter-.

межа (*pl* -и, меж, -ам) boundary.

междоме́тие interjection.

ме́жду *prep+instr* between; among; ~ про́чим incidentally, by the way; ~ тем meanwhile; ~ тем, как while.

между- *in comb* inter-. **междугоро́дный** inter-city. **~наро́дный** international.

межконтинента́льный intercontinental. **межплане́тный** interplanetary.

мезони́н attic (storey); mezzanine (floor).

Ме́ксика Mexico.

мел (*loc* -ý) chalk.

мёл *etc.*: *see* **мести́**

меланхо́лия melancholy.

меле́ть (-éет) *impf* (*pf* **об~**) grow shallow.

мелиора́ция land improvement.

ме́лкий (-лок, -лка́, -о) small; shallow; fine; petty. **ме́лко** *adv* fine, small. **мелкобуржуа́зный** petty bourgeois. **мелково́дный** shallow.

мелоди́чный melodious, melodic. **мело́дия** melody.

ме́лочный petty. **ме́лочь** (*pl* -и, -éй) small items; (small) change; *pl* trifles, trivialities.

мель (*loc* -и́) shoal; bank; **на мели́** aground.

мелька́ть *impf*, **мелькну́ть** (-ну́, -нёшь) *pf* be glimpsed fleetingly. **ме́льком** *adv* in passing; fleetingly.

ме́льник miller. **ме́льница** mill.

мельча́йший *superl of* **ме́лкий**. **ме́льче** *comp of* **ме́лкий**, **ме́лко**.

мелюзга́ small fry.

мелю́ *etc.*: *see* **моло́ть**

мембра́на membrane; diaphragm.

меморандум memorandum.

мемуа́ры (-ов) *pl* memoirs.

ме́на exchange, barter.

ме́неджер manager.

ме́нее *adv* less; **тем не ~** none the less.

мензу́рка measuring-glass.

менево́й exchange; barter.

менуэ́т minuet.

ме́ньше smaller; less. **меньшеви́к** (-á) Menshevik. **ме́ньший** lesser, smaller; younger. **меньшинство́** minority.

меню́ *neut indecl* menu.

меня́ *see* **я** *pron*

меня́ть *impf* (*pf* **об~, по~**) change; exchange; **~ся** change; +*instr* exchange.

ме́ра measure.

мере́щиться (-щусь) *impf* (*pf* **по~**) seem, appear.

мерза́вец (-вца) swine, bastard. **ме́рзкий** (-зок, -зка́, -о) disgusting.

мерзлота́: ве́чная ~ permafrost. **мёрзнуть** (-ну; мёрз) *impf* (*pf* **за~**) freeze.

ме́рзость vileness; abomination.

меридиа́н meridian.

мери́ло standard, criterion.

ме́рин gelding.

ме́рить *impf* (*pf* **по~, с~**) measure; try on. **ме́рка** measure.

ме́рный measured; rhythmical. **мероприя́тие** measure.

мертве́ть (-е́ю) *impf* (*pf* **о~, по~**) grow numb; be benumbed. **мертве́ц** (-á) corpse, dead man. **мёртвый** (мёртв, -á, мёртво) dead.

мерца́ть *impf* twinkle; flicker.

меси́ть (мешу́, ме́сишь) *impf* (*pf* **с~**) knead.

ме́сса Mass.

места́ми *adv* here and there. **месте́чко** (*pl* -и, -чек) small town.

мести́ (мету́, -тёшь; мёл, -á) *impf* sweep; whirl.

ме́стность locality; area. **ме́стный** local; locative. **-ме́стный** *in comb* -berth, -seater. **ме́сто** (*pl* -á) place; site; seat; room; job. **местожи́тельство** (place of) residence. **местоиме́ние** pronoun. **местонахожде́ние** location, whereabouts. **месторожде́ние** deposit; layer.

месть vengeance, revenge.

ме́сяц month; moon. **ме́сячный** monthly.

мета́лл metal. **металли́ческий** metal, metallic. **металлу́ргия** metallurgy.

мета́н methane.

мета́ние throwing, flinging. **мета́ть**[1] (мечу́, ме́чешь) *impf* (*pf* **метну́ть**) throw, fling; **~ся** rush about; toss (and turn).

мета́ть[2] *impf* (*pf* **на~, с~**) tack.

метафи́зика metaphysics.

мета́фора metaphor.

метёлка panicle.

метéль snow-storm.

метеóр meteor. метеорúт meteorite. метеорóлог meteorologist. метеорологúческий meteorological. метеоролóгия meteorology. метеосвóдка weather report. метеостáнция weather-station.

мéтить¹ (мéчу) *impf* (*pf* на~, по~) mark.

мéтить² (мéчу) *impf* (*pf* на~) aim; mean.

мéтка marking, mark.

мéткий (-ток, -ткá, -о) well-aimed, accurate.

метлá (*pl* мётлы, -тел) broom.

метнýть (-нý, -нёшь) *pf of* метáть¹

мéтод method. метóдика method(s); methodology. методúчный methodical. методолóгия methodology.

метр metre.

мéтрика birth certificate. метрúческ|ий¹: ~ое свидéтельство birth certificate.

метрúческий² metric; metrical.

метрó *neut indecl*, метрополитéн Metro; underground.

метý *etc.: see* местú

мех¹ (*loc* -ý; *pl* -á) fur.

мех² (*pl* -и́) wine-skin, water-skin; *pl* bellows.

механизáция mechanization. механúзм mechanism; gear(ing). мехáник mechanic. механика mechanics; trick; knack. механúческий mechanical; mechanistic.

меховóй fur.

меч (-á) sword.

мéченый marked.

мечéть mosque.

мечтá (day-)dream. мечтáтельный dreamy. мечтáть *impf* dream.

мéчу *etc.: see* мéтить. мечý *etc.: see* метáть

мешáлка mixer.

мешáть¹ *impf* (*pf* по~) +*dat* hinder; prevent; disturb.

мешáть² *impf* (*pf* по~, с~) stir; mix; mix up; ~ся (в+*acc*) interfere (in), meddle (with).

мешóк (-шкá) bag; sack. мешковúна sacking, hessian.

мещанúн (*pl* -áне, -áн) petty bourgeois; Philistine. мещáнский bourgeois, narrow-minded; Philistine. мещáнство petty bourgeoisie; philistinism, narrow-mindedness.

миг moment, instant.

мигáть *impf*, мигнýть (-нý, -нёшь) *pf* blink; wink, twinkle.

мúгом *adv* in a flash.

мигрáция migration.

мигрéнь migraine.

мизантрóп misanthrope.

мизúнец (-нца) little finger; little toe.

микрóб microbe.

микроволнóвая печь microwave oven.

микрóн micron.

микроорганúзм micro-organism.

микроскóп microscope. микроскопúческий microscopic.

микросхéма microchip.

микрофóн (*gen pl* -н) microphone.

мúксер (*cul*) mixer, blender.

микстýра medicine, mixture.

мúленький pretty; nice; sweet; dear.

милитарúзм militarism.

милиционéр militiaman, policeman. милúция militia, police force.

миллиáрд billion, a thousand million. миллимéтр millimetre. миллиóн million. миллионéр millionaire.

милосéрдие mercy, charity. милосéрдный merciful, charitable.

мúлостивый gracious, kind. мúлостыня alms. мúлость favour, grace. мúлый (мил, -á, -о) nice; kind; sweet; dear.

мúля mile.

мúмика (facial) expression; mimicry.

мúмо *adv* & *prep* +*gen* by, past. мимолётный fleeting. мимохóдом *adv* in passing.

мúна¹ mine; bomb.

мúна² expression, mien.

миндáль (-я́) *m* almond(-tree); almonds.

минерáл mineral. минералóгия mineralogy. минерáльный mineral.

миниатюра miniature. миниатюрный miniature; tiny.

минимáльный minimum. мúнимум minimum.

министéрство ministry. минúстр minister.

миновáть *impf* & *pf* pass; *impers*+*dat* escape.

миномёт mortar. минонóсец (-сца)

torpedo-boat.
мино́р minor (key); melancholy.
мину́вш|ий past; **~ee** sb the past.
ми́нус minus.
мину́та minute. **мину́тный** minute; momentary.
мину́ть (-нешь; ми́нул) pf pass.
мир[1] (pl -ы́) world.
мир[2] peace.
мира́ж mirage.
мири́ть impf (pf по~, при~) reconcile; **~ся** be reconciled. **ми́рный** peace; peaceful.
мировоззре́ние (world-)outlook; philosophy. **мирово́й** world. **мирозда́ние** universe.
миролюби́вый peace-loving.
ми́ска basin, bowl.
мисс f indecl Miss.
миссионе́р missionary.
ми́ссия mission.
ми́стер Mr.
ми́стика mysticism.
мистифика́ция hoax, leg-pull.
ми́тинг mass meeting; rally.
митрополи́т metropolitan.
миф myth. **мифи́ческий** mythical. **мифологи́ческий** mythological. **мифоло́гия** mythology.
ми́чман warrant officer.
мише́нь target.
ми́шка (Teddy) bear.
младе́нец (-нца) baby; infant. **мла́дший** younger; youngest; junior.
млекопита́ющие sb pl mammals. **Мле́чный Путь** Milky Way.
мне see я pron
мне́ние opinion.
мни́мый imaginary; sham. **мни́тельный** hypochondriac; mistrustful.
мнить (мню) impf think.
мно́гие sb pl many (people); **~ое** sb much, a great deal. **мно́го** adv+gen much; many; **на ~** by far.
много- in comb many-, poly-, multi-, multiple-. **многобо́рье** combined event. **~гра́нный** polyhedral; many-sided. **~де́тный** having many children. **~же́нство** polygamy. **~значи́тельный** significant. **~кра́тный** repeated; frequentative. **~ле́тний** lasting, living, many years; of many years' standing; perennial. **~лю́дный** crowded. **~национа́льный** multi-national. **~обеща́ющий** prom-

ising. **~обра́зие** diversity. **~сло́вный** verbose. **~сторо́нний** multilateral; many-sided; versatile. **~то́чие** dots, omission points. **~уважа́емый** respected; Dear. **~уго́льный** polygonal. **~цве́тный** multi-coloured; multiflorous. **~чи́сленный** numerous. **~эта́жный** many-storeyed. **~язы́чный** polyglot.
мно́жественный plural. **мно́жество** great number. **мно́жить** (-жу) impf (pf y~) multiply; increase.
мной etc.: see я pron. **мну** etc.: see мять
мобилиза́ция mobilization. **мобилизова́ть** impf & pf mobilize.
мог etc.: see мочь
моги́ла grave. **моги́льный** (of the) grave; sepulchral.
могу́ etc.: see мочь. **могу́чий** mighty. **могу́щественный** powerful. **могу́щество** power, might.
мо́да fashion.
модели́ровать impf & pf design. **моде́ль** model; pattern. **модельер** fashion designer. **моде́льный** model; fashionable.
модернизи́ровать impf & pf modernize.
моди́стка milliner.
модифика́ция modification. **модифици́ровать** impf & pf modify.
мо́дный (-ден, -дна́, -о) fashionable; fashion.
мо́жет see мочь
можжеве́льник juniper.
мо́жно one may, one can; it is permissible; it is possible; **как ~+comp** as ... as possible; **как ~ скоре́е** as soon as possible.
моза́ика mosaic; jigsaw.
мозг (loc -ý; pl -и́) brain; marrow. **мозгово́й** cerebral.
мозо́ль corn; callus.
мой (моего́) m, **моя́** (мое́й) f, **моё** (моего́) neut, **мои́** (-и́х) pl pron my; mine; **по-мо́ему** in my opinion; in my way.
мо́йка washing.
мо́кнуть (-ну; мок) impf get wet; soak. **мокро́та** phlegm. **мо́крый** wet, damp.
мол (loc -ý) mole, pier.
молва́ rumour, talk.
моле́бен (-бна) church service.

молékула molecule. **молекулярный** molecular.

молитва prayer. **молить** (-лю́, -лишь) *impf* pray; beg; ~**ся** (*pf* по~**ся**) pray.

моллю́ск mollusc.

молниенóсный lightning. **мóлния** lightning; zip(-fastener).

молодёжь youth, young people. **молодéть** (-éю) *impf* (*pf* по~) get younger, look younger. **молодéц** (-дца́) fine fellow *or* girl; ~! well done! **молодожёны** (-ов) *pl* newly-weds. **молодóй** (мóлод, -а́, -о) young. **мóлодость** youth. **молóже** *comp of* **молодóй**

молокó milk.

мóлот hammer. **молоти́ть** (-очу́, -óтишь) *impf* (*pf* с~) thresh; hammer. **молотóк** (-тка́) hammer. **мóлотый** ground. **молóть** (мелю́, мéлешь) *impf* (*pf* с~) grind, mill.

молóчная *sb* dairy. **молóчный** milk; dairy; milky.

мóлча *adv* silently, in silence. **молчали́вый** silent, taciturn; tacit. **молча́ние** silence. **молча́ть** (-чу́) *impf* be *or* keep silent.

моль moth.

мольба́ entreaty.

мольбéрт easel.

момéнт moment; feature. **момента́льно** *adv* instantly. **момента́льный** instantaneous.

мона́рх monarch. **монархи́ст** monarchist.

монасты́рь (-я́) *m* monastery; convent. **мона́х** monk. **мона́хиня** nun.

монгóл, ~**ка** Mongol.

монéта coin.

монографи́я monograph.

моноли́тный monolithic.

монолóг monologue.

монопóлия monopoly.

монотóнный monotonous.

монта́ж (-á) assembling, mounting; editing. **монта́жник** rigger, fitter. **монтёр** fitter, mechanic. **монти́ровать** *impf* (*pf* с~) mount; install, fit; edit.

монумéнт monument. **монумента́льный** monumental.

мора́ль moral; morals, ethics. **мора́льный** moral; ethical.

морг morgue.

морга́ть *impf*, **моргну́ть** (-ну́, -нёшь) *pf* blink; wink.

мóрда snout, muzzle; (ugly) mug.

мóре (*pl* -я́, -éй) sea.

морепла́вание navigation. **морепла́ватель** *m* seafarer. **морехóдный** nautical.

морж (-á), **моржи́ха** walrus.

Мóрзе *indecl* Morse; а́збука ~ Morse code.

мори́ть *impf* (*pf* у~) exhaust; ~ гóлодом starve.

моркóвка carrot. **моркóвь** carrots.

морóженое *sb* ice-cream. **морóженый** frozen, chilled. **морóз** frost; *pl* intensely cold weather. **моро́зилка** freezer compartment; freezer. **морози́льник** deep-freeze. **моро́зить** (-óжу) freeze. **моро́зный** frosty.

мороси́ть *impf* drizzle.

морск|óй sea; maritime; marine, nautical; ~**а́я сви́нка** guinea-pig; ~**óй флот** navy, fleet.

мóрфий morphine.

морщи́на wrinkle; crease. **мóрщить** (-щу) *impf* (*pf* на~, по~, с~) wrinkle; pucker; ~**ся** knit one's brow; wince; crease, wrinkle.

моря́к (-á) sailor, seaman.

москви́ч (-á), ~**ка** Muscovite. **моско́вский** (of) Moscow.

мост (мóста́, *loc* -ý; *pl* -ы́) bridge. **мóстик** bridge. **мости́ть** (-ощу́) *impf* (*pf* вы́~) pave. **мостки́** (-óв) *pl* planked footway. **мостова́я** *sb* roadway; pavement. **мостовóй** bridge.

мота́ть[1] *impf* (*pf* мотну́ть, на~) wind, reel.

мота́ть[2] *impf* (*pf* про~) squander. **мота́ться** *impf* dangle; wander; rush about.

моти́в motive; reason; tune; motif. **мотиви́ровать** *impf* & *pf* give reasons for, justify. **мотивирóвка** reason(s); justification.

мотну́ть (-ну́, -нёшь) *pf of* **мота́ть**

мото- *in comb* motor-, engine-. **мотогóнки** (-нок) *pl* motor-cycle races. ~**пéд** moped. ~**пехóта** motorized infantry. ~**póллер** (motor-)scooter. ~**ци́кл** motor cycle.

мотóк (-тка́) skein, hank.

мотóр motor, engine. **мотори́ст** motor-mechanic. **мотóрный** motor; engine.

моты́га hoe, mattock.

мотылёк (-лька́) butterfly, moth.

мох (мха *or* мо́ха, *loc* мху; *pl* мхи, мхов) moss. **мохна́тый** hairy, shaggy.

моча́ urine.

моча́лка loofah.

мочево́й пузы́рь bladder. **мочи́ть** (-чу́, -чишь) *impf* (*pf* за~, на~) wet, moisten; soak; ~ся (*pf* по~ся) urinate.

мо́чка ear lobe.

мочь (могу́, мо́жешь; мог, -ла́) *impf* (*pf* с~) be able; **мо́жет (быть)** perhaps.

моше́нник rogue. **моше́нничать** *impf* (*pf* с~) cheat, swindle. **моше́ннический** rascally.

мо́шка midge. **мошкара́** (swarm of) midges.

мо́щность power; capacity. **мо́щный** (-щен, -щна́, -о) powerful.

мощу́ *etc.: see* **мости́ть**

мощь power.

мо́ю *etc.: see* **мыть. мо́ющий** washing; detergent.

мрак darkness, gloom. **мракобе́с** obscurantist.

мра́мор marble. **мра́морный** marble.

мра́чный dark; gloomy.

мсти́тельный vindictive. **мстить** (мщу) *impf* (*pf* ото~) take vengeance on; +за+*acc* avenge.

мудре́ц (-а́) sage, wise man. **му́дрость** wisdom. **му́дрый** (-др, -а́, -о) wise, sage.

муж (*pl* -жья́ *or* -и́) husband. **мужа́ть** *impf* grow up; mature; ~ся take courage. **мужеподо́бный** mannish; masculine. **му́жественный** manly, steadfast. **му́жество** courage.

мужи́к (-а́) peasant; fellow.

мужско́й masculine; male. **мужчи́на** *m* man.

му́за muse.

музе́й museum.

му́зыка music. **музыка́льный** musical. **музыка́нт** musician.

му́ка¹ torment.

мука́² flour.

мультиплика́ция, мультфи́льм cartoon film.

му́мия mummy.

мунди́р (full-dress) uniform.

мундшту́к (-а́) mouthpiece; cigarette-holder.

муниципа́льный municipal.

мураве́й (-вья́) ant. **мураве́йник** ant-hill.

мурлы́кать (-ы́чу *or* -каю) *impf* purr.

муска́т nutmeg.

му́скул muscle. **му́скульный** muscular.

му́сор refuse; rubbish. **му́сорный я́щик** dustbin.

мусульма́нин (*pl* -ма́не, -ма́н), -а́нка Muslim.

мути́ть (мучу́, му́тишь) *impf* (*pf* вз~) make muddy; stir up, upset. **му́тный** (-тен, -тна́, -о) turbid, troubled; dull. **муть** sediment; murk.

му́ха fly.

муче́ние torment, torture. **му́ченик, му́ченица** martyr. **мучи́тельный** agonizing. **му́чить** (-чу) *impf* (*pf* за~, из~) torment; harass; ~ся torment o.s.; suffer agonies.

мучно́й flour, meal; starchy.

мха *etc.: see* **мох**

мча́ть (мчу) *impf* rush along, whirl along; ~ся rush.

мщу *etc.: see* **мстить**

мы (нас, нам, на́ми, нас) *pron* we; **мы с ва́ми** you and I.

мы́лить *impf* (*pf* на~) soap; ~ся wash o.s. **мы́ло** (*pl* -а́) soap. **мы́льница** soap-dish. **мы́льный** soap, soapy.

мыс cape, promontory.

мы́сленный mental. **мы́слимый** conceivable. **мысли́тель** *m* thinker. **мы́слить** *impf* think; conceive. **мысль** thought; idea. **мы́слящий** thinking.

мыть (мо́ю) *impf* (*pf* вы́~, по~) wash; ~ся wash (o.s.).

мыча́ть (-чу́) *impf* (*pf* про~) low, moo; bellow; mumble.

мышело́вка mousetrap.

мы́шечный muscular.

мышле́ние thinking, thought.

мы́шца muscle.

мышь (*gen pl* -е́й) mouse.

мэр mayor. **мэ́рия** town hall.

мя́гкий (-гок, -гка́, -о) soft; mild; **знак** soft sign, the letter **ь**. **мя́гче** *comp* of **мя́гкий, мя́гко. мя́коть** fleshy part, flesh; pulp.

мяси́стый fleshy; meaty. **мясни́к** (-а́) butcher. **мясно́й** meat. **мя́со** meat;

flesh. **мясору́бка** mincer.

мя́та mint; peppermint.

мяте́ж (-á) mutiny, revolt. **мяте́жник** mutineer, rebel. **мяте́жный** rebellious; restless.

мя́тный mint, peppermint.

мять (мну, мнёшь) *impf* (*pf* из~, раз~, с~) work up; knead; crumple; ~ся become crumpled; crush (easily).

мяу́кать *impf* miaow.

мяч (-á), **мя́чик** ball.

Н

на¹ *prep* I. +*acc* on; on to, to, into; at; till, until; for; by. II. +*prep* on, upon; in; at.

на² *partl* here; here you are.

наба́вить (-влю) *pf*, **набавля́ть** *impf* add (to), increase.

наба́т alarm-bell.

набе́г raid, foray.

набекре́нь *adv* aslant.

на|бели́ть (-éлишь) *pf*. **на́бело** *adv* without corrections.

на́бережная *sb* embankment, quay.

наберу́ *etc.: see* **набра́ть**

набива́ть(ся *impf of* **наби́ть(ся**. **наби́вка** stuffing, padding; (textile) printing.

набира́ть(ся *impf of* **набра́ть(ся**

наби́тый packed, stuffed; crowded.

наби́ть (-бью, -бьёшь) *pf* (*impf* **набива́ть**) stuff, pack, fill; smash; print; hammer, drive; ~ся crowd in.

наблюда́тель *m* observer. **наблюда́тельный** observant; observation.

наблюда́ть *impf* observe, watch; +*за*+*instr* look after; supervise. **наблюде́ние** observation; supervision.

на́божный devout, pious.

на́бок *adv* on one side, crooked.

наболе́вший sore, painful.

набо́р recruiting; collection, set; typesetting.

набра́сывать(ся *impf of* **наброса́ть**, **набро́сить(ся**

набра́ть (-беру́, -берёшь; -áл, -á, -о) *pf* (*impf* **набира́ть**) gather; enlist; compose, set up; ~ но́мер dial a number; ~ся assemble, collect; +*gen* find, acquire, pick up; ~ся сме́лости

pluck up courage.

набрести́ (-еду́, -дёшь; -ёл, -елá) *pf* +*на*+*acc* come across.

наброса́ть *pf* (*impf* **набра́сывать**) throw (down); sketch; jot down. **набро́сить** (-óшу) *pf* (*impf* **набра́сывать**) throw; ~ся throw o.s.; ~ся на attack. **набро́сок** (-ска) sketch, draft.

набу́хать *impf*, **набу́хнуть** (-нет; -у́х) *pf* swell.

набью́ *etc.: see* **наби́ть**

наважде́ние delusion.

нава́ливать *impf*, **навали́ть** (-лю́, -лишь) *pf* heap, pile up; load; ~ся lean; +*на*+*acc* fall (up)on.

наведе́ние laying (on); placing.

наведу́ *etc.: see* **навести́**

наве́к, наве́ки *adv* for ever.

навёл *etc.: see* **навести́**

наве́рно, наве́рное *adv* probably. **наверняка́** *adv* certainly, for sure.

наверста́ть *pf*, **навёрстывать** *impf* make up for.

наве́рх *adv* up(wards); upstairs. **наверху́** *adv* above; upstairs.

наве́с awning.

наве́сить (-éшу) *pf* (*impf* **наве́шивать**) hang (up). **навесно́й** hanging.

навести́ (-еду́, -едёшь; -вёл, -á) *pf* (*impf* **наводи́ть**) direct; aim; cover (with), spread; introduce, bring; make.

навести́ть (-ещу́) *pf* (*impf* **навеща́ть**) visit.

наве́шать *pf*, **наве́шивать¹** *impf* hang (out); weigh out.

наве́шивать² *impf of* **наве́сить**.

навеща́ть *impf of* **навести́ть**

на́взничь *adv* backwards, on one's back.

навзры́д *adv*: пла́кать ~ sob.

навига́ция navigation.

нависа́ть *impf*, **нави́снуть** (-нет; -вис) *pf* overhang, hang (over); threaten. **нави́сший** beetling.

навлека́ть *impf*, **навле́чь** (-еку́, -ечёшь; -ёк, -лá) *pf* bring, draw; incur.

наводи́ть (-ожу́, -óдишь) *impf of* **навести́**; **наводя́щий** вопро́с leading question. **наво́дка** aiming; applying.

наводне́ние flood. **наводни́ть** *pf*,

наводнять *impf* flood; inundate.
навóз dung, manure.
нáволочка pillowcase.
на|врáть (-рý, -рёшь; -áл, -á, -о) *pf* tell lies, romance; talk nonsense; +**в**+*prep* make mistake(s) in.
навредить (-ежý) *pf* +*dat* harm.
навсегдá *adv* for ever.
навстрéчу *adv* to meet; **идти ~** go to meet; meet halfway.
навы|ворот *adv* inside out; back to front.
нáвык experience, skill.
навы|нос *adv* to take away.
навы|пуск *adv* worn outside.
навьючивать *impf*, **на|вьючить** (-чу) *pf* load.
навязáть (-яжý, -яжешь) *pf*, **навязывать** *impf* tie, fasten; thrust, foist; **~ся** thrust o.s. **навязчивый** importunate; obsessive.
на|гáдить (-áжу) *pf*.
нагáн revolver.
нагибáть(ся *impf of* **нагнýть(ся**
нагишóм *adv* stark naked.
наглéц (-á) impudent fellow. **нáглость** impudence. **нáглый** (нагл, -á, -о) impudent.
наглядный clear, graphic; visual.
нагнáть (-гоню, -гóнишь; -áл, -á, -о) *pf* (*impf* **нагонять**) overtake, catch up (with); inspire, arouse.
нагнести (-етý, -етёшь) *pf*, **нагнетáть** *impf* compress; supercharge.
нагноéние suppuration. **нагноиться** *pf* suppurate.
нагнýть (-нý, -нёшь) *pf* (*impf* **нагибáть**) bend; **~ся** bend, stoop.
наговáривать *impf*, **наговорить** *pf* slander; talk a lot (of); record.
нагóй (наг, -á, -о) naked, bare.
нáголо *adv* naked, bare.
нагонять *impf of* **нагнáть**
нагорáть *impf*, **нагорéть** (-рит) *pf* be consumed; *impers*+*dat* be scolded.
нагóрный upland, mountain; mountainous.
наготá nakedness, nudity.
награбить (-блю) *pf* amass by dishonest means.
нагрáда reward; decoration; prize.
наградить (-ажý) *pf*, **награждáть** *impf* reward; decorate; award prize to.
нагревáтельный heating. **нагре-**

вáть *impf*, **нагрéть** (-éю) *pf* warm, heat; **~ся** get hot, warm up.
нагромождáть *impf*, **на|громоздить** (-зжý) *pf* heap up, pile up.
нагромождéние heaping up; conglomeration.
на|грубить (-блю) *pf*.
нагружáть *impf*, **на|грузить** (-ужý, -ýзишь) *pf* load; **~ся** load o.s.
нагрýзка loading; load; work; commitments.
нагрянуть (-ну) *pf* appear unexpectedly.
над, надо *prep*+*instr* over, above; on, at.
надавить (-влю, -вишь) *pf*, **надáвливать** *impf* press; squeeze out; crush.
надбáвка addition, increase.
надвигáть *impf*, **надвинуть** (-ну) *pf* move, pull, push; **~ся** approach.
нáдвое *adv* in two.
надгрóбие epitaph. **надгрóбный** (*on or over a*) grave.
надевáть *impf of* **надéть**
надéжда hope. **надёжность** reliability. **надёжный** reliable.
надéл allotment.
надéлать *pf* make; cause; do.
наделить (-лю, -лишь) *pf*, **наделять** *impf* endow, provide.
надéть (-éну) *pf* (*impf* **надевáть**) put on.
надéяться (-éюсь) *impf* (*pf* **по~**) hope; rely.
надзирáтель *m* overseer, supervisor.
надзирáть *impf* +**за**+*instr* supervise, oversee. **надзóр** supervision; surveillance.
надлáмывать(ся *impf of* **над-лом́ить(ся**
надлежáщий fitting, proper, appropriate. **надлежит** (-жáло) *impers* (+*dat*) it is necessary, required.
надлóм break; crack; breakdown.
надломить (-млю, -мишь) *pf* **надлáмывать** break; crack; breakdown; **~ся** break, crack, breakdown.
надлóмленный broken.
надмéнный haughty, arrogant.
нáдо[1] (+*dat*) it is necessary; I (*etc.*) must, ought to; I (*etc.*) need. **нáдобность** necessity, need.
надо[2]: *see* **над**.
надоедáть *impf*, **надоéсть** (-éм, -éшь,

-ést, -еди́м) pf +dat bore, pester.
надое́дливый boring, tiresome.
надо́лго adv for a long time.
надорва́ть (-ву́, -вёшь; -а́л, -а́, -о)
pf (impf **надрыва́ть**) tear; strain;
~**ся** tear; overstrain o.s.
на́дпись inscription.
надре́з cut, incision. **надре́зать**
(-е́жу) pf, **надреза́ть** impf, **над-
ре́зывать** impf make an incision in.
надруга́тельство outrage. **надру-
га́ться** pf +над+instr outrage, insult.
надры́в tear; strain; breakdown; outburst. **надрыва́ть(ся** impf of **надо-
рва́ть(ся. надры́вный** hysterical;
heartrending.
надста́вить (-влю) pf, **надста-
вля́ть** impf lengthen.
надстра́ивать impf, **надстро́ить**
(-о́ю) pf build on top; extend upwards. **надстро́йка** building upwards; superstructure.
надува́тельство swindle. **надувать(ся** impf. of **надуть(ся. на-
дувно́й** pneumatic, inflatable.
наду́манный far-fetched.
наду́тый swollen; haughty; sulky.
наду́ть (-у́ю) pf (impf **надува́ть**) inflate; swindle; ~**ся** swell out; sulk.
на|души́ть(ся (-шу́(сь, -шишь(ся) pf.
наеда́ться impf of **нае́сться**
наедине́ adv privately, alone.
нае́зд flying visit; raid. **нае́здник,
-ица** rider. **наезжа́ть** impf of
нае́здить, нае́хать; pay occasional
visits.
наём (на́йма) hire; renting; **взять в
~ rent; сдать в ~** let. **наёмник** hire-
ling; mercenary. **наёмный** hired,
rented.
нае́сться (-е́мся, -е́шься, -е́стся,
-еди́мся) pf (impf **наеда́ться**) eat
one's fill; stuff o.s.
нае́хать (-е́ду) pf (impf **наезжа́ть**)
arrive unexpectedly; +на+acc run
into, collide with.
нажа́ть (-жму́, -жмёшь) pf (impf
нажима́ть) press; put pressure (on).
нажда́к (-а́) emery. **нажда́чная
бума́га** emery paper.
нажи́ва profit, gain.
нажива́ть(ся impf of **нажи́ть(ся
нажи́м** pressure; clamp. **нажима́ть**
impf of **нажа́ть.**
нажи́ть (-иву́, -ивёшь; на́жил, -а́, -о)

pf (impf **нажива́ть**) acquire; contract, incur; ~**ся** (-жи́лся, -а́сь) get
rich.
нажму́ etc.: see **нажа́ть**
наза́втра adv (the) next day.
наза́д adv back(wards); **(тому́) ~**
ago.
назва́ние name; title. **назва́ть** (-зову́,
-зовёшь; -а́л, -а́, -о) pf (impf **назы-
ва́ть**) call, name; ~**ся** be called.
назе́мный ground, surface.
на́зло́ adv out of spite; to spite.
назнача́ть impf, **назна́чить** (-чу) pf
appoint; fix, set; prescribe. **назна-
че́ние** appointment; fixing, setting;
prescription.
назову́ etc.: see **назва́ть**
назо́йливый importunate.
назрева́ть impf, **назре́ть** (-е́ет) pf
ripen, mature; become imminent.
называ́емый: так ~ so-called. **на-
зыва́ть(ся** impf of **назва́ть(ся.**
наибо́лее adv (the) most. **наибо́ль-
ший** greatest, biggest.
наи́вный naive.
наивы́сший highest.
наигра́ть pf, **наи́грывать** impf win;
play, pick out.
наизна́нку adv inside out.
наизу́сть adv by heart.
наилу́чший best.
наименова́ние name; title.
на́искось adv obliquely.
найму́ etc.: see **наня́ть**
найти (-йду́, -йдёшь; нашёл, -шла́,
-шло́) pf (impf **находи́ть**) find; ~**сь**
be found; be, be situated.
наказа́ние punishment. **наказа́ть**
(-ажу́, -а́жешь) pf, **нака́зывать**
impf punish.
нака́л incandescence. **нака́ливать**
impf, **накали́ть, накаля́ть** impf
heat; make red-hot; strain, make
tense; ~**ся** glow, become incandescent; become strained.
нака́лывать(ся impf of **наколо́ть(ся**
накану́не adv the day before.
нака́пливать(ся impf of **накопи́ть(ся**
накача́ть pf, **нака́чивать** impf
pump (up).
наки́дка cloak, cape; extra charge.
наки́нуть (-ну) pf, **наки́дывать**
impf throw; throw on; ~**ся** throw

o.s.; ~ся на attack.

на́кипь scum; scale.

накладна́я *sb* invoice. **накладн|о́й** laid on; false; ~ые расхо́ды overheads. **накла́дывать** *impf of* **на|ложи́ть**

на|клевета́ть (-ещу́, -е́щешь) *pf*.

накле́ивать *impf*, **накле́ить** *pf* stick on. **накле́йка** sticking (on, up); label.

накло́н slope, incline. **наклоне́ние** inclination; mood. **наклони́ть** (-ню́, -нишь) *pf*, **наклоня́ть** *impf* incline, bend; ~ся stoop, bend. **накло́нный** inclined, sloping.

нако́лка pinning; (*pinned-on*) ornament for hair; tattoo. **наколо́ть¹** (-лю́, -лешь) *pf* (*impf* **нака́лывать**) prick; pin; ~ся prick o.s.

наколо́ть² (-лю́, -лешь) *pf* (*impf* **нака́лывать**) chop.

наконе́ц *adv* at last. **наконе́чник** tip, point.

на|копи́ть (-плю́, -пишь) *pf*, **накопля́ть** *impf* (*impf also* **нака́пливать**) accumulate; ~ся accumulate. **накопле́ние** accumulation.

на|копти́ть (-пчу́) *pf*. **на|корми́ть** (-млю́, -мишь) *pf*.

накра́сить (-а́шу) *pf* paint; make up. **на|кра́ситься** (-а́шусь) *pf*.

на|крахма́лить *pf*.

на|крени́ть *pf*. **накрени́ться** (-ни́тся) *pf*, **накреня́ться** *impf* tilt; list.

накрича́ть (-чу́) *pf* (+на+*acc*) shout (at).

накро́ю *etc.*: *see* **накры́ть**

накрыва́ть *impf*, **накры́ть** (-ро́ю) *pf* cover; catch; ~ (на) стол lay the table; ~ся cover o.s.

накури́ть (-рю́, -ришь) *pf* fill with smoke.

налага́ть *impf of* **наложи́ть**

нала́дить (-а́жу) *pf*, **нала́живать** *impf* regulate, adjust; repair; organize; ~ся come right; get going.

на|лга́ть (-лгу́, -лжёшь; -а́л, -á, -о) *pf*.

нале́во *adv* to the left.

налёг *etc.*: *see* **нале́чь**. **налега́ть** *impf of* **нале́чь**

налегке́ *adv* lightly dressed; without luggage.

налёт raid; flight; thin coating. **налета́ть¹** *pf* have flown. **налета́ть²** *impf*, **налете́ть** (-лечу́) *pf*

swoop down; come flying; spring up.

нале́чь (-ля́гу, -ля́жешь; -лёг, -лá) *pf* (*impf* **налега́ть**) lean, apply one's weight; lie; apply o.s.

налжёшь *etc.*: *see* **налга́ть**

налива́ть(ся *impf of* **нали́ть(ся**. **нали́вка** fruit liqueur.

нали́ть (-лью́, -льёшь; на́лил, -á, -о) *pf* (*impf* **налива́ть**) pour (out), fill; ~ся (-и́лся, -а́сь, -и́ло́сь) pour in; ripen.

налицо́ *adv* present; available.

нали́чие presence. **нали́чн|ый** on hand; cash; ~ые (де́ньги) ready money.

нало́г tax. **налогоплате́льщик** taxpayer. **нало́женн|ый**: ~ым платежо́м C.O.D. **наложи́ть** (-жу́, -жишь) *pf* (*impf* **накла́дывать**, **налага́ть**) lay (in, on), put (in, on); apply; impose.

налью́ *etc.*: *see* **нали́ть**

наля́гу *etc.*: *see* **нале́чь**

нам *etc.*: *see* **мы**

на|ма́зать (-а́жу) *pf*, **нама́зывать** *impf* oil, grease; smear, spread.

нама́тывать *impf of* **намота́ть**. **нама́чивать** *impf of* **намочи́ть**

намёк hint. **намека́ть** *impf*, **намекну́ть** (-ну́, -нёшь) *pf* hint.

намерева́ться *impf* +*inf* intend to. **наме́рен** *predic*: я ~(а)+*inf* I intend to. **наме́рение** intention. **наме́ренный** intentional.

на|мета́ть *pf*. **на|ме́тить¹** (-е́чу) *pf*. **наме́тить²** (-е́чу) *pf* (*impf* **намеча́ть**) plan; outline; nominate; ~ся be outlined, take shape.

намно́го *adv* much, far.

намока́ть *impf*, **намо́кнуть** (-ну) *pf* get wet.

намо́рдник muzzle.

на|мо́рщить(ся (-щу(сь) *pf*.

на|мота́ть *pf* (*impf also* **нама́тывать**) wind, reel.

на|мочи́ть (-очу́, -о́чишь) *pf* (*impf also* **нама́чивать**) wet; soak; splash, spill.

намы́ливать *impf*, **на|мы́лить** *pf* soap.

нанести́ (-су́, -сёшь; -ёс, -лá) *pf* (*impf* **наноси́ть**) carry, bring; draw, plot; inflict.

на|низа́ть (-ижу́, -и́жешь) *pf*, **нани́зывать** *impf* string, thread.

нанима́тель *m* tenant; employer. **нанима́ть(ся** *impf of* **наня́ть(ся**

наноси́ть (-ошу́, -о́сишь) *impf of* **нанести́**

наня́ть (найму́, -мёшь; на́нял, -а́, -о) *pf* (*impf* **нанима́ть**) hire; rent; **~ся** get a job.

наоборо́т *adv* on the contrary; back to front; the other, the wrong, way (round); vice versa.

на́отмашь *adv* violently.

наотре́з *adv* flatly, point-blank.

напада́ть *impf of* **напа́сть. напада́ющий** *sb* forward. **нападе́ние** attack; forwards.

напа́рник co-driver, (work)mate.

напа́сть (-аду́, -адёшь; -а́л) *pf* (*impf* **напада́ть**) на+*acc* attack; descend on; seize; come upon. **напа́сть** misfortune.

напе́в tune. **напева́ть** *impf of* **напе́ть**

наперебо́й *adv* interrupting, vying with, one another.

наперёд *adv* in advance.

напереко́р *adv*+*dat* in defiance of, counter to.

напёрсток (-тка) thimble.

напе́ть (-пою́, -поёшь) *pf* (*impf* **напева́ть**) sing; hum, croon.

на|печа́тать(ся *pf.* **напива́ться** *impf of* **напи́ться**

напи́льник file.

на|писа́ть (-ишу́, -и́шешь) *pf.*

напи́ток (-тка) drink. **напи́ться** (-пью́сь, -пьёшься; -и́лся, -а́сь, -и́ло́сь) *pf* (*impf* **напива́ться**) quench one's thirst, drink; get drunk.

напиха́ть *pf*, **напи́хивать** *impf* cram, stuff.

на|плева́ть (-люю́, -люёшь) *pf*; **~!** to hell with it! who cares?

наплы́в influx; accumulation; canker.

наплюю́ *etc.*: *see* **наплева́ть**

напова́л outright.

наподо́бие *prep*+*gen* like, not unlike.

на|пои́ть (-ою́, -о́ишь) *pf.*

напока́з *adv* for show.

наполни́тель *m* filler. **напо́лнить(ся** *pf*, **наполня́ть(ся** *impf* fill.

наполови́ну *adv* half.

напомина́ние reminder. **напомина́ть** *impf*, **напо́мнить** *pf* remind.

напо́р pressure. **напо́ристый** energetic, pushing.

напосле́док *adv* in the end; after all.

напою́ *etc.*: *see* **напе́ть, напои́ть**

напр. *abbr* (*of* **наприме́р**) e.g., for example.

напра́вить (-влю) *pf*, **направля́ть** *impf* direct; send; sharpen; **~ся** make (for), go (towards). **направле́ние** direction; trend; warrant; order. **напра́вленный** purposeful.

напра́во *adv* to the right.

напра́сно *adv* in vain, for nothing; unjustly, mistakenly.

напра́шиваться *impf of* **напроси́ться**

наприме́р for example.

на|прока́зничать *pf.*

напрока́т *adv* for, on, hire.

напролёт *adv* through, without a break.

напроло́м *adv* straight, regardless of obstacles.

напроси́ться (-ошу́сь, -о́сишься) *pf* (*impf* **напра́шиваться**) thrust o.s.; suggest itself; **~ на** ask for, invite.

напро́тив *adv* opposite; on the contrary. **напро́тив** *prep*+*gen* opposite.

напряга́ть(ся *impf of* **напря́чь(ся. напряже́ние** tension; exertion; voltage. **напряжённый** tense; intense; intensive.

напрями́к *adv* straight (out).

напря́чь (-ягу́, -яжёшь; -яг, -ла́) *pf* (*impf* **напряга́ть**) strain; **~ся** strain o.s.

на|пуга́ть(ся *pf.* **на|пу́дриться** *pf.*

напуска́ть *impf*, **напусти́ть** (-ущу́, -у́стишь) *pf* let in; let loose; **~ся** +на+*acc* fly at, go for.

напу́тать *pf* +в+*prep* make a mess of.

на|пыли́ть *pf.*

напью́сь *etc.*: *see* **напи́ться**

наравне́ *adv* level; equally.

нараспа́шку *adv* unbuttoned.

нараста́ние growth, accumulation. **нараста́ть** *impf*, **нарасти́** (-тёт; -ро́с, -ла́) *pf* grow; increase.

нарасхва́т *adv* very quickly, like hot cakes.

нарва́ть[1] (-рву́, -рвёшь; -а́л, -а́, -о) *pf* (*impf* **нарыва́ть**) pick; tear up.

нарва́ть[2] (-вёт; -а́л, -а́, -о) *pf* (*impf* **нарыва́ть**) gather.

нарва́ться (-ву́сь, -вёшься; -а́лся, -ала́сь, -а́ло́сь) *pf* (*impf* **нарыва́ться**) +на+*acc* run into, run up against.

наре́зать (-е́жу) *pf*, **нареза́ть** *impf* cut (up), slice, carve; thread, rifle.

наре́чие[1] dialect.

наре́чие[2] adverb.

на|рисова́ть *pf*.

нарко́з narcosis. **наркома́н, -ма́нка** drug addict. **наркома́ния** drug addiction. **нарко́тик** narcotic.

наро́д people. **наро́дность** nationality; national character. **наро́дный** national; folk; popular; people's.

наро́с *etc.*: *see* **нарасти́**

наро́чно *adv* on purpose, deliberately. **на́рочный** *sb* courier.

нару́жность exterior. **нару́жный** external, outward. **нару́жу** *adv* outside.

нару́чник handcuff. **нару́чный** wrist.

наруше́ние breach; infringement. **нару́шитель** *m* transgressor. **нару́шить** (-шу) *pf*, **наруша́ть** *impf* break; disturb, infringe, violate.

нарци́сс narcissus; daffodil.

на́ры (нар) *pl* plank-bed.

нары́в abscess, boil. **нарыва́ть(ся** *impf of* **нарва́ть(ся**

наря́д[1] order, warrant.

наря́д[2] attire; dress. **наряди́ть** (-яжу́) *pf* (*impf* **наряжа́ть**) dress (up); ~**ся** dress up. **наря́дный** well-dressed.

наряду́ *adv* alike, equally; side by side.

наряжа́ть(ся *impf of* **наряди́ть(ся.** нас *see* мы

насади́ть (-ажу́, -а́дишь) *pf*, **насажда́ть** *impf* (*impf also* **наса́живать**) plant; propagate; implant. **наса́дка** setting, fixing. **насажде́ние** planting; plantation; propagation. **наса́живать** *impf of* **насади́ть**

насеко́мое *sb* insect.

населе́ние population. **населённость** density of population. **населённый** populated; ~ пункт settlement; built-up area. **насели́ть** *pf*, **населя́ть** *impf* settle, people.

наси́лие violence, force. **наси́ловать** *impf* (*pf* из~) coerce; rape. **наси́лу** *adv* with difficulty. **наси́льник** aggressor; rapist; violator. **наси́льно** *adv* by force. **наси́льственный** violent, forcible.

наска́кивать *impf of* **наскочи́ть**

насквозь *adv* through, throughout.

наско́лько *adv* how much?, how far?; as far as.

на́скоро *adv* hastily.

наскочи́ть (-очу́, -о́чишь) *pf* (*impf* **наска́кивать**) +на+*acc* run into, collide with; fly at.

наску́чить (-чу) *pf* bore.

наслади́ться (-ажу́сь) *pf*, **наслажда́ться** *impf* enjoy, take pleasure. **наслажде́ние** pleasure, enjoyment.

насле́дие legacy; heritage. **на|следи́ть** (-ежу́) *pf*. **насле́дник** heir; successor. **насле́дница** heiress. **насле́дный** next in succession. **насле́довать** *impf & pf* (*pf also* у~) inherit, succeed to. **насле́дственность** heredity. **насле́дственный** hereditary, inherited. **насле́дство** inheritance; heritage.

на́смерть *adv* to (the) death.

на|смеши́ть (-шу́) *pf* **насме́шка** mockery; gibe. **насме́шливый** mocking.

на́сморк cold in the head.

на|сори́ть *pf*.

насо́с pump.

на́спех *adv* hastily.

на|спле́тничать *pf*. **настава́ть** (-та́ёт) *impf of* **наста́ть**

наставле́ние exhortation; directions, manual.

наста́вник tutor, mentor.

наста́ивать[1] *impf of* **настоя́ть**[1]. **наста́ивать**[2](ся *impf of* **настоя́ть**[2](ся

наста́ть (-а́нет) *pf* (*impf* **настава́ть**) come, begin, set in.

на́стежь *adv* wide (open).

настелю́ *etc.*: *see* **настла́ть**

настига́ть *impf*, **насти́гнуть, насти́чь** (-и́гну; -и́г) *pf* catch up with, overtake.

насти́л flooring, planking. **настила́ть** *impf of* **настла́ть**

насти́чь *see* **настига́ть**

настла́ть (-телю́, -те́лешь) *pf* (*impf* **настила́ть**) lay, spread.

насто́йка liqueur, cordial.

насто́йчивый persistent; urgent.

насто́лько *adv* so, so much.

насто́льный table, desk; reference.

настора́живать *impf*, **насторожи́ть** (-жу́) *pf* set; prick up; ~**ся** prick up one's ears. **насторо́жен-**

ный (-ен, -енна) guarded; alert.
настоя́тельный insistent; urgent.
настоя́ть[1] (-ою́) *pf* (*impf* **наста́ивать**[1]) insist.
настоя́ть[2] (-ою́) *pf* (*impf* **наста́ивать**[2]) brew; **~ся** draw, stand.
настоя́щее *sb* the present. **настоя́щий** (the) present, this; real, genuine.
настра́ивать(ся *impf of* **настро́ить(ся**
настри́чь (-игу́, -ижёшь; -и́г) *pf* shear, clip.
настрое́ние mood. **настро́ить** (-о́ю) *pf* (*impf* **настра́ивать**) tune (in); dispose; **~ся** dispose o.s. **настро́йка** tuning. **настро́йщик** tuner.
на|строчи́ть (-чу́) *pf*.
наступа́тельный offensive. **наступа́ть**[1] *impf of* **наступи́ть**[1]
наступа́ть[2] *impf of* **наступи́ть**[2]. **наступа́ющий**[1] coming.
наступа́ющий[2] *sb* attacker.
наступи́ть[1] (-плю́, -пишь) *pf* (*impf* **наступа́ть**[1]) tread; attack; advance.
наступи́ть[2] (-у́пит) *pf* (*impf* **наступа́ть**[2]) come, set in. **наступле́ние**[1] coming.
наступле́ние[2] offensive, attack.
насу́питься (-плюсь) *pf*, **насу́пливаться** *impf* frown.
на́сухо *adv* dry. **насуши́ть** (-шу́, -шишь) *pf* dry.
насу́щный urgent, vital; **хлеб ~** daily bread.
насчёт *prep+gen* about, concerning; as regards. **насчита́ть** *pf*, **насчи́тывать** *impf* count; hold; **~ся** +*gen* number.
насы́пать (-плю) *pf*, **насыпа́ть** *impf* pour in, on; fill; spread; heap up. **на́сыпь** embankment.
насы́тить (-ы́щу) *pf*, **насыща́ть** *impf* satiate; saturate; **~ся** be full; be saturated.
ната́лкивать(ся *impf of* **натолкну́ть(ся. ната́пливать** *impf of* **натопи́ть**
натаска́ть *pf*, **ната́скивать** *impf* train; coach, cram; bring in, lay in.
натвори́ть *pf* do, get up to.
натере́ть (-тру́, -трёшь; -тёр) *pf* (*impf* **натира́ть**) rub on, in; polish; chafe; grate; **~ся** rub o.s.
на́тиск onslaught.

наткну́ться (-ну́сь, -нёшься) *pf* (*impf* **натыка́ться**) +**на**+*acc* run into; strike, stumble on.
натолкну́ть (-ну́, -нёшь) *pf* (*impf* **ната́лкивать**) push; lead; **~ся** run against, across.
натопи́ть (-плю́, -пишь) *pf* (*impf* **ната́пливать**) heat (up); stoke up; melt.
на|точи́ть (-чу́, -чишь) *pf*.
натоща́к *adv* on an empty stomach.
натрави́ть (-влю́, -вишь) *pf*, **натра́вливать** *impf*, **натравля́ть** *impf* set (on); stir up.
на|трениро́ва́ть(ся *pf*.
на́трий sodium.
нату́ра nature. **натура́льный** natural; genuine. **нату́рщик, -щица** artist's model.
натыка́ть(ся *impf of* **наткну́ть(ся**
натюрмо́рт still life.
натя́гивать *impf*, **натяну́ть** (-ну́, -нешь) *pf* stretch; draw; pull (on); **~ся** stretch. **натя́нутость** tension. **натя́нутый** tight; strained.
науга́д *adv* at random.
нау́ка science; learning.
нау́тро *adv* (the) next morning.
на|учи́ть (-чу́, -чишь) *pf*.
нау́чный scientific; **~ая фанта́стика** science fiction.
нау́шник ear-flap; ear-phone; informer.
нафтали́н naphthalene.
наха́л, -ха́лка impudent creature. **наха́льный** impudent. **наха́льство** impudence.
нахвата́ть *pf*, **нахва́тывать** *impf* pick up, get hold of; **~ся** +*gen* pick up.
нахле́бник hanger-on.
нахлы́нуть (-нет) *pf* well up; surge; gush.
на|хму́рить(ся *pf*.
находи́ть(ся (-ожу́(сь, -о́дишь(ся) *impf of* **найти́(сь. нахо́дка** find. **нахо́дчивый** resourceful, quickwitted.
наце́ливать *impf*, **на|це́лить** *pf* aim; **~ся** (take) aim.
наце́нка extra, addition; additional charge.
нации́зм Nazism. **национализа́ция** nationalization. **национализи́ровать** *impf* & *pf* nationalize.

национали́зм nationalism. **нациoналисти́ческий** nationalist(ic). **национáльность** nationality; ethnic group. **национáльный** national. **нацúст, -úстка** Nazi. **нáция** nation. **нацмéн, -мéнка** abbr member of national minority.

начáло beginning; origin; principle, basis. **начáльник** head, chief; boss. **начáльный** initial; primary. **начáльство** the authorities; command. **начáть** (-чну́, -чнёшь; нáчал, -á, -о) pf (impf **начинáть**) begin; ~**ся** begin.

начертáть pf trace, inscribe. **на|черти́ть** (-рчу́, -рти́шь) pf.

начинáние undertaking. **начинáть(ся** impf of **начáть(ся. начинáющий** sb beginner.

начини́ть pf, **начиня́ть** impf stuff, fill. **начи́нка** stuffing, filling.

начи́стить (-и́щу) pf (impf **начищáть**) clean. **нáчисто** adv clean; flatly, decidedly; openly, frankly. **начистоту́** adv openly, frankly.

начи́танность learning; wide reading. **начи́танный** well-read.

начищáть impf of **начи́стить**

наш (-его) m, **нáша** (-ей) f, **нáше** (-его) neut, **нáши** (-их) pl, pron our, ours.

нашаты́рный спирт ammonia. **нашаты́рь** (-я́) m sal-ammoniac; ammonia.

нашёл etc.: see **найти́**

нашéствие invasion.

нашивáть impf, **наши́ть** (-шью, -шьёшь) pf sew on. **наши́вка** stripe, chevron; tab.

нашлёпать impf slap.

нашумéть (-млю) pf make a din; cause a sensation.

нашью́ etc.: see **наши́ть**

нащу́пать pf, **нащу́пывать** impf grope for.

на|электризовáть pf.

наяву́ adv awake; in reality.

не partl not.

не- pref un-, in-, non-, mis-, dis-; -less; not. **неаккурáтный** careless; untidy; unpunctual. **небезразли́чный** not indifferent. **небезызвéстный** not unknown; notorious; well-known.

небесá etc.: see **нéбо**[2]. **небéсный** heavenly; celestial.

не-. **неблагодáрный** ungrateful;

thankless. **неблагонадёжный** unreliable. **неблагополу́чный** unsuccessful, bad, unfavourable. **неблагоприя́тный** unfavourable. **неблагорaзу́мный** imprudent. **неблагорóдный** ignoble, base.

нéбо[1] palate.

нéбо[2] (pl -бесá, -бéс) sky; heaven.

не-. **небогáтый** of modest means, modest. **небольшóй** small, not great; **с небольши́м** a little over.

небосвóд firmament. **небосклóн** horizon. **небоскрёб** skyscraper.

небóсь adv I dare say; probably. не-. **небрéжный** careless. **небывáлый** unprecedented; fantastic. **небыли́ца** fable, cock-and-bull story. **небытиé** non-existence. **небью́щийся** unbreakable. **невáжно** adv not too well, indifferently. **невáжный** unimportant; indifferent. **невдалекé** adv not far away. **невéдение** ignorance. **невéдомый** unknown; mysterious. **невéжа** m & f boor, lout. **невéжда** m & f ignoramus. **невéжественный** ignorant. **невéжество** ignorance. **невéжливый** rude. **невели́кий** (-и́к, -á, -и́кó) small. **невéрие** unbelief, atheism; scepticism. **невéрный** (-рен, -рнá, -о) incorrect, wrong; inaccurate, unsteady; unfaithful. **невероя́тный** improbable; incredible. **невéрующий** unbelieving; sb atheist. **невесёлый** joyless, sad. **невесóмый** weightless; imponderable.

невéста fiancée; bride. **невéстка** daughter-in-law; brother's wife, sister-in-law.

не-. **невзгóда** adversity. **невзирáя на** prep+acc regardless of. **невзначáй** adv by chance. **невзрáчный** unattractive, plain. **неви́данный** unprecedented, unheard-of. **неви́димый** invisible. **неви́нность** innocence. **неви́нный, невинóвный** innocent. **невменя́емый** irresponsible. **невмешáтельство** non-intervention; non-interference. **невмоготу́, невмóчь** advs unbearable, too much (for). **невнимáтельный** inattentive, thoughtless.

нéвод seine(-net).

не-. **невозврати́мый, невозврáтный** irrevocable, irrecoverable. **не-**

возмо́жный impossible. **невозму-
ти́мый** imperturbable.
невольник, -ница slave. **нево́ль-
ный** involuntary; unintentional;
forced. **нево́ля** captivity; necessity.
не-. невообрази́мый unimaginable,
inconceivable. **невооружённ|ый**
unarmed; **~ным гла́зом** with the
naked eye. **невоспи́танный** ill-bred,
bad-mannered. **невоспламеня́ю-
щийся** non-flammable. **невоспри-
и́мчивый** unreceptive; immune.
невралги́я neuralgia.
невреди́мый safe, unharmed.
невро́з neurosis. **неврологи́ческий**
neurological. **невроти́ческий** neurotic.
не-. невы́годный disadvantageous;
unprofitable. **невы́держанный**
lacking self-control; unmatured. **не-
выноси́мый** unbearable. **невыпол-
ни́мый** impracticable. **невысо́кий**
(-со́к, -а́, -око́) low; short.
не́га luxury; bliss.
негати́вный negative.
не́где adv (there is) nowhere.
не-. неги́бкий (-бок, -бка́, -о) inflexible, stiff. **негла́сный** secret. **не-
глубо́кий** (-о́к, -а́, -о) shallow. **не-
глу́пый** (-у́п, -а́, -о) sensible, quite
intelligent. **него́дный** (-ден, -дна́,
-о) unfit, unsuitable; worthless. **не-
годова́ние** indignation. **негодо-
ва́ть** impf be indignant. **негодя́й**
scoundrel. **негостеприи́мный** inhospitable.
негр Negro, black man.
негра́мотность illiteracy. **негра́-
мотный** illiterate.
негритя́нка Negress, black woman.
негритя́нский Negro.
не-. негро́мкий (-мок, -мка́, -о)
quiet. **неда́вний** recent. **неда́вно**
adv recently. **недалёкий** (-ёк, -а́,
-ёко́) near; short; not bright, dull-
witted. **недалеко́** adv not far, near.
неда́ром adv not for nothing, not
without reason. **недви́жимость** real
estate. **недви́жимый** immovable.
недвусмы́сленный unequivocal.
недействи́тельный ineffective;
invalid. **недели́мый** indivisible.
неде́льный of a week, week's.
неде́ля week.
не-. недёшево adv dear(ly).

недоброжела́тель m ill-wisher.
недоброжела́тельность hostility.
недоброка́чественный of poor
quality. **недобросо́вестный** unscrupulous; careless. **недо́брый** (-о́бр,
-бра́, -о) unkind; bad. **недове́рие**
distrust. **недове́рчивый** distrustful
недово́льный dissatisfied. **недо-
во́льство** dissatisfaction. **недоеда́-
ние** malnutrition. **недоеда́ть** impf
be undernourished.
не-. недо́лгий (-лог, -лга́, -о) short,
brief. **недо́лго** adv not long. **не-
долгове́чный** short-lived. **недомо-
га́ние** indisposition. **недомога́ть**
impf be unwell. **недомы́слие**
thoughtlessness. **недоно́шенный**
premature. **недооце́нивать** impf,
недооцени́ть (-ню́, -нишь) pf underestimate; underrate. **недооце́нка**
underestimation. **недопусти́мый**
inadmissible, intolerable. **недоразу-
ме́ние** misunderstanding. **недо-
рого́й** (-до́рог, -а́, -о) inexpensive.
недосмотре́ть (-рю́,-ришь) pf overlook. **недоспа́ть** (-плю́; -а́л, -а́, -о)
pf (impf **недосыпа́ть**) not have
enough sleep.
недостава́ть (-таёт) impf, **недо-
ста́ть** (-а́нет) pf impers be missing,
be lacking. **недоста́ток** (-тка) shortage, deficiency. **недоста́точный** in-
sufficient, inadequate. **недоста́ча**
lack, shortage.
не-. недостижи́мый unattainable.
недосто́йный unworthy, **недо-
сту́пный** inaccessible. **недо-
счита́ться** pf, **недосчи́тываться**
impf miss, find missing, be short (of).
недосыпа́ть impf of **недоспа́ть**.
недосяга́емый unattainable.
недоумева́ть impf be at a loss, be
bewildered. **недоуме́ние** bewilderment.
не-. недоу́чка m & f half-educated
person. **недочёт** deficit; defect.
не́дра (недр) pl depths, heart, bowels.
не-. не́друг enemy. **недружелю́б-
ный** unfriendly.
неду́г illness, disease.
недурно́й not bad; not bad-looking.
не-. неесте́ственный unnatural. **не-
жда́нный** unexpected. **нежела́ние**
unwillingness. **нежела́тельный** undesirable.

не́жели than.

нежена́тый unmarried.

не́женка *m & f* mollycoddle.

нежило́й uninhabited; uninhabitable.

не́житься (-жусь) *impf* luxuriate, bask. **не́жность** tenderness; *pl* endearments. **не́жный** tender; affectionate.

не-. незабве́нный unforgettable. **незабу́дка** forget-me-not. **незабыва́емый** unforgettable. **незави́симость** independence. **незави́симый** independent. **незадо́лго** *adv* not long. **незаконнорождённый** illegitimate. **незако́нный** illegal, illicit; illegitimate. **незако́нченный** unfinished. **незамени́мый** irreplaceable. **незамерза́ющий** ice-free; anti-freeze. **незаме́тный** imperceptible. **незаму́жняя** unmarried. **незапа́мятный** immemorial. **незаслу́женный** unmerited. **незауря́дный** uncommon, outstanding.

не́зачем *adv* there is no need.

не-. незащищённый unprotected. **незва́ный** uninvited. **нездоро́виться** *impf*, *impers* +dat: **мне нездоро́вится** I don't feel well. **нездоро́вый** unhealthy. **нездоро́вье** ill health. **незнако́мец** (-мца), **незнако́мка** stranger. **незнако́мый** unknown, unfamiliar. **незна́ние** ignorance. **незначи́тельный** insignificant. **незре́лый** unripe, immature. **незри́мый** invisible. **незы́блемый** unshakable, firm. **неизбе́жность** inevitability. **неизбе́жный** inevitable. **неизве́данный** unknown.

неизве́стность uncertainty; ignorance; obscurity. **неизве́стный** unknown; *sb* stranger.

не-. неизлечи́мый incurable. **неизме́нный** unchanged, unchanging; devoted. **неизменя́емый** unalterable. **неизмери́мый** immeasurable, immense. **неизу́ченный** unstudied; unexplored. **неиму́щий** poor. **неинтере́сный** uninteresting. **неискренний** insincere. **неискушённый** inexperienced, unsophisticated. **неисполни́мый** impracticable. **неисправи́мый** incorrigible; irreparable. **неиспра́вный** out of order, defect-ive; careless. **неиссле́дованный** unexplored. **неиссяка́емый** inexhaustible. **нейстовство** fury, frenzy; atrocity. **нейстовый** furious, frenzied, uncontrolled. **неистощи́мый, неисчерпа́емый** inexhaustible. **неисчисли́мый** innumerable.

нейло́н, нейло́новый nylon.

нейро́н neuron.

нейтрализа́ция neutralization. **нейтрализова́ть** *impf & pf* neutralize. **нейтралите́т** neutrality. **нейтра́льный** neutral. **нейтро́н** neutron.

неквалифици́рованный unskilled.

не́кий *pron* a certain, some.

не́когда[1] *adv* once, formerly.

не́когда[2] *adv* there is no time; **мне ~** I have no time.

не́кого (**не́кому, не́кем, не́ о ком**) *pron* there is nobody.

некомпете́нтный not competent, unqualified.

не́котор|ый *pron* some; **~ые** *sb pl* some (people).

некраси́вый plain, ugly; not nice.

некроло́г obituary.

некста́ти *adv* at the wrong time, out of place.

не́кто *pron* somebody; a certain.

не́куда *adv* there is nowhere.

не-. некульту́рный uncivilized, uncultured. **некуря́щий** *sb* nonsmoker. **нела́дный** wrong. **нелега́льный** illegal. **нелёгкий** not easy; heavy. **неле́пость** absurdity, nonsense. **неле́пый** absurd. **нело́вкий** awkward. **нело́вкость** awkwardness.

нельзя́ *adv* it is impossible; it is not allowed.

не-. нелюби́мый unloved. **нелюди́мый** unsociable. **нема́ло** *adv* quite a lot (of). **нема́лый** considerable. **неме́дленно** *adv* immediately. **неме́дленный** immediate.

неме́ть (-е́ю) *impf* (*pf* о~) become dumb. **не́мец** (-мца) German. **неме́цкий** German.

неминуемый inevitable.

не́мка German woman.

немно́гие *sb pl* (a) few. **немно́го** *adv* a little; some; a few. **немно́жко** *adv* a little.

немо́й (нем, -а́, -о) dumb, mute, silent. **немота́** dumbness.

не́мощный feeble.

немы́слимый unthinkable.

ненави́деть (-**и́жу**) *impf* hate. **ненави́стный** hated; hateful. **не́нависть** hatred.

не-. ненагля́дный beloved. **ненадёжный** unreliable. **ненадо́лго** *adv* for a short time. **нена́стье** bad weather. **ненасы́тный** insatiable. **ненорма́льный** abnormal. **нену́жный** unnecessary, unneeded. **необду́манный** thoughtless, hasty. **необеспе́ченный** without means, unprovided for. **необита́емый** uninhabited. **необозри́мый** boundless, immense. **необосно́ванный** unfounded, groundless. **необрабо́танный** uncultivated; crude; unpolished. **необразо́ванный** uneducated. **необходи́мость** necessity. **необходи́мый** necessary.

не-. необъясни́мый inexplicable. **необъя́тный** immense. **необыкнове́нный** unusual. **необыча́йный** extraordinary. **необы́чный** unusual. **необяза́тельный** optional. **неограни́ченный** unlimited. **неоднокра́тный** repeated. **неодобри́тельный** disapproving. **неодушевлённый** inanimate.

неожи́данность unexpectedness. **неожи́данный** unexpected, sudden.

неокласси́цизм neoclassicism.

не-. неоко́нченный unfinished. **неопла́ченный** unpaid. **неопра́вданный** unjustified. **неопределённый** indefinite; infinitive; vague. **неопровержи́мый** irrefutable. **неопублико́ванный** unpublished. **нео́пытный** inexperienced. **неоргани́ческий** inorganic. **неоспори́мый** incontestable. **неосторо́жный** careless. **неосуществи́мый** impracticable. **неотврати́мый** inevitable. **не́откуда** *adv* there is nowhere.

не-. неотло́жный urgent. **неотрази́мый** irresistible. **неотсту́пный** persistent. **неотъе́млемый** inalienable. **неофициа́льный** unofficial. **неохо́та** reluctance. **неохо́тно** *adv* reluctantly. **неоцени́мый** inestimable, invaluable. **непарти́йный** nonparty; unbefitting a member of the (Communist) Party. **непереводи́мый** untranslatable. **непереходный** intransitive. **неплатёжеспосо́бный** insolvent.

не-. непло́хо *adv* not badly, quite well. **неплохо́й** not bad, quite good. **непобеди́мый** invincible. **неповинове́ние** insubordination. **непово́ротливый** clumsy. **неповтори́мый** inimitable, unique. **непого́да** bad weather. **непогреши́мый** infallible. **неподалёку** *adv* not far (away). **неподви́жный** motionless, immovable; fixed. **неподде́льный** genuine; sincere. **неподку́пный** incorruptible. **неподража́емый** inimitable. **неподходя́щий** unsuitable, inappropriate. **непоколеби́мый** unshakable, steadfast. **непоко́рный** recalcitrant, unruly.

не-. непола́дки (-**док**) *pl* defects. **неполноце́нность; ко́мплекс неполноце́нности** inferiority complex. **неполноце́нный** defective; inadequate. **непо́лный** incomplete; not (a) full. **непоме́рный** excessive. **непонима́ние** incomprehension, lack of understanding. **непоня́тный** incomprehensible. **непопра́вимый** irreparable. **непоря́док** (-**дка**) disorder. **непоря́дочный** dishonourable. **непосе́да** *m & f* fidget. **непоси́льный** beyond one's strength. **непосле́довательный** inconsistent. **непослуша́ние** disobedience. **непослу́шный** disobedient. **непосре́дственный** immediate; spontaneous. **непостижи́мый** incomprehensible. **непостоя́нный** inconstant, changeable. **непохо́жий** unlike; different.

не-. непра́вда untruth. **неправдоподо́бный** improbable. **непра́вильно** *adv* wrong. **непра́вильный** irregular; wrong. **непра́вый** wrong. **непракти́чный** unpractical. **превзойдённый** unsurpassed. **непредви́денный** unforeseen. **непредубеждённый** unprejudiced. **непредусмо́тренный** unforeseen. **непредусмотри́тельный** short-sighted. **непрекло́нный** inflexible; adamant. **непрело́жный** immutable.

не-. непреме́нно *adv* without fail. **непреме́нный** indispensable. **непреодоли́мый** insuperable. **непререка́емый** unquestionable. **непре-**

ры́вно *adv* continuously. **непре-ры́вный** continuous. **непреста́н-ный** incessant. **неприве́тливый** unfriendly; bleak. **непривлека́тель-ный** unattractive. **непривы́чный** unaccustomed. **непригля́дный** un-attractive. **неприго́дный** unfit, use-less. **неприе́млемый** unacceptable. **неприкоснове́нность** inviolability, immunity. **неприкоснове́нный** in-violable; reserve. **неприли́чный** in-decent. **непримири́мый** irreconcil-able. **непринуждённый** uncon-strained; relaxed. **неприспосо́блен-ный** unadapted; maladjusted. **не-присто́йный** obscene. **непристу́п-ный** inaccessible. **непритяза́тель-ный, неприхотли́вый** unpreten-tious, simple. **неприя́зненный** hos-tile, inimical. **неприя́знь** hostility. **неприя́тель** *m* enemy. **неприя́-тельский** enemy. **неприя́тность** unpleasantness; trouble. **неприя́т-ный** unpleasant.

не-. непрове́ренный unverified. **непрогля́дный** pitch-dark. **непро-е́зжий** impassable. **непрозра́чный** opaque. **непроизводи́тельный** un-productive. **непроизво́льный** in-voluntary. **непромока́емый** water-proof. **непроница́емый** impene-trable. **непрости́тельный** unfor-givable. **непроходи́мый** impass-able. **непро́чный** (-чен, -чна́, -о) fragile, flimsy.

не прочь *predic* not averse.

не-. непро́шеный uninvited, unsoli-cited. **неработоспосо́бный** dis-abled. **нерабо́чий:** ~ **день** day off. **нера́венство** inequality. **нерав-номе́рный** uneven. **нера́вный** un-equal. **неради́вый** lackadaisical. **неразбери́ха** muddle. **неразбо́р-чивый** not fastidious; illegible. **не-развито́й** (-ра́звит, -а́, -о) undevel-oped; backward. **неразгово́рчивый** taciturn. **неразделённый:** ~ая лю-бо́вь unrequited love. **неразличи́-мый** indistinguishable. **неразлу́чный** inseparable. **неразрешённый** un-solved; forbidden. **неразреши́мый** insoluble. **неразры́вный** indissolu-uble. **неразу́мный** unwise; unrea-sonable. **нераствори́мый** insoluble. **нерв** nerve. **не́рвничать** *impf* fret,

be nervous. **нервнобольно́й** *sb* neurotic. **не́рвный** (-вен, -вна́, -о) nervous; nerve; irritable. **нерво́з-ный** nervy, irritable.

не-. нереа́льный unreal; unrealistic. **нере́дкий** (-док, -дка́, -о) not infre-quent, not uncommon. **нереши́-тельность** indecision. **нереши́-тельный** indecisive, irresolute. **не-ржаве́ющая сталь** stainless steel. **неро́вный** (-вен, -вна́, -о) uneven, rough; irregular. **неруши́мый** inviol-able.

неря́ха *m & f* sloven. **неря́шливый** slovenly.

не-. несбы́точный unrealizable. **несваре́ние желу́дка** indigestion. **несве́жий** (-éж, -á) not fresh; tainted; weary. **несвоевре́менный** ill-timed; overdue. **несво́йствен-ный** not characteristic. **несгора́е-мый** fireproof. **несерьёзный** not serious.

несессе́р case.

несимметри́чный asymmetrical.

нескла́дный incoherent; awkward.

несклоня́емый indeclinable.

не́сколько (-их) *pron* some, several; *adv* somewhat.

не-. несконча́емый interminable. **нескро́мный** (-мен, -мна́, -о) im-modest; indiscreet. **несло́жный** sim-ple. **неслы́ханный** unprecedented. **неслы́шный** inaudible. **несме́тный** countless, incalculable. **несмолка́е-мый** ceaseless.

несмотря́ на *prep+acc* in spite of.

не-. несно́сный intolerable. **несо-блюде́ние** non-observance. **несо-вершенноле́тний** under-age; *sb* mi-nor. **несоверше́нный** imperfect, in-complete; imperfective. **несовер-ше́нство** imperfection. **несовме-сти́мый** incompatible. **несогла́сие** disagreement. **несогласо́ванный** uncoordinated. **несозна́тельный** ir-responsible. **несоизмери́мый** in-commensurable. **несокруши́мый** indestructible. **несомне́нный** un-doubted, unquestionable. **несооб-ра́зный** incongruous. **несоотве́т-ствие** disparity. **несостоя́тельный** insolvent; of modest means; unten-able. **неспе́лый** unripe. **неспоко́й-ный** restless; uneasy. **неспосо́бный**

not bright; incapable. **несправедли́вость** injustice. **несправедли́вый** unjust, unfair; incorrect. **несравнённый** (-ёнен, -éнна) incomparable. **несравни́мый** incomparable. **нестерпи́мый** unbearable.

нести́ (-су́, -сёшь; нёс, -ла́) *impf* (*pf* по~, с~) carry; bear; bring, take; suffer; incur; lay; ~сь rush, fly; float, be carried.

не-. нестойкий unstable. **несуще́ственный** immaterial, inessential.

несу́ *etc.*: see **нести́**

несхо́дный unlike, dissimilar.

несчастли́вый unfortunate, unlucky; unhappy. **несча́стный** unhappy, unfortunate; ~ слу́чай accident. **несча́стье** misfortune; к **несча́стью** unfortunately.

несчётный innumerable.

нет *partl* no, not; nothing. **нет, не́ту** there is not, there are not.

не-. нетакти́чный tactless. **нетвёрдый** (-ёрд, -á, -о) unsteady, shaky. **нетерпели́вый** impatient. **нетерпе́ние** impatience. **нетерпи́мый** intolerable, intolerant. **неторопли́вый** leisurely. **нето́чный** (-чен, -чна́, -о) inaccurate, inexact. **нетре́звый** drunk. **нетро́нутый** untouched; chaste, virginal. **нетрудово́й дохо́д** unearned income. **нетрудоспосо́бность** disability.

не́тто *indecl adj & adv* net(t).

не́ту see **нет**

не-. неубеди́тельный unconvincing. **неуваже́ние** disrespect. **неуве́ренность** uncertainty. **неуве́ренный** uncertain. **неувяда́емый, неувяда́ющий** unfading. **неугомо́нный** indefatigable. **неуда́ча** failure. **неуда́чливый** unlucky. **неуда́чник, -ница** unlucky person, failure. **неуда́чный** unsuccessful, unfortunate. **неудержи́мый** irrepressible. **неудо́бный** uncomfortable; inconvenient; embarrassing. **неудо́бство** discomfort; inconvenience; embarrassment. **неудовлетворе́ние** dissatisfaction. **неудовлетворённый** dissatisfied. **неудовлетвори́тельный** unsatisfactory. **неудово́льствие** displeasure.

неуже́ли? *partl* really?

не-. неузнава́емый unrecognizable. **неукло́нный** steady; undeviating. **неуклю́жий** clumsy. **неулови́мый** elusive; subtle. **неуме́лый** inept; clumsy. **неуме́ренный** immoderate. **неуме́стный** inappropriate; irrelevant. **неумоли́мый** implacable, inexorable. **неумы́шленный** unintentional.

не-. неупла́та non-payment. **неуравнове́шенный** unbalanced. **неурожа́й** bad harvest. **неуро́чный** untimely, inopportune. **неуря́дица** disorder, mess. **неуспева́емость** poor progress. **неусто́йка** forfeit. **неусто́йчивый** unstable; unsteady. **неусту́пчивый** unyielding. **неуте́шный** inconsolable. **неутоли́мый** unquenchable. **неутоми́мый** tireless. **не́уч** ignoramus. **неучти́вый** discourteous. **неуязви́мый** invulnerable.

нефри́т jade.

нефте- *in comb* oil, petroleum. **нефтено́сный** oil-bearing. **~перего́нный заво́д** oil refinery. **~прово́д** (oil) pipeline. **~проду́кты** (-ов) *pl* petroleum products.

нефть oil, petroleum. **нефтяно́й** oil, petroleum.

не-. нехва́тка shortage. **нехорошо́** *adv* badly. **нехоро́ш|ий** (-о́ш, -á) bad; ~о́ it is bad, it is wrong. **не́хотя** *adv* unwillingly; unintentionally. **нецелесообра́зный** inexpedient; pointless. **нецензу́рный** unprintable. **неча́янный** unexpected; accidental.

не́чего (не́чему, -чем, не́ о чем) *pron* (*with separable pref*) (there is) nothing.

нечелове́ческий inhuman, superhuman.

нече́стный dishonest, unfair.

нечётный odd.

нечистопло́тный dirty; slovenly; unscrupulous. **нечистота́** (*pl* -о́ты, -о́т) dirtiness, filth; *pl* sewage. **нечи́стый** (-и́ст, -á, -о) dirty, unclean; impure; unclear. **не́чисть** evil spirits; scum.

нечленоразде́льный inarticulate.

не́что *pron* something.

не-. неэконо́мный uneconomical. **неэффекти́вный** ineffective; inefficient. **нея́вка** failure to appear. **не-**

я́ркий dim, faint; dull, subdued. **нея́сный** (-сен, -сна́, -о) not clear; vague.

ни *partl* not a; **ни оди́н** (одна́, одно́) not a single; (*with prons and pronominal advs*) -ever; **кто... ни** whoever. **ни** *conj*: **ни... ни** neither ... nor; **ни то ни сё** neither one thing nor the other.

ни́ва cornfield, field.

нивели́р level.

нигде́ *adv* nowhere.

нидерла́ндец (-дца; *gen pl* -дцев) Dutchman. **нидерла́ндка** Dutchwoman. **нидерла́ндский** Dutch. **Нидерла́нды** (-ов) *pl* the Netherlands.

ни́же *adj* lower, humbler; *adv* below; *prep+gen* below, beneath. **нижесле́дующий** following. **ни́жн|ий** lower, under-; ~ее бельё underclothes; ~ий эта́ж ground floor. **низ** (*loc* -ý, *pl* -ы́) bottom; *pl* lower classes; low notes.

низа́ть (нижу́, ни́жешь) *impf* (*pf* **на**~) string, thread.

низверга́ть *impf*, **низве́ргнуть** (-ну; -éрг) *pf* throw down, overthrow; ~ся crash down; be overthrown. **низверже́ние** overthrow.

низи́на low-lying place. **ни́зкий** (-зок, -зка́, -о) low; base, mean. **низкопокло́нство** servility. **низкопро́бный** base; low-grade. **низкоро́слый** undersized. **низкосо́ртный** low-grade.

ни́зменность lowland; baseness. **ни́зменный** low-lying; base.

низо́вье (*gen pl* -ьев) the lower reaches. **ни́зость** baseness, meanness. **ни́зш|ий** lower, lowest; ~ее образова́ние primary education.

ника́к *adv* in no way. **никако́й** *pron* no; no ... whatever.

ни́кель *m* nickel.

ниќем *see* **никто́. никогда́** *adv* never. **никто́** (-кого́, -кому́, -кем, ни о ко́м) *pron* (*with separable pref*) nobody, no one. **никуда́** nowhere. **ничёмный** useless. **нима́ло** *adv* not in the least.

нимб halo, nimbus.

ни́мфа nymph; pupa.

ниотку́да *adv* from nowhere.

нипочём *adv* it is nothing; dirt cheap;

in no circumstances.

ниско́лько *adv* not at all.

ниспроверга́ть *impf*, **ниспрове́ргнуть** (-ну; -éрг) *pf* overthrow. **ниспроверже́ние** overthrow.

нисходя́щий descending.

ни́тка thread; string; **до ни́тки** to the skin; **на живу́ю ни́тку** hastily, anyhow. **ни́точка** thread. **нить** thread; filament.

ничего́ *etc.*: *see* **ничто́. ничего́** *adv* all right; it doesn't matter, never mind; *as indecl adj* not bad, pretty good. **ниче́й** (-чья́, -чьё) *pron* nobody's; **ничья́ земля́** no man's land. **ничья́** *sb* draw; tie.

ничко́м *adv* face down, prone.

ничто́ (-чего́, -чему́, -чём, ни о чём) *pron* (*with separable pref*) nothing. **ничто́жество** nonentity, nobody. **ничто́жный** insignificant; worthless.

ничу́ть *adv* not a bit.

ничьё *etc.*: *see* **ниче́й**

ни́ша niche, recess.

ни́щенка beggar-woman. **ни́щенский** beggarly. **нищета́** poverty. **ни́щий** (нищ, -á, -е) destitute, poor; *sb* beggar.

но *conj* but; still.

нова́тор innovator. **нова́торский** innovative. **нова́торство** innovation.

Но́вая Зела́ндия New Zealand.

нове́йший newest, latest.

нове́лла short story.

но́венький brand-new.

новизна́ novelty; newness. **нови́нка** novelty. **новичо́к** (-чка́) novice.

ново- *in comb* new(ly). **новобра́нец** (-нца) new recruit. ~**бра́чный** *sb* newly-wed. ~**введе́ние** innovation. ~**го́дний** new year's. ~**зела́ндец** (- дца; *gen pl* -дцев), ~**зела́ндка** New-Zealander. ~**зела́ндский** New Zealand. ~**лу́ние** new moon. ~**прибы́вший** newly-arrived; *sb* newcomer. ~**рождённый** newborn. ~**сёл** new settler. ~**се́лье** new home; housewarming. **новостро́йка** new building.

но́вость news; novelty. **но́вшество** innovation, novelty. **но́вый** (нов, -á, -о) new; modern; ~ **год** New Year's Day.

нога́ (*acc* но́гу; *pl* но́ги, ног, нога́м) foot, leg.

но́готь (-гтя; pl -и) m finger-nail, toe-nail.

нож (-а́) knife.

но́жка small foot or leg; leg; stem, stalk.

но́жницы (-иц) pl scissors, shears.

но́жны (-жен) pl sheath, scabbard.

ножо́вка saw, hacksaw.

ноздря́ (pl -и, -е́й) nostril.

нока́ут knock-out. **нокаути́ровать** impf & pf knock out.

нолево́й, нулево́й zero. **ноль** (-я́), **нуль** (-я́) m nought, zero, nil.

номенклату́ра nomenclature; top positions in government.

но́мер (pl -а́) number; size; (hotel-) room; item; trick. **номеро́к** (-рка́) tag; label, ticket.

номина́л face value. **номина́льный** nominal.

нора́ (pl -ы) burrow, hole.

Норве́гия Norway. **норве́жец** (-жца), **норве́жка** Norwegian. **норве́жский** Norwegian.

норд (naut) north; north wind.

но́рка mink.

но́рма standard, norm; rate. **нормализа́ция** standardization. **норма́льно** all right, OK. **норма́льный** normal; standard. **нормирова́ние, нормиро́вка** regulation; rate-fixing; rationing. **нормирова́ть** impf & pf regulate, standardize; ration.

нос (loc -у́; pl -ы́) nose; beak; bow, prow. **но́сик** (small) nose; spout.

носи́лки (-лок) pl stretcher; litter.

носи́льщик porter. **носи́тель** m, **~ница** (fig) bearer; (med) carrier.

носи́ть (-ошу́, -о́сишь) impf carry, bear; wear; **~ся** rush, tear along, fly; float, drift, be carried; wear. **но́ска** carrying, wearing. **но́ский** hard-wearing.

носово́й nose; nasal; **~ плато́к** (pocket) handkerchief. **носо́к** (-ска́) little nose; toe; sock. **носоро́г** rhinoceros.

но́та note; pl music. **нота́ция** notation; lecture, reprimand.

нота́риус notary.

ночева́ть (-чу́ю) impf (pf пере~) spend the night. **ночёвка** spending the night. **ночле́г** place to spend the night; passing the night. **ночле́жка** doss-house. **ночни́к** (-а́) night-light.

ночно́й night, nocturnal; **~ горшо́к** potty; chamber-pot. **ночь** (loc -и́; gen pl -е́й) night. **но́чью** adv at night.

но́ша burden. **но́шеный** worn; second-hand.

но́ю etc.: see ныть

ноя́брь (-я́) m November. **ноя́брьский** November.

нрав disposition, temper; pl customs, ways. **нра́виться** (-влюсь) impf (pf по~) +dat please; **мне нра́вится** I like. **нра́вственность** morality, morals. **нра́вственный** moral.

ну int & partl well, well then.

ну́дный tedious.

нужда́ (pl -ы) need. **нужда́ться** impf be in need; +в+prep need, require. **ну́жн|ый** (-жен, -жна́, -о, -ы) necessary; **~о** it is necessary; +dat I, etc., must, ought to, need.

нулево́й, нуль see нолево́й, ноль

нумера́ция numeration; numbering. **нумерова́ть** impf (pf про~) number.

нутро́ inside, interior; instinct(s).

ны́не adv now; today. **ны́нешний** present; today's. **ны́нче** adv today; now.

нырну́ть (-ну́, -нёшь) pf, **ныря́ть** impf dive.

ныть (но́ю) impf ache; whine. **нытьё** whining.

н.э. abbr (of на́шей э́ры) AD.

нюх scent; flair. **ню́хать** impf (pf по~) smell, sniff.

ня́нчить (-чу) impf nurse, look after; **~ся** c+instr nurse; fuss over. **ня́нька** nanny. **ня́ня** (children's) nurse, nanny.

О

о, об, обо prep I. +prep of, about, concerning. II. +acc against; on, upon.

о int oh!

оа́зис oasis.

об see о prep.

о́ба (обо́их) m & neut, **о́бе** (обе́их) f both.

обалдева́ть impf, **обалде́ть** (-е́ю) pf go crazy; become dulled; be stunned.

обанкро́титься (-о́чусь) pf go bankrupt.

обая́ние fascination, charm. **обая́тельный** fascinating, charming.

обва́л fall(ing); crumbling; collapse; caving-in; landslide; (**сне́жный**) ~ avalanche. **обвали́ть** (-лю́, -лишь) pf (impf **обва́ливать**) cause to fall or collapse; crumble; heap round; ~**ся** collapse, cave in; crumble.

обваля́ть pf (impf **обва́ливать**) roll.

обва́ривать impf, **обвари́ть** (-рю́, -ришь) pf pour boiling water over; scald; ~**ся** scald o.s.

обведу́ etc.: see **обвести́**. **обвёл** etc.: see **обвести́**. **об|венча́ть(ся** pf.

обверну́ть (-ну́, -нёшь) pf, **обвёртывать** impf wrap, wrap up.

обве́с short weight. **обве́сить** (-ешу) pf (impf **обве́шивать**) cheat in weighing.

обвести́ (-еду́, -едёшь; -ёл, -ела́) pf (impf **обводи́ть**) lead round, take round; encircle; surround; outline; dodge.

обве́тренный weather-beaten.

обветша́лый decrepit. **об|ветша́ть** pf.

обве́шивать impf of **обве́сить**.

обвива́ть(ся impf of **обви́ть(ся**

обвине́ние charge, accusation; prosecution. **обвини́тель** m accuser; prosecutor. **обвини́тельный** accusatory; ~ **акт** indictment; ~ **пригово́р** verdict of guilty. **обвини́ть** pf, **обвиня́ть** impf prosecute, indict; +**в**+prep accuse of, charge with. **обвиня́емый** sb the accused; defendant.

обви́ть (обовью́, обовьёшь; обви́л, -а́, -о) pf (impf **обвива́ть**) wind round; ~**ся** wind round.

обводи́ть (-ожу́, -о́дишь) impf of **обвести́**

обвора́живать impf, **обворожи́ть** (-жу́) pf charm, enchant. **обворо-жи́тельный** charming, enchanting.

обвяза́ть (-яжу́, -я́жешь) pf, **об-вя́зывать** impf tie round; ~**ся** +instr tie round o.s.

обго́н passing. **обгоня́ть** impf of **обогна́ть**

обгора́ть impf, **обгоре́ть** (-рю́) pf be burnt, be scorched. **обгоре́лый** burnt, charred, scorched.

обде́лать pf (impf **обде́лывать**) fin-ish; polish; set; manage, arrange.

обдели́ть (-лю́, -лишь) pf (impf **обделя́ть**) +instr do out of one's (fair) share of.

обде́лывать impf of **обде́лать**. **обделя́ть** impf of **обдели́ть**

обдеру́ etc.: see **ободра́ть**. **обди-ра́ть** impf of **ободра́ть**

обду́манный deliberate, well-consid-ered. **обду́мать** pf, **обду́мывать** impf consider, think over.

о́бе: see **о́ба**. **обега́ть** impf of **обежа́ть**. **обегу́** etc.: see **обежа́ть**

обе́д dinner. **обе́дать** impf (pf по~) have dinner, dine. **обе́денный** din-ner.

обедне́вший impoverished. **обедне́ние** impoverishment. **о|бедне́ть** (-е́ю) pf.

обе́дня (gen pl -ден) mass.

обежа́ть (-егу́) pf (impf **обега́ть**) run round; run past; outrun.

обезбо́ливание anaesthetization. **обезбо́ливать** impf, **обезбо́лить** pf anaesthetize.

обезвре́дить (-е́жу) pf, **обез-вре́живать** impf render harmless.

обездо́ленный unfortunate, hapless.

обеззара́живающий disinfectant.

обезли́ченный depersonalized; robbed of individuality.

обезобра́живать impf, **о|безобра́-зить** (-а́жу) pf disfigure.

обезопа́сить (-а́шу) pf secure.

обезору́живать impf, **обезору́-жить** (-жу) pf disarm.

обезу́меть (-ею) pf lose one's senses, lose one's head.

обезья́на monkey; ape.

обели́ть pf, **обеля́ть** impf vindicate; clear of blame.

оберега́ть impf, **обере́чь** (-егу́, -ежёшь; -рёг, -ла́) pf guard; protect.

оберну́ть (-ну́, -нёшь) pf, **обёрты-вать** impf (impf also **обора́чивать**) twist; wrap up; turn; ~**ся** turn (round); turn out; +instr or **в**+acc turn into. **обёртка** wrapper; (dust-) jacket, cover. **обёрточный** wrapping.

оберу́ etc.: see **обобра́ть**

обескура́живать impf, **обескура́-жить** (-жу) pf discourage; dis-hearten.

обескро́вить (-влю) pf, **обес-кро́вливать** impf drain of blood,

bleed white; render lifeless.
обеспе́чение securing, guaranteeing; ensuring; provision; guarantee; security. **обеспе́ченность** security; +*instr* provision of. **обеспе́ченный** well-to-do; well provided for. **обеспе́чивать** *impf*, **обеспе́чить** (-чу) *pf* provide for; secure; ensure; protect; +*instr* provide with.

о|беспоко́ить(ся *pf*.

обесси́леть (-ею) *pf* grow weak, lose one's strength. **обесси́ливать** *impf*, **обесси́лить** *pf* weaken.

о|бесслáвить (-влю) *pf*.

обессме́ртить (-рчу) *pf* immortalize.

обесцене́ние depreciation. **обесце́нивать** *impf*, **обесце́нить** *pf* depreciate; cheapen; ~ся depreciate.

о|бесче́стить (-е́щу) *pf*.

обе́т vow, promise. **обетовáнный** promised. **обещáние** promise. **обещáть** *impf* & *pf* (*pf also* по~) promise.

обжáлование appeal. **обжáловать** *pf* appeal against.

обже́чь (обожгу́, обожжёшь; обжёг, обожглá) *pf*, **обжигáть** *impf* burn; scorch; bake; ~ся burn o.s.; burn one's fingers.

обжóра *m* & *f* glutton. **обжóрство** gluttony.

обзавести́сь (-еду́сь, -еде́шься; -вёлся, -лáсь) *pf*, **обзаводи́ться** (-ожу́сь, -óдишься) *impf* +*instr* provide o.s. with; acquire.

обзову́ *etc.*: *see* обозвáть

обзóр survey, review.

обзывáть *impf of* обозвáть

обивáть *impf of* оби́ть. **оби́вка** upholstering; upholstery.

оби́да offence, insult; nuisance. **оби́деть** (-и́жу) *pf*, **обижáть** *impf* offend; hurt; wound; ~ся take offence; feel hurt. **оби́дный** offensive; annoying. **оби́дчивый** touchy. **оби́женный** offended.

оби́лие abundance. **оби́льный** abundant.

обирáть *impf of* обобрáть

обитáемый inhabited. **обитáтель** *m* inhabitant. **обитáть** *impf* live.

оби́ть (обобью́, -ьёшь) *pf* (*impf* **обивáть**) upholster; knock off.

обихóд custom, (general) use, practice. **обихóдный** everyday.

обклáдывать(ся *impf of* обложи́ть(ся

обкрáдывать *impf of* обокрáсть

облáва raid; cordon, cordoning off.

облагáемый taxable. **облагáть(ся** *impf of* обложи́ть(ся: ~ся налóгом be liable to tax.

облáдание possession. **облáдатель** *m* possessor. **обладáть** *impf* +*instr* possess.

óблако (*pl* -á, -óв) cloud.

облáмывать(ся *impf of* обломáть(ся, обломи́ть(ся

областнóй regional. **óбласть** (*gen pl* -е́й) region; field, sphere.

óблачность cloudiness. **óблачный** cloudy.

облёг *etc.*: *see* обле́чь. **облегáть** *impf of* обле́чь

облегчáть *impf*, **облегчи́ть** (-чу́) *pf* lighten; relieve; alleviate; facilitate. **облегче́ние** relief.

обледене́лый ice-covered. **обледене́ние** icing over. **обледене́ть** (-е́ет) *pf* become covered with ice.

обле́злый shabby; mangy.

облекáть(ся *impf of* обле́чь² (ся. **облеку́** *etc.*: *see* обле́чь²

облепи́ть (-плю́, -пишь) *pf*, **облеплáть** *impf* stick to, cling to; throng round; plaster.

облетáть *impf*, **облете́ть** (-лечу́) *pf* fly (round); spread (all over); fall.

обле́чь¹ (-ля́жет; -лёг, -лá) *pf* (*impf* **облегáть**) cover, envelop; fit tightly.

обле́чь² (-еку́, -ече́шь; -ёк, -клá) *pf* (*impf* **облекáть**) clothe, invest; ~ся clothe o.s.; +*gen* take the form of.

обливáть(ся *impf of* обли́ть(ся

облигáция bond.

облизáть (-ижу́, -и́жешь) *pf*, **обли́зывать** *impf* lick (all over); ~ся smack one's lips.

óблик look, appearance.

óбли́тый (óбли́т, -á, -о) covered, enveloped. **обли́ть** (оболью́, -льёшь; óбли́л, -илá, -о) *pf* (*impf* **обливáть**) pour, sluice, spill; ~ся sponge down, take a shower; pour over o.s.

облицевáть (-цую́) *pf*, **облицóвывать** *impf* face. **облицóвка** facing; lining.

обличáть *impf*, **обличи́ть** (-чу́) *pf* expose; reveal; point to. **обличе́ние** exposure, denunciation. **обличи́-**

тельный denunciatory.

обложе́ние taxation; assessment.

обложи́ть (-жу́, -жишь) pf (impf **обкла́дывать, облага́ть**) edge; face; cover; surround; assess; **круго́м обло́жило** (**не́бо**) the sky is overcast; ~ **нало́гом** tax; ~**ся** +instr surround o.s. with. **обло́жка** (dust-) cover; folder.

облока́чиваться impf, **облоко-ти́ться** (-очу́сь, -о́тишься) pf **на**+acc lean one's elbows on.

облома́ть pf (impf **обла́мывать**) break off; ~**ся** break off. **обло-ми́ться** (-ло́мится) pf (impf **обла́мываться**) break off. **обло́мок** (-мка) fragment.

облу́пленный chipped.

облучи́ть (-чу́) pf, **облуча́ть** impf irradiate. **облуче́ние** irradiation.

об|лысе́ть (-е́ю) pf.

обля́жет etc.: see **обле́чь**[1]

обма́зать (-а́жу) pf, **обма́зывать** impf coat; putty; besmear; ~**ся** +instr get covered with.

обма́кивать impf, **обмакну́ть** (-ну́, -нёшь) pf dip.

обма́н deceit; illusion; ~ **зре́ния** optical illusion. **обма́нный** deceitful. **обману́ть** (-ну́, -нешь) pf, **обма́ны-вать** impf deceive; cheat; ~**ся** be deceived. **обма́нчивый** deceptive. **об-ма́нщик** deceiver; fraud.

обма́тывать(ся impf of **обмо-та́ть(ся**

обма́хивать impf, **обмахну́ть** (-ну́, -нёшь) pf brush off; fan; ~**ся** fan o.s.

обмёл etc.: see **обмести́**

обмеле́ние shallowing. **об|меле́ть** (-е́ет) pf become shallow.

обме́н exchange; barter; **в** ~ **за**+acc in exchange for; ~ **веще́ств** metabolism. **обме́нивать** impf, **обмени́ть** (-ню́, -нишь) pf, **об|меня́ть** pf exchange; ~**ся** +instr exchange. **об-ме́нный** exchange.

обме́р measurement; false measure.

обмере́ть (обомру́, -рёшь; о́бмер, -ла́, -ло) pf (impf **обмира́ть**) faint; ~ **от у́жаса** be horror-struck.

обме́ривать impf, **обме́рить** pf measure; cheat in measuring.

обмести́ (-ету́, -етёшь; -мёл, -а́) pf, **обмета́ть**[1] impf sweep off, dust.

обмета́ть[2] (-ечу́ or -а́ю, -е́чешь or

-а́ешь) pf (impf **обмётывать**) oversew.

обмету́ etc.: see **обмести́. обмёты-вать** impf of **обмета́ть. обмира́ть** impf of **обмере́ть**

обмо́лвиться (-влюсь) pf make a slip of the tongue; +instr say, utter. **обмо́лвка** slip of the tongue.

обморо́женный frost-bitten.

о́бморок fainting-fit, swoon.

обмота́ть pf (impf **обма́тывать**) wind round; ~**ся** +instr wrap o.s. in. **обмо́тка** winding; pl puttees.

обмо́ю etc.: see **обмы́ть**

обмундирова́ние fitting out (with uniform); uniform. **обмундирова́ть** pf, **обмундиро́вывать** impf fit out (with uniform).

обмыва́ть impf, **обмы́ть** (-мо́ю) pf bathe, wash; ~**ся** wash, bathe.

обмяка́ть impf, **обмя́кнуть** (-ну; -мя́к) pf become soft or flabby.

обнадёживать impf, **обнадёжить** (-жу) pf reassure.

обнажа́ть impf, **обнажи́ть** (-жу́) pf bare, uncover; reveal. **обнажённый** (-ён, -ена́) naked, bare; nude.

обнаро́довать impf & pf promulgate.

обнаруже́ние revealing; discovery; detection. **обнару́живать** impf, **обнару́жить** (-жу) pf display; reveal; discover; ~**ся** come to light.

обнести́ (-су́, -сёшь; -нёс, -ла́) pf (impf **обноси́ть**) enclose; +instr serve round; pass over, leave out.

обнима́ть(ся impf of **обня́ть(ся. обниму́** etc.: see **обня́ть**

обнища́ние impoverishment.

обнови́ть (-влю́) pf, **обновля́ть** impf renovate; renew. **обно́вка** new acquisition; new garment. **обно-вле́ние** renovation, renewal.

обноси́ть (-ошу́, -о́сишь) impf of **обнести́;** ~**ся** pf have worn out one's clothes.

обня́ть (-ниму́, -ни́мешь; о́бнял, -а́, -о) pf (impf **обнима́ть**) embrace; clasp; ~**ся** embrace; hug one another.

обо see **о** prep.

обобра́ть (оберу́, -рёшь; обобра́л, -а́, -о) pf (impf **обира́ть**) rob; pick.

обобща́ть impf, **обобщи́ть** (-щу́) pf generalize. **обобще́ние** generalization. **обобществи́ть** (-влю́) pf, обобществля́ть *impf* socialize; collectivize. обобществле́ние socialization; collectivization.

обобью́ *etc.*: see обби́ть. обовью́ *etc.*: *see* обви́ть

обогати́ть (-ащу́) *pf*, обогаща́ть *impf* enrich; ～ся become rich; enrich o.s. обогаще́ние enrichment.

обогна́ть (обгоню́, -о́нишь; обогна́л, -а́, -о) *pf* (*impf* обгоня́ть) pass; outstrip.

обогну́ть (-ну́, -нёшь) *pf* (*impf* огиба́ть) round, skirt; bend round.

обогрева́тель *m* heater. обогрева́ть *impf*, обогре́ть (-е́ю) *pf* heat, warm; ～ся warm up.

о́бод (*pl* -о́дья, -ьев) rim. ободо́к (-дка́) thin rim, narrow border.

обо́дранный ragged. ободра́ть (обдеру́, -рёшь; -а́л, -а́, -о) *pf* (*impf* обдира́ть) skin, flay; peel; fleece.

ободре́ние encouragement, reassurance. ободри́тельный encouraging, reassuring. ободри́ть *pf*, ободря́ть *impf* encourage, reassure; ～ся cheer up, take heart.

обожа́ть *impf* adore.

обожгу́ *etc.*: *see* обжечь

обожестви́ть (-влю́) *pf*, обожествля́ть *impf* deify.

обожжённый (-ён, -ена́) burnt, scorched.

обо́з string of vehicles; transport.

обозва́ть (обзову́, -вёшь; -а́л, -а́, -о) *pf* (*impf* обзыва́ть) call; call names.

обозлённый (-ён, -а́) angered; embittered. обо|зли́ть *pf*, о|зли́ть *pf* anger; embitter; ～ся get angry.

обозна́ться *pf* mistake s.o. for s.o. else.

обознача́ть *impf*, обозна́чить (-чу) *pf* mean; mark; ～ся appear, reveal o.s. обозначе́ние sign, symbol.

обозрева́тель *m* reviewer; columnist. обозрева́ть *impf*, обозре́ть (-рю́) *pf* survey. обозре́ние survey; review; revue. обозри́мый visible.

обо́и (-ев) *pl* wallpaper.

обо́йма (*gen pl* -о́йм) cartridge clip.

обойти́ (-йду́, -йдёшь; обошёл, -ошла́) *pf* (*impf* обходи́ть) go round; pass; avoid; pass over; ～сь manage, make do; +c+*instr* treat.

обокра́сть (обкраду́, -дёшь) *pf* (*impf* обкра́дывать) rob.

оболо́чка casing; membrane; cover, envelope, jacket; shell.

обольсти́тель *m* seducer. обольсти́тельный seductive. обольсти́ть (-льщу́) *pf*, обольща́ть *impf* seduce. обольще́ние seduction; delusion.

оболью́ *etc.*: *see* обли́ть

обомру́ *etc.*: *see* обмере́ть

обоня́ние (sense of) smell. обоня́тельный olfactory.

обопру́ *etc.*: *see* опере́ть

обора́чивать(ся *impf* of оберну́ть(ся, обороти́ть(ся

обо́рванный torn, ragged. оборва́ть (-ву́, -вёшь; -а́л, -а́, -о) *pf* (*impf* обрыва́ть) tear off; break; snap; cut short; ～ся break; snap; fall; stop suddenly.

обо́рка frill, flounce.

оборо́на defence. оборони́тельный defensive. обороня́ть *pf*, обороня́ть *impf* defend; ～ся defend o.s. оборо́нный defence, defensive.

оборо́т turn; revolution; circulation; turnover; back; ～ ре́чи (turn of) phrase; смотри́ на ～е P.T.O. обороти́ть (-рочу́, -ро́тишь) *pf* (*impf* обора́чивать) turn; ～ся turn (round); +*instr* or в+*acc* turn into. оборо́тный circulating; reverse; ～ капита́л working capital.

обору́дование equipping; equipment. обору́довать *impf* & *pf* equip.

обоснова́ние basing; basis, ground. обосно́ванный well-founded. обоснова́ть *pf*, обосно́вывать *impf* ground, base; substantiate; ～ся settle down.

обосо́бленный isolated, solitary.

обостре́ние aggravation. обострённый keen; strained; sharp, pointed. обостри́ть *pf*, обостря́ть *impf* sharpen; strain; aggravate; ～ся become strained; be aggravated; become acute.

оботру́ *etc.*: *see* обтере́ть

обо́чина verge; shoulder, edge.

обошёл *etc.*: *see* обойти́. обошью́ *etc.*: *see* обши́ть

обою́дный mutual, reciprocal.

обраба́тывать *impf*, обрабо́тать *pf* till, cultivate; work, work up; treat, process. **обрабóтка** working (up); processing; cultivation.

об|рáдовать(ся *pf.*

óбраз shape, form; image; manner; way; icon; **глáвным ~ом** mainly; **такúм ~ом** thus. **образéц** (-зцá) model; pattern; sample. **óбразный** graphic; figurative. **образовáние** formation; education. **образóванный** educated. **образовáтельный** educational. **образовáть** *impf & pf,* **образóвывать** *impf* form; **~ся** form; arise; turn out well.

образýмить (-млю) *pf* bring to reason; **~ся** see reason.

образцóвый model. **обрáзчик** specimen, sample.

обрáмить (-млю) *pf,* **обрамлять** *impf* frame.

обрастáть *impf,* **обрастú** (-тý, -тёшь; -рóс, -лá) *pf* be overgrown.

обратúмый reversible, convertible. **обратúть** (-ащý) *pf,* **обращáть** *impf* turn; convert; ~ **внимáние на**+*acc* pay *or* draw attention to; **~ся** turn; appeal; apply; address; **+в**+*acc* turn into; **+с**+*instr* treat; handle. **обрáтно** *adv* back; backwards; conversely; ~ **пропорционáльный** inversely proportional. **обрáтный** reverse; return; opposite; inverse. **обращéние** appeal, address; conversion; (+**с**+*instr*) treatment (of); handling (of); use (of).

обрéз edge; sawn-off gun; **в ~**+*gen* only just enough. **обрéзать** (-éжу) *pf,* **обрезáть** *impf* cut (off); clip, trim; pare; prune; circumcise; **~ся** cut o.s. **обрéзок** (-зка) scrap; *pl* ends; clippings.

обрекáть *impf of* **обрéчь. обрекý** *etc.: see* **обрéчь. обрёл** *etc.: see* **обрестú**

обременúтельный onerous. **о|бременúть** *pf,* **обременять** *impf* burden.

обрестú (-етý, -етёшь; -рёл, -á) *pf,* **обретáть** *impf* find.

обречéние doom. **обречённый** doomed. **обрéчь** (-екý, -ечёшь; -ёк, -лá) *pf* (*impf* **обрекáть**) doom.

обрисовáть *pf,* **обрисóвывать** *impf* outline, depict; **~ся** appear (in outline).

обронúть (-ню, -нишь) *pf* drop; let drop.

обрóс *etc.: see* **обрастú.**

обрубáть *impf,* **обрубúть** (-блю, -бишь) *pf* chop off; cut off. **обрýбок** (-бка) stump.

об|ругáть *pf.*

óбруч (*pl* -и, -éй) hoop. **обручáльный** engagement; **~ое кольцó** betrothal ring, wedding ring. **обручáть** *impf,* **обручúть** (-чý) betroth; **~ся** **+с**+*instr* become engaged to. **обручéние** engagement.

обрýшивать *impf,* **об|рýшить** (-шу) *pf* bring down; **~ся** come down, collapse.

обрыв precipice. **обрывáть(ся** *impf of* **оборвáть(ся. обрывок** (-вка) scrap; snatch.

обрызгать *pf,* **обрызгивать** *impf* splash; sprinkle.

обрюзглый flabby.

обряд rite, ceremony.

обсерватóрия observatory.

обслýживание service; maintenance. **обслýживать** *impf,* **обслужúть** (-жý, -жишь) *pf* serve; service; operate.

обслéдование inspection. **обслéдователь** *m* inspector. **обслéдовать** *impf & pf* inspect.

обсóхнуть (-ну; -óх) *pf* (*impf* **обсыхáть**) dry (off).

обстáвить (-влю) *pf,* **обставлять** *impf* surround; furnish; arrange. **обстанóвка** furniture; situation, conditions; set.

обстоятельный thorough, reliable; detailed. **обстоятельство** circumstance. **обстоять** (-ойт) *impf* be; go; **как обстоúт дéло?** how is it going?

обстрéл firing, fire; **под ~ом** under fire. **обстрéливать** *impf,* **обстрелять** *impf* fire at; bombard.

обступáть *impf,* **обступúть** (-ýпит) *pf* surround.

обсудúть (-ужý, -ýдишь) *pf,* **обсуждáть** *impf* discuss. **обсуждéние** discussion.

обсчитáть *pf,* **обсчúтывать** *impf* shortchange; **~ся** miscount, miscalculate.

обсыпать (-плю) *pf,* **обсыпáть** *impf* strew; sprinkle.

обсыхáть *impf of* **обсóхнуть. обтáчивать** *impf of* **оточúть**

обтекáемый streamlined.

обтере́ть (оботру́, -трёшь; обтёр) *pf* (*impf* **обтира́ть**) wipe; rub; ~**ся** dry o.s.; sponge down.

о(б)теса́ть (-ешу́, -е́шешь) *pf*, **о(б)тёсывать** *impf* rough-hew; teach good manners to; trim.

обтира́ние sponge-down. **обтира́ть(ся** *pf of* **обтере́ть(ся**

обточи́ть (-чу́, -чишь) *pf* (*impf* **обта́чивать**) grind; machine.

обтрёпанный frayed; shabby.

обтя́гивать *impf*, **обтяну́ть** (-ну́, -нешь) *pf* cover; fit close. **обтя́жка** cover; skin; **в обтя́жку** close-fitting.

обува́ть(ся *impf of* **обу́ть(ся. обувь** footwear; boots, shoes.

обу́гливать *impf*, **обу́глить** *pf* char; carbonize; ~**ся** char, become charred.

обу́за burden.

обузда́ть *pf*, **обу́здывать** *impf* bridle, curb.

обурева́ть *impf* grip; possess.

обусло́вить (-влю) *pf*, **обусло́вливать** *impf* cause; +*instr* make conditional on; ~**ся** +*instr* be conditional on; depend on.

обу́тый shod. **обу́ть** (-у́ю) *pf* (*impf* **обува́ть**) put shoes on; ~**ся** put on one's shoes.

о́бух butt, back.

обуча́ть *impf*, **об|учи́ть** (-чу́, -чишь) *pf* teach; train; ~**ся** +*dat or inf* learn. **обуче́ние** teaching; training.

обхва́т girth; **в** ~**е** in circumference. **обхвати́ть** (-ачу́, -а́тишь) *pf*, **обхва́тывать** *impf* embrace; clasp.

обхо́д round(s); roundabout way; by-pass. **обходи́тельный** courteous; pleasant. **обходи́ть(ся** (-ожу́(сь, -о́дишь(ся) *impf of* **обойти́(сь. обхо́дный** roundabout.

обша́ривать *impf*, **обша́рить** *pf* rummage through, ransack.

обшива́ть *impf of* **обши́ть. обши́вка** edging; trimming; boarding, panelling; plating.

обши́рный extensive; vast.

обши́ть (обошью́, -шьёшь) *pf* (*impf* **обшива́ть**) edge; trim; make outfit(s) for; plank.

обшла́г (-а́; *pl* -а́, -о́в) cuff.

обща́ться *impf* associate.

обще- *in comb* common(ly), general(ly). **общедосту́пный** mod-

erate in price; popular. ~**жи́тие** hostel. ~**изве́стный** generally known. ~**наро́дный** national, public. ~**образова́тельный** of general education. ~**при́нятый** generally accepted. ~**сою́зный** All-Union. ~**челове́ческий** common to all mankind; universal.

обще́ние contact; social intercourse. **обще́ственность** (the) public; public opinion; community. **обще́ственный** social, public; voluntary. **о́бщество** society; company.

о́бщ|ий general; common; **в** ~**ем** on the whole, in general. **общи́на** community; commune.

об|щипа́ть (-плю́, -плешь) *pf*. **общи́тельный** sociable. **о́бщность** community.

объеда́ть(ся *impf of* **объе́сть(ся**

объедине́ние unification; merger; union, association. **объединённый** (-ён, -а́) united. **объедини́тельный** unifying. **объедини́ть** *pf*, **объединя́ть** *impf* unite; join; combine; ~**ся** unite.

объе́дки (-ов) *pl* leftovers, scraps.

объе́зд riding round; detour.

объе́здить (-зжу, -здишь) *pf* (*impf* **объезжа́ть**) travel over; break in.

объезжа́ть *impf of* **объе́здить**, **объе́хать**

объе́кт object; objective; establishment, works. **объекти́в** lens. **объекти́вность** objectivity. **объекти́вный** objective.

объём volume; scope. **объёмный** by volume, volumetric.

объе́сть (-е́м, -е́шь, -е́ст, -еди́м) *pf* (*impf* **объеда́ть**) gnaw (round), nibble; ~**ся** overeat.

объе́хать (-е́ду) *pf* (*impf* **объезжа́ть**) drive or go round; go past; travel over.

объяви́ть (-влю́, -вишь) *pf*, **объявля́ть** *impf* declare, announce; ~**ся** turn up; +*instr* declare o.s. **объявле́ние** declaration, announcement; advertisement.

объясне́ние explanation. **объясни́мый** explainable. **объясни́ть** *pf*, **объясня́ть** *impf* explain; ~**ся** be explained; make o.s. understood; +**с**+*instr* have it out with.

объя́тие embrace.

обыва́тель *m* Philistine. **обыва́тельский** narrow-minded.

обыгра́ть *pf*, **обы́грывать** *impf* beat (*in a game*).

обы́денный ordinary; everyday.

обыкнове́ние habit. **обыкнове́нно** *adv* usually. **обыкнове́нный** usual; ordinary.

о́быск search. **обыска́ть** (-ыщу́, -ы́щешь) *pf*, **обы́скивать** *impf* search.

обы́чай custom; usage. **обы́чно** *adv* usually. **обы́чный** usual.

обя́занность duty; responsibility. **обя́занный** (+*inf*) obliged; +*dat* indebted to (+*instr* for). **обяза́тельно** *adv* without fail. **обяза́тельный** obligatory. **обяза́тельство** obligation; commitment. **обяза́ть** (-яжу́, -я́жешь) *pf*, **обя́зывать** *impf* bind; commit; oblige; ~**ся** pledge o.s., undertake.

ова́л oval. **ова́льный** oval.

ова́ция ovation.

овдове́ть (-е́ю) *pf* become a widow, widower.

ове́с (овса́) oats.

ове́чка *dim of* **овца́**; harmless person.

овладева́ть *impf*, **овладе́ть** (-е́ю) *pf* +*instr* seize; capture; master.

о́вод (*pl* -ы *or* -á) gadfly.

о́вощ (*pl* -и, -е́й) vegetable. **овощно́й** vegetable.

овра́г ravine, gully.

овся́нка oatmeal; porridge. **овся́ный** oat, oatmeal.

овца́ (*pl* -ы, ове́ц, о́вцам) sheep; ewe. **овча́рка** sheep-dog. **овчи́на** sheepskin.

ога́рок (-рка) candle-end.

огиба́ть *impf of* **обогну́ть**

оглавле́ние table of contents.

огласи́ть (-ашу́) *pf*, **оглаша́ть** *impf* announce; fill (with sound); ~**ся** resound. **огла́ска** publicity. **оглаше́ние** publication.

огло́бля (*gen pl* -бель) shaft.

о|гло́хнуть (-ну; -о́х) *pf*.

оглуша́ть *impf*, **о|глуши́ть** (-шу́) *pf* deafen; stun. **оглуши́тельный** deafening.

огляде́ть (-яжу́) *pf*, **огля́дывать** *impf*, **огляну́ть** (-ну́, -нешь) *pf* look round; look over; ~**ся** look round; look back. **огля́дка** looking back.

огнево́й fire; fiery. **о́гненный** fiery.

огнеопа́сный inflammable. **огнеприпа́сы** (-ов) *pl* ammunition. **огнесто́йкий** fire-proof. **огнестре́льн|ый**: ~**ое ору́жие** firearm(s). **огнетуши́тель** *m* fire-extinguisher. **огнеупо́рный** fire-resistant.

ого́ *int* oho!

огова́ривать *impf*, **оговори́ть** *pf* slander; stipulate (for); ~**ся** make a proviso; make a slip (of the tongue). **огово́р** slander. **огово́рка** reservation, proviso; slip of the tongue.

оголе́нный bare, nude. **оголи́ть** *pf* (*impf* **оголя́ть**) bare; strip; ~**ся** strip o.s.; become exposed.

оголя́ть(ся *impf of* **оголи́ть(ся**

огоне́к (-нька́) (*small*) light; zest. **ого́нь** (огня́) *m* fire; light.

огора́живать *impf*, **огороди́ть** (-рожу́, -ро́дишь) *pf* fence in, enclose; ~**ся** fence o.s. in. **огоро́д** kitchen-garden. **огоро́дный** kitchen-garden.

огорча́ть *impf*, **огорчи́ть** (-чу́) *pf* grieve; pain; ~**ся** grieve, be distressed. **огорче́ние** grief; chagrin.

о|гра́бить (-блю) *pf*. **ограбле́ние** robbery; burglary.

огра́да fence. **огради́ть** (-ажу́) *pf*, **огражда́ть** *impf* guard, protect.

ограниче́ние limitation, restriction. **ограни́ченный** limited. **ограни́чивать** *impf*, **ограни́чить** (-чу) *pf* limit, restrict; ~**ся** +*instr* limit *or* confine o.s. to; be limited to.

огро́мный huge; enormous.

о|гру́бе́ть (-е́ю) *pf*.

огры́зок (-зка) bit, end; stub.

огуре́ц (-рца́) cucumber.

ода́лживать *impf of* **одолжи́ть**

одарённый gifted. **ода́ривать** *impf*, **одари́ть** *pf*, **одаря́ть** *impf* give presents (to); +*instr* endow with.

одева́ть(ся *impf of* **оде́ть(ся**

оде́жда clothes; clothing.

одеколо́н eau-de-Cologne.

одели́ть *pf*, **оделя́ть** *impf* (+*instr*) present (with); endow (with).

оде́ну *etc.*: *see* **оде́ть**. **одёргивать** *impf of* **одёрнуть**

о|деревене́ть (-е́ю) *pf*.

одержа́ть (-жу́, -жишь) *pf*, **оде́рживать** *impf* gain. **одержи́мый** possessed.

одёрнуть (-ну) *pf* (*impf* **одёргивать**) pull down, straighten.

оде́тый dressed; clothed. **оде́ть** (-е́ну) *pf* (*impf* **одева́ть**) dress; clothe; **~ся** dress (o.s.). **одея́ло** blanket. **одея́ние** garb, attire.

оди́н (одного́), **одна́** (одно́й), **одно́** (одного́); *pl* **одни́** (одни́х) one; a, an; a certain; alone; only; nothing but; same; **одно́ и то же** the same thing; **оди́н на оди́н** in private; **оди́н раз** once; **одни́м сло́вом** in a word; **по одному́** one by one.

одина́ковый identical, the same, equal.

оди́ннадцатый eleventh. **оди́ннадцать** eleven.

одино́кий solitary; lonely; single. **одино́чество** solitude; loneliness. **одино́чка** *m & f* (one) person alone. **одино́чн|ый** individual; one-man; single; **~ое заключе́ние** solitary confinement.

одича́лый wild.

одна́жды *adv* once; one day; once upon a time.

одна́ко *conj* however.

одно- *in comb* single, one; uni-, mono-, homo-. **однобо́кий** one-sided. **~вре́менно** *adv* simultaneously, at the same time. **~вре́менный** simultaneous. **~зву́чный** monotonous. **~зна́чащий** synonymous. **~зна́чный** synonymous; one-digit. **~имённый** of the same name. **~кла́ссник** classmate. **~кле́точный** unicellular. **~кра́тный** single. **~ле́тний** one-year; annual. **~ме́стный** single-seater. **~обра́зие, ~обра́зность** monotony. **~обра́зный** monotonous. **~ро́дность** homogeneity, uniformity. **~ро́дный** homogeneous; similar. **~сторо́нний** one-sided; unilateral; one-way. **~фами́лец** (-льца) person of the same surname. **~цве́тный** one-colour; monochrome. **~эта́жный** one-storeyed.

одобре́ние approval. **одобри́тельный** approving. **одо́брить** *pf*, **одобря́ть** *impf* approve (of).

одолева́ть *impf*, **одоле́ть** (-е́ю) *pf* overcome.

одолжа́ть *impf*, **одолжи́ть** (-жу́) *pf* lend; **+у+gen** borrow from. **одолже́ние** favour.

о|дряхле́ть (-е́ю) *pf*.

одува́нчик dandelion.

оду́маться *pf*, **оду́мываться** *impf* change one's mind.

одуре́лый stupid. **о|дуре́ть** (-е́ю) *pf*.

одурма́нивать *impf*, **о|дурма́нить** *pf* stupefy. **одуря́ть** *impf* stupefy.

одухотворённый inspired; spiritual. **одухотвори́ть** *pf*, **одухотворя́ть** *impf* inspire.

одушеви́ть (-влю́) *pf*, **одушевля́ть** *impf* animate. **одушевле́ние** animation.

оды́шка shortness of breath.

ожере́лье necklace.

ожесточа́ть *impf*, **ожесточи́ть** (-чу́) *pf* embitter, harden. **ожесточе́ние** bitterness. **ожесточённый** bitter; hard.

ожива́ть *impf of* **ожи́ть**

оживи́ть (-влю́) *pf*, **оживля́ть** *impf* revive; enliven; **~ся** become animated. **оживле́ние** animation; reviving; enlivening. **оживлённый** animated, lively.

ожида́ние expectation; waiting. **ожида́ть** *impf* **+gen** wait for; expect.

ожире́ние obesity. **о|жире́ть** (-е́ю) *pf*.

ожи́ть (-иву́, -ивёшь; о́жил, -а́, -о) *pf* (*impf* **ожива́ть**) come to life, revive.

ожо́г burn, scald.

озабо́ченность preoccupation; anxiety. **озабо́ченный** preoccupied; anxious.

озагла́вить (-лю) *pf*, **озагла́вливать** *impf* entitle; head. **озада́чивать** *impf*, **озада́чить** (-чу) *pf* perplex, puzzle.

озари́ть *pf*, **озаря́ть** *impf* light up, illuminate; **~ся** light up.

оздорови́тельный бег jogging. **оздоровле́ние** sanitation.

озелени́ть *pf*, **озеленя́ть** *impf* plant (with trees etc.).

о́зеро (*pl* озёра) lake.

ози́мые *sb* winter crops. **ози́мый** winter. **о́зимь** winter crop.

озира́ться *impf* look round; look back.

о|зли́ть(ся: *see* **обозли́ть(ся**

озло́бить (-блю) *pf*, **озлобля́ть** *impf* embitter; **~ся** grow bitter. **озлобле́ние** bitterness, animosity.

озлобленный embittered.

о|знакомить (-млю) pf, ознакомлять impf с+instr acquaint with; ~ся с+instr familiarize o.s. with.

ознаменовать pf, ознаменовывать impf mark; celebrate.

означать impf mean, signify.

озноб shivering, chill.

озон ozone.

озорник (-а) mischief-maker. озорной naughty, mischievous. озорство mischief.

озябнуть (-ну; озяб) pf be cold, be freezing.

ой int oh.

оказать (-ажу, -ажешь) pf (impf оказывать) render, provide, show; ~ся turn out, prove; find o.s., be found.

оказия unexpected event, funny thing.

оказывать(ся impf of оказать(ся

окаменелость fossil. окаменелый fossilized; petrified. о|каменеть (-ею) pf.

окантовать mount.

оканчивать(ся impf of окончить(ся. окапывать(ся impf of окопать(ся

окаянный damned, cursed.

океан ocean. океанский ocean; oceanic.

окидывать impf, окинуть (-ну) pf; ~ взглядом take in at a glance, glance over.

окисел (-сла) oxide. окисление oxidation. окись oxide.

оккупант invader. оккупация occupation. оккупировать impf & pf occupy.

оклад salary scale; (basic) pay.

оклеветать (-ещу, -ещешь) pf slander.

оклеивать impf, оклеить pf cover; paste over; ~ обоями paper.

окно (pl окна) window.

око (pl очи, очей) eye.

оковы (оков) pl fetters.

околдовать pf, околдовывать impf bewitch.

около adv & prep+gen by; close (to), near; around; about.

окольный roundabout.

оконный window.

окончание end; conclusion; termination; ending. окончательный

final. окончить (-чу) pf (impf оканчивать) finish, end; ~ся finish, end.

окоп trench. окопать pf (impf окапывать) dig round; ~ся entrench o.s., dig in. окопный trench.

окорок (pl -а, -ов) ham, gammon.

окоченелый stiff with cold. о|коченеть (-ею) pf.

окошечко, окошко (small) window.

окраина outskirts, outlying districts.

о|красить (-ашу) pf, окрашивать impf paint, colour; dye. окраска painting; colouring; dyeing; colouration.

о|крепнуть (-ну) pf. о|крестить(ся (-ещу(сь, -естишь(ся) pf.

окрестность environs. окрестный neighbouring.

окрик hail; shout. окрикивать impf, окрикнуть (-ну) pf hail, call, shout to.

окровавленный blood-stained.

округ (pl ~а) district. округа neighbourhood. округлить pf, округлять impf round; round off. округлый rounded. окружать impf, окружить (-жу) pf surround; encircle. окружающ|ий surrounding; ~ее sb environment; ~ие sb pl associates. окружение encirclement; environment. окружной district. окружность circumference.

окрылить pf, окрылять impf inspire, encourage.

октава octave.

октан octane.

октябрь (-я) m October. октябрьский October.

окулист oculist.

окунать impf, окунуть (-ну, -нёшь) pf dip; ~ся dip; plunge; become absorbed.

окунь (pl -и, -ей) m perch.

окупать impf, окупить (-плю, -пишь) pf compensate, repay; ~ся be repaid, pay for itself.

окурок (-рка) cigarette-end.

окутать pf, окутывать impf wrap up; shroud, cloak.

окучивать impf, окучить (-чу) pf earth up.

оладья (gen pl -ий) fritter; dropscone.

оледенелый frozen. о|леденеть (-ею) pf.

оле́ний deer, deer's; reindeer.
оле́нина venison. **оле́нь** *m* deer; reindeer.

оли́ва olive. **оли́вковый** olive; olive-coloured.

олига́рхия oligarchy.

олимпиа́да olympiad; Olympics. **олимпи́йск|ий** Olympic; Olympian; ~ие и́гры Olympic games.

оли́фа drying oil (*e.g. linseed oil*).

олицетворе́ние personification; embodiment. **олицетвори́ть** *pf*, **олицетворя́ть** *impf* personify, embody.

о́лово tin. **оловя́нный** tin.

ом ohm.

ома́р lobster.

омерзе́ние loathing. **омерзи́тельный** loathsome.

омертве́лый stiff, numb; necrotic. **о|мертве́ть** (-е́ю) *pf.*

омле́т omelette.

омоложе́ние rejuvenation.

омо́ним homonym.

омо́ю *etc.: see* **омы́ть**

омрача́ть *impf*, **омрачи́ть** (-чу́) *pf* darken, cloud.

о́мут whirlpool; maelstrom.

омыва́ть *impf*, **омы́ть** (омо́ю) *pf* wash; ~ся be washed.

он (его́, ему́, им, о нём) *pron* he. **она́** (её, ей, ей (е́ю), о ней) *pron* she.

онда́тра musk-rat.

онеме́лый numb. **о|неме́ть** (-е́ю) *pf.*

они́ (их, им, и́ми, о них) *pron* they. **оно́** (его́, ему́, им, о нём) *pron* it; this, that.

опада́ть *impf of* **опа́сть**

опа́здывать *impf of* **опозда́ть**

опа́ла disgrace.

о|пали́ть *pf.*

опа́ловый opal.

опа́лубка casing.

опаса́ться *impf* +*gen* fear; avoid, keep off. **опасе́ние** fear; apprehension.

опа́сность danger; peril. **опа́сный** dangerous.

опа́сть (-адёт) *pf* (*impf* **опада́ть**) fall, fall off; subside.

опе́ка guardianship; trusteeship. **опека́емый** *sb* ward. **опека́ть** *impf* be guardian of; take care of. **опеку́н** (-а́), **-у́нша** guardian; tutor; trustee.

о́пера opera.

операти́вный efficient, operative,

---

surgical; operation(s), operational.

опера́тор operator; cameraman.

операцио́нн|ый operating; ~ая *sb* operating theatre. **опера́ция** operation.

опереди́ть (-режу́) *pf*, **опережа́ть** *impf* outstrip, leave behind.

опере́ние plumage.

опере́тта, -е́тка operetta.

опере́ть (обопру́, -прёшь; опёр, -ла́) *pf* (*impf* **опира́ть**) +о+*acc* lean against; ~ся на *or* о+*acc* lean on, lean against.

опери́ровать *impf & pf* operate on; operate, act; +*instr* use.

о́перный opera; operatic.

о|печа́лить(ся *pf.*

опеча́тать *pf* (*impf* **опеча́тывать**) seal up.

опеча́тка misprint.

опеча́тывать *impf of* **опеча́тать**

опеши́ть (-шу) *pf* be taken aback.

опи́лки (-лок) *pl* sawdust; filings.

опира́ть(ся *impf of* **опере́ть(ся**

описа́ние description. **описа́тельный** descriptive. **описа́ть** (-ишу́, -и́шешь) *pf*, **опи́сывать** *impf* describe; ~ся make a slip of the pen. **опи́ска** slip of the pen. **о́пись** inventory.

о́пиум opium.

опла́кать (-а́чу) *pf*, **опла́кивать** *impf* mourn for; bewail.

опла́та payment. **оплати́ть** (-ачу́, -а́тишь) *pf*, **опла́чивать** *impf* pay (for).

оплачу́ *etc.: see* **опла́кать**. **оплачу́** *etc.: see* **оплати́ть**

оплеу́ха slap in the face.

оплодотвори́ть *pf*, **оплодотворя́ть** *impf* impregnate; fertilize.

о|пломбирова́ть *pf.*

опло́т stronghold, bulwark.

опло́шность blunder, mistake.

оповести́ть (-ещу́) *pf*, **оповеща́ть** *impf* notify. **оповеще́ние** notification.

опозда́вший *sb* late-comer. **опозда́ние** lateness; delay. **опозда́ть** *pf* (*impf* **опа́здывать**) be late; +на+*acc* miss.

опознава́тельный distinguishing; ~ знак landmark. **опознава́ть** (-наю́, -наёшь) *impf*, **опозна́ть** *pf* identify. **опозна́ние** identification.

о|позо́рить(ся *pf*.

ополза́ть *impf*, оползти́ (-зёт; -о́лз, -ла́) *pf* slip, slide. о́ползень (-зня) *m* landslide.

ополче́ние militia.

опо́мниться *pf* come to one's senses.

опо́р: во весь ~ at full speed.

опо́ра support; pier; то́чка опо́ры fulcrum, foothold.

опора́жнивать *impf of* опорожни́ть

опо́рный support, supporting, supported; bearing.

опоро́жнить *pf*, опорожня́ть *impf* (*impf also* опора́жнивать) empty.

о|поро́чить (-чу) *pf*.

опохмели́ться *pf*, опохмеля́ться *impf* take a hair of the dog that bit you.

опо́шлить *pf*, опошля́ть *impf* vulgarize, debase.

опоя́сать (-я́шу) *pf*, опоя́сывать *impf* gird; girdle.

оппозицио́нный opposition. оппози́ция opposition.

оппортуни́зм opportunism.

опра́ва setting, mounting; spectacle frames.

оправда́ние justification; excuse; acquittal. оправда́тельный пригово́р verdict of not guilty. оправда́ть *pf*, опра́вдывать *impf* justify; excuse; acquit; ~ся justify o.s.; be justified.

опра́вить (-влю) *pf*, оправля́ть *impf* set right, adjust; mount; ~ся put one's dress in order; recover; +от+*gen* get over.

опра́шивать *impf of* опроси́ть

определе́ние definition; determination; decision. определённый definite; certain. определи́мый definable. определи́ть *pf*, определя́ть *impf* define; determine; appoint; ~ся be formed; be determined; find one's position.

опроверга́ть *impf*, опрове́ргнуть (-ну; -ве́рг) *pf* refute, disprove. опроверже́ние refutation; denial.

опроки́дывать *impf*, опроки́нуть (-ну) *pf* overturn; topple; ~ся overturn; capsize.

опроме́тчивый rash, hasty.

опро́с (cross-)examination; (opinion) poll. опроси́ть (-ошу́, -о́сишь) *pf* (*impf* опра́шивать) question; (cross-)

examine. опро́сный лист questionnaire.

опры́скать *pf*, опры́скивать *impf* sprinkle; spray.

опря́тный neat, tidy.

о́птик optician. о́птика optics. опти́ческий optic, optical.

оптима́льный optimal. оптими́зм optimism. оптими́ст optimist. оптимисти́ческий optimistic.

опто́вый wholesale. о́птом *adv* wholesale.

опубликова́ние publication; promulgation. о|публикова́ть *pf*, опублико́вывать *impf* publish; promulgate.

опуска́ть(ся *impf of* опусти́ть(ся

опусте́лый deserted. о|пусте́ть (-е́ет) *pf*.

опусти́ть (-ущу́, -у́стишь) *pf* (*impf* опуска́ть) lower; let down; turn down; omit; post; ~ся lower o.s.; sink; fall; go down; go to pieces.

опустоша́ть *impf*, опустоши́ть (-шу́) *pf* devastate. опустоше́ние devastation. опустоши́тельный devastating.

опу́тать *pf*, опу́тывать *impf* entangle; ensnare.

опуха́ть *impf*, о|пу́хнуть (-ну; опу́х) *pf* swell, swell up. о́пухоль swelling; tumour.

опу́шка edge of a forest; trimming.

опущу́ *etc.*: *see* опусти́ть

опыле́ние pollination. опыли́ть *pf*, опыля́ть *impf* pollinate.

о́пыт experience; experiment. о́пытный experienced; experimental.

опьяне́ние intoxication. о|пьяне́ть (-е́ю) *pf*, о|пьяни́ть *pf*, опьяня́ть *impf* intoxicate, make drunk.

опя́ть *adv* again.

ора́ва crowd, horde.

ора́кул oracle.

орангута́нг orangutan.

ора́нжевый orange. оранжере́я greenhouse, conservatory.

ора́тор orator. орато́рия oratorio.

ора́ть (ору́, орёшь) *impf* yell.

орби́та orbit; (eye-)socket.

о́рган[1] organ; body. орга́н[2] (*mus*) organ. организа́тор organizer. организацио́нный organization(al). организа́ция organization. органи́зм organism. организо́ванный organized. **организова́ть** *impf & pf* (*pf also* с~) organize; ~**ся** be organized; organize. **органи́ческий** organic.

óргия orgy.

орда́ (*pl* -ы) horde.

óрден (*pl* -á) order.

óрдер (*pl* -á) order; warrant; writ.

ордина́та ordinate.

ордина́тор house-surgeon.

орёл (орла́) eagle; ~ и́ли ре́шка? heads or tails?

орео́л halo.

оре́х nut, nuts; walnut. **оре́ховый** nut; walnut. **оре́шник** hazel; hazel-thicket.

оригина́л original; eccentric. **оригина́льный** original.

ориента́ция orientation. **ориенти́р** landmark; reference point. **ориенти́роваться** *impf & pf* orient o.s.; +на+*acc* head for; aim at. **ориенти́ро́вка** orientation. **ориентиро́вочный** reference; tentative; approximate.

орке́стр orchestra.

орли́ный eagle; aquiline.

орна́мент ornament; ornamental design.

о|робе́ть (-е́ю) *pf.*

ороси́тельный irrigation. **ороси́ть** (-ошу́) *pf,* **ороша́ть** *impf* irrigate. **ороше́ние** irrigation; поля́ ороше́ния sewage farm.

ору́ *etc.: see* **ора́ть**

ору́дие instrument; tool; gun. **ору́дийный** gun. **ору́довать** *impf* +*instr* handle; run. **оруже́йный** arms; gun. **ору́жие** arm, arms; weapons.

орфографи́ческий orthographic(al). **орфогра́фия** orthography, spelling.

оса́ (*pl* -ы) wasp.

оса́да siege. **осади́ть**[1] (-ажу́) *pf* (*impf* **осажда́ть**) besiege.

осади́ть[2] (-ажу́, -а́дишь) *pf* (*impf* **оса́живать**) check; force back; rein in; take down a peg.

оса́дный siege.

оса́док (-дка) sediment; fall-out; aftertaste; *pl* precipitation, fall-out. **оса́дочный** sedimentary.

осажда́ть *impf of* **осади́ть**[1]

оса́живать *impf of* **осади́ть**[2]. **осажу́** *see* **осади́ть**[1,2]

оса́нка carriage, bearing.

осва́ивать(ся *impf of* **осво́ить(ся**

осведоми́тельный informative; information. **осведоми́ть** (-млю) *pf,* **осведомля́ть** *impf* inform; ~**ся** о+*prep* inquire about, ask after. **осведомле́ние** notification. **осведомлённый** well-informed, knowledgeable.

освежа́ть *impf,* **освежи́ть** (-жу́) *pf* refresh; air. **освежи́тельный** refreshing.

освети́тельный illuminating. **освети́ть** (-ещу́) *pf,* **освеща́ть** *pf* light up; illuminate; throw light on; ~**ся** light up. **освеще́ние** lighting, illumination. **освещённый** (-ён, -á) lit.

о|свиде́тельствовать *pf.*

освиста́ть (-ищу́, -и́щешь) *pf,* **осви́стывать** *impf* hiss (off); boo.

освободи́тель *m* liberator. **освободи́тельный** liberation, emancipation. **освободи́ть** (-ожу́) *pf,* **освобожда́ть** *impf* liberate; emancipate; dismiss; vacate; empty; ~**ся** free o.s.; become free. **освобожде́ние** liberation; release; emancipation; vacation. **освобождённый** (-ён, -á) freed, free; exempt.

освое́ние mastery; opening up. **осво́ить** (*impf* **осва́ивать**) master; become familiar with; ~**ся** familiarize o.s.

освящённый (-ён, -ена́) consecrated; sanctified; ~ века́ми time-honoured.

оседа́ть *impf of* **осе́сть**

о|седла́ть *pf,* **осёдлывать** *impf* saddle.

осе́длый settled.

осека́ться *impf of* **осе́чься**

осёл (-сла́) donkey; ass.

осело́к (-лка́) touchstone; whetstone.

осени́ть *pf* (*impf* **осеня́ть**) overshadow; dawn upon.

осе́нний autumn(al). **óсень** autumn. **óсенью** *adv* in autumn.

осеня́ть *impf of* **осени́ть**

осе́сть (осяду; осёл) *pf* (*impf* **оседа́ть**) settle; subside.

осётр (-á) sturgeon. **осетри́на** sturgeon.

осе́чка misfire. **осе́чься** (-еку́сь, -ечёшься; -ёкся, -екла́сь) *pf* (*impf* **осека́ться**) stop short.

оси́ливать *impf,* **оси́лить** *pf* overpower; master.

осина aspen.

о|сипнуть (-ну; осип) get hoarse.

осиротелый orphaned. осиротеть (-ею) pf be orphaned.

оскаливать impf, о|скалить pf, ~ зубы, ~ся bare one's teeth.

о|скандалить(ся pf.

осквернить pf, осквернять impf profane; defile.

осколок (-лка) splinter; fragment.

оскомина bitter taste (in the mouth); набить оскомину set the teeth on edge.

оскорбительный insulting, abusive. оскорбить (-блю) pf, оскорблять impf insult; offend; ~ся take offence. оскорбление insult. оскорблённый (-ён, -á) insulted.

ослабевать impf, о|слабеть (-ею) pf weaken; slacken. ослабить (-блю) pf, ослаблять impf weaken; slacken. ослабление weakening; slackening; relaxation.

ослепительный blinding, dazzling. ослепить (-плю) pf, ослеплять impf blind, dazzle. ослепление blinding, dazzling; blindness. о|слепнуть (-ну; -éп) pf.

ослиный donkey; asinine. ослица she-ass.

осложнение complication. осложнить pf, осложнять impf complicate; ~ся become complicated.

ослышаться (-шусь) pf mishear.

осматривать(ся impf of осмотреть(ся. осмеивать impf of осмеять.

о|смелеть (-ею) pf. осмеливаться impf, осмелиться pf dare; venture.

осмеять (-ею, -еёшь) pf (impf осмеивать) ridicule.

осмотр examination, inspection. осмотреть (-рю, -ришь) pf (impf осматривать) examine, inspect; look round; ~ся look round. осмотрительный circumspect.

осмысленный sensible, intelligent. осмысливать impf, осмыслить pf, осмыслять impf interpret; comprehend.

оснастить (-ащу) pf, оснащать impf fit out, equip. оснастка rigging. оснащение fitting out; equipment.

основа base, basis, foundation; pl fundamentals; stem (of a word).

основание founding, foundation; base; basis; reason; на каком основании? on what grounds? основатель m founder. основательный well-founded; solid; thorough. основать pf, основывать impf found; base; ~ся settle; be founded, be based. основной fundamental, basic; main; в основном in the main, on the whole. основоположник founder.

особа person. особенно adv especially. особенность peculiarity; в особенности in particular. особенный special, particular, peculiar. особняк (-á) private residence; detached house. особняком adv by o.s. особо adv apart; especially. особый special; particular.

осознавать (-наю, -наёшь) impf, осознать pf realize.

осока sedge.

óспа smallpox; pock-marks.

оспаривать impf, оспорить pf dispute; contest.

о|срамить(ся (-млю(сь) pf. оставаться (-таюсь, -таёшься) impf of остаться.

ост (naut) east; east wind.

оставить (-влю) pf, оставлять impf leave; abandon; reserve.

остальной the rest of; ~ое sb the rest; ~ые sb pl the others.

останавливать(ся impf of остановить(ся.

останки (-ов) pl remains.

остановить (-влю, -вишь) pf (impf останавливать) stop; restrain; ~ся stop, halt; stay; +на+prep dwell on; settle on. остановка stop.

остаток (-тка) remainder; rest; residue; pl remains; leftovers. остаться (-áнусь) pf (impf оставаться) remain; stay; impers it remains, it is necessary; нам не остаётся ничего другого, как we have no choice but.

остеклить pf, остеклять impf glaze.

остервенеть pf become enraged.

остерегать impf, остеречь (-регу, -режёшь; -рёг, -лá) pf warn; ~ся (+gen) beware (of).

óстов frame, framework; skeleton.

о|столбенеть (-ею) pf.

осторожно adv carefully; ~! look

out! **осторо́жность** care, caution. **осторо́жный** careful, cautious.

острига́ть(ся *impf of* **остри́чь(ся**
остриё point; spike; (cutting) edge. **остри́ть**[1] *impf* sharpen. **остри́ть**[2] *impf* (*pf* **с~**) be witty.

о|стри́чь (-игу́, -ижёшь; -и́г) *pf* (*impf also* **острига́ть**) cut, clip; **~ся** have one's hair cut.

о́стров (*pl* -á) island. **островóк** (-вка́) islet; **~ безопа́сности** (traffic) island.

остро́та[1] witticism, joke. **острота́**[2] sharpness; keenness; pungency. **остроу́мие** wit. **остроу́мный** witty.

о́стрый (остр, -á, -о) sharp; pointed; acute; keen. **остря́к** (-á) wit.

о|студи́ть (-ужу́, -у́дишь) *pf*, **осту-жа́ть** *impf* cool.

оступа́ться *impf*, **оступи́ться** (-плю́сь, -пишься) *pf* stumble.

остыва́ть *impf*, **осты́ть** (-ы́ну) *pf* get cold; cool down.

осуди́ть (-ужу́, -у́дишь) *pf*, **осужда́ть** *impf* condemn; convict. **осужде́ние** condemnation; conviction. **осуждённый** (-ён, -á) condemned, convicted; *sb* convict.

осу́нуться (-нусь) *pf* grow thin, become drawn.

осуша́ть *impf*, **осуши́ть** (-шу́, -шишь) *pf* drain; dry. **осуше́ние** drainage.

осуществи́мый feasible. **осуществи́ть** (-влю́) *pf*, **осуществля́ть** *impf* realize, bring about; accomplish; **~ся** be fulfilled, come true. **осуществле́ние** realization; accomplishment.

осчастли́вить (-влю) *pf*, **осчастли́вливать** *impf* make happy.

осы́пать (-плю) *pf*, **осыпа́ть** *impf* strew; shower; **~ся** crumble; fall. **о́сыпь** scree.

ось (*gen pl* -е́й) axis; axle.

осьмино́г octopus.

ося́ду *etc.: see* **осе́сть**

осяза́емый tangible. **осяза́ние** touch. **осяза́тельный** tactile; tangible. **осяза́ть** *impf* feel.

от, ото *prep+gen* from; of; against.

ота́пливать *impf of* **отопи́ть**

ота́ра flock (*of sheep*).

отба́вить (-влю) *pf*, **отбавля́ть** *impf* pour off; **хоть отбавля́й** more than enough.

отбега́ть *impf*, **отбежа́ть** (-егу́) *pf*

run off.

отберу́ *etc.: see* **отобра́ть**

отбива́ть(ся *impf of* **отби́ть(ся**

отбивна́я котле́та cutlet, chop.

отбира́ть *impf of* **отобра́ть**

отби́ть (отобью́, -ёшь) *pf* (*impf* **отбива́ть**) beat (off), repel; win over; break off; **~ся** break off; drop behind; **+от+**gen defend o.s. against.

о́тблеск reflection.

отбо́й repelling; retreat; ringing off. **бить ~** beat a retreat; **дать ~** ring off.

отбо́йный молото́к (-тка́) pneumatic drill.

отбо́р selection. **отбо́рный** choice, select(ed).

отбра́сывать *impf*, **отбро́сить** (-о́шу) *pf* throw off *or* away; hurl back; reject; **~ тень** cast a shadow. **отбро́сы** (-ов) *pl* garbage.

отбыва́ть *impf*, **отбы́ть** (-бу́ду; о́тбыл, -á, -о) *pf* depart; serve (*a sentence*).

отва́га courage, bravery.

отва́живаться *impf*, **отва́житься** (-жусь) *pf* dare. **отва́жный** courageous.

отва́л dump, slag-heap; casting off; **до ~а** to satiety. **отва́ливать** *impf*, **отвали́ть** (-лю́, -лишь) *pf* push aside; cast off; fork out.

отва́р broth; decoction. **отва́ривать** *impf*, **отвари́ть** (-рю́, -ришь) *pf* boil. **отварно́й** boiled.

отве́дать *pf* (*impf* **отве́дывать**) taste, try.

отведу́ *etc.: see* **отвести́**

отве́дывать *impf of* **отве́дать**

отвезти́ (-зу́, -зёшь; -вёз, -ла́) *pf* (*impf* **отвози́ть**) take *or* cart away.

отвёл *etc.: see* **отвести́**

отверга́ть *impf*, **отве́ргнуть** (-ну; -ве́рг) *pf* reject; repudiate.

отве́рженный outcast.

отверну́ть (-ну́, -нёшь) *pf* (*impf* **отвёртывать, отвора́чивать**) turn aside; turn down; turn on; unscrew; screw off; **~ся** turn away; come unscrewed.

отве́рстие opening; hole.

отверте́ть (-рчу́, -ртишь) *pf* (*impf* **отвёртывать**) unscrew; twist off; **~ся** come unscrewed; get off. **отвёртка** screwdriver.

отвёртывать(ся *impf of* **отвернуть(ся, отвертеть(ся**

отвес plumb; vertical slope. **отвесить** (-ёшу) *pf* (*impf* **отвешивать**) weigh out. **отвесный** perpendicular, sheer.

отвести (-еду́, -едёшь; -вёл, -á) *pf* (*impf* **отводить**) lead, take; draw *or* take aside; deflect; draw off; reject; allot.

ответ answer.

ответвиться *pf*, **ответвляться** *impf* branch off. **ответвление** branch, offshoot.

ответить (-éчу) *pf*, **отвечать** *impf* answer; +**на**+*acc* reply to; +**за**+*acc* answer for. **ответный** in reply, return. **ответственность** responsibility. **ответственный** responsible. **ответчик** defendant.

отвешивать *impf of* **отвесить**. **отвешу** *etc.: see* **отвесить**

отвинтить (-нчу́) *pf*, **отвинчивать** *impf* unscrew.

отвисать *impf*, **отвиснуть** (-нет; -ис) *pf* hang down, sag. **отвислый** hanging, baggy.

отвлекать *impf*, **отвлечь** (-еку́, -ечёшь; -влёк, -ла́) *pf* distract, divert; ~**ся** be distracted. **отвлечённый** abstract.

отвод taking aside; diversion; leading, taking; rejection; allotment. **отводить** (-ожу́, -óдишь) *impf of* **отвести**.

отвоевать (-оюю) *pf*, **отвоёвывать** *impf* win back; spend in fighting.

отвозить (-ожу́, -óзишь) *impf of* **отвезти**. **отворачивать(ся** *impf of* **отвернуть(ся**

отворить (-рю́, -ришь) *pf* (*impf* **отворять**) open; ~**ся** open.

отворять(ся *impf of* **отворить(ся. отвоюю** *etc.: see* **отвоевать**

отвратительный disgusting. **отвращение** disgust, repugnance.

отвыкать *impf*, **отвыкнуть** (-ну; -вык) *pf* +**от** *or* +inf lose the habit of; grow out of.

отвязать (-яжу́, -я́жешь) *pf*, **отвязывать** *impf* untie, unfasten; ~**ся** come untied, come loose; +**от**+*gen* get rid of; leave alone.

отгадать *pf*, **отгадывать** *impf* guess. **отгадка** answer.

отгибать(ся *impf of* **отогнуть(ся**

отгладить (-áжу) *pf*, **отглаживать** *impf* iron (out).

отговаривать *impf*, **отговорить** *pf* dissuade; ~**ся** +*instr* plead. **отговорка** excuse, pretext.

отголосок (-ска) echo.

отгонять *impf of* **отогнать**

отгораживать *impf*, **отгородить** (-ожу́, -óдишь) *pf* fence off; partition off; ~**ся** shut o.s. off.

отдавать[1](**ся** (-даю́(сь) *impf of* **отдать(ся. отдавать**[2] (-аёт) *impf impers*+*instr* taste of; smell of; smack of; **от него отдаёт водкой** he reeks of vodka.

отдаление removal; distance. **отдалённый** remote. **отдалить** *pf*, **отдалять** *impf* remove; estrange; postpone; ~**ся** move away; digress.

отдать (-áм, -áшь, -áст, -адим; óтдал, -á, -о) *pf* (*impf* **отдавать**[1]) give back, return; give; give up; give away; recoil; cast off; ~**ся** give o.s. (up); resound. **отдача** return; payment; casting off; efficiency; output; recoil.

отдел department; section.

отделать *pf* (*impf* **отделывать**) finish, put the finishing touches to; trim; ~**ся** +**от**+*gen* get rid of; +*instr* get off with.

отделение separation; department; compartment; section. **отделить** (-елю́, -éлишь) *pf* (*impf* **отделять**) separate; detach; ~**ся** separate; detach o.s.; get detached.

отделка finishing; finish, decoration. **отделывать(ся** *impf of* **отделать(ся**

отдельно separately; apart. **отдельный** separate. **отделять(ся** *impf of* **отделить(ся**

отдёргивать *impf*, **отдёрнуть** (-ну) *pf* draw *or* pull aside *or* back.

отдеру *etc.: see* **отодрать. отдирать** *impf of* **отодрать**

отдохнуть (-ну́, -нёшь) *pf* (*impf* **отдыхать**) rest.

отдушина air-hole, vent.

отдых rest. **отдыхать** *impf* (*pf* **отдохнуть**) rest; be on holiday.

отдышаться (-шу́сь, -шишься) *pf* recover one's breath.

отекать *impf of* **отечь. о|телиться** (-éлится) *pf*.

отéль *m* hotel.

отесáть *etc.*: see **обтесáть**

отéц (отцá) father. **отéческий** fatherly, paternal. **отéчественный** home, native. **отéчество** native land, fatherland.

отéчь (-екý, -ечёшь; отёк, -лá) *pf* (*impf* **отекáть**) swell (up).

отживáть *impf*, **отжúть** (-ивý, -ивёшь; óтжил, -á, -о) *pf* become obsolete *or* outmoded. **отжúвший** obsolete; outmoded.

óтзвук echo.

óтзыв[1] opinion; reference; review; response. **отзыв**[2] recall. **отзывáть(ся** *impf of* **отозвáть(ся. отзывчивый** responsive.

откáз refusal; repudiation; failure; natural. **отказáть** (-ажý, -áжешь) *pf*, **откáзывать** *impf* break down; (+*dat* в+*prep*) refuse, deny (*s.o. sth*); ~**ся** (+*от*+*gen or* +*inf*) refuse; turn down; renounce, give up.

откáлывать(ся *impf of* **отколóть(ся. откáлывать** *impf of* **отколóть. откáрмливать** *impf of* **откормúть. откатúть** (-ачý, -áтишь) *pf*, **откáтывать** *impf* roll away; ~**ся** roll away *or* back; be forced back.

откачáть *pf*, **откáчивать** *impf* pump out; give artificial respiration to.

откáшливаться *impf*, **откáшляться** *pf* clear one's throat.

откиднóй folding, collapsible. **откúдывать** *impf*, **откúнуть** (-ну) *pf* fold back; throw aside.

отклáдывать *impf of* **отложúть**

отклéивать *impf*, **отклéить** (-éю) *pf* unstick; ~**ся** come unstuck.

óтклик response; comment; echo. **откликáться** *impf*, **откликнуться** (-нусь) *pf* answer, respond.

отклонéние deviation; declining, refusal; deflection. **отклонúть** (-ню, -нишь) *pf*, **отклонять** *impf* deflect; decline; ~**ся** deviate; diverge.

отключáть *impf*, **отключúть** (-чý) *pf* cut off, disconnect.

отколотúть (-очý, -óтишь) *pf* knock off; beat up.

отколóть (-лю, -лешь) *pf* (*impf* **откáлывать**) break off; chop off; unpin; ~**ся** break off; come unpinned; break away.

откопáть *pf* (*impf* **откáпывать**) dig

up; exhume.

откормúть (-млю, -мишь) *pf* (*impf* **откáрмливать**) fatten.

откóс slope.

открепúть (-плю) *pf*, **открепля́ть** *impf* unfasten; ~**ся** become unfastened.

откровéние revelation. **откровéнный** frank; outspoken; unconcealed.

открóю *etc.*: see **открыть**

открутúть (-учý, -ýтишь) *pf*, **открýчивать** *impf* untwist, unscrew.

открывáть *impf*, **открыть** (-рóю) *pf* open; reveal; discover; turn on; ~**ся** open; come to light, be revealed. **открытие** discovery; revelation; opening. **открытка** postcard. **открыто** openly. **открытый** open.

откýда *adv* from where; from which; how; ~ **ни возьмúсь** from out of nowhere. **откýда-либо, -нибудь** from somewhere or other. **откýда-то** from somewhere.

откýпоривать *impf*, **откýпорить** *pf* uncork.

откусúть (-ушý, -ýсишь) *pf*, **откýсывать** *impf* bite off.

отлагáтельство delay. **отлагáть** *impf of* **отложúть**

от|лакировáть *pf*. **отлáмывать** *impf of* **отломáть, отломúть**

отлепúть (-плю, -пишь) *pf* unstick, take off; ~**ся** come unstuck, come off.

отлёт flying away; departure. **отлетáть** *impf*, **отлетéть** (-лечý) *pf*, fly, fly away, fly off; rebound.

отлúв ebb, ebb-tide; tint; play of colours. **отливáть** *impf*, **отлúть** (отолью; óтлúл, -á, -о) *pf* pour off; pump out; cast, found; (*no pf*) +*instr* be shot with. **отлúвка** casting; moulding.

отличáть *impf*, **отличúть** (-чý) *pf* distinguish; ~**ся** distinguish o.s.; differ; +*instr* be notable for. **отлúчие** difference; distinction; **знак отлúчия** order, decoration; **с отлúчием** with honours. **отлúчник** outstanding student, worker, etc. **отличúтельный** distinctive; distinguishing. **отлúчный** different; excellent.

отлóгий sloping.

отложéние sediment; deposit. **отложúть** (-ожý, -óжишь) *pf* (*impf*

откла́дывать, отлага́ть) put aside; postpone; deposit.

отлома́ть, отломи́ть (-млю́, -мишь) *pf* (*impf* **отла́мывать**) break off. **от|лупи́ть** *pf*.

отлуча́ть *impf*, **отлучи́ть** (-чу́) *pf* (**от це́ркви**) excommunicate; ~**ся** absent o.s. **отлу́чка** absence.

отлы́нивать *impf* +*от*+*gen* shirk.

отма́хиваться *impf*, **отмахну́ться** (-ну́сь, -нёшься) *pf* *от*+*gen* brush off; brush aside.

отмежева́ться (-жу́юсь) *pf*, **отмежёвываться** *impf* *от*+*gen* dissociate o.s. from.

о́тмель (sand-)bank.

отме́на abolition; cancellation. **отмени́ть** (-ню́, -нишь) *pf*, **отменя́ть** *impf* repeal; abolish; cancel.

отмере́ть (отомрёт; о́тмер, -ла́, -ло) *pf* (*impf* **отмира́ть**) die off; die out.

отме́ривать *impf*, **отме́рить** *pf*, **отмеря́ть** *impf* measure off.

отмести́ (-ету́, -етёшь; -ёл, -а́) *pf* (*impf* **отмета́ть**) sweep aside.

отмета́ть *impf of* **отмести́**

отме́тить (-е́чу) *pf*, **отмеча́ть** *impf* mark, note; celebrate; ~**ся** sign one's name; sign out. **отме́тка** note; mark.

отмира́ть *impf of* **отмере́ть**

отмора́живать *impf*, **отморо́зить** (-о́жу) *pf* injure by frost-bite. **отморо́жение** frost-bite. **отморо́женный** frost-bitten.

отмо́ю *etc.*: *see* **отмы́ть**

отмыва́ть *impf*, **отмы́ть** (-мо́ю) *pf* wash clean; wash off; ~**ся** wash o.s. clean; come out.

отмыка́ть *impf of* **отомкну́ть**

отмы́чка master key.

отнести́ (-су́, -сёшь; -нёс, -ла́) *pf* (*impf* **относи́ть**) take; carry away; ascribe, attribute; ~**сь** *к*+*dat* treat; regard; apply to; concern, have to do with.

отнима́ть(ся *impf of* **отня́ть(ся**

относи́тельно *adv* relatively; *prep* +*gen* concerning. **относи́тельность** relativity. **относи́тельный** relative. **относи́ть(ся** (-ошу́(сь, -о́сишь(ся) *impf of* **отнести́(сь. отноше́ние** attitude; relation; respect; ratio; **в отноше́нии**+*gen*, **по отноше́нию к**+*dat* with regard to; **в прямо́м (обра́тном) отноше́нии** in direct (in-

verse) ratio.

отны́не *adv* henceforth.

отню́дь not at all.

отня́тие taking away; amputation. **отня́ть** (-ниму́, -ни́мешь; о́тнял, -а, -о) *pf* (*impf* **отнима́ть**) take (away); amputate; ~ **от груди́** wean; ~**ся** be paralysed.

ото: *see* **от**

отобража́ть *impf*, **отобрази́ть** (-ажу́) *pf* reflect; represent. **отображе́ние** reflection; representation.

отобра́ть (отберу́, -рёшь; отобра́л, -а́, -о) *pf* (*impf* **отбира́ть**) take (away); select.

отобью́ *etc.*: *see* **отби́ть**

отовсю́ду *adv* from everywhere.

отогна́ть (отгоню́, -о́нишь; отогна́л, -а́, -о) *pf* (*impf* **отгоня́ть**) drive away, off.

отогну́ть (-ну́, -нёшь) *pf* (*impf* **отгиба́ть**) bend back; ~**ся** bend.

отогрева́ть *impf*, **отогре́ть** (-е́ю) *pf* warm.

отодвига́ть *impf*, **отодви́нуть** (-ну) *pf* move aside; put off.

отодра́ть (отдеру́, -рёшь; отодра́л, -а́, -о) *pf* (*impf* **отдира́ть**) tear off, rip off.

отож(д)естви́ть (-влю́) *pf*, **отож(д)ествля́ть** *impf* identify.

отозва́ть (отзову́, -вёшь; отозва́л, -а́, -о)*pf* (*impf* **отзыва́ть**) take aside; recall; ~**ся** *на*+*acc* answer; *на*+*acc or prep* tell on; have an affect on.

отойти́ (-йду́, -йдёшь; отошёл, -шла́) *pf* (*impf* **отходи́ть**) move away; depart; withdraw; digress; come out; recover.

отолью́ *etc.*: *see* **отли́ть. отомрёт** *etc.*: *see* **отмере́ть. ото|мсти́ть** (-мщу́) *pf*.

отомкну́ть (-ну́, -нёшь) *pf* (*impf* **отмыка́ть**) unlock, unbolt.

отопи́тельный heating. **отопи́ть** (-плю́, -пишь) *pf* (*impf* **ота́пливать**) heat. **отопле́ние** heating.

отопру́ *etc.*: *see* **отпере́ть. отопью́** *etc.*: *see* **отпи́ть**

ото́рванный cut off, isolated. **оторва́ть** (-ву́, -вёшь) *pf* (*impf* **отрыва́ть**) tear off; tear away; ~**ся** come off, be torn off; be cut off, lose touch; break away; tear o.s. away; ~**ся от земли́** take off.

оторопе́ть (-е́ю) *pf* be struck dumb.

отосла́ть (-ошлю́, -ошлёшь) *pf* (*impf* **отсыла́ть**) send (off); send back; **+к**+*dat* refer to.

отоспа́ться (-сплю́сь; -а́лся, -ала́сь, -ось) *pf* (*impf* **отсыпа́ться**) catch up on one's sleep.

отошёл *etc.*: *see* **отойти́. отошлю́** *etc.*: *see* **отосла́ть**

отпада́ть *impf of* **отпа́сть**.

от|пари́ровать *pf.* **отпа́рывать** *impf of* **отпоро́ть**

отпа́сть (-адёт) *pf* (*impf* **отпада́ть**) fall off; fall away; pass.

отпева́ние funeral service.

отпере́ть (отопру́, -прёшь; о́тпер, -ла́, -ло) *pf* (*impf* **отпира́ть**) unlock; **~ся** open; **+от**+*gen* deny; disown.

от|печа́тать *pf*, **отпеча́тывать** *impf* print (off); type (out); imprint. **отпеча́ток** (-тка) imprint, print.

отпива́ть *impf of* **отпи́ть**

отпи́ливать *impf*, **отпили́ть** (-лю́, -лишь) *pf* saw off.

от|пира́тельство denial. **отпира́ть(ся** *impf of* **отпере́ть(ся**

отпи́ть (отопью́, -пьёшь; о́тпил, -а́, -о) *pf* (*impf* **отпива́ть**) take a sip of.

отпи́хивать *impf*, **отпихну́ть** (-ну́, -нёшь) *pf* push off; shove aside.

отплати́ть (-ачу́, -а́тишь) *pf*, **отпла́чивать** *impf* +*dat* pay back.

отплыва́ть *impf*, **отплы́ть** (-ыву́, -ывёшь; -ы́л, -а́, -о) *pf* (set) sail; swim off. **отплы́тие** sailing, departure.

о́тповедь rebuke.

отполза́ть *impf*, **отползти́** (-зу́, -зёшь; -о́лз, -ла́) *pf* crawl away.

от|полирова́ть *pf.* **от|полоска́ть** (-ощу́) *pf.*

отпо́р repulse; rebuff.

отпоро́ть (-рю́, -решь) *pf* (*impf* **отпа́рывать**) rip off.

отправи́тель *m* sender. **отпра́вить** (-влю) *pf*, **отправля́ть** *impf* send, dispatch; **~ся** set off, start. **отпра́вка** dispatch. **отправле́ние** sending; departure; performance. **отправн|о́й**: **~о́й пункт**, **~а́я то́чка** starting-point.

от|пра́здновать *pf.*

отпра́шиваться *impf*, **отпроси́ться** (-ошу́сь, -о́сишься) *pf* ask for leave, get leave.

отпры́гивать *impf*, **отпры́гнуть** (-ну) *pf* jump *or* spring back *or* aside.

о́тпрыск offshoot, scion.

отпряга́ть *impf of* **отпря́чь**

отпря́нуть (-ну) *pf* recoil, start back.

отпря́чь (-ягу́, -яжёшь; -я́г, -ла́) (*impf* **отпряга́ть**) unharness.

отпу́гивать *impf*, **отпугну́ть** (-ну́, -нёшь) *pf* frighten off.

о́тпуск (*pl* -а́) leave, holiday(s). **отпуска́ть** *impf*, **отпусти́ть** (-ущу́, -у́стишь) *pf* let go, let off; set free; release; slacken; (let) grow; allot; re-mit. **отпускни́к** (-а́) person on leave. **отпускно́й** holiday; leave. **отпуще́ние** remission; **козёл отпуще́ния** scapegoat.

отраба́тывать *impf*, **отрабо́тать** *pf* work off; master. **отрабо́танный** worked out; waste, spent, exhaust.

отра́ва poison. **отрави́ть** (-влю́, -вишь) *pf*, **отравля́ть** *impf* poison.

отра́да joy, delight. **отра́дный** grati-fying, pleasing.

отража́тель *m* reflector; scanner. **отража́ть** *impf*, **отрази́ть** (-ажу́) *pf* reflect; repulse; **~ся** be reflected; **+на**+*prep* affect. **отраже́ние** reflec-tion; repulse.

о́трасль branch.

отраста́ть *impf*, **отрасти́** (-тёт; отро́с, -ла́) *pf* grow. **отрасти́ть** (-ащу́) *pf*, **отра́щивать** *impf* (let) grow.

от|реаги́ровать *pf.* **от|регули́-ровать** *pf.* **от|редакти́ровать** *pf.*

отре́з cut; length. **отреза́ть** (-е́жу) *pf*, **отреза́ть** *impf* cut off; snap.

о|трезве́ть (-е́ю) *pf.* **отрезви́ть** (-влю́, -ви́шь) *pf*, **отрезвля́ть** *impf* sober; **~ся** sober up.

отре́зок (-зка) piece; section; seg-ment.

отрека́ться *impf of* **отре́чься**

от|рекомендова́ть(ся *pf.* **отрёкся** *etc.*: *see* **отре́чься. от|ремонти́-ровать** *pf.* **от|репети́ровать** *pf.*

отре́пье, отре́пья (-ьев) *pl* rags.

от|реставри́ровать *pf.*

отрече́ние renunciation; **~ от пре-сто́ла** abdication. **отре́чься** (-еку́сь, -ечёшься) *pf* (*impf* **отрека́ться**) re-nounce.

отреша́ться *impf*, **отреши́ться** (-шу́сь) *pf* renounce; get rid of.

отрица́ние denial; negation. **отри-ца́тельный** negative. **отрица́ть** *impf* deny.

отро́с *etc.*: *see* **отрасти́. отро́сток** (-тка) shoot, sprout; appendix.

о́трочество adolescence.

отруба́ть *impf of* **отруби́ть**

о́труби (-е́й) *pl* bran.

отруби́ть (-блю́, -бишь) *pf* (*impf* **отруба́ть**) chop off; snap back.

от|руга́ть *pf.*

отры́в tearing off; alienation, isolation; **в ~е от**+*gen* out of touch with; **~ (от земли́)** take-off. **отрыва́ть(ся** *impf of* **оторва́ть(ся. отры́вистый** staccato; disjointed. **отрывно́й** tear-off. **отры́вок** (-вка) fragment, excerpt. **отры́вочный** fragmentary, scrappy.

отры́жка belch; throw-back.

от|ры́ть (-ро́ю) *pf.*

отря́д detachment; order.

отря́хивать *impf*, **отряхну́ть** (-ну́, -нёшь) *pf* shake down *or* off.

от|салютова́ть *pf.*

отса́сывание suction. **отса́сывать** *impf of* **отсоса́ть**

отсве́чивать *impf* be reflected; +*instr* shine with.

отсе́в sifting, selection; dropping out. **отсева́ть(ся, отсе́ивать(ся** *impf of* **отсе́ять(ся**

отсе́к compartment. **отсека́ть** *impf*, **отсе́чь** (-еку́, -ечёшь; -сёк, -ла́) *pf* chop off.

отсе́ять (-е́ю) *pf* (*impf* **отсева́ть, отсе́ивать**) sift, screen; eliminate; **~ся** drop out.

отсиде́ть (-ижу́) *pf*, **отси́живать** *impf* make numb by sitting; sit through; serve out.

отска́кивать *impf*, **отскочи́ть** (-чу́, -чишь) *pf* jump aside *or* away; rebound; come off.

отслу́живать *impf*, **отслужи́ть** (-жу́, -жишь) *pf* serve one's time; be worn out.

отсоса́ть (-осу́, -осёшь) *pf* (*impf* **отса́сывать**) suck off, draw off.

отсо́хнуть (-ну) *pf* (*impf* **отсыха́ть**) wither.

отсро́чивать *impf*, **отсро́чить** *pf* postpone, defer. **отсро́чка** postponement; deferment.

отстава́ние lag; lagging behind. **отстава́ть** (-таю́, -аёшь) *impf of* **отста́ть**

отста́вить (-влю) *pf*, **отставля́ть** *impf* set *or* put aside. **отста́вка** resignation; retirement; **в отста́вке** retired; **вы́йти в отста́вку** resign, retire. **отставно́й** retired.

отста́ивать(ся *impf of* **отстоя́ть(ся**

отста́лость backwardness. **отста́лый** backward. **отста́ть** (-а́ну) *pf* (*impf* **отстава́ть**) fall behind; lag behind; become detached; lose touch; break (off); be slow. **отстаю́щий** *sb* backward pupil.

от|стега́ть *pf.*

отстёгивать *impf*, **отстегну́ть** (-ну́, -нёшь) *pf* unfasten, undo; **~ся** come unfastened *or* undone.

отстоя́ть[1] (-ою́) *pf* (*impf* **отста́ивать**) defend; stand up for.

отстоя́ть[2] (-ои́т) *impf* **на**+*acc* be ... distant (**от**+*gen* from). **отстоя́ться** *pf* (*impf* **отста́иваться**) settle; become stabilized.

отстра́ивать(ся *impf of* **отстро́ить(ся**

отстране́ние pushing aside; dismissal. **отстрани́ть** *pf*, **отстраня́ть** *impf* push aside; remove; suspend; **~ся** move away; keep aloof; **~ся от** dodge.

отстре́ливаться *impf*, **отстре́ля́ться** *pf* fire back.

отстрига́ть *impf*, **отстри́чь** (-игу́, -ижёшь; -ри́г) *pf* cut off.

отстро́ить *pf* (*impf* **отстра́ивать**) finish building; build up.

отступа́ть *impf*, **отступи́ть** (-плю́, -пишь) *pf* step back; recede; retreat; back down; **~ от**+*gen* give up; deviate from; **~ся от**+*gen* give up; go back on. **отступле́ние** retreat; deviation; digression. **отступн|о́й**: **~ые де́ньги, ~о́е** *sb* indemnity, compensation. **отступя́** *adv* (farther) off, away (**от**+*gen* from).

отсу́тствие absence; lack. **отсу́тствовать** *impf* be absent. **отсу́тствующий** absent; *sb* absentee.

отсчита́ть *pf*, **отсчи́тывать** *impf* count off.

отсыла́ть *impf of* **отосла́ть**

отсы́пать (-плю) *pf*, **отсыпа́ть** *impf* pour out; measure off.

отсыпа́ться *impf of* **отоспа́ться**

отсыре́лый damp. **от|сыре́ть** (-е́ет) *pf.*

отсыха́ть *impf of* **отсо́хнуть**

отсю́да *adv* from here; hence.

отта́ивать *impf of* **отта́ять**

отта́лкивать *impf of* **оттолкну́ть**.
отта́лкивающий repulsive, repellent.

отта́чивать *impf of* **отточи́ть**

отта́ять (-а́ю) *pf* (*impf* **отта́ивать**) thaw out.

отте́нок (-нка) shade, nuance; tint.

о́ттепель thaw.

оттесни́ть *pf*, **оттесня́ть** *impf* drive back; push aside.

о́ттиск impression; off-print, reprint.

оттого́ *adv* that is why; ~, **что** because.

оттолкну́ть (-ну́, -нёшь) *pf* (*impf* **отта́лкивать**) push away; antagonize; ~**ся** push off.

оттопы́ренный protruding. **оттопы́ривать** *impf*, **оттопы́рить** *pf* stick out; ~**ся** protrude; bulge.

отточи́ть (-чу́, -чишь) *pf* (*impf* **отта́чивать**) sharpen.

оттуда *adv* from there.

оття́гивать *impf*, **оттяну́ть** (-ну́, -нешь) *pf* draw out; draw off; delay. **оття́жка** delay.

отупе́ние stupefaction. **о|тупе́ть** (-е́ю) *pf* sink into torpor.

от|утю́жить (-жу) *pf*.

отуча́ть *impf*, **отучи́ть** (-чу́, -чишь) *pf* break (of); ~**ся** break o.s. (of).

отха́ркать *pf*, **отха́ркивать** *impf* expectorate.

отхвати́ть (-чу́, -тишь) *pf*, **отхва́тывать** *impf* snip *or* chop off.

отхлебну́ть (-ну́, -нёшь) *pf*, **отхлёбывать** *impf* sip, take a sip of.

отхлы́нуть (-нет) *pf* flood *or* rush back.

отхо́д departure; withdrawal. **отходи́ть** (-ожу́, -о́дишь) *impf of* **отойти́**. **отхо́ды** (-ов) *pl* waste.

отцвести́ (-ету́, -етёшь; -ёл, -а́) *pf*, **отцвета́ть** *impf* finish blossoming, fade.

отцепи́ть (-плю́, -пишь) *pf*, **отцепля́ть** *impf* unhook; uncouple.

отцо́вский father's; paternal.

отча́иваться *impf of* **отча́яться**

отча́ливать *impf*, **отча́лить** *pf* cast off.

отча́сти *adv* partly.

отча́яние despair. **отча́янный** desperate. **отча́яться** (-а́юсь) *pf* (*impf* **отча́иваться**) despair.

отчего́ *adv* why. **отчего́-либо, -нибу́дь** *adv* for some reason or other. **отчего́-то** *adv* for some reason.

от|чека́нить *pf*.

о́тчество patronymic.

отчёт account; **отда́ть себе́ ~ в**+*prep* be aware of, realize. **отчётливый** distinct; clear. **отчётность** bookkeeping; accounts. **отчётный** *adj*: ~ **год** financial year, current year; ~ **докла́д** report.

отчи́зна native land. **о́тчий** paternal. **о́тчим** step-father.

отчисле́ние deduction; dismissal. **отчи́слить** *pf*, **отчисля́ть** *impf* deduct; dismiss.

отчита́ть *pf*, **отчи́тывать** *impf* tell off; ~**ся** report back.

отчужде́ние alienation; estrangement.

отшатну́ться (-ну́сь, -нёшься) *pf*, **отша́тываться** *impf* start back, recoil; +**от**+*gen* give up, forsake.

отшвы́ривать *impf*, **отшвырну́ть** (-ну́, -нёшь) *pf* fling away; throw off.

отше́льник hermit; recluse.

отшлёпать *pf* spank.

от|шлифова́ть *pf*. **от|штукату́рить** *pf*.

отщепе́нец (-нца) renegade.

отъе́зд departure. **отъезжа́ть** *impf*, **отъе́хать** (-е́ду) *pf* drive off, go off.

отъя́вленный inveterate.

отыгра́ть *pf*, **оты́грывать** *impf* win back; ~**ся** win back what one has lost.

отыска́ть (-ыщу́, -ы́щешь) *pf*, **оты́скивать** *impf* find; look for; ~**ся** turn up, appear.

отяготи́ть (-ощу́) *pf*, **отягоща́ть** *impf* burden.

офице́р officer. **офице́рский** officer's, officers'.

официа́льный official.

официа́нт waiter. **официа́нтка** waitress.

официо́з semi-official organ. **официо́зный** semi-official.

оформи́тель *m* designer; stagepainter. **офо́рмить** (-млю) *pf*, **оформля́ть** *impf* design; put into shape; make official; process; ~**ся** take shape; go through the formalities. **оформле́ние** design; mount-

ing, staging; processing.
ох *int* oh! ah!
оха́пка armful.
о|характеризова́ть *pf.*
о́хать *impf* (*pf* **о́хнуть**) moan; sigh.
охва́т scope; inclusion; outflanking.
охвати́ть (-ачу́, -а́тишь) *pf*, **охва́-**
тывать *impf* envelop; seize; comprehend.
охладева́ть *impf*, **охладе́ть** (-е́ю)
pf grow cold. **охлади́ть** (-ажу́) *pf*,
охлажда́ть *impf* cool; ~**ся** become
cool, cool down. **охлажде́ние** cooling; coolness.
о|хмеле́ть (-е́ю) *pf*. **о́хнуть** (-ну) *pf*
of **о́хать**
охо́та[1] hunt, hunting; chase.
охо́та[2] wish, desire.
охо́титься (-о́чусь) *impf* hunt. **охо́т-**
ник[1] hunter.
охо́тник[2] volunteer; enthusiast.
охо́тничий hunting.
охо́тно *adv* willingly, gladly.
о́хра ochre.
охра́на guarding; protection; guard.
охрани́ть *pf*, **охраня́ть** *impf* guard,
protect.
охри́плый, **охри́пший** hoarse.
о|хри́пнуть (-ну; охри́п) *pf* become
hoarse.
о|цара́пать(ся *pf.*
оце́нивать *impf*, **оцени́ть** (-ню́, -нишь)
pf estimate; appraise. **оце́нка** estimation; appraisal; estimate. **оце́н-**
щик valuer.
о|цепене́ть (-е́ю) *pf.*
оцепи́ть (-плю́, -пишь) *pf*, **оцепля́ть**
impf surround; cordon off.
оча́г (-а́) hearth; centre; breeding
ground; hotbed.
очарова́ние charm, fascination. **оча-**
рова́тельный charming. **очаро-**
ва́ть *pf*, **очаро́вывать** *impf* charm,
fascinate.
очеви́дец (-дца) eye-witness. **оче-**
ви́дно *adv* obviously, evidently.
очеви́дный obvious.
о́чень *adv* very; very much.
очередно́й next in turn; usual, regular; routine. **о́чередь** (*gen pl* -е́й)
turn; queue.
о́черк essay, sketch.
о|черни́ть *pf.*
о|черстве́ть (-е́ю) *pf.*
очерта́ние outline(s), contour(s).

очерти́ть (-рчу́, -ртишь) *pf*, **очер-**
чивать *impf* outline.
о́чи *etc.: see* **о́ко**
очисти́тельный cleansing. **о|чи́-**
стить (-и́щу) *pf*, **очища́ть** *impf*
clean; refine; peel; clear; ~**ся**
o.s.; become clear (**от**+*gen* of).
очи́стка cleaning; purification; clearance. **очи́стки** (-ов) *pl* peelings.
очище́ние cleansing; purification.
очки́ (-о́в) *pl* spectacles. **очко́** (*gen*
pl -о́в) pip; point. **очко́вая змея́** cobra.
очну́ться (-ну́сь, -нёшься) *pf* wake
up; regain consciousness.
о́чн|ый: ~**ое обуче́ние** classroom instruction; ~**ая ста́вка** confrontation.
очути́ться (-у́тишься) *pf* find o.s.
оше́йник collar.
ошеломи́тельный stunning. **ошело-**
ми́ть (-млю́) *pf*, **ошеломля́ть**
impf stun.
ошиба́ться *impf*, **ошиби́ться** (-бу́сь,
-бёшься; -и́бся) *pf* be mistaken, make
a mistake; be wrong. **оши́бка** mistake; error. **оши́бочный** erroneous.
ошпа́ривать *impf*, **о|шпа́рить** *pf*
scald.
о|штрафова́ть *pf.* **о|штукату́рить**
pf.
ощети́ниваться *impf*, **о|щети́-**
ниться *pf* bristle (up).
о|щипа́ть (-плю́, -плешь) *pf*, **ощи-**
пывать *impf* pluck.
ощу́пать, **ощу́пывать** *impf* feel;
grope about. **о́щупь: на** ~ to the
touch; by touch. **о́щупью** *adv* gropingly; by touch.
ощути́мый, **ощути́тельный** perceptible; appreciable. **ощути́ть** (-ущу́)
pf, **ощуща́ть** *impf* feel, sense. **ощу-**
ще́ние sensation; feeling.

П

па *neut indecl* dance step.
павильо́н pavilion; film studio.
павли́н peacock.
па́водок (-дка) (sudden) flood.
па́вший fallen.
па́губный pernicious, ruinous.
па́даль carrion.
па́дать *impf* (*pf* **пасть**, **упа́сть**) fall;
~ **ду́хом** lose heart. **паде́ж** (-а́) case.

паде́ние fall; degradation; incidence.

па́дкий на+*acc or* до+*gen* having a weakness for.

па́дчерица step-daughter.

паёк (пайка́) ration.

па́зуха bosom; sinus; axil.

пай (*pl* -и́, -ёв) share. па́йщик shareholder.

паке́т package; packet; paper bag.

Пакиста́н Pakistan. пакиста́нец (-нца), -а́нка Pakistani. пакиста́нский Pakistani.

па́кля tow; oakum.

пакова́ть *impf* (*pf* за~, у~) pack.

па́костный dirty, mean. па́кость dirty trick; obscenity.

пакт pact.

пала́та chamber, house. пала́тка tent; stall, booth.

пала́ч (-а́) executioner.

па́лец (-льца) finger; toe.

палиса́дник (*small*) front garden.

палиса́ндр rosewood.

пали́тра palette.

пали́ть[1] *impf* (*pf* о~, с~) burn; scorch.

пали́ть[2] *impf* (*pf* вы́~, пальну́ть) fire, shoot.

па́лка stick; walking-stick.

пало́мник pilgrim. пало́мничество pilgrimage.

па́лочка stick; bacillus; wand; baton.

па́луба deck.

пальба́ fire.

па́льма palm(-tree). па́льмовый palm.

пальну́ть (-ну́, -нёшь) *pf of* пали́ть

пальто́ *neut indecl* (over)coat.

паля́щий burning, scorching.

па́мятник monument; memorial. па́мятный memorable; memorial. па́мять memory; consciousness; на ~ as a keepsake.

панаце́я panacea.

пане́ль footpath; panel(ling); wainscot(ing). пане́льный panelling.

па́ника panic. паникёр alarmist.

панихи́да requiem.

пани́ческий panic; panicky.

панно́ *neut indecl* panel.

панора́ма panorama.

пансио́н boarding-house; board and lodging. пансиона́т holiday hotel. пансионе́р boarder; guest.

пантало́ны (-о́н) *pl* knickers.

панте́ра panther.

пантоми́ма mime.

па́нцирь *m* armour, coat of mail.

па́па[1] *m* pope.

па́па[2] *m*, папа́ша *m* daddy.

папа́ха tall fur cap.

папиро́са (*Russian*) cigarette.

па́пка file; folder.

па́поротник fern.

пар[1] (*loc* -у́; *pl* -ы́) steam.

пар[2] (*loc* -у́; *pl* -ы́) fallow.

па́ра pair; couple; (two-piece) suit.

пара́граф paragraph.

пара́д parade; review. пара́дн|ый parade; gala; main, front; ~ая фо́рма full dress (uniform).

парадо́кс paradox. парадокса́льный paradoxical.

парази́т parasite.

парализова́ть *impf & pf* paralyse. парали́ч (-а́) paralysis.

паралле́ль parallel. паралле́льный parallel.

пара́метр parameter.

парано́йя paranoia.

парашю́т parachute.

паре́ние soaring.

па́рень (-рня; *gen pl* -рней) *m* lad; fellow.

пари́ *neut indecl* bet; держа́ть ~ bet, lay a bet.

пари́к (-а́) wig. парикма́хер hairdresser. парикма́херская *sb* hairdresser's.

пари́ровать *impf & pf* (*pf also* от~) parry, counter.

парите́т parity.

пари́ть[1] *impf* soar, hover.

па́рить[2] *impf* steam; stew; *impers* па́рит it is sultry; ~ся (*pf* по~ся) steam, sweat; stew.

парк park; depot; stock.

парке́т parquet.

парла́мент parliament. парламента́рный parliamentarian. парламентёр envoy; bearer of flag of truce. парла́ментский parliamentary; ~ зако́н Act of Parliament.

парни́к (-а́) hotbed; seed-bed. парнико́в|ый *adj*: ~ые расте́ния hothouse plants.

парни́шка *m* boy, lad.

парно́й fresh; steamy.

па́рный (forming a) pair; twin.

паро- *in comb* steam-. парово́з

(steam-)engine, locomotive. **~обра́зный** vaporous. **~ход** steamer; steamship. **~хо́дство** steamship-line.
парово́й steam; steamed.
паро́дия parody.
паро́ль *m* password.
паро́м ferry(-boat).
парт- *abbr in comb* Party. **партбиле́т** Party (membership) card. **~ком** Party committee. **~организа́ция** Party organization.
па́рта (*school*) desk.
партёр stalls; pit.
партиза́н (*gen pl* -а́н) partisan; guerilla. **партиза́нский** partisan, guerilla; unplanned.
парти́йный party; Party; *sb* Party member.
партиту́ра (*mus*) score.
па́ртия party; group; batch; game, set; part.
партнёр partner.
па́рус (*pl* -а́, -о́в) sail. **паруси́на** canvas. **па́русник** sailing vessel. **па́русный** sail; ~ **спорт** sailing.
парфюме́рия perfumes.
парча́ (*gen pl* -е́й) brocade. **парчо́вый** brocade.
па́сека apiary, beehive.
пасётся *see* **пасти́сь**
па́сквиль *m* lampoon; libel.
па́смурный overcast; gloomy.
па́спорт (*pl* -а́) passport.
пасса́ж passage; arcade.
пассажи́р passenger.
пасси́вный passive.
па́ста paste.
па́стбище pasture.
па́ства flock.
пасте́ль pastel.
пастерна́к parsnip.
пасти́ (-су́, -сёшь; пас, -ла́) *impf* graze; tend.
пасти́сь (-сётся; па́сся, -ла́сь) *impf* graze. **пасту́х** (-а́) shepherd. **па́стырь** *m* pastor.
пасть[1] mouth; jaws.
пасть[2] (паду́, -дёшь; пал) *pf of* **па́дать**
Па́сха Easter; Passover.
па́сынок (-нка) stepson, stepchild.
пат stalemate.
пате́нт patent.
патети́ческий passionate.
па́тока treacle; syrup.

патоло́гия pathology.
патриа́рх patriarch.
патрио́т patriot. **патриоти́зм** patriotism. **патриоти́ческий** patriotic.
патро́н cartridge; chuck; lamp-socket.
патру́ль (-я́) *m* patrol.
па́уза pause; (*also mus*) rest.
пау́к (-а́) spider. **паути́на** cobweb; gossamer; web.
па́фос zeal, enthusiasm.
пах (*loc* -ý) groin.
па́харь *m* ploughman. **паха́ть** (пашу́, па́шешь) *impf* (*pf* вс~) plough.
па́хнуть[1] (-ну; пах) *impf* smell (+*instr* of).
пахну́ть[2] (-нёт) *pf* puff, blow.
па́хота ploughing. **па́хотный** arable.
паху́чий odorous, strong-smelling.
пацие́нт, ~ка patient.
пацифи́зм pacifism. **пацифи́ст** pacifist.
па́чка bundle; packet, pack; tutu.
па́чкать *impf* (*pf* за~, ис~) dirty, soil, stain.
пашу́ *etc.: see* **паха́ть. па́шня** (*gen pl* -шен) ploughed field.
паште́т pâté.
пая́льная ла́мпа blow-lamp. **пая́льник** soldering iron. **пая́ть** (-я́ю) *impf* solder.
пая́ц clown, buffoon.
певе́ц (-вца́), **певи́ца** singer. **певу́чий** melodious. **пе́вчий** singing; *sb* chorister.
пе́гий piebald.
педаго́г teacher; pedagogue. **педаго́гика** pedagogy. **педагоги́ческий** pedagogical; educational; ~ **институ́т** (teachers') training college.
педа́ль pedal.
педиа́тр paediatrician. **педиатри́ческий** paediatric.
пейза́ж landscape; scenery.
пёк *see* **печь. пека́рный** baking. **пека́рня** (*gen pl* -рен) bakery. **пе́карь** (*pl* -я, -е́й) *m* baker. **пе́кло** scorching heat; hell-fire. **пеку́** *etc.: see* **печь**
пелена́ (*gen pl* -лён) shroud. **пелена́ть** *impf* (*pf* за~) swaddle; put a nappy on.
пе́ленг bearing. **пеленгова́ть** *impf* & *pf* take the bearings of.
пелёнка nappy.
пельме́нь *m* meat dumpling.

пе́на foam; scum; froth.

пена́л pencil-case.

пе́ние singing.

пе́нистый foamy; frothy. **пе́ниться** *impf* (*pf* вс~) foam.

пе́нка skin. **пенопла́ст** plastic foam.

пеницилли́н penicillin.

пенсионе́р pensioner. **пенсио́нный** pensionable. **пе́нсия** pension.

пень (пня) *m* stump, stub.

пенька́ hemp.

пе́пел (-пла) ash, ashes. **пе́пельница** ashtray.

перве́йший the first; first-class. **пе́рвенец** (-нца) first-born. **пе́рвенство** first place; championship. **пе́рвенствовать** *impf* take first place; take priority. **перви́чный** primary.

перво- *in comb* first; prime. **~бы́тный** primitive; primeval. **~исто́чник** source; origin. **~кла́ссный** first-class. **~ку́рсник** first-year student. **~нача́льный** original; primary. **~со́ртный** best-quality; first-class. **~степе́нный** paramount.

пе́рвое *sb* first course. **пе́рвый** first; former.

перга́мент parchment.

перебега́ть *impf*, **перебежа́ть** (-бегу́) *pf* cross, run across; desert. **перебе́жчик** deserter; turncoat.

переберу́ *etc.*: *see* перебра́ть

перебива́ть(ся *impf of* переби́ть(ся **перебира́ть(ся** *impf of* перебра́ть(ся

переби́ть (-бью́, -бьёшь) *pf* (*impf* перебива́ть) interrupt; slaughter; beat; break; re-upholster; **~ся** break; make ends meet. **перебо́й** interruption; stoppage; irregularity.

перебо́рка sorting out; partition; bulkhead.

перебоpо́ть (-рю́, -решь) *pf* overcome.

переборщи́ть (-щу́) *pf* go too far; overdo it.

перебра́сывать(ся *impf of* переброси́ть(ся

перебра́ть (-беру́, -берёшь; -а́л, -а́, -о) *pf* (*impf* перебира́ть) sort out; look through; turn over in one's mind; finger; **~ся** get over, cross; move.

перебро́сить (-о́шу) *pf* (*impf* пере-

бра́сывать) throw over; transfer; **~ся** fling o.s.; spread. **перебро́ска** transfer.

перебью́ *etc.*: *see* переби́ть

перева́л crossing; pass. **перева́ливать** *impf*, **перевали́ть** (-лю́, -лишь) *pf* transfer, shift; cross, pass.

перева́ривать *impf*, **перевари́ть** (-рю́, -ришь) *pf* reheat; overcook; digest; tolerate.

переведу́ *etc.*: *see* перевести́

перевезти́ (-зу́, -зёшь; -вёз, -ла́) *pf* (*impf* перевози́ть) take across; transport; (re)move.

переверну́ть (-ну́, -нёшь) *pf*, **переве́ртывать** *impf* (*impf also* перевора́чивать) turn (over); upset; turn inside out; **~ся** turn (over).

переве́с preponderance; advantage. **переве́сить** (-е́шу) *pf* (*impf* переве́шивать) re-weigh; outweigh; tip the scales; hang elsewhere.

перевести́ (-веду́, -ведёшь; -вёл, -а́) *pf* (*impf* переводи́ть) take across; transfer, move, shift; translate; convert; **~сь** be transferred; run out; become extinct.

переве́шивать *impf of* переве́сить. **перевира́ть** *impf of* перевра́ть

перево́д transfer, move, shift; translation; conversion; waste. **переводи́ть(ся** (-ожу́(сь, -о́дишь(ся *impf of* перевести́(сь. **переводн|о́й**: **~а́я бума́га** carbon paper; **~а́я карти́нка** transfer. **перево́дный** transfer; translated. **перево́дчик, ~ица** translator; interpreter.

перево́з transporting; ferry. **перевози́ть** (-ожу́, -о́зишь) *impf of* перевезти́. **перево́зка** conveyance. **перево́зчик** ferryman; removal man.

перевооружа́ть *impf*, **перевооружи́ть** (-жу́) *pf* rearm; **~ся** rearm. **перевооруже́ние** rearmament.

перевоплоти́ть (-лощу́) *pf*, **перевоплоща́ть** *impf* reincarnate; **~ся** be reincarnated. **перевоплоще́ние** reincarnation.

перевора́чивать(ся *impf of* переверну́ть(ся. **переворо́т** revolution; overturn; cataclysm; **госуда́рственный ~** coup d'état.

перевоспита́ние re-education. **перевоспита́ть** *pf*, **перевоспи́тывать**

impf re-educate.
перевра́ть (-ру́, -рёшь; -а́л, -а́, -о) *pf*
(*impf* **перевира́ть**) garble; misquote.
перевыполне́ние over-fulfilment.
перевы́полнить *pf,* **перевыпол-
ня́ть** *impf* over-fulfil.
перевяза́ть (-яжу́, -я́жешь) *pf,* **пере-
вя́зывать** *impf* bandage; tie up; re-
tie. **перевя́зка** dressing, bandage.
переги́б bend; excess, extreme.
перегиба́ть(ся *impf of* **пере-
гну́ть(ся**
перегля́дываться *impf,* **пере-
гляну́ться** (-ну́сь, -нешься) *pf* exchange glances.
перегна́ть (-гоню́, -го́нишь; -а́л, -а́,
-о) *pf* (*impf* **перегоня́ть**) outdis-
tance; surpass; drive; distil.
перегно́й humus.
перегну́ть (-ну́, -нёшь) *pf* (*impf*
перегиба́ть) bend; ~ па́лку go too
far; ~ся bend; lean over.
перегова́ривать *impf,* **перегово-
ри́ть** *pf* talk; out-talk; ~ся (c+*instr*)
exchange remarks (with). **пере-
гово́ры** (-ов) *pl* negotiations, par-
ley. **перегово́рный** *adj:* ~ пункт
public call-boxes; trunk-call office.
перего́н driving; stage. **перего́нка**
distillation. **перего́нный** distilling,
distillation. **перегоню́** *etc.: see* **пере-
гна́ть**. **перегоня́ть** *impf of* **пере-
гна́ть**
перегора́живать *impf of* **пере-
городи́ть**
перегора́ть *impf,* **перегоре́ть** (-ри́т)
pf burn out, fuse.
перегороди́ть (-рожу́, -ро́дишь) *pf*
(*impf* **перегора́живать**) partition
off; block. **перегоро́дка** partition.
перегре́в overheating. **перегрева́ть**
impf, **перегре́ть** (-е́ю) *pf* overheat;
~ся overheat.
перегружа́ть *impf,* **перегрузи́ть**
(-ужу́, -у́зишь) *pf* overload; transfer.
перегру́зка overload; transfer.
перегрыза́ть *impf,* **перегры́зть**
(-зу́, -зёшь; -гры́з) *pf* gnaw through.
пе́ред, пе́редо, пред, пре́до
prep+*instr* before; in front of; compared to. **перёд** (пе́реда; *pl* -а́)
front, forepart.
передава́ть (-даю́, -даёшь) *impf,*
переда́ть (-а́м, -а́шь, -а́ст, -ади́м;
пе́редал, -а́, -о) *pf* pass, hand, hand

over; transfer; hand down; make
over; tell; communicate; convey; give
too much; ~ся pass; be transmitted;
be communicated; be inherited.
переда́тчик transmitter. **переда́ча**
passing; transmission; communication; transfer; broadcast; drive; gear,
gearing.
передвига́ть *impf,* **передви́нуть**
(-ну) *pf* move, shift; ~ся move, shift.
передвиже́ние movement; transportation. **передви́жка** movement;
in comb travelling; itinerant. **пере-
движно́й** movable, mobile.
переде́лать *pf,* **переде́лывать**
impf alter; refashion. **переде́лка** alteration.
передёргивать(ся *impf of* **передёр-
нуть(ся**
передержа́ть (-жу́, -жишь) *pf,* **пере-
де́рживать** *impf* overdo; overcook;
overexpose.
передёрнуть (-ну) *pf* (*impf* **пере-
дёргивать**) pull aside *or* across;
cheat; distort; ~ся wince.
пере́дний front; ~ план foreground.
пере́дник apron. **пере́дняя** *sb* (entrance) hall, lobby. **пе́редо:** *see*
пе́ред. передови́к (-а́) exemplary
worker. **передови́ца** leading article.
передово́й advanced; foremost;
leading.
передохну́ть (-ну́, -нёшь) *pf* pause
for breath.
передра́знивать *impf,* **передраз-
ни́ть** (-ню́, -нишь) *pf* mimic.
переду́мать *pf,* **переду́мывать**
impf change one's mind.
переды́шка respite.
перее́зд crossing; move. **переез-
жа́ть** *impf,* **перее́хать** (-е́ду) *pf*
cross; run over, knock down; move
(house).
пережа́ривать *impf,* **пережа́рить**
pf overdo, overcook.
пережда́ть (-жду́, -ждёшь; -а́л, -а́,
-о) *pf* (*impf* **пережида́ть**) wait for
the end of.
пережёвывать *impf* chew; repeat
over and over again.
пережива́ние experience. **пере-
жива́ть** *impf of* **пережи́ть**
пережида́ть *impf of* **пережда́ть**
пережито́е *sb* the past. **пережи́ток**
(-тка) survival; vestige. **пережи́ть**

(-иву́, -иве́шь; пе́режи́л, -а́, -о) *pf*
(*impf* **пережива́ть**) experience; go
through; endure; outlive.

перезаряди́ть (-яжу́, -яди́шь) *pf*,
перезаряжа́ть *impf* recharge, re-
load.

перезва́нивать *impf*, **перезвони́ть**
pf +*dat* ring back.

пере|зимова́ть *pf*.

перезре́лый overripe.

переигра́ть *pf*, **переи́грывать** *impf*
play again; overact.

переизбира́ть *impf*, **переизбра́ть**
(-беру́, -берёшь; -бра́л, -а́, -о) *pf* re-
elect. **переизбра́ние** re-election.

переиздава́ть (-даю́, -даёшь) *impf*,
переизда́ть (-а́м, -а́шь, -а́ст, -ади́м;
-а́л, -а́, -о) *pf* republish, reprint.
переизда́ние republication; new
edition.

переименова́ть *pf*, **переимено́вы-
вать** *impf* rename.

перейму́ *etc.*: see **переня́ть**

перейти́ (-йду́, -йдёшь; перешёл,
-шла́) *pf* (*impf* **переходи́ть**) cross;
pass; turn (**в**+*acc* to, into).

перекантова́ть *pf* transfer (*a load*).

перека́пывать *impf of* **перекопа́ть**

перекати́ть (-чу́, -тишь) *pf*, **пере-
ка́тывать** *impf* roll; ~**ся** roll.

перекача́ть *pf*, **перека́чивать** *impf*
pump (across).

переквалифици́роваться *impf* &
pf retrain.

переки́дывать *impf*, **переки́нуть**
(-ну) *pf* throw over; ~**ся** leap.

пе́рекись peroxide.

перекла́дина cross-beam; joist; horizontal bar.

перекла́дывать *impf of* **перело-
жи́ть**

перекли́чка roll-call.

переключа́тель *m* switch. **пере-
ключа́ть** *impf*, **переключи́ть** (-чу́)
pf switch (over). ~**ся** switch (over).

перекова́ть (-кую́, -куёшь) *pf*, **пере-
ко́вывать** *impf* re-shoe; re-forge.

перекопа́ть *pf* (*impf* **перека́пы-
вать**) dig (all of); dig again.

перекоси́ть (-ошу́, -о́сишь) *pf* warp;
distort; ~**ся** warp; become distorted.

перекочева́ть (-чу́ю) *pf*, **переко-
чёвывать** *impf* migrate.

переко́шенный distorted, twisted.

перекра́ивать *impf of* **перекро́йть**

перекра́сить (-а́шу) *pf*, **перекра́-
шивать** *impf* (re-)paint; (re-)dye;
~**ся** change colour; turn one's coat.

пере|крести́ть (-ещу́, -е́стишь) *pf*,
перекре́щивать *impf* cross; ~**ся**
cross, intersect; cross o.s. **пере-
кре́стн|ый** cross; ~**ый допро́с**
cross-examination; ~**ый ого́нь** cross-
fire; ~**ая ссы́лка** cross-reference.

перекрёсток (-тка) cross-roads,
crossing.

перекри́кивать *impf*, **перекрича́ть**
(-чу́) *pf* shout down.

перекро́йть (-о́ю) *pf* (*impf* **пере-
кра́ивать**) cut out again; reshape.

перекрыва́ть *impf*, **перекры́ть**
(-ро́ю) *pf* re-cover; exceed. **пере-
кры́тие** ceiling.

перекую́ *etc.*: see **перекова́ть**

перекупа́ть *impf*, **перекупи́ть**
(-плю́, -пишь) *pf* buy up; buy by out-
bidding s.o. **переку́пщик** second-
hand dealer.

перекуси́ть (-ушу́, -у́сишь) *pf*, **пере-
ку́сывать** *impf* bite through; have a
snack.

перелага́ть *impf of* **переложи́ть**

перела́мывать *impf of* **переломи́ть**

перелеза́ть *impf*, **переле́зть** (-зу;
-ёз) *pf* climb over.

переле́сок (-ска) copse.

перелёт migration; flight. **переле-
та́ть** *impf*, **перелете́ть** (-лечу́) *pf*
fly over. **перелётный** migratory.

перелива́ние decanting; transfusion.
перелива́ть *impf of* **перели́ть**.
перелива́ться *impf of* **перели́ться**;
gleam; modulate.

перелиста́ть *pf*, **перели́стывать**
impf leaf through.

перели́ть (-лью́, -льёшь; -и́л, -а́, -о)
pf (*impf* **перелива́ть**) pour; decant;
let overflow; transfuse. **перели́ться**
(-льётся; -ли́лся, -лила́сь, -ли́ло́сь)
pf (*impf* **перелива́ться**) flow; overflow.

перелицева́ть (-цу́ю) *pf*, **пере-
лицо́вывать** *impf* turn; have turned.

переложе́ние arrangement. **пере-
ложи́ть** (-жу́, -жишь) *pf* (*impf* **пере-
кла́дывать**, **перелага́ть**) put elsewhere; shift; transfer; interlay; put in
too much; set; arrange; transpose.

перело́м breaking; fracture; turning-
point; crisis; sudden change.

переломáть *pf* break; **~ся** break, be broken. **переломи́ть** (-млю́, -мишь) *pf* (*impf* **перелáмывать**) break in two; master. **перело́мный** critical.

перелью́ *etc.*: *see* **перели́ть**

перемáнивать *impf*, **перемани́ть** (-ню́, -нишь) *pf* win over; entice.

перемежáться *impf* alternate.

переме́на change; break. **перемени́ть** (-ню́, -нишь) *pf*, **переменя́ть** *impf* change; **~ся** change. **переме́нный** variable; **~ ток** alternating current. **переме́нчивый** changeable.

перемести́ть (-мещу́) *pf* (*impf* **перемещáть**) move; transfer; **~ся** move.

перемешáть *pf*, **переме́шивать** *impf* mix; mix up; shuffle; **~ся** get mixed (up).

перемещáть(ся *impf of* **перемести́ть(ся. перемеще́ние** transference; displacement. **перемещён|ый** displaced; **~ые ли́ца** displaced persons.

переми́рие armistice, truce.

перемывáть *impf*, **перемы́ть** (-мо́ю) *pf* wash (up) again.

перенапрягáть *impf*, **перенапря́чь** (-ягу́, -яжёшь: -я́г, -ла́) *pf* overstrain.

перенаселе́ние overpopulation. **перенаселённый** (-лён, -á) overpopulated; overcrowded.

перенести́ (-су́, -сёшь; -нёс, -ла́) *pf* (*impf* **переноси́ть**) carry, move, take; transfer; take over; postpone; endure, bear; **~сь** be carried; be carried away.

перенимáть *impf of* **переня́ть**

перено́с transfer; word division; **знак ~a** end-of-line hyphen. **переноси́мый** endurable. **переноси́ть(ся** (-ошу́(сь, -о́сишь(ся) *impf of* **перенести́(сь**

перено́сица bridge (*of the nose*).

перено́ска carrying over; transporting; carriage. **перено́сный** portable; figurative. **перено́счик** carrier.

пере|ночевáть (-чу́ю) *pf.* **переношу́** *etc.*: *see* **переноси́ть**

переня́ть (-ейму́, -еймёшь; пе́реня́л, -á, -о) *pf* (*impf* **перенимáть**) imitate; adopt.

переобору́довать *impf* & *pf* re-equip.

переобувáться *impf*, **переобу́ться** (-у́юсь, -у́ешься) *pf* change one's shoes.

переодевáться *impf*, **переоде́ться** (-е́нусь) *pf* change (one's clothes).

переосвиде́тельствовать *impf* & *pf* re-examine.

переоце́нивать *impf*, **переоцени́ть** (-ню́, -нишь) *pf* overestimate; revalue. **переоце́нка** overestimation; revaluation.

перепáчкать *pf* make dirty; **~ся** get dirty.

пе́репел (*pl* -á) quail.

перепеленáть *pf* change (*a baby*).

перепечáтать *pf*, **перепечáтывать** *impf* reprint. **перепечáтка** reprint.

перепи́ливать *impf*, **перепили́ть** (-лю́, -лишь) *pf* saw in two.

переписáть (-ишу́, -и́шешь) *pf*, **перепи́сывать** *impf* copy; re-write; make a list of. **перепи́ска** copying; correspondence. **перепи́сываться** *impf* correspond. **пе́репись** census.

переплáвить (-влю) *pf*, **переплавля́ть** *impf* smelt.

переплати́ть (-ачу́, -áтишь) *pf*, **переплáчивать** *impf* overpay.

переплести́ (-лету́, -летёшь; -лёл, -á) *pf*, **переплетáть** *impf* bind; interlace, intertwine; re-plait; **~ся** interlace, interweave; get mixed up. **переплёт** binding. **переплётчик** bookbinder.

переплывáть *impf*, **переплы́ть** (-ыву́, -ывёшь; -ы́л, -á, -о) *pf* swim *or* sail across.

переподгото́вка further training; refresher course.

переползáть *impf*, **переползти́** (-зу́, -зёшь; -о́лз, -ла́) *pf* crawl *or* creep across.

переполне́ние overfilling; overcrowding. **перепо́лненный** overcrowded; too full. **перепо́лнить** *pf*, **переполня́ть** *impf* overfill; overcrowd.

переполо́х commotion.

перепо́нка membrane; web.

переправа crossing; ford.

переправить (-влю) *pf*, **переправля́ть** *impf* convey; take across; forward; **~ся** cross, get across.

перепродавáть (-даю́, -даёшь) *impf*, **перепродáть** (-áм, -áшь, -áст, -адим; -про́дáл, -á, -о) *pf* re-sell. **перепродáжа** re-sale.

перепроизво́дство overproduction.

перепры́гивать *impf,* **перепры́гнуть** (-ну) *pf* jump (over).

перепуга́ть *pf* frighten, scare; ~**ся** get a fright.

пере|пу́тать *pf,* **перепу́тывать** *impf* tangle; confuse, mix up.

перепу́тье cross-roads.

перераба́тывать *impf,* **перерабо́тать** *pf* convert; treat; re-make; recast; process; work overtime; overwork; ~**ся** overwork. **перерабо́тка** processing; reworking; overtime work.

перераспределе́ние redistribution. **перераспредели́ть** *pf,* **перераспределя́ть** *impf* redistribute.

перераста́ние outgrowing; escalation; development (into). **перераста́ть** *impf,* **перерасти́** (-ту́, -тёшь; -ро́с, -ла́) *pf* outgrow; develop.

перерасхо́д over-expenditure; overdraft. **перерасхо́довать** *impf & pf* expend too much of.

перерасчёт recalculation.

перерва́ть (-ву́, -вёшь; -а́л, -а́, -о) *pf* (*impf* **перерыва́ть**) break, tear asunder; ~**ся** break, come apart.

перере́зать (-е́жу) *pf,* **перереза́ть** *impf,* **перере́зывать** *impf* cut; cut off; kill.

перероди́ть (-ожу́) *pf,* **перерожда́ть** *impf* regenerate; ~**ся** be reborn; be regenerated; degenerate. **перерожде́ние** regeneration; degeneration.

переро́с *etc.*: *see* **перерасти́**. **переро́ю** *etc.*: *see* **переры́ть**

переруба́ть *impf,* **переруби́ть** (-блю́, -бишь) *pf* chop in two.

переры́в interruption; interval.

перерыва́ть[1](**ся** *impf of* **перерва́ть**(**ся**

перерыва́ть[2] *impf,* **переры́ть** (-ро́ю) *pf* dig up; rummage through.

пересади́ть (-ажу́, -а́дишь) *pf,* **переса́живать** *impf* transplant; graft; seat somewhere else. **переса́дка** transplantation; grafting; change.

переса́живаться *impf of* **пересе́сть**. **переса́ливать** *impf of* **пересоли́ть**

пересдава́ть (-даю́сь) *impf,* **пересда́ть** (-а́м, -а́шь, -а́ст, -ади́м; -да́л, -а́, -о) *pf* sublet; re-sit.

пересека́ть(**ся** *impf of* **пересе́чь**(**ся** **переселе́нец** (-нца) settler; immigrant. **переселе́ние** migration; immigration, resettlement; moving.

пересели́ть *pf,* **переселя́ть** *impf* move; ~**ся** move; migrate.

пересе́сть (-ся́ду) *pf* (*impf* **переса́живаться**) change one's seat; change (*trains etc.*).

пересече́ние crossing, intersection.

пересе́чь (-секу́, -сечёшь; -сёк, -ла́) *pf* (*impf* **пересека́ть**) cross; intersect; ~**ся** cross, intersect.

переси́ливать *impf,* **переси́лить** *pf* overpower.

переска́з (re)telling; exposition. **пересказа́ть** (-ажу́, -а́жешь) *pf,* **переска́зывать** *impf* retell.

переска́кивать *impf,* **перескочи́ть** (-чу́, -чишь) *pf* jump *or* skip (over).

пересла́ть (-ешлю́, -шлёшь) *pf* (*impf* **пересыла́ть**) send; forward.

пересма́тривать *impf,* **пересмо́треть** (-трю́, -тришь) *pf* look over; reconsider. **пересмо́тр** revision; reconsideration; review.

пересоли́ть (-олю́, -о́ли́шь) *pf* (*impf* **переса́ливать**) over-salt; overdo it.

пересо́хнуть (-нет; -о́х) *pf* (*impf* **пересыха́ть**) dry up, become parched.

переспа́ть (-плю́; -а́л, -а́, -о) *pf* oversleep; spend the night.

переспе́лый overripe.

переспра́шивать *impf,* **переспроси́ть** (-ошу́, -о́сишь) *pf* ask again.

переставáть (-таю́, -таёшь) *impf of* **переста́ть**

переста́вить (-влю) *pf,* **переставля́ть** *impf* move; re-arrange; transpose. **перестано́вка** rearrangement; transposition.

переста́ть (-а́ну) *pf* (*impf* **перестава́ть**) stop, cease.

перестрада́ть *pf* have suffered.

перестра́ивать(**ся** *impf of* **перестро́ить**(**ся**

перестрахо́вка re-insurance; overcautiousness.

перестре́лка exchange of fire. **перестреля́ть** *pf* shoot (down).

перестро́ить *pf* (*impf* **перестра́ивать**) rebuild; reorganize; retune; ~**ся** re-form; reorganize o.s.; switch over (**на**+*acc* to). **перестро́йка** reconstruction; reorganization; retuning; perestroika.

переступа́ть *impf*, переступи́ть (-плю́, -пишь) *pf* step over; cross; overstep.

пересчита́ть *pf*, пересчи́тывать *impf* (*pf also* пересче́сть) re-count; count.

пересыла́ть *impf of* пересла́ть. пересы́лка sending, forwarding.

пересыпа́ть *impf*, пересы́пать (-плю, -плешь) *pf* pour; sprinkle; pour too much.

пересыха́ть *impf of* пересо́хнуть. переся́ду *etc.*: *see* пересе́сть. перета́пливать *impf of* перетопи́ть

перета́скивать *impf*, перетащи́ть (-щу́, -щишь) *pf* drag (over, through); move.

перетере́ть (-тру́, -трёшь; -тёр) *pf*, перетира́ть *impf* wear out, wear down; grind; wipe; ∼ся wear out *or* through.

перетопи́ть (-плю́, -пишь) *pf* (*impf* перета́пливать) melt.

перетру́ *etc.*: *see* перетере́ть

переть (пру, прёшь; пёр, -ла) *impf* go; make *or* force one's way; haul; come out.

перетя́гивать *impf*, перетяну́ть (-ну́, -нешь) *pf* pull, draw; win over; outweigh.

переубеди́ть *pf*, переубежда́ть *impf* make change one's mind.

переу́лок (-лка) side street, alley.

переустро́йство reconstruction, re-organization.

переутоми́ть (-млю́) *pf*, переутомля́ть *impf* overtire; ∼ся overtire o.s. переутомле́ние overwork.

переучёт stock-taking.

переу́чивать *impf*, переучи́ть (-чу́, -чишь) *pf* teach again.

перефрази́ровать *impf & pf* paraphrase.

перехвати́ть (-ачу́, -а́тишь) *pf*, перехва́тывать *impf* intercept; snatch a bite (of); borrow.

перехитри́ть *pf* outwit.

перехо́д transition; crossing; conversion. переходи́ть (-ожу́, -о́дишь) *impf of* перейти́. перехо́дный transitional; transitive. переходя́щий transient; intermittent; brought forward.

пе́рец (-рца) pepper.

перечёл *etc.*: *see* перечесть

пе́речень (-чня) *m* list, enumeration.

перечёркивать *impf*, перечеркну́ть (-ну́, -нёшь) *pf* cross out, cancel.

перече́сть (-чту́, -чтёшь; -чёл, -чла́) *pf*: *see* пересчита́ть, перечита́ть

перечисле́ние enumeration; transfer. перечи́слить *pf*, перечисля́ть *impf* enumerate; transfer.

перечита́ть *pf*, перечи́тывать *impf* (*pf also* перече́сть) re-read.

пере́чить (-чу) *impf* contradict; cross, go against.

пе́речница pepper-pot.

перечту́ *etc.*: *see* перече́сть. пере́чу *etc.*: *see* пере́чить

перешага́ть *impf*, перешагну́ть (-ну́, -нёшь) *pf* step over.

переше́ек (-е́йка) isthmus, neck.

перешёл *etc.*: *see* перейти́

перешива́ть *impf*, переши́ть (-шью, -шьёшь) *pf* alter; have altered.

перешлю́ *etc.*: *see* пересла́ть

переэкзаменова́ть *pf.*, переэкзамено́вывать *impf* re-examine; ∼ся retake an exam.

пери́ла (-и́л) *pl* railing(s); banisters.

пери́на feather-bed.

пери́од period. перио́дика periodicals. периоди́ческий periodical; recurring.

пе́ристый feathery; cirrus.

перифери́я periphery.

перламу́тр mother-of-pearl. перламу́тровый mother-of-pearl. перло́в|ый: ∼ая крупа́ pearl barley.

перма́нент perm. перма́нентный permanent.

перна́тый feathered. перна́тые *sb pl* birds. перо́ (*pl* пе́рья, -ьев) feather; pen. перочи́нный нож, но́жик penknife.

перпендикуля́рный perpendicular.

перро́н platform.

перс Persian. перси́дский Persian.

пе́рсик peach.

персия́нка Persian woman.

персо́на person; со́бственной персо́ной in person. персона́ж character; personage. персона́л personnel, staff. персона́льный personal.

перспекти́ва perspective; vista; prospect. перспекти́вный perspective; long-term; promising.

пе́рстень (-тня) *m* ring.

перфока́рта punched card.

пе́рхоть dandruff.

перча́тка glove.

пе́рчить (-чу) *impf* (*pf* по~) pepper.

пёс (пса) dog.

пе́сенник song-book; (choral) singer; song-writer. **пе́сенный** song; of songs.

песе́ц (-сца́) (polar) fox.

песнь (*gen pl* -ей) song; canto. **пе́сня** (*gen pl* -сен) song.

песо́к (-ска́) sand. **песо́чный** sand; sandy.

пессими́зм pessimism. **пессими́ст** pessimist. **пессимисти́ческий** pessimistic.

пестрота́ diversity of colours; diversity. **пёстрый** variegated; diverse; colourful.

песча́ник sandstone. **песча́ный** sandy. **песчи́нка** grain of sand.

петербу́ргский (of) St Petersburg.

пети́ция petition.

петли́ца buttonhole; tab. **пе́тля** (*gen pl* -тель) loop; noose; buttonhole; stitch; hinge.

петру́шка¹ parsley.

петру́шка² *m* Punch; *f* Punch-and-Judy show.

пету́х (-á) cock. **петушо́к** (-шка́) cockerel.

петь (пою́, поёшь) *impf* (*pf* про~, с~) sing.

пехо́та infantry, foot. **пехоти́нец** (-нца) infantryman. **пехо́тный** infantry.

печа́лить *impf* (*pf* о~) sadden; ~ся grieve, be sad. **печа́ль** sorrow. **печа́льный** sad.

печа́тать *impf* (*pf* на~, от~) print; ~ся write, be published; be at the printer's. **печа́тн|ый** printing; printer's; printed; ~ые бу́квы block capitals; ~ый стано́к printing-press. **печа́ть** seal, stamp; print; printing; press.

пече́ние baking.

печёнка liver.

печёный baked.

пе́чень liver.

пече́нье pastry; biscuit. **пе́чка** stove.

печно́й stove; oven; kiln. **печь** (*loc* -и́; *gen pl* -е́й) stove; oven; kiln. **печь** (пеку́, -чёшь; пёк, -ла́) *impf* (*pf* ис~) bake; ~ся bake.

пешехо́д pedestrian. **пешехо́дный** pedestrian; foot-. **пе́ший** pedestrian; foot. **пе́шка** pawn. **пешко́м** *adv* on foot.

пеще́ра cave. **пеще́рный** cave; ~ челове́к cave-dweller.

пиани́но *neut indecl* (upright) piano. **пиани́ст**, ~ка pianist.

пивна́я *sb* pub. **пивно́й** beer. **пи́во** beer. **пивова́р** brewer.

пигме́й pygmy.

пиджа́к (-á) jacket.

пижа́ма pyjamas.

пижо́н dandy.

пик peak; часы́ пик rush-hour.

пи́ка lance.

пика́нтный piquant; spicy.

пика́п pick-up (van).

пике́ *neut indecl* dive.

пике́т picket. **пике́тчик** picket.

пи́ки (пик) *pl* (*cards*) spades.

пики́ровать *impf* & *pf* (*pf also* с~) dive.

пики́ровщик, пики́рующий бомбардиро́вщик dive-bomber.

пикни́к (-á) picnic.

пи́кнуть (-ну) *pf* squeak; make a sound.

пи́ковый of spades.

пила́ (*pl* -ы) saw; nagger. **пилёный** sawed, sawn. **пили́ть** (-лю́, -лишь) *impf* saw; nag (at). **пи́лка** sawing; fret-saw; nail-file.

пило́т pilot.

пило́тка forage-cap.

пилоти́ровать *impf* pilot.

пилю́ля pill.

пина́ть *impf* (*pf* пнуть) kick. **пино́к** (-нка́) kick.

пингви́н penguin.

пинце́т tweezers.

пио́н peony.

пионе́р pioneer. **пионе́рский** pioneer.

пипе́тка pipette.

пир (*loc* -ý; *pl* -ы́) feast, banquet. **пирова́ть** *impf* feast.

пирами́да pyramid.

пира́т pirate.

пиро́г (-á) pie. **пиро́жное** *sb* cake, pastry. **пирожо́к** (-жка́) pasty.

пирс pier.

пируэ́т pirouette.

пи́ршество feast; celebration.

пи́саный handwritten. **пи́сарь** (*pl*

-я) *m* clerk. **писа́тель** *m*, **писа́-
тельница** writer, author. **писа́ть**
(пишу́, пи́шешь) *impf* (*pf* на~) write;
paint; ~ ма́слом paint in oils; ~ся
be spelt.

писк squeak, chirp. **пискли́вый**
squeaky. **пи́скнуть** (-ну) *pf of* пища́ть.

пистоле́т pistol; gun; ~-пулемёт
sub-machine gun.

писто́н (percussion-)cap; piston.

писчебума́жный stationery. **пи́счая
бума́га** writing paper. **пи́сьменно**
adv in writing. **пи́сьменность** literature. **пи́сьменный** writing, written. **письмо́** (*pl* -а, -сем) letter.

пита́ние nourishment; feeding. **пита́-
тельный** nutritious; alimentary; feed.
пита́ть *impf* (*pf* на~) feed; nourish;
supply; ~ся be fed, eat; +*instr* feed
on.

пито́мец (-мца) charge; pupil; alum-
nus. **пито́мник** nursery.

пить (пью, пьёшь; пил, -а́, -о) *impf*
(*pf* вы́~) drink. **питьё** (*pl* -тья́, -тей,
-тья́м) drinking; drink. **питьево́й**
drinkable; drinking.

пиха́ть *impf*, **пихну́ть** (-ну́, -нёшь)
pf push, shove.

пи́хта (silver) fir.

пи́чкать *impf* (*pf* на~) stuff.

пи́шущ|ий writing; ~ая маши́нка
typewriter.

пи́ща food.

пища́ть (-щу́) *impf* (*pf* **пи́скнуть**)
squeak; cheep.

пищеваре́ние digestion. **пищево́д**
oesophagus, gullet. **пищево́й** food.

пия́вка leech.

пла́вание swimming; sailing; voyage.
пла́вательный swimming; ~ бас-
се́йн swimming-pool. **пла́вать** *impf*
swim; float; sail. **плавба́за** depot
ship, factory ship.

плави́льный melting, smelting. **пла-
ви́льня** foundry. **пла́вить** (-влю)
impf (*pf* рас~) melt, smelt; ~ся
melt. **пла́вка** fusing; melting.

пла́вки (-вок) *pl* bathing trunks.

пла́вкий fusible; fuse. **плавле́ние**
melting.

плавни́к (-а́) fin; flipper. **пла́вный**
smooth, flowing; liquid. **плаву́чий**
floating.

плагиа́т plagiarism. **плагиа́тор** pla-
giarist.

пла́зма plasma.

плака́т poster; placard.

пла́кать (-а́чу) *impf* cry, weep; ~ся
complain, lament; +на+*acc* complain
of; bemoan.

пла́кса cry-baby. **плакси́вый** whining. **плаку́чий** weeping.

пла́менный flaming; ardent. **пла́мя**
(-мени) *neut* flame; blaze.

план plan.

планёр glider. **планери́зм** gliding.
планери́ст glider-pilot.

плане́та planet. **плане́тный** plan-
etary.

плани́рование[1] planning.

плани́рование[2] gliding; glide.

плани́ровать[1] *impf* (*pf* за~) plan.

плани́ровать[2] *impf* (*pf* с~) glide
(down).

пла́нка lath, slat.

пла́новый planned, systematic; planning. **планоме́рный** systematic,
planned.

планта́ция plantation.

пласт (-а́) layer; stratum. **пласти́на**
plate. **пласти́нка** plate; (*gramophone*) record.

пласти́ческий, **пласти́чный** plastic. **пластма́сса** plastic. **пластма́с-
совый** plastic.

пла́стырь *m* plaster.

пла́та pay; charge; fee. **платёж** (-а́)
payment. **платёжеспосо́бный** solvent. **платёжный** pay.

пла́тина platinum. **пла́тиновый**
platinum.

плати́ть (-ачу́, -а́тишь) *impf* (*pf* за~,
у~) pay; ~ся (*pf* по~ся) за+*acc* pay
for. **пла́тный** paid; requiring payment.

плато́к (-тка́) shawl; head-scarf;
handkerchief.

платони́ческий platonic.

платфо́рма platform; truck.

пла́тье (*gen pl* -ьев) clothes, clothing; dress; gown. **платяно́й** clothes.

плафо́н ceiling; lamp shade.

плацда́рм bridgehead, beach-head;
base; springboard.

плацка́рта reserved-seat ticket.

плач weeping. **плаче́вный** lamentable. **пла́чу** *etc.*: *see* **пла́кать**

плачу́ *etc.*: *see* **плати́ть**

плашмя́ *adv* flat, prone.

плащ (-а́) cloak; raincoat.

плебе́й plebeian.

плева́тельница spittoon. **плева́ть** (плюю́, плюёшь) *impf* (*pf* на~, плю́нуть) spit; *inf+dat*: мне ~ I don't give a damn (на+*acc* about); ~ся spit. **плево́к** (-вка́) spit, spittle.

плеври́т pleurisy.

плед rug; plaid.

плёл *etc.*: *see* **плести́**

племенно́й tribal; pedigree. **пле́мя** (-мени; *pl* -мена́, -мён) *neut* tribe. **племя́нник** nephew. **племя́нница** niece.

плен (*loc* -у́) captivity.

плена́рный plenary.

плени́тельный captivating. **плени́ть** *pf* (*impf* **пленя́ть**) captivate; ~ся be captivated.

плёнка film; tape; pellicle.

пле́нник prisoner. **пле́нный** captive.

пле́нум plenary session.

пленя́ть(ся *impf of* **плени́ть(ся**

пле́сень mould.

плеск splash, lapping. **плеска́ть** (-ещу́, -е́щешь) *impf* (*pf* **плесну́ть**) splash; lap; ~ся splash; lap.

пле́сневеть (-еет) *impf* (*pf* за~) go mouldy, grow musty.

плесну́ть (-ну́, -нёшь) *pf of* **плеска́ть**

плести́ (-ету́, -етёшь; плёл, -а́) *impf* (*pf* с~) plait; weave; ~сь trudge along. **плете́ние** plaiting; wickerwork. **плетёный** wattled; wicker. **плете́нь** (-тня́) *m* wattle fencing. **плётка, плеть** (*gen pl* -е́й) lash.

пле́чико (*pl* -и, -ов) shoulder-strap; *pl* coat-hanger. **плечи́стый** broad-shouldered. **плечо́** (*pl* -и, -а́м) shoulder.

плеши́вый bald. **плеши́на, плешь** bald patch.

плещу́ *etc.*: *see* **плеска́ть**

пли́нтус plinth; skirting-board.

плис velveteen.

плиссиро́вать *impf* pleat.

плита́ (*pl* -ы) slab; flag-(stone); stove, cooker; **моги́льная** ~ gravestone. **пли́тка** tile; (thin) slab; stove, cooker; ~ **шокола́да** bar of chocolate. **пли́точный** tiled.

плове́ц (-вца́), **пловчи́ха** swimmer. **плову́чий** floating; buoyant.

плод (-а́) fruit. **плоди́ть** (-ожу́) *impf* (*pf* **рас**~) produce, procreate; ~ся propagate.

плодо- *in comb* fruit-. **плодови́тый** fruitful, prolific; fertile. ~**во́дство** fruit-growing. ~**но́сный** fruit-bearing, fruitful. ~**овощно́й** fruit and vegetable. ~**ро́дный** fertile. ~**тво́рный** fruitful.

пло́мба seal; filling. **пломбирова́ть** *impf* (*pf* за~, о~) fill; seal.

пло́ский (-сок, -ска́, -о) flat; trivial.

плоско- *in comb* flat. **плоского́рье** plateau. ~**гу́бцы** (-ев) *pl* pliers. ~**до́нный** flat-bottomed.

пло́скость (*gen pl* -е́й) flatness; plane; platitude.

плот (-а́) raft.

плоти́на dam; weir; dyke.

пло́тник carpenter.

пло́тность solidity; density. **пло́тный** (-тен, -тна́, -о) thick; compact; dense; solid, strong; hearty.

плотоя́дный carnivorous. **плоть** flesh.

плохо́й bad; poor.

площа́дка area, (sports) ground, court, playground; site; landing; platform. **пло́щадь** (*gen pl* -е́й) area; space; square.

плуг (*pl* -и́) plough.

плут (-а́) cheat, swindler; rogue. **плутова́тый** cunning. **плутовско́й** roguish; picaresque.

плуто́ний plutonium.

плыть (-ыву́, -ывёшь; плыл, -а́, -о) *impf* swim; float; sail.

плю́нуть (-ну) *pf of* **плева́ть**

плюс plus; advantage.

плюш plush.

плющ (-а́) ivy.

плюю́ *etc.*: *see* **плева́ть**

пляж beach.

пляса́ть (-яшу́, -я́шешь) *impf* (*pf* с~) dance. **пля́ска** dance; dancing.

пневмати́ческий pneumatic.

пневмони́я pneumonia.

пнуть (пну, пнёшь) *pf of* **пина́ть**

пня *etc.*: *see* **пень**

по *prep* I. +*dat* on; along; round, about; by; over; according to; in accordance with; for; in; at; by (reason of); on account of; from; no **понеде́льникам** on Mondays; **по профе́ссии** by profession; **по ра́дио** over the radio. II. +*dat or acc of cardinal number, forms distributive number*: **по два, по дво́е** in twos, two by two; **по пять рублей штука** at five roubles each. +*acc* to, up to; for, to get; **идти по воду** go to get water; **по первое сентября** up to (and including) 1st September. **IV.** +*prep* on, (immediately) after; **по прибытии** on arrival.

по- *pref* **I.** *in comb* +*dat of adjs, or with advs in* **-и,** *indicates manner, use of a named language, or accordance with the opinion or wish of:* **говорить по-русски** speak Russian; **жить по-старому** live in the old style; **по-моему** in my opinion. **II.** *in comb with adjs and nn, indicates situation along or near a thing:* **поморье** seaboard, coastal region. **III.** *in comb with comp of adjs indicates a smaller degree of comparison:* **поменьше** a little less.

побаиваться *impf* be rather afraid.

побег[1] flight; escape.

побег[2] shoot; sucker.

побегушки: быть на побегушках run errands.

победа victory. **победитель** *m* victor; winner. **победить** *pf* (*impf* **побеждать**) conquer; win. **победный, победоносный** victorious, triumphant.

по|бежать *pf*.

побеждать *impf of* **победить**

по|белеть (-ею) *pf*. **по|белить** *pf*. **побелка** whitewashing.

побережный coastal. **побережье** (sea-)coast.

по|беспокоить(ся *pf*.

побираться *impf* beg; live by begging.

по|бить(ся (-бью(сь, -бьёшь(ся) *pf*. **по|благодарить** *pf*.

поблажка indulgence.

по|бледнеть (-ею) *pf*.

поблёскивать *impf* gleam.

поблизости *adv* nearby.

побои (-ев) *pl* beating. **побоище** slaughter; bloody battle.

поборник champion, advocate. **по|бороть** (-рю, -решь) *pf* overcome.

побочный secondary; done on the side; ~ **продукт** by-product.

по|браниться *pf*.

по|брататься *pf*. **побратим** twin town.

по|брезгать *pf*. **по|брить(ся** (-брею(сь) *pf*.

побудительный stimulating. **побудить** (-ужу) *pf*, **побуждать** *impf* induce, prompt. **побуждение** motive; inducement.

побывать *pf* have been, have visited; look in, visit. **побывка** leave. **по|быть** (-буду, -дешь; побыл, -а, -о) *pf* stay (for a short time).

побью(сь *etc.: see* **побить(ся**

повадиться (-ажусь) get into the habit (of). **повадка** habit.

по|валить(ся (-лю(сь, -лишь(ся) *pf*.

повально *adv* without exception. **повальный** general, mass.

повар (*pl* -а) cook, chef. **поваренный** culinary; cookery, cooking.

по-вашему *adv* in your opinion.

поведать *pf* disclose; relate.

поведение behaviour.

поведу *etc.: see* **повести. по|везти** (-зу, -зёшь; -вёз, -ла) *pf*. **повёл** *etc.: see* **повести**

повелевать *impf* +*instr* rule (over); +*dat* command. **повеление** command. **повелительный** imperious; imperative.

по|венчать(ся *pf*.

повергать *impf*, **повергнуть** (-ну; -верг) *pf* throw down; plunge.

поверенная *sb* confidante. **поверенный** *sb* attorney; confidant; ~ **в делах** chargé d'affaires. **по|верить**[1].

поверить[2] *pf* (*impf* **поверять**) check; confide. **поверка** check; roll-call.

повернуть (-ну, -нёшь) *pf*, **повёртывать** *impf* (*impf also* **поворачивать**) turn; ~**ся** turn.

поверх *prep*+*gen* over. **поверхностный** surface, superficial. **поверхность** surface.

поверье (*gen pl* -ий) popular belief, superstition. **поверять** *impf of* **поверить**[2]

повеса playboy.

по|веселеть (-ею) *pf*.

повеселить *pf* cheer (up), amuse; ~**ся** have fun.

повесить(ся (-вешу(сь) *pf of* **вешать(ся**

повествование narrative, narration. **повествовательный** narrative. **повествовать** *impf* +**о**+*prep* narrate, relate.

по|вести (-еду, -едёшь; -вёл, -а) *pf*

(*impf* **поводи́ть**) +*instr* move.

пове́стка notice; summons; ~ (дня) agenda.

по́весть (*gen pl* -**е́й**) story, tale.

пове́трие epidemic; craze.

пове́шу *etc.: see* **пове́сить. по|вздо́рить** *pf*.

повзросле́ть (-**е́ю**) *pf* grow up.

по|вида́ть(ся *pf*.

по-ви́димому apparently.

пови́дло jam.

по|вини́ться *pf*.

пови́нность duty, obligation; **во́инская** ~ conscription. **пови́нный** guilty.

повинова́ться *impf & pf* obey. **повинове́ние** obedience.

повиса́ть *impf*, **по|ви́снуть** (-**ну**; -**вис**) *pf* hang (on); hang down, droop.

повле́чь (-**еку́**, -**ече́шь**; -**ёк**, -**ла́**) *pf* (**за собо́й**) entail, bring in its train.

по|влия́ть *pf*.

по́вод[1] occasion, cause; **по** ~**у**+*gen* as regards, concerning.

по́вод[2] (*loc* -**у́**; *pl* -**о́дья**, -**ев**) rein; **быть на** ~**у́ у**+*gen* be under the thumb of. **поводи́ть** (-**ожу́**, -**о́дишь**) *impf of* **повести́. поводо́к** (-**дка́**) leash. **поводы́рь** (-**я́**) *m* guide.

пово́зка cart; vehicle.

повора́чивать(ся *impf of* **поверну́ть(ся, повороти́ть(ся; повора́чивайся, -айтесь!** get a move on!

поворо́т turn, turning; bend; turning-point. **повороти́ть(ся** (-**рочу́(сь**, -**ро́тишь(ся**) *pf* (*impf* **повора́чивать(ся**) turn. **поворо́тливый** agile, nimble; manoeuvrable. **поворо́тный** turning; rotary; revolving.

по|вреди́ть (-**ежу́**) *pf*, **поврежда́ть** *impf* damage; injure; ~**ся** be damaged; be injured. **поврежде́ние** damage, injury.

повремени́ть *pf* wait a little; +**с**+*instr* delay over.

повседне́вный daily; everyday.

повсеме́стно *adv* everywhere. **повсеме́стный** universal, general.

повста́нец (-**нца**) rebel, insurgent. **повста́нческий** rebel; insurgent.

повсю́ду *adv* everywhere.

повторе́ние repetition. **повтори́ть** *pf*, **повторя́ть** *impf* repeat; ~**ся** repeat o.s.; be repeated; recur. **по-**

вто́рный repeated.

повы́сить (-**ы́шу**) *pf*, **повыша́ть** *impf* raise, heighten; ~**ся** rise. **повыше́ние** rise; promotion. **повы́шенный** heightened, high.

повяза́ть (-**яжу́**, -**я́жешь**) *pf*, **повя́зывать** *impf* tie. **повя́зка** band; bandage.

по|гада́ть *pf*.

пога́нка toadstool. **пога́ный** foul; unclean.

погаса́ть *impf*, **по|га́снуть** (-**ну**) *pf* go out, be extinguished. **по|гаси́ть** (-**ашу́**, -**а́сишь**) *pf*. **погаша́ть** *impf* liquidate, cancel. **пога́шенный** used, cancelled, cashed.

погиба́ть *impf*, **по|ги́бнуть** (-**ну**; -**ги́б**) *pf* perish; be lost. **поги́бель** ruin. **поги́бший** lost; ruined; killed.

по|гла́дить (-**а́жу**) *pf*.

поглоти́ть (-**ощу́**, -**о́тишь**) *pf*, **поглоща́ть** *impf* swallow up; absorb. **поглоще́ние** absorption.

по|глупе́ть (-**е́ю**) *pf*.

по|гляде́ть (-**яжу́**) *pf*. **погля́дывать** *impf* glance (from time to time); +**за**+*instr* keep an eye on.

погна́ть (-**гоню́**, -**го́нишь**; -**гна́л**, -**а́**, -**о**) *pf* drive; ~**ся за**+*instr* run after; start in pursuit of.

по|гну́ть(ся (-**ну́(сь**, -**нёшь(ся**) *pf*. **по|гнуша́ться** *pf*.

поговори́ть *pf* have a talk.

погово́рка saying, proverb.

пого́да weather.

погоди́ть (-**ожу́**) *pf* wait a little; **немно́го погодя́** a little later.

поголо́вно *adv* one and all. **поголо́вный** general; capitation. **поголо́вье** number.

пого́н (*gen pl* -**о́н**) shoulder-strap.

пого́нщик driver. **пого́ню** *etc.: see* **погна́ть. пого́ня** pursuit, chase. **погоня́ть** *impf* urge on, drive.

погорячи́ться (-**чу́сь**) *pf* get worked up.

пого́ст graveyard.

погра́ничник frontier guard. **погра́ничный** frontier.

по́греб (*pl* -**á**) cellar. **погреба́льный** funeral. **погреба́ть** *impf of* **погрести́. погребе́ние** burial.

погрему́шка rattle.

погрести́[1] (-**ебу́**, -**ебёшь**; -**рёб**, -**ла́**) *pf* (*impf* **погреба́ть**) bury.

погрести́² (-ебу́, -ебёшь; -рёб, -ла́) *pf* row for a while.

погре́ть (-е́ю) *pf* warm; **~ся** warm o.s.

по|греши́ть (-шу́) *pf* sin; err. **погре́шность** error, mistake.

по|грози́ть(ся (-ожу́(сь) *pf*. **по|грубе́ть** (-е́ю) *pf*.

погружа́ть *impf*, **по|грузи́ть** (-ужу́, -у́зишь) *pf* load; ship; dip, plunge, immerse; **~ся** sink, plunge; dive; be plunged, absorbed. **погруже́ние** submergence; immersion; dive. **погру́зка** loading; shipment.

погряза́ть *impf*, **по|гря́знуть** (-ну; -я́з) *pf* be bogged down; wallow.

по|губи́ть (-блю́, -бишь) *pf*. **по|гуля́ть** *pf*.

под, подо *prep* **I.** +*acc or instr* under; near, close to; **взять по́д руку**+*acc* take the arm of; **~ ви́дом**+*gen* under the guise of; **под го́ру** downhill; **~ Москво́й** in the environs of Moscow. **II.** +*instr* occupied by, used as; (meant, implied) by; in, with; **говя́дина ~ хре́ном** beef with horse-radish. **III.** +*acc* towards; to (the accompaniment of); in imitation of; on; for, to serve as; **ему́ ~ пятьдеся́т (лет)** he is getting on for fifty.

подава́ть(ся (-даю́(сь, -даёшь(ся) *impf of* **пода́ть(ся**

подави́ть (-влю́, -вишь) *pf*, **подавля́ть** *impf* suppress; depress; overwhelm. **по|дави́ться** (-влю́сь, -вишься) *pf*. **подавле́ние** suppression; repression. **пода́вленность** depression. **пода́вленный** suppressed; depressed. **подавля́ющий** overwhelming.

пода́вно *adv* all the more.

пода́гра gout.

пода́льше *adv* a little further.

по|дари́ть (-рю́, -ришь) *pf*. **пода́рок** (-рка) gift.

пода́тливый pliant, pliable. **по́дать** (*gen pl* -е́й) tax. **пода́ть** (-а́м, -а́шь, -а́ст, -ади́м; по́дал, -а́, -о) *pf* (*impf* **подава́ть**) serve; give; put, move, turn; put forward, present, hand in; **~ся** move; give way; yield; +**на**+*acc* set out for. **пода́ча** giving, presenting; serve; feed, supply. **пода́чка** handout, crumb. **подаю́** *etc.*: *see*

подава́ть. пода́яние alms.

подбега́ть *impf*, **подбежа́ть** (-егу́) *pf* come running (up).

подбива́ть *impf of* **подби́ть**

подберу́ *etc.*: *see* **подобра́ть. подбира́ть(ся** *impf of* **подобра́ть(ся**

подби́ть (-добью́, -добьёшь) *pf* (*impf* **подбива́ть**) line; re-sole; bruise; put out of action; incite.

подбодри́ть *pf*, **подбодря́ть** *impf* cheer up, encourage; **~ся** cheer up, take heart.

подбо́р selection, assortment. **подборо́док** (-дка) chin.

подбоче́нившись *adv* with hands on hips.

подбра́сывать *impf*, **подбро́сить** (-ро́шу) *pf* throw up.

подва́л cellar; basement. **подва́льный** basement, cellar.

подведу́ *etc.*: *see* **подвести́**

подвезти́ (-зу́, -зёшь; -вёз, -ла́) *pf* (*impf* **подвози́ть**) bring, take; give a lift.

подвене́чный wedding.

подверга́ть *impf*, **подве́ргнуть** (-ну; -ве́рг) *pf* subject; expose; **~ся** +*dat* undergo. **подве́рженный** subject, liable.

подверну́ть (-ну́, -нёшь) *pf*, **подвёртывать** *impf* turn up; tuck under; sprain; tighten; **~ся** be sprained; be turned up; be tucked under.

подве́сить (-е́шу) *pf* (*impf* **подве́шивать**) hang up, suspend. **подвесно́й** hanging, suspended.

подвести́ (-еду́, -едёшь; -вёл, -а́) *pf* (*impf* **подводи́ть**) lead up, bring up; place (under); bring under, subsume; let down; **~ ито́ги** reckon up; sum up.

подве́шивать *impf of* **подве́сить**

по́двиг exploit, feat.

подвига́ть(ся *impf of* **подви́нуть(ся** **подви́жник** religious ascetic; champion.

подвижно́й mobile; **~ соста́в** rolling-stock. **подви́жность** mobility. **подви́жный** mobile; lively; agile.

подвиза́ться *impf* (**в** *or* **на**+*prep*) work (in).

подви́нуть (-ну) *pf* (*impf* **подвига́ть**) move; push; advance; **~ся** move; advance.

подвла́стный +*dat* subject to; under

the control of.

подвóда cart. **подводúть** (-ожý, -óдишь) *impf of* **подвестú**

подвóдн|ый submarine; underwater; ~**ая скалá** reef.

подвóз transport; supply. **подвозúть** (-ожý, -óзишь) *impf of* **подвезтú**

подворóтня (*gen pl* -тен) gateway.

подвóх trick.

подвы́пивший tipsy.

подвязáть (-яжý, -я́жешь) *pf*, **подвя́зывать** *impf* tie up. **подвя́зка** garter; suspender.

подгибáть *impf of* **подогнýть**

подглядéть (-яжý) *pf*, **подгля́дывать** *impf* peep; spy.

подговáривать *impf*, **подговорúть** *pf* incite.

подгоню́ *etc.: see* **подогнáть. подгоня́ть** *impf of* **подогнáть**

подгорáть *impf*, **подгорéть** (-рúт) *pf* get a bit burnt. **подгорéлый** slightly burnt.

подготовúтельный preparatory. **подготóвить** (-влю) *pf*, **подготовля́ть** *impf* prepare; ~**ся** prepare, get ready. **подготóвка** preparation, training.

поддавáться (-даю́сь, -даёшься) *impf of* **поддáться**

поддáкивать *impf* agree, assent.

пóдданный *sb* subject; citizen. **пóдданство** citizenship. **поддáться** (-áмся, -áшься, -áстся, -адúмся, -áлся, -лáсь) *pf* (*impf* **поддавáться**) yield, give way.

поддéлать *pf*, **поддéлывать** *impf* counterfeit; forge. **поддéлка** falsification; forgery; imitation. **поддéльный** false, counterfeit.

поддержáть (-жý, -жишь) *pf*, **поддéрживать** *impf* support; maintain. **поддéржка** support.

по|дéйствовать *pf*.

подéлать *pf* do; **ничегó не подéлаешь** it can't be helped.

по|делúть(ся (-лю́(сь, -лишь(ся) *pf*.

подéлка *pl* small (hand-made) articles.

подéлом *adv*: ~ **емý** (*etc.*) it serves him (*etc.*) right.

подённый by the day. **подёнщик, -ица** day-labourer.

подёргиваться *impf* twitch.

подéржанный second-hand.

подёрнуть (-нет) *pf* cover.

подерý *etc.: see* **подрáть. по|дешевéть** (-éет) *pf*.

поджáривать(ся *impf*, **поджáрить(ся** *pf* fry, roast, grill; toast. **поджáристый** brown(ed).

поджáрый lean, wiry.

поджáть (-дожмý, -дожмёшь) *pf* (*impf* **поджимáть**) draw in, draw under; ~ **гýбы** purse one's lips.

поджéчь (-дожгý, -ожжёшь; -жёг, -дожглá) *pf*, **поджигáть** *impf* set fire to; burn. **поджигáтель** *m* arsonist; instigator.

поджидáть *impf* (+*gen*) wait (for).

поджимáть *impf of* **поджáть**

поджóг arson.

подзаголóвок (-вка) subtitle, subheading.

подзащúтный *sb* client.

подземéлье (*gen pl* -лий) cave; dungeon. **подзéмный** underground.

подзову́ *etc.: see* **подозвáть**

подзóрная трубá telescope.

подзывáть *impf of* **подозвáть**

по|дивúться (-влю́сь) *pf*.

подкáпывать(ся *impf of* **подкопáть(ся**

подкарáуливать *impf*, **подкарáулить** *pf* be on the watch (for).

подкатúть (-ачý, -áтишь) *pf*, **подкáтывать** *impf* roll up, drive up; roll.

подкáшивать(ся *impf of* **подкосúть(ся**

подкúдывать *impf*, **подкúнуть** (-ну) *pf* throw up. **подкúдыш** foundling.

подклáдка lining. **подклáдывать** *impf of* **подложúть**

подклéивать *impf*, **подклéить** *pf* glue (up); mend.

подкóва (horse-)shoe. **под|ковáть** (-кую́, -ёшь) *pf*, **подкóвывать** *impf* shoe.

подкóжный hypodermic.

подкомúссия, подкомитéт subcommittee.

подкóп undermining; underground passage. **подкопáть** *pf* (*impf* **подкáпывать**) undermine; ~**ся** **под**+*acc* undermine; burrow under.

подкосúть (-ошý, -óсишь) *pf* (*impf* **подкáшивать**) cut down; ~**ся** give way.

подкра́дываться *impf of* **подкра́сться**

подкра́сить (-а́шу) *pf* (*impf* **подкра́шивать**) touch up; ~**ся** make up lightly.

подкра́сться (-аду́сь, -аде́шься) *pf* (*impf* **подкра́дываться**) sneak up.

подкра́шивать(ся *impf of* **подкра́сить(ся. подкра́шу** *etc.: see* **подкра́сить**

подкрепи́ть (-плю́) *pf*, **подкрепля́ть** *impf* reinforce; support; corroborate; fortify; ~**ся** fortify o.s. **подкрепле́ние** confirmation; sustenance; reinforcement.

подкрути́ть (-учу́, -у́тишь) *pf* (*impf* **подкру́чивать**) tighten up.

по́дкуп bribery. **подкупа́ть** *impf*, **подкупи́ть** (-плю́, -пишь) *pf* bribe; win over.

подла́диться (-а́жусь) *pf*, **подла́живаться** *impf* +к+*dat* adapt o.s. to; make up to.

подла́мываться *impf of* **подломи́ться**

по́дле *prep*+*gen* by the side of, beside.

подлежа́ть (-жу́) *impf* +*dat* be subject to; **не подлежи́т сомне́нию** it is beyond doubt. **подлежа́щее** *sb* subject. **подлежа́щий** +*dat* subject to.

подлеза́ть *impf*, **подле́зть** (-зу; -éз) *pf* crawl (under).

подле́сок (-ска) undergrowth.

подле́ц (-á) scoundrel.

подлива́ть *impf of* **подли́ть. подли́вка** sauce, dressing; gravy.

подли́за *m & f* toady. **подлиза́ться** (-ижу́сь, -и́жешься) *pf*, **подли́зываться** *impf* +к+*dat* suck up to.

по́длинник original. **по́длинно** *adv* really. **по́длинный** genuine; authentic; original; real.

подли́ть (-долью́, -дольёшь; по́длил, -á, -о) *pf* (*impf* **подлива́ть**) pour; add.

подло́г forgery.

подло́дка submarine.

подложи́ть (-жу́, -жишь) *pf* (*impf* **подкла́дывать**) add; +под+*acc* lay under; line.

подло́жный false, spurious; counterfeit, forged.

подлоко́тник arm (*of chair*).

подломи́ться (-о́мится) *pf* (*impf* **подла́мываться**) break; give way.

по́длость meanness, baseness; mean trick. **по́длый** (подл, -á, -о) mean, base.

подма́зать (-а́жу) *pf*, **подма́зывать** *impf* grease; bribe.

подмасте́рье (*gen pl* -ьев) *m* apprentice.

подме́н, подме́на replacement. **подме́нивать** *impf*, **подмени́ть** (-ню́, -нишь) *pf*, **подменя́ть** *impf* replace.

подмести́ (-ету́, -ете́шь; -мёл, -á) *pf*, **подмета́ть**[1] *impf* sweep.

подмета́ть[2] *pf* (*impf* **подмётывать**) tack.

подме́тить (-éчу) *pf* (*impf* **подмеча́ть**) notice.

подмётка sole.

подмётывать *impf of* **подмета́ть**[2]. **подмеча́ть** *impf of* **подме́тить**

подмеша́ть *pf*, **подме́шивать** *impf* mix in, stir in.

подми́гивать *impf*, **подмигну́ть** (-ну́, -нёшь) *pf* +*dat* wink at.

подмо́га help.

подмока́ть *impf*, **подмо́кнуть** (-нет; -мо́к) *pf* get damp, get wet.

подмора́живать *impf*, **подморо́зить** *pf* freeze.

подмоско́вный (situated) near Moscow.

подмо́стки (-ов) *pl* scaffolding; stage.

подмо́ченный damp; tarnished.

подмыва́ть *impf*, **подмы́ть** (-мо́ю) *pf* wash; wash away; **его́ так и подмыва́ет** he feels an urge (to).

подмы́шка armpit.

поднево́льный dependent; forced.

поднести́ (-су́, -сёшь; -ёс, -лá) *pf* (*impf* **подноси́ть**) present; take, bring.

поднима́ть(ся *impf of* **подня́ть(ся**

поднови́ть (-влю́) *pf*, **подновля́ть** *impf* renew, renovate.

подного́тная *sb* ins and outs.

подно́жие foot; pedestal. **подно́жка** running-board. **подно́жный корм** pasture.

подно́с tray. **подноси́ть** (-ошу́, -о́сишь) *impf of* **поднести́. подноше́ние** giving; present.

подня́тие raising. **подня́ть** (-ниму́, -ни́мешь; по́днял, -á, -о) *pf* (*impf* **поднима́ть, подыма́ть**) raise; lift (up); rouse; ~ся rise; go up.

подо see **под**

подоба́ть impf befit, become. **подоба́ющий** proper.

подо́бие likeness; similarity. **подо́бн|ый** like, similar; **и тому́ ~ое** and so on, and such like; **ничего́ ~ого!** nothing of the sort!

подобостра́стие servility. **подобостра́стный** servile.

подобра́ть (-дберу́, -дберёшь; -бра́л, -а́, -о) pf (impf **подбира́ть**) pick up; tuck up, put up; pick; ~ся steal up.

подо́бью etc.: see **подби́ть**

подогна́ть (-дгоню́, -дго́нишь; -а́л, -а́, -о) pf (impf **подгоня́ть**) drive; urge on; adjust.

подогну́ть (-ну́, -нёшь) pf (impf **подгиба́ть**) tuck in; bend under.

подогрева́ть impf, **подогре́ть** (-е́ю) pf warm up.

пододвига́ть impf, **пододви́нуть** (-ну) pf move up.

пододея́льник blanket cover; top sheet.

подожгу́ etc.: see **поджёчь**

подожда́ть (-ду́, -дёшь; -а́л, -а́, -о) pf wait (+gen or acc for).

подожму́ etc.: see **поджа́ть**

подозва́ть (-дзову́, -дзовёшь; -а́л, -а́, -о) pf (impf **подзыва́ть**) call to; beckon.

подозрева́емый suspected; suspect. **подозрева́ть** impf suspect. **подозре́ние** suspicion. **подозри́тельный** suspicious.

по|до́ить (-ою́, -о́йшь) pf.

подойти́ (-йду́, -йдёшь; -ошёл, -шла́) pf (impf **подходи́ть**) approach; come up; +dat suit, fit.

подоко́нник window-sill.

подо́л hem.

подо́лгу adv for ages; for hours (etc.) on end.

подолью́ etc.: see **подли́ть**

подо́нки (-ов) pl dregs; scum.

подоплёка underlying cause.

подопру́ etc.: see **подпере́ть**

подо́пытный experimental.

подорва́ть (-рву́, -рвёшь; -а́л, -а́, -о) pf (impf **подрыва́ть**) undermine; blow up.

по|дорожа́ть pf.

подоро́жник plantain. **подоро́жный** roadside.

подосла́ть (-ошлю́, -ошлёшь) pf (impf **подсыла́ть**) send (secretly).

подоспева́ть impf, **подоспе́ть** (-е́ю) pf arrive, appear (in time).

подостла́ть (-дстелю́, -дсте́лешь) pf (impf **подстила́ть**) lay under.

подотде́л section, subdivision.

подотру́ etc.: see **подтере́ть**

подотчётный accountable.

по|до́хнуть (-ну) pf (impf also **подыха́ть**).

подохо́дный нало́г income-tax.

подо́шва sole; foot.

подошёл etc.: see **подойти́**. **подошлю́** etc.: see **подосла́ть подошью́** etc.: see **подши́ть**.

подпада́ть impf, **подпа́сть** (-аду́, -адёшь; -а́л) pf **под**+acc fall under.

подпева́ть impf (+dat) sing along (with).

подпере́ть (-допру́; -пёр) pf (impf **подпира́ть**) prop up.

подпи́ливать impf, **подпили́ть** (-лю́, -лишь) pf saw; saw a little off.

подпира́ть impf of **подпере́ть**

подписа́ние signing. **подписа́ть** (-ишу́, -и́шешь) pf, **подпи́сывать** impf sign; ~ся sign; subscribe. **подпи́ска** subscription. **подписно́й** subscription. **подпи́счик** subscriber. **по́дпись** signature.

подплыва́ть impf, **подплы́ть** (-ыву́, -ывёшь; -плы́л, -а́, -о) pf **к**+dat swim or sail up to.

подполза́ть impf, **подползти́** (-зу́, -зёшь; -по́лз, -ла́) pf creep up (**к**+dat to); +**под**+acc crawl under.

подполко́вник lieutenant-colonel.

подпо́лье cellar; underground. **подпо́льный** underfloor; underground.

подпо́ра, подпо́рка prop, support.

подпо́чва subsoil.

подпра́вить (-влю) pf, **подправля́ть** impf touch up, adjust.

подпры́гивать impf, **подпры́гнуть** (-ну) pf jump up (and down).

подпуска́ть impf, **подпусти́ть** (-ущу́, -у́стишь) pf allow to approach.

подраба́тывать impf, **подрабо́тать** pf earn on the side; work up.

подра́внивать impf of **подровня́ть подража́ние** imitation. **подража́ть** impf imitate.

подразделе́ние subdivision. **подраздели́ть** pf, **подразделя́ть** impf subdivide.

подразумева́ть *impf* imply, mean; **~ся** be meant, be understood.

подраста́ть *impf*, **подрасти́** (-ту́, -тёшь; -ро́с, -ла́) *pf* grow.

по|дра́ть(ся (-деру́(сь, -дерёшь(ся, -а́л(ся, -ла́(сь, -о́(сь *or* -о́(сь) *pf*.

подре́зать (-е́жу) *pf*, **подреза́ть** *impf* cut; clip, trim.

подро́бно *adv* in detail. **подро́бность** detail. **подро́бный** detailed.

подровня́ть *pf* (*impf* **подра́внивать**) level, even; trim.

подро́с *etc.*: *see* **подрасти́**. **подро́сток** (-тка) adolescent; youth.

подро́ю *etc.*: *see* **подры́ть**

подруба́ть¹ *impf*, **подруби́ть** (-блю́, -бишь) *pf* chop down; cut short(er).

подруба́ть² *impf*, **подруби́ть** (-блю́, -бишь) *pf* hem.

подру́га friend. **по-дру́жески** *adv* in a friendly way. **по|дружи́ться** (-жу́сь) *pf*.

по-друго́му *adv* in a different way.

подру́чный at hand; improvised; *sb* assistant.

подры́в undermining; injury.

подрыва́ть¹ *impf of* **подорва́ть**

подрыва́ть² *impf*, **подры́ть** (-ро́ю) *pf* undermine, sap. **подрывно́й** blasting, demolition; subversive.

подря́д¹ *adv* in succession.

подря́д² contract. **подря́дчик** contractor.

подса́живаться *impf of* **подсе́сть**

подса́ливать *impf of* **подсоли́ть**

подсве́чник candlestick.

подсе́сть (-ся́ду; -се́л) *pf* (*impf* **подса́живаться**) sit down (**к**+*dat* near).

подсказа́ть (-ажу́, -а́жешь) *pf*, **подска́зывать** *impf* prompt; suggest. **подска́зка** prompting.

подска́кивать *impf*, **подскочи́ть** (-чу́, -чишь) *pf* jump (up); soar; come running.

подласти́ть (-ащу́) *pf*, **подсла́щивать** *impf* sweeten.

подсле́дственный under investigation.

подслу́шать *pf*, **подслу́шивать** *impf* overhear; eavesdrop, listen.

подсма́тривать *impf*, **подсмотре́ть** (-рю́, -ришь) *pf* spy (on).

подсне́жник snowdrop.

подсо́бный subsidiary; auxiliary.

подсо́вывать *impf of* **подсу́нуть**

подсозна́ние subconscious (mind). **подсозна́тельный** subconscious.

подсоли́ть (-со́лишь) *pf* (*impf* **подса́ливать**) add salt to.

подсо́лнечник sunflower. **подсо́лнечный** sunflower.

подсо́хнуть (-ну) *pf* (*impf* **подсыха́ть**) dry out a little.

подспо́рье help.

подста́вить (-влю) *pf*, **подставля́ть** *impf* put (under); bring up; expose; ~ **но́жку** +*dat* trip up. **подста́вка** stand; support. **подставно́й** false.

подстака́нник glass-holder.

подстелю́ *etc.*: *see* **подстла́ть**

подстерега́ть *impf*, **подстере́чь** (-егу́, -ежёшь; -рёг, -ла́) *pf* lie in wait for.

подстила́ть *impf of* **подостла́ть**. **подсти́лка** litter.

подстра́ивать *impf of* **подстро́ить**

подстрека́тель *m* instigator. **подстрека́тельство** instigation. **подстрека́ть** *impf*, **подстрекну́ть** (-ну́, -нёшь) *pf* instigate, incite.

подстре́ливать *impf*, **подстрели́ть** (-лю́, -лишь) *pf* wound.

подстрига́ть *impf*, **подстри́чь** (-игу́, -ижёшь; -и́г) *pf* cut; clip, trim; **~ся** have a hair-cut.

подстро́ить *pf* (*impf* **подстра́ивать**) build on; cook up.

по́дступ approach. **подступа́ть** *impf*, **подступи́ть** (-плю́, -пишь) *pf* approach; **~ся к**+*dat* approach.

подсуди́мый *sb* defendant; the accused. **подсу́дный**+*dat* under the jurisdiction of.

подсу́нуть (-ну) *pf* (*impf* **подсо́вывать**) put, shove; palm off.

подсчёт calculation; count. **подсчита́ть** *pf*, **подсчи́тывать** count (up); calculate.

подсыла́ть *impf of* **подосла́ть**. **подсыха́ть** *impf of* **подсо́хнуть**. **подся́ду** *etc.*: *see* **подсе́сть**. **подта́лкивать** *impf of* **подтолкну́ть**

подта́скивать *impf of* **подтащи́ть**

подтасова́ть *pf*, **подтасо́вывать** *impf* shuffle unfairly; juggle with.

подта́чивать *impf of* **подточи́ть**

подтащи́ть (-щу́, -щишь) *pf* (*impf* **подта́скивать**) drag up.

подтверди́ть (-ржу́) *pf*, **подтвержда́ть** *impf* confirm; corroborate. **подтвержде́ние** confirmation, corroboration.

подтёк bruise. **подтека́ть** *impf of* **подте́чь**; leak.

подтере́ть (-дотру́, -дотрёшь; подтёр) *pf* (*impf* **подтира́ть**) wipe (up).

подте́чь (-ечёт; -тёк, -ла́) *pf* (*impf* **подтека́ть**) **под**+*acc* flow under.

подтира́ть *impf of* **подтере́ть**

подтолкну́ть (-ну́, -нёшь) *pf* (*impf* **подта́лкивать**) push; urge on.

подточи́ть (-чу́, -чишь) *pf* (*impf* **подта́чивать**) sharpen; eat away; undermine.

подтру́нивать *impf*, **подтруни́ть** *pf* **над**+*instr* tease.

подтя́гивать *impf*, **подтяну́ть** (-ну́, -нешь) *pf* tighten; pull up; move up; **~ся** tighten one's belt *etc.*; pull o.s. together. **подтя́жки** (-жек) *pl* braces, suspenders. **подтя́нутый** smart.

по|ду́мать *pf* think (for a while). **поду́мывать** *impf*+*inf* or **o**+*prep* think about.

по|ду́ть (-у́ю) *pf*.

поду́шка pillow; cushion.

подхали́м *m* toady. **подхали́мство** grovelling.

подхвати́ть (-ачу́, -а́тишь) *pf*, **подхва́тывать** *impf* catch (up), pick up, take up.

подхлестну́ть (-ну́, -нёшь) *pf*, **подхлёстывать** *impf* whip up.

подхо́д approach. **подходи́ть** (-ожу́, -о́дишь) *impf of* **подойти́**. **подходя́щий** suitable.

подцепи́ть (-плю́, -пишь) *pf*, **подцепля́ть** *impf* hook on; pick up.

подча́с *adv* sometimes.

подчёркивать *impf*, **подчеркну́ть** (-ну́, -нёшь) *pf* underline; emphasize.

подчине́ние subordination; submission. **подчинённый** subordinate.

подчини́ть *pf*, **подчиня́ть** *impf* subordinate, subject; **~ся** +*dat* submit to.

подшива́ть *impf of* **подши́ть**. **подши́вка** hemming; lining; soling.

подши́пник bearing.

подши́ть (-дошью́, -дошьёшь) *pf* (*impf* **подшива́ть**) hem, line; sole.

подшути́ть (-учу́, -у́тишь) *pf*, **подшу́чивать** *impf* **над**+*instr* mock; play a trick on.

подъе́ду *etc.*: *see* **подъе́хать**

подъе́зд entrance, doorway; approach. **подъезжа́ть** *impf of* **подъе́хать**

подъём lifting; raising; ascent; climb; enthusiasm; instep; reveille. **подъёмник** lift, elevator, hoist. **подъёмный** lifting; **~ кран** crane; **~ мост** drawbridge.

подъе́хать (-е́ду) *pf* (*impf* **подъезжа́ть**) drive up.

подыма́ть(ся *impf of* **подня́ть(ся**

подыска́ть (-ыщу́, -ы́щешь) *pf*, **поды́скивать** *impf* seek (out).

подыто́живать *impf*, **подыто́жить** (-жу) *pf* sum up.

подыха́ть *impf of* **подо́хнуть**

подыша́ть (-шу́, -шишь) *pf* breathe.

поеда́ть *impf of* **пое́сть**

поеди́нок (-нка) duel.

по́езд (*pl* -а́) train. **пое́здка** trip.

пое́сть (-е́м, -е́шь, -е́ст, -еди́м; -е́л) *pf* (*impf* **поеда́ть**) eat, eat up; have a bite to eat.

по|е́хать (-е́ду) *pf* go; set off.

по|жале́ть (-е́ю) *pf*.

по|жа́ловать(ся *pf*. **пожа́луй** *adv* perhaps. **пожа́луйста** *partl* please; you're welcome.

пожа́р fire. **пожа́рище** scene of a fire. **пожа́рник**, **пожа́рный** *sb* fireman. **пожа́рный** fire; **~ая кома́нда** fire-brigade; **~ая ле́стница** fire-escape; **~ая маши́на** fire-engine.

пожа́тие handshake. **пожа́ть**[1] (-жму́, -жмёшь) *pf* (*impf* **пожима́ть**) press; **~ ру́ку**+*dat* shake hands with; **~ плеча́ми** shrug one's shoulders.

пожа́ть[2] (-жну́, -жнёшь) *pf* (*impf* **пожина́ть**) reap.

пожела́ние wish, desire. **по|жела́ть** *pf*.

по|желте́ть (-е́ю) *pf*.

по|жени́ть (-ню́, -нишь) *pf*. **пожени́ться** (-же́нимся) *pf* get married.

поже́ртвование donation. **по|же́ртвовать** *pf*.

пожива́ть *impf* live; **как (вы) пожива́ете?** how are you (getting on)? **пожи́зненный** life(long). **пожило́й** elderly.

пожима́ть *impf of* **пожа́ть**¹. **пожина́ть** *impf of* **пожа́ть**². **пожира́ть** *impf of* **пожра́ть**

пожи́тки (-ов) *pl* belongings.

пожи́ть (-иву́, -ивёшь; по́жил, -а́, -о) *pf.* live for a while; stay.

пожму́ *etc.*: *see* **пожа́ть**¹. **пожну́** *etc.*: *see* **пожа́ть**²

пожра́ть (-ру́, -рёшь; -а́л, -а́, -о) *pf* (*impf* **пожира́ть**) devour.

по́за pose.

по|забо́титься (-о́чусь) *pf.*

позабыва́ть *impf*, **позабы́ть** (-у́ду) *pf* forget all about.

позавчера́ *adv* the day before yesterday.

позади́ *adv & prep+gen* behind.

по|займствовать *pf.*

позапро́шлый before last.

по|зва́ть (-зову́, -зовёшь; -а́л, -а́, -о) *pf.*

позволе́ние permission. **позволи́тельный** permissible. **позво́лить** *pf*, **позволя́ть** *impf +dat or acc* allow, permit; **позво́ль(те)** allow me; excuse me.

по|звони́ть *pf.*

позвоно́к (-нка́) vertebra. **позвоно́чник** spine. **позвоно́чн|ый** spinal; vertebrate; ~ые *sb pl* vertebrates.

поздне́е *adv* later. **по́здний** late; **по́здно** it is late.

по|здоро́ваться *pf.* **поздра́вить** (-влю) *pf*, **поздравля́ть** *impf c+instr* congratulate on. **поздравле́ние** congratulation.

по|зелене́ть (-е́ет) *pf.*

по́зже *adv* later (on).

пози́ровать *impf* pose.

позити́в positive. **позити́вный** positive.

пози́ция position.

познава́тельный cognitive. **познава́ть** (-наю́, -наёшь) *impf of* **позна́ть**

по|знако́мить(ся (-млю(сь) *pf.*

позна́ние cognition. **позна́ть** *pf* (*impf* **познава́ть**) get to know.

позоло́та gilding. **по|золоти́ть** (-очу́) *pf.*

позо́р shame, disgrace. **позо́рить** *impf* (*pf* **о~**) disgrace; ~**ся** disgrace o.s. **позо́рный** shameful.

позы́в urge; inclination.

поигра́ть *pf* play (for a while).

поимённо *adv* by name.

по́имка capture.

поинтересова́ться *pf* be curious.

поиска́ть (-ищу́, -и́щешь) *pf* look for. **по́иски** (-ов) *pl* search.

пои́стине *adv* indeed.

пои́ть (пою́, по́ишь) *impf* (*pf* **на~**) give something to drink; water.

пойду́ *etc.*: *see* **пойти́**

по́йло swill.

пойма́ть *pf of* **лови́ть**. **пойму́** *etc.*: *see* **поня́ть**

пойти́ (-йду́, -йдёшь; пошёл, -шла́) *pf of* **идти́**, **ходи́ть**; go, walk; begin to walk; +*inf* begin; **пошёл!** off you go! I'm off; **пошёл вон!** be off!

пока́ *adv* for the present; cheerio; ~ **что** in the meanwhile. **пока́** *conj* while; ~ **не** until.

пока́з showing, demonstration. **показа́ние** testimony, evidence; reading. **показа́тель** *m* index. **показа́тельный** significant; model; demonstration. **показа́ть** (-ажу́, -а́жешь) *pf*, **пока́зывать** *impf* show. **по|каза́ться** (-ажу́сь, -а́жешься) *pf*, **пока́зываться** *impf* show o.s.; appear. **показно́й** for show; ostentatious. **показу́ха** show.

по|кале́чить(ся (-чу(сь) *pf.*

пока́мест *adv & conj* for the present; while; meanwhile.

по|кара́ть *pf.*

покати́ть (-чу́, -тишь) *pf* start (rolling); ~**ся** start rolling.

пока́тый sloping; slanting.

покача́ть *pf* rock, swing; ~ **голово́й** shake one's head. **пока́чивать** rock slightly; ~**ся** rock; stagger. **покачну́ть** (-ну́, -нёшь) *pf* shake; rock; ~**ся** sway, totter, lurch.

пока́шливать *impf* have a slight cough.

покая́ние confession; repentance. **по|ка́яться** *pf.*

поквита́ться *pf* be quits; get even.

покида́ть *impf*, **поки́нуть** (-ну) *pf* leave; abandon. **поки́нутый** deserted.

поклада́|я: не ~ рук untiringly.

покла́дистый complaisant, obliging.

покло́н bow; greeting; regards. **поклоне́ние** worship. **поклони́ться**

(-ню́сь, -ни́шься) *pf of* **кла́няться.**
покло́нник admirer; worshipper.
поклоня́ться *impf +dat* worship.
по|кля́сться (-яну́сь, -нёшься; -я́лся, -ла́сь) *pf.*
поко́иться *impf* rest, repose. **поко́й** rest, peace; room. **поко́йник, -ица** the deceased. **поко́йный** calm, quiet; deceased.
по|колеба́ть(ся (-е́блю(сь) *pf.*
поколе́ние generation.
по|колоти́ть(ся (-очу́(сь, -о́тишь(ся) *pf.*
поко́нчить (-чу) *pf* с+*instr* finish; put an end to; ~ с собо́й commit suicide.
покоре́ние conquest. **покори́ть** *pf* (*impf* **покоря́ть**) subdue; conquer; ~ся submit.
по|корми́ть(ся (-млю́(сь, -мишь(ся) *pf.*
поко́рный humble; submissive, obedient.
по|коро́бить(ся (-блю(сь) *pf.*
покоря́ть(ся *impf of* **покори́ть(ся**
поко́с mowing; meadow(-land).
покоси́вшийся rickety, ramshackle.
по|коси́ть(ся (-ошу́(сь) *pf.*
по|кра́сить (-а́шу) *pf.* **покра́ска** painting, colouring.
по|красне́ть (-е́ю) *pf.* **по|криви́ть(ся** (-влю́(сь) *pf.*
покро́в cover. **покрови́тель** *m,* **покрови́тельница** patron; sponsor. **покрови́тельственный** protective; patronizing. **покрови́тельство** protection, patronage. **покрови́тельствовать** *impf +dat* protect, patronize.
покро́й cut.
покроши́ть (-шу́, -шишь) *pf* crumble; chop.
покрути́ть (-учу́, -у́тишь) *pf* twist.
покрыва́ло cover; bedspread; veil. **покрыва́ть** *impf,* **по|кры́ть** (-ро́ю) *pf* cover; ~ся cover o.s.; get covered. **покры́тие** covering; surfacing; payment. **покры́шка** cover; tyre.
покупа́тель *m* buyer; customer. **покупа́ть** *impf of* **купи́ть. поку́пка** purchase. **покупно́й** bought, purchased; purchase.
по|кури́ть (-рю́, -ришь) *pf* have a smoke.
по|ку́шать *pf.*

покуше́ние +на+*acc* attempted assassination of.
пол[1] (*loc* -у́; *pl* -ы́) floor.
пол[2] sex.
пол- *in comb with n in gen, in oblique cases* **полу-,** half.
пола́ (*pl* -ы) flap; **из-под полы́** on the sly.
полага́ть *impf* suppose, think. **полага́ться** *impf of* **положи́ться; полага́ется** *impers* one is supposed to; +*dat* it is due to.
по|ла́комить(ся (-млю(сь) *pf.*
полго́да (полуго́да) *m* half a year.
по́лдень (-дня *or* -лу́дня) *m* noon. **полдне́вный** *adj.*
по́ле (*pl* -я́, -е́й) field; ground; margin; brim. **полев|о́й** field; ~ы́е цветы́ wild flowers.
полежа́ть (-жу́) *pf* lie down for a while.
поле́зн|ый useful; helpful; good, wholesome; ~ая нагру́зка payload.
по|ле́зть (-зу; -ле́з) *pf.*
полемизи́ровать *impf* debate, engage in controversy. **поле́мика** controversy; polemics. **полеми́ческий** polemical.
по|лени́ться (-ню́сь, -нишься) *pf.*
поле́но (*pl* -е́нья, -ьев) log.
полёт flight. **по|лете́ть** (-лечу́) *pf.*
по́лзать *indet impf,* **ползти́** (-зу́, -зёшь; полз, -ла́) *det impf* crawl, creep; ooze; fray. **ползу́чий** creeping.
поли- *in comb* poly-.
полива́ть(ся *impf of* **поли́ть(ся. поли́вка** watering.
полига́мия polygamy.
полигло́т polyglot.
полиграфи́ческий printing. **полиграфи́я** printing.
полиго́н range.
поликли́ника polyclinic.
полиме́р polymer.
полиня́лый faded. **по|линя́ть** *pf.*
полиомиели́т poliomyelitis
полирова́льный polishing. **полирова́ть** *impf* (*pf* от~) polish. **полиро́вка** polishing; polish. **полиро́вщик** polisher.
полит- *abbr in comb* (*of* **полити́ческий**) political. **политбюро́** *neut indecl* Politburo. ~заключённый *sb* political prisoner.
политехни́ческий polytechnic.

поли́тик politician. **поли́тика** policy; politics. **полити́ческий** political.

поли́ть (-лью́, -льёшь; по́лил, -а́, -о) *pf* (*impf* **полива́ть**) pour over; water; **~ся** +*instr* pour over o.s.

полице́йский police; *sb* policeman. **поли́ция** police.

поли́чн|ое *sb*: **с ~ым** red-handed.

полк (-а́, *loc* -у́) regiment.

по́лка shelf; berth.

полко́вник colonel. **полково́дец** (-дца) commander; general. **полково́й** regimental.

пол-ли́тра half a litre.

полне́ть (-е́ю) *impf* (*pf* **по~**) put on weight.

по́лно *adv* that's enough! stop it!

полно- *in comb* full; completely. **полнолу́ние** full moon. **~метра́жный** full-length. **~пра́вный** enjoying full rights; competent. **~це́нный** of full value.

полномо́чие (*usu pl*) authority, power. **полномо́чный** plenipotentiary.

по́лностью *adv* in full; completely. **полнота́** completeness; corpulence. **по́лночь** (-л(у́)ночи) midnight.

по́лный (-лон, -лна́, по́лно) full; complete; plump.

полови́к (-а́) mat, matting.

полови́на half; **два с полови́ной** two and a half; **~ шесто́го** half-past five. **полови́нка** half.

полови́ца floor-board.

полово́дье high water.

полово́й[1] floor.

полово́й[2] sexual.

поло́гий gently sloping.

положе́ние position; situation; status; regulations; thesis; provisions. **поло́женный** agreed; determined. **поло́жим** let us assume; suppose. **положи́тельный** positive. **положи́ть** (-жу́, -жишь) *pf* (*impf* **класть**) put; lay (down); **~ся** (*impf* **полага́ться**) rely.

по́лоз (*pl* -о́зья, -ьев) runner.

по|лома́ть(ся *pf*. **поло́мка** breakage.

полоса́ (*acc* по́лосу; *pl* по́лосы, -ло́с, -а́м) stripe; strip; band; region; belt; period. **полоса́тый** striped.

полоска́ть (-ощу́, -о́щешь) *impf* (*pf* вы́~, от~, про~) rinse; gargle; **~ся** paddle; flap.

по́лость[1] (*gen pl* -е́й) cavity.

по́лость[2] (*gen pl* -е́й) travelling rug.

полоте́нце (*gen pl* -нец) towel.

полотёр floor-polisher.

полоти́ще width; panel. **полотно́** (*pl* -а, -тен) linen; canvas. **полотня́ный** linen.

поло́ть (-лю́, -лешь) *impf* (*pf* вы́~) weed.

полощу́ *etc.*: *see* **полоска́ть**

полти́нник fifty copecks.

полтора́ (-лу́тора) *m & neut*, **полторы́** (-лу́тора) *f* one and a half. **полтора́ста** (полу́т-) a hundred and fifty.

полу-[1] *see* **пол-**

полу-[2] *in comb* half-, semi-, demi-. **полуботи́нок** (-нка; *gen pl* -нок) shoe. **~го́дие** half a year. **~годи́чный** half-year's, lasting six months. **~годова́лый** six-month-old. **~годово́й** half-yearly, six-monthly. **~гра́мотный** semi-literate. **~защи́тник** half-back. **~круг** semicircle. **~кру́глый** semicircular. **~ме́сяц** crescent (moon). **~мра́к** semi-darkness. **~но́чный** midnight. **~о́стров** peninsula. **~откры́тый** ajar. **~проводни́к** (-а́) semi-conductor, transistor. **~ста́нок** (-нка) halt. **~тьма́** semi-darkness. **~фабрика́т** semi-finished product, convenience food. **~фина́л** semi-final. **~часово́й** half-hourly. **~ша́рие** hemisphere. **~шу́бок** (-бка) sheepskin coat.

полу́денный midday.

получа́тель *m* recipient. **получа́ть** *impf*, **получи́ть** (-чу́, -чишь) *pf* get, receive, obtain; **~ся** come, turn up; turn out; **из э́того ничего́ не получи́лось** nothing came of it. **получе́ние** receipt. **полу́чка** receipt; pay(-packet).

полу́чше *adv* a little better.

полчаса́ (получа́са) *m* half an hour.

по́лчище horde.

по́лый hollow; flood.

по|лысе́ть (-е́ю) *pf*.

по́льза use; benefit, profit; **в по́льзу**+*gen* in favour of, on behalf of. **по́льзование** use. **по́льзоваться** *impf* (*pf* вос~) +*instr* make use of,

utilize; profit by; enjoy.
по́лька Pole; polka. **по́льский** Polish; *sb* polonaise.
по|льсти́ть(ся (-льщу́(сь) *pf.* **полью** *etc. see* **поли́ть**
По́льша Poland.
полюби́ть (-блю́, -бишь) *pf* come to like; fall in love with.
по|любова́ться (-бу́юсь) *pf.*
полюбо́вный amicable.
по|любопы́тствовать *pf.*
по́люс pole.
поля́к Pole.
поля́на glade, clearing.
поляриза́ция polarization. **поля́р-ник** polar explorer. **поля́рн|ый** polar; ~**ая звезда́** pole-star.
пом- *abbr in comb (of* **помо́щник)** assistant. ~**на́ч** assistant chief, assistant head.
пома́да pomade; lipstick.
помаза́ние anointment. **по|ма́зать-(ся** (-а́жу(сь) *pf.* **помазо́к** (-зка́) small brush.
помале́ньку *adv* gradually; gently; modestly; so-so.
пома́лкивать *impf* hold one's tongue.
по|мани́ть (-ню́, -нишь) *pf.*
пома́рка blot; pencil mark; correction.
по|ма́слить *pf.*
помаха́ть (-машу́, -ма́шешь) *pf,* **пома́хивать** *impf* +*instr* wave; wag.
поме́длить *pf* +*c+instr* delay.
поме́ньше a little smaller; a little less.
по|меня́ть(ся *pf.*
помере́ть (-мру́, -мрёшь; -мер, -ла́, -ло) *pf* (*impf* **помира́ть**) die.
по|мере́щиться (-щусь) *pf.* **по|ме́рить** *pf.*
помертве́лый deathly pale. **по|мерт-ве́ть** (-е́ю) *pf.*
помести́ть (-ещу́) *pf* (*impf* **поме-ща́ть**) accommodate; place, locate; invest; ~**ся** lodge; find room. **поме́стье** (*gen pl* -тий, -тьям) estate.
по́месь cross(-breed), hybrid.
помёт dung; droppings; litter, brood.
поме́та, поме́тка mark, note. **по|ме́-тить** (-е́чу) *pf* (*impf also* **помеча́ть**) mark; date; ~ **га́лочкой** tick.
поме́ха hindrance; obstacle; *pl* interference.

помеча́ть *impf of* **поме́тить**
поме́шанный mad; *sb* lunatic. **по-меша́тельство** madness; craze. **по|меша́ть** *pf.* **помеша́ться** *pf* go mad.
помеща́ть *impf of* **помести́ть.** **помеща́ться** *impf of* **помести́ться**; be (situated); be accommodated, find room. **помеще́ние** premises; apartment, room, lodging; location; investment. **поме́щик** landowner.
помидо́р tomato.
поми́лование forgiveness. **поми́-ловать** *pf* forgive.
поми́мо *prep*+*gen* apart from; besides; without the knowledge of.
помина́ть *impf of* **помяну́ть;** не ~ ли́хом remember kindly. **поми́нки** (-нок) *pl* funeral repast.
помира́ть *impf of* **помере́ть**
по|мири́ть(ся *pf.*
по́мнить *impf* remember.
помога́ть *impf of* **помо́чь**
по-мо́ему *adv* in my opinion.
помо́и (-ев) *pl* slops. **помо́йка** (*gen pl* -о́ек) rubbish dump. **помо́йный** slop.
помо́л grinding.
помо́лвка betrothal.
по|моли́ться (-лю́сь, -лишься) *pf.* **по|молоде́ть** (-е́ю) *pf.*
помолча́ть (-чу́) *pf* be silent for a time.
помо́рье: *see* **по- II.**
по|мо́рщиться (-щусь) *pf.*
помо́ст dais; rostrum.
по|мо́чи́ться (-чу́сь, -чишься) *pf.*
помо́чь (-огу́, -о́жешь; -ог, -ла́) (*impf* **помога́ть**) help. **помо́щник, помо́щница** assistant. **по́мощь** help; на ~! help!
помо́ю *etc.: see* **помы́ть**
по́мпа pump.
помутне́ние dimness, clouding.
помча́ться (-чу́сь) *pf* rush; dart off.
помыка́ть *impf* +*instr* order about.
по́мысел (-сла) intention; thought.
по|мы́ть(ся (-мо́ю(сь) *pf.*
помяну́ть (-ну́, -нешь) *pf* (*impf* **помина́ть**) mention; pray for.
помя́тый crumpled. **по|мя́ться** (-мнётся) *pf.*
по|наде́яться (-е́юсь) *pf* count, rely.
пона́добиться (-блюсь) *pf* be *or* become necessary; **е́сли пона́добится** if necessary.

понапра́сну *adv* in vain.

понаслы́шке *adv* by hearsay.

по-настоя́щему *adv* properly, truly.

понача́лу *adv* at first.

понево́ле *adv* willynilly; against one's will.

понеде́льник Monday.

понемно́гу, понемно́жку *adv* little by little.

по|нести́(сь (-су́(сь, -сёшь(ся; -нёс(ся, -ла́(сь) *pf.*

понижа́ть *impf*, **пони́зить** (-ни́жу) *pf* lower; reduce; **~ся** fall, drop, go down. **пониже́ние** fall; lowering; reduction.

поника́ть *impf*, **по|ни́кнуть** (-ну; -ник) *pf* droop, wilt.

понима́ние understanding. **понима́ть** *impf of* **поня́ть**

по-но́вому *adv* in a new fashion.

поно́с diarrhoea.

поноси́ть¹ (-ошу́, -о́сишь) *pf* carry; wear.

поноси́ть² (-ошу́, -о́сишь) *impf* abuse (*verbally*).

поно́шенный worn; threadbare.

по|нра́виться (-влюсь) *pf.*

понто́н pontoon.

пону́дить (-у́жу) *pf*, **понужда́ть** *impf* compel.

понука́ть *impf* urge on.

пону́рить *pf*: **~ го́лову** hang one's head. **пону́рый** downcast.

по|ню́хать *pf.* **поню́шка**: **~ табаку́** pinch of snuff.

поня́тие concept; notion, idea. **поня́тливый** bright, quick. **поня́тный** understandable; **~о** naturally; **~о?** (do you) see? **поня́ть** (пойму́, -мёшь; по́нял, -а́, -о) *pf* (*impf* **понима́ть**) understand; realize.

по|обе́дать *pf.* **по|обеща́ть** *pf.*

поо́даль *adv* at some distance.

поодино́чке *adv* one by one.

поочерёдно *adv* in turn.

поощре́ние encouragement. **поощри́ть** *pf*, **поощря́ть** *impf* encourage.

поп (-а́) priest.

попада́ние hit. **попада́ть(ся** *impf of* **попа́сть(ся**

попа́дья priest's wife.

попа́ло: *see* **попа́сть. по|па́риться** *pf.*

попа́рно *adv* in pairs, two by two.

попа́сть (-аду́, -адёшь; -а́л) *pf* (*impf* **попада́ть**) **+в+**acc hit; get (in)to, find o.s. in; **+на+**acc hit upon, come on; **не туда́ ~** get the wrong number; **~ся** be caught; find o.s.; turn up; **что попадётся** anything. **попа́ло** *with prons & advs*: **где ~** anywhere; **как ~** anyhow; **что ~** the first thing to hand.

поперёк *adv & prep+*gen across.

попереме́нно *adv* in turns.

попере́чник diameter. **попере́чный** transverse, diametrical, cross; **~ый разре́з, ~ое сече́ние** cross-section.

поперхну́ться (-ну́сь, -нёшься) *pf* choke.

по|пе́рчить (-чу) *pf.*

попече́ние care; charge; **на попече́нии+**gen in the care of. **попечи́тель** *m* guardian, trustee.

попира́ть *impf* (*pf* **попра́ть**) trample on; flout.

попи́ть (-пью, -пьёшь; по́пил, -ла, по́пило) *pf* have a drink.

поплаво́к (-вка́) float.

попла́кать (-а́чу) *pf* cry a little.

по|плати́ться (-чу́сь, -тишься) *pf.*

поплы́ть (-ыву́, -ывёшь; -ы́л, -ыла́, -о) *pf.* start swimming.

попо́йка drinking-bout.

пополáм *adv* in two, in half; half-and-half.

поползнове́ние half a mind; pretension(s).

пополне́ние replenishment; reinforcement. **по|полне́ть** (-е́ю) *pf.* **попо́лнить** *pf*, **пополня́ть** *impf* replenish; re-stock; reinforce.

пополу́дни *adv* in the afternoon; p.m.

попо́на horse-cloth.

по|по́тчевать (-чую) *pf.*

поправи́мый rectifiable. **попра́вить** (-влю) *pf*, **поправля́ть** *impf* repair; correct, put right; set straight; **~ся** correct o.s.; get better, recover; improve. **попра́вка** correction; repair; adjustment; recovery.

попра́ть *pf of* **попира́ть**

по-пре́жнему *adv* as before.

попрёк reproach. **попрека́ть** *impf*, **попрекну́ть** (-ну́, -нёшь) *pf* reproach.

по́прище field; walk of life.

по|про́бовать *pf.* **по|проси́ть(ся**

(-ошу́(сь, -о́сишь(ся) *pf.*

по́просту *adv* simply; without ceremony.

попроша́йка *m & f* cadger. **попроша́йничать** *impf* cadge.

попроща́ться *pf* (+с+*instr*) say goodbye (to).

попры́гать *pf* jump, hop.

попуга́й parrot.

популя́рность popularity. **популя́рный** popular.

попусти́тельство connivance.

по-пусто́му, по́пусту *adv* in vain.

попу́тно *adv* at the same time; in passing. **попу́тный** passing. **попу́тчик** fellow-traveller.

по|пыта́ться *pf* попы́тка attempt.

по|пя́титься (-я́чусь) *pf.* **попя́тный** backward; **идти́ на ~** go back on one's word.

по́ра¹ pore.

пора́² (*acc* -у; *pl* -ы, пор, -а́м) time; it is time; **до каки́х пор?** till when?; **до сих пор** till now; **с каки́х пор?** since when?

порабо́тать *pf* do some work.

поработи́ть (-ощу́) *pf,* **порабоща́ть** *impf* enslave. **порабоще́ние** enslavement.

поравня́ться *pf* come alongside.

**по|ра́доваться)ся *pf.*

поража́ть *impf,* **по|рази́ть** (-ажу́) *pf* hit; strike; defeat; affect; astonish; **~ся** be astounded. **пораже́ние** defeat. **порази́тельный** striking; astonishing.

по-ра́зному *adv* differently.

пора́нить *pf* wound; injure.

порва́ть (-ву́, -вёшь; -ва́л, -а́, -о) *pf* (*impf* **порыва́ть**) tear (up); break, break off; **~ся** tear; break (off).

по|реде́ть (-е́ет) *pf.*

поре́з cut. **поре́зать** (-е́жу) *pf* cut; **~ся** cut o.s.

поре́й leek.

по|рекомендова́ть *pf.* **по|ржа́веть** (-е́ет) *pf.*

по́ристый porous.

порица́ние censure; blame. **порица́ть** *impf* blame; censure.

по́рка flogging.

по́ровну *adv* equally.

поро́г threshold; rapids.

поро́да breed, race, species. **поро́дистый** thoroughbred. **породи́ть**

(-ожу́) *pf* (*impf* **порожда́ть**) give birth to; give rise to.

по|родни́ть(ся *pf.* **поро́дный** pedigree.

порожда́ть *impf of* **породи́ть**

поро́жний empty.

по́рознь *adv* separately, apart.

поро́й, поро́ю *adv* at times.

поро́к vice; defect.

поросёнок (-нка; *pl* -ся́та, -ся́т) piglet.

по́росль shoots; young wood.

поро́ть¹ (-рю́, -решь) *impf* (*pf* **вы́~**) thrash; whip.

поро́ть² (-рю́, -решь) *impf* (*pf* **рас~**) undo, unpick; **~ся** come unstitched.

по́рох (*pl* ~а́) gunpowder, powder. **порохово́й** powder.

поро́чить (-чу) *impf* (*pf* **о~**) discredit; smear. **поро́чный** vicious, depraved; faulty.

пороши́ть (-ши́т) *impf* snow slightly.

порошо́к (-шка́) powder.

порт (*loc* -у́; *pl* -ы, -о́в) port.

порта́тивный portable.

портве́йн port (wine).

по́ртик portico.

по́ртить (-чу) *impf* (*pf* **ис~**) spoil; corrupt; **~ся** deteriorate; go bad.

портни́ха dressmaker. **портно́вский** tailor's. **портно́й** *sb* tailor.

порто́вый port.

портре́т portrait.

портсига́р cigarette-case.

португа́лец (-льца), **-лка** Portuguese. **Португа́лия** Portugal. **португа́льский** Portuguese.

портфе́ль *m* brief-case; portfolio.

портье́ра curtain(s), portière.

портя́нка foot-binding.

поруга́ние desecration; humiliation. **пору́ганный** desecrated; outraged. **поруга́ть** *pf* scold, swear at; **~ся** swear; fall out.

пору́ка bail; guarantee; surety; **на пору́ки** on bail.

по-ру́сски *adv* (in) Russian.

поруча́ть *impf of* **поручи́ть**. **поруче́ние** assignment; errand; message.

по́ручень (-чня) *m* handrail.

поручи́тельство guarantee; bail.

поручи́ть (-чу́, -чишь) *pf* (*impf* **поруча́ть**) entrust; instruct.

поручи́ться (-чу́сь, -чишься) *pf of* **руча́ться**

порхáть *impf*, **порхнýть** (-нý, -нёшь) *pf* flutter, flit.

пóрция portion; helping.

пóрча spoiling; damage; curse.

пóршень (-шня) *m* piston.

порыв[1] gust; rush; fit

порыв[2] breaking. **порывáть(ся**[1] *impf of* **порвáть(ся**

порывáться[2] *impf* make jerky movements; endeavour. **порывистый** gusty; jerky; impetuous; fitful.

порядковый ordinal. **порядок** (-дка) order; sequence; manner, way; procedure; **всё в порядке** everything is alright; ~ **дня** agenda, order of the day. **порядочный** decent; honest; respectable; fair, considerable.

посадить (-ажý, -áдишь) *pf of* **садить**, **сажáть**. **посáдка** planting; embarkation; boarding; landing. **посáдочный** planting; landing.

посажу *etc.: see* **посадить**. **по|свáтать(ся** *pf*. **по|свежéть** (-éет) *pf*. **по|светить** (-ечý, -éтишь) *pf*. **по|светлéть** (-éет) *pf*.

посвистывать *impf* whistle.

по-своéму *adv* (in) one's own way.

посвятить (-ящý) *pf*, **посвящáть** *impf* devote; dedicate; let in; ordain. **посвящéние** dedication; initiation; ordination.

посéв sowing; crops. **посевн|óй** sowing; ~áя **площадь** area under crops.

по|седéть (-éю) *pf*.

поселéнец (-нца) settler; exile. **поселéние** settlement; exile. **по|селить** *pf*, **поселять** *impf* settle; lodge; arouse; ~**ся** settle, take up residence. **посёлок** (-лка) settlement; housing estate.

посеребрённый (-рён, -á) silver-plated. **по|серебрить** *pf*.

посередине *adv & prep+gen* in the middle (of).

посетитель *m* visitor. **посетить** (-ещý) *pf* (*impf* **посещáть**) visit; attend.

по|сéтовать *pf*.

посещáемость attendance. **посещáть** *impf of* **посетить**. **посещéние** visit.

по|сéять (-éю) *pf*.

посидéть (-ижý) *pf* sit (for a while).

посильный within one's powers; feasible.

посинéлый gone blue. **по|синéть** (-éю) *pf*.

по|скакáть (-ачý, -áчешь) *pf*.

поскользнýться (-нýсь, -нёшься) *pf* slip.

поскóльку *conj* as far as, (in) so far as.

по|скромничать *pf*. **по|скупиться** (-плюсь) *pf*.

послáнец (-нца) messenger, envoy. **послáние** message; epistle. **послáнник** envoy, minister. **послáть** (-шлю, -шлёшь) *pf* (*impf* **посылáть**) send.

пóсле *adv & prep+gen* after; afterwards.

после- *in comb* post-; after-. **послевоéнный** post-war. ~**зáвтра** *adv* the day after tomorrow. ~**родовóй** post-natal. ~**слóвие** epilogue; concluding remarks.

послéдний last; recent; latest; latter. **послéдователь** *m* follower. **послéдовательность** sequence; consistency. **послéдовательный** consecutive; consistent. **по|слéдовать** *pf*. **послéдствие** consequence. **послéдующий** subsequent; consequent.

пословица proverb, saying.

по|служить (-жý, -жишь) *pf*. **послужнóй** service.

послушáние obedience. **по|слýшать(ся** *pf*. **послýшный** obedient.

по|слышаться (-шится) *pf*.

посмáтривать *impf* look from time to time.

посмéиваться *impf* chuckle.

посмéртный posthumous.

по|смéть (-éю) *pf*.

посмеяние ridicule. **посмеяться** (-еюсь, -еёшься) *pf* laugh; +**над**+*instr* laugh at.

по|смотрéть(ся (-рю(сь, -ришь(ся) *pf*.

пособие aid; allowance, benefit; textbook. **пособник** accomplice.

по|совéтовать(ся *pf*. **по|содéйствовать** *pf*.

посóл (-слá) ambassador.

по|солить (-олю, -óлишь) *pf*.

посóльство embassy.

поспáть (-сплю; -áл, -á, -о) *pf* sleep; have a nap.

поспевáть[1] *impf*, **по|спéть**[1] (-éет) *pf* ripen.

поспевáть[2] *impf*, **поспéть**[2] (-éю) *pf*

have time; be in time (**к**+*dat*, **на**+*acc*
for); +**за**+*instr* keep up with.
по|спешить (-шу) *pf*. **поспешный**
hasty, hurried.
по|спорить *pf*. **по|способствовать**
pf.
посрамить (-млю) *pf*, **посрамлять**
impf disgrace.
посреди, посредине *adv & prep+gen*
in the middle (of). **посредник** mediator. **посредничество** mediation.
посредственный mediocre. **посредством** *prep+gen* by means of.
по|ссорить(ся *pf*.
пост[1] (-á, *loc* -ý) post.
пост[2] (-á, *loc* -ý) fast(ing).
по|ставить[1] (-влю) *pf*.
по|ставить[2] (-влю) *pf*, **поставлять**
impf supply. **поставка** delivery.
поставщик (-á) supplier.
постамент pedestal.
постановить (-влю, -вишь) *pf* (*impf*
постановлять) decree; decide.
постановка production; arrangement; putting, placing.
постановление decree; decision.
постановлять *impf of* **постановить**
постановщик producer; (film) director.
по|стараться *pf*.
по|стареть (-ею) *pf*. **по-старому**
adv as before.
постель bed. **постелю** etc.: see **постлать**
постепенный gradual.
по|стесняться *pf*.
постигать *impf of* **постичь**. **постигнуть**: *see* **постичь**. **постижение**
comprehension, grasp. **постижи-
мый** comprehensible.
постилать *impf of* **постлать**
постирать *pf* do some washing.
поститься (-щусь) *impf* fast.
постичь, постигнуть (-йгну; -йг(нул))
pf (*impf* **постигать**) comprehend,
grasp; befall.
по|стлать (-стелю, -стелешь) *pf*
(*impf also* **постилать**) spread; make
(bed).
постн|ый lenten; lean; glum; ~ое
масло vegetable oil.
постовой on point duty.
постой billeting.
постольку: ~, **поскольку** *conj* to

that extent, insofar as.
по|сторониться (-нюсь, -нишься) *pf*.
посторонний strange; foreign; extraneous, outside; *sb* stranger, outsider.
постоянный permanent; constant;
continual; ~ый **ток** direct current.
постоянство constancy.
по|стоять (-ою) *pf* stand (for a
while); +**за**+*acc* stand up for.
пострадавший *sb* victim. **по|стра-
дать** *pf*.
постригаться *impf*, **постричься**
(-игусь, -ижёшься; -йгся) *pf* take mo-
nastic vows; get one's hair cut.
построение construction; building;
formation. **по|строить(ся** (-рою(сь)
pf. **постройка** building.
постскриптум postscript.
постулировать *impf & pf* postulate.
поступательный forward. **посту-
пать** *impf*, **поступить** (-плю, -пишь)
pf act; do; be received; +**в** *or* **на**+*acc*
enter, join; +**с**+*instr* treat; ~**ся** +*instr*
waive, forgo. **поступление** entering,
joining; receipt. **поступок** (-пка) act,
deed. **поступь** gait; step.
по|стучать(ся (-чу(сь) *pf*.
по|стыдиться (-ыжусь) *pf*. **постыд-
ный** shameful.
посуда crockery; dishes. **посудный**
china; dish.
по|сулить *pf*.
посчастливиться *pf impers* (+*dat*)
be lucky; **ей посчастливилось** +*inf*
she had the luck to.
посчитать *pf* count (up). **по|счи-
таться** *pf*.
посылать *impf of* **послать**. **посылка** sending; parcel; errand;
premise. **посыльный** *sb* messenger.
посыпать (-плю, -плешь) *pf*, **посыпать** *impf* strew. **посыпаться**
(-плется) *pf* begin to fall; rain down.
посягательство encroachment; infringement. **посягать** *impf*, **посяг-
нуть** (-ну, -нёшь) *pf* encroach, infringe.
пот (*loc* -ý; *pl* -ы́) sweat.
потайной secret.
потакать *impf* +*dat* indulge.
потасовка brawl.
поташ (-á) potash.
по-твоему *adv* in your opinion.
потворствовать *impf* (+*dat*) be in-

dulgent (towards), pander (to).
потёк damp patch.
потёмки (-мок) pl darkness. **по|темне́ть** (-е́ет) pf.
потенциа́л potential. **потенциа́льный** potential.
по|тепле́ть (-е́ет) pf.
потерпе́вший sb victim. **по|терпе́ть** (-плю́, -пишь) pf.
поте́ря loss; waste; pl casualties. **по|теря́ть(ся** pf.
по|тесни́ть pf. **по|тесни́ться** pf sit closer, squeeze up.
поте́ть (-е́ю) impf (pf вс~, за~) sweat; mist over.
поте́ха fun. **по|те́шить(ся** (-шу(сь) pf. **поте́шный** amusing.
поте́чь (-чёт, -тёк, -ла́) pf begin to flow.
потира́ть impf rub.
потихо́ньку adv softly; secretly; slowly.
по́тный (-тен, -тна́, -тно) sweaty.
пото́к stream; torrent; flood.
потоло́к (-лка́) ceiling.
по|толсте́ть (-е́ю) pf.
пото́м adv later (on); then. **пото́мок** (-мка) descendant. **пото́мство** posterity.
потому́ adv that is why; ~ что conj because.
по|тону́ть (-ну́, -нешь) pf. **пото́п** flood, deluge. **по|топи́ть** (-плю́, -пишь) pf, **потопля́ть** impf sink.
по|топта́ть (-пчу́, -пчешь) pf. **по|торопи́ть(ся** (-плю́(сь, -пишь(ся) pf.
пото́чный continuous; production-line.
по|тра́тить (-а́чу) pf.
потреби́тель m consumer, user. **потреби́тельский** consumer; consumers'. **потреби́ть** (-блю́) pf, **потребля́ть** impf consume. **потребле́ние** consumption. **потре́бность** need, requirement. **по|тре́бовать(ся** pf.
по|трево́жить(ся (-жу(сь) pf.
потрёпанный shabby; tattered. **по|трепа́ть(ся** (-плю́(сь, -плешь(ся) pf.
по|тре́скаться pf. **потре́скивать** impf crackle.
потро́гать pf touch, feel, finger.
потроха́ (-о́в) pl giblets. **потроши́ть** (-шу́) impf (pf вы́~) disembowel, clean.

потруди́ться (-ужу́сь, -у́дишься) pf do some work; take the trouble.
потряса́ть impf, **потрясти́** (-су́, -сёшь; -яс, -ла́) pf shake; rock; stagger; +acc or instr brandish, shake. **потряса́ющий** staggering, tremendous. **потрясе́ние** shock.
поту́ги f pl vain attempts; **родовы́е** ~ labour.
поту́пить (-плю) pf, **потупля́ть** impf lower; ~ся look down.
по|тускне́ть (-е́ет) pf.
потусторо́ний мир the next world.
потуха́ть impf, **по|ту́хнуть** (-нет, -ух) pf go out; die out. **поту́хший** extinct; lifeless.
по|туши́ть (-шу́, -шишь) pf.
по́тчевать (-чую) impf (pf по~) +instr treat to.
потя́гиваться impf, **по|тяну́ться** (-ну́сь, -нешься) pf stretch o.s. **по|тяну́ть** (-ну́, -нешь) pf.
по|у́жинать pf. **по|умне́ть** (-е́ю) pf.
поуча́ть impf preach at.
поучи́тельный instructive.
поха́бный obscene.
похвала́ praise. **по|хвали́ть(ся** (-лю́(сь, -лишь(ся) pf. **похва́льный** laudable; laudatory.
по|хва́стать(ся pf.
похити́тель m kidnapper; abductor; thief. **похи́тить** (-и́щу) pf, **похища́ть** impf kidnap; abduct; steal. **похище́ние** theft; kidnapping; abduction.
похлёбка broth, soup.
похло́пать pf slap; clap.
по|хлопота́ть (-очу́, -о́чешь) pf.
похме́лье hangover.
похо́д campaign; march; hike; excursion.
по|хода́тайствовать pf.
походи́ть (-ожу́, -о́дишь) impf на+acc resemble.
похо́дка gait, walk. **похо́дный** mobile; field; marching. **похожде́ние** adventure.
похо́жий alike; ~ на like.
похолода́ние drop in temperature.
по|холоде́ть (-е́ю) pf. **похоро́нить** (-ню́, -нишь) pf. **похоро́нный** funeral. **по́хороны** (-ро́н) pl funeral.
по|хороше́ть (-е́ю) pf.
по́хоть lust.
по|худе́ть (-е́ю) pf.

по|**целова́ть(ся** *pf.* **поцелу́й** kiss.

поча́ток (-тка) ear; (corn) cob.

по́чва soil; ground; basis. **по́чвенный** soil; ~ **покро́в** top-soil.

почём *adv* how much; how; ~ **знать?** who can tell?; ~ **я зна́ю?** how should I know?

почему́ *adv* why. **почему́-либо, -нибудь** *advs* for some reason or other. **почему́-то** *adv* for some reason.

по́черк hand(writing).

почерне́лый blackened, darkened. **по**|**черне́ть** (-е́ю) *pf.*

почерпну́ть (-ну́, -нёшь) *pf* draw, scoop up; glean.

по|**черстве́ть** (-е́ю) *pf.* **по**|**чеса́ть(ся** (-ешу́(сь, -е́шешь(ся) *pf.*

по́честь honour. **почёт** honour; respect. **почётный** of honour; honourable; honorary.

по́чечный renal; kidney.

почива́ть *impf of* **почи́ть**

почи́н initiative.

по|**чини́ть** (-ню́, -нишь) *pf,* **починя́ть** *impf* repair, mend. **почи́нка** repair.

по|**чи́стить(ся** (-и́щу(сь) *pf.*

почита́ть[1] *impf* honour; revere.

почита́ть[2] *pf* read for a while.

почи́ть (-и́ю, -и́ешь) *pf (impf* **почива́ть)** rest; pass away; ~ **на ла́врах** rest on one's laurels.

по́чка[1] bud.

по́чка[2] kidney.

по́чта post, mail; post-office. **почта́льо́н** postman. **почта́мт** (*main*) post-office.

почте́ние respect. **почте́нный** venerable; considerable.

почти́ *adv* almost.

почти́тельный respectful. **почти́ть** (-чту́) *pf* honour.

почто́в|**ый** postal; ~**ая ка́рточка** postcard; ~**ый перево́д** postal order; ~**ый я́щик** letter-box.

по|**чу́вствовать(ся** *pf.*

по|**чу́диться** (-ишься) *pf.*

пошатну́ть (-ну́, -нёшь) *pf* shake; ~**ся** shake; stagger.

по|**шевели́ть(ся** (-елю́(сь, -е́ли́шь(ся) *pf.* **пошёл** *etc.: see* **пойти́**

поши́вочный sewing.

по́шлина duty.

по́шлость vulgarity; banality. **по́шлый** vulgar; banal.

пошту́чный by the piece.

по|**шути́ть** (-учу́, -у́тишь) *pf.*

поща́да mercy. **по**|**щади́ть** (-ажу́) *pf.*

по|**щекота́ть** (-очу́, -о́чешь) *pf.*

пощёчина slap in the face.

по|**щу́пать** *pf.*

поэ́зия poetry. **поэ́ма** poem. **поэ́т** poet. **поэти́ческий** poetic.

поэ́тому *adv* therefore.

пою́ *etc.: see* **петь, по́ить**

появи́ться (-влю́сь, -вишься) *pf,* **появля́ться** *impf* appear. **появле́ние** appearance.

по́яс (*pl* -а́) belt; girdle; waist-band; waist; zone.

поясне́ние explanation. **поясни́тельный** explanatory. **поясни́ть** *pf* (*impf* **поясня́ть)** explain, elucidate.

поясни́ца small of the back. **поясно́й** waist; to the waist; zonal.

пояснять *impf of* **поясни́ть**

пра- *pref* first; great-. **праба́бушка** great-grandmother.

пра́вда (the) truth. **правди́вый** true; truthful. **правдоподо́бный** likely; plausible. **пра́ведный** righteous; just.

пра́вило rule; principle.

пра́вильн|**ый** right, correct; regular; ~**о!** that's right!

прави́тель *m* ruler. **прави́тельственный** government(al). **прави́тельство** government. **пра́вить**[1] (-влю) +*instr* rule, govern; drive.

пра́вить[2] (-влю) *impf* correct. **пра́вка** correcting.

правле́ние board; administration; government.

пра́|**внук**, ~**внучка** great-grandson, -granddaughter.

пра́во[1] (*pl* -а́) law; right; **(води́тельские)** driving licence; **на права́х**+*gen* in the capacity of, as.

пра́во[2] *adv* really.

право-[1] *in comb* law; right. **правове́рный** orthodox. ~**ме́рный** lawful, rightful. ~**мо́чный** competent. ~**наруше́ние** infringement of the law, offence. ~**наруши́тель** *m* offender, delinquent. ~**писа́ние** spelling, orthography. ~**сла́вный** orthodox; *sb* member of the Orthodox Church. ~**су́дие** justice.

право-[2] *in comb* right, right-hand. **правосторо́нний** right; right-hand.

правово́й legal.

правота́ rightness; innocence.

пра́вый[1] right; right-hand; right-wing.

пра́вый[2] (прав, -а́, -о) right, correct; just.

пра́вящий ruling.

пра́дед great-grandfather; pl ancestors. **праде́душка** m great-grandfather.

пра́здник (public) holiday. **пра́здничный** festive. **пра́зднование** celebration. **пра́здновать** impf (pf от~) celebrate. **пра́здность** idleness. **пра́здный** idle; useless.

пра́ктика practice; practical work. **практикова́ть** impf practise; ~ся (pf на~ся) be practised; +в+prep practise. **практи́ческий, практи́чный** practical.

пра́отец (-тца) forefather.

пра́порщик ensign.

прапра́дед great-great-grandfather. **прароди́тель** m forefather.

прах dust; remains.

пра́чечная sb laundry. **пра́чка** laundress.

пребыва́ние stay. **пребыва́ть** impf be; reside.

превзойти́ (-йду́, -йдёшь; -ошёл, -шла́) pf (impf **превосходи́ть**) surpass; excel.

превозмога́ть impf, **превозмо́чь** (-огу́, -о́жешь; -о́г, -ла́) pf overcome.

превознести́ (-су́, -сёшь; -ёс, -ла́) pf, **превозноси́ть** (-ошу́, -о́сишь) impf extol, praise.

превосходи́тельство Excellency. **превосходи́ть** (-ожу́, -о́дишь) impf of превзойти́. **превосхо́дный** superlative; superb, excellent. **превосхо́дство** superiority. **превосходя́щий** superior.

преврати́ть (-ащу́) pf, **превраща́ть** impf convert, turn, reduce; ~ся turn, change. **превра́тный** wrong; changeful. **превраще́ние** transformation.

превы́сить (-ы́шу) pf, **превыша́ть** impf exceed. **превыше́ние** exceeding, excess.

прегра́да obstacle; barrier. **прегради́ть** (-ажу́) pf, **прегражда́ть** impf bar, block.

пред prep+instr: see пе́ред

предава́ть(ся (-даю́(сь, -даёшь(ся)

impf of преда́ть(ся

преда́ние legend; tradition; handing over, committal. **пре́данность** devotion. **пре́данный** devoted. **преда́тель** m, ~ница betrayer, traitor. **преда́тельский** treacherous. **преда́тельство** treachery. **преда́ть** (-а́м, -а́шь, -а́ст, -ади́м; пре́дал, -а́, -о) pf (impf **предава́ть**) hand over, commit; betray; ~ся abandon o.s.; give way, indulge.

предаю́ etc.: see предава́ть

предвари́тельный preliminary; prior. **предвари́ть** pf, **предваря́ть** impf forestall, anticipate.

предве́стник forerunner; harbinger. **предвеща́ть** impf portend; augur.

предвзя́тый preconceived; biased.

предви́деть (-и́жу) impf foresee.

предвкуси́ть (-ушу́, -у́сишь) pf, **предвкуша́ть** impf look forward to.

предводи́тель m leader. **предводи́тельствовать** impf +instr lead.

предвое́нный pre-war.

предвосхи́тить (-и́щу) pf, **предвосхища́ть** impf anticipate.

предвы́борный (pre-)election.

предго́рье foothills.

преддве́рие threshold.

преде́л limit; bound. **преде́льный** boundary; maximum; utmost.

предзнаменова́ние omen, augury.

предисло́вие preface.

предлага́ть impf of предложи́ть. **предло́г**[1] pretext.

предло́г[2] preposition.

предложе́ние[1] sentence; clause.

предложе́ние[2] offer; proposition; proposal; motion; suggestion; supply. **предложи́ть** (-жу́, -жишь) pf (impf **предлага́ть**) offer; propose; suggest; order.

предло́жный prepositional.

предме́стье suburb.

предме́т object; subject.

предназнача́ть impf, **предназна́чить** (-чу) pf destine, intend; earmark.

преднаме́ренный premeditated.

пре́до: see пе́ред

пре́док (-дка) ancestor.

предопределе́ние predetermination. **предопредели́ть** pf, **предопределя́ть** impf predetermine, predestine.

предоста́вить (-влю) *pf*, **предоставля́ть** *impf* grant; leave; give.

предостерега́ть *impf*, **предостере́чь** (-егу́, -ежёшь; -ёг, -ла́) *pf* warn. **предостереже́ние** warning. **предосторо́жность** precaution.

предосуди́тельный reprehensible.

предотврати́ть (-ащу́) *pf*, **предотвраща́ть** *impf* avert, prevent.

предохране́ние protection; preservation. **предохрани́тель** *m* guard; safety device, safety-catch; fuse. **предохрани́тельный** preservative; preventive; safety. **предохрани́ть** *pf*, **предохраня́ть** *impf* preserve, protect.

предписа́ние order; *pl* directions, instructions. **предписа́ть** (-ишу́, -и́шешь) *pf*, **предпи́сывать** *impf* order, direct; prescribe.

предпле́чье forearm.

предполага́емый supposed. **предполага́ется** *impers* it is proposed. **предполага́ть** *impf*, **предположи́ть** (-жу́, -о́жишь) *pf* suppose, assume. **предположе́ние** supposition, assumption. **предположи́тельный** conjectural; hypothetical.

предпосле́дний penultimate, last-but-one.

предпосы́лка precondition; premise.

предпоче́сть (-чту́, -чтёшь; -чёл, -чла́) *pf*, **предпочита́ть** *impf* prefer. **предпочте́ние** preference. **предпочти́тельный** preferable.

предприи́мчивый enterprising.

предпринима́тель *m* owner; entrepreneur; employer. **предпринима́тельство: свобо́дное ~** free enterprise. **предпринима́ть** *impf*, **предприня́ть** (-иму́, -и́мешь; -и́нял, -а́, -о) *pf* undertake. **предприя́тие** undertaking, enterprise.

предрасположе́ние predisposition.

предрассу́док (-дка) prejudice.

предрека́ть *impf*, **предре́чь** (-еку́, -ечёшь; -рёк, -ла́) *pf* foretell.

предреша́ть *impf*, **предреши́ть** (-шу́) *pf* decide beforehand; predetermine.

председа́тель *m* chairman.

предсказа́ние prediction. **предсказа́ть** (-ажу́, -а́жешь) *pf*, **предска́зывать** *impf* predict; prophesy.

предсме́ртный dying.

представа́ть (-таю́, -таёшь) *impf of* **предста́ть**

представи́тель *m* representative. **представи́тельный** representative; imposing. **представи́тельство** representation.

предста́вить (-влю) *pf*, **представля́ть** *impf* present; submit; introduce; represent; **~ себе́** imagine; **представля́ть собо́й** represent, be; **~ся** present itself, occur; seem; introduce o.s.; +*instr* pretend to be. **представле́ние** presentation; performance; idea, notion.

предста́ть (-а́ну) *pf* (*impf* **представа́ть**) appear.

предстоя́ть (-ои́т) *impf* be in prospect, lie ahead. **предстоя́щий** forthcoming; imminent.

предте́ча *m & f* forerunner, precursor.

предубежде́ние prejudice.

предугада́ть *pf*, **предуга́дывать** *impf* guess; foresee.

предупреди́тельный preventive; warning; courteous, obliging. **предупреди́ть** (-ежу́) *pf*, **предупрежда́ть** *impf* warn; give notice; prevent; anticipate. **предупрежде́ние** notice; warning; prevention.

предусма́тривать *impf*, **предусмотре́ть** (-рю́, -ришь) *pf* envisage, foresee; provide for. **предусмотри́тельный** prudent; far-sighted.

предчу́вствие presentiment; foreboding. **предчу́вствовать** *impf* have a presentiment (about).

предше́ственник predecessor. **предше́ствовать** *impf* +*dat* precede.

предъяви́тель *m* bearer. **предъяви́ть** (-влю́, -вишь) *pf*, **предъявля́ть** *impf* show, produce; bring (*lawsuit*); **~ пра́во на**+*acc* lay claim to.

предыду́щий previous.

прее́мник successor. **прее́мственность** succession; continuity.

пре́жде *adv* first; formerly; *prep*+*gen* before; **~ всего́** first of all; first and foremost; **~ чем** *conj* before. **преждевре́менный** premature. **пре́жний** previous, former.

презервати́в condom.

президе́нт president. **президе́нтский** presidential. **прези́диум** presidium.

презира́ть *impf* despise. **презре́ние** contempt. **презре́нный** contemptible. **презри́тельный** scornful.

преиму́щественно *adv* mainly, chiefly, principally. **преиму́щественный** main, primary; preferential. **преиму́щество** advantage; preference; **по преиму́ществу** for the most part.

преиспо́дняя *sb* the underworld.

прейскура́нт price list, catalogue.

преклоне́ние admiration. **преклони́ть** *pf*, **преклоня́ть** *impf* bow, bend; **~ся** bow down; **перед**+*instr* admire, worship. **прекло́нный**: ~ во́зраст old age.

прекра́сный beautiful; fine; excellent.

прекрати́ть (-ащу́) *pf*, **прекраща́ть** *impf* stop, discontinue; **~ся** cease, end. **прекраще́ние** halt; cessation.

преле́стный delightful. **пре́лесть** charm, delight.

преломи́ть (-млю́, -мишь) *pf*, **преломля́ть** *impf* refract. **преломле́ние** refraction.

прельсти́ть (-льщу́) *pf*, **прельща́ть** *impf* attract; entice; **~ся** be attracted; fall (+*instr* for).

прелюбодея́ние adultery.

прелю́дия prelude.

преми́нуть (-ну) *pf with neg* not fail.

премирова́ть *impf & pf* award a prize to; give a bonus. **пре́мия** prize; bonus; premium.

премье́р prime minister; lead(ing actor). **премье́ра** première. **премье́р-мини́стр** prime minister. **премье́рша** leading lady.

пренебрега́ть *impf*, **пренебре́чь** (-егу́, -ежёшь; -ёг, -ла́) *pf* +*instr* scorn; neglect. **пренебреже́ние** scorn; neglect. **пренебрежи́тельный** scornful.

пре́ния (-ий) *pl* debate.

преоблада́ние predominance. **преоблада́ть** *impf* predominate; prevail.

преобража́ть *impf*, **преобрази́ть** (-ажу́) *pf* transform. **преображе́ние** transformation; Transfiguration. **преобразова́ние** transformation; reform. **преобразова́ть** *pf*, **преобразо́вывать** *impf* transform; reform, reorganize.

преодолева́ть *impf*, **преодоле́ть** (-е́ю) *pf* overcome.

препара́т preparation.

препина́ние: **зна́ки препина́ния** punctuation marks.

препира́тельство altercation, wrangling.

преподава́ние teaching. **преподава́тель** *m*, **~ница** teacher. **преподава́тельский** teaching. **преподава́ть** (-даю́, -даёшь) *impf* teach.

преподнести́ (-су́, -сёшь; -ёс, -ла́) *pf*, **преподноси́ть** (-ошу́, -о́сишь) present with, give.

препроводи́ть (-вожу́, -во́дишь) *pf*, **препровожда́ть** *impf* send, forward.

препя́тствие obstacle; hurdle. **препя́тствовать** *impf* (*pf* **вос~**) +*dat* hinder.

прерва́ть (-ву́, -вёшь; -а́л, -а́, -о) *pf* (*impf* **прерыва́ть**) interrupt; break off; **~ся** be interrupted; break.

пререка́ние argument. **пререка́ться** *impf* argue.

прерыва́ть(ся *impf of* **прерва́ть(ся**

пресека́ть *impf*, **пресе́чь** (-еку́, -ечёшь; -ёк, -екла́) *pf* stop; put an end to; **~ся** stop; break.

пресле́дование pursuit; persecution; prosecution. **пресле́довать** *impf* pursue; haunt; persecute; prosecute.

пресловý́тый notorious.

пресмыка́ться *impf* grovel. **пресмыка́ющееся** *sb* reptile.

пресново́дный freshwater. **пре́сный** fresh; unleavened; insipid; bland.

пресс press. **пре́сса** the press. **пресс-конфере́нция** press-conference.

престаре́лый aged.

прести́ж prestige.

престо́л throne.

преступле́ние crime. **престу́пник** criminal. **престу́пность** criminality; crime, delinquency. **престу́пный** criminal.

пресы́титься (-ы́щусь) *pf*, **пресыща́ться** *impf* be satiated. **пресыще́ние** surfeit, satiety.

претвори́ть *pf*, **претворя́ть** *impf* (в+*acc*) turn, change, convert; ~ в жизнь realize, carry out.

претенде́нт claimant; candidate; преtender. **претендова́ть** *impf* на+*acc* lay claim to; have pretensions to. **прете́нзия** claim; pretension; **быть в прете́нзии** на+*acc* have a grudge, a grievance, against.

претерпева́ть *impf*, **претерпе́ть** (-плю́, -пишь) *pf* undergo; suffer.

преть (пре́ет) *impf* (*pf* со∼) rot.

преувеличе́ние exaggeration. **преувели́чивать** *impf*, **преувели́чить** (-чу) *pf* exaggerate.

преуменьша́ть *impf*, **преуме́ньшить** (-е́ньшу) *pf* underestimate; understate.

преуспева́ть *impf*, **преуспе́ть** (-е́ю) *pf* be successful; thrive.

преходя́щий transient.

прецеде́нт precedent.

при *prep* +*prep* by, at; in the presence of; attached to, affiliated to; with; about; on; in the time of; under; during; when, in case of; ∼ **всём том** for all that.

приба́вить (-влю) *pf*, **прибавля́ть** add; increase; ∼**ся** increase; rise; wax; **день прибавился** the days are getting longer. **приба́вка** addition; increase. **прибавле́ние** addition; supplement, appendix. **приба́вочный** additional; surplus.

Приба́лтика the Baltic States.

прибау́тка humorous saying.

прибега́ть[1] *impf of* **прибежа́ть**

прибега́ть[2] *impf*, **прибе́гнуть** (-ну; -бег) *pf* +к+*dat* resort to.

прибежа́ть (-егу́) *pf* (*impf* **прибега́ть**) come running.

прибе́жище refuge.

прибере́га́ть *impf*, **прибере́чь** (-егу́, -ежёшь; -ёг, -ла́) *pf* save (up), reserve.

приберу́ *etc.: see* **прибра́ть. прибива́ть** *impf of* **приби́ть. прибира́ть** *impf of* **прибра́ть**

приби́ть (-бью, -бьёшь) *pf* (*impf* **прибива́ть**) nail; flatten; drive.

приближа́ть *impf*, **прибли́зить** (-и́жу) *pf* bring *or* move nearer; ∼**ся** approach; draw nearer. **приближе́ние** approach. **приблизи́тельный** approximate.

прибо́й surf, breakers.

прибо́р instrument, device, apparatus; set. **прибо́рная доска́** instrument panel; dashboard.

прибра́ть (-беру́, -берёшь; -а́л, -а́, -о) *pf* (*impf* **прибира́ть**) tidy (up); put away.

прибре́жный coastal; offshore.

прибыва́ть *impf*, **прибы́ть** (-бу́ду; при́был, -а́, -о) *pf* arrive; increase, grow; rise; wax. **при́быль** profit, gain; increase, rise. **при́быльный** profitable. **прибы́тие** arrival.

прибью́ *etc.: see* **приби́ть**

прива́л halt.

прива́ривать *impf*, **привари́ть** (-рю́, -ришь) *pf* weld on.

приватиза́ция privatization. **приватизи́ровать** *impf* & *pf* privatize.

приведу́ *etc.: see* **привести́**

привезти́ (-зу́, -зёшь; -ёз, -ла́) (*impf* **привози́ть**) bring.

привере́дливый pernickety.

приве́рженец (-нца) adherent. **приве́рженный** devoted.

приве́сить (-е́шу) *pf* (*impf* **приве́шивать**) hang up, suspend.

привести́ (-еду́, -едёшь; -ёл, -а́) *pf* (*impf* **приводи́ть**) bring; lead; take; reduce; cite; put in(to), set.

приве́т greeting(s); regards. **приве́тливый** friendly; affable. **приве́тствие** greeting; speech of welcome. **приве́тствовать** *impf* & *pf* greet, salute; welcome.

приве́шивать *impf of* **приве́сить**

привива́ть(ся *impf of* **приви́ть(ся. приви́вка** inoculation.

привиде́ние ghost; apparition. **при|ви́деться** (-дится) *pf*.

привилегиро́ванный privileged. **привиле́гия** privilege.

привинти́ть (-нчу́) *pf*, **приви́нчивать** *impf* screw on.

приви́ть (-вью, -вьёшь; -и́л, -а́, -о) *pf* (*impf* **привива́ть**) inoculate; graft; inculcate; foster; ∼**ся** take; become established. **при́вкус** after-taste; smack.

привлека́тельный attractive. **привлека́ть** *impf*, **привле́чь** (-еку́, -ечёшь; -ёк, -ла́) *pf* attract; draw; draw in, win over; (*law*) have up; ∼ **к суду́** sue. **привлече́ние** attraction.

приво́д drive, gear. **приводи́ть** (-ожу́, -о́дишь) *impf of* **привести́. приводно́й** driving.

привожу́ *etc.: see* **приводи́ть, привози́ть**

привоз bringing; importation; load. **привозить** (-ожу, -озишь) *impf of* **привезти**. **привозной**, **привозный** imported.

привольный free.

привставать (-таю, -таёшь) *impf*, **привстать** (-ану) *pf* half-rise; rise.

привыкать *impf*, **привыкнуть** (-ну; -ык) *pf* get accustomed. **привычка** habit. **привычный** habitual, usual.

привью *etc.: see* **привить**

привязанность attachment; affection. **привязать** (-яжу, -яжешь) *pf*, **привязывать** *impf* attach; tie, bind; ∼ся become attached; attach o.s.; +к+*dat* pester. **привязчивый** annoying; affectionate. **привязь** tie; lead, leash; tether.

пригибать *impf of* **пригнуть**

пригласить (-ашу) *pf*, **приглашать** *impf* invite. **приглашение** invitation.

приглядеться (-яжусь) *pf*, **приглядываться** *impf* look closely; +к+*dat* scrutinize; get used to.

пригнать (-гоню, -гонишь; -ал, -а, -о) *pf* (*impf* **пригонять**) bring in; fit, adjust.

пригнуть (-ну, -нёшь) *pf* (*impf* **пригибать**) bend down.

приговаривать[1] *impf* keep saying.

приговаривать[2] *impf*, **приговорить** *pf* sentence, condemn. **приговор** verdict, sentence.

пригодиться (-ожусь) *pf* prove useful. **пригодный** fit, suitable.

пригонять *impf of* **пригнать**

пригорать *impf*, **пригореть** (-рит) *pf* be burnt.

пригород suburb. **пригородный** suburban.

пригорок (-рка) hillock.

пригоршня (*gen pl* -ей) handful.

приготовительный preparatory. **приготовить** (-влю) *pf*, **приготовлять** *impf* prepare; ∼ся prepare. **приготовление** preparation.

пригревать *impf*, **пригреть** (-ею) *pf* warm; cherish.

пригрозить (-ожу) *pf*.

придавать (-даю, -даёшь) *impf*, **придать** (-ам, -ашь, -аст, -адим; придал, -а, -о) *pf* add; give; attach. **придача** adding; addition; **в придачу** into the bargain.

придавить (-влю, -вишь) *pf*, **придавливать** *impf* press (down).

приданое *sb* dowry. **придаток** (-тка) appendage.

придвигать *impf*, **придвинуть** (-ну) *pf* move up, draw up; ∼ся move up, draw near.

придворный court.

приделать *pf*, **приделывать** *impf* attach.

придерживаться *impf* hold on; hold; +*gen* keep to.

придерусь *etc.: see* **придраться**.

придираться *impf of* **придраться**. **придирка** quibble; fault-finding. **придирчивый** fault-finding.

придорожный roadside.

придраться (-дерусь, -дерёшься; -ался, -ась, -алось) *pf* (*impf* **придираться**) find fault.

приду *etc.: see* **прийти**

придумать *pf*, **придумывать** *impf* think up, invent.

приеду *etc.: see* **приехать**. **приезд** arrival. **приезжать** *impf of* **приехать**. **приезжий** newly arrived; *sb* newcomer.

приём receiving; reception; surgery; welcome; admittance; dose; go; movement; method, way; trick. **приемлемый** acceptable. **приёмная** *sb* waiting-room; reception room. **приёмник** (radio) receiver. **приёмный** receiving; reception; entrance; foster, adopted.

приехать (-еду) *pf* (*impf* **приезжать**) arrive, come.

прижать (-жму, -жмёшь) *pf* (*impf* **прижимать**) press; clasp; ∼ся nestle up.

прижечь (-жгу, -жжёшь; -жёг, -жгла) *pf* (*impf* **прижигать**) cauterize.

приживаться *impf of* **прижиться**

прижигание cauterization. **прижигать** *impf of* **прижечь**

прижимать(ся *impf of* **прижать(ся**

прижиться (-ивусь, -ивёшься; -жился, -ась) *pf* (*impf* **приживаться**) become acclimatized.

прижму *etc.: see* **прижать**

приз (*pl* -ы) prize.

призвание vocation. **призвать** (-зову, -зовёшь; -ал, -а, -о) *pf* (*impf* **призывать**) call; call upon; call up.

приземистый stocky, squat.

приземле́ние landing. приземли́ться pf, приземля́ться impf land.

призёр prizewinner.

при́зма prism.

признава́ть (-наю́, -наёшь) impf, призна́ть pf recognize; admit; ~ся confess. при́знак sign, symptom; indication. призна́ние confession, declaration; acknowledgement; recognition. при́знанный acknowledged, recognized. призна́тельный grateful.

призову́ etc.: see призва́ть

при́зрак spectre, ghost. при́зрачный ghostly; illusory, imagined. призы́в call, appeal; slogan; call-up. призыва́ть impf of призва́ть. призывно́й conscription.

при́иск mine.

прийти́ (приду́, -дёшь; пришёл, -шла́) pf (impf приходи́ть) come; arrive; ~ в себя́ regain consciousness; ~сь +по+dat fit; suit; +на+acc fall on; impers+dat have to; happen (to), fall to the lot (of).

прика́з order, command. приказа́ние order, command. приказа́ть (-ажу́, -а́жешь) pf, прика́зывать impf order, command.

прика́лывать impf of приколо́ть. прикаса́ться impf of прикосну́ться

прика́нчивать impf of прико́нчить

прикати́ть (-ачу́, -а́тишь) pf, прика́тывать impf roll up.

прики́дывать impf, прики́нуть (-ну) pf throw in, add; weigh; estimate; ~ся +instr pretend (to be).

прикла́д[1] butt.

прикла́д[2] trimmings. прикладно́й applied. прикла́дывать(ся impf of приложи́ть(ся

прикле́ивать impf, прикле́ить pf stick; glue.

приключа́ться impf, приключи́ться pf happen, occur. приключе́ние adventure. приключе́нческий adventure.

прикова́ть (-кую́, -куёшь) pf, прико́вывать impf chain; rivet.

прикола́чивать impf, приколоти́ть (-очу́, -о́тишь) pf nail.

приколо́ть (-лю́, -лешь) pf (impf прика́лывать) pin; stab.

прикомандирова́ть pf, прикомандиро́вывать impf attach.

прико́нчить (-чу) pf (impf прика́нчивать) use up; finish off.

прикоснове́ние touch; concern. прикосну́ться (-ну́сь, -нёшься) pf (impf прикаса́ться) к+dat touch.

прикрепи́ть (-плю́) pf, прикрепля́ть impf fasten, attach. прикрепле́ние fastening; registration.

прикрыва́ть impf, прикры́ть (-ро́ю) pf cover; screen; shelter. прикры́тие cover; escort.

прику́ривать impf, прикури́ть (-рю́, -ришь) pf get a light.

прикуси́ть (-ушу́, -у́сишь) pf, прику́сывать impf bite.

прила́вок (-вка) counter.

прилага́тельное sb adjective. прилага́ть impf of приложи́ть

прила́дить (-а́жу) pf, прила́живать impf fit, adjust.

приласка́ть pf caress, pet; ~ся snuggle up.

прилега́ть impf (pf приле́чь) к+dat fit; adjoin. прилега́ющий close-fitting; adjoining, adjacent.

приле́жный diligent.

прилепи́ть(ся (-плю́(сь, -пишь(ся) pf, прилепля́ть(ся impf stick.

прилёт arrival. прилета́ть impf, прилете́ть (-ечу́) pf arrive, fly in; come flying.

приле́чь (-ля́гу, -ля́жешь; -ёг, -гла́) pf (impf прилега́ть) lie down.

прили́в flow, flood; rising tide; surge. прилива́ть impf of прили́ть. прили́вный tidal.

прилипа́ть impf, прили́пнуть (-нет; -ли́п) pf stick.

прили́ть (-льёт; -и́л, -а́, -о) pf (impf прилива́ть) flow; rush.

прили́чие decency. прили́чный decent.

приложе́ние application; enclosure; supplement; appendix. приложи́ть (-жу́, -жишь) pf (impf прикла́дывать, прилага́ть) put; apply; affix; add; enclose; ~ся take aim; +instr put, apply; +к+dat kiss.

прильёт etc.: see прили́ть. при|льну́ть (-ну́, -нёшь) pf. приля́гу etc.: see приле́чь

прима́нивать impf, примани́ть (-ню́, -нишь) pf lure; entice. прима́нка bait, lure.

применéние application; use. **применить** (-ню, -нишь) pf, **применять** impf apply; use; ~ся adapt o.s., conform.

примéр example.

при|мéрить pf (impf also **примéрять**) try on. **примéрка** fitting.

примéрно adv approximately. **примéрный** exemplary; approximate. **примерять** impf of **примéрить**

примесь admixture.

примéта sign, token. **примéтный** perceptible; conspicuous.

примечáние note, footnote; pl comments. **примечáтельный** notable.

примешáть pf, **примéшивать** impf add, mix in.

приминáть impf of **примять**

примирéние reconciliation. **примирительный** conciliatory. **при|мирить** pf, **примирять** impf reconcile; conciliate; ~ся be reconciled.

примитивный primitive.

примкнýть (-нý, -нёшь) pf (impf **примыкáть**) join; fix, attach.

примнý etc.: see **примять**

примóрский seaside; maritime. **примóрье** seaside.

примóчка wash, lotion.

примý etc.: see **принять**

примчáться (-чýсь) pf come tearing along.

примыкáть impf of **примкнýть**; +к+dat adjoin. **примыкáющий** affiliated.

примять (-мнý, -мнёшь) pf (impf **приминáть**) crush; trample down.

принадлежáть (-жý) impf belong. **принадлéжность** belonging; membership; pl accessories; equipment.

принести (-сý, -сёшь) pf (impf **приносить**) bring; fetch.

принижáть impf, **принизить** (-ижу) pf humiliate; belittle.

принимáть(ся impf of **принять(ся**

приносить (-ошý, -осишь) impf of **принести**. **приношéние** gift, offering.

принтер (comput) printer.

принудительный compulsory. **принýдить** (-ýжу) pf, **принуждáть** impf compel. **принуждéние** compulsion, coercion. **принуждённый** constrained, forced.

принц prince. **принцéсса** princess.

принцип principle. **принципиáльно** adv on principle; in principle. **принципиáльный** of principle; general.

принятие taking; acceptance; admission. **принято** it is accepted, it is usual; не ~ it is not done. **принять** (-имý, -имешь; прйнял, -á, -о) pf (impf **принимáть**) take; accept; take over; receive; +за+acc take for; ~ учáстие take part; take; take root; ~ за рабóту set to work.

приободрить pf, **приободрять** impf cheer up; ~ся cheer up.

приобрести (-етý, -етёшь; -рёл, -á) pf, **приобретáть** impf acquire. **приобретéние** acquisition.

приобщáть impf, **приобщить** (-щý) pf join, attach, unite; ~ся к+dat join in.

приоритéт priority.

приостанáвливать impf, **приостановить** (-влю, -вишь) pf stop, suspend; ~ся stop. **приостанóвка** halt, suspension.

приоткрывáть impf, **приоткрыть** (-рóю) pf open slightly.

припáдок (-дка) fit; attack.

припáсы (-ов) pl stores, supplies.

припéв refrain.

приписáть (-ишý, -ишешь) pf, **приписывать** impf add; attribute. **приписка** postscript; codicil.

приплóд offspring; increase.

приплывáть impf, **приплыть** (-ывý, -ывёшь; -ýл, -á, -о) pf swim up; sail up.

приплюснуть (-ну) pf, **приплющивать** impf flatten.

приподнимáть impf, **приподнять** (-нимý, -нимешь; -óднял, -á, -о) pf raise (a little); ~ся raise o.s. (a little).

припóй solder.

приползáть impf, **приползти** (-зý, -зёшь; -полз, -лá) pf creep up, crawl up.

припоминáть impf, **припóмнить** pf recollect.

приправа seasoning, flavouring. **приправить** (-влю) pf, **приправлять** impf season, flavour.

припрятать (-ячу) pf, **припрятывать** impf secrete, put by.

припýгивать impf, **припугнýть** (-нý, -нёшь) pf scare.

прираба́тывать *impf*, **прирабо́тать** *pf* earn ... extra. **при́работок** (-тка) additional earnings.

прира́внивать *impf*, **приравня́ть** *pf* equate (with к+*dat*).

прираста́ть *impf*, **прирасти́** (-тёт; -ро́с, -ла́) *pf* adhere; take; increase; accrue.

приро́да nature. **приро́дный** natural; by birth; innate. **прирождё́нный** innate; born.

приро́с *etc.*: *see* прирасти́. **прирост** increase.

прируча́ть *impf*, **приручи́ть** (-чу́) *pf* tame; domesticate.

приса́живаться *impf of* присе́сть

присва́ивать *impf*, **присво́ить** *pf* appropriate; award.

приседа́ть *impf*, **присе́сть** (-ся́ду) *pf* (*impf also* **приса́живаться**) sit down, take a seat.

прискака́ть (-ачу́, -а́чешь) *pf* come galloping.

приско́рбный sorrowful.

присла́ть (-ишлю́, -ишлёшь) *pf* (*impf* **присыла́ть**) send.

прислони́ть(ся (-оню́(сь, -о́ни́шь(ся) *pf*, **прислоня́ть(ся** *impf* lean, rest.

прислу́га servant; crew. **прислу́живать** *impf* (к+*dat*) wait (on), attend.

прислу́шаться *pf*, **прислу́шиваться** *impf* listen; +к+*dat* listen to; heed.

присма́тривать *impf*, **присмотре́ть** (-рю́, -ришь) *pf* +за+*instr* look after, keep an eye on; ~ся (к+*dat*) look closely (at). **присмо́тр** supervision.

при|сни́ться *pf*.

присоедине́ние joining; addition; annexation. **присоедини́ть** *pf*, **присоединя́ть** *impf* join; add; annex; ~ся к+*dat* join; subscribe to (*an opinion*).

приспосо́бить (-блю) *pf*, **приспособля́ть** *impf* fit, adjust, adapt; ~ся adapt o.s. **приспособле́ние** adaptation; device; appliance. **приспособля́емость** adaptability.

приставáть (-таю́, -таёшь) *impf of* **приста́ть**

приста́вить (-влю) *pf* (*impf* **приставля́ть**) к+*dat* place, set, *or* lean against; add; appoint to look after.

приста́вка prefix.

приставля́ть *impf of* приста́вить

при́стальный intent.

приста́нище refuge, shelter.

при́стань (*gen pl* -е́й) landing-stage; pier; wharf.

приста́ть (-а́ну) *pf* (*impf* **приставáть**) stick, adhere (к+*dat* to); pester.

пристёгивать *impf*, **пристегну́ть** (-ну́, -нёшь) *pf* fasten.

присто́йный decent, proper.

пристра́ивать(ся *impf of* пристро́ить(ся

пристра́стие predilection, passion; bias. **пристра́стный** biased.

пристре́ливать *impf*, **пристрели́ть** *pf* shoot (down).

пристро́ить (-о́ю) *pf* (*impf* **пристра́ивать**) add, build on; fix up; ~ся be fixed up, get a place. **пристро́йка** annexe, extension.

при́ступ assault; fit, attack. **приступа́ть** *impf*, **приступи́ть** (-плю́, -пишь) *pf* к+*dat* set about, start.

при|стыди́ть (-ыжу́) *pf*.

при|стыкова́ться *pf*.

присуди́ть (-ужу́, -у́дишь) *pf*, **присужда́ть** *impf* sentence, condemn; award; confer. **присужде́ние** awarding; conferment.

прису́тствие presence. **прису́тствовать** be present, attend. **прису́тствующие** *sb pl* those present.

прису́щий inherent; characteristic.

присыла́ть *impf of* присла́ть

прися́га oath. **присяга́ть** *impf*, **присягну́ть** (-ну́, -нёшь) *pf* swear.

прися́ду *etc.*: *see* присе́сть

прися́жный *sb* juror.

притаи́ться *pf* hide.

прита́птывать *impf of* притопта́ть

прита́скивать *impf*, **притащи́ть** (-ащу́, -а́щишь) *pf* bring, drag, haul; ~ся drag o.s.

притвори́ться *pf*, **притворя́ться** *impf* +*instr* pretend to be. **притво́рный** pretended, feigned. **притво́рство** pretence, sham. **притво́рщик** sham; hypocrite.

притека́ть *impf of* прите́чь

притесне́ние oppression. **притесни́ть** *pf*, **притесня́ть** *impf* oppress.

прите́чь (-ечёт, -еку́т; -ёк, -ла́) *pf* (*impf* притека́ть) pour in.

притиха́ть *impf*, **прити́хнуть** (-ну; -и́х) *pf* quiet down.

прито́к tributary; influx.

при́толока lintel.

прито́м *conj* (and) besides.

прито́н den, haunt.

притопта́ть (-пчу́, -пчешь) *pf* (*impf* **прита́птывать**) trample down.

при́торный sickly-sweet, luscious, cloying.

притра́гиваться *impf*, **притро́нуться** (-нусь) *pf* touch.

притупи́ть (-плю́, -пишь) *pf*, **притупля́ть** *impf* blunt, dull; deaden; ~**ся** become blunt *or* dull.

при́тча parable.

притяга́тельный attractive, magnetic. **притя́гивать** *impf of* **притяну́ть**

притяжа́тельный possessive.

притяже́ние attraction.

притяза́ние claim, pretension. **притяза́тельный** demanding.

притяну́тый far-fetched. **притяну́ть** (-ну́, -нешь) *pf* (*impf* **притя́гивать**) attract; drag (up).

приуро́чивать *impf*, **приуро́чить** (-чу) *pf* **к**+*dat* time for.

приуса́дебный: ~ уча́сток individual plot (*in kolkhoz*).

приуча́ть *impf*, **приучи́ть** (-чу́, -чишь) *pf* train, school.

прихлеба́тель *m* sponger.

прихо́д coming, arrival; receipts; parish. **приходи́ть(ся** (-ожу́(сь, -о́дишь(ся) *impf of* **прийти́(сь. прихо́дный** receipt. **приходя́щий** nonresident; ~ больно́й outpatient.

прихожа́нин (*pl* -а́не, -а́н), -а́нка parishioner.

прихо́жая *sb* hall, lobby.

прихотли́вый capricious; fanciful, intricate. **при́хоть** whim, caprice.

прихра́мывать limp (slightly).

прице́л sight; aiming. **прице́ливаться** *impf*, **прице́литься** *pf* take aim.

прице́ниваться *impf*, **прицени́ться** (-ню́сь, -нишься) *pf* (**к**+*dat*) ask the price of.

прице́п trailer. **прицепи́ть** (-плю́, -пишь) *pf*, **прицепля́ть** *impf* hitch, hook on; ~**ся к**+*dat* stick to, cling to. **прице́пка** hitching, hooking on; quibble. **прицепно́й**: ~ ваго́н trailer.

прича́л mooring; mooring line. **прича́ливать** *impf*, **прича́лить** *pf*

moor.

прича́стие¹ participle. **прича́стие**² communion. **причасти́ть** (-ащу́) *pf* (*impf* **причаща́ть**) give communion to; ~**ся** receive communion.

прича́стный¹ participial. **прича́стный**² concerned; privy.

причаща́ть *impf of* **причасти́ть**

причём *conj* moreover, and.

причеса́ть (-ешу́, -е́шешь) *pf*, **причёсывать** *impf* comb; do the hair (of); ~**ся** do one's hair, have one's hair done. **причёска** hair-do; haircut.

причи́на cause; reason. **причини́ть** *pf*, **причиня́ть** *impf* cause.

причи́слить *pf*, **причисля́ть** *impf* number, rank (**к**+*dat* among); add on.

причита́ние lamentation. **причита́ть** *impf* lament.

причита́ться *impf* be due.

причмо́кивать *impf*, **причмо́кнуть** (-ну) *pf* smack one's lips.

причу́да caprice, whim.

при|чу́диться *pf*.

причу́дливый odd; fantastic; whimsical.

при|швартова́ть *pf*. **пришёл** *etc.*: *see* **прийти́**

пришеле́ц (-ьца) newcomer.

прише́ствие coming; advent.

пришива́ть *impf*, **приши́ть** (-шью, -шьёшь) *pf* sew on.

пришлю́ *etc.*: *see* **присла́ть**

пришпи́ливать *impf*, **пришпи́лить** *pf* pin on.

пришпо́ривать *impf*, **пришпо́рить** *pf* spur (on).

прищеми́ть (-млю́) *pf*, **прищемля́ть** *impf* pinch.

прище́пка clothes-peg.

прищу́риваться *impf*, **прищу́риться** *pf* screw up one's eyes.

прию́т shelter, refuge. **приюти́ть** (-ючу́) *pf* shelter; ~**ся** take shelter.

прия́тель *m*, **прия́тельница** friend. **прия́тельский** friendly. **прия́тный** nice, pleasant.

про *prep*+*acc* about; for; ~ себя́ to o.s.

про|анализи́ровать *pf*.

про́ба trial, test; hallmark; sample.

пробе́г run; race. **пробега́ть** *impf*, **пробежа́ть** (-егу́) *pf* run; cover; run past.

пробе́л blank, gap; flaw.

проберу́ etc.: see **пробра́ть**. **про|би́ва́ть(ся** impf of **проби́ть(ся.**

пробира́ть(ся impf of **пробра́ть(ся**

пробирка test-tube. **пробировать** impf test, assay.

про|би́ть (-бью́, -бьёшь) pf (impf also **пробива́ть**) make a hole in; pierce; punch; ~**ся** force, make, one's way.

про́бка cork; stopper; fuse; (traffic) jam, congestion. **про́бковый** cork.

пробле́ма problem.

про́блеск flash; gleam, ray.

про́бный trial, test; ~ **ка́мень** touch-stone. **про́бовать** impf (pf ис~, по~) try; attempt.

пробо́ина hole.

пробо́р parting.

про|бормота́ть (-очу́, -о́чешь) pf.

пробра́ть (-беру́, -берёшь; -а́л, -а́, -о) pf (impf **пробира́ть**) penetrate; scold; ~**ся** make or force one's way.

пробу́ду etc.: see **пробы́ть**

про|буди́ть (-ужу́, -у́дишь) pf, **пробужда́ть** impf wake (up); arouse; ~**ся** wake up. **пробужде́ние** awakening.

про|бура́вить (-влю) pf, **пробура́вливать** impf bore (through), drill.

про|бури́ть pf.

пробы́ть (-бу́ду; про́бы́л, -а́, -о) pf stay; be.

пробью́ etc.: see **проби́ть**

прова́л failure; downfall; gap. **прова́ливать** impf, **провали́ть** (-лю́, -лишь) pf bring down; ruin; reject; fail; ~**ся** collapse; fall in; fail; disappear.

прове́дать pf, **прове́дывать** impf call on; learn.

проведе́ние conducting; construction; installation.

провезти́ (-зу́, -зёшь; -ёз, -ла́) pf (impf **провози́ть**) convey, transport.

прове́рить pf, **проверя́ть** impf check, test. **прове́рка** checking, check; testing.

про|вести́ (-еду́, -едёшь; -ёл, -а́) pf (impf also **проводи́ть**) lead, take; build; install; carry out; conduct; pass; draw; spend; +instr pass over.

прове́тривать impf, **прове́трить** pf air.

про|ве́ять (-е́ю) pf.

провиде́ние Providence.

прови́зия provisions.

провини́ться pf be guilty; do wrong.

провинциа́льный provincial. **прови́нция** province; the provinces.

про́вод (pl -á) wire, lead, line. **проводи́мость** conductivity. **проводи́ть**[1] (-ожу́, -о́дишь) impf of **провести́**; conduct.

проводи́ть[2] (-ожу́, -о́дишь) pf (impf **провожа́ть**) accompany; see off.

прово́дка leading, taking; building; installation; wiring, wires.

проводни́к[1] (-á) guide; conductor.

проводни́к[2] (-á) conductor; bearer; transmitter.

про́воды (-ов) pl send-off. **провожа́тый** sb guide, escort. **провожа́ть** impf of **проводи́ть**

прово́з conveyance, transport.

провозгласи́ть (-ашу́) pf, **провозглаша́ть** impf proclaim; propose. **провозглаше́ние** proclamation.

провози́ть (-ожу́, -о́зишь) impf of **провезти́**

провока́тор agent provocateur. **провока́ция** provocation.

про́волока wire. **про́волочный** wire.

прово́рный quick; agile. **прово́рство** quickness; agility.

провоци́ровать impf & pf (pf с~) provoke.

прогада́ть pf, **прога́дывать** impf miscalculate.

прога́лина glade; space.

прогиба́ть(ся impf of **прогну́ть(ся**

прогла́тывать impf, **проглоти́ть** (-очу́, -о́тишь) pf swallow.

прогляде́ть (-яжу́) pf, **прогля́дывать**[1] impf overlook; look through.

прогляну́ть (-я́нет) pf, **прогля́дывать**[2] impf show, peep through, appear.

прогна́ть (-гоню́, -го́нишь; -а́л, -а́, -о) pf (impf **прогоня́ть**) drive away; banish; drive; sack.

прогнива́ть impf, **прогни́ть** (-ниёт; -и́л, -а́, -о) pf rot through.

прогно́з prognosis; (weather) forecast.

прогну́ть (-ну́, -нёшь) pf (impf **прогиба́ть**) cause to sag; ~**ся** sag, bend.

проговаривать impf, **проговори́ть** pf say, utter; talk; ~**ся** let the cat out of the bag.

проголода́ться *pf* get hungry.

про|голосова́ть *pf.*

прого́н purlin; girder; stairwell.

прогоня́ть *impf of* **прогна́ть**

прогора́ть *impf,* **прогоре́ть** (-рю́) *pf* burn (through); burn out; go bankrupt.

прого́рклый rancid, rank.

програ́мма programme; syllabus. **программи́ровать** *impf* (*pf* за~) programme.

прогрева́ть *impf,* **прогре́ть** (-е́ю) *pf* heat; warm up; **~ся** warm up.

про|греме́ть (-млю́) *pf.* **про|грохота́ть** (-очу́, -о́чешь) *pf.*

прогре́сс progress. **прогресси́вный** progressive. **прогресси́ровать** *impf* progress.

прогрыза́ть *impf,* **прогры́зть** (-зу́, -зёшь; -ы́з) *pf* gnaw through.

про|гуде́ть (-гужу́) *pf.*

прогу́л truancy; absenteeism. **прогу́ливать** *impf,* **прогуля́ть** *pf* play truant, be absent, (from); miss; take for a walk; **~ся** take a walk. **прогу́лка** walk, stroll; outing. **прогу́льщик** absentee; truant.

продава́ть (-даю́, -даёшь) *impf,* **прода́ть** (-а́м, -а́шь, -а́ст, -ади́м; про́дал, -а́, -о) *pf* sell. **продава́ться** (-даётся) *impf* be for sale; sell. **продаве́ц** (-вца́) seller, vendor; salesman. **продавщи́ца** seller, vendor; saleswoman. **прода́жа** sale. **прода́жный** for sale; corrupt.

продвига́ть *impf,* **продви́нуть** (-ну) *pf* move on, push forward; advance; **~ся** advance; move forward; push on. **продвиже́ние** advancement.

продева́ть *impf of* **проде́ть**

про|деклами́ровать *pf.*

проде́лать *pf,* **проде́лывать** *impf* do, perform, make. **проде́лка** trick; prank.

продемонстри́ровать *pf* demonstrate, show.

продёргивать *impf of* **продёрнуть**

продержа́ть (-жу́, -жишь) *pf* hold; keep; **~ся** hold out.

продёрнуть (-ну, -нешь) *pf* (*impf* **продёргивать**) pass, run; criticize severely.

проде́ть (-е́ну) *pf* (*impf* **продева́ть**) pass; **~ ни́тку в иго́лку** thread a needle.

продешеви́ть (-влю́) *pf* sell too cheap.

про|диктова́ть *pf.*

продлева́ть *impf,* **продли́ть** *pf* prolong. **продле́ние** extension. **про|дли́ться** *pf.*

продма́г grocery. **продово́льственный** food. **продово́льствие** food; provisions.

продолгова́тый oblong.

продолжа́тель *m* continuer. **продолжа́ть** *impf,* **продо́лжить** (-жу) *pf* continue; prolong; **~ся** continue, last, go on. **продолже́ние** continuation; sequel; **в ~**+*gen* in the course of. **продолжи́тельность** duration. **продолжи́тельный** long; prolonged.

продо́льный longitudinal.

продро́гнуть (-ну; -ог) *pf* be chilled to the bone.

продтова́ры (-ов) *pl* food products.

продува́ть *impf* **проду́ть**

проду́кт product; *pl* food-stuffs. **продукти́вность** productivity. **продукти́вный** productive. **продукто́вый** food. **проду́кция** production.

проду́манный well thought-out; considered. **проду́мать** *pf,* **проду́мывать** *impf* think over; think out.

проду́ть (-у́ю, -у́ешь) *pf* (*impf* **продува́ть**) blow through.

продыря́вить (-влю) *pf* make a hole in.

проеда́ть *impf of* **прое́сть. прое́ду** *etc.: see* **прое́хать**

прое́зд passage, thoroughfare; trip. **прое́здить** (-зжу) *pf* (*impf* **проезжа́ть**) spend travelling. **прое́зд|н|о́й** travelling; **~о́й биле́т** ticket; **~ая пла́та** fare; **~ы́е** *sb pl* travelling expenses. **проезжа́ть** *impf of* **прое́здить, прое́хать. прое́зжий** passing (by); *sb* passer-by.

прое́кт project, plan, design; draft. **проекти́ровать** *impf* (*pf* с~) project; plan. **прое́ктный** planning; planned. **прое́ктор** projector.

проекцио́нный фона́рь *m* projector. **прое́кция** projection.

прое́сть (-е́м, -е́шь, -е́ст, -еди́м; -е́л) *pf* (*impf* **проеда́ть**) eat through, corrode; spend on food.

проéхать (-éду) *pf* (*impf* **проезжáть**) pass, ride, drive (by, through); cover.

прожáренный (*cul*) well-done.

прожевáть (-жую, -жуёшь) *pf*, **прожёвывать** *impf* chew well.

прожéктор (*pl* -ы *or* -á) searchlight.

прожéчь (-жгу, -жжёшь; -жёг, -жглá) *pf* (*impf* **прожигáть**) burn (through).

проживáть *impf of* **прожить**. **прожигáть** *impf of* **прожéчь**

прожи́точный ми́нимум living wage. **прожи́ть** (-иву, -ивёшь; -óжи́л, -á, -о) *pf* (*impf* **прожива́ть**) live; spend.

прожóрливый gluttonous.

прóза prose. **прозаи́ческий** prose; prosaic.

прозвáние, прóзвище nickname. **прозвáть** (-зову, -зовёшь; -áл, -á, -о) *pf* (*impf* **прозывáть**) nickname, name.

про|звучáть *pf*.

про|зевáть *pf*. **про|зимовáть** *pf*. **прозову́** *etc.: see* **прозвáть**

прозорли́вый perspicacious.

прозрáчный transparent.

прозревáть *impf*, **прозрéть** *pf* regain one's sight; see clearly. **прозрéние** recovery of sight; insight.

прозывáть *impf of* **прозвáть**

прозябáние vegetation. **прозябáть** *impf* vegetate.

проигрáть *pf*, **прои́грывать** *impf* lose; play; ~ся gamble away all one's money. **прои́грыватель** *m* recordplayer. **прóигрыш** loss.

произведéние work; production; product. **произвести́** (-еду, -едёшь; -ёл, -á) *pf*, **производи́ть** (-ожу, -óдишь) *impf* make; carry out; produce; +в+*acc/nom pl* promote to (the rank of). **производи́тель** *m* producer. **производи́тельность** productivity. **производи́тельный** productive. **произвóдный** derivative. **произвóдственный** industrial; production. **произвóдство** production.

произвóл arbitrariness; arbitrary rule. **произвóльный** arbitrary.

произнести́ (-су, -сёшь; -ёс, -лá) *pf*, **произноси́ть** (-ошу, -óсишь) *impf* pronounce; utter. **произношéние** pronunciation.

произойти́ (-ойдёт; -ошёл, -шлá) *pf* (*impf* **происходи́ть**) happen, occur;

result; be descended.

произрастáть *impf*, **произрасти́** (-ту́; -тёшь; -рос, -лá) *pf* sprout; grow.

прóиски (-ов) *pl* intrigues.

проистекáть *impf*, **проистéчь** (-ечёт; -ёк, -лá) *pf* spring, result.

происходи́ть (-ожу, -óдишь) *impf of* **произойти́**. **происхождéние** origin; birth.

происшéствие event, incident.

пройдóха *m* & *f* sly person.

пройти́ (-йду, -йдёшь; -ошёл, -шлá) *pf* (*impf* **проходи́ть**) pass; go; go past; cover; study; get through; ~сь (*impf* **прохáживаться**) take a stroll.

прок use, benefit.

прокажённый *sb* leper. **прокáза**[1] leprosy.

прокáза[2] mischief, prank. **прокáзничать** *impf* (*pf* на~) be up to mischief. **прокáзник** prankster.

прокáлывать *impf of* **проколóть**

прокáпывать *impf of* **прокопáть**

прокáт hire.

прокати́ться (-ачусь, -áтишься) *pf* roll; go for a drive.

прокáтный rolling; rolled.

прокипяти́ть (-ячу́) *pf* boil (thoroughly).

прокисáть *impf*, **про|ки́снуть** (-нет) *pf* turn (sour).

проклáдка laying; construction; washer; packing. **проклáдывать** *impf of* **проложи́ть**

прокламáция leaflet.

проклинáть *impf*, **прокля́сть** (-яну́, -янёшь; -óклял, -á, -о) *pf* curse, damn. **прокля́тие** curse; damnation. **прокля́тый** (-я́т, -á, -о) damned.

прокóл puncture.

проколóть (-лю́, -лешь) *pf* (*impf* **прокáлывать**) prick, pierce.

прокомменти́ровать *pf* comment (upon).

про|компости́ровать *pf*. **про|конспекти́ровать** *pf*. **про|консульти́ровать(ся** *pf*. **про|контроли́ровать** *pf*.

прокопáть *pf* (*impf* **прокáпывать**) dig, dig through.

прокóрм nourishment, sustenance. **про|корми́ть(ся** (-млю́(сь, -мишь(ся) *pf*.

про|корректи́ровать *pf*.

прокрáдываться *impf*, **прокрáсть-**

ся (-аду́сь, -аде́шься) *pf* steal in.
прокурату́ра office of public prosecutor. **прокуро́р** public prosecutor.
прокуси́ть (-ушу́, -у́сишь) *pf*, **проку́сывать** *impf* bite through.
прокути́ть (-учу́, -у́тишь) *pf*, **проку́чивать** *impf* squander; go on a binge.
пролага́ть *impf of* **проложи́ть**
прола́мывать *impf of* **пролома́ть**
пролега́ть *impf* lie, run.
пролеза́ть *impf*, **проле́зть** (-зу; -ле́з) *pf* get through, climb through.
про|лепета́ть (-ечу́, -е́чешь) *pf*.
пролёт span; stairwell; bay.
пролетариа́т proletariat. **пролета́рий** proletarian. **пролета́рский** proletarian.
пролета́ть *impf*, **пролете́ть** (-ечу́) *pf* fly; cover; fly by, past, through.
проли́в strait. **пролива́ть** *impf*, **проли́ть** (-лью́, -льёшь; -о́лил, -а́, -о) *pf* spill, shed; **~ся** be spilt.
проло́г prologue.
проложи́ть (-жу́, -жишь) *pf* (*impf* **прокла́дывать**, **пролага́ть**) lay; build; interlay.
проло́м breach, break. **проломи́ть**, **проломи́ть** (-млю́, -мишь) *pf* (*impf* **прола́мывать**) break (through).
пролью́ *etc.: see* **проли́ть**
про|ма́зать (-а́жу) *pf*. **прома́тывать(ся** *impf of* **промота́ть(ся**
про́мах miss; slip, blunder. **прома́хиваться** *impf*, **промахну́ться** (-ну́сь, -нёшься) *pf* miss; make a blunder.
прома́чивать *impf of* **промочи́ть**
промедле́ние delay. **проме́длить** *pf* delay; procrastinate.
промежу́ток (-тка) interval; space. **промежу́точный** intermediate
промелькну́ть (-ну́, -нёшь) *pf* flash (past, by).
проме́нивать *impf*, **променя́ть** *pf* exchange.
промерза́ть *impf*, **промёрзнуть** (-ну; -ёрз) *pf* freeze through. **промёрзлый** frozen.
промока́ть *impf*, **промо́кнуть** (-ну; -мо́к) *pf* get soaked; let water in.
промо́лвить (-влю) *pf* say, utter.
промолча́ть (-чу́) *pf* keep silent.
про|мота́ть *pf* (*impf also* **прома́тывать**) squander.

промочи́ть (-чу́, -чишь) *pf* (*impf* **прома́чивать**) soak, drench.
промо́ю *etc.: see* **промы́ть**
промтова́ры (-ов) *pl* manufactured goods.
промча́ться (-чу́сь) *pf* rush by.
промыва́ть *impf of* **промы́ть**
про́мысел (-сла) trade, business; *pl* works. **промысло́вый** producers'; business; game.
промы́ть (-мо́ю) *pf* (*impf* **промыва́ть**) wash (thoroughly); bathe; **~ мозги́**+*dat* brain-wash.
про|мыча́ть (-чу́) *pf*.
промы́шленник industrialist. **промы́шленность** industry. **промы́шленный** industrial.
пронести́ (-су́, -сёшь; -ёс, -ла́) *pf* (*impf* **проноси́ть**) carry (past, through); pass (over); **~сь** rush past, through; scud (past); fly; spread.
пронза́ть *impf*, **пронзи́ть** (-нжу́) *pf* pierce, transfix. **пронзи́тельный** piercing.
прониза́ть (-ижу́, -и́жешь) *pf*, **прони́зывать** *impf* pierce; permeate.
проника́ть *impf*, **прони́кнуть** (-ну; -и́к) *pf* penetrate; percolate; **~ся** be imbued. **проникнове́ние** penetration; feeling. **проникнове́нный** heartfelt.
проница́емый permeable. **проница́тельный** perspicacious.
проноси́ть(ся (-ошу́(сь, -о́сишь(ся) *impf of* **пронести́(сь**. **про|нумерова́ть** *pf*.
пронюхать *pf*, **проню́хивать** *impf* smell out, get wind of.
прообраз prototype.
пропага́нда propaganda. **пропаганди́ст** propagandist.
пропада́ть *impf of* **пропа́сть**. **пропа́жа** loss.
пропа́лывать *impf of* **прополо́ть**
про́пасть precipice; abyss; lots of.
пропа́сть (-аду́, -аде́шь) *pf* (*impf* **пропада́ть**) be missing; be lost; disappear; be done for, die; be wasted. **пропа́щий** lost; hopeless.
пропека́ть(ся *impf of* **пропе́чь(ся**. **про|пе́ть** (-пою́, -поёшь) *pf*.
пропе́чь (-еку́, -ечёшь; -ёк, -ла́) *pf* (*impf* **пропека́ть**) bake thoroughly; **~ся** get baked through.
пропива́ть *impf of* **пропи́ть**

прописа́ть (-ишу́, -и́шешь) *pf*, про-
пи́сывать *impf* prescribe; register;
~ся register. пропи́ска registration;
residence permit. пропис́н|о́й: ~а́я
бу́ква capital letter; ~а́я и́стина truism. про́писью *adv* in words.
пропита́ние subsistence, sustenance.
пропита́ть *pf*, пропи́тывать *impf*
impregnate, saturate.
пропи́ть (-пью́, -пьёшь; -о́пил, -á, -о)
pf (*impf* пропива́ть) spend on drink.
проплыва́ть *impf*, проплы́ть (-ыву́,
-ывёшь; -ы́л, -á, -о) *pf* swim, sail, *or*
float past *or* through.
пропове́дник preacher; advocate.
пропове́довать *impf* preach; advocate. про́поведь sermon; advocacy.
пропол́зти́ *impf*, пропол́зти́ (-зу́,
-зёшь; -по́лз, -лá) *pf* crawl, creep.
пропо́лка weeding. прополо́ть (-лю́,
-лешь) *pf* (*impf* пропа́лывать) weed.
про|полоска́ть (-ощу́, -о́щешь) *pf*.
пропорциона́льный proportional,
proportionate. пропо́рция proportion.
про́пуск (*pl* -á *or* -и, -о́в *or* -ов) pass,
permit; password; admission; omis-
sion; non-attendance; blank, gap.
пропуска́ть *impf*, пропусти́ть (-ущу́,
-у́стишь) *pf* let pass; let in; pass; leave
out; miss. пропускн|о́й: ~а́я
спосо́бность capacity.
пропью́ *etc.*: *see* пропи́ть
прора́б works superintendent.
прораба́тывать *impf*, прорабо́тать
pf work (through, at); study; pick
holes in.
прораста́ние germination; sprouting.
прораста́ть *impf*, прорасти́ (-тёт;
-ро́с, -лá) *pf* germinate, sprout.
прорва́ть (-ву́, -вёшь; -áл, -á, -о) *pf*
(*impf* прорыва́ть) break through;
~ся burst open; break through.
про|реаги́ровать *pf*.
проре́ди́ть (-ежу́) *pf*, проре́живать
impf thin out.
проре́з cut; slit; notch. про|ре́зать
(-éжу) *pf*, прореза́ть *impf* (*impf*
also проре́зывать) cut through; ~ся
be cut, come through.
проре́зывать(ся *impf of* про-
ре́зать(ся. про|репети́ровать *pf*.
проре́ха tear, slit; flies; deficiency.
про|рецензи́ровать *pf*.
проро́к prophet.

пророни́ть *pf* utter.
проро́с *etc.*: *see* прорасти́
проро́ческий prophetic. проро́че-
ство prophecy.
проро́ю *etc.*: *see* прорыть
проруба́ть *impf*, проруби́ть (-блю́,
-бишь) *pf* cut *or* hack through.
про́рубь ice-hole.
проры́в break; break-through; hitch.
прорыва́ть¹(ся *impf of* про-
рва́ть(ся
прорыва́ть² *impf*, проры́ть (-ро́ю)
pf dig through; ~ся dig one's way
through.
проса́чиваться *impf of* просо́-
чи́ться
просве́рливать *impf*, просвер-
ли́ть *pf* drill, bore; perforate.
просве́т (clear) space; shaft of light;
ray of hope; opening. просвети́-
тельный educational. просвети́ть¹
(-ещу́) *pf* (*impf* просвеща́ть) enlighten.
просвети́ть² (-ечу́, -éтишь) *pf* (*impf*
просве́чивать) X-ray.
просветле́ние brightening (up); lu-
cidity. про|светле́ть (-éет) *pf*.
просве́чивание radioscopy. про-
све́чивать *impf of* просвети́ть; be
translucent; be visible.
просвеща́ть *impf of* просвети́ть.
просвеще́ние enlightenment.
просви́ра communion bread.
про́седь streak(s) of grey.
просе́ивать *impf of* просе́ять
про́сека cutting, ride.
просёлок (-лка) country road.
просе́ять (-éю) *pf* (*impf* просе́и-
вать) sift.
про|сигнализи́ровать *pf*.
просиде́ть (-ижу́) *pf*, проси́живать
impf sit.
проси́тельный pleading. проси́ть
(-ошу́, -о́сишь) *impf* (*pf* по~) ask;
beg; invite; ~ся ask; apply.
проска́кивать *impf of* проскочи́ть
проска́льзывать *impf*, проскольз-
ну́ть (-ну́, -нёшь) *pf* slip, creep.
проскочи́ть (-чу́, -чишь) *pf* (*impf*
проска́кивать) rush by; slip through;
creep in.
просла́вить (-влю) *pf*, просла-
вля́ть *impf* glorify; make famous;
~ся become famous. просла́влен-
ный renowned.

проследить (-ежу) *pf*, **прослёживать** *impf* track (down); trace.

прослезиться (-ежусь) *pf* shed a few tears.

прослойка layer, stratum.

прослужить (-жу, -жишь) *pf* serve (for a certain time).

про|слушать *pf*, **прослушивать** *impf* hear; listen to; miss, not catch.

про|слыть (-ыву, -ывёшь; -ыл, -а, -о) *pf*.

просматривать *impf*, **просмотреть** (-рю, -ришь) *pf* look over; overlook. **просмотр** survey; view, viewing; examination.

проснуться (-нусь, -нёшься) *pf* (*impf* **просыпаться**) wake up.

просо millet.

просовывать(ся *impf of* **просунуть(ся**

про|сохнуть (-ну; -ох) *pf* (*impf also* **просыхать**) dry out.

просочиться (-ится) *pf* (*impf* **просачиваться**) percolate; seep (out); leak (out).

проспать (-плю; -ал, -а, -о) *pf* (*impf* **просыпать**) sleep (through); oversleep.

проспект avenue.

про|спрягать *pf*.

просроченный overdue; expired. **просрочить** (-чу) *pf* allow to run out; be behind with; overstay. **просрочка** delay; expiry of time limit.

простаивать *impf of* **простоять**

простак (-а) simpleton.

простенок (-нка) pier (*between windows*).

простереться (-трётся; -тёрся) *pf*, **простираться** *impf* extend.

простительный pardonable, excusable. **простить** (-ощу) *pf* (*impf* **прощать**) forgive; excuse; ~ся (с+*instr*) say goodbye (to).

проститутка prostitute. **проституция** prostitution.

просто *adv* simply.

простоволосый bare-headed. **простодушный** simple-hearted; ingenuous.

простой[1] downtime.

прост|ой[2] simple; plain; mere; ~ым глазом with the naked eye; ~ое число prime number.

простокваша thick sour milk.

просто-напросто *adv* simply.

простонародный of the common people.

простор spaciousness; space. **просторный** spacious.

просторечие popular speech. **простосердечный** simple-hearted.

простота simplicity.

простоять (-ою) *pf* (*impf* **простаивать**) stand (idle).

пространный extensive, vast. **пространственный** spatial. **пространство** space.

прострел lumbago. **простреливать** *impf*, **прострелить** (-лю, -лишь) *pf* shoot through.

про|строчить (-очу, -очишь) *pf*.

простуда cold. **простудиться** (-ужусь, -удишься) *pf*, **простужаться** *impf* catch (a) cold.

проступать *impf*, **проступить** (-ит) *pf* appear.

проступок (-пка) misdemeanour.

простыня (*pl* простыни, -ынь, -ням) sheet.

простыть (-ыну) *pf* get cold.

просунуть (-ну) *pf* (*impf* **просовывать**) push, thrust.

просушивать *impf*, **просушить** (-шу, -шишь) *pf* dry out; ~ся (get) dry.

просуществовать *pf* exist; endure.

просчёт error. **просчитаться** *pf*, **просчитываться** *impf* miscalculate.

просыпать (-плю), **просыпать**[1] *impf* spill; ~ся get spilt.

просыпать[2] *impf of* **проспать**.

просыпаться *impf of* **проснуться**.

просыхать *impf of* **просохнуть**

просьба request.

проталкивать *impf of* **протолкнуть**.

протапливать *impf of* **протопить**

протаптывать *impf of* **протоптать**

протаскивать *impf*, **протащить** (-щу, -щишь) *pf* drag, push (through).

протез artificial limb, prosthesis; зубной ~ denture.

протеин protein.

протекать *impf of* **протечь**

протекция patronage.

протереть (-тру, -трёшь; -тёр) *pf* (*impf* **протирать**) wipe (over); wear (through).

протест protest. **протестант**, ~**ка** Protestant. **протестовать** *impf* & *pf* protest.

проте́чь (-ечёт; -тёк, -ла́) *pf* (*impf* **протека́ть**) flow; leak; seep; pass; take its course.

про́тив *prep+gen* against; opposite; contrary to, as against.

про́тивень (-вня) *m* baking-tray; meat-pan.

проти́виться (-влюсь) *impf* (*pf* **вос~**) +*dat* oppose; resist. **проти́вник** opponent; the enemy. **проти́вный**[1] opposite; contrary. **проти́вный**[2] nasty, disgusting.

противо- *in comb* anti-, contra-, counter-. **противове́с** counterbalance. **~возду́шный** anti-aircraft. **~га́з** gas-mask. **~де́йствие** opposition. **~де́йствовать** *impf* +*dat* oppose, counteract. **~есте́ственный** unnatural. **~зако́нный** illegal. **~зача́точный** contraceptive. **~поло́жность** opposite; opposition, contrast. **~поло́жный** contrary. **~поста́вить** (-влю) *pf*, **~поставля́ть** *impf* oppose; contrast. **~речи́вый** contradictory; conflicting. **~ре́чие** contradiction. **~ре́чить** (-чу) *impf* +*dat* contradict. **~стоя́ть** (-ою́) *impf* +*dat* resist, withstand. **~та́нковый** anti-tank. **~я́дие** antidote.

протира́ть *impf of* **протере́ть**

проти́скивать *impf*, **проти́снуть** (-ну) *pf* force, squeeze (through, into).

проткну́ть (-ну́, -нёшь) *pf* (*impf* **протыка́ть**) pierce; skewer.

протоко́л minutes; report; protocol.

протолкну́ть (-ну́, -нёшь) *pf* (*impf* **прота́лкивать**) push through.

прото́н proton.

протопи́ть (-плю́, -пишь) *pf* (*impf* **прота́пливать**) heat (thoroughly).

протопта́ть (-пчу́, -пчешь) *pf* (*impf* **прота́птывать**) tread; wear out.

проторённый beaten, well-trodden.

прототи́п prototype.

прото́чный flowing, running.

про|тра́лить *pf*. **протру́** *etc.*: *see* **протере́ть**. **про|труби́ть** (-блю́) *pf*.

протрезви́ться (-влюсь) *pf*, **протрезвля́ться** *impf* sober up.

протуха́ть *impf*, **проту́хнуть** (-нет; -у́х) *pf* become rotten; go bad.

протыка́ть *impf of* **проткну́ть**

протя́гивать *impf*, **протяну́ть** (-ну́, -нешь) *pf* stretch; extend; hold out;

~ся stretch out; extend; last. **протяже́ние** extent, stretch; period. **протя́жный** long-drawn-out; drawling.

проу́чивать *impf*, **проучи́ть** (-чу́, -чишь) *pf* study; teach a lesson.

профа́н ignoramus.

профана́ция profanation.

профессиона́л professional. **профессиона́льный** professional; occupational. **профе́ссия** profession. **профе́ссор** (*pl* -а́) professor.

профила́ктика prophylaxis; preventive measures.

про́филь *m* profile; type.

про|фильтрова́ть *pf*.

профсою́з trade-union.

проха́живаться *impf of* **пройти́сь**

прохво́ст scoundrel.

прохла́да coolness. **прохлади́тельный** refreshing, cooling. **прохла́дный** cool, chilly.

прохо́д passage; gangway, aisle; duct. **проходи́мец** (-мца) rogue. **проходи́мый** passable. **проходи́ть** (-ожу́, -о́дишь) *impf of* **пройти́**. **проходно́й** entrance; communicating. **проходя́щий** passing. **прохо́жий** passing, in transit; *sb* passer-by.

процвета́ние prosperity. **процвета́ть** *impf* prosper, flourish.

процеди́ть (-ежу́, -е́дишь) *pf* (*impf* **проце́живать**) filter, strain.

процеду́ра procedure; (*usu in pl*) treatment.

проце́живать *impf of* **процеди́ть**

проце́нт percentage; per cent; interest.

проце́сс process; trial; legal proceedings. **проце́ссия** procession.

про|цити́ровать *pf*.

прочёска screening; combing.

проче́сть (-чту́, -чтёшь; -чёл, -чла́) *pf of* **чита́ть**

про́чий other.

прочи́стить (-и́щу) *pf* (*impf* **прочища́ть**) clean; clear.

про|чита́ть *pf*, **прочи́тывать** *impf* read (through).

прочища́ть *impf of* **прочи́стить**

про́чность firmness, stability, durability. **про́чный** (-чен, -чна́, -о) firm, sound, solid; durable.

прочте́ние reading. **прочту́** *etc.*: *see* **проче́сть**

прочу́вствовать *pf* feel deeply;

experience, go through.

прочь adv away, off; averse to.

проше́дший past; last. **прошёл** etc.: see **пройти́**

проше́ние application, petition.

прошепта́ть (-пчу́, -пчешь) pf whisper.

проше́ствие: по проше́ствии +gen after.

прошива́ть impf, **проши́ть** (-шью, -шьёшь) pf sew, stitch.

прошлого́дний last year's. **про́шл|ый** past; last; ~oe sb the past.

про|штудирова́ть pf. **прошью́** etc.: see **прошить**

проща́й(те) goodbye. **проща́льный** parting; farewell. **проща́ние** farewell; parting. **проща́ть(ся** impf of **прости́ть(ся**

про́ще simpler, plainer.

проще́ние forgiveness, pardon.

прощу́пать pf, **прощу́пывать** impf feel.

про|экзаменова́ть pf.

проявитель m developer. **прояви́ть** (-влю́, -вишь) pf, **проявля́ть** impf show, display; develop; ~ся reveal itself. **проявле́ние** display; manifestation; developing.

проясни́ться pf, **проясня́ться** impf clear, clear up.

пруд (-а́, loc -у́) pond. **пруди́ть** (-ужу́, -у́ди́шь) impf (pf за~) dam.

пружи́на spring. **пружи́нистый** springy. **пружи́нный** spring.

пру́сский Prussian.

прут (-а́ or -а; pl -тья) twig.

пры́гать impf, **пры́гнуть** (-ну) pf jump, leap; bounce; ~ с шесто́м pole-vault. **прыгу́н** (-а́), **прыгу́нья** (gen pl -ний) jumper. **прыжо́к** (-жка́) jump; leap; **прыжки́** jumping; прыжки́ в во́ду diving; ~ в высоту́ high jump; ~ в длину́ long jump.

пры́скать impf, **пры́снуть** (-ну) pf spurt; sprinkle; burst out laughing.

прыть speed; energy.

прыщ (-а́), **пры́щик** pimple.

пряди́льный spinning. **пряди́льня** (gen pl -лен) (spinning-)mill. **пряди́льщик** spinner. **пряду́** etc.: see **прясть**. **прядь** lock; strand. **пря́жа** yarn, thread.

пря́жка buckle, clasp.

пря́лка distaff; spinning-wheel.

пряма́я sb straight line. **пря́мо** adv straight; straight on; frankly; really.

прямоду́шие directness, straightforwardness. ~**ду́шный** direct, straightforward.

прямо́й (-ям, -а́, -о) straight; upright, erect; through; direct; straightforward; real.

прямолине́йный rectilinear; straightforward. **прямоуго́льник** rectangle. **прямоуго́льный** rectangular.

пря́ник spice cake. **пря́ность** spice. **пря́ный** spicy; heady.

прясть (-яду́, -ядёшь; -ял, -яла́, -о) impf (pf с~) spin.

пря́тать (-я́чу) impf (pf с~) hide; ~ся hide. **пря́тки** (-ток) pl hide-and-seek.

пса etc.: see **пёс**

псало́м (-лма́) psalm. **псалты́рь** Psalter.

псевдони́м pseudonym.

псих madman, lunatic. **психиатри́я** psychiatry. **пси́хика** psyche; psychology. **психи́ческий** mental, psychical.

психоана́лиз psychoanalysis. **психо́з** psychosis. **психо́лог** psychologist. **психологи́ческий** psychological. **психоло́гия** psychology. **психопа́т** psychopath. **психопати́ческий** psychopathic. **психосомати́ческий** psychosomatic. **психотерапе́вт** psychotherapist. **психотерапи́я** psychotherapy. **психоти́ческий** psychotic.

птене́ц (-нца́) nestling; fledgeling. **пти́ца** bird. **птицефе́рма** poultry-farm. **пти́чий** bird, bird's, poultry. **пти́чка** bird; tick.

пу́блика public; audience. **публика́ция** publication; notice, advertisement. **публикова́ть** impf (pf о~) publish. **публици́стика** writing on current affairs. **публи́чность** publicity. **публи́чный** public; ~ дом brothel.

пу́гало scarecrow. **пуга́ть** impf (pf ис~, на~) frighten, scare; ~ся (+gen) be frightened (of). **пуга́ч** (-а́) toy pistol. **пугли́вый** fearful.

пу́говица button.

пуд (pl -ы́) pood (= 16.38 kg). **пудово́й, пудо́вый** one pood in weight.

пу́дель *m* poodle.

пу́динг blancmange.

пу́дра powder. **пу́дреница** powder compact. **пу́дреный** powdered. **пу́дриться** *impf* (*pf* на~) powder one's face.

пуза́тый pot-bellied.

пузырёк (-рька́) vial; bubble. **пузы́рь** (-я́) *m* bubble; blister; bladder.

пук (*pl* -и́) bunch, bundle; tuft.

пу́кать *impf*, **пу́кнуть** *pf* fart.

пулемёт machine-gun. **пулемётчик** machine-gunner. **пуленепробива́емый** bullet-proof.

пульвериза́тор atomizer; spray.

пульс pulse. **пульса́р** pulsar. **пульси́ровать** *impf* pulsate.

пульт desk, stand; control panel.

пу́ля bullet.

пункт point; spot; post; item. **пункти́р** dotted line. **пункти́рный** dotted, broken.

пунктуа́льный punctual.

пунктуа́ция punctuation.

пунцо́вый crimson.

пуп (-а́) navel. **пупови́на** umbilical cord. **пупо́к** (-пка́) navel; gizzard.

пурга́ blizzard.

пурита́нин (*pl* -та́не, -та́н), **-а́нка** Puritan.

пу́рпур purple, crimson. **пурпу́р|ный**, ~**овый** purple.

пуск starting (up). **пуска́й** *see* пусть. **пуска́ть(ся** *impf of* пусти́ть(ся. **пусково́й** starting.

пусте́ть (-е́ет) *impf* (*pf* о~) empty; become deserted.

пусти́ть (пущу́, пу́стишь) *pf* (*impf* **пуска́ть**) let go; let in; let; start; send; set in motion; throw; put forth; ~**ся** set out; start.

пустова́ть *impf* be *or* stand empty. **пусто́й** (-ст, -а́, -о) empty; uninhabited; idle; shallow. **пустота́** (*pl* -ы) emptiness; void; vacuum; futility. **пустоте́лый** hollow.

пусты́нный uninhabited; deserted; desert. **пусты́ня** desert. **пусты́рь** (-я́) *m* waste land; vacant plot.

пусты́шка blank; hollow object; dummy.

пусть, пуска́й *partl* let; all right; though, even if.

пустя́к (-а́) trifle. **пустяко́вый** trivial.

пу́таница muddle, confusion. **пу́таный** muddled, confused. **пу́тать** *impf* (*pf* за~, пере~, с~) tangle; confuse; mix up; ~**ся** get confused *or* mixed up.

путёвка pass; place on a group tour.

путеводи́тель *m* guide, guide-book. **путево́й** travelling; road. **путём** *prep+gen* by means of. **путеше́ственник** traveller. **путеше́ствие** journey; voyage. **путеше́ствовать** *impf* travel; voyage.

пу́ты (пут) *pl* shackles.

путь (-и́, *instr* -ём, *prep* -и́) way; track; path; course; journey; voyage; means; **в пути́** en route, on one's way.

пух (*loc* -у́) down; fluff.

пу́хлый (-хл, -а́, -о) plump. **пу́хнуть** (-ну; пух) *impf* (*pf* вс~, о~) swell.

пухови́к (-а́) feather-bed. **пухо́вка** powder-puff. **пухо́вый** downy.

пучи́на abyss; the deep.

пучо́к (-чка́) bunch, bundle.

пу́шечный gun, cannon.

пуши́нка bit of fluff. **пуши́стый** fluffy.

пу́шка gun, cannon.

пушни́на furs, pelts. **пушно́й** fur; fur-bearing.

пу́ще *adv* more; ~ **всего́** most of all.

пущу́ *etc.*: *see* пусти́ть

пчела́ (*pl* -ёлы) bee. **пчели́ный** bee, bees'. **пчелово́д** bee-keeper. **пче́льник** apiary.

пшени́ца wheat. **пшени́чный** wheat(en).

пшённый millet. **пшено́** millet.

пыл (*loc* -у́) heat, ardour. **пыла́ть** *impf* blaze; burn.

пылесо́с vacuum cleaner. **пылесо́сить** *impf* vacuum (-clean). **пыли́нка** speck of dust. **пыли́ть** *impf* (*pf* за~, на~) raise a dust; cover with dust; ~**ся** get dusty.

пы́лкий ardent; fervent.

пыль (*loc* -и́) dust. **пы́льный** (-лен, -льна́, -о) dusty. **пыльца́** pollen.

пыре́й couch grass.

пырну́ть (-ну́, -нёшь) *pf* jab.

пыта́ть *impf* torture. **пыта́ться** *impf* (*pf* по~) try. **пы́тка** torture, torment. **пытли́вый** inquisitive.

пыхте́ть (-хчу́) *impf* puff, pant.

пы́шка bun.

пы́шность splendour. **пы́шный**

(-шен, -шна́, -шно) splendid; lush.
пьедеста́л pedestal.
пье́са play; piece.
пью *etc.*: *see* **пить**
пьяне́ть (-е́ю) *impf* (*pf* **о~**) get drunk. **пьяни́ть** *impf* (*pf* **о~**) intoxicate, make drunk. **пья́ница** *m & f* drunkard. **пья́нство** drunkenness. **пья́нствовать** *impf* drink heavily. **пья́ный** drunk.
пюпи́тр lectern; stand.
пюре́ *neut indecl* purée.
пядь (*gen pl* -е́й) span; **ни пя́ди** not an inch.
пя́льцы (-лец) *pl* embroidery frame.
пята́ (*pl* -ы, -а́м) heel.
пята́к (-а́), **пятачо́к** (-чка́) five-copeck piece. **пятёрка** five; figure 5; No. 5; fiver (5-*rouble note*)
пяти- *in comb* five; penta-. **пятибо́рье** pentathlon. **~десятиле́тие** fifty years; fiftieth anniversary, birthday. П**~деся́тница** Pentecost. **~деся́тый** fiftieth; **~деся́тые го́ды** the fifties. **~коне́чный** five-pointed. **~ле́тие** five years; fifth anniversary. **~ле́тка** five-year plan. **~со́тый** five-hundredth. **~уго́льник** pentagon. **~уго́льный** pentagonal.
пя́титься (пя́чусь) *impf* (*pf* **по~**) move backwards; back.
пя́тка heel.
пятна́дцатый fifteenth. **пятна́дцать** fifteen.
пятна́ть *impf* (*pf* **за~**) spot, stain. **пятна́шки** (-шек) *pl* tag. **пятни́стый** spotted.
пя́тница Friday.
пятно́ (*pl* -а, -тен) stain; spot; blot; **роди́мое ~** birth-mark.
пя́тый fifth. **пять** (-й, *instr* -ью) five. **пятьдеся́т** (-и́десяти, *instr* -ью́десятью) fifty. **пятьсо́т** (-тисо́т, -тиста́м) five hundred. **пя́тью** *adv* five times.

Р

раб (-а́), **раба́** slave. **рабовладе́лец** (-льца) slave-owner. **раболе́пие** servility. **рабо́лепный** servile. **раболе́пствовать** cringe, fawn.
рабо́та work; job; functioning. **рабо́тать** *impf* work; function; be open;

~ над+instr work on. **рабо́тник**, **-ица** worker. **работоспосо́бность** capacity for work, efficiency. **работоспосо́бный** able-bodied, hardworking. **работя́щий** hardworking. **рабо́чий** *sb* worker. **рабо́ч|ий** worker's; working; **~ая си́ла** manpower.
ра́бский slave; servile. **ра́бство** slavery. **рабы́ня** female slave.
равви́н rabbi.
ра́венство equality. **равне́ние** alignment. **равни́на** plain.
равно́ *adv* alike; equally; **~ как** as well as. **равно́** *predic*: *see* **ра́вный**
равно- *in comb* equi-, iso-. **равнобе́дренный** isosceles. **~ве́сие** equilibrium; balance. **~де́нствие** equinox. **~ду́шие** indifference. **~ду́шный** indifferent. **~ме́рный** even; uniform. **~пра́вие** equality of rights. **~пра́вный** having equal rights. **~си́льный** of equal strength; equal, equivalent, tantamount. **~сторо́нний** equilateral. **~це́нный** of equal value; equivalent.
ра́вный (-вен, -вна́) equal. **равно́** *predic* make(s), equals; **всё ~о́** (it is) all the same. **равня́ть** *impf* (*pf* **с~**) make even; treat equally; **+с+**instr compare with, treat as equal to; **~ся** compete, compare; be equal; be tantamount.
рад (-а, -о) *predic* glad.
рада́р radar.
ра́ди *prep+gen* for the sake of.
радиа́тор radiator. **радиа́ция** radiation.
ра́дий radium.
радика́льный radical.
ра́дио *neut indecl* radio.
ра́дио- *in comb* radio-; radioactive. **радиоакти́вный** radioactive. **~веща́ние** broadcasting. **~волна́** radiowave. **~гра́мма** radio-telegram. **радио́лог** radiologist. **~ло́гия** radiology. **~лока́тор** radar (set). **~люби́тель** *m* radio amateur, ham. **~мая́к** (-а́) radio beacon. **~переда́тчик** transmitter. **~переда́ча** broadcast. **~приёмник** radio (set). **~связь** radio communication. **~слу́шатель** *m* listener. **~ста́нция** radio station. **~электро́ника** radio-electronics.

радио́ла radiogram.
ради́ровать *impf & pf* radio. **ради́ст** radio operator.
ра́диус radius.
ра́довать *impf* (*pf* об~, по~) gladden, make happy; ~ся be glad, rejoice. **ра́достный** joyful. **ра́дость** gladness, joy.
ра́дуга rainbow. **ра́дужн|ый** iridescent; cheerful; ~ая оболо́чка iris.
раду́шие cordiality. **раду́шный** cordial.
ражу́ *etc.: see* рази́ть
раз (*pl* -ы́, раз) time, occasion; one; ещё ~ (once) again; как ~ just, exactly; не ~ more than once; ни ~у not once. **раз** *adv* once, one day. **раз** *conj* if; since.
разба́вить (-влю) *pf*, **разбавля́ть** *impf* dilute.
разба́зоривать *impf*, **разбаза́рить** *pf* squander.
разба́лтывать(ся *impf of* разболта́ть(ся
разбе́г running start. **разбега́ться** *impf*, **разбежа́ться** (-егу́сь) *pf* take a run, run up; scatter.
разберу́ *etc.: see* разобра́ть
разбива́ть(ся *impf of* разби́ть(ся. **разби́вка** laying out; spacing (out).
разбинтова́ть *pf*, **разбинто́вывать** *impf* unbandage.
разбира́тельство investigation. **разбира́ть** *impf of* разобра́ть; ~ся *impf of* разобра́ться
разби́ть (-зобью́, -зобьёшь) *pf* (*impf* разбива́ть) break; smash; divide (up); damage; defeat; mark out; space (out); ~ся break, get broken; hurt o.s. **разби́тый** broken; jaded.
раз|богате́ть (-е́ю) *pf*.
разбо́й robbery. **разбо́йник** robber. **разбо́йничий** robber.
разболе́ться[1] (-ли́тся) *pf* begin to ache badly.
разболе́ться[2] (-е́юсь) *pf* become ill.
разболта́ть[1] *pf* (*impf* разба́лтывать) divulge, give away.
разболта́ть[2] *pf* (*impf* разба́лтывать) shake up; loosen; ~ся work loose; get out of hand.
разбомби́ть (-блю) *pf* bomb, destroy by bombing.
разбо́р analysis; critique; discrimination; investigation. **разбо́рка** sorting

out; dismantling. **разбо́рный** collapsible. **разбо́рчивый** legible; discriminating.
разбра́сывать *impf of* разброса́ть
разбреда́ться *impf*, **разбрести́сь** (-еду́тся; -ёлся, -ла́сь) *pf* disperse; straggle. **разбро́д** disorder.
разбро́санный scattered; disconnected, incoherent. **разброса́ть** *pf* (*impf* разбра́сывать) throw about; scatter.
раз|буди́ть (-ужу́, -у́дишь) *pf*.
разбуха́ть *impf*, **разбу́хнуть** (-нет; -бу́х) *pf* swell.
разбушева́ться (-шу́юсь) *pf* fly into a rage; blow up; rage.
разва́л breakdown, collapse. **разва́ливать** *impf*, **развали́ть** (-лю́, -лишь) *pf* pull down; mess up; ~ся collapse; go to pieces; tumble down; sprawl. **разва́лина** ruin; wreck.
ра́зве *partl* really?; ~ (то́лько), ~ (что) except that, only.
развева́ться *impf* fly, flutter.
разве́дать *pf* (*impf* разве́дывать) find out; reconnoitre.
разведе́ние breeding; cultivation.
разведённ|ый divorced; ~ый, ~ая *sb* divorcee.
разве́дка intelligence (service); reconnaissance; prospecting. **разве́дочный** prospecting, exploratory.
разведу́ *etc.: see* развести́
разве́дчик intelligence officer; scout; prospector. **разве́дывать** *impf of* разве́дать
развезти́ (-зу́, -зёшь; -ёз, -ла́) *pf* (*impf* развози́ть) convey, transport; deliver.
разве́ивать(ся *impf of* разве́ять(ся. **развёл** *etc.: see* развести́
развенча́ть *pf*, **развенчивать** *impf* dethrone; debunk.
развёрнутый extensive, all-out; detailed. **разверну́ть** (-ну́, -нёшь) *pf* (*impf* развёртывать, развора́чивать) unfold, unwrap; unroll; unfurl; deploy; expand; develop; turn; scan; display; ~ся unfold, unroll, come unwrapped; deploy; develop; spread; turn.
развёрстка allotment, apportionment.
развёртывать(ся *impf of* разверну́ть(ся

раз|весели́ть *pf* cheer up, amuse; **~ся** cheer up.

разве́сить[1] (-ёшу) *pf* (*impf* **разве́шивать**) spread; hang (out).

разве́сить[2] (-ёшу) *pf* (*impf* **разве́шивать**) weigh out. **разве́ска** weighing. **развесно́й** sold by weight.

развести́ (-еду́, -едёшь; -ёл, -а́) *pf* (*impf* **разводи́ть**) take; separate; divorce; dilute; dissolve; start; breed; cultivate; **~сь** get divorced; breed, multiply.

разветви́ться (-ви́тся) *pf*, **разветвля́ться** *impf* branch; fork. **разветвле́ние** branching, forking; branch; fork.

разве́шать *pf*, **разве́шивать** *impf* hang.

разве́шивать *impf of* **разве́сить**, **разве́шать**. **разве́шу** *etc.*: *see* **разве́сить**

разве́ять (-ею) *pf* (*impf* **разве́ивать**) scatter, disperse; dispel; **~ся** disperse; be dispelled.

развива́ть(ся *impf of* **разви́ть(ся** **разви́лка** fork.

развинти́ть (-нчу́) *pf*, **разви́нчивать** *impf* unscrew.

разви́тие development. **развито́й** (ра́звит, -а́, -о) developed; mature. **разви́ть** (-зовью́, -зовьёшь; -и́л, -а́, -о) *pf* (*impf* **развива́ть**) develop; unwind; **~ся** develop.

развлека́ть *impf*, **развле́чь** (-еку́, -ечёшь; -ёк, -ла́) *pf* entertain, amuse; **~ся** have a good time; amuse o.s. **развлече́ние** entertainment, amusement.

разво́д divorce. **разводи́ть(ся** (-ожу́(сь, -о́дишь(ся) *impf of* **развести́(сь**. **разво́дка** separation. **разводно́й**: **~ ключ** adjustable spanner; **~ мост** drawbridge.

развози́ть (-ожу́, -о́зишь) *impf of* **развезти́**

разволнова́ть(ся *pf* get excited, be agitated.

развора́чивать(ся *impf of* **разверну́ть(ся**

разворова́ть *pf*, **разворо́вывать** *impf* loot; steal.

разворо́т U-turn; turn; development.

развра́т depravity, corruption. **развра́тить** (-ащу́) *pf*. **развраща́ть** *impf* corrupt; deprave. **развра́т-**

ничать *impf* lead a depraved life. **развра́тный** debauched, corrupt. **развращённый** (-ён, -а́) corrupt.

развяза́ть (-яжу́, -я́жешь) *pf*, **развя́зывать** *impf* untie; unleash; **~ся** come untied; **~ся** с+*instr* rid o.s. of. **развя́зка** dénouement; outcome. **развя́зный** overfamiliar.

разгада́ть *pf*, **разга́дывать** *impf* solve, guess, interpret. **разга́дка** solution.

разга́р height, climax.

разгиба́ть(ся *impf of* **разогну́ть(ся**

разглаго́льствовать *impf* hold forth.

разгла́дить (-а́жу) *pf*, **разгла́живать** *impf* smooth out; iron (out).

разгласи́ть (-ашу́) *pf*, **разглаша́ть** *impf* divulge; +*o*+*prep* trumpet. **разглаше́ние** disclosure.

разгляде́ть (-яжу́) *pf*, **разгля́дывать** *impf* make out, discern.

разгне́вать *pf* anger. **раз|гне́ваться** *pf*.

разгова́ривать *impf* talk, converse. **разгово́р** conversation. **разгово́рник** phrase-book. **разгово́рный** colloquial. **разгово́рчивый** talkative.

разго́н dispersal; running start; distance. **разгоня́ть(ся** *impf of* **разогна́ть(ся**

разгора́живать *impf of* **разгороди́ть**

разгора́ться *impf*, **разгоре́ться** (-рю́сь) *pf* flare up.

разгороди́ть (-ожу́, -о́ди́шь) *pf* (*impf* **разгора́живать**) partition off.

раз|горячи́ть(ся (-чу́(сь) *pf*.

разгра́бить (-блю) *pf* plunder, loot. **разграбле́ние** plunder, looting.

разграниче́ние demarcation; differentiation. **разграни́чивать** *impf*, **разграни́чить** (-чу) *pf* delimit; differentiate.

разгреба́ть *impf*, **разгрести́** (-ебу́, -ебёшь; -ёб, -ла́) *pf* rake *or* shovel (away).

разгро́м crushing defeat; devastation; havoc. **разгроми́ть** (-млю́) *pf* rout, defeat.

разгружа́ть *impf*, **разгрузи́ть** (-ужу́, -у́зишь) *pf* unload; relieve; **~ся** unload; be relieved. **разгру́зка** unloading; relief.

разгрыза́ть *impf,* **раз|гры́зть** (-зу́, -зёшь; -ы́з) *pf* crack.

разгу́л revelry; outburst. **разгу́ливать** *impf* stroll about. **разгу́ливаться** *impf,* **разгуля́ться** *pf* spread o.s.; become wide awake; clear up. **разгу́льный** wild, rakish.

раздава́ть(ся (-даю́(сь, -даёшь(ся) *impf of* **разда́ть(ся**

раз|дави́ть (-влю́, -вишь) *pf.* **разда́вливать** *impf* crush; run over.

разда́ть (-а́м, -а́шь, -а́ст, -ади́м; ро́з*or* разда́л, -а́, -о) *pf* (*impf* **раздава́ть**) distribute, give out; ~**ся** be heard; resound; ring out; make way; expand; put on weight. **разда́ча** distribution. **раздаю́** *etc.: see* **раздава́ть**

раздва́ивать(ся *impf of* **раздвои́ть(ся**

раздвига́ть *impf,* **раздви́нуть** (-ну) *pf* move apart; ~**ся** move apart. **раздвижно́й** expanding; sliding.

раздвое́ние division; split; ~ ли́чности split personality. **раздво́енный** forked; cloven; split. **раздво́ить** *pf* (*impf* **раздва́ивать**) divide into two; bisect; ~**ся** fork; split.

раздева́лка cloakroom. **раздева́ть(ся** *impf of* **разде́ть(ся**

разде́л division; section.

разде́латься *pf* +c+*instr* finish with; settle accounts with.

разделе́ние division. **раздели́мый** divisible. **раз|дели́ть** (-лю́, -лишь) *pf,* **разделя́ть** *impf* divide; separate; share; ~**ся** divide; be divided; be divisible; separate. **разде́льный** separate.

разде́ну *etc.: see* **разде́ть. раздеру́** *etc.: see* **раздра́ть**

разде́ть (-де́ну) *pf* (*impf* **раздева́ть**) undress; ~**ся** undress; take off one's coat.

раздира́ть *impf of* **раздра́ть**

раздобыва́ть *impf,* **раздобы́ть** (-бу́ду) *pf* get, get hold of.

раздо́лье expanse; liberty. **раздо́льный** free.

раздо́р discord.

раздоса́довать *pf* vex.

раздража́ть *impf,* **раздражи́ть** (-жу́) *pf* irritate; annoy; ~**ся** get annoyed. **раздраже́ние** irritation. **раздражи́тельный** irritable.

раз|дроби́ть (-блю́) *pf,* **раздробля́ть** *impf* break; smash to pieces.

раздува́ть(ся *impf of* **разду́ть(ся**

разду́мать *pf,* **разду́мывать** *impf* change one's mind; ponder. **разду́мье** meditation; thought.

разду́ть (-у́ю) *pf* (*impf* **раздува́ть**) blow; fan; exaggerate; whip up; swell; ~**ся** swell.

разева́ть *impf of* **рази́нуть**

разжа́лобить (-блю) *pf* move (to pity).

разжа́ловать *pf* demote.

разжа́ть (-зожму́, -мёшь) *pf* (*impf* **разжима́ть**) unclasp, open; release.

разжева́ть (-жую́, -жуёшь) *pf,* **разжёвывать** *impf* chew.

разже́чь (-зожгу́, -зожжёшь; -жёг, -зожгла́) *pf,* **разжига́ть** *impf* kindle; rouse.

разжима́ть *impf of* **разжа́ть. раз|жире́ть** (-е́ю) *pf.*

рази́нуть (-ну) *pf* (*impf* **разева́ть**) open; ~ **рот** gape. **рази́ня** *m* & *f* scatter-brain.

рази́тельный striking. **рази́ть** (ражу́) *impf* (*pf* **по~**) strike.

разлага́ть(ся *impf of* **разложи́ть(ся разла́д** discord; disorder.

разла́мывать(ся *impf of* **разлома́ть(ся, разломи́ть(ся. разлёгся** *etc.: see* **разле́чься**

разлеза́ться *impf,* **разле́зться** (-зется; -ле́зся) *pf* come to pieces; fall apart.

разлета́ться *impf,* **разлете́ться** (-лечу́сь) *pf* fly away; scatter; shatter; rush.

разле́чься (-ля́гусь; -лёгся, -гла́сь) *pf* stretch out.

разли́в bottling; flood; overflow. **разлива́ть** *impf,* **разли́ть** (-золью́, -зольёшь; -и́л, -а́, -о) *pf* pour out; spill; flood (with); ~**ся** spill; overflow; spread. **разливно́й** draught.

различа́ть *impf,* **различи́ть** (-чу́) *pf* distinguish; discern; ~**ся** differ. **разли́чие** distinction; difference. **различи́тельный** distinctive, distinguishing. **разли́чный** different.

разложе́ние decomposition; decay; disintegration. **разложи́ть** (-жу́, -жишь) *pf* (*impf* **разлага́ть, раскла́дывать**) put away; spread (out); distribute; break down; decompose;

resolve; corrupt; **~ся** decompose; become demoralized; be corrupted; disintegrate, go to pieces.

разло́м breaking; break. **разлома́ть**, **разломи́ть** (-млю́, -мишь) *pf* (*impf* **разла́мывать**) break to pieces; pull down; **~ся** break to pieces.

разлу́ка separation. **разлуча́ть** *impf*, **разлучи́ть** (-чу́) *pf* separate, part; **~ся** separate, part.

разлюби́ть (-блю́, -бишь) *pf* stop loving *or* liking.

разля́гусь *etc.*: see **разле́чься**

разма́зать (-а́жу) *pf*, **разма́зывать** *impf* spread, smear.

разма́лывать *impf of* **размоло́ть**

разма́тывать *impf of* **размота́ть**

разма́х sweep; swing; span; scope. **разма́хивать** *impf* +*instr* swing; brandish. **разма́хиваться** *impf*, **размахну́ться** (-ну́сь, -нёшься) *pf* swing one's arm. **разма́шистый** sweeping.

размежева́ние demarcation, delimitation. **размежева́ть** (-жу́ю) *pf*, **размежёвывать** *impf* delimit.

размёл *etc.*: see **размести́**

размельча́ть *impf*, **раз|мельчи́ть** (-чу́) *pf* crush, pulverize.

размелю́ *etc.*: see **размоло́ть**

разме́н exchange. **разме́нивать** *impf*, **разменя́ть** *pf* change; **~ся** +*instr* exchange; dissipate. **разме́нная моне́та** (small) change.

разме́р size; measurement; amount; scale, extent; *pl* proportions. **разме́ренный** measured. **разме́рить** *pf*, **размеря́ть** *impf* measure.

размести́ (-ету́, -етёшь; -мёл, -а́) *pf* (*impf* **размета́ть**) sweep clear; sweep away.

размести́ть (-ещу́) *pf* (*impf* **размеща́ть**) place, accommodate; distribute; **~ся** take one's seat.

размета́ть *impf of* **размести́**

разме́тить (-е́чу) *pf*, **размеча́ть** *impf* mark.

размеша́ть *pf*, **разме́шивать** *impf* stir (in).

размеща́ть(ся *impf of* **размести́ть(ся. размеще́ние** placing; accommodation; distribution. **размещу́** *etc.*: see **размести́ть**

размина́ть(ся *impf of* **размя́ть(ся**

разми́нка limbering up.

размину́ться (-ну́сь, -нёшься) *pf* pass; +*c*+*instr* pass; miss.

размножа́ть *impf*, **размно́жить** (-жу) *pf* multiply, duplicate; breed; **~ся** multiply; breed.

размозжи́ть (-жу́) *pf* smash.

размо́лвка tiff.

размоло́ть (-мелю́, -ме́лешь) *pf* (*impf* **разма́лывать**) grind.

размора́живать *impf*, **разморо́зить** (-о́жу) *pf* unfreeze, defrost; **~ся** unfreeze; defrost.

размота́ть *pf* (*impf* **разма́тывать**) unwind.

размыва́ть *impf*, **размы́ть** (-о́ет) *pf* wash away; erode.

размыка́ть *impf of* **разомкну́ть**

размышле́ние reflection; meditation. **размышля́ть** *impf* reflect, ponder.

размягча́ть *impf*, **размягчи́ть** (-чу́) *pf* soften; **~ся** soften.

размяка́ть *impf*, **размя́кнуть** (-ну; -мяк) *pf* soften.

раз|мя́ть (-зомну́, -зомнёшь) *pf* (*impf also* **размина́ть**) knead; mash; **~ся** stretch one's legs; limber up.

разна́шивать *impf of* **разноси́ть**

разнести́ (-су́, -сёшь; -ёс, -ла́) *pf* (*impf* **разноси́ть**) carry; deliver; spread; note down; smash; scold; scatter; *impers* make puffy, swell.

разнима́ть *impf of* **разня́ть**

ра́зниться *impf* differ. **ра́зница** difference.

разно- *in comb* different, vari-, hetero-. **разнобо́й** lack of co-ordination; difference. **~ви́дность** variety. **~гла́сие** disagreement; discrepancy. **~обра́зие** variety, diversity. **~обра́зный** various, diverse. **~речи́вый** contradictory. **~ро́дный** heterogeneous. **~сторо́нний** many-sided; versatile. **~цве́тный** variegated. **~шёрстный** of different colours; ill-assorted.

разноси́ть[1] (-ошу́, -о́сишь) *pf* (*impf* **разна́шивать**) wear in.

разноси́ть[2] (-ошу́, -о́сишь) *impf of* **разнести́. разно́ска** delivery.

ра́зность difference.

разно́счик pedlar.

разношу́ *etc.*: see **разноси́ть**

разну́зданный unbridled.

ра́зн|ый different; various; **~ое** *sb*

various things.

разню́хать pf, **разню́хивать** impf smell out.

разня́ть (-ниму́, -ни́мешь; ро́з- or разня́л, -á, -о) pf (impf **разнима́ть**) take to pieces; separate.

разоблача́ть impf, **разоблачи́ть** (-чу́) pf expose. **разоблаче́ние** exposure.

разобра́ть (-зберу́, -рёшь; -áл, -á, -о) pf (impf **разбира́ть**) take to pieces; buy up; sort out; investigate; analyse; understand; ~**ся** sort things out; +в+prep investigate, look into; understand.

разобью́ etc.: see **разби́ть**. **разовью́** etc.: see **разви́ть**

ра́зовый single.

разогна́ть (-згоню́, -о́нишь; -гна́л, -á, -о) pf (impf **разгоня́ть**) scatter; disperse; dispel; drive fast; ~**ся** gather speed.

разогну́ть (-ну́, -нёшь) pf (impf **разгиба́ть**) unbend, straighten; ~**ся** straighten up.

разогрева́ть impf, **разогре́ть** (-éю) pf warm up.

разоде́ть(ся (-е́ну(сь) pf dress up.

разодра́ть (-здеру́, -рёшь; -áл, -á, -о) pf (impf **раздира́ть**) tear (up); lacerate.

разожгу́ etc.: see **разже́чь**. **разожму́** etc.: see **разжа́ть**

разо|зли́ть pf.

разойти́сь (-йду́сь, -йдёшься; -ошёлся, -ошла́сь) pf (impf **расходи́ться**) disperse; diverge; radiate; differ; conflict; part; be spent; be sold out.

разолью́ etc.: see **разли́ть**

ра́зом adv at once, at one go.

разомкну́ть (-ну, -нёшь) pf (impf **размыка́ть**) open; break.

разомну́ etc.: see **размя́ть**

разорва́ть (-ву́, -вёшь; -áл, -á, -о) pf (impf **разрыва́ть**) tear; break (off); blow up; ~**ся** tear; break; explode.

разоре́ние ruin; destruction. **разори́тельный** ruinous; wasteful. **разори́ть** pf (impf **разоря́ть**) ruin; destroy; ~**ся** ruin o.s.

разоружа́ть impf, **разоружи́ть** (-жу́) pf disarm; ~**ся** disarm. **разоруже́ние** disarmament.

разоря́ть(ся impf of **разори́ть(ся**

разосла́ть (-ошлю́, -ошлёшь) pf (impf **рассыла́ть**) distribute, circulate.

разостла́ть, расстели́ть (-сстелю́, -те́лешь) pf (impf **расстила́ть**) spread (out); lay; ~**ся** spread.

разотру́ etc.: see **растере́ть**

разочарова́ние disappointment.

разочарова́ть pf, **разочаро́вывать** impf disappoint; ~**ся** be disappointed.

разочту́ etc.: see **расчесть**. **разошёлся** etc.: see **разойти́сь**. **разошлю́** etc.: see **разосла́ть**. **разошью́** etc.: see **расшить**

разраба́тывать impf, **разрабо́тать** pf cultivate; work, exploit; work out; develop. **разрабо́тка** cultivation; exploitation; working out; mining; quarry.

разража́ться impf, **разрази́ться** (-ажу́сь) pf break out; burst out.

разраста́ться impf, **разрасти́сь** (-тётся; -ро́сся, -ла́сь) pf grow; spread.

разрежённый (-ён, -á) rarefied.

разре́з cut; section; point of view. **разре́зать** (-е́жу) pf, **разреза́ть** impf cut; slit.

разреша́ть impf, **разреши́ть** (-шу́) pf (+dat) allow; solve; settle; ~**ся** be allowed; be solved; be settled. **разреше́ние** permission; permit; solution; settlement. **разреши́мый** solvable.

разро́зненный uncoordinated; odd; incomplete.

разро́сся etc.: see **разрасти́сь**. **разро́ю** etc.: see **разры́ть**

разруба́ть impf, **разруби́ть** (-блю́, -бишь) pf cut; chop up.

разру́ха ruin, collapse. **разруша́ть** impf, **разру́шить** (-шу) pf destroy; demolish; ruin; ~**ся** go to ruin, collapse. **разруше́ние** destruction. **разруши́тельный** destructive.

разры́в break; gap; rupture; burst. **разрыва́ть**[1]**(ся** impf of **разорва́ть(ся**

разрыва́ть[2] impf of **разры́ть**

разрывно́й explosive.

разрыда́ться pf burst into tears.

разры́ть (-ро́ю) pf (impf **разрыва́ть**) dig (up).

раз|рыхли́ть pf, **разрыхля́ть** impf loosen; hoe.

разря́д[1] category; class.

разря́д[2] discharge. **разряди́ть** (-яжу́, -я́дишь) *pf* (*impf* **разряжа́ть**) unload; discharge; space out; **~ся** run down; clear, ease. **разря́дка** spacing (out); discharging; unloading; relieving.

разряжа́ть(ся *impf of* **разряди́ть(ся**

разубеди́ть (-ежу́) *pf*, **разубежда́ть** *impf* dissuade; **~ся** change one's mind.

разува́ться *impf of* **разу́ться**

разуве́рить *pf*, **разуверя́ть** *impf* dissuade, undeceive; **~ся** (в+*prep*) lose faith (in).

разузнава́ть (-наю́, -наёшь) *impf*, **разузна́ть** *pf* (try to) find out.

разукра́сить (-а́шу) *pf*, **разукра́шивать** *impf* adorn, embellish.

ра́зум reason; intellect. **разуме́ться** (-е́ется) *impf* be understood, be meant; **(само́ собо́й) разуме́ется** of course; it goes without saying. **разу́мный** rational, intelligent; sensible; reasonable; wise.

разу́ться (-у́юсь) *pf* (*impf* **разува́ться**) take off one's shoes.

разу́чивать *impf*, **разучи́ть** (-чу́, -чишь) *pf* learn (up). **разу́чиваться** *impf*, **разучи́ться** (-чу́сь, -чишься) *pf* forget (how to).

разъеда́ть *impf of* **разъе́сть**

разъедини́ть *pf*, **разъединя́ть** *impf* separate; disconnect.

разъе́дусь *etc.*: *see* **разъе́хаться**

разъе́зд departure; siding (track); mounted patrol; *pl* travel; journeys. **разъездно́й** travelling. **разъезжа́ть** drive or ride about; travel; **~ся** *impf of* **разъе́хаться**

разъе́сть (-е́ст, -едя́т; -е́л) *pf* (*impf* **разъеда́ть**) eat away; corrode.

разъе́хаться (-е́дусь) *pf* (*impf* **разъезжа́ться**) depart; separate; pass (one another); miss one another.

разъярённый (-ён, -а́) furious. **разъяри́ть** *pf*, **разъяря́ть** *impf* infuriate; **~ся** get furious.

разъясне́ние explanation; interpretation. **разъясни́тельный** explanatory. **разъясни́ть** *pf*, **разъясня́ть** *impf* explain; interpret; **~ся** become clear, be cleared up.

разыгра́ть *pf*, **разы́грывать** *impf* perform; draw; raffle; play a trick on;

~ся get up; run high.

разыска́ть (-ыщу́, -ы́щешь) *pf* find. **разы́скивать** *impf* search for.

рай (*loc* -ю́) paradise; garden of Eden.

райко́м district committee.

райо́н region. **райо́нный** district.

ра́йский heavenly.

рак crayfish; cancer; Cancer.

раке́та[1], **раке́тка** racket.

раке́та[2] rocket; missile; flare.

ра́ковина shell; sink.

ра́ковый cancer; cancerous.

раку́шка cockle-shell, mussel.

ра́ма frame. **ра́мка** frame; *pl* framework.

ра́мпа footlights.

ра́на wound. **ране́ние** wounding; wound. **ра́неный** wounded; injured.

ранг rank.

ра́нец (-нца) knapsack; satchel.

ра́нить *impf & pf* wound; injure.

ра́нний early. **ра́но** *adv* early. **ра́ньше** *adv* earlier; before; formerly.

рапи́ра foil.

ра́порт report. **рапортова́ть** *impf & pf* report.

ра́са race. **раси́зм** racism. **раси́стский** racist.

раска́иваться *impf of* **раска́яться**

раскалённый (-ён, -а́) scorching; incandescent. **раскали́ть** *pf* (*impf* **раскаля́ть**) make red-hot; **~ся** become red-hot. **раска́лывать(ся** *impf of* **расколо́ть(ся**. **раскаля́ть(ся** *impf of* **раскали́ть(ся**. **раска́пывать** *impf of* **раскопа́ть**

раска́т roll, peal. **раската́ть** *pf*, **раска́тывать** *impf* roll (out); smooth out, level; drive or ride (about). **раска́тистый** rolling, booming. **раскати́ться** (-ачу́сь, -а́тишься) *pf*, **раска́тываться** *impf* gather speed; roll away; peal, boom.

раскача́ть *pf*, **раска́чивать** *impf* swing; rock; **~ся** swing, rock.

раска́яние repentance. **рас|ка́яться** *pf* (*impf also* **раска́иваться**) repent.

расквита́ться *pf* settle accounts.

раски́дывать *impf*, **раски́нуть** (-ну) *pf* stretch (out); spread; pitch; **~ся** spread out; sprawl.

раскладно́й folding. **раскладу́шка** camp-bed. **раскла́дывать** *impf of* **разложи́ть**

раскла́няться *pf* bow; take leave.

раскле́ивать *impf*, **раскле́ить** *pf* unstick; stick (up); **~ся** come unstuck.

раско́л split; schism. **рас|коло́ть** (-лю́, -лешь) *pf* (*impf also* **раска́лывать**) split; break; disrupt; **~ся** split. **раско́льник** dissenter.

раскопа́ть *pf* (*impf* **раска́пывать**) dig up, unearth, excavate. **раско́пки** (-пок) *pl* excavations.

раско́сый slanting.

раскра́ивать *impf of* **раскро́ить**

раскра́сить (-а́шу) *pf*, **раскра́шивать** paint, colour.

раскрепости́ть (-ощу́) *pf*, **раскрепоща́ть** *impf* liberate. **раскрепоще́ние** emancipation.

раскритикова́ть *pf* criticize harshly.

раскро́ить *pf* (*impf* **раскра́ивать**) cut out.

раскро́ю *etc.: see* **раскры́ть**

раскрути́ть (-учу́, -у́тишь) *pf*, **раскру́чивать** *impf* untwist; **~ся** come untwisted.

раскрыва́ть *impf*, **раскры́ть** (-о́ю) *pf* open; expose; reveal; discover; **~ся** open; uncover o.s.; come to light.

раскупа́ть *impf*, **раскупи́ть** (-у́пит) *pf* buy up.

раску́поривать *impf*, **раску́порить** *pf* uncork, open.

раскуси́ть (-ушу́, -у́сишь) *pf*, **раску́сывать** *impf* bite through; see through.

ра́совый racial.

распа́д disintegration; collapse. **распада́ться** *impf of* **распа́сться**

распакова́ть *pf*, **распако́вывать** *impf* unpack.

распа́рывать(ся *impf of* **распоро́ть(ся**

распа́сться (-адётся) *pf* (*impf* **распада́ться**) disintegrate, fall to pieces.

распаха́ть (-ашу́, -а́шешь) *pf*, **распа́хивать**[1] *impf* plough up.

распа́хивать[2] *impf*, **распахну́ть** (-ну́, -нёшь) *pf* throw open; **~ся** fly open, swing open.

распашо́нка baby's vest.

распева́ть *impf* sing.

распеча́тать *pf*, **распеча́тывать** *impf* open; unseal.

распи́ливать *impf*, **распили́ть** (-лю́,

-лишь) *pf* saw up.

распина́ть *impf of* **распя́ть**

расписа́ние time-table. **расписа́ть** (-ишу́, -и́шешь) *pf*, **распи́сывать** *impf* enter; assign; paint; **~ся** sign; register one's marriage; +в+*prep* sign for; acknowledge. **распи́ска** receipt. **расписно́й** painted, decorated.

распиха́ть *pf*, **распи́хивать** *impf* push, shove, stuff.

рас|пла́вить (-влю) *pf*, **расплавля́ть** *impf* melt, fuse. **распла́вленный** molten.

распла́каться (-а́чусь) *pf* burst into tears.

распласта́ть *pf*, **распла́стывать** *impf* spread; flatten; split; **~ся** sprawl.

распла́та payment; retribution. **расплати́ться** (-ачу́сь, -а́тишься) *pf*, **распла́чиваться** *impf* (+с+*instr*) pay off; get even; +за+*acc* pay for.

расплеска́ть(ся (-ещу́(сь, -е́щешь(ся) *pf*, **расплёскивать(ся** *impf* spill.

расплести́ (-ету́, -етёшь; -ёл, -а́) *pf*, **расплета́ть** *impf* unplait; untwist.

рас|плоди́ть(ся (-ожу́(сь) *pf*

расплыва́ться *impf*, **расплы́ться** (-ывётся; -ы́лся, -а́сь) *pf* run. **расплы́вчатый** indistinct; vague.

расплю́щивать *impf*, **расплю́щить** (-щу) *pf* flatten out, hammer out.

распну́ *etc.: see* **распя́ть**

распознава́ть (-наю́, -наёшь) *impf*, **распозна́ть** *pf* recognize, identify; diagnose.

располага́ть *impf* (*pf* **расположи́ть**) +*instr* have at one's disposal. **располага́ться** *impf of* **расположи́ться**

располза́ться *impf*, **расползти́сь** (-зётся; -о́лзся, -зла́сь) *pf* crawl (away); give at the seams.

расположе́ние disposition; arrangement; situation; tendency; liking; mood. **располо́женный** disposed, inclined. **расположи́ть** (-жу́, -жишь) *pf* (*impf* **располага́ть**) dispose; set out; win over; **~ся** settle down.

распо́рка cross-bar, strut.

рас|поро́ть (-рю́, -решь) *pf* (*impf also* **распа́рывать**) unpick, rip; **~ся** rip, come undone.

распоряди́тель *m* manager. **распоряди́тельный** capable; efficient.

распоряди́ться (-яжу́сь) *pf*, **распоряжа́ться** *impf* order, give orders; see; +*instr* manage, deal with.

распоря́док (-дка) order; routine.

распоряже́ние order; instruction; disposal, command.

распра́ва violence; reprisal.

распра́вить (-влю) *pf*, **расправля́ть** *impf* straighten; smooth out; spread.

распра́виться (-влюсь) *pf*, **расправля́ться** *impf* с+*instr* deal with severely; make short work of.

распределе́ние distribution; allocation. **распредели́тель** *m* distributor. **распредели́тельный** distributive, distributing; ~ **щит** switchboard. **распредели́ть** *pf*, **распределя́ть** *impf* distribute; allocate.

распродава́ть (-даю́, -даёшь) *impf*, **распрода́ть** (-а́м, -а́шь, -а́ст, -ади́м; -о́дал, -а́, -о) *pf* sell off; sell out. **распрода́жа** (clearance) sale.

распростёртый outstretched; prostrate.

распростране́ние spreading; dissemination. **распространённый** (-ён, -а́) widespread, prevalent. **расространи́ть** *pf*, **распространя́ть** *impf* spread; ~**ся** spread.

ра́спря (*gen pl* -ей) quarrel.

распряга́ть *impf*, **распря́чь** (-ягу́, -яжёшь; -яг, -ла́) *pf* unharness.

распрями́ться *pf*, **распрямля́ться** *impf* straighten up.

распуска́ть *impf*, **распусти́ть** (-ущу́, -у́стишь) *pf* dismiss; dissolve; let out; relax; let get out of hand; melt; spread; ~**ся** open; come loose; dissolve; melt; get out of hand; let o.s. go.

распу́тать *pf* (*impf* **распу́тывать**) untangle; unravel.

распу́тица season of bad roads.

распу́тный dissolute. **распу́тство** debauchery.

распу́тывать *impf of* **распу́тать**

распу́тье crossroads.

распуха́ть *impf*, **распу́хнуть** (-ну; -у́х) *pf* swell (up).

распу́щенный undisciplined; spoilt; dissolute.

распыли́тель *m* spray, atomizer.

распыли́ть *pf*, **распыля́ть** *impf* spray; pulverize; disperse.

распя́тие crucifixion; crucifix. **распя́ть** (-пну́, -пнёшь) *pf* (*impf* **распина́ть**) crucify.

расса́да seedlings. **рассади́ть** (-ажу́, -а́дишь) *pf*, **расса́живать** *impf* plant out; seat; separate, seat separately.

расса́живаться *impf of* **рассе́сться**.

расса́сываться *impf of* **рассоса́ться**

рассвести́ (-етёт; -ело́) *pf*, **рассвета́ть** *impf* dawn. **рассве́т** dawn.

рас|свирипе́ть (-е́ю) *pf*.

расседла́ть *pf* unsaddle.

рассе́ивание dispersal, scattering. **рассе́ивать(ся** *impf of* **рассе́ять(ся**

рассека́ть *impf of* **рассе́чь**

расселе́ние settling, resettlement; separation.

рассе́лина cleft, fissure.

рассели́ть *pf*, **расселя́ть** *impf* settle, resettle; separate.

рас|серди́ть(ся (-жу́(сь, -рдишь(ся) *pf*.

рассе́сться (-ся́дусь) *pf* (*impf* **расса́живаться**) take seats; sprawl.

рассе́чь (-еку́, -ечёшь; -ёк, -ла́) *pf* (*impf* **рассека́ть**) cut (through); cleave.

рассе́янность absent-mindedness; dispersion. **рассе́янный** absent-minded; diffused; scattered. **рассе́ять** (-е́ю) *pf* (*impf* **рассе́ивать**) disperse, scatter; dispel; ~**ся** disperse, scatter; clear; divert o.s.

расска́з story; account. **рассказа́ть** (-ажу́, -а́жешь) *pf*, **расска́зывать** *impf* tell, recount. **расска́зчик** story-teller, narrator.

рассла́бить (-блю) *pf*, **расслабля́ть** *impf* weaken.

рассла́ивать(ся *impf of* **расслои́ть(ся**

рассле́дование investigation, examination; inquiry; **произвести́** ~+*gen* hold an inquiry into. **рассле́довать** *impf* & *pf* investigate, look into, hold an inquiry into.

рассло́ить *pf* (*impf* **рассла́ивать**) divide into layers; ~**ся** become stratified; flake off.

рассл́ышать (-шу) *pf* catch.

рассма́тривать *impf of* **рассмотре́ть**; examine; consider.

рас|смеши́ть (-шу́) *pf*.

рассме́яться (-ею́сь, -еёшься) *pf*

burst out laughing.

рассмотре́ние examination; consideration. **рассмотре́ть** (-рю́, -ришь) *pf* (*impf* **рассма́тривать**) examine, consider; discern, make out.

рассова́ть (-су́ю, -су́ёшь) *pf*, **рассо́вывать** *impf* по+*dat* shove into.

рассо́л brine; pickle.

рассо́риться *pf* c+*instr* fall out with.

рас|сортирова́ть *pf*, **рассорти-ро́вывать** *impf* sort out.

рассоса́ться (-сётся) *pf* (*impf* **расса́сываться**) resolve.

рассо́хнуться (-нется; -о́хся) *pf* (*impf* **рассыха́ться**) crack.

расспра́шивать *impf*, **расспроси́ть** (-ошу́, -о́сишь) *pf* question; make inquiries of.

рассро́чить (-чу) *pf* spread (over a period). **рассро́чка** instalment.

расстава́ние parting. **расстава́ться** (-таю́сь, -таёшься) *impf of* **расста́ться**

расста́вить (-влю) *pf*, **расставля́ть** *impf* place, arrange; move apart. **расстано́вка** arrangement; pause.

расста́ться (-а́нусь) *pf* (*impf* **расстава́ться**) part, separate.

расстёгивать *impf*, **расстегну́ть** (-ну́, -нёшь) *pf* undo, unfasten; **~ся** come undone; undo one's coat.

расстели́ть(ся, *etc.*: *see* **разостла́ть(ся. расстила́ть(ся, -а́ю(сь** *impf of* **разостла́ть(ся**

расстоя́ние distance.

расстра́ивать(ся *impf of* **расстро́-ить(ся**

расстре́л execution by firing squad. **расстре́ливать** *impf*, **расстреля́ть** *pf* shoot.

расстро́енный disordered; upset; out of tune. **расстро́ить** *pf* (*impf* **расстра́ивать**) upset; thwart; disturb; throw into confusion; put out of tune; **~ся** be upset; get out of tune; fall into confusion; fall through. **расстро́йство** upset; disarray; confusion; frustration.

расступа́ться *impf*, **расступи́ться** (-у́пится) *pf* part, make way.

рассуди́тельный reasonable; sensible. **рассуди́ть** (-ужу́, -у́дишь) *pf* judge; think; decide. **рассу́док** (-дка) reason; intellect. **рассужда́ть** *impf* reason; +о+*prep* discuss. **рассу-**

жде́ние reasoning; discussion; argument.

рассую́ *etc.*: *see* **рассова́ть**

рассчи́танный deliberate; intended. **рассчита́ть** *pf*, **рассчи́тывать** *impf*, **расче́сть** (разочту́, -тёшь; расчёл, разочла́) *pf* calculate; count; depend; **~ся** settle accounts.

рассыла́ть *impf of* **разосла́ть. рассы́лка** distribution. **рассы́льный** *sb* delivery man.

рассы́пать (-плю) *pf*, **рассыпа́ть** *impf* spill; scatter; **~ся** spill, scatter; spread out; crumble. **рассы́пчатый** friable; crumbly.

рассыха́ться *impf of* **рассо́хнуться. расся́дусь** *etc.*: *see* **рассе́сться. раста́лкивать** *impf of* **растолкну́ть. раста́пливать(ся** *impf of* **расто-пи́ть(ся**

растаска́ть *pf*, **раста́скивать** *impf*, **растащи́ть** (-щу́, -щишь) *pf* pilfer, filch.

растащи́ть *see* **растаска́ть. рас|та́-ять** (-а́ю) *pf*.

раство́р² opening, span. **раство́р¹** solution; mortar. **раствори́мый** soluble. **раствори́тель** *m* solvent. **раствори́ть¹** *pf* (*impf* **растворя́ть**) dissolve; **~ся** dissolve.

раствори́ть² (-рю́, -ришь) *pf* (*impf* **растворя́ть**) open; **~ся** open.

растворя́ть(ся *impf of* **раствори́ть(ся. растека́ться** *impf of* **расте́чься**

расте́ние plant.

растере́ть (разотру́, -трёшь; растёр) *pf* (*impf* **растира́ть**) grind; spread; rub; massage.

растерза́ть *pf*, **расте́рзывать** *impf* tear to pieces.

расте́рянность confusion, dismay. **расте́рянный** confused, dismayed. **растеря́ть** *pf* lose; **~ся** get lost; lose one's head.

расте́чься (-ечётся, -еку́тся; -тёкся, -ла́сь) *pf* (*impf* **растека́ться**) run; spread.

расти́ (-ту́, -тёшь; рос, -ла́) *impf* grow; grow up.

растира́ние grinding; rubbing, massage. **растира́ть(ся** *impf of* **расте-ре́ть(ся**

расти́тельность vegetation; hair. **расти́тельный** vegetable. **расти́ть**

(ращу) *impf* bring up; train; grow.
растлевать *impf*, **растлить** *pf* seduce; corrupt.
растолкать *pf* (*impf* **расталкивать**) push apart; shake.
растолковать *pf*, **растолковывать** *impf* explain.
рас|толочь (-лку, -лчёшь; -лок, -лкла) *pf*.
растолстеть (-ею) *pf* put on weight.
растопить[1] (-плю, -пишь) *pf* (*impf* **растапливать**) melt; thaw; ∼**ся** melt.
растопить[2] (-плю, -пишь) *pf* (*impf* **растапливать**) light, kindle; ∼**ся** begin to burn.
растоптать (-пчу, -пчешь) *pf* trample, stamp on.
расторгать *impf*, **расторгнуть** (-ну; -орг) *pf* annul, dissolve. **расторжение** annulment, dissolution.
расторопный quick; efficient.
расточать *impf*, **расточить** (-чу) *pf* squander, dissipate. **расточительный** extravagant, wasteful.
растравить (-влю, -вишь) *pf*, **растравлять** *impf* irritate.
растрата spending; waste; embezzlement. **растратить** (-ачу) *pf*, **растрачивать** *impf* spend; waste; embezzle.
растрёпанный dishevelled; tattered.
рас|трепать (-плю, -плешь) *pf* disarrange; tatter.
растрескаться *pf*, **растрескиваться** *impf* crack, chap.
растрогать *pf* move, touch; ∼**ся** be moved.
растущий growing.
растягивать *impf*, **растянуть** (-ну, -нешь) *pf* stretch (out); strain, sprain; drag out; ∼**ся** stretch; drag on; sprawl. **растяжение** tension; strain, sprain. **растяжимый** tensile; stretchable. **растянутый** stretched; long-winded.
рас|фасовать *pf*.
расформировать *pf*, **расформировывать** *impf* break up; disband.
расхаживать *impf* walk about; pace up and down.
расхваливать *impf*, **расхвалить** (-лю, -лишь) *pf* lavish praises on.
расхватать *pf*, **расхватывать** *impf* seize on, buy up.

расхититель *m* embezzler. **расхитить** (-ищу) *pf*, **расхищать** *impf* steal, misappropriate. **расхищение** misappropriation.
расхлябанный loose; lax.
расход expenditure; consumption; *pl* expenses, outlay. **расходиться** (-ожусь, -одишься) *impf of* **разойтись. расходование** expense, expenditure. **расходовать** *impf* (*pf* **из**∼) spend; consume. **расхождение** divergence.
расхолаживать *impf*, **расхолодить** (-ожу) *pf* damp the ardour of.
расхотеть (-очу, -очешь, -отим) *pf* no longer want.
расхохотаться (-очусь, -очешься) *pf* burst out laughing.
расцарапать *pf* scratch (all over).
расцвести (-ету, -етёшь; -ёл, -а) *pf*, **расцветать** *impf* blossom; flourish. **расцвет** blossoming (out); flowering, heyday.
расцветка colours; colouring.
расценивать *impf*, **расценить** (-ню, -нишь) *pf* estimate, value; consider. **расценка** valuation; price; (wage-) rate.
расцепить (-плю, -пишь) *pf*, **расцеплять** *impf* uncouple, unhook.
расчесать (-ешу, -ешешь) *pf* (*impf* **расчёсывать**) comb; scratch. **расчёска** comb.
расчесть *etc.*: *see* **рассчитать.**
расчёсывать *impf of* **расчесать**
расчёт[1] calculation; estimate; gain; settlement. **расчётливый** thrifty; careful. **расчётный** calculation; pay; accounts; calculated.
расчистить (-ищу) *pf*, **расчищать** *impf* clear; ∼**ся** clear. **расчистка** clearing.
рас|членить *pf*, **расчленять** *impf* dismember; divide.
расшатать *pf*, **расшатывать** *impf* shake loose, make rickety; impair.
расшевелить (-лю, -елишь) *pf* stir; rouse.
расшибать *impf*, **расшибить** (-бу, -бёшь; -иб) *pf* smash to pieces; hurt; stub; ∼**ся** hurt o.s.
расшивать *impf of* **расшить**
расширение widening; expansion; dilation, dilatation. **расширить** *pf*, **расширять** *impf* widen; enlarge;

expand; ~ся broaden, widen; expand, dilate.

расши́ть (разошью́, -шьёшь) pf (impf расшива́ть) embroider; unpick.

расшифрова́ть pf, расшифро́вывать impf decipher.

расшнурова́ть pf, расшнуро́вывать impf unlace.

расще́лина crevice.

расщепи́ть (-плю́) pf, расщепля́ть impf split; ~ся split. расщепле́ние splitting; fission.

ратифици́ровать impf & pf ratify.

рать army, battle.

ра́унд round.

рафини́рованный refined.

рацио́н ration.

рационализа́ция rationalization. рационализи́ровать impf & pf rationalize. рациона́льный rational; efficient.

ра́ция walkie-talkie.

рвану́ться (-ну́сь, -нёшься) pf dart, dash.

рва́ный torn; lacerated. рвать¹ (рву, рвёшь; рвал, -á, -о) impf tear (out); pull out; pick; blow up; break off; ~ся break; tear; burst, explode; be bursting.

рвать² (рвёт; рва́ло) impf (pf вы́~) impers+acc vomit.

рвач (-á) self-seeker.

рве́ние zeal.

рво́та vomiting.

реабилита́ция rehabilitation. реабилити́ровать impf & pf rehabilitate.

реаги́ровать impf (pf от~, про~) react.

реакти́в reagent. реакти́вный reactive; jet-propelled. реа́ктор reactor.

реакционе́р reactionary. реакцио́нный reactionary. реа́кция reaction.

реализа́ция realization. реали́зм realism. реализова́ть impf & pf realize. реали́ст realist. реалисти́ческий realistic.

реа́льность reality; practicability. реа́льный real; practicable.

ребёнок (-нка; pl ребя́та, -я́т and де́ти, -е́й) child; infant.

ребро́ (pl рёбра, -бер) rib; edge.

ребя́та (-я́т) pl children; guys; lads. ребя́ческий child's; childish. ребя́чество childishness. ребя́читься

(-чусь) impf be childish.

рёв roar; howl.

рева́нш revenge; return match.

ревера́нс curtsey.

реве́ть (-ву́, -вёшь) impf roar; bellow; howl.

ревизио́нный inspection; auditing. реви́зия inspection; audit; revision. ревизо́р inspector.

ревмати́зм rheumatism.

ревни́вый jealous. ревнова́ть impf (pf при~) be jealous. ре́вностный zealous. ре́вность jealousy.

револьве́р revolver.

революционе́р revolutionary. револю́цио́нный revolutionary. револю́ция revolution.

рега́та regatta.

ре́гби neut indecl rugby.

ре́гент regent.

регио́н region. региона́льный regional.

регистра́тор registrar. регистрату́ра registry. регистра́ция registration. регистри́ровать impf & pf (pf also за~) register, record; ~ся register; register one's marriage.

регла́мент standing orders; time-limit. регламента́ция regulation. регламенти́ровать impf & pf regulate.

регресси́ровать impf regress.

регули́ровать impf (pf от~, у~) regulate; adjust. регулиро́вщик traffic controller. регуля́рный regular. регуля́тор regulator.

редакти́ровать impf (pf от~) edit. реда́ктор editor. реда́кторский editorial. редакцио́нный editorial, editing. реда́кция editorial staff; editorial office; editing.

реде́ть (-е́ет) impf (pf по~) thin (out).

реди́с radishes. реди́ска radish.

ре́дкий (-док, -дка́, -о) thin; sparse; rare. ре́дко adv sparsely; rarely, seldom. ре́дкость rarity.

редколле́гия editorial board.

рее́стр register.

режи́м régime; routine; procedure; regimen; conditions.

режиссёр-(постано́вщик) producer; director.

ре́жущий cutting, sharp. ре́зать (ре́жу) impf (pf за~, про~, с~) cut;

engrave; kill, slaughter.
резвиться (-влюсь) *impf* gambol,
play. **резвый** frisky, playful.
резерв reserve. **резервный** reserve;
back-up.
резервуар reservoir.
резец (-зца) cutter; chisel; incisor.
резиденция residence.
резина rubber. **резинка** rubber;
elastic band. **резиновый** rubber.
резкий sharp; harsh; abrupt; shrill.
резной carved. **резня** carnage.
резолюция resolution.
резонанс resonance; response.
результат result.
резьба carving, fretwork.
резюме *neut indecl* résumé.
рейд[1] roads, roadstead.
рейд[2] raid.
рейка lath, rod.
рейс trip; voyage; flight.
рейтузы (-уз) *pl* leggings; riding
breeches.
река (*acc* реку, *pl* -и, рекам) river.
реквием requiem.
реквизит props.
реклама advertising, advertisement.
рекламировать *impf & pf* advertise. **рекламный** publicity.
рекомендательный of recommendation. **рекомендация** recommendation; reference. **рекомендовать**
impf & pf (*pf also* **от~, по~**) recommend; **~ся** introduce o.s.; be advisable.
реконструировать *impf & pf* reconstruct. **реконструкция** reconstruction.
рекорд record. **рекордный** record,
record-breaking. **рекордсмен, -енка**
record-holder.
ректор principal (*of university*).
религиозный religious. **религия** religion.
реле (*electr*) *neut indecl* relay.
реликвия relic.
рельеф relief. **рельефный** relief;
raised, bold.
рельс rail.
ремарка stage direction.
ремень (-мня) *m* strap; belt.
ремесленник artisan, craftsman.
ремесленный handicraft; mechanical. **ремесло** (*pl* -ёсла, -ёсел) craft;
trade.

ремонт repair(s); maintenance. **ре-
монтировать** *impf & pf* (*pf also*
от~) repair; recondition. **ремонт-
ный** repair.
рента rent; income. **рентабельный**
paying, profitable.
рентген X-rays. **рентгеновский** X-
ray. **рентгенолог** radiologist. **рент-
генология** radiology.
реорганизация reorganization. **ре-
организовать** *impf & pf* reorganize.
репа turnip.
репатриировать *impf & pf* repatriate.
репертуар repertoire.
репетировать *impf* (*pf* **от~, про~,
с~**) rehearse; coach. **репетитор**
coach. **репетиция** rehearsal.
реплика retort; cue.
репортаж report; reporting. **репор-
тёр** reporter.
репрессия repression.
репродуктор loud-speaker. **репродукция** reproduction.
репутация reputation.
ресница eyelash.
республика republic. **республиканский** republican.
рессора spring.
реставрация restoration. **реставри-
ровать** *impf & pf* (*pf also* **от~**) restore.
ресторан restaurant.
ресурс resort; *pl* resources.
ретранслятор (radio-)relay.
реферат synopsis, abstract; paper,
essay.
референдум referendum.
рефлекс reflex. **рефлектор** reflect-
or.
реформа reform. **реформировать**
impf & pf reform.
рефрижератор refrigerator.
рецензировать *impf* (*pf* **про~**) review. **рецензия** review.
рецепт prescription; recipe.
рецидив relapse. **рецидивист** re-
cidivist.
речевой speech; vocal.
речка river. **речной** river.
речь (*gen pl* -ей) speech.
решать(ся *impf of* **решить(ся. решающий** decisive, deciding. **решение** decision; solution.
решётка grating; grille; railing; lattice; trellis; fender, (fire)guard; (fire-)

grate; tail. **решето́** (*pl* -ёта) sieve.
решётчатый lattice, latticed.
реши́мость resoluteness; resolve.
реши́тельно *adv* resolutely; definitely; absolutely. **реши́тельность** determination. **реши́тельный** definite; decisive. **реши́ть** (-шу́) *pf* (*impf* **реша́ть**) decide; solve; ~**ся** make up one's mind.
ржа́веть (-еет) *impf* (*pf* **за**~, **по**~) rust. **ржа́вчина** rust. **ржа́вый** rusty.
ржано́й rye.
ржать (ржу, ржёшь) *impf* neigh.
ри́млянин (*pl* -яне, -ян), **ри́млянка** Roman. **ри́мский** Roman.
ринг boxing ring.
ри́нуться (-нусь) *pf* rush, dart.
рис rice.
риск risk. **риско́ванный** risky; risqué. **рискова́ть** *impf* run risks; +*instr or inf* risk.
рисова́ние drawing. **рисова́ть** *impf* (*pf* **на**~) draw; paint, depict; ~**ся** be silhouetted; appear; pose.
ри́совый rice.
рису́нок (-нка) drawing; figure; pattern, design.
ритм rhythm. **ритми́ческий**, **ритми́чный** rhythmic.
ритуа́л ritual.
риф reef.
ри́фма rhyme. **рифмова́ть** *impf* rhyme; ~**ся** rhyme.
робе́ть (-е́ю) *impf* (*pf* **о**~) be timid. **ро́бкий** (-бок, -бка́, -о) timid, shy. **ро́бость** shyness.
ро́бот robot.
ров (рва, *loc* -у́) ditch.
рове́сник coeval. **ро́вно** *adv* evenly; exactly; absolutely. **ро́вный** flat; even; level; equable; exact; equal. **ровня́ть** *impf* (*pf* **с**~) even, level.
рог (*pl* -а́, -о́в) horn; antler. **рога́тка** catapult. **рога́тый** horned. **рогови́ца** cornea. **рогово́й** horn; horny; horn-rimmed.
рого́жа bast mat(ting).
род (*loc* -у́; *pl* -ы́) family, kin, clan; birth, origin, stock; generation; genus; sort, kind. **роди́льный** maternity. **ро́дина** native land; homeland. **ро́динка** birth-mark. **роди́тели** (-ей) *pl* parents. **роди́тельный** genitive. **роди́тельский** parental. **роди́ть** (рожу́, -и́л, -ила́, -о) *impf* &

pf (*impf also* **рожа́ть**, **рожда́ть**) give birth to; ~**ся** be born.
родни́к (-а́) spring.
родни́ть (*pf* **по**~) make related, link; ~**ся** become related. **родн|о́й** own; native; home; ~**о́й брат** brother; ~**ы́е** *sb pl* relatives. **родня́** relative(s); kinsfolk. **родово́й** tribal; ancestral; generic; gender. **родонача́льник** ancestor. **родосло́вн|ый** genealogical; ~**ая** *sb* genealogy, pedigree. **ро́дственник** relative. **ро́дственный** related. **родство́** relationship; kinship. **ро́ды** (-ов) *pl* childbirth; labour.
ро́жа (ugly) mug.
рожа́ть, **рожда́ть(ся** *impf of* **роди́ть(ся**. **рожда́емость** birthrate. **рожде́ние** birth. **рожде́ственский** Christmas. **Рождество́** Christmas.
рожь (ржи) rye.
ро́за rose.
ро́зга (*gen pl* -зог) birch.
ро́здал *etc.*: *see* **разда́ть**
розе́тка electric socket; rosette.
ро́зница retail; в ~у retail. **ро́зничный** retail. **рознь** difference; dissension.
ро́знял *etc.*: *see* **разня́ть**
ро́зовый pink.
ро́зыгрыш draw; drawn game.
ро́зыск search; inquiry.
ро́иться swarm. **рой** (*loc* -ю́; *pl* -и́, -ёв) swarm.
рок fate.
рокиро́вка castling.
рок-му́зыка rock music.
роково́й fateful; fatal.
ро́кот roar, rumble. **рокота́ть** (-о́чет) *impf* roar, rumble.
ро́лик roller; castor; *pl* roller skates.
роль (*gen pl* -е́й) role.
ром rum.
рома́н novel; romance. **романи́ст** novelist.
рома́нс (*mus*) romance.
рома́нтик romantic. **рома́нтика** romance. **романти́ческий**, **романти́чный** romantic.
рома́шка camomile.
ромб rhombus.
роня́ть *impf* (*pf* **урони́ть**) drop.
ро́пот murmur, grumble. **ропта́ть** (-пщу́, -пщешь) *impf* murmur, grumble.

рос etc.: see расти́

роса́ (pl -ы) dew. **роси́стый** dewy.

роско́шный luxurious; luxuriant. **ро́скошь** luxury; luxuriance.

ро́слый strapping.

ро́спись painting(s), mural(s).

ро́спуск dismissal; disbandment.

росси́йский Russian. **Росси́я** Russia.

ро́ссыпи f pl deposit.

рост growth; increase; height, stature.

ро́стбиф roast beef.

ростовщи́к (-á) usurer, money-lender.

росто́к (-тка́) sprout, shoot.

ро́счерк flourish.

рот (рта, loc рту) mouth.

ро́та company.

рота́тор duplicator.

ро́тный company; sb company commander.

ротозе́й, -зе́йка gaper, rubberneck; scatter-brain.

ро́ща grove.

ро́ю etc.: see рыть

роя́ль m (grand) piano.

ртуть mercury.

руба́нок (-нка) plane.

руба́ха, руба́шка shirt.

рубе́ж (-á) boundary, border(line); line; **за ~о́м** abroad.

рубе́ц (-бца́) scar; weal; hem; tripe.

руби́н ruby. **руби́новый** ruby; ruby-coloured.

руби́ть (-блю́, -бишь) impf (pf c~) fell; hew, chop; mince; build (of logs).

ру́бище rags.

ру́бка[1] felling; chopping; mincing.

ру́бка[2] deck house; **боева́я ~** conning-tower; **рулева́я ~** wheelhouse.

рублёвка one-rouble note. **рублёвый** (one-)rouble.

ру́бленый minced, chopped; of logs.

рубль (-я́) m rouble.

ру́брика rubric, heading.

ру́бчатый ribbed. **ру́бчик** scar; rib.

ру́гань abuse, swearing. **руга́тельный** abusive. **руга́тельство** oath, swear-word. **руга́ть** impf (pf вы́~, об~, от~) curse, swear at; abuse; **~ся** curse, swear; swear at one another.

руда́ (pl -ы) ore. **рудни́к** (-á) mine, pit. **рудни́чный** mine, pit; **~ газ** fire-damp. **рудоко́п** miner.

руже́йный rifle, gun. **ружьё** (pl -ья, -жей, -ьям) gun, rifle.

руи́на usu pl ruin.

рука́ (acc -у; pl -и, рук, -áм) hand; arm; **идти́ под руку** c+instr walk arm in arm with; **под руко́й** at hand; **руко́й пода́ть** a stone's throw away; **э́то мне на́ руку** that suits me.

рука́в (-á; pl -á, -о́в) sleeve. **рукави́ца** mitten; gauntlet.

руководи́тель m leader; manager; instructor; guide. **руководи́ть** (-ожу́) impf +instr lead; guide; direct, manage. **руково́дство** leadership; guidance; direction; guide; handbook, manual; leaders. **руково́дствоваться**+instr follow; be guided by. **руководя́щий** leading; guiding.

рукоде́лие needlework.

рукомо́йник washstand.

рукопа́шный hand-to-hand.

рукопи́сный manuscript. **ру́копись** manuscript.

рукоплеска́ние applause. **рукоплеска́ть** (-ещу́, -е́щешь) impf +dat applaud.

рукопожа́тие handshake.

руко́ятка handle.

рулево́й steering; sb helmsman.

руле́тка tape-measure; roulette.

рули́ть impf (pf вы́~) taxi.

руль (-я́) m rudder; helm; (steering-)wheel; handlebar.

румы́н (gen pl -ы́н), **~ка** Romanian. **Румы́ния** Romania. **румы́нский** Romanian.

румя́на (-я́н) pl rouge. **румя́нец** (-нца) (high) colour; flush; blush. **румя́ный** rosy, ruddy.

ру́пор megaphone; mouthpiece.

руса́к (-á) hare.

руса́лка mermaid.

русифици́ровать impf & pf Russify.

ру́сло river-bed, channel; course.

ру́сский Russian; sb Russian.

ру́сый light brown.

Русь (hist)Russia.

рути́на routine.

ру́хлядь junk.

ру́хнуть (-ну) pf crash down.

руча́тельство guarantee. **руча́ться** impf (pf поручи́ться) +за+acc vouch for, guarantee.

руче́й (-чья́) brook.

ру́чка handle; (door-)knob; (chair-)arm. **ручн|о́й** hand; arm; manual;

tame; ~ые часы́ wrist-watch.

ру́шить (-у) *impf* (*pf* об~) pull down; ~ся collapse.

ры́ба fish. **рыба́к** (-а́) fisherman. **рыба́лка** fishing. **рыба́цкий, рыба́чий** fishing. **ры́бий** fish; fishy; ~ жир cod-liver oil. **ры́бный** fish. **рыболо́в** fisherman. **рыболо́вный** fishing.

рыво́к (-вка́) jerk.

рыда́ние sobbing. **рыда́ть** *impf* sob.

ры́жий (рыж, -а́, -е) red, red-haired; chestnut.

ры́ло snout; mug.

ры́нок (-нка) market; market-place. **ры́ночный** market.

рыса́к (-а́) trotter.

рысь[1] (*loc* -и́) trot; ~ю, на рыся́х at a trot.

рысь[2] lynx.

ры́твина rut, groove. **ры́ть(ся** (ро́ю(сь) *impf* (*pf* вы́~, от~) dig; rummage.

рыхли́ть *impf* (*pf* вз~, раз~) loosen. **ры́хлый** (-л, -а́, -о) friable; loose.

ры́царский chivalrous. **ры́царь** *m* knight.

рыча́г (-а́) lever.

рыча́ть (-чу́) *impf* growl, snarl.

рья́ный zealous.

рюкза́к rucksack.

рю́мка wineglass.

ряби́на[1] rowan, mountain ash.

ряби́на[2] pit, pock. **ряби́ть** (-и́т) *impf* ripple; *impers*: у меня́ ряби́т в глаза́х I am dazzled. **рябо́й** pock-marked. **ря́бчик** hazel hen, hazel grouse. **рябь** ripples; dazzle.

ря́вкать *impf*, **ря́вкнуть** (-ну) *pf* bellow, roar.

ряд (*loc* -у́; *pl* -ы́) row; line; file, rank; series; number. **рядово́й** ordinary; common; ~ соста́в rank and file; *sb* private. **ря́дом** *adv* alongside; close by; +с+*instr* next to.

ря́са cassock.

С

с, со *prep* I. +*gen* from; since; off; for, with; on; by; с ра́дости for joy; с утра́ since morning. II. +*acc* about; the size of; с неде́лю for about a week. III. +*instr* with; and; мы с

ва́ми you and I; что с ва́ми? what is the matter?

са́бля (*gen pl* -бель) sabre.

сабота́ж sabotage. **саботи́ровать** *impf* & *pf* sabotage.

са́ван shroud; blanket.

с|агити́ровать *pf*.

сад (*loc* -у́; *pl* -ы́) garden. **сади́ть** (сажу́, са́дишь) *impf* (*pf* по~) plant. **сади́ться** (сажу́сь) *impf* of **сесть**. **садо́вник, -ница** gardener. **садо́водство** gardening; horticulture. **садо́вый** garden; cultivated.

сади́зм sadism. **сади́ст** sadist. **сади́стский** sadistic.

са́жа soot.

сажа́ть *impf* (*pf* посади́ть) plant; seat; set, put. **са́женец** (-нца) seedling; sapling.

са́жень (*pl* -и, -жен *or* -же́ней) sazhen (2.13 *metres*).

сажу́ *etc.*: see **сади́ть**

са́йка roll.

с|акти́ровать *pf*.

сала́зки (-зок) *pl* toboggan.

сала́т lettuce; salad.

са́ло fat, lard; suet; tallow.

сало́н salon; saloon.

салфе́тка napkin.

са́льный greasy; tallow; obscene.

салю́т salute. **салютова́ть** *impf* & *pf* (*pf also* от~) +*dat* salute.

сам (-ого́) *m*, **сама́** (-о́й, *acc* -оё) *f*, **само́** (-ого́) *neut*, **са́ми** (-и́х) *pl*, *pron* -self, -selves; myself, *etc.*, ourselves, *etc.*; ~ по себе́ in itself; by o.s.; ~ собо́й of itself, of its own accord; ~о́ собо́й (разуме́ется) of course; it goes without saying.

са́мбо *neut indecl abbr* (*of* самозащи́та без ору́жия) unarmed combat.

саме́ц (-мца́) male. **са́мка** female.

само- *in comb* self-, auto-. **самобы́тный** original, distinctive. ~**внуше́ние** auto-suggestion. ~**возгора́ние** spontaneous combustion. ~**во́льный** wilful; unauthorized. ~**де́льный** home-made. ~**держа́вие** autocracy. ~**держа́вный** autocratic. ~**де́ятельность** amateur work, amateur performance; initiative. ~**дово́льный** self-satisfied. ~**ду́р** petty tyrant. ~**ду́рство** high-handedness. ~**забве́ние** selflessness. ~**забве́нный** selfless. ~**защи́та**

self-defence. ~зва́нец (-нца) impostor, pretender. ~ка́т scooter. ~кри́тика self-criticism. ~люби́вый proud; touchy. ~любие pride, self-esteem. ~мне́ние conceit, self-importance. ~надёянный presumptuous. ~облада́ние self-control. ~обма́н self-deception. ~оборо́на self-defence. ~образова́ние self-education. ~обслу́живание self-service. ~определе́ние self-determination. ~отве́рженность self-lessness. ~отве́рженный selfless. ~поже́ртвование self-sacrifice. ~ро́док (-дка) nugget; person with natural talent. ~свал tip-up lorry. ~созна́ние (self-)consciousness. ~сохране́ние self-preservation. ~стоя́тельность independence. ~стоя́тельный independent. ~суд lynch law, mob law. ~тёк drift. ~тёком adv by gravity; of its own accord. ~убийственный suicidal. ~убийство suicide. ~убийца m & f suicide. ~уваже́ние self-respect. ~уве́ренность self-confidence. ~уве́ренный self-confident. ~униже́ние self-abasement. ~управле́ние self-government. ~управля́ющийся self-governing. ~упра́вный arbitrary. ~учи́тель m self-instructor, manual. ~у́чка m & f self-taught person. ~хо́дный self-propelled. ~чу́вствие general state; как ва́ше ~чу́вствие? how do you feel?

самова́р samovar.
самого́н home-made vodka.
самолёт aeroplane.
самоцве́т semi-precious stone.
са́мый pron (the) very, (the) right; (the) same; (the) most.
сан dignity, office.
санато́рий sanatorium.
санда́лия sandal.
са́ни (-е́й) pl sledge, sleigh.
санита́р medical orderly; stretcher-bearer. **санита́рия** sanitation. **санита́рка** nurse. **санита́рн|ый** medical; health; sanitary; ~ая маши́на ambulance; ~ый у́зел = сану́зел.
са́нки (-нок) pl sledge; toboggan.
санкциони́ровать impf & pf sanction. **са́нкция** sanction.
сано́вник dignitary.

санпу́нкт medical centre.
санскри́т Sanskrit.
санте́хник plumber.
сантиме́тр centimetre; tape-measure.
сану́зел (-зла́) sanitary arrangements; WC.
санча́сть (gen pl -е́й) medical unit.
сапёр sapper.
сапо́г(-а́; gen pl -о́г) boot. **сапо́жник** shoemaker; cobbler. **сапо́жный** shoe.
сапфи́р sapphire.
сара́й shed; barn.
саранча́ locust(s).
сарафа́н sarafan; pinafore dress.
сарде́лька small fat sausage.
сарди́на sardine.
сарка́зм sarcasm. **саркасти́ческий** sarcastic.
сатана́ m Satan. **сатани́нский** satanic.
сателли́т satellite.
сати́н sateen.
сати́ра satire. **сати́рик** satirist. **сатири́ческий** satirical.
Сау́довская Ара́вия Saudi Arabia.
сафья́н morocco. **сафья́новый** morocco.
са́хар sugar. **сахари́н** saccharine. **са́харистый** sugary. **са́харница** sugar-basin. **са́харн|ый** sugar; sugary; ~ый заво́д sugar-refinery; ~ый песо́к granulated sugar; ~ая пу́дра castor sugar; ~ая свёкла sugar-beet.
сачо́к (-чка́) net.
сба́вить (-влю) pf, **сбавля́ть** impf take off; reduce.
с|баланси́ровать pf.
сбе́гать[1] pf run; +за+instr run for. **сбега́ть**[2] impf, **сбежа́ть** (-егу́) pf run down (from); run away; disappear; ~ся come running.
сберега́тельная ка́сса savings bank. **сберега́ть** impf, **сбере́чь** (-егу́, -ежёшь; -ёг, -ла́) pf save; save up; preserve. **сбереже́ние** economy; saving; savings. **сберка́сса** savings bank.
сбива́ть impf, **с|бить** (собью́, -бьёшь) pf bring down, knock down; knock off; distract; wear down; knock together; churn; whip, whisk; ~ся be dislodged; slip; go wrong; be confused; ~ся с пути́ lose one's way; ~ся с ног be run off one's feet.
сби́вчивый confused; inconsistent.

сближа́ть *impf*, **сбли́зить** (-и́жу) *pf* bring (closer) together, draw together; **~ся** draw together; become good friends. **сближе́ние** rapprochement; closing in.

сбо́ку *adv* from one side; on one side.

сбор collection; duty; fee, toll; takings; gathering. **сбо́рище** crowd, mob. **сбо́рка** assembling, assembly; gather. **сбо́рник** collection. **сбо́рный** assembly; mixed, combined; prefabricated; detachable. **сбо́рочный** assembly. **сбо́рщик** collector; assembler.

сбра́сывать(ся *impf of* **сбро́сить(ся**

сбрива́ть *impf*, **сбрить** (сбре́ю) *pf* shave off.

сброд riff-raff.

сброс fault, break. **сбро́сить** (-о́шу) *pf* (*impf* **сбра́сывать**) throw down, drop; throw off; shed; discard.

сбру́я (*collect*) (riding) tack.

сбыва́ть *impf*, **сбыть** (сбу́ду; сбыл, -á, -о) *pf* sell, market; get rid of; **~ся** come true, be realized. **сбыт** (*no pl*) sale; market.

св. *abbr* (*of* **свято́й**) Saint.

сва́дебный wedding. **сва́дьба** (*gen pl* -де́б) wedding.

сва́ливать *impf*, **с**|**вали́ть** (-лю́, -лишь) *pf* throw down; overthrow; pile up; **~ся** fall (down), collapse. **сва́лка** dump; scuffle.

с|**валя́ть** *pf*.

сва́ривать *impf*, **с**|**вари́ть** (-рю́, -ришь) *pf* boil; cook; weld. **сва́рка** welding.

сварли́вый cantankerous.

сварно́й welded. **сва́рочный** welding. **сва́рщик** welder.

сва́стика swastika.

сва́тать *impf* (*pf* **по~**, **со~**) propose as a husband or wife; propose to; **~ся** к+*dat or* за+*acc* propose to.

сва́я pile.

све́дение piece of information; knowledge; *pl* information, intelligence; knowledge. **све́дущий** knowledgeable; versed.

сведу́ *etc.: see* **свести́**

свежезаморо́женный fresh-frozen; chilled. **све́жесть** freshness. **свеже́ть** (-е́ет) *impf* (*pf* **по~**) become cooler; freshen. **све́жий** (-еж, -á) fresh; new.

свезти́ (-зу́, -зёшь; свёз, -лá) *pf* (*impf* **свози́ть**) take; bring *or* take down *or* away.

свёкла beet, beetroot.

свёкор (-кра) father-in-law. **свекро́вь** mother-in-law.

свёл *etc.: see* **свести́**

сверга́ть *impf*, **све́ргнуть** (-ну; сверг) *pf* throw down, overthrow. **сверже́ние** overthrow.

све́рить *pf* (*impf* **сверя́ть**) collate.

сверка́ть *impf* sparkle, twinkle; glitter; gleam. **сверкну́ть** (-ну́, -нёшь) *pf* flash.

сверли́льный drill, drilling; boring. **сверли́ть** *impf* (*pf* **про~**) drill; bore (through); nag. **сверло́** drill. **сверля́щий** gnawing, piercing.

сверну́ть (-ну́, -нёшь) *pf* (*impf* **свёртывать, свора́чивать**) roll (up); turn; curtail, cut down; **~ шею**+*dat* wring the neck of; **~ся** roll up, curl up; curdle, coagulate; contract.

све́рстник contemporary.

свёрток (-тка) package, bundle. **свёртывание** rolling (up); curdling, coagulation; curtailment, cuts. **свёртывать(ся** *impf of* **сверну́ть(ся**

сверх *prep*+*gen* over, above, on top of; beyond; in addition to; **~ того́** moreover.

сверх- *in comb* super-, over-, hyper-. **сверхзвуково́й** supersonic. **~пла́новый** over and above the plan. **~при́быль** excess profit. **~проводни́к** (-á) superconductor. **~секре́тный** top secret. **~уро́чный** overtime. **~уро́чные** *sb pl* overtime. **~челове́к** superman. **~челове́ческий** superhuman. **~ъесте́ственный** supernatural.

све́рху *adv* from above; **~ до́низу** from top to bottom.

сверчо́к (-чка́) cricket.

сверше́ние achievement.

сверя́ть *impf of* **све́рить**

све́сить (-е́шу) *pf* (*impf* **све́шивать**) let down, lower; **~ся** hang over, lean over.

свести́ (-еду́, -еде́шь; -ёл, -á) *pf* (*impf* **своди́ть**) take; take down; take away; remove; bring together; reduce, bring; cramp.

свет[1] light; daybreak.

свет[2] world; society.

светать *impf impers* dawn. **светило** luminary. **светить** (-ечу, -етишь) *impf* (*pf* по~) shine; +*dat* light; light the way for; ~**ся** shine, gleam. **светлеть** (-еет) *impf* (*pf* по~, про~) brighten (up); grow lighter. **светлость** brightness; Grace. **светлый** light; bright; joyous. **светлячок** (-чка) glow-worm.

свето- *in comb* light, photo-. **светонепроницаемый** light-proof. ~**фильтр** light filter. ~**фор** traffic light(s).

световой light; luminous; ~ **день** daylight hours.

светопреставление end of the world.

светский fashionable; refined; secular.

светящийся luminous, fluorescent. **свеча** (*pl* -и, -ей) candle; (spark-) plug. **свечение** luminescence, fluorescence. **свечка** candle. **свечу** *etc.*: *see* **светить**

с|вешать *pf.* **свешивать(ся** *impf of* **свесить(ся. свивать** *impf of* **свить**

свидание meeting; appointment; до свидания! goodbye!

свидетель *m*, -**ница** witness. **свидетельство** evidence; testimony; certificate. **свидетельствовать** *impf* (*pf* за~, о~) give evidence, testify; be evidence (of); witness.

свинарник pigsty.

свинец (-нца) lead.

свинина pork. **свинка** mumps. **свиной** pig; pork. **свинство** despicable act; outrage; squalor.

свинцовый lead; leaden.

свинья (*pl* -и, -ей, -ям) pig, swine.

свирель (reed-)pipe.

свирепеть (-ею) *impf* (*pf* рас~) grow savage; become violent. **свирепствовать** *impf* rage; be rife. **свирепый** fierce, ferocious.

свисать, *impf* **свиснуть** (-ну; -ис) *pf* hang down, dangle; trail.

свист whistle; whistling. **свистать** (-ищу, -ищешь) *impf* whistle. **свистеть** (-ищу) *impf*, **свистнуть** (-ну) *pf* whistle; hiss. **свисток** (-тка) whistle.

свита suite; retinue.

свитер sweater.

свиток (-тка) roll, scroll. **с|вить**

(совью, совьёшь; -ил, -а́, -о) *pf* (*impf also* **свивать**) twist, wind; ~**ся** roll up.

свихнуться (-нусь, -нёшься) *impf* go mad; go astray.

свищ (-а́) flaw; (knot-)hole; fistula.

свищу *etc.*: *see* **свистать**, **свистеть**

свобода freedom. **свободно** *adv* freely; easily; fluently; loose(ly). **свободный** free; easy; vacant; spare; loose; flowing. **свободолюбивый** freedom-loving. **свободомыслие** free-thinking.

свод code; collection; arch, vault.

сводить (-ожу, -одишь) *impf of* **свести**

сводка summary; report. **сводный** composite; step-.

сводчатый arched, vaulted.

своеволие self-will, wilfulness. **своевольный** wilful.

своевременно *adv* in good time; opportunely. **своевременный** timely, opportune.

своенравие capriciousness. **своенравный** wilful, capricious.

своеобразие originality; peculiarity. **своеобразный** original; peculiar.

свожу *etc.*: *see* **сводить**, **свозить**.

свозить (-ожу, -озишь) *impf of* **свезти**

свой (своего) *m*, **своя** (своей) *f*, **своё** (своего) *neut*, **свои** (своих) *pl*, *pron* one's (own); my, his, her, its; our, your, their. **свойственный** peculiar, characteristic. **свойство** property, attribute, characteristic.

сволочь swine; riff-raff.

свора leash; pack.

сворачивать *impf of* **свернуть**, **своротить**. **с|воровать** *pf.*

своротить (-очу, -отишь) *pf* (*impf* **сворачивать**) dislodge, shift; turn; twist.

свояк brother-in-law (*husband of wife's sister*). **свояченица** sister-in-law (*wife's sister*).

свыкаться *impf*, **свыкнуться** (-нусь; -ыкся) *pf* get used.

свысока *adv* haughtily. **свыше** *adv* from above. **свыше** *prep*+*gen* over; beyond.

связанный constrained; combined; bound; coupled; **с|вязать** (-яжу, -яжешь) *pf*, **связывать** *impf* tie, bind; connect; **~ся** get in touch; get involved. **связи́ст, -ы́стка** signaller; worker in communication services. **свя́зка** sheaf, bundle; ligament. **свя́зный** connected, coherent. **связь** (*loc* -и́) connection; link, bond; liaison; communication(s).

святи́лище sanctuary. **свя́тки** (-ток) *pl* Christmas-tide. **свя́то** *adv* piously; religiously. **свят|о́й** (-ят, -а́, -о) holy; **~о́й, ~а́я** *sb* saint. **святы́ня** sacred object *or* place. **свяще́нник** priest. **свяще́нный** sacred.

сгиб bend. **сгиба́ть** *impf of* **согну́ть**
сгла́|дить (-а́жу) *pf*, **сгла́живать** *impf* smooth out; smooth over, soften.
сгла́зить (-а́жу) *pf* put the evil eye on.
сгнива́ть *impf*, **с|гни́ть** (-ию́, -иёшь; -и́л, -а́, -о) *pf* rot.
с|гнои́ть *pf*.
сгова́риваться *impf*, **сговори́ться** *pf* come to an arrangement; arrange. **сго́вор** agreement. **сгово́рчивый** compliant.
сгоня́ть *impf of* **согна́ть**
сгора́ние combustion; **дви́гатель вну́треннего сгора́ния** internal-combustion engine. **сгора́ть** *impf of* **сгоре́ть**
с|го́рбить(ся (-блю(сь) *pf*.
с|горе́ть (-рю́) *pf* (*impf also* **сгора́ть**) burn down; be burnt down; be used up; burn; burn o.s. out. **сгоряча́** *adv* in the heat of the moment.
с|гото́вить (-влю) *pf*.
сгреба́ть *impf*, **сгрести́** (-ебу́, -ебёшь; -ёб, -ла́) *pf* rake up, rake together.
сгружа́ть *impf*, **сгрузи́ть** (-ужу́, -у́зи́шь) *pf* unload.
с|группирова́ть(ся *pf*.
сгусти́ть (-ущу́) *pf*, **сгуща́ть** *impf* thicken; condense; **~ся** thicken; condense; clot. **сгу́сток** (-тка) clot. **сгуще́ние** thickening, condensation; clotting.
сдава́ть (сдаю́, сдаёшь) *impf of* **сдать**; **~ экза́мен** take an examination; **~ся** *impf of* **сда́ться**
сда́вить (-влю, -вишь) *pf*, **сда́вливать** *impf* squeeze.
сдать (-ам, -ашь, -аст, -ади́м; -ал, -а́, -о) *pf* (*impf* **сдава́ть**) hand over; pass; let, hire out; surrender, give up;

deal; **~ся** surrender, yield. **сда́ча** handing over; hiring out; surrender; change; deal.
сдвиг displacement; fault; change, improvement. **сдвига́ть** *impf*, **сдви́нуть** (-ну) *pf* shift, move; move together; **~ся** move, budge; come together.
с|де́лать(ся *pf*. **сде́лка** transaction; deal, bargain. **сде́льн|ый** piece-work; **~ая рабо́та** piece-work. **сде́льщина** piece-work.
сде́ргивать *impf of* **сдёрнуть**
сде́ржанный restrained, reserved.
сдержа́ть (-жу́, -жишь) *pf*, **сде́рживать** *impf* hold back; restrain; keep.
сдёрнуть (-ну) *pf* (*impf* **сде́ргивать**) pull off.
сдеру́ *etc.*: *see* **содра́ть. сдира́ть** *impf of* **содра́ть**
сдо́ба shortening; fancy bread, bun(s). **сдо́бный** (-бен, -бна́, -о) rich, short.
с|до́хнуть (-нет; сдох) *pf* die; kick the bucket.
сдружи́ться (-жу́сь) *pf* become friends.
сдува́ть *impf*, **сду́нуть** (-ну) *pf*, **сдуть** (-у́ю) *pf* blow away *or* off.
сеа́нс performance; showing; sitting.
себесто́имость prime cost; cost (price).
себя́ (*dat & prep* себе́, *instr* собо́й *or* собо́ю) *refl pron* oneself; myself, yourself, himself, *etc.*; **ничего́ себе́** not bad; **собо́й** -looking, in appearance.
себялю́бие selfishness.
сев sowing.
се́вер north. **се́верный** north, northern; northerly. **се́веро-восто́к** north-east **се́веро-восто́чный** north-east(ern). **се́веро-за́пад** north-west. **се́веро-за́падный** north-west(ern). **северя́|нин** (*pl* -я́не, -я́н) northerner.
севооборо́т crop rotation.
сего́ *see* **сей. сего́дня** *adv* today. **сего́дняшний** of today, today's.
седе́ть (-е́ю) *impf* (*pf* по~) turn grey. **седина́** (*pl* -ы) grey hair(s).
седла́ть *impf* (*pf* о~) saddle. **седло́** (*pl* сёдла, -дел) saddle.
седоборо́дый grey-bearded. **седоволо́сый** grey-haired. **седо́й** (сед, -а́, -о) grey(-haired).
седо́к (-а́) passenger; rider.

седьмой seventh.

сезон season. **сезонный** seasonal.

сей (сего) *m*, **сия** (сей) *f*, **сиё** (сего) *neut*, **сий** (сих) *pl*, *pron* this; these; **сию минуту** at once, instantly.

сейсмический seismic.

сейф safe.

сейчас *adv* (just) now; soon; immediately.

сёк *etc.*: *see* **сечь**

секрет secret.

секретариат secretariat.

секретарский secretarial. **секретарша**, **секретарь** (-я́) *m* secretary. **секретный** secret.

секс sex. **сексуальный** sexual; sexy.

секстет sextet.

секта sect. **сектант** sectarian.

сектор sector.

секу *etc.*: *see* **сечь**

секуляризация secularization.

секунда second. **секундант** second. **секундный** second. **секундомер** stop-watch.

секционный sectional. **секция** section.

селёдка herring.

селезёнка spleen.

селезень (-зня) *m* drake.

селекция breeding.

селение settlement, village.

селитра saltpetre, nitre.

селить(ся *impf* (*pf* по~) settle. **село** (*pl* сёла) village.

сельдерей celery.

сельдь (*pl* -и, -ей) herring.

сельский rural; village; ~ое хозяйство agriculture. **сельскохозяйственный** agricultural.

сельсовет village soviet.

семантика semantics. **семантический** semantic.

семафор semaphore; signal.

сёмга (smoked) salmon.

семейный family; domestic. **семейство** family.

семени *etc.*: *see* **семя**

семенить *impf* mince.

семенить *impf* seed. **семенник** (-á) testicle; seed-vessel. **семенной** seed; seminal.

семёрка seven; figure 7; No. 7. **семеро** (-ых) seven.

семестр term, semester.

семечко (*pl* -и) seed; *pl* sunflower seeds.

семидесятилетие seventy years; seventieth anniversary, birthday. **семидесятый** seventieth; ~ые годы the seventies. **семилётка** seven-year school. **семилётний** seven-year; seven-year-old.

семинар seminar. **семинария** seminary.

семисотый seven-hundredth. **семнадцатый** seventeenth. **семнадцать** seventeen. **семь** (-ми́, -мью) seven. **семьдесят** (-ми́десяти, -мью́десятью) seventy. **семьсот** (-мисо́т, *instr* -мьюста́ми) seven hundred. **семью** *adv* seven times.

семья (*pl* -и, -ей, -ям) family. **семьянин** family man.

семя (-мени; *pl* -мена́, -мя́н, -мена́м) seed; semen, sperm.

сенат senate. **сенатор** senator.

сени (-ей) *pl* (entrance-)hall.

сено hay. **сеновал** hayloft. **сенокос** haymaking; hayfield. **сенокосилка** mowing-machine.

сенсационный sensational. **сенсация** sensation.

сентенция maxim.

сентиментальный sentimental.

сентябрь (-я́) *m* September. **сентябрьский** September.

сепсис sepsis.

сера sulphur; ear-wax.

серб, ~ка Serb. **Сербия** Serbia. **сербский** Serb(ian). **сербскохорватский** Serbo-Croat(ian).

сервант sideboard.

сервиз service, set. **сервировать** *impf* & *pf* serve; lay (a table). **сервировка** laying; table lay-out.

сердечник core. **сердечность** cordiality; warmth. **сердечный** heart; cardiac; cordial; warm(-hearted). **сердитый** angry. **сердить** (-ржу́, -рдишь) *impf* (*pf* рас~) anger; ~ся be angry. **сердобольный** tender-hearted. **сердце** (*pl* -а́, -де́ц) heart; в сердцах in anger; от всего сердца from the bottom of one's heart. **сердцебиение** palpitation. **сердцевидный** heart-shaped. **сердцевина** core, pith, heart.

серебрёный silver-plated. **серебристый** silvery. **серебрить** *impf* (*pf* по~) silver, silver-plate; ~ся become silvery. **серебро́** silver. **сере́бряный** silver.

середи́на middle.

серёжка earring; catkin.

серена́да serenade.

се́ренький grey; dull.

сержа́нт sergeant.

сери́йный serial; mass. **се́рия** series; part.

се́рный sulphur; sulphuric.

серогла́зый grey-eyed.

се́рость uncouthness; ignorance.

серп (-á) sickle; ~ **луны́** crescent moon.

серпанти́н streamer.

сертифика́т certificate.

се́рый (сер, -á, -о) grey; dull; uneducated.

серьга́ (pl -и, -рёг) earring.

серьёзность seriousness. **серьёзный** serious.

се́ссия session.

сестра́ (pl сёстры, сестёр, сёстрам) sister.

сесть (ся́ду) pf (impf **сади́ться**) sit down; land; set; shrink; +**на**+acc board, get on.

се́тка net, netting; (luggage-)rack; string bag; grid.

се́товать impf (pf **по~**) complain.

сетча́тка retina. **сеть** (loc -и́; pl -и, -е́й) net; network.

сече́ние section. **сечь** (секу́, сечёшь; сёк) impf (pf **вы́~**) cut to pieces; flog; **~ся** split.

се́ялка seed drill. **се́ять** (се́ю) impf (pf **по~**) sow.

сжа́литься pf take pity (**над**+instr) on.

сжа́тие pressure; grasp, grip; compression. **сжа́тый** compressed; compact; concise.

с|жать[1] (сожну́, -нёшь) pf.

сжать[2] (сожму́, -мёшь) pf (impf **сжима́ть**) squeeze; compress; grip; clench; **~ся** tighten, clench; shrink, contract.

с|жечь (сожгу́, сожжёшь; сжёг, сожгла́) pf (impf **сжига́ть**) burn (down); cremate.

сжива́ться impf of **сжи́ться**

сжига́ть impf of **сжечь**

сжима́ть(ся impf of **сжать**[2](ся

сжи́ться (-иву́сь, -ивёшься; -и́лся, -а́сь) pf (impf **сжива́ться**) с+instr

get used to.

с|жу́льничать pf.

сза́ди adv from behind; behind. **сза́ди** prep+gen behind.

сзыва́ть impf of **созва́ть**

сиби́рский Siberian. **Сиби́рь** Siberia. **сибиря́к** (-á), **сибиря́чка** Siberian.

сига́ра cigar. **сигаре́та** cigarette.

сигна́л signal. **сигнализа́ция** signalling. **сигнализи́ровать** impf & pf (pf also **про~**) signal. **сигна́льный** signal. **сигна́льщик** signal-man.

сиде́лка sick-nurse. **сиде́ние** sitting. **сиде́нье** seat. **сиде́ть** (-ижу́) impf sit; be; fit. **сидя́чий** sitting, sedentary.

сие́ etc.: see **сей**

си́зый (сиз, -á, -о) (blue-)grey.

сий see **сей**

си́ла strength; force; power; **в си́лу** +gen on the strength of, because of; **не по ~ам** beyond one's powers; **си́лой** by force. **сила́ч** (-á) strong man. **си́литься** impf try, make efforts. **силово́й** power; of force.

сило́к (-лка́) noose, snare.

си́лос silo; silage.

силуэ́т silhouette.

си́льно adv strongly, violently; very much, greatly. **си́льный** (-лен or -лён, -льна́, -о) strong; powerful; intense, hard.

симбио́з symbiosis.

си́мвол symbol. **символизи́ровать** impf symbolize. **символи́зм** symbolism. **символи́ческий** symbolic.

симме́трия symmetry.

симпатизи́ровать impf +dat like, sympathize with. **симпати́чный** likeable, nice. **симпа́тия** liking; sympathy.

симпо́зиум symposium.

симпто́м symptom.

симули́ровать impf & pf simulate, feign. **симуля́нт** malingerer, sham. **симуля́ция** simulation, pretence.

симфо́ния symphony.

синаго́га synagogue.

синева́ blue. **синева́тый** bluish. **синегла́зый** blue-eyed. **сине́ть** (-е́ю) impf (pf **по~**) turn blue; show blue. **си́ний** (синь, -ня, -не) (dark) blue.

сини́ца titmouse.

синóд synod. синóним synonym. сúнтаксис syntax.

сúнтез synthesis. синтезúровать *impf & pf* synthesize. синтетúческий synthetic.

сúнус sine; sinus.

синхронизúровать *impf & pf* synchronize.

синь[1] blue. синь[2] *see* сúний. сúнька blueing; blue-print. синя́к (-á) bruise.

сионúзм Zionism.

сúплый hoarse, husky. сúпнуть (-ну; сип) *impf* (*pf* о~) become hoarse, husky.

сирéна siren; hooter.

сирéневый lilac(-coloured). сирéнь lilac.

Сúрия Syria.

сирóп syrup.

сиротá (*pl* -ы) *m & f* orphan. сиротлúвый lonely. сирóтский orphan's, orphans'.

систéма system. систематизúровать *impf & pf* systematize. систематúческий, систематúчный systematic.

сúтец (-тца) (printed) cotton; chintz. сúто sieve.

ситуáция situation.

сúтцевый print, chintz.

сúфилис syphilis.

сифóн siphon.

сия́ *see* сей

сия́ние radiance. сия́ть *impf* shine, beam.

сказ tale. сказáние story, legend. сказáть (-ажу́, -áжешь) *pf* (*impf* говорúть) say; speak; tell. сказáться (-ажу́сь, -áжешься) *pf*, скáзываться *impf* tell (on); declare o.s. сказúтель *m* story-teller. скáзка (fairy-)tale; fib. скáзочный (fairy-)tale; fantastic. сказу́емое *sb* predicate.

скакáлка skipping-rope. скакáть (-ачу́, -áчешь) *impf* (*pf* по~) skip, jump; gallop. скаковóй race, racing.

скалá (*pl* -ы) rock face; cliff. скалúстый rocky.

скáлить *impf* (*pf* о~); ~ зу́бы bare one's teeth; grin; ~ся bare one's teeth.

скáлка rolling-pin.

скалолáз rock-climber.

скáлывать *impf of* сколóть

скальп scalp.

скáльпель *m* scalpel.

скамéечка footstool; small bench. скамéйка bench. скамья́ (*pl* скáмьи, -éй) bench; ~ подсудúмых dock.

скандáл scandal; brawl, rowdy scene. скандалúст trouble-maker. скандáлиться *impf* (*pf* о~) disgrace o.s. скандáльный scandalous.

скандинáвский Scandinavian.

скандúровать *impf & pf* declaim.

скáпливать(ся *impf of* скопúть(ся

скарб goods and chattels.

скáредный stingy.

скарлатúна scarlet fever.

скат slope; pitch.

с|катáть *pf* (*impf* скáтывать) roll (up).

скáтерть (*pl* -и, -éй) table-cloth.

скатúть (-ачу́, -áтишь) *pf*, скáтывать[1] *impf* roll down; slip, slide. скáтывать[2] *impf of* скатáть

скафáндр diving-suit; space-suit.

скáчка gallop, galloping. скáчки (-чек) *pl* horse-race; races. скачóк (-чкá) jump, leap.

скáшивать *impf of* скосúть

сквáжина slit, chink; well.

сквер public garden.

сквéрно badly; bad. сквернослóвить (-влю) *impf* use foul language. сквéрный foul; bad.

сквозúть *impf* be transparent; show through; сквозúт *impers* there is a draught. сквознóй through; transparent. сквозня́к (-á) draught. сквозь *prep+gen* through.

скворéц (-рцá) starling.

скелéт skeleton.

скéптик sceptic. скептицúзм scepticism. скептúческий sceptical.

скетч sketch.

скúдка reduction. скúдывать *impf*, скúнуть (-ну) *pf* throw off *or* down; knock off.

скúпетр sceptre.

скипидáр turpentine.

скирд (-á; *pl* -ы́), скирдá (*pl* -ы, -áм) stack, rick.

скисáть *impf*, скúснуть (-ну; скис) *pf* go sour.

скитáлец (-льца) wanderer. скитáться *impf* wander.

скиф Scythian.

склад[1] depot; store.

склад[2] mould; turn; logical connection; ~ ума́ mentality.

скла́дка fold; pleat; crease; wrinkle.

скла́дно adv smoothly.

складно́й folding, collapsible.

скла́дный (-ден, -дна, -о) well-knit, well-built; smooth, coherent.

скла́дчина: в скла́дчину by clubbing together. скла́дывать(ся impf of сложи́ть(ся

скле́ивать impf, с|кле́ить pf stick together; ~ся stick together.

склеп (burial) vault, crypt.

склепа́ть pf, склёпывать impf rivet. склёпка riveting.

склеро́з sclerosis.

скло́ка squabble.

склон slope; на ~е лет in one's declining years. склоне́ние inclination; declension. склони́ть (-ню́, -нишь) pf, склоня́ть impf incline; bow; win over; decline; ~ся bend, bow; yield; be declined. скло́нность inclination; tendency. скло́нный (-нен, -нна́, -нно) inclined, disposed. склоня́емый declinable.

скля́нка phial; bottle; (naut) bell.

скоба́ (pl -ы, -а́м) cramp, clamp; staple.

ско́бка dim of скоба́; bracket; pl parenthesis, parentheses.

скобли́ть (-облю́, -о́бли́шь) impf scrape, plane.

ско́ванность constraint. ско́ванный constrained; bound. скова́ть (скую́, скуёшь) pf (impf ско́вывать) forge; chain; fetter; pin down, hold, contain.

сковорода́ (pl ско́вороды, -ро́д, -а́м), сковоро́дка frying-pan.

ско́вывать impf of скова́ть

скола́чивать impf, сколоти́ть (-очу́, -о́тишь) pf knock together.

сколо́ть (-лю́, -лешь) pf (impf ска́лывать) chop off; pin together.

скольже́ние sliding, slipping; glide. скользи́ть (-льжу́) impf, скользну́ть (-ну́, -нёшь) pf slide; slip; glide. ско́льзкий (-зок, -зка́, -о) slippery. скользя́щий sliding.

ско́лько adv how much; how many; as far as.

с|кома́ндовать pf. с|комбини́ро-

вать pf. с|ко́мкать pf. с|комплектова́ть pf. с|компромети́ровать pf. с|конструи́ровать pf.

сконфу́женный embarrassed, confused, disconcerted. с|конфу́зить(ся (-у́жу(сь) pf.

с|концентри́ровать pf.

сконча́ться pf pass away, die.

с|копи́ровать pf.

скопи́ть (-плю́, -пишь) pf (impf ска́пливать) save (up); amass; ~ся accumulate. скопле́ние accumulation; crowd.

ско́пом adv in a crowd, en masse.

скорбе́ть (-блю́) impf grieve. ско́рбный sorrowful. скорбь (pl -и, -е́й) sorrow.

скоре́е, скоре́й comp of ско́ро, ско́рый; adv rather, sooner; как мо́жно ~ as soon as possible; ~ всего́ most likely.

скорлупа́ (pl -ы) shell.

скорня́к (-а́) furrier.

ско́ро adv quickly; soon.

скоро- in comb quick-, fast-. скорова́рка pressure-cooker. ~гово́рка patter; tongue-twister. ~ро́пись cursive; shorthand. ~по́ртящийся perishable. ~пости́жный sudden. ~спе́лый early; fast-ripening; premature; hasty. ~сшива́тель m binder, file. ~те́чный transient, short-lived.

скоростно́й high-speed. ско́рость (gen pl -е́й) speed; gear.

скорпио́н scorpion; Scorpio.

с|корректи́ровать pf. с|ко́рчить(ся (-чу(сь) pf.

ско́рый (скор, -а́, -о) quick, fast; near; forthcoming; ~ая по́мощь first-aid; ambulance.

с|коси́ть[1] (-ошу́, -о́сишь) pf (impf also ска́шивать) mow.

с|коси́ть[2] (-ошу́) pf (impf also ска́шивать) squint; cut on the cross.

скот (-а́), скоти́на cattle; livestock; beast. ско́тный cattle.

ското- in comb cattle. скотобо́йня (gen pl -оен) slaughter-house. ~во́д cattle-breeder. ~во́дство cattle-raising.

ско́тский cattle; brutish. ско́тство brutish condition; brutality.

скра́сить (-а́шу) pf, скра́шивать impf smooth over; relieve.

скребо́к (-бка́) scraper. **скребу́** etc.: see **скрести́**

скре́жет grating; gnashing. **скре-жета́ть** (-ещу́, -е́щешь) impf grate; +instr gnash.

скре́па clamp, brace; counter-signature.

скрепи́ть (-плю́) pf, **скрепля́ть** impf fasten (together), make fast; clamp; countersign, ratify; **скрепя́ се́рдце** reluctantly. **скре́пка** paperclip. **скрепле́ние** fastening; clamping; tie, clamp.

скрести́ (-ебу́, -ебёшь; -ёб, -ла́) impf scrape; scratch; ~**сь** scratch.

скрести́ть (-ещу́) pf, **скре́щивать** impf cross; interbreed. **скреще́ние** crossing. **скре́щивание** crossing; interbreeding.

с|криви́ть(ся (-влю́(сь) pf.

скрип squeak, creak. **скрипа́ч** (-а́) violinist. **скрипе́ть** (-плю́) impf, **скри́пнуть** (-ну) pf squeak, creak; scratch. **скрипи́чный** violin; ~ **ключ** treble clef. **скри́пка** violin. **скри-пу́чий** squeaky, creaking.

с|кро́ить(ся pf.

скро́мничать impf (pf по~) be (too) modest. **скро́мность** modesty. **скро́мный** (-мен, -мна́, -о) modest.

скро́ю etc.: see **скрыть**. **скрою́** etc.: see **скрои́ть**

скрупулёзный scrupulous.

с|крути́ть (-учу́, -у́тишь) pf, **скру́чивать** impf twist; roll; tie up.

скрыва́ть impf, **скрыть** (-о́ю) pf hide, conceal; ~**ся** hide, go into hiding, be hidden; steal away; disappear. **скры́тничать** impf be secretive. **скры́тный** secretive. **скры́тый** secret, hidden; latent.

скря́га m & f miser.

ску́дный (-ден, -дна́, -о) scanty; meagre. **ску́дость** scarcity, paucity.

ску́ка boredom.

скула́ (pl -ы) cheek-bone. **скула́стый** with high cheek-bones.

скули́ть impf whine, whimper.

ску́льптор sculptor. **скульпту́ра** sculpture.

ску́мбрия mackerel.

скунс skunk.

скупа́ть impf of **скупи́ть**

скупе́ц (-пца́) miser.

скупи́ть (-плю́, -пишь) pf (impf **ску-пать**) buy (up).

скупи́ться (-плю́сь) impf (pf по~) be stingy; skimp; be sparing (of +на+acc).

ску́пка buying (up).

ску́по adv sparingly. **скупо́й** (-п, -а́, -о) stingy, meagre. **ску́пость** stinginess.

ску́пщик buyer(-up).

ску́тер (pl -а́) outboard speed-boat.

скуча́ть impf be bored; +по~+dat or prep miss, yearn for.

ску́ченность density, overcrowding. **ску́ченный** dense, overcrowded. **ску́чить** (-чу) pf crowd (together); ~**ся** cluster; crowd together.

ску́чный (-чен, -чна́, -о) boring; **мне ску́чно** I'm bored.

с|ку́шать pf. **скую́** etc.: see **скова́ть**

слабе́ть (-е́ю) impf (pf о~) weaken, grow weak. **слаби́тельн|ый** laxative; ~**ое** sb laxative. **сла́бить** impf impers: **его́ сла́бит** he has diarrhoea.

слабо- in comb weak, feeble, slight. **слабово́лие** weakness of will. ~**во́льный** weak-willed. ~**не́рв-ный** nervy, nervous. ~**разви́тый** under-developed. ~**у́мие** feeble-mindedness. ~**у́мный** feeble-minded. **сла́бость** weakness. **сла́бый** (-б, -а́, -о) weak.

сла́ва glory; fame; **на сла́ву** wonderfully well. **сла́вить** (-влю) impf celebrate, sing the praises of; ~**ся** (+instr) be famous (for). **сла́вный** glorious, renowned; nice.

славяни́н (pl -я́не, -я́н), **славя́нка** Slav. **славянофи́л** Slavophil(e). **славя́нский** Slav, Slavonic.

слага́емое sb component, term, member. **слага́ть** impf of **сложи́ть**

сла́дить (-а́жу) pf с+instr cope with; handle; manage.

сла́дк|ий (-док, -дка́, -о) sweet; ~**ое** sb sweet course. **сладостра́стник** voluptuary. **сладостра́стный** voluptuous. **сла́дость** joy; sweetness; pl sweets.

сла́женность harmony. **сла́жен-ный** co-ordinated, harmonious.

сла́мывать impf of **сломи́ть**

сла́нец (-нца) shale, slate.

сласть *m & f* person with a sweet tooth. **сласть** (pl -и, -е́й) delight; pl sweets, sweet things.

слать (шлю, шлёшь) *impf* send.

слаща́вый sugary, sickly-sweet. **сла́-ще** *comp of* **сла́дкий**

сле́ва *adv* from *or* on the left; ~ **напра́во** from left to right.

слёг *etc.: see* **слечь**

слегка́ *adv* slightly; lightly.

след (следа́, *dat* -у, *loc* -ý; *pl* -ы́) track; footprint; trace. **следи́ть**[1] (-ежу́) *impf* +**за**+*instr* watch; follow; keep up with; look after; keep an eye on. **следи́ть**[2] (-ежу́) *impf* (*pf* **на**~) leave footprints. **сле́дование** movement. **сле́дователь** *m* investigator. **сле́довательно** *adv* consequently. **сле́довать** *impf* (*pf* **по**~) I. +*dat or* **за**+*instr* follow; go, be bound; II. *impers* (+*dat*) ought, be owing, be owed; **вам сле́дует** +*inf* you ought to; **как сле́дует** properly; as it should be; **ско́лько с меня́ сле́дует?** how much do I owe (you)? **сле́дом** *adv* (**за**+*instr*) immediately after, close behind. **сле́дственный** investigation, inquiry. **сле́дствие**[1] consequence. **сле́дствие**[2] investigation. **сле́дующий** following, next. **слёжка** shadowing.

слеза́ (*pl* -ёзы, -а́м) tear.

слеза́ть *impf of* **слезть**

слези́ться (-и́тся) *impf* water. **слезли́вый** tearful. **слёзный** tear; tearful. **слезоточи́вый** watering; ~ **газ** tear-gas.

слезть (-зу; слез) *pf* (*impf* **слеза́ть**) climb *or* get down; dismount; get off; come off.

слепе́нь (-пня́) *m* horse-fly.

слепе́ц (-пца́) blind man. **слепи́ть**[1] *impf* blind; dazzle.

с|лепи́ть[2] (-плю́, -пишь) *pf* stick together.

слепну́ть (-ну; слеп) *impf* (*pf* **о**~) go blind. **сле́по** *adv* blindly. **слеп|о́й** (-п, -а́, -о) blind; ~**ые** *sb pl* the blind.

слепо́к (-пка) cast.

слепота́ blindness.

сле́сарь (*pl* -я́ *or* -и) *m* metalworker; locksmith.

слёт gathering; rally. **слета́ть** *impf*, **слете́ть** (-ечу́) *pf* fly down *or* away; fall down *or* off; ~**ся** fly together; congregate.

слечь (сля́гу, -я́жешь; слёг, -ла́) *pf*

take to one's bed.

сли́ва plum; plum-tree.

слива́ть(ся *impf of* **сли́ть(ся. сли́в-ки** (-вок) *pl* cream. **сли́вочн|ый** cream; creamy; ~**ое ма́сло** butter; ~**ое моро́женое** dairy ice-cream.

сли́зистый slimy. **слизня́к** (-á) slug. **слизь** mucus; slime.

с|линя́ть *pf.*

слипа́ться *impf*, **сли́пнуться** (-нет-ся; -и́пся) *pf* stick together.

сли́тно together, as one word. **сли́-ток** (-тка) ingot, bar. **с|лить** (солью́, -ьёшь; -ил, -á, -о) *pf* (*impf also* **слива́ть**) pour, pour out *or* off; fuse, amalgamate; ~**ся** flow together; blend; merge.

слича́ть *impf*, **сличи́ть** (-чу́) *pf* collate; check. **сличе́ние** collation, checking.

сли́шком *adv* too; too much.

слия́ние confluence; merging; merger.

слова́к, -а́чка Slovak. **слова́цкий** Slovak.

слова́рный lexical; dictionary. **слова́рь** (-я́) *m* dictionary; vocabulary. **слове́сность** literature; philology. **слове́сный** verbal, oral. **сло́вно** *conj* as if; like, as. **сло́во** (*pl* -á) word; **одни́м ~м** in a word. **сло́вом** *adv* in a word. **словообразова́ние** word-formation. **словоохо́тливый** talkative. **словосочета́ние** word combination, phrase. **словоупотребле́ние** usage.

слог[1] style.

слог[2] (*pl* -и, -о́в) syllable.

слоёный flaky.

сложе́ние composition; addition; build, constitution. **сложи́ть** (-жу́, -жишь) *pf* (*impf* **класть, скла́дывать, слага́ть**) put *or* lay (together); pile, stack; add, add up; fold (up); compose; take off, put down; lay down; ~**ся** turn out; take shape; arise; club together. **сло́жность** complication; complexity. **сло́жный** (-жен, -жна́, -о) complicated; complex; compound.

сло́истый stratified; flaky. **слой** (*pl* -и́, -ёв) layer; stratum.

слом demolition, pulling down. **с|лома́ть(ся** *pf.* **сломи́ть** (-млю́, -мишь) *pf* (*impf* **сла́мывать**) break (off); overcome; **сломя́ го́лову** at breakneck speed; ~ся break.

слон (-á) elephant; bishop. **слони́ха** she-elephant. **слоно́в|ый** elephant; ~ая кость ivory.

слоня́ться *impf* loiter, mooch (about).

слуга́ (*pl* -и) *m* (man)servant. **служа́нка** servant, maid. **служа́щий** *sb* employee. **слу́жба** service; work. **служе́бный** office; official; auxiliary; secondary. **служе́ние** service, serving. **служи́ть** (-жу́, -жишь) *impf* (*pf* по~) serve; work.

с|лука́вить (-влю) *pf*.

слух hearing; ear; rumour; по ~у by ear. **слухов|о́й** acoustic, auditory, aural; ~о́й аппара́т hearing aid; ~о́е окно́ dormer (window).

слу́чай incident, event; case; opportunity; chance; ни в ко́ем слу́чае in no circumstances. **случа́йно** *adv* by chance, accidentally; by any chance. **случа́йность** chance. **случа́йный** accidental; chance; incidental. **случа́ться** *impf*, **случи́ться** *pf* happen.

слу́шание listening; hearing. **слу́шатель** *m* listener; student; *pl* audience. **слу́шать** *impf* (*pf* по~, про~) listen (to); hear; attend lectures on; (я) слу́шаю! hello!; very well; ~ся +*gen* obey, listen to.

слыть (-ыву́, -ывёшь; -ыл, -á, -о) *impf* (*pf* про~) have the reputation (+*instr or* за+*acc* for).

слыха́ть *impf*, **слы́шать** (-шу) *impf* (*pf* у~) hear; sense. **слы́шаться** (-шится) *impf* (*pf* по~) be heard. **слы́шимость** audibility. **слы́шимый** audible. **слы́шный** audible.

слюда́ mica.

слюна́ (*pl* -и, -е́й) saliva; spit; *pl* spittle. **слюня́вый** dribbling.

сля́гу *etc*.: *see* слечь

сля́коть slush.

см. *abbr* (*of* смотри́) see, vide.

сма́зать (-а́жу) *pf*, **сма́зывать** *impf* lubricate; grease; slur over. **сма́зка** lubrication; greasing; grease. **сма́зочный** lubricating.

смак relish. **смакова́ть** *impf* relish; savour.

с|маневри́ровать *pf*.

сма́нивать *impf*, **смани́ть** (-ню́, -нишь) *pf* entice.

с|мастери́ть *pf*. **сма́тывать** *impf of*

смота́ть

сма́хивать *impf*, **смахну́ть** (-ну́, -нёшь) *pf* brush away *or* off.

сма́чивать *impf of* **смочи́ть**

сме́жный adjacent.

смека́лка native wit.

смёл *etc*.: *see* смести́

смеле́ть (-е́ю) *impf* (*pf* о~) grow bolder. **сме́лость** boldness, courage. **сме́лый** bold, courageous. **смельча́к** (-á) daredevil.

смелю́ *etc*.: *see* смоло́ть

сме́на changing; change; replacement(s); relief; shift. **смени́ть** (-ню́, -нишь) *pf*, **сменя́ть**[1] *impf* change; replace; relieve; ~ся hand over; be relieved; take turns; +*instr* give place to. **сме́нный** shift; changeable. **сме́нщик** relief; *pl* new shift. **сменя́ть**[2] *pf* exchange.

с|ме́рить *pf*.

смерка́ться *impf*, **сме́ркнуться** (-нется) *pf* get dark.

смерте́льный mortal, fatal, death; extreme. **сме́ртность** mortality. **сме́ртный** mortal; death; deadly, extreme. **смерть** (*gen pl* -е́й) death.

смерч whirlwind; waterspout; sandstorm.

смеси́тельный mixing. **с|меси́ть** (-ешу́, -е́сишь) *pf*.

смести́ (-ету́, -етёшь; -ёл, -á) *pf* (*impf* смета́ть) sweep off, away.

смести́ть (-ещу́) *pf* (*impf* смеща́ть) displace; remove.

смесь mixture; medley.

сме́та estimate.

смета́на sour cream.

с|мета́ть[1] *pf* (*impf also* смётывать) tack (together).

смета́ть[2] *impf of* смести́

сме́тливый quick, sharp.

смету́ *etc*.: *see* смести́. **смётывать** *impf of* смета́ть

сметь (-е́ю) *impf* (*pf* по~) dare.

смех laughter; laugh. **смехотво́рный** laughable.

сме́шанный mixed; combined. **с|меша́ть** *pf*, **сме́шивать** *impf* mix, blend; confuse; ~ся mix, (inter)blend; get mixed up. **смеше́ние** mixture; mixing up.

смеши́ть (-шу́) *impf* (*pf* на~, рас~) make laugh. **смешли́вый** given to laughing. **смешно́й** funny; ridiculous.

смешу́ *etc.*: see **смеси́ть, смеши́ть**

смеща́ть(ся *impf of* **смести́ть(ся. смеще́ние** displacement, removal. **смещу́** *etc.*: see **смести́ть**

смея́ться (-ею́сь, -еёшься) *impf* laugh (at +**над**+*instr*).

смире́ние humility, meekness. **смире́нный** humble, meek. **смири́тельный: ~ая руба́шка** straitjacket. **смири́ть** *pf*, **смиря́ть** *impf* restrain, subdue; **~ся** submit; resign o.s. **сми́рно** *adv* quietly; **~!** attention! **сми́рный** quiet; submissive.

смогу́ *etc.*: see **смочь**

смола́ (*pl* -ы) resin; pitch, tar; rosin. **смоли́стый** resinous.

смолка́ть *impf*, **смо́лкнуть** (-ну; -олк) *pf* fall silent.

смо́лоду *adv* from one's youth.

с|молоти́ть (-очу́, -о́тишь) *pf*. **с|моло́ть** (смелю́, сме́лешь) *pf*.

смоляно́й pitch, tar, resin.

с|монти́ровать *pf*.

сморка́ть *impf* (*pf* **вы́~**) blow; **~ся** blow one's nose.

сморо́дина (*no pl*; *usu collect*) currant; currants; currant-bush.

смо́рщенный wrinkled. **с|мо́рщить(ся** (-щу(сь) *pf*.

смота́ть *pf* (*impf* **сма́тывать**) wind, reel.

смотр (*loc* -у́; *pl* -о́тры) review, inspection. **смотре́ть** (-рю́, -ришь) *impf* (*pf* **по~**) look (at **на**+*acc*); see; watch; look through; examine; +**за**+*instr* look after; +**в**+*acc*, **на**+*acc* look on to; +*instr* look (like); **смотри́(те)!** take care!; **смотря́** it depends; **смотря́ по**+*dat* depending on; **~ся** look at o.s. **смотрово́й** observation, inspection.

смочи́ть (-чу́, -чишь) *pf* (*impf* **сма́чивать**) moisten.

с|мочь (-огу́, -о́жешь; смог, -ла́) *pf*.

с|моше́нничать *pf*. **смо́ю** *etc.*: see **смыть**

смрад stench. **сма́дный** stinking.

сму́глый (-гл, -а́, -о) dark-complexioned, swarthy.

смути́ть (-ущу́) *pf*, **смуща́ть** *impf* embarrass, confuse; **~ся** be embarrassed, be confused. **сму́тный** vague; dim; troubled. **смуще́ние** embarrassment, confusion. **смущённый** (-ён, -а́) embarrassed, confused.

смыва́ть *impf of* **смыть**

смыка́ть(ся *impf of* **сомкну́ть(ся**

смысл sense; meaning. **смы́слить** *impf* understand. **смыслово́й** semantic.

смыть (смо́ю) *pf* (*impf* **смыва́ть**) wash off, away.

смычо́к (-чка́) bow.

смышлёный clever.

смягча́ть *impf*, **смягчи́ть** (-чу́) *pf* soften; alleviate; **~ся** soften; relent; grow mild.

смяте́ние confusion; commotion.

с|мять(ся (сомну́(сь, -нёшь(ся) *pf*.

снабди́ть (-бжу́) *pf*, **снабжа́ть** *impf* +*instr* supply with. **снабже́ние** supply, supplying.

сна́йпер sniper.

снару́жи *adv* on *or* from (the) outside.

снаря́д projectile, missile; shell; contrivance; tackle, gear. **снаряди́ть** (-яжу́) *pf*, **снаряжа́ть** *impf* equip, fit out. **снаряже́ние** equipment, outfit.

снасть (*gen pl* -е́й) tackle; *pl* rigging.

снача́ла *adv* at first; all over again.

сна́шивать *impf of* **сноси́ть**

СНГ *abbr* (*of* **Содру́жество незави́симых госуда́рств**) CIS.

снег (*pl* -а́) snow.

снеги́рь (-я́) bullfinch.

снегово́й snow. **снегопа́д** snowfall. **Снегу́рочка** Snow Maiden. **сне́жинка** snow-flake. **сне́жный** snow(y); **~ая ба́ба** snowman. **снежо́к** (-жка́) light snow; snowball.

снести́¹ (-су́, -сёшь; -ёс, -ла́) *pf* (*impf* **сноси́ть**) take; bring together; bring *or* fetch down; carry away; blow off; demolish; endure; **~сь** communicate (**с**+*instr* with).

с|нести́²(сь (-су́(сь, -сёшь(ся; снёс(ся, -сла́(сь) *pf*.

снижа́ть *impf*, **сни́зить** (-и́жу) *pf* lower; bring down; reduce; **~ся** come down; fall. **сниже́ние** lowering; loss of height.

снизойти́ (-йду́, -йдёшь; -ошёл, -шла́) *pf* (*impf* **снисходи́ть**) condescend.

сни́зу *adv* from below.

снима́ть(ся *impf of* **снять(ся. сни́мок** (-мка) photograph. **сниму́** *etc.*: see **снять**

сниска́ть (-ищу́, -и́щешь) *pf*, **сни́скивать** *impf* gain, win.

снисходи́тельность condescension; leniency. **снисходи́тельный** condescending; lenient. **снисходи́ть** (-ожу́, -о́дишь) *impf of* **снизойти́**. **снисхожде́ние** indulgence, leniency. **сни́ться** *impf (pf* при~) *impers+dat* dream.

сноби́зм snobbery.

сно́ва *adv* again, anew.

снова́ть (сную́, снуёшь) *impf* rush about.

сновиде́ние dream.

сноп (-а́) sheaf.

сноро́вка knack, skill.

снос demolition; drift; wear. **сноси́ть**[1] (-ошу́, -о́сишь) *pf (impf* сна́шивать) wear out. **сноси́ть**[2](ся (-ошу́(сь, -о́сишь(ся) *impf of* снести́(сь. сно́ска footnote. **сно́сно** *adv* tolerably, so-so. **сно́сный** tolerable; fair.

снотво́рный soporific.

сноха́ (*pl* -и) daughter-in-law.

сноше́ние intercourse; relations, dealings.

сношу́ *etc.: see* **сноси́ть**

сня́тие taking down; removal; making. **снять** (сниму́, -и́мешь; -ял, -а́, -о) *pf (impf* снима́ть) take off; take down; gather in; remove; rent; take; make; photograph; ~ся come off; move off; be photographed.

со *see* **с** *prep*.

со- *pref* co-, joint. **соа́втор** co-author.

соба́ка dog. **соба́чий** dog's; canine. **соба́чка** little dog; trigger.

соберу́ *etc.: see* **собра́ть**

собе́с *abbr (of* социа́льное обеспе́чение) social security (department).

собесе́дник interlocutor, companion. **собесе́дование** conversation.

собира́тель *m* collector. **собира́ть(ся** *impf of* **собра́ть(ся**

собла́зн temptation. **соблазни́тель** *m*, ~ница tempter; seducer. **соблазни́тельный** tempting; seductive. **соблазни́ть** *pf*, **соблазня́ть** *impf* tempt; seduce.

соблюда́ть *impf*, **со**|**блюсти́** (-юду́, -дёшь; -юл, -а́) *pf* observe; keep (to). **соблюде́ние** observance; maintenance.

собо́й, собо́ю *see* **себя́**

соболе́знование sympathy, condolence(s). **соболе́зновать** *impf +dat* sympathize *or* commiserate with.

со́боль (*pl* -и *or* -я́) *m* sable.

собо́р cathedral; council, synod. **собо́рный** cathedral.

собра́ние meeting; assembly; collection. **со́бранный** collected; concentrated.

собра́т (*pl* -ья, -ьев) colleague.

собра́ть (-беру́, -берёшь; -а́л, -а́, -о) *pf (impf* собира́ть) gather; collect; ~ся prepare; intend, be going; +c+*instr* collect.

со́бственник owner, proprietor. **со́бственнический** proprietary; proprietorial. **со́бственно** *adv*: ~ (говоря́) strictly speaking, as a matter of fact. **собственнору́чно** *adv* personally, with one's own hand. **со́бственность** property; ownership. **со́бственн**|**ый** (one's) own; proper; true; и́мя ~ое proper name; ~ой персо́ной in person.

собы́тие event.

собью́ *etc.: see* **сбить**

сова́ (*pl* -ы) owl.

сова́ть (сую́, -ёшь) *impf (pf* су́нуть) thrust, shove; ~ся push, push in; butt in.

соверша́ть *impf*, **соверши́ть** (-шу́) *pf* accomplish; carry out; commit; complete; ~ся happen; be accomplished. **соверше́ние** accomplishment; perpetration. **соверше́нно** *adv* perfectly; absolutely, completely. **совершенноле́тие** majority. **совершенноле́тний** of age. **соверше́нный**[1] perfect; absolute, complete. **соверше́нный**[2] perfective. **соверше́нство** perfection. **соверше́нствование** perfecting; improvement. **соверше́нствовать** *impf (pf* у~) perfect; improve; ~ся в+*instr* perfect o.s. in; improve.

со́вестливый conscientious. **со́вестно** *impers+dat* be ashamed. **со́весть** conscience.

сове́т advice, counsel; opinion; council; soviet, Soviet. **сове́тник** adviser. **сове́товать** *impf (pf* по~) advise; ~ся с+*instr* consult, ask advice of. **совето́лог** Kremlinologist. **сове́т**|**ский** Soviet; ~ая власть the Soviet regime; ~ий Сою́з the Soviet Union. сове́тчик adviser.

совеща́ние conference. совеща́тельный consultative, deliberative. совеща́ться *impf* deliberate; consult.

совлада́ть *pf* с+*instr* control, cope with.

совмести́мый compatible. совмести́тель *m* person holding more than one office. совмести́ть (-ещу́) *pf*, совмеща́ть *impf* combine; ~ся coincide; be combined, combine. совме́стно jointly. совме́стный joint, combined.

сово́к (-вка́) shovel; scoop; dust-pan.

совокупи́ться (-плю́сь) *pf*, совокупля́ться *impf* copulate. совокупле́ние copulation. совоку́пно *adv* jointly. совоку́пность aggregate, sum total.

совпада́ть *impf*, совпа́сть (-адёт) *pf* coincide; agree, tally. совпаде́ние coincidence.

соврати́ть (-ащу́) *pf* (*impf* совраща́ть) pervert, seduce.

со|вра́ть (-вру́, -врёшь; -а́л, -а́, -о) *pf*.

совраща́ть(ся *impf of* соврати́ть(ся. совраще́ние perverting, seduction.

совреме́нник contemporary. совреме́нность the present (time); contemporaneity. совреме́нный contemporary; modern.

совру́ *etc.*: *see* совра́ть

совсе́м *adv* quite; entirely.

совхо́з State farm.

совью́ *etc.*: *see* свить

согла́сие consent; assent; agreement; harmony. согласи́ться (-ашу́сь) *pf* (*impf* соглаша́ться) consent; agree.

согла́сно *adv* in accord, in harmony; *prep*+*dat* in accordance with. согла́сн|ый[1] agreeable (to); in agreement; harmonious. согла́сный[2] consonant(al); *sb* consonant.

согласова́ние co-ordination; agreement. согласо́ванность co-ordination. согласова́ть *pf*, согласо́вывать *impf* co-ordinate; make agree; ~ся conform; agree.

соглаша́ться *impf of* согласи́ться. соглаше́ние agreement. соглашу́ *etc.*: *see* согласи́ть

согна́ть (сгоню́, сго́нишь; -а́л, -а́, -о)

pf (*impf* сгоня́ть) drive away; drive together.

со|гну́ть (-ну́, -нёшь) *pf* (*impf also* сгиба́ть) bend, curve; ~ся bend (down).

согрева́ть *impf*, согре́ть (-е́ю) *pf* warm, heat; ~ся get warm; warm o.s.

со|греши́ть (-шу́) *pf*.

со́да soda.

соде́йствие assistance. соде́йствовать *impf* & *pf* (*pf also* по~) +*dat* assist; promote; contribute to.

содержа́ние maintenance, upkeep; content(s); pay. содержа́тельный rich in content; pithy. содержа́ть (-жу́, -жишь) *impf* keep; maintain; contain; ~ся be kept; be maintained; be; be contained. содержи́мое *sb* contents.

со|дра́ть (сдеру́, -рёшь; -а́л, -а́, -о) *pf* (*impf also* сдира́ть) tear off, strip off; fleece.

содрога́ние shudder. содрога́ться *impf*, содрогну́ться (-ну́сь, -нёшься) *pf* shudder.

содру́жество concord; commonwealth.

соедине́ние joining, combination; joint; compound; formation. Соединённое Короле́вство United Kingdom. Соединённые Шта́ты (Аме́рики) *m pl* United States (of America). соединённый (-ён, -а́) united, joint. соедини́тельный connective, connecting. соедини́ть *pf*, соединя́ть *impf* join, unite; connect; combine; ~ся join, unite; combine.

сожале́ние regret; pity; к сожале́нию unfortunately. сожале́ть (-е́ю) *impf* regret, deplore.

сожгу́ *etc.*: *see* сжечь. сожже́ние burning; cremation.

сожи́тель *m*, ~ница room-mate, flat-mate; lover. сожи́тельство cohabitation.

сожму́ *etc.*: *see* сжать[2]. сожну́ *etc.*: *see* сжать[1]. созва́ниваться *impf of* созвони́ться

созва́ть (-зову́, -зовёшь; -а́л, -а́, -о) *pf* (*impf* сзыва́ть, созыва́ть) call together; call; invite.

созве́здие constellation.

созвони́ться *pf* (*impf* созва́ниваться) ring up; speak on the telephone.

созву́чие accord; assonance. **созву́чный** harmonious; +*dat* in keeping with.

создава́ть (-даю́, -даёшь) *impf*, **созда́ть** (-а́м, -а́шь, -а́ст, -ади́м; со́здал, -а́, -о) *pf* create; establish; ∼ся be created; arise, spring up. **созда́ние** creation; work; creature. **созда́тель** *m* creator; originator.

созерца́ние contemplation. **созерца́тельный** contemplative. **созерца́ть** *impf* contemplate.

созида́ние creation. **созида́тельный** creative.

сознава́ть (-наю́, -наёшь) *impf*, **созна́ть** *pf* be conscious of, realize; acknowledge; ∼ся confess. **созна́ние** consciousness; acknowledgement; confession. **созна́тельность** awareness, consciousness. **созна́тельный** conscious; deliberate.

созову́ *etc.: see* **созва́ть**

созрева́ть *impf*, **со|зре́ть** (-е́ю) *pf* ripen, mature.

созы́в summoning, calling. **созыва́ть** *impf of* **созва́ть**

соизмери́мый commensurable.

соиска́ние competition. **соиска́тель** *m*, ∼ница competitor, candidate.

сойти́ (-йду́, -йдёшь; сошёл, -шла́) *pf* (*impf* **сходи́ть**) go *or* come down; get off; leave; come off; pass, go off; ∼ с ума́ go mad, go out of one's mind; ∼сь meet; gather; become friends; become intimate; agree.

сок (*loc* -ý) juice.

со́кол falcon.

сократи́ть (-ащу́) *pf*, **сокраща́ть** *impf* shorten; abbreviate; reduce; ∼ся grow shorter; decrease; contract. **сокраще́ние** shortening; abridgement; abbreviation; reduction.

сокрове́нный secret; innermost. **сокро́вище** treasure. **сокро́вищница** treasure-house.

сокруша́ть *impf*, **сокруши́ть** (-шу́) *pf* shatter; smash; distress; ∼ся grieve, be distressed. **сокруше́ние** smashing; grief. **сокрушённый** (-ён, -á) grief-stricken. **сокруши́тельный** shattering.

сокры́тие concealment.

со|лга́ть (-лгу́, -лжёшь; -а́л, -á, -о) *pf*.

солда́т (*gen pl* -а́т) soldier. **солда́т-**

ский soldier's.

соле́ние salting; pickling. **солёный** (со́лон, -á, -о) salt(y); salted; pickled. **соле́нье** salted food(s); pickles.

солида́рность solidarity. **соли́дный** solid; strong; reliable; respectable; sizeable.

соли́ст, соли́стка soloist.

соли́ть (-лю́, со́лишь) *impf* (*pf* по∼) salt; pickle.

со́лнечный sun; solar; sunny; ∼ свет sunlight; sunshine; ∼ уда́р sunstroke. **со́лнце** sun. **солнцепёк: на** ∼е in the sun. **солнцестоя́ние** solstice.

со́ло *neut indecl* solo; *adv* solo.

солове́й (-вья́) nightingale.

со́лод malt.

солодко́вый liquorice.

соло́ма straw; thatch. **соло́менный** straw; thatch. **соло́минка** straw.

со́лон *etc.: see* **солёный. солони́на** corned beef. **соло́нка** salt-cellar.

солонча́к (-á) saline soil; *pl* salt marshes. **соль** (*pl* -и, -е́й) salt.

со́льный solo.

солью́ *etc.: see* **слить**

соляно́й, соля́ный salt, saline; **соля́ная кислота́** hydrochloric acid.

со́мкнутый close. **сомкну́ть** (-ну́, -нёшь) *pf* (*impf* **смыка́ть**) close; ∼ся close.

сомнева́ться *impf* doubt, have doubts. **сомне́ние** doubt. **сомни́тельный** doubtful.

сомну́ *etc.: see* **смять**

сон (сна) sleep; dream. **сонли́вость** sleepiness; somnolence. **сонли́вый** sleepy. **со́нный** sleepy; sleeping.

сона́та sonata.

соне́т sonnet.

сообража́ть *impf*, **сообрази́ть** (-ажу́) *pf* consider, think out; weigh; understand. **соображе́ние** consideration; understanding; notion. **сообрази́тельный** quick-witted.

сообра́зный с+*instr* conforming to, in keeping with.

сообща́ *adv* together. **сообща́ть** *impf*, **сообщи́ть** (-щу́) *pf* communicate, report, announce; impart; +*dat* inform. **сообще́ние** communication, report; announcement. **соо́бщество** association. **соо́бщник** accomplice.

сооруди́ть (-ужу́) *pf*, **сооружа́ть** *impf* build, erect. **сооруже́ние**

building; structure.
соотве́тственно *adv* accordingly, correspondingly; *prep+dat* according to, in accordance with. **соотве́тственный** corresponding. **соотве́тствие** accordance, correspondence. **соотве́тствовать** *impf* correspond, conform. **соотве́тствующий** corresponding; suitable.

соотéчественник fellow-countryman.

соотноше́ние correlation.

сопе́рник rival. **сопе́рничать** *impf* compete, vie. **сопе́рничество** rivalry.

сопе́ть (-плю́) *impf* wheeze; snuffle.

со́пка hill, mound.

сопли́вый snotty.

сопоста́вить (-влю) *pf*, **сопоставля́ть** *impf* compare. **сопоставле́ние** comparison.

сопреде́льный contiguous.

со|пре́ть *pf*.

соприкаса́ться *impf*, **соприкосну́ться** (-ну́сь, -нёшься) *pf* adjoin; come into contact. **соприкоснове́ние** contact.

сопроводи́тельный accompanying. **сопроводи́ть** (-ожу́) *pf*, **сопровожда́ть** *impf* accompanying; escort. **сопровожде́ние** accompaniment; escort.

сопротивле́ние resistance. **сопротивля́ться** *impf +dat* resist, oppose. **сопу́тствовать** *impf +dat* accompany.

сопью́сь *etc.*: see **спи́ться**

сор litter, rubbish.

соразме́рить *pf*, **соразмеря́ть** *impf* balance, match. **соразме́рный** proportionate, commensurate.

сора́тник comrade-in-arms.

сорва́ть (-ву́, -вёшь; -а́л, -а́, -о) *pf* (*impf* **срыва́ть**) tear off, away, down; break off; pick; get; break; ruin, spoil; vent; ~**ся** break away, break loose; fall, come down; fall through.

с|организова́ть *pf*.

соревнова́ние competition; contest. **соревнова́ться** *impf* compete.

сори́ть *impf* (*pf* **на~**) *+acc or instr* litter; throw about. **со́рный** rubbish, refuse; ~**ая трава́** weed(s). **сорня́к** (-а́) weed.

со́рок (-а́) forty.

соро́ка magpie.

сороков|о́й fortieth; ~**ые го́ды** the forties.

соро́чка shirt; blouse; shift.

сорт (*pl* -а́) grade, quality; sort. **сортирова́ть** *impf* (*pf* **рас~**) sort, grade. **сортиро́вка** sorting. **сортиро́вочн|ый** sorting; ~**ая** *sb* marshalling-yard. **сортиро́вщик** sorter. **со́ртный** high quality.

соса́ть (-су́, -сёшь) *impf* suck.

со|сва́тать *pf*.

сосе́д (*pl* -и), **сосе́дка** neighbour. **сосе́дний** neighbouring; adjacent, next. **сосе́дский** neighbours'. **сосе́дство** neighbourhood. **соси́ска** frankfurter, sausage.

со́ска (*baby's*) dummy.

соска́кивать *impf of* **соскочи́ть**

соска́льзывать *impf*, **соскользну́ть** (-ну́, -нёшь) *pf* slide down, slide off.

соскочи́ть (-чу́, -чишь) *pf* (*impf* **соска́кивать**) jump off *or* down; come off.

соску́читься (-чусь) *pf* get bored; ~ **по+**dat miss.

сослага́тельный subjunctive.

сосла́ть (сошлю́, -лёшь) *pf* (*impf* **ссыла́ть**) exile, deport; ~**ся на+**acc refer to; cite; plead, allege.

сосло́вие estate; class.

сослужи́вец (-вца) colleague.

сосна́ (*pl* -ы, -сен) pine(-tree). **сосно́вый** pine; deal.

сосо́к (-ска́) nipple, teat.

сосредото́ченный concentrated. **сосредото́чивать** *impf*, **сосредото́чить** (-чу) *pf* concentrate; focus; ~**ся** concentrate.

соста́в composition; structure; compound; staff; strength; train; в ~**е** **+**gen consisting of. **состави́тель** *m* compiler. **соста́вить** (-влю) *pf*, **составля́ть** *impf* put together; make (up); draw up; compile; be, constitute; total; ~**ся** form, be formed. **составно́й** compound; component, constituent.

со|ста́рить(ся *pf*.

состоя́ние state, condition; fortune. **состоя́тельный** well-to-do; well-grounded. **состоя́ть** (-ою́) *impf* be; **+из+**gen consist of; **+в+**prep consist in, be. **состоя́ться** (-ойтся) *pf* take place.

сострада́ние compassion. состра-
да́тельный compassionate.
с|остри́ть pf. со|стря́пать pf.
со|стыкова́ть pf, состыко́вывать
impf dock; ~ся dock.
состяза́ние competition, contest.
состяза́ться impf compete.
сосу́д vessel.
сосу́лька icicle.
сосуществова́ние co-existence.
со|счита́ть pf. сот see сто.
сотворе́ние creation. со|твори́ть pf.
со|тка́ть (-ку́, -кёшь; -а́л, -а́ла́, -о) pf.
со́тня (gen pl -тен) a hundred.
сотру́ etc.: see стере́ть
сотру́дник collaborator; colleague;
employee. сотру́дничать impf collaborate; +в+prep contribute to. со-
тру́дничество collaboration.
сотряса́ть impf, сотрясти́ (-су́, -сёшь;
-я́с, -ла́) pf shake; ~ся tremble.
сотрясе́ние shaking; concussion.
со́ты (-ов) pl honeycomb.
со́тый hundredth.
соумы́шленник accomplice.
со́ус sauce; gravy; dressing.
соуча́стие participation; complicity.
соуча́стник participant; accomplice.
софа́ (pl -ы) sofa.
соха́ (pl -и) (wooden) plough.
со́хнуть (-ну; сох) impf (pf вы́~,
за~, про~) (get) dry; wither.
сохране́ние preservation; conservation; (safe)keeping; retention. со-
храни́ть pf, сохраня́ть impf preserve, keep; ~ся remain (intact); last
out; be well preserved. сохра́нный
safe.
социа́л-демокра́т Social Democrat.
социа́л-демократи́ческий Social
Democratic. социали́зм socialism.
социали́ст socialist. социалисти́-
ческий socialist. социа́льн|ый so-
cial; ~ое обеспече́ние social security. социо́лог sociologist. социо-
ло́гия sociology.
соцреали́зм socialist realism.
сочета́ние combination. сочета́ть
impf & pf combine; ~ся combine;
harmonize; match.
сочине́ние composition; work. со-
чини́ть pf, сочиня́ть impf compose;
write; make up.
сочи́ться (-и́тся) impf ooze (out),
trickle; ~ кро́вью bleed.

со́чный (-чен, -чна́, -о) juicy; rich.
сочту́ etc.: see счесть
сочу́вствие sympathy. сочу́вство-
вать impf +dat sympathize with.
сошёл etc.: see сойти́. сошлю́ etc.:
see сосла́ть. сошью́ etc.: see сшить
сощу́ривать impf, со|щу́рить pf
screw up, narrow; ~ся screw up
one's eyes; narrow.
сою́з[1] union; alliance; league. сою́з[2]
conjunction. сою́зник ally. сою́з-
ный allied; Union.
спад recession; abatement. спада́ть
impf of спасть
спазм spasm.
спа́ивать impf of спая́ть, спои́ть
спа́йка soldered joint; solidarity,
unity.
с|пали́ть pf.
спа́льн|ый sleeping; ~ый ваго́н
sleeping car; ~ое ме́сто berth.
спа́льня (gen pl -лен) bedroom.
спа́ржа asparagus.
спартакиа́да sports meeting.
спаса́тельный rescue; ~ жиле́т life
jacket; ~ круг lifebuoy; ~ по́яс
lifebelt. спаса́ть(ся impf of спа-
сти́(сь. спасе́ние rescue, escape;
salvation. спаси́бо thank you. спа-
си́тель m rescuer; saviour. спаси́-
тельный saving; salutary.
спасти́ (-су́, -сёшь; спас, -ла́) pf (impf
спаса́ть) save; rescue; ~сь escape;
be saved.
спасть (-адёт) pf (impf спада́ть) fall
(down); abate.
спать (сплю; -ал, -а́, -о) impf sleep;
лечь ~ go to bed.
спа́янность cohesion, unity. спа́-
янный united. спая́ть pf (impf
спа́ивать) solder, weld; unite.
спекта́кль m performance; show.
спектр spectrum.
спекули́ровать impf speculate. спе-
куля́нт speculator, profiteer. спеку-
ля́ция speculation; profiteering.
спе́лый ripe.
сперва́ adv at first; first.
спе́реди adv in front, from the front;
prep+gen (from) in front of.
спёртый close, stuffy.
спеси́вый arrogant, haughty. спесь
arrogance, haughtiness.
спеть[1] (-е́ет) impf (pf по~) ripen.
с|петь[2] (спою́, споёшь) pf.

спец- *abbr in comb* (*of* **специа́льный**) special. **спецко́р** special correspondent. **~оде́жда** protective clothing; overalls.

специализа́ция specialization. **специализи́роваться** *impf & pf* specialize. **специали́ст, ~ка** specialist, expert. **специа́льность** speciality; profession. **специа́льный** special; specialist.

специ́фика specific character. **специфи́ческий** specific.

спе́ция spice.

спецо́вка protective clothing; overall(s).

спеши́ть (-шу́) *impf* (*pf* по**~**) hurry, be in a hurry; be fast.

спе́шка hurry, haste. **спе́шный** urgent.

спива́ться *impf of* **спи́ться**

СПИД *abbr* (*of* **синдро́м приобретённого имму́нного дефици́та**) Aids.

с|пики́ровать *pf.*

спи́ливать *impf*, **спили́ть** (-лю́, -лишь) *pf* saw down, off.

спина́ (*acc* -у, *pl* -ы) back. **спи́нка** back. **спинно́й** spinal; **~ мозг** spinal cord.

спира́ль spiral.

спирт alcohol, spirit(s). **спиртн|о́й** alcoholic; **~о́е** *sb* alcohol. **спирто́вка** spirit-stove. **спиртово́й** spirit, alcoholic.

списа́ть (-ишу́, -и́шешь) *pf*, **спи́сывать** *impf* copy; **~ся** exchange letters. **спи́сок** (-ска) list; record.

спи́ться (сопью́сь, -ьёшься; -и́лся, -а́сь) *pf* (*impf* **спива́ться**) take to drink.

спи́хивать *impf*, **спихну́ть** (-ну́, -нёшь) *pf* push aside, down.

спи́ца knitting-needle; spoke.

спи́чечн|ый match; **~ая коро́бка** match-box. **спи́чка** match.

спишу́ *etc.: see* **списа́ть**

сплав[1] floating. **сплав**[2] alloy. **спла́вить**[1] (-влю) *pf*, **сплавля́ть**[1] *impf* float; raft; get rid of. **спла́вить**[2] (-влю) *pf*, **сплавля́ть**[2] *impf* alloy; **~ся** fuse.

с|плани́ровать *pf*. **спла́чивать(ся** *impf of* **сплоти́ть(ся. сплёвывать** *impf of* **сплю́нуть**

с|плести́ (-ету́, -етёшь; -ёл, -а́) *pf*,

сплета́ть *impf* weave; plait; interlace. **сплете́ние** interlacing; plexus.

спле́тник, -ница gossip, scandalmonger. **спле́тничать** *impf* (*pf* на**~**) gossip. **спле́тня** (*gen pl* -тен) gossip, scandal.

сплоти́ть (-очу́) *pf* (*impf* **спла́чивать**) join; unite, rally; **~ся** unite, rally; close ranks. **сплоче́ние** uniting. **сплочённость** cohesion, unity. **сплочённый** (-ён, -а́) united; firm; unbroken.

сплошно́й solid; complete; continuous; utter. **сплошь** *adv* all over; completely; **~ да ря́дом** pretty often.

сплю *see* **спать**

сплю́нуть (-ну) *pf* (*impf* **сплёвывать**) spit; spit out.

сплю́щивать *impf*, **сплю́щить** (-щу) *pf* flatten; **~ся** become flat.

с|пляса́ть (-яшу́, -я́шешь) *pf.*

сподви́жник comrade-in-arms.

спо́ить (-ою, -о́ишь) *pf* (*impf* **спа́ивать**) make a drunkard of.

споко́йн|ый quiet; calm; **~ой но́чи** good night! **споко́йствие** quiet; calm; serenity.

спола́скивать *impf of* **сполосну́ть**

сполза́ть *impf*, **сползти́** (-зу́, -зёшь; -олз, -ла́) *pf* climb down; slip (down); fall away.

сполна́ *adv* in full.

сполосну́ть (-ну́, -нёшь) *pf* (*impf* **спола́скивать**) rinse.

спо́нсор sponsor, backer.

спор argument; controversy; dispute. **спо́рить** *impf* (*pf* по**~**) argue; dispute; debate. **спо́рный** debatable, questionable; disputed; moot.

спо́ра spore.

спорт sport. **спорти́вный** sports; **~ зал** gymnasium. **спортсме́н, ~ка** athlete, player.

спо́соб way, method; **таки́м ~ом** in this way. **спосо́бность** ability, aptitude; capacity. **спосо́бный** able; clever; capable. **спосо́бствовать** *impf* (*pf* по**~**) +*dat* assist; further.

споткну́ться (-ну́сь, -нёшься) *pf*, **спотыка́ться** *impf* stumble.

спохвати́ться (-ачу́сь, -а́тишься) *pf*, **спохва́тываться** *impf* remember suddenly.

спою́ *etc.: see* **спеть, спои́ть**

спра́ва *adv* from *or* on the right.

справедли́вость justice; fairness; truth. **справедли́вый** just; fair; justified.

спра́вить (-влю) *pf*, **справля́ть** *impf* celebrate. **спра́виться¹** (-влюсь) *pf*, **справля́ться** *impf* c+*instr* cope with, manage. **спра́виться²** (-влюсь) *pf*, **справля́ться** *impf* inquire; +в+*prep* consult. **спра́вка** information; reference; certificate; **наводи́ть спра́вку** make inquiries. **спра́вочник** reference-book, directory. **спра́вочный** inquiry, information.

спра́шивать(ся *impf of* **спроси́ть(ся**

спринт sprint. **спри́нтер** sprinter.

с|провоци́ровать *pf*. **с|проекти́ровать** *pf*.

спрос demand; asking; **без ~у** without permission. **спроси́ть** (-ошу́, -о́сишь) *pf* (*impf* **спра́шивать**) ask (for); inquire; **~ся** ask permission.

спрут octopus.

спры́гивать *impf*, **спры́гнуть** (-ну) *pf* jump off, jump down.

спры́скивать *impf*, **спры́снуть** (-ну) *pf* sprinkle.

спряга́ть *impf* (*pf* **про~**) conjugate. **спряже́ние** conjugation.

с|прясть (-яду́, -ядёшь; -ял, -яла́, -о) *pf*. **с|пря́тать(ся** (-я́чу(сь) *pf*.

спу́гивать *impf*, **спугну́ть** (-ну́, -нёшь) *pf* frighten off.

спуск lowering; descent; slope. **спуска́ть** *impf*, **спусти́ть** (-ущу́, -у́стишь) *pf* let down, lower; let go, release; let out; send out; go down; forgive; squander; **~ кора́бль** launch a ship; **~ куро́к** pull the trigger; **~ пе́тлю** drop a stitch; **~ся** go down, descend. **спускно́й** drain. **спусково́й** trigger. **спустя́** *prep*+*acc* after; later.

с|пу́тать(ся *pf*.

спу́тник satellite, sputnik; (travelling) companion.

спущу́ *etc.*: *see* **спусти́ть**

спя́чка hibernation; sleepiness.

ср. *abbr* (*of* **сравни́**) cf.

сраба́тывать *impf*, **срабо́тать** *pf* make; work, operate.

сравне́ние comparison; simile. **сра́внивать** *impf of* **сравни́ть**, **сравня́ть**. **сравни́мый** comparable. **сравни́тельно** *adv* comparatively. **сравни́тельный** comparative. **сравни́ть** *pf* (*impf* **сра́внивать**) compare; **~ся** c+*instr* compare with. **с|равня́ть** *pf* (*impf also* **сра́внивать**) make even, equal; level.

сража́ть *impf*, **срази́ть** (-ажу́) *pf* strike down; overwhelm, crush; **~ся** fight. **сраже́ние** battle.

сра́зу *adv* at once.

срам shame. **срами́ть** (-млю) *impf* (*pf* **о~**) shame; **~ся** cover o.s. with shame. **срамота́** shame.

сраста́ние growing together. **сраста́ться** *impf*, **срасти́сь** (-тётся; сро́сся, -ла́сь) *pf* grow together; knit.

среда́¹ (*pl* -ы) environment, surroundings; medium. **среда́²** (*acc* -у; *pl* -ы, -а́м *or* -ам) Wednesday. **среди́** *prep*+*gen* among; in the middle of; **~ бе́ла дня** in broad daylight. **средиземномо́рский** Mediterranean. **сре́дне** *adv* so-so. **средневеко́вый** medieval. **средневеко́вье** the Middle Ages. **сре́дний** middle; medium; mean; average; middling; secondary; neuter; **~ее** *sb* mean, average. **средото́чие** focus. **сре́дство** means; remedy.

срез cut; section; slice. **с|ре́зать** (-е́жу) *pf*. **среза́ть** *impf* cut off; slice; fail; **~ся** fail.

с|репети́ровать *pf*.

срисова́ть *pf*, **срисо́вывать** *impf* copy.

с|ровня́ть *pf*.

сродство́ affinity.

срок date; term; time, period; **в ~, к ~у** in time, to time.

сро́сся *etc.*: *see* **срасти́сь**

сро́чно *adv* urgently. **сро́чность** urgency. **сро́чный** urgent; for a fixed period.

сро́ю *etc.*: *see* **срыть**

сруб felling; framework. **сруба́ть** *impf*, **с|руби́ть** (-блю́, -бишь) *pf* cut down; build (*of logs*).

срыв disruption; breakdown; ruining. **срыва́ть¹(ся** *impf of* **сорва́ть(ся**

срыва́ть² *impf*, **срыть** (сро́ю) *pf* raze to the ground.

сря́ду *adv* running.

сса́дина scratch. **ссади́ть** (-ажу́, -а́дишь) *pf*, **сса́живать** *impf* set down; help down; turn off.

ссо́ра quarrel. **ссо́рить** *impf* (*pf* **по~**) cause to quarrel; **~ся** quarrel.

СССР abbr (of Сою́з Сове́тских Социалисти́ческих Респу́блик) USSR.

ссу́да loan. **ссуди́ть** (-ужу́, -у́дишь) pf, **ссужа́ть** impf lend, loan.

ссыла́ть(ся impf of **сосла́ть(ся. ссы́лка**[1] exile. **ссы́лка**[2] reference. **ссы́льный, ссы́льная** sb exile.

ссы́пать (-плю) pf, **ссыпа́ть** impf pour.

стабилиза́тор stabilizer; tail-plane. **стабилизи́ровать(ся** impf & pf stabilize. **стаби́льность** stability. **стаби́льный** stable, firm.

ста́вень (-вня; gen pl -вней) m, **ста́вня** (gen pl -вен) shutter.

ста́вить (-влю) impf (pf по~) put, place, set; stand; station; erect; install; apply; present, stage. **ста́вка**[1] rate; stake. **ста́вка**[2] headquarters.

ста́вня see **ста́вень**

стадио́н stadium.

ста́дия stage.

ста́дность herd instinct. **ста́дный** gregarious. **ста́до** (pl -á) herd, flock.

стаж length of service; probation. **стажёр** probationer; student on a special non-degree course. **стажиро́вка** period of training.

стака́н glass.

сталелите́йный steel-founding; ~ заво́д steel foundry. **сталепла-ви́льный** steel-making; ~ заво́д steel works. **сталепрока́тный** (steel-)rolling; ~ стан rolling-mill.

ста́лкивать(ся impf of **столк-ну́ть(ся**

ста́ло быть conj consequently.

сталь steel. **стально́й** steel.

стаме́ска chisel.

стан[1] figure, torso.

стан[2] camp.

стан[3] mill.

станда́рт standard. **станда́ртный** standard.

стани́ца Cossack village.

станкостроéние machine-tool engineering.

станови́ться (-влю́сь, -вишься) impf of **стать**[1]

стано́к (-нка́) machine tool, machine.

ста́ну etc.: see **стать**[2]

станцио́нный station. **ста́нция** station.

ста́пель (pl -я) m stocks.

ста́птывать(ся impf of **стопта́ть(ся**

стара́ние effort. **стара́тельность** diligence. **стара́тельный** diligent.

стара́ться impf (pf по~) try.

старе́ть impf (pf по~, у~) grow old. **ста́рец** (-рца) elder, (venerable) old man. **стари́к** (-á) old man. **старина́** antiquity, olden times; antique(s); old fellow. **стари́нный** ancient; old; antique. **ста́рить** impf (pf со~) age, make old; ~ся age, grow old.

старо- in comb old. **старове́р** Old Believer. **~жи́л** old resident. **~мо́дный** old-fashioned. **~славя́нский** Old Slavonic.

ста́роста head; monitor; churchwarden. **ста́рость** old age.

старт start; на ~! on your marks! **старте́р** starter. **стартова́ть** impf & pf start. **ста́ртовый** starting.

стару́ха, стару́шка old woman. **ста́рческий** old man's; senile. **ста́рше** comp of **ста́рый. ста́рш|ий** oldest, eldest; senior; head; **~ие** sb pl (one's) elders; **~ий** sb chief; man in charge. **старшина́** m sergeant-major; petty officer; leader, senior representative. **ста́рый** (-ар, -á, -о) old. **старьё** old things, junk.

ста́скивать impf of **стащи́ть**

с|тасова́ть pf.

стати́ст extra.

стати́стика statistics. **статисти́ческий** statistical.

ста́тный stately.

ста́тский civil, civilian.

ста́тус status. **ста́тус-кво́** neut indecl status quo.

статуэ́тка statuette.

ста́туя statue.

стать[1] (-áну) pf (impf станови́ться) stand; take up position; stop; cost; begin; +instr become; +c+instr become of; не ~ impers+gen cease to be; disappear; его́ не ста́ло he is no more; ~ на коле́ни kneel.

стать[2] physique, build.

ста́ться (-áнется) pf happen.

статья́ (gen pl -е́й) article; clause; item; matter.

стациона́р permanent establishment; hospital. **стациона́рный** stationary; permanent; ~ больно́й in-patient.

ста́чечник striker. **ста́чка** strike.

с|тащи́ть (-щу́, -щишь) pf (impf also

ста́скивать) drag off, pull off.

ста́я flock; school, shoal; pack.

ствол (-á) trunk; barrel.

ство́рка leaf, fold.

сте́бель (-бля; *gen pl* -бле́й) *m* stem, stalk.

стёган|ый quilted; ~ое одея́ло quilt. **стега́ть**[1] *impf* (*pf* вы~) quilt.

стега́ть[2] *impf*, **стегну́ть** (-ну́) *pf* (*pf also* от~) whip, lash.

стежо́к (-жка́) stitch.

стезя́ path, way.

стёк *etc.: see* стечь. **стека́ть(ся** *impf of* сте́чь(ся

стекло́ (*pl* -ёкла, -кол) glass; lens; (window-)pane.

стекло- *in comb* glass. **стекловоло-кно́** glass fibre. **~очисти́тель** *m* windscreen-wiper. **~ре́з** glass-cutter. **~тка́нь** fibreglass.

стекля́нный glass; glassy. **стеко́ль-щик** glazier.

стели́ть *see* стлать

стелла́ж (-á) shelves, shelving.

сте́лька insole.

стелю́ *etc.: see* стлать

с|темне́ть (-éет) *pf*.

стена́ (*acc* -у; *pl* -ы, -áм) wall. **стен-газе́та** wall newspaper.

стенд stand.

сте́нка wall; side. **стенно́й** wall.

стеногра́мма shorthand record. **сте-но́граф, стенографи́ст, ~ка** ste-nographer. **стенографи́ровать** *impf* & *pf* take down in shorthand. **сте-нографи́ческий** shorthand. **стено-гра́фия** shorthand.

стенокарди́я angina.

степе́нный staid; middle-aged.

сте́пень (*gen pl* -éй) degree; extent; power.

степно́й steppe. **степь** (*loc* -и́; *gen pl* -éй) steppe.

стервя́тник vulture.

стерегу́ *etc.: see* стере́чь

сте́рео *indecl adj* stereo. **сте́рео-** *in comb* stereo. **стереоти́п** stereotype. **стереоти́пный** stereotype(d). **сте-реофони́ческий** stereo(phonic). **~фо́ния** stereo(phony).

стере́ть (сотру́, сотрёшь; стёр) *pf* (*impf* стира́ть[1]) wipe off; rub out, rub sore; **~ся** rub off; wear down; be effaced.

стере́чь (-регу́, -режёшь; -ёг, -ла́)

impf guard; watch for.

сте́ржень (-жня) *m* pivot; rod; core.

стерилизова́ть *impf* & *pf* sterilize. **стери́льный** sterile.

сте́рлинг sterling.

сте́рлядь (*gen pl* -éй) sterlet.

стерпе́ть (-плю́, -пишь) *pf* bear, en-dure.

стёртый worn, effaced.

стесне́ние constraint. **стесни́тель-ный** shy; inconvenient. **с|тесни́ть** *pf*, **стесня́ть** *impf* constrain; ham-per; inhibit. **с|тесни́ться** *pf*, **стес-ня́ться** *impf* (*pf also* по~) +*inf* feel too shy (to), be ashamed to.

стече́ние confluence; gathering; com-bination. **стечь** (-чёт; -ёк, -ла́) *pf* (*impf* стека́ть) flow down; **~ся** flow together; gather.

стилисти́ческий stylistic. **стиль** *m* style. **сти́льный** stylish; period.

сти́мул stimulus, incentive. **стиму-ли́ровать** *impf* & *pf* stimulate.

стипе́ндия grant.

стира́льный washing.

стира́ть[1]**(ся** *impf of* стере́ть(ся

стира́ть[2] *impf* (*pf* вы~) wash, laun-der; **~ся** wash. **сти́рка** washing, wash, laundering.

сти́скивать *impf*, **сти́снуть** (-ну) *pf* squeeze; clench; hug.

стих (-á) verse; line; *pl* poetry.

стиха́ть *impf of* сти́хнуть

стихи́йный elemental; spontaneous. **стихи́я** element.

сти́хнуть (-ну; стих) *pf* (*impf* сти-ха́ть) subside; calm down.

стихотворе́ние poem. **стихотво́р-ный** in verse form.

стлать, стели́ть (стелю́, сте́лешь) *impf* (*pf* по~) spread; ~ **посте́ль** make a bed; **~ся** spread; creep.

сто (ста; *gen pl* сот) a hundred.

стог (*loc* -е & -ý; *pl* -á) stack, rick.

сто́имость cost; value. **сто́ить** *impf* cost; be worth(while); deserve.

стой *see* стоя́ть

сто́йка counter, bar; prop; upright; strut. **сто́йкий** firm; stable; steadfast. **сто́йкость** firmness, stability; stead-fastness. **сто́йло** stall. **стоймя́** *adv* upright.

сток flow; drainage; drain, gutter; sewer.

стол (-á) table; desk; cuisine.

столб (-á) post, pole, pillar, column. **столбене́ть** (-éю) *impf* (*pf* **о~**) be rooted to the ground. **столбня́к** (-á) stupor; tetanus.

столе́тие century; centenary. **столе́тний** hundred-year-old; of a hundred years.

столи́ца capital; metropolis. **столи́чный** (of the) capital.

столкнове́ние collision; clash. **столкну́ть** (-ну́, -нёшь) *pf* (*impf* **ста́лкивать**) push off, away; cause to collide; bring together; **~ся** collide, clash; **+с**+*instr* run into.

столо́вая *sb* dining-room; canteen. **столо́вый** table.

столп (-á) pillar.

столпи́ться *pf* crowd.

столь *adv* so. **сто́лько** *adv* so much, so many.

столя́р (-á) joiner, carpenter. **столя́рный** joiner's.

стомато́лог dentist.

стометро́вка (the) hundred metres.

стон groan. **стона́ть** (-ну́, -нешь) *impf* groan.

стоп! *int* stop!

стопа́[1] foot.

стопа́[2] (*pl* -ы́) ream; pile.

сто́пка[1] pile.

сто́пка[2] small glass.

сто́пор stop, catch. **сто́пориться** *impf* (*pf* **за~**) come to a stop.

стопроце́нтный hundred-per-cent.

стоп-сигна́л brake-light.

стопта́ть (-пчу́, -пчешь) *pf* (*impf* **ста́птывать**) wear down; **~ся** wear down.

с|торгова́ть(ся *pf*.

сто́рож (*pl* -á) watchman, guard. **сторожево́й** watch; patrol-. **сторожи́ть** (-жу́) *impf* guard, watch (over).

сторона́ (*acc* сто́рону, *pl* сто́роны, -ро́н, -áм) side; direction; hand; feature; part; land; **в сто́рону** aside; **с мое́й стороны́** for my part; **с одно́й стороны́** on the one hand. **сторони́ться** (-ню́сь, -ни́шься) *impf* (*pf* **по~**) stand aside; +*gen* avoid. **сторо́нник** supporter, advocate.

сто́чный sewage, drainage.

стоя́нка stop; parking; stopping place, parking space; stand; rank. **стоя́ть** (-ою́) *impf* (*pf* **по~**) stand; be; stay; stop; have stopped; +**за**+*acc* stand up for; **~ на коле́нях** kneel. **стоя́чий** standing; upright; stagnant. **сто́ящий** deserving; worthwhile.

стр. *abbr* (*of* **страни́ца**) page.

страда́ (*pl* -ды) (hard work at) harvest time.

страда́лец (-льца) sufferer. **страда́ние** suffering. **страда́тельный** passive. **страда́ть** (-áю *or* -áжду) *impf* (*pf* **по~**) suffer; **~ за** +*gen* feel for.

стра́жа guard, watch; **под стра́жей** under arrest, in custody; **стоя́ть на стра́же** +*gen* guard.

страна́ (*pl* -ы) country; land; **~ све́та** cardinal point.

страни́ца page.

стра́нник, стра́нница wanderer.

стра́нно *adv* strangely. **стра́нность** strangeness; eccentricity. **стра́нн|ый** (-áнен, -анна́, -о) strange.

стра́нствие wandering. **стра́нствовать** *impf* wander.

Страстн|о́й of Holy Week; **~áя пя́тница** Good Friday.

стра́стный (-тен, -тна́, -о) passionate. **страсть**[1] (*gen pl* -е́й) passion. **страсть**[2] *adv* awfully, frightfully.

стратеги́ческий strategic(al). **страте́гия** strategy.

стратосфе́ра stratosphere.

стра́ус ostrich.

страх fear.

страхова́ние insurance; **~ жи́зни** life insurance. **страхова́ть** *impf* (*pf* **за~**) insure (**от**+*gen* against); **~ся** insure o.s. **страхо́вка** insurance.

страши́ться (-шу́сь) *impf* +*gen* be afraid of. **стра́шно** *adv* awfully. **стра́шный** (-шен, -шна́, -о) terrible, awful.

стрекоза́ (*pl* -ы) dragonfly.

стрекота́ть (-очу́, -о́чешь) *impf* chirr.

стрела́ (*pl* -ы) arrow; shaft; boom. **стреле́ц** (-льца́) Sagittarius. **стре́лка** pointer; hand; needle; arrow; spit; points. **стрелко́вый** rifle; shooting; infantry. **стрело́к** (-лка́) shot; rifleman, gunner. **стре́лочник** pointsman. **стрельба́** (*pl* -ы) shooting, firing. **стре́льчатый** lancet; arched. **стреля́ть** *impf* shoot; fire; **~ся** shoot o.s.; fight a duel.

стремгла́в *adv* headlong.

стреми́тельный swift; impetuous.

стреми́ться (-млю́сь) *impf* strive. **стремле́ние** striving, aspiration.

стремни́на rapid(s).

стре́мя (-мени; *pl* -мена́, -мя́н, -а́м) *neut* stirrup. **стремя́нка** step-ladder.

стресс stress.

стри́женый short; short-haired, cropped; shorn. **стри́жка** hair-cut; shearing. **стричь** (-игу́, -ижёшь; -иг) *impf* (*pf* о~) cut, clip; cut the hair of; shear; ~ся have one's hair cut.

строга́ть *impf* (*pf* вы~) plane, shave. **стро́гий** strict; severe. **стро́гость** strictness.

строево́й combatant; line; drill. **строе́ние** building; structure; composition.

строжа́йший, стро́же *superl* & *comp of* **стро́гий**

строи́тель *m* builder. **строи́тельный** building, construction. **строи́тельство** building, construction; building site. **стро́ить** *impf* (*pf* по~) build; construct; make; base; draw up; ~ся be built, be under construction; draw up. **строй** (*loc* -ю́; *pl* -и́ *or* -й, -ёв *or* -ёв) system; régime; structure; pitch; formation. **стро́йка** building; building-site. **стро́йность** proportion; harmony; balance, order. **стро́йный** (-о́ен, -ойна́, -о) harmonious, orderly, well-proportioned, shapely.

строка́ (асс -о́ку́; *pl* -и, -а́м) line; **кра́сная** ~ new paragraph.

строп, стро́па sling; shroud line.

стропи́ло rafter, beam.

стропти́вый refractory.

строфа́ (*pl* -ы, -а́м) stanza.

строчи́ть (-чу́, -о́чишь) *impf* (*pf* на~, про~) stitch; scribble, dash off. **стро́чка** stitch; line.

стро́ю *etc.*: *see* **стро́ить**

струга́ть *impf* (*pf* вы~) plane. **стру́жка** shaving.

струи́ться *impf* stream.

структу́ра structure.

струна́ (*pl* -ы) string. **стру́нный** stringed.

струп (*pl* -пья, -пьев) scab.

с|тру́сить (-у́шу) *pf*.

стручо́к (-чка́) pod.

струя́ (*pl* -и, -уй) jet, spurt, stream.

стря́пать *impf* (*pf* со~) cook; concoct. **стряпня́** cooking.

стря́хивать *impf*, **стряхну́ть** (-ну́, -нёшь) *pf* shake off.

студени́стый jelly-like.

студе́нт, студе́нтка student. **студе́нческий** student.

сту́день (-дня) *m* jelly; aspic.

студи́ть (-ужу́, -у́дишь) *impf* (*pf* о~) cool.

сту́дия studio.

сту́жа severe cold, hard frost.

стук knock; clatter. **сту́кать** *impf*, **сту́кнуть** (-ну) *pf* knock; bang; strike; ~ся knock (o.s.), bang. **стука́ч** (-а́) informer.

стул (*pl* -лья, -льев) chair. **стульча́к** (-а́) (*lavatory*) seat. **сту́льчик** stool.

сту́па mortar.

ступа́ть *impf*, **ступи́ть** (-плю́, -пишь) *pf* step; tread. **ступе́нчатый** stepped, graded. **ступе́нь** (*gen pl* -éней) step, rung; stage, grade. **ступе́нька** step. **ступня́** foot; sole.

стуча́ть (-чу́) *impf* (*pf* по~) knock; chatter; pound; ~ся в+*acc* knock at.

стушева́ться (-шу́юсь) *pf*, **стушёвываться** *impf* efface o.s.

с|туши́ть (-шу́, -шишь) *pf*.

стыд (-а́) shame. **стыди́ть** (-ыжу́) *impf* (*pf* при~) put to shame; ~ся (*pf* по~ся) be ashamed. **стыдли́вый** bashful. **сты́дн|ый** shameful; ~о! shame! ~о *impers*+*dat* ему́ ~о he is ashamed; **как тебе́ не ~о!** you ought to be ashamed of yourself!

стык joint; junction. **стыкова́ть** *impf* (*pf* со~) join end to end; ~ся (*pf* при~ся) dock. **стыко́вка** docking.

сты́нуть, стыть (-ы́ну; стыл) *impf* cool; get cold.

сты́чка skirmish; squabble.

стюарде́сса stewardess.

стя́гивать *impf*, **стяну́ть** (-ну́, -нешь) *pf* tighten; pull together; assemble; pull off; steal; ~ся tighten; assemble.

стяжа́тель (-я) *m* money-grubber. **стяжа́ть** *impf* & *pf* gain, win.

суббо́та Saturday.

субсиди́ровать *impf* & *pf* subsidize. **субси́дия** subsidy.

субъе́кт subject; ego; person; character, type. **субъекти́вный** subjective.

сувени́р souvenir.

суверените́т sovereignty. **суверен- ный** sovereign.

сугли́нок (-нка) loam.

сугро́б snowdrift.

сугу́бо adv especially.

суд (-á) court; trial; verdict.

суда́ etc.: see **суд, су́дно**[1]

суда́к (-á) pike-perch.

суде́бный judicial; legal; forensic. **суде́йский** judge's; referee's, um- pire's. **суди́мость** previous convic- tions. **суди́ть** (сужу́, су́дишь) impf judge; try; referee, umpire; foreor- dain; ~ся go to law.

су́дно[1] (pl -дá, -óв) vessel, craft.

су́дно[2] (gen pl -ден) bed-pan. **судово́й** ship's; marine.

судомо́йка kitchen-maid; scullery.

судопроизво́дство legal proceed- ings.

су́дорога cramp, convulsion. **су́до- рожный** convulsive.

судостро́ение shipbuilding. **судо- стро́ительный** shipbuilding. **судо- хо́дный** navigable; shipping.

судьба́ (pl -ы, -дéб) fate, destiny.

судья́ (pl -и, -éй, -ям) m judge; ref- eree; umpire.

суеве́рие superstition. **суеве́рный** superstitious.

суета́ bustle, fuss. **суети́ться** (-ечу́сь) impf bustle, fuss. **суетли́вый** fussy, bustling.

сужде́ние opinion; judgement.

суже́ние narrowing; constriction. **су́- живать** impf, **су́зить** (-у́жу) pf nar- row, contract; ~ся narrow; taper.

сук (-á, loc -ý, pl су́чья, -ьев or -и́, -óв) bough.

су́ка bitch. **су́кин** adj: ~ **сын** son of a bitch.

сукно́ (pl -а, -кон) cloth; **положи́ть под ~** shelve. **суко́нный** cloth; clumsy, crude.

сули́ть impf (pf по~) promise.

султа́н plume.

сумасбро́д, сумасбро́дка nutcase. **сумасбро́дный** wild, mad. **сума- сбро́дство** wild behaviour. **сума- сше́дш|ий** mad; ~**ий** sb, ~**ая** sb lu- natic. **сумасше́ствие** madness.

суматóха turmoil; bustle.

сумбу́р confusion. **сумбу́рный** con- fused.

су́меречный twilight. **су́мерки** (-рек) pl twilight, dusk.

суме́ть (-éю) pf +inf be able to, man- age to.

су́мка bag.

су́мма sum. **сумма́рный** summary; total. **сумми́ровать** impf & pf add up; summarize.

су́мрак twilight; murk. **су́мрачный** gloomy.

су́мчатый marsupial.

сунду́к (-á) trunk, chest.

су́нуть(ся (-ну(сь) pf of **сова́ть(ся**

суп (pl -ы́) soup.

суперма́ркет supermarket.

суперобло́жка dust-jacket.

супру́г husband, spouse; pl husband and wife, (married) couple. **супру́га** wife, spouse. **супру́жеский** conju- gal. **супру́жество** matrimony.

сургу́ч (-á) sealing-wax.

сурди́нка mute; **под сурди́нку** on the sly.

суро́вость severity, sternness. **суро́- вый** severe, stern; bleak; unbleached.

суро́к (-рка́) marmot.

суррога́т substitute.

су́слик ground-squirrel.

суста́в joint, articulation.

су́тки (-ток) pl twenty-four hours; a day.

су́толока commotion.

су́точн|ый daily; round-the-clock; ~**ые** sb pl per diem allowance.

суту́литься impf stoop. **суту́лый** round-shouldered.

суть essence, main point.

суфлёр prompter. **суфли́ровать** impf +dat prompt.

су́ффикс suffix.

суха́рь (-я́) m rusk; pl bread-crumbs. **су́хо** adv drily; coldly.

сухожи́лие tendon.

сухо́й (сух, -á, -о) dry; cold. **сухо- пу́тный** land. **су́хость** dryness; coldness. **сухоща́вый** lean, skinny.

сучкова́тый knotty; gnarled. **сучо́к** (-чка́) twig; knot.

су́ша (dry) land. **су́ше** comp of **сухо́й. суше́ный** dried. **суши́лка** dryer; drying-room. **суши́ть** (-шу́, -шишь) impf (pf вы́~) dry, dry out, up; ~ся (get) dry.

суще́ственный essential, vital. **су-ществи́тельное** sb noun. **сущест-**

во being, creature; essence. **существование** existence. **существовать** *impf* exist. **сущий** absolute, downright. **сущность** essence.

сую *etc.*: see **совать**. **с|фабриковать** *pf*. **с|фальшивить** (-влю) *pf*. **с|фантазировать** *pf*.

сфера sphere. **сферический** spherical.

сфинкс sphinx.

с|формировать(ся *pf*. **с|формовать** *pf*. **с|формулировать** *pf*. **с|фотографировать(ся** *pf*.

схватить (-ачу, -атишь) *pf*, **схватывать** *impf* (*impf also* **хватать**) seize; catch; grasp; **~ся** snatch, catch; grapple. **схватка** skirmish; *pl* contractions.

схема diagram; outline, plan; circuit. **схематический** schematic; sketchy. **схематичный** sketchy.

с|хитрить *pf*.

схлынуть (-нет) *pf* (break and) flow back; subside.

сход coming off; descent; gathering. **сходить**[1] (-ожу(сь, -одишь(ся) *impf of* **сойти**(сь. **с|ходить**[2] (-ожу, -одишь) *pf* go; +**за**+*instr* go to fetch. **сходка** gathering, meeting. **сходный** (-ден, -дна, -о) similar; reasonable. **сходня** (*gen pl* -ей) (*usu pl*) gang-plank. **сходство** similarity.

с|хоронить(ся (-ню(сь, -нишь(ся) *pf*.

сцедить (-ежу, -едишь) *pf*, **сцеживать** *impf* strain off, decant.

сцена stage; scene. **сценарий** scenario; script. **сценарист** script-writer. **сценический** stage.

сцепить (-плю, -пишь) *pf*, **сцеплять** *impf* couple; **~ся** be coupled; grapple. **сцепка** coupling. **сцепление** coupling; clutch.

счастливец (-вца), **счастливчик** lucky man. **счастливица** lucky woman. **счастливый** (счастлив) happy; lucky; **~о!** all the best!; **~ого пути** bon voyage. **счастье** happiness; good fortune.

счесть(ся (сочту(сь, -тёшь(ся; счёл(ся, сочла(сь) *pf of* **считать(ся**. **счёт** (*loc* -ý; *pl* -á) account; counting, calculation; score; expense. **счётный** calculating; accounts. **счетовод** book-keeper, accountant. **счётчик** counter; meter. **счёты** (-ов) *pl* abacus.

счистить (-ищу) *pf* (*impf* **счищать**) clean off; clear away.

считать *impf* (*pf* **со~, счесть**) count; reckon; consider; **~ся** (*pf also* **по~ся**) settle accounts; be considered; +**с**+*instr* take into consideration; reckon with.

счищать *impf of* **счистить**

США *pl indecl abbr* (*of* **Соединённые Штаты Америки**) USA.

сшибать *impf*, **сшибить** (-бý, -бёшь; сшиб) *pf* strike, hit, knock (off); **~ с ног** knock down; **~ся** collide; come to blows.

сшивать *impf*, **с|шить** (сошью, -ьёшь) *pf* sew (together).

съедать *impf of* **съесть**. **съедобный** edible; nice.

съеду *etc.*: see **съехать**

съёживаться *impf*, **съ|ёжиться** (-жусь) *pf* shrivel, shrink.

съезд congress; conference; arrival. **съездить** (-зжу) *pf* go, drive, travel.

съезжать(ся *impf of* **съехать(ся**. **съел** *etc.*: see **съесть**

съёмка removal; survey, surveying; shooting. **съёмный** detachable, removable. **съёмщик, съёмщица** tenant; surveyor.

съестной food; **~ое** *sb* food (supplies). **съесть** (-ем, -ешь, -ест, -едим; съел) *pf* (*impf also* **съедать**) go down; come down; move; **~ся** meet; assemble.

съехать (-еду) *pf* (*impf* **съезжать**) go down; come down; move; **~ся** meet; assemble.

съ|язвить (-влю) *pf*.

сыворотка whey; serum.

сыграть *pf of* **играть**; **~ся** play (well) together.

сын (*pl* сыновья, -ей *or* -ы, -ов) son. **сыновний** filial. **сынок** (-нка) little son; sonny.

сыпать (-плю) *impf* pour; pour forth; **~ся** fall; pour out; rain down; fray. **сыпной тиф** typhus. **сыпучий** friable; free-flowing; shifting. **сыпь** rash, eruption.

сыр (*loc* -ý; *pl* -ы) cheese.

сыреть (-ею) *impf* (*pf* **от~**) become damp.

сырец (-рца) raw product.

сыр|ой (сыр, -á, -о) damp; raw; uncooked; unboiled; unfinished; unripe. **сырость** dampness. **сырьё** raw material(s).

сыска́ть (сыщу́, сы́щешь) *pf* find.

сы́тный (-тен, -тна́, -о) filling. **сы́-тость** satiety. **сы́тый** (сыт, -а́, -о) full.

сыч (-а́) little owl.

сы́щик detective.

с|эконо́мить (-млю) *pf.*

сэр sir.

сюда́ *adv* here, hither.

сюже́т subject; plot; topic. **сюже́т-ный** subject; having a theme.

сюи́та suite.

сюрпри́з surprise.

сюрреали́зм surrealism. **сюрреали-сти́ческий** surrealist.

сюрту́к (-а́) frock-coat.

сяк *adv*: *see* **так**. **сям** *adv*: *see* **там**

Т

та *see* **тот**

таба́к (-а́) tobacco. **табаке́рка** snuff-box. **таба́чный** tobacco.

табле́тка tablet.

табли́ца table; ~ **умноже́ния** multi-plication table.

та́бор (gipsy) camp.

табу́н (-а́) herd.

табуре́т, табуре́тка stool.

тавро́ (*pl* -а, -а́м) brand.

тавтоло́гия tautology.

таджи́к, -и́чка Tadzhik. **Таджикиста́н** Tadzhikistan.

таёжный taiga.

таз (*loc* -у́; *pl* -ы́) basin; pelvis. **тазо-бе́дренный** hip. **та́зовый** pelvic.

таи́нственный mysterious; secret. **таи́ть** *impf* hide, harbour; ~**ся** hide; lurk.

Тайва́нь *m* Taiwan.

тайга́ taiga.

тайко́м *adv* secretly, surreptitiously; ~ **от**+*gen* behind the back of.

тайм half; period of play.

та́йна secret; mystery. **тайни́к** (-а́) hiding-place; *pl* recesses. **та́йный** se-cret; privy.

тайфу́н typhoon.

так *adv* so; like this; as it should be; just like that; **и** ~ even so; as it is; **и** ~ **да́лее** and so on; ~ **и сяк** this way and that; **не** ~ wrong; ~ **же** in the same way; ~ **же... как** as ... as;

~ **и есть** I thought so!; ~ **ему́ и на́до** serves him right; ~ **и́ли ина́че** one way or another; ~ **себе́** so-so. **так** *conj* then; so; ~ **как** as, since.

такела́ж rigging.

та́кже *adv* also, too, as well.

тако́в *m* (-а́ *f*, -о́ *neut*, -ы́ *pl*) *pron* such.

так|о́й *pron* such (а); **в** ~**о́м слу́чае** in that case; **кто он** ~**о́й?** who is he?; ~**о́й же** the same; ~**и́м о́бразом** in this way; **что э́то** ~**о́е?** what is this? **тако́й-то** *pron* so-and-so; such-and-such.

та́кса fixed *or* statutory price; tariff.

таксёр taxi-driver. **такси́** *neut indecl* taxi. **такси́ст** taxi-driver. **таксо-па́рк** taxi depot.

такт time; bar; beat; tact.

та́к-таки after all, really.

та́ктика tactics. **такти́ческий** tac-tical.

такти́чность tact. **такти́чный** tactful.

та́ктов|ый time, timing; ~**ая черта́** bar-line.

тала́нт talent. **тала́нтливый** tal-ented.

талисма́н talisman.

та́лия waist.

тало́н, тало́нчик coupon.

та́лый thawed, melted.

тальк talc; talcum powder.

там *adv* there; ~ **и сям** here and there; ~ **же** in the same place; ibid.

тамада́ *m* toast-master.

та́мбур¹ tambour; lobby; platform. **та́мбур**² chain-stitch.

тамо́женник customs official. **тамо́-женный** customs. **тамо́жня** custom-house.

та́мошний of that place, local.

тампо́н tampon.

та́нгенс tangent.

та́нго *neut indecl* tango.

та́нец (-нца) dance; dancing.

тани́н tannin.

танк tank. **та́нкер** tanker. **танки́ст** member of a tank crew. **та́нковый** tank, armoured.

танцева́льный dancing; ~ **ве́чер** dance. **танцева́ть** (-цу́ю) *impf* dance. **танцо́вщик, танцо́вщица** (ballet) dancer. **танцо́р, танцо́рка** dancer.

та́пка, та́почка slipper.

та́ра packing; tare.

тарака́н cockroach.

тара́н battering-ram.

тара́нтул tarantula.

таре́лка plate; cymbal; satellite dish.

тари́ф tariff.

таска́ть *impf* drag, lug; carry; pull; take; pull out; swipe; wear; **~ся** drag; hang about.

тасова́ть *impf* (*pf* **c~**) shuffle.

ТАСС *abbr* (*of* **Телегра́фное аге́нтство Сове́тского Сою́за**) Tass (Telegraph Agency of the Soviet Union).

тата́рин, тата́рка Tatar.

татуиро́вка tattooing, tattoo.

тафта́ taffeta.

тахта́ ottoman.

та́чка wheelbarrow.

тащи́ть (-щу́, -щишь) *impf* (*pf* **вы́~, с~**) pull; drag, lug; carry; take; pull out; swipe; **~ся** drag o.s. along; drag.

та́ять (та́ю) *impf* (*pf* **рас~**) melt; thaw; dwindle.

тварь creature(s); wretch.

тверде́ть (-е́ет) *impf* (*pf* **за~**) harden, become hard. **тверди́ть** (-ржу́) *impf* (*pf* **вы́~**) repeat, say again and again; memorize. **твёрдо** *adv* hard; firmly, firm. **твердоло́бый** thick-skulled; diehard. **твёрдый** hard; firm; solid; steadfast; **~знак** hard sign, ъ; **~ое те́ло** solid. **тверды́ня** stronghold.

твой (-его́) *m*, **твоя́** (-е́й) *f*, **твоё** (-его́) *neut*, **твои́** (-и́х) *pl* your, yours.

творе́ние creation, work; creature. **творе́ц** (-рца́) creator. **твори́тельный** instrumental. **твори́ть** *impf* (*pf* **со~**) create; do; make; **~ся** happen.

творо́г (-а́) curds; cottage cheese. **тво́рческий** creative. **тво́рчество** creation; creative work; works.

те *see* **тот**

т.е. *abbr* (*of* **то есть**) that is, i.e.

теа́тр theatre. **театра́льный** theatre; theatrical.

тебя́ *etc.*: *see* **ты**

те́зис thesis.

тёзка *m & f* namesake.

тёк *see* **течь**

текст text; libretto, lyrics.

тексти́ль *m* textiles. **тексти́льный** textile.

факту́ра texture.

теку́чий fluid; unstable. **теку́щий** current; routine.

теле- *in comb* tele-; television. **телеателье́** *neut indecl* television maintenance workshop. **~ви́дение** television. **~визио́нный** television. **~ви́зор** television (set). **~гра́мма** telegram. **~гра́ф** telegraph (office). **~графи́ровать** *impf & pf* telegraph. **~гра́фный** telegraph(ic). **~зри́тель** *m* (television) viewer. **~объекти́в** telephoto lens. **~пати́ческий** telepathic. **~па́тия** telepathy. **~ско́п** telescope. **~ста́нция** television station. **~сту́дия** television studio. **~фо́н** telephone; (telephone) number; **(по)звони́ть по ~фо́ну** +*dat* ring up. **~фон-автома́т** public telephone, call-box. **~фони́ст, -и́стка** (telephone) operator. **~фо́нный** (telephone); **~фо́нная кни́га** telephone directory; **~фо́нная ста́нция** telephone exchange; **~фо́нная тру́бка** telephone receiver. **~фон-отве́тчик** answering machine. **~фотогра́фия** telephotography. **~це́нтр** television centre.

теле́га cart, wagon. **теле́жка** small cart; trolley.

телёнок (-нка; *pl* -я́та, -я́т) calf.

теле́сн|ый bodily; corporal; **~ого цве́та** flesh-coloured.

Теле́ц (-льца́) Taurus.

тели́ться *impf* (*pf* **о~**) calve. **тёлка** heifer.

те́ло (*pl* -а́) body. **телогре́йка** padded jacket. **телосложе́ние** build. **телохрани́тель** *m* bodyguard.

теля́та *etc.*: *see* **телёнок. теля́тина** veal. **теля́чий** calf; veal.

тем *conj* (so much) the; **~ лу́чше** so much the better; **~ не ме́нее** nevertheless.

тем *see* **тот, тьма**

те́ма subject; theme. **тема́тика** subject-matter; themes. **темати́ческий** subject; thematic.

тембр timbre.

темне́ть (-е́ет) *impf* (*pf* **по~, с~**) become dark. **темни́ца** dungeon. **темно́** *predic* it is dark. **темноко́жий** dark-skinned, swarthy. **тёмно-си́ний** dark blue. **темнота́** darkness. **тёмный** dark.

темп tempo; rate.

темпера́мент temperament. **темпера́ментный** temperamental.

температу́ра temperature.

те́мя (-мени) *neut* crown, top of the head.

тенде́нция tendency; bias.

теневой, тени́стый shady.

те́ннис tennis. **теннисист, -и́стка** tennis-player. **те́нниси|ый** tennis; ~ая площа́дка tennis-court.

те́нор (*pl* -á) tenor.

тент awning.

тень (*loc* -и́; *pl* -и, -ей) shade; shadow; phantom; ghost; particle, vestige, atom; suspicion; те́ни для век *pl* eyeshadow.

тео́лог theologian. **теологи́ческий** theological. **теоло́гия** theology.

теоре́ма theorem. **теоре́тик** theoretician. **теорети́ческий** theoretical. **тео́рия** theory.

тепе́решн|ий present. **тепе́рь** *adv* now; today.

тепле́ть (-éет) *impf* (*pf* по~) get warm. **те́плиться** (-ится) *impf* flicker; glimmer. **тепли́ца** greenhouse, conservatory. **тепли́чный** hothouse. **тепло́** heat; warmth. **тепло́** *adv* warmly; *predic* it is warm. **тепло-** *in comb* heat; thermal; thermo-. **теплово́з** diesel locomotive. ~ёмкость thermal capacity. ~кро́вный warm-blooded. ~обме́н heat exchange. ~прово́дный heat-conducting. ~сто́йкий heat-resistant. ~хо́д motor ship. ~центра́ль heat and power station. **теплово́й** heat; thermal. **теплота́** heat; warmth. **тёплый** (-пел, -пла́, тёпло́) warm.

терапе́вт therapeutist. **терапи́я** therapy.

тереби́ть (-блю́) *impf* pull (at); pester.

тере́ть (тру, трёшь; тёр) *impf* rub; grate; ~ся rub o.s.; ~ся о́коло+*gen* hang about, hang around; ~ся среди́ +*gen* mix with.

терза́ть *impf* tear to pieces; torment; ~ся +*instr* suffer; be a prey to.

тёрка grater.

те́рмин term. **терминоло́гия** terminology.

терми́ческий thermic, thermal. **термо́метр** thermometer. **те́рмос** thermos (flask). **термоста́т** thermostat. **термоя́дерный** thermonuclear.

терно́вник sloe, blackthorn. **терни́стый** thorny.

терпели́вый patient. **терпе́ние** patience. **терпе́ть** (-плю́, -пишь) *impf* (*pf* по~) suffer; bear, endure. **терпе́ться** (-пится) *impf impers+dat*: ему́ не те́рпится +*inf* he is impatient to. **терпи́мость** tolerance. **терпи́мый** tolerant; tolerable.

те́рпкий (-пок, -пка́, -о) astringent; tart.

терра́са terrace.

территориа́льный territorial. **террито́рия** territory.

терро́р terror. **терроризи́ровать** *impf & pf* terrorize. **террори́ст** terrorist.

тёртый grated; experienced.

терье́р terrier.

теря́ть *impf* (*pf* по~, у~) lose; shed; ~ся get lost; disappear; fail, decline; become flustered.

тёс boards, planks. **теса́ть** (тешу́, те́шешь) *impf* cut, hew.

тесёмка ribbon, braid.

тесни́ть *impf* (*pf* по~, с~) crowd; squeeze, constrict; be too tight; ~ся press through; move up; crowd, jostle. **теснота́** crowded state; crush. **те́сн|ый** crowded; (too) tight; close; compact; ~о it is crowded.

тесо́вый board, plank.

тест test.

те́сто dough; pastry.

тесть *m* father-in-law.

тесьма́ ribbon, braid.

те́терев (*pl* -á) black grouse. **тетёрка** grey hen.

тётка aunt.

тетра́дка, тетра́дь exercise book.

тётя (*gen pl* -ей) aunt.

тех- *abbr in comb* (*of* техни́ческий) technical.

те́хник technician. **те́хника** technical equipment; technology; technique. **те́хникум** technical college. **техни́ческий** technical; ~ие усло́вия specifications. **техно́лог** technologist. **технологи́ческий** technological. **техноло́гия** technology. **техперсона́л** technical personnel.

тече́ние flow; course; current; stream; trend.

течь[1] (-чёт; тёк, -ла́) *impf* flow; stream; leak. **течь**[2] leak.

те́шить (-шу) *impf* (*pf* по~) amuse; gratify; ~ся (+*instr*) amuse o.s. (with).

тешу́ *etc.*: *see* теса́ть

тёща mother-in-law.

тигр tiger. тигри́ца tigress.

тик[1] tic.

тик[2] teak.

ти́на slime, mud.

тип type. типи́чный typical. типово́й standard; model. типогра́фия printing-house, press. типогра́фский typographical.

тир shooting-range, -gallery. тира́ж (-á) draw; circulation; edition.

тира́н tyrant. тира́нить *impf* tyrannize. тирани́ческий tyrannical. тирани́я tyranny.

тире́ *neut indecl* dash.

ти́скать *impf*, ти́снуть (-ну) *pf* press, squeeze. тиски́ (-о́в) *pl* vice; в тиска́х +*gen* in the grip of. тисне́ние stamping; imprint; design. тиснёный stamped.

тита́н[1] titanian.

тита́н[2] boiler.

тита́н[3] titan.

титр title, sub-title.

ти́тул title; title-page. ти́тульный title.

тиф (*loc* -у́) typhus.

ти́хий (тих, -á, -о) quiet; silent; calm; slow. тихоокеа́нский Pacific. ти́ше *comp* of ти́хий, ти́хо; ти́ше! quiet! тишина́ quiet, silence.

т. к. *abbr* (*of* так как) as, since.

тка́ный woven. ткань fabric, cloth; tissue. ткать (тку, ткёшь; -ал, -ала́, -о) *impf* (*pf* со~) weave. тка́цкий weaving; ~ стано́к loom. ткач, ткачи́ха weaver.

ткну́ть(ся (-у́(сь, -ёшь(ся) *pf of* ты́-кать(ся

тле́ние decay; smouldering. тлеть (-éет) *impf* rot, decay; smoulder; ~ся smoulder.

тля aphis.

тмин caraway(-seeds).

то *pron* that; а не то́ or else, otherwise; (да) и то́ and even then, and that; то́ есть that is (to say); то и де́ло every now and then. то *conj* then; не то..., не то either ... or; half ..., half; то..., то now ..., now; то ли..., то ли whether ... or.

-то *partl* just, exactly; в то́м-то и де́ло that's just it.

тобо́й *see* ты

това́р goods; commodity.

това́рищ comrade; friend; colleague. това́рищеский comradely; friendly. това́рищество comradeship; company; association.

това́рный goods; commodity.

товаро- *in comb* commodity; goods. ~обме́н barter. ~оборо́т (sales) turnover. ~отправи́тель *m* consignor. ~получа́тель *m* consignee.

тогда́ *adv* then; ~ как whereas. тогда́шний of that time.

того́ *see* тот

тожде́ственный identical. то́ждество identity.

то́же *adv* also, too.

ток (*pl* -и) current.

тока́рный turning; ~ стано́к lathe. то́карь (*pl* -я, -е́й *or* -и, -ей) *m* turner, lathe operator.

токси́ческий toxic.

толк sense; use; без ~у senselessly; знать ~ в+*prep* know well; сбить с ~у confuse; с ~ом intelligently.

толка́ть *impf* (*pf* толкну́ть) push, shove; jog; ~ся jostle.

то́лки (-ов) *pl* rumours, gossip.

толкну́ть(ся (-ну́(сь, -нёшь(ся) *pf of* толка́ть(ся

толкова́ние interpretation; *pl* commentary. толкова́ть *impf* interpret; explain; talk. толко́вый intelligent; clear; ~ слова́рь defining dictionary. то́лком *adv* plainly; seriously.

толкотня́ crush, squash.

толку́ *etc.*: *see* толо́чь

толку́чка crush, squash; second-hand market.

толокно́ oatmeal.

толо́чь (-лку́, -лчёшь; -лóк, -лкла́) *impf* (*pf* ис~, рас~) pound, crush.

толпа́ (*pl* -ы) crowd. толпи́ться *impf* crowd; throng.

толсте́ть (-е́ю) *impf* (*pf* по~) grow fat; put on weight. толстоко́жий thick-skinned; pachydermatous. то́лстый (-á, -о) fat; thick. толстя́к (-á) fat man *or* boy.

толчёный crushed; ground. толчёт *etc.*: *see* толо́чь

толчея́ crush, squash.

толчо́к (-чка́) push, shove; (*sport*) put; jolt; shock, tremor.

то́лща thickness; thick. **то́лще** *comp of* **то́лстый**. **толщина́** thickness; fatness.

толь *m* roofing felt.

то́лько *adv* only, merely; ~ что (only) just; *conj* only, but; (как) ~, (лишь) ~ as soon as; ~ бы if only.

том (*pl* -а́) volume. **то́мик** small volume.

тома́т tomato. **тома́тный** tomato.

томи́тельный tedious, wearing; agonizing. **томи́ть** (-млю́) *impf* (*pf* ис~) tire; torment; ~ся languish; be tormented. **томле́ние** languor. **то́мный** (-мен, -мна́, -о) languid, languorous.

тон (*pl* -а́ *or* -ы, -о́в) tone; note; shade; form. **тона́льность** key.

то́ненький thin; slim. **то́нкий** (-нок, -нка́, -о) thin; slim; fine; refined; subtle; keen. **то́нкость** thinness; slimness; fineness; subtlety.

то́нна ton.

тонне́ль *see* **тунне́ль**

то́нус tone.

тону́ть (-ну́, -нешь) *impf* (*pf* по~, у~) sink; drown.

то́ньше *comp of* **то́нкий**

то́пать *impf* (*pf* то́пнуть) stamp.

топи́ть[1] (-плю́, -пишь) *impf* (*pf* по~, у~) sink; drown; ruin; ~ся drown o.s.

топи́ть[2] (-плю́ -пишь) *impf* stoke; heat; melt (down); ~ся burn; melt. **то́пка** stoking; heating; melting (down); furnace.

то́пкий boggy, marshy.

то́пливный fuel. **то́пливо** fuel.

то́пнуть (-ну) *pf of* **то́пать**

топографи́ческий topographical. **топогра́фия** topography.

то́поль (*pl* -я́ *or* -и) *m* poplar.

топо́р (-а́) axe. **топо́рик** hatchet. **топори́ще** axe-handle. **топо́рный** axe; clumsy, crude.

то́пот tramp; clatter. **топта́ть** (-пчу́, -пчешь) *impf* (*pf* по~) trample (down); ~ся stamp; ~ся на ме́сте mark time.

топча́н (-а́) trestle-bed.

топь bog, marsh.

торг (*loc* -у́; *pl* -и́) trading; bargaining; *pl* auction. **торгова́ть** *impf* (*pf* с~) trade; ~ся bargain, haggle.

торго́вец (-вца) merchant; tradesman. **торго́вка** market-woman; stallholder. **торго́вля** trade. **торго́вый** trade, commercial; merchant. **торгпре́д** *abbr* trade representative.

торе́ц (-рца́) butt-end; wooden paving-block.

торже́ственный solemn; ceremonial. **торжество́** celebration; triumph. **торжествова́ть** *impf* celebrate; triumph.

торможе́ние braking. **то́рмоз** (*pl* -а́ *or* -ы) brake. **тормози́ть** (-ожу́) *impf* (*pf* за~) brake; hamper.

тормоши́ть (-шу́) *impf* pester; bother.

торопи́ть (-плю́, -пишь) *impf* (*pf* по~) hurry; hasten; ~ся hurry. **торопли́вый** hasty.

торпе́да torpedo.

торс torso.

торт cake.

торф peat. **торфяно́й** peat.

торча́ть (-чу́) *impf* stick out; protrude; hang about.

торше́р standard lamp.

тоска́ melancholy; boredom; nostalgia; ~ по+*dat* longing for. **тоскли́вый** melancholy; depressed; dreary. **тоскова́ть** *impf* be melancholy, depressed; long; ~ по+*dat* miss.

тост toast.

тот *m* (та *f*, то *neut*, те *pl*) *pron* that; the former; the other; the one; the same; the right; и ~ и друго́й both; к тому́ же moreover; не ~ the wrong; ни ~ ни друго́й neither; тот, кто the one who, the person who. **то́тчас** *adv* immediately.

тоталитари́зм totalitarianism. **тоталита́рный** totalitarian.

тота́льный total.

точи́лка sharpener; pencil-sharpener. **точи́ло** whetstone, grindstone. **точи́льный** grinding, sharpening; ~ ка́мень whetstone, grindstone. **точи́льщик** (knife-)grinder. **точи́ть** (-чу́, -чишь) *impf* (*pf* вы~, на~) sharpen; hone; turn; eat away; gnaw at.

то́чка spot; dot; full stop; point; ~ зре́ния point of view; ~ с запято́й semicolon. **то́чно**[1] *adv* exactly, precisely; punctually. **то́чно**[2] *conj* as though, as if. **то́чность** punctuality; precision; accuracy; **в то́чности** exactly, precisely. **то́чный** (-чен, -чна́, -о) exact, precise; accurate; punctual. **то́чь-в-то́чь** *adv* exactly; word for word.

тошни́ть *impf impers*: **меня́ тошни́т** I feel sick. **тошнота́** nausea. **тошнотво́рный** sickening, nauseating.

то́щий (тощ, -á, -е) gaunt, emaciated; skinny; empty; poor.

трава́ (*pl* -ы) grass; herb. **трави́нка** blade of grass.

трави́ть (-влю́, -вишь) *impf* (*pf* вы́~, за~) poison; exterminate, destroy; etch; hunt; torment; badger. **травле́ние** extermination; etching. **тра́вля** hunting; persecution; badgering.

тра́вма trauma, injury.

травоя́дный herbivorous. **травяни́стый, травяно́й** grass; herbaceous; grassy.

траге́дия tragedy. **тра́гик** tragedian. **траги́ческий, траги́чный** tragic.

традицио́нный traditional. **тради́ция** tradition.

траекто́рия trajectory.

тракта́т treatise; treaty.

тракти́р inn, tavern.

трактова́ть *impf* interpret; treat, discuss. **тракто́вка** treatment; interpretation.

тра́ктор tractor. **тракторист** tractor driver.

трал trawl. **тра́лить** *impf* (*pf* про~) trawl; sweep. **тра́льщик** trawler; mine-sweeper.

трамбова́ть *impf* (*pf* у~) ram, tamp. **трамва́й** tram. **трамва́йный** tram.

трампли́н spring-board; ski-jump.

транзи́стор transistor; transistor radio.

транзи́тный transit.

транс trance.

трансатланти́ческий transatlantic.

трансли́ровать *impf* & *pf* broadcast, transmit. **трансляцио́нный** transmission; broadcasting. **трансля́ция** broadcast, transmission.

тра́нспорт transport; consignment. **транспортёр** conveyor. **транспорти́р** protractor. **транспорти́ровать** *impf* & *pf* transport. **тра́нспортный** transport.

трансформа́тор transformer.

транше́я trench.

трап ladder.

тра́пеза meal.

трапе́ция trapezium; trapeze.

тра́сса line, course, direction; route, road.

тра́та expenditure; waste. **тра́тить** (-а́чу) *impf* (*pf* ис~, по~) spend, expend; waste.

тра́улер trawler.

тра́ур mourning. **тра́урный** mourning; funeral; mournful.

трафаре́т stencil; stereotype; cliché. **трафаре́тный** stencilled; conventional, stereotyped.

тра́чу *etc.*: *see* **тра́тить**

тре́бование demand; request; requirement; requisition, order; *pl* needs. **тре́бовательный** demanding. **тре́бовать** *impf* (*pf* по~) summon; +*gen* demand, require; need; ~ся be needed, be required.

трево́га alarm; anxiety. **трево́жить** (-жу) *impf* (*pf* вс~, по~) alarm; disturb; worry; ~ся worry, be anxious; trouble o.s. **трево́жный** worried, anxious; alarming; alarm.

тре́звенник teetotaller. **трезве́ть** (-е́ю) *impf* (*pf* о~) sober up.

трезво́н peal (*of bells*); rumours; row.

тре́звость sobriety. **тре́звый** (-зв, -á, -о) sober; teetotal.

тре́йлер trailer.

трель trill; warble.

тре́нер trainer, coach.

тре́ние friction.

трениро́вать *impf* (*pf* на~) train, coach; ~ся be in training. **трениро́вка** training, coaching. **трениро́вочный** training.

трепа́ть (-плю́, -плешь) *impf* (*pf* ис~, по~, рас~) blow about; dishevel; wear out; pat; ~ся fray; wear out; flutter. **тре́пет** trembling; trepidation. **трепета́ть** (-ещу́, -е́щешь) *impf* tremble; flicker; palpitate. **тре́петный** trembling; flickering; palpitating; timid.

треск crack; crackle; fuss.

треска́ cod.

тре́скаться[1] *impf* (*pf* по~) crack; chap.

тре́скаться[2] *impf of* **тре́снуться**

тре́снуть (-нет) *pf* snap, crackle;

crack; chap; bang; ~**ся** (*impf* **тре́-
скаться**) +*instr* bang.

трест trust.

тре́т|ий (-ья, -ье) third; ~**ье** *sb* sweet
(course).

трети́ровать *impf* slight.

треть (*gen pl* -е́й) third. **тре́тье** *etc.*:
see **тре́тий**. **треуго́льник** triangle.
треуго́льный triangular.

тре́фы (треф) *pl* clubs.

трёх- *in comb* three-, tri-. **трёх-
го́дичный** three-year. ~**голо́сный**
three-part. ~**гра́нный** three-edged;
trihedral. ~**колёсный** three-wheeled.
~**ле́тний** three-year; three-year old.
~**ме́рный** three-dimensional. ~**ме́-
сячный** three-month; quarterly;
three-month-old. ~**по́лье** three-field
system. ~**со́тый** three-hundredth.
~**сторо́нний** three-sided; trilateral;
tripartite. ~**эта́жный** three-storeyed.

треща́ть (-щу́) *impf* crack; crackle;
creak; chirr; crack up; chatter.
тре́щина crack, split; fissure; chap.

три (трёх, -ём, -емя́, -ёх) three.

трибу́на platform, rostrum; stand.
трибуна́л tribunal.

тригономе́трия trigonometry.

тридцатиле́тний thirty-year; thirty-
year old. **тридца́тый** thirtieth. **три́д-
цать** (-и, *instr* -ью) thirty. **три́жды**
adv three times; thrice.

трико́ *neut indecl* tricot; tights; knickers. **трикота́ж** knitted fabric; knitwear. **трикота́жный** jersey, tricot;
knitted.

трина́дцатый thirteenth. **трина́д-
цать** thirteen. **трио́ль** triplet.

три́ппер gonorrhoea.

три́ста (трёхсо́т, -ёмста́м, -емяста́ми,
-ёхста́х) three hundred.

трито́н *zool* triton.

триу́мф triumph.

тро́гательный touching, moving.
тро́гать(ся *impf of* **тро́нуть(ся**

тро́е (-и́х) *pl* three. **троебо́рье**
triathlon. **троекра́тный** thrice-re-
peated. **Тро́ица** Trinity; **тро́ица**
trio. **Тро́ицын день** Whit Sunday.
тро́йка three; figure 3; troika; No.
3; three-piece suit. **тройно́й** triple,
treble; three-ply. **тро́йственный**
triple; tripartite.

тролле́йбус trolley-bus.

тромб blood clot.

тромбо́н trombone.

трон throne.

тро́нуть (-ну) *pf* (*impf* **тро́гать**)
touch; disturb; affect; ~**ся** start, set
out; be touched; be affected.

тропа́ path.

тро́пик tropic.

тропи́нка path.

тропи́ческий tropical.

трос rope, cable.

тростни́к (-á) reed, rush. **тро́сточ-
ка**, **трость** (*gen pl* ~е́й) cane, walking-stick.

тротуа́р pavement.

трофе́й trophy; *pl* spoils (*of war*),
booty.

трою́родн|ый: ~**ый брат**, ~**ая
сестра́** second cousin.

тру *etc.*: *see* **тере́ть**

труба́ (*pl* -ы) pipe; chimney; funnel;
trumpet; tube. **труба́ч** (-á) trumpeter; trumpet-player. **труби́ть** (-блю́)
impf (*pf* **про**~) blow, sound; blare.
тру́бка tube; pipe; (*telephone*) receiver. **трубопрово́д** pipe-line; piping; manifold. **трубочи́ст** chimney-
sweep. **тру́бочный** pipe. **тру́бча-
тый** tubular.

труд (-á) labour; work; effort; **с** ~**о́м**
with difficulty. **труди́ться** (-ужу́сь,
-у́дишься) *impf* toil, labour; work;
trouble. **тру́дно** *predic* it is difficult.
тру́дность difficulty. **тру́дный** (-ден,
-дна́, -о) difficult; hard.

трудо- *in comb* labour, work. **тру-
додéнь** (-дня́) *m* work-day (*unit*).
~**ёмкий** labour-intensive. ~**люби́-
вый** industrious. ~**люби́е** industry.
~**спосо́бность** ability to work.
~**спосо́бный** able-bodied; capable
of working.

трудово́й work; working; earned;
hard-earned. **трудя́щ|ийся** working;
~**иеся** *sb pl* the workers. **тру́-
женик**, **тру́женица** toiler.

труп corpse; carcass.

тру́ппа troupe, company.

трус coward.

тру́сики (-ов) *pl* shorts; trunks; pants.

труси́ть¹ (-ушу́) *impf* trot, jog along.

тру́сить² (-ушу) *impf* (*pf* **с**~) be a
coward; lose one's nerve; be afraid.

труси́ха coward. **трусли́вый** cowardly. **тру́сость** cowardice.

трусы́ (-о́в) *pl* shorts; trunks; pants.

труха́ dust; trash.

тру́шу etc.: see **труси́ть**[1], **тру́сить**[2]

трущо́ба slum; godforsaken hole.

трюк stunt; trick.

трюм hold.

трюмо́ neut indecl pier-glass.

трю́фель (gen pl **-ле́й**) m truffle.

тря́пка rag; spineless creature; pl clothes. **тряпьё** rags; clothes.

тряси́на quagmire. **тря́ска** shaking, jolting. **трясти́** (**-су́, -сёшь; -яс, -ла́**) impf, **тряхну́ть** (**-ну́, -нёшь**) pf (pf also **вы́~**) shake; shake out; jolt; **~сь** shake; tremble, shiver; jolt.

тсс int sh! hush!

туале́т dress; toilet. **туале́тный** toilet.

туберкулёз tuberculosis.

ту́го adv tight(ly), taut; with difficulty. **туго́й** (**туг, -а́, -о**) tight; taut; tightly filled; difficult.

туда́ adv there, thither; that way; to the right place; **ни ~ ни сюда́** neither one way nor the other; **~ и обра́тно** there and back.

ту́же comp of **ту́го**, **туго́й**

тужу́рка (double-breasted) jacket.

туз (**-а́**, acc **-а́**) ace; bigwig.

тузе́мец (**-мца**), **-мка** native.

ту́ловище trunk; torso.

тулу́п sheepskin coat.

тума́н fog; mist; haze. **тума́нить** impf (pf **за~**) dim, cloud, obscure; **~ся** grow misty; be befogged. **тума́нность** fog, mist; nebula; obscurity. **тума́нный** foggy; misty; hazy; obscure, vague.

ту́мба post; bollard; pedestal. **ту́мбочка** bedside table.

ту́ндра tundra.

тунея́дец (**-дца**) sponger.

туни́ка tunic.

тунне́ль m, **тонне́ль** m tunnel.

тупе́ть (**-е́ю**) impf (pf **о~**) become blunt; grow dull. **тупи́к** (**-а́**) cul-de-sac, dead end; impasse; **поста́вить в ~** stump, nonplus. **тупи́ться** (**-пится**) impf (pf **за~**, **ис~**) become blunt. **тупи́ца** m & f blockhead, dimwit. **тупо́й** (**туп, -а́, -о**) blunt; obtuse; dull; vacant, stupid. **ту́пость** bluntness; vacancy; dullness, slowness.

тур turn; round.

тура́ rook, castle.

турба́за holiday village; campsite.

турби́на turbine.

туре́цкий Turkish; **~ бараба́н** bass drum.

тури́зм tourism. **тури́ст, -и́стка** tourist. **тури́ст(иче)ский** tourist.

туркме́н (gen pl **-ме́н**), **~ка** Turkmen. **Туркмениста́н** Turkmenistan.

турне́ neut indecl tour.

турне́пс swede.

турни́р tournament.

ту́рок (**-рка**) Turk. **турча́нка** Turkish woman. **Ту́рция** Turkey.

ту́склый dim, dull; lacklustre. **тускне́ть** (**-е́ет**) impf (pf **по~**) grow dim.

тут adv here; now; **~ же** there and then.

ту́фля shoe.

ту́хлый (**-хл, -а́, -о**) rotten, bad. **ту́хнуть**[1] (**-нет; тух**) go bad.

ту́хнуть[2] (**-нет; тух**) impf (pf **по~**) go out.

ту́ча cloud; storm-cloud.

ту́чный (**-чен, -чна́, -чно**) fat; rich, fertile.

туш flourish.

ту́ша carcass.

тушева́ть (**-шу́ю**) impf (pf **за~**) shade.

тушёный stewed. **туши́ть**[1] (**-шу́, -шишь**) impf (pf **с~**) stew.

туши́ть[2] (**-шу́, -шишь**) impf (pf **за~**, **по~**) extinguish.

тушу́ю etc.: see **тушева́ть**. **тушь** Indian ink; **~ (для ресни́ц)** mascara.

тща́тельность care. **тща́тельный** careful; painstaking.

тщеду́шный feeble, frail.

тщесла́вие vanity, vainglory. **тщесла́вный** vain. **тщета́** vanity. **тще́тный** vain, futile.

ты (**тебя́, тебе́, тобо́й, тебе́**) you; thou; **быть на ты** c+instr be on intimate terms with.

ты́кать (**ты́чу**) impf (pf **ткнуть**) poke; prod; stick.

ты́ква pumpkin; gourd.

тыл (loc **-у́**; pl **-ы́**) back; rear. **ты́льный** back; rear.

тын paling; palisade.

ты́сяча (instr **-ей** or **-ью**) thousand. **тысячеле́тие** millennium; thousandth anniversary. **ты́сячный** thousandth; of (many) thousands.

тычи́нка stamen.

тьма[1] dark, darkness.

тьма[2] host, multitude.

тюбетейка skull-cap.

тюбик tube.

тюк (-á) bale, package.

тюлень *m* seal.

тюльпан tulip.

тюремный prison. **тюремщик** gaoler. **тюрьма** (*pl* -ы, -рем) prison, gaol.

тюфяк (-á) mattress.

тяга traction; thrust; draught; attraction; craving. **тягаться** *impf* vie, contend. **тягач** (-á) tractor.

тягостный burdensome; painful. **тягость** burden. **тяготение** gravity, gravitation; bent, inclination. **тяготеть** (-ею) *impf* gravitate; be attracted; ~ **над** hang over. **тяготить** (-ощу) *impf* be a burden on; oppress.

тягучий malleable, ductile; viscous; slow.

тяжба lawsuit; competition.

тяжело *adv* heavily; seriously. **тяжело** *predic* it is hard; it is painful. **тяжелоатлет** weight-lifter. **тяжеловес** heavyweight. **тяжеловесный** heavy; ponderous. **тяжёлый** (- ёл, -á) heavy; hard; serious; painful. **тяжесть** gravity; weight; heaviness; severity. **тяжкий** heavy; severe; grave.

тянуть (-ну, -нешь) *impf* (*pf* по~) pull; draw; drag; drag out; weigh; *impers* attract; be tight; ~ся stretch; extend; stretch out; stretch o.s.; drag on; crawl; drift; move along one after another; last out; reach.

тянучка toffee.

У

у *prep+gen* by; at; with; from, of; belonging to; **у меня (есть)** I have; **у нас** at our place; in our country.

убавить (-влю) *pf*, **убавлять** *impf* reduce, diminish.

убаюкать *pf*, **убаюкивать** *impf* lull (to sleep).

убегать *impf of* **убежать**

убедительный convincing; earnest. **убедить** (-ишь) *pf* (*impf* **убеждать**) convince, persuade; ~ся be convinced; make certain.

убежать (-егу) *pf* (*impf* **убегать**) run away; escape; boil over.

убеждать(ся *impf of* **убедить(ся.**

убеждение persuasion; conviction, belief. **убеждённость** conviction. **убеждённый** (-ён, -á) convinced; staunch.

убежище refuge, asylum; shelter.

уберегать *impf*, **уберечь** (-регу, -режёшь; -рёг, -гла) *pf* protect, preserve; ~ся от+*gen* protect o.s. against.

уберу *etc.: see* **убрать**

убивать(ся *impf of* **убить(ся. убийственный** deadly; murderous; killing. **убийство** murder. **убийца** *m* & *f* murderer.

убирать(ся *impf of* **убрать(ся; убирайся!** clear off!

убитый killed; crushed; *sb* dead man. **убить** (убью, -бьёшь) *pf* (*impf* **убивать**) kill; murder; ~ся hurt o.s.

убогий wretched. **убожество** poverty; squalor.

убой slaughter.

убор dress, attire.

уборка harvesting; clearing up. **уборная** *sb* lavatory; dressing-room. **уборочн|ый** harvesting; ~**ая машина** harvester. **уборщик, уборщица** cleaner. **убранство** furniture. **убрать** (уберу, -рёшь; -áл, -á, -о) *pf* (*impf* **убирать**) remove; take away; put away; harvest; clear up; decorate; ~ **постель** make a bed; ~ **со стола** clear the table; ~ся tidy up, clean up; clear off.

убывать *impf*, **убыть** (убуду; убыл, -á, -о) *pf* diminish; subside; wane; leave. **убыль** diminution; casualties. **убыток** (-тка) loss; *pl* damages. **убыточный** unprofitable.

убью *etc.: see* **убить**

уважаемый respected; dear. **уважать** *impf* respect. **уважение** respect; **с ~м** yours sincerely. **уважительный** valid; respectful.

уведомить (-млю) *pf*, **уведомлять** *impf* inform. **уведомление** notification.

уведу *etc.: see* **увести**

увезти (-зу, -зёшь; увёз, -лá) *pf* (*impf* **увозить**) take (away); steal; abduct.

увековечивать *impf*, **увековечить** (-чу) *pf* immortalize; perpetuate.

увёл *etc.: see* **увести**

увеличение increase; magnification; enlargement. **увеличивать** *impf*,

увели́чить (-чу) *pf* increase; magnify; enlarge; **~ся** increase, grow. **увеличи́тель** *m* enlarger. **увеличи́тельн|ый** magnifying; enlarging; **~ое стекло́** magnifying glass.

у|венча́ть *pf*, **увенчивать** *impf* crown; **~ся** be crowned.

уве́ренность confidence; certainty. **уве́ренный** confident; sure; certain. **уве́рить** *pf* (*impf* **уверя́ть**) assure; convince; **~ся** satisfy o.s.; be convinced.

уверну́ться (-ну́сь, -нёшься) *pf*, **увёртываться** *impf* от+*gen* evade. **уве́ртка** dodge, evasion; subterfuge; *pl* wiles. **увёртливый** evasive, shifty. **увертю́ра** overture.

уверя́ть(ся *impf of* **уве́рить(ся**

увеселе́ние amusement, entertainment. **увеселительный** entertainment; pleasure. **увеселя́ть** *impf* amuse, entertain.

уве́систый weighty.

увести́ (-еду́, -едёшь; -ёл, -á) *pf* (*impf* **уводи́ть**) take (away); walk off with. **уве́чить** (-чу) *impf* maim, cripple. **уве́чный** maimed, crippled; *sb* cripple. **уве́чье** maiming; injury.

уве́шать *pf*, **уве́шивать** *impf* hang (+*instr* with).

увеща́ть *impf*, **увещева́ть** *impf* exhort, admonish.

у|ви́дать *pf see.* **у|ви́деть(ся** (-и́жу(сь) *pf*.

уви́ливать *impf*, **увильну́ть** (-ну́, -нёшь) *pf* от+*gen* dodge; evade.

увлажни́ть *pf*, **увлажня́ть** *impf* moisten.

увлека́тельный fascinating. **увлека́ть** *impf*, **увле́чь** (-еку́, -ечёшь; -ёк, -ла́) *pf* carry away; fascinate; **~ся** be carried away; become mad (+*instr* about). **увлече́ние** animation; passion; crush.

уво́д withdrawal; stealing. **уводи́ть** (-ожу́, -о́дишь) *impf of* **увести́**

увози́ть (-ожу́, -о́дишь) *impf of* **увезти́**

уво́лить *pf*, **увольня́ть** *impf* discharge, dismiss; retire; **~ся** be discharged, retire. **увольне́ние** discharge, dismissal.

увы́ *int* alas!

увяда́ть *impf of* **увя́нуть. увя́дший**

withered.

увяза́ть[1] *impf of* **увя́знуть**

увяза́ть[2] (-яжу́, -я́жешь) *pf* (*impf* **увя́зывать**) tie up; pack up; co-ordinate; **~ся** pack; tag along. **увя́зка** tying up; co-ordination.

у|вя́знуть (-ну; -я́з) *pf* (*impf also* **увяза́ть**) get bogged down.

увя́зывать(ся *impf of* **увяза́ть(ся**

у|вя́нуть (-ну) *pf* (*impf also* **увяда́ть**) fade, wither.

угада́ть *pf*, **уга́дывать** *impf* guess.

уга́р carbon monoxide (poisoning); ecstasy. **уга́рный газ** carbon monoxide.

угаса́ть *impf*, **у|га́снуть** (-нет; -áс) *pf* go out; die down.

угле- *in comb* coal; charcoal; carbon. **углево́д** carbohydrate. **~водоро́д** hydrocarbon. **~добы́ча** coal extraction. **~кислота́** carbonic acid; carbon dioxide. **~ки́слый** carbonate (of). **~ро́д** carbon.

угловой corner; angular.

углуби́ть (-блю́) *pf*, **углубля́ть** *impf* deepen; **~ся** deepen; delve deeply; become absorbed. **углубле́ние** depression, dip; deepening. **углублённый** deepened; profound; absorbed.

угна́ть (угоню́, -о́нишь; -а́л, -á, -о) *pf* (*impf* **угоня́ть**) drive away; despatch; steal; **~ся за**+*instr* keep pace with.

угнета́тель *m* oppressor. **угнета́ть** *impf* oppress; depress. **угнете́ние** oppression; depression. **угнетённый** oppressed; depressed.

угова́ривать *impf*, **уговори́ть** *pf* persuade; **~ся** arrange, agree. **угово́р** persuasion; agreement.

уго́да: в уго́ду +*dat* to please. **угоди́ть** (-ожу́) *pf*, **угожда́ть** *impf* fall, get; bang; (+*dat*) hit; +*dat or* на+*acc* please. **уго́дливый** obsequious. **уго́дно** *predic*+*dat*: **как вам ~** as you wish; **что вам ~?** what would you like?; *partl* **кто ~** anyone (you like); **что ~** anything (you like).

уго́дье (*gen pl* -ий) land.

у́гол (угла́, *loc* -ý) corner; angle.

уголо́вник criminal. **уголо́вный** criminal.

уголо́к (-лка́, *loc* -ý) corner.

у́голь (у́гля́; *pl* у́гли, -ей *or* -éй) *m* coal; charcoal.

уго́льник set square.
у́гольный coal; carbon(ic).
угомони́ть *pf* calm down; **~ся** calm down.
уго́н driving away; stealing. **угоня́ть** *impf of* **угна́ть**
угора́ть *impf*, **угоре́ть** (-рю́) *pf* get carbon monoxide poisoning; be mad. **угоре́лый** mad; possessed.
у́горь[1] (угря́) *m* eel.
у́горь[2] (угря́) *m* blackhead.
угости́ть (-ощу́) *pf*, **угоща́ть** *impf* entertain; treat. **угоще́ние** entertaining, treating; refreshments.
угрожа́ть *impf* threaten. **угро́за** threat, menace.
угро́зыск *abbr* criminal investigation department.
угрызе́ние pangs.
угрю́мый sullen, morose.
удава́ться (удаётся) *impf of* **уда́ться**
у|дави́ть(ся (-влю́(сь, -вишь(ся) *pf*. **уда́вка** running-knot, half hitch.
удале́ние removal; sending away; moving off. **удали́ть** *pf* (*impf* **удаля́ть**) remove; send away; move away; **~ся** move off, away; retire.
удало́й, уда́лый (-а́л, -а́, -о) daring, bold. **у́даль, удальство́** daring, boldness.
удаля́ть(ся *impf of* **удали́ть(ся**
уда́р blow; stroke; attack; kick; thrust; seizure; bolt. **ударе́ние** accent; stress; emphasis. **уда́рить** *pf*, **ударя́ть** *impf* (*impf also* **бить**) strike; hit; beat; **~ся** strike, hit; **+в+**acc break into; burst into. **уда́рник, -ница** shock-worker. **уда́рный** percussion; shock; stressed; urgent.
уда́ться (-а́стся, -аду́тся, -а́лся, -ла́сь) *pf* (*impf* **удава́ться**) succeed, be a success; *impers* **+**dat **+**inf succeed, manage; **мне удало́сь найти́ рабо́ту** I managed to find a job. **уда́ча** good luck; success. **уда́чный** successful; felicitous.
удва́ивать *impf*, **удво́ить** (-о́ю) *pf* double, redouble. **удвое́ние** (re)doubling.
уде́л lot, destiny.
удели́ть *pf* (*impf* **уделя́ть**) spare, give.
уделя́ть *impf of* **удели́ть**
удержа́ние deduction; retention,

keeping. **удержа́ть** (-жу́, -жишь) *pf*, **уде́рживать** *impf* hold (on to); retain; restrain; suppress; deduct; **~ся** hold out; stand firm; refrain (from).
удеру́ *etc.: see* **удра́ть**
удешеви́ть (-влю́) *pf*, **удешевля́ть** *impf* reduce the price of.
удиви́тельный surprising, amazing; wonderful. **удиви́ть** (-влю́) *pf*, **удивля́ть** *impf* surprise, amaze; **~ся** be surprised, be amazed. **удивле́ние** surprise, amazement.
удила́ (-и́л) *pl* bit.
уди́лище fishing-rod.
удира́ть *impf of* **удра́ть**
уди́ть (ужу́, у́дишь) *impf* fish for; **~ ры́бу** fish; **~ся** bite.
удлине́ние lengthening; extension. **удлини́ть** *pf*, **удлиня́ть** *impf* lengthen; extend; **~ся** become longer; be extended.
удо́бно *adv* comfortably; conveniently. **удо́бный** comfortable; convenient.
удобовари́мый digestible.
удобре́ние fertilization; fertilizer. **удо́брить** *pf*, **удобря́ть** *impf* fertilize.
удо́бство comfort; convenience.
удовлетворе́ние satisfaction; gratification. **удовлетворённый** (-рён, -а́) satisfied. **удовлетвори́тельный** satisfactory. **удовлетвори́ть** *pf*, **удовлетворя́ть** *impf* satisfy; **+**dat meet; **+**instr supply with; **~ся** be satisfied.
удово́льствие pleasure. **у|дово́льствоваться** *pf*.
удо́й milk-yield; milking.
удоста́ивать(ся *impf of* **удосто́ить(ся**
удостовере́ние certification; certificate; **~ ли́чности** identity card. **удостове́рить** *pf*, **удостоверя́ть** *impf* certify, witness; **~ся** make sure (**в+**prep of), assure o.s.
удосто́ить *pf* (*impf* **удоста́ивать**) make an award to; **+**gen award; **+**instr favour with; **~ся** **+**gen be awarded; be favoured with.
у́дочка (fishing-)rod.
удра́ть (удеру́, -ёшь; удра́л, -а́, -о) *pf* (*impf* **удира́ть**) make off.
удруча́ть *impf*, **удручи́ть** (-чу́) *pf* depress. **удручённый** (-чён, -а́) depressed.

удуша́ть *impf*, **удуши́ть** (-шу́, -шишь) *pf* stifle, suffocate. **удуше́ние** suffocation. **уду́шливый** stifling. **уду́шье** asthma; asphyxia.

уедине́ние solitude; seclusion. **уединённый** secluded; lonely. **уедини́ться** *pf*, **уединя́ться** *impf* seclude o.s.

уе́зд uyezd, District.

уезжа́ть *impf*, **уе́хать** (уе́ду) *pf* go away, depart.

уж[1] (-а́) grass-snake.

уж[2]: *see* **уже́**[2]. **уж**[3], **уже́**[3] *partl* indeed; really.

у|жа́лить *pf*.

у́жас horror, terror; *predic* it is awful. **ужаса́ть** *impf*, **ужасну́ть** (-ну́, -нёшь) *pf* horrify; ~ся be horrified, be terrified. **ужа́сно** *adv* terribly; awfully. **ужа́сный** awful, terrible.

у́же[1] *comp of* **у́зкий**

уже́[2], **уж**[2] *adv* already; ~ не no longer. **уже́**[3]: *see* **уж**[3]

уже́ние fishing.

ужива́ться *impf of* **ужи́ться**. **ужи́вчивый** easy to get on with.

ужи́мка grimace.

у́жин supper. **у́жинать** *impf* (*pf* по~) have supper.

ужи́ться (-иву́сь, -ивёшься; -и́лся, -ла́сь) *pf* (*impf* **ужива́ться**) get on.

ужу́ *see* **удить**

узако́нивать *impf*, **узако́нить** *pf* legalize.

узбе́к, **-е́чка** Uzbek. **Узбекиста́н** Uzbekistan.

узда́ (*pl* -ы) bridle.

у́зел (узла́) knot; junction; centre; node; bundle.

у́зкий (у́зок, узка́, -о) narrow; tight; narrow-minded. **узкоколе́йка** narrow-gauge railway.

узлова́тый knotty. **узлов|о́й** junction; main, key; ~а́я ста́нция junction.

узнава́ть (-наю́, -наёшь) *impf*, **узна́ть** *pf* recognize; get to know; find out.

у́зник, **у́зница** prisoner.

узо́р pattern, design. **узо́рчатый** patterned.

у́зость narrowness; tightness.

узурпа́тор usurper. **узурпи́ровать** *impf* & *pf* usurp.

у́зы (уз) *pl* bonds, ties.

уйду́ *etc.*: *see* **уйти́**.

у́йма lots (of).

уйму́ *etc.*: *see* **уня́ть**

уйти́ (уйду́, -дёшь; ушёл, ушла́) *pf* (*impf* **уходи́ть**) go away, leave, depart; escape; retire; bury o.s.; be used up; pass away.

ука́з decree; edict. **указа́ние** indication; instruction. **ука́занный** appointed, stated. **указа́тель** *m* indicator; gauge; index; directory. **указа́тельный** indicating; demonstrative; ~ па́лец index finger. **указа́ть** (-ажу́, -а́жешь) *pf*, **ука́зывать** *impf* show; indicate; point; point out. **ука́зка** pointer; orders.

ука́лывать *impf of* **уколо́ть**

уката́ть *pf*, **ука́тывать**[1] *impf* roll; flatten; wear out. **укати́ть** (-ачу́, -а́тишь) *pf*, **ука́тывать**[2] *impf* roll away; drive off; ~ся roll away.

укача́ть *pf*, **ука́чивать** *impf* rock to sleep; make sick.

укла́д structure; style; organization. **укла́дка** packing; stacking; laying; setting. **укла́дчик** packer; layer. **укла́дывать(ся**[1] *impf of* **уложи́ть(ся**

укла́дываться[2] *impf of* **уле́чься**

укло́н slope; incline; gradient; bias; deviation. **уклоне́ние** deviation; digression. **уклони́ться** *pf*, **уклоня́ться** *impf* deviate; +от+*gen* turn (off, aside); avoid; evade. **укло́нчивый** evasive.

уклю́чина rowlock.

уко́л prick; injection; thrust. **уколо́ть** (-лю́, -лешь) *pf* (*impf* **ука́лывать**) prick; wound.

у|комплектова́ть *pf*, **укомплекто́вывать** *impf* complete; bring up to (full) strength; man; +*instr* equip with.

уко́р reproach.

укора́чивать *impf of* **укороти́ть**

укорени́ть *pf*, **укореня́ть** *impf* implant, inculcate; ~ся take root.

укори́зна reproach. **укори́зненный** reproachful. **укори́ть** *pf* (*impf* **укоря́ть**) reproach (в+*prep* with).

укороти́ть (-очу́) *pf* (*impf* **укора́чивать**) shorten.

укоря́ть *impf of* **укори́ть**

уко́с (hay-)crop.

укра́дкой *adv* stealthily. **украду́** *etc.*: *see* **укра́сть**

Украи́на Ukraine. **украи́нец** (-нца), **украи́нка** Ukrainian. **украи́нский** Ukrainian.

укра́сить (-а́шу) *pf* (*impf* **украша́ть**) adorn, decorate; ~**ся** be decorated; adorn o.s.

у|кра́сть (-аду́, -дёшь) *pf*.

украша́ть(ся *impf of* **укра́сить(ся. украше́ние** decoration; adornment.

укрепи́ть (-плю́) *pf*, **укрепля́ть** *impf* strengthen; fix; fortify; ~**ся** become stronger; fortify one's position. **укрепле́ние** strengthening; reinforcement; fortification.

укро́мный secluded, cosy.

укро́п dill.

укроти́тель *m* (animal-)tamer. **укроти́ть** (-ощу́) *pf*, **укроща́ть** *impf* tame; curb; ~**ся** become tame; calm down. **укроще́ние** taming.

укро́ю *etc.: see* **укры́ть**

укрупне́ние enlargement; amalgamation. **укрупни́ть** *pf*, **укрупня́ть** *impf* enlarge; amalgamate.

укрыва́тель *m* harbourer. **укрыва́тельство** *n* harbouring; receiving. **укрыва́ть** *impf*, **укры́ть** (-ро́ю) *pf* cover; conceal, harbour; shelter; receive; ~**ся** cover o.s.; take cover. **укры́тие** cover; shelter.

у́ксус vinegar.

уку́с bite; sting. **укуси́ть** (-ушу́, -у́сишь) *pf* bite; sting.

уку́тать *pf*, **уку́тывать** *impf* wrap up; ~**ся** wrap o.s. up.

укушу́ *etc.: see* **укуси́ть**

ул. *abbr* (*of* **у́лица**) street, road.

ула́вливать *impf of* **улови́ть**

ула́дить (-а́жу) *pf*, **ула́живать** *impf* settle, arrange.

у́лей (у́лья) (bee)hive.

улета́ть *impf*, **улете́ть** (улечу́) *pf* fly (away). **улету́чиваться**, *impf*, **улету́читься** (-чусь) *pf* evaporate; vanish.

уле́чься (уля́гусь, -я́жешься; улёгся, -гла́сь) *pf* (*impf* **укла́дываться**) lie down; settle; subside.

ули́ка clue; evidence.

ули́тка snail.

у́лица street; **на у́лице** in the street; outside.

улича́ть *impf*, **уличи́ть** (-чу́) *pf* establish the guilt of.

у́личный street.

уло́в catch. **улови́мый** perceptible; audible. **улови́ть** (-влю́, -вишь) *pf* (*impf* **ула́вливать**) catch; seize. **уло́вка** trick, ruse.

уложе́ние code. **уложи́ть** (-жу́, -жишь) *pf* (*impf* **укла́дывать**) lay; pile; ~ **спать** put to bed; ~**ся** pack (up); fit in.

улуча́ть *impf*, **улучи́ть** (-чу́) *pf* find, seize.

улучша́ть *impf*, **улу́чшить** (-шу) *pf* improve; better; ~**ся** improve; get better. **улучше́ние** improvement.

улыба́ться *impf*, **улыбну́ться** (-ну́сь, -нёшься) *pf* smile. **улы́бка** smile.

ультима́тум ultimatum.

ультра- *in comb* ultra-. **ультразвуково́й** supersonic. ~**фиоле́товый** ultra-violet.

уля́гусь *etc.: see* **уле́чься**

ум (-а́) mind, intellect; head; **сойти́ с** ~**а́** go mad.

умали́ть *pf* (*impf* **умаля́ть**) belittle.

умалишённый mad; *sb* lunatic.

ума́лчивать *impf of* **умолча́ть**

умаля́ть *impf of* **умали́ть**

уме́лец (-льца) skilled craftsman. **уме́лый** able, skilful. **уме́ние** ability, skill.

уменьша́ть *impf*, **уме́ньшить** (-шу) *pf* reduce, diminish, decrease; ~**ся** diminish, decrease; abate. **уменьше́ние** decrease, reduction; abatement. **уменьши́тельный** diminutive.

уме́ренность moderation. **уме́ренный** moderate; temperate.

умере́ть (умру́, -рёшь; у́мер, -ла́, -о) *pf* (*impf* **умира́ть**) die.

уме́рить *pf* (*impf* **умеря́ть**) moderate; restrain.

умертви́ть (-рщвлю́, -ртви́шь) *pf*, **умерщвля́ть** *impf* kill, destroy; mortify. **у́мерший** dead; *sb* the deceased. **умерщвле́ние** killing, destruction; mortification.

умеря́ть *impf of* **уме́рить**

умести́ть (-ещу́) *pf* (*impf* **умеща́ть**) fit in, find room for; ~**ся** fit in. **уме́стный** appropriate; pertinent; timely.

уме́ть (-е́ю) *impf* be able, know how.

умеща́ть(ся *impf of* **умести́ть(ся**

умиле́ние tenderness; emotion. **умили́ть** *pf*, **умиля́ть** *impf* move, touch; ~ся be moved.

умира́ние dying. умира́ть *impf of* умере́ть. умира́ющий dying; *sb* dying person.

умиротворе́ние pacification; appeasement. умиротвори́ть *pf*, умиротворя́ть *impf* pacify; appease.

умне́ть (-е́ю) *impf* (*pf* по~) grow wiser. у́мница good girl; *m & f* clever person.

умножа́ть *impf*, у|мно́жить (-жу) *pf* multiply; increase; ~ся increase, multiply. умноже́ние multiplication; increase. умножи́тель *m* multiplier.

у́мный (умён, умна́, у́мно́) clever, wise, intelligent. умозаключе́ние deduction; conclusion.

умоли́ть *pf* (*impf* умоля́ть) move by entreaties.

умолка́ть *impf*, умо́лкнуть (-ну; -о́лк) *pf* fall silent; stop. умолча́ть (-чу́) *pf* (*impf* ума́лчивать) fail to mention; hush up.

умоля́ть *impf of* умоли́ть; beg, entreat.

умопомеша́тельство derangement. умори́тельный incredibly funny, killing. у|мори́ть *pf* kill; exhaust.

умо́ю *etc.: see* умы́ть. умру́ *etc.: see* умере́ть

у́мственный mental, intellectual.

умудри́ть *pf*, умудря́ть *impf* make wiser; ~ся contrive.

умыва́льная *sb* wash-room. умыва́льник wash-stand, wash-basin. умыва́ть(ся *impf of* умы́ть(ся

у́мысел (-сла) design, intention.

умы́ть (умо́ю) *pf* (*impf* умыва́ть) wash; ~ся wash (o.s.).

умы́шленный intentional.

у|насле́довать *pf*.

унести́ (-су́, -сёшь; -ёс, -ла́) *pf* (*impf* уноси́ть) take away; carry off, make off with; ~сь speed away; fly by; be carried (away).

универма́г *abbr* department store. универса́льн|ый universal; allround; versatile; all-purpose; ~ мага́зин department store; ~ое сре́дство panacea. универса́м *abbr* supermarket.

университе́т university. университе́тский university.

унижа́ть *impf*, уни́зить (-и́жу) *pf* humiliate; ~ся humble o.s.; stoop.

униже́ние humiliation. уни́женный humble. унизи́тельный humiliating.

уника́льный unique.

унима́ть(ся *impf of* уня́ть(ся

унисо́н unison.

унита́з lavatory pan.

унифици́ровать *impf & pf* standardize.

уничижи́тельный pejorative.

уничтожа́ть *impf*, уничто́жить (-жу) *pf* destroy, annihilate; abolish; do away with. уничтоже́ние destruction, annihilation; abolition.

уноси́ть(ся (-ошу́(сь, -о́сишь(ся) *impf of* унести́(сь

у́нция ounce.

уныва́ть *impf* be dejected. уны́лый dejected; doleful, cheerless. уны́ние dejection, despondency.

уня́ть (уйму́, -мёшь; -я́л, -а́, -о) *pf* (*impf* унима́ть) calm, soothe; ~ся calm down.

упа́док (-дка) decline; decay; ~ ду́ха depression. упа́дочнический decadent. упа́дочный depressive; decadent. упаду́ *etc.: see* упа́сть

у|пакова́ть *pf*, упако́вывать *impf* pack (up). упако́вка packing; wrapping. упако́вщик packer.

упа́сть (-аду́, -адёшь) *pf of* па́дать

упере́ть (упру́, -рёшь; -ёр) *pf*, упира́ть *impf* rest, lean; ~ на+*acc* stress; ~ся rest, lean; resist; +в+*acc* come up against.

упи́танный well-fed; fattened.

упла́та payment. у|плати́ть (-ачу́, -а́тишь) *pf*, упла́чивать *impf* pay.

уплотне́ние compression; condensation; consolidation; sealing. уплотни́ть *pf*, уплотня́ть *impf* condense; compress; pack more into.

уплыва́ть *impf*, уплы́ть (-ыву́, -ывёшь; -ы́л, -а́, -о) *pf* swim *or* sail away; pass.

упова́ть *impf* +на+*acc* put one's trust in.

уподо́биться (-блюсь) *pf*, уподобля́ться *impf* +*dat* become like.

упое́ние ecstasy, rapture. упои́тельный intoxicating, ravishing.

уполза́ть *impf*, уползти́ (-зу́, -зёшь; -о́лз, -зла́) *pf* creep away, crawl away.

уполномо́ченный *sb* (authorized)

agent, representative; proxy. **уполномóчивать**, **уполномóчивать** *impf*, **уполномóчить** (-чу) *pf* authorize, empower.

упоминáние mention. **упоминáть** *impf*, **упомянýть** (-нý, -нешь) *pf* mention, refer to.

упóр prop, support; в ~ point-blank; **сдéлать** ~ **на**+*acc or prep* lay stress on. **упóрный** stubborn; persistent. **упóрство** stubbornness; persistence. **упóрствовать** *impf* be stubborn; persist (в+*prep* in).

упорядочивать *impf*, **упорядочить** (-чу) *pf* regulate, put in order.

употребительный (widely-)used; common. **употребить** (-блю) *pf*, **употреблять** *impf* use. **употреблéние** use; usage.

упрáва justice.

управдóм *abbr* manager (*of block of flats*). **упрáвиться** (-влюсь) *pf*, **управляться** *impf* cope, manage; +*с*+*instr* deal with. **управлéние** management; administration; direction; control; driving, steering; government. **управляемый снаряд** guided missile. **управлять** *impf* +*instr* manage, direct, run; govern; be in charge of; operate; drive. **управляющий** *sb* manager.

упражнéние exercise. **упражнять** *impf* exercise, train; ~**ся** practise, train.

упразднить *pf*, **упразднять** *impf* abolish.

упрáшивать *impf of* **упросить**

упрёк reproach. **упрекáть** *impf*, **упрекнýть** (-нý, -нёшь) *pf* reproach.

упросить (-ошý, -óсишь) *pf* (*impf* **упрáшивать**) entreat; prevail upon.

упростить (-ощý) *pf* (*impf* **упрощáть**) (over-)simplify.

упрóчивать *impf*, **упрóчить** (-чу) *pf* strengthen, consolidate; ~**ся** be firmly established.

упрошý *etc.: see* **упросить**

упрощáть *impf of* **упростить**. **упрощённый** (-щён, -á) (over-)simplified.

упрý *etc.: see* **уперéть**

упрýгий elastic; springy. **упрýгость** elasticity; spring. **упрýже** *comp of* **упрýгий**

упряжка harness; team. **упряжнóй** draught. **ýпряжь** harness.

упрямиться (-млюсь) *impf* be obstinate; persist. **упрямство** obstinacy. **упрямый** obstinate; persistent.

упускáть *impf*, **упустить** (-ущý, -ýстишь) *pf* let go, let slip; miss. **упущéние** omission; slip; negligence.

урá *int* hurrah!

уравнéние equalization; equation. **урáвнивать** *impf*, **уравнять** *pf* equalize. **уравнительный** equalizing, levelling. **уравновéсить** (-éшу) *pf*, **уравновéшивать** *impf* balance; counterbalance. **уравновéшенность** composure. **уравновéшенный** balanced, composed.

урагáн hurricane; storm.

урáльский Ural.

урáн uranium; Uranus. **урáновый** uranium.

урвáть (-вý, -вёшь; -áл, -á, -о) *pf* (*impf* **урывáть**) snatch.

урегулировáние regulation; settlement. **у|регулировать** *pf*.

урéзать (-éжу) *pf*, **урезáть**, **урéзывать** *impf* cut off; shorten; reduce.

ýрка *m & f* (*sl*) lag, convict.

ýрна urn; litter-bin.

ýровень (-вня) *m* level; standard.

урóд freak, monster.

уродиться (-ожýсь) *pf* ripen; grow. **урóдливость** deformity; ugliness. **урóдливый** deformed; ugly; bad. **урóдовать** *impf* (*pf* **из~**) disfigure; distort. **урóдство** disfigurement; ugliness.

урожáй harvest; crop; abundance. **урожáйность** yield; productivity. **урожáйный** productive, high-yield. **урождённый** *née*. **урожéнец** (-нца), **урожéнка** native. **урожýсь** *see* **уродиться**

урóк lesson.

урóн losses; damage. **уронить** (-ню, -нишь) *pf of* **ронять**

урчáть (-чý) *impf* rumble.

урывáть *impf of* **урвáть**. **урывками** *adv* in snatches, by fits and starts.

ус (*pl* -ы́) whisker; tendril; *pl* moustache.

усадить (-ажý, -áдишь) *pf*, **усáживать** *impf* seat, offer a seat; plant. **усáдьба** (*gen pl* -деб *or* -дьб) country estate; farmstead. **усáживаться** *impf of* **усéсться**

усáтый moustached; whiskered.

усва́ивать *impf*, **усво́ить** *pf* master; assimilate; adopt. **усвое́ние** mastering; assimilation; adoption.

усе́рдие zeal; diligence. **усе́рдный** zealous; diligent.

усе́сться (уся́дусь; -е́лся) *pf* (*impf* **уса́живаться**) take a seat; settle down (to).

усиде́ть (-ижу́) *pf* remain seated; hold down a job. **уси́дчивый** assiduous.

у́сик tendril; runner; antenna; *pl* small moustache.

усиле́ние strengthening; reinforcement; intensification; amplification. **уси́ленный** intensified, increased; earnest. **уси́ливать** *impf*, **уси́лить** *pf* intensify, increase; amplify; strengthen, reinforce; ~ся increase, intensify; become stronger. **уси́лие** effort. **усили́тель** *m* amplifier; booster.

ускака́ть (-ачу́, -а́чешь) *pf* skip off; gallop off.

ускольза́ть *impf*, **ускользну́ть** (-ну́, -нёшь) *pf* slip off; steal away; escape.

ускоре́ние acceleration. **ускоре́нный** accelerated; rapid; crash. **ускори́тель** accelerator. **уско́рить** *pf*, **ускоря́ть** *impf* quicken; accelerate; hasten; ~ся accelerate, be accelerated; quicken.

усло́вие condition. **усло́виться** (-влюсь) *pf*, **усло́вливаться, усла́вливаться** *impf* agree; arrange. **усло́вленный** agreed, fixed. **усло́вность** convention. **усло́вный** conditional; conditioned; conventional; agreed; relative.

усложне́ние complication. **усложни́ть** *pf*, **усложня́ть** *impf* complicate; ~ся become complicated.

услу́га service; good turn. **услу́жливый** obliging.

услыха́ть (-ышу) *pf*, **у|слы́шать** (-ышу) *pf* hear; sense; scent.

усма́тривать *impf of* **усмотре́ть**

усмеха́ться *impf*, **усмехну́ться** (-ну́сь, -нёшься) *pf* smile; grin; smirk. **усме́шка** smile; grin; sneer.

усмире́ние pacification; suppression. **усмири́ть** *pf*, **усмиря́ть** *impf* pacify; calm; suppress.

усмотре́ние discretion, judgement. **усмотре́ть** (-рю́, -ришь) *pf* (*impf*

усма́тривать) perceive; see; regard; +за+*instr* keep an eye on.

усну́ть (-ну́, -нёшь) *pf* go to sleep.

усоверше́нствование advanced studies; improvement, refinement. **у|соверше́нствовать(ся** *pf*.

усомни́ться *pf* doubt.

успева́емость progress. **успева́ть** *impf*, **успе́ть** (-е́ю) *pf* have time; manage; succeed. **успе́х** success; progress. **успе́шный** successful.

успока́ивать *impf*, **успоко́ить** *pf* calm, quiet, soothe; ~ся calm down; abate. **успока́ивающий** calming, sedative. **успокое́ние** calming, soothing; calm; peace. **успокои́тель|ный** calming; reassuring; ~ое *sb* sedative, tranquillizer.

уста́ (-т, -та́м) *pl* mouth.

уста́в regulations, statutes; charter.

устава́ть (-таю́, -ёшь) *impf of* **уста́ть**; **не устава́я** incessantly.

уста́вить (-влю) *pf*, **уставля́ть** *impf* set, arrange; cover, fill; direct; ~ся find room, go in; stare.

уста́лость tiredness. **уста́лый** tired.

устана́вливать *impf*, **установи́ть** (-влю́, -вишь) *pf* put, set up; install; set; establish; fix; ~ся dispose o.s.; be established; set in. **устано́вка** putting, setting up; installation; setting; plant, unit; directions. **установле́ние** establishment. **устано́вленный** established, prescribed.

устану́ *etc.*: *see* **уста́ть**

устарева́ть *impf*, **у|старе́ть** (-е́ю) *pf* become obsolete; become antiquated. **устаре́лый** obsolete; antiquated; out-of-date.

уста́ть (-а́ну) *pf* (*impf* **устава́ть**) get tired.

устила́ть *impf*, **устла́ть** (-телю́, -те́лешь) *pf* cover; pave.

у́стный oral, verbal.

усто́й abutment; foundation; support. **усто́йчивость** stability, steadiness. **усто́йчивый** stable, steady. **устоя́ть** (-ою́) *pf* keep one's balance; stand firm; ~ся settle; become fixed.

устра́ивать(ся *impf of* **устро́ить(ся**

устране́ние removal, elimination. **устрани́ть** *pf*, **устраня́ть** *impf* remove; eliminate; ~ся resign, retire.

устраша́ть *impf*, **устраши́ть** (-шу́) *pf* frighten; ~ся be frightened.

устреми́ть (-млю́) pf, **устремля́ть** impf direct, fix; ~**ся** rush; be directed; concentrate. **устремле́ние** rush; aspiration.

у́стрица oyster.

устро́итель m, ~**ница** organizer. **устро́ить** pf (impf **устра́ивать**) arrange, organize; make; cause; settle, put in order; place, fix up; get; suit; ~**ся** work out; manage; settle down; be found, get fixed up. **устро́йство** arrangement; construction; mechanism, device; system.

усту́п shelf, ledge. **уступа́ть** impf, **уступи́ть** (-плю́, -пишь) pf yield; give up; ~ **доро́гу** make way. **усту́пка** concession. **усту́пчивый** pliable; compliant.

устыди́ться (-ыжу́сь) pf (+gen) be ashamed (of).

у́стье (gen pl -ьев) mouth; estuary.

усугуби́ть (-блю́) pf, **усугубля́ть** impf increase; aggravate.

усы́ see **ус**

усынови́ть (-влю́) pf, **усыновля́ть** impf adopt. **усыновле́ние** adoption.

усы́пать (-плю) pf, **усыпа́ть** impf strew, scatter.

усыпи́тельный soporific. **усыпи́ть** (-плю́) pf, **усыпля́ть** impf put to sleep; lull; weaken.

уся́дусь etc.: see **усе́сться**

ута́ивать impf, **утаи́ть** pf conceal; keep secret.

ута́птывать impf of **утопта́ть**

ута́скивать impf, **утащи́ть** (-щу́, -щишь) pf drag off.

у́тварь utensils.

утверди́тельный affirmative. **утверди́ть** (-ржу́) pf, **утвержда́ть** impf confirm; approve; ratify; establish; assert; ~**ся** gain a foothold; become established; be confirmed. **утвержде́ние** approval; confirmation; ratification; assertion; establishment.

утека́ть impf of **уте́чь**

утёнок (-нка; pl утя́та, -я́т) duckling.

утепли́ть pf, **утепля́ть** impf warm.

утере́ть (утру́, -рёшь; утёр) pf (impf **утира́ть**) wipe (off, dry).

утерпе́ть (-плю́, -пишь) pf restrain o.s.

утёс cliff, crag.

уте́чка leak, leakage; escape; loss.

уте́чь (-еку́, -ечёшь; утёк, -ла́) pf (impf **утека́ть**) leak, escape; pass.

утеша́ть impf, **уте́шить** (-шу) pf console; ~**ся** console o.s. **утеше́ние** consolation. **утеши́тельный** comforting.

утилизи́ровать impf & pf utilize.

ути́ль m, **утильсырьё** scrap.

ути́ный duck, duck's.

утира́ть(ся impf of **утере́ть(ся**

утиха́ть impf, **ути́хнуть** (-ну; -их) pf abate, subside; calm down.

у́тка duck; canard.

уткну́ть (-ну́, -нёшь) pf bury; fix; ~**ся** bury o.s.

утоли́ть pf (impf **утоля́ть**) quench; satisfy; relieve.

утолще́ние thickening; bulge.

утоля́ть impf of **утоли́ть**

утоми́тельный tedious; tiring. **утоми́ть** (-млю́) pf, **утомля́ть** impf tire, fatigue; ~**ся** get tired. **утомле́ние** weariness. **утомлённый** weary.

у|тону́ть (-ну́, -нешь) pf drown, be drowned; sink.

утончённый refined.

у|топи́ть(ся (-плю́(сь, -пишь(ся) pf. **уто́пленник** drowned man.

утопи́ческий utopian. **уто́пия** Utopia.

утопта́ть (-пчу́, -пчешь) pf (impf **ута́птывать**) trample down.

уточне́ние more precise definition; amplification. **уточни́ть** pf, **уточня́ть** impf define more precisely; amplify.

утра́ивать impf of **утро́ить**

у|трамбова́ть pf, **утрамбо́вывать** impf ram, tamp; ~**ся** become flat.

утра́та loss. **утра́тить** (-а́чу) pf, **утра́чивать** impf lose.

у́тренний morning. **у́тренник** morning performance; early-morning frost.

утри́ровать impf & pf exaggerate.

у́тро (-а or -а́, -у or -у́, pl -а, -ам or -а́м) morning.

утро́ба womb; belly.

утро́ить pf (impf **утра́ивать**) triple, treble.

утру́ etc.: see **утере́ть, у́тро**

утружда́ть impf trouble, tire.

утю́г (-а́) iron. **утю́жить** (-жу) impf (pf **вы́~, от~**) iron.

ух int oh, ooh, ah.

уха́ fish soup.

уха́б pot-hole. **уха́бистый** bumpy.

ухáживать *impf* **за**+*instr* tend; look after; court.

ухвати́ть (-ачý, -а́тишь) *pf*, **ухва́тывать** *impf* seize; grasp; ~**ся за**+*acc* grasp, lay hold of; set to; seize; jump at. **ухва́тка** grip; skill; trick; manner.

ухитри́ться *pf*, **ухитря́ться** *impf* manage, contrive. **ухищре́ние** device, trick.

ухмы́лка smirk. **ухмыльну́ться** (-нýсь, -нёшься) *pf*, **ухмыля́ться** *impf* smirk.

у́хо (*pl* у́ши, ушéй) ear; ear-flap.

ухóд¹ +**за**+*instr* care of; tending, looking after.

ухóд² leaving, departure. **уходи́ть** (-ожý, -о́дишь) *impf of* **уйти́**

ухудша́ть *impf*, **уху́дшить** (-шу) *pf* make worse; ~**ся** get worse. **ухудше́ние** deterioration.

уцеле́ть (-éю) *pf* remain intact; survive.

уце́нивать *impf*, **уцени́ть** (-ню́, -нишь) *pf* reduce the price of.

уцепи́ть (-плю́, -пишь) *pf* catch hold of, seize; ~**ся за**+*acc* catch hold of, seize; jump at.

уча́ствовать *impf* take part; hold shares. **уча́ствующий** *sb* participant. **уча́стие** participation; share; sympathy.

участи́ть (-ащу́) *pf* (*impf* **учаща́ть**) make more frequent; ~**ся** become more frequent, quicken.

уча́стливый sympathetic. **уча́стник** participant. **уча́сток** (-тка) plot; part, section; sector; district; field, sphere. **у́часть** lot, fate.

учаща́ть(ся *impf of* **участи́ть(ся**

уча́щийся *sb* student; pupil. **уче́ба** studies; course; training. **уче́бник** text-book. **уче́бный** educational; school; training. **уче́ние** learning; studies; apprenticeship; teaching; doctrine; exercise.

учени́к (-á), **учени́ца** pupil; apprentice; disciple. **учени́ческий** pupil('s); apprentice('s); unskilled; crude. **учёность** learning, erudition. **учён|ый** learned; scholarly; academic; scientific; ~**ая сте́пень** (*university*) degree; ~**ый** *sb* scholar; scientist.

уче́сть (учту́, -тёшь; учёл, учла́) *pf* (*impf* **учи́тывать**) take stock of; take

into account; discount. **учёт** stock-taking; calculation; taking into account; registration; discount; **без** ~**а** +*gen* disregarding; **взять на** ~ register. **учётный** registration; discount.

учи́лище (*specialist*) school.

у|чини́ть *pf*, **учиня́ть** *impf* make; carry out; commit.

учи́тель (*pl* -я́) *m*, **учи́тельница** teacher. **учи́тельск|ий** teacher's, teachers'; ~**ая** *sb* staff-room.

учи́тывать *impf of* **уче́сть**

учи́ть (учу́, у́чишь) *impf* (*pf* **вы́~**, **на~**, **об~**) teach; be a teacher; learn; ~**ся** be a student; +*dat or inf* learn, study.

учреди́тельный constituent. **учреди́ть** (-ежу́) *pf*, **учрежда́ть** *impf* found, establish. **учрежде́ние** founding; establishment; institution.

учти́вый civil, courteous.

учту́ *etc.*: *see* **уче́сть**

уша́нка hat with ear-flaps.

ушёл *etc.*: *see* **уйти́**. **у́ши** *etc.*: *see* **у́хо**

уши́б injury; bruise. **ушиба́ть** *impf*, **ушиби́ть** (-бу́, -бёшь; уши́б) *pf* injure; bruise; hurt; ~**ся** hurt o.s.

ушко́ (*pl* -и́, -о́в) eye; tab.

ушно́й ear, aural.

уще́лье ravine, gorge, canyon.

ущеми́ть (-млю́) *pf*, **ущемля́ть** *impf* pinch, jam; limit; encroach on; hurt. **ущемле́ние** pinching, jamming; limitation; hurting.

уще́рб detriment; loss; damage; prejudice. **уще́рбный** waning.

ущипну́ть (-ну́, -нёшь) *pf of* **щипа́ть**

Уэ́льс Wales. **уэ́льский** Welsh.

ую́т cosiness, comfort. **ую́тный** cosy, comfortable.

язви́мый vulnerable. **язви́ть** (-влю́) *pf*, **язвля́ть** *impf* wound, hurt.

уясни́ть *pf*, **уясня́ть** *impf* understand, make out.

Ф

фа́брика factory. **фабрика́нт** manufacturer. **фабрика́т** finished product, manufactured product. **фабрикова́ть** *impf* (*pf* **с~**) fabricate, forge. **фабри́чн|ый** factory; manufacturing; factory-made; ~**ая ма́рка**, ~**ое клеймо́** trade-mark.

фа́була plot, story.

фаго́т bassoon.

фа́за phase; stage.

фаза́н pheasant.

фа́зис phase.

файл (*comput*) file.

фа́кел torch, flare.

факс fax.

факси́миле *neut indecl* facsimile.

факт fact; **соверши́вшийся ~ fait** accompli. **факти́чески** *adv* in fact; virtually. **факти́ческий** actual; real; virtual.

фа́ктор factor.

факту́ра texture; style, execution.

факультати́вный optional. **факульте́т** faculty, department.

фа́лда tail (*of coat*).

фальсифика́тор falsifier, forger. **фальсифика́ция** falsification; adulteration; forgery. **фальсифици́ровать** *impf & pf* falsify; forge; adulterate. **фальши́вить** (-влю) *impf* (*pf* с~) be a hypocrite; sing *or* play out of tune. **фальши́вка** forged document. **фальши́вый** false; spurious; forged; artificial; out of tune. **фальшь** deception; falseness.

фами́лия surname. **фамилья́рничать** be over-familiar. **фамилья́рность** (over-)familiarity. **фамилья́рный** (over-)familiar; unceremonious.

фанати́зм fanaticism. **фана́тик** fanatic.

фане́ра veneer; plywood.

фантазёр dreamer, visionary. **фантази́ровать** *impf* (*pf* с~) dream; make up, dream up; improvise. **фанта́зия** fantasy; fancy; imagination; whim. **фанта́стика** fiction, fantasy. **фантасти́ческий**, **фантасти́чный** fantastic.

фа́ра headlight.

фарао́н pharaoh; faro.

фарва́тер fairway, channel.

фармазо́н freemason.

фармаце́вт pharmacist.

фарс farce.

фа́ртук apron.

фарфо́р china; porcelain. **фарфо́ровый** china.

фарцо́вщик currency speculator.

фарш stuffing; minced meat. **фарширова́ть** *impf* (*pf* за~) stuff.

фаса́д façade.

фасова́ть *impf* (*pf* рас~) package.

фасо́ль kidney bean(s), French bean(s); haricot beans.

фасо́н cut; fashion; style; manner. **фасо́нный** shaped.

фата́ veil.

фатали́зм fatalism. **фата́льный** fatal.

фаши́зм Fascism. **фаши́ст** Fascist. **фаши́стский** Fascist.

фая́нс faience, pottery.

февра́ль (-я́) *m* February. **февра́льский** February.

федера́льный federal. **федера́ция** federation.

фееpи́ческий fairy-tale.

фейерве́рк firework.

фе́льдшер (*pl* -á), **-шери́ца** (*partly-qualified*) medical assistant.

фельето́н feuilleton, feature.

фемини́зм feminism. **феминисти́ческий**, **фемини́стский** feminist.

фен (hair-)dryer.

фено́мен phenomenon. **феноме́нальный** phenomenal.

феода́л feudal lord. **феодали́зм** feudalism. **феода́льный** feudal.

ферзь (-я́) *m* queen.

фе́рма[1] farm.

фе́рма[2] girder, truss.

ферма́та (*mus*) pause.

ферме́нт ferment.

фе́рмер farmer.

фестива́ль *m* festival.

фетр felt. **фе́тровый** felt.

фехтова́льщик, **-щица** fencer. **фехтова́ние** fencing. **фехтова́ть** *impf* fence.

фе́я fairy.

фиа́лка violet.

фиа́ско *neut indecl* fiasco.

фи́бра fibre.

фигля́р buffoon.

фигу́ра figure; court-card; (chess-) piece. **фигура́льный** figurative, metaphorical. **фигури́ровать** *impf* figure, appear. **фигури́ст**, **-и́стка** figure-skater. **фигу́рка** figurine, statuette; figure. **фигу́рн|ый** figured; **~ое ката́ние** figure-skating.

фи́зик physicist. **фи́зика** physics. **физио́лог** physiologist. **физиологи́ческий** physiological. **физиоло́гия** physiology. **физионо́мия** physi-

ognomy; face, expression. **физио-
терапе́вт** physiotherapist. **физи́-
ческий** physical; physics. **физкульту́ра** *abbr* P.E., gymnastics. **физкульту́рный** *abbr* gymnastic; athletic; ~ **зал** gymnasium.

фикса́ж fixer. **фикса́ция** fixing. **фикси́ровать** *impf & pf* (*pf also* за~) fix; record.

фикти́вный fictitious. ~ **брак** marriage of convenience. **фи́кция** fiction.

филантро́п philanthropist. **филантро́пия** philanthropy.

филармо́ния philharmonic society; concert hall.

филатели́ст philatelist.

филе́ *neut indecl* sirloin; fillet.

филиа́л branch.

фили́стер philistine.

фило́лог philologist. **филологи́ческий** philological. **филоло́гия** philology.

фило́соф philosopher. **филосо́фия** philosophy. **филосо́фский** philosophical.

фильм film. **фильмоско́п** projector.

фильтр filter. **фильтрова́ть** *impf* (*pf* про~) filter.

фина́л finale; final. **фина́льный** final.

финанси́ровать *impf & pf* finance. **фина́нсовый** financial. **фина́нсы** (-ов) *pl* finance, finances.

фи́ник date.

фи́ниш finish; finishing post.

финн Finn. **Финля́ндия** Finland. **финля́ндский** Finnish. **финн** Finn. **фи́нский** Finnish.

фиоле́товый violet.

фи́рма firm; company. **фи́рменное блю́до** speciality of the house.

фисгармо́ния harmonium.

фити́ль (-я́) *m* wick; fuse.

флаг flag. **фла́гман** flagship.

флако́н bottle, flask.

фланг flank; wing.

флане́ль flannel.

флегмати́чный phlegmatic.

фле́йта flute.

фле́ксия inflexion. **флекти́вный** inflected.

фли́гель (*pl* -я́) *m* wing; annexe.

флирт flirtation. **флиртова́ть** *impf* flirt.

флома́стер felt-tip pen.

фло́ра flora.

флот fleet. **фло́тский** naval.

флю́гер (*pl* -а́) weather-vane.

флюоресце́нтный fluorescent.

флюс[1] gumboil, abscess.

флюс[2] (*pl* -ы́) flux.

фля́га flask; churn. **фля́жка** flask.

фойе́ *neut indecl* foyer.

фо́кус[1] trick.

фо́кус[2] focus. **фокуси́ровать** *impf* focus.

фо́кусник conjurer, juggler.

фолиа́нт folio.

фольга́ foil.

фолькло́р folklore.

фон background.

фона́рик small lamp; torch. **фона́рный** lamp; ~ **столб** lamp-post. **фона́рь** (-я́) *m* lantern; lamp; light.

фонд fund; stock; reserves.

фоне́тика phonetics. **фонети́ческий** phonetic.

фонта́н fountain.

форе́ль trout.

фо́рма form; shape; mould, cast; uniform. **форма́льность** formality. **форма́льный** formal. **форма́т** format. **форма́ция** structure; stage; formation; mentality. **фо́рменный** uniform; proper, regular. **формирова́ние** forming; unit, formation. **формирова́ть** *impf* (*pf* с~) form; organize; ~**ся** form, develop. **формова́ть** *impf* (*pf* с~) form, shape; mould, cast.

фо́рмула formula. **формули́ровать** *impf & pf* (*pf also* с~) formulate. **формулиро́вка** formulation; wording; formula. **формуля́р** log-book; library card.

форси́ровать *impf & pf* force; speed up.

форсу́нка sprayer; injector.

фортепья́но *neut indecl* piano.

фо́рточка small hinged (window-) pane.

форту́на fortune.

фо́рум forum

фо́сфор phosphorus.

фо́то *neut indecl* photo(graph).

фото- *in comb* photo-, photo-electric. **фотоаппара́т** camera. ~**бума́га** photographic paper. ~**гени́чный** photogenic. **фото́граф** photographer.

~графи́ровать *impf* (*pf* **с~**) photograph. **~графи́роваться** be photographed, have one's photograph taken. **~графи́ческий** photographic. **~гра́фия** photography; photograph; photographer's studio. **~ко́пия** photocopy. **~люби́тель** *m* amateur photographer. **~объекти́в** (camera) lens. **~репортёр** press photographer. **~хро́ника** news in pictures. **~элеме́нт** photoelectric cell.

фрагме́нт fragment.

фра́за sentence; phrase. **фразеоло́гия** phraseology.

фрак tail-coat, tails.

фракцио́нный fractional; factional. **фра́кция** fraction; faction.

франк franc.

франкмасо́н Freemason.

франт dandy.

Фра́нция France. **францу́женка** Frenchwoman. **францу́з** Frenchman. **францу́зский** French.

фрахт freight. **фрахтова́ть** *impf* (*pf* **за~**) charter.

фрега́т frigate.

фрезеро́вщик milling machine operator.

фре́ска fresco.

фронт (*pl* **-ы́**, **-о́в**) front. **фронтови́к** (**-а́**) front-line soldier. **фронтово́й** front(-line).

фронто́н pediment.

фрукт fruit. **фрукто́вый** fruit; **~ сад** orchard.

фтор fluorine. **фто́ристый** fluorine; fluoride. **~ ка́льций** calcium fluoride.

фу *int* ugh! oh!

фуга́нок (**-нка**) smoothing-plane.

фуга́с landmine. **фуга́сный** high-explosive.

фунда́мент foundation. **фундамента́льный** solid, sound; main; basic.

функциона́льный functional. **функциони́ровать** *impf* function. **фу́нкция** function.

фунт pound.

фура́ж (**-а́**) forage, fodder. **фура́жка** peaked cap, forage-cap.

фурго́н van; caravan.

фут foot; foot-rule. **футбо́л** football. **футболи́ст** footballer. **футбо́лка** football jersey, sports shirt. **футбо́льный** football; **~ мяч** football.

футля́р case, container.

футури́зм futurism.

фуфа́йка jersey; sweater.

фы́ркать *impf*, **фы́ркнуть** (**-ну**) *pf* snort.

фюзеля́ж fuselage.

X

хала́т dressing-gown. **хала́тный** careless, negligent.

халту́ра pot-boiler; hackwork; money made on the side. **халту́рщик** hack.

хам boor, lout. **ха́мский** boorish, loutish. **ха́мство** boorishness, loutishness.

хамелео́н chameleon.

хан khan.

хандра́ depression. **хандри́ть** *impf* be depressed.

ханжа́ hypocrite. **ха́нжеский** sanctimonious, hypocritical.

хао́с chaos. **хаоти́чный** chaotic.

хара́ктер character. **характеризова́ть** *impf & pf* (*pf also* **о~**) describe; characterize; **~ся** be characterized. **характери́стика** reference; description. **характе́рный** characteristic; distinctive; character.

ха́ркать *impf*, **ха́ркнуть** (**-ну**) *pf* spit.

ха́ртия charter.

ха́та peasant hut.

хвала́ praise. **хвале́бный** laudatory. **хвалёный** highly-praised. **хвали́ть** (**-лю́**, **-лишь**) *impf* (*pf* **по~**) praise; **~ся** boast.

хва́стать(ся *impf* (*pf* **по~**) boast. **хвастли́вый** boastful. **хвастовство́** boasting. **хвасту́н** (**-а́**) boaster.

хвата́ть[1] *impf*, **хвати́ть** (**-ачу́**, **-а́тишь**) *pf* (*pf also* **схвати́ть**) snatch, seize; grab; **~ся** remember; +*gen* realize the absence of; +**за**+*acc* snatch at, clutch at; take up.

хвата́ть[2] *impf*, **хвати́ть** (**-а́тит**) *pf*, *impers* (+*gen*) suffice, be enough; last out; **вре́мени не хвата́ло** there was not enough time; **у нас не хвата́ет де́нег** we haven't enough money; **хва́тит!** that will do!; **э́того ещё не хвата́ло!** that's all we needed! **хва́тка** grasp, grip; method; skill.

хво́йн|ый coniferous; **~ые** *sb pl* conifers.

хвора́ть *impf* be ill.

хво́рост brushwood; (*pastry*) straws. **хворости́на** stick, switch.

хвост (-á) tail; tail-end. **хво́стик** tail. **хвостово́й** tail.

хво́я needle(s); (*coniferous*) branch(es).

херуви́м cherub.

хиба́р(к)а shack, hovel.

хи́жина shack, hut.

хи́лый (-л, -á, -о) sickly.

химе́ра chimera.

хи́мик chemist. **химика́т** chemical. **хими́ческий** chemical. **хи́мия** chemistry.

химчи́стка dry-cleaning; dry-cleaner's.

хи́на, хини́н quinine.

хиру́рг surgeon. **хирурги́ческий** surgical. **хирурги́я** surgery.

хитре́ц (-á) cunning person. **хитри́ть** *impf* (*pf* c~) use cunning, be crafty. **хи́трость** cunning; ruse; skill; intricacy. **хи́трый** cunning; skilful; intricate.

хихи́кать *impf*, **хихи́кнуть** (-ну) *pf* giggle, snigger.

хище́ние theft; embezzlement. **хи́щник** predator, bird *or* beast of prey. **хи́щнический** predatory. **хи́щные пти́цы** predatory; rapacious; ~ые пти́цы birds of prey.

хладнокро́вие coolness, composure. **хладнокро́вный** cool, composed.

хлам rubbish.

хлеб (*pl* -ы, -ов *or* -á, -о́в) bread; loaf; grain. **хлеба́ть** *impf*, **хлебну́ть** (-ну́, -нёшь) *pf* gulp down. **хле́бный** bread; baker's; grain. **хлебозаво́д** bakery. **хлебопека́рня** (*gen pl* -рен) bakery.

хлев (*loc* -ý; *pl* -á) cow-shed.

хлеста́ть (-ещу́, -е́щешь) *impf*, **хлестну́ть** (-ну́, -нёшь) *pf* lash; whip.

хлоп *int* bang! **хло́пать** *impf* (*pf* **хло́пнуть**) bang; slap; ~ (в ладо́ши) clap.

хлопково́дство cotton-growing. **хло́пковый** cotton.

хло́пнуть (-ну) *pf of* **хло́пать**

хлопо́к[1] (-пка́) clap.

хло́пок[2] (-пка) cotton.

хлопота́ть (-очу́, -о́чешь) *impf* (*pf* по~) busy o.s.; bustle about; take trouble; +о+*prep or* за+*acc* petition for. **хлопотли́вый** troublesome; ex-

acting; busy, bustling. **хло́поты** (-о́т) *pl* trouble; efforts.

хлопчатобума́жный cotton.

хло́пья (-ьев) *pl* flakes.

хлор chlorine. **хло́ристый, хло́рный** chlorine; chloride. **хло́рка** bleach. **хлорофи́лл** chlorophyll. **хлорофо́рм** chloroform.

хлы́нуть (-нет) *pf* gush, pour.

хлыст (-á) whip, switch.

хмеле́ть (-е́ю) *impf* (*pf* за~, о~) get tipsy. **хмель** (*loc* -ю́) *m* hop, hops; drunkenness; **во хмелю́** tipsy. **хмельно́й** (-лён, -льна́) drunk; intoxicating.

хму́рить *impf* (*pf* на~): ~ бро́ви knit one's brows; ~ся frown; become gloomy; be overcast. **хму́рый** gloomy; overcast.

хны́кать (-ы́чу *or* -аю) *impf* whimper, snivel.

хо́бби *neut indecl* hobby.

хо́бот trunk. **хобото́к** (-тка́) proboscis.

ход (*loc* -ý; *pl* -ы, -ов *or* -ы́ *or* -á, -о́в) motion; going; speed; course; operation; stroke; move; manoeuvre; entrance; passage; в ~ý in demand; дать за́дний ~ reverse; дать ~ set in motion; на ~ý in transit, on the move; in motion; in operation; по́лным ~ом at full speed; пусти́ть в ~ start, set in motion; три часа́ ~у three hours' journey.

хода́тайство petitioning; application. **хода́тайствовать** *impf* (*pf* по~) petition, apply.

ходи́ть (хожу́, хо́дишь) *impf* walk; go; run; pass, go round; lead, play; move; +в+*prep* wear; +за+*instr* look after. **хо́дкий** (-док, -дка́, -о) fast; marketable; popular. **ходьба́** walking; walk. **ходя́чий** walking; able to walk; popular; current.

хозрасчёт *abbr* (*of* **хозя́йственный расчёт**) self-financing system.

хозя́ин (*pl* -я́ева, -я́ев) owner, proprietor; master; boss; landlord; host; **хозя́ева по́ля** home team. **хозя́йка** owner; mistress; hostess; landlady. **хозя́йничать** *impf* keep house; be in charge; lord it. **хозя́йственник** financial manager. **хозя́йственный** economic; household; economical. **хозя́йство** economy; housekeeping;

equipment; farm; **дома́шнее** ~ housekeeping; **се́льское** ~ agriculture.

хоккеи́ст (ice-)hockey-player. **хокке́й** hockey, ice-hockey.

холе́ра cholera.

холестери́н cholesterol.

холл hall, vestibule.

холм (-á) hill. **холми́стый** hilly.

хо́лод (pl -á, -óв) cold; coldness; cold weather. **холоди́льник** refrigerator. **хо́лодно** adv coldly. **холо́дн|ый** (хо́лоден, -дна́, -о) cold; inadequate, thin; ~ое ору́жие cold steel.

холо́п serf.

холосто́й (хо́лост, -á) unmarried, single; bachelor; idle; blank. **холостя́к** (-á) bachelor.

холст (-á) canvas; linen.

холу́й (-луя́) m lackey.

хому́т (-á) (horse-)collar; burden.

хомя́к (-á) hamster.

хор (pl хо́ры) choir; chorus.

хорва́т, ~ка Croat. **Хорва́тия** Croatia. **хорва́тский** Croatian.

хорёк (-рька́) polecat.

хореографи́ческий choreographic. **хореогра́фия** choreography.

хори́ст member of a choir or chorus.

хорони́ть (-ню́, -нишь) impf (pf за~, по~, с~) bury.

хоро́шенький pretty; nice. **хоро́шенько** adv properly, thoroughly. **хороше́ть** (-е́ю) impf (pf по~) grow prettier. **хоро́ший** (-óш, -á, -о) good; nice; pretty, nice-looking; **хорошо́** predic it is good; it is nice. **хорошо́** adv well; nicely; all right! good.

хо́ры (хор or -ов) pl gallery.

хоте́ть (хочу́, хо́чешь, хоти́м) impf (pf за~) wish; +gen, acc want; ~ пить be thirsty; ~ сказа́ть mean; ~ся impers +dat want; мне хоте́лось бы I should like; мне хо́чется I want.

хоть conj although; even if; partl at least, if only; for example; ~ бы if only. **хотя́** conj although; ~ бы even if; if only.

хо́хот loud laugh(ter). **хохота́ть** (-очу́, -о́чешь) impf laugh loudly.

хочу́ etc.: see **хоте́ть**

храбре́ц (-á) brave man. **храбри́ться** make a show of bravery; pluck up courage. **хра́брость** brav-

ery. **хра́брый** brave.

храм temple, church.

хране́ние keeping; storage; **ка́мера хране́ния** cloakroom, left-luggage office. **храни́лище** storehouse, depository. **храни́тель** m keeper, custodian; curator. **храни́ть** impf keep; preserve; ~ся be, be kept.

храпе́ть (-плю́) impf snore; snort.

хребе́т (-бта́) spine; (mountain) range; ridge.

хрен horseradish.

хрестома́тия reader.

хрип wheeze. **хрипе́ть** (-плю́) impf wheeze. **хри́плый** (-пл, -á, -о) hoarse. **хри́пнуть** (-ну; хрип) impf (pf о~) become hoarse. **хрипота́** hoarseness.

христиани́н (pl -а́не, -а́н), **христиа́нка** Christian. **христиа́нский** Christian. **христиа́нство** Christianity. **Христо́с** (-ста́) Christ.

хром chromium; chrome.

хромати́ческий chromatic.

хрома́ть impf limp; be poor. **хромо́й** (хром, -á, -о) lame; sb lame person.

хромосо́ма chromosome.

хромота́ lameness.

хро́ник chronic invalid. **хро́ника** chronicle; news items; newsreel.

хрони́ческий chronic.

хронологи́ческий chronological. **хроноло́гия** chronology.

хру́пкий (-пок, -пка́, -о) fragile; frail. **хру́пкость** fragility; frailness.

хруст crunch; crackle.

хруста́ль (-я́) m cut glass; crystal. **хруста́льный** cut-glass; crystal; crystal-clear.

хрусте́ть (-ущу́) impf, **хру́стнуть** (-ну) pf crunch; crackle.

хрю́кать impf, **хрю́кнуть** (-ну) pf grunt.

хрящ (-á) cartilage, gristle. **хрящево́й** cartilaginous, gristly.

худе́ть (-е́ю) impf (pf по~) grow thin.

ху́до harm; evil. **ху́до** adv ill, badly.

худоба́ thinness.

худо́жественный art, arts; artistic; ~ фильм feature film. **худо́жник** artist.

худо́й[1] (худ, -á, -о) thin, lean.

худо́й[2] (худ, -á, -о) bad; full of holes; worn; **ему́ ху́до** he feels bad.

худоща́вый thin, lean.

худший *superl of* **худой, плохой** (the) worst. **хуже** *comp of* **худой, худо, плохой, плохо** worse.

хула abuse, criticism.

хулиган hooligan. **хулиганить** *impf* behave like a hooligan. **хулиганство** hooliganism.

хунта junta.

хутор (*pl* -á) farm; small village.

Ц

цапля (*gen pl* -пель) heron.

царапать *impf*, **царапнуть** (-ну) *pf* (*pf also* **на~, о~**) scratch; scribble; **~ся** scratch; scratch one another. **царапина** scratch.

царизм tsarism. **царить** *impf* reign, prevail. **царица** tsarina; queen. **царский** tsar's; royal; tsarist; regal. **царство** kingdom; realm; reign. **царствование** reign. **царствовать** *impf* reign. **царь** (-я́) *m* tsar; king.

цвести (-ету́, -етёшь; -ёл, -á) *impf* flower, blossom; flourish.

цвет[1] (*pl* -á) colour; ~ лицá complexion.

цвет[2] (*loc* -ý; *pl* -ы́) flower; prime; **в цвету́** in blossom. **цветник** (-á) flower-bed, flower-garden.

цветн|о́й coloured; colour; non-ferrous; **~áя капу́ста** cauliflower; **~о́е стекло́** stained glass.

цветов|о́й colour; **~áя слепотá** colour-blindness.

цвето́к (-ткá; *pl* цветы́ *or* цветки́, -о́в) flower. **цвето́чный** flower. **цвету́щий** flowering; prosperous.

цеди́ть (цежу́, це́дишь) *impf* strain, filter.

целе́бный curative, healing.

целево́й earmarked for a specific purpose. **целенапра́вленный** purposeful. **целесообра́зный** expedient. **целеустремлённый** (-ён, -ённа *or* -енá) purposeful.

целико́м *adv* whole; entirely.

целинá virgin lands, virgin soil. **цели́нн|ый** virgin; **~ые зе́мли** virgin lands.

цели́тельный healing, medicinal.

це́лить(ся *impf* (*pf* **на~**) aim, take aim.

целлофáн cellophane.

целовáть *impf* (*pf* **по~**) kiss; **~ся** kiss.

це́лое *sb* whole; integer. **целому́дренный** chaste. **целому́дрие** chastity. **це́лостность** integrity. **це́лый** (цел, -á, -о) whole; safe, intact.

цель target; aim, object, goal.

це́льный (-лен, -льнá, -о) of one piece, solid; whole; integral; single. **це́льность** wholeness.

цеме́нт cement. **цементи́ровать** *impf & pf* cement. **цеме́нтный** cement.

ценá (*acc* -у; *pl* -ы) price, cost; worth.

ценз qualification. **це́нзор** censor. **цензу́ра** censorship.

цени́тель *m* judge, connoisseur. **цени́ть** (-ню́, -нишь) *impf* value; appreciate. **це́нность** value; price; *pl* valuables; values. **це́нный** valuable.

цент cent. **це́нтнер** centner (*100kg*).

центр centre. **централизáция** centralization. **централизовáть** *impf & pf* centralize. **центрáльный** central.

центробе́жный centrifugal.

цепене́ть (-е́ю) *impf* (*pf* **о~**) freeze; become rigid. **це́пкий** tenacious; prehensile; sticky; obstinate. **це́пкость** tenacity. **цепля́ться** *impf* **за**+*acc* clutch at; cling to.

цепно́й chain. **цепо́чка** chain; file. **цепь** (*loc* -и́; *gen pl* -е́й) chain; series; circuit.

церемо́ниться *impf* (*pf* **по~**) stand on ceremony. **церемо́ния** ceremony. **церковнославя́нский** Church Slavonic. **церко́вный** church; ecclesiastical. **це́рковь** (-кви; *gen pl* -е́й) church.

цех (*loc* -ý; *pl* -и *or* -á) shop; section; guild.

цивилизáция civilization. **цивилизо́ванный** civilized. **цивилизовáть** *impf & pf* civilize.

циге́йка beaver lamb.

цикл cycle.

цико́рий chicory.

цили́ндр cylinder; top hat. **цилиндри́ческий** cylindrical.

цимбáлы (-áл) *pl* cymbals.

цингá scurvy.

цини́зм cynicism. **ци́ник** cynic. **цини́чный** cynical.

цинк zinc. **ци́нковый** zinc.

цино́вка mat.

цирк circus.

циркули́ровать *impf* circulate. **ци́ркуль** *m* (pair of) compasses; dividers. **циркуля́р** circular. **циркуля́ция** circulation.

цисте́рна cistern, tank.

цитаде́ль citadel.

цита́та quotation. **цити́ровать** *impf* (*pf* **про~**) quote.

ци́трус citrus. **ци́трусов|ый** citrus; **~ые** *sb pl* citrus plants.

цифербла́т dial, face.

ци́фра figure; number, numeral. **цифрово́й** numerical, digital.

цо́коль *m* socle, plinth.

цыга́н (*pl* **-е, -а́н** *or* **-ы, -ов**), **цыга́нка** gipsy. **цыга́нский** gipsy.

цыплёнок (**-нка** *pl* **-ля́та, -ля́т**) chicken; chick.

цы́почки: на ~, на цы́почках on tip-toe.

Ч

чаба́н (**-а́**) shepherd.

чад (*loc* **-у́**) fumes, smoke.

чадра́ yashmak.

чай (*pl* **-и́, -ёв**) tea. **чаевы́е** (**-ы́х**) *sb pl* tip.

ча́йка (*gen pl* **ча́ек**) (sea-)gull.

ча́йная *sb* tea-shop. **ча́йник** teapot; kettle. **ча́йный** tea. **чайхана́** tea-house.

чалма́ turban.

чан (*loc* **-у́, *pl* **-ы́**) vat, tub.

чарова́ть *impf* bewitch; charm.

час (*with numerals* **-а́**, *loc* **-у́**; *pl* **-ы́**) hour; *pl* guard-duty; **кото́рый час?** what's the time?; **~** one o'clock; **в два ~а́** at two o'clock; **стоя́ть на ~а́х** stand guard; **~ы́ пик** rush-hour. **часо́вня** (*gen pl* **-вен**) chapel. **часово́й** *sb* sentry. **часово́й** clock, watch; of one hour, hour-long. **часовщи́к** (**-а́**) watchmaker.

части́ца small part; particle. **части́чно** *adv* partly, partially. **части́чный** partial.

ча́стник private trader.

ча́стность detail; **в ча́стности** in particular. **ча́стный** private; personal; particular, individual.

ча́сто *adv* often; close, thickly. **частоко́л** paling, palisade. **частота́** (*pl* **-ы**) frequency. **часто́тный** frequency.

часту́шка ditty. **ча́стый** (**част, -а́, -о**) frequent; close (together); dense; close-woven; rapid.

часть (*gen pl* **-е́й**) part; department; field; unit.

часы́ (**-о́в**) *pl* clock, watch.

ча́хлый stunted; sickly, puny. **чахо́тка** consumption.

ча́ша bowl; chalice; **~ весо́в** scale, pan. **ча́шка** cup; scale, pan.

ча́ща thicket.

ча́ще *comp of* **ча́сто, ча́стый**; **~ всего́** most often, mostly.

ча́яние expectation; hope. **ча́ять** (**ча́ю**) *impf* hope, expect.

чва́нство conceit, arrogance.

чего́ *see* **что**

чей *m*, **чья** *f*, **чьё** *neut*, **чьи** *pl pron* whose. **чей-либо, чей-нибудь** anyone's. **чей-то** someone's.

чек cheque; bill; receipt.

чека́нить *impf* (*pf* **вы́~, от~**) mint, coin; stamp, engrave; enunciate. **чека́нка** coinage, minting. **чека́нный** stamping, engraving; stamped, engraved; precise, expressive.

чёлка fringe; forelock.

чёлн (**-а́**; *pl* **чёлны́**) dug-out (canoe); boat. **челно́к** (**-а́**) dug-out (canoe); shuttle.

челове́к (*pl* **лю́ди**; with numerals, *gen* **-ве́к, -ам**) man, person.

человеко- *in comb* man-, anthropo-. **человеколюби́вый** philanthropic. **~лю́бие** philanthropy. **~ненави́стнический** misanthropic. **челове́ко-ча́с** (*pl* **-ы**) man-hour.

челове́чек (**-чка**) little man. **челове́ческий** human; humane. **челове́чество** mankind. **челове́чность** humaneness. **челове́чный** humane.

че́люсть jaw(-bone); dentures, false teeth.

чем, чём *see* **что**. **чем** *conj* than; **~..., тем...+comp** the more ..., the more.

чемода́н suitcase.

чемпио́н, ~ка champion, title-holder. **чемпиона́т** championship.

чему́ *see* **что**

чепуха́ nonsense; trifle.

че́пчик cap; bonnet.

че́рви (**-е́й**), **че́рвы** (**черв**) *pl* hearts. **черво́нн|ый** of hearts; **~ое зо́лото** pure gold.

червь (-я́; *pl* -и, -е́й) *m* worm; bug. **червя́к** (-а́) worm.

черда́к (-а́) attic, loft.

черёд (-а́, *loc* -ý) turn; **идти́ свои́м ~о́м** take its course. **чередова́ние** alternation. **чередова́ть** *impf* alternate; **~ся** alternate, take turns.

че́рез, чрез *prep+acc* across; over; through; via; in; after; every other.

черёмуха bird cherry.

черено́к (-нка́) handle; graft, cutting. **че́реп** (*pl* -а́) skull. **черепа́ха** tortoise; turtle; tortoise-shell. **черепа́ховый** tortoise; turtle; tortoiseshell. **черепа́ший** tortoise, turtle; very slow.

черепи́ца tile. **черепи́чный** tile; tiled.

черепо́к (-пка́) potsherd, fragment of pottery.

чересчу́р *adv* too; too much.

чере́шневый cherry. **чере́шня** (*gen pl* -шен) cherry(-tree).

черке́с, черке́шенка Circassian.

черкну́ть (-ну́, -нёшь) *pf* scrape; leave a mark on; scribble.

черне́ть (-е́ю) *impf* (*pf* по~) turn black; show black. **черни́ка** (*no pl; usu collect*) bilberry; bilberries. **черни́ла** (-и́л) *pl* ink. **черни́льный** ink. **черни́ть** *impf* (*pf* o~) blacken; slander. **черно-** *in comb* black; unskilled; rough. **чёрно-бе́лый** black-and-white. **~бу́рый** dark-brown; **~бу́рая лиса́** silver fox. **~воло́сый** black-haired. **~гла́зый** black-eyed. **~зём** chernozem, black earth. **~ко́жий** black; *sb* black. **~мо́рский** Black-Sea. **~рабо́чий** *sb* unskilled worker, labourer. **~сли́в** prunes. **~сморо́динный** blackcurrant.

чернови́к (-а́) rough copy, draft. **черново́й** rough; draft. **чернота́** blackness; darkness. **чёрн|ый** (-рен, -рна́) black; back; unskilled; ferrous; gloomy; *sb* (*derog*) black person; **~ая сморо́дина** (*no pl; usu collect*) blackcurrant(s).

черпа́к (-а́) scoop. **че́рпать** *impf*, **черпну́ть** (-ну́, -нёшь) *pf* draw; scoop; extract.

черстве́ть (-е́ю) *impf* (*pf* за~, о~, по~) get stale; become hardened. **чёрствый** (чёрств, -а́, -о) stale; hard.

чёрт (*pl* че́рти, -е́й) devil.

черта́ line; boundary; trait, characteristic. **чертёж** (-а́) drawing; blueprint, plan. **чертёжник** draughtsman. **чертёжный** drawing. **черти́ть** (-рчу́, -ртишь) *impf* (*pf* на~) draw. **чёртов** *adj* devil's; devilish. **чёрто́вский** devilish.

чертополо́х thistle.

чёрточка line; hyphen. **черче́ние** drawing. **черчу́** *etc.: see* **черти́ть**

чеса́ть (чешу́, -шешь) *impf* (*pf* по~) scratch; comb; card; **~ся** scratch o.s.; itch; comb one's hair.

чесно́к (-а́) garlic.

че́ствование celebration. **че́ствовать** *impf* celebrate; honour. **че́стность** honesty. **че́стный** (-тен, -тна́, -о) honest. **честолюби́вый** ambitious. **честолю́бие** ambition. **честь** (*loc* -и́) honour; **отда́ть ~** +*dat* salute.

чета́ pair, couple.

четве́рг (-а́) Thursday. **четве́реньки: на ~, на четве́реньках** on hands and knees. **четвёрка** four; figure 4; No. 4. **че́тверо** (-ы́х) four. **четвероно́г|ий** four-legged; **~ое** *sb* quadruped. **четверости́шие** quatrain. **четвёртый** fourth. **че́тверть** (*gen pl* -е́й) quarter; quarter of an hour; **без че́тверти час** a quarter to one. **че́тверть-фина́л** quarter-final.

чёткий (-ток, -тка́, -о) precise; clear-cut; clear; distinct. **чёткость** precision; clarity; distinctness.

чётный even.

четы́ре (-рёх, -рьмя́, -рёх) four. **четы́реста** (-рёхсо́т, -ьмяста́ми, -ёхста́х) four hundred. **четырёх-** *in comb* four-, tetra-. **четырёхкра́тный** fourfold. **~ме́стный** four-seater. **~со́тый** four-hundredth. **~уго́льник** quadrangle. **~уго́льный** quadrangular. **четы́рнадцатый** fourteenth. **четы́рнадцать** fourteen.

чех Czech.

чехо́л (-хла́) cover, case.

чечеви́ца lentil; lens.

че́шка Czech. **че́шский** Czech.

чешу́ *etc.: see* **чеса́ть**

чешу́йка scale. **чешуя́** scales.

чиж (-а́) siskin.

чин (*pl* -ы́) rank.

чини́ть[1] (-ню́, -нишь) *impf* (*pf* по~) repair, mend.

чинить[2] *impf* (*pf* у~) carry out; cause; ~ **препятствия** +*dat* put obstacles in the way of.

чиновник civil servant; official.

чип (micro)chip.

чипсы (-ов) *pl* (potato) crisps.

чирикать *impf*, **чирикнуть** (-ну) *pf* chirp.

чиркать *impf*, **чиркнуть** (-ну) *pf* +*instr* strike.

численность numbers; strength. **численный** numerical. **числитель** *m* numerator. **числительное** *sb* numeral. **числить** *impf* count, reckon; ~**ся** be; +*instr* be reckoned. **число** (*pl* -а, -сел) number; date, day; **в числе** +*gen* among; **в том числе** including; **единственное** ~ singular; **множественное** ~ plural. **числовой** numerical.

чистилище purgatory.

чистильщик cleaner. **чистить** (чищу) *impf* (*pf* вы~, о~, по~) clean; peel; clear. **чистка** cleaning; purge. **чисто** *adv* cleanly, clean; purely; completely. **чистовой** fair, clean. **чистокровный** thoroughbred. **чистописание** calligraphy. **чистоплотный** clean; neat; decent. **чистосердечный** frank, sincere. **чистота** cleanness; neatness; purity. **чистый** clean; neat; pure; complete.

читаемый widely-read, popular. **читальный** reading. **читатель** *m* reader. **читать** *impf* (*pf* про~, прочесть) read; recite; ~ **лекции** lecture; ~**ся** be legible; be discernible. **читка** reading.

чихать *impf*, **чихнуть** (-ну, -нёшь) *pf* sneeze.

чище *comp of* **чисто**, **чистый**

чищу *etc.: see* **чистить**

член member; limb; term; part; article. **членить** *impf* (*pf* рас~) divide; articulate. **член-корреспондент** corresponding member, associate. **членораздельный** articulate. **членский** membership. **членство** membership.

чмокать *impf*, **чмокнуть** (-ну) *pf* smack; squelch; kiss noisily; ~ **губами** smack one's lips.

чокаться *impf*, **чокнуться** (-нусь) *pf* clink glasses.

чопорный prim; stand-offish.

чреватый +*instr* fraught with. **чрево** belly, womb. **чревовещатель** *m* ventriloquist. **чревоугодие** gluttony.

чрез *see* **через**. **чрезвычайный** extraordinary; extreme; ~**ое положение** state of emergency. **чрезмерный** excessive.

чтение reading. **чтец** (-а) reader; reciter.

чтить (чту) *impf* honour.

что, чего, чему, чем, о чём *pron* what?; how?; why?; how much?; which, what, who; anything; **в чём дело?** what is the matter? **для чего?** what ... for? why?; ~ **ему до этого?** what does it matter to him?; ~ **с тобой?** what's the matter (with you)?; ~ **за** what? what sort of?; what (a) ..!; **что** *conj* that. **что (бы) ни** *pron* whatever, no matter what.

чтоб, чтобы *conj* in order (to), so as; that; to. **что-либо, что-нибудь** *prons* anything. **что-то**[1] *pron* something. **что-то**[2] *adv* somewhat, slightly; somehow, for some reason.

чувственность sensuality. **чувствительность** sensitivity; perceptibility; sentimentality. **чувствительный** sensitive; perceptible; sentimental. **чувство** feeling; sense; senses; **прийти в** ~ come round. **чувствовать** *impf* (*pf* по~) feel; realize; appreciate; ~**ся** be perceptible; make itself felt.

чугун (-а) cast iron. **чугунный** cast-iron.

чудак (-а), **чудачка** eccentric, crank. **чудачество** eccentricity.

чудеса *etc.: see* **чудо**. **чудесный** miraculous; wonderful.

чудиться (-ишься) *impf* (*pf* по~, при~) seem.

чудно *adv* wonderfully; wonderful! **чудной** (-дён, -дна) odd, strange. **чудный** wonderful; magical. **чудо** (*pl* доса) miracle; wonder. **чудовище** monster. **чудовищный** monstrous. **чудодейственный** miracle-working; miraculous. **чудом** *adv* miraculously. **чудотворный** miraculous, miracle-working.

чужбина foreign land. **чуждаться** *impf* +*gen* avoid; stand aloof from. **чуждый** (-жд, -а, -о) alien (to); +*gen* free from, devoid of. **чужеземец** (-мца), **-земка** foreigner. **чужезем-**

ный foreign. **чужо́й** someone else's, others'; strange, alien; foreign.

чула́н store-room; larder.

чуло́к (-лка́; *gen pl* -ло́к) stocking.

чума́ plague.

чума́зый dirty.

чурба́н block. **чу́рка** block, lump.

чу́ткий (-ток, -тка́, -о) keen; sensitive; sympathetic; delicate. **чу́ткость** keenness; delicacy.

чу́точка: ни чу́точки not in the least; **чу́точку** a little (bit).

чу́тче *comp of* **чу́ткий**

чуть *adv* hardly; just; very slightly; **~ не** almost; **~чуть** a tiny bit.

чутьё scent; flair.

чу́чело stuffed animal, stuffed bird; scarecrow.

чушь nonsense.

чу́ять (чу́ю) *impf* scent; sense.

чьё *etc.: see* **чей**

Ш

ша́баш sabbath.

шабло́н template; mould, stencil; cliché. **шабло́нный** stencil; trite; stereotyped.

шаг (with numerals -á, *loc* -ý; *pl* -и́) step; footstep; pace. **шага́ть** *impf*, **шагну́ть** (-ну́, -нёшь) *pf* step; stride; pace; make progress. **ша́гом** *adv* at walking pace.

ша́йба washer; puck.

ша́йка[1] tub.

ша́йка[2] gang, band.

шака́л jackal.

шала́ш (-á) cabin, hut.

шали́ть *impf* be naughty; play up. **шаловли́вый** mischievous, playful. **ша́лость** prank; *pl* mischief. **шалу́н** (-á), **шалу́нья** (*gen pl* -ний) naughty child.

шаль shawl.

шально́й mad, crazy.

ша́мкать *impf* mumble.

шампа́нское *sb* champagne.

шампиньо́н field mushroom.

шампу́нь *m* shampoo.

шанс chance.

шанта́ж (-á) blackmail. **шантажи́ровать** *impf* blackmail.

ша́пка hat; banner headline. **ша́почка** hat.

шар (with numerals -á; *pl* -ы́) sphere; ball; balloon.

шара́хать *impf*, **шара́хнуть** (-ну) hit; **~ся** dash; shy.

шарж caricature.

ша́рик ball; corpuscle. **ша́риков|ый: ~ая (авто)ру́чка** ball-point pen; **~ый подши́пник** ball-bearing. **шарикоподши́пник** ball-bearing.

ша́рить *impf* grope; sweep.

ша́ркать *impf*, **ша́ркнуть** (-ну) *pf* shuffle; scrape.

шарлата́н charlatan.

шарма́нка barrel-organ. **шарма́нщик** organ-grinder.

шарни́р hinge, joint.

шарова́ры (-áр) *pl* (*wide*) trousers.

шарови́дный spherical. **шаровой** ball; globular. **шарообра́зный** spherical.

шарф scarf.

шасси́ *neut indecl* chassis.

шата́ть *impf* rock, shake; *impers +acc* **его́ шата́ет** he is reeling; **~ся** sway; reel, stagger; come loose, be loose; be unsteady; loaf about.

шатёр (-трá) tent; marquee.

ша́ткий unsteady; shaky.

шату́н (-á) connecting-rod.

ша́фер (*pl* -á) best man.

шах check; **~ и мат** checkmate. **шахмати́ст** chess-player. **ша́хматы** (-ат) *pl* chess; chessmen.

ша́хта mine, pit; shaft. **шахтёр** miner. **шахтёрский** miner's; mining.

ша́шка[1] draught; *pl* draughts.

ша́шка[2] sabre.

шашлы́к (-á) kebab; barbecue.

шва *etc.: see* **шов**

шва́бра mop.

шваль rubbish; riff-raff.

шварто́в mooring-line; *pl* moorings. **швартова́ть** *impf* (*pf* при**~**) moor; **~ся** moor.

швед, ~ка Swede. **шве́дский** Swedish.

швейн|ый sewing; **~ая маши́на** sewing-machine.

швейца́р porter, doorman.

швейца́рец (-рца), -ца́рка Swiss. **Швейца́рия** Switzerland. **швейца́рский** Swiss.

Шве́ция Sweden.

швея́ seamstress.

швырну́ть (-ну́, -нёшь) *pf*, **швыря́ть**

impf throw, fling; ~ся +*instr* throw (about); treat carelessly.

шевели́ть (-елю́, -е́ли́шь) *impf*, **шевельну́ть** (-ну́, -нёшь) *pf* (*pf also* по~) (+*instr*) move, stir; ~ся move, stir.

шеде́вр masterpiece.

ше́йка (*gen pl* ше́ек) neck.

шёл *see* идти́

ше́лест rustle. **шелесте́ть** (-сти́шь) *impf* rustle.

шёлк (*loc* -у́, *pl* -а́) silk. **шелкови́стый** silky. **шелкови́ца** mulberry (-tree). **шелкови́чный** mulberry; ~ червь silkworm. **шёлковый** silk.

шелохну́ть (-ну́, -нёшь) *pf* stir, agitate; ~ся stir, move.

шелуха́ skin; peelings; pod. **шелуши́ть** (-шу́) peel; shell; ~ся peel (off), flake off.

шепеля́вить (-влю) *impf* lisp. **шепеля́вый** lisping.

шепну́ть (-ну́, -нёшь) *pf*, **шепта́ть** (-пчу́, -пчешь) *impf* whisper; ~ся whisper (together). **шёпот** whisper. **шёпотом** *adv* in a whisper.

шере́нга rank; file.

шерохова́тый rough; uneven.

шерсть wool; hair, coat. **шерстяно́й** wool(len).

шерша́вый rough.

шест (-а́) pole; staff.

ше́ствие procession. **ше́ствовать** process; march.

шестёрка six; figure 6; No. 6.

шестерня́ (*gen pl* -рён) gear-wheel, cogwheel.

ше́стеро (-ы́х) six.

шести- *in comb* six-, hexa-, sex(i)-.

шестигра́нник hexahedron. ~**дне́вка** six-day (*working*) week. ~**деся́тый** sixtieth. ~**ме́сячный** six-month; six-month-old. ~**со́тый** six-hundredth. ~**уго́льник** hexagon.

шестнадцатиле́тний sixteen-year; sixteen-year-old. **шестна́дцатый** sixteenth. **шестна́дцать** sixteen. **шесто́й** sixth. **шесть** (-и́, *instr* -ью́) six. **шестьдеся́т** (-и́десяти, *instr* -ью́десятью) sixty. **шестьсо́т** (-исо́т, -иста́м, -ьюста́ми, -иста́х) six hundred. **ше́стью** *adv* six times.

шеф boss, chief; patron, sponsor. **шеф-по́вар** chef. **ше́фство** patronage, adoption. **ше́фствовать** *impf*

+над+*instr* adopt; sponsor.

ше́я neck.

ши́ворот collar.

шика́рный chic, smart; splendid.

ши́ло (*pl* -ья, -ьев) awl.

шимпанзе́ *m indecl* chimpanzee.

ши́на tyre; splint.

шине́ль overcoat.

шинкова́ть *impf* shred, chop.

ши́нный tyre.

шип (-а́) thorn, spike, crampon; pin; tenon.

шипе́ние hissing; sizzling. **шипе́ть** (-плю́) *impf* hiss; sizzle; fizz.

шипо́вник dog-rose.

шипу́чий sparkling; fizzy. **шипу́чка** fizzy drink. **шипя́щий** sibilant.

ши́ре *comp of* широ́кий, широко́. **ширина́** width; gauge. **ши́рить** *impf* extend, expand; ~ся spread, extend.

ши́рма screen.

широ́к|ий (-о́к, -а́, -о́ко́) wide, broad; това́ры ~ого потребле́ния consumer goods. **широко́** *adv* wide, widely, broadly.

широко- *in comb* wide-, broad-. **широковеща́ние** broadcasting. ~**веща́тельный** broadcasting. ~**экра́нный** wide-screen.

широта́ (*pl* -ы) width, breadth; latitude. **широ́тный** of latitude; latitudinal. **широча́йший** *superl of* широ́кий. **ширпотре́б** *abbr* consumption; consumer goods. **ширь** (wide) expanse.

шить (шью, шьёшь) *impf* (*pf* с~) sew; make; embroider. **шитьё** sewing; embroidery.

ши́фер slate.

шифр cipher, code; shelf-mark. **шифро́ванный** in cipher, coded. **шифрова́ть** *impf* (*pf* за~) encipher. **шифро́вка** enciphering; coded communication.

ши́шка cone; bump; lump; (*sl*) big shot.

шкала́ (*pl* -ы) scale; dial.

шкату́лка box, casket, case.

шкаф (*loc* -у́; *pl* -ы́) cupboard; wardrobe. **шка́фчик** cupboard, locker.

шквал squall.

шкив (*pl* -ы́) pulley.

шко́ла school. **шко́льник** schoolboy. **шко́льница** schoolgirl. **шко́льный** school.

шку́ра skin, hide, pelt. шку́рка skin; rind; emery paper, sandpaper.

шла *see* идти́

шлагба́ум barrier.

шлак slag; dross; clinker. шлако-бло́к breeze-block.

шланг hose.

шлейф train.

шлем helmet.

шлёпать *impf*, шлёпнуть (-ну) *pf* smack, spank; shuffle; tramp; ~ся fall flat, plop down.

шли *see* идти́

шлифова́льный polishing; grinding. шлифова́ть *impf* (*pf* от~) polish; grind. шлифо́вка polishing.

шло *see* идти́. шлю *etc.*: *see* слать

шлюз lock, sluice.

шлю́пка boat.

шля́па hat. шля́пка hat; head.

шмель (-я́) *m* bumble-bee.

шмон *sl* search, frisking.

шмы́гать *impf*, шмыгну́ть (-ыгну́, -ыгнёшь) *pf* dart, rush; +*instr* rub, brush; ~ но́сом sniff.

шни́цель *m* schnitzel.

шнур (-а́) cord; lace; flex, cable. шнурова́ть *impf* (*pf* за~, про~) lace up; tie. шнуро́к (-рка́) lace.

шов (шва) seam; stitch; joint.

шовини́зм chauvinism. шовини́ст chauvinist. шовинисти́ческий chauvinistic.

шок shock. шоки́ровать *impf* shock.

шокола́д chocolate. шокола́дка chocolate, bar of chocolate. шокола́дный chocolate.

шо́рох rustle.

шо́рты (шорт) *pl* shorts.

шо́ры (шор) *pl* blinkers.

шоссе́ *neut indecl* highway.

шотла́ндец (-дца) Scotsman, Scot. Шотла́ндия Scotland. шотла́ндка[1] Scotswoman. шотла́ндка[2] tartan. шотла́ндский Scottish, Scots.

шофёр driver; chauffeur. шофёрский driver's; driving.

шпа́га sword.

шпага́т cord; twine; string; splits.

шпаклева́ть (-люю) *impf* (*pf* за~) caulk; fill, putty. шпаклёвка filling, puttying; putty.

шпа́ла sleeper.

шпана́ (*sl*) hooligan(s); riff-raff.

шпарга́лка crib.

шпа́рить *impf* (*pf* о~) scald.

шпат spar.

шпиль *m* spire; capstan. шпи́лька hairpin; hat-pin; tack; stiletto heel.

шпина́т spinach.

шпингале́т (vertical) bolt; catch, latch.

шпио́н spy. шпиона́ж espionage. шпио́нить *impf* spy (за+*instr* on). шпио́нский spy's; espionage.

шпо́ра spur.

шприц syringe.

шпро́та sprat.

шпу́лька spool, bobbin.

шрам scar.

шрапне́ль shrapnel.

шрифт (*pl* -ы́) type, print.

шт. *abbr* (*of* шту́ка) item, piece.

штаб (*pl* -ы́) staff; headquarters.

шта́бель (*pl* -я́) *m* stack.

штабно́й staff; headquarters.

штамп die, punch; stamp; cliché. штампо́ванный punched, stamped, pressed; trite; stock.

шта́нга bar, rod, beam; weight. штанги́ст weight-lifter.

штани́шки (-шек) *pl* (*child's*) shorts. штаны́ (-о́в) *pl* trousers.

штат[1] State.

штат[2], шта́ты (-ов) *pl* staff, establishment.

штати́в tripod, base, stand.

шта́тный staff; established.

шта́тск|ий civilian; ~ое (пла́тье) civilian clothes; ~ий *sb* civilian.

штемпель (*pl* -я́) *m* stamp; почто́вый ~ postmark.

ште́псель (*pl* -я́) *m* plug, socket.

штиль *m* calm.

штифт (-а́) pin, dowel.

што́льня (*gen pl* -лен) gallery.

што́пать *impf* (*pf* за~) darn. што́пка darning; darning wool.

што́пор corkscrew; spin.

што́ра blind.

шторм gale.

штраф fine. штрафно́й penal; penalty. штрафова́ть *impf* (*pf* о~) fine.

штрих (-а́) stroke; feature. штрихова́ть *impf* (*pf* за~) shade, hatch.

штуди́ровать *impf* (*pf* про~) study.

шту́ка item, one; piece; trick.

штукату́р plasterer. штукату́рить *impf* (*pf* от~, о~) plaster. штукату́рка plastering; plaster.

штурва́л (steering-)wheel, helm.

штурм storm, assault.

штурман (pl -ы or -á) navigator.

штурмовать impf storm, assault.
штурмов|ой assault; storming; ~áя
авиáция ground-attack aircraft.
штурмовщина rushed work.

штучный piece, by the piece.

штык (-á) bayonet.

штырь (-я) m pintle, pin.

шуба fur coat.

шулер (pl -á) card-sharper.

шум noise; uproar, racket; stir. шу-
меть (-млю) impf make a noise; row;
make a fuss. шумный (-мен, -мнá, -о)
noisy; loud; sensational.

шумов|ой sound; ~ые эффекты
sound effects. шумок (-мкá) noise;
под ~ on the quiet.

шурин brother-in-law (wife's brother).

шурф prospecting shaft.

шуршать (-шу) impf rustle.

шустрый (-тёр, -трá, -о) smart, bright,
sharp.

шут (-á) fool; jester. шутить (-чу,
-тишь) impf (pf по~) joke; play,
trifle; +над+instr make fun of. шут-
ка joke, jest. шутливый humorous;
joking, light-hearted. шуточный
comic; joking. шутя adv for fun, in
jest; easily.

шушукаться impf whisper together.

шхуна schooner.

шью etc.: see шить

Щ

щавель (-я) m sorrel.

щадить (щажу) impf (pf по~) spare.

щебёнка, щебень (-бня) m crushed
stone, ballast; road-metal.

щебет twitter, chirp. щебетать (-ечу,
-ечешь) impf twitter, chirp.

щегол (-глá) goldfinch.

щёголь (-гля) m dandy, fop. щегольнуть
(-ну, -нёшь) pf, щеголять impf dress
fashionably; strut about; +instr show
off, flaunt. щегольской foppish.

щедрость generosity. щедрый (-др,
-á, -о) generous; liberal.

щека (acc щёку; pl щёки, -áм) cheek.

щеколда latch, catch.

щекотать (-очу, -очешь) impf (pf по~)
tickle. щекотка tickling, tickle. ще-
котливый ticklish, delicate.

щёлкать impf, щёлкнуть (-ну) pf
crack; flick; trill; +instr click, snap,
pop.

щёлок bleach. щелочной alkaline.
щёлочь (gen pl -ей) alkali.

щелчок (-чкá) flick; slight; blow.

щель (gen pl -ей) crack; chink; slit;
crevice; slit trench.

щемить (-млю) impf constrict; ache;
oppress.

щенок (-нкá; pl -нки, -ов or -нята, -ят)
pup; cub.

щепá (pl -ы, -áм), щепка splinter, chip;
kindling.

щепетильный punctilious.

щепка see щепá

щепотка, щепоть pinch.

щетина bristle; stubble. щетини-
стый bristly. щетиниться impf (pf
о~) bristle. щётка brush; fetlock.

щи (щей or щец, щам, щáми) pl shchi,
cabbage soup.

щиколотка ankle.

щипать (-плю, -плешь) impf, щип-
нуть (-ну, -нёшь) pf (pf also о~,
о~, ущипнуть) pinch, nip; sting, bite;
burn; pluck; nibble; ~ся pinch. щип-
ком adv pizzicato. щипок (-пкá)
pinch, nip. щипцы (-ов) pl tongs,
pincers, pliers; forceps.

щит (-á) shield; screen; sluice-gate; (tor-
toise-)shell; board; panel. щитовид-
ный thyroid. щиток (-ткá) dashboard.

щука pike.

щуп probe. щупальце (gen pl -лец)
tentacle; antenna. щупать impf (pf
по~) feel, touch.

щуплый (-пл, -á, -о) weak, puny.

щурить impf (pf со~) screw up, narrow; ~ся screw up one's eyes; narrow.

Э

эбеновый ebony.

эвакуáция evacuation. эвакуиро-
ванный sb evacuee. эвакуировать
impf & pf evacuate.

эвкалипт eucalyptus.

эволюционировать impf & pf evolve.
эволюционный evolutionary. эво-
люция evolution.

эгида aegis.

эгоизм egoism, selfishness. эгоист,
~ка egoist. эгоистический, эгои-

сти́чный egoistic, selfish.

эй *int* hi! hey!

эйфори́я euphoria.

эква́тор equator.

эквивале́нт equivalent.

экзальта́ция exaltation.

экза́мен examination; **вы́держать, сдать ~** pass an examination. **экзамена́тор** examiner. **экзаменова́ть** *impf* (*pf* **про~**) examine; **~ся** take an examination.

экзеку́ция (corporal) punishment.

экзе́ма eczema.

экземпля́р specimen; copy.

экзистенциали́зм existentialism.

экзоти́ческий exotic.

э́кий what (a).

экипа́ж[1] carriage.

экипа́ж[2] crew. **экипирова́ть** *impf* & *pf* equip. **экипиро́вка** equipping; equipment.

эклекти́зм eclecticism.

экле́р éclair.

экологи́ческий ecological. **эколо́гия** ecology.

эконо́мика economics; economy. **экономи́ст** economist. **эконо́мить** (-млю) *impf* (*pf* **с~**) use sparingly; save; economize. **экономи́ческий** economic; economical. **экономи́чный** economical. **эконо́мия** economy; saving. **эконо́мка** housekeeper. **эконо́мный** economical; thrifty.

экра́н screen. **экраниза́ция** filming; film version.

экскава́тор excavator.

экскурса́нт tourist. **экскурсио́нный** excursion. **экску́рсия** (conducted) tour; excursion. **экскурсово́д** guide.

экспанси́вный effusive.

экспатриа́нт expatriate. **экспатрии́ровать** *impf* & *pf* expatriate.

экспеди́ция expedition; dispatch; forwarding office.

эксперимент experiment. **экспериме́нтальный** experimental. **эксперименти́ровать** *impf* experiment.

экспе́рт expert. **эксперти́за** (expert) examination; commission of experts.

эксплуата́тор exploiter. **эксплуатацио́нный** operating. **эксплуата́ция** exploitation; operation. **эксплуати́ровать** *impf* exploit; operate, run.

экспози́ция lay-out; exposition; ex-

posure. **экспона́т** exhibit. **экспоно́метр** exposure meter.

э́кспорт export. **экспорти́ровать** *impf* & *pf* export. **э́кспортный** export.

экспре́сс express (train etc.).

экспро́мт impromptu. **экспро́мтом** *adv* impromptu.

экспроприа́ция expropriation. **экспроприи́ровать** *impf* & *pf* expropriate.

экста́з ecstasy.

экстраваѓа́нтный eccentric, bizarre.

экстра́кт extract.

экстреми́ст extremist. **экстреми́стский** extremist.

э́кстренный urgent; emergency; special.

эксцентри́чный eccentric.

эксце́сс excess.

эласти́чный elastic; supple.

элева́тор grain elevator; hoist.

элега́нтный elegant, smart.

эле́гия elegy.

электризова́ть *impf* (*pf* **на~**) electrify. **эле́ктрик** electrician. **электрифика́ция** electrification. **электрифици́ровать** *impf* & *pf* electrify. **электри́ческий** electric(al). **электри́чество** electricity. **электри́чка** electric train.

электро- *in comb* electro-, electric, electrical. **~во́з** electric locomotive. **~дви́гатель** *m* electric motor. **электро́лиз** electrolysis. **~магни́тный** electromagnetic. **~монтёр** electrician. **~одея́ло** electric blanket. **~по́езд** electric train. **~прибо́р** electrical appliance. **~про́вод** (*pl* **-а́**) electric cable. **~прово́дка** electric wiring. **~ста́нция** power-station. **~те́хник** electrical engineer. **~те́хника** electrical engineering. **~шо́к** electric-shock treatment. **~эне́ргия** electrical energy.

электро́д electrode.

электро́н electron. **электро́ника** electronics.

электро́нный electron; electronic.

элеме́нт element; cell; character. **элемента́рный** elementary.

эли́та élite.

э́ллипс elipse.

эма́левый enamel. **эмалирова́ть**

impf enamel. **эма́ль** enamel.

эмансипа́ция emancipation.

эмба́рго *neut indecl* embargo.

эмбле́ма emblem.

эмбрио́н embryo.

эмигра́нт emigrant, émigré. **эмигра́ция** emigration. **эмигри́ровать** *impf & pf* emigrate.

эмоциона́льный emotional. **эмо́ция** emotion.

эмпири́ческий empirical.

эму́льсия emulsion.

э́ндшпиль *m* end-game.

энерге́тика power engineering. **энергети́ческий** energy. **энерги́чный** energetic. **эне́ргия** energy.

энтомоло́гия entomology.

энтузиа́зм enthusiasm. **энтузиа́ст** enthusiast.

энциклопеди́ческий encyclopaedic. **энциклопе́дия** encyclopaedia.

эпигра́мма epigram. **эпи́граф** epigraph.

эпиде́мия epidemic.

эпизо́д episode. **эпизоди́ческий** episodic; sporadic.

эпиле́псия epilepsy. **эпиле́птик** epileptic.

эпило́г epilogue. **эпита́фия** epitaph. **эпи́тет** epithet. **эпице́нтр** epicentre.

эпопе́я epic.

эпо́ха epoch, era.

э́ра era; **до на́шей э́ры** BC; **на́шей э́ры** AD.

эре́кция erection.

эро́зия erosion.

эроти́зм eroticism. **эро́тика** sensuality. **эроти́ческий, эроти́чный** erotic, sensual.

эруди́ция erudition.

эска́дра (*naut*) squadron. **эскадри́лья** (*gen pl* -лий) (*aeron*) squadron. **эскадро́н** (*mil*) squadron. **эскадро́нный** squadron.

эскала́тор escalator. **эскала́ция** escalation.

эски́з sketch; draft. **эски́зный** sketch; draft.

эскимо́с, эскимо́ска Eskimo.

эско́рт escort.

эсми́нец (-нца) *abbr* (*of* эска́дренный миноно́сец) destroyer.

эссе́нция essence.

эстака́да trestle bridge; overpass; pier, boom.

эста́мп print, engraving, plate.

эстафе́та relay race; baton.

эсте́тика aesthetics. **эстети́ческий** aesthetic.

эсто́нец (-нца), **эсто́нка** Estonian. **Эсто́ния** Estonia. **эсто́нский** Estonian.

эстра́да stage, platform; variety. **эстра́дный** stage; variety; ~ конце́рт variety show.

эта́ж (-а́) storey, floor. **этаже́рка** shelves.

э́так *adv* so, thus; about. **э́такий** such (a), what (a).

этало́н standard.

эта́п stage; halting-place.

э́тика ethics.

этике́т etiquette.

этике́тка label.

эти́л ethyl.

этимоло́гия etymology.

эти́ческий, эти́чный ethical.

этни́ческий ethnic. **этногра́фия** ethnography.

э́то *partl* this (is), that (is), it (is). **э́тот** *m*, **э́та** *f*, **э́то** *neut*, **э́ти** *pl pron* this, these.

этю́д study, sketch; étude.

эфеме́рный ephemeral.

эфио́п, ~ка Ethiopian. **эфио́пский** Ethiopian.

эфи́р ether; air. **эфи́рный** ethereal; ether, ester.

эффе́кт effect. **эффекти́вность** effectiveness. **эффекти́вный** effective. **эффе́ктный** effective; striking.

эх *int* eh! oh!

э́хо echo.

эшафо́т scaffold.

эшело́н echelon; special train.

Ю

юбиле́й anniversary; jubilee. **юбиле́йный** jubilee.

ю́бка skirt. **ю́бочка** short skirt.

ювели́р jeweller. **ювели́рный** jeweller's, jewellery; fine, intricate.

юг south; **на ~е** in the south. **ю́го-восто́к** south-east. **ю́го-за́пад** south-west. **югосла́в, ~ка** Yugoslav. **Югосла́вия** Yugoslavia. **югосла́вский** Yugoslav.

юдофо́б anti-Semite. **юдофо́бство**

anti-Semitism.

южа́нин (*pl* -а́не, -а́н), южа́нка southerner. ю́жный south, southern; southerly.

юла́ top; fidget. юли́ть *impf* fidget.

ю́мор humour. юмори́ст humourist. юмористи́ческий humorous.

ю́ность youth. ю́ноша (*gen pl* -шей) *m* youth. ю́ношеский youthful. ю́ношество youth; young people. ю́ный (юн, -а́, -о) young; youthful.

юпи́тер floodlight.

юриди́ческий legal, juridical. юриско́нсульт legal adviser. юри́ст lawyer.

ю́ркий (-рок, -рка́, -рко) quick-moving, brisk; smart.

юро́дивый crazy.

ю́рта yurt, nomad's tent.

юсти́ция justice.

юти́ться (ючу́сь) *impf* huddle (together).

Я

я (меня́, мне, мной (-о́ю), (обо) мне) *pron* I.

я́беда *m & f*, tell-tale; informer.

я́блоко (*pl* -и, -ок) apple; глазно́е ~ eyeball. я́блоневый, я́блочный apple. я́блоня apple-tree.

яви́ться (явлю́сь, я́вишься) *pf*, явля́ться *impf* appear; arise; +*instr* be, serve as. я́вка appearance, attendance; secret rendez-vous. явле́ние phenomenon; appearance; occurrence; scene. я́вный obvious; overt. я́вственный clear. я́вствовать be clear, be obvious.

ягнёнок (-нка; *pl* -ня́та, -я́т) lamb.

я́года berry; berries.

я́годица buttock(s).

ягуа́р jaguar.

яд poison; venom.

я́дерный nuclear.

ядови́тый poisonous; venomous.

ядрёный healthy; bracing; juicy.

ядро́ (*pl* -а, я́дер) kernel, core; nucleus; (cannon-)ball; shot.

я́зва ulcer, sore. я́звенн|ый ulcerous; ~ая боле́знь ulcers. язви́тельный

caustic, sarcastic. язви́ть (-влю́) *impf* (*pf* съ~) be sarcastic.

язы́к (-а́) tongue; clapper; language. языкове́д linguist. языкове́дение, языкозна́ние linguistics. языково́й linguistic. языко́вый tongue; lingual. язычко́вый reed. язы́чник heathen, pagan. язычо́к (-чка́) tongue; reed; catch.

яи́чко (*pl* -и, -чек) egg; testicle. яи́чник ovary. яи́чница fried eggs. яйцо́ (*pl* я́йца, яи́ц) egg; ovum.

я́кобы *conj* as if; *partl* supposedly.

я́корн|ый anchor; ~ая стоя́нка anchorage. я́корь (*pl* -я́) *m* anchor.

я́лик skiff.

я́ма pit, hole.

ямщи́к (-а́) coachman.

янва́рский January. янва́рь (-я́) *m* January.

янта́рный amber. янта́рь (-я́) *m* amber.

япо́нец (-нца), япо́нка Japanese. Япо́ния Japan. япо́нский Japanese.

ярд yard.

я́ркий (я́рок, ярка́, -о) bright; colourful, striking.

ярлы́к (-а́) label; tag.

я́рмарка fair.

ярмо́ (*pl* -а) yoke.

ярово́й spring.

я́ростный furious, fierce. я́рость fury.

я́рус circle; tier; layer.

я́рче *comp of* я́ркий

я́рый fervent; furious; violent.

я́сень *m* ash(-tree).

я́сли (-ей) *pl* manger; crèche, day nursery.

ясне́ть (-е́ет) *impf* become clear, clear. я́сно *adv* clearly. яснови́дение clairvoyance. яснови́дец (-дца), яснови́дица clairvoyant. я́сность clarity; clearness. я́сный (я́сен, ясна́, -о) clear; bright; fine.

я́ства (яств) *pl* victuals.

я́стреб (*pl* -а́) hawk.

я́хта yacht.

яче́йка cell.

ячме́нь[1] (-я́) *m* barley.

ячме́нь[2] (-я́) *m* stye.

я́щерица lizard.

я́щик box; drawer.

A

a, an *indef article, not usu translated*; **twice a week** два ра́за в неде́лю.

aback *adv*: **take ~** озада́чивать *impf*, озада́чить *pf*.

abacus *n* счёты *m pl*.

abandon *vt* покида́ть *impf*, поки́нуть *pf*; (*give up*) отка́зываться *impf*, отказа́ться *pf* от+*gen*; **~ o.s. to** предава́ться *impf*, преда́ться *pf* +*dat*. **abandoned** *adj* поки́нутый; (*profligate*) распу́тный.

abase *vt* унижа́ть *impf*, уни́зить *pf*. **abasement** *n* униже́ние.

abate *vi* затиха́ть *impf*, зати́хнуть *pf*. **abattoir** *n* скотобо́йня.

abbey *n* абба́тство.

abbreviate *vt* сокраща́ть *impf*, сократи́ть *pf*. **abbreviation** *n* сокраще́ние.

abdicate *vi* отрека́ться *impf*, отре́чься *pf* от престо́ла. **abdication** *n* отрече́ние (от престо́ла).

abdomen *n* брюшна́я по́лость. **abdominal** *adj* брюшно́й.

abduct *vt* похища́ть *impf*, похити́ть *pf*. **abduction** *n* похище́ние.

aberration *n* (*mental*) помутне́ние рассу́дка.

abet *vt* подстрека́ть *impf*, подстрекну́ть *pf* (к соверше́нию преступле́ния *etc.*).

abhor *vt* ненави́деть *impf*. **abhorrence** *n* отвраще́ние. **abhorrent** *adj* отврати́тельный.

abide *vt* (*tolerate*) выноси́ть *impf*, вы́нести *pf*; **~ by** (*rules etc.*) сле́довать *impf*, по~ *pf*. **ability** *n* спосо́бность.

abject *adj* (*wretched*) жа́лкий; (*humble*) уни́женный; **~ poverty** кра́йняя нищета́.

ablaze *predic* охва́ченный огнём.

able *adj* спосо́бный, уме́лый; **be ~ to** мочь *impf*, с~ *pf*; (*know how to*) уме́ть *impf*, с~ *pf*.

abnormal *adj* ненорма́льный. **abnormality** *n* ненорма́льность.

aboard *adv* на борт(у́); (*train*) в по́езд(е).

abode *n* жили́ще; **of no fixed ~** без постоя́нного местожи́тельства.

abolish *vt* отменя́ть *impf*, отмени́ть *pf*. **abolition** *n* отме́на.

abominable *adj* отврати́тельный. **abomination** *n* ме́рзость.

aboriginal *adj* коренно́й; *n* абориге́н, коренно́й жи́тель *m*. **aborigine** *n* абориге́н, коренно́й жи́тель *m*.

abort *vi* (*med*) выки́дывать *impf*, вы́кинуть *pf*; *vt* (*terminate*) прекраща́ть *impf*, прекрати́ть *pf*. **abortion** *n* або́рт; **have an ~** де́лать *impf*, с~ *pf* або́рт. **abortive** *adj* безуспе́шный.

abound *vi* быть в изоби́лии; **~ in** изоби́ловать *impf* +*instr*.

about *adv & prep* (*approximately*) о́коло+*gen*; (*concerning*) о+*prep*, насчёт+*gen*; (*up and down*) по+*dat*; (*in the vicinity*) круго́м; **be ~ to** собира́ться *impf*, собра́ться *pf* +*inf*.

above *adv* наверху́; (*higher up*) вы́ше; **from ~** све́рху; свы́ше; *prep* над+*instr*, выше; (*more than*) свы́ше+*gen*. **above-board** *adj* че́стный. **above-mentioned** *adj* вышеупомя́нутый.

abrasion *n* истира́ние; (*wound*) сса́дина. **abrasive** *adj* абрази́вный; (*manner*) колю́чий; *n* абрази́вный материа́л.

abreast *adv* в ряд; **keep ~ of** идти́ в но́гу с+*instr*.

abridge *vt* сокраща́ть *impf*, сократи́ть *pf*. **abridgement** *n* сокраще́ние.

abroad *adv* за грани́цей, за грани́цу; **from ~** из-за грани́цы.

abrupt *adj* (*steep*) круто́й; (*sudden*) внеза́пный; (*curt*) ре́зкий.

abscess *n* абсце́сс.

abscond *vi* скрыва́ться *impf*, скры́ться *pf*.

absence *n* отсу́тствие. **absent** *adj* отсу́тствующий; **be ~** отсу́тствовать *impf*; *vt*: ~ **o.s.** отлучаться *impf*, отлучиться *pf*. **absentee** *n* отсутствующий *sb*. **absenteeism** *n* прогул. **absent-minded** *adj* рассеянный.

absolute *adj* абсолютный; (*complete*) полный, совершенный.

absolution *n* отпущение грехов. **absolve** *vt* прощать *impf*, простить *pf*.

absorb *vt* впитывать *impf*, впитать *pf*. **absorbed** *adj* поглощённый. **absorbent** *adj* всасывающий. **absorption** *n* впитывание; (*mental*) погружённость.

abstain *vi* воздерживаться *impf*, воздержаться *pf* (**from** от+*gen*). **abstemious** *adj* воздержанный. **abstention** *n* воздержание; (*person*) воздержавшийся *sb*. **abstinence** *n* воздержание.

abstract *adj* абстрактный, отвлечённый; *n* реферат.

absurd *adj* абсурдный. **absurdity** *n* абсурд.

abundance *n* обилие. **abundant** *adj* обильный.

abuse *vt* (*insult*) ругать *impf*, вы~, об~, от~ *pf*; (*misuse*) злоупотреблять *impf*, злоупотребить *pf*; *n* (*curses*) ругань, ругательства *neut pl*; (*misuse*) злоупотребление. **abusive** *adj* оскорбительный, ругательный.

abut *vi* примыкать *impf* (**on** к+*dat*).

abysmal *adj* (*extreme*) безграничный; (*bad*) ужасный. **abyss** *n* бездна.

academic *adj* академический. **academician** *n* академик. **academy** *n* академия.

accede *vi* вступать *impf*, вступить *pf* (**to** в, на+*acc*); (*assent*) соглашаться *impf*, согласиться *pf*.

accelerate *vt & i* ускорять(ся) *impf*, ускорить(ся) *pf*; (*motoring*) давать *impf*, дать *pf* газ. **acceleration** *n* ускорение. **accelerator** *n* ускоритель *m*; (*pedal*) акселератор.

accent *n* акцент; (*stress*) ударение; *vt* делать *impf*, с~ *pf* ударение на+*acc*. **accentuate** *vt* акцентировать *impf & pf*.

accept *vt* принимать *impf*, принять *pf*. **acceptable** *adj* приемлемый. **acceptance** *n* принятие.

access *n* доступ. **accessible** *adj* доступный. **accession** *n* вступление (на престол). **accessories** *n* принадлежности *f pl*. **accessory** *n* (*accomplice*) соучастник, -ица.

accident *n* (*chance*) случайность; (*mishap*) несчастный случай; (*crash*) авария; **by** ~ случайно. **accidental** *adj* случайный.

acclaim *vt* (*praise*) восхвалять *impf*, восхвалить *pf*; *n* восхваление.

acclimatization *n* акклиматизация. **acclimatize** *vt* акклиматизировать *impf & pf*.

accommodate *vt* помещать *impf*, поместить *pf*; (*hold*) вмещать *impf*, вместить *pf*. **accommodating** *adj* услужливый. **accommodation** *n* (*hotel*) номер; (*home*) жильё.

accompaniment *n* сопровождение; (*mus*) аккомпанемент. **accompanist** *n* аккомпаниатор. **accompany** *vt* сопровождать *impf*, сопроводить *pf*; (*escort*) провожать *impf*, проводить *pf*; (*mus*) аккомпанировать *impf* +*dat*.

accomplice *n* соучастник, -ица.

accomplish *vt* совершать *impf*, совершить *pf*. **accomplished** *adj* законченный. **accomplishment** *n* выполнение; (*skill*) совершенство.

accord *n* согласие; **of one's own** ~ добровольно; **of its own** ~ сам собой, сам по себе. **accordance** *n*: **in** ~ **with** в соответствии с+*instr*, согласно+*dat*. **according** *adv*: ~ **to** по+*dat*, ~ **to him** по его словам. **accordingly** *adv* соответственно.

accordion *n* аккордеон.

accost *vt* приставать *impf*, пристать *pf* к+*dat*.

account *n* (*comm*) счёт; (*report*) отчёт; (*description*) описание; **on no** ~ ни в коем случае; **on** ~ в счёт причитающейся суммы; **on** ~ **of** из-за+*gen*, по причине+*gen*; **take into** ~ принимать *impf*, принять *pf* в расчёт; *vi*: ~ **for** объяснять *impf*, объяснить *pf*. **accountable** *adj* ответственный.

accountancy *n* бухгалтерия. **accountant** *n* бухгалтер.

accrue *vi* нарастать *impf*, нарасти *pf*.

accumulate *vt & i* накапливать(ся)

impf, копи́ть(ся) *impf*, на~ *pf*. **accumulation** *n* накопле́ние. **accumulator** *n* аккумуля́тор.

accuracy *n* то́чность. **accurate** *adj* то́чный.

accusation *n* обвине́ние. **accusative** *adj* (*n*) вини́тельный (паде́ж). **accuse** *vt* обвиня́ть *impf*, обвини́ть *pf* (**of**+*prep*); **the** ~**d** обвиня́емый *sb*.

accustom *vt* приуча́ть *impf*, приучи́ть *pf* (**to** к+*dat*). **accustomed** *adj* привы́чный; **be, get** ~ привыка́ть *impf*, привы́кнуть *pf* (**to** к+*dat*).

ace *n* туз; (*pilot*) ас.

ache *n* боль; *vi* боле́ть *impf*.

achieve *vt* достига́ть *impf*, дости́чь & дости́гнуть *pf* +*gen*. **achievement** *n* достиже́ние.

acid *n* кислота́; *adj* ки́слый; ~ **rain** кисло́тный дождь. **acidity** *n* кислота́.

acknowledge *vt* признава́ть *impf*, призна́ть *pf*; (~ **receipt of**) подтвержда́ть *impf*, подтверди́ть *pf* получе́ние+*gen*. **acknowledgement** *n* призна́ние; подтвержде́ние.

acne *n* прыщи́ *m pl*.

acorn *n* жёлудь *m*.

acoustic *adj* акусти́ческий. **acoustics** *n pl* аку́стика.

acquaint *vt* знако́мить *impf*, по~ *pf*. **acquaintance** *n* знако́мство; (*person*) знако́мый *sb*. **acquainted** *adj* знако́мый.

acquiesce *vi* соглаша́ться *impf*, согласи́ться *pf*. **acquiescence** *n* согла́сие.

acquire *vt* приобрета́ть *impf*, приобрести́ *pf*. **acquisition** *n* приобрете́ние. **acquisitive** *adj* стяжа́тельский.

acquit *vt* опра́вдывать *impf*, оправда́ть *pf*; ~ **o.s.** вести́ *impf* себя́. **acquittal** *n* оправда́ние.

acre *n* акр.

acrid *adj* е́дкий.

acrimonious *adj* язви́тельный.

acrobat *n* акроба́т. **acrobatic** *adj* акробати́ческий.

across *adv* & *prep* че́рез+*acc*; (*athwart*) поперёк (+*gen*); (*to, on, other side*) на ту сто́рону (+*gen*), на той стороне́ (+*gen*); (*crosswise*) крест-на́крест.

acrylic *n* акри́л; *adj* акри́ловый.

act *n* (*deed*) акт, посту́пок; (*law*)

акт, зако́н; (*of play*) де́йствие; (*item*) но́мер; *vi* поступа́ть *impf*, поступи́ть *pf*; де́йствовать *impf*, по~ *pf*; *vt* игра́ть *impf*, сыгра́ть *pf*. **acting** *n* игра́; (*profession*) актёрство; *adj* исполня́ющий обя́занности+*gen*. **action** *n* де́йствие, посту́пок; (*law*) иск, проце́сс; (*battle*) бой; ~ **replay** повто́р; **be out of** ~ не рабо́тать *impf*. **activate** *vt* приводи́ть *impf*, привести́ *pf* в де́йствие. **active** *adj* акти́вный; ~ **service** действи́тельная слу́жба; ~ **voice** действи́тельный зало́г. **activity** *n* де́ятельность. **actor** *n* актёр. **actress** *n* актри́са.

actual *adj* действи́тельный. **actuality** *n* действи́тельность. **actually** *adv* на са́мом де́ле, факти́чески.

acumen *n* проница́тельность.

acupuncture *n* иглоука́лывание.

acute *adj* о́стрый.

AD *abbr* н.э. (на́шей э́ры).

adamant *adj* непрекло́нный.

adapt *vt* приспособля́ть *impf*, приспосо́бить *pf*; (*theat*) инсцени́ровать *impf* & *pf*; ~ **o.s.** приспособля́ться *impf*, приспосо́биться *pf*. **adaptable** *adj* приспособля́ющийся. **adaptation** *n* приспособле́ние; (*theat*) инсцениро́вка. **adapter** *n* ада́птер.

add *vt* прибавля́ть *impf*, приба́вить *pf*; (*say*) добавля́ть *impf*, доба́вить *pf*; ~ **together** скла́дывать *impf*, сложи́ть *pf*; ~ **up** сумми́ровать *impf* & *pf*; ~ **up to** составля́ть *impf*, соста́вить *pf*; (*fig*) своди́ться *impf*, свести́сь *pf* к+*dat*. **addenda** *n* приложе́ния *pl*.

adder *n* гадю́ка.

addict *n* наркома́н, ~ка. **addicted** *adj*: **be** ~ **to** быть рабо́м+*gen*; **become** ~ **to** пристрасти́ться *pf* к+*dat*. **addiction** *n* (*passion*) пристра́стие; (*to drugs*) наркома́ния.

addition *n* прибавле́ние; дополне́ние; (*math*) сложе́ние; **in** ~ вдоба́вок, кро́ме того́. **additional** *adj* доба́вочный. **additive** *n* доба́вка.

address *n* а́дрес; (*speech*) речь; ~ **book** записна́я кни́жка; *vt* адресова́ть *impf* & *pf*; (*speak to*) обраща́ться *impf*, обрати́ться *pf* к+*dat*; ~ **a meeting** выступа́ть *impf*, вы́ступить *pf* на собра́нии. **addressee**

n адреса́т.

adept *adj* све́дущий; *n* ма́стер.

adequate *adj* доста́точный.

adhere *vi* прилипа́ть *impf*, прили́пнуть *pf* (**to** к+*dat*); (*fig*) приде́рживаться *impf* +*gen*. **adherence** *n* приве́рженность. **adherent** *n* приве́рженец. **adhesive** *adj* ли́пкий; *n* кле́йкое вещество́.

ad hoc *adj* специа́льный.

ad infinitum *adv* до бесконе́чности.

adjacent *adj* сме́жный.

adjective *n* (и́мя) прилага́тельное.

adjoin *vt* прилега́ть *impf* к+*dat*.

adjourn *vt* откла́дывать *impf*, отложи́ть *pf*; *vi* объявля́ть *impf*, объяви́ть *pf* переры́в; (*move*) переходи́ть *impf*, перейти́ *pf*.

adjudicate *vi* выноси́ть *impf*, вы́нести *pf* реше́ние (**in** по+*dat*); суди́ть *impf*.

adjust *vt & i* приспособля́ть(ся) *impf*, приспосо́бить(ся) *pf*; *vt* пригоня́ть *impf*, пригна́ть *pf*; (*regulate*) регули́ровать *impf*, от~ *pf*. **adjustable** *adj* регули́руемый. **adjustment** *n* регули́рование, подго́нка.

ad lib *vt & i* импровизи́ровать *impf*, сымпровизи́ровать *pf*.

administer *vt* (*manage*) управля́ть *impf* +*instr*; (*give*) дава́ть *impf*, дать *pf*. **administration** *n* управле́ние; (*government*) прави́тельство. **administrative** *adj* администрати́вный. **administrator** *n* администра́тор.

admirable *adj* похва́льный.

admiral *n* адмира́л.

admiration *n* восхище́ние. **admire** *vt* (*look at*) любова́ться *impf*, по~ *pf* +*instr*, на+*acc*; (*respect*) восхища́ться *impf*, восхити́ться *pf* +*instr*. **admirer** *n* покло́нник.

admissible *adj* допусти́мый. **admission** *n* (*access*) до́ступ; (*entry*) вход; (*confession*) призна́ние. **admit** *vt* (*allow in*) впуска́ть *impf*, впусти́ть *pf*; (*confess*) признава́ть *impf*, призна́ть *pf*. **admittance** *n* до́ступ. **admittedly** *adv* призна́ться.

admixture *n* при́месь.

adolescence *n* о́трочество. **adolescent** *adj* подро́стковый; *n* подро́сток.

adopt *vt* (*child*) усыновля́ть *impf*, усынови́ть *pf*; (*thing*) усва́ивать *impf*, усво́ить *pf*; (*accept*) принима́ть *impf*, приня́ть *pf*. **adoptive** *adj* приёмный. **adoption** *n* усыновле́ние; приня́тие.

adorable *adj* преле́стный. **adoration** *n* обожа́ние. **adore** *vt* обожа́ть *impf*.

adorn *vt* украша́ть *impf*, укра́сить *pf*. **adornment** *n* украше́ние.

adrenalin *n* адреналин.

adroit *adj* ло́вкий.

adulation *n* преклоне́ние.

adult *adj & n* взро́слый (*sb*).

adulterate *vt* фальсифици́ровать *impf & pf*.

adultery *n* супру́жеская изме́на.

advance *n* (*going forward*) продвиже́ние (вперёд); (*progress*) прогре́сс; (*mil*) наступле́ние; (*of pay etc.*) ава́нс; **in ~** зара́нее; *pl* (*overtures*) ава́нсы *m pl*; *vi* (*go forward*) продвига́ться *impf*, продви́нуться *pf* вперёд; идти́ *impf* вперёд; (*mil*) наступа́ть *impf*; *vt* продвига́ть *impf*, продви́нуть *pf*; (*put forward*) выдвига́ть *impf*, вы́двинуть *pf*. **advanced** *adj* (*modern*) передово́й.

advancement *n* продвиже́ние.

advantage *n* преиму́щество; (*profit*) вы́года, по́льза; **take ~ of** по́льзоваться *impf*, вос~ *pf* +*instr*. **advantageous** *adj* вы́годный.

adventure *n* приключе́ние. **adventurer** *n* иска́тель *m* приключе́ний. **adventurous** *adj* предприи́мчивый.

adverb *n* наре́чие.

adversary *n* проти́вник. **adverse** *adj* неблагоприя́тный. **adversity** *n* несча́стье.

advertise *vt* (*publicize*) реклами́ровать *impf & pf*; *vt & i* (**~ for**) дава́ть *impf*, дать *pf* объявле́ние о+*prep*. **advertisement** *n* объявле́ние, рекла́ма.

advice *n* сове́т. **advisable** *adj* жела́тельный. **advise** *vt* сове́товать *impf*, по~ *pf* +*dat & inf*; (*notify*) уведомля́ть *impf*, уве́домить *pf*. **advisedly** *adv* наме́ренно. **adviser** *n* сове́тник. **advisory** *adj* совеща́тельный.

advocate *n* (*supporter*) сторо́нник; *vt* выступа́ть *impf*, вы́ступить *pf* за+*acc*; (*advise*) сове́товать *impf*, по~ *pf*.

aegis *n* эги́да.

aerial *n* анте́нна; *adj* возду́шный.

aerobics *n* аэро́бика.

aerodrome *n* аэродро́м. **aerodynamics** *n* аэродина́мика. **aeroplane** *n* самолёт. **aerosol** *n* аэрозо́ль *m*.

aesthetic *adj* эстети́ческий. **aesthetics** *n pl* эсте́тика.

afar *adv*: **from ~** издалека́.

affable *adj* приве́тливый.

affair *n* (*business*) де́ло; (*love*) рома́н.

affect *vt* влия́ть *impf*, по~ *pf* на+*acc*; (*touch*) тро́гать *impf*, тро́нуть *pf*; (*concern*) затра́гивать *impf*, затро́нуть *pf*; **affectation** *n* жема́нство. **affected** *adj* жема́нный. **affection** *n* привя́занность. **affectionate** *adj* не́жный.

affiliated *adj* свя́занный (**to** c+*instr*).

affinity *n* (*relationship*) родство́; (*resemblance*) схо́дство; (*attraction*) влече́ние.

affirm *vt* утвержда́ть *impf*. **affirmation** *n* утвержде́ние. **affirmative** *adj* утверди́тельный.

affix *vt* прикрепля́ть *impf*, прикрепи́ть *pf*.

afflict *vt* постига́ть *impf*, пости́чь *pf*; **be afflicted with** страда́ть *impf* +*instr*. **affliction** *n* боле́знь.

affluence *n* бога́тство. **affluent** *adj* бога́тый.

afford *vt* позволя́ть *impf*, позво́лить *pf* себе́; (*supply*) предоставля́ть *impf*, предоста́вить *pf*.

affront *n* оскорбле́ние; *vt* оскорбля́ть *impf*, оскорби́ть *pf*.

afield *adv*: **far ~** далеко́; **farther ~** да́льше.

afloat *adv & predic* на воде́.

afoot *predic*: **be ~** гото́виться *impf*.

aforesaid *adj* вышеупомя́нутый.

afraid *predic*: **be ~** боя́ться *impf*.

afresh *adv* сно́ва.

Africa *n* А́фрика. **African** *n* африка́нец, -ка́нка; *adj* африка́нский.

after *adv* пото́м; *prep* по́сле+*gen*; (*time*) че́рез+*acc*; (*behind*) за+*acc*, *instr*; **~ all** в конце́ концо́в; *conj* по́сле того́, как.

aftermath *n* после́дствия *neut pl*.

afternoon *n* втора́я полови́на дня; **in the ~** днём. **aftershave** *n* лосьо́н по́сле бритья́. **afterthought** *n* запозда́лая мысль.

afterwards *adv* пото́м.

again *adv* опя́ть; (*once more*) ещё раз; (*anew*) сно́ва.

against *prep* (*opposing*) про́тив+*gen*; (*touching*) к+*dat*; (*hitting*) о+*acc*.

age *n* во́зраст; (*era*) век, эпо́ха; *vt* ста́рить *impf*, со~ *pf*; *vi* старе́ть *impf*, по~ *pf*. **aged** *adj* престаре́лый.

agency *n* аге́нтство. **agenda** *n* пове́стка дня. **agent** *n* аге́нт.

aggravate *vt* ухудша́ть *impf*, уху́дшить *pf*; (*annoy*) раздража́ть *impf*, раздражи́ть *pf*.

aggregate *adj* совоку́пный; *n* совоку́пность.

aggression *n* агре́ссия. **aggressive** *adj* агресси́вный. **aggressor** *n* агре́ссор.

aggrieved *adj* оби́женный.

aghast *predic* в у́жасе (**at** от+*gen*).

agile *adj* прово́рный. **agility** *n* прово́рство.

agitate *vt* волнова́ть *impf*, вз~ *pf*; *vi* агити́ровать *impf*. **agitation** *n* волне́ние; агита́ция.

agnostic *n* агно́стик. **agnosticism** *n* агностици́зм.

ago *adv* (тому́) наза́д; **long ~** давно́.

agonize *vi* му́читься *impf*. **agonizing** *adj* мучи́тельный. **agony** *n* аго́ния.

agrarian *adj* агра́рный.

agree *vi* соглаша́ться *impf*, согласи́ться *pf*; (*arrange*) догова́риваться *impf*, договори́ться *pf*. **agreeable** *adj* (*pleasant*) прия́тный. **agreement** *n* согла́сие; (*treaty*) соглаше́ние; **in ~** согла́сен (-сна).

agricultural *adj* сельскохозя́йственный. **agriculture** *n* се́льское хозя́йство.

aground *predic* на мели́; *adv*: **run ~** сади́ться *impf*, сесть *pf* на мель.

ahead *adv* (*forward*) вперёд; (*in front*) впереди́; **~ of time** досро́чно.

aid *vt* помога́ть *impf*, помо́чь *pf* +*dat*; *n* по́мощь; (*teaching*) посо́бие; **in ~ of** в по́льзу+*gen*.

Aids *n* СПИД.

ailing *adj* (*ill*) больно́й.

ailment *n* неду́г.

aim *n* цель, наме́рение; **take ~** прице́ливаться *impf*, прице́литься *pf* (**at** в+*acc*); *vi* це́литься *impf*, на~ *pf* (**at** в+*acc*); (*also fig*) ме́тить *impf*, на~ pf (at в+acc); vt нацеливать impf, нацелить pf; (also fig) наводить impf, навести pf. **aimless** adj бесцельный.

air n воздух; (look) вид; **by** ~ самолётом; **on the** ~ в эфире; attrib воздушный; vt (ventilate) проветривать impf, проветрить pf; (make known) выставлять impf, выставить pf напоказ. **air-conditioning** n кондиционирование воздуха. **aircraft** n самолёт. **aircraft-carrier** n авианосец. **airfield** n аэродром. **air force** n ВВС (военно-воздушные силы) f pl. **air hostess** n стюардесса. **airless** adj душный. **airlift** n воздушные перевозки f pl; vt перевозить impf, перевезти pf по воздуху. **airline** n авиалиния. **airlock** n воздушная пробка. **airmail** n авиа(почта). **airman** n лётчик. **airport** n аэропорт. **air raid** n воздушный налёт. **airship** n дирижабль m. **airstrip** n взлётно-посадочная полоса. **airtight** adj герметичный. **air traffic controller** n диспетчер. **airwaves** n pl радиоволны f pl.

aisle n боковой неф; (passage) проход.

ajar predic приоткрытый.

akin predic (similar) похожий; **be** ~ **to** быть сродни к+dat.

alabaster n алебастр.

alacrity n быстрота.

alarm n тревога; vt тревожить impf, вс~ pf; ~ **clock** будильник. **alarming** adj тревожный. **alarmist** n паникёр; adj паникёрский.

alas int увы!

album n альбом.

alcohol n алкоголь m, спирт; спиртные напитки m pl. **alcoholic** adj алкогольный; n алкоголик, -ичка.

alcove n альков.

alert adj бдительный; n тревога; vt предупреждать impf, предупредить pf.

algebra n алгебра.

alias adv иначе (называемый); n кличка, вымышленное имя neut.

alibi n алиби neut indecl.

alien n иностранец, -нка; adj иностранный; ~ **to** чуждый +dat. **alienate** vt отчуждать impf. **alienation** n отчуждение.

alight[1] vi сходить impf, сойти pf; (bird) садиться impf, сесть pf.

alight[2] predic: **be** ~ гореть impf; (shine) сиять impf.

align vt выравнивать impf, выровнять pf. **alignment** n выравнивание.

alike predic похож; adv одинаково.

alimentary adj: ~ **canal** пищеварительный канал.

alimony n алименты m pl.

alive predic жив, в живых.

alkali n щёлочь. **alkaline** adj щелочной.

all adj весь; n всё, pl все; adv совсем, совершенно; ~ **along** всё время; ~ **right** хорошо, ладно; (not bad) так себе; неплохо; ~ **the same** всё равно; **in** ~ всего; **two** ~ по два; **not at** ~ нисколько.

allay vt успокаивать impf, успокоить pf.

allegation n утверждение. **allege** vt утверждать impf. **allegedly** adv якобы.

allegiance adv верность.

allegorical adj аллегорический. **allegory** n аллегория.

allergic adj аллергический; **be** ~ **to** иметь аллергию к+dat. **allergy** n аллергия.

alleviate vt облегчать impf, облегчить pf. **alleviation** n облегчение.

alley n переулок.

alliance n союз. **allied** adj союзный.

alligator n аллигатор.

allocate vt (distribute) распределять impf, распределить pf; (allot) выделять impf, выделить pf. **allocation** n распределение; выделение.

allot vt выделять impf, выделить pf; (distribute) распределять impf, распределить pf. **allotment** n выделение; (land) участок.

allow vt разрешать impf, разрешить pf; (let happen; concede) допускать impf, допустить pf; ~ **for** учитывать impf, учесть pf. **allowance** n (financial) пособие; (deduction, also fig) скидка; **make** ~**(s) for** учитывать impf, учесть pf.

alloy n сплав.

all-round adj разносторонний.

allude vi ссылаться impf, сослаться pf (**to** на+acc).

allure vt заманивать impf, заманить

pf. **allure(ment)** *n* прима́нка. **alluring** *adj* зама́нчивый.

allusion *n* ссы́лка.

ally *n* сою́зник; *vt* соединя́ть *impf*, соедини́ть *pf*; ~ **oneself with** вступа́ть *impf*, вступи́ть *pf* в сою́з c+*instr*.

almighty *adj* всемогу́щий.

almond *n* (*tree*; *pl collect*) минда́ль *m*; (*nut*) минда́льный оре́х.

almost *adv* почти́, едва́ не.

alms *n pl* ми́лостыня.

aloft *adv* наве́рх(-у́).

alone *predic* оди́н; (*lonely*) одино́к; *adv* то́лько; **leave** ~ оставля́ть *impf*, оста́вить *pf* в поко́е; **let** ~ не говоря́ уже́ о+*prep*.

along *prep* по+*dat*, (*position*) вдоль +*gen*; *adv* (*onward*) да́льше; **all** ~ всё вре́мя; ~ **with** вме́сте c+*instr*.

alongside *adv* & *prep* ря́дом (c+*instr*).

aloof *predic* & *adv* (*distant*) сде́ржанный; (*apart*) в стороне́.

aloud *adv* вслух.

alphabet *n* алфави́т. **alphabetical** *adj* алфави́тный.

alpine *adj* альпи́йский.

already *adv* уже́.

also *adv* та́кже, то́же.

altar *n* алта́рь *m*.

alter *vt* (*modify*) переде́лывать *impf*, переде́лать *pf*; *vt* & *i* (*change*) изменя́ть(ся) *impf*, измени́ть(ся) *pf*. **alteration** *n* переде́лка; измене́ние.

alternate *adj* череду́ющийся; *vt* & *i* чередова́ть(ся) *impf*; **alternating current** переме́нный ток; **on** ~ **days** че́рез день. **alternation** *n* чередова́ние. **alternative** *n* альтернати́ва; *adj* альтернати́вный.

although *conj* хотя́.

altitude *n* высота́.

alto *n* альт.

altogether *adv* (*fully*) совсе́м; (*in total*) всего́.

altruistic *adj* альтруисти́ческий.

aluminium *n* алюми́ний.

always *adv* всегда́; (*constantly*) посто́я́нно.

Alzheimer's disease *n* боле́знь Альцге́ймера.

a.m. *abbr* (*morning*) утра́; (*night*) но́чи.

amalgamate *vt* & *i* слива́ть(ся) *impf*, сли́ть(ся) *pf*; (*chem*) амальгами́ровать(ся) *impf* & *pf*. **amalgamation** *n* слия́ние; (*chem*) амальгами́рование.

amass *vt* копи́ть *impf*, на~ *pf*.

amateur *n* люби́тель *m*, ~ница; *adj* люби́тельский. **amateurish** *adj* дилета́нтский.

amaze *vt* изумля́ть *impf*, изуми́ть *pf*. **amazement** *n* изумле́ние. **amazing** *adj* изуми́тельный.

ambassador *n* посо́л.

amber *n* янта́рь *m*.

ambience *n* среда́; атмосфе́ра.

ambiguity *n* двусмы́сленность. **ambiguous** *adj* двусмы́сленный.

ambition *n* (*quality*) честолю́бие; (*aim*) мечта́. **ambitious** *adj* честолю́бивый.

amble *vi* ходи́ть *indet*, идти́ *det* неторопли́вым ша́гом.

ambulance *n* маши́на ско́рой по́мощи.

ambush *n* заса́да; *vt* напада́ть *impf*, напа́сть *pf* из заса́ды на+*acc*.

ameliorate *vt* & *i* улучша́ть(ся) *impf*, улу́чшить(ся) *pf*. **amelioration** *n* улучше́ние.

amen *int* ами́нь!

amenable *adj* сгово́рчивый (**to** +*dat*).

amend *vt* (*correct*) исправля́ть *impf*, испра́вить *pf*; (*change*) вноси́ть *impf*, внести́ *pf* из попра́вки в+*acc*. **amendment** *n* попра́вка, исправле́ние. **amends** *n pl*: **make** ~ **for** загла́живать *impf*, загла́дить *pf*.

amenities *n pl* удо́бства *neut pl*.

America *n* Аме́рика. **American** *adj* америка́нский; *n* америка́нец, -нка. **Americanism** *n* американи́зм.

amiable *adj* любе́зный. **amicable** *adj* дружелю́бный.

amid(st) *prep* среди́+*gen*.

amino acid *n* аминокислота́.

amiss *adv* нела́дный; **take** ~ обижа́ться *impf*, оби́деться *pf* на+*acc*.

ammonia *n* аммиа́к; (*liquid* ~) нашаты́рный спирт.

ammunition *n* боеприпа́сы *m pl*.

amnesia *n* амнези́я.

amnesty *n* амни́стия.

among(st) *prep* (*amidst*) среди́+*gen*, (*between*) ме́жду+*instr*.

amoral *adj* амора́льный.

amorous *adj* влюбчивый.

amorphous *adj* бесфо́рменный.

amortization *n* амортиза́ция.

amount *n* коли́чество; *vi*: ~ **to** составля́ть *impf*, соста́вить *pf*; (*be equivalent to*) быть равноси́льным+*dat*.

ampere *n* ампе́р.

amphetamine *n* амфетами́н.

amphibian *n* амфи́бия. **amphibious** *adj* земново́дный; (*mil*) пла́вающий.

amphitheatre *n* амфитеа́тр.

ample *adj* доста́точный. **amplification** *n* усиле́ние. **amplifier** *n* усили́тель *m*. **amplify** *vt* уси́ливать *impf*, уси́лить *pf*. **amply** *adv* доста́точно.

amputate *vt* ампути́ровать *impf & pf*. **amputation** *n* ампута́ция.

amuse *vt* забавля́ть *impf*; развлека́ть *impf*, развле́чь *pf*. **amusement** *n* заба́ва, развлече́ние; *pl* аттракцио́ны *m pl*. **amusing** *adj* заба́вный; (*funny*) смешно́й.

anachronism *n* анахрони́зм. **anachronistic** *adj* анахрони́ческий.

anaemia *n* анеми́я. **anaemic** *adj* анеми́чный.

anaesthesia *n* анестези́я. **anaesthetic** *n* обезбо́ливающее сре́дство. **anaesthetist** *n* анестезио́лог. **anaesthetize** *vt* анестези́ровать *impf & pf*.

anagram *n* анагра́мма.

analogous *adj* аналоги́чный. **analogue** *n* ана́лог. **analogy** *n* анало́гия.

analyse *vt* анализи́ровать *impf & pf*. **analysis** *n* ана́лиз. **analyst** *n* анали́тик; психоанали́тик. **analytical** *adj* аналити́ческий

anarchic *adj* анархи́ческий. **anarchist** *n* анархи́ст, ~ка; *adj* анархи́стский. **anarchy** *n* ана́рхия.

anathema *n* ана́фема.

anatomical *adj* анатоми́ческий. **anatomy** *n* анато́мия.

ancestor *n* пре́док. **ancestry** *n* происхожде́ние.

anchor *n* я́корь *m*; *vt* ста́вить *impf*, по~ *pf* на я́корь; *vi* станови́ться *impf*, стать *pf* на я́корь. **anchorage** *n* я́корная стоя́нка.

anchovy *n* анчо́ус.

ancient *adj* дре́вний, стари́нный.

and *conj* и, (*but*) а; с+*instr*; **you** ~ **I** мы с ва́ми; **my wife** ~ **I** мы с жено́й.

anecdote *n* анекдо́т.

anew *adv* сно́ва.

angel *n* а́нгел. **angelic** *adj* а́нгельский.

anger *n* гнев; *vt* серди́ть *impf*, рас~ *pf*.

angina *n* стенокарди́я.

angle[1] *n* у́гол; (*fig*) то́чка зре́ния.

angle[2] *vi* уди́ть *impf* ры́бу. **angler** *n* рыболо́в.

angry *adj* серди́тый.

anguish *n* страда́ние, му́ка. **anguished** *adj* отча́янный.

angular *adj* углово́й; (*sharp*) углова́тый.

animal *n* живо́тное *sb*; *adj* живо́тный. **animate** *adj* живо́й. **animated** *adj* оживлённый; ~ **cartoon** мультфи́льм. **animation** *n* оживле́ние.

animosity *n* вражде́бность.

ankle *n* лоды́жка.

annals *n pl* ле́топись.

annex *vt* аннекси́ровать *impf & pf*. **annexation** *n* анне́ксия. **annexe** *n* пристро́йка.

annihilate *vt* уничтожа́ть *impf*, уничто́жить *pf*. **annihilation** *n* уничтоже́ние.

anniversary *n* годовщи́на.

annotate *vt* комменти́ровать *impf & pf*. **annotated** *adj* снабжённый коммента́риями. **annotation** *n* аннота́ция.

announce *vt* объявля́ть *impf*, объяви́ть *pf*; заявля́ть *impf*, заяви́ть *pf*; (*radio*) сообща́ть *impf*, сообщи́ть *pf*. **announcement** *n* объявле́ние; сообще́ние. **announcer** *n* ди́ктор.

annoy *vt* досажда́ть *impf*, досади́ть *pf*; раздража́ть *impf*, раздражи́ть *pf*. **annoyance** *n* доса́да. **annoying** *adj* доса́дный.

annual *adj* ежего́дный, (*of a given year*) годово́й; *n* (*book*) ежего́дник; (*bot*) одноле́тник. **annually** *adv* ежего́дно. **annuity** *n* (ежего́дная) ре́нта.

annul *vt* аннули́ровать *impf & pf*. **annulment** *n* аннули́рование.

anoint *vt* пома́зывать *impf*, пома́зать *pf*.

anomalous *adj* анома́льный. **anomaly** *n* анома́лия.

anonymous *adj* анони́мный. **ano-**

nymity *n* анони́мность.

anorak *n* ку́ртка.

anorexia *n* аноре́ксия.

another *adj*, *pron* друго́й; ~ **one** ещё (оди́н); **in** ~ **ten years** ещё че́рез де́сять лет.

answer *n* отве́т; *vt* отвеча́ть *impf*, отве́тить *pf* (*person*) +*dat*, (*question*) на+*acc*; ~ **the door** отворя́ть *impf*, отвори́ть *pf* дверь; ~ **the phone** подходи́ть *impf*, подойти́ *pf* к телефо́ну. **answerable** *adj* отве́тственный. **answering machine** *n* телефо́н-отве́тчик.

ant *n* мураве́й.

antagonism *n* антагони́зм. **antagonistic** *adj* антагонисти́ческий. **antagonize** *vt* настра́ивать *impf*, настро́ить *pf* про́тив себя́.

Antarctic *n* Анта́рктика.

antelope *n* антило́па.

antenna *n* у́сик; (*also radio*) анте́нна.

anthem *n* гимн.

anthology *n* антоло́гия.

anthracite *n* антраци́т.

anthropological *adj* антропологи́ческий. **anthropologist** *n* антропо́лог. **anthropology** *n* антрополо́гия.

anti-aircraft *adj* зени́тный. **antibiotic** *n* антибио́тик. **antibody** *n* антите́ло. **anticlimax** *n* разочарова́ние. **anticlockwise** *adj* & *adv* про́тив часово́й стре́лки. **antidepressant** *n* антидепресса́нт. **antidote** *n* противоя́дие. **antifreeze** *n* антифри́з. **antipathy** *n* антипа́тия. **anti-Semitic** *adj* антисеми́тский. **anti-Semitism** *n* антисемити́зм. **antiseptic** *adj* антисепти́ческий; *n* антисе́птик. **antisocial** *adj* асоциа́льный. **antitank** *adj* противота́нковый. **antithesis** *n* противополо́жность; (*philos*) антите́зис.

anticipate *vt* ожида́ть *impf* +*gen*; (*with pleasure*) предвкуша́ть *impf*, предвкуси́ть *pf*; (*forestall*) предупрежда́ть *impf*, предупреди́ть *pf*. **anticipation** *n* ожида́ние; предвкуше́ние; предупрежде́ние.

antics *n* вы́ходки *f pl*.

antiquarian *adj* антиква́рный. **antiquated** *adj* устаре́лый. **antique** *adj* стари́нный; *n* антиква́рная вещь; ~ **shop** антиква́рный магази́н. **antiquity** *n* дре́вность.

antler *n* оле́ний рог.

anus *n* за́дний прохо́д.

anvil *n* накова́льня.

anxiety *n* беспоко́йство. **anxious** *adj* беспоко́йный; **be** ~ беспоко́иться *impf*; тревожи́ться *impf*.

any *adj*, *pron* (*some*) како́й-нибудь; ско́лько-нибудь; (*every*) вся́кий, любо́й; (*anybody*) кто́-нибудь; (*anything*) что́-нибудь; (*with neg*) никако́й, ни оди́н; ниско́лько; никто́; ничто́; *adv* ско́лько-нибудь; (*with neg*) ниско́лько, ничу́ть. **anybody**, **anyone** *pron* кто́-нибудь; (*everybody*) вся́кий, любо́й; (*with neg*) никто́. **anyhow** *adv* ка́к-нибудь; ко́е-как; (*with neg*) ника́к; *conj* во вся́ком слу́чае; всё равно́. **anyone** *see* **anybody**. **anything** *pron* что́-нибудь; всё (что уго́дно); (*with neg*) ничего́. **anyway** *adv* во вся́ком слу́чае; как бы то ни́ было. **anywhere** *adv* где/куда́ уго́дно; (*with neg*, *interrog*) где́-нибудь, куда́-нибудь.

apart *adv* (*aside*) в стороне́, в сто́рону; (*separately*) врозь; (*distant*) друг от дру́га; (*into pieces*) на ча́сти; ~ **from** кро́ме+*gen*.

apartheid *n* апартеи́д.

apartment *n* (*flat*) кварти́ра.

apathetic *adj* апати́чный. **apathy** *n* апа́тия.

ape *n* обезья́на; *vt* обезья́нничать *impf*, с~ *pf* с+*gen*.

aperture *n* отве́рстие.

apex *n* верши́на.

aphorism *n* афори́зм.

apiece *adv* (*per person*) на ка́ждого; (*per thing*) за шту́ку; (*amount*) по+*dat or acc with numbers*.

aplomb *n* апло́мб.

Apocalypse *n* Апока́липсис. **apocalyptic** *adj* апокалипти́ческий.

apologetic *adj* извиня́ющийся; **be** ~ извиня́ться *impf*. **apologize** *vi* извиня́ться *impf*, извини́ться *pf* (**to** пе́ред+*instr*; **for** за+*acc*). **apology** *n* извине́ние.

apostle *n* апо́стол.

apostrophe *n* апостро́ф.

appal *vi* ужаса́ть *impf*, ужасну́ть *pf*. **appalling** *adj* ужа́сный.

apparatus *n* аппара́т; прибо́р; (*gymnastic*) гимнасти́ческие снаря́ды *m pl*.

apparel *n* одея́ние.

apparent *adj* (*seeming*) ви́димый; (*manifest*) очеви́дный. **apparently** *adv* ка́жется, по-ви́димому.

apparition *n* виде́ние.

appeal *n* (*request*) призы́в, обраще́ние; (*law*) апелля́ция, обжа́лование; (*attraction*) привлека́тельность; ~ **court** апелляцио́нный суд; *vi* (*request*) взыва́ть *impf*, воззва́ть *pf* (**to** к+*dat*; **for** о+*prep*); обраща́ться *impf*, обрати́ться *pf* (с призы́вом); (*law*) апелли́ровать *impf & pf*; ~ **to** (*attract*) привлека́ть *impf*, привле́чь *pf*.

appear *vi* появля́ться *impf*, появи́ться *pf*; (*in public*) выступа́ть *impf*, вы́ступить *pf*; (*seem*) каза́ться *impf*, по~ *pf*. **appearance** *n* появле́ние; выступле́ние; (*aspect*) вид.

appease *vt* умиротворя́ть *impf*, умиротвори́ть *pf*.

append *vt* прилага́ть *impf*, приложи́ть *pf*. **appendicitis** *n* аппендици́т. **appendix** *n* приложе́ние; (*anat*) аппенди́кс.

appertain *vi*: ~ **to** относи́ться *impf* +*dat*.

appetite *n* аппети́т. **appetizing** *adj* аппети́тный.

applaud *vt* аплоди́ровать *impf* +*dat*. **applause** *n* аплодисме́нты *m pl*.

apple *n* я́блоко; *adj* я́блочный; ~ **tree** я́блоня.

appliance *n* прибо́р. **applicable** *adj* примени́мый. **applicant** *n* кандида́т. **application** *n* (*use*) примене́ние; (*putting on*) наложе́ние; (*request*) заявле́ние. **applied** *adj* прикладно́й. **apply** *vt* (*use*) применя́ть *impf*, примени́ть *pf*; (*put on*) накла́дывать *impf*, наложи́ть *pf*; *vi* (*request*) обраща́ться *impf*, обрати́ться *pf* (**to** к+*dat*; **for** за+*acc*); **for** (*job*) подава́ть *impf*, пода́ть *pf* заявле́ние на+*acc*; ~ **to** относи́ться *impf* к+*dat*.

appoint *vt* назнача́ть *impf*, назна́чить *pf*. **appointment** *n* назначе́ние; (*job*) до́лжность; (*meeting*) свида́ние.

apposite *adj* уме́стный.

appraise *vt* оце́нивать *impf*, оцени́ть *pf*.

appreciable *adj* заме́тный; (*consid-erable*) значи́тельный. **appreciate** *vt* цени́ть *impf*; (*understand*) понима́ть *impf*, поня́ть *pf*; *vi* повыша́ться *impf*, повы́ситься *pf* в цене́. **appreciation** *n* (*estimation*) оце́нка; (*gratitude*) призна́тельность; (*rise in value*) повыше́ние цены́. **appreciative** *adj* призна́тельный (**of** за+*acc*).

apprehension *n* (*fear*) опасе́ние. **apprehensive** *adj* опаса́ющийся.

apprentice *n* учени́к; *vt* отдава́ть *impf*, отда́ть *pf* в уче́ние. **apprenticeship** *n* учени́чество.

approach *vt & i* подходи́ть *impf*, подойти́ *pf* (к+*dat*); приближа́ться *impf*, прибли́зиться *pf* (к+*dat*); *vt* (*apply to*) обраща́ться *impf*, обрати́ться *pf* к+*dat*; *n* приближе́ние; подхо́д; подъе́зд; (*access*) по́дступ.

approbation *n* одобре́ние.

appropriate *adj* подходя́щий; *vt* присва́ивать *impf*, присво́ить *pf*. **appropriation** *n* присвое́ние.

approval *n* одобре́ние; **on** ~ на про́бу. **approve** *vt* утвержда́ть *impf*, утверди́ть *pf*; *vt & i* (~ **of**) одобря́ть *impf*, одо́брить *pf*.

approximate *adj* приблизи́тельный; *vi* приближа́ться *impf* (**to** к+*dat*). **approximation** *n* приближе́ние.

apricot *n* абрико́с.

April *n* апре́ль *m*; *adj* апре́льский.

apron *n* пере́дник.

apropos *adv*: ~ **of** по по́воду+*gen*.

apt *adj* (*suitable*) уда́чный; (*inclined*) скло́нный. **aptitude** *n* спосо́бность.

aqualung *n* аквала́нг. **aquarium** *n* аква́риум. **Aquarius** *n* Водоле́й. **aquatic** *adj* водяно́й; (*of sport*) во́дный. **aqueduct** *n* акведу́к.

aquiline *adj* орли́ный.

Arab *n* ара́б, ~ка; *adj* ара́бский. **Arabian** *adj* арави́йский. **Arabic** *adj* ара́бский.

arable *adj* па́хотный.

arbitrary *adj* произво́льный. **arbitrate** *vi* де́йствовать *impf* в ка́честве трете́йского судьи́. **arbitration** *n* арбитра́ж, трете́йское реше́ние. **arbitrator** *n* арби́тр, трете́йский судья́ *m*.

arc *n* дуга́. **arcade** *n* арка́да, (*shops*) пасса́ж.

arch[1] *n* а́рка, свод; (*of foot*) свод стопы́; *vt & i* выгиба́ть(ся) *impf*,

вы́гнуть(ся) *pf*.
arch² *adj* игри́вый.
archaeological *adj* археологи́ческий. **archaeologist** *n* архео́лог. **archaeology** *n* археоло́гия.
archaic *adj* архаи́ческий.
archangel *n* арха́нгел.
archbishop *n* архиепи́скоп.
arched *adj* сво́дчатый.
arch-enemy *n* закля́тый враг.
archer *n* стрело́к из лука. **archery** *n* стрельба́ из лука.
archipelago *n* архипела́г.
architect *n* архите́ктор. **architectural** *adj* архитекту́рный. **architecture** *n* архитекту́ра.
archive(s) *n* архи́в.
archway *n* сво́дчатый прохо́д.
Arctic *adj* аркти́ческий; *n* А́рктика.
ardent *adj* горя́чий. **ardour** *n* пыл.
arduous *adj* тру́дный.
area *n* (*extent*) пло́щадь; (*region*) райо́н; (*sphere*) о́бласть.
arena *n* аре́на.
argue *vt* (*maintain*) утвержда́ть *impf*; дока́зывать *impf*; *vi* спо́рить *impf*, по~ *pf*. **argument** *n* (*dispute*) спор; (*reason*) до́вод. **argumentative** *adj* любящий спо́рить.
aria *n* а́рия.
arid *adj* сухо́й.
Aries *n* Ове́н.
arise *vi* возника́ть *impf*, возни́кнуть *pf*.
aristocracy *n* аристокра́тия. **aristocrat** *n* аристокра́т, ~ка. **aristocratic** *adj* аристократи́ческий.
arithmetic *n* арифме́тика. **arithmetical** *adj* арифмети́ческий.
ark *n* (Но́ев) ковче́г.
arm¹ *n* (*of body*) рука́; (*of chair*) ру́чка; ~ **in** ~ под руку; **at** ~'s **length** (*fig*) на почти́тельном расстоя́нии; **with open** ~s с распростёртыми объя́тиями.
arm² *n pl* (*weapons*) ору́жие; *pl* (*coat of* ~s) герб; *vt* вооружа́ть *impf*, вооружи́ть *pf*. **armaments** *n pl* вооруже́ние.
armchair *n* кре́сло.
Armenia *n* Арме́ния. **Armenian** *n* армяни́н, армя́нка; *adj* армя́нский.
armistice *n* переми́рие.
armour *n* (*for body*) доспе́хи *m pl*; (*for vehicles*; *fig*) броня́. **armoured**

adj брониро́ванный; (*vehicles etc.*) бронета́нковый, броне-; ~ **car** броневи́к. **armoury** *n* арсена́л.
armpit *n* подмы́шка.
army *n* а́рмия; *adj* арме́йский.
aroma *n* арома́т. **aromatic** *adj* аромати́чный.
around *adv* круго́м; *prep* вокру́г+*gen*; **all** ~ повсю́ду.
arouse *vt* (*wake up*) буди́ть *impf*, раз~ *pf*; (*stimulate*) возбужда́ть *impf*, возбуди́ть *pf*.
arrange *vt* расставля́ть *impf*, расста́вить *pf*; (*plan*) устра́ивать *impf*, устро́ить *pf*; (*mus*) аранжи́ровать *impf* & *pf*; *vi*: ~ **to** догова́риваться *impf*, договори́ться *pf* +*inf*. **arrangement** *n* расположе́ние; устро́йство; (*agreement*) соглаше́ние; (*mus*) аранжиро́вка; *pl* приготовле́ния *neut pl*.
array *vt* выставля́ть *impf*, вы́ставить *pf*; *n* (*dress*) наря́д; (*display*) колле́кция.
arrears *n pl* задо́лженность.
arrest *vt* аресто́вывать *impf*, арестова́ть *pf*; *n* аре́ст.
arrival *n* прибы́тие, прие́зд; (*new* ~) вновь прибы́вший *sb*. **arrive** *vi* прибыва́ть *impf*, прибы́ть *pf*; приезжа́ть *impf*, прие́хать *pf*.
arrogance *n* высокоме́рие. **arrogant** *adj* высокоме́рный.
arrow *n* стрела́; (*pointer*) стре́лка.
arsenal *n* арсена́л.
arsenic *n* мышья́к.
arson *n* поджо́г.
art *n* иску́сство; *pl* гуманита́рные нау́ки *f pl*; *adj* худо́жественный.
arterial *adj*: ~ **road** магистра́ль. **artery** *n* арте́рия.
artful *adj* хи́трый.
arthritis *n* артри́т.
article *n* (*literary*) статья́; (*clause*) пункт; (*thing*) предме́т; (*gram*) арти́кль *m*.
articulate *vt* произноси́ть *impf*, произнести́ *pf*; (*express*) выража́ть *impf*, вы́разить *pf*; *adj* (*of speech*) членоразде́льный; **be** ~ чётко выража́ть *impf* свои́ мы́сли. **articulated lorry** *n* грузово́й автомоби́ль с прице́пом.
artifice *n* хи́трость. **artificial** *adj* иску́сственный.
artillery *n* артилле́рия.

artisan *n* ремéсленник.

artist *n* худóжник. **artiste** *n* артúст, **~ка. artistic** *adj* худóжественный.

artless *adj* простодýшный.

as *adv* как; *conj* (*when*) когдá; в то врéмя как; (*because*) так как; (*manner*) как; (*though, however*) как ни; *rel pron* какóй; котóрый; что; **as ... as** так (же)... как; **as for, to** относúтельно+*gen*; что касáется +*gen*; **as if** как бýдто; **as it were** кáк бы; так сказáть; **as soon as** как тóлько; **as well** тáкже; тóже.

asbestos *n* асбéст.

ascend *vt* (*go up*) поднимáться *impf*, поднятся *pf* по+*dat*; (*throne*) всходúть *impf*, взойтú *pf* на+*acc*; *vi* возносúться *impf*, вознестúсь *pf*. **ascendancy** *n* власть. **Ascension** *n* (*eccl*) Вознесéние. **ascent** *n* восхождéние (**of** на+*acc*).

ascertain *vt* устанáвливать *impf*, установúть *pf*.

ascetic *adj* аскетúческий; *n* аскéт. **asceticism** *n* аскетúзм.

ascribe *vt* припúсывать *impf*, приписáть *pf* (**to** +*dat*).

ash[1] *n* (*tree*) ясень *m*.

ash[2], **ashes** *n* в золá, пéпел; (*human remains*) прах. **ashtray** *n* пéпельница.

ashamed *predic*: **he is ~** емý стыдно; **be, feel, ~ of** стыдúться *impf*, по~ *pf* +*gen*.

ashen *adj* (*pale*) мéртвенно-блéдный.

ashore *adv* на бéрег(ý).

Asia *n* Áзия. **Asian, Asiatic** *adj* азиáтский; *n* азиáт, **~ка.**

aside *adv* в стóрону.

ask *vt & i* (*enquire of*) спрáшивать *impf*, спросúть *pf*; (*request*) просúть *impf*, по~ *pf* (**for** *acc, gen,* о+*prep*); (*invite*) приглашáть *impf*, приглáсúть *pf*; (*demand*) трéбовать *impf* +*gen* (**of** от+*gen*); **~ after** освéдомляться *impf*, освéдомиться *pf* о+*prep*; **~ a question** задавáть *impf*, задáть *pf* вопрóс.

askance *adv* кóсо.

askew *adv* крúво.

asleep *predic & adv*: **be ~** спать *impf*; **fall ~** засыпáть *impf*, заснýть *pf*.

asparagus *n* спáржа.

aspect *n* вид; (*side*) сторонá.

aspersion *n* клеветá.

asphalt *n* асфáльт.

asphyxiate *vt* удушáть *impf*, удушúть *pf*.

aspiration *n* стремлéние. **aspire** *vi* стремúться *impf* (**to** к+*dat*).

aspirin *n* аспирúн; (*tablet*) таблéтка аспирúна.

ass *n* осёл.

assail *vt* нападáть *impf*, напáсть *pf* на+*acc*; (*with questions*) забрáсывать *impf*, забросáть *pf* вопрóсами. **assailant** *n* нападáющий *sb*.

assassin *n* убúйца *m & f*. **assassinate** *vt* убивáть *impf*, убúть *pf*. **assassination** *n* убúйство.

assault *n* нападéние; (*mil*) штурм; **~ and battery** оскорблéние дéйствием; *vt* нападáть *impf*, напáсть *pf* на+*acc*.

assemblage *n* сбóрка. **assemble** *vt & i* собирáть(ся) *impf*, собрáть(ся) *pf*. **assembly** *n* собрáние; (*of machine*) сбóрка.

assent *vi* соглашáться *impf*, согласúться *pf* (**to** на+*acc*); *n* соглáсие.

assert *vt* утверждáть *impf*; **~ o.s.** отстáивать *impf*, отстоять *pf* свой правá. **assertion** *n* утверждéние. **assertive** *adj* настóйчивый.

assess *vt* (*amount*) определять *impf*, определúть *pf*; (*value*) оцéнивать *impf*, оценúть *pf*. **assessment** *n* определéние; оцéнка.

asset *n* цéнное кáчество; (*comm; also pl*) актúв.

assiduous *adj* прилéжный.

assign *vt* (*appoint*) назначáть *impf*, назнáчить *pf*; (*allot*) отводúть *impf*, отвестú *pf*. **assignation** *n* свидáние. **assignment** *n* (*task*) задáние; (*mission*) командирóвка.

assimilate *vt* усвáивать *impf*, усвóить *pf*. **assimilation** *n* усвоéние.

assist *vt* помогáть *impf*, помóчь *pf* +*dat*. **assistance** *n* пóмощь. **assistant** *n* помóщник, ассистéнт.

associate *vt* ассоциúровать *impf & pf*; *vi* общáться *impf* (**with** c+*instr*); *n* коллéга *m & f*. **association** *n* óбщество, ассоциáция.

assorted *adj* рáзный. **assortment** *n* ассортимéнт.

assuage *vt* (*calm*) успокáивать *impf*,

успокоить pf; (alleviate) смягчать impf, смягчить pf.

assume vt (take on) принимать impf, принять pf; (suppose) предполагать impf, предположить pf; ~d name вымышленное имя neut; let us ~ допустим. **assumption** n (taking on) принятие на себе; (supposition) предположение.

assurance n заверение; (self-~) самоуверенность; (insurance) страхование. **assure** vt уверять impf, уверить pf.

asterisk n звёздочка.

asthma n астма. **asthmatic** adj астматический.

astonish vt удивлять impf, удивить pf. **astonishing** adj удивительный. **astonishment** n удивление.

astound vt изумлять impf, изумить pf. **astounding** adj изумительный.

astray adv: go ~ сбиваться impf, сбиться pf с пути; lead ~ сбивать impf, сбить pf с пути.

astride prep верхом на+prep.

astringent adj вяжущий; терпкий.

astrologer n астролог. **astrology** n астрология. **astronaut** n астронавт. **astronomer** n астроном. **astronomical** adj астрономический. **astronomy** n астрономия.

astute adj проницательный.

asunder adv (apart) врозь; (in pieces) на части.

asylum n сумасшедший дом; (refuge) убежище.

asymmetrical adj асимметричный. **asymmetry** n асимметрия.

at prep (position) на+prep, в+prep, у+gen: **at a concert** на концерте; **at the cinema** в кино; **at the window** у окна; (time) в+acc: **at two o'clock** в два часа; на+acc: **at Easter** на Пасху; (price) по+dat: **at 5p a pound** по пяти пенсов за фунт; (speed): **at 60 mph** со скоростью шестьдесят миль в час; ~ **first** сначала, сперва; ~ **home** дома; ~ **last** наконец; ~ **least** по крайней мере; ~ **that** в том, (moreover) к тому же.

atheism n атеизм. **atheist** n атеист, ~ка.

athlete n спортсмен, ~ка. **athletic** adj атлетический. **athletics** n (лёгкая) атлетика.

atlas n атлас.

atmosphere n атмосфера. **atmospheric** adj атмосферный.

atom n атом; ~ **bomb** атомная бомба. **atomic** adj атомный.

atone vi искупать impf, искупить pf (for +acc). **atonement** n искупление.

atrocious adj ужасный. **atrocity** n зверство.

attach vt (fasten) прикреплять impf, прикрепить pf; (append) прилагать impf, приложить pf; (attribute) придавать impf, придать pf; **attached to** (devoted) привязанный к+dat. **attaché** n атташе m indecl. **attachment** n прикрепление; привязанность; (tech) принадлежность.

attack vt нападать impf, напасть pf на+acc; n нападение; (of illness) припадок.

attain vt достигать impf, достичь & достигнуть pf +gen. **attainment** n достижение.

attempt vt пытаться impf, по~ pf +inf; n попытка.

attend vt & i (be present at) присутствовать impf (на+prep); vt (accompany) сопровождать impf, сопроводить pf; (go to regularly) посещать impf, посетить pf; ~ **to** заниматься impf, заняться pf. **attendance** n (presence) присутствие; (number) посещаемость. **attendant** adj сопровождающий; n дежурный sb; (escort) провожатый sb.

attention n внимание; pay ~ обращать impf, обратить pf внимание (to на+acc); int (mil) смирно! **attentive** adj внимательный; (solicitous) заботливый.

attest vt & i (also ~ to) заверять impf, заверить pf; свидетельствовать impf, за~ pf (o+prep).

attic n чердак.

attire vt наряжать impf, нарядить pf; n наряд.

attitude n (posture) поза; (opinion) отношение (towards к+dat).

attorney n поверенный sb; power of ~ доверенность.

attract vt привлекать impf, привлечь pf. **attraction** n привлекательность; (entertainment) аттракцион. **attractive** adj привлекательный.

attribute vt припи́сывать impf, приписа́ть pf; n (quality) сво́йство. **attribution** n припи́сывание. **attributive** adj атрибути́вный.

attrition n: war of ~ война́ на истоще́ние.

aubergine n баклажа́н.

auburn adj тёмно-ры́жий.

auction n аукцио́н; vt продава́ть impf, прода́ть pf с аукцио́на. **auctioneer** n аукциони́ст.

audacious adj (bold) сме́лый; (impudent) де́рзкий. **audacity** n сме́лость; де́рзость.

audible adj слы́шный. **audience** n пу́блика, аудито́рия; (listeners) слу́шатели m pl, (viewers, spectators) зри́тели m pl; (interview) аудие́нция. **audit** n прове́рка счето́в, реви́зия; vt прове́рять impf, прове́рить pf (счета́+gen). **audition** n про́ба; vt устра́ивать impf, устро́ить pf про́бу +gen. **auditor** n ревизо́р. **auditorium** n зри́тельный зал.

augment vt увели́чивать impf, увели́чить pf.

augur vt & i предвеща́ть impf.

August n а́вгуст; adj а́вгустовский. **august** adj величе́ственный.

aunt n тётя, тётка.

au pair n домрабо́тница иностра́нного происхожде́ния.

aura n орео́л.

auspices n pl покрови́тельство. **auspicious** adj благоприя́тный.

austere adj стро́гий. **austerity** n стро́гость.

Australia n Австра́лия. **Australian** n австрали́ец, -и́йка; adj австрали́йский.

Austria n А́встрия. **Austrian** n австри́ец, -и́йка; adj австри́йский.

authentic adj по́длинный. **authenticate** vt устана́вливать impf, установи́ть pf по́длинность+gen. **authenticity** n по́длинность.

author, authoress n а́втор.

authoritarian adj авторита́рный. **authoritative** adj авторите́тный. **authority** n (power) власть, полномо́чие; (weight; expert) авторите́т; (source) авторите́тный исто́чник. **authorization** n уполномо́чивание; (permission) разреше́ние. **authorize** vt (action) разреша́ть impf, раз-

реши́ть pf; (person) уполномо́чивать impf, уполномо́чить pf.

authorship n а́вторство.

autobiographical автобиографи́ческий. **autobiography** n автобиогра́фия. **autocracy** n автокра́тия. **autocrat** n автокра́т. **autocratic** adj автократи́ческий. **autograph** n авто́граф. **automatic** adj автомати́ческий. **automation** n автоматиза́ция. **automaton** n автома́т. **automobile** n автомоби́ль m. **autonomous** adj автоно́мный. **autonomy** n автоно́мия. **autopilot** n автопило́т. **autopsy** n вскры́тие; ауто́псия.

autumn n о́сень. **autumn(al)** adj осе́нний.

auxiliary adj вспомога́тельный; n помо́щник, -ица.

avail n: to no ~ напра́сно; vt: ~ o.s. of по́льзоваться impf, вос~ pf +instr. **available** adj досту́пный, нали́чный.

avalanche n лави́на.

avant-garde n аванга́рд; adj аванга́рдный.

avarice n жа́дность. **avaricious** adj жа́дный.

avenge vt мстить impf, ото~ pf за+acc. **avenger** n мсти́тель m.

avenue n (of trees) алле́я; (wide street) проспе́кт; (means) путь m.

average n сре́днее число́, сре́днее sb; on ~ в сре́днем; adj сре́дний; vt де́лать impf в сре́днем; vt & i: ~ (out at) составля́ть impf, соста́вить pf в сре́днем.

averse adj: not ~ to не прочь+inf, не про́тив+gen. **aversion** n отвраще́ние. **avert** vt (ward off) предотвраща́ть impf, предотврати́ть pf; (turn away) отводи́ть impf, отвести́ pf.

aviary n пти́чник.

aviation n авиа́ция.

avid adj жа́дный; (keen) стра́стный.

avocado n авока́до neut indecl.

avoid vt избега́ть impf, избежа́ть pf +gen; (evade) уклоня́ться impf, уклони́ться pf от+gen. **avoidance** n избежа́ние, уклоне́ние.

avowal n призна́ние. **avowed** adj при́знанный.

await vt ждать impf +gen.

awake predic: be ~ не спать impf.

awake(n) vt пробужда́ть impf, пробуди́ть pf; vi просыпа́ться impf, просну́ться pf.

award vt присужда́ть impf, присуди́ть pf (person dat, thing acc); награжда́ть impf, награди́ть pf (person acc, thing instr); n награ́да.

aware predic: be ~ of сознава́ть impf; знать impf. **awareness** n созна́ние.

away adv прочь; be ~ отсу́тствовать impf; far ~ (from) далеко́ (от+gen); 5 miles ~ в пяти́ ми́лях отсю́да; ~ game игра́ на чужо́м по́ле.

awe n благогове́йный страх. **awful** adj ужа́сный. **awfully** adv ужа́сно.

awhile adv не́которое вре́мя.

awkward adj нело́вкий. **awkwardness** n нело́вкость.

awning n наве́с, тент.

awry adv ко́со.

axe n топо́р; vt уре́зывать, уреза́ть impf, уре́зать pf.

axiom n аксио́ма. **axiomatic** adj аксиомати́ческий.

axis, axle n ось.

ay int да!; n (in vote) го́лос „за“.

Azerbaijan n Азербайджа́н. **Azerbaijani** n азербайджа́нец (-нца), -а́нка; adj азербайджа́нский.

azure n лазу́рь; adj лазу́рный.

B

BA abbr (univ) бакала́вр.

babble n (voices) болтовня́; (water) журча́ние; vi болта́ть impf; (water) журча́ть impf.

baboon n павиа́н.

baby n младе́нец; ~-sit присма́тривать за детьми́ в отсу́тствие роди́телей; ~-sitter приходя́щая ня́ня. **babyish** adj ребя́ческий.

bachelor n холостя́к; (univ) бакала́вр.

bacillus n баци́лла.

back n (of body) спина́; (rear) за́дняя часть; (reverse) оборо́т; (of seat) спи́нка; (sport) защи́тник; adj за́дний; vt (support) подде́рживать impf, поддержа́ть pf; (car) отодвига́ть impf, отодви́нуть pf; (horse) ста́вить impf, по~ pf на+acc; (finance) финанси́ровать impf & pf; vi ото-

двига́ться impf, отодви́нуться pf наза́д; **backed out of the garage** вы́ехал за́дом из гаража́; ~ **down** уступа́ть impf, уступи́ть pf; ~ **out** уклоня́ться impf, уклони́ться pf (of от+gen); ~ **up** (support) подде́рживать impf, поддержа́ть pf; (confirm) подкрепля́ть impf, подкрепи́ть pf. **backbiting** n спле́тня.

backbone n позвоно́чник; (support) гла́вная опо́ра; (firmness) твёрдость хара́ктера. **backcloth, backdrop** n за́дник; (fig) фон. **backer** n спо́нсор; (supporter) сторо́нник. **backfire** vi дава́ть impf, дать pf отсе́чку. **background** n фон, за́дний план; (person's) происхожде́ние. **backhand(er)** n уда́р сле́ва. **backhanded** adj (fig) сомни́тельный. **backhander** n (bribe) взя́тка. **backing** n подде́ржка. **backlash** n реа́кция. **backlog** n задо́лженность. **backside** n зад. **backstage** adv за кули́сами; adj закули́сный. **backstroke** n пла́вание на спине́. **back-up** n подде́ржка; (copy) резе́рвная ко́пия; adj вспомога́тельный. **backward** adj отста́лый. **backward(s)** adv наза́д. **backwater** n за́водь.

back yard n за́дний двор.

bacon n беко́н.

bacterium n бакте́рия.

bad adj плохо́й; (food etc.) испо́рченный; (language) гру́бый; ~-mannered невоспи́танный; ~ **taste** безвку́сица; ~-tempered раздражи́тельный.

badge n значо́к.

badger n барсу́к; vt трави́ть impf, за~ pf.

badly adv пло́хо; (very much) о́чень.

badminton n бадминто́н.

baffle vt озада́чивать impf, озада́чить pf.

bag n (handbag) су́мка; (plastic ~, sack, under eyes) мешо́к; (paper ~) бума́жный паке́т; pl (luggage) бага́ж.

baggage n бага́ж.

baggy adj мешкова́тый.

bagpipe n волы́нка.

bail[1] n (security) поручи́тельство; **release on ~** отпуска́ть impf, отпусти́ть pf на пору́ки; vt (~ out) брать impf, взять pf на пору́ки; (help)

выруча́ть *impf*, вы́ручить *pf*.
bail², **bale²** *vt* вычёрпывать *impf*, вы́черпнуть *pf* (во́ду из+*gen*); ~ **out** *vi* выбра́сываться *impf*, вы́броситься *pf* с парашю́том.
bailiff *n* суде́бный исполни́тель.
bait *n* нажи́вка; прима́нка (*also fig*); *vt* (*torment*) трави́ть *impf*, за~ *pf*.
bake *vt & i* печь(ся) *impf*, ис~ *pf*. **baker** *n* пе́карь *m*, бу́лочник. **bakery** *n* пека́рня; (*shop*) бу́лочная *sb*.
balalaika *n* балала́йка.
balance *n* (*scales*) весы́ *m pl*; (*equilibrium*) равнове́сие; (*econ*) бала́нс; (*remainder*) оста́ток; ~ **sheet** бала́нс; *vt* (*make equal*) уравнове́шивать *impf*, уравнове́сить *pf*; *vt & i* (*econ*; *hold steady*) баланси́ровать *impf*, с~ *pf*.
balcony *n* балко́н.
bald *adj* лы́сый; ~ **patch** лы́сина. **balding** *adj* лысе́ющий. **baldness** *n* плеши́вость.
bale¹ *n* (*bundle*) ки́па.
bale² *see* bail²
balk *vi* арта́читься *impf*, за~ *pf*; she balked at the price цена́ её испуга́ла.
ball¹ *n* (*in games*) мяч; (*sphere*; *billiards*) шар; (*wool*) клубо́к; ~**bearing** шарикоподши́пник; ~**point (pen)** ша́риковая ру́чка.
ball² *n* (*dance*) бал.
ballad *n* балла́да.
ballast *n* балла́ст.
ballerina *n* балери́на.
ballet *n* бале́т. **ballet-dancer** *n* арти́ст, ~ка, бале́та.
balloon *n* возду́шный шар.
ballot *n* голосова́ние. **ballot-paper** *n* избира́тельный бюллете́нь *m*; *vt* держа́ть *impf* голосова́ние между +*instr*.
balm *n* бальза́м. **balmy** *adj* (*soft*) мя́гкий.
Baltic *n* Балти́йское мо́ре; ~ **States** прибалти́йские госуда́рства, Приба́лтика.
balustrade *n* балюстра́да.
bamboo *n* бамбу́к.
bamboozle *vt* надува́ть *impf*, наду́ть *pf*.
ban *n* запре́т; *vt* запреща́ть *impf*, запрети́ть *pf*.
banal *adj* бана́льный. **banality** *n* бана́льность.

banana *n* бана́н.
band *n* (*stripe, strip*) полоса́; (*braid, tape*) тесьма́; (*category*) катего́рия; (*of people*) гру́ппа; (*gang*) ба́нда; (*mus*) орке́стр; (*radio*) диапазо́н; *vi*: ~ **together** объединя́ться *impf*, объедини́ться *pf*.
bandage *n* бинт; *vt* бинтова́ть *impf*, за~ *pf*.
bandit *n* банди́т.
bandstand *n* эстра́да для орке́стра.
bandwagon *n*: jump on the ~ по́льзоваться *impf*, вос~ *pf* благоприя́тными обстоя́тельствами.
bandy-legged *adj* кривоно́гий.
bane *n* отра́ва.
bang *n* (*blow*) уда́р; (*noise*) стук; (*of gun*) вы́стрел; *vt* (*strike*) ударя́ть *impf*, уда́рить *pf*; *vi* хло́пать *impf*, хло́пнуть *pf*; (*slam shut*) захло́пываться *impf*, захло́пнуться *pf*; ~ **one's head** уда́риться *impf*, уда́риться *pf* голово́й; ~ **the door** хло́пать *impf*, хло́пнуть *pf* две́рью.
bangle *n* брасле́т.
banish *vt* изгоня́ть *impf*, изгна́ть *pf*.
banister *n* пери́ла *neut pl*.
banjo *n* ба́нджо *neut indecl*.
bank¹ *n* (*of river*) бе́рег; (*of earth*) вал; *vt* сгреба́ть *impf*, сгрести́ *pf* в ку́чу; *vi* (*aeron*) накреня́ться *impf*, накрени́ться *pf*.
bank² *n* (*econ*) банк; ~ **account** счёт в ба́нке; ~ **holiday** устано́вленный пра́здник; *vi* (*keep money*) держа́ть *impf* де́ньги (в ба́нке); *vt* (*put in* ~) класть *impf*, положи́ть *pf* в банк; ~ **on** полага́ться *impf*, положи́ться *pf* на+*acc*. **banker** *n* банки́р. **banknote** *n* банкно́та.
bankrupt *n* банкро́т; *adj* обанкро́тившийся; *vt* доводи́ть *impf*, довести́ *pf* до банкро́тства. **bankruptcy** *n* банкро́тство.
banner *n* зна́мя *neut*.
banquet *n* банке́т, пир.
banter *n* подшу́чивание.
baptism *n* креще́ние. **baptize** *vt* крести́ть *impf*, о~ *pf*.
bar *n* (*beam*) брус; (*of cage*) решётка; (*of chocolate*) пли́тка; (*of soap*) кусо́к; (*barrier*) прегра́да; (*law*) адвокату́ра; (*counter*) сто́йка; (*room*) бар; (*mus*) такт; *vt* (*obstruct*) прегражда́ть *impf*, прегради́ть *pf*;

(*prohibit*) запрещáть *impf*, за-
претúть *pf*.
barbarian *n* вáрвар. **barbaric, bar-
barous** *adj* вáрварский.
barbecue *n* (*party*) шашлы́к; *vt* жá-
рить *impf*, за~ *pf* на вéртеле.
barbed wire *n* колю́чая прóволока.
barber *n* парикмáхер; ~'s **shop** па-
рикмáхерская *sb*.
bar code *n* маркирóвка.
bard *n* бард.
bare *adj* (*naked*) гóлый; (*empty*)
пустóй; (*small*) минимáльный; *vt*
обнажáть *impf*, обнажúть *pf*; ~
one's teeth скáлить *impf*, о~ *pf*
зу́бы. **barefaced** *adj* нáглый. **barefoot** *adj* босóй. **barely** *adv* едвá.
bargain *n* (*deal*) сдéлка; (*good buy*)
вы́годная сдéлка; *vi* торговáться
impf, с~ *pf*; ~ **for, on** (*expect*)
ожидáть *impf* +*gen*.
barge *n* бáржа; *vi*: ~ **into** (*room etc.*)
вры́ваться *impf*, ворвáться *pf*
в+*acc*.
baritone *n* баритóн.
bark[1] *n* (*of dog*) лай; *vi* лáять *impf*.
bark[2] *n* (*of tree*) корá.
barley *n* ячмéнь *m*.
barmaid *n* буфéтчица. **barman** *n*
буфéтчик.
barmy *adj* трóнутый.
barn *n* амбáр.
barometer *n* барóметр.
baron *n* барóн. **baroness** *n* баро-
нéсса.
baroque *n* барóкко *neut indecl; adj*
барóчный.
barrack[1] *n* казáрма.
barrack[2] *vt* освúстывать *impf*, освн-
стáть *pf*.
barrage *n* (*in river*) запру́да; (*gun-
fire*) огневóй вал; (*fig*) град.
barrel *n* бóчка; (*of gun*) ду́ло.
barren *adj* бесплóдный.
barricade *n* баррикáда; *vt* барри-
кадúровать *impf*, за~ *pf*.
barrier *n* барьéр.
barring *prep* исключáя.
barrister *n* адвокáт.
barrow *n* телéжка.
barter *n* товарообмéн; *vi* обмéниваться *impf*, обменя́ться *pf* товá-
рами.
base[1] *adj* нúзкий; (*metal*) неблагорóдный.

base[2] *n* оснóва; (*also mil*) бáза; *vt*
оснóвывать *impf*, основáть *pf*.
baseball *n* бейсбóл. **baseless** *adj*
необоснóванный. **basement** *n* под-
вáл.
bash *vt* трéснуть *pf*; *n*: **have a** ~!
попрóбуй(те)!
bashful *adj* застéнчивый.
basic *adj* оснóвнóй. **basically** *adv* в
оснóвнóм.
basin *n* таз; (*geog*) бассéйн.
basis *n* оснóва, бáзис.
bask *vi* грéться *impf*; (*fig*) насла-
ждáться *impf*, наслади́ться *pf* (**in**
+*instr*).
basket *n* корзи́на. **basketball** *n*
баскетбóл.
bass *n* бас; *adj* басóвый.
bassoon *n* фагóт.
bastard *n* (*sl*) негодя́й.
baste *vt* (*cul*) поливáть *impf*, поли́ть
pf жи́ром.
bastion *n* бастиóн.
bat[1] *n* (*zool*) летýчая мышь.
bat[2] *n* (*sport*) битá; *vi* бить *impf*, по-
pf по мячý.
bat[3] *vt*: **he didn't** ~ **an eyelid** он и
глáзом не моргнýл.
batch *n* пáчка; (*of loaves*) вы́печка.
bated *adj*: **with** ~ **breath** затаи́в
дыхáние.
bath *n* (*vessel*) вáнна; *pl* плáва-
тельный бассéйн; **have a bath**
принимáть *impf*, приня́ть *pf* вáнну;
vt купáть *impf*, вы́~, ис~ *pf*. **bathe**
vi купáться *impf*, вы́~, ис~ *pf; vt*
омывáть *impf*, омы́ть *pf*. **bather** *n*
купáльщик, -ица. **bath-house** *n*
бáня. **bathing** *n*: ~ **cap** купáльная
шáпочка; ~ **costume** купáльный
костю́м. **bathroom** *n* вáнная *sb*.
baton *n* (*staff of office*) жезл; (*sport*)
эстафéта; (*mus*) (дирижёрская)
пáлочка.
battalion *n* батальóн.
batten *n* рéйка.
batter *n* взби́тое тéсто; *vt* колоти́ть
impf, по~ *pf*.
battery *n* батарéя.
battle *n* би́тва; (*fig*) борьбá; *vi*
борóться *impf*. **battlefield** *n* пóле
бóя. **battlement** *n* зубчáтая стенá.
battleship *n* линéйный корáбль *m*.
bawdy *adj* непристóйный.
bawl *vi* орáть *impf*.

bay[1] *n* (*bot*) лавр; *adj* лавро́вый.

bay[2] *n* (*geog*) зали́в.

bay[3] *n* (*recess*) пролёт; ~ **window** фона́рь *m*.

bay[4] *vi* (*bark*) ла́ять *impf*; (*howl*) выть *impf*.

bay[5] *adj* (*colour*) гнедо́й.

bayonet *n* штык.

bazaar *n* база́р.

BC *abbr* до н.э. (до на́шей э́ры).

be[1] *v* 1. быть: *usually omitted in pres*: **he is a teacher** он учи́тель. 2. (*exist*) существова́ть *impf*. 3. (*frequentative*) быва́ть *impf*. 4. (~ *situated*) находи́ться *impf*; (*stand*) стоя́ть *impf*; (*lie*) лежа́ть *impf*. 5. (*in general definitions*) явля́ться *impf* +*instr*: **Moscow is the capital of Russia** столи́цей Росси́и явля́ется го́род Москва́. 6.: **there is, are** име́ется, име́ются; (*emph*) есть.

be[2] *v aux* 1. *be+inf, expressing duty, plan*: до́лжен+*inf*. 2. *be+past participle passive, expressing passive*: быть+*past participle passive in short form*: **it was done** бы́ло сде́лано; *impers construction of 3 pl+acc*: **I was beaten** меня́ би́ли; *reflexive construction*: **music was heard** слы́шалась му́зыка. 3. *be+pres participle active, expressing continuous tenses*: *imperfective aspect*: **I am reading** я чита́ю.

beach *n* пляж.

beacon *n* мая́к, сигна́льный ого́нь *m*.

bead *n* бу́сина; (*drop*) ка́пля; *pl* бу́сы *f pl*.

beak *n* клюв.

beaker *n* (*child's*) ча́шка с но́сиком; (*chem*) мензу́рка.

beam *n* ба́лка; (*ray*) луч; *vi* (*shine*) сия́ть *impf*.

bean *n* фасо́ль, боб.

bear[1] *n* медве́дь *m*.

bear[2] *vt* (*carry*) носи́ть *indet*, нести́ *det*, по~ *pf*; (*endure*) терпе́ть *impf*; (*child*) роди́ть *impf* & *pf*; ~ **out** подтвержда́ть *impf*, подтверди́ть *pf*; ~ **up** держа́ться *impf*. **bearable** *adj* терпи́мый.

beard *n* борода́. **bearded** *adj* борода́тый.

bearer *n* носи́тель *m*; (*of cheque*) предъяви́тель *m*; (*of letter*) пода́тель *m*.

bearing *n* (*deportment*) оса́нка; (*relation*) отноше́ние; (*position*) пе́ленг; (*tech*) подши́пник; **get one's** ~**s** ориенти́роваться *impf* & *pf*; **lose one's** ~**s** потеря́ть *pf* ориенти́ровку.

beast *n* живо́тное *sb*; (*fig*) скоти́на *m* & *f*. **beastly** *adj* (*coll*) проти́вный.

beat *n* бой; (*round*) обхо́д; (*mus*) такт; *vt* бить *impf*, по~ *pf*; (*cul*) взбива́ть *impf*, взбить *pf*; *vi* би́ться *impf*, ~ **off** отбива́ть *impf*, отби́ть *pf*; ~ **up** избива́ть *impf*, изби́ть *pf*. **beating** *n* битьё; (*defeat*) пораже́ние; (*of heart*) бие́ние.

beautiful *adj* краси́вый. **beautify** *vt* украша́ть *impf* укра́сить *pf*. **beauty** *n* красота́; (*person*) краса́вица.

beaver *n* бобр.

because *conj* потому́, что; так как; *adv*: ~ **of** из-за+*gen*.

beckon *vt* мани́ть *impf*, по~ *pf* к себе́.

become *vi* станови́ться *impf*, стать *pf* +*instr*; ~ **of** ста́ться *pf* с+*instr*. **becoming** *adj* (*dress*) иду́щий к лицу́ +*dat*.

bed *n* крова́ть, посте́ль; (*garden*) гря́дка; (*sea*) дно; (*river*) ру́сло; (*geol*) пласт; **go to** ~ ложи́ться *impf*, лечь *pf* спать; **make the** ~ стели́ть *impf*, по~ *pf* посте́ль. **bed and breakfast** *n* (*hotel*) ма́ленькая гости́ница. **bedclothes** *n pl*, **bedding** *n* посте́льное бельё. **bedridden** *adj* прико́ванный к посте́ли. **bedroom** *n* спа́льня. **bedside table** *n* ту́мбочка. **bedsitter** *n* одноко́мнатная кварти́ра. **bedspread** *n* покрыва́ло. **bedtime** *n* вре́мя *neut* ложи́ться спать.

bedevil *vt* му́чить *impf*, за~ *pf*.

bedlam *n* бедла́м.

bedraggled *adj* растрёпанный.

bee *n* пчела́. **beehive** *n* у́лей.

beech *n* бук.

beef *n* говя́дина. **beefburger** *n* котле́та.

beer *n* пи́во.

beetle *n* жук.

beetroot *n* свёкла.

befall *vt* & *i* случа́ться *impf*, случи́ться *pf* (+*dat*).

befit *vt* подходи́ть *impf*, подойти́ *pf* +*dat*.

before *adv* ра́ньше; *prep* пе́ред+*instr*,

до+*gen*; *conj* до того́ как; пре́жде
чем; (*rather than*) скоре́е чем; **the
day ~ yesterday** позавчера́. **beforehand** *adv* зара́нее.

befriend *vt* дружи́ться *impf*, по~ *pf*
с+*instr*.

beg *vt* (*ask*) о́чень проси́ть *impf*,
по~ *pf* (*person+acc*; *thing+acc* or
gen); *vi* ни́щенствовать *impf*; (*of
dog*) служи́ть *impf*; **~ for** проси́ть
impf, по~ *pf* +*acc* or *gen*; **~ pardon**
проси́ть *impf* проще́ние.

beggar *n* ни́щий *sb*.

begin *vt* (& *i*) начина́ть(ся) *impf*,
нача́ть(ся) *pf*. **beginner** *n* начи-
на́ющий *sb*. **beginning** *n* нача́ло.

begrudge *vt* (*give reluctantly*) жале́ть
impf, со~ *pf* o+*prep*.

beguile *vt* (*charm*) очаро́вывать
impf, очарова́ть *pf*; (*seduce, delude*)
обольща́ть *impf*, обольсти́ть *pf*.

behalf *n*: **on ~ of** от и́мени+*gen*; (*in
interest of*) в по́льзу+*gen*.

behave *vi* вести́ *impf* себя́. **behaviour** *n* поведе́ние.

behest *n* заве́т.

behind *adv*, *prep* сза́ди (+*gen*), поза-
ди́ (+*gen*), за (+*acc, instr*); *n* зад; **be,
fall, ~** отстава́ть *impf*, отста́ть *pf*.

behold *vt* смотре́ть *impf*, по~ *pf*. **be-
holden** *predic*: **~ to** обя́зан+*dat*.

beige *adj* бе́жевый.

being *n* (*existence*) бытие́; (*creature*)
существо́.

Belarus *n* Белару́сь.

belated *adj* запозда́лый.

belch *vi* рыга́ть *impf*, рыгну́ть *pf*; *vt*
изверга́ть *impf*, изве́ргнуть *pf*.

beleaguer *vt* осажда́ть *impf*, осади́ть
pf.

belfry *n* колоко́льня.

Belgian *n* белги́ец, -ги́йка; *adj* бель-
ги́йский. **Belgium** *n* Бе́льгия.

belie *vt* противоре́чить *impf*+*dat*.

belief *n* (*faith*) ве́ра; (*confidence*)
убежде́ние. **believable** *adj* правдо-
подо́бный. **believe** *vt* ве́рить *impf*,
по~ *pf* +*dat*; **~ in** ве́рить *impf* в+*acc*.
believer *n* ве́рующий *sb*.

belittle *vt* умаля́ть *impf*, умали́ть *pf*.

bell *n* ко́локол; (*doorbell*) звоно́к;
~ tower колоко́льня.

bellicose *adj* вои́нственный. **bel-
ligerence** *n* вои́нственность. **bel-
ligerent** *adj* вою́ющий; (*aggressive*)

вои́нственный.

bellow *vt* & *i* реве́ть *impf*.

bellows *n pl* мехи́ *m pl*.

belly *n* живо́т.

belong *vi* принадлежа́ть *impf* (**to**
(к)+*dat*). **belongings** *n pl* пожи́тки
(-ков) *pl*.

Belorussian *n* белору́с, ~ка; *adj*
белору́сский.

beloved *adj* & *sb* возлю́бленный.

below *adv* (*position*) вниз, (*place*)
внизу́, ни́же; *prep* ни́же+*gen*.

belt *n* (*strap*) по́яс, (*also tech*) ре-
ме́нь; (*zone*) зо́на, полоса́.

bench *n* скаме́йка; (*for work*) ста-
но́к.

bend *n* изги́б; *vt* (& *i, also* **~ down**)
сгиба́ть(ся) *impf*, согну́ть(ся) *pf*; **~
over** склоня́ться *impf*, склони́ться
pf над+*instr*.

beneath *prep* под+*instr*.

benediction *n* благослове́ние.

benefactor *n* благоде́тель *m*. **benefactress** *n* благоде́тельница

beneficial *adj* поле́зный. **beneficiary**
n получа́тель *m*; (*law*) насле́дник.
benefit *n* по́льза; (*allowance*) по-
со́бие; (*theat*) бенефи́с; *vt* прино-
си́ть *impf*, принести́ *pf* по́льзу +*dat*;
vi извлека́ть *impf*, извле́чь *pf* вы́-
году.

benevolence *n* благожела́тельность.
benevolent *adj* благожела́тельный.

benign *adj* до́брый, мя́гкий; (*tumour*) доброка́чественный.

bent *n* скло́нность.

bequeath *vt* завеща́ть *impf* & *pf*
(**to**+*dat*). **bequest** *n* посме́ртный
дар.

berate *vt* руга́ть *impf*, вы́~ *pf*.

bereave *vt* лиша́ть *impf*, лиши́ть *pf*
(**of** +*gen*). **bereavement** *n* тяжёлая
утра́та.

berry *n* я́года.

berserk *adj*: **go ~** взбеси́ться *pf*.

berth *n* (*bunk*) ко́йка; (*naut*) сто-
я́нка; *vi* прича́ливать *impf*, при-
ча́лить *pf*.

beseech *vt* умоля́ть *impf*, умоли́ть
pf.

beset *vt* осажда́ть *impf*, осади́ть *pf*.

beside *prep* о́коло+*gen*, ря́дом
с+*instr*; **~ the point** некста́ти; **~ o.s.**
вне себя́. **besides** *adv* кро́ме того́;
prep кро́ме+*gen*.

besiege vt осажда́ть impf, осади́ть pf.

besotted adj одурма́ненный.

bespoke adj сде́ланный на зака́з.

best adj лу́чший, са́мый лу́чший; adv лу́чше всего́, бо́льше всего́; **all the ~!** всего́ наилу́чшего! **at ~** в лу́чшем слу́чае; **do one's ~** де́лать impf, с~ pf всё возмо́жное; **~ man** ша́фер.

bestial adj зве́рский. **bestiality** n зве́рство.

bestow vt дарова́ть impf & pf.

bestseller n бестсе́ллер.

bet n пари́ neut indecl; (stake) ста́вка; vi держа́ть impf пари́ (**on** на+acc); vt (stake) ста́вить impf, по~ pf; **he bet me £5** он поспо́рил со мной 5 фу́нтов.

betray vt изменя́ть impf, измени́ть pf+dat. **betrayal** n изме́на.

better adj лу́чший; adv лу́чше; (more) бо́льше; vt улучша́ть impf, улу́чшить pf; **all the ~** тем лу́чше; **~ off** бо́лее состоя́тельный; **~ o.s.** выдвига́ть impf, вы́двинуться pf; **get ~** (health) поправля́ться impf, попра́виться pf; **get the ~ of** брать impf, взять pf верх над+instr; **had ~: you had ~ go** вам (dat) лу́чше бы пойти́; **think ~ of** переду́мывать impf, переду́мать pf. **betterment** n улучше́ние.

between prep ме́жду+instr.

bevel vt ска́шивать impf, скоси́ть pf.

beverage n напи́ток.

bevy n ста́йка.

beware vi остерега́ться impf, остере́чься pf (**of** +gen).

bewilder vt сбива́ть impf, сбить pf с то́лку. **bewildered** adj озада́ченный. **bewilderment** n замеша́тельство.

bewitch vt заколдо́вывать impf, заколдова́ть pf; (fig) очаро́вывать impf, очарова́ть pf. **bewitching** adj очарова́тельный.

beyond prep за+acc & instr; по ту сто́рону+gen; (above) сверх+gen; (outside) вне+gen; **the back of ~** край све́та.

bias n (inclination) укло́н; (prejudice) предупрежде́ние. **biased** adj предупреждённый.

bib n нагру́дник.

Bible n Би́блия. **biblical** adj библе́йский.

bibliographical n библиографи́ческий. **bibliography** n библиогра́фия.

bicarbonate (of soda) n питьева́я со́да.

biceps n би́цепс.

bicker vi пререка́ться impf.

bicycle n велосипе́д.

bid n предложе́ние цены́; (attempt) попы́тка; vt & i предлага́ть impf, предложи́ть pf (це́ну) (**for** за+acc); vt (command) прика́зывать impf, приказа́ть pf +dat. **bidding** n предложе́ние цены́; (command) приказа́ние.

bide vt: **~ one's time** ожида́ть impf благоприя́тного слу́чая.

biennial adj двухле́тний; n двухле́тник.

bier n катафа́лк.

bifocals n pl бифока́льные очки́ pl.

big adj большо́й; (also important) кру́пный.

bigamist n (man) двоежёнец; (woman) двуму́жница. **bigamy** n двубра́чие.

bigwig n ши́шка.

bike n велосипе́д. **biker** n мотоцикли́ст.

bikini n бики́ни neut indecl.

bilateral adj двусторо́нний.

bilberry n черни́ка (no pl; usu collect).

bile n жёлчь. **bilious** adj жёлчный.

bilingual adj двуязы́чный.

bill[1] n счёт; (parl) законопрое́кт; (~ of exchange) ве́ксель; (poster) афи́ша; vt (announce) объявля́ть impf, объяви́ть pf в афи́шах; (charge) присыла́ть impf, присла́ть pf счёт +dat.

bill[2] n (beak) клюв.

billet vt расквартиро́вывать impf, расквартирова́ть pf.

billiards n billiá́рд.

billion n биллио́н.

billow n вал; vi вздыма́ться impf.

bin n му́сорное ведро́; (corn) за́кром.

bind vt (tie) свя́зывать impf, связа́ть pf; (oblige) обя́зывать impf, обяза́ть pf; (book) переплета́ть impf, переплести́ pf. **binder** n (person) переплётчик; (*agric*) вязáльщик; (*for papers*) пáпка. **binding** n переплёт.

binge n кутёж.

binoculars n pl бинóкль m.

biochemistry n биохúмия. **biographer** n биóграф. **biographical** adj биографúческий. **biography** n биогрáфия. **biological** adj биологúческий. **biologist** n биóлог. **biology** n биолóгия.

bipartisan adj двухпартúйный.

birch n берёза; (*rod*) рóзга.

bird n птúца; ~ **of prey** хúщная птúца.

birth n рождéние; (*descent*) происхождéние; ~ **certificate** мéтрика; ~ **control** противозачáточные мéры f pl. **birthday** n день m рождéния; **fourth** ~ четырёхлéтие. **birthplace** n мéсто рождéния. **birthright** n прáво по рождéнию.

biscuit n печéнье.

bisect vt разрезáть impf, разрéзать pf попол́ам.

bisexual adj бисексуáльный.

bishop n епúскоп; (*chess*) слон.

bit[1] n (*piece*) кусóчек; **a** ~ немнóго; **not a** ~ ничýть.

bit[2] n (*tech*) сверлó; (*bridle*) удилá (-л) pl.

bitch n (*coll*) стéрва. **bitchy** adj стервóзный.

bite n укýс; (*snack*) закýска; (*fishing*) клёв; vt кусáть impf, укусúть pf; vi (*fish*) клевáть impf, клю́нуть pf. **biting** adj éдкий.

bitter adj гóрький; **bitterness** n гóречь.

bitumen n битýм.

bivouac n бивáк.

bizarre adj стрáнный.

black adj чёрный; ~ **eye** подбúтый глаз; ~ **market** чёрный ры́нок; v: ~ **out** (vt) затемня́ть impf, затемнúть pf; (vi) теря́ть impf, по~ pf сознáние; n (*colour*) чёрный цвет; (~ *person*) негр, ~итя́нка; (*mourning*) трáур. **blackberry** n ежевúка (*no pl; usu collect*). **blackbird** n чёрный дрозд. **blackboard** n доскá. **blackcurrant** n чёрная сморóдина (*no pl; usu collect*). **blacken** vt (*fig*) чернúть impf, о~ pf. **blackleg** n штрейкбрéхер. **blacklist** vt вносúть

impf, внестú pf в чёрный спúсок. **blackmail** n шантáж; vt шантажúровать impf. **blackout** n затемнéние; (*faint*) потéря сознáния. **blacksmith** n кузнéц.

bladder n пузы́рь m.

blade n (*knife*) лéзвие; (*oar*) лóпасть; (*grass*) былúнка.

blame n винá, порицáние; vt винúть impf (**for** в+prep); **be to** ~ быть виновáтым. **blameless** adj безупрéчный.

blanch vt (*vegetables*) ошпáривать impf, ошпáрить pf; vi бледнéть impf, по~ pf.

bland adj мя́гкий; (*dull*) прéсный.

blandishments n pl лесть.

blank adj (*look*) отсýтствующий; (*paper*) чúстый; n (*space*) прóпуск; (*form*) бланк; (*cartridge*) холостóй патрóн; ~ **cheque** незапóлненный чек.

blanket n одея́ло.

blare vi трубúть impf, про~ pf.

blasé adj пресы́щенный.

blasphemous adj богохýльный. **blasphemy** n богохýльство.

blast n (*wind*) пóрыв вéтра; (*explosion*) взрыв; vt взорвáть pf; ~ **off** стартовáть impf & pf. **blast-furnace** n дóмна.

blatant adj я́вный.

blaze n (*flame*) плáмя neut; (*fire*) пожáр; vi пылáть impf.

blazer n лёгкий пиджáк.

bleach n хлóрка, отбéливатель m; vt отбéливать impf, отбелúть pf.

bleak adj пусты́нный; (*dreary*) уны́лый.

bleary-eyed adj с затумáненными глазáми.

bleat vi блéять impf.

bleed vi кровоточúть impf.

bleeper n персонáльный сигнализáтор.

blemish n пятнó.

blend n смесь; vt смéшивать impf, смешáть pf; vi гармонúровать impf. **blender** n мúксер.

bless vt благословля́ть impf, благословúть pf. **blessed** adj благословéнный. **blessing** n (*action*) благословéние; (*object*) блáго.

blight vt губúть impf, по~ pf.

blind adj слепóй; ~ **alley** тупúк; n

штора; *vt* ослепля́ть *impf*, ослепи́ть *pf*. **blindfold** *vt* завя́зывать *impf*, завяза́ть *pf* глаза́+*dat*. **blindness** *n* слепота́.

blink *vi* мига́ть *impf*, мигну́ть *pf*. **blinkers** *n pl* шо́ры (-р) *pl*.

bliss *n* блаже́нство. **blissful** *adj* блаже́нный.

blister *n* пузы́рь *m*, волды́рь *m*.

blithe *adj* весёлый; (*carefree*) беспе́чный.

blitz *n* бомбёжка.

blizzard *n* мете́ль.

bloated *adj* взду́тый.

blob *n* (*liquid*) ка́пля; (*colour*) кля́кса.

bloc *n* блок.

block *n* (*wood*) чурба́н; (*stone*) глы́ба; (*flats*) жило́й дом; *vt* прегражда́ть *impf*, прегради́ть *pf*; ~ **up** забива́ть *impf*, заби́ть *pf*.

blockade *n* блока́да; *vt* блоки́ровать *impf & pf*.

blockage *n* зато́р.

bloke *n* па́рень *m*.

blond *n* блонди́н, ~ка; *adj* белоку́рый.

blood *n* кровь; ~ **donor** до́нор; ~ **poisoning** *n* зараже́ние кро́ви; ~ **pressure** кровяно́е давле́ние; ~ **relation** бли́зкий ро́дственник, -ая ро́дственница; ~ **transfusion** перелива́ние кро́ви. **bloodhound** *n* ище́йка. **bloodshed** *n* кровопроли́тие. **bloodshot** *adj* нали́тый кро́вью. **bloodthirsty** *adj* кровожа́дный. **bloody** *adj* крова́вый.

bloom *n* расцве́т; *vi* цвести́ *pf*. **blossom** *n* цвет; **in** ~ в цвету́.

blot *n* кля́кса; пятно́; *vt* (*dry*) промока́ть *impf*, промокну́ть *pf*; (*smudge*) па́чкать *impf*, за~ *pf*.

blotch *n* пятно́.

blotting-paper *n* промока́тельная бума́га.

blouse *n* ко́фточка, блу́зка.

blow[1] *n* уда́р.

blow[2] *vt & i* дуть *impf*; ~ **away** сноси́ть *impf*, снести́ *pf*; ~ **down** вали́ть *impf*, по~ *pf*; ~ **one's nose** сморка́ться *impf*, сморкну́ться *pf*; ~ **out** задува́ть *impf*, заду́ть *pf*; ~ **over** (*fig*) проходи́ть *impf*, пройти́ *pf*; ~ **up** взрыва́ть *impf*, взорва́ть *pf*; (*inflate*) надува́ть *impf*, наду́ть *pf*. **blow-lamp** *n* пая́льная ла́мпа.

blubber[1] *n* во́рвань.

blubber[2] *vi* реве́ть *impf*.

bludgeon *n* дуби́нка; *vt* (*compel*) вынужда́ть *impf*, вы́нудить *pf*.

blue *adj* (*dark*) си́ний; (*light*) голубо́й; *n* си́ний, голубо́й, цвет. **bluebell** *n* колоко́льчик. **bluebottle** *n* си́няя му́ха. **blueprint** *n* си́нька, светоко́пия; (*fig*) прое́кт.

bluff *n* блеф; *vi* блефова́ть *impf*.

blunder *n* опло́шность; *vi* оплоша́ть *pf*.

blunt *adj* тупо́й; (*person*) прямо́й; *vt* тупи́ть *impf*, за~, ис~ *pf*.

blur *vt* затума́нивать *impf*, затума́нить *pf*. **blurred** *adj* расплы́вчатый.

blurt *vt*: ~ **out** выба́лтывать *impf*, вы́болтать *pf*.

blush *vi* красне́ть *impf*, по~ *pf*.

bluster *vi* бушева́ть *impf*; *n* пусты́е слова́ *neut pl*.

boar *n* бо́ров; (*wild*) каба́н.

board *n* доска́; (*committee*) правле́ние, сове́т; **on** ~ на борт(у́); *vi* сади́ться *impf*, сесть *pf* (на кора́бль, в по́езд и т.д.); ~ **up** забива́ть *impf*, заби́ть *pf*. **boarder** *n* пансионе́р. **boarding-house** *n* пансио́н. **boarding-school** *n* интерна́т.

boast *vi* хва́статься *impf*, по~ *pf*; *vt* горди́ться *impf* +*instr*. **boaster** *n* хвасту́н. **boastful** *adj* хвастли́вый.

boat *n* (*small*) ло́дка; (*large*) кора́бль *m*.

bob *vi* подпры́гивать *impf*, подпры́гнуть *pf*.

bobbin *n* кату́шка.

bobsleigh *n* бо́бслей.

bode *vt*: ~ **well/ill** предвеща́ть *impf* хоро́шее/недо́брое.

bodice *n* лиф, корса́ж.

bodily *adv* целико́м; *adj* теле́сный.

body *n* те́ло, ту́ловище; (*corpse*) труп; (*group*) о́рган; (*main part*) основна́я часть. **bodyguard** *n* телохрани́тель *m*. **bodywork** *n* ку́зов.

bog *n* боло́то; **get ~ged down** увяза́ть *impf*, увя́знуть *pf*. **boggy** *adj* боло́тистый.

bogus *adj* подде́льный.

boil[1] *n* (*med*) фуру́нкул.

boil[2] *vi* кипе́ть *impf*, вс~ *pf*; *vt* кипяти́ть *impf*, с~ *pf*; (*cook*) вари́ть *impf*, с~ *pf*; ~ **down to** сходи́ться *impf*, сойти́сь *pf* к тому́, что; ~**over** выкипа́ть *impf*, вы́кипеть *pf*; *n* кипе́ние; **bring to the** ~ доводи́ть *impf*, довести́ *pf* до кипе́ния. **boiled** *adj* варёный. **boiler** *n* котёл; ~ **suit** комбинезо́н. **boiling** *adj* кипя́щий; ~ **point** то́чка кипе́ния; ~ **water** кипято́к.

boisterous *adj* шумли́вый.

bold *adj* сме́лый; (*type*) жи́рный.

bollard *n* (*in road*) столб; (*on quay*) пал.

bolster *n* ва́лик; *vt*: ~ **up** подпира́ть *impf*, подпере́ть *pf*.

bolt *n* засо́в; (*tech*) болт; *vt* запира́ть *impf*, запере́ть *pf* на засо́в; скрепля́ть *impf*, скрепи́ть *pf* болта́ми; *vi* (*flee*) удира́ть *impf*, удра́ть *pf*; (*horse*) понести́ *pf*.

bomb *n* бо́мба; *vt* бомби́ть *impf*. **bombard** *vt* бомбарди́ровать *impf*. **bombardment** *n* бомбарди́ровка. **bomber** *n* бомбардиро́вщик.

bombastic *adj* напы́щенный.

bond *n* (*econ*) облига́ция; (*link*) связь; *pl* око́вы (-в) *pl*, (*fig*) у́зы (уз) *pl*.

bone *n* кость.

bonfire *n* костёр.

bonnet *n* ка́пор; (*car*) капо́т.

bonus *n* пре́мия.

bony *adj* кости́стый.

boo *vt* освисты́вать *impf*, освиста́ть *pf*; *vi* улюлю́кать *impf*.

booby trap *n* лову́шка.

book *n* кни́га; *vt* (*order*) зака́зывать *impf*, заказа́ть *pf*; (*reserve*) брони́ровать *impf*, за~ *pf*. **bookbinder** *n* переплётчик. **bookcase** *n* кни́жный шкаф. **booking** *n* зака́з; ~ **office** ка́сса. **bookkeeper** *n* бухга́лтер. **bookmaker** *n* букме́кер. **bookshop** *n* кни́жный магази́н.

boom[1] *n* (*barrier*) бон.

boom[2] *n* (*sound*) гул; (*econ*) бум; *vi* гуде́ть *impf*; (*fig*) процвета́ть *impf*.

boon *n* бла́го.

boor *n* хам. **boorish** *adj* ха́мский.

boost *n* соде́йствие; *vt* увели́чивать *impf*, увели́чить *pf*.

boot *n* боти́нок; (*high*) сапо́г; (*football*) бу́тса; (*car*) бага́жник.

booth *n* кио́ск, бу́дка; (*polling*) каби́на.

booty *n* добы́ча.

booze *n* вы́пивка; *vi* выпива́ть *impf*.

border *n* (*frontier*) грани́ца; (*trim*) кайма́; (*gardening*) бордю́р; *vi* грани́чить *impf* (**on** с+*instr*). **borderline** *n* грани́ца.

bore[1] *n* (*calibre*) кана́л (ствола́); *vt* сверли́ть *impf*, про~ *pf*.

bore[2] *n* (*thing*) ску́ка; (*person*) ску́чный челове́к; *vt* надоеда́ть *impf*, надое́сть *pf*. **boredom** *n* ску́ка. **boring** *adj* ску́чный.

born *adj* прирождённый; **be** ~ роди́ться *impf* & *pf*.

borough *n* райо́н.

borrow *vt* одолжа́ть *impf*, одолжи́ть *pf* (**from** у+*gen*).

Bosnia *n* Бо́сния. **Bosnian** *n* босни́ец, -и́йка; *adj* босни́йский.

bosom *n* грудь.

boss *n* нача́льник; *vt* кома́ндовать *impf*, с~ *pf* +*instr*. **bossy** *adj* команди́рский.

botanical *adj* ботани́ческий. **botanist** *n* бота́ник. **botany** *n* бота́ника.

botch *vt* зала́тывать *impf*, залата́ть *pf*.

both *adj* & *pron* о́ба *m* & *neut*, о́бе *f*; ~ ... **and** и... и.

bother *n* доса́да; *vt* беспоко́ить *impf*.

bottle *n* буты́лка; ~**-neck** суже́ние; *vt* разлива́ть *impf*, разли́ть *pf* по буты́лкам; ~ **up** сде́рживать *impf*, сдержа́ть *pf*.

bottom *n* ни́жняя часть; (*of river etc.*) дно; (*buttocks*) зад; **at the** ~ **of** (*stairs*) внизу́+*gen*; **get to the** ~ **of** добира́ться *impf*, добра́ться *pf* до су́ти +*gen*; *adj* са́мый ни́жний. **bottomless** *adj* бездо́нный.

bough *n* сук.

boulder *n* валу́н.

bounce *vi* подпры́гивать *impf*, подпры́гнуть *pf*; (*cheque*) верну́ться *pf*.

bound[1] *n* (*limit*) преде́л; *vt* ограни́чивать *impf*, ограни́чить *pf*.

bound[2] *n* (*spring*) прыжо́к; *vi* пры́гать *impf*, пры́гнуть *pf*.

bound[3] *adj*: **he is** ~ **to be there** он обяза́тельно там бу́дет.

bound[4] *adj*: **to be** ~ **for** направля́ться *impf*, напра́виться *pf* в+*acc*.

boundary *n* грани́ца.

boundless *adj* безграни́чный.

bountiful *adj* (*generous*) ще́дрый;

(*ample*) оби́льный. **bounty** *n* щедрость; (*reward*) пре́мия.
bouquet *n* буке́т.
bourgeois *adj* буржуа́зный. **bourgeoisie** *n* буржуази́я.
bout *n* (*med*) при́ступ; (*sport*) схва́т-
ка.
bow[1] *n* (*weapon*) лук; (*knot*) бант;
(*mus*) смычо́к.
bow[2] *n* (*obeisance*) покло́н; *vi* кла́-
няться *impf*, поклони́ться *pf*; *vt*
склоня́ть *impf*, склони́ть *pf*.
bow[3] *n* (*naut*) нос.
bowel *n* кишка́; (*depths*) не́дра (-р)
pl.
bowl[1] *n* ми́ска.
bowl[2] *n* (*ball*) шар; *vi* подава́ть *impf*,
пода́ть *pf* мяч. **bowler** *n* подаю́щий
sb мяч; (*hat*) котело́к. **bowling-al-
ley** *n* кегельба́н. **bowls** *n* игра́ в
шары́.
box[1] *n* коро́бка, я́щик; (*theat*) ло́жа;
~ **office** ка́сса.
box[2] *vi* бокси́ровать *impf*. **boxer** *n*
боксёр. **boxing** *n* бокс. **Boxing Day**
n второ́й день Рождества́.
boy *n* ма́льчик. **boyfriend** *n* молодо́й
до́й челове́к. **boyhood** *n* о́тро-
чество. **boyish** *adj* мальчи́шеский.
boycott *n* бойко́т; *vt* бойкоти́ровать
impf & *pf*.
bra *n* ли́фчик.
brace *n* (*clamp*) скре́па; *pl* подтя́жки
f pl; (*dental*) ши́на; *vt* скрепля́ть
impf, скрепи́ть *pf*; ~ **o.s.** соби-
ра́ться *impf*, собра́ться *pf* с си́лами.
bracelet *n* брасле́т.
bracing *adj* бодря́щий.
bracket *n* (*support*) кронште́йн; *pl*
ско́бки *f pl*; (*category*) катего́рия.
brag *vi* хва́статься *impf*, по~ *pf*.
braid *n* тесьма́.
braille *n* шрифт Бра́йля.
brain *n* мозг. **brainstorm** *n* припа́док
безу́мия. **brainwash** *vt* промыва́ть
impf, промы́ть *pf* мозги́+*dat*. **brain-
wave** *n* блестя́щая иде́я.
braise *vt* туши́ть *impf*, с~ *pf*.
brake *n* то́рмоз; *vt* тормози́ть *impf*,
за~ *pf*.
bramble *n* ежеви́ка.
bran *n* о́труби (-бе́й) *pl*.
branch *n* ве́тка; (*fig*) о́трасль;
(*comm*) филиа́л; *vi* разветвля́ться
impf, разветви́ться *pf*; ~ **out** (*fig*)

расширя́ть *impf*, расши́рить *pf*
де́ятельность.
brand *n* (*mark*) клеймо́; (*make*) ма́р-
ка; (*sort*) сорт; *vt* клейми́ть *impf*,
за~ *pf*.
brandish *vt* разма́хивать *impf*+*instr*.
brandy *n* конья́к.
brash *adj* наха́льный.
brass *n* лату́нь, жёлтая медь; (*mus*)
ме́дные инструме́нты *m pl*; *adj*
лату́нный, ме́дный; ~ **band** ме́дный
духово́й орке́стр; **top** ~ вы́сшее на-
ча́льство.
brassière *n* бюстга́лтер.
brat *n* чертёнок.
bravado *n* брава́да.
brave *adj* хра́брый; *vt* покоря́ть
impf, покори́ть *pf*. **bravery** *n* хра́б-
рость.
bravo *int* бра́во.
brawl *n* сканда́л; *vi* дра́ться *impf*,
по~ *pf*.
brawny *adj* му́скулистый.
bray *n* крик осла́; *vi* крича́ть *impf*.
brazen *adj* бессты́дный.
brazier *n* жаро́вня.
breach *n* наруше́ние; (*break*) про-
ло́м; (*mil*) брешь; *vt* прорыва́ть
impf, прорва́ть *pf*; (*rule*) наруша́ть
impf, нару́шить *pf*.
bread *n* хлеб; (*white*) бу́лка. **bread-
crumb** *n* кро́шка. **breadwinner** *n*
корми́лец.
breadth *n* ширина́; (*fig*) широта́.
break *n* проло́м, разры́в; (*pause*)
переры́в, па́уза; *vt* (& *i*) лома́ть(ся)
impf, с~ *pf*; разбива́ть(ся) *impf*,
разби́ть(ся) *pf*; *vt* (*violate*) на-
руша́ть *impf*, нару́шить *pf*; ~ **away**
вырыва́ться *impf*, вы́рваться *pf*; ~
down (*vi*) (*tech*) лома́ться *impf*, с~
pf; (*talks*) срыва́ться *impf*, со-
рва́ться *pf*; (*vt*) (*door*) выла́мывать
impf, вы́ломать *pf*; ~ **in(to)** вла́-
мываться *impf*, вломи́ться *pf* в+*acc*;
~ **off** (*vt* & *i*) отла́мывать(ся) *impf*,
отломи́ть(ся) *pf*; (*vi*) (*speaking*) за-
молча́ть *pf*; (*vt*) (*relations*) пору-
ва́ть *impf*, порва́ть *pf*; ~ **out** вырыва́-
ва́ться *impf*, вы́рваться *pf*; (*fire*,
war) вспы́хнуть *pf*; ~ **through** про-
бива́ться *impf*, проби́ться *pf*; ~ **up**
(*vi*) (*marriage*) распада́ться *impf*,
распа́сться *pf*; (*meeting*) преры-
ва́ться *impf*, прерва́ться *pf*; (*vt*)

(*disperse*) разгоня́ть *impf*, разогна́ть *pf*; (*vt & i*) разбива́ть(ся) *impf*, разби́ть(ся) *pf*; ~ **with** порыва́ть *impf*, порва́ть *pf* c+*instr*. **breakage** *n* поло́мка. **breakdown** *n* поло́мка; (*med*) не́рвный срыв. **breaker** *n* бурун. **breakfast** *n* за́втрак; *vi* за́втракать *impf*, по~ *pf*. **breakneck** *adj*: **at** ~ **speed** сломя́ го́лову. **breakthrough** *n* проры́в. **breakwater** *n* волноре́з.

breast *n* грудь; ~-**feeding** *n* кормле́ние гру́дью; ~ **stroke** *n* брасс.

breath *n* дыха́ние; **be out of** ~ запыха́ться *impf & pf*. **breathe** *vi* дыша́ть *impf*; ~ **in** вдыха́ть *impf*, вдохну́ть *pf*; ~ **out** выдыха́ть *impf*, вы́дохнуть *pf*. **breather** *n* переды́шка. **breathless** *adj* запыха́вшийся.

breeches *n pl* бри́джи (-жей) *pl*.

breed *n* поро́да; *vi* размножа́ться *impf*, размно́житься *pf*; *vt* разводи́ть *impf*, развести́ *pf*. **breeder** *n* -во́д: **cattle** ~ скотово́д. **breeding** *n* разведе́ние, -во́дство; (*upbringing*) воспи́танность.

breeze *n* ветеро́к; (*naut*) бриз. **breezy** *adj* све́жий.

brevity *n* кра́ткость.

brew *vt* (*beer*) вари́ть *impf*, c~ *pf*; (*tea*) зава́ривать *impf*, завари́ть *pf*; (*beer*) ва́рка; (*tea*) зава́рка. **brewer** *n* пивова́р. **brewery** *n* пивова́ренный заво́д.

bribe *n* взя́тка; *vt* подкупа́ть *impf*, подкупи́ть *pf*. **bribery** *n* по́дкуп.

brick *n* кирпи́ч; *adj* кирпи́чный. **bricklayer** *n* ка́менщик.

bridal *adj* сва́дебный. **bride** *n* неве́ста. **bridegroom** *n* жени́х. **bridesmaid** *n* подру́жка неве́сты.

bridge[1] *n* мост; (*of nose*) перено́сица; *vt* (*gap*) заполня́ть *impf*, запо́лнить *pf*; (*overcome*) преодолева́ть *impf*, преодоле́ть *pf*.

bridge[2] *n* (*game*) бридж.

bridle *n* узда́; *vi* возмуща́ться *impf*, возмути́ться *pf*.

brief *adj* недо́лгий; (*concise*) кра́ткий; *n* инстру́кция; *vt* инструкти́ровать *impf & pf*. **briefcase** *n* портфе́ль *m*. **briefing** *n* инструкта́ж. **briefly** *adv* кра́тко. **briefs** *n pl* трусы́ (-со́в) *pl*.

brigade *n* брига́да. **brigadier** *n*

генера́л-майо́р.

bright *adj* я́ркий. **brighten** (*also* ~ **up**) *vi* проясня́ться *impf*, проясни́ться *pf*; *vt* оживля́ть *impf*, оживи́ть *pf*. **brightness** *n* я́ркость.

brilliant *adj* блестя́щий.

brim *n* край; (*hat*) поля́ (-ле́й) *pl*.

brine *n* рассо́л.

bring *vt* (*carry*) приноси́ть *impf*, принести́ *pf*; (*lead*) приводи́ть *impf*, привести́ *pf*; (*transport*) привози́ть *impf*, привезти́ *pf*; ~ **about** приноси́ть *impf*, принести́ *pf*; ~ **back** возвраща́ть *impf*, возврати́ть *pf*; ~ **down** сва́ливать *impf*, свали́ть *pf*; ~ **round** (*unconscious person*) приводи́ть *impf*, привести́ *pf* в себя́; (*deliver*) доставля́ть *impf*, доста́вить *pf*; ~ **up** (*educate*) воспи́тывать *impf*, воспита́ть *pf*; (*question*) поднима́ть *impf*, подня́ть *pf*.

brink *n* край.

brisk *adj* (*lively*) оживлённый; (*air etc.*) све́жий; (*quick*) бы́стрый.

bristle *n* щети́на; *vi* щети́ниться *impf*, o~ *pf*.

Britain *n* Великобрита́ния, А́нглия. **British** *adj* брита́нский, англи́йский; ~ **Isles** Брита́нские острова́ *m pl*. **Briton** *n* брита́нец, -нка *pl*; англича́нин, -а́нка.

brittle *adj* хру́пкий.

broach *vt* затра́гивать *impf*, затро́нуть *pf*.

broad *adj* широ́кий; **in** ~ **daylight** средь бе́ла дня; **in** ~ **outline** в о́бщих черта́х. **broad-minded** *adj* с широ́кими взгля́дами. **broadly** *adv*: ~ **speaking** вообще́ говоря́.

broadcast *n* переда́ча; *vt* передава́ть *impf*, переда́ть *pf* по ра́дио, по телеви́дению; (*seed*) се́ять *impf*, по~ *pf* вразбро́с. **broadcaster** *n* ди́ктор. **broadcasting** *n* радио-, теле-, веща́ние.

brocade *n* парча́.

broccoli *n* бро́кколи *neut indecl*.

brochure *n* брошю́ра.

broke *predic* без гроша́. **broken** *adj* сло́манный; ~-**hearted** с разби́тым се́рдцем.

broker *n* комиссионе́р.

bronchitis *n* бронхи́т.

bronze *n* бро́нза; *adj* бро́нзовый.

brooch *n* брошь, бро́шка.

brood n вы́водок; vi мра́чно раз-
мышля́ть impf.
brook[1] n ручей.
brook[2] vt терпе́ть impf.
broom n метла́. **broomstick** n
(witches') помело́.
broth n бульо́н.
brothel n публи́чный дом.
brother n брат; ~-in-law n (sister's
husband) зять; (husband's brother)
де́верь; (wife's brother) шу́рин;
(wife's sister's husband) своя́к.
brotherhood n бра́тство. **brotherly**
adj бра́тский.
brow n (eyebrow) бровь; (forehead)
лоб; (of hill) гре́бень m. **brow-
beaten** adj запу́ганный.
brown adj кори́чневый; (eyes) ка́рий;
n кори́чневый цвет; vt (cul) под-
румя́нивать impf, подрумя́нить pf.
browse vi (look around) осма́три-
ваться impf, осмотре́ться pf; (in
book) просма́тривать impf просмо-
тре́ть pf кни́гу.
bruise n синя́к; vt ушиба́ть impf,
ушиби́ть pf.
brunette n брюне́тка.
brunt n основна́я тя́жесть.
brush n щётка; (paint) кисть; vt
(clean) чи́стить impf, вы́~, по~ pf
(щёткой); (touch) легко́ каса́ться
impf, косну́ться pf +gen; (hair) расчёсывать impf, расчеса́ть pf щёткой; ~ aside, off отма́хиваться impf,
отмахну́ться pf от+gen; ~ up сме-
та́ть impf, смести́ pf; (renew) под-
чища́ть impf, подчи́стить pf.
brushwood n хво́рост.
Brussels sprouts n pl брюссе́льская
капу́ста.
brutal adj жесто́кий. **brutality** n
жесто́кость. **brutalize** vt ожесто-
ча́ть impf, ожесточи́ть pf. **brute** n
живо́тное sb; (person) скоти́на.
brutish adj ха́мский.
B.Sc. abbr бакала́вр нау́к.
bubble n пузы́рь m; vi пузы́риться
impf; кипе́ть impf, вс~ pf.
buck n саме́ц оле́ня, кро́лика etc.;
vi брыка́ться impf.
bucket n ведро́.
buckle n пря́жка; vt застёгивать
impf, застегну́ть pf (пря́жкой); vi
(warp) коро́биться impf, по~, с~
pf.

bud n по́чка.
Buddhism n будди́зм. **Buddhist** n
будди́ст; adj будди́йский.
budge vt & i шевели́ть(ся) impf,
по~ pf.
budget n бюдже́т; vi: ~ for преду-
сма́тривать impf, предусмотре́ть pf
в бюдже́те.
buff adj све́тло-кори́чневый.
buffalo n бу́йвол.
buffet[1] n буфе́т.
buffet[2] vt броса́ть impf (impers).
buffoon n шут.
bug n (insect) бука́шка; (germ) ин-
фе́кция; (in computer) оши́бка в
програ́мме; (microphone) потайно́й
микрофо́н; vt (install ~) устана́вли-
вать impf, установи́ть pf аппара-
ту́ру для подслу́шивания в+prep;
(listen) подслу́шивать impf.
bugle n горн.
build n (of person) телосложе́ние;
vt стро́ить impf, по~ pf; ~ on при-
стра́ивать impf, пристро́ить pf (to
к+dat); ~ up (vt) создава́ть impf,
созда́ть pf; (vi) накопля́ться impf;
накопи́ться pf. **builder** n строи́тель
m. **building** n (edifice) зда́ние; (action) строи́тельство; ~ site стро́й-
ка; ~ society жили́щно-строи́тель-
ный кооперати́в.
built-up area n застро́енный райо́н.
bulb n (of plant) лу́ковица; (electric) ла́мпоч-
ка. **bulbous** adj лу́ковичный.
Bulgaria n Болга́рия. **Bulgarian** n
болга́рин, -га́рка; adj болга́рский.
bulge n вы́пуклость; vi выпя́чи-
ваться impf; выпира́ть impf. **bulging** adj разбу́хший, оттопы́ри-
вающийся.
bulk n (size) объём; (greater part)
бо́льшая часть; in ~ гурто́м. **bulky**
adj громо́здкий.
bull n бык; (male) саме́ц. **bulldog** n
бульдо́г. **bulldoze** vt расчища́ть
impf, расчи́стить pf бульдо́зером.
bulldozer n бульдо́зер. **bullfinch** n
снеги́рь m. **bullock** n вол. **bull's-
eye** n я́блоко.
bullet n пу́ля. **bullet-proof** adj пуле-
сто́йкий.
bulletin n бюллете́нь m.
bullion n: gold ~ зо́лото в сли́тках.
bully n зади́ра m & f; vt запу́гивать
impf, запуга́ть pf.

bum n зад.

bumble-bee n шмель m.

bump n (blow) уда́р, толчо́к; (swelling) ши́шка; (in road) уха́б; vi ударя́ться impf, уда́риться pf; ~ into ната́лкиваться impf, натолкну́ться pf на+acc. **bumper** n ба́мпер.

bumpkin n дереве́нщина m & f.

bumptious adj самоуве́ренный.

bumpy adj уха́бистый.

bun n сдо́бная бу́лка; (hair) пучо́к.

bunch n (of flowers) буке́т; (grapes) гроздь; (keys) свя́зка.

bundle n у́зел; vt свя́зывать impf, связа́ть pf в у́зел; ~ off спрова́живать impf, спрова́дить pf.

bungalow n бу́нгало neut indecl.

bungle vt по́ртить impf, ис~ pf.

bunk n ко́йка.

bunker n бу́нкер.

buoy n буй. **buoyancy** n плаву́честь; (fig) бо́дрость. **buoyant** adj плаву́чий; (fig) бо́дрый.

burden n бре́мя neut; vt обременя́ть impf, обремени́ть pf.

bureau n бюро́ neut indecl. **bureaucracy** n бюрокра́тия. **bureaucrat** n бюрокра́т. **bureaucratic** adj бюрократи́ческий.

burger n котле́та.

burglar n взло́мщик. **burglary** n кра́жа со взло́мом. **burgle** vt гра́бить impf, о~ pf.

burial n погребе́ние.

burlesque n бурле́ск.

burly adj здорове́нный.

burn vt жечь impf, c~ pf; vt & i (injure) обжига́ть(ся) impf, обже́чь(ся) pf; vi горе́ть impf, c~ pf; (by sun) загора́ть impf, загоре́ть pf; n ожо́г. **burner** n горе́лка.

burnish vt полирова́ть impf, от~ pf.

burp vi рыга́ть impf, рыгну́ть pf.

burrow n нора́; vi рыть impf, вы́~ pf нору́; (fig) ры́ться impf.

bursar n казначе́й. **bursary** n стипе́ндия.

burst n разры́в, вспы́шка; vi разрыва́ться impf, разорва́ться pf; (bubble) ло́паться impf, ло́пнуть pf; vt разрыва́ть impf, разорва́ть pf; ~ into tears распла́каться pf.

bury vt (dead) хорони́ть impf, по~ pf; (hide) зарыва́ть impf, зары́ть pf.

bus n авто́бус.

bush n куст. **bushy** adj густо́й.

busily adv энерги́чно.

business n (affair, dealings) де́ло; (firm) предприя́тие; **mind your own** ~ не ва́ше де́ло; **on** ~ по де́лу. **businesslike** adj делово́й. **businessman** n бизнесме́н.

busker n у́личный музыка́нт.

bust n бюст; (bosom) грудь.

bustle n суета́; vi суети́ться impf.

busy adj заня́той; vt: ~ o.s. занима́ться impf, заня́ться pf (with +instr). **busybody** n назо́йливый челове́к.

but conj но, а; ~ **then** зато́; prep кро́ме+gen.

butcher n мясни́к; vt ре́зать impf, за~ pf; ~**'s shop** мясна́я sb.

butler n дворе́цкий sb.

butt[1] n (cask) бо́чка.

butt[2] n (of gun) прикла́д; (cigarette) оку́рок.

butt[3] n (target) мише́нь.

butt[4] vt бода́ть impf, за~ pf; ~ **in** вме́шиваться impf, вмеша́ться pf.

butter n (сли́вочное) ма́сло; vt нама́зывать impf, нама́зать pf ма́слом; ~ **up** льстить impf, по~ pf. **buttercup** n лю́тик. **butterfly** n ба́бочка.

buttock n я́годица.

button n пу́говица; (knob) кно́пка; vt застёгивать impf, застегну́ть pf. **buttonhole** n пе́тля.

buttress n контрфо́рс; vt подпира́ть impf, подпере́ть pf.

buxom adj полногру́дая.

buy n поку́пка; vt покупа́ть impf, купи́ть pf. **buyer** n покупа́тель m.

buzz n жужжа́ние; vi жужжа́ть impf.

buzzard n каню́к.

buzzer n зу́ммер.

by adv ми́мо; prep (near) о́коло+gen, у+gen; (beside) ря́дом с+instr; (past) ми́мо+gen; (time) к+dat; (means) instr without prep; ~ **and large** в це́лом.

bye int пока́!

by-election n дополни́тельные вы́боры m pl.

Byelorussian see **Belorussian**

bygone adj мину́вший; **let** ~**s be** ~**s** что прошло́, то прошло́. **by-law** n постановле́ние. **bypass** n обхо́д; vt обходи́ть impf, обойти́ pf. **by-product** n побо́чный проду́кт. **byroad** n

небольша́я доро́га. **bystander** *n* свиде́тель *m*. **byway** *n* просёлочная доро́га. **byword** *n* олицетворе́ние (**for** +*gen*).
Byzantine *adj* византи́йский.

C

cab *n* (*taxi*) такси́ *neut indecl*; (*of lorry*) каби́на.
cabaret *n* кабаре́ *neut indecl*.
cabbage *n* капу́ста.
cabin *n* (*hut*) хи́жина; (*aeron*) каби́на; (*naut*) каю́та.
cabinet *n* (*Cabinet*) кабине́т; ~**-maker** краснодере́вец; ~**-minister** мини́стр-член кабине́та.
cable *n* (*rope*) кана́т; (*electric*) ка́бель *m*; (*cablegram*) телегра́мма; *vt & i* телеграфи́ровать *impf & pf*.
cache *n* потайно́й склад.
cackle *vi* гогота́ть *impf*.
cactus *n* ка́ктус.
caddy *n* (*box*) ча́йница.
cadet *n* новобра́нец.
cadge *vt* стреля́ть *impf*, стрельну́ть *pf*.
cadres *n pl* ка́дры *m pl*.
Caesarean (section) *n* ке́сарево-сече́ние.
cafe *n* кафе́ *neut indecl*. **cafeteria** *n* кафете́рий.
caffeine *n* кофе́ин.
cage *n* кле́тка.
cajole *vt* зада́бривать *impf*, задо́брить *pf*.
cake *n* (*large*) торт, (*small*) пиро́жное *sb*; (*fruit-*~) кекс; *vt*: ~d обле́пленный (**in** +*instr*).
calamitous *adj* бе́дственный. **calamity** *n* бе́дствие.
calcium *n* ка́льций.
calculate *vt* вычисля́ть *impf*, вы́числить *pf*, *vi* рассчи́тывать *impf*, рассчита́ть *pf* (**on** на+*acc*). **calculation** *n* вычисле́ние, расчёт. **calculator** *n* калькуля́тор.
calendar *n* календа́рь *m*.
calf[1] *n* (*cow*) телёнок.
calf[2] *n* (*leg*) икра́.
calibrate *vt* калиброва́ть *impf*. **calibre** *n* кали́бр.
call *v* звать *impf*, по~ *pf*; (*name*) называ́ть *impf*, назва́ть *pf*; (*cry*)

крича́ть *impf*, кри́кнуть *pf*; (*wake*) буди́ть *impf*, раз~ *pf*; (*visit*) заходи́ть *impf*, зайти́ *pf* (**on** к+*dat*; **at** в+*acc*); (*stop at*) остана́вливаться *impf*, останови́ться *pf* (**at** в, на, +*prep*); (*summon*) вызыва́ть *impf*, вы́звать *pf*; (*ring up*) звони́ть *impf*, по~ *pf* +*dat*; **for** (*require*) тре́бовать *impf*, по~ *pf* +*gen*; (*fetch*) заходи́ть *impf*, зайти́ *pf* за+*instr*; ~ **off** отменя́ть *impf*, отмени́ть *pf*; ~ **out** вскри́кивать *impf*, вскри́кнуть *pf*; ~ **up** призыва́ть *impf*, призва́ть *pf*; *n* (*cry*) крик; (*summons*) зов, при́зыв; (*telephone*) (телефо́нный) вы́зов, разгово́р; (*visit*) визи́т; (*signal*) сигна́л; ~**-box** телефо́н-автома́т; ~**-up** при́зыв. **caller** *n* посети́тель *m*, ~ница; (*tel*) позвони́вший *sb*. **calling** *n* (*vocation*) призва́ние.
callous *adj* (*person*) чёрствый.
callus *n* мозо́ль.
calm *adj* споко́йный; *n* споко́йствие; *vt & i* (~ **down**) успока́ивать(ся) *impf*, успоко́ить(ся) *pf*.
calorie *n* кало́рия.
camber *n* скат.
camcorder *n* камко́рдер.
camel *n* верблю́д.
camera *n* фотоаппара́т. **cameraman** *n* киноопера́тор.
camouflage *n* камуфля́ж; *vt* маскирова́ть *impf*, за~ *pf*.
camp *n* ла́герь *m*; *vi* (*set up* ~) располага́ться *impf*, расположи́ться *pf* ла́герем; (*go camping*) жить *impf* в пала́тках; ~**-bed** раскладу́шка; ~**-fire** костёр.
campaign *n* кампа́ния; *vi* проводи́ть *impf*, провести́ *pf* кампа́нию.
campsite *n* ла́герь *m*, ке́мпинг.
campus *n* университе́тский городо́к.
can[1] *n* ба́нка; *vt* консерви́ровать *impf*, за~ *pf*.
can[2] *v aux* (*be able*) мочь *impf*, с~ *pf* +*inf*; (*know how*) уме́ть *impf*, с~ *pf* +*inf*.
Canada *n* Кана́да. **Canadian** *n* кана́дец, -дка; *adj* кана́дский.
canal *n* кана́л.
canary *n* канаре́йка.
cancel *vt* (*make void*) аннули́ровать *impf & pf*; (*call off*) отменя́ть *impf*, отмени́ть *pf*; (*stamp*) гаси́ть *impf*, по~ *pf*. **cancellation** *n* аннули́рова

ние; отме́на.

cancer *n* рак; (**C~**) Рак. **cancerous** *adj* ра́ковый.

candelabrum *n* канделя́бр.

candid *adj* открове́нный.

candidate *n* кандида́т.

candied *adj* заса́харенный.

candle *n* свеча́. **candlestick** *n* подсве́чник.

candour *n* открове́нность.

candy *n* сла́дости *f pl*.

cane *n* (*plant*) тростни́к; (*stick*) трость, па́лка; *vt* бить *impf*, по~ *pf* па́лкой.

canine *adj* соба́чий; *n* (*tooth*) клык.

canister *n* ба́нка, коро́бка.

canker *n* рак.

cannabis *n* гаши́ш.

cannibal *n* людое́д. **cannibalism** *n* людое́дство.

cannon *n* пу́шка; **~-ball** пу́шечное ядро́.

canoe *n* кано́э *neut indecl*; *vi* пла́вать *indet*, плыть *det* на кано́э.

canon *n* кано́н; (*person*) кано́ник. **canonize** *vt* канонизова́ть *impf* & *pf*.

canopy *n* балдахи́н.

cant *n* (*hypocrisy*) ха́нжество; (*jargon*) жарго́н.

cantankerous *adj* сварли́вый.

cantata *n* канта́та.

canteen *n* столо́вая *sb*.

canter *n* лёгкий гало́п; *vi* (*rider*) е́здить *indet*, е́хать *det* лёгким гало́пом; (*horse*) ходи́ть *indet*, идти́ *det* лёгким гало́пом.

canvas *n* (*art*) холст; (*naut*) паруси́на; (*tent material*) брезе́нт.

canvass *vi* агити́ровать *impf*, с~ *pf* (**for** за+*acc*); *n* собира́ние голосо́в; агита́ция. **canvasser** *n* собира́тель *m* голосо́в.

canyon *n* каньо́н.

cap *n* (*of uniform*) фура́жка; (*cloth*) ке́пка; (*woman's*) чепе́ц; (*lid*) кры́шка; *vt* превосходи́ть *impf*, превзойти́ *pf*.

capability *n* спосо́бность. **capable** *adj* спосо́бный (**of** на+*acc*).

capacious *adj* вмести́тельный. **capacity** *n* ёмкость; (*ability*) спосо́бность; **in the ~ of** в ка́честве +*gen*.

cape[1] *n* (*geog*) мыс.

cape[2] *n* (*cloak*) наки́дка.

caper *vi* скака́ть *impf*.

capers[1] *n pl* (*cul*) ка́персы *m pl*.

capillary *adj* капилля́рный.

capital *adj* (*letter*) прописно́й; **~ punishment** сме́ртная казнь; *n* (*town*) столи́ца; (*letter*) прописна́я бу́ква; (*econ*) капита́л. **capitalism** *n* капитали́зм. **capitalist** *n* капитали́ст; *adj* капиталисти́ческий. **capitalize** *vt* извлека́ть *impf*, извле́чь *pf* вы́году (**on** из+*gen*).

capitulate *vi* капитули́ровать *impf* & *pf*. **capitulation** *n* капитуля́ция.

caprice *n* капри́з. **capricious** *adj* капри́зный.

Capricorn *n* Козеро́г.

capsize *vt* & *i* опроки́дывать(ся) *impf*, опроки́нуть(ся) *pf*.

capsule *n* ка́псула.

captain *n* капита́н; *vt* быть капита́ном +*gen*.

caption *n* по́дпись; (*cin*) титр.

captious *adj* приди́рчивый.

captivate *vt* пленя́ть *impf*, плени́ть *pf*. **captivating** *adj* плени́тельный.

captive *adj* & *n* пле́нный. **captivity** *n* нево́ля; (*esp mil*) плен. **capture** *n* взя́тие, захва́т, пойма́ка; *vt* (*person*) брать *impf*, взять *pf* в плен; (*seize*) захва́тывать *impf*, захвати́ть *pf*.

car *n* маши́на; автомоби́ль *m*; **~ park** стоя́нка.

carafe *n* графи́н.

caramel(s) *n* караме́ль.

carat *n* кара́т.

caravan *n* фурго́н; (*convoy*) карава́н.

caraway (seeds) *n* тмин.

carbohydrate *n* углево́д. **carbon** *n* углеро́д; **~ copy** ко́пия; **~ dioxide** углекислота́; **~ monoxide** о́кись углеро́да; **~ paper** копирова́льная бума́га.

carburettor *n* карбюра́тор.

carcass *n* ту́ша.

card *n* (*stiff paper*) карто́н; (*visiting* ~) ка́рточка; (*playing* ~) ка́рта; (*greetings* ~) откры́тка; (*ticket*) биле́т. **cardboard** *n* карто́н; *adj* карто́нный.

cardiac *adj* серде́чный.

cardigan *n* кардига́н.

cardinal *adj* кардина́льный; **~ number** коли́чественное числи́тельное *sb*; *n* кардина́л.

care n (*trouble*) забóта; (*caution*) осторóжность; (*tending*) ухóд; **in the ~ of** на попечéнии +*gen*; **take ~** осторóжно!; **смотри́(те)!; take ~ of** забóтиться *impf*, по~ *pf* о+*prep*; *vi*: **I don't ~** мне всё равнó; **~ for** (*look after*) уха́живать *impf* за+*instr*; (*like*) нрáвиться *impf*, по~ *pf impers* +*dat*.

career n карьéра.

carefree adj беззабóтный. **careful** adj (*cautious*) осторóжный; (*thorough*) тщáтельный. **careless** adj (*negligent*) небрéжный; (*incautious*) неосторóжный.

caress n лáска; *vt* ласка́ть *impf*.

caretaker n смотри́тель m, ~ница; *attrib* врéменный.

cargo n груз.

caricature n карикату́ра; *vt* изобража́ть *impf*, изобрази́ть *pf* в карикату́рном ви́де.

carnage n резня́.

carnal adj плóтский.

carnation n гвозди́ка.

carnival n карнавáл.

carnivorous adj плотоя́дный.

carol n (*рождéственский*) гимн.

carouse vi кути́ть *impf*, кутну́ть *pf*.

carp[1] n карп.

carp[2] vi придира́ться *impf*, придра́ться *pf* (**at** к+*dat*).

carpenter n плóтник. **carpentry** n плóтничество.

carpet n ковёр; *vt* покрыва́ть *impf*, покры́ть *pf* коврóм.

carping adj приди́рчивый.

carriage n (*vehicle*) карéта; (*rly*) вагóн; (*conveyance*) перевóзка; (*bearing*) осáнка. **carriageway** n проéзжая часть дорóги. **carrier** n (*on bike*) багáжник; (*firm*) трáнспортная кампáния; (*med*) бацилло-носи́тель m.

carrot n морко́вка; *pl* морко́вь (*collect*).

carry vt (*by hand*) носи́ть *indet*, нести́ *det*; переноси́ть *impf*, перенести́ *pf*; (*in vehicle*) вози́ть *indet*, везти́ *det*; (*sound*) передавáть *impf*, передáть *pf*; vi (*sound*) быть слы́шен; **be carried away** увлека́ться *impf*, увлéчься *pf*; ~ **on** (*continue*) продолжáть *impf*; ~ **out** выполня́ть *impf*, вы́полнить *pf*; ~ **over** пере-

носи́ть *impf*, перенести́ *pf*.

cart n телéга; *vt* (*lug*) тащи́ть *impf*.

cartilage n хрящ.

carton n картóнка.

cartoon n карикату́ра; (*cin*) мультфи́льм. **cartoonist** n карикату́рист, ~ка.

cartridge n патрóн; (*of record player*) звукоснимáтель m.

carve vt рéзать *impf* по+*dat*; (*in wood*) вырезáть *impf*, вы́резать *pf*; (*in stone*) высекáть *impf*, вы́сечь; (*slice*) нарезáть *impf*, нарéзать *pf*. **carving** n резьба́; ~ **knife** нож для нареза́ния мя́са.

cascade n каскáд; *vi* пáдать *impf*.

case[1] n (*instance*) слу́чай; (*law*) дéло; (*med*) больнóй *sb*; (*gram*) падéж; **in ~** (в слу́чае) éсли; **in any ~** во вся́ком слу́чае; **in no ~** не в кóем слу́чае; **just in ~** на вся́кий слу́чай.

case[2] n (*box*) я́щик; (*suitcase*) чемодáн; (*small box*) футля́р; (*cover*) чехóл; (*display ~*) витри́на.

cash n нали́чные *sb*; (*money*) дéньги *pl*; ~ **on delivery** налóженным платежóм; ~ **desk, register** кáсса; *vt*: ~ **a cheque** получáть *impf*, получи́ть *pf* дéньги по чéку. **cashier** n касси́р.

casing n (*tech*) кожу́х.

casino n казинó *neut indecl*.

cask n бóчка.

casket n шкату́лка.

casserole n (*pot*) лáтка; (*stew*) рагу́ *neut indecl*.

cassette n кассéта; ~ **recorder** кассéтный магнитофóн.

cassock n ря́са.

cast vt (*throw*) бросáть *impf*, брóсить *pf*; (*shed*) сбрáсывать *impf*, сбрóсить *pf*; (*theat*) распределя́ть *impf*, распредели́ть *pf* рóли +*dat*; (*found*) лить *impf*, с~ *pf*; ~ **off** (*knitting*) спускáть *impf*, спусти́ть *pf* пéтли; (*naut*) отплывáть *impf*, отплы́ть *pf*; ~ **on** (*knitting*) набирáть *impf*, набрáть *pf* пéтли; n (*of mind etc.*) склад; (*mould*) фóрма; (*moulded object*) слéпок; (*med*) ги́псовая повя́зка; (*theat*) дéйствующие ли́ца (-ц) *pl*. **castaway** n потерпéвший *sb* кораблекрушéние. **cast iron** n чугу́н. **cast-iron** adj чугу́нный. **cast-offs** n pl нóшеное плáтье.

castanet *n* кастанье́та.

caste *n* ка́ста.

castigate *vt* бичева́ть *impf*.

castle *n* за́мок; (*chess*) ладья́.

castor *n* (*wheel*) ро́лик; ~ **sugar** са́харная пу́дра.

castrate *vt* кастри́ровать *impf & pf*. **castration** *n* кастра́ция.

casual *adj* (*chance*) случа́йный; (*offhand*) небре́жный; (*clothes*) обы́денный; (*unofficial*) неофициа́льный; (*informal*) лёгкий; (*labour*) подённый; ~ **labourer** подёнщик, -ица.

casualty *n* (*wounded*) ра́неный *sb*; (*killed*) уби́тый *sb*; *pl* поте́ри (-рь) *pl*; ~ **ward** пала́та ско́рой по́мощи.

cat *n* ко́шка, (*tom*) кот; ~'**s-eye** (*on road*) (доро́жный) рефле́ктор.

catalogue *n* катало́г; (*price list*) прейскура́нт; *vt* каталогизи́ровать *impf & pf*.

catalyst *n* катализа́тор. **catalytic** *adj* каталити́ческий.

catapult *n* (*toy*) рога́тка; (*hist, aeron*) катапу́льта; *vt & i* катапульти́ровать(ся) *impf & pf*.

cataract *n* (*med*) катара́кта.

catarrh *n* ката́р.

catastrophe *n* катастро́фа. **catastrophic** *adj* катастрофи́ческий.

catch *vt* (*ball, fish, thief*) лови́ть *impf*, пойма́ть *pf*; (*surprise*) застава́ть *impf*, заста́ть *pf*; (*disease*) заража́ться *impf*, зарази́ться *pf* +*instr*; (*be in time for*) успева́ть *impf*, успе́ть *pf* на+*acc*; *vt & i* (*snag*) зацепля́ть(ся) *impf*, зацепи́ть(ся) *pf* (*on* за+*acc*); ~ **on** (*become popular*) привива́ться *impf*, приви́ться *pf*; ~ **up with** догоня́ть *impf*, догна́ть *pf*; *n* (*of fish*) уло́в; (*trick*) уло́вка; (*on door etc.*) защёлка. **catching** *adj* зара́зный. **catchword** *n* мо́дное слове́чко. **catchy** *adj* прили́пчивый.

categorical *adj* категори́ческий. **category** *n* катего́рия.

cater *vi*: ~ **for** поставля́ть *impf*, поста́вить *pf* прови́зию для+*gen*; (*satisfy*) удовлетворя́ть *impf*, удовлетвори́ть *pf*. **caterer** *n* поставщи́к (прови́зии).

caterpillar *n* гу́сеница.

cathedral *n* собо́р.

catheter *n* кате́тер.

Catholic *adj* католи́ческий; *n* като́-

лик, -и́чка. **Catholicism** *n* католи́чество.

cattle *n* скот.

Caucasus *n* Кавка́з.

cauldron *n* котёл.

cauliflower *n* цветна́я капу́ста.

cause *n* причи́на, по́вод; (*law etc.*) де́ло; *vt* причиня́ть *impf*, причини́ть *pf*; вызыва́ть *impf*, вы́звать *pf*; (*induce*) заставля́ть *impf*, заста́вить *pf*.

caustic *adj* е́дкий.

cauterize *vt* прижига́ть *impf*, прижё́чь *pf*.

caution *n* осторо́жность; (*warning*) предостереже́ние; *vt* предостерега́ть *impf*, предостере́чь *pf*. **cautious** *adj* осторо́жный. **cautionary** *adj* предостерега́ющий.

cavalcade *n* кавалька́да. **cavalier** *adj* бесцеремо́нный. **cavalry** *n* кавале́рия.

cave *n* пеще́ра; *vi*: ~ **in** обва́ливаться *impf*, обвали́ться *pf*; (*yield*) сдава́ться *impf*, сда́ться *pf*. **caveman** *n* пеще́рный челове́к. **cavern** *n* пеще́ра. **cavernous** *adj* пеще́ристый.

caviare *n* икра́.

cavity *n* впа́дина, по́лость; (*in tooth*) дупло́.

cavort *vi* скака́ть *impf*.

caw *vi* ка́ркать *impf*, ка́ркнуть *pf*.

CD *abbr* (*of compact disc*) компа́кт-ди́ск; ~ **player** прои́грыватель *m* компа́кт-ди́сков.

cease *vt & i* прекраща́ть(ся) *impf*, прекрати́ть(ся) *pf*; *vi* перестава́ть *impf*, переста́ть *pf* (+*inf*); ~-**fire** прекраще́ние огня́. **ceaseless** *adj* непреста́нный.

cedar *n* кедр.

cede *vt* уступа́ть *impf*, уступи́ть *pf*.

ceiling *n* потоло́к; (*fig*) макси́мальный у́ровень *m*.

celebrate *vt & i* пра́здновать *impf*, от~ *pf*; (*extol*) прославля́ть *impf*, просла́вить *pf*. **celebrated** *adj* знамени́тый. **celebration** *n* пра́зднование. **celebrity** *n* знамени́тость.

celery *n* сельдере́й.

celestial *adj* небе́сный.

celibacy *n* безбра́чие. **celibate** *adj* холосто́й; *n* холостя́к.

cell *n* (*prison*) ка́мера; (*biol*) кле́тка.

cellar *n* подва́л.

cello *n* виолончéль.

cellophane *n* целлофáн. **cellular** *adj* клéточный. **celluloid** *n* целлулóид.

Celt *n* кельт. **Celtic** *adj* кéльтский.

cement *n* цемéнт; *vt* цементи́ровать *impf*, за~ *pf*.

cemetery *n* клáдбище.

censor *n* цéнзор; *vt* подвергáть *impf*, подвéргнуть *pf* цензýре. **censorious** *adj* сверхкрити́ческий. **censorship** *n* цензýра. **censure** *n* порицáние; *vt* порицáть *impf*.

census *n* пéрепись.

cent *n* цент; **per** ~ процéнт.

centenary *n* столéтие. **centennial** *adj* столéтний. **centigrade** *adj*: 10° ~ 10° по Цéльсию. **centimetre** *n* сантимéтр. **centipede** *n* сороконóжка.

central *adj* центрáльный; ~ **heating** центрáльное отоплéние. **centralization** *n* централизáция. **centralize** *vt* централизовáть *impf* & *pf*. **centre** *n* центр; середи́на; ~ **forward** центр нападéния; *vi* & *i*: ~ **on** сосредотóчивать(ся) *impf*, сосредотóчить(ся) *pf* на+*prep*. **centrifugal** *adj* центробéжный.

century *n* столéтие, век.

ceramic *adj* керами́ческий. **ceramics** *n pl* керáмика.

cereals *n pl* хлéбные злáки *m pl*; **breakfast** ~ зерновы́е хлóпья (-ев) *pl*.

cerebral *adj* мозговóй.

ceremonial *adj* церемониáльный; *n* церемониáл. **ceremonious** *adj* церемóнный. **ceremony** *n* церемóния.

certain *adj* (*confident*) увéрен (-нна); (*undoubted*) несомнéнный; (*unspecified*) извéстный; (*inevitable*) вéрный; **for** ~ навернякá. **certainly** *adv* (*of course*) конéчно, безуслóвно; (*without doubt*) несомнéнно; ~ **not!** ни в кóем слýчае. **certainty** *n* (*conviction*) увéренность; (*fact*) несомнéнный факт.

certificate *n* свидéтельство; сертификáт. **certify** *vt* удостоверя́ть *impf*, удостовéрить *pf*.

cervical *n* шéйный. **cervix** *n* шéйка мáтки.

cessation *n* прекращéние.

cf. *abbr* ср., сравни́.

CFCs *abbr* (*of* **chlorofluorocarbons**) хлори́рованные фтороуглерóды *m pl*.

chafe *vt* (*rub*) терéть *impf*; (*rub sore*) натирáть *impf*, натерéть *pf*.

chaff *n* (*husks*) мяки́на; (*straw*) сéчка.

chaffinch *n* зя́блик.

chagrin *n* огорчéние.

chain *n* цепь; ~ **reaction** цепнáя реáкция; ~ **smoker** зая́длый кури́льщик.

chair *n* стул, (*armchair*) крéсло; (*univ*) кáфедра; *vt* (*preside*) председáтельствовать *impf* на+*prep*. **chairman, -woman** *n* председáтель *m*, ~ница.

chalice *n* чáша.

chalk *n* мел. **chalky** *adj* меловóй.

challenge *n* (*summons, fig*) вы́зов; (*sentry's*) óклик; (*law*) отвóд; *vt* вызывáть *impf*, вы́звать *pf*; (*sentry*) окликáть *impf*, окли́кнуть *pf*; (*law*) отводи́ть *impf*, отвести́ *pf*. **challenger** *n* претендéнт. **challenging** *adj* интригýющий.

chamber *n* (*cavity*) кáмера; (*hall*) зал; (*polit*) палáта; *pl* (*law*) адвокáтская контóра, (*judge's*) кабинéт (судьи́); ~ **music** кáмерная мýзыка; ~ **pot** ночнóй горшóк. **chambermaid** *n* гóрничная *sb*.

chameleon *n* хамелеóн.

chamois *n* (*animal*) сéрна; (~ *leather*) зáмша.

champagne *n* шампáнское *sb*.

champion *n* чемпиóн, ~ка; (*upholder*) побóрник, -ица; *vt* боро́ться *impf* за +*acc*. **championship** *n* пéрвенство, чемпионáт.

chance *n* случáйность; (*opportunity*) возмóжность, (*favourable*) слýчай; (*likelihood*) шанс (*usu pl*); **by** ~ случáйно; *adj* случáйный; *vi*: ~ **it** рискнýть *pf*.

chancellery *n* канцеля́рия. **chancellor** *n* кáнцлер; (*univ*) рéктор; **C~ of the Exchequer** кáнцлер казначéйства.

chancy *adj* рискóванный.

chandelier *n* лю́стра.

change *n* перемéна; изменéние; (*of clothes etc.*) смéна; (*money*) сдáча; (*of trains etc.*) пересáдка; **for a** ~ для разнообрáзия; *vt* & *i* меня́ть(ся) *impf*; изменя́ть(ся) *impf*, измени́ть(ся) *pf*; *vi* (*one's clothes*) переодева́ться *impf*, переоде́ться *pf*; (*trains etc.*) переса́живаться *impf*, пересе́сть *pf*; *vt* (*a baby*) перепелёнывать *impf*, перепелена́ть *pf*; (*money*) обме́нивать *impf*, обменя́ть *pf*; (*give ~ for*) разме́нивать *impf*, разменя́ть *pf*; ~ **into** превраща́ться *impf*, преврати́ться *pf* в+*acc*; ~ **over to** переходи́ть *impf*, перейти́ *pf* на+*acc*. **changeable** *adj* изме́нчивый.

channel *n* (*water*) проли́в; (*also TV*) кана́л; (*fig*) путь *m*; **the (English) C~** Ла-Ма́нш; *vt* (*fig*) направля́ть *impf*.

chant *n* (*eccl*) песнопе́ние; *vt & i* петь *impf*; (*slogans*) сканди́ровать *impf & pf*.

chaos *n* ха́ос. **chaotic** *adj* хаоти́чный.

chap *n* (*person*) па́рень *m*.

chapel *n* часо́вня; (*Catholic*) капе́лла.

chaperone *n* компаньо́нка.

chaplain *n* капелла́н.

chapped *adj* потреска́вшийся.

chapter *n* глава́.

char *vt & i* обу́гливать(ся) *impf*, обу́глить(ся) *pf*.

character *n* хара́ктер; (*theat*) де́йствующее лицо́; (*letter*) бу́ква; (*Chinese etc.*) иеро́глиф. **characteristic** *adj* характе́рный; *n* сво́йство; (*of person*) черта́ хара́ктера. **characterize** *vt* характеризова́ть *impf & pf*.

charade *n* шара́да.

charcoal *n* древе́сный у́голь *m*.

charge *n* (*for gun; electr*) заря́д; (*fee*) пла́та; (*person*) пито́мец, -мица; (*accusation*) обвине́ние; (*mil*) ата́ка; **be in ~ of** заве́довать *impf* +*instr*; **in the ~ of** на попече́нии +*gen*; *vt* (*gun; electr*) заряжа́ть *impf*, заряди́ть *pf*; (*accuse*) обвиня́ть *impf*, обвини́ть *pf* (**with** в+*prep*); (*mil*) атакова́ть *impf & pf*; *vi* броса́ться *impf*, бро́ситься *pf* в ата́ку; ~ (**for**) брать *impf*, взять *pf* (за+*acc*); ~ **to (the account of**) запи́сывать *impf*, записа́ть *pf* на счёт+*gen*.

chariot *n* колесни́ца.

charisma *n* обая́ние. **charismatic** *adj* обая́тельный.

charitable *adj* благотвори́тельный; (*kind, merciful*) милосе́рдный. **char-**

-ity *n* (*kindness*) милосе́рдие; (*organization*) благотвори́тельная организа́ция.

charlatan *n* шарлата́н.

charm *n* очарова́ние; пре́лесть; (*spell*) за́говор; *pl* ча́ры (чар) *pl*; (*amulet*) талисма́н; (*trinket*) брело́к; *vt* очаро́вывать *impf*, очарова́ть *pf*. **charming** *adj* очарова́тельный, преле́стный.

chart *n* (*naut*) морска́я ка́рта; (*table*) гра́фик; *vt* наноси́ть *impf*, нанести́ *pf* на гра́фик. **charter** *n* (*document*) ха́ртия; (*statutes*) уста́в; *vt* нанима́ть *impf*, наня́ть *pf*.

charwoman *n* приходя́щая убо́рщица.

chase *vt* гоня́ться *indet*, гна́ться *det* за+*instr*; *n* пого́ня; (*hunting*) охо́та.

chasm *n* (*abyss*) бе́здна.

chassis *n* шасси́ *neut indecl*.

chaste *adj* целому́дренный.

chastise *vt* кара́ть *impf*, по~ *pf*.

chastity *n* целому́дрие.

chat *n* бесе́да; *vi* бесе́довать *impf*; ~ **show** телевизио́нная бесе́да-интервью́ *f*.

chatter *n* болтовня́; *vi* болта́ть *impf*; (*teeth*) стуча́ть *impf*. **chatterbox** *n* болту́н. **chatty** *adj* разгово́рчивый.

chauffeur *n* шофёр.

chauvinism *n* шовини́зм. **chauvinist** *n* шовини́ст; *adj* шовинисти́ческий.

cheap *adj* дешёвый. **cheapen** *vt* (*fig*) опошля́ть *impf*, опошли́ть *pf*. **cheaply** *adv* дёшево.

cheat *vt* обма́нывать *impf*, обману́ть *pf*; *vi* плутова́ть *impf*, на~, с~ *pf*; *n* (*person*) обма́нщик, -ица; плут; (*act*) обма́н.

check[1] *n* контро́ль *m*, прове́рка; (*chess*) шах; ~**mate** шах и мат; *vt* (*examine*) проверя́ть *impf*, прове́рить *pf*; (*control*) контроли́ровать *impf*, про~ *pf*; (*restrain*) сде́рживать *impf*, сдержа́ть *pf*; ~ **in** регистри́роваться *impf*, за~ *pf*; ~ **out** выпи́сываться *impf*, вы́писаться *pf*; ~**-out** ка́сса. ~**-up** осмо́тр.

check[2] *n* (*pattern*) кле́тка. **check(ed)** *adj* кле́тчатый.

cheek *n* щека́; (*impertinence*) на́глость. **cheeky** *adj* на́глый.

cheep *vi* пища́ть *impf*, пи́скнуть *pf*.

cheer *n* ободря́ющий во́зглас; ~s! за (ва́ше) здоро́вье!; *vt* (*applaud*) приве́тствовать *impf* & *pf*; ~ up ободря́ть(ся) *impf*, ободри́ть(ся) *pf*. **cheerful** *adj* весёлый. **cheerio** *int* пока́. **cheerless** *adj* уны́лый.

cheese *n* сыр; ~-cake ватру́шка.

cheetah *n* гепа́рд.

chef *n* (шеф-)по́вар.

chemical *adj* хими́ческий; *n* химика́т. **chemist** *n* хи́мик; (*druggist*) апте́карь *m*; ~'s (*shop*) апте́ка. **chemistry** *n* хи́мия.

cheque *n* чек; ~-book че́ковая кни́жка.

cherish *vt* (*foster*) леле́ять *impf*; (*hold dear*) дорожи́ть *impf* +*instr*; (*love*) не́жно люби́ть *impf*.

cherry *n* ви́шня; *adj* вишнёвый.

cherub *n* херуви́м.

chess *n* ша́хматы (-т) *pl*; ~-board ша́хматная доска́; ~-men *n* ша́хматы (-т) *pl*.

chest *n* сунду́к; (*anat*) грудь; ~ of drawers комо́д.

chestnut *n* кашта́н; (*horse*) гнеда́я *sb*.

chew *vt* жева́ть *impf*. **chewing-gum** *n* жева́тельная рези́нка.

chic *adj* элега́нтный.

chick *n* цыплёнок. **chicken** *n* ку́рица; цыплёнок; *adj* трусли́вый; ~ out тру́сить *impf*, с~ *pf*. **chicken-pox** *n* ветря́нка.

chicory *n* цико́рий.

chief *n* глава́ *m* & *f*; (*boss*) нача́льник; (*of tribe*) вождь *m*; *adj* гла́вный. **chiefly** *adv* гла́вным о́бразом. **chieftain** *n* вождь *m*.

chiffon *n* шифо́н.

child *n* ребёнок; ~-birth ро́ды (-дов) *pl*. **childhood** *n* де́тство. **childish** *adj* де́тский. **childless** *adj* безде́тный. **childlike** *adj* де́тский. **childrens'** *adj* де́тский.

chill *n* стручко́вый пе́рец.

chill *n* хо́лод; (*ailment*) просту́да; *vt* охлажда́ть *impf*, охлади́ть *pf*. **chilly** *adj* прохла́дный.

chime *n* (*set of bells*) набо́р колоко́лов; *pl* (*sound*) перезво́н; (*of clock*) бой; *vt* & *i* (*clock*) бить *impf*, про~ *pf*; *vi* (*bell*) звони́ть *impf*, по~ *pf*.

chimney *n* труба́; ~-sweep трубочи́ст.

chimpanzee *n* шимпанзе́ *m indecl*.

chin *n* подборо́док.

china *n* фарфо́р.

China *n* Кита́й. **Chinese** *n* кита́ец, -ая́нка; *adj* кита́йский.

chink[1] *n* (*sound*) звон; *vi* звене́ть *impf*, про~ *pf*.

chink[2] *n* (*crack*) щель.

chintz *n* си́тец.

chip *vt* & *i* отка́лывать(ся) *impf*, отколо́ть(ся) *pf*; *n* (*of wood*) ще́пка; (*in cup*) щерби́на; (*in games*) фи́шка; *pl* карто́фель-соло́мка (*collect*); (*electron*) чип, микросхе́ма.

chiropodist *n* челове́к, занима́ющийся педикю́ром. **chiropody** *n* педикю́р.

chirp *vi* чири́кать *impf*.

chisel *n* (*wood*) стаме́ска; (*masonry*) зуби́ло; *vt* высека́ть *impf*, вы́сечь *pf*.

chit *n* (*note*) запи́ска.

chivalrous *adj* ры́царский. **chivalry** *n* ры́царство.

chlorine *n* хлор. **chloroform** *n* хлорофо́рм. **chlorophyll** *n* хлорофи́лл.

chock-full *adj* битко́м наби́тый.

chocolate *n* шокола́д; (*sweet*) шокола́дка.

choice *n* вы́бор; *adj* отбо́рный.

choir *n* хор *m*; ~-boy пе́вчий *sb*.

choke *n* (*valve*) дро́ссель *m*; *vi* дави́ться *impf*, по~ *pf*; (*with anger etc.*) задыха́ться *impf*, задохну́ться *pf* (*with* от+*gen*); *vt* (*suffocate*) души́ть *impf*, за~ *pf*; (*of plants*) заглуша́ть, глуши́ть *impf*, заглуши́ть *pf*.

cholera *n* холе́ра.

cholesterol *n* холестери́н.

choose *vt* (*select*) выбира́ть *impf*, вы́брать *pf*; (*decide*) реша́ть *impf*, реши́ть *pf*. **choosy** *adj* разбо́рчивый.

chop *vt* (*also* ~ down) руби́ть *impf*, рубну́ть, рубану́ть *pf*; ~ off отруба́ть *impf*, отруби́ть *pf*; *n* (*cul*) отбивна́я котле́та.

chopper *n* топо́р. **choppy** *adj* бурли́вый.

chop-sticks *n* па́лочки *f pl* для еды́.

choral *adj* хорово́й. **chorale** *n* хора́л.

chord *n* (*mus*) акко́рд.

chore *n* обя́занность.

choreographer *n* хорео́граф. **chore-**

ography n хореогра́фия.
chorister n пе́вчий sb.
chortle vi фы́ркать impf, фы́ркнуть pf.
chorus n хор; (refrain) припе́в.
christen vt крести́ть impf & pf. **Christian** n христиани́н, -а́нка; adj христиа́нский; ~ **name** и́мя neut. **Christianity** n христиа́нство. **Christmas** n Рождество́; ~ **Day** пе́рвый день Рождества́; ~ **Eve** соче́льник; ~ **tree** ёлка.
chromatic adj хромати́ческий. **chrome** n хром. **chromium** n хром. **chromosome** n хромосо́ма.
chronic adj хрони́ческий.
chronicle n хро́ника, ле́топись.
chronological adj хронологи́ческий.
chrysalis n ку́колка.
chrysanthemum n хризанте́ма.
chubby adj пу́хлый.
chuck vt броса́ть impf, бро́сить pf; ~ **out** вышиба́ть impf, вы́шибить pf.
chuckle vi посме́иваться impf.
chum n това́рищ.
chunk n ломо́ть m.
church n це́рковь. **churchyard** n кла́дбище.
churlish adj гру́бый.
churn n маслобо́йка; vt сбива́ть impf, сбить pf; vi (foam) пе́ниться impf, вс~ pf; (stomach) крути́ть impf; ~ **out** выпека́ть impf, вы́печь pf; ~ **up** взбить pf.
chute n жёлоб.
cider n сидр.
cigar n сига́ра. **cigarette** n сигаре́та; папиро́са; ~ **lighter** зажига́лка.
cinder n шлак; pl зола́.
cine-camera n киноаппара́т. **cinema** n кино́ neut indecl.
cinnamon n кори́ца.
cipher n нуль m; (code) шифр.
circle n круг; (theatre) я́рус; vi кружи́ться impf; vt (walking) обходи́ть impf, обойти́ pf; (flying) облета́ть impf, облете́ть pf. **circuit** n кругооборо́т; объе́зд, обхо́д; (electron) схе́ма; (electr) цепь. **circuitous** adj окружно́й. **circular** adj кру́глый; (moving in a circle) круговой; n циркуля́р. **circulate** vi циркули́ровать impf, vt распространя́ть impf, распространи́ть pf. **circulation** n (air)

циркуля́ция; (distribution) распростране́ние; (of newspaper) тира́ж; (med) кровообраще́ние.
circumcise vt обреза́ть impf, обре́зать pf. **circumcision** n обреза́ние.
circumference n окру́жность.
circumspect adj осмотри́тельный.
circumstance n обстоя́тельство; **under the** ~**s** при да́нных обстоя́тельствах, в тако́м слу́чае; **under no** ~**s** ни при каки́х обстоя́тельствах, ни в ко́ем слу́чае.
circumvent vt обходи́ть impf, обойти́ pf.
circus n цирк.
cirrhosis n цирро́з.
CIS abbr (of **Commonwealth of Independent States**) СНГ.
cistern n бачо́к.
citadel n цитаде́ль.
cite vt ссыла́ться impf, сосла́ться pf на+acc.
citizen n граждани́н, -а́нка. **citizenship** n гражда́нство.
citrus n ци́трус; adj ци́трусовый.
city n го́род.
civic adj гражда́нский. **civil** adj гражда́нский; (polite) ве́жливый; ~ **engineer** гражда́нский инжене́р; ~ **engineering** гражда́нское строи́тельство; **C~ Servant** госуда́рственный слу́жащий sb; чино́вник; **C~ Service** госуда́рственная слу́жба. **civilian** n шта́тский sb; adj шта́тский. **civility** n ве́жливость.
civilization n цивилиза́ция. **civilize** vt цивилизова́ть impf & pf. **civilized** adj цивилизо́ванный.
clad adj оде́тый.
claim n (demand) тре́бование, притяза́ние; (assertion) утвержде́ние; vt (demand) тре́бовать impf +gen; (assert) утвержда́ть impf, утверди́ть pf. **claimant** n претенде́нт.
clairvoyant n яснови́дец, -дица; adj яснови́дящий.
clam n моллю́ск; vi: ~ **up** отка́зываться impf, отказа́ться pf разгова́ривать.
clamber vi кара́бкаться impf, вс~ pf.
clammy adj вла́жный.
clamour n шум; vi: ~ **for** шу́мно тре́бовать impf, по~ pf +gen.
clamp n зажи́м; vt скрепля́ть impf, скрепи́ть pf; ~ **down on** прижа́ть pf.

clan *n* клан.

clandestine *adj* тайный.

clang, clank *n* лязг; *vt & i* ля́згать *impf*, ля́згнуть *pf* (+*instr*).

clap *vt & i* хло́пать *impf*, хло́пнуть *pf* +*dat*; *n* хлопо́к; (*thunder*) уда́р.

claret *n* бордо́ *neut indecl*.

clarification *n* (*explanation*) разъясне́ние. **clarify** *vt* разъясня́ть *impf*, разъясни́ть *pf*.

clarinet *n* кларне́т.

clarity *n* я́сность.

clash *n* (*conflict*) столкнове́ние; (*disharmony*) дисгармо́ния; *vi* ста́лкиваться *impf*, столкну́ться *pf*; (*coincide*) совпада́ть *impf*, совпа́сть *pf*; не гармони́ровать *impf*.

clasp *n* застёжка; (*embrace*) объя́тие; *vt* обхва́тывать *impf*, обхвати́ть *pf*; ~ one's hands сплести́ *pf* па́льцы рук.

class *n* класс; ~-room класс; *vt* классифици́ровать *impf & pf*.

classic *adj* класси́ческий; *n* кла́ссик; *pl* (*literature*) кла́ссика; (*Latin and Greek*) класси́ческие языки́ *m pl*. **classical** *adj* класси́ческий.

classification *n* классифика́ция. **classified** *adj* засекре́ченный. **classify** *vt* классифици́ровать *impf & pf*.

classy *adj* кла́ссный.

clatter *n* стук; *vi* стуча́ть *impf*, по~ *pf*.

clause *n* статья́; (*gram*) предложе́ние.

claustrophobia *n* клаустрофо́бия.

claw *n* ко́готь; *vt* цара́пать *impf* когтя́ми.

clay *n* гли́на; *adj* гли́няный.

clean *adj* чи́стый; *adv* (*fully*) соверше́нно; ~-shaven гла́дко вы́бритый; *vt* чи́стить *impf*, вы~, по~ *pf*. **cleaner** *n* убо́рщик, -ица. **cleaner's** *n* химчи́стка. **clean(li)ness** *n* чистота́. **cleanse** *vt* очища́ть *impf*, очи́стить *pf*.

clear *adj* я́сный; (*transparent*) прозра́чный; (*distinct*) отчётливый; (*free*) свобо́дный (of от+*gen*); (*pure*) чи́стый; *vt & i* очища́ть(ся) *impf*, очи́стить(ся) *pf*; *vt* (*jump over*) перепры́гивать *impf*, перепры́гнуть *pf*; (*acquit*) опра́вдывать *impf*, оправда́ть *pf*; ~ away убира́ть *impf*,

убра́ть *pf* со стола́; ~ off (*go away*) убира́ться *impf*, убра́ться *pf*; ~ out (*vt*) вычища́ть *impf*, вы́чистить *pf*, (*vi*) (*make off*) убира́ться *pf*; ~ up (*tidy away*) убира́ть *impf*, убра́ть *pf*; (*weather*) проясня́ться *impf*, проясни́ться *pf*; (*explain*) выясня́ть *impf*, вы́яснить *pf*. **clearance** *n* расчи́стка; (*permission*) разреше́ние. **clearing** *n* (*glade*) поля́на. **clearly** *adv* я́сно.

cleavage *n* разре́з груди́.

clef *n* (*mus*) ключ.

cleft *n* тре́щина.

clemency *n* милосе́рдие.

clench *vt* (*fist*) сжима́ть *impf*, сжать *pf*; (*teeth*) сти́скивать *impf*, сти́снуть *pf*.

clergy *n* духове́нство. **clergyman** *n* свяще́нник. **clerical** *adj* (*eccl*) духо́вный; (*of clerk*) канцеля́рский. **clerk** *n* конто́рский слу́жащий *sb*.

clever *adj* у́мный. **cleverness** *n* уме́ние.

cliche *n* клише́ *neut indecl*.

click *vt* щёлкать *impf*, щёлкнуть *pf* +*instr*.

client *n* клие́нт. **clientele** *n* клиенту́ра.

cliff *n* утёс.

climate *n* кли́мат. **climatic** *adj* климати́ческий.

climax *n* кульмина́ция.

climb *vt & i* ла́зить *indet*, лезть *det* на+*acc*; влеза́ть *impf*, влезть *pf* на+*acc*; поднима́ться *impf*, подня́ться *pf* на+*acc*; ~ down (*tree*) слеза́ть *impf*, слезть *pf* (с+*gen*); (*mountain*) спуска́ться *impf*, спусти́ться *pf* (с+*gen*); (*give in*) отступа́ть *impf*, отступи́ть *pf* и подъём. **climber** *n* альпини́ст, ~ка; (*plant*) вью́щееся расте́ние. **climbing** *n* альпини́зм.

clinch *vt*: ~ a deal закрепи́ть *pf* сде́лку.

cling *vi* (*stick*) прилипа́ть *impf*, прили́пнуть *pf* (to к+*dat*); (*grasp*) цепля́ться *impf*, цепи́ться *pf* (to за+*acc*).

clinic *n* кли́ника. **clinical** *adj* клини́ческий.

clink *vt & i* звене́ть *impf*, про~ *pf* (+*instr*); ~ glasses чо́каться *impf*, чо́кнуться *pf*; *n* звон.

clip[1] *n* скре́пка; зажи́м; *vt* скрепля́ть

impf, скрепи́ть *pf*.

clip² *vt* (*cut*) подстрига́ть *impf*, подстри́чь *pf*. **clippers** *n pl* но́жницы *f pl*. **clipping** *n* (*extract*) вы́резка.

clique *n* кли́ка.

cloak *n* плащ. **cloakroom** *n* гардеро́б; (*lavatory*) убо́рная *sb*.

clock *n* часы́ *m pl*; ~**wise** по часово́й стре́лке; ~**work** часово́й механи́зм; *vi*: ~ **in, out** отмеча́ться *impf*, отме́титься *pf* приходя́ на рабо́ту/ уходя́ с рабо́ты.

clod *n* ком.

clog *vt*: ~ **up** засоря́ть *impf*, засори́ть *pf*.

cloister *n* арка́да.

close *adj* (*near*) бли́зкий; (*stuffy*) ду́шный; *vt & i* (*also* ~ *down*) закрыва́ть(ся) *impf*, закры́ть(ся) *pf*; (*conclude*) зака́нчивать *impf*, зако́нчить *pf*; *adv* бли́зко (**to** от+*gen*). **closed** *adj* закры́тый. **closeted** *adj*: **be** ~ **together** совеща́ться *impf* наедине́. **close-up** *n* фотогра́фия сня́тая кру́пным пла́ном. **closing** *n* закры́тие; *adj* заключи́тельный. **closure** *n* закры́тие.

clot *n* сгу́сток; *vi* сгуща́ться *impf*, сгусти́ться *pf*.

cloth *n* ткань; (*duster*) тря́пка; (*table-*~) ска́терть.

clothe *vt* одева́ть *impf*, оде́ть (**in** +*instr*, в+*acc*) *pf*. **clothes** *n pl* оде́жда, пла́тье.

cloud *n* о́блако; (*rain* ~) ту́ча; *vt* затемня́ть *impf*, затемни́ть *pf*; омрача́ть *impf*, омрачи́ть *pf*; ~ **over** покрыва́ться *impf*, покры́ться *pf* облака́ми, ту́чами. **cloudy** *adj* о́блачный; (*liquid*) му́тный.

clout *vt* ударя́ть *impf*, уда́рить *pf*; *n* затре́щина; (*fig*) влия́ние.

clove *n* гвозди́ка; (*of garlic*) зубо́к.

cloven *adj* раздво́енный.

clover *n* кле́вер.

clown *n* кло́ун.

club *n* (*stick*) дуби́нка; *pl* (*cards*) тре́фы (треф) *pl*; (*association*) клуб; *vt* колоти́ть *impf*, по~ *pf* дуби́нкой; *vi*: ~ **together** скла́дываться *impf*, сложи́ться *pf*.

cluck *vi* куда́хтать *impf*.

clue *n* (*evidence*) ули́ка; (*to puzzle*) ключ; (*hint*) намёк.

clump *n* гру́ппа.

clumsiness *n* неуклю́жесть. **clumsy** *adj* неуклю́жий.

cluster *n* гру́ппа; *vi* собира́ться *impf*, собра́ться *pf* гру́ппами.

clutch *n* (*grasp*) хва́тка; ко́гти *m pl*; (*tech*) сцепле́ние; *vt* зажима́ть *impf*, зажа́ть *pf*; *vi*: ~ **at** хвата́ться *impf*, хвати́ться *pf* за+*acc*.

clutter *n* беспоря́док; *vt* загроможда́ть *impf*, загромозди́ть *pf*.

c/o *abbr* (*of care of*) по а́дресу +*gen*; че́рез+*acc*.

coach *n* (*horse-drawn*) каре́та; (*rly*) ваго́н; (*bus*) авто́бус; (*tutor*) репети́тор; (*sport*) тре́нер; *vt* репети́ровать *impf*; тренирова́ть *impf*, на~ *pf*.

coagulate *vi* сгуща́ться *impf*, сгусти́ться *pf*.

coal *n* у́голь *m*; ~**mine** у́гольная ша́хта.

coalition *n* коали́ция.

coarse *adj* гру́бый.

coast *n* побере́жье, бе́рег; ~ **guard** берегова́я охра́на; *vi* (*move without power*) дви́гаться *impf*, дви́нуться *pf* по ине́рции. **coastal** *adj* берегово́й, прибре́жный.

coat *n* пальто́ *neut indecl*; (*layer*) слой; (*animal*) шерсть, мех; ~ **of arms** герб; *vt* покрыва́ть *impf*, покры́ть *pf*.

coax *vt* угова́ривать *impf*, уговори́ть *pf*.

cob *n* (*corn-*~) поча́ток кукуру́зы.

cobble *n* булы́жник (*also collect*). **cobbled** *adj* булы́жный. **cobbler** *n* сапо́жник.

cobweb *n* паути́на.

Coca-Cola *n* (*propr*) ко́ка-ко́ла.

cocaine *n* кокаи́н.

cock *n* (*bird*) пету́х; (*tap*) кран; (*of gun*) куро́к; *vt* (*gun*) взводи́ть *impf*, взвести́ *pf* куро́к+*gen*.

cockerel *n* петушо́к.

cockle *n* сердцеви́дка.

cockpit *n* (*aeron*) каби́на.

cockroach *n* тарака́н.

cocktail *n* кокте́йль *m*.

cocky *adj* чва́нный.

cocoa *n* кака́о *neut indecl*.

coco(a)nut *n* коко́с.

cocoon *n* ко́кон.

cod *n* треска́.

code *n* (*of laws*) ко́декс; (*cipher*) код;

vt шифровать *impf*, за~ *pf.* **codify**
vt кодифицировать *impf & pf.*

co-education *n* совместное обучение.

coefficient *n* коэффициент.

coerce *vt* принуждать *impf*, принудить *pf.* **coercion** *n* принуждение.

coexist *vi* сосуществовать *impf.* **co-existence** *n* сосуществование.

coffee *n* кофе *m indecl*; ~-**mill** *n* кофейница; ~-**pot** *n* кофейник.

coffer *n pl* казна.

coffin *n* гроб.

cog *n* зубец. **cogwheel** *n* зубчатое колесо.

cogent *adj* убедительный.

cohabit *vi* сожительствовать *impf.*

coherent *adj* связный. **cohesion** *n* сплочённость. **cohesive** *adj* сплочённый.

coil *vt & i* свёртывать(ся) *impf*, свернуть(ся) *pf* кольцом; *n* кольцо; (*electr*) катушка.

coin *n* монета; *vt* чеканить *impf*, от~ *pf.*

coincide *vi* совпадать *impf*, совпасть *pf.* **coincidence** *n* совпадение. **coincidental** *adj* случайный.

coke *n* кокс.

colander *n* дуршлаг.

cold *n* холод; (*med*) простуда, насморк; *adj* холодный; ~-**blooded** *adj* жестокий; (*zool*) холоднокровный.

colic *n* колики *f pl.*

collaborate *vi* сотрудничать *impf.* **collaboration** *n* сотрудничество. **collaborator** *n* сотрудник, -ица; (*traitor*) коллаборационист, -истка.

collapse *vi* рухнуть *pf*; *n* падение; крушение.

collar *n* воротник; (*dog's*) ошейник; ~-**bone** ключица.

colleague *n* коллега *m & f.*

collect *vt* собирать *impf*, собрать *pf*; (*as hobby*) коллекционировать *impf*; (*fetch*) забирать *impf*, забрать *pf.* **collected** *adj* (*calm*) собранный; ~ **works** собрание сочинений. **collection** *n* (*stamps etc.*) коллекция; (*church etc.*) сбор; (*post*) выемка. **collective** *n* коллектив; *adj* коллективный; ~ **farm** колхоз; ~ **noun** собирательное существительное *sb.* **collectivization** *n* коллективиза

ция. **collector** *n* сборщик; коллекционер.

college *n* колледж, училище.

collide *vi* сталкиваться *impf*, столкнуться *pf.* **collision** *n* столкновение.

colliery *n* каменноугольная шахта.

colloquial *adj* разговорный. **colloquialism** *n* разговорное выражение.

collusion *n* тайный сговор.

colon[1] *n* (*anat*) толстая кишка.

colon[2] *n* (*gram*) двоеточие.

colonel *n* полковник.

colonial *adj* колониальный. **colonialism** *n* колониализм. **colonize** *vt* колонизовать *impf & pf.* **colony** *n* колония.

colossal *adj* колоссальный.

colour *n* цвет, краска; (*pl*) (*flag*) знамя *neut*; ~-**blind** страдающий дальтонизмом; ~ **film** цветная плёнка; *vt* раскрашивать *impf*, раскрасить *pf*; *vi* краснеть *impf*, по~ *pf.* **coloured** *adj* цветной. **colourful** *adj* яркий. **colourless** *adj* бесцветный.

colt *n* жеребёнок.

column *n* (*archit, mil*) колонна; (*of smoke etc.*) столб; (*of print*) столбец. **columnist** *n* журналист.

coma *n* кома.

comb *n* гребёнка; *vt* причёсывать *impf*, причесать *pf.*

combat *n* бой; *vt* бороться *impf* с+*instr*, против+*gen.*

combination *n* сочетание; комбинация. **combine** *n* комбинат; (~*harvester*) комбайн; *vt & i* совмещать(ся) *impf*, совместить(ся) *pf.* **combined** *adj* совместный.

combustion *n* горение.

come *vi* (*on foot*) приходить *impf*, прийти *pf*; (*by transport*) приезжать *impf*, приехать *pf*; ~ **about** случаться *impf*, случиться *pf*; ~ **across** случайно наталкиваться *impf*, натолкнуться *pf* на+*acc*; ~ **back** возвращаться *impf*, возвратиться *pf*; ~ **in** входить *impf*, войти *pf*; ~ **out** выходить *impf*, выйти *pf*; ~ **round** (*revive*) приходить *impf*, прийти *pf* в себя; (*visit*) заходить *impf*, зайти *pf*; (*agree*) соглашаться *impf*, согласиться *pf*; ~ **up to** (*approach*) подходить *impf*, подойти *pf* к+*dat*;

(*reach*) доходи́ть *impf*, дойти́ *pf* до+*gen*. **come-back** *n* возвраще́ние. **come-down** *n* униже́ние.

comedian *n* комедиа́нт. **comedy** *n* коме́дия.

comet *n* коме́та.

comfort *n* комфо́рт; (*convenience*) удо́бство; (*consolation*) утеше́ние; *vt* утеша́ть *impf*, уте́шить *pf*. **comfortable** *adj* удо́бный.

comic *adj* коми́ческий; *n* ко́мик; (*magazine*) ко́микс. **comical** *adj* смешно́й.

coming *adj* сле́дующий.

comma *n* запята́я *sb*.

command *n* (*order*) прика́з; (*order, authority*) кома́нда; **have ~ of** (*master*) владе́ть *impf* +*instr*; *vt* прика́зывать *impf*, приказа́ть *pf* +*dat*; (*mil*) кома́ндовать *impf*, c~ *pf* +*instr*. **commandant** *n* коменда́нт. **commandeer** *vt* реквизи́ровать *impf* & *pf*. **commander** *n* команди́р; **~in-chief** главнокома́ндующий *sb*. **commandment** *n* за́поведь. **commando** *n* деса́нтник.

commemorate *vt* ознамено́вывать *impf*, ознаменова́ть *pf*. **commemoration** *n* ознаменова́ние. **commemorative** *adj* па́мятный.

commence *vt* & *i* начина́ть(ся) *impf*, нача́ть(ся) *pf*. **commencement** *n* нача́ло.

commend *vt* хвали́ть *impf*, по~ *pf*; (*recommend*) рекомендова́ть *impf* & *pf*. **commendable** *adj* похва́льный. **commendation** *n* похвала́.

commensurate *adj* соразме́рный.

comment *n* замеча́ние; *vi* де́лать *impf*, c~ *pf* замеча́ния; **~ on** комменти́ровать *impf* & *pf*, про~ *pf*. **commentary** *n* коммента́рий. **commentator** *n* коммента́тор.

commerce *n* комме́рция. **commercial** *adj* торго́вый; *n* рекла́ма.

commiserate *vi*: **~ with** соболе́зновать *impf* +*dat*. **commiseration** *n* соболе́знование.

commission *n* (*order for work*) зака́з; (*agent's fee*) комиссио́нные *sb*; (*of inquiry etc.*) коми́ссия; (*mil*) офице́рское зва́ние; *vt* зака́зывать *impf*, заказа́ть *pf*. **commissionaire** *n* швейца́р. **commissioner** *n* комисса́р.

commit *vt* соверша́ть *impf*, соверши́ть *pf*; **~ o.s.** обя́зываться *impf*, обяза́ться *pf*. **commitment** *n* обяза́тельство.

committee *n* комите́т.

commodity *n* това́р.

commodore *n* (*officer*) коммодо́р.

common *adj* о́бщий; (*ordinary*) просто́й; *n* общи́нная земля́; **~ sense** здра́вый смысл. **commonly** *adv* обы́чно. **commonplace** *adj* бана́льный. **commonwealth** *n* содру́жество.

commotion *n* сумато́ха.

communal *adj* общи́нный, коммуна́льный. **commune** *n* комму́на; *vi* обща́ться *impf*.

communicate *vt* передава́ть *impf*, переда́ть *pf*; сообща́ть *impf*, сообщи́ть *pf*. **communication** *n* сообще́ние; связь. **communicative** *adj* разгово́рчивый.

communion *n* (*eccl*) прича́стие.

communiqué *n* коммюнике́ *neut indecl*.

Communism *n* коммуни́зм. **Communist** *n* коммуни́ст, **~ка**; *adj* коммунисти́ческий.

community *n* общи́на.

commute *vt* заменя́ть *impf*, замени́ть *pf*; (*travel*) добира́ться *impf*, добра́ться *pf* тра́нспортом. **commuter** *n* регуля́рный пассажи́р.

compact[1] *n* (*agreement*) соглаше́ние. **compact**[2] *adj* компа́ктный; **~ disc** компа́кт-ди́ск; *n* пу́дреница.

companion *n* това́рищ; (*handbook*) спра́вочник. **companionable** *adj* общи́тельный. **companionship** *n* дру́жеское обще́ние. **company** *n* о́бщество, (*also firm*) компа́ния; (*theat*) тру́ппа; (*mil*) ро́та.

comparable *adj* сравни́мый. **comparative** *adj* сравни́тельный; *n* сравни́тельная сте́пень. **compare** *vt* & *i* сра́внивать(ся) *impf*, сравни́ть(ся) *pf* (**to, with** c+*instr*). **comparison** *n* сравне́ние.

compartment *n* отделе́ние; (*rly*) купе́ *neut indecl*.

compass *n* ко́мпас; *pl* ци́ркуль *m*.

compassion *n* сострада́ние. **compassionate** *adj* сострада́тельный.

compatibility *n* совмести́мость. **compatible** *adj* совмести́мый.

compatriot *n* соотече́ственник, **-ица**.

compel vt заставля́ть impf, заста́вить pf.

compensate vt компенси́ровать impf & pf (for за+acc). **compensation** n компенса́ция.

compete vi конкури́ровать impf; соревнова́ться impf.

competence n компете́нтность. **competent** adj компете́нтный.

competition n (contest) соревнова́ние, состяза́ние; (rivalry) конку́ренция. **competitive** adj (comm) конкурентоспосо́бный. **competitor** n конкуре́нт, ~ка.

compilation n (result) компиля́ция; (act) составле́ние. **compile** vt составля́ть impf, соста́вить pf. **compiler** n состави́тель m, ~ница.

complacency n самодово́льство. **complacent** adj самодово́льный.

complain vi жа́ловаться impf, по~ pf. **complaint** n жа́лоба.

complement n дополне́ние; (full number) (ли́чный) соста́в; vt дополня́ть impf, допо́лнить pf. **complementary** adj дополни́тельный.

complete vt заверша́ть impf, заверши́ть pf; adj (entire, thorough) по́лный; (finished) зако́нченный. **completion** n заверше́ние.

complex adj сло́жный; n ко́мплекс. **complexity** n сло́жность.

complexion n цвет лица́.

compliance n усту́пчивость. **compliant** adj усту́пчивый.

complicate vt осложня́ть impf, осложни́ть pf. **complicated** adj сло́жный. **complication** n осложне́ние.

complicity n соуча́стие.

compliment n комплиме́нт; pl приве́т; vt говори́ть impf комплиме́нт(ы) +dat; хвали́ть impf, по~ pf. **complimentary** adj ле́стный; (free) беспла́тный.

comply vi - with (fulfil) исполня́ть impf, испо́лнить pf; (submit to) подчиня́ться impf, подчини́ться pf +dat.

component n дета́ль; adj составно́й.

compose vt (music etc.) сочиня́ть impf, сочини́ть pf; (draft; constitute) составля́ть impf, соста́вить pf. **composed** adj споко́йный; be ~ of состоя́ть impf из+gen. **composer** n композ
и́тор. **composition** n сочи-

не́ние; (make-up) соста́в.

compost n компо́ст.

composure n самооблада́ние.

compound[1] n (chem) соедине́ние; adj сло́жный.

compound[2] n (enclosure) огоро́женное ме́сто.

comprehend vt понима́ть impf, поня́ть pf. **comprehensible** adj поня́тный. **comprehension** n понима́ние. **comprehensive** adj всеобъе́млющий; ~ school общеобразова́тельная шко́ла.

compress vt сжима́ть impf, сжать pf. **compressed** adj сжа́тый. **compression** n сжа́тие. **compressor** n компре́ссор.

comprise vt состоя́ть impf из+gen.

compromise n компроми́сс; vt компромети́ровать impf, с~ pf; vi идти́ impf, пойти́ pf на компроми́сс.

compulsion n принужде́ние. **compulsory** adj обяза́тельный.

compunction n угрызе́ние со́вести.

computer n компью́тер.

comrade n това́рищ. **comradeship** n това́рищество.

con[1] see pro[1]

con[2] vt надува́ть impf, наду́ть pf.

concave adj во́гнутый.

conceal vt скрыва́ть impf, скрыть pf.

concede vt уступа́ть impf, уступи́ть pf; (admit) признава́ть impf, призна́ть pf; (goal) пропуска́ть impf, пропусти́ть pf.

conceit n самомне́ние. **conceited** adj самовлюблённый.

conceivable adj мы́слимый. **conceive** vt (plan, imagine) заду́мывать impf, заду́мать pf; (biol) зачина́ть impf, зача́ть pf; vi забере́менеть pf.

concentrate vt & i сосредото́чивать(ся) impf, сосредото́чить(ся) pf (on на+prep); vt (also chem) концентри́ровать impf, с~ pf. **concentration** n сосредото́ченность, концентра́ция.

concept n поня́тие. **conception** n поня́тие; (biol) зача́тие.

concern n (worry) забо́та; (comm) предприя́тие; vt каса́ться impf +gen; ~ o.s. with занима́ться impf, заня́ться pf +instr. **concerned** adj озабо́ченный; as far as I'm ~ что каса́ется меня́. **concerning** prep относительно+*gen*.

concert *n* концерт. **concerted** *adj* согласованный.

concertina *n* гармоника.

concession *n* уступка; (*econ*) концессия. **concessionary** *adj* концессионный.

conciliation *n* примирение. **conciliatory** *adj* примирительный.

concise *adj* краткий. **conciseness** *n* сжатость, краткость.

conclude *vt* заключать *impf*, заключить *pf*. **concluding** *adj* заключительный. **conclusion** *n* заключение; (*deduction*) вывод. **conclusive** *adj* решающий.

concoct *vt* стряпать *impf*, со~ *pf*. **concoction** *n* стряпня.

concourse *n* зал.

concrete *n* бетон; *adj* бетонный; (*fig*) конкретный.

concur *vi* соглашаться *impf*, согласиться *pf*. **concurrent** *adj* одновременный.

concussion *n* сотрясение.

condemn *vt* осуждать *impf*, осудить *pf*; (*as unfit for use*) браковать *impf*, за~ *pf*. **condemnation** *n* осуждение.

condensation *n* конденсация. **condense** *vt* (*liquid etc.*) конденсировать *impf* & *pf*; (*text etc.*) сокращать *impf*, сократить *pf*. **condensed** *adj* сжатый; (*milk*) сгущённый. **condenser** *n* конденсатор.

condescend *vi* снисходить *impf*, снизойти *pf*. **condescending** *adj* снисходительный. **condescension** *n* снисхождение.

condiment *n* приправа.

condition *n* условие; (*state*) состояние; *vt* (*determine*) обусловливать *impf*, обусловить *pf*; (*psych*) приучать *impf*, приучить *pf*. **conditional** *adj* условный.

condolence *n*: *pl* соболезнование.

condom *n* презерватив.

condone *vt* закрывать *impf*, закрыть *pf* глаза на+*acc*.

conducive *adj* способствующий (**to** +*dat*).

conduct *n* (*behaviour*) поведение; *vt* вести *impf*, по~ *pf*; (*mus*) дирижировать *impf* +*instr*; (*phys*) проводить *impf*. **conduction** *n* про-

водимость. **conductor** *n* (*bus*) кондуктор; (*phys*) проводник; (*mus*) дирижёр.

conduit *n* трубопровод.

cone *n* конус; (*bot*) шишка.

confectioner *n* кондитер; ~**'s** (*shop*) кондитерская *sb*. **confectionery** *n* кондитерские изделия *neut pl*.

confederation *n* конфедерация.

confer *vt* присуждать *impf*, присудить (**on** +*dat*) *pf*; *vi* совещаться *impf*. **conference** *n* совещание; конференция.

confess *vt* & *i* (*acknowledge*) признавать(ся) *impf*, признать(ся) *pf* (**to** в+*prep*); (*eccl*) исповедовать(ся) *impf* & *pf*. **confession** *n* признание; исповедь. **confessor** *n* духовник.

confidant(e) *n* близкий собеседник.

confide *vt* доверять *impf*, доверить *pf*; ~ **in** делиться *impf*, по~ *pf* c+*instr*. **confidence** *n* (*trust*) доверие; (*certainty*) уверенность; (*self-*~) самоуверенность. **confident** *adj* уверенный. **confidential** *adj* секретный.

confine *vt* ограничивать *impf*, ограничить *pf*; (*shut in*) заключать *impf*, заключить *pf*. **confinement** *n* заключение. **confines** *n pl* пределы *m pl*.

confirm *vt* подтверждать *impf*, подтвердить *pf*. **confirmation** *n* подтверждение; (*eccl*) конфирмация. **confirmed** *adj* закоренелый.

confiscate *vt* конфисковать *impf* & *pf*. **confiscation** *n* конфискация.

conflict *n* конфликт; противоречие; *vi*: ~ **with** противоречить *impf* +*dat*. **conflicting** *adj* противоречивый.

conform *vi*: ~ **to** подчиняться *impf*, подчиниться *pf* +*dat*. **conformity** *n* соответствие; (*compliance*) подчинение.

confound *vt* сбивать *impf*, сбить *pf* с толку. **confounded** *adj* проклятый.

confront *vt* стоять *impf* лицом к лицу c+*instr*; ~ (*person*) **with** ставить *impf*, по~ *pf* лицом к лицу c+*instr*. **confrontation** *n* конфронтация.

confuse *vt* смущать *impf*, смутить *pf*; (*also mix up*) путать *impf*, за~, с~ *pf*. **confusion** *n* смущение;

пу́таница.
congeal vt густе́ть impf, за~ pf; (blood) свёртываться impf, сверну́ться pf.
congenial adj прия́тный.
congenital adj врождённый.
congested adj перепо́лненный. **congestion** n (traffic) зато́р.
congratulate vt поздравля́ть impf, поздра́вить pf (on c+instr). **congratulation** n поздравле́ние; ~s! поздравля́ю!
congregate vi собира́ться impf, собра́ться pf. **congregation** n (eccl) прихожа́не (-н) pl.
congress n съезд. **Congressman** n конгрессме́н.
conic(al) adj кони́ческий.
conifer n хвойное де́рево. **coniferous** adj хвойный.
conjecture n дога́дка; vt гада́ть impf.
conjugal adj супру́жеский.
conjugate vt спряга́ть impf, про~ pf. **conjugation** n спряже́ние.
conjunction n (gram) сою́з; in ~ with совме́стно c+instr.
conjure vi: ~ up (in mind) вызыва́ть impf, вы́звать pf в воображе́нии. **conjurer** n фо́кусник. **conjuring trick** n фо́кус.
connect vt & i свя́зывать(ся) impf, связа́ть(ся) pf; соединя́ть(ся) impf, соедини́ть(ся) pf. **connected** adj свя́занный. **connection, -exion** n связь; (rly etc.) переса́дка.
connivance n попусти́тельство. **connive** vi: ~ at попусти́тельствовать impf +dat.
connoisseur n знато́к.
conquer vt (country) завоёвывать impf, завоева́ть pf; (enemy) побежда́ть impf, победи́ть pf; (habit) преодолева́ть impf, преодоле́ть pf. **conqueror** n завоева́тель m. **conquest** n завоева́ние.
conscience n со́весть. **conscientious** adj добросо́вестный. **conscious** adj созна́тельный; predic в созна́нии; be ~ of сознава́ть impf +acc. **consciousness** n созна́ние.
conscript vt призыва́ть impf, призва́ть pf на вое́нную слу́жбу; n призывни́к. **conscription** n во́инская пови́нность.
consecrate vt освяща́ть impf, освя-

ти́ть pf. **consecration** n освяще́ние.
consecutive adj после́довательный.
consensus n согла́сие.
consent vi соглаша́ться impf, согласи́ться pf (to +inf, на+acc); n согла́сие.
consequence n после́дствие; of great ~ большо́го значе́ния; of some ~ дово́льно ва́жный. **consequent** adj вытека́ющий. **consequential** adj ва́жный. **consequently** adv сле́довательно.
conservation n сохране́ние; (of nature) охра́на приро́ды. **conservative** adj консервати́вный; n консерва́тор. **conservatory** n оранжере́я. **conserve** vt сохраня́ть impf, сохрани́ть pf.
consider vt (think over) обду́мывать impf, обду́мать pf; (examine) рассма́тривать impf, рассмотре́ть pf; (regard as, be of opinion that) счита́ть impf, счесть pf +instr, за+acc, что; (take into account) счита́ться impf c+instr. **considerable** adj значи́тельный. **considerate** adj внима́тельный. **consideration** n рассмотре́ние; внима́ние; (factor) фа́ктор; take into ~ принима́ть impf, приня́ть pf во внима́ние. **considering** prep принима́я +acc во внима́ние.
consign vt передава́ть impf, переда́ть pf. **consignment** n (goods) па́ртия; (consigning) отпра́вка това́ров.
consist vi: ~ of состоя́ть impf из +gen. **consistency** n после́довательность; (density) консисте́нция. **consistent** adj после́довательный; ~ with совмести́мый c+instr.
consolation n утеше́ние. **console**[1] vt утеша́ть impf, уте́шить pf.
console[2] n (control panel) пульт управле́ния.
consolidate vt укрепля́ть impf, укрепи́ть pf. **consolidation** n укрепле́ние.
consonant n согла́сный sb.
consort n супру́г, ~a.
conspicuous adj заме́тный.
conspiracy n за́говор. **conspirator** n загово́рщик, -ица. **conspiratorial** adj загово́рщицкий. **conspire** vi устра́ивать impf, устро́ить pf за́говор.

constable n полицейский sb.

constancy n постоянство. **constant** adj постоянный. **constantly** adv постоянно.

constellation n созвездие.

consternation n тревога.

constipation n запор.

constituency n избирательный округ. **constituent** n (component) составная часть; (voter) избиратель m; adj составной. **constitute** vt составлять impf, составить pf. **constitution** n (polit, med) конституция; (composition) составление. **constitutional** adj (polit) конституционный.

constrain vt принуждать impf, принудить pf. **constrained** adj (inhibited) стеснённый. **constraint** n принуждение; (inhibition) стеснение.

constrict vt (compress) сжимать impf, сжать pf; (narrow) суживать impf, сузить pf. **constriction** n сжатие; сужение.

construct vt строить impf, по~ pf. **construction** n строительство; (also gram) конструкция; (interpretation) истолкование; ~ site стройка. **constructive** adj конструктивный.

construe vt истолковывать impf, истолковать pf.

consul n консул. **consulate** n консульство.

consult vt советоваться impf, по~ pf c+instr. **consultant** n консультант. **consultation** n консультация.

consume vt потреблять impf, потребить pf; (eat or drink) съедать impf, съесть pf. **consumer** n потребитель m; ~ **goods** товары m pl широкого потребления.

consummate vt завершать impf, завершить pf; ~ **a marriage** осуществлять impf, осуществить pf брачные отношения. **consummation** n завершение; (of marriage) осуществление.

consumption n потребление.

contact n контакт; (person) связь; ~ **lens** контактная линза; vt связываться impf, связаться pf c+instr.

contagious adj заразный.

contain vt содержать impf; (restrain) сдерживать impf, сдержать pf. **con-**tainer n (vessel) сосуд; (transport) контейнер.

contaminate vt загрязнять impf, загрязнить pf. **contamination** n загрязнение.

contemplate vt (gaze) созерцать impf; размышлять impf; (consider) предполагать impf, предположить pf. **contemplation** n созерцание; размышление. **contemplative** adj созерцательный.

contemporary n современник; adj современный.

contempt n презрение; ~ **of court** неуважение к суду; **hold in** ~ презирать impf. **contemptible** adj презренный. **contemptuous** adj презрительный.

contend vi (compete) состязаться impf; ~ **for** оспаривать impf; ~ **with** справляться impf, справиться pf c+instr; vt утверждать impf. **contender** n претендент.

content[1] n содержание; pl содержимое sb; (table of) ~s содержание.

content[2] predic доволен (-льна); vt: ~ **o.s. with** довольствоваться impf, у~ pf +instr. **contented** adj довольный.

contention n (claim) утверждение. **contentious** adj спорный.

contest n состязание; vt (dispute) оспаривать impf, оспорить pf. **contestant** n участник, -ица, состязания.

context n контекст.

continent n материк. **continental** adj материковый.

contingency n возможный случай; ~ **plan** вариант плана. **contingent** adj случайный; n контингент.

continual adj непрестанный. **continuation** n продолжение. **continue** vt & i продолжать(ся) impf, продолжить(ся) pf. **continuous** adj непрерывный.

contort vt искажать impf, исказить pf. **contortion** n искажение.

contour n контур; ~ **line** горизонталь.

contraband n контрабанда.

contraception n предупреждение зачатия. **contraceptive** n противозачаточное средство; adj противозачаточный.

contract n контра́кт, до́гово́р; vi (make a ~) заключа́ть impf, заключи́ть pf контра́кт; vt & i (shorten, reduce) сокраща́ть(ся) impf, сократи́ть(ся) pf; vt (illness) заболева́ть impf, заболе́ть pf +instr. **contraction** n сокраще́ние; pl (med) схва́тки f pl. **contractor** n подря́дчик.

contradict vt противоре́чить impf +dat. **contradiction** n противоре́чие. **contradictory** adj противоре́чивый.

contraflow n встре́чное движе́ние.

contralto n контра́льто (voice) neut & (person) f indecl.

contraption n приспособле́ние.

contrary adj (opposite) противополо́жный; (perverse) капри́зный; ~ **to** вопреки́+dat; n: on the ~ наоборо́т.

contrast n контра́ст, противополо́жность; vt противопоставля́ть impf, противопоста́вить pf (with +dat); vi контрасти́ровать impf.

contravene vt наруша́ть impf, нару́шить pf. **contravention** n наруше́ние.

contribute vt (to fund etc.) же́ртвовать impf, по~ pf (to в+acc); ~ to (further) соде́йствовать impf & pf, по~ pf +dat; (write for) сотру́дничать impf в+prep. **contribution** n (money) поже́ртвование; (fig) вклад. **contributor** n (donor) же́ртвователь m; (writer) сотру́дник.

contrite adj ка́ющийся.

contrivance n приспособле́ние. **contrive** vt ухитря́ться impf, ухитри́ться pf +inf.

control n (mastery) контро́ль m; (operation) управле́ние; pl управле́ния pl; vt (dominate; verify) контроли́ровать impf, про~ pf; (regulate) управля́ть impf +instr; ~ **o.s.** сде́рживаться impf, сдержа́ться pf. **controversial** adj спо́рный. **controversy** n спор.

convalesce vi выздора́вливать impf. **convalescence** n выздоровле́ние.

convection n конве́кция. **convector** n конве́ктор.

convene vt созыва́ть impf, созва́ть pf.

convenience n удо́бство; (public ~)

убо́рная sb. **convenient** adj удо́бный.

convent n же́нский монасты́рь m.

convention n (assembly) съезд; (agreement) конве́нция; (custom) обы́чай; (conventionality) усло́вность. **conventional** adj общепри́нятый; (also mil) обы́чный.

converge vi сходи́ться impf, сойти́сь pf. **convergence** n схо́димость.

conversant predic: ~ **with** знако́м с+instr.

conversation n разгово́р. **conversational** adj разгово́рный. **converse**[1] vi разгова́ривать impf.

converse[2] n обра́тное sb. **conversely** adv наоборо́т. **conversion** n (change) превраще́ние; (of faith) обраще́ние; (of building) перестро́йка. **convert** vt (change) превраща́ть impf, преврати́ть pf (into в+acc); (to faith) обраща́ть impf, обрати́ть pf (to в+acc); (a building) перестра́ивать impf, перестро́ить pf. **convertible** adj обрати́мый; n автомоби́ль m со снима́ющейся кры́шей.

convex adj вы́пуклый.

convey vt (transport) перевози́ть impf, перевезти́ pf; (communicate) передава́ть impf, переда́ть pf. **conveyance** n перево́зка; переда́ча. **conveyancing** n нотариа́льная переда́ча. **conveyor belt** n транспортёрная ле́нта.

convict n осуждённый sb; vt осужда́ть impf, осуди́ть pf. **conviction** n (law) осужде́ние; (belief) убежде́ние. **convince** vt убежда́ть impf, убеди́ть pf. **convincing** adj убеди́тельный.

convivial adj весёлый.

convoluted adj изви́листый; (fig) запу́танный.

convoy n конво́й.

convulse vt: be ~d with содрога́ться impf, содрогну́ться pf от+gen. **convulsion** n (med) конву́льсия.

cook n куха́рка, по́вар; vt гото́вить impf; vi вари́ться impf; с~ pf. **cooker** n плита́, печь. **cookery** n кулина́рия.

cool adj прохла́дный; (calm) хладнокро́вный; (unfriendly) холо́дный; vt охлажда́ть impf, охлади́ть pf; ~

down, off остывать *impf*, осты-(ну)ть *pf*. **coolness** *n* прохлада; (*calm*) хладнокровие; (*manner*) холодок.

coop *n* курятник; *vt*: ~ **up** держать *impf* взаперти.

cooperate *vi* сотрудничать *impf*. **cooperation** *n* сотрудничество. **cooperative** *n* кооператив; *adj* кооперативный; (*helpful*) услужливый.

co-opt *vt* кооптировать *impf & pf*.

coordinate *vt* координировать *impf & pf*; *n* координата. **coordination** *n* координация.

cope *vi*: ~ **with** справляться *impf*, справиться *pf* с+*instr*.

copious *adj* обильный.

copper *n* (*metal*) медь; *adj* медный.

coppice, copse *n* рощица.

copulate *vi* совокупляться *impf*, совокупиться *pf*.

copy *n* копия; (*book*) экземпляр; *vt* (*reproduce*) копировать *impf*, с~ *pf*; (*transcribe*) переписывать *impf*, переписать *pf*; (*imitate*) подражать *impf* +*dat*. **copyright** *n* авторское право.

coral *n* коралл.

cord *n* (*string*) верёвка; (*electr*) шнур.

cordial *adj* сердечный.

corduroy *n* рубчатый вельвет.

core *n* сердцевина; (*fig*) суть.

cork *n* (*material; stopper*) пробка; (*float*) поплавок. **corkscrew** *n* штопор.

corn[1] *n* зерно; (*wheat*) пшеница; (*maize*) кукуруза. **cornflakes** *n pl* кукурузные хлопья (-пьев) *pl*. **cornflour** *n* кукурузная мука. **corny** *adj* (*coll*) банальный.

corn[2] *n* (*med*) мозоль.

cornea *n* роговая оболочка.

corner *n* угол; ~**stone** *n* краеугольный камень *m*; *vt* загонять *impf*, загнать *pf* в угол.

cornet *n* (*mus*) корнет; (*ice-cream*) рожок.

cornice *n* карниз.

coronary (thrombosis) *n* коронаротромбоз. **coronation** *n* коронация.

coroner *n* медик судебной экспертизы.

corporal[1] *n* капрал.

corporal[2] *adj* телесный; ~ **punishment** телесное наказание.

corporate *adj* корпоративный. **corporation** *n* корпорация.

corps *n* корпус.

corpse *n* труп.

corpulent *adj* тучный.

corpuscle *n* кровяной шарик.

correct *adj* правильный; (*conduct*) корректный; *vt* исправлять *impf*, исправить *pf*. **correction** *n* исправление.

correlation *n* соотношение.

correspond *vi* соответствовать *impf* (**to, with** +*dat*); (*by letter*) переписываться *impf*. **correspondence** *n* соответствие; (*letters*) корреспонденция. **correspondent** *n* корреспондент. **corresponding** *adj* соответствующий (**to** +*dat*).

corridor *n* коридор.

corroborate *vt* подтверждать *impf*, подтвердить *pf*.

corrode *vt* разъедать *impf*, разъесть *pf*. **corrosion** *n* коррозия. **corrosive** *adj* едкий.

corrugated iron *n* рифлёное железо.

corrupt *adj* (*person*) развращённый; (*government*) продажный; *vt* развращать *impf*, развратить *pf*. **corruption** *n* развращение; коррупция.

corset *n* корсет.

cortège *n* кортеж.

cortex *n* кора.

corundum *n* корунд.

cosmetic *adj* косметический. **cosmetics** *n pl* косметика.

cosmic *adj* космический. **cosmonaut** *n* космонавт.

cosmopolitan *adj* космополитический.

cosmos *n* космос.

Cossack *n* казак, -ачка.

cosset *vt* нежить *impf*.

cost *n* стоимость, цена; *vt* стоить *impf*.

costly *adj* дорогой.

costume *n* костюм.

cosy *adj* уютный.

cot *n* детская кроватка.

cottage *n* коттедж; ~ **cheese** творог.

cotton *n* хлопок; (*cloth*) хлопчатобумажная ткань; (*thread*) нитка; ~ **wool** вата; *adj* хлопковый; хлопчатобумажный.

couch *n* диван.

couchette n спа́льное ме́сто.

cough n ка́шель m; vi ка́шлять impf.

council n сове́т; ~ **tax** ме́стный нало́г; ~ **house** жильё из обще́ственного фо́нда. **councillor** n член сове́та.

counsel n (advice) сове́т; (lawyer) адвока́т; vt сове́товать impf, по~ pf +dat.

count¹ vt счита́ть impf, со~, счесть pf; ~ **on** рассчи́тывать impf на+acc; n счёт. **countdown** n отсчёт вре́мени.

count² n (title) граф.

countenance n лицо́; vt одобря́ть impf, одо́брить pf.

counter n прила́вок; (token) фи́шка; adv: run ~ **to** идти́ impf вразре́з с+instr; vt пари́ровать impf, от~ pf. **counteract** vt противоде́йствовать impf +dat. **counterbalance** n противове́с; vt уравнове́шивать impf, уравнове́сить pf. **counterfeit** adj подде́льный. **counterpart** n соотве́тственная часть. **counterpoint** n контрапу́нкт. **counter-revolutionary** n контрреволюционе́р; adj контрреволюцио́нный. **countersign** vt ста́вить impf, по~ pf втору́ю по́дпись на+prep.

countess n графи́ня.

countless adj бесчи́сленный.

country n (nation) страна́; (native land) ро́дина; (rural areas) дере́вня; adj дереве́нский, се́льский. **countryman** n (compatriot) соотéчественник; (rural) се́льский жи́тель m. **countryside** n приро́дный ландша́фт.

county n гра́фство.

coup n (polit) переворо́т.

couple n па́ра; (a few) не́сколько +gen; vt сцепля́ть impf, сцепи́ть pf.

coupon n купо́н; тало́н; ва́учер.

courage n хра́брость. **courageous** adj хра́брый.

courier n (messenger) курье́р; (guide) гид.

course n курс; (process) ход, тече́ние; (of meal) блю́до; **of** ~ коне́чно.

court n двор; (sport) корт, площа́дка; (law) суд; ~ **martial** вое́нный суд; vt уха́живать impf за+instr.

courteous adj ве́жливый. **courtesy** n ве́жливость. **courtier** n придво́рный sb. **courtyard** n двор.

cousin n двою́родный брат, -ная сестра́.

cove n бу́хточка.

covenant n догово́р.

cover n (covering; lid) покры́шка; (shelter) укры́тие; (chair ~; soft case) чехо́л; (bed) покрыва́ло; (book) переплёт, обло́жка; **under separate** ~ в отде́льном конве́рте; vt покрыва́ть impf, покры́ть pf; (hide, protect) закрыва́ть impf, закры́ть pf. **coverage** n освеще́ние. **covert** adj скры́тый.

covet vt пожела́ть pf +gen.

cow¹ n коро́ва. **cowboy** n ковбо́й. **cowshed** n хлев.

cow² vt запу́гивать impf, запуга́ть pf.

coward n трус. **cowardice** n тру́сость. **cowardly** adj трусли́вый.

cower vi съёживаться impf, съёжиться pf.

cox(swain) n рулево́й m.

coy adj жема́нно стыдли́вый.

crab n краб.

crack n (in cup, ice) тре́щина; (in wall) щель; (noise) треск; adj первокла́ссный; vt (break) коло́ть impf, рас~ pf; (china) де́лать impf, с~ pf тре́щину в+acc; vi тре́снуть pf. **crackle** vi потре́скивать impf.

cradle n колыбе́ль.

craft n (trade) ремесло́; (boat) су́дно. **craftiness** n хи́трость. **craftsman** n ремéсленник. **crafty** adj хи́трый.

crag n утёс. **craggy** adj скали́стый.

cram vt (fill) набива́ть impf, наби́ть pf; (stuff in) впи́хивать impf, впихну́ть pf; vi (study) зубри́ть impf.

cramp¹ n (med) су́дорога.

cramp² vt стесня́ть impf, стесни́ть pf. **cramped** adj те́сный.

cranberry n клю́ква.

crane n (bird) жура́вль m; (machine) кран; vt вытя́гивать impf, вы́тянуть pf (ше́ю).

crank¹ n заводна́я ру́чка; ~-**shaft** колéнчатый вал; vt заводи́ть impf, завести́ pf.

crank² n (eccentric) чуда́к. **cranky** adj чуда́ческий.

cranny n щель.

crash n (noise) гро́хот, треск; (accident) ава́рия; (financial) крах; ~ **course** уско́ренный курс; ~ **helmet**

защи́тный шлем; ~ **landing** ава-
ри́йная поса́дка; *vi* (~ *into*) врезать-
ся *impf*, вре́заться *pf* в+*acc*; (*aeron*)
разбива́ться *impf*, разби́ться *pf*;
(*fall with* ~) гро́хнуться *pf*; *vt* (*bang
down*) гро́хнуть *pf*.
crass *adj* гру́бый.
crate *n* я́щик.
crater *n* кра́тер.
crave *vi*: ~ **for** жа́ждать *impf* +*gen*.
craving *n* стра́стное жела́ние.
crawl *vi* по́лзать *indet*, ползти́ *det*;
~ **with** кише́ть+*instr*; *n* (*sport*)
кроль *m*.
crayon *n* цветно́й каранда́ш.
craze *n* ма́ния. **crazy** *adj* поме́-
шанный (*about* на+*prep*).
creak *n* скрип; *vi* скрипе́ть *impf*.
cream *n* сли́вки (-вок) *pl*; (*cosmetic*;
cul) крем; ~ **cheese** сли́вочный
сыр; ~ **soured** ~ смета́на; *vt* сбива́ть
impf, сбить *pf*; *adj* (*of cream*)
сли́вочный; (*colour*) кре́мовый.
creamy *adj* сли́вочный, кре́мовый.
crease *n* скла́дка; *vt* мять *impf*, из~,
с~ *pf*. **creased** *adj* мя́тый.
create *vt* создава́ть *impf*, созда́ть *pf*.
creation *n* созда́ние. **creative** *adj*
тво́рческий. **creator** *n* созда́тель *m*.
creature *n* созда́ние.
crèche *n* (де́тские) я́сли (-лей) *pl*.
credence *n* ве́ра; **give** ~ ве́рить *impf*
(**to** +*dat*). **credentials** *n pl* удосто-
вере́ние; (*diplomacy*) вери́тельные
гра́моты *f pl*. **credibility** *n* правдо-
подо́бие; (*of person*) спосо́бность
вызыва́ть дове́рие. **credible** *adj* (*of
thing*) правдоподо́бный; (*of person*)
заслу́живающий дове́рия.
credit *n* дове́рие; (*comm*) креди́т;
(*honour*) честь; **give** ~ кредитова́ть
impf & *pf* +*acc*; отдава́ть *impf*,
отда́ть *pf* до́лжное+*dat*; ~ **card** кре-
ди́тная ка́рточка; *vt*: ~ **with** припи́-
сывать *impf*, приписа́ть *pf* +*dat*.
creditable *adj* похва́льный. **cred-
itor** *n* кредито́р.
credulity *n* легкове́рие. **credulous**
adj легкове́рный.
creed *n* убежде́ния *neut pl*; (*eccl*)
вероиспове́дание.
creep *vi* по́лзать *indet*, ползти́ *det*.
creeper *n* (*plant*) ползу́чее расте́-
ние.
cremate *vt* креми́ровать *impf* & *pf*.

cremation *n* крема́ция. **crematorium** *n* кремато́рий.
crêpe *n* креп.
crescendo *adv*, *adj*, & *n* креще́ндо
indecl.
crescent *n* полуме́сяц.
crest *n* гре́бень *m*; (*heraldry*) герб.
crevasse, crevice *n* расще́лина, рас-
се́лина.
crew *n* брига́да; (*of ship*, *plane*)
экипа́ж.
crib *n* (*bed*) де́тская крова́тка; *vi*
спи́сывать *impf*, списа́ть *pf*.
crick *n* растяже́ние мышц.
cricket[1] *n* (*insect*) сверчо́к.
cricket[2] *n* (*sport*) кри́кет; ~ **bat** бита́.
crime *n* преступле́ние.
Crimea *n* Крым. **Crimean** *adj* кры́м-
ский.
criminal *n* престу́пник; *adj* престу́п-
ный; (*of crime*) уголо́вный.
crimson *adj* мали́новый.
cringe *vi* (*cower*) съёживаться *impf*,
съёжиться *pf*.
crinkle *n* морщи́на; *vt* & *i* мо́р-
щить(ся) *impf*, на~, с~ *pf*.
cripple *n* кале́ка *m* & *f*; *vt* кале́чить
impf, ис~ *pf*; (*fig*) расша́тывать
impf, расша́тать *pf*.
crisis *n* кри́зис.
crisp *adj* (*brittle*) хрустя́щий; (*fresh*)
све́жий. **crisps** *n pl* хрустя́щий кар-
то́фель *m*.
criss-cross *adv* крест-на́крест.
criterion *n* крите́рий.
critic *n* кри́тик. **critical** *adj* крити́че-
ский. **critically** *adv* (*ill*) тяжело́.
criticism *n* кри́тика. **criticize** *vt*
критикова́ть *impf*. **critique** *n* кри́-
тика.
croak *vi* ква́кать *impf*, ква́кнуть *pf*;
хрипе́ть *impf*.
Croat *n* хорва́т, ~ка. **Croatia** *n*
Хорва́тия. **Croatian** *adj* хорва́т-
ский.
crochet *n* вяза́ние крючко́м; *vt*
вяза́ть *impf*, с~ *pf* (крючко́м).
crockery *n* посу́да.
crocodile *n* крокоди́л.
crocus *n* кро́кус.
crony *n* закады́чный друг.
crook *n* (*staff*) по́сох; (*swindler*)
моше́нник. **crooked** *adj* криво́й;
(*dishonest*) нече́стный.
crop *n* (*yield*) урожа́й; *pl* культу́ры

f pl; (*bird's*) зоб; *vt* (*cut*) подстригать *impf*, подстричь *pf*; ~ **up** возникать *impf*, возникнуть *pf*.

croquet *n* крокет.

cross *n* крест; (*biol*) помесь; *adj* (*angry*) злой; *vt* пересекать *impf*, пересечь *pf*; (*biol*) скрещивать *impf*, скрестить *pf*; ~ **off, out** вычёркивать *impf*, вычеркнуть *pf*; ~ **o.s.** креститься *impf*, пере~ *pf*; ~ **over** переходить *impf*, перейти *pf* (через) +*acc*. **~bar** поперечина. **~breed** помесь; **~-country race** кросс; **~-examination** перекрёстный допрос; **~-examine, ~-question** подвергать *impf*, подвергнуть *pf* перекрёстному допросу; **~-eyed** косоглазый; **~-legged:** sit ~ сидеть *impf* по-турецки; **~-reference** перекрёстная ссылка; **~road(s)** перекрёсток; (*fig*) распутье; **~-section** перекрёстное сечение; **~wise** *adv* крест-накрест; **~word (puzzle)** кроссворд. **crossing** *n* (*intersection*) перекрёсток; (*foot*) переход; (*transport*; *rly*) переезд.

crotch *n* (*anat*) промежность.

crotchet *n* (*mus*) четвертная нота.

crotchety *adj* раздражительный.

crouch *vi* приседать *impf*, присесть *pf*.

crow *n* ворона; **as the ~ flies** по прямой линии; *vi* кукарекать *impf*. **crowbar** *n* лом.

crowd *n* толпа; *vi* тесниться *impf*, с~ *pf*; ~ **into** втискиваться *impf*, втиснуться *pf*. **crowded** *adj* переполненный.

crown *n* корона; (*tooth*) коронка; (*head*) тема; (*hat*) тулья; *vt* короновать *impf* & *pf*.

crucial *adj* (*important*) очень важный; (*decisive*) решающий; (*critical*) критический.

crucifix, crucifixion *n* распятие. **crucify** *vt* распинать *impf*, распять *pf*.

crude *adj* (*rude*) грубый; (*raw*) сырой. **crudeness, crudity** *n* грубость.

cruel *adj* жестокий. **cruelty** *n* жестокость.

cruise *n* круиз; *vi* крейсировать *impf*. **cruiser** *n* крейсер.

crumb *n* крошка.

crumble *vt* крошить *impf*, рас~ *pf*; *vi* обваливаться *impf*, обвалиться

pf. **crumbly** *adj* рассыпчатый.

crumple *vt* мять *impf*, с~ *pf*; (*intentionally*) комкать *impf*, с~ *pf*.

crunch *n* (*fig*) решающий момент; *vt* грызть *impf*, раз~ *pf*; *vi* хрустеть *impf*, хрустнуть *pf*.

crusade *n* крестовый поход; (*fig*) кампания. **crusader** *n* крестоносец; (*fig*) борец (**for** за+*acc*).

crush *n* давка; (*infatuation*) сильное увлечение; *vt* давить *impf*, за~, раз~ *pf*; (*crease*) мять *impf*, с~ *pf*; (*fig*) подавлять *impf*, подавить *pf*.

crust *n* (*of earth*) кора; (*bread etc.*) корка.

crutch *n* костыль *m*.

crux *n*: ~ **of the matter** суть дела.

cry *n* крик; **a far ~ from** далеко от+*gen*; *vi* (*weep*) плакать *impf*; (*shout*) кричать *impf*.

crypt *n* склеп. **cryptic** *adj* загадочный.

crystal *n* кристалл; (*glass*) хрусталь *m*. **crystallize** *vt* & *i* кристаллизовать(ся) *impf* & *pf*.

cub *n* детёныш; **bear ~** медвежонок; **fox ~** лисёнок; **lion ~** львёнок; **wolf ~** волчёнок.

cube *n* куб. **cubic** *adj* кубический.

cubicle *n* кабина.

cuckoo *n* кукушка.

cucumber *n* огурец.

cuddle *vt* обнимать *impf*, обнять *pf*; *vi* обниматься *impf*, обняться *pf*; ~ **up** прижиматься *impf*, прижаться *pf* (**to** к+ *dat*).

cudgel *n* дубинка.

cue[1] *n* (*theat*) реплика.

cue[2] *n* (*billiards*) кий.

cuff[1] *n* манжета; **off the ~** экспромтом; **~-link** запонка.

cuff[2] *vt* (*hit*) шлёпать *impf*, шлёпнуть *pf*.

cul-de-sac *n* тупик.

culinary *adj* кулинарный.

cull *vt* (*select*) отбирать *impf*, отобрать *pf*; (*slaughter*) бить *impf*.

culminate *vi* кончаться *impf*, кончиться *pf* (**in** +*instr*). **culmination** *n* кульминационный пункт.

culpability *n* виновность. **culpable** *adj* виновный. **culprit** *n* виновник.

cult *n* культ.

cultivate *vt* (*land*) обрабатывать *impf*, обработать *pf*; (*crops*) выращивать

impf; вы́растить *impf*; (*develop*)
развива́ть *impf*, разви́ть *pf*.
cultural *adj* культу́рный. **culture** *n*
культу́ра. **cultured** *adj* культу́рный.
cumbersome *adj* громо́здкий.
cumulative *adj* кумуляти́вный.
cunning *n* хи́трость; *adj* хи́трый.
cup *n* ча́шка; (*prize*) ку́бок.
cupboard *n* шкаф.
cupola *n* ку́пол.
curable *adj* излечи́мый.
curative *adj* целе́бный.
curator *n* храни́тель *m*.
curb *vt* обу́здывать *impf*, обузда́ть
pf.
curd (*cheese*) *n* творо́г. **curdle** *vt & i*
свёртывать(ся) *impf*, сверну́ть(ся)
pf.
cure *n* сре́дство (**for** про́тив+*gen*); *vt*
выле́чивать *impf*, вы́лечить *pf*;
(*smoke*) копти́ть *impf*, за~ *pf*; (*salt*)
соли́ть *impf*, по~ *pf*.
curfew *n* коменда́нтский час.
curiosity *n* любопы́тство. **curious**
adj любопы́тный.
curl *n* ло́кон; *vt* завива́ть *impf*, за-
ви́ть *pf*; ~ **up** свёртываться *impf*,
сверну́ться *pf*. **curly** *adj* кудря́вый.
currants *n pl* (*dried*) изю́м (*collect*).
currency *n* валю́та; (*prevalence*)
хожде́ние. **current** *adj* теку́щий; *n*
тече́ние; (*air*) струя́; (*water*; *electr*)
ток.
curriculum *n* курс обуче́ния; ~ **vitae**
автобиогра́фия.
curry[1] *n* кэ́рри *neut indecl*.
curry[2] *vt*: ~ **favour with** зайски́вать
impf пе́ред+*instr*, у+*gen*.
curse *n* прокля́тие; (*oath*) руга́тель-
ство; *vt* проклина́ть *impf*, про-
кля́сть *pf*; *vi* руга́ться *impf*, по~ *pf*.
cursory *adj* бе́глый.
curt *adj* ре́зкий.
curtail *vt* сокраща́ть *impf*, сократи́ть
pf.
curtain *n* занаве́ска.
curts(e)y *n* реверанс; *vi* де́лать *impf*,
с~ *pf* реверанс.
curve *n* изги́б; (*line*) крива́я *sb*; *vi*
изгиба́ться *impf*, изогну́ться *pf*.
cushion *n* поду́шка; *vt* смягча́ть
impf, смягчи́ть *pf*.
custard *n* сла́дкий заварно́й крем.
custodian *n* храни́тель *m*. **custody**
n опе́ка; (*of police*) аре́ст; **to take**

into ~ арестова́ть *pf*.
custom *n* обы́чай; (*comm*) клиен-
ту́ра; *pl* (*duty*) тамо́женные по́ш-
лины *f pl*; **go through** ~**s** проходи́ть
impf, пройти́ *pf* тамо́женный
осмо́тр; ~**-house** тамо́жня; ~ **officer**
тамо́женник. **customary** *adj* обы́ч-
ный. **customer** *n* клие́нт; покупа́-
тель *m*.
cut *vt* ре́зать *impf*, по~ *pf*; (*hair*)
стричь *impf*, о~ *pf*; (*mow*) коси́ть
impf, с~ *pf*; (*price*) снижа́ть *impf*,
сни́зить *pf*; (*cards*) снима́ть *impf*,
снять *pf* коло́ду; ~ **back** (*prune*)
подреза́ть *impf*, подре́зать *pf*; (*re-*
duce) сокраща́ть *impf*, сократи́ть
pf; ~ **down** сруба́ть *impf*, сруби́ть
pf; ~ **off** отреза́ть *impf*, отре́зать
pf; (*interrupt*) прерыва́ть *impf*, пре-
рва́ть *pf*; (*disconnect*) отключа́ть
impf, отключи́ть *pf*; ~ **out** выре́-
зывать *impf*, вы́резать *pf*; ~ **out for**
со́зданный для+*gen*; ~ **up** раз-
реза́ть *impf*, разре́зать *pf*; *n* (*gash*)
поре́з; (*clothes*) покро́й; (*reduction*)
сниже́ние; ~ **glass** хруста́ль *m*.
cute *adj* симпати́чный.
cutlery *n* ножи́, ви́лки и ло́жки *pl*.
cutlet *n* отбивна́я котле́та.
cutting *n* (*press*) вы́резка; (*plant*)
черено́к; *adj* ре́зкий.
CV *abbr* (*of* **curriculum vitae**) авто-
биогра́фия.
cycle *n* цикл; (*bicycle*) велосипе́д; *vi*
е́здить *impf* на велосипе́де. **cyclic**
(al) *adj* цикли́ческий. **cyclist** *n* ве-
лосипеди́ст.
cylinder *n* цили́ндр. **cylindrical** *adj*
цилиндри́ческий.
cymbals *n pl* таре́лки *f pl*.
cynic *n* ци́ник. **cynical** *adj* цини́ч-
ный. **cynicism** *n* цини́зм.
cypress *n* кипари́с.
Cyrillic *n* кири́ллица.
cyst *n* киста́.
Czech *n* чех, че́шка; *adj* че́шский;
~ **Republic** Че́шская Респу́блика.

D

dab *n* мазо́к; *vt* (*eyes etc.*)
прикла́дывать *impf* плато́к к+*dat*;
~ **on** накла́дывать *impf*, наложи́ть
pf мазка́ми.

dabble *vi*: ~ **in** поверхностно заниматься *impf*, заняться *pf* +*instr*.

dachshund *n* такса.

dad, daddy *n* папа; **~-long-legs** *n* долгоножка.

daffodil *n* жёлтый нарцисс.

daft *adj* глупый.

dagger *n* кинжал.

dahlia *n* георгин.

daily *adv* ежедневно; *adj* ежедневный; *n* (*charwoman*) приходящая уборщица; (*newspaper*) ежедневная газета.

dainty *adj* изящный.

dairy *n* маслобойня; (*shop*) молочная *sb*; *adj* молочный.

dais *n* помост.

daisy *n* маргаритка.

dale *n* долина.

dally *vi* (*dawdle*) мешкать *impf*; (*toy*) играть *impf* +*instr*; (*flirt*) флиртовать *impf*.

dam *n* (*barrier*) плотина; *vt* запруживать *impf*, запрудить *pf*.

damage *n* повреждение; *pl* убытки *m pl*; *vt* повреждать *impf*, повредить *pf*.

damn *vt* (*curse*) проклинать *impf*, проклясть *pf*; (*censure*) осуждать *impf*, осудить *pf*; *int* чёрт возьми!; **I don't give a ~** мне наплевать. **damnation** *n* проклятие. **damned** *adj* проклятый.

damp *n* сырость; *adj* сырой; *vt* (*also* **dampen**) смачивать *impf*, смочить *pf*; (*fig*) охлаждать *impf*, охладить *pf*.

dance *vi* танцевать *impf*; *n* танец; (*party*) танцевальный вечер. **dancer** *n* танцор, ~ка; (*ballet*) танцовщик, -ица; балерина.

dandelion *n* одуванчик.

dandruff *n* перхоть.

Dane *n* датчанин, -анка; **Great ~** дог. **Danish** *adj* датский.

danger *n* опасность. **dangerous** *adj* опасный.

dangle *vt* &*i* покачивать(ся) *impf*.

dank *adj* промозглый.

dapper *adj* выхоленный.

dare *vi* (*have courage*) осмеливаться *impf*, осмелиться *pf*; (*have impudence*) сметь *impf*, по~ *pf*; *vt* вызывать *impf*, вызвать *pf*; *n* вызов.

daredevil *n* лихач; *adj* отчаянный.

daring *n* отвага; *adj* отчаянный.

dark *adj* тёмный; ~ **blue** тёмно-синий; *n* темнота. **darken** *vt* затемнять *impf*, затемнить *pf*; *vi* темнеть *impf*, по~ *pf*. **darkly** *adv* мрачно. **darkness** *n* темнота.

darling *n* дорогой *sb*, милый *sb*; *adj* дорогой.

darn *vt* штопать *impf*, за~ *pf*.

dart *n* стрела; (*for game*) метательная стрела; (*tuck*) вытачка; *vi* броситься *pf*.

dash *n* (*hyphen*) тире *neut indecl*; (*admixture*) примесь; *vt* швырять *impf*, швырнуть *pf*; *vi* бросаться *impf*, броситься *pf*. **dashboard** *n* приборная доска. **dashing** *adj* лихой.

data *n pl* данные *sb pl*. **database** *n* база данных.

date[1] *n* (*fruit*) финик.

date[2] *n* число, дата; (*engagement*) свидание; **out of ~** устарелый; **up to ~** современный; **в курсе дела**; *vt* датировать *impf* & *pf*; (*go out with*) встречаться *impf* c+*instr*; *vi* (*originate*) относиться *impf* (**from** к+*instr*).

dative *adj* (*n*) дательный (падеж).

daub *vt* мазать *impf*, на~ *pf* (**with** +*instr*).

daughter *n* дочь; **~-in-law** невестка (*in relation to mother*), сноха (*in relation to father*).

daunting *adj* угрожающий.

dawdle *vi* мешкать *impf*.

dawn *n* рассвет; (*also fig*) заря; *vi* (*day*) рассветать *impf*, рассвести *pf impers*; ~ (**up)on** осенять *impf*, осенить *pf*; **it ~ed on me** меня осенило.

day *n* день *m*; (*24 hours*) сутки *pl* (*period*) период, время *neut*; ~ **after** ~ изо дня в день; **the ~ after tomorrow** послезавтра; **the ~ before** накануне; **the ~ before yesterday** позавчера; **the other ~** на днях; **by ~** днём; **every other ~** через день; ~ **off** выходной день *m*; **one ~** однажды; **these ~s** в наши дни. **daybreak** *n* рассвет. **day-dreams** *n pl* мечты *f pl*. **daylight** *n* дневной свет; **in broad ~** средь бела дня. **daytime** *n*: **in the ~** днём.

daze *n*: **in a ~, dazed** *adj* оглушён (-ена).

dazzle vt ослепля́ть impf, ослепи́ть pf.

deacon n дья́кон.

dead adj мёртвый; (animals) до́хлый; (plants) увя́дший; (numb) онемёвший; n: the ~ мёртвые sb pl; at ~ of night глубо́кой но́чью; adv соверше́нно; ~ **end** тупи́к; ~ **heat** одновреме́нный фи́ниш; ~line преде́льный срок; ~**lock** тупи́к.

deaden vt заглуша́ть impf, заглуши́ть pf.

deadly adj смерте́льный.

deaf adj глухо́й; ~ **and dumb** глухонемо́й. **deafen** vt оглуша́ть impf, оглуши́ть pf. **deafness** n глухота́.

deal[1] n: **a great, good,** ~ мно́го (+gen); (with comp) гора́здо.

deal[2] n (bargain) сде́лка; (cards) сда́ча; vt (cards) сдава́ть impf, сдать pf; (blow) наноси́ть impf, нанести́ pf; ~ **in** торгова́ть impf +instr; ~ **out** распределя́ть impf, распредели́ть pf; ~ **with** (take care of) занима́ться impf, заня́ться pf +instr; (handle a person) поступа́ть impf, поступи́ть pf c+instr; (treat a subject) рассма́тривать impf, рассмотре́ть pf; (cope with) справля́ться impf, спра́виться pf c+instr. **dealer** n торго́вец (in +instr).

dean n дека́н.

dear adj дорого́й; (also n) ми́лый (sb).

dearth n недоста́ток.

death n смерть; **put to** ~ казни́ть impf & pf; ~bed n сме́ртное ло́же; ~ **certificate** свиде́тельство о сме́рти; ~ **penalty** сме́ртная казнь. **deathly** adj смерте́льный.

debar vt: ~ **from** не допуска́ть impf до+gen.

debase vt унижа́ть impf, уни́зить pf; (coinage) понижа́ть impf, пони́зить pf ка́чество +gen.

debatable adj спо́рный. **debate** n пре́ния (-ий) pl; vt обсужда́ть impf, обсуди́ть pf.

debauched adj развращённый. **debauchery** n разврат.

debilitate vt ослабля́ть; impf, осла́бить pf. **debility** n сла́бость.

debit n де́бет; vt дебетова́ть impf & pf.

debris n обло́мки m pl.

debt n долг. **debtor** n должни́к.

début n дебю́т; **make one's** ~ дебюти́ровать impf & pf.

decade n десятиле́тие.

decadence n декаде́нтство. **decadent** adj декаде́нтский.

decaffeinated adj без кофеи́на.

decant vt перелива́ть impf, перели́ть pf. **decanter** n графи́н.

decapitate vt обезгла́вливать impf, обезгла́вить pf.

decay vi гнить impf, с~ pf; (tooth) разруша́ться impf, разру́шиться pf; n гние́ние; (tooth) разруше́ние.

decease n кончи́на. **deceased** adj поко́йный; n поко́йник, -ица.

deceit n обма́н. **deceitful** adj лжи́вый. **deceive** vt обма́нывать impf, обману́ть pf.

deceleration n замедле́ние.

December n дека́брь m; adj дека́брьский.

decency n прили́чие. **decent** adj прили́чный.

decentralization n децентрализа́ция. **decentralize** vt децентрализова́ть impf & pf.

deception n обма́н. **deceptive** adj обма́нчивый.

decibel n дециба́л.

decide vt реша́ть impf, реши́ть pf. **decided** adj реши́тельный.

deciduous adj листопа́дный.

decimal n десяти́чная дробь; adj десяти́чный; ~ **point** запята́я sb.

decimate vt (fig) коси́ть impf, с~ pf.

decipher vt расшифро́вывать impf, расшифрова́ть pf.

decision n реше́ние. **decisive** adj (firm) реши́тельный, (deciding) реша́ющий.

deck n па́луба; (bus etc.) эта́ж; ~chair n шезло́нг; vt: ~ **out** украша́ть impf, укра́сить pf.

declaim vt деклами́ровать impf, про~ pf.

declaration n объявле́ние; (document) деклара́ция. **declare** vt (proclaim) объявля́ть impf, объяви́ть pf; (assert) заявля́ть impf, заяви́ть pf.

declension n склоне́ние. **decline** n упа́док; vi приходи́ть impf, прийти́ pf в упа́док; vt отклоня́ть impf, отклони́ть pf; (gram) склоня́ть impf, про~ pf.

decode *vt* расшифро́вывать *impf*, расшифрова́ть *pf*.

decompose *vi* разлага́ться *impf*, разложи́ться *pf*.

décor *n* эстети́ческое оформле́ние.

decorate *vt* украша́ть *impf*, укра́сить *pf*; (*room*) ремонти́ровать *impf*, от~ *pf*; (*with medal etc.*) награжда́ть *impf*, награди́ть *pf*. **decoration** *n* украше́ние; (*medal*) о́рден. **decorative** *adj* декорати́вный. **decorator** *n* маля́р.

decorous *adj* прили́чный. **decorum** *n* прили́чие.

decoy *n* (*bait*) прима́нка; *vt* зама́нивать *impf*, замани́ть *pf*.

decrease *vt & i* уменьша́ть(ся) *impf*, уме́ньшить(ся) *pf*; *n* уменьше́ние.

decree *n* ука́з; *vt* постановля́ть *impf*, постанови́ть *pf*.

decrepit *adj* дря́хлый.

dedicate *vt* посвяща́ть *impf*, посвяти́ть *pf*. **dedication** *n* посвяще́ние.

deduce *vt* заключа́ть *impf*, заключи́ть *pf*.

deduct *vt* вычита́ть *impf*, вы́честь *pf*. **deduction** *n* (*subtraction*) вы́чет; (*inference*) вы́вод.

deed *n* посту́пок; (*heroic*) по́двиг; (*law*) акт.

deem *vt* счита́ть *impf*, счесть *pf* +*acc & instr*.

deep *adj* глубо́кий; (*colour*) тёмный; (*sound*) ни́зкий; ~ **freeze** морози́льник. **deepen** *vt & i* углубля́ть(ся) *impf*, углуби́ть(ся) *pf*.

deer *n* оле́нь *m*.

deface *vt* обезобра́живать *impf*, обезобра́зить *pf*.

defamation *n* диффама́ция. **defamatory** *adj* клеветни́ческий.

default *n* (*failure to pay*) неупла́та; (*failure to appear*) нея́вка; (*comput*) автомати́ческий вы́бор; *vi* не выполня́ть *impf* обяза́тельств.

defeat *n* пораже́ние; *vt* побежда́ть *impf*, победи́ть *pf*. **defeatism** *n* пораже́нчество. **defeatist** *n* пораже́нец; *adj* пораже́нческий.

defecate *vi* испражня́ться *impf*, испражни́ться *pf*.

defect *n* дефе́кт; *vi* перебега́ть *impf*, перебежа́ть *pf*. **defective** *adj* неиспра́вный. **defector** *n* перебе́жчик.

defence *n* защи́та. **defenceless** *adj* беззащи́тный. **defend** *vt* защища́ть *impf*, защити́ть *pf*. **defendant** *n* подсуди́мый *sb*. **defender** *n* защи́тник. **defensive** *adj* оборони́тельный.

defer[1] *vt* (*postpone*) отсро́чивать *impf*, отсро́чить *pf*.

defer[2] *vi*: ~ **to** подчиня́ться *impf* +*dat*. **deference** *n* уваже́ние. **deferential** *adj* почти́тельный.

defiance *n* неповинове́ние; **in** ~ **of** вопреки́+*dat*. **defiant** *adj* вызыва́ющий.

deficiency *n* недоста́ток. **deficient** *adj* недоста́точный. **deficit** *n* дефици́т.

defile *vt* оскверня́ть *impf*, оскверни́ть *pf*.

define *vt* определя́ть *impf*, определи́ть *pf*. **definite** *adj* определённый **definitely** *adv* несомне́нно. **definition** *n* определе́ние. **definitive** *adj* оконча́тельный.

deflate *vt & i* спуска́ть *impf*, спусти́ть *pf*; *vt* (*person*) сбива́ть *impf*, сбить *pf* спесь с+*gen*. **deflation** *n* дефля́ция.

deflect *vt* отклоня́ть *impf*, отклони́ть *pf*.

deforestation *n* обезле́сение.

deformed *adj* уро́дливый. **deformity** *n* уро́дство.

defraud *vt* обма́нывать *impf*, обману́ть *pf*; ~ **of** выма́нивать *impf*, вы́манить *pf* +*acc & y*+*gen* (*of person*).

defray *vt* опла́чивать *impf*, оплати́ть *pf*.

defrost *vt* размора́живать *impf*, разморо́зить *pf*.

deft *adj* ло́вкий.

defunct *adj* бо́льше не существу́ющий.

defy *vt* (*challenge*) вызыва́ть *impf*, вы́звать *pf*; (*disobey*) идти́ *impf*, по~ *pf* про́тив+*acc*; (*fig*) не поддава́ться *impf* +*dat*.

degenerate *vi* вырожда́ться *impf*, вы́родиться *pf*; *adj* вы́родившийся.

degradation *n* униже́ние. **degrade** *vt* унижа́ть *impf*, уни́зить *pf*. **degrading** *adj* унизи́тельный.

degree *n* сте́пень; (*math etc.*) гра́дус; (*univ*) учёная сте́пень.

dehydrate *vt* обезво́живать *impf*,

обезво́дить *pf.* **dehydration** *n* обезво́живание.

deign *vi* снисходи́ть *impf*, снизойти́ *pf.*

deity *n* божество́.

dejected *adj* удручённый.

delay *n* заде́ржка; **without ~** неме́дленно; *vt* заде́рживать *impf*, задержа́ть *pf.*

delegate *n* делега́т; *vt* делеги́ровать *impf* & *pf.* **delegation** *n* делега́ция.

delete *vt* вычёркивать *impf*, вы́черкнуть *pf.*

deliberate *adj* (*intentional*) преднаме́ренный; (*careful*) осторо́жный; *vt* & *i* размышля́ть *impf*, размы́слить *pf* (o+*prep*); (*discuss*) совеща́ться *impf* (o+*prep*). **deliberation** *n* размышле́ние; (*discussion*) совеща́ние.

delicacy *n* (*tact*) делика́тность; (*dainty*) ла́комство. **delicate** *adj* то́нкий; (*tactful, needing tact*) делика́тный; (*health*) боле́зненный.

delicatessen *n* гастроно́м.

delicious *adj* о́чень вку́сный.

delight *n* наслажде́ние; (*delightful thing*) пре́лесть. **delightful** *adj* преле́стный.

delinquency *n* престу́пность. **delinquent** *n* правонаруши́тель *m*, ~ница; *adj* вино́вный.

delirious *adj*: **be ~** бре́дить *impf.* **delirium** *n* бред.

deliver *vt* (*goods*) доставля́ть *impf*, доста́вить *pf*; (*save*) избавля́ть *impf*, изба́вить *pf* (**from** от+*gen*); (*lecture*) прочита́ть *impf*, проче́сть *pf*; (*letters*) разноси́ть *impf*, разнести́ *pf*; (*speech*) произноси́ть *impf*, произнести́ *pf*; (*blow*) наноси́ть *impf*, нанести́ *pf.* **deliverance** *n* избавле́ние. **delivery** *n* доста́вка.

delta *n* де́льта.

delude *vt* вводи́ть *impf*, ввести́ *pf* в заблужде́ние.

deluge *n* (*flood*) пото́п; (*rain*) ли́вень *m*; (*fig*) пото́к.

delusion *n* заблужде́ние; **~s of grandeur** ма́ния вели́чия.

de luxe *adj* -люкс (*added to noun*).

delve *vi* углубля́ться *impf*, углуби́ться *pf* (**into** в+*acc*).

demand *n* тре́бование; (*econ*) спрос (**for** на+*acc*); *vt* тре́бовать *impf*, по~

pf +*gen.* **demanding** *adj* тре́бовательный.

demarcation *n* демарка́ция.

demean *vt*: **~ o.s.** унижа́ться *impf*, уни́зиться *pf.*

demeanour *n* мане́ра вести́ себя́.

demented *adj* сумасше́дший. **dementia** *n* слабоу́мие.

demise *n* кончи́на.

demobilize *vt* демобилизова́ть *impf* & *pf.*

democracy *n* демокра́тия. **democrat** *n* демокра́т. **democratic** *adj* демократи́ческий. **democratization** *n* демократиза́ция.

demolish *vt* (*destroy*) разруша́ть *impf*, разру́шить *pf*; (*building*) сноси́ть *impf*, снести́ *pf*; (*refute*) опроверга́ть *impf*, опрове́ргнуть *pf.* **demolition** *n* разруше́ние; снос.

demon *n* де́мон.

demonstrable *adj* дока́зуемый. **demonstrably** *adv* нагля́дно. **demonstrate** *vt* демонстри́ровать *impf* & *pf*; *vi* уча́ствовать *impf* в демонстра́ции. **demonstration** *n* демонстра́ция. **demonstrative** *adj* экспанси́вный; (*gram*) указа́тельный. **demonstrator** *n* демонстра́тор; (*polit*) демонстра́нт.

demoralize *vt* демонстрализова́ть *impf* & *pf.*

demote *vt* понижа́ть *impf*, пони́зить *pf* в до́лжности.

demure *adj* скро́мный.

den *n* берло́га.

denial *n* отрица́ние; (*refusal*) отка́з.

denigrate *vt* черни́ть *impf*, o~ *pf.*

denim *adj* джинсо́вый; *n* джинсо́вая ткань.

Denmark *n* Да́ния.

denomination *n* (*money*) досто́инство; (*relig*) вероисповеда́ние. **denominator** *n* знамена́тель *m*.

denote *vt* означа́ть *impf*, озна́чить *pf.*

denounce *vt* (*condemn*) осужда́ть *impf*, осуди́ть *pf*; (*inform on*) доноси́ть *impf*, донести́ *pf* на+*acc*.

dense *adj* густо́й; (*stupid*) тупо́й. **density** *n* пло́тность.

dent *n* вмя́тина; *vt* де́лать *impf*, с~ *pf* вмя́тину в+*prep*.

dental *adj* зубно́й. **dentist** *n* зубно́й врач. **dentures** *n pl* зубно́й проте́з.

denunciation n (condemnation) осуждéние; (informing) донóс.

deny vt отрицáть impf; (refuse) откáзывать impf, отказáть pf +dat (person) в+prep.

deodorant n дезодорáнт.

depart vi отбывáть impf, отбы́ть pf; (deviate) отклоня́ться impf, отклони́ться pf (from от+gen).

department n отдéл; (univ) кáфедра; ~ **store** универмáг.

departure n отбы́тие; (deviation) отклонéние.

depend vi зави́сеть impf (on от+gen); (rely) полагáться impf, положи́ться pf (on на+acc). **dependable** adj надёжный. **dependant** n иждивéнец. **dependence** n зави́симость. **dependent** adj зави́симый.

depict vt изображáть impf, изобрази́ть pf.

deplete vt истощáть impf, истощи́ть pf. **depleted** adj истощённый. **depletion** n истощéние.

deplorable adj плачéвный. **deplore** vt сожалéть impf о+prep.

deploy vt развёртывать impf, разверну́ть pf. **deployment** n развёртывание.

deport vt депорти́ровать impf & pf; высылáть impf, вы́слать pf. **deportation** n депортáция; вы́сылка.

deportment n осáнка.

depose vt сверráть impf, свéргнуть pf. **deposit** n (econ) вклад; (advance) задáток; (sediment) осáдок; (coal etc.) месторождéние; vt (econ) вноси́ть impf, внести́ pf.

depot n (transport) депó neut indecl; (store) склад.

deprave vt развращáть impf, разврати́ть pf. **depraved** adj развращённый. **depravity** n разврáт.

deprecate vt осуждáть impf, осуди́ть pf.

depreciate vt & i (econ) обесцéнивать(ся) impf, обесцéнить(ся) pf. **depreciation** n обесцéнение.

depress vt (dispirit) удручáть impf, удручи́ть pf. **depressed** adj удручённый. **depressing** adj угнетáющий. **depression** n (hollow) впáдина; (econ, med, meteorol, etc.) депрéссия.

deprivation n лишéние. **deprive** vt

лишáть impf, лиши́ть pf (of +gen).

depth n глубинá; **in the** ~ **of winter** в разгáре зимы́.

deputation n депутáция. **deputize** vi замещáть impf, замести́ть pf (for +acc). **deputy** n замести́тель m; (parl) депутáт.

derail vt: **be derailed** сходи́ть impf, сойти́ pf с рéльсов. **derailment** n сход с рéльсов.

deranged adj сумасшéдший.

derelict adj забрóшенный.

deride vt высмéивать impf, вы́смеять pf. **derision** n высмéивание. **derisive** adj (mocking) насмéшливый. **derisory** adj (ridiculous) смехотвóрный.

derivation n происхождéние. **derivative** n произвóдное sb; adj произвóдный. **derive** vt извлекáть impf, извлéчь pf; vi: ~ **from** происходи́ть impf, произойти́ pf от+gen.

derogatory adj отрицáтельный.

descend vi (& t) (go down) спускáться impf, спусти́ться pf (c+gen); **be descended from** происходи́ть impf, произойти́ pf из, от, +gen. **descendant** n потóмок. **descent** n спуск; (lineage) происхождéние.

describe vt опи́сывать impf, описáть pf. **description** n описáние. **descriptive** adj описáтельный.

desecrate vt оскверня́ть impf, оскверни́ть pf. **desecration** n осквернéние.

desert[1] n (waste) пусты́ня.

desert[2] vt покидáть impf, поки́нуть pf; (mil) дезерти́ровать impf & pf. **deserter** n дезерти́р. **desertion** n дезерти́рство.

deserts n pl заслу́ги f pl. **deserve** vt заслу́живать impf, заслужи́ть pf. **deserving** adj достóйный (of +gen).

design n (pattern) узóр; (of car etc.) констру́кция, проéкт; (industrial) дизáйн; (aim) у́мысел; vt проекти́ровать impf, c~ pf; (intend) предназначáть impf, предназнáчить pf.

designate vt (indicate) обозначáть impf, обознáчить pf; (appoint) назначáть impf, назнáчить pf.

designer n (tech) констру́ктор; (industrial) дизáйнер; (of clothes) модельéр.

desirable adj желáтельный. **desire**

n жела́ние; *vt* жела́ть *impf*, по~ *pf* +*gen*.

desist *vi* (*refrain*) возде́рживаться *impf*, воздержа́ться *pf* (**from** от+*gen*).

desk *n* пи́сьменный стол; (*school*) па́рта.

desolate *adj* забро́шенный. **desolation** *n* забро́шенность.

despair *n* отча́яние; *vi* отча́иваться *impf*, отча́яться *pf*. **desperate** *adj* отча́янный. **desperation** *n* отча́яние.

despicable *adj* презре́нный. **despise** *vt* презира́ть *impf*, презре́ть *pf*.

despite *prep* несмотря́ на+*acc*.

despondency *n* уны́ние. **despondent** *adj* уны́лый.

despot *n* де́спот.

dessert *n* десе́рт.

destination *n* (*of goods*) ме́сто назначе́ния; (*of journey*) цель. **destiny** *n* судьба́.

destitute *adj* без вся́ких средств.

destroy *vt* разруша́ть *impf*, разру́шить *pf*. **destroyer** *n* (*naut*) эсми́нец. **destruction** *n* разруше́ние. **destructive** *adj* разруши́тельный.

detach *vt* отделя́ть *impf*, отдели́ть *pf*. **detached** *adj* отде́льный; (*objective*) беспристра́стный; ~ **house** особня́к. **detachment** *n* (*objectivity*) беспристра́стие; (*mil*) отря́д.

detail *n* дета́ль, подро́бность; **in detail** подро́бно; *vt* подро́бно расска́зывать *impf*, рассказа́ть *pf*. **detailed** *adj* подро́бный.

detain *vt* заде́рживать *impf*, задержа́ть *pf*. **detainee** *n* заде́ржанный *sb*.

detect *vt* обнару́живать *impf*, обнару́жить *pf*. **detection** *n* обнаруже́ние; (*crime*) рассле́дование. **detective** *n* детекти́в; ~ **film, story,** *etc*. детекти́в. **detector** *n* дете́ктор.

detention *n* задержа́ние; (*school*) заде́ржка в наказа́ние.

deter *vt* уде́рживать *impf*, удержа́ть *pf* (**from** от+*gen*).

detergent *n* мо́ющее сре́дство.

deteriorate *vi* ухудша́ться *impf*, уху́дшиться *pf*. **deterioration** *n* ухудше́ние.

determination *n* реши́мость. **determine** *vt* (*ascertain*) устана́вливать *impf*, установи́ть *pf*; (*be decisive fac-*

tor) определя́ть *impf*, определи́ть *pf*; (*decide*) реша́ть *impf*, реши́ть *pf*. **determined** *adj* реши́тельный.

deterrent *n* сре́дство устраше́ния.

detest *vt* ненави́деть *impf*. **detestable** *adj* отврати́тельный.

detonate *vt* & *i* взрыва́ть(ся) *impf*, взорва́ть(ся) *pf*. **detonator** *n* детона́тор.

detour *n* объе́зд.

detract *vi*: ~ **from** умаля́ть *impf*, умали́ть *pf* +*acc*.

detriment *n* уще́рб. **detrimental** *adj* вре́дный.

deuce *n* (*tennis*) ра́вный счёт.

devaluation *n* девальва́ция. **devalue** *vt* девальви́ровать *impf* & *pf*.

devastate *vt* опустоша́ть *impf*, опустоши́ть *pf*. **devastated** *adj* потрясённый. **devastating** *adj* уничтожа́ющий. **devastation** *n* опустоше́ние.

develop *vt* & *i* развива́ть(ся) *impf*, разви́ть(ся) *pf*; *vt* (*phot*) проявля́ть *impf*, прояви́ть *pf*. **developer** *n* (*of land etc.*) застро́йщик. **development** *n* разви́тие.

deviant *adj* ненорма́льный. **deviate** *vi* отклоня́ться *impf*, отклони́ться *pf* (**from** от+*gen*). **deviation** *n* отклоне́ние.

device *n* прибо́р.

devil *n* чёрт. **devilish** *adj* черто́вский.

devious *adj* (*circuitous*) окружно́й; (*person*) непоря́дочный.

devise *vt* приду́мывать *impf*, приду́мать *pf*.

devoid *adj* лишённый (**of** +*gen*).

devolution *n* переда́ча (вла́сти).

devote *vt* посвяща́ть *impf*, посвяти́ть *pf*. **devoted** *adj* пре́данный. **devotee** *n* покло́нник. **devotion** *n* пре́данность.

devour *vt* пожира́ть *impf*, пожра́ть *pf*.

devout *adj* на́божный.

dew *n* роса́.

dexterity *n* ло́вкость. **dext(e)rous** *adj* ло́вкий.

diabetes *n* диабе́т. **diabetic** *n* диабе́тик; *adj* диабети́ческий.

diabolic(al) *adj* дья́вольский.

diagnose *vt* диагности́ровать *impf* & *pf*. **diagnosis** *n* диа́гноз.

diagonal n диагона́ль; adj диаго-
на́льный. **diagonally** adv по диа-
гона́ли.

diagram n диагра́мма.

dial n (clock) цифербла́т; (tech) шка-
ла́; vt набира́ть impf, набра́ть pf.

dialect n диале́кт.

dialogue n диало́г.

diameter n диа́метр. **diametric(al)**
adj диаметра́льный; ~ly opposed
диаметра́льно противополо́жный.

diamond n алма́з; (shape) ромб; pl
(cards) бу́бны (-бён, -бна́м) pl.

diaper n пелёнка.

diaphragm n диафра́гма.

diarrhoea n поно́с.

diary n дневни́к.

dice see **die¹**

dicey adj риско́ванный.

dictate vt диктова́ть impf, про~ pf.
dictation n дикто́вка. **dictator** n
дикта́тор. **dictatorial** adj дикта́тор-
ский. **dictatorship** n диктату́ра.

diction n ди́кция.

dictionary n слова́рь m.

didactic adj дидакти́ческий.

die¹ n (pl **dice**) игра́льная кость; (pl
dies) (stamp) штамп.

die² vi (person) умира́ть impf, уме-
ре́ть pf; (animal) до́хнуть impf, из~,
по~ pf; (plant) вя́нуть impf, за~ pf;
be dying to о́чень хоте́ть impf; ~
down (fire, sound) угаса́ть impf,
уга́снуть pf; ~ **out** вымира́ть impf,
вы́мереть pf.

diesel n (engine) ди́зель m; attrib
ди́зельный.

diet n дие́та; (habitual food) пи́ща;
vi быть на дие́те. **dietary** adj дие́ти-
ческий.

differ vi отлича́ться impf; разли-
ча́ться impf; (disagree) расходи́ться
impf, разойти́сь pf. **difference** n
ра́зница; (disagreement) разногла́-
сие. **different** adj разли́чный, раз-
ный. **differential** n (math, tech)
дифференциа́л; (difference) ра́зни-
ца. **differentiate** vt различа́ть impf,
различи́ть pf.

difficult adj тру́дный. **difficulty** n
тру́дность; (difficult situation) за-
трудне́ние; **without** ~ без труда́.

diffidence n неуве́ренность в себе́.
diffident adj неуве́ренный в себе́.

diffused adj рассе́янный.

dig n (archaeol) раско́пки f pl; (poke)
тычо́к; (gibe) шпи́лька; pl (lodg-
ings) кварти́ра; **give a ~ in the ribs**
ткнуть pf ло́ктем под ребро́; vt ко-
па́ть impf, вы́~ pf; рыть impf, вы́~
pf; ~ **up** (bone) выка́пывать impf,
вы́копать pf; (land) вска́пывать
impf, вскопа́ть pf.

digest vt перева́ривать impf, пере-
вари́ть pf. **digestible** adj удобова-
ри́мый. **digestion** n пищеваре́ние.

digger n (tech) экскава́тор.

digit n (math) знак.

dignified adj велича́вый. **dignitary**
n сано́вник. **dignity** n досто́инство.

digress vi отклоня́ться impf, откло-
ни́ться pf. **digression** n откло-
не́ние.

dike n да́мба; (ditch) ров.

dilapidated adj ве́тхий.

dilate vt & i расширя́ть(ся) impf,
расши́рить(ся) pf.

dilemma n диле́мма.

dilettante n дилета́нт.

diligence n прилежа́ние. **diligent** adj
приле́жный.

dilute vt разбавля́ть impf, разба́вить
pf.

dim adj (not bright) ту́склый; (vague)
сму́тный; (stupid) тупо́й.

dimension n (pl) разме́ры m pl;
(math) измере́ние. **-dimensional** in
comb -ме́рный; **three-~** трёхме́р-
ный.

diminish vt & i уменьша́ть(ся) impf,
уме́ньшить(ся) pf. **diminutive** adj
ма́ленький; n уменьши́тельное sb.

dimness n ту́склость.

dimple n я́мочка.

din n гро́хот; (voices) гам.

dine vi обе́дать impf, по~ pf. **diner**
n обе́дающий sb.

dinghy n шлю́пка; (rubber ~) на-
дувна́я ло́дка.

dingy adj (drab) ту́склый; (dirty)
гря́зный.

dining-car n ваго́н-рестора́н. **dining-
room** n столо́вая sb. **dinner** n обе́д;
~-**jacket** смо́кинг.

dinosaur n диноза́вр.

diocese n епа́рхия.

dip vt (immerse) окуна́ть impf, оку-
ну́ть pf; (partially) обма́кивать impf,
обмакну́ть pf; vi (slope) понижа́ть-
ся impf, пони́зиться pf; n (depres-

sion) впáдина; (*slope*) уклóн; **have a ~** (*bathe*) купáться *impf*, вы~ *pf*.

diphtheria *n* дифтерúя.

diphthong *n* дифтóнг.

diploma *n* д."плóм. **diplomacy** *n* дипломáтия. **diplomat** *n* дипломáт. **diplomatic** *adj* дипломатúческий.

dire *adj* стрáшный; (*ominous*) зловéщий.

direct *adj* прямóй; **~ current** постоя́нный ток; *vt* направля́ть *impf*, напрáвить *pf*; (*guide, manage*) руководúть *impf* +*instr*; (*film*) режиссúровать *impf*. **direction** *n* направлéние; (*guidance*) руковóдство; (*instruction*) указáние; (*film*) режиссу́ра; **stage ~** ремáрка. **directive** *n* директúва. **directly** *adv* пря́мо; (*at once*) срáзу. **director** *n* дирéктор; (*film etc.*) режиссёр(-постанóвщик).

directory *n* спрáвочник, указáтель *m*; (*tel*) телефóнная кнúга.

dirt *n* грязь. **dirty** *adj* гря́зный; *vt* пáчкать *impf*, за~ *pf*.

disability *n* физúческий/психúческий недостáток; (*disablement*) инвалúдность. **disabled** *adj*: **he is ~** он инвалúд.

disadvantage *n* невы́годное положéние; (*defect*) недостáток. **disadvantageous** *adj* невы́годный.

disaffected *adj* недовóльный.

disagree *vi* не соглашáться *impf*, согласúться *pf*; (*not correspond*) не соответствовать *impf* +*dat*. **disagreeable** *adj* неприя́тный. **disagreement** *n* разноглáсие; (*quarrel*) ссóра.

disappear *vi* исчезáть *impf*, исчéзнуть *pf*. **disappearance** *n* исчезновéние.

disappoint *vt* разочарóвывать *impf*, разочаровáть *pf*. **disappointed** *adj* разочарóванный. **disappointing** *adj* разочарóвывающий. **disappointment** *n* разочарованúе.

disapproval *n* неодобрéние. **disapprove** *vt & i* не одобря́ть *impf*.

disarm *vt* (*mil*) разоружáть *impf*, разоружúть *pf*; (*criminal; also fig*) обезору́живать *impf*, обезору́жить *pf*. **disarmament** *n* разоружéние.

disarray *n* беспоря́док.

disaster *n* бéдствие. **disastrous** *adj* катастрофúческий.

disband *vt* распускáть *impf*, распустúть *pf*; *vi* расходúться *impf*, разойтúсь *pf*.

disbelief *n* невéрие.

disc, disk *n* диск; **~ jockey** веду́щий *sb* передáчу.

discard *vt* отбрáсывать *impf*, отбрóсить *pf*.

discern *vt* различáть *impf*, различúть *pf*. **discernible** *adj* различúмый. **discerning** *adj* проницáтельный.

discharge *vt* (*ship etc.*) разгружáть *impf*, разгрузúть *pf* (*gun; electr*) разряжáть *impf*, разрядúть *pf*; (*dismiss*) увольня́ть *impf*, уволить *pf*; (*prisoner*) освобождáть *impf*, освободúть *pf*; (*debt; duty*) выполня́ть *impf*, вы́полнить *pf*; (*from hospital*) выпúсывать *impf*, вы́писать *pf*; *n* разгру́зка; (*electr*) разря́д; увольнéние; освобождéние; выполнéние; (*matter discharged*) выделéния *neut pl*.

disciple *n* ученúк.

disciplinarian *n* сторóнник дисциплúны. **disciplinary** *adj* дисциплинáрный. **discipline** *n* дисциплúна; *vt* дисциплинúровать *impf & pf*.

disclaim *vt* (*deny*) отрицáть *impf*; **~ responsibility** слагáть *impf*, сложúть *pf* с себя́ отвéтственность.

disclose *vt* обнáруживать *impf*, обнáружить *pf*. **disclosure** *n* обнаружéние.

discoloured *adj* обесцвéченный.

discomfit *vt* смущáть *impf*, смутúть *pf*. **discomfiture** *n* смущéние.

discomfort *n* неудóбство.

disconcert *vt* смущáть *impf*, смутúть *pf*.

disconnect *vt* разъединя́ть *impf*, разъединúть *pf*; (*switch off*) выключáть *impf*, вы́ключить *pf*. **disconnected** *adj* (*incoherent*) бессвя́зный.

disconsolate *adj* неутéшный.

discontent *n* недовóльство. **discontented** *adj* недовóльный.

discontinue *vt* прекращáть *impf*, прекратúть *pf*.

discord *n* разноглáсие; (*mus*) диссонáнс. **discordant** *adj* несогласу́ющийся; диссонúрующий.

discotheque *n* дискотéка.

discount n скидка; vt (disregard) не принимать impf, принять pf в расчёт.

discourage vt обескураживать impf, обескуражить pf; (dissuade) отговаривать impf, отговорить pf.

discourse n речь.

discourteous adj невежливый.

discover vt открывать impf, открыть pf; (find out) обнаруживать impf, обнаружить pf. **discovery** n открытие.

discredit n позор; vt дискредитировать impf & pf.

discreet adj тактичный. **discretion** n (judgement) усмотрение; (prudence) благоразумие; **at one's ~** по своему усмотрению.

discrepancy n несоответствие.

discriminate vt различать impf, различить pf; **~ against** дискриминировать impf & pf. **discrimination** n (taste) разборчивость; (bias) дискриминация.

discus n диск.

discuss vt обсуждать impf, обсудить pf. **discussion** n обсуждение.

disdain n презрение. **disdainful** adj презрительный.

disease n болезнь. **diseased** adj больной.

disembark vi высаживаться impf, высадиться pf.

disenchantment n разочарование.

disengage vt освобождать impf, освободить pf; (clutch) отпускать impf, отпустить pf.

disentangle vt распутывать impf, распутать pf.

disfavour n немилость.

disfigure vt уродовать impf, из~ pf.

disgrace n позор; (disfavour) немилость; vt позорить impf, о~ pf. **disgraceful** adj позорный.

disgruntled adj недовольный.

disguise n маскировка; vt маскировать impf, за~ pf; (conceal) скрывать impf, скрыть pf. **disguised** adj замаскированный.

disgust n отвращение; vt внушать impf, внушить pf. отвращение +dat. **disgusting** adj отвратительный.

dish n блюдо; pl посуда collect; **~washer** (посудо)моечная машина; vt: **~ up** подавать impf, подать pf.

dishearten vt обескураживать impf, обескуражить pf.

dishevelled adj растрёпанный.

dishonest adj нечестный. **dishonesty** n нечестность. **dishonour** n бесчестье; vt бесчестить impf, о~ pf. **dishonourable** adj бесчестный.

disillusion vt разочаровывать impf, разочаровать pf. **disillusionment** n разочарованность.

disinclination n несклонность, неохота. **disinclined** adj **be ~** не хотеться impers+dat.

disinfect vt дезинфицировать impf & pf. **disinfectant** n дезинфицирующее средство.

disingenuous adj неискренний.

disinherit vt лишать impf, лишить pf наследства.

disintegrate vi распадаться impf, распасться pf. **disintegration** n распад.

disinterested adj бескорыстный.

disjointed adj бессвязный.

disk see disc

dislike n нелюбовь (**for** к+dat); vt не любить impf.

dislocate vt (med) вывихнуть pf.

dislodge vt смещать impf, сместить pf.

disloyal adj нелояльный. **disloyalty** n нелояльность.

dismal adj мрачный.

dismantle vt разбирать impf, разобрать pf.

dismay vt смущать impf, смутить pf; n смущение.

dismiss vt (sack) увольнять impf, уволить pf; (disband) распускать impf, распустить pf. **dismissal** n увольнение; роспуск.

dismount vi спешиваться impf, спешиться pf.

disobedience n непослушание. **disobedient** adj непослушный. **disobey** vt не слушаться impf +gen.

disorder n беспорядок. **disorderly** adj (untidy) беспорядочный; (unruly) буйный.

disorganized adj неорганизованный.

disorientation n дезориентация. **disoriented** adj: **I am/was ~** я потерял(а) направление.

disown vt отказываться impf, отказаться pf от+gen.

disparaging adj оскорби́тельный.

disparity n нера́венство.

dispassionate adj беспристра́стный.

dispatch vt (send) отправля́ть impf, отпра́вить pf; (deal with) расправля́ться impf, распра́виться pf с+instr; n отпра́вка; (message) донесе́ние; (rapidity) быстрота́; ~ **rider** мотоцикли́ст свя́зи.

dispel vt рассе́ивать impf, рассе́ять pf.

dispensable adj необяза́тельный.

dispensary n апте́ка.

dispensation n (exemption) освобожде́ние (от обяза́тельства). **dispense** vt (distribute) раздава́ть impf, разда́ть pf; ~ **with** обходи́ться impf, обойти́сь pf без+gen.

dispersal n распростране́ние. **disperse** vt (drive away) разгоня́ть impf, разогна́ть pf; (scatter) рассе́ивать impf, рассе́ять pf; vi расходи́ться impf, разойти́сь pf.

dispirited adj удручённый.

displaced adj: ~ **persons** переме́щённые ли́ца neut pl.

display n пока́з; vt пока́зывать impf, показа́ть pf.

displeased predic недово́лен (-льна). **displeasure** n недово́льство.

disposable adj однора́зовый. **disposal** n удале́ние; **at your** ~ в ва́шем распоряже́нии. **dispose** vi: ~ **of** избавля́ться impf, изба́виться pf от+gen. **disposed** predic: ~ **to** располо́жен (-ена) к+dat or +inf. **disposition** n расположе́ние; (temperament) нрав.

disproportionate adj непропорциона́льный.

disprove vt опроверга́ть impf, опрове́ргнуть pf.

dispute n (debate) спор; (quarrel) ссо́ра; vt оспа́ривать impf, оспо́рить pf.

disqualification n дисквалифика́ция. **disqualify** vt дисквалифици́ровать impf & pf.

disquieting adj трево́жный.

disregard n пренебреже́ние +instr; vt игнори́ровать impf & pf; пренебрега́ть impf, пренебре́чь pf +instr.

disrepair n неиспра́вность.

disreputable adj по́льзующийся дурно́й сла́вой. **disrepute** n дурна́я сла́ва.

disrespect n неуваже́ние. **disrespectful** adj непочти́тельный.

disrupt vt срыва́ть impf, сорва́ть pf. **disruptive** adj подрывно́й.

dissatisfaction n недово́льство. **dissatisfied** adj недово́льный.

dissect vt разреза́ть impf, разре́зать pf; (med) вскрыва́ть impf, вскрыть pf.

disseminate vt распространя́ть impf, распространи́ть pf; **dissemination** n распростране́ние.

dissension n раздо́р. **dissent** n расхожде́ние; (eccl) раско́л.

dissertation n диссерта́ция.

disservice n плоха́я услу́га.

dissident n диссиде́нт.

dissimilar adj несхо́дный.

dissipate vt (dispel) рассе́ивать impf, рассе́ять pf; (squander) прома́тывать impf, промота́ть pf. **dissipated** adj распу́тный.

dissociate vt: ~ **o.s.** отмежёвываться impf, отмежева́ться pf (**from** от+gen).

dissolute adj распу́тный. **dissolution** n расторже́ние; (parl) ро́спуск. **dissolve** vt & i (in liquid) растворя́ть(ся) impf, раствори́ть(ся) pf; vt (annul) расторга́ть impf, расто́ргнуть pf; (parl) распуска́ть impf, распусти́ть pf.

dissonance n диссона́нс. **dissonant** adj диссони́рующий.

dissuade vt отгова́ривать impf, отговори́ть pf.

distance n расстоя́ние; **from a** ~ и́здали; **in the** ~ вдалеке́. **distant** adj далёкий, (also of relative) да́льний; (reserved) сде́ржанный.

distaste n отвраще́ние. **distasteful** adj проти́вный.

distended adj наду́тый.

distil vt (whisky) перегоня́ть impf, перегна́ть pf; (water) дистилли́ровать impf & pf. **distillation** n перего́нка; дистилля́ция. **distillery** n перего́нный заво́д.

distinct adj (different) отли́чный; (clear) отчётливый; (evident) заме́тный. **distinction** n (difference; excellence) отли́чие; (discrimination) разли́чие. **distinctive** adj отличи́тельный. **distinctly** adv я́сно.

distinguish vt различа́ть impf,

различи́ть *pf*; ~ **o.s.** отлича́ться *impf*, отличи́ться *pf*. **distinguished** *adj* выдаю́щийся.

distort *vt* искажа́ть *impf*, искази́ть *pf*; (*misrepresent*) извраща́ть *impf*, изврати́ть *pf*. **distortion** *n* искаже́ние; извраще́ние.

distract *vt* отвлека́ть *impf*, отвле́чь *pf*. **distraction** *n* (*amusement*) развлече́ние; (*madness*) безу́мие.

distraught *adj* обезу́мевший.

distress *n* (*suffering*) огорче́ние; (*danger*) бе́дствие; *vt* огорча́ть *impf*, огорчи́ть *pf*.

distribute *vt* распределя́ть *impf*, распредели́ть *pf*. **distribution** *n* распределе́ние. **distributor** *n* распредели́тель *m*.

district *n* райо́н.

distrust *n* недове́рие; *vt* не доверя́ть *impf*. **distrustful** *adj* недове́рчивый.

disturb *vt* беспоко́ить *impf*, о~ *pf*. **disturbance** *n* наруше́ние поко́я; *pl* (*polit etc.*) беспоря́дки *m pl*.

disuse *n* неупотребле́ние; **fall into** ~ выходи́ть *impf*, вы́йти *pf* из употребле́ния. **disused** *adj* вы́шедший из употребле́ния.

ditch *n* кана́ва, ров.

dither *vi* колеба́ться *impf*.

ditto *n* то же са́мое; *adv* так же.

divan *n* дива́н.

dive *vi* ныря́ть *impf*, нырну́ть *pf*; (*aeron*) пики́ровать *impf & pf*; *n* ныро́к, прыжо́к в во́ду. **diver** *n* водола́з.

diverge *vi* расходи́ться *impf*, разойти́сь *pf*. **divergent** *adj* расходя́щийся.

diverse *adj* разнообра́зный. **diversification** *n* расшире́ние ассортиме́нта. **diversify** *vt* разнообра́зить *impf*. **diversion** *n* (*detour*) объе́зд; (*amusement*) развлече́ние. **diversity** *n* разнообра́зие. **divert** *vt* отклоня́ть *impf*, отклони́ть *pf*; (*amuse*) развлека́ть *impf*, развле́чь *pf*. **diverting** *adj* заба́вный.

divest *vt* (*deprive*) лиша́ть *impf*, лиши́ть *pf* (**of** +*gen*); ~ **o.s.** отка́зываться *impf*, отказа́ться *pf* (**of** от+*gen*).

divide *vt* (*share; math*) дели́ть *impf*, по~ *pf*; (*separate*) разделя́ть *impf*, раздели́ть *pf*. **dividend** *n* дивиде́нд.

divine *adj* боже́ственный.

diving *n* ныря́ние; ~-**board** трампли́н.

divinity *n* (*quality*) боже́ственность; (*deity*) божество́; (*theology*) богосло́вие.

divisible *adj* дели́мый. **division** *n* (*dividing*) деле́ние, разделе́ние; (*section*) отде́л; (*mil*) диви́зия.

divorce *n* разво́д; *vi* разводи́ться *impf*, развести́сь *pf*. **divorced** *adj* разведённый.

divulge *vt* разглаша́ть *impf*, разгласи́ть *pf*.

DIY *abbr* (*of* **do-it-yourself**): **he is good at** ~ у него́ золоты́е ру́ки; ~ **shop** магази́н «сде́лай сам».

dizziness *n* головокруже́ние. **dizzy** *adj* (*causing dizziness*) головокружи́тельный; **I am** ~ у меня́ кру́жится голова́.

DNA *abbr* (*of* **deoxyribonucleic acid**) ДНК.

do *vt* де́лать *impf*, с~ *pf*; *vi* (*be suitable*) годи́ться *impf*; (*suffice*) быть доста́точным; ~-**it-yourself** *see* DIY; **that will** ~ хва́тит!; **how** ~ **you** ~? здра́вствуйте!; из вы пожива́ете?; ~ **away with** (*abolish*) уничтожа́ть *impf*, уничто́жить *pf*; ~ **in** (*kill*) убива́ть *impf*, уби́ть *pf*; ~ **up** (*restore*) ремонти́ровать *impf*, от~ *pf*; (*wrap up*) завёртывать *impf*, заверну́ть *pf*; (*fasten*) застёгивать *impf*, застегну́ть *pf*; ~ **without** обходи́ться *impf*, обойти́сь *pf* без+*gen*.

docile *adj* поко́рный. **docility** *n* поко́рность.

dock[1] *n* (*naut*) док; *vt* ста́вить *impf*, по~ *pf* в док; *vi* входи́ть *impf*, войти́ *pf* в док; *vi* (*spacecraft*) стыкова́ться *impf*, со~ *pf*. **docker** *n* до́кер. **dockyard** *n* верфь.

dock[2] *n* (*law*) скамья́ подсуди́мых.

docket *n* квита́нция; (*label*) ярлы́к.

doctor *n* врач; (*also univ*) до́ктор; *vt* (*castrate*) кастри́ровать *impf & pf*; (*spay*) удаля́ть *impf*, удали́ть *pf* я́йчники у+*gen*; (*falsify*) фальсифици́ровать *impf & pf*. **doctorate** *n* сте́пень до́ктора.

doctrine *n* доктри́на.

document *n* докуме́нт; *vt* документи́ровать *impf & pf*. **documentary** *n* документа́льный фильм. **docu-**

mentation n документация.

doddery adj дряхлый.

dodge n увёртка; vt уклоняться impf, уклониться pf от+gen; (jump to avoid) отскакивать impf, отскочить pf (от+gen). **dodgy** adj каверзный.

doe n самка.

dog n собака, пёс; (fig) преследовать impf. **dog-eared** adj захватанный.

dogged adj упорный.

dogma n догма. **dogmatic** adj догматический.

doings n pl дела neut pl.

doldrums n: be in the ~ хандрить impf.

dole n пособие по безработице; vt (~ out) выдавать impf, выдать pf.

doleful adj скорбный.

doll n кукла.

dollar n доллар.

dollop n солидная порция.

dolphin n дельфин.

domain n (estate) владение; (field) область.

dome n купол.

domestic adj (of household; animals) домашний; (of family) семейный; (polit) внутренний; n прислуга. **domesticate** vt приручать impf, приручить pf. **domesticity** n домашняя, семейная, жизнь.

domicile n местожительство.

dominance n господство. **dominant** adj преобладающий; господствующий. **dominate** vt господствовать impf над+instr. **domineering** adj властный.

dominion n владычество; (realm) владение.

domino n кость домино; pl (game) домино neut indecl.

don vt надевать impf, надеть pf.

donate vt жертвовать impf, по~ pf. **donation** n пожертвование.

donkey n осёл.

donor n жертвователь m; (med) донор.

doom n (ruin) гибель; vt обрекать impf, обречь pf.

door n дверь. **doorbell** n (дверной) звонок. **doorman** n швейцар. **doormat** n половик. **doorstep** n порог. **doorway** n дверной проём.

dope n (drug) наркотик; vt дурманить impf, о~ pf.

dormant adj (sleeping) спящий; (inactive) бездействующий.

dormer window n слуховое окно.

dormitory n общая спальня.

dormouse n соня.

dorsal adj спинной.

dosage n дозировка. **dose** n доза.

dossier n досье neut indecl.

dot n точка; vt ставить impf, по~ pf точки на+acc; (scatter) усеивать impf, усеять pf (with +instr); ~ted line пунктир.

dote vi: ~ on обожать impf.

double adj двойной; (doubled) удвоенный; ~-bass контрабас; ~ bed двуспальная кровать; ~-breasted двубортный; ~-cross обманывать impf, обмануть pf; ~-dealer двурушник; ~-dealing двурушничество; ~-decker двухэтажный автобус; ~-edged обоюдоострый; ~ glazing двойные рамы f pl; ~ room комната на двоих; adv вдвое; (two together) вдвоём; n двойное количество; (person's) двойник; pl (sport) парная игра; vt & i удваивать(ся) impf, удвоить(ся) pf; ~ back возвращаться impf, вернуться pf назад; ~ up (in pain) скрючиваться impf, скрючиться pf; (share a room) помещаться impf, поместиться pf вдвоём в одной комнате; (~ up as) работать impf + instr по совместительству.

doubt n сомнение; vt сомневаться impf в+prep. **doubtful** adj сомнительный. **doubtless** adv несомненно.

dough n тесто. **doughnut** n пончик.

douse vt (drench) заливать impf, залить pf.

dove n голубь m. **dovetail** n ласточкин хвост.

dowdy adj неэлегантный.

down¹ n (fluff) пух.

down² adv (motion) вниз; (position) внизу; be ~ with (ill) болеть impf +instr; prep вниз с+gen, по+dat; (along) (вдоль) по+dat; vt: (gulp) опрокидывать impf, опрокинуть pf; ~-and-out бродяга m; ~cast, ~hearted унылый. **downfall** n гибель. **downhill** adv под гору. **downpour**

n ли́вень *m*. **downright** *adj* я́вный;
adv совершéнно. **downstairs** *adv*
(*motion*) вниз; (*position*) внизу́.
downstream *adv* вниз по течéнию.
down-to-earth *adj* реалисти́ческий.
downtrodden *adj* угнетённый.
dowry *n* прида́ное *sb*.
doze *vi* дрема́ть *impf*.
dozen *n* дю́жина.
drab *adj* бесцвéтный; (*boring*) ску́ч-
ный.
draft *n* (*outline, rough copy*) набро́-
сок; (*document*) проéкт; (*econ*)
тра́тта; *see also* **draught**; *vt* состав-
ля́ть *impf*, соста́вить *pf* план, проéкт, +*gen*.
drag *vt* тащи́ть *impf*; (*river etc.*)
драги́ровать *impf* & *pf*; ~ **on** (*vi*)
затя́гиваться *impf*, затяну́ться *pf*; *n*
(*burden*) обу́за; (*on cigarette*) затя́ж-
ка; **in** ~ в жéнской одéжде.
dragon *n* драко́н. **dragonfly** *n* стре-
коза́.
drain *n* водосто́к; (*leakage; fig*) утéч-
ка; *vt* осуша́ть *impf*, осуши́ть *pf*; *vi*
спуска́ться *impf*, спусти́ться *pf*.
drainage *n* дренáж; (*system*) канали-
за́ция.
drake *n* сéлезень *m*.
drama *n* дра́ма; (*quality*) драмати́зм.
dramatic *adj* драмати́ческий. **drama-
tist** *n* драмату́рг. **dramatize** *vt* драма-
тизи́ровать *impf* & *pf*.
drape *vt* драпирова́ть *impf*, за~ *pf*;
n драпиро́вка.
drastic *adj* радика́льный.
draught *n* (*air*) сквозня́к; (*traction*)
тя́га; *pl* (*game*) ша́шки *f pl*; *see also*
draft; **there is a** ~ сквози́т; ~ **beer**
пи́во из бо́чки. **draughtsman** *n* чертёжник. **draughty** *adj*: **it is** ~ **here**
здесь ду́ет.
draw *n* (*in lottery*) ро́зыгрыш; (*attraction*) прима́нка; (*drawn game*)
ничья́; *vt* (*pull*) тяну́ть *impf*, по~
pf; таска́ть *indet*, тащи́ть *det*; (*cur-
tains*) задёргивать *impf*, задёрнуть
pf (занавéски); (*attract*) привлека́ть
impf, привлéчь *pf*; (*pull out*) выта́-
скивать *impf*, вы́тащить *pf*; (*sword*)
обнажа́ть *impf*, обнажи́ть *pf*; (*lots*)
броса́ть *impf*, бро́сить *pf* (жрéбий);
(*water; inspiration*) чéрпать *impf*,
черпну́ть *pf*; (*evoke*) вызыва́ть *impf*,
вы́звать *pf*; (*conclusion*) выводи́ть

impf, вы́вести *pf* (заключéние);
(*diagram*) черти́ть *impf*, на~ *pf*;
(*picture*) рисова́ть *impf*, на~ *pf*; *vi*
(*sport*) сыгра́ть *pf* вничью́; ~ **aside**
отводи́ть *impf*, отвести́ *pf* в сто́-
рону; ~ **back** (*withdraw*) отступа́ть
impf, отступи́ть *pf*; ~ **in** втя́гивать
impf, втяну́ть *pf*; (*train*) входи́ть
impf, войти́ *pf* в ста́нцию; (*car*)
подходи́ть *impf*, подойти́ *pf* (**to** к +
dat); (*days*) станови́ться *impf* ко-
ро́че; ~ **out** выта́гивать *impf*,
вы́тянуть *pf*; (*money*) выпи́сывать
impf, вы́писать *pf* (*train/car*) вы-
ходи́ть *impf*, вы́йти *pf* (со ста́нции/
на доро́гу); ~ **up** (*car*) подходи́ть
impf, подойти́ *pf* (**to** к + *dat*); (*document*) составля́ть *impf*, соста́вить
pf. **drawback** *n* недоста́ток. **drawbridge** *n* подъёмный мост. **drawer**
n я́щик. **drawing** *n* (*action*) рисо-
ва́ние, черчéние; (*object*) рису́нок,
чертёж; ~**-board** чертёжная доска́;
~**-pin** кно́пка; ~**-room** гости́ная *sb*.
drawl *n* протя́жное произношéние.
dread *n* страх; *vt* боя́ться *impf* +*gen*.
dreadful *adj* ужа́сный.
dream *n* сон; (*fantasy*) мечта́; *vi*
ви́деть *impf*, y~ *pf* сон; ~ **of** ви́деть
impf, y~ *pf* во снé; (*fig*) мечта́ть
impf o+*prep*.
dreary *adj* (*weather*) па́смурный;
(*boring*) ску́чный.
dredge *vt* (*river etc.*) драги́ровать
impf & *pf*. **dredger** *n* дра́га.
dregs *n pl* оса́дки (-ков) *pl*.
drench *vt* прома́чивать *impf*, про-
мочи́ть *pf*; **get ~ed** промока́ть *impf*,
промо́кнуть *pf*.
dress *n* пла́тье; (*apparel*) одéжда; ~
circle бельэта́ж; ~**maker** портни́ха;
~ **rehearsal** генера́льная репети́ция;
vt & *i* одева́ть(ся) *impf*, одéть(ся)
pf; *vt* (*cul*) приправля́ть *impf*, при-
пра́вить *pf*; (*med*) перевя́зывать *impf*,
перевяза́ть *pf*; ~ **up** наряжа́ться
impf, наряди́ться *pf* (**as** + *instr*).
dresser *n* ку́хонный шкаф.
dressing *n* (*cul*) припра́ва; (*med*)
перевя́зка; ~**-gown** хала́т; ~**-room**
убо́рная *sb*; ~**-table** туалéтный сто́-
лик.
dribble *vi* (*person*) пуска́ть *impf*,
пусти́ть *pf* слю́ни; (*sport*) вести́
impf мяч.

dried adj сушёный. **drier** n сушилка.

drift n (meaning) смысл; (snow) сугроб; vi плыть impf по течению; (naut) дрейфовать impf; (snow etc.) скопляться impf, скопиться pf; ~ **apart** расходиться impf, разойтись pf.

drill[1] n сверло; (dentist's) бур; vt сверлить impf, про~ pf.

drill[2] vt (mil) обучать impf, обучить pf строю; vi проходить impf, пройти pf строевую подготовку; n строевая подготовка.

drink n напиток; vt пить impf, вы~ pf; ~-**driving** вождение в нетрезвом состоянии. **drinking-water** n питьевая вода.

drip n (action) капанье; (drop) капля; vi капать impf, капнуть pf.

drive n (journey) езда; (excursion) прогулка; (campaign) поход, кампания; (energy) энергия; (tech) привод; (driveway) подъездная дорога; vt (urge; chase) гонять indet, гнать det; (vehicle) водить indet, везти det; управлять impf +instr; (convey) возить indet, везти det, по~ pf; vi (travel) ездить indet, ехать det, по~ pf; vi доводить impf, довести pf (**to** до+gen); (nail etc.) вбивать impf, вбить pf (**into** в+acc); ~ **away** vt прогонять impf, прогнать pf; vi уезжать impf, уехать pf; ~ **up** подъезжать impf, подъехать pf (**to** к+dat).

driver n (of vehicle) водитель m, шофёр. **driving** adj (force) движущий; (rain) проливной; ~-**licence** водительские права neut pl; ~-**test** экзамен на получение водительских прав; ~-**wheel** ведущее колесо.

drizzle n мелкий дождь m; vi моросить impf.

drone n (bee; idler) трутень m; (of voice) жужжание; (of engine) гул; vi (buzz) жужжать impf; (~ **on**) бубнить impf.

drool vi пускать impf, пустить pf слюни.

droop vi поникать impf, поникнуть pf.

drop n (of liquid) капля; (fall) падение, понижение; vt & i (price) снижать(ся) impf, снизить(ся) pf; vi (fall) падать impf, упасть pf; vt (let fall) ронять impf, уронить pf; (aban-

don) бросать impf, бросить pf; ~ **behind** отставать impf, отстать pf; ~ **in** заходить impf, зайти pf (**on** к+dat); ~ **off** (fall asleep) засыпать impf, заснуть pf; (from car) высаживать impf, высадить pf; ~ **out** выбывать impf, выбыть pf (**of** из+gen). **droppings** n pl помёт.

drought n засуха.

droves n pl: **in** ~ толпами.

drown vt топить impf, y~ pf; (sound) заглушать impf, заглушить pf; vi тонуть impf, y~ pf.

drowsy adj сонливый.

drudgery n нудная работа.

drug n медикамент; (narcotic) наркотик; ~ **addict** наркоман, ~ка; vt давать impf, дать pf наркотик+dat.

drum n барабан; vi бить impf в барабан; барабанить impf; ~ **sth into s.o.** вдалбливать impf, вдолбить pf + dat of person в голову. **drummer** n барабанщик.

drunk adj пьяный. **drunkard** n пьяница m & f. **drunken** adj пьяный; ~ **driving** вождение в нетрезвом состоянии. **drunkenness** n пьянство.

dry adj сухой; ~ **land** суша; vt сушить impf, вы~ pf; (wipe dry) вытирать impf, вытереть pf; vi сохнуть impf, вы~, про~ pf. **dry-cleaning** n химчистка. **dryness** n сухость.

dual adj двойной; (joint) совместный; ~-**purpose** двойного назначения.

dub[1] vt (nickname) прозывать impf, прозвать pf.

dub[2] vt (cin) дублировать impf & pf.

dubious adj сомнительный.

duchess n герцогиня. **duchy** n герцогство.

duck[1] n (bird) утка.

duck[2] vt (immerse) окунать impf, окунуть pf; (one's head) нагнуть pf; (evade) увёртываться impf, увернуться pf от+gen; vi (~ **down**) наклоняться impf, наклониться pf. **duckling** n утёнок.

duct n проход; (anat) проток.

dud n (forgery) подделка; (shell) неразорвавшийся снаряд; adj поддельный; (worthless) негодный.

due n (credit) должное sb; pl взносы m pl; adj (proper) должный, надлежащий; predic (expected) должен

(-жна́); in ~ course со вре́менем; ~ south пря́мо на юг; ~ to благодаря́ +dat.

duel n дуэ́ль.

duet n дуэ́т.

duke n ге́рцог.

dull adj (tedious) ску́чный; (colour) ту́склый, (weather) па́смурный; (not sharp; stupid) тупо́й; vt притупля́ть impf, притупи́ть pf.

duly adv надлежа́щим о́бразом; (punctually) своевре́менно.

dumb adj немо́й. **dumbfounded** adj ошара́шенный.

dummy n (tailor's) манеке́н; (baby's) со́ска; ~ run испыта́тельный рейс.

dump n сва́лка; vt сва́ливать impf, свали́ть pf.

dumpling n клёцка.

dumpy adj призе́мистый.

dune n дю́на.

dung n наво́з.

dungarees n pl комбинезо́н.

dungeon n темни́ца.

dunk vt мака́ть impf, макну́ть pf.

duo n па́ра; (mus) дуэ́т.

dupe vt надува́ть impf, наду́ть pf; n простофи́ля m & f.

duplicate n ко́пия; in ~ в двух экземпля́рах; adj (double) двойно́й; (identical) идентичный; vt размножа́ть impf, размно́жить pf **duplicity** n двули́чность.

durability n про́чность. **durable** adj про́чный. **duration** n продолжи́тельность.

duress n принужде́ние; under ~ под давле́нием.

during prep во вре́мя +gen; (throughout) в тече́ние +gen.

dusk n су́мерки (-рек) pl.

dust n пыль; ~bin му́сорный я́щик; ~-jacket суперобло́жка; ~man му́сорщик; ~pan сово́к; vt & i (clean) стира́ть impf, стере́ть pf пыль (c+gen); (sprinkle) посыпа́ть impf, посы́пать pf sth +acc, with +instr. **duster** n пы́льная тря́пка. **dusty** adj пы́льный.

Dutch adj голла́ндский; n: the ~ голла́ндцы m pl. **Dutchman** n голла́ндец. **Dutchwoman** n голла́ндка.

dutiful adj послу́шный. **duty** n (obligation) долг; обя́занность; (office) дежу́рство; (tax) по́шлина; be on ~

дежу́рить impf; ~-free adj беспо́шлинный.

dwarf n ка́рлик; vt (tower above) возвыша́ться impf, возвы́ситься pf над +instr.

dwell vi обита́ть impf; ~ upon остана́вливаться impf на+prep. **dweller** n жи́тель m. **dwelling** n жили́ще.

dwindle vi убыва́ть impf, убы́ть pf.

dye n краси́тель m; vt окра́шивать impf, окра́сить pf.

dynamic adj динами́ческий. **dynamics** n pl дина́мика.

dynamite n динами́т.

dynamo n дина́мо neut indecl.

dynasty n дина́стия.

dysentery n дизентери́я.

dyslexia n дисле́ксия. **dyslexic** adj: he is ~ он дисле́ктик.

E

each adj & pron ка́ждый; ~ other друг дру́га (dat -гу, etc.).

eager adj (pupil) усе́рдный; I am ~ to мне не те́рпится +inf; о́чень жела́ю +inf. **eagerly** adv с нетерпе́нием; жа́дно. **eagerness** n си́льное жела́ние.

eagle n орёл.

ear[1] n (corn) ко́лос.

ear[2] n (anat) у́хо; (sense) слух; ~ache боль в у́хе; ~drum бараба́нная перепо́нка; ~mark (assign) предназнача́ть impf, предназна́чить pf; ~phone нау́шник; ~ring серьга́; (clip-on) клипс; ~shot: within ~ в преде́лах слы́шимости; out of ~ вне преде́лов слы́шимости.

earl n граф.

early adj ра́нний; adv ра́но.

earn vt зараба́тывать impf, зарабо́тать pf; (deserve) заслу́живать impf, заслужи́ть pf; earnings n pl за́работок.

earnest adj серьёзный; n: in ~ всерьёз.

earth n (ground) земля́; (soil) по́чва; vt заземля́ть impf, заземли́ть pf. **earthenware** n гли́няный. **earthly** adj земно́й. **earthquake** n землетрясе́ние. **earthy** adj земли́стый; (coarse) гру́бый.

earwig n уховёртка.

ease n (*facility*) лёгкость; (*unconstraint*) непринуждённость; **with ~** легко; vt облегчáть *impf*, облегчи́ть *pf*; vi успокáиваться *impf*, успокóиться *pf*.
easel n мольбéрт.
east n востóк; (*naut*) ост; *adj* востóчный. **easterly** *adj* востóчный. **eastern** *adj* востóчный. **eastward(s)** *adv* на востóк, к востóку.
Easter n Пáсха.
easy *adj* лёгкий; (*unconstrained*) непринуждённый; **~-going** уживчивый.
eat vt есть *impf*, с~ *pf*; по~, с~ *pf*; **~ away** разъедáть *impf*, разъéсть *pf*; **~ into** въедáться *impf*, въéсться *pf* в+*acc*; **~ up** доедáть *impf*, доéсть *pf*. **eatable** *adj* съедóбный.
eaves n pl стрехá. **eavesdrop** vi подслýшивать *impf*.
ebb n (*tide*) отли́в; (*fig*) упáдок.
ebony n чёрное дéрево.
ebullient *adj* кипýчий.
EC *abbr* (*of European Community*) Европéйское соббщество.
eccentric n чудáк; *adj* эксцентри́чный.
ecclesiastical *adj* церкóвный.
echo n э́хо; vi (*resound*) отражáться *impf*, отрази́ться *pf*; vt (*repeat*) повторя́ть *impf*, повтори́ть *pf*.
eclipse n затмéние; vt затмевáть *impf*, затми́ть *pf*.
ecological *adj* экологи́ческий. **ecology** n эколóгия.
economic *adj* экономи́ческий. **economical** *adj* экономный. **economist** n экономи́ст. **economize** vt & i экономить *impf*, с~ *pf*. **economy** n экономика; (*saving*) эконóмия.
ecstasy n экстáз. **ecstatic** *adj* экстати́ческий.
eddy n водоворóт.
edge n край; (*blade*) лéзвие; **on ~** в нéрвном состоя́нии; **have the ~ on** имéть *impf* преимýщество над+*instr*; vt (*border*) окаймля́ть *impf*, окайми́ть *pf*; vi пробирáться *impf*, пробрáться *pf*. **edging** n каймá. **edgy** *adj* раздражи́тельный.
edible *adj* съедóбный.
edict n укáз.
edifice n здáние. **edifying** *adj* назидáтельный.

edit vt редакти́ровать *impf*, от~ *pf*; (*cin*) монти́ровать *impf*, с~ *pf*. **edition** n издáние; (*number of copies*) тирáж. **editor** n редáктор. **editorial** n передовáя статья́; *adj* редáкторский, редакцио́нный.
educate vt давáть *impf*, дать *pf* образовáние +*dat*; **where was he educated?** где он получи́л образовáние? **educated** *adj* образóванный. **education** n образовáние. **educational** *adj* образовáтельный; (*instructive*) учéбный.
eel n ýгорь m.
eerie *adj* жýткий.
effect n (*result*) слéдствие; (*validity*; *influence*) дéйствие; (*impression*; *theat*) эффéкт; **in ~** факти́чески; **take ~** вступáть *impf*, вступи́ть *pf* в си́лу; (*medicine*) начинáть *impf*, начáть *pf* дéйствовать; vt производи́ть *impf*, произвести́ *pf*. **effective** *adj* эффекти́вный; (*striking*) эффéктный; (*actual*) факти́ческий. **effectiveness** n эффекти́вность.
effeminate *adj* женоподóбный.
effervesce vi пузыри́ться *impf*. **effervescent** *adj* (*fig*) и́скря́щийся.
efficiency n эффекти́вность. **efficient** *adj* эффекти́вный; (*person*) организóванный.
effigy n изображéние.
effort n уси́лие.
effrontery n нáглость.
effusive *adj* экспанси́вный.
e.g. *abbr* напр.
egalitarian *adj* эгалитáрный.
egg[1] n яйцó; **~cup** рюмка для яйцá; **~shell** яи́чная скорлупá.
egg[2] vt: **~ on** подстрекáть *impf*, подстрекнýть *pf*.
ego n «Я». **egocentric** *adj* эгоцентри́ческий. **egoism** n эгои́зм. **ego(t)ist** n эгои́ст, **~ка**. **ego(t)istical** *adj* эгоцентри́ческий. **egotism** n эготи́зм.
Egypt n Еги́пет. **Egyptian** n египтя́нин, **-я́нка**; *adj* еги́петский.
eiderdown n пуховое одея́ло.
eight *adj* & n вóсемь; (*number 8*) восьмёрка. **eighteen** *adj* & n восемнáдцать. **eighteenth** *adj* & n восемнáдцатый. **eighth** *adj* & n восьмóй; (*fraction*) восьмáя sb. **eightieth** *adj* & n восьмидеся́тый.

eighty adj & n восемьдесят; pl (decade) восьмидесятые годы (-дов) m pl.

either adj & pron (one of two) один из двух, тот или другой; (both) и тот, и другой; оба; (one or other) любой; adv & conj: ~ ... or или... или, либо... либо.

eject vt выбрасывать impf, выбросить pf; vi (pilot) катапультироваться impf & pf.

eke vt: ~ out a living перебиваться impf, перебиться pf кое-как.

elaborate adj (ornate) витиеватый; (detailed) подробный; vt разрабатывать impf, разработать pf; (detail) уточнять impf, уточнить pf.

elapse vi проходить impf, пройти pf; (expire) истекать impf, истечь pf.

elastic n резинка; adj эластичный, ~ **band** резинка. **elasticity** n эластичность.

elated adj в восторге. **elation** n восторг.

elbow n локоть m; vt: ~ (one's way) **through** проталкиваться impf, протолкнуться pf через+acc.

elder[1] n (tree) бузина.

elder[2] n (person) старец, pl старшие sb; adj старший. **elderly** adj пожилой. **eldest** adj старший.

elect adj избранный; vt избирать impf, избрать pf. **election** n выборы m pl. **elector** n избиратель m. **electoral** adj избирательный. **electorate** n избиратели m pl.

electric(al) adj электрический; ~ **shock** удар электрическим током. **electrician** n электрик. **electricity** n электричество. **electrify** vt (convert to electricity) электрифицировать impf & pf; (charge with electricity; fig) электризовать impf, наpf. **electrode** n электрод. **electron** n электрон. **electronic** adj электронный. **electronics** n электроника.

electrocute vt убивать impf, убить pf электрическим током; (execute) казнить impf & pf на электрическом стуле. **electrolysis** n электролиз.

elegance n элегантность. **elegant** adj элегантный.

elegy n элегия.

element n элемент; (earth, wind, etc.) стихия; be in one's ~ быть в своей стихии. **elemental** adj стихийный. **elementary** adj элементарный; (school etc.) начальный.

elephant n слон.

elevate vt поднимать impf, поднять pf. **elevated** adj возвышенный. **elevation** n (height) высота. **elevator** n (lift) лифт.

eleven adj & n одиннадцать. **eleventh** adj & n одиннадцатый; at the ~ **hour** в последнюю минуту.

elf n эльф.

elicit vt (obtain) выявлять impf, выявить pf; (evoke) вызывать impf, вызвать pf.

eligible adj имеющий право (**for** на+acc); (bachelor) подходящий.

eliminate vt (do away with) устранять impf, устранить pf; (rule out) исключать impf, исключить pf.

élite n элита.

ellipse n эллипс. **elliptic(al)** adj эллиптический.

elm n вяз.

elocution n ораторское искусство.

elongate vt удлинять impf, удлинить pf.

elope vi бежать det (с возлюбленным).

eloquence n красноречие. **eloquent** adj красноречивый.

else adv (besides) ещё; (instead) другой; (with neg) больше; **nobody** ~ никто больше; **or** ~ иначе; а (не) то; или же; **s.o.** ~ кто-нибудь другой; **something** ~? ещё что-нибудь?

elsewhere adv (place) в другом месте; (direction) в другое место.

elucidate vt разъяснять impf, разъяснить pf.

elude vt избегать impf +gen. **elusive** adj неуловимый.

emaciated adj истощённый.

emanate vi исходить impf (**from** из, от, +gen).

emancipate vt эмансипировать impf & pf. **emancipation** n эмансипация.

embankment n (river) набережная sb; (rly) насыпь.

embargo n эмбарго neut indecl.

embark vi садиться impf, сесть pf на корабль; ~ **upon** предпринимать impf, предпринять pf. **embarkation**

n посáдка (на корáбль).

embarrass *vt* смущáть *impf*, смутúть *pf*; be ~ed чýвствовать *impf* себя́ неудóбно. **embarrassing** *adj* неудóбный. **embarrassment** *n* смущéние.

embassy *n* посóльство.

embedded *adj* врéзанный.

embellish *vt* (*adorn*) украшáть *impf*, укрáсить *pf*; (*story*) прикрáшивать *impf*, прикрáсить *pf*. **embellishment** *n* украшéние.

embers *n pl* тлéющие уголькú *m pl*.

embezzle *vt* растрáчивать *impf*, растрáтить *pf*. **embezzlement** *n* растрáта.

embitter *vt* ожесточáть *impf*, ожесточúть *pf*.

emblem *n* эмблéма.

embodiment *n* воплощéние. **embody** *vt* воплощáть *impf*, воплотúть *pf*.

emboss *vt* чекáнить *impf*, вы́~, от~ *pf*.

embrace *n* объя́тие; *vi* обнимáться *impf*, обня́ться *pf*; *vt* обнимáть *impf*, обня́ть *pf*; (*accept*) принимáть *impf*, приня́ть *pf*; (*include*) охвáтывать *impf*, охватúть *pf*.

embroider *vt* вышивáть *impf*, вы́шить *pf*; (*story*) прикрáшивать *impf*, прикрáсить *pf*. **embroidery** *n* вы́шивка.

embroil *vt* впу́тывать *impf*, впу́тать *pf*.

embryo *n* эмбриóн.

emerald *n* изумрýд.

emerge *vi* появля́ться *impf*, появúться *pf*. **emergence** *n* появлéние. **emergency** *n* крáйняя необходúмость; state of ~ чрезвычáйное положéние; ~ exit запаснóй вы́ход.

emery paper *n* наждáчная бумáга.

emigrant *n* эмигрáнт, ~ка. **emigrate** *vi* эмигрúровать *impf & pf*. **emigration** *n* эмигрáция.

eminence *n* (*fame*) знаменúтость. **eminent** *adj* выдаю́щийся. **eminently** *adv* чрезвычáйно.

emission *n* испускáние. **emit** *vt* испускáть *impf*, испустúть *pf*; (*light*) излучáть *impf*, излучúть *pf*; (*sound*) издавáть *impf*, издáть *pf*.

emotion *n* эмóция, чýвство. **emotional** *adj* эмоционáльный.

empathize *vt* сопережива́ть *impf*, сопережúть *pf*. **empathy** *n* эмпáтия.

emperor *n* имперáтор.

emphasis *n* ударéние. **emphasize** *vt* подчёркивать *impf*, подчеркнýть *pf*. **emphatic** *adj* вырази́тельный; категорúческий.

empire *n* импéрия.

empirical *adj* эмпирúческий.

employ *vt* (*use*) пóльзоваться *impf* +*instr*; (*person*) нанимáть *impf*, наня́ть *pf*. **employee** *n* сотрýдник, рабóчий *sb*. **employer** *n* работодáтель *m*. **employment** *n* рабóта, слýжба; (*use*) использование.

empower *vt* уполномóчивать *impf*, уполномóчить *pf* (to на+*acc*).

empress *n* императрúца.

emptiness *n* пустотá. **empty** *adj* пустóй; ~-headed пустоголóвый; *vt* (*container*) опорожня́ть *impf*, опорóжнить *pf*; (*solid*) высыпáть *impf*, вы́сыпать *pf*; (*liquid*) выливáть *impf*, вы́лить *pf*; *vi* пустéть *impf*, о~ *pf*.

emulate *vt* достигáть *impf*, достúгнуть, достúчь *pf* +*gen*; (*copy*) подражáть *impf* +*dat*.

emulsion *n* эмýльсия.

enable *vt* давáть *impf*, дать *pf* возмóжность +*dat* & *inf*.

enact *vt* (*law*) принимáть *impf*, приня́ть *pf*; (*theat*) разы́грывать *impf*, разыгрáть *pf*. **enactment** *n* (*law*) постановлéние; (*theat*) игрá.

enamel *n* эмáль; *adj* эмáлевый; *vt* эмалировáть *impf & pf*.

encampment *n* лáгерь *m*.

enchant *vt* очарóвывать *impf*, очаровáть *pf*. **enchanting** *adj* очаровáтельный. **enchantment** *n* очаровáние.

encircle *vt* окружáть *impf*, окружúть *pf*.

enclave *n* анклáв.

enclose *vt* огорáживать *impf*, огородúть *pf*; (*in letter*) прилагáть *impf*, приложúть *pf*; please find ~d прилагáется (-áются) +*nom*. **enclosure** *n* огорóженное мéсто; (*in letter*) приложéние.

encode *vt* шифровáть *impf*, за~ *pf*.

encompass *vt* (*encircle*) окружáть *impf*, окружúть *pf*; (*contain*) заключáть *impf*, заключúть *pf*.

encore *int* бис!; *n* вы́зов на бис.

encounter *n* встре́ча; (*in combat*) столкнове́ние; *vt* встреча́ть *impf*, встре́тить *pf*; (*fig*) ста́лкиваться *impf*, столкну́ться *pf* c+*instr*.

encourage *vt* ободря́ть *impf*, ободри́ть *pf*. **encouragement** *n* ободре́ние. **encouraging** *adj* ободри́тельный.

encroach *vt* вторга́ться *impf*, вто́ргнуться *pf* (**on** в+*acc*). **encroachment** *n* вторже́ние.

encumber *vt* обременя́ть *impf*, обремени́ть *pf*. **encumbrance** *n* обу́за.

encyclopaedia *n* энциклопе́дия. **encyclopaedic** *adj* энциклопеди́ческий.

end *n* коне́ц; (*death*) смерть; (*purpose*) цель; **an ~ in itself** самоце́ль; **in the ~** в конце́ концо́в; **make ~s meet** своди́ть *impf*, свести́ *pf* концы́ с конца́ми; **no ~ of** ма́сса+*gen*; **on ~** (*upright*) стоймя́, ды́бом; (*continuously*) подря́д; **put an ~to** класть *impf*, положи́ть *pf* коне́ц +*dat*; *vt* конча́ть *impf*, ко́нчить *pf*; (*halt*) прекраща́ть *impf*, прекрати́ть *pf*; *vi* конча́ться *impf*, ко́нчиться *pf*.

endanger *vt* подверга́ть *impf*, подве́ргнуть *pf* опа́сности.

endearing *adj* привлека́тельный. **endearment** *n* ла́ска.

endeavour *n* попы́тка; (*exertion*) уси́лие; (*undertaking*) де́ло; *vi* стара́ться *impf*, по~ *pf*.

endemic *adj* эндеми́ческий.

ending *n* оконча́ние. **endless** *adj* бесконе́чный.

endorse *vt* (*document*) подпи́сывать *impf*, подписа́ть *pf*; (*support*) подде́рживать *impf*, поддержа́ть *pf*. **endorsement** *n* по́дпись; подде́ржка; (*on driving licence*) проко́л.

endow *vt* обеспе́чивать *impf*, обеспе́чить *pf* постоя́нным дохо́дом; (*fig*) одаря́ть *impf*, одари́ть *pf*. **endowment** *n* поже́ртвование; (*talent*) дарова́ние.

endurance *n* (*of person*) выно́сливость; (*of object*) про́чность. **endure** *vt* выноси́ть *impf*, вы́нести *pf*; терпе́ть *impf*, по~ *pf*; *vi* продолжа́ться *impf*, продо́лжиться *pf*.

enemy *n* враг; *adj* вра́жеский.

energetic *adj* энерги́чный. **energy** *n*

эне́ргия; *pl* си́лы *f pl*.

enforce *vt* (*law etc.*) следи́ть *impf* за выполне́нием +*gen*. **enforcement** *n* наблюде́ние за выполне́нием +*gen*.

engage *vt* (*hire*) нанима́ть *impf*, наня́ть *pf*; (*tech*) зацепля́ть *impf*, зацепи́ть *pf*. **engaged** *adj* (*occupied*) за́нятый; **be ~ in** занима́ться *impf*, заня́ться *pf* +*instr*; **become ~** обруча́ться *impf*, обручи́ться *pf* (**to** c+*instr*). **engagement** *n* (*appointment*) свида́ние; (*betrothal*) обруче́ние; (*battle*) бой; **~ ring** обруча́льное кольцо́. **engaging** *adj* привлека́тельный.

engender *vt* порожда́ть *impf*, породи́ть *pf*.

engine *n* дви́гатель *m*; (*rly*) локомоти́в; **~-driver** (*rly*) машини́ст. **engineer** *n* инжене́р; *vt* (*fig*) организова́ть *impf* & *pf*. **engineering** *n* инжене́рное де́ло, те́хника.

England *n* А́нглия. **English** *adj* англи́йский; *n*: **the ~** *pl* англича́не (-н) *pl*. **Englishman, -woman** *n* англича́нин, -а́нка.

engrave *vt* гравирова́ть *impf*, вы́~ *pf*; (*fig*) вреза́ть *impf*, вре́зать *pf*. **engraver** *n* граве́р. **engraving** *n* гравю́ра.

engross *vt* поглоща́ть *impf*, поглоти́ть *pf*; **be ~ed in** быть поглощённым +*instr*.

engulf *vt* поглоща́ть *impf*, поглоти́ть *pf*.

enhance *vt* увели́чивать *impf*, увели́чить *pf*.

enigma *n* зага́дка. **enigmatic** *adj* зага́дочный.

enjoy *vt* получа́ть *impf*, получи́ть *pf* удово́льствие от+*gen*; наслажда́ться *impf*, наслади́ться *pf* +*instr*; (*health etc.*) облада́ть *impf* +*instr*; **~ o.s.** хорошо́ проводи́ть *impf*, провести́ *pf* вре́мя. **enjoyable** *adj* прия́тный. **enjoyment** *n* удово́льствие.

enlarge *vt* увели́чивать *impf*, увели́чить *pf*; **~ upon** распространя́ться *impf*, распространи́ться *pf* о+*prep*. **enlargement** *n* увеличе́ние.

enlighten *vt* просвеща́ть *impf*, просвети́ть *pf*. **enlightenment** *n* просвеще́ние.

enlist *vi* поступа́ть *impf*, поступи́ть *pf* на вое́нную слу́жбу; *vt* (*mil*) вербова́ть *impf*, за~ *pf*; (*support etc.*) заруча́ться *impf*, заручи́ться *pf* +*instr*.

enliven *vt* оживля́ть *impf*, оживи́ть *pf*.

enmity *n* вражда́.

ennoble *vt* облагора́живать *impf*, облагоро́дить *pf*.

ennui *n* тоска́.

enormity *n* чудо́вищность. **enormous** *adj* огро́мный. **enormously** *adv* чрезвыча́йно.

enough *adj* доста́точно +*gen*; *adv* доста́точно, дово́льно; **be** ~ хвата́ть *impf*, хвати́ть *pf impers*+*gen*.

enquire, enquiry *see* **inquire, inquiry**

enrage *vt* беси́ть *impf*, вз~ *pf*.

enrapture *vt* восхища́ть *impf*, восхити́ть *pf*.

enrich *vt* обогаща́ть *impf*, обогати́ть *pf*.

enrol *vt & i* запи́сывать(ся) *impf*, записа́ть(ся) *pf*. **enrolment** *n* за́пись.

en route *adv* по пути́ (**to, for** в+*acc*).

ensconce *vt*: ~ **o.s.** заса́живаться *impf*, засе́сть *pf* (**with** за+*acc*).

ensemble *n* (*mus*) анса́мбль *m*.

enshrine *vt* (*fig*) охраня́ть *impf*, охрани́ть *pf*.

ensign *n* (*flag*) флаг.

enslave *vt* порабоща́ть *impf*, поработи́ть *pf*.

ensue *vi* сле́довать *impf*. **ensuing** *adj* после́дующий.

ensure *vt* обеспе́чивать *impf*, обеспе́чить *pf*.

entail *vt* (*necessitate*) влечь *impf* за собо́й.

entangle *vt* запу́тывать *impf*, запу́тать *pf*.

enter *vt & i* входи́ть *impf*, войти́ *pf* в+*acc*; (*by transport*) въезжа́ть *impf*, въе́хать *pf* в+*acc*; *vt* (*join*) поступа́ть *impf*, поступи́ть *pf* в, на, +*acc*; (*competition*) вступа́ть *impf*, вступи́ть *pf* в+*acc*; (*in list*) вноси́ть *impf*, внести́ *pf* в+*acc*.

enterprise *n* (*undertaking*) предприя́тие; (*initiative*) предприи́мчивость. **enterprising** *adj* предприи́мчивый.

entertain *vt* (*amuse*) развлека́ть *impf*, развле́чь *pf*; (*guests*) принима́ть *impf*, приня́ть *pf*; угоща́ть *impf*, угости́ть *pf* (**to** +*instr*); (*hopes*) пита́ть *impf*. **entertaining** *adj* зани-ма́тельный. **entertainment** *n* развлече́ние; (*show*) представле́ние.

enthral *vt* порабоща́ть *impf*, поработи́ть *pf*.

enthusiasm *n* энтузиа́зм. **enthusiast** *n* энтузиа́ст, ~ка. **enthusiastic** *adj* восто́рженный; по́лный энтузиа́зма.

entice *vt* зама́нивать *impf*, замани́ть *pf*. **enticement** *n* прима́нка. **enticing** *adj* зама́нчивый.

entire *adj* по́лный, це́лый, весь. **entirely** *adv* вполне́, соверше́нно; (*solely*) исключи́тельно. **entirety** *n*: **in its** ~ по́лностью.

entitle *vt* (*authorize*) дава́ть *impf*, дать *pf* пра́во+*dat* (**to** на+*acc*); **be** ~d (*book*) называ́ться *impf*; **be** ~d **to** име́ть *impf* пра́во на+*acc*.

entity *n* объе́кт; фено́мен.

entomology *n* энтомоло́гия.

entourage *n* сви́та.

entrails *n pl* вну́тренности (-тей) *pl*.

entrance[1] *n* вход, въезд; (*theat*) вы́ход; ~ **exam** вступи́тельный экза́мен; ~ **hall** вестибю́ль *m*.

entrance[2] *vt* (*charm*) очаро́вывать *impf*, очарова́ть *pf*. **entrancing** *adj* очарова́тельный.

entrant *n* уча́стник (**for** +*gen*).

entreat *vt* умоля́ть *impf*, умоли́ть *pf*. **entreaty** *n* мольба́.

entrench *vt* **be, become** ~ed (*fig*) укореня́ться *impf*, укорени́ться *pf*.

entrepreneur *n* предпринима́тель *m*.

entrust *vt* (*secret*) вверя́ть *impf*, вве́рить *pf* (**to** +*dat*); (*object*; *person*) поруча́ть *impf*, поручи́ть *pf* (**to** +*dat*).

entry *n* вход, въезд; вступле́ние; (*theat*) вы́ход; (*note*) за́пись; (*in reference book*) статья́.

entwine *vt* (*interweave*) сплета́ть *impf*, сплести́ *pf*; (*wreathe*) обвива́ть *impf*, обви́ть *pf*.

enumerate *vt* перечисля́ть *impf*, перечи́слить *pf*.

enunciate *vt* (*express*) излага́ть *impf*, изложи́ть *pf*; (*pronounce*) произноси́ть *impf*, произнести́ *pf*. **enunciation** *n* изложе́ние; произноше́ние.

envelop *vt* оку́тывать *impf*, оку́тать *pf*. **envelope** *n* конве́рт.

enviable *adj* зави́дный. **envious** *adj* зави́стливый.

environment n среда́; (the ~) окружа́ющая среда́. **environs** n pl окре́стности f pl.

envisage vt предусма́тривать impf, предусмотре́ть pf.

envoy n посла́нник, аге́нт.

envy n за́висть; vt зави́довать impf, по~ pf +dat.

enzyme n энзи́м.

ephemeral adj эфеме́рный.

epic n эпопе́я; adj эпи́ческий.

epidemic n эпиде́мия.

epilepsy n эпиле́псия. **epileptic** n эпиле́птик; adj эпилепти́ческий.

epilogue n эпило́г.

episode n эпизо́д. **episodic** adj эпизоди́ческий.

epistle n посла́ние.

epitaph n эпита́фия.

epithet n эпи́тет.

epitome n воплоще́ние. **epitomize** vt воплоща́ть impf, воплоти́ть pf.

epoch n эпо́ха.

equal adj ра́вный, одина́ковый; (capable of) спосо́бный (to на+acc, +inf); n ра́вный sb; vt равня́ться impf +dat. **equality** n ра́венство.

equalize vt ура́внивать impf, уравня́ть pf; vi (sport) равня́ть impf, с~ pf счёт. **equally** adv равно́, ра́вным о́бразом.

equanimity n хладнокро́вие.

equate vt прира́внивать impf, приравня́ть pf (with к+dat).

equation n (math) уравне́ние.

equator n эква́тор. **equatorial** adj экваториа́льный.

equestrian adj ко́нный.

equidistant adj равностоя́щий. **equilibrium** n равнове́сие.

equip vt обору́довать impf & pf; (person) снаряжа́ть impf, снаряди́ть pf; (fig) вооружа́ть impf, вооружи́ть pf. **equipment** n обору́дование, снаряже́ние.

equitable adj справедли́вый. **equity** n справедли́вость; pl (econ) обыкнове́нные а́кции f pl.

equivalent adj эквивале́нтный; n эквивале́нт.

equivocal adj двусмы́сленный.

era n э́ра.

eradicate vt искореня́ть impf, искорени́ть pf.

erase vt стира́ть impf, стере́ть pf; (from memory) вычёркивать impf, вы́черкнуть pf (из па́мяти). **eraser** n ла́стик.

erect adj прямо́й; vt сооружа́ть impf, сооруди́ть pf. **erection** n сооруже́ние; (biol) эре́кция.

erode vt разруша́ть impf, разру́шить pf. **erosion** n эро́зия; (fig) разруше́ние.

erotic adj эроти́ческий.

err vi ошиба́ться impf, ошиби́ться pf; (sin) греши́ть impf, со~ pf.

errand n поруче́ние; run ~s быть на посы́лках (for y+gen).

erratic adj неро́вный.

erroneous adj оши́бочный. **error** n оши́бка.

erudite adj учёный. **erudition** n эруди́ция.

erupt vi взрыва́ться impf, взорва́ться pf; (volcano) изверга́ться impf, изве́ргнуться pf. **eruption** n изверже́ние.

escalate vi возраста́ть impf, возрасти́ pf; vt интенсифици́ровать impf & pf.

escalator n эскала́тор.

escapade n вы́ходка. **escape** n (from prison) побе́г; (from danger) спасе́ние; (leak) уте́чка; have a narrow ~ едва́ спасти́сь; vi (flee) бежа́ть impf & pf; убега́ть impf, убежа́ть pf; (save o.s.) спаса́ться impf, спасти́сь pf; (leak) утека́ть impf, уте́чь pf; vt избега́ть impf, избежа́ть pf +gen; (groan) вырыва́ться impf, вы́рваться pf из, у, +gen.

escort n (mil) эско́рт; (of lady) кавале́р; vt сопровожда́ть impf, сопроводи́ть pf; (mil) эскорти́ровать impf & pf.

Eskimo n эскимо́с, ~ка.

esoteric adj эзотери́ческий.

especially adv осо́бенно.

espionage n шпиона́ж.

espousal n подде́ржка. **espouse** vt (fig) подде́рживать impf, поддержа́ть pf.

essay n о́черк.

essence n (philos) су́щность; (gist) суть; (extract) эссе́нция. **essential** adj (fundamental) суще́ственный; (necessary) необходи́мый; n pl (necessities) необходи́мое sb; (crux) суть; (fundamentals) осно́вы f pl.

essentially *adv* по существу́.

establish *vt* (*set up*) учрежда́ть *impf*, учреди́ть *pf*; (*fact etc.*) устана́вливать *impf*, установи́ть *pf*. **establishment** *n* (*action*) учрежде́ние, установле́ние; (*institution*) учрежде́ние.

estate *n* (*property*) име́ние; (*after death*) насле́дство; (*housing ~*) жило́й масси́в; ~ **agent** аге́нт по прода́же недви́жимости; ~ **car** автомоби́ль *m* с ку́зовом «универса́л».

esteem *n* уваже́ние; *vt* уважа́ть *impf*. **estimate** *n* (*of quality*) оце́нка; (*of cost*) сме́та; *vt* оце́нивать *impf*, оцени́ть *pf*. **estimation** *n* оце́нка, мне́ние.

Estonia *n* Эсто́ния. **Estonian** *n* эсто́нец, -нка; *adj* эсто́нский.

estranged *adj* отчуждённый. **estrangement** *n* отчужде́ние.

estuary *n* у́стье.

etc. *abbr* и т.д. **etcetera** и так да́лее.

etch *vt* трави́ть *impf*, вы́- *pf*. **etching** *n* (*action*) травле́ние; (*object*) офо́рт.

eternal *adj* ве́чный. **eternity** *n* ве́чность.

ether *n* эфи́р. **ethereal** *adj* эфи́рный.

ethical *adj* эти́ческий, эти́чный. **ethics** *n* э́тика.

ethnic *adj* этни́ческий.

etiquette *n* этике́т.

etymology *n* этимоло́гия.

EU *abbr* (*of* European Union) ЕС.

eucalyptus *n* эвкали́пт.

Eucharist *n* прича́стие.

eulogy *n* похвала́.

euphemism *n* эвфеми́зм. **euphemistic** *adj* эвфемисти́ческий.

Europe *n* Евро́па. **European** *n* европе́ец; *adj* европе́йский; ~ **Community** Европе́йское соо́бщество; ~ **Union** Европе́йский сою́з.

evacuate *vt* (*person, place*) эваку́ировать *impf & pf*. **evacuation** *n* эвакуа́ция.

evade *vt* уклоня́ться *impf*, уклони́ться *pf* от+*gen*.

evaluate *vt* оце́нивать *impf*, оцени́ть *pf*. **evaluation** *n* оце́нка.

evangelical *adj* ева́нгельский. **evangelist** *n* евангели́ст.

evaporate *vt & i* испаря́ть(ся) *impf*, испари́ть(ся) *pf*. **evaporation** *n* испаре́ние.

evasion *n* уклоне́ние (**of** от+*gen*). **evasive** *adj* укло́нчивый.

eve *n* кану́н; **on the ~** накану́не.

even *adj* ро́вный; (*number*) чётный; **get ~** расквита́ться *pf* (**with** c+*instr*); *adv* да́же; (*just*) как раз; (*with comp*) ещё; ~ **if** да́же е́сли; ~ **though** хотя́; ~ **so** всё-таки; **not ~** да́же не; *vt* выра́внивать *impf*, вы́ровнять *pf*.

evening *n* ве́чер; *adj* вече́рний; ~ **class** вече́рние ку́рсы *m pl*.

evenly *adv* по́ровну, ро́вно. **evenness** *n* ро́вность.

event *n* собы́тие, происше́ствие; **in the ~ of** в слу́чае+*gen*; **in any ~** во вся́ком слу́чае; **in the ~** в коне́чном счёте. **eventful** *adj* по́лный собы́тий. **eventual** *adj* коне́чный. **eventuality** *n* возмо́жность. **eventually** *adv* в конце́ концо́в.

ever *adv* (*at any time*) когда́-либо, когда́-нибудь; (*always*) всегда́; (*emph*) же; ~ **since** с тех пор (как); ~ **so** о́чень; **for ~** навсегда́; **hardly ~** почти́ никогда́. **evergreen** *adj* вечнозелёный; *n* вечнозелёное расте́ние. **everlasting** *adj* ве́чный. **evermore** *adv*: **for ~** навсегда́.

every *adj* ка́ждый, вся́кий, все (*pl*); ~ **now and then** вре́мя от вре́мени; ~ **other** ка́ждый второ́й; ~ **other day** че́рез день. **everybody, everyone** *pron* ка́ждый, все (*pl*). **everyday** *adj* (*daily*) ежедне́вный; (*commonplace*) повседне́вный. **everything** *pron* всё. **everywhere** *adv* всю́ду, везде́.

evict *vt* выселя́ть *impf*, вы́селить *pf*. **eviction** *n* выселе́ние.

evidence *n* свиде́тельство, доказа́тельство; **give ~** свиде́тельствовать *impf* (о+*prep*; +*acc*; +что). **evident** *adj* очеви́дный.

evil *n* зло; *adj* злой.

evoke *vt* вызыва́ть *impf*, вы́звать *pf*.

evolution *n* эволю́ция. **evolutionary** *adj* эволюцио́нный. **evolve** *vt & i* развива́ть(ся) *impf*, разви́ть(ся) *pf*.

ewe *n* овца́.

ex- *in comb* бы́вший.

exacerbate *vt* обостря́ть *impf*, обостри́ть *pf*.

exact *adj* то́чный; *vt* взы́скивать

impf, взыскáть *pf* (**from, of** с+*gen*).
exacting *adj* трéбовательный. **ex-
actitude, exactness** *n* тóчность.
exactly *adv* тóчно; (*just*) как раз;
(*precisely*) úменно.
exaggerate *vt* преувелúчивать *impf*,
преувелúчить *pf*. **exaggeration** *n*
преувеличéние.
exalt *vt* возвышáть *impf*, возвы́сить
pf; (*extol*) превозносúть *impf*, пре-
вознестú *pf*.
examination *n* (*inspection*) осмóтр;
(*exam*) экзáмен; (*law*) допрóс. **examine** *vt* (*inspect*) осмáтривать
impf, осмотрéть *pf*; (*test*) экзаме-
новáть *impf*, про~ *pf*; (*law*) допрá-
шивать *impf*, допросúть *pf*. **examiner** *n* экзаменáтор.
example *n* примéр; **for ~** напримéр.
exasperate *vt* раздражáть *impf*, раз-
дражúть *pf*. **exasperation** *n* раздра-
жéние.
excavate *vt* раскáпывать *impf*, рас-
копáть *pf*. **excavations** *n pl* рас-
кóпки *f pl*. **excavator** *n* экскавáтор.
exceed *vt* превышáть *impf*, пре-
вы́сить *pf*. **exceedingly** *adv* чрезвычáйно.
excel *vt* превосходúть *impf*, пре-
взойтú *pf*; *vi* отличáться *impf*,
отличúться *pf* (**at, in** в+*prep*). **excellence** *n* превосхóдство. **excellency** *n* превосходúтельство. **excellent** *adj* отлúчный.
except *vt* исключáть *impf*, исклю-
чúть *pf*; *prep* крóме+*gen*. **exception**
n исключéние; **take ~ to** возражáть
impf, возразúть *pf* прóтив+*gen*. **exceptional** *adj* исключúтельный.
excerpt *n* отры́вок.
excess *n* избы́ток. **excessive** *adj*
чрезмéрный.
exchange *n* обмéн (**of** +*instr*); (*of
currency*) размéн; (*building*) бúржа;
(*telephone*) центрáльная телефóнная стáнция; **~ rate** курс; *vt* обмé-
нивать *impf*, обменя́ть *pf* (**for**
на+*acc*); обмéниваться *impf*, обмé-
ня́ться *pf* +*instr*.
Exchequer *n* казначéйство.
excise[1] *n* (*duty*) акцúз(ный сбор).
excise[2] *vt* (*cut out*) вырезáть *impf*,
вы́резать *pf*.
excitable *adj* возбудúмый. **excite** *vt*
(*cause, arouse*) возбуждáть *impf*,

возбудúть *pf*; (*thrill, agitate*) вол-
новáть *impf*, вз~ *pf*. **excitement** *n*
возбуждéние; волнéние.
exclaim *vi* восклицáть *impf*, вос-
клúкнуть *pf*. **exclamation** *n* воскли-
цáние; **~ mark** восклицáтельный
знак.
exclude *vt* исключáть *impf*, исклю-
чúть *pf*. **exclusion** *n* исключéние.
exclusive *adj* исключúтельный.
excommunicate *vt* отлучáть *impf*,
отлучúть *pf* (**от** цéркви).
excrement *n* экскремéнты (-тов) *pl*.
excrete *vt* выделя́ть *impf*, вы́делить
pf. **excretion** *n* выделéние.
excruciating *adj* мучúтельный.
excursion *n* экскýрсия.
excusable *adj* простúтельный. **excuse** *n* оправдáние; (*pretext*) отго-
вóрка; *vt* (*forgive*) извиня́ть *impf*,
извинúть *pf*; (*justify*) опрáвдывать
impf, оправдáть *pf*; (*release*) освобождáть *impf*, освободúть *pf* (**from**
от+*gen*); **~ me!** извинúте!; прос-
тúте!
execute *vt* исполня́ть *impf*, испóлнить *pf*; (*criminal*) казнúть *impf* &
pf. **execution** *n* исполнéние; казнь.
executioner *n* палáч. **executive** *n*
исполнúтельный óрган; (*person*)
руководúтель *m*; *adj* исполнúтельный.
exemplary *adj* примéрный. **exem-
plify** *vt* (*illustrate by example*) при-
водúть *impf*, привестú *pf* примéр
+*gen*; (*serve as example*) служúть
impf, по~ *pf* примéром +*gen*.
exempt *adj* освобождённый; *vt* освобождáть *impf*, освободúть *pf* (**from**
от+*gen*). **exemption** *n* освобождéние.
exercise *n* (*use*) применéние; (*physical ~; task*) упражнéние; **take ~**
упражня́ться *impf*; **~ book** тетрáдь;
vt (*use*) применя́ть *impf*, применúть
pf; (*dog*) прогýливать *impf*; (*train*)
упражня́ть *impf*.
exert *vt* окáзывать *impf*, оказáть *pf*;
~ o.s. старáться *impf*, по~ *pf*. **exertion** *n* напряжéние.
exhale *vt* выдыхáть *impf*, вы́дохнуть
pf.
exhaust *n* вы́хлоп; **~ fumes** выхлоп-
нúе гáзы *m pl*; **~ pipe** выхлопнáя
трубá; *vt* (*use up*) истощáть *impf*,

exhibit 323 export

истощи́ть *pf*; (*person*) изнуря́ть *impf*, изнури́ть *pf*; (*subject*) исчёрпывать *impf*, исчёрпать *pf*. **exhausted** *adj*: be ~ (*person*) быть измождённым. **exhausting** *adj* изнури́тельный. **exhaustion** *n* изнуре́ние; (*depletion*) истоще́ние. **exhaustive** *adj* исчёрпывающий.

exhibit *n* экспона́т; (*law*) веще́ственное доказа́тельство; *vt* (*manifest*) проявля́ть *impf*, прояви́ть *pf*; (*publicly*) выставля́ть *impf*, вы́ставить *pf*. **exhibition** *n* проявле́ние; (*public* ~) вы́ставка. **exhibitor** *n* экспоне́нт.

exhilarated *adj* в припо́днятом настрое́нии. **exhilarating** *adj* возбужда́ющий. **exhilaration** *n* возбужде́ние.

exhort *vt* увещева́ть *impf*. **exhortation** *n* увещева́ние.

exhume *vt* выка́пывать *impf*, вы́копать *pf*.

exile *n* изгна́ние; (*person*) изгна́нник; *vt* изгоня́ть *impf*, изгна́ть *pf*.

exist *vi* существова́ть *impf*. **existence** *n* существова́ние. **existing** *adj* существу́ющий.

exit *n* вы́ход; (*theat*) ухо́д (со сце́ны); ~ **visa** выездна́я ви́за; *vi* уходи́ть *impf*, уйти́ *pf*.

exonerate *vt* опра́вдывать *impf*, оправда́ть *pf*.

exorbitant *adj* непоме́рный.

exorcize *vt* (*spirits*) изгоня́ть *impf*, изгна́ть *pf*.

exotic *adj* экзоти́ческий.

expand *vt & i* расширя́ть(ся) *impf*, расши́рить(ся) *pf*; ~ on распространя́ться *impf*, распространи́ться *pf* o+*prep*. **expanse** *n* простра́нство. **expansion** *n* расшире́ние. **expansive** *adj* экспанси́вный.

expatriate *n* экспатриа́нт, ~ка.

expect *vt* (*await*) ожида́ть *impf* +*gen*; ждать *impf* +*gen*, что; (*suppose*) полага́ть *impf*; (*require*) тре́бовать *impf* +*gen*, что́бы. **expectant** *adj* выжида́тельный; ~ **mother** бере́менная же́нщина. **expectation** *n* ожида́ние.

expediency *n* целесообра́зность. **expedient** *n* приём; *adj* целесообра́зный. **expedite** *vt* ускоря́ть *impf*, уско́рить *pf*. **expedition** *n* экспе-

ди́ция. **expeditionary** *adj* экспедицио́нный.

expel *vt* (*drive out*) выгоня́ть *impf*, вы́гнать *pf*; (*from school etc.*) исключа́ть *impf*, исключи́ть *pf*; (*from country etc.*) изгоня́ть *impf*, изгна́ть *pf*.

expend *vt* тра́тить *impf*, ис~, по~ *pf*. **expendable** *adj* необяза́тельный. **expenditure** *n* расхо́д. **expense** *n* расхо́д; *pl* расхо́ды *m pl*, at the ~ of за счёт+*gen*; (*fig*) цено́ю+*gen*. **expensive** *adj* дорого́й.

experience *n* о́пыт; (*incident*) пережива́ние; *vt* испы́тывать *impf*, испыта́ть *pf*; (*undergo*) пережива́ть *impf*, пережи́ть *pf*. **experienced** *adj* о́пытный.

experiment *n* экспериме́нт; *vi* эксперименти́ровать *impf* (**on, with** над, с+*instr*). **experimental** эксперимента́льный.

expert *n* экспе́рт; *adj* о́пытный. **expertise** *n* специа́льные зна́ния *neut pl*.

expire *vi* (*period*) истека́ть *impf*, исте́чь *pf*. **expiry** *n* истече́ние.

explain *vt* объясня́ть *impf*, объясни́ть *pf*. **explanation** *n* объясне́ние. **explanatory** *adj* объясни́тельный.

expletive *n* (*oath*) бра́нное сло́во.

explicit *adj* я́вный; (*of person*) прямо́й.

explode *vt & i* взрыва́ть(ся) *impf*, взорва́ть(ся) *pf*; *vt* (*discredit*) опроверга́ть *impf*, опрове́ргнуть *pf*; *vi* (*with anger etc.*) разража́ться *impf*, разрази́ться *pf*.

exploit *n* по́двиг; *vt* эксплуати́ровать *impf*; (*use to advantage*) испо́льзовать *impf & pf*. **exploitation** *n* эксплуата́ция. **exploiter** *n* эксплуата́тор.

exploration *n* иссле́дование. **exploratory** *adj* иссле́довательский. **explore** *vt* иссле́довать *impf & pf*. **explorer** *n* иссле́дователь *m*.

explosion *n* взрыв. **explosive** *n* взры́вчатое вещество́; *adj* взры́вчатый; (*fig*) взрывно́й.

exponent *n* (*interpreter*) истолкова́тель *m*; (*advocate*) сторо́нник.

export *n* вы́воз, э́кспорт; *vt* вывози́ть *impf*, вы́везти *pf*; экспорти́ровать *impf & pf*. **exporter** *n* экспортёр.

expose vt (*bare*) раскрывать *impf*, раскрыть *pf*; (*subject*) подвергать *impf*, подвергнуть *pf* (**to** +*dat*); (*discredit*) разоблачать *impf*, разоблачить *pf*; (*phot*) экспонировать *impf* & *pf*.

exposition n изложение.

exposure n подвергание (**to** +*dat*); (*phot*) выдержка; (*unmasking*) разоблачение; (*med*) холод.

expound vt излагать *impf*, изложить *pf*.

express n (*train*) экспресс; *adj* (*clear*) точный; (*purpose*) специальный; (*urgent*) срочный; vt выражать *impf*, выразить *pf*. **expression** n выражение; (*expressiveness*) выразительность. **expressive** *adj* выразительный. **expressly** *adv* (*clearly*) ясно; (*specifically*) специально.

expropriate vt экспроприировать *impf* & *pf*. **expropriation** n экспроприация.

expulsion n (*from school etc.*) исключение; (*from country etc.*) изгнание.

exquisite *adj* утончённый.

extant *adj* сохранившийся.

extempore *adv* экспромптом. **extemporize** vt & i импровизировать *impf*, сымпровизировать *pf*.

extend vt (*stretch out*) протягивать *impf*, протянуть *pf*; (*enlarge*) расширять *impf*, расширить *pf*; (*prolong*) продлевать *impf*, продлить *pf*; vi простираться *impf*, простереться *pf*. **extension** n (*enlarging*) расширение; (*time*) продление; (*to house*) пристройка; (*tel*) добавочный. **extensive** *adj* обширный. **extent** n (*degree*) степень.

extenuating *adj*: ~ **circumstances** смягчающие вину обстоятельства *neut pl*.

exterior n внешность; *adj* внешний.

exterminate vt истреблять *impf*, истребить *pf*. **extermination** n истребление.

external *adj* внешний.

extinct *adj* (*volcano*) потухший; (*species*) вымерший; **become** ~ вымирать *impf*, вымереть *pf*. **extinction** n вымирание.

extinguish vt гасить *impf*, по~ *pf*. **extinguisher** n огнетушитель *m*.

extol vt превозносить *impf*, превознести *pf*.

extort vt вымогать *impf* (**from** y+*gen*). **extortion** n вымогательство. **extortionate** *adj* вымогательский.

extra n (*theat*) статист, ~ка; (*payment*) приплата; *adj* дополнительный; (*special*) особый; *adv* особенно.

extract n экстракт; (*from book etc.*) выдержка; vt извлекать *impf*, извлечь *pf*. **extraction** n извлечение; (*origin*) происхождение. **extradite** vt выдавать *impf*, выдать *pf*. **extradition** n выдача.

extramarital *adj* внебрачный.

extraneous *adj* посторонний.

extraordinary *adj* чрезвычайный.

extrapolate vt & i экстраполировать *impf* & *pf*.

extravagance *adj* расточительность. **extravagant** *adj* расточительный; (*fantastic*) сумасбродный.

extreme n крайность; *adj* крайний. **extremity** n (*end*) край; (*adversity*) крайность; *pl* (*hands & feet*) конечности *f pl*.

extricate vt выпутывать *impf*, выпутать *pf*.

exuberance n жизнерадостность. **exuberant** *adj* жизнерадостный.

exude vt & i выделять(ся) *impf*, выделить(ся) *pf*; (*fig*) излучать(ся) *impf*, излучить(ся) *pf*.

exult vi ликовать *impf*. **exultant** *adj* ликующий. **exultation** n ликование.

eye n глаз; (*needle etc.*) ушко; vt разглядывать *impf*, разглядеть *pf*. **eyeball** n глазное яблоко. **eyebrow** n бровь. **eyelash** n ресница. **eyelid** n веко. **eyeshadow** n тени *f pl* для век. **eyesight** n зрение. **eyewitness** n очевидец.

F

fable n басня.

fabric n (*structure*) структура; (*cloth*) ткань. **fabricate** vt (*invent*) выдумывать *impf*, выдумать *pf*. **fabrication** n выдумка.

fabulous *adj* сказочный.

façade n фасад.

face n лицо; (*expression*) выражение;

(*grimace*) грима́са; (*side*) сторона́; (*surface*) пове́рхность; (*clock etc.*) цифербла́т; **make ~s** ко́рчить *impf* ро́жи; **~ down** лицо́м вниз; **~ to ~** лицо́м к лицу́; **in the ~ of** пе́ред лицо́м+*gen*, вопреки́+*dat*; **on the ~ of it** на пе́рвый взгляд; *vt* (*be turned towards*) быть обращённым к+*dat*; (*of person*) стоя́ть *impf* лицо́м к+*dat*; (*meet firmly*) смотре́ть *impf* в лицо́+*dat*; (*cover*) облицо́вывать *impf*, облицева́ть *pf*; **I can't ~ it** я да́же ду́мать об э́том не могу́. **faceless** *adj* безли́чный.

facet *n* грань; (*fig*) аспе́кт.

facetious *adj* шутли́вый.

facial *adj* лицево́й.

facile *adj* пове́рхностный. **facilitate** *vt* облегча́ть *impf*, облегчи́ть *pf*. **facility** *n* (*ease*) лёгкость; (*ability*) спосо́бность; *pl* (*conveniences*) удо́бства *neut pl*, (*opportunities*) возмо́жности *f pl*.

facing *n* облицо́вка; (*of garment*) отде́лка.

facsimile *n* факси́миле *neut indecl*.

fact *n* факт; **the ~ is that ...** де́ло в том, что...; **as a matter of ~** со́бственно говоря́; **in ~** на са́мом де́ле.

faction *n* фра́кция.

factor *n* фа́ктор.

factory *n* фа́брика, заво́д.

factual *adj* факти́ческий.

faculty *n* спосо́бность; (*univ*) факульте́т.

fade *vi* (*wither*) вя́нуть *impf*, за~ *pf*; (*colour*) выцвета́ть *impf*, вы́цвести *pf*; (*sound*) замира́ть *impf*, замере́ть *pf*.

faeces *n pl* кал.

fag *n* (*cigarette*) сигаре́тка.

fail *n*: **without ~** обяза́тельно; *vi* (*weaken*) слабе́ть *impf*; (*break down*) отка́зывать *impf*, отказа́ть *pf*; (*not succeed*) терпе́ть *impf*, по~ *pf* неуда́чу; не удава́ться *impf*, уда́ться *pf impers*+*dat*; *vt* & *i* (*exam*) прова́ливать(ся) *impf*, провали́ть(ся) *pf*.; *vt* (*disappoint*) подводи́ть *impf*, подвести́ *pf*. **failing** *n* недоста́ток; *prep* за неиме́нием +*gen*. **failure** *n* неуда́ча; (*person*) неуда́чник, -ица.

faint *n* о́бморок; *adj* (*weak*) сла́бый; (*pale*) бле́дный; **I feel ~** мне ду́рно;

~-hearted малоду́шный; *vi* па́дать *impf*, упа́сть *pf* в о́бморок.

fair[1] *n* я́рмарка.

fair[2] *adj* (*hair, skin*) све́тлый; (*weather*) я́сный; (*just*) справедли́вый; (*average*) сно́сный; **a ~ amount** дово́льно мно́го+*gen*. **fairly** *adv* дово́льно.

fairy *n* фе́я; **~-tale** ска́зка.

faith *n* ве́ра; (*trust*) дове́рие. **faithful** *adj* ве́рный; **yours ~ly** с уваже́нием.

fake *n* подде́лка; *vt* подде́лывать *impf*, подде́лать *pf*.

falcon *n* со́кол.

fall *n* паде́ние; *vi* па́дать *impf*, (у)па́сть *pf*; **~ apart** распада́ться *impf*, распа́сться *pf*; **~ asleep** засыпа́ть *impf*, засну́ть *pf*; **~ back on** прибега́ть *impf*, прибе́гнуть *pf* к+*dat*; **~ down** упа́сть *pf*; (*building*) разва́ливаться *impf*, развали́ться *pf*; **~ in** ру́хнуть *pf*; **~ in love with** влюбля́ться *impf*, влюби́ться *pf* в+*acc*; **~ off** отпада́ть *impf*, отпа́сть *pf*; **~ out** выпада́ть *impf*, вы́пасть *pf*; (*quarrel*) поссо́риться *pf*; **~ over** опроки́дываться *impf*, опроки́нуться *pf*; **~ through** прова́ливаться *impf*, провали́ться *pf*; **~-out** радиоакти́вные оса́дки (-ков) *pl*.

fallacy *n* оши́бка.

fallible *adj* подве́рженный оши́бкам.

fallow *adj*: **lie ~** лежа́ть *impf* под па́ром.

false *adj* ло́жный; (*teeth*) иску́сственный; **~ start** неве́рный старт. **falsehood** *n* ложь. **falsification** *n* фальсифика́ция. **falsify** *vt* фальсифици́ровать *impf* & *pf*. **falsity** *n* ло́жность.

falter *vi* спотыка́ться *impf*, споткну́ться *pf*; (*stammer*) запина́ться *impf*, запну́ться *pf*.

fame *n* сла́ва. **famed** *adj* изве́стный.

familiar *adj* (*well known*) знако́мый; (*usual*) обы́чный; (*informal*) фамилья́рный. **familiarity** *n* знако́мство; фамилья́рность. **familiarize** *vt* ознакомля́ть *impf*, ознако́мить *pf* (**with** c+*instr*).

family *n* семья́; *attrib* семе́йный; **~ tree** родосло́вная *sb*.

famine *n* го́лод. **famished** *adj*: **be ~** голода́ть *impf*.

famous *adj* знамени́тый.

fan[1] *n* ве́ер; (*ventilator*) вентиля́тор;

~-belt ремéнь *m* вентилятора; *vt* обмáхивать *impf*, обмахнýть *pf*; (*flame*) раздувáть *impf*, раздýть *pf*.
fan² *n* поклóнник, -ица; (*sport*) болéльщик. fanatic *n* фанáтик. fanatical *adj* фанатический.
fanciful *adj* причýдливый. fancy *n* фантáзия; (*whim*) причýда; take a ~ to увлекáться *impf*, увлéчься *pf* +*instr*; *adj* витиевáтый; *vt* (*imagine*) представлять *impf*, предстáвить *pf* себé; (*suppose*) полагáть *impf*; (*like*) нрáвиться *impf*, по~ *pf impers*+*dat*; ~ dress маскарáдный костюм; ~-dress костюмированный.
fanfare *n* фанфáра.
fang *n* клык; (*serpent's*) ядовитый зуб.
fantasize *vi* фантазировать *impf*.
fantastic *adj* фантастический. fantasy *n* фантáзия.
far *adj* дáльний; Russia is ~ away Россия óчень далекó; *adv* далёко; (*fig*) намнóго; as ~ as (*prep*) до +*gen*; (*conj*) поскóльку; by ~ намнóго; (*in*) so ~ as поскóльку; so ~ до сих пор; ~-fetched притянутый зá волосы; ~-reaching далекó идущий; ~-sighted дальновидный.
farce *n* фарс. farcical *adj* смехотвóрный.
fare *n* (*price*) проезднáя плáта; (*food*) пища; *vi* поживáть *impf*.
farewell *int* прощáй(те)!; *n* прощáние; *attrib* прощáльный; bid ~ прощáться *impf*, проститься *pf* (to c+*instr*).
farm *n* фéрма. farmer *n* фéрмер. farming *n* сéльское хозяйство.
fart (*vulg*) *n* пýкание; *vi* пýкать *impf*, пýкнуть *pf*.
farther see further. farthest see furthest.
fascinate *vt* очарóвывать *impf*, очарóвать *pf*. fascinating *adj* очаровáтельный. fascination *n* очаровáние.
Fascism *n* фашизм. Fascist *n* фашист, ~ка; *adj* фашистский.
fashion *n* мóда; (*manner*) манéра; after a ~ нéкоторым óбразом; *vt* придавáть *impf*, придáть *pf* фóрму +*dat*. fashionable *adj* мóдный.
fast¹ *n* пост; *vi* поститься *impf*.
fast² *adj* (*rapid*) скóрый, быстрый;

(*colour*) стóйкий; (*shut*) плóтно закрытый; be ~ (*timepiece*) спешить *impf*.
fasten *vt* (*attach*) прикреплять *impf*, прикрепить *pf* (to к+*dat*); (*tie*) привязывать *impf*, привязáть *pf* (to к+*dat*); (*garment*) застёгивать *impf*, застегнýть *pf*. fastener, fastening *n* запóр, задвижка; (*on garment*) застёжка.
fastidious *adj* брезгливый.
fat *n* жир; *adj* (*greasy*) жирный; (*plump*) тóлстый; get ~ толстéть *impf*, по~ *pf*.
fatal *adj* рокóвóй; (*deadly*) смертéльный. fatalism *n* фатализм. fatality *n* (*death*) смертéльный слýчай. fate *n* судьбá. fateful *adj* рокóвóй.
father *n* отéц; ~-in-law (*husband's* ~) свёкор; (*wife's* ~) тесть *m*. fatherhood *n* отцóвство. fatherland *n* отéчество. fatherly *adj* отéческий.
fathom *n* морскáя сáжень; *vt* (*fig*) понимáть *impf*, понять *pf*.
fatigue *n* утомлéние; *vt* утомлять *impf*, утомить *pf*.
fatten *vt* откáрмливать *impf*, откормить *pf*; *vi* толстéть *impf*, по~ *pf*. fatty *adj* жирный.
fatuous *adj* глýпый.
fault *n* недостáток; (*blame*) винá; (*geol*) сброс. faultless *adj* безупрéчный. faulty *adj* дефéктный.
fauna *n* фáуна.
favour *n* (*kind act*) любéзность; (*goodwill*) благосклóнность; in (*s.o.'s*) ~ в пóльзу +*gen*; be in ~ of быть за+*acc*; *vt* (*support*) благоприятствовать *impf* +*dat*; (*treat with partiality*) оказывать *impf*, оказáть *pf* предпочтéние +*dat*. favourable *adj* (*propitious*) благоприятный; (*approving*) благосклóнный. favourite *n* любимец, -мица; (*also sport*) фаворит, ~ка; *adj* любимый.
fawn¹ *n* оленёнок; *adj* желтовáтокоричневый.
fawn² *vi* подлизываться *impf*, подлизáться *pf* (on к+*dat*).
fax *n* факс; *vt* посылáть *impf*, послáть *pf* по фáксу.
fear *n* страх, боязнь, опасéние; *vt* & *i* боя́ться *impf* +*gen*; опасáться *impf* +*gen*. fearful *adj* (*terrible*) стра́ш-

ный; (*timid*) пугли́вый. **fearless** *adj* бесстра́шный. **fearsome** *adj* гро́зный.

feasibility *n* осуществи́мость. **feasible** *adj* осуществи́мый.

feast *n* (*meal*) пир; (*festival*) пра́здник; *vi* пирова́ть *impf*.

feat *n* по́двиг.

feather *n* перо́.

feature *n* черта́; (*newspaper*) (темати́ческая) статья́; ~ **film** худо́жественный фильм; *vt* помеща́ть *impf*, помести́ть *pf* на ви́дном ме́сте; (*in film*) пока́зывать *impf*, показа́ть *pf*; *vi* игра́ть *impf* сыгра́ть *pf* роль.

February *n* февра́ль *m*; *adj* февра́льский.

feckless *adj* безала́берный.

federal *adj* федера́льный. **federation** *n* федера́ция.

fee *n* гонора́р; (*entrance* ~ *etc.*) взнос; *pl* (*regular payment, school, etc.*) пла́та.

feeble *adj* сла́бый.

feed *n* корм; *vt* корми́ть *impf*, на~, по~ *pf*; *vi* корми́ться *impf*, по~ *pf*; ~ **up** отка́рмливать *impf*, откорми́ть *pf*; **I am fed up with** мне надое́л (-а, -о; -и) +*nom*. **feedback** *n* обра́тная связь.

feel *vt* чу́вствовать *impf*, по~ *pf*; (*think*) счита́ть *impf*, счесть *pf*; *vi* (~ *bad etc.*) чу́вствовать *impf*, по~ *pf* себя́ +*adv*, +*instr*; ~ **like** хоте́ться *impf impers*+*dat*. **feeling** *n* (*sense*) ощуще́ние; (*emotion*) чу́вство; (*impression*) впечатле́ние; (*mood*) настрое́ние.

feign *vt* притворя́ться *impf*, притвори́ться *pf* +*instr*. **feigned** *adj* притво́рный.

feline *adj* коша́чий.

fell *vt* (*tree*) сруба́ть *impf*, сруби́ть *pf*; (*person*) сбива́ть *impf*, сбить *pf* с ног.

fellow *n* па́рень *m*; (*of society etc.*) член; ~ **countryman** соотéчественник. **fellowship** *n* това́рищество.

felt *n* фетр; *adj* фе́тровый; ~-**tip pen** флома́стер.

female *n* (*animal*) са́мка; (*person*) же́нщина; *adj* же́нский. **feminine** *adj* же́нский, же́нственный; (*gram*) же́нского ро́да. **femininity** *n* же́нст-

венность. **feminism** *n* femini3м. **feminist** *n* femини́ст, ~ка; *adj* femини́стский.

fence *n* забо́р; *vt*: ~ **in** огора́живать *impf*, огороди́ть *pf*; ~ **off** отгора́живать *impf*, отгороди́ть *pf*; *vi* (*sport*) фехтова́ть *impf*. **fencer** *n* фехтова́льщик, -ица. **fencing** *n* (*enclosure*) забо́р; (*sport*) фехтова́ние.

fend *vt*: ~ **off** отража́ть *impf*, отрази́ть *pf*; *vi*: ~ **for o.s.** забо́титься *impf*, по~ *pf* о себе́. **fender** *n* решётка.

fennel *n* фе́нхель *m*.

ferment *n* броже́ние; *vi* броди́ть *impf*; *vt* ква́сить *impf*, за~ *pf*; (*excite*) возбужда́ть *impf*, возбуди́ть *pf*. **fermentation** *n* броже́ние; (*excitement*) возбужде́ние.

fern *n* па́поротник.

ferocious *adj* свире́пый. **ferocity** *n* свире́пость.

ferret *n* хорёк; *vt*: ~ **out** (*search out*) разню́хивать *impf*, разню́хать *pf*; *vi*: ~ **about** (*rummage*) ры́ться *impf*.

ferry *n* паро́м; *vt* перевози́ть *impf*, перевезти́ *pf*.

fertile *adj* плодоро́дный. **fertility** *n* плодоро́дие. **fertilize** *vt* (*soil*) удобря́ть *impf*, удо́брить *pf*; (*egg*) оплодотворя́ть *impf*, оплодотвори́ть *pf*. **fertilizer** *n* удобре́ние.

fervent *adj* горя́чий. **fervour** *n* жар.

fester *vi* гнои́ться *impf*.

festival *n* пра́здник, (*music etc.*) фестива́ль *m*. **festive** *adj* пра́здничный. **festivities** *n pl* торжества́ *neut pl*.

festoon *vt* украша́ть *impf*, укра́сить *pf*.

fetch *vt* (*carrying*) приноси́ть *impf*, принести́ *pf*; (*leading*) приводи́ть *impf*, привести́ *pf*; (*go and come back with*) (*on foot*) идти́ *impf*, по~ *pf* за+*instr*; (*by vehicle*) заезжа́ть *impf*, зае́хать *pf* за+*instr*; (*price*) выруча́ть *impf*, вы́ручить *pf*. **fetching** *adj* привлека́тельный.

fetid *adj* злово́нный.

fetish *n* фети́ш.

fetter *vt* ско́вывать *impf*, скова́ть *pf*; *n*: *pl* кандалы́ (-ло́в) *pl*; (*fig*) око́вы (-в) *pl*.

fettle *n* состоя́ние.

feud *n* кро́вная месть.

feudal *adj* феода́льный. **feudalism** *n* феодали́зм.

fever *n* лихора́дка. **feverish** *adj* лихора́дочный.

few *adj & pron* немно́гие *pl*; ма́ло +*gen*; **a ~** не́сколько +*gen*; **quite a ~** нема́ло +*gen*.

fiancé *n* жени́х. **fiancée** *n* неве́ста.

fiasco *n* прова́л.

fib *n* враньё; *vi* привира́ть *impf*, приврать *pf*.

fibre *n* волокно́. **fibreglass** *n* стекловолокно́. **fibrous** *adj* волокни́стый.

fickle *adj* непостоя́нный.

fiction *n* худо́жественная литерату́ра; (*invention*) вы́думка. **fictional** *adj* беллетристи́ческий. **fictitious** *adj* вы́мышленный.

fiddle *n* (*violin*) скри́пка; (*swindle*) обма́н; *vi*: **~ about** безде́льничать *impf*; **~ with** верте́ть *impf*; *vt* (*falsify*) подде́лывать *impf*, подде́лать *pf*; (*cheat*) жи́лить *impf*, у~ *pf*.

fidelity *n* ве́рность.

fidget *n* непосе́да *m & f*; *vi* ёрзать *impf*; не́рвничать *impf*. **fidgety** *adj* непосе́дливый.

field *n* по́ле; (*sport*) площа́дка; (*sphere*) о́бласть; **~-glasses** полево́й бино́кль *m*. **~work** полевы́е рабо́ты *f pl*.

fiend *n* дья́вол. **fiendish** *adj* дья́вольский.

fierce *adj* свире́пый; (*strong*) си́льный.

fiery *adj* о́гненный.

fifteen *adj & n* пятна́дцать. **fifteenth** *adj & n* пятна́дцатый. **fifth** *adj & n* пя́тый; (*fraction*) пя́тая *sb*. **fiftieth** *adj & n* пятидеся́тый. **fifty** *adj & n* пятьдеся́т; *pl* (*decade*) пятидеся́тые го́ды (-до́в) *m pl*.

fig *n* инжи́р.

fight *n* дра́ка; (*battle*) бой; (*fig*) борьба́; *vt* боро́ться *impf* с+*instr*; *vi* дра́ться *impf*; *vt & i* (*wage war*) воева́ть *impf* с+*instr*. **fighter** *n* бое́ц; (*aeron*) истреби́тель *m*. **fighting** *n* бой *m pl*.

figment *n* плод воображе́ния.

figurative *adj* перено́сный. **figure** *n* (*form, body, person*) фигу́ра; (*number*) ци́фра; (*diagram*) рису́нок; (*image*) изображе́ние; (*of speech*)

оборо́т ре́чи; **~-head** (*naut*) носово́е украше́ние; (*person*) номина́льная глава́; *vt* (*think*) полага́ть *impf*; *vi* фигури́ровать *impf*; **~ out** вычисля́ть *impf*, вы́числить *pf*.

filament *n* волокно́; (*electr*) нить.

file¹ *n* (*tool*) напи́льник; *vt* подпи́ливать *impf*, подпили́ть *pf*.

file² *n* (*folder*) па́пка; (*comput*) файл; *vt* подшива́ть *impf*, подши́ть *pf*; (*complaint*) поддава́ть *impf*, подда́ть *pf*.

file³ *n* (*row*) ряд; **in (single) ~** гусько́м.

filigree *n* филигра́нь; *adj* филигра́нный.

fill *vt & i* (*also* **~ up**) наполня́ть(ся) *impf*, напо́лнить(ся) *pf*; vt заполня́ть *impf*, запо́лнить *pf*; (*tooth*) пломбирова́ть *impf*, за~ *pf*; (*occupy*) занима́ть *impf*, заня́ть *pf*; (*satiate*) насыща́ть *impf*, насы́тить *pf*; **~ in** (*vt*) заполня́ть *impf*, запо́лнить *pf*; (*vi*) замеща́ть *impf*, замести́ть *pf*.

fillet *n* (*cul*) филе́ *neut indecl*.

filling *n* (*tooth*) пло́мба; (*cul*) начи́нка.

filly *n* кобы́лка.

film *n* (*layer; phot*) плёнка; (*cin*) фильм; **~ star** кинозвезда́; *vt* снима́ть *impf*, снять *pf*.

filter *n* фильтр; *vt* фильтрова́ть *impf*, про~ *pf*; **~ through, out** проса́чиваться *impf*, просочи́ться *pf*.

filth *n* грязь. **filthy** *adj* гря́зный.

fin *n* плавни́к.

final *n* фина́л; *pl* выпускны́е экза́мены *m pl*; *adj* после́дний; (*decisive*) оконча́тельный. **finale** *n* фина́л. **finalist** *n* финали́ст. **finality** *n* зако́нченность. **finalize** *vt* (*complete*) заверша́ть *impf*, заверши́ть *pf*; (*settle*) ула́живать *impf*, ула́дить *pf*. **finally** *adv* наконе́ц.

finance *n* фина́нсы (-сов) *pl*; *vt* финанси́ровать *impf & pf*. **financial** *adj* фина́нсовый. **financier** *n* финанси́ст.

finch *n see comb, e.g.* bullfinch

find *n* нахо́дка; *vt* находи́ть *impf*, найти́ *pf*; (*person*) застава́ть *impf*, заста́ть *pf*; **~ out** узнава́ть *impf*, узна́ть *pf*; **~ fault with** придира́ться *impf*, придра́ться *pf* к+*dat*. **finding**

n pl (*of inquiry*) вы́воды *m pl.*

fine¹ *n* (*penalty*) штраф; *vt* штрафова́ть *impf*, o~ *pf.*

fine² *adj* (*weather*) я́сный; (*excellent*) прекра́сный; (*delicate*) то́нкий; (*of sand etc.*) ме́лкий; ~ **arts** изобрази́тельные иску́сства *neut pl*; *adv* хорошо́. **finery** *n* наря́д. **finesse** *n* то́нкость.

finger *n* па́лец; ~**-nail** но́готь; ~**-print** отпеча́ток па́льца; ~**-tip** ко́нчик па́льца; **have at (one's)** ~**s** знать *impf* как свои́ пять па́льцев; *vt* щу́пать *impf*, по~ *pf.*

finish *n* коне́ц; (*polish*) отде́лка; (*sport*) фи́ниш; *vt & i* конча́ть(ся) *impf*, ко́нчить(ся) *pf*; *vt* ока́нчивать *impf*, око́нчить *pf.*

finite *adj* коне́чный.

Finland *n* Финля́ндия. **Finn** *n* финн, фи́нка. **Finnish** *adj* фи́нский.

fir *n* ель, пи́хта.

fire *vt* (*bake*) обжига́ть *impf*, обже́чь *pf*; (*excite*) воспламеня́ть *impf*, воспламени́ть *pf*; (*gun*) стреля́ть *impf* из+*gen* (at в+*acc*, по+*dat*); (*dismiss*) увольня́ть *impf*, уво́лить *pf*; *n* ого́нь *m*; (*grate*) ками́н; (*conflagration*) пожа́р; (*bonfire*) костёр; (*fervour*) пыл; **be on** ~ горе́ть *impf*; **catch** ~ загора́ться *impf*, загоре́ться *pf*; **set** ~ **to, set on** ~ поджига́ть *impf*, подже́чь *pf*; ~**-alarm** пожа́рная трево́га; ~**arm(s)** огнестре́льное ору́жие; ~ **brigade** пожа́рная кома́нда; ~**-engine** пожа́рная маши́на; ~**-escape** пожа́рная ле́стница; ~**-extinguisher** огнетуши́тель *m*; ~**-guard** ками́нная решётка; ~**man** пожа́рный *sb*; ~ **place** ками́н; ~**side** ме́сто у ками́на; ~ **station** пожа́рное депо́ *neut indecl*; ~**-wood** дрова́ (-в) *pl*; ~**work** фейерве́рк. **firing** *n* (*shooting*) стрельба́.

firm¹ *n* (*business*) фи́рма.

firm² *adj* твёрдый. **firmness** *n* твёрдость.

first *adj* пе́рвый; *n* пе́рвый *sb*; *adv* сперва́, снача́ла; (*for the* ~ *time*) впервы́е; **in the** ~ **place** во-пе́рвых; ~ **of all** пре́жде всего́; **at** ~ **sight** на пе́рвый взгляд; ~ **aid** пе́рвая по́мощь; ~**-class** первокла́ссный; ~**hand** из пе́рвых рук; ~**-rate** первокла́ссный.

fiscal *adj* фина́нсовый.

fish *n* ры́ба; *adj* ры́бный; *vi* лови́ть *impf* ры́бу; ~ **for** (*compliments etc.*) напра́шиваться *impf*, напроси́ться *pf* на+*acc*; ~ **out** выта́скивать *impf*, вы́таскать *pf*. **fisherman** *n* рыба́к. **fishery** *n* ры́бный про́мысел. **fishing** *n* ры́бная ло́вля; ~ **boat** рыболо́вное су́дно; ~ **line** леса́; ~ **rod** у́дочка. **fishmonger** *n* торго́вец ры́бой. **fishy** *adj* ры́бный; (*dubious*) подозри́тельный.

fissure *n* тре́щина.

fist *n* кула́к.

fit¹ *n*: **be a good** ~ хорошо́ сиде́ть *impf*; *adj* (*suitable*) подходя́щий, го́дный; (*healthy*) здоро́вый; *vt* (*be suitable*) годи́ться *impf* +*dat*, на+*acc*, для+*gen*; *vt & i* (*be the right size (for)*) подходи́ть *impf*, подойти́ *pf* (+*dat*); (*adjust*) прила́живать *impf*, прила́дить *pf* (**to** к+*dat*); (*be small enough for*) входи́ть *impf*, войти́ *pf* в+*acc*; ~ **out** снабжа́ть *impf*, снабди́ть *pf.*

fit² *n* (*attack*) припа́док; (*fig*) поры́в. **fitful** *adj* поры́вистый.

fitter *n* монтёр. **fitting** *n* (*of clothes*) приме́рка; *pl* армату́ра; *adj* подходя́щий.

five *adj & n* пять; (*number 5*) пятёрка; ~**-year plan** пятиле́тка.

fix *n* (*dilemma*) переде́лка; (*drugs*) уко́л; *vt* (*repair*) чини́ть *impf*, по~ *pf*; (*settle*) назнача́ть *impf*, назна́чить *pf*; (*fasten*) укрепля́ть *impf*, укрепи́ть *pf*; ~ **up** (*organize*) организова́ть *impf & pf*; (*install*) устана́вливать *impf*, установи́ть *pf.* **fixation** *n* фикса́ция. **fixed** *adj* устано́вленный. **fixture** *n* (*sport*) предстоя́щее спорти́вное мероприя́тие; (*fitting*) приспособле́ние.

fizz, fizzle *vi* шипе́ть *impf*; **fizzle out** выдыха́ться *impf*, вы́дохнуться *pf*. **fizzy** *adj* шипу́чий.

flabbergasted *adj* ошеломлённый.

flabby *adj* дря́блый.

flag¹ *n* флаг, зна́мя *neut*; *vt*: ~ **down** остана́вливать *impf*, останови́ть *pf.* **flag**² *vi* (*weaken*) ослабева́ть *impf*, ослабе́ть *pf.*

flagon *n* кувши́н.

flagrant *adj* вопию́щий.

flagship *n* фла́гман.

flagstone *n* плита́.

flair *n* чутьё.

flake *n* слой; *pl* хло́пья (-ьев) *pl*; *vi* шелуши́ться *impf*. **flaky** *adj* сло́истый.

flamboyant *adj* цвети́стый.

flame *n* пла́мя *neut*, ого́нь *m*; *vi* пыла́ть *impf*.

flange *n* фла́нец.

flank *n* (*of body*) бок; (*mil*) фланг; *vt* быть сбо́ку +*gen*.

flannel *n* фла́нель; (*for face*) моча́лка для лица́.

flap *n* (*board*) откидна́я доска́; (*pocket, tent* ~) кла́пан; (*panic*) па́ника; *vt* взма́хивать *impf*, взмахну́ть *pf* +*instr*; *vi* развева́ться *impf*.

flare *n* (*signal*) сигна́льная раке́та; *vi* вспы́хивать *impf*, вспы́хнуть *pf*; ~ **up** (*fire*) возгора́ться *impf*, возгоре́ться *pf*; (*fig*) вспыли́ть *pf*.

flash *n* вспы́шка; **in a** ~ ми́гом; *vi* сверка́ть *impf*, сверкну́ть *pf*. **flashback** *n* ретроспе́кция. **flashy** *adj* показно́й.

flask *n* фля́жка.

flat[1] *n* (*dwelling*) кварти́ра.

flat[2] *n* (*mus*) бемо́ль *m*; (*tyre*) спу́щенная ши́на; **on the** ~ на пло́скости; *adj* пло́ский; ~**-fish** ка́мбала. **flatly** *adv* наотре́з. **flatten** *vt* & *i* выра́внивать(ся) *impf*, вы́ровнять(ся) *pf*.

flatmate *n* сосе́д, ~ка по кварти́ре.

flatter *vt* льстить *impf*, по~ *pf* +*dat*. **flattering** *adj* льсти́вый. **flattery** *n* лесть.

flaunt *vt* щеголя́ть *impf*, щегольну́ть *pf* +*instr*.

flautist *n* флейти́ст.

flavour *n* вкус; (*fig*) при́вкус; *vt* приправля́ть *impf*, припра́вить *pf*.

flaw *n* изъя́н.

flax *n* лён. **flaxen** *adj* (*colour*) соло́менный.

flea *n* блоха́; ~ **market** барахо́лка.

fleck *n* кра́пинка.

flee *vi* бежа́ть *impf* & *pf* (**from** от+*gen*); *vt* бежа́ть *impf* из+*gen*.

fleece *n* руно́; *vt* (*fig*) обдира́ть *impf*, ободра́ть *pf*. **fleecy** *adj* шерсти́стый.

fleet *n* флот; (*vehicles*) парк.

fleeting *adj* мимолётный.

flesh *n* (*as opposed to mind*) плоть;

(*meat*) мя́со; **in the** ~ во плоти́. **fleshy** *adj* мяси́стый.

flex *n* шнур; *vt* сгиба́ть *impf*, согну́ть *pf*. **flexibility** *adj* ги́бкость. **flexible** *adj* ги́бкий.

flick *vt* & *i* щёлкать *impf*, щёлкнуть *pf* (+*instr*); ~ **through** пролиста́ть *pf*.

flicker *n* мерца́ние; *vi* мерца́ть *impf*.

flier *see* **flyer**

flight[1] *n* (*fleeing*) бе́гство; **put** (**take**) **to** ~ обраща́ть(ся) *impf*, обрати́ть(ся) *pf* в бе́гство.

flight[2] *n* (*flying*) полёт; (*trip*) рейс; ~ **of stairs** ле́стничный марш. **flighty** *adj* ве́треный.

flimsy *adj* (*fragile*) непро́чный; (*dress*) лёгкий; (*excuse*) сла́бый.

flinch *vi* (*recoil*) отпря́дывать *impf*, отпря́нуть *pf*; (*fig*) уклоня́ться *impf*, уклони́ться *pf* (**from** от+*gen*).

fling *vt* швыря́ть *impf*, швырну́ть *pf*; *vi* (*also* ~ *o.s.*) броса́ться *impf*, бро́ситься *pf*.

flint *n* креме́нь *m*.

flip *vt* щёлкать *impf*, щёлкнуть *pf* +*instr*.

flippant *adj* легкомы́сленный.

flipper *n* ласт.

flirt *n* коке́тка; *vi* флиртова́ть *impf* (**with** с+*instr*). **flirtation** *n* флирт.

flit *vi* порха́ть *impf*, порхну́ть *pf*.

float *n* поплаво́к; *vi* пла́вать *indet*, плыть *det*; *vt* (*company*) пуска́ть *impf*, пусти́ть *pf* в ход.

flock *n* (*animals*) ста́до; (*birds*) ста́я; *vi* стека́ться *impf*, сте́чься *pf*.

flog *vt* сечь *impf*, вы́~ *pf*.

flood *n* наводне́ние; (*bibl*) пото́п; (*fig*) пото́к; *vi* (*river etc.*) выступа́ть *impf*, вы́ступить *pf* из берего́в; *vt* затопля́ть *impf*, затопи́ть *pf*. **floodgate** *n* шлюз. **floodlight** *n* прожектор.

floor *n* пол; (*storey*) эта́ж; ~**board** полови́ца; *vt* (*confound*) ста́вить *impf*, по~ *pf* в тупи́к.

flop *vi* (*fall*) плю́хаться *impf*, плюхнуться *pf*; (*fail*) прова́ливаться *impf*, провали́ться *pf*.

flora *n* фло́ра. **floral** *adj* цвето́чный.

florid *adj* цвети́стый; (*ruddy*) румя́ный. **florist** *n* торго́вец цвета́ми.

flounce[1] *vi* броса́ться *impf*, бро́ситься *pf*.

flounce[2] *n* (*of skirt*) обо́рка.

flounder[1] *n* (*fish*) ка́мбала.

flounder[2] *vi* бара́хтаться *impf*.

flour *n* мука́.

flourish *n* (*movement*) разма́хивание (+*instr*); (*of pen*) ро́счерк; *vi* (*thrive*) процвета́ть *impf*; *vt* (*wave*) разма́хивать *impf*, размахну́ть *impf* +*instr*.

flout *n* попира́ть *impf*, попра́ть *pf*.

flow *vi* течь *impf*; ли́ться *impf*; *n* тече́ние.

flower *n* цвето́к; **~-bed** клу́мба; **~pot** цвето́чный горшо́к; *vi* цвести́ *impf*. **flowery** *adj* цвети́стый.

fluctuate *vi* колеба́ться *impf*, по~ *pf*. **fluctuation** *n* колеба́ние.

flue *n* дымохо́д.

fluent *adj* бе́глый. **fluently** *adv* свобо́дно.

fluff *n* пух. **fluffy** *adj* пуши́стый.

fluid *n* жи́дкость; *adj* жи́дкий.

fluke *n* случа́йная уда́ча.

fluorescent *adj* флюоресце́нтный.

fluoride *n* фтори́д.

flurry *n* (*squall*) шквал; (*fig*) волна́.

flush *n* (*redness*) румя́нец; *vi* (*redden*) красне́ть *impf*, по~ *pf*; *vt* спуска́ть *impf*, спусти́ть *pf* во́ду в+*acc*.

flustered *adj* сконфу́женный.

flute *n* фле́йта.

flutter *vi* (*flit*) порха́ть *impf*, порхну́ть *pf*; (*wave*) развева́ться *impf*.

flux *n*: **in a state of ~** в состоя́нии измене́ния.

fly[1] *n* (*insect*) му́ха.

fly[2] *vi* лета́ть *indet*, лете́ть *det*, по~ *pf*; (*flag*) развева́ться *impf*; (*hasten*) нести́сь *impf*, по~ *pf*; *vt* (*aircraft*) управля́ть *impf* +*instr*; (*transport*) перевози́ть *impf*, перевезти́ *pf* (*самолётом*); (*flag*) поднима́ть *impf*, подня́ть *pf*. **flyer, flier** *n* лётчик. **flying** *n* полёт.

foal *n* (*horse*) жеребёнок.

foam *n* пе́на; **~ plastic** пенопла́ст; **~ rubber** пенорези́на; *vi* пе́ниться *impf*, вс~ *pf*. **foamy** *adj* пе́нистый.

focal *adj* фо́кусный. **focus** *n* фо́кус; (*fig*) центр; *vt* фокуси́ровать *impf*, с~ *pf*; (*concentrate*) сосредото́чивать *impf*, сосредото́чить *pf*.

fodder *n* корм.

foe *n* враг.

foetus *n* заро́дыш.

fog *n* тума́н. **foggy** *adj* тума́нный.

foible *n* сла́бость.

foil[1] *n* (*metal*) фольга́; (*contrast*) контра́ст.

foil[2] *vt* (*thwart*) расстра́ивать *impf*, расстро́ить *pf*.

foil[3] *n* (*sword*) рапи́ра.

foist *vt* навя́зывать *impf*, навяза́ть *pf* (**on** +*dat*).

fold[1] *n* (*sheep-*~) овча́рня.

fold[2] *n* скла́дка, сгиб; *vt* скла́дывать *impf*, сложи́ть *pf*. **folder** *n* па́пка. **folding** *adj* складно́й.

foliage *n* листва́.

folk *n* наро́д, лю́ди *pl*; *pl* (*relatives*) родня́ *collect*; *attrib* наро́дный. **folklore** *n* фолькло́р.

follow *vt* сле́довать *impf*, по~ *pf* +*dat*, за+*instr*; (*walk behind*) идти́ *det* за+*instr*; (*fig*) следи́ть *impf* за+*instr*. **follower** *n* после́дователь *m*. **following** *adj* сле́дующий.

folly *n* глу́пость.

fond *adj* не́жный; **be ~ of** люби́ть *impf* +*acc*.

fondle *vt*ласка́ть *impf*.

fondness *n* любо́вь.

font *n* (*eccl*) купе́ль.

food *n* пи́ща, еда́. **foodstuff** *n* пищево́й проду́кт.

fool *n* дура́к; *vt* дура́чить *impf*, о~ *pf*; *vi*: **~ about** дура́читься *impf*. **foolhardy** *adj* безрассу́дно хра́брый. **foolish** *adj* глу́пый. **foolishness** *n* глу́пость. **foolproof** *adj* абсолю́тно надёжный.

foot *n* нога́; (*measure*) фут; (*of hill etc.*) подно́жие; **on ~** пешко́м; **put one's ~ in it** сесть *pf* в лу́жу. **football** *n* футбо́л; *attrib* футбо́льный. **footballer** *n* футболи́ст. **foothills** *n pl* предго́рье. **footing** *n* (*fig*) ба́зис; **lose one's ~** оступи́ться *pf*; **on an equal ~** на ра́вной ноге́. **footlights** *n pl* ра́мпа. **footman** *n* лаке́й. **footnote** *n* сно́ска. **footpath** *n* тропи́нка; (*pavement*) тротуа́р. **footprint** *n* след. **footstep** *n* (*sound*) шаг; (*footprint*) след. **footwear** *n* о́бувь.

for *prep* (*of time*) в тече́ние +*gen*, на +*acc*; (*of purpose*) для+*gen*, за+*acc*, +*instr*; (*price*) за+*acc*; (*on account of*) из-за +*gen*; (*in place of*) вме́сто+*gen*; **~ the sake of** ра́ди+*gen*; **as ~** что каса́ется+*gen*; *conj* так как.

forage n фура́ж; vi: ~ **for** разы́скивать impf.

foray n набе́г.

forbearance n возде́ржанность.

forbid vt запреща́ть impf, запрети́ть pf (+dat (person) & acc (thing)). **forbidding** adj гро́зный.

force n (strength, validity) си́ла; (meaning) смысл; pl (armed ~) вооружённые си́лы f pl; **by** ~ си́лой; vt (compel) заставля́ть impf, заста́вить pf; (lock etc.) взла́мывать impf, взлома́ть pf. **forceful** adj си́льный; (speech) убеди́тельный. **forcible** adj наси́льственный.

forceps n щипцы́ (-цо́в) pl.

ford n брод; vt переходи́ть impf, перейти́ pf вброд+acc.

fore n: **come to the ~** выдвига́ться impf, вы́двинуться pf на пере́дний план.

forearm n предпле́чье. **foreboding** n предчу́вствие. **forecast** n предсказа́ние; (of weather) прогно́з; vt предска́зывать impf, предсказа́ть pf. **forecourt** n пере́дний двор. **forefather** n пре́док. **forefinger** n указа́тельный па́лец. **forefront** n (foreground) пере́дний план; (leading position) аванга́рд. **foregone** adj: ~ **conclusion** предрешённый исхо́д. **foreground** n пере́дний план. **forehead** n лоб.

foreign adj (from abroad) иностра́нный; (alien) чу́ждый; (external) вне́шний; ~ **body** иноро́дное те́ло; ~ **currency** валю́та. **foreigner** n иностра́нец, -нка.

foreman n ма́стер.

foremost adj выдаю́щийся; **first and ~** пре́жде всего́.

forename n и́мя.

forensic adj суде́бный.

forerunner n предве́стник. **foresee** vt предви́деть impf. **foreshadow** vt предвеща́ть impf. **foresight** n предви́дение; (caution) предусмотри́тельность.

forest n лес.

forestall vt предупрежда́ть impf, предупреди́ть pf.

forester n лесни́чий sb. **forestry** n лесово́дство.

foretaste n предвкуше́ние; vt предвкуша́ть impf, предвкуси́ть pf. **fore-**

foretell vt предска́зывать impf, предсказа́ть pf. **forethought** n предусмотри́тельность. **forewarn** vt предостерега́ть impf, предостере́чь pf.

foreword n предисло́вие.

forfeit n (in game) фант; vt лиша́ться impf, лиши́ться pf +gen.

forge¹ n (smithy) ку́зница; (furnace) горн; vt кова́ть impf, вы́~ pf; (fabricate) подде́лывать impf, подде́лать pf.

forge² vi: ~ **ahead** продвига́ться impf, продви́нуться pf вперёд.

forger n фальшивомоне́тчик. **forgery** n подде́лка.

forget vt забыва́ть impf, забы́ть pf. **forgetful** adj забы́вчивый.

forgive n проща́ть impf, прости́ть pf. **forgiveness** n проще́ние.

forgo vt возде́рживаться impf, воздержа́ться pf от+gen.

fork n (eating) ви́лка; (digging) ви́лы (-л) pl; (in road) разветвле́ние; vi (road) разветвля́ться impf, разветви́ться pf.

forlorn adj жа́лкий.

form n (shape; kind) фо́рма; (class) класс; (document) анке́та; vt (make, create) образо́вывать impf, образова́ть pf; (develop; make up) составля́ть impf, соста́вить pf; vi образо́вываться impf, образова́ться pf. **formal** adj форма́льный; (official) официа́льный. **formality** n форма́льность. **format** n форма́т. **formation** n образова́ние. **formative** adj: ~ **years** молоды́е го́ды (-до́в) m pl.

former adj (earlier) пре́жний; (ex) бы́вший; **the ~** (of two) пе́рвый. **formerly** adv пре́жде.

formidable adj (dread) гро́зный; (arduous) тру́дный.

formless adj бесфо́рменный.

formula n фо́рмула. **formulate** vt формули́ровать impf, с~ pf. **formulation** n формулиро́вка.

forsake vt (desert) покида́ть impf, поки́нуть pf; (renounce) отка́зываться impf, отказа́ться pf от+gen.

fort n форт.

forth adv вперёд, да́льше; **back and ~** взад и вперёд; **and so ~** и так да́лее. **forthcoming** adj предстоя́щий; **be ~** (available) поступа́ть *impf,* поступи́ть *pf.* **forthwith** *adv* неме́дленно.

fortieth *adj & n* сороково́й.

fortification *n* укрепле́ние. **fortify** *vt* укрепля́ть *impf,* укрепи́ть *pf;* (*fig*) подкрепля́ть *impf,* подкрепи́ть *pf.* **fortitude** *n* сто́йкость.

fortnight *n* две неде́ли *f pl.* **fortnightly** *adj* двухнеде́льный; *adv* раз в две неде́ли.

fortress *n* кре́пость.

fortuitous *adj* случа́йный.

fortunate *adj* счастли́вый. **fortunately** *adv* к сча́стью. **fortune** *n* (*destiny*) судьба́; (*good* ~) сча́стье; (*wealth*) состоя́ние.

forty *adj & n* со́рок; *pl* (*decade*) сороковы́е го́ды (-до́в) *m pl.*

forward *adj* пере́дний; (*presumptuous*) развя́зный; *n* (*sport*) напада́ющий *sb; adv* вперёд; *vt* (*letter*) пересыла́ть *impf,* пересла́ть *pf.*

fossil *n* ископа́емое *sb; adj* ископа́емый. **fossilized** *adj* ископа́емый.

foster *vt* (*child*) приюти́ть *pf;* (*idea*) вына́шивать *impf,* вы́носить *pf;* (*create*) создава́ть *impf,* созда́ть *pf;* (*cherish*) леле́ять *impf;* ~-**child** приёмыш.

foul *adj* (*dirty*) гря́зный; (*repulsive*) отврати́тельный; (*obscene*) непристо́йный; *n* (*sport*) наруше́ние пра́вил; *vt* (*dirty*) па́чкать *impf,* за~, ис~ *pf;* (*entangle*) запу́тывать *impf,* запу́тать *pf.*

found *vt* осно́вывать *impf,* основа́ть *pf.*

foundation *n* (*of building*) фунда́мент; (*basis*) осно́ва; (*institution*) учрежде́ние; (*fund*) фонд. **founder**[1] *n* основа́тель *m.*

founder[2] *vi* (*naut, fig*) тону́ть *impf,* по~ *pf.*

foundry *n* лите́йная *sb.*

fountain *n* фонта́н; ~-**pen** авторучка.

four *adj & n* четы́ре; (*number 4*) четвёрка; **on all** ~**s** на четвере́ньках. **fourteen** *adj & n* четы́рнадцать. **fourteenth** *adj & n* четы́рнадцатый. **fourth** *adj & n* четвёртый; (*quarter*) че́тверть.

fowl *n* (*domestic*) дома́шняя пти́ца; (*wild*) дичь *collect.*

fox *n* лиса́, лиси́ца; *vt* озада́чивать

impf, озада́чить *pf.*

foyer *n* фойе́ *neut indecl.*

fraction *n* (*math*) дробь; (*portion*) части́ца.

fractious *adj* раздражи́тельный.

fracture *n* перело́м; *vt & i* лома́ть(ся) *impf,* с~ *pf.*

fragile *adj* ло́мкий.

fragment *n* обло́мок; (*of conversation*) отры́вок; (*of writing*) фрагме́нт. **fragmentary** *adj* отры́вочный.

fragrance *n* арома́т. **fragrant** *adj* арома́тный, души́стый.

frail *adj* хру́пкий.

frame *n* о́стов; (*build*) телосложе́ние; (*picture*) ра́ма; (*cin*) кадр; ~ **of mind** настрое́ние; *vt* (*devise*) создава́ть *impf,* созда́ть *pf;* (*formulate*) формули́ровать *impf,* с~ *pf;* (*picture*) вставля́ть *impf,* вста́вить *pf* в ра́му; (*incriminate*) фабрикова́ть *impf,* с~ *pf* обвине́ние про́тив+*gen.* **framework** *n* о́стов; (*fig*) ра́мки *f pl.*

franc *n* франк.

France *n* Фра́нция.

franchise *n* (*comm*) привиле́гия; (*polit*) пра́во го́лоса.

frank[1] *adj* открове́нный.

frank[2] *vt* (*letter*) франки́ровать *impf & pf.*

frantic *adj* нейстовый.

fraternal *adj* бра́тский. **fraternity** *n* бра́тство.

fraud *n* обма́н; (*person*) обма́нщик. **fraudulent** *adj* обма́нный.

fraught *adj:* ~ **with** чрева́тый +*instr.*

fray[1] *vt & i* обтрёпывать(ся) *impf,* обтрепа́ть(ся) *pf.*

fray[2] *n* бой.

freak *n* уро́д; *attrib* необы́чный.

freckle *n* весну́шка. **freckled** *adj* весну́шчатый.

free *adj* свобо́дный; (*gratis*) беспла́тный; ~ **kick** штрафно́й уда́р; ~ **speech** свобо́да сло́ва; *vt* освобожда́ть *impf,* освободи́ть *pf.* **freedom** *n* свобо́да. **freehold** *n* неограни́ченное пра́во со́бственности на недви́жимость. **freelance** *adj* внешта́тный. **Freemason** *n* франкмасо́н.

freeze *vi* замерза́ть *impf,* мёрзнуть *impf,* замёрзнуть *pf; vt* замора́живать *impf,* заморо́зить *pf.* **freezer** *n*

морози́льник; (*compartment*) морози́лка. **freezing** *adj* моро́зный;
below ~ ни́же нуля́.
freight *n* фрахт. **freighter** *n* (*ship*)
грузово́е су́дно.
French *adj* францу́зский; ~ **bean**
фасо́ль; ~ **horn** валто́рна; ~ **windows** двуство́рчатое окно́ до по́ла.
Frenchman *n* францу́з. **Frenchwoman** *n* францу́женка.
frenetic *adj* нейстовый.
frenzied *adj* нейстовый. **frenzy** *n*
нейстовство.
frequency *n* частота́. **frequent** *adj*
ча́стый; *vt* ча́сто посеща́ть *impf*.
fresco *n* фре́ска.
fresh *adj* све́жий; (*new*) но́вый; ~
water пре́сная вода́. **freshen** *vt* освежа́ть *impf*, освежи́ть *pf*; *vi* свежеть
impf, по~ *pf*. **freshly** *adv* свежо́; (*recently*) неда́вно. **freshness** *n* све́
жесть. **freshwater** *adj* пресново́дный.
fret¹ *vi* му́читься *impf*. **fretful** *adj*
раздражи́тельный.
fret² *n* (*mus*) лад.
fretsaw *n* ло́бзик.
friar *n* мона́х.
friction *n* тре́ние; (*fig*) тре́ния *neut
pl*.
Friday *n* пя́тница.
fridge *n* холоди́льник.
fried *adj*: ~ **egg** яи́чница.
friend *n* друг, подру́га; прия́тель *m*,
~ница. **friendly** *adj* дру́жеский.
friendship *n* дру́жба.
frieze *n* фриз.
frigate *n* фрега́т.
fright *n* испу́г. **frighten** *vt* пуга́ть
impf, ис~, на~ *pf*. **frightful** *adj*
стра́шный.
frigid *adj* холо́дный.
frill *n* обо́рка.
fringe *n* бахрома́; (*of hair*) чёлка;
(*edge*) край.
frisk *vi* (*frolic*) резви́ться *impf*; *vt*
(*search*) шмона́ть *impf*. **frisky** *adj*
ре́звый.
fritter *vt*: ~ **away** растра́чивать *impf*,
растра́тить *pf*.
frivolity *n* легкомы́сленность. **frivolous** *adj* легкомы́сленный.
fro *adv*: **to and** ~ взад и вперёд.
frock *n* пла́тье.
frog *n* лягу́шка.

frolic *vi* резви́ться *impf*.
from *prep* от+*gen*; (~ *off, down* ~;
in time) с+*gen*; (*out of*) из+*gen*; (*according to*) по+*dat*; (*because of*) изза+*gen*; ~ **above** све́рху; ~ **abroad**
из-за грани́цы; ~ **afar** и́здали; ~
among из числа́+*gen*; ~ **behind** изза+*gen*; ~ **day to day** изо дня́ в день;
~ **everywhere** отовсю́ду; ~ **here**
отсю́да; ~ **memory** по па́мяти; ~
now on отны́не; ~ **there** отту́да; ~
time to time вре́мя от вре́мени; ~
under из-под+*gen*.
front *n* фаса́д, пере́дняя сторона́;
(*mil*) фронт; **in** ~ **of** впереди́+*gen*,
пе́ред+*instr*; *adj* пере́дний; (*first*)
пе́рвый.
frontier *n* грани́ца.
frost *n* моро́з; ~-**bite** отмороже́ние;
~-**bitten** отморо́женный. **frosted**
adj: ~ **glass** ма́товое стекло́. **frosty**
adj моро́зный; (*fig*) ледяно́й.
froth *n* пе́на; *vi* пе́ниться *impf*, вс~
pf. **frothy** *adj* пе́нистый.
frown *n* хму́рый взгляд; *vi* хму́риться *impf*, на~ *pf*.
frugal *adj* (*careful*) бережли́вый;
(*scanty*) ску́дный.
fruit *n* плод; *collect* фру́кты *m pl*;
adj фрукто́вый. **fruitful** *adj* плодотво́рный. **fruition** *n*: **come to** ~ осуществи́ться *pf*. **fruitless** *adj* беспло́дный.
frustrate *vt* фрустри́ровать *impf* &
pf. **frustrating** *adj* фрустри́рующий.
frustration *n* фрустра́ция.
fry¹ *n*: **small** ~ мелюзга́.
fry² *vt* & *i* жа́рить(ся) *impf*, за~, из~
pf. **frying-pan** *n* сковорода́.
fuel *n* то́пливо.
fugitive *n* бегле́ц.
fulcrum *n* то́чка опо́ры.
fulfil *vt* (*perform*) выполня́ть *impf*,
вы́полнить *pf*; (*dreams*) осуществля́ть *impf*, осуществи́ть *pf*. **fulfilling** *adj* удовлетворя́ющий. **fulfilment** *n* выполне́ние; осуществле́
ние; удовлетворе́ние.
full *adj* по́лный; (*of* +*gen*, *instr*); (*replete*) сы́тый; ~ **stop** то́чка; *n*: **time:**
I work ~ **time** я рабо́таю на по́лную
ста́вку; *n*: **in** ~ по́лностью; **to the** ~
в по́лной ме́ре. **fullness** *n* полнота́.
fully *adv* вполне́.
fulsome *adj* чрезме́рный.

fumble vi: ~ **for** нащу́пывать impf +acc; ~ **with** вози́ться impf c+instr.

fume vi (with anger) кипе́ть impf, вс~ pf гне́вом. **fumes** n pl испаре́ния neut pl. **fumigate** vt оку́ривать impf, окури́ть pf.

fun n заба́ва; **it was** ~ бы́ло заба́вно; **have** ~ забавля́ться impf; **make** ~ **of** смея́ться impf, по~ pf над+instr.

function n фу́нкция; (event) ве́чер; vi функциони́ровать impf; де́йствовать impf. **functional** adj функциона́льный. **functionary** n чино́вник.

fund n фонд; (store) запа́с.

fundamental adj основно́й; n: pl осно́вы f pl.

funeral n по́хороны (-о́н, -она́м) pl.

fungus n гриб.

funnel n воро́нка; (chimney) дымова́я труба́.

funny adj смешно́й; (odd) стра́нный.

fur n мех; ~ **coat** шу́ба.

furious adj бе́шеный.

furnace n горн, печь.

furnish vt (provide) снабжа́ть impf, снабди́ть pf (with c+instr); (house) обставля́ть impf, обста́вить pf. **furniture** n ме́бель.

furrow n борозда́.

furry adj пуши́стый.

further, farther comp adj дальне́йший; adv да́льше; vt продвига́ть impf, продви́нуть pf. **furthermore** adv к тому́ же. **furthest, farthest** superl adj са́мый да́льний.

furtive adj скры́тый, та́йный.

fury n я́рость.

fuse[1] vt & i (of metal) сплавля́ть(ся) impf, спла́вить(ся) pf.

fuse[2] n (in bomb) запа́л; (detonating device) взрыва́тель m.

fuse[3] n (electr) про́бка; vi перегора́ть impf, перегоре́ть pf.

fuselage n фюзеля́ж.

fusion n пла́вка, слия́ние.

fuss n суета́; vi суети́ться impf. **fussy** adj суетли́вый; (fastidious) разбо́рчивый.

futile adj тще́тный. **futility** n тще́тность.

future n бу́дущее sb; (gram) бу́дущее вре́мя neut; adj бу́дущий. **futuristic** adj футуристи́ческий.

fuzzy adj (hair) пуши́стый; (blurred) расплы́вчатый.

G

gabble vi тарато́рить impf.

gable n щипе́ц.

gad vi: ~ **about** шата́ться impf.

gadget n приспособле́ние.

gaffe n опло́шность.

gag n кляп; vt засо́вывать impf, засу́нуть pf кляп в рот+dat.

gaiety n весёлость. **gaily** adv ве́село.

gain n при́быль; pl дохо́ды m pl; (increase) приро́ст; vt (acquire) получа́ть impf, получи́ть pf; ~ **on** нагоня́ть impf, нагна́ть pf.

gait n похо́дка.

gala n пра́зднество; adj пра́здничный.

galaxy n гала́ктика; (fig) плея́да.

gale n бу́ря, шторм.

gall[1] n (bile) желчь; (cheek) на́глость; ~**-bladder** жёлчный пузы́рь m.

gall[2] vt (vex) раздража́ть impf, раздражи́ть pf.

gallant adj (brave) хра́брый; (courtly) гала́нтный. **gallantry** n хра́брость; гала́нтность.

gallery n галере́я.

galley n (ship) гале́ра; (kitchen) ка́мбуз.

gallon n галло́н.

gallop n гало́п; vi галопи́ровать impf.

gallows n pl ви́селица.

gallstone n жёлчный ка́мень m.

galore adv в изоби́лии.

galvanize vt гальванизи́ровать impf & pf.

gambit n гамби́т.

gamble n (undertaking) риско́ванное предприя́тие; vi игра́ть impf в аза́ртные и́гры; (fig) рискова́ть impf (with +instr); ~ **away** прои́грывать impf, проигра́ть pf. **gambler** n игро́к. **gambling** n аза́ртные и́гры f pl.

game n игра́; (single ~) па́ртия; (collect, animals) дичь; adj (ready) гото́вый. **gamekeeper** n лесни́к.

gammon n о́корок.

gamut n га́мма.

gang n ба́нда; (workmen) брига́да.

gangrene n гангре́на.

gangster n га́нгстер.

gangway n (passage) прохо́д; (naut) схо́дни (-ней) pl.

gaol *n* тюрьма́; *vt* заключа́ть *impf*, заключи́ть *pf* в тюрьму́. **gaoler** *n* тюре́мщик.

gap *n* (*empty space*; *deficiency*) пробе́л; (*in wall etc.*) брешь; (*fig*) разры́в.

gape *vi* (*person*) зева́ть *impf* (*at* на +*acc*); (*chasm*) зия́ть *impf*.

garage *n* гара́ж.

garb *n* одея́ние.

garbage *n* му́сор.

garbled *adj* искажённый.

garden *n* сад; *attrib* садо́вый. **gardener** *n* садо́вник. **gardening** *n* садово́дство.

gargle *vi* полоска́ть *impf*, про~ *pf* го́рло.

gargoyle *n* горгу́лья.

garish *adj* крича́щий.

garland *n* гирля́нда.

garlic *n* чесно́к.

garment *n* предме́т оде́жды.

garnish *n* гарни́р; *vt* гарни́ровать *impf* & *pf*.

garret *n* манса́рда.

garrison *n* гарнизо́н.

garrulous *adj* болтли́вый.

gas *n* газ; *attrib* га́зовый; *vt* отравля́ть *impf*, отрави́ть *pf* га́зом. **gaseous** *adj* газообра́зный.

gash *n* поре́з; *vt* поре́зать *pf*.

gasket *n* прокла́дка.

gasp *vi* задыха́ться *impf*, задохну́ться *pf*.

gastric *adj* желу́дочный.

gate *n* (*large*) воро́та (-т) *pl*; (*small*) кали́тка. **gateway** *n* (*gate*) воро́та (-т) *pl*; (*entrance*) вход.

gather *vt* & *i* собира́ть(ся) *impf*, собра́ть(ся) *pf*; *vt* заключа́ть *impf*, заключи́ть *pf*. **gathering** *n* (*assembly*) собра́ние.

gaudy *adj* крича́щий.

gauge *n* (*measure*) ме́ра; (*instrument*) кали́бр, измери́тельный прибо́р; (*rly*) коле́я; (*criterion*) крите́рий; *vt* измеря́ть *impf*, изме́рить *pf*; (*estimate*) оце́нивать *impf*, оцени́ть *pf*.

gaunt *adj* то́щий.

gauntlet *n* рукави́ца.

gauze *n* ма́рля.

gay *adj* весёлый; (*bright*) пёстрый; (*homosexual*) гомосексуа́льный.

gaze *n* при́стальный взгляд; *vi* при́стально гляде́ть *impf* (*at* на+*acc*).

gazelle *n* газе́ль.

GCSE *abbr* (*of General Certificate of Secondary Education*) аттеста́т о сре́днем образова́нии.

gear *n* (*equipment*) принадле́жности *f pl*; (*in car*) ско́рость; ~ **lever** рыча́г; *vt* приспособля́ть *impf*, приспосо́бить *pf* (**to** к+*dat*). **gearbox** *n* коро́бка переда́ч.

gel *n* космети́ческое желе́ *neut indecl.* **gelatine** *n* желати́н.

gelding *n* ме́рин.

gelignite *n* гелигни́т.

gem *n* драгоце́нный ка́мень *m*.

Gemini *n* Близнецы́ *m pl.*

gender *n* род.

gene *n* ген.

genealogy *n* генеало́гия.

general *n* генера́л; *adj* о́бщий; (*nationwide*) всео́бщий; **in** ~ вообще́.

generalization *n* обобще́ние. **generalize** *vi* обобща́ть *impf*, обобщи́ть *pf*. **generally** *adv* (*usually*) обы́чно; (*in general*) вообще́.

generate *vt* порожда́ть *impf*, породи́ть *pf*. **generation** *n* (*in descent*) поколе́ние. **generator** *n* генера́тор.

generic *adj* родово́й; (*general*) о́бщий.

generosity *n* (*magnanimity*) великоду́шие; (*munificence*) ще́дрость. **generous** *adj* великоду́шный; ще́дрый.

genesis *n* происхожде́ние; (**G**~) Кни́га Бытия́.

genetic *adj* генети́ческий. **genetics** *n* гене́тика.

genial *adj* (*of person*) доброду́шный.

genital *adj* полово́й. **genitals** *n pl* половы́е о́рганы *m pl.*

genitive *adj* (*n*) роди́тельный (паде́ж).

genius *n* (*person*) ге́ний; (*ability*) гениа́льность.

genocide *n* геноци́д.

genre *n* жанр.

genteel *adj* благовоспи́танный.

gentile *adj* нееврейский; *n* нееврей, ~ка.

gentility *n* благовоспи́танность.

gentle *adj* (*mild*) мя́гкий; (*quiet*) ти́хий; (*light*) лёгкий. **gentleman** *n* джентльме́н. **gentleness** *n* мя́гкость. **gents** *n pl* мужска́я убо́рная *sb.*

genuine *adj* (*authentic*) по́длинный;

(*sincere*) и́скренний.

genus *n* род.

geographical *adj* географи́ческий. **geography** *n* геогра́фия. **geological** *adj* геологи́ческий. **geologist** *n* гео́лог. **geology** *n* геоло́гия. **geometric(al)** *adj* геометри́ческий. **geometry** *n* геоме́трия.

Georgia *n* Гру́зия. **Georgian** *n* грузи́н, ~ка; *adj* грузи́нский.

geranium *n* гера́нь.

geriatric *adj* гериатри́ческий.

germ *m* микро́б.

German *n* не́мец, не́мка; *adj* неме́цкий; ~ **measles** красну́ха.

germane *adj* уме́стный.

Germanic *adj* герма́нский.

Germany *n* Герма́ния.

germinate *vi* прораста́ть *impf*, прорасти́ *pf*.

gesticulate *vi* жестикули́ровать *impf*. **gesture** *n* жест.

get *vt* (*obtain*) достава́ть *impf*, доста́ть *pf*; (*receive*) получа́ть *impf*, получи́ть *pf*; (*understand*) понима́ть *impf*, поня́ть *pf*; (*disease*) заража́ться *impf*, зарази́ться *pf* +*instr*; (*induce*) угова́ривать *impf*, уговори́ть *pf* (**to do** +*inf*); (*fetch*) приноси́ть *impf*, принести́ *pf*; *vi* (*become*) станови́ться *impf*, стать *pf* +*instr*; **have got** (*have*) име́ть *impf*; **have got to** быть до́лжен (-жна́) +*inf*; ~ **about** (*spread*) распространя́ться *impf*, распространи́ться *pf*; (*move around*) передвига́ться *impf*; (*travel*) разъезжа́ть *impf*; ~ **at** (*mean*) хоте́ть *impf* сказа́ть; ~ **away** (*slip off*) ускольза́ть *impf*, ускользну́ть *pf*; (*escape*) убега́ть *impf*, убежа́ть *pf*; (*leave*) уезжа́ть *impf*, уе́хать *pf*; ~ **away with** избега́ть *impf*, избежа́ть *pf* отве́тственности за+*acc*; ~ **back** (*recover*) получа́ть *impf*, получи́ть *pf* обра́тно; (*return*) возвраща́ться *impf*, верну́ться *pf*; ~ **by** (*manage*) справля́ться *impf*, спра́виться *pf*; ~ **down** сходи́ть *impf*, сойти́ *pf*; ~ **down to** принима́ться *impf*, приня́ться *pf* за+*acc*; ~ **off** слеза́ть *impf*, слезть *pf* с+*gen*; ~ **on** сади́ться *impf*, сесть *pf* в, на, +*acc*; (*prosper*) преуспева́ть *impf*, преуспе́ть *pf*; ~ **on with** (*person*) ужи-

ва́ться *impf*, ужи́ться *pf* с+*instr*; ~ **out of** (*avoid*) избавля́ться *impf*, изба́виться *pf* от+*gen*; (*car*) выходи́ть *impf*, вы́йти *pf* из+*gen*; ~ **round to** успева́ть *impf*, успе́ть *pf*; ~ **to** (*reach*) достига́ть *impf*, дости́гнуть & дости́чь *pf* +*gen*; ~ **up** (*from bed*) встава́ть *impf*, встать *pf*.

geyser *n* (*spring*) ге́йзер; (*waterheater*) коло́нка.

ghastly *adj* ужа́сный.

gherkin *n* огуре́ц.

ghetto *n* ге́тто *neut indecl*.

ghost *n* привиде́ние. **ghostly** *adj* при́зрачный.

giant *n* гига́нт; *adj* гига́нтский.

gibberish *n* тараба́рщина.

gibbet *n* ви́селица.

gibe *n* насме́шка; *vi* насмеха́ться *impf* (**at** над+*instr*).

giblets *n pl* потроха́ (-хо́в) *pl*.

giddiness *n* головокруже́ние. **giddy** *predic*: **I feel** ~ у меня́ кру́жится голова́.

gift *n* (*present*) пода́рок; (*donation*; *ability*) дар. **gifted** *adj* одарённый.

gig *n* (*theat*) выступле́ние.

gigantic *adj* гига́нтский.

giggle *n* хихи́канье; *vi* хихи́кать, хихи́кнуть *pf*.

gild *vt* золоти́ть *impf*, вы́~, по~ *pf*.

gill *n* (*of fish*) жа́бра.

gilt *n* позоло́та; *adj* золочённый.

gimmick *n* трюк.

gin *n* (*spirit*) джин.

ginger *n* имби́рь *m*; *adj* (*colour*) ры́жий.

gingerly *adv* осторо́жно.

gipsy *n* цыга́н, ~ка.

giraffe *n* жира́ф.

girder *n* ба́лка. **girdle** *n* по́яс.

girl *n* (*child*) де́вочка; (*young woman*) де́вушка. **girlfriend** *n* подру́га. **girlish** *adj* де́вичий.

girth *n* обхва́т; (*on saddle*) подпру́га.

gist *n* суть.

give *vt* дава́ть *impf*, дать *pf*; ~ **away** выдава́ть *impf*, вы́дать *pf*; ~ **back** возвраща́ть *impf*, возврати́ть *pf*; ~ **in** (*yield*, *vi*) уступа́ть *impf*, уступи́ть *pf* (**to** +*dat*); (*hand in*, *vt*) вруча́ть *impf*, вручи́ть *pf*; ~ **out** (*emit*) издава́ть *impf*, изда́ть *pf*; (*distribute*) раздава́ть *impf*, разда́ть *pf*; ~ **up** отка́зываться *impf*, отказа́ться

pf от+*gen*; (*habit etc.*) броса́ть *impf*, бро́сить *pf*; ~ **o.s. up** сдава́ться *impf*, сда́ться *pf*. **given** *predic* (*inclined*) скло́нен (-онна́, -о́нно) (**to** к+*dat*).
glacier *n* ледни́к.
glad *adj* ра́достный; *predic* рад. **gladden** *vt* ра́довать *impf*, об~ *pf*.
glade *n* поля́на.
gladly *adv* охо́тно.
glamorous *adj* я́ркий; (*attractive*) привлека́тельный.
glamour *n* я́ркость; привлека́тельность.
glance *n* (*look*) бе́глый взгляд; *vi*: ~ **at** взгля́дывать *impf*, взгляну́ть *pf* на+*acc*.
gland *n* железа́. **glandular** *adj* желе́зистый.
glare *n* (*light*) ослепи́тельный блеск; (*look*) свире́пый взгляд; *vi* свире́по смотре́ть *impf* (**at** на+*acc*). **glaring** *adj* (*dazzling*) ослепи́тельный; (*mistake*) гру́бый.
glasnost *n* гла́сность.
glass *n* (*substance*) стекло́; (*drinking vessel*) стака́н; (*wine* ~) рю́мка; (*mirror*) зе́ркало; *pl* (*spectacles*) очки́ (-ко́в) *pl*; *attrib* стекля́нный. **glassy** *adj* (*look*) ту́склый.
glaze *n* глазу́рь; *vt* (*with glass*) застекля́ть *impf*, застекли́ть *pf*; (*pottery*) глазурова́ть *impf & pf*; (*cul*) глази́ровать *impf & pf*. **glazier** *n* стеко́льщик.
gleam *n* про́блеск; *vi* свети́ться *impf*.
glean *vt* собира́ть *impf*, собра́ть *pf* по крупи́цам.
glee *n* весе́лье. **gleeful** *adj* лику́ющий.
glib *adj* бо́йкий.
glide *vi* скользи́ть *impf*; (*aeron*) плани́ровать *impf*, с~ *pf*. **glider** *n* планёр.
glimmer *n* мерца́ние; *vi* мерца́ть *impf*.
glimpse *vt* мелько́м ви́деть *impf*, у~ *pf*.
glint *n* блеск; *vi* блесте́ть *impf*.
glisten, glitter *vi* блесте́ть *impf*.
gloat *vi* злора́дствовать *impf*.
global *adj* (*world-wide*) мирово́й; (*total*) всео́бщий. **globe** *n* (*sphere*) шар; (*the earth*) земно́й шар; (*chart*) гло́бус. **globule** *n* ша́рик.
gloom *n* мрак. **gloomy** *adj* мра́чный.

glorify *vt* прославля́ть *impf*, просла́вить *pf*. **glorious** *adj* сла́вный; (*splendid*) великоле́пный. **glory** *n* сла́ва; *vi* торжествова́ть *impf*.
gloss *n* лоск; *vi*: ~ **over** зама́зывать *impf*, зама́зать *pf*.
glossary *n* глосса́рий.
glove *n* перча́тка.
glow *n* за́рево; (*of cheeks*) румя́нец; *vi* (*incandesce*) накаля́ться *impf*, накали́ться *pf*; (*shine*) сия́ть *impf*.
glucose *n* глюко́за.
glue *n* клей; *vt* прикле́ивать *impf*, прикле́ить *pf* (**to** к+*dat*).
glum *adj* угрю́мый.
glut *n* избы́ток.
glutton *n* обжо́ра *m & f*. **gluttonous** *adj* обжо́рливый. **gluttony** *n* обжо́рство.
gnarled *adj* (*hands*) шишкова́тый; (*tree*) сучкова́тый.
gnash *vt* скрежета́ть *impf* +*instr*.
gnat *n* кома́р.
gnaw *vt* грызть *impf*.
gnome *n* гном.
go *n* (*energy*) эне́ргия; (*attempt*) попы́тка; **be on the** ~ быть в движе́нии; **have a** ~ пыта́ться *impf*, по~ *pf*; *vi* (*on foot*) ходи́ть *indet*, идти́ *det*, пойти́ *pf*; (*by transport*) е́здить *indet*, е́хать *det*, по~ *pf*; (*work*) рабо́тать *impf*; (*become*) станови́ться *impf*, стать *pf* +*instr*; (*belong*) идти́ *impf*; **be** ~**ing** (**to do**) собира́ться *impf*, собра́ться *pf* (+*inf*); ~ **about** (*set to work at*) бра́ться *impf*, взя́ться *pf* за+*acc*; (*wander*) броди́ть *indet*; ~ **away** (*on foot*) уходи́ть *impf*, уйти́ *pf*; (*by transport*) уезжа́ть *impf*, уе́хать *pf*; ~ **down** спуска́ться *impf*, спусти́ться *pf* (+*gen*); ~ **in(to)** (*enter*) входи́ть *impf*, войти́ *pf* (в+*acc*); (*investigate*) рассле́довать *impf & pf*; ~ **off** (*go away*) уходи́ть *impf*, уйти́ *pf*; (*deteriorate*) по́ртиться *impf*, ис~ *pf*; ~ **on** (*continue*) продолжа́ть(ся) *impf*, продо́лжить(ся) *pf*; ~ **out** выходи́ть *impf*, вы́йти *pf*; (*flame etc.*) га́снуть *impf*, по~ *pf*; ~ **over** (*inspect*) пересма́тривать *impf*, пересмотре́ть *pf*; (*rehearse*) повторя́ть *impf*, повтори́ть *pf*; (*change allegiance etc.*) переходи́ть *impf*, перейти́ *pf* (**to** в, на, +*acc*, к+*dat*);

~ **through** (*scrutinize*) разбира́ть *impf*, разобра́ть *pf*; ~ **through with** доводи́ть *impf*, довести́ *pf* до конца́; ~ **without** обходи́ться *impf*, обойти́сь *pf* без+*gen*; ~-**ahead** предприи́мчивый; ~-**between** посре́дник.

goad *vt* (*instigate*) подстрека́ть *impf*, подстрекну́ть *pf* (**into** к+*dat*); (*taunt*) раздража́ть *impf*.

goal *n* (*aim*) цель; (*sport*) воро́та (-т) *pl*; (*point won*) гол. **goalkeeper** *n* врата́рь *m*.

goat *n* коза́; (*male*) козёл.

gobble *vt* (*eat*) жрать *impf*; ~ **up** пожира́ть *impf*, пожра́ть *pf*.

goblet *n* бока́л, ку́бок.

god *n* бог; (G~) Бог. **godchild** *n* кре́стник, -ица. **god-daughter** *n* кре́стница. **goddess** *n* боги́ня. **godfather** *n* крёстный *sb*. **God-fearing** *adj* богобоя́зненный. **godless** *adj* безбо́жный. **godly** *adj* на́божный. **godmother** *n* крёстная *sb*. **godparent** *n* крёстный *sb*. **godsend** *n* бо́жий дар. **godson** *n* кре́стник.

goggle *vi* тара́щить *impf* глаза́ (**at** на+*acc*); *n*: *pl* защи́тные очки́ (-ко́в) *pl*.

going *adj* де́йствующий. **goings-on** *n pl* дела́ *neut pl*.

gold *n* зо́лото; *adj* золото́й; ~-**plated** накладно́го зо́лота; ~-**smith** золоты́х дел ма́стер. **golden** *adj* золото́й; ~ **eagle** бе́ркут. **goldfish** *n* золота́я ры́бка.

golf *n* гольф; ~ **club** (*implement*) клю́шка; ~ **course** площа́дка для го́льфа. **golfer** *n* игро́к в гольф.

gondola *n* гондо́ла.

gong *n* гонг.

gonorrhoea *n* три́ппер.

good *n* добро́; *pl* (*wares*) това́р(ы); **do** ~ (*benefit*) идти́ *impf*, пойти́ *pf* на по́льзу +*dat*; *adj* хоро́ший, до́брый; ~-**humoured** добродушный; ~-**looking** краси́вый; ~ **morning** до́брое у́тро!; ~ **night** споко́йной но́чи! **goodbye** *int* проща́й(те)!; до свида́ния! **goodness** *n* доброта́.

goose *n* гусь *m*; ~-**flesh** гуси́ная ко́жа.

gooseberry *n* крыжо́вник.

gore[1] *n* (*blood*) запёкшаяся кровь.
gore[2] *vt* (*pierce*) бода́ть *impf*, за~ *pf*.
gorge *n* (*geog*) ущелье; *vi* & *t* объ-

еда́ться *impf*, объе́сться *pf* (**on** +*instr*).

gorgeous *adj* великоле́пный.

gorilla *n* гори́лла.

gorse *n* уте́сник.

gory *adj* крова́вый.

gosh *int* бо́же мой!

Gospel *n* Ева́нгелие.

gossip *n* спле́тня; (*person*) спле́тник, -ица; *vi* спле́тничать *impf*, на~ *pf*.

Gothic готи́ческий.

gouge *vt*: ~ **out** выда́лбливать *impf*, вы́долбить *pf*; (*eyes*) выка́лывать *impf*, вы́колоть *pf*.

goulash *n* гуля́ш.

gourmet *n* гурма́н.

gout *n* пода́гра.

govern *vt* пра́вить *impf* +*instr*; (*determine*) определя́ть *impf*, определи́ть *pf*. **governess** *n* гуверна́нтка. **government** *n* прави́тельство. **governmental** *adj* прави́тельственный. **governor** *n* губерна́тор; (*of school etc.*) член правле́ния.

gown *n* пла́тье; (*official's*) ма́нтия.

grab *vt* захва́тывать *impf*, захвати́ть *pf*.

grace *n* (*gracefulness*) гра́ция; (*refinement*) изя́щество; (*favour*) ми́лость; (*at meal*) моли́тва; **have the** ~ **to** быть насто́лько такти́чен, что; **with bad** ~ нелюбе́зно; **with good** ~ с досто́инством; *vt* (*adorn*) украша́ть *impf*, укра́сить *pf*; (*favour*) удоста́ивать *impf*, удосто́ить *pf* (**with** +*gen*). **graceful** *adj* грацио́зный.

gracious *adj* ми́лостивый.

gradation *n* града́ция.

grade *n* (*level*) сте́пень; (*quality*) сорт; *vt* сортирова́ть *impf*, рас~ *pf*.

gradient *n* укло́н.

gradual *adj* постепе́нный.

graduate *n* око́нчивший *sb* университе́т, вуз; *vi* конча́ть *impf*, око́нчить *pf* (университе́т, вуз); *vt* градуи́ровать *impf* & *pf*.

graffiti *n* на́дписи *f pl*.

graft *n* (*bot*) черено́к; (*med*) переса́дка (живо́й тка́ни); *vt* (*bot*) привива́ть *impf*, приви́ть *pf* (**to** +*dat*); (*med*) переса́живать *impf*, пересади́ть *pf*.

grain *n* (*seed*; *collect*) зерно́; (*particle*)

крупи́нка; (*of sand*) песчи́нка; (*of wood*) (древе́сное) волокно́; **against the** ~ не по нутру́.

gram(me) *n* грамм.

grammar *n* грамма́тика; ~ **school** гимна́зия. **grammatical** *adj* граммати́ческий.

gramophone *n* прои́грыватель *m*; ~ **record** грампласти́нка.

granary *n* амба́р.

grand *adj* великоле́пный; ~ **piano** роя́ль *m*. **grandchild** *n* внук, вну́чка. **granddaughter** *n* вну́чка. **grandfather** *n* де́душка *m*. **grandmother** *n* ба́бушка. **grandparents** *n* ба́бушка и де́душка. **grandson** *n* внук. **grandstand** *n* трибу́на.

grandeur *n* вели́чие.

grandiose *adj* грандио́зный.

granite *n* грани́т.

granny *n* ба́бушка.

grant *n* (*financial*) дота́ция; (*univ*) стипе́ндия; *vt* дарова́ть *impf* & *pf*; (*concede*) допуска́ть *impf*, допусти́ть *pf*; **take for** ~**ed** (*assume*) счита́ть *impf*, счесть *pf* само́ собо́й разуме́ющимся; (*not appreciate*) принима́ть *impf* как до́лжное.

granular *adj* зерни́стый.

granulated *adj*: ~ **sugar** са́харный песо́к.

granule *n* зёрнышко.

grape *n* виногра́д. **grapefruit** *n* гре́йпфрут.

graph *n* гра́фик.

graphic *adj* графи́ческий; (*vivid*) я́ркий.

graphite *n* графи́т.

grapple *vi* (*struggle*) боро́ться *impf* (**with** с+*instr*).

grasp *n* (*grip*) хва́тка; (*comprehension*) понима́ние; *vt* (*clutch*) хвата́ть *impf*, схвати́ть *pf*; (*comprehend*) понима́ть *impf*, поня́ть *pf*. **grasping** *adj* жа́дный.

grass *n* трава́. **grasshopper** *n* кузне́чик. **grassy** *adj* травяни́стый.

grate[1] *n* (*in fireplace*) решётка.

grate[2] *vt* (*rub*) тере́ть *impf*, на- *pf*; *vi* (*sound*) скрипе́ть *impf*; ~ (**up**)**on** (*irritate*) раздража́ть *impf*, раздражи́ть *pf*.

grateful *n* благода́рный.

grater *n* тёрка.

gratify *vt* удовлетворя́ть *impf*, удовлетвори́ть *pf*.

grating *n* решётка.

gratis *adv* беспла́тно.

gratitude *n* благода́рность.

gratuitous *adj* (*free*) даровой; (*motiveless*) беспричи́нный.

gratuity *n* (*tip*) чаевы́е *sb pl*.

grave[1] *n* моги́ла. **gravedigger** *n* моги́льщик. **gravestone** *n* надгро́бный ка́мень *m*. **graveyard** *n* кла́дбище.

grave[2] *adj* серьёзный.

gravel *n* гра́вий.

gravitate *vi* тяготе́ть *impf* (**towards** к+*dat*). **gravitational** *adj* гравитацио́нный. **gravity** *n* (*seriousness*) серьёзность; (*force*) тя́жесть.

gravy *n* (мясна́я) подли́вка.

graze[1] *vi* (*feed*) пасти́сь *impf*.

graze[2] *n* (*abrasion*) цара́пина; *vt* (*touch*) задева́ть *impf*, заде́ть *pf*; (*abrade*) цара́пать *impf*, о~ *pf*.

grease *n* жир; (*lubricant*) сма́зка; ~ **paint** грим; *vt* сма́зывать *impf*, сма́зать *pf*. **greasy** *adj* жи́рный.

great *adj* (*large*) большой; (*eminent*) вели́кий; (*splendid*) замеча́тельный; **to a** ~ **extent** в большо́й сте́пени; **a** ~ **deal** мно́го (+*gen*); **a** ~ **many** мно́гие; ~-**aunt** двою́родная ба́бушка; ~-**granddaughter** пра́внучка; ~-**grandfather** пра́дед; ~-**grandmother** праба́бка; ~-**grandson** пра́внук; ~-**uncle** двою́родный де́душка *m*. **greatly** *adv* о́чень.

Great Britain *n* Великобрита́ния.

Greece *n* Гре́ция.

greed *n* жа́дность (**for** к+*dat*). **greedy** *adj* жа́дный (**for** к+*dat*).

Greek *n* грек, греча́нка; *adj* гре́ческий.

green *n* (*colour*) зелёный цвет; (*piece of land*) лужо́к; *pl* зе́лень *collect*; *adj* зелёный; (*inexperienced*) неопы́тный. **greenery** *n* зе́лень. **greenfly** *n* тля. **greengrocer** *n* зеленщи́к. **greenhouse** *n* тепли́ца; ~ **effect** парнико́вый эффе́кт.

greet *vt* здоро́ваться *impf*, по~ *pf* с +*instr*; (*meet*) встреча́ть *impf*, встре́тить *pf*. **greeting** *n* приве́т(ствие).

gregarious *adj* общи́тельный.

grenade *n* грана́та.

grey *adj* се́рый; (*hair*) седо́й.

greyhound *n* борзая *sb*.

grid n (*grating*) решётка; (*electr*) сеть; (*map*) координа́тная се́тка.

grief n го́ре; **come to ~** терпе́ть *impf*, по~ *pf* неуда́чу.

grievance n жа́лоба, оби́да.

grieve vt огорча́ть *impf*, огорчи́ть *pf*; vi горева́ть *impf* (**for** o+*prep*).

grievous adj тя́жкий.

grill n ра́шпер; vt (*cook*) жа́рить *impf*, за~, из~ *pf* (на ра́шпере); (*question*) допра́шивать *impf*, допроси́ть *pf*.

grille n (*grating*) решётка.

grim adj (*stern*) суро́вый; (*unpleasant*) неприя́тный.

grimace n грима́са; vi грима́сничать *impf*.

grime n грязь. **grimy** adj гря́зный.

grin n усме́шка; vi усмеха́ться *impf*, усмехну́ться *pf*.

grind vt (*flour etc.*) моло́ть *impf*, с~ *pf*; (*axe*) точи́ть *impf*, на~ *pf*; **~ one's teeth** скрежета́ть *impf* зуба́ми.

grip n хва́тка; vt схва́тывать *impf*, схвати́ть *pf*.

gripe vi ворча́ть *impf*.

gripping adj захва́тывающий.

grisly adj жу́ткий.

gristle n хрящ.

grit n песо́к; (*for building*) гра́вий; (*firmness*) вы́держка.

grizzle vi хны́кать *impf*.

groan n стон; vi стона́ть *impf*.

grocer n бакале́йщик; **~'s (shop)** бакале́йная ла́вка, гастроно́м. **groceries** n pl бакале́я collect.

groggy adj разби́тый.

groin n (*anat*) пах.

groom n ко́нюх; (*bridegroom*) жени́х; vt (*horse*) чи́стить *impf*, по~ *pf*; (*prepare*) гото́вить *impf*, под~ *pf* (**for** k+*dat*); **well-groomed** хорошо́ вы́глядящий.

groove n желобо́к.

grope vi нащу́пывать *impf* (**for, after** +*acc*).

gross¹ n (*12 dozen*) гросс.

gross² adj (*fat*) ту́чный; (*coarse*) гру́бый; (*total*) валово́й; **~ weight** вес бру́тто.

grotesque adj гроте́скный.

grotto n грот.

ground n земля́; (*earth*) по́чва; pl (*dregs*) гу́ща; (*sport*) площа́дка; pl (*of house*) парк; (*reason*) основа́ние;

~ floor пе́рвый эта́ж; vt (*instruct*) обуча́ть *impf*, обучи́ть *pf* осно́вам (**in** +*gen*); (*aeron*) запреща́ть *impf*, запрети́ть *pf* полёты +*gen*; vi (*naut*) сади́ться *impf*, сесть *pf* на мель.

groundless adj необосно́ванный.

groundwork n фунда́мент.

group n гру́ппа; vt & i группирова́ть(ся) *impf*, с~ *pf*.

grouse¹ n шотла́ндская куропа́тка.

grouse² vi (*grumble*) ворча́ть *impf*.

grove n ро́ща.

grovel vi пресмыка́ться *impf* (**before** пе́ред+*instr*).

grow vi расти́ *impf*; (*become*) станови́ться *impf*, стать *pf* +*instr*; vt (*cultivate*) выра́щивать *impf*, вы́растить *pf*; (*hair*) отра́щивать *impf*, отрасти́ть *pf*; **~ up** (*person*) выраста́ть *impf*, вы́расти *pf*; (*custom*) возника́ть *impf*, возни́кнуть *pf*.

growl n ворча́ние; vi ворча́ть *impf* (**at** на+*acc*).

grown-up adj взро́слый sb.

growth n рост; (*med*) о́пухоль.

grub n (*larva*) личи́нка; (*food*) жратва́; vi: **~ about** ры́ться *impf*. **grubby** adj запа́чканный.

grudge n зло́ба; **have a ~ against** име́ть *impf* зуб про́тив+*gen*; vt жале́ть *impf*, по~ *pf* +*acc*, +*gen*. **grudgingly** adv неохо́тно.

gruelling adj изнури́тельный.

gruesome adj жу́ткий.

gruff adj (*surly*) грубова́тый; (*voice*) хри́плый.

grumble vi ворча́ть *impf* (**at** на+*acc*).

grumpy adj брюзгли́вый.

grunt n хрю́канье; vi хрю́кать *impf*, хрю́кнуть *pf*.

guarantee n гара́нтия; vt гаранти́ровать *impf* & *pf* (**against** от+*gen*). **guarantor** n поручи́тель m.

guard n (*device*) предохрани́тель; (*watch; soldiers*) карау́л; (*sentry*) часово́й m; (*watchman*) сто́рож; (*rly*) конду́ктор; pl (*prison*) надзира́тель m; vt охраня́ть *impf*, охрани́ть *pf*; vi: **~ against** остерега́ться *impf*, остере́чься *pf* +*gen*, inf. **guardian** n храни́тель m; (*law*) опеку́н.

guer(r)illa n партиза́н; **~ warfare** партиза́нская война́.

guess n дога́дка; vt & i дога́дываться

impf, догада́ться *pf* (o+*prep*); *vt* (~ *correctly*) уга́дывать *impf*, угада́ть *pf*. **guesswork** *n* дога́дки *f pl*.

guest *n* гость *m*; ~ **house** ма́ленькая гости́ница.

guffaw *n* хо́хот; *vi* хохота́ть *impf*.

guidance *n* руково́дство. **guide** *n* проводни́к, гид; (*guidebook*) путеводи́тель *m*; *vt* води́ть indet, вести́ det; (*direct*) руководи́ть *impf* +*instr*; ~**ed missile** управля́емая раке́та. **guidelines** *n pl* инстру́кции *f pl*; (*advice*) сове́т.

guild *n* ги́льдия, цех.

guile *n* кова́рство. **guileless** *adj* простоду́шный.

guillotine *n* гильоти́на.

guilt *n* вина́; (*guiltiness*) вино́вность. **guilty** *adj* (*of crime*) вино́вный (**of** в+*prep*); (*of wrong*) винова́тый.

guinea-pig *n* морска́я сви́нка; (*fig*) подо́пытный кро́лик.

guise *n*: **under the** ~ **of** под ви́дом +*gen*.

guitar *n* гита́ра. **guitarist** *n* гитари́ст.

gulf *n* (*geog*) зали́в; (*chasm*) про́пасть.

gull *n* ча́йка.

gullet *n* (*oesophagus*) пищево́д; (*throat*) го́рло.

gullible *adj* легкове́рный.

gully *n* (*ravine*) овра́г.

gulp *n* глото́к; *vt* жа́дно глота́ть *impf*.

gum[1] *n* (*anat*) десна́.

gum[2] *n* каме́дь; (*glue*) клей; *vt* скле́ивать *impf*, скле́ить *pf*.

gumption *n* инициати́ва.

gun *n* (*piece of ordnance*) ору́дие, пу́шка; (*rifle etc.*) ружьё; (*pistol*) пистоле́т; *vt*: ~ **down** расстре́ливать *impf*, расстреля́ть *pf*. **gunner** *n* артиллери́ст. **gunpowder** *n* по́рох.

gurgle *vi* бу́лькать *impf*.

gush *vi* хлы́нуть *pf*.

gusset *n* клин.

gust *n* поры́в. **gusty** *adj* поры́вистый.

gusto *n* смак.

gut *n* кишка́; *pl* (*entrails*) кишки́ *f pl*; (*bravery*) му́жество; *vt* потроши́ть *impf*, вы́~ *pf*; (*devastate*) опустоша́ть *impf*, опустоши́ть *pf*.

gutter *n* (*of roof*) (водосто́чный) жёлоб; (*of road*) сто́чная кана́ва.

guttural *adj* горта́нный.

guy[1] *n* (*rope*) оття́жка.

guy[2] *n* (*fellow*) па́рень *m*.

guzzle *vt* (*food*) пожира́ть *impf*, пожра́ть *pf*; (*liquid*) хлеба́ть *impf*, хлебну́ть *pf*.

gym *n* (*gymnasium*) гимнасти́ческий зал; (*gymnastics*) гимна́стика. **gymnasium** *n* гимнасти́ческий зал. **gymnast** *n* гимна́ст. **gymnastic** *adj* гимнасти́ческий. **gymnastics** *n* гимна́стика.

gynaecologist *n* гинеко́лог. **gynaecology** *n* гинеколо́гия.

gyrate *vi* враща́ться *impf*.

H

haberdashery *n* галантере́я; (*shop*) галантере́йный магази́н.

habit *n* привы́чка; (*monk's*) ря́са.

habitable *adj* приго́дный для жилья́. **habitat** *n* есте́ственная среда́. **habitation** *n*: **unfit for** ~ неприго́дный для жилья́.

habitual *adj* привы́чный.

hack[1] *vt* руби́ть *impf*; ~**saw** ножо́вка.

hack[2] *n* (*hired horse*) наёмная ло́шадь; (*writer*) халту́рщик. **hackneyed** *adj* изби́тый.

haddock *n* пи́кша.

haemophilia *n* гемофили́я. **haemorrhage** *n* кровотече́ние. **haemorrhoids** *n pl* геморро́й *collect*.

hag *n* карга́.

haggard *adj* изможднённый.

haggle *vi* торгова́ться *impf*, с~ *pf*.

hail[1] *n* град; *vi* **it is** ~**ing** идёт град. **hailstone** *n* гра́дина.

hail[2] *vt* (*greet*) приве́тствовать *impf* (& *pf* in past); (*taxi*) подзыва́ть *impf*, подозва́ть *pf*; *vi*: ~ **from** быть ро́дом из+*gen*.

hair *n* (*single* ~) во́лос; *collect* (*human*) во́лосы (-о́с, -оса́м) *pl*; (*animal*) шерсть. **hairbrush** *n* щётка для воло́с. **haircut** *n* стри́жка; **have a** ~ постри́чься *pf*. **hair-do** *n* причёска. **hairdresser** *n* парикма́хер. **hair-dryer** *n* фен. **hairstyle** *n* причёска. **hairy** *adj* волоса́тый.

hale *adj*: ~ **and hearty** здоро́вый и бо́дрый.

half *n* полови́на; (*sport*) тайм; *adj*

полови́нный; in ~ попола́м; one and a ~ полтора́; ~ past (one etc.) полови́на (второ́го и т.д.); ~-hearted равноду́шный; ~ an hour полчаса́; ~-time переры́в ме́жду та́ймами; ~-way на полпути́; ~-witted слабоу́мный.

hall n (large room) зал; (entrance ~) холл, вестибю́ль m; (~ of residence) общежи́тие. **hallmark** n про́бирное клеймо́; (fig) при́знак.

hallo int здра́сте, приве́т; (on telephone) алло́.

hallucination n галлюцина́ция.

halo n (around Saint) нимб; (fig) орео́л.

halt n остано́вка; vt & i остана́вливать(ся) impf, останови́ть(ся) pf; int (mil) стой(те)! **halting** adj запина́ющий.

halve vt дели́ть impf, раз~ pf попола́м.

ham n (cul) ветчина́.

hamlet n деревушка.

hammer n молото́к; vt бить impf молотко́м.

hammock n гама́к.

hamper[1] n (basket) корзи́на с крышкой.

hamper[2] vt (hinder) меша́ть impf, по~ pf +dat.

hamster n хомя́к.

hand n рука́; (worker) рабо́чий sb; (writing) по́черк; (clock ~) стре́лка; at ~ под руко́й; on ~s and knees на четвере́ньках; vt передава́ть impf, переда́ть pf; ~ in подава́ть impf, пода́ть pf; ~ out раздава́ть impf, разда́ть pf. **handbag** n су́мка. **handbook** n руково́дство. **handcuffs** n pl нару́чники m pl. **handful** n горсть.

handicap n (sport) гандика́п; (hindrance) поме́ха. **handicapped** adj: ~ person инвали́д.

handicraft n ремесло́.

handiwork n ручна́я рабо́та.

handkerchief n носово́й плато́к.

handle n ру́чка, рукоя́тка; vt (people) обраща́ться impf c+instr; (situations) справля́ться impf, спра́виться pf c+instr; (touch) тро́гать impf, тро́нуть pf руко́й, рука́ми. **handlebar(s)** n руль m.

handmade adj ручно́й рабо́ты.

handout n пода́чка; (document) лифле́т.

handrail n пери́ла (-л) pl.

handshake n рукопожа́тие.

handsome adj краси́вый; (generous) ще́дрый.

handwriting n по́черк.

handy adj (convenient) удо́бный; (skilful) ло́вкий; come in ~ пригоди́ться pf.

hang vt ве́шать impf, пове́сить pf; vi висе́ть impf; ~ about слоня́ться impf; ~ on (cling) держа́ться impf; (tel) не ве́шать impf тру́бку; (persist) упо́рствовать impf; ~ out выве́шивать impf, вы́весить pf; (spend time) болта́ться impf; ~ up ве́шать impf, пове́сить pf; (tel) ве́шать impf, пове́сить pf тру́бку. **hanger** n ве́шалка. **hanger-on** n прилипа́ла m & f. **hangman** n пала́ч.

hangar n анга́р.

hangover n похме́лье.

hang-up n ко́мплекс.

hanker vi: ~ after мечта́ть impf o+prep.

haphazard adj случа́йный.

happen vi (occur) случа́ться impf, случи́ться pf; происходи́ть impf, произойти́ pf; ~ to be somewhere ока́зываться impf, оказа́ться pf; ~ upon ната́лкиваться impf, натолкну́ться pf на+acc.

happiness n сча́стье. **happy** adj счастли́вый; ~-go-lucky беззабо́тный.

harass vt (pester) дёргать impf; (persecute) пресле́довать impf. **harassment** n тра́вля; пресле́дование.

harbinger n предве́стник.

harbour n га́вань, порт; vt (person) укрыва́ть impf, укры́ть pf; (thoughts) зата́ивать impf, затаи́ть pf.

hard adj твёрдый; (difficult) тру́дный; (difficult to bear) тяжёлый; (severe) суро́вый; ~-boiled egg яйцо́ вкруту́ю; ~-headed практи́чный; ~-hearted жестокосе́рдный; ~-up стеснённый в сре́дствах; ~-working трудолюби́вый. **hardboard** n стро́ительный карто́н.

harden vi затвердева́ть impf, затверде́ть pf; (fig) ожесточа́ться impf, ожесточи́ться pf.

hardly adv едва́ (ли).

hardship *n* (*privation*) нужда́.

hardware *n* скобяны́е изде́лия *neut pl*; (*comput*) аппарату́ра.

hardy *adj* (*robust*) выно́сливый; (*plant*) морозосто́йкий.

hare *n* за́яц.

hark *vi*: ~ **back to** возвраща́ться *impf*, верну́ться *pf* к+*dat*; *int* слу́шай(те)!

harm *n* вред; *vt* вреди́ть *impf*, по~ *pf* +*dat*. **harmful** *adj* вре́дный. **harmless** *adj* безвре́дный.

harmonic *adj* гармони́ческий. **harmonica** *n* губна́я гармо́ника. **harmonious** *adj* гармони́чный. **harmonize** *vi* гармони́ровать *impf* (**with** с+*instr*). **harmony** *n* гармо́ния.

harness *n* у́пряжь; *vt* запряга́ть *impf*, запря́чь *pf*; (*fig*) испо́льзовать *impf* & *pf*.

harp *n* а́рфа; *vi*: ~ **on** тверди́ть *impf* о+*prep*.

harpoon *n* гарпу́н.

harpsichord *n* клавеси́н.

harrow *n* борона́. **harrowing** *adj* душераздира́ющий.

harsh *adj* (*sound*, *colour*) ре́зкий; (*cruel*) суро́вый.

harvest *n* жа́тва, сбор (плодо́в); (*yield*) урожа́й; (*fig*) плоды́ *m pl*; *vt* & *abs* собира́ть *impf*, собра́ть *pf* (урожа́й).

hash *n*: **make a** ~ **of** напу́тать *pf* +*acc*, в+*prep*.

hashish *n* гаши́ш.

hassle *n* беспоко́йство.

hassock *n* поду́шечка.

haste *n* спе́шка. **hasten** *vi* спеши́ть *impf*, по~ *pf*; *vt* & *i* торопи́ть(ся) *impf*, по~ *pf*; *vt* ускоря́ть *impf*, уско́рить *pf*. **hasty** *adj* (*hurried*) поспе́шный; (*quick-tempered*) вспы́льчивый.

hat *n* ша́пка; (*stylish*) шля́па.

hatch[1] *n* люк; ~**back** маши́на-пика́п.

hatch[2] *vi* вылупли́ваться, вылупля́ться *impf*, вы́лупиться *pf*.

hatchet *n* топо́рик.

hate *n* не́нависть; *vt* ненави́деть *impf*. **hateful** *adj* ненави́стный. **hatred** *n* не́нависть.

haughty *adj* надме́нный.

haul *n* (*fish*) уло́в; (*loot*) добы́ча; (*distance*) езда́; *vt* (*drag*) тяну́ть *impf*; таска́ть *indet*, тащи́ть *det*.

haulage *n* перево́зка.

haunt *n* люби́мое ме́сто; *vt* (*ghost*) обита́ть *impf*; (*memory*) пресле́довать *impf*. **haunted** *adj*: ~ **house** дом с привиде́ниями. **haunting** *adj* навя́зчивый.

have *vt* име́ть *impf*; **I** ~ (*possess*) у меня́ (есть; был, -а́, -о) +*nom*; **I** ~ **not** у меня́ нет (*past* не́ было) +*gen*; **I** ~ (**got**) **to** я до́лжен +*inf*; **you had better** вам лу́чше бы +*inf*; ~ **on** (*wear*) быть оде́тым в +*prep*; (*be engaged in*) быть за́нятым +*instr*.

haven *n* (*refuge*) убе́жище.

haversack *n* рюкза́к.

havoc *n* (*devastation*) опустоше́ние; (*disorder*) беспоря́док.

hawk[1] *n* (*bird*) я́стреб.

hawk[2] *vt* (*trade*) торгова́ть *impf* вразно́с+*instr*. **hawker** *n* разно́счик.

hawser *n* трос.

hawthorn *n* боя́рышник.

hay *n* се́но; ~ **make** ~ коси́ть *impf*, с~ *pf* се́но; ~ **fever** сенна́я лихора́дка. **haystack** *n* стог.

hazard *n* риск; *vt* рискова́ть *impf* +*instr*. **hazardous** *adj* риско́ванный. **haze** *n* ды́мка.

hazel *n* лещи́на. **hazelnut** *n* лесно́й оре́х.

hazy *adj* тума́нный; (*vague*) сму́тный.

he *pron* он.

head *n* голова́; (*mind*) ум; (~ **of coin**) лицева́я сторона́ моне́ты; ~ **or tails?** орёл и́ли ре́шка?; (*chief*) глава́ *m*, нача́льник; *attrib* гла́вный; *vt* (*lead*) возглавля́ть *impf*, возгла́вить *pf*; (*ball*) забива́ть *impf*, заби́ть *pf* голово́й; *vi*: ~ **for** направля́ться *impf*, напра́виться *pf* в, на, +*acc*, к+*dat*. **headache** *n* головна́я боль. **head-dress** *n* головно́й убо́р. **header** *n* уда́р голово́й. **heading** *n* (*title*) заголо́вок. **headland** *n* мыс. **headlight** *n* фа́ра. **headline** *n* заголо́вок. **headlong** *adv* стремгла́в. **headmaster, -mistress** *n* дире́ктор шко́лы. **head-on** *adj* голово́й; *adv* в лоб. **headphone** *n* нау́шник. **headquarters** *n* штаб-кварти́ра. **headscarf** *n* косы́нка. **headstone** *n* надгро́бный ка́мень *m*. **headstrong** *adj* своево́льный. **headway** *n* движе́ние вперёд. **heady** *adj* опьяня́ющий.

heal *vt* изле́чивать *impf*, излечи́ть

pf; vi зажива́ть *impf*, зажи́ть *pf.*
healing *adj* целе́бный.
health *n* здоро́вье; ~ care здраво-
охране́ние. **healthy** *adj* здоро́вый;
(*beneficial*) поле́зный.
heap *n* ку́ча; *vt* нагроможда́ть *impf*,
нагромозди́ть *pf.*
hear *vt* слы́шать *impf*, y~ *pf*; (*listen
to*) слу́шать *impf*, по~ *pf*; ~ out
выслу́шивать *impf*, вы́слушать *pf.*
hearing *n* слух; (*law*) слу́шание.
hearsay *n* слух.
hearse *n* катафа́лк.
heart *n* се́рдце; (*essence*) суть; *pl*
(*cards*) че́рви (-ве́й) *pl*; by ~ на-
изу́сть; ~ attack серде́чный приступ. **heartburn** *n* изжо́га. **hearten**
vt ободря́ть *impf*, ободри́ть *pf.*
heartfelt *adj* серде́чный. **heartless**
adj бессерде́чный. **heart-rending**
adj душераздира́ющий. **hearty** *adj*
(*cordial*) серде́чный; (*vigorous*)
здоро́вый.
hearth *n* оча́г.
heat *n* жара́; (*phys*) теплота́; (*of feeling*) пыл; (*sport*) забе́г, зае́зд; *vt
& i* (*heat up*) нагрева́ть(ся) *impf*,
нагре́ть(ся) *pf*; *vt* (*house*) топи́ть
impf. **heater** *n* нагрева́тель *m.* **heating** *n* отопле́ние.
heath *n* пу́стошь.
heathen *n* язы́чник; *adj* язы́ческий.
heather *n* ве́реск.
heave *vt* (*lift*) поднима́ть *impf*, под-
ня́ть *pf*; (*pull*) тяну́ть *impf*, по~ *pf.*
heaven *n* (*sky*) не́бо; (*paradise*) рай;
pl небеса́ *neut pl.* **heavenly** *adj*
небе́сный; (*divine*) боже́ственный.
heavy *adj* тяжёлый; (*strong, intense*)
си́льный. **heavyweight** *n* тяжело-
ве́с.
Hebrew *adj* (дре́вне)евре́йский.
heckle *vt* перека́ться *impf* c+*instr.*
hectic *adj* лихора́дочный.
hedge *n* жива́я и́згородь. **hedgerow**
n шпале́ра.
hedgehog *n* ёж.
heed *vt* обраща́ть *impf*, обрати́ть *pf*
внима́ние на+*acc.* **heedless** *adj* не-
бре́жный.
heel[1] *n* (*of foot*) пята́; (*of foot, sock*)
пя́тка; (*of shoe*) каблу́к.
heel[2] *vi* крени́ться *impf*, на~ *pf.*
hefty *adj* дю́жий.
heifer *n* тёлка.

height *n* высота́; (*of person*) рост.
heighten *vt* (*strengthen*) уси́ливать
impf, уси́лить *pf.*
heinous *adj* гну́сный.
heir *n* насле́дник. **heiress** *n* насле́д-
ница. **heirloom** *n* фами́льная вещь.
helicopter *n* вертолёт.
helium *n* ге́лий.
hell *n* ад. **hellish** *adj* а́дский.
hello *see* hallo
helm *n* руль.
helmet *n* шлем.
help *n* по́мощь; *vt* помога́ть *impf*,
помо́чь *pf +dat*; (*can't* ~) не мочь
impf не +*inf*; ~ o.s. брать *impf*,
взять *pf* себе́; ~ yourself! бери́те!
helpful *adj* поле́зный; (*obliging*)
услу́жливый. **helping** *n* (*of food*)
по́рция. **helpless** *adj* беспо́мощ-
ный.
helter-skelter *adv* как попа́ло.
hem *n* рубе́ц; *vt* подруба́ть *impf*,
подруби́ть *pf*; ~ in окружа́ть *impf*,
окружи́ть *pf.*
hemisphere *n* полуша́рие.
hemp *n* (*plant*) конопля́; (*fibre*)
пенька́.
hen *n* (*female bird*) са́мка; (*domestic
fowl*) ку́рица.
hence *adv* (*from here*) отсю́да; (*as a
result*) сле́довательно; 3 years ~
че́рез три го́да. **henceforth** *adv*
отны́не.
henchman *n* приспе́шник.
henna *n* хна.
hepatitis *n* гепати́т.
her *poss pron* её; свой.
herald *n* ве́стник; *vt* возвеща́ть *impf*,
возвести́ть *pf.*
herb *n* трава́. **herbaceous** *adj* травя-
но́й; ~ border цвето́чный бордю́р.
herbal *adj* травяно́й.
herd *n* ста́до; (*people*) толпи́ться
impf, c~ *pf*; *vt* (*tend*) пасти́ *impf*;
(*drive*) загоня́ть *impf*, загна́ть *pf* в
ста́до.
here *adv* (*position*) здесь, тут; (*direction*) сюда́; ~ is ... вот (+*nom*);
~ and there там и сям; ~ you are!
пожа́луйста. **hereabout(s)** *adv* по-
бли́зости. **hereafter** *adv* в бу́дущем.
hereby *adv* э́тим. **hereupon** *adv* (*in
consequence*) всле́дствие э́того; (*after*) по́сле э́того. **herewith** *adv* при
сём.

hereditary *adj* насле́дственный. **heredity** *n* насле́дственность.

heresy *n* е́ресь. **heretic** *n* ерети́к. **heretical** *adj* ерети́ческий.

heritage *n* насле́дие.

hermetic *adj* гермети́ческий.

hermit *n* отше́льник.

hernia *n* гры́жа.

hero *n* геро́й. **heroic** *adj* герои́ческий. **heroin** *n* герои́н.

heroine *n* герои́ня. **heroism** *n* герои́зм.

heron *n* ца́пля.

herpes *n* лиша́й.

herring *n* сельдь; (*food*) селёдка.

hers *poss pron* её; свой.

herself *pron* (*emph*) (она́) сама́; (*refl*) себя́.

hertz *n* герц.

hesitant *adj* нереши́тельный. **hesitate** *vi* колеба́ться *impf*, по~ *pf*; (*in speech*) запина́ться *impf*, запну́ться *pf*. **hesitation** *n* колеба́ние.

hessian *n* мешкови́на.

heterogeneous *adj* разноро́дный.

heterosexual *adj* гетеросексуа́льный.

hew *vt* руби́ть *impf*.

hexagon *n* шестиуго́льник.

hey *int* эй!

heyday *n* расцве́т.

hi *int* приве́т!

hiatus *n* пробе́л.

hibernate *vi* быть *impf* в спя́чке; впада́ть *impf*, впасть *pf* в спя́чку. **hibernation** *n* спя́чка.

hiccup *vi* ика́ть *impf*, икну́ть *pf*; *n*: *pl* ико́та.

hide[1] *n* (*skin*) шку́ра.

hide[2] *vt & i* (*conceal*) пря́тать(ся) *impf*, с~ *pf*; скрыва́ть(ся) *impf*, скры́ть(ся) *pf*.

hideous *adj* отврати́тельный.

hideout *n* укры́тие.

hiding *n* (*flogging*) по́рка.

hierarchy *n* иера́рхия.

hieroglyphics *n pl* иеро́глифы *m pl*.

hi-fi *n* прои́грыватель *m* с высоко-ка́чественным воспроизведе́нием зву́ка за́писи.

higgledy-piggledy *adv* как придётся.

high *adj* высо́кий; (*wind*) си́льный; (*on drugs*) в наркоти́ческом дурма́не; ~**er education** вы́сшее образова́ние; ~**-handed** своево́льный;

~**-heeled** на высо́ких каблука́х; ~**jump** прыжо́к в высоту́; ~**-minded** благоро́дный; иде́йный; ~**-pitched** высо́кий; ~**-rise** высо́тный. **high-brow** *adj* интеллектуа́льный. **highland(s)** *n* го́рная страна́. **highlight** *n* (*fig*) вы́сшая то́чка; *vt* обраща́ть *impf*, обрати́ть *pf* внима́ние на+*acc*. **highly** *adv* весьма́; ~**-strung** легко́ возбужда́емый. **highness** *n* (*title*) высо́чество. **highstreet** *n* гла́вная у́лица. **highway** *n* магистра́ль.

hijack *vt* похища́ть *impf*, похи́тить *pf*. **hijacker** *n* похити́тель *m*.

hike *n* похо́д.

hilarious *adj* умори́тельный. **hilarity** *n* весе́лье.

hill *n* холм. **hillock** *n* хо́лмик. **hillside** *n* склон холма́. **hilly** *adj* холми́стый.

hilt *n* рукоя́тка.

himself *pron* (*emph*) (он) сам; (*refl*) себя́.

hind *adj* (*rear*) за́дний.

hinder *vt* меша́ть *impf*, по~ *pf* +*dat*. **hindrance** *n* поме́ха.

Hindu *n* инду́с; *adj* инду́сский.

hinge *n* шарни́р; *vi* (*fig*) зави́сеть *impf* от+*gen*.

hint *n* намёк; *vi* намека́ть *impf*, намекну́ть *pf* (**at** на+*acc*)

hip *n* (*anat*) бедро́.

hippie *n* хи́ппи *neut indecl*.

hippopotamus *n* гиппопота́м.

hire *n* наём, прока́т; ~**-purchase** поку́пка в рассро́чку; *vt* нанима́ть *impf*, наня́ть *pf*; ~ **out** сдава́ть *impf*, сдать *pf* напрока́т.

his *poss pron* его́; свой.

hiss *n* шипе́ние; *vi* шипе́ть *impf*; *vt* (*performer*) осви́стывать *impf*, освиста́ть *pf*.

historian *n* исто́рик. **historic(al)** *adj* истори́ческий. **history** *n* исто́рия.

histrionic *adj* театра́льный.

hit *n* (*blow*) уда́р; (*on target*) попада́ние (в цель); (*success*) успе́х; *vt* (*strike*) ударя́ть *impf*, уда́рить *pf*; (*target*) попада́ть *impf*, попа́сть *pf* (в цель); ~ (**up**)**on** находи́ть *impf*, найти́ *pf*.

hitch *n* (*stoppage*) заде́ржка; *vt* (*fasten*) привя́зывать *impf*, привяза́ть *pf*; ~ **up** подтя́гивать *impf*, подтяну́ть *pf*; ~**hike** е́здить *indet*, е́хать

det, по~ *pf* автостóпом.
hither *adv* сюдá. **hitherto** *adv* до сих пор.
HIV *abbr* (*of* **human immunodeficiency virus**) ВИЧ.
hive *n* улей.
hoard *n* запáс; *vt* скáпливать *impf*, скопи́ть *pf*.
hoarding *n* реклáмный щит.
hoarse *adj* хри́плый.
hoax *n* надувáтельство.
hobble *vi* ковыля́ть *impf*.
hobby *n* хóбби *neut indecl*.
hock *n* (*wine*) рейнвéйн.
hockey *n* хоккéй.
hoe *n* мотыга; *vt* мотыжить *impf*.
hog *n* бóров.
hoist *n* подъёмник; *vt* поднимáть *impf*, подня́ть *pf*.
hold[1] *n* (*naut*) трюм.
hold[2] *n* (*grasp*) захвáт; (*influence*) влия́ние (**on** на+*acc*); **catch ~ of** ухвати́ться *pf* за+*acc*; *vt* (*grasp*) держáть *impf*; (*contain*) вмещáть *impf*, вмести́ть *pf*; (*possess*) владéть *impf* +*instr*; (*conduct*) проводи́ть *impf*, провести́ *pf*; (*consider*) считáть *impf*, счесть *pf* (+*acc* & *instr*, за+*acc*); *vi* держáться *impf*; (*weather*) продéрживаться *impf*, продержáться *pf*; **~ back** сдéрживать(ся) *impf*, сдержáть(ся) *pf*; **~ forth** разглагóльствовать *impf*; **~ on** (*wait*) подождáть *pf*; (*tel*) не вéшать *impf* трýбку; (*grip*) держáться *impf* (**to** за+*acc*); **~ out** (*stretch out*) протя́гивать *impf*, протяну́ть *pf*; (*resist*) не сдавáться *impf*; **~ up** (*support*) поддéрживать *impf*, поддержáть *pf*; (*impede*) задéрживать *impf*, задержáть *pf*. **holdall** *n* сýмка. **hold-up** *n* (*robbery*) налёт; (*delay*) задéржка.
hole *n* дырá; (*animal's*) норá; (*golf*) лýнка.
holiday *n* (*day off*) выходнóй день; (*festival*) прáздник; (*annual leave*) óтпуск; *pl* (*school*) кани́кулы (-л) *pl*; **~-maker** тури́ст; **on ~** в óтпуске.
holiness *n* свя́тость.
Holland *n* Голлáндия.
hollow *n* впáдина; (*valley*) лощи́на; *adj* пустóй; (*sunken*) впáлый; (*sound*) глухóй; *vt* (**~ out**) выдáлбливать *impf*, выдолбить *pf*.
holly *n* остроли́ст.

holocaust *n* мáссовое уничтожéние.
holster *n* кобурá.
holy *adj* святóй, свящéнный.
homage *n* почтéние; **pay ~ to** преклоня́ться *impf*, преклони́ться *pf* пéред+*instr*.
home *n* дом; (*native land*) рóдина; **at ~** дóма; **feel at ~** чýвствовать *impf* себя́ как дóма; *adj* домáшний; (*native*) роднóй; **H~ Affairs** внýтренние делá *neut pl*; *adv* (*direction*) домóй; (*position*) дóма. **homeland** *n* рóдина. **homeless** *adj* бездóмный. **homemade** *adj* (*food*) домáшний; (*object*) самодéльный. **homesick** *adj*: **be ~** скучáть *impf* по дóму. **homewards** *adv* домóй, восвоя́си.
homely *adj* простóй.
homicide *n* (*action*) уби́йство.
homogeneous *adj* однорóдный.
homosexual *n* гомосексуали́ст; *adj* гомосексуáльный.
honest *adj* (*fair*) чéстный. **honesty** *n* чéстность.
honey *n* мёд. **honeymoon** *n* медóвый мéсяц. **honeysuckle** *n* жи́молость.
honk *vi* гудéть *impf*.
honorary *adj* почётный.
honour *n* честь; *vt* (*respect*) почитáть *impf*; (*confer*) удостáивать *impf*, удостóить *pf* (**with** +*gen*); (*fulfil*) выполня́ть *impf*, вы́полнить *pf*. **honourable** *adj* чéстный.
hood *n* капюшóн; (*tech*) капóт.
hoodwink *vt* обмáнывать *impf*, обманýть *pf*.
hoof *n* копы́то.
hook *n* крючóк; *vt* (*hitch*) зацепля́ть *impf*, зацепи́ть *pf*; (*fasten*) застёгивать *impf*, застегнýть *pf*.
hooligan *n* хулигáн.
hoop *n* óбруч.
hoot *vi* (*owl*) ýхать *impf*, ýхнуть *pf*; (*horn*) гудéть *impf*. **hooter** *n* гудóк.
hop[1] *n* (*plant*; *collect*) хмель *m*.
hop[2] *n* (*jump*) прыжóк; *vi* прыгать *impf*, прыгнуть *pf* (на однóй ногé).
hope *n* надéжда; *vi* надéяться *impf*, по~ *pf* (**for** на+*acc*). **hopeful** *adj* (*promising*) обнадёживающий; **I am ~** я надéюсь. **hopefully** *adv* с надéждой; (*it is hoped*) нáдо надéяться. **hopeless** *adj* безнадёжный.
horde *n* (*hist*; *fig*) ордá.

horizon n горизо́нт. **horizontal** adj горизонта́льный.

hormone n гормо́н.

horn n рог; (mus) рожо́к; (car) гудо́к.

hornet n ше́ршень m.

horny adj (calloused) мозо́листый.

horoscope n гороско́п.

horrible, horrid adj ужа́сный. **horrify** vt ужаса́ть impf, ужасну́ть pf. **horror** n у́жас.

hors-d'oeuvre n заку́ска.

horse n ло́шадь. **horse-chestnut** n ко́нский кашта́н. **horseman, -woman** n вса́дник, -ица. **horseplay** n возня́. **horsepower** n лошади́ная си́ла. **horse-racing** n ска́чки (-чек) pl. **horse-radish** n хрен. **horseshoe** n подко́ва.

horticulture n садово́дство.

hose n (~-pipe) шланг.

hosiery n чуло́чные изде́лия neut pl.

hospitable adj гостеприи́мный.

hospital n больни́ца.

hospitality n гостеприи́мство.

host[1] n (multitude) мно́жество.

host[2] n (entertaining) хозя́ин.

hostage n зало́жник.

hostel n общежи́тие.

hostess n хозя́йка; (air ~) стюарде́сса.

hostile adj вражде́бный. **hostility** n вражде́бность; pl вое́нные де́йствия neut pl.

hot adj горя́чий, жа́ркий; (pungent) о́стрый; ~-headed вспы́льчивый; ~-water bottle гре́лка. **hotbed** n (fig) оча́г. **hothouse** n тепли́ца. **hotplate** n пли́тка.

hotel n гости́ница.

hound n охо́тничья соба́ка; vt трави́ть impf, за~ pf.

hour n час. **hourly** adj ежеча́сный.

house n дом; (parl) пала́та; attrib дома́шний; vt помеща́ть impf, помести́ть pf. **household** n семья́, adj хозя́йственный; дома́шний. **housekeeper** n эконо́мка. **house-warming** n новосе́лье. **housewife** n хозя́йка. **housework** n дома́шняя рабо́та. **housing** n (accommodation) жильё; (casing) кожу́х; ~ **estate** жило́й масси́в.

hovel n лачу́га.

hover vi (bird) пари́ть impf; (helicopter) висе́ть impf; (person) мая́чить impf. **hovercraft** n су́дно на возду́шной поду́шке, СВП.

how adv как, каки́м о́бразом; ~ **do you do?** здра́вствуйте!; ~ **many, much** ско́лько (+gen). **however** adv как бы ни (+past); conj одна́ко, тем не ме́нее; ~ **much** ско́лько бы ни (+gen & past).

howl n вой; vi выть impf. **howler** n грубе́йшая оши́бка.

hub n (of wheel) ступи́ца; (fig) центр, средото́чие.

hubbub n шум, гам.

huddle vi: ~ **together** прижима́ться impf, прижа́ться pf друг к дру́гу.

hue n (tint) отте́нок.

huff n: **in a** ~ оскорблённый.

hug n объя́тие; vt (embrace) обнима́ть impf, обня́ть pf.

huge adj огро́мный.

hulk n ко́рпус (корабля́). **hulking** adj (bulky) грома́дный; (clumsy) неуклю́жий.

hull n (of ship) ко́рпус.

hum n жужжа́ние; vi (buzz) жужжа́ть impf; vt & i (person) напева́ть impf.

human adj челове́ческий, людско́й; n челове́к. **humane, humanitarian** adj челове́чный. **humanity** n (human race) челове́чество; (humaneness) гума́нность; **the Humanities** гуманита́рные нау́ки f pl.

humble adj (person) смире́нный; (abode) скро́мный; vt унижа́ть impf, уни́зить pf.

humdrum adj однообра́зный.

humid adj вла́жный. **humidity** n вла́жность.

humiliate vt унижа́ть impf, уни́зить pf. **humiliation** n униже́ние.

humility n смире́ние.

humorous adj юмористи́ческий. **humour** n ю́мор; (mood) настрое́ние; vt потака́ть impf +dat.

hump n горб; (of earth) буго́р.

humus n перегно́й.

hunch n (idea) предчу́вствие; vt го́рбить impf, с~ pf. **hunchback** n (person) горбу́н, ~ья. **hunchbacked** adj горба́тый.

hundred adj & n сто; ~s **of** со́тни f pl +gen; **two** ~ две́сти; **three** ~ три́ста; **four** ~ четы́реста; **five** ~ пятьсо́т. **hundredth** adj & n со́тый.

Hungarian *n* венгр, венге́рка; *adj* венге́рский. **Hungary** *n* Ве́нгрия.

hunger *n* го́лод; (*fig*) жа́жда (for +gen); ~ **strike** голодо́вка; *vi* голода́ть *impf*; ~ **for** жа́ждать *impf* +gen.

hungry *adj* голо́дный.

hunk *n* ломо́ть *m*.

hunt *n* охо́та; (*fig*) по́иски *m pl* (for +gen); *vt* охо́титься *impf* на+*acc*, за+*instr*; (*persecute*) трави́ть *impf*, за~ *pf*; ~ **down** вы́следить *pf*; ~ **for** иска́ть *impf* +*acc or gen*; ~ **out** отыска́ть *pf*. **hunter** *n* охо́тник. **hunting** *n* охо́та.

hurdle *n* (*sport*, *fig*) барье́р. **hurdler** *n* барьери́ст. **hurdles** *n pl* (*sport*) барье́рный бег.

hurl *vt* швыря́ть *impf*, швырну́ть *pf*.

hurly-burly *n* сумато́ха.

hurrah, hurray *int* ура́!

hurricane *n* урага́н.

hurried *adj* торопли́вый. **hurry** *n* спе́шка; **be in a** ~ спеши́ть *impf*; *vt* & *i* торопи́ть(ся) *impf*, по~ *pf*; *vi* спеши́ть *impf*, по~ *pf*.

hurt *n* уще́рб; *vi* боле́ть *impf*; *vt* поврежда́ть *impf*, повреди́ть *pf*; (*offend*) обижа́ть *impf*, оби́деть *pf*.

hurtle *vi* нести́сь *impf*, по~ *pf*.

husband *n* муж.

hush *n* тишина́; *vt*: ~ **up** замина́ть *impf*, замя́ть *pf*; *int* ти́ше!

husk *n* шелуха́.

husky *adj* (*voice*) хри́плый.

hustle *n* толкотня́; *vt* (*push*) затолка́ть *impf*, затолкну́ть *pf*; (*herd people*) загоня́ть *impf*, загна́ть *pf*; *vt* & *i* (*hurry*) торопи́ть(ся) *impf*, по~ *pf*.

hut *n* хи́жина.

hutch *n* кле́тка.

hyacinth *n* гиаци́нт.

hybrid *n* гибри́д; *adj* гибри́дный.

hydrangea *n* горте́нзия.

hydrant *n* гидра́нт.

hydraulic *adj* гидравли́ческий.

hydrochloric acid *n* соля́ная кислота́. **hydroelectric** *adj* гидроэлектри́ческий; ~ **power station** гидроэлектроста́нция, ГЭС *f indecl*. **hydrofoil** *n* су́дно на подво́дных кры́льях, СПК.

hydrogen *n* водоро́д.

hyena *n* гие́на.

hygiene *n* гигие́на. **hygienic** *adj* гиги-

ени́ческий.

hymn *n* гимн.

hyperbole *n* гипе́рбола.

hyphen *n* дефи́с. **hyphen(ate)** *vt* писа́ть *impf*, на~ *pf* че́рез дефи́с.

hypnosis *n* гипно́з. **hypnotic** *adj* гипноти́ческий. **hypnotism** *n* гипноти́зм. **hypnotist** *n* гипнотизёр. **hypnotize** *vt* гипнотизи́ровать *impf*, за~ *pf*.

hypochondria *n* ипохо́ндрия. **hypochondriac** *n* ипохо́ндрик.

hypocrisy *n* лицеме́рие. **hypocrite** *n* лицеме́р. **hypocritical** *adj* лицеме́рный.

hypodermic *adj* подко́жный.

hypothesis *n* гипо́теза. **hypothesize** *vi* стро́ить *impf*, по~ *pf* гипоте́зу. **hypothetical** *adj* гипотети́ческий.

hysterectomy *n* гистерэктоми́я, удале́ние ма́тки.

hysteria *n* истери́я. **hysterical** *adj* истери́ческий. **hysterics** *n pl* исте́рика.

I

I *pron* я.

ibid(em) *adv* там же.

ice *n* лёд; ~**-age** леднико́вый пери́од; ~**-axe** ледору́б; ~**-cream** моро́женое *sb*; ~ **hockey** хокке́й (с ша́йбой); ~ **rink** като́к; ~ **skate** конёк; *vi* ката́ться *impf* на конька́х; *vt* (*chill*) замора́живать *impf*, заморо́зить *pf*; (*cul*) глазирова́ть *impf* & *pf*; *vi*: ~ **over, up** обледенева́ть *impf*, обледене́ть *pf*. **iceberg** *n* а́йсберг. **icicle** *n* сосу́лька. **icing** *n* (*cul*) глазу́рь. **icy** *adj* ледяно́й.

icon *n* ико́на.

ID *abbr* (*of* **identification**) удостовере́ние ли́чности.

idea *n* иде́я, мысль; (*conception*) поня́тие.

ideal *n* идеа́л; *adj* идеа́льный. **idealism** *n* идеали́зм. **idealist** *n* идеали́ст. **idealize** *vt* идеализи́ровать *impf* & *pf*.

identical *adj* тожде́ственный, одина́ковый. **identification** *n* (*recognition*) опозна́ние; (*of person*) установле́ние ли́чности. **identify** *vt* опознава́ть *impf*, опозна́ть *pf*. **identity** *n*

(*of person*) ли́чность; ~ **card** удостовере́ние ли́чности.
ideological *adj* идеологи́ческий. **ideology** *n* идеоло́гия.
idiom *n* идио́ма. **idiomatic** *adj* идиомати́ческий.
idiosyncrasy *n* идиосинкразия.
idiot *n* идио́т. **idiotic** *adj* идио́тский.
idle *adj* (*unoccupied*) lazy; *purposeless*) пра́здный; (*vain*) тще́тный; (*empty*) пусто́й; (*machine*) недействующий; *vi* безде́льничать *impf*; (*engine*) рабо́тать *impf* вхолосту́ю; *vt*: ~ **away** пра́здно проводи́ть *impf*, провести́ *pf*. **idleness** *n* пра́здность.
idol *n* и́дол. **idolatry** *n* идолопокло́нство; (*fig*) обожа́ние. **idolize** *vt* боготвори́ть *impf*.
idyll *n* иди́ллия. **idyllic** *adj* идилли́ческий.
i.e. *abbr* т.е., то есть.
if *conj* е́сли, е́сли бы; (*whether*) ли; **as** ~ как бу́дто; **even** ~ да́же е́сли; ~ **only** е́сли бы то́лько.
ignite *vt* зажига́ть *impf*, заже́чь *pf*; *vi* загора́ться *impf*, загоре́ться *pf*. **ignition** *n* зажига́ние.
ignoble *adj* ни́зкий.
ignominious *adj* позо́рный.
ignoramus *n* неве́жда *m*. **ignorance** *n* неве́жество, (*of certain facts*) неве́дение. **ignorant** *adj* неве́жественный; (*uninformed*) несве́дущий (**of** в+*prep*).
ignore *vt* не обраща́ть *impf* внима́ния на+*acc*; игнори́ровать *impf & pf*.
ilk *n*: **of that** ~ тако́го ро́да.
ill *n* (*evil*) зло; (*harm*) вред; *pl* (*misfortunes*) несча́стья (-тий) *pl*; *adj* (*sick*) больно́й; (*bad*) дурно́й; *adv* пло́хо, ду́рно; **fall** ~ заболева́ть *impf*, заболе́ть *pf*; **~-advised** неблагоразу́мный; **~-mannered** неве́жливый; **~-treat** *vt* пло́хо обраща́ться *impf* с+*instr*.
illegal *adj* нелега́льный. **illegality** *n* незако́нность, нелега́льность.
illegible *adj* неразбо́рчивый.
illegitimacy *n* незако́нность; (*of child*) незаконнорождённость. **illegitimate** *adj* незако́нный; незаконнорождённый.
illicit *adj* незако́нный, недозво́ленный.

illiteracy *n* негра́мотность. **illiterate** *adj* негра́мотный.
illness *n* боле́знь.
illogical *adj* нелоги́чный.
illuminate *vt* освеща́ть *impf*, освети́ть *pf*. **illumination** *n* освеще́ние.
illusion *n* иллю́зия. **illusory** *adj* иллюзо́рный.
illustrate *vt* иллюстри́ровать *impf & pf*, про-~ *pf*. **illustration** *n* иллюстра́ция. **illustrative** *adj* иллюстрати́вный.
illustrious *adj* знамени́тый.
image *n* (*phys; statue etc.*) изображе́ние; (*optical* ~) отраже́ние; (*likeness*) ко́пия; (*metaphor; conception*) о́браз; (*reputation*) репута́ция. **imagery** *n* о́бразность.
imaginable *adj* вообрази́мый. **imaginary** *adj* вообража́емый. **imagination** *n* воображе́ние. **imagine** *vt* вообража́ть *impf*, вообрази́ть *pf*; (*conceive*) представля́ть *impf*, предста́вить *pf* себе́.
imbecile *n* слабоу́мный *sb*; (*fool*) глупе́ц.
imbibe *vt* (*absorb*) впи́тывать *impf*, впита́ть *pf*.
imbue *vt* внуша́ть *impf*, внуши́ть *pf* +*dat* (**with** +*acc*).
imitate *vt* подража́ть *impf* +*dat*. **imitation** *n* подража́ние (**of** +*dat*); *attrib* иску́сственный. **imitative** *adj* подража́тельный.
immaculate *adj* безупре́чный.
immaterial *adj* (*unimportant*) несуще́ственный.
immature *adj* незре́лый.
immeasurable *adj* неизмери́мый.
immediate *adj* (*direct*) непосре́дственный; (*swift*) неме́дленный. **immediately** *adv* то́тчас, сра́зу.
immemorial *adj*: **from time** ~ с незапа́мятных времён.
immense *adj* огро́мный.
immerse *vt* погружа́ть *impf*, погрузи́ть *pf*. **immersion** *n* погруже́ние.
immigrant *n* иммигра́нт, ~ка. **immigration** *n* иммигра́ция.
imminent *adj* надвига́ющийся; (*danger*) грозя́щий.
immobile *adj* неподви́жный. **immobilize** *vt* парализова́ть *impf & pf*.
immoderate *adj* неуме́ренный.
immodest *adj* нескро́мный.

immoral *adj* безнра́вственный. **immorality** *n* безнра́вственность.

immortal *adj* бессме́ртный. **immortality** *n* бессме́ртие. **immortalize** *vt* обессме́ртить *pf*.

immovable *adj* неподви́жный; (*fig*) непоколеби́мый.

immune *adj* (*to illness*) невосприи́мчивый (**to** к+*dat*); (*free from*) свобо́дный (**from** от+*gen*). **immunity** *n* иммуните́т (**from** к+*dat*); освобожде́ние (**from** от+*gen*). **immunize** *vt* иммунизи́ровать *impf* & *pf*.

immutable *adj* неизме́нный.

imp *n* бесёнок.

impact *n* уда́р; (*fig*) влия́ние.

impair *vt* вреди́ть *impf*, по~ *pf*.

impale *vt* протыка́ть *impf*, проткну́ть *pf*.

impart *vt* дели́ться *impf*, по~ *pf* +*instr* (**to** с+*instr*).

impartial *adj* беспристра́стный.

impassable *adj* непроходи́мый; (*for vehicles*) непрое́зжий.

impasse *n* тупи́к.

impassioned *adj* стра́стный.

impassive *adj* бесстра́стный.

impatience *n* нетерпе́ние. **impatient** *adj* нетерпели́вый.

impeach *vt* обвиня́ть *impf*, обвини́ть *pf* (**for** в+*prep*).

impeccable *adj* безупре́чный.

impecunious *adj* безде́нежный.

impedance *n* по́лное сопротивле́ние. **impede** *vt* препя́тствовать *impf*, вос~ *pf* +*dat*. **impediment** *n* препя́тствие; (*in speech*) заика́ние.

impel *vt* побужда́ть *impf*, побуди́ть *pf* (**to** +*inf*, к+*dat*).

impending *adj* предстоя́щий.

impenetrable *adj* непроница́емый.

imperative *adj* необходи́мый; *n* (*gram*) повели́тельное наклоне́ние.

imperceptible *adj* незаме́тный.

imperfect *n* имперфе́кт; *adj* несоверше́нный. **imperfection** *n* несоверше́нство; (*fault*) недоста́ток. **imperfective** *adj* (*n*) несоверше́нный (вид).

imperial *adj* импе́рский. **imperialism** *n* империали́зм. **imperialist** *n* империали́ст; *attrib* империалисти́ческий.

imperil *vt* подверга́ть *impf*, подве́ргнуть *pf* опа́сности.

imperious *adj* вла́стный.

impersonal *adj* безли́чный.

impersonate *vt* (*imitate*) подража́ть *impf*; (*pretend to be*) выдава́ть *impf*, вы́дать *pf* себя́ за+*acc*. **impersonation** *n* подража́ние.

impertinence *n* де́рзость. **impertinent** *adj* де́рзкий.

imperturbable *adj* невозмути́мый.

impervious *adj* (*fig*) глухо́й (**to** к +*dat*).

impetuous *adj* стреми́тельный.

impetus *n* дви́жущая си́ла.

impinge *vi*: ~ (**up)on** ока́зывать *impf*, оказа́ть *pf* (отрица́тельный) эффе́кт на+*acc*.

implacable *adj* неумоли́мый.

implant *vt* вводи́ть *impf*, ввести́ *pf*; (*fig*) се́ять *impf*, по~ *pf*.

implement[1] *n* ору́дие, инструме́нт.
implement[2] *vt* (*fulfil*) выполня́ть *impf*, вы́полнить *pf*.

implicate *vt* впу́тывать *impf*, впу́тать *pf*. **implication** *n* (*inference*) намёк; *pl* значе́ние.

implicit *adj* подразумева́емый; (*absolute*) безоговоро́чный.

implore *vt* умоля́ть *impf*.

imply *vt* подразумева́ть *impf*.

impolite *adj* неве́жливый.

imponderable *adj* неопределённый.

import *n* (*meaning*) значе́ние; (*of goods*) и́мпорт; *vt* импорти́ровать *impf* & *pf*. **importer** *n* импортёр.

importance *n* ва́жность. **important** *adj* ва́жный.

impose *vt* (*tax*) облага́ть *impf*, обложи́ть *pf* +*instr* (**on** +*acc*); (*obligation*) налага́ть *impf*, наложи́ть *pf* (**on** на+*acc*); ~ (**o.s.**) **on** налега́ть *impf* на+*acc*. **imposing** *adj* внуши́тельный. **imposition** *n* обложе́ние, наложе́ние.

impossibility *n* невозмо́жность. **impossible** *adj* невозмо́жный.

impostor *n* самозва́нец.

impotence *n* бесси́лие; (*med*) импоте́нция. **impotent** *adj* бесси́льный; (*med*) импоте́нтный.

impound *vt* (*confiscate*) конфискова́ть *impf* & *pf*.

impoverished *adj* обедне́вший.

impracticable *adj* невыполни́мый.

imprecise *adj* нето́чный.

impregnable *adj* непристу́пный.

impregnate vt (fertilize) оплодотворя́ть impf, оплодотвори́ть pf; (saturate) пропи́тывать impf, пропита́ть pf.

impresario n аге́нт.

impress vt производи́ть impf, произвести́ pf (како́е-либо) впечатле́ние на+acc; ~ **upon** (s.o.) внуша́ть impf, внуши́ть pf (+dat). **impression** n впечатле́ние; (imprint) отпеча́ток; (reprint) (стереоти́пное) изда́ние.

impressionism n импрессиони́зм. **impressionist** n импрессиони́ст.

impressive adj впечатля́ющий.

imprint n отпеча́ток; vt отпеча́тывать impf, отпеча́тать pf; (on memory) запечатлева́ть impf, запечатле́ть pf.

imprison vt заключа́ть impf, заключи́ть pf (в тюрьму́). **imprisonment** n тюре́мное заключе́ние.

improbable adj невероя́тный.

impromptu adj импровизи́рованный; adv без подгото́вки, экспро́мтом.

improper adj (incorrect) непра́вильный; (indecent) неприли́чный. **impropriety** n неуме́стность.

improve vt & i улучша́ть(ся) impf, улу́чшить(ся) pf. **improvement** n улучше́ние.

improvisation n импровиза́ция. **improvise** vt импровизи́ровать impf, сымпровизи́ровать pf.

imprudent adj неосторо́жный.

impudence n на́глость. **impudent** adj на́глый.

impulse n толчо́к, и́мпульс; (sudden tendency) поры́в. **impulsive** adj импульси́вный.

impunity n: **with** ~ безнака́занно.

impure adj нечи́стый.

impute vt припи́сывать impf, приписа́ть pf (to +dat).

in prep (place) в+prep, на+prep; (into) в+acc, на+acc; (point in time) в+prep, на+prep; **in the morning** (etc.) у́тром (instr); **in spring** (etc.) весно́й (instr); (at some stage in; throughout) во вре́мя +gen; (duration) за+acc; (after interval of) че́рез+acc; (during course of) в тече́ние+gen; (circumstance) в+prep, при+prep; adv (place) внутри́; (motion) внутрь; (at home) до́ма; (in

fashion) в мо́де; **in here, there** (place) здесь, там; (motion) сюда́, туда́; adj вну́тренний; (fashionable) мо́дный; n: **the ins and outs** все ходы́ и вы́ходы.

inability n неспосо́бность.

inaccessible adj недосту́пный.

inaccurate adj нето́чный.

inaction n безде́йствие. **inactive** adj безде́йственный. **inactivity** n безде́йственность.

inadequate adj недоста́точный.

inadmissible adj недопусти́мый.

inadvertent adj неча́янный.

inalienable adj неотъе́млемый.

inane adj глу́пый.

inanimate adj неодушевлённый.

inappropriate adj неуме́стный.

inarticulate adj (person) косноязы́чный; (indistinct) невня́тный.

inasmuch adv: ~ **as** так как; ввиду́ того́, что.

inattentive adj невнима́тельный.

inaudible adj неслы́шный.

inaugural adj вступи́тельный. **inaugurate** vt (admit to office) торже́ственно вводи́ть impf, ввести́ pf в до́лжность; (open) открыва́ть impf, откры́ть pf; (introduce) вводи́ть impf, ввести́ pf. **inauguration** n введе́ние в до́лжность; откры́тие; нача́ло.

inauspicious adj неблагоприя́тный.

inborn, inbred adj врождённый.

incalculable adj неисчисли́мый.

incandescent adj накалённый.

incantation n заклина́ние.

incapability n неспосо́бность. **incapable** adj неспосо́бный (of к+dat, на+acc).

incapacitate vt де́лать impf, с~ pf неспосо́бным. **incapacity** n неспосо́бность.

incarcerate vt заключа́ть impf, заключи́ть pf (в тюрьму́). **incarceration** n заключе́ние (в тюрьму́).

incarnate adj воплощённый. **incarnation** n воплоще́ние.

incendiary adj зажига́тельный.

incense[1] n фимиа́м, ла́дан.

incense[2] vt разгнева́ть pf.

incentive n побужде́ние.

inception n нача́ло.

incessant adj непреста́нный.

incest n кровосмеше́ние.

inch n дюйм; ~ **by** ~ ма́ло-пома́лу; vi ползти́ impf.

incidence n (phys) паде́ние; (prevalence) распростране́ние. **incident** n слу́чай, инциде́нт. **incidental** adj (casual) случа́йный; (inessential) несуще́ственный. **incidentally** adv ме́жду про́чим.

incinerate vt испепеля́ть impf, испепели́ть pf. **incinerator** n мусоросжига́тельная печь.

incipient adj начина́ющийся.

incision n надре́з (**in** на+acc). **incisive** adj (fig) о́стрый. **incisor** n резе́ц.

incite vt подстрека́ть impf, подстрекну́ть pf (**to** к+dat). **incitement** n подстрека́тельство.

inclement adj суро́вый.

inclination n (slope) накло́н; (propensity) скло́нность (**for, to** к+dat). **incline** n накло́н; vt & i склоня́ть(ся) impf, склони́ть(ся) pf. **inclined** predic (disposed) скло́нен (-онна́, -о́нно) (**to** к+dat).

include vt включа́ть impf, включи́ть pf (**in** в+acc); (contain) заключа́ть impf, заключи́ть pf в себе́. **including** prep включа́я+acc. **inclusion** n включе́ние. **inclusive** adj включа́ющий (в себе́); adv включи́тельно.

incognito adv инко́гнито.

incoherent adj бессвя́зный.

income n дохо́д; ~ **tax** подохо́дный нало́г.

incommensurate adj несоразме́рный.

incomparable adj несравни́мый (**to, with** c+instr); (matchless) несравне́нный.

incompatible adj несовмести́мый.

incompetence n некомпете́нтность. **incompetent** adj некомпете́нтный.

incomplete adj непо́лный, незако́нченный.

incomprehensible adj непоня́тный.

inconceivable adj невообрази́мый.

inconclusive adj (evidence) недоста́точный; (results) неопределённый.

incongruity n несоотве́тствие. **incongruous** adj несоотве́тствующий.

inconsequential adj незначи́тельный.

inconsiderable adj незначи́тельный.

inconsiderate adj невнима́тельный.

inconsistency n непосле́довательность. **inconsistent** adj непосле́довательный.

inconsolable adj безуте́шный.

inconspicuous adj незаме́тный.

incontinence n (med) недержа́ние. **incontinent** adj: **be** ~ страда́ть impf недержа́нием.

incontrovertible adj неопровержи́мый.

inconvenience n неудо́бство; vt затрудня́ть impf, затрудни́ть pf. **inconvenient** adj неудо́бный.

incorporate vt (include) включа́ть impf, включи́ть pf; (unite) объединя́ть impf, объедини́ть pf.

incorrect adj непра́вильный.

incorrigible adj неисправи́мый.

incorruptible adj неподку́пный.

increase n рост, увеличе́ние; (in pay etc.) приба́вка; vt & i увели́чивать(ся) impf, увели́чить(ся) pf.

incredible adj невероя́тный.

incredulous adj недове́рчивый.

increment n приба́вка.

incriminate vt изоблича́ть impf, изобличи́ть pf.

incubate vt (eggs) выводи́ть impf, вы́вести pf (в инкуба́торе). **incubator** n инкуба́тор.

inculcate vt внедря́ть impf, внедри́ть pf.

incumbent adj (in office) стоя́щий у вла́сти; **it is** ~ (**up**)**on you** вы обя́заны.

incur vt навлека́ть impf, навле́чь pf на себя́.

incurable adj неизлечи́мый.

incursion n (invasion) вторже́ние; (attack) набе́г.

indebted predic в долгу́ (**to** y+gen).

indecency n неприли́чие. **indecent** adj неприли́чный.

indecision n нереши́тельность. **indecisive** adj нереши́тельный.

indeclinable adj несклоня́емый.

indeed adv в са́мом де́ле, действи́тельно; (interrog) неуже́ли?

indefatigable adj неутоми́мый.

indefensible adj не име́ющий оправда́ния.

indefinable adj неопредели́мый. **indefinite** adj неопределённый.

indelible adj несмыва́емый.

indemnify vt: ~ **against** страхова́ть

impf, за~ *pf* от+*gen*; ~ **for** (*compensate*) компенси́ровать *impf* & *pf*.
indemnity *n* (*against loss*) гара́нтия от убы́тков; (*compensation*) компенса́ция.

indent *vt* (*printing*) писа́ть *impf*, с~ *pf* с о́тступом. **indentation** *n* (*notch*) зубе́ц; (*printing*) о́тступ.

independence *n* незави́симость, самостоя́тельность. **independent** *adj* незави́симый, самостоя́тельный.

indescribable *adj* неопису́емый.

indestructible *adj* неразруши́мый.

indeterminate *adj* неопределённый.

index *n* (*alphabetical*) указа́тель *m*; (*econ*) и́ндекс; (*pointer*) стре́лка; ~ **finger** указа́тельный па́лец.

India *n* И́ндия. **Indian** *n* инди́ец, индиа́нка; (*American*) индее́ц, индиа́нка; *adj* инди́йский; (*American*) инде́йский; ~ **summer** ба́бье ле́то.

indicate *vt* ука́зывать *impf*, указа́ть *pf*; (*be a sign of*) свиде́тельствовать *impf* о+*prep*. **indication** *n* указа́ние; (*sign*) при́знак. **indicative** *adj* ука́зывающий; (*gram*) изъяви́тельный; *n* изъяви́тельное наклоне́ние. **indicator** *n* указа́тель *m*.

indict *vt* обвиня́ть *impf*, обвини́ть *pf* (**for** в+*prep*).

indifference *n* равноду́шие. **indifferent** *adj* равноду́шный; (*mediocre*) посре́дственный.

indigenous *adj* тузе́мный.

indigestible *adj* неудобовари́мый. **indigestion** *n* несваре́ние желу́дка.

indignant *adj* негоду́ющий; **be** ~ негодова́ть *impf* (**with** на+*acc*). **indignation** *n* негодова́ние.

indignity *n* оскорбле́ние.

indirect *adj* непрямо́й; (*econ*; *gram*) ко́свенный.

indiscreet *adj* нескро́мный. **indiscretion** *n* нескро́мность.

indiscriminate *adj* неразбо́рчивый. **indiscriminately** *adv* без разбо́ра.

indispensible *adj* необходи́мый.

indisposed *predic* (*unwell*) нездоро́в.

indisputable *adj* бесспо́рный.

indistinct *adj* нея́сный.

indistinguishable *adj* неразличи́мый.

individual *n* ли́чность; *adj* индивидуа́льный. **individualism** *n* индивидуали́зм. **individualist** *n* индивидуали́ст. **individualistic** *adj* индивидуа-

алисти́ческий. **individuality** *n* индивидуа́льность.

indivisible *adj* недели́мый.

indoctrinate *vt* внуша́ть *impf*, внуши́ть *pf* +*dat* (**with** +*acc*).

indolence *n* ле́ность. **indolent** *adj* лени́вый.

indomitable *adj* неукроти́мый.

Indonesia *n* Индоне́зия.

indoor *adj* ко́мнатный. **indoors** *adv* (*position*) в до́ме; (*motion*) в дом.

induce *vt* (*prevail on*) убежда́ть *impf*, убеди́ть *pf*; (*bring about*) вызыва́ть *impf*, вы́звать *pf*. **inducement** *n* побужде́ние.

induction *n* (*logic, electr*) инду́кция; (*in post*) введе́ние в до́лжность.

indulge *vt* потво́рствовать *impf* +*dat*; *vi* предава́ться *impf*, преда́ться *pf* (**in** +*dat*). **indulgence** *n* потво́рство; (*tolerance*) снисходи́тельность. **indulgent** *adj* снисходи́тельный.

industrial *adj* промы́шленный. **industrialist** *n* промы́шленник. **industrious** *adj* трудолюби́вый. **industry** *n* промы́шленность; (*zeal*) трудолю́бие.

inebriated *adj* пья́ный.

inedible *adj* несъедо́бный.

ineffective, ineffectual *adj* безрезульта́тный; (*person*) неспосо́бный.

inefficiency *n* неэффекти́вность. **inefficient** *adj* неэффекти́вный.

ineligible *adj* не име́ющий пра́во (**for** на+*acc*).

inept *adj* неуме́лый.

inequality *n* нера́венство.

inert *adj* ине́ртный. **inertia** *n* (*phys*) ине́рция; (*sluggishness*) ине́ртность.

inescapable *adj* неизбе́жный.

inevitability *n* неизбе́жность. **inevitable** *adj* неизбе́жный.

inexact *adj* нето́чный.

inexcusable *adj* непрости́тельный.

inexhaustible *adj* неистощи́мый.

inexorable *adj* неумоли́мый.

inexpensive *adj* недорого́й.

inexperience *n* нео́пытность. **inexperienced** *adj* нео́пытный.

inexplicable *adj* необъясни́мый.

infallible *adj* непогреши́мый.

infamous *adj* позо́рный. **infamy** *n* позо́р.

infancy *n* младе́нчество. **infant** *n* младе́нец. **infantile** *adj* де́тский.

infantry n пехо́та.

infatuate vt вскружи́ть pf го́лову +dat. **infatuation** n увлече́ние.

infect vt заража́ть impf, зарази́ть pf (with +instr). **infection** n зара́за, инфе́кция. **infectious** adj зара́зный; (fig) зарази́тельный.

infer vt заключа́ть impf, заключи́ть pf. **inference** n заключе́ние.

inferior adj (in rank) ни́зший; (in quality) ху́дший, плохо́й; n подчинённый sb. **inferiority** n бо́лее ни́зкое ка́чество; ~ **complex** ко́мплекс неполноце́нности.

infernal adj а́дский. **inferno** n ад.

infertile adj неплодоро́дный.

infested adj: be ~ with кише́ть impf +instr.

infidelity n неве́рность.

infiltrate vt постепе́нно проника́ть impf, прони́кнуть pf в+acc.

infinite adj бесконе́чный. **infinitesimal** adj бесконе́чно ма́лый. **infinitive** n инфинити́в. **infinity** n бесконе́чность.

infirm adj не́мощный. **infirmary** n больни́ца. **infirmity** n не́мощь.

inflame vt & i (excite) возбужда́ть(ся) impf, возбуди́ть(ся) pf; (med) воспаля́ть(ся) impf, воспали́ть(ся) pf. **inflammable** adj огнеопа́сный. **inflammation** n воспале́ние. **inflammatory** adj подстрека́тельский.

inflate vt надува́ть impf, наду́ть pf. **inflation** n (econ) инфля́ция.

inflection n (gram) фле́ксия.

inflexible adj неги́бкий; (fig) непрекло́нный.

inflict vt (blow) наноси́ть impf, нанести́ pf ((up)on +dat); (suffering) причиня́ть impf, причини́ть pf ((up)on +dat); (penalty) налага́ть impf, наложи́ть pf ((up)on на+acc); ~ **o.s. (up)on** навя́зываться impf, навяза́ться pf +dat.

inflow n втека́ние, прито́к.

influence n влия́ние; vt влия́ть impf, по~ pf на+acc. **influential** adj влия́тельный.

influenza n грипп.

influx n (fig) наплы́в.

inform vt сообща́ть impf, сообщи́ть pf +dat (of, about +acc, о+prep); vi доноси́ть impf, донести́ pf (against на+acc).

informal adj (unofficial) неофициа́льный; (casual) обы́денный.

informant n осведоми́тель m. **information** n информа́ция. **informative** adj поучи́тельный. **informer** n доно́счик.

infra-red adj инфракра́сный.

infrequent adj ре́дкий.

infringe vt (violate) наруша́ть impf, нару́шить pf; vi: ~ (up)on посяга́ть impf, посягну́ть pf на+acc. **infringement** n наруше́ние; посяга́тельство.

infuriate vt разъяря́ть impf, разъяри́ть pf.

infuse vt (fig) внуша́ть impf, внуши́ть pf (into +dat). **infusion** n (fig) внуше́ние; (herbs etc) настой.

ingenious adj изобрета́тельный. **ingenuity** n изобрета́тельность.

ingenuous adj бесхи́тростный.

ingot n сли́ток.

ingrained adj закорене́лый.

ingratiate vt ~ **o.s.** вкра́дываться impf, вкра́сться pf в ми́лость (with +dat).

ingratitude n неблагода́рность.

ingredient n ингредие́нт, составля́ющее sb.

inhabit vt жить impf в, на, +prep; обита́ть impf в, на, +prep. **inhabitant** n жи́тель m, ~ница.

inhalation n вдыха́ние. **inhale** vt вдыха́ть impf, вдохну́ть pf.

inherent adj прису́щий (in +dat).

inherit vt насле́довать impf & pf, у~ pf. **inheritance** n насле́дство.

inhibit vt стесня́ть impf, стесни́ть pf. **inhibited** adj стесни́тельный. **inhibition** n стесне́ние.

inhospitable adj негостеприи́мный; (fig) недружелю́бный.

inhuman(e) adj бесчелове́чный.

inimical adj вражде́бный; (harmful) вре́дный.

inimitable adj неподража́емый.

iniquity n несправедли́вость.

initial adj (перво)нача́льный; n нача́льная бу́ква; pl инициа́лы m pl; vt ста́вить impf, по~ pf инициа́лы на+acc. **initially** adv в нача́ле.

initiate vt вводи́ть impf, ввести́ pf (into в+acc). **initiation** n введе́ние.

initiative n инициати́ва.

inject vt вводи́ть impf, ввести́ pf (person +dat, substance +acc). **injection** n укóл; (*fig*) инъéкция.

injunction *n* (*law*) судéбный запрéт.

injure *vt* поврежда́ть *impf*, повреди́ть *pf*. **injury** *n* ра́на.

injustice *n* несправедли́вость.

ink *n* черни́ла (-л).

inkling *n* представлéние.

inland *adj* внýтренний; *adv* (*motion*) внутрь страны́; (*place*) внутри́ страны́; I~ **Revenue** управлéние нало́говых сбо́ров.

in-laws *n pl* ро́дственники *m pl* супрýга, -ги.

inlay *n* инкруста́ция; *vt* инкрусти́ровать *impf* & *pf*.

inlet *n* (*of sea*) ýзкий зали́в.

inmate *n* (*prison*) заключённый *sb*; (*hospital*) больно́й *sb*.

inn *n* гости́ница.

innate *adj* врождённый.

inner *adj* внýтренний. **innermost** *adj* глубоча́йший; (*fig*) сокровéннейший.

innocence *n* неви́нность; (*guiltlessness*) невино́вность. **innocent** *adj* неви́нный; (*not guilty*) невино́вный (**of** в+*prep*).

innocuous *adj* безврéдный.

innovate *vi* вводи́ть *impf*, ввести́ *pf* но́вшества. **innovation** *n* нововведéние. **innovative** *adj* нова́торский. **innovator** *n* нова́тор.

innuendo *n* намёк, инсинуа́ция.

innumerable *adj* бесчи́сленный.

inoculate *vt* привива́ть *impf*, приви́ть *pf* +*dat* (**against** +*acc*). **inoculation** *n* приви́вка.

inoffensive *adj* безоби́дный.

inopportune *adj* несвоеврéменный.

inordinate *adj* чрезмéрный.

inorganic *adj* неоргани́ческий.

in-patient *n* стациона́рный больно́й *sb*.

input *n* ввод.

inquest *n* судéбное слéдствие, дозна́ние.

inquire *vt* спра́шивать *impf*, спроси́ть *pf*; *vi* справля́ться *impf*, спра́виться *pf* (**about** о+*prep*); расслéдовать *impf* & *pf* (**into** +*acc*). **inquiry** *n* вопро́с, спра́вка; (*investigation*) расслéдование.

inquisition *n* инквизи́ция. **inquisitive** *adj* пытли́вый, любозна́тельный.

inroad *n* (*attack*) набéг; (*fig*) посяга́тельство (**on, into** на+*acc*).

insane *adj* безýмный. **insanity** *n* безýмие.

insatiable *adj* ненасы́тный.

inscribe *vt* надпи́сывать *impf*, надписа́ть *pf*; (*engrave*) выреза́ть *impf*, вы́резать *pf*. **inscription** *n* на́дпись.

inscrutable *adj* непостижи́мый, непроница́емый.

insect *n* насеко́мое *sb*. **insecticide** *n* инсектици́д.

insecure *adj* (*unsafe*) небезопа́сный; (*not confident*) неувéренный (в себé).

insemination *n* оплодотворéние.

insensible *adj* (*unconscious*) потеря́вший созна́ние.

insensitive *adj* нечувстви́тельный.

inseparable *adj* неотдели́мый; (*people*) неразлýчный.

insert *vt* вставля́ть *impf*, вста́вить *pf*; вкла́дывать *impf*, вложи́ть *pf*; (*coin*) опуска́ть *impf*, опусти́ть *pf*. **insertion** *n* (*inserting*) вставлéние, вкла́дывание; (*thing inserted*) вста́вка.

inshore *adj* прибрéжный; *adv* бли́зко к бéрегу.

inside *n* внýтренняя часть; *pl* (*anat*) внýтренности *f pl*; **turn ~ out** вывёртывать *impf*, вы́вернуть *pf* наизна́нку; *adj* внýтренний; *adv* (*place*) внутри́; (*motion*) внутрь; *prep* (*place*) внутри́+*gen*, в+*prep*; (*motion*) внутрь+*gen*, в+*acc*.

insidious *adj* кова́рный.

insight *n* проница́тельность.

insignia *n* зна́ки *m pl* разли́чия.

insignificant *adj* незначи́тельный.

insincere *adj* нейскренний.

insinuate *vt* (*hint*) намека́ть *impf*, намекнýть *pf* на+*acc*. **insinuation** *n* инсинуа́ция.

insipid *adj* прéсный.

insist *vt* & *i* наста́ивать *impf*, настоя́ть *pf* (**on** на+*prep*). **insistence** *n* насто́йчивость. **insistent** *adj* насто́йчивый.

insolence *n* на́глость. **insolent** *adj* на́глый.

insoluble *adj* (*problem*) неразреши́мый; (*in liquid*) нераствори́мый.

insolvent *adj* несостоя́тельный.

insomnia *n* бессо́нница.

inspect *vt* инспекти́ровать *impf*,

про~ *pf.* **inspection** *n* инспе́кция.

inspector *n* инспе́ктор; (*ticket* ~) контролёр.

inspiration *n* вдохнове́ние. **inspire** *vt* вдохновля́ть *impf*, вдохнови́ть *pf*; внуша́ть *impf*, внуши́ть *pf* +*dat* (**with** +*acc*).

instability *n* неусто́йчивость; (*of character*) неуравнове́шенность.

install *vt* (*person in office*) вводи́ть *impf*, ввести́ *pf* в до́лжность; (*apparatus*) устана́вливать *impf*, установи́ть *pf.* **installation** *n* введе́ние в до́лжность; устано́вка; *pl* сооруже́ния *neut pl.*

instalment *n* (*comm*) взнос; (*publication*) вы́пуск; часть; **by** ~**s** в рассро́чку.

instance *n* (*example*) приме́р; (*case*) слу́чай; **for** ~ наприме́р.

instant *n* мгнове́ние, моме́нт; *adj* немме́дленный; (*coffee etc.*) раствори́мый. **instantaneous** *adj* мгнове́нный. **instantly** *adv* немме́дленно, то́тчас.

instead *adv* вме́сто (**of** +*gen*); ~ **of going** вме́сто того́, чтобы пойти́.

instep *n* подъём.

instigate *vt* подстрека́ть *impf*, подстрекну́ть *pf* (**to** к+*dat*). **instigation** *n* подстрека́тельство. **instigator** *n* подстрека́тель *m*, ~ница.

instil *vt* (*ideas etc.*) внуша́ть *impf*, внуши́ть *pf* (**into** +*dat*).

instinct *n* инсти́нкт. **instinctive** *adj* инстинкти́вный.

institute *n* институ́т; *vt* (*establish*) устана́вливать *impf*, установи́ть *pf*; (*introduce*) вводи́ть *impf*, ввести́ *pf*; (*reforms*) проводи́ть *impf*, провести́ *pf.* **institution** *n* учрежде́ние.

instruct *vt* (*teach*) обуча́ть *impf*, обучи́ть *pf* (**in** +*dat*); (*inform*) сообща́ть *impf*, сообщи́ть *pf* +*dat*; (*command*) прика́зывать *impf*, приказа́ть *pf* +*dat*. **instruction** *n* инстру́кция; (*teaching*) обуче́ние. **instructive** *adj* поучи́тельный. **instructor** *n* инстру́ктор.

instrument *n* ору́дие, инструме́нт. **instrumental** *adj* (*mus*) инструмента́льный; (*gram*) твори́тельный; **be** ~ **in** спосо́бствовать *impf*, по~ *pf* +*dat*; *n* (*gram*) твори́тельный паде́ж. **instrumentation** *n*

(*mus*) инструменто́вка.

insubordinate *adj* неподчиня́ющийся.

insufferable *adj* невыноси́мый.

insular *adj* (*fig*) ограни́ченный.

insulate *vt* изоли́ровать *impf* & *pf.* **insulation** *n* изоля́ция. **insulator** *n* изоля́тор.

insulin *n* инсули́н.

insult *n* оскорбле́ние; *vt* оскорбля́ть *impf*, оскорби́ть *pf.* **insulting** *adj* оскорби́тельный.

insuperable *adj* непреодоли́мый.

insurance *n* страхова́ние; *attrib* страхово́й. **insure** *vt* страхова́ть *impf*, за~ *pf* (**against** от+*gen*).

insurgent *n* повста́нец.

insurmountable *adj* непреодоли́мый.

insurrection *n* восста́ние.

intact *adj* це́лый.

intake *n* (*of persons*) набо́р; (*consumption*) потребле́ние.

intangible *adj* неосяза́емый.

integral *adj* неотъе́млемый. **integrate** *vt* & *i* интегри́роваться *impf* & *pf.* **integration** *n* интегра́ция.

integrity *n* (*honesty*) че́стность.

intellect *n* интелле́кт. **intellectual** *n* интеллиге́нт; *adj* интеллектуа́льный.

intelligence *n* (*intellect*) ум; (*information*) све́дения *neut pl*; (~ *service*) разве́дка. **intelligent** *adj* у́мный.

intelligentsia *n* интеллиге́нция.

intelligible *adj* поня́тный.

intemperate *adj* невозде́ржанный.

intend *vt* собира́ться *impf*, собра́ться *pf*; (*design*) предназнача́ть *impf*, предназна́чить *pf* (**for** для +*gen*, на+*acc*).

intense *adj* си́льный. **intensify** *vt* & *i* уси́ливать(ся) *impf*, уси́лить(ся) *pf.* **intensity** *n* интенси́вность, си́ла. **intensive** *adj* интенси́вный.

intent *n* наме́рение; *adj* (*resolved*) стремя́щийся (**on** к+*dat*); (*occupied*) погружённый (**on** в+*acc*); (*earnest*) внима́тельный. **intention** *n* наме́рение. **intentional** *adj* наме́ренный.

inter *vt* хорони́ть *impf*, по~ *pf.*

interact *vi* взаимоде́йствовать *impf.* **interaction** *n* взаимоде́йствие.

intercede *vi* хода́тайствовать *impf*, по~ *pf* (**for** за+*acc*; **with** пе́ред+*instr*).

intercept *vt* перехва́тывать *impf*,

перехвати́ть *pf.* **interception** *n* перехва́т.

interchange *n* обме́н (of +*instr*); (*junction*) тра́нспортная развя́зка; *vt* обме́ниваться *impf*, обменя́ться *pf* +*instr*. **interchangeable** *adj* взаимозаменя́емый.

inter-city *adj* междугоро́дный.

intercom *n* вну́тренняя телефо́нная связь.

interconnected *adj* взаимосвя́занный. **interconnection** *n* взаимосвя́зь.

intercourse *n* (*social*) обще́ние; (*trade*; *sexual*) сноше́ния *neut pl*.

interdisciplinary *adj* межотраслево́й.

interest *n* интере́с (in к+*dat*); (*econ*) проце́нты *m pl*; *vt* интересова́ть *impf*; (~ *person in*) заинтересо́вывать *impf*, заинтересова́ть *pf* (in +*instr*); be ~ed in интересова́ться *impf* +*instr*. **interesting** *adj* интере́сный.

interfere *vi* вме́шиваться *impf*, вмеша́ться *pf* (in в+*acc*). **interference** *n* вмеша́тельство; (*radio*) поме́хи *f pl*.

interim *n*: in the ~ тем вре́менем; *adj* промежу́точный; (*temporary*) вре́менный.

interior *n* вну́тренность; *adj* вну́тренний.

interjection *n* восклица́ние; (*gram*) междоме́тие.

interlock *vt & i* сцепля́ть(ся) *impf*, сцепи́ть(ся) *pf*.

interloper *n* незва́ный гость *m*.

interlude *n* (*theat*) антра́кт; (*mus*, *fig*) интерлю́дия.

intermediary *n* посре́дник.

intermediate *adj* промежу́точный.

interminable *adj* бесконе́чный.

intermission *n* переры́в; (*theat*) антра́кт.

intermittent *adj* преры́вистый.

intern *vt* интерни́ровать *impf & pf*.

internal *adj* вну́тренний; ~ combustion engine дви́гатель *m* вну́треннего сгора́ния.

international *adj* междунаро́дный; *n* (*contest*) междунаро́дные состяза́ния *neut pl*.

internment *n* интерни́рование.

interplay *n* взаимоде́йствие.

interpret *vt* (*explain*) толкова́ть *impf*; (*understand*) истолко́вывать *impf*, истолкова́ть *pf*; *vi* переводи́ть *impf*, перевести́ *pf*. **interpretation** *n* толкова́ние. **interpreter** *n* перево́дчик, -ица.

interrelated *adj* взаимосвя́занный. **interrelationship** *n* взаи́мная связь.

interrogate *vt* допра́шивать *impf*, допроси́ть *pf*. **interrogation** *n* допро́с. **interrogative** *adj* вопроси́тельный.

interrupt *vt* прерыва́ть *impf*, прерва́ть *pf*. **interruption** *n* переры́в.

intersect *vt & i* пересека́ть(ся) *impf*, пересе́чь(ся) *pf*. **intersection** *n* пересече́ние.

intersperse *vt* (*scatter*) рассыпа́ть *impf*, рассы́пать *pf* (between, among ме́жду+*instr*, среди́+*gen*).

intertwine *vt & i* переплета́ть(ся) *impf*, переплести́(сь) *pf*.

interval *n* интерва́л; (*theat*) антра́кт.

intervene *vi* (*occur*) происходи́ть *impf*, произойти́ *pf*; ~ in вме́шиваться *impf*, вмеша́ться *pf* в+*acc*. **intervention** *n* вмеша́тельство; (*polit*) интерве́нция.

interview *n* интервью́ *neut indecl*; *vt* интервьюи́ровать *impf & pf*, про~ *pf*. **interviewer** *n* интервьюе́р.

interweave *vt* воткать́ *pf*.

intestate *adj* без завеща́ния.

intestine *n* кишка́; *pl* кише́чник.

intimacy *n* инти́мность. **intimate**[1] *adj* инти́мный.

intimate[2] *vt* (*hint*) намека́ть *impf*, намекну́ть *pf* на+*acc*. **intimation** *n* намёк.

intimidate *vt* запу́гивать *impf*, запуга́ть *pf*.

into *prep* в, во+*acc*, на+*acc*.

intolerable *adj* невыноси́мый. **intolerance** *n* нетерпи́мость. **intolerant** *adj* нетерпи́мый.

intonation *n* интона́ция.

intoxicated *adj* пья́ный. **intoxication** *n* опьяне́ние.

intractable *adj* непода́тливый.

intransigent *adj* непримири́мый.

intransitive *adj* неперехо́дный.

intrepid *adj* неустраши́мый.

intricacy *n* запу́танность. **intricate** *adj* запу́танный.

intrigue *n* интри́га; *vi* интригова́ть *impf*; *vt* интригова́ть *impf*, за~ *pf*.

intrinsic *adj* прису́щий; (*value*) вну́тренний.

introduce *vt* вводи́ть *impf*, ввести́ *pf*; (*person*) представля́ть *impf*, предста́вить *pf*. **introduction** *n* введе́ние; представле́ние; (*to book*) предисло́вие. **introductory** *adj* вступи́тельный.

introspection *n* интроспе́кция.

intrude *vi* вторга́ться *impf*, вто́ргнуться *pf* (**into** в+*acc*); (*disturb*) меша́ть *impf*, по~ *pf*. **intruder** *n* (*burglar*) граби́тель *m*. **intrusion** *n* вторже́ние.

intuition *n* интуи́ция. **intuitive** *adj* интуити́вный.

inundate *vt* наводня́ть *impf*, наводни́ть *pf*. **inundation** *n* наводне́ние.

invade *vt* вторга́ться *impf*, вто́ргнуться *pf* в+*acc*. **invader** *n* захва́тчик.

invalid[1] *n* (*person*) инвали́д.

invalid[2] *adj* недействи́тельный. **invalidate** *vt* де́лать *impf*, с~ *pf* недействи́тельным.

invaluable *adj* неоцени́мый.

invariable *adj* неизме́нный.

invasion *n* вторже́ние.

invective *n* брань.

invent *vt* изобрета́ть *impf*, изобрести́ *pf*; (*think up*) выду́мывать *impf*, вы́думать *pf*. **invention** *n* изобрете́ние; вы́думка. **inventive** *adj* изобрета́тельный. **inventor** *n* изобрета́тель *m*.

inventory *n* инвента́рь *m*.

inverse *adj* обра́тный; *n* противоположность. **invert** *vt* перевора́чивать *impf*, переверну́ть *pf*. **inverted commas** *n pl* кавы́чки *f pl*.

invest *vt & i* (*econ*) вкла́дывать *impf*, вложи́ть *pf* (де́ньги) (**in** в+*acc*).

investigate *vt* иссле́довать *impf & pf*; (*law*) рассле́довать *impf & pf*. **investigation** *n* иссле́дование; рассле́дование.

investment *n* (*econ*) вклад. **investor** *n* вкла́дчик.

inveterate *adj* закоренéлый.

invidious *adj* оскорби́тельный.

invigorate *vt* оживля́ть *impf*, оживи́ть *pf*.

invincible *adj* непобеди́мый.

inviolable *adj* неруши́мый.

invisible *adj* неви́димый.

invitation *n* приглаше́ние. **invite** *vt* приглаша́ть *impf*, пригласи́ть *pf*. **inviting** *adj* привлека́тельный.

invoice *n* факту́ра.

invoke *vt* обраща́ться *impf*, обрати́ться *pf* к+*dat*.

involuntary *adj* нево́льный.

involve *vt* (*entangle*) вовлека́ть *impf*, вовле́чь *pf*; (*entail*) влечь *impf* за собо́й. **involved** *adj* сло́жный.

invulnerable *adj* неуязви́мый.

inward *adj* вну́тренний. **inwardly** *adv* внутри́. **inwards** *adv* внутрь.

iodine *n* йод.

iota *n*: **not an ~** ни на йо́ту.

IOU *n* долгова́я распи́ска.

Iran *n* Ира́н. **Iranian** *n* ира́нец, -нка; *adj* ира́нский.

Iraq *n* Ира́к. **Iraqi** *n* ира́кец; жи́тель *m*, ~ница Ира́ка; *adj* ира́кский.

irascible *adj* раздражи́тельный.

irate *adj* гне́вный.

Ireland *n* Ирла́ндия.

iris *n* (*anat*) ра́дужная оболо́чка; (*bot*) каса́тик.

Irish *adj* ирла́ндский. **Irishman** *n* ирла́ндец. **Irishwoman** *n* ирла́ндка.

irk *vt* раздража́ть *impf*, раздражи́ть *pf* +*dat*. **irksome** *adj* раздражи́тельный.

iron *n* желе́зо; (*for clothes*) утю́г; *adj* желе́зный; *vt* гла́дить *impf*, вы́~ *pf*. **ironic(al)** *adj* ирони́ческий. **irony** *n* иро́ния.

irradiate *vt* (*subject to radiation*) облуча́ть *impf*, облучи́ть *pf*. **irradiation** *n* облуче́ние.

irrational *adj* неразу́мный.

irreconcilable *adj* непримири́мый.

irrefutable *adj* неопровержи́мый.

irregular *adj* нерегуля́рный; (*gram*) непра́вильный; (*not even*) неро́вный.

irrelevant *adj* неуме́стный.

irreparable *adj* непоправи́мый.

irreplaceable *adj* незамени́мый.

irrepressible *adj* неудержи́мый.

irreproachable *adj* безупре́чный.

irresistible *adj* неотрази́мый.

irresolute *adj* нереши́тельный.

irrespective *adj*: **~ of** несмотря́ на +*acc*.

irresponsible *adj* безотве́тственный.

irretrievable *adj* непоправи́мый.

irreverent *adj* непочти́тельный.

irreversible *adj* необрати́мый.

irrevocable *adj* неотменя́емый.

irrigate *vt* ороша́ть *impf*, ороси́ть *pf*. **irrigation** *n* ороше́ние.

irritable *adj* раздражи́тельный. **irritate** *vt* раздража́ть *impf*, раздражи́ть *pf*. **irritation** *n* раздраже́ние.

Islam *n* исла́м. **Islamic** *adj* мусульма́нский.

island, isle *n* о́стров. **islander** *n* островитя́нин, -я́нка.

isolate *vt* изоли́ровать *impf & pf*. **isolation** *n* изоля́ция.

Israel *n* Изра́иль *m*. **Israeli** *n* израильтя́нин, -я́нка; *adj* изра́ильский.

issue *n* (*question*) (спо́рный) вопро́с; (*of bonds etc.*) вы́пуск; (*of magazine*) но́мер; *vi* выходи́ть *impf*, вы́йти *pf*; (*flow*) вытека́ть *impf*, вы́течь *pf*; *vt* выпуска́ть *impf*, вы́пустить *pf*; (*give out*) выдава́ть *impf*, вы́дать *pf*.

isthmus *n* переше́ек.

it *pron* он, она́, оно́; *demonstrative* э́то.

Italian *n* италья́нец, -нка; *adj* италья́нский.

italics *n pl* курси́в; **in ~** курси́вом. **italicize** *vt* выделя́ть *impf*, вы́делить *pf* курси́вом.

Italy *n* Ита́лия.

ITAR-Tass *abbr* ИТА́Р-ТА́СС.

itch *n* зуд; *vi* чеса́ться *impf*.

item *n* (*on list*) предме́т; (*in account*) статья́; (*on agenda*) пункт; (*in programme*) но́мер. **itemize** *vt* перечисля́ть *impf*, перечи́слить *pf*.

itinerant *adj* стра́нствующий. **itinerary** *n* маршру́т.

its *poss pron* его́, её; свой.

itself *pron* (*emph*) (он(о́)) сам(о́), (она́) сама́; (*refl*) себя́; -ся (*suffixed to vt*).

ivory *n* слоно́вая кость.

ivy *n* плющ.

J

jab *n* толчо́к; (*injection*) уко́л; *vt* ты́кать *impf*, ткнуть *pf*.

jabber *vi* тарато́рить *impf*.

jack *n* (*cards*) вале́т; (*lifting device*) домкра́т; *vt* (**~ up**) поднима́ть *impf*, подня́ть *pf* домкра́том.

jackdaw *n* га́лка.

jacket *n* (*tailored*) пиджа́к; (*anorak*) ку́ртка; (*on book*) (су́пер)обло́жка.

jackpot *n* банк.

jade *n* (*mineral*) нефри́т.

jaded *adj* утомлённый.

jagged *adj* зазу́бренный.

jaguar *n* ягуа́р.

jail *see* gaol

jam¹ *n* (*crush*) да́вка; (*in traffic*) про́бка; *vt* (*thrust*) впи́хивать *impf*, впихну́ть *pf* (**into** в+*acc*); (*wedge open; block*) закли́нивать *impf*, закли́нить *pf*; (*radio*) заглуша́ть *impf*, заглуши́ть *pf*; *vi* (*machine*) закли́нивать *impf*, заклини́ть *pf impers*+*acc*.

jam² *n* (*conserve*) варе́нье, джем.

jangle *vi* (& *t*) звя́кать (+*instr*).

janitor *n* привра́тник.

January *n* янва́рь; *adj* янва́рский.

Japan *n* Япо́ния. **Japanese** *n* япо́нец, -нка; *adj* япо́нский.

jar¹ *n* (*container*) ба́нка.

jar² *vi* (*irritate*) раздража́ть *impf*, раздражи́ть *pf* (**upon** +*acc*).

jargon *n* жарго́н.

jasmin(e) *n* жасми́н.

jaundice *n* желту́ха. **jaundiced** *adj* (*fig*) цини́чный.

jaunt *n* прогу́лка.

jaunty *adj* бо́дрый.

javelin *n* копьё.

jaw *n* че́люсть; *pl* пасть, рот.

jay *n* со́йка.

jazz *n* джаз; *adj* джа́зовый.

jealous *adj* ревни́вый; (*envious*) зави́стливый; **be ~ of** (*person*) ревнова́ть *impf*; (*thing*) зави́довать *impf*, по~ *pf* +*dat*; (*rights*) ревни́во оберега́ть *impf*, обере́чь *pf*. **jealousy** *n* ре́вность; за́висть.

jeans *n pl* джи́нсы (-сов) *pl*.

jeer *n* насме́шка; *vt & i* насмеха́ться *impf* (**at** над+*instr*).

jelly *n* (*sweet*) желе́ *neut indecl*; (*aspic*) сту́день *m*. **jellyfish** *n* меду́за.

jeopardize *vt* подверга́ть *impf*, подве́ргнуть *pf* опа́сности. **jeopardy** *n* опа́сность.

jerk *n* рыво́к; *vt* дёргать *impf* +*instr*; *vi* (*twitch*) дёргаться *impf*, дёрнуться *pf*. **jerky** *adj* неро́вный.

jersey *n* (*garment*) дже́мпер; (*fabric*) джерси́ *neut indecl*.

jest *n* шу́тка; **in ~** в шу́тку; *vi* шути́ть

impf, по~ *pf*. **jester** *n* шут.

jet¹ *n* (*stream*) струя́; (*nozzle*) сопло́; ~ **engine** реакти́вный дви́гатель *m*; ~ **plane** реакти́вный самолёт.

jet² *n* (*mineralogy*) гага́т; ~**-black** чёрный как смоль.

jettison *vt* выбра́сывать *impf*, вы́бросить *pf* за́ борт.

jetty *n* при́стань.

Jew *n* евре́й, евре́йка. **Jewish** *adj* евре́йский.

jewel *n* драгоце́нность, драгоце́нный ка́мень *m*. **jeweller** *n* ювели́р. **jewellery** *n* драгоце́нности *f pl*.

jib *n* (*naut*) кли́вер; *vi*: ~ **at** уклоня́ться *impf* от+*gen*.

jigsaw *n* (*puzzle*) моза́ика.

jingle *n* звя́канье; *vi* (*& t*) звя́кать *impf*, звя́кнуть *pf* (+*instr*).

job *n* (*work*) рабо́та; (*task*) зада́ние; (*position*) ме́сто. **jobless** *adj* безрабо́тный.

jockey *n* жоке́й; *vi* оттира́ть *impf* друг дру́га.

jocular *adj* шутли́вый.

jog *n* (*push*) толчо́к; *vt* подта́лкивать *impf*, подтолкну́ть *pf*; *vi* бе́гать *impf* трусцо́й. **jogger** *n* занима́ющийся оздорови́тельным бе́гом. **jogging** *n* оздорови́тельный бег.

join *vt & i* соединя́ть(ся) *impf*, соедини́ть(ся) *pf*; *vt* (*a group of people*) присоединя́ть *impf*, присоедини́ться *pf* к+*dat*; (*as member*) вступа́ть *impf*, вступи́ть *pf* в+*acc*; *vi*: ~ **in** принима́ть *impf*, приня́ть *pf* уча́стие (в+*prep*); ~ **up** вступа́ть *impf*, вступи́ть *pf* в а́рмию.

joiner *n* столя́р.

joint *n* соедине́ние; (*anat*) суста́в; (*meat*) кусо́к; *adj* совме́стный; (*common*) о́бщий.

joist *n* перекла́дина.

joke *n* шу́тка; *vi* шути́ть *impf*, по~ *pf*. **joker** *n* шутни́к; (*cards*) джо́кер.

jollity *n* весе́лье. **jolly** *adj* весёлый; *adv* о́чень.

jolt *n* толчо́к; *vt & i* трясти́(сь) *impf*.

jostle *vt & i* толка́ть(ся) *impf*, толкну́ть(ся) *pf*.

jot *n* йо́та; **not a** ~ ни на йо́ту; *vt* (~ **down**) запи́сывать *impf*, записа́ть *pf*.

journal *n* журна́л; (*diary*) дневни́к.

journalese *n* газе́тный язы́к. **journalism** *n* журнали́стика. **journalist** *n* журнали́ст.

journey *n* путеше́ствие; *vi* путеше́ствовать *impf*.

jovial *adj* весёлый.

joy *n* ра́дость. **joyful, joyous** *adj* ра́достный. **joyless** *adj* безра́достный. **joystick** *n* рыча́г управле́ния; (*comput*) джо́йстик.

jubilant *adj* лику́ющий; **be** ~ ликова́ть *impf*. **jubilation** *n* ликова́ние.

jubilee *n* юбиле́й.

Judaism *n* юдаи́зм.

judge *n* судья́ *m*; (*connoisseur*) цени́тель *m*; *vt & i* суди́ть *impf*. **judgement** *n* (*legal decision*) реше́ние; (*opinion*) мне́ние; (*discernment*) рассуди́тельность.

judicial *adj* суде́бный. **judiciary** *n* судьи́ *m pl*. **judicious** *adj* здравомы́слящий.

judo *n* дзюдо́ *neut indecl*.

jug *n* кувши́н.

juggernaut *n* (*lorry*) многото́нный грузови́к; (*fig*) неумоли́мая си́ла.

juggle *vi* жонгли́ровать *impf*. **juggler** *n* жонглёр.

jugular *n* яре́мная ве́на.

juice *n* сок. **juicy** *adj* со́чный.

July *n* ию́ль *m*; *adj* ию́льский.

jumble *n* (*disorder*) беспоря́док; (*articles*) барахло́; *vt* перепу́тывать *impf*, перепу́тать *pf*.

jump *n* прыжо́к, скачо́к; *vi* пры́гать *impf*, пры́гнуть *pf*; скака́ть *impf*; (*from shock*) вздра́гивать *impf*, вздро́гнуть *pf*; *vt* (~ **over**) перепры́гивать *impf*, перепры́гнуть *pf*; ~ **at** (*offer*) ухва́тываться *impf*, ухвати́ться *pf* за+*acc*; ~ **up** вска́кивать *impf*, вскочи́ть *pf*.

jumper *n* джéмпер.

jumpy *adj* не́рвный.

junction *n* (*rly*) у́зел; (*roads*) перекрёсток.

juncture *n*: **at this** ~ в э́тот моме́нт.

June *n* ию́нь *m*; *adj* ию́ньский.

jungle *n* джу́нгли (-лей) *pl*.

junior *adj* мла́дший; ~ **school** нача́льная шко́ла.

juniper *n* можжеве́льник.

junk *n* (*rubbish*) барахло́.

jurisdiction *n* юрисди́кция.

jurisprudence *n* юриспруде́нция.

juror *n* прися́жный *sb.* **jury** *n* прися́жные *sb*; (*in competition*) жюри́ *neut indecl.*

just *adj* (*fair*) справедли́вый; (*deserved*) заслу́женный; *adv* (*exactly*) как раз, и́менно; (*simply*) про́сто; (*barely*) едва́; (*very recently*) то́лько что; ~ **in case** на вся́кий слу́чай.

justice *n* (*proceedings*) правосу́дие; (*fairness*) справедли́вость; **do** ~ **to** отдава́ть *impf*, отда́ть *pf* до́лжное +*dat.*

justify *vt* опра́вдывать *impf*, оправда́ть *pf.* **justification** *n* оправда́ние.

jut *vi* (~ *out*) выдава́ться *impf*; выступа́ть *impf.*

juvenile *n & adj* несовершенноле́тний *sb & adj.*

juxtapose *vt* помеща́ть *impf*, помести́ть *pf* ря́дом; (*for comparison*) сопоставля́ть *impf*, сопоста́вить *pf* (**with** c+*instr*).

K

kaleidoscope *n* калейдоско́п.

kangaroo *n* кенгуру́ *m indecl.*

Kazakhstan *n* Казахста́н.

keel *n* киль *m*; *vi*: ~ **over** опроки́дываться *impf*, опроки́нуться *pf.*

keen *adj* (*enthusiastic*) по́лный энтузиа́зма; (*sharp*) о́стрый; (*strong*) си́льный; **be** ~ **on** увлека́ться *impf*, увле́чься *pf* +*instr*; (*want to do*) о́чень хоте́ть *impf* +*inf.*

keep[1] *n* (*tower*) гла́вная ба́шня; (*maintenance*) содержа́ние.

keep[2] *vt* (*possess, maintain*) держа́ть *impf*; храни́ть *impf*; (*observe*) соблюда́ть *impf*, соблюсти́ *pf* (*the law*); сде́рживать *impf*, сдержа́ть *pf* (*one's word*); (*family*) содержа́ть *impf*; (*diary*) вести́ *impf*; (*detain*) заде́рживать *impf*, задержа́ть *pf*; (*retain, reserve*) сохраня́ть *impf*, сохрани́ть *pf*; *vi* (*remain*) остава́ться *impf*, оста́ться *pf*; (*of food*) не по́ртиться *impf*; ~ **back** (*vt*) (*hold back*) уде́рживать *impf*, удержа́ть *pf*; (*vi*) держа́ться *impf* сза́ди; ~ **doing sth** всё +*verb*: **she** ~**s** giggling она́ всё хихи́кает; ~ **from** уде́рживаться *impf*, удержа́ться *pf* от+*gen*; ~ **on** продолжа́ть *impf*, продол-

жи́ть *pf* (+*inf*); ~ **up (with)** (*vi*) не отстава́ть *impf* (от+*gen*).

keepsake *n* пода́рок на па́мять.

keg *n* бочо́нок.

kennel *n* конура́.

kerb *n* край тротуа́ра.

kernel *n* (*nut*) ядро́; (*grain*) зерно́; (*fig*) суть.

kerosene *n* кероси́н.

kettle *n* ча́йник.

key *n* ключ; (*piano, typewriter*) кла́виш(а); (*mus*) тона́льность; *attrib* веду́щий, ключево́й. **keyboard** *n* клавиату́ра. **keyhole** *n* замо́чная сква́жина.

KGB *abbr* КГБ.

khaki *n & adj* ха́ки *neut, adj indecl.*

kick *n* уда́р ного́й, пино́к; *vt* ударя́ть *impf*, уда́рить *pf* ного́й; пина́ть *impf*, пнуть *pf*; *vi* (*of horse etc.*) ляга́ться *impf.* **kick-off** *n* нача́ло (игры́).

kid[1] *n* (*goat*) козлёнок; (*child*) малы́ш.

kid[2] *vt* (*deceive*) обма́нывать *impf*, обману́ть *pf*; *vi* (*joke*) шути́ть *impf*, по~ *pf.*

kidnap *vt* похища́ть *impf*, похи́тить *pf.*

kidney *n* по́чка.

kill *vt* убива́ть *impf*, уби́ть *pf.* **killer** *n* уби́йца *m & f.* **killing** *n* уби́йство; *adj* (*murderous, fig*) уби́йственный; (*amusing*) уморительный.

kiln *n* обжиговая печь.

kilo *n* кило́ *neut indecl.* **kilohertz** *n* килоге́рц. **kilogram(me)** *n* килогра́мм. **kilometre** *n* киломе́тр. **kilowatt** *n* килова́тт.

kilt *n* шотла́ндская ю́бка.

kimono *n* кимоно́ *neut indecl.*

kin *n* (*family*) семья́; (*collect, relatives*) родня́.

kind[1] *n* сорт, род; **a** ~ **of** что́-то вро́де+*gen*; **this** ~ **of** тако́й; **what** ~ **of** что (э́то, он, *etc.*) за +*nom*; ~ **of** (*adv*) как бу́дто, ка́к-то.

kind[2] *adj* до́брый.

kindergarten *n* де́тский сад.

kindle *vt* зажига́ть *impf*, заже́чь *pf.* **kindling** *n* расто́пка.

kindly *adj* до́брый; *adv* любе́зно; (*with imper*) (*request*) бу́дьте добры́, +*imper.* **kindness** *n* доброта́.

kindred *adj*: ~ **spirit** родна́я душа́.

kinetic adj кинети́ческий.

king n коро́ль m (also chess, cards, fig); (draughts) да́мка. **kingdom** n короле́вство; (fig) ца́рство. **king-fisher** n зиморо́док.

kink n переги́б.

kinship n родство́; (similarity) схо́дство. **kinsman, -woman** n ро́дственник, -ица.

kiosk n кио́ск; (telephone) бу́дка.

kip n сон; vi дры́хнуть impf.

kipper n копчёная селёдка.

Kirghizia n Кирги́зия.

kiss n поцелу́й; vt & i целова́ть(ся) impf, по~ pf.

kit n (clothing) снаряже́ние; (tools) набо́р, компле́кт; vt: ~ **out** снаряжа́ть impf, снаряди́ть pf. **kitbag** n вещево́й мешо́к.

kitchen n ку́хня; attrib ку́хонный; ~ **garden** огоро́д.

kite n (toy) змей.

kitsch n дешёвка.

kitten n котёнок.

knack n сноро́вка.

knapsack n ра́нец.

knead vt меси́ть impf, с~ pf.

knee n коле́но. **kneecap** n коле́нная ча́шка.

kneel vi стоя́ть impf на коле́нях; (~ down) станови́ться impf, стать pf на коле́ни.

knickers n pl тру́сики (-ов) pl.

knick-knack n безделу́шка.

knife n нож; vt коло́ть impf, за~ pf ножо́м.

knight n (hist) ры́царь m; (holder of order) кавале́р; (chess) конь m. **knighthood** n ры́царское зва́ние.

knit vt (garment) вяза́ть impf, с~ pf; vi (bones) сраста́ться impf, срасти́сь pf; ~ **one's brows** хму́рить impf, на~ pf бро́ви. **knitting** n (action) вяза́ние; (object) вяза́нье; ~**needle** спи́ца. **knitwear** n трикота́ж.

knob n ши́шка, кно́пка; (door handle) ру́чка. **knobb(l)y** adj шишкова́тый.

knock n (noise) стук; (blow) уда́р; vt & i (strike) ударя́ть impf, уда́рить pf; (strike door etc.) по~ pf (at в+acc); ~ **about** (treat roughly) колоти́ть impf, по~ pf; (wander) шата́ться impf; ~ **down** (person) сбива́ть impf, сбить pf с

ног; (building) сноси́ть impf, снести́ pf; ~ **off** сбива́ть impf, сбить pf; (stop work) шаба́шить impf (рабо́ту); (deduct) сбавля́ть impf, сба́вить pf; ~ **out** выбива́ть impf, вы́бить pf; (sport) нокаути́ровать impf & pf; ~**out** нока́ут; ~ **over** опроки́дывать impf, опроки́нуть impf. **knocker** n дверно́й молото́к.

knoll n буго́р.

knot n у́зел; vt завя́зывать impf, завяза́ть pf узло́м. **knotty** adj (fig) запу́танный.

know vt знать impf; (~ how to) уме́ть impf, с~ pf +inf; ~**how** уме́ние. **knowing** adj многозначи́тельный. **knowingly** adv созна́тельно. **knowledge** n зна́ние; **to my** ~ наско́лько мне изве́стно.

knuckle n суста́в па́льца; vi: ~ **down to** впряга́ться impf, впря́чься pf в+acc; ~ **under** уступа́ть impf, уступи́ть pf (**to** +dat).

Korea n Коре́я.

ko(w)tow vi (fig) раболе́пствовать impf (**to** пе́ред+instr).

Kremlin n Кремль m.

kudos n сла́ва.

L

label n этике́тка, ярлы́к; vt прикле́ивать impf, прикле́ить pf ярлы́к к+dat.

laboratory n лаборато́рия.

laborious adj кропотли́вый.

labour n труд; (med) ро́ды (-дов) pl; attrib трудово́й; ~ **force** рабо́чая си́ла; ~**intensive** трудоёмкий; **L~ Party** лейбори́стская па́ртия; vi труди́ться impf; vt: ~ **a point** входи́ть impf, войти́ pf в изли́шние подро́бности. **laboured** adj затруднённый; (style) вы́мученный. **labourer** n чернорабо́чий sb. **labourite** n лейбори́ст.

labyrinth n лабири́нт.

lace n (fabric) кру́жево; (cord) шнуро́к; vt (~ up) шнурова́ть impf, за~ pf.

lacerate vt (also fig) терза́ть impf, ис~ pf. **laceration** n (wound) рва́ная ра́на.

lack n недоста́ток (**of** +gen, в+prep),

отсу́тствие; vt & i не хвата́ть impf, хвати́ть pf impers +dat (person), +gen (object).

lackadaisical adj то́мный.

laconic adj лакони́чный.

lacquer n лак; vt лакирова́ть impf, от~ pf.

lad n па́рень m.

ladder n ле́стница.

laden adj нагружённый.

ladle n (spoon) поло́вник; vt че́рпать impf, черпну́ть pf.

lady n да́ма, ле́ди f indecl. **ladybird** n бо́жья коро́вка.

lag¹ vi: ~ **behind** отстава́ть impf, отста́ть pf (от+gen).

lag² vt (insulate) изоли́ровать impf & pf.

lagoon n лагу́на.

lair n ло́говище.

laity n (in religion) миря́не (-н) pl.

lake n о́зеро.

lamb n ягнёнок.

lame adj хромо́й; **be** ~ хрома́ть impf; **go** ~ хроме́ть impf, о~ pf; vt кале́чить impf, о~ pf.

lament n плач; vt сожале́ть impf о+prep. **lamentable** adj прискорбный.

laminated adj слои́стый.

lamp n ла́мпа; (in street) фона́рь m. **lamp-post** n фона́рный столб. **lampshade** n абажу́р.

lance n пи́ка; vt (med) вскрыва́ть impf, вскрыть pf (ланце́том).

land n земля́; (dry ~) су́ша; (country) страна́; vi (naut) прича́ливать impf, прича́лить pf; vt & i (aeron) приземля́ть(ся) impf, приземли́ть(ся) pf; (find o.s.) попада́ть impf, попа́сть pf. **landing** n (aeron) поса́дка; (on stairs) площа́дка; ~**stage** при́стань. **landlady** n хозя́йка. **landlord** n хозя́ин. **landmark** n (conspicuous object) ориенти́р; (fig) ве́ха. **landowner** n землевладе́лец. **landscape** n ландша́фт; (also picture) пейза́ж. **landslide** n о́ползень m.

lane n (in country) доро́жка; (street) переу́лок; (passage) прохо́д; (on road) ряд; (in race) доро́жка.

language n язы́к; (style, speech) речь.

languid adj то́мный.

languish vi томи́ться impf.

languor n то́мность.

lank adj (hair) гла́дкий. **lanky** adj долговя́зый.

lantern n фона́рь m.

lap¹ n (of person) коле́ни (-ней) pl; (sport) круг.

lap² vt (drink) лака́ть impf, вы́~ pf; vi (water) плеска́ться impf.

lapel n отворо́т.

lapse n (mistake) оши́бка; (interval) промежу́ток; (expiry) истече́ние; vi впада́ть impf, впасть pf (into в+acc); (expire) истека́ть impf, исте́чь pf.

lapwing n чи́бис.

larch n ли́ственница.

lard n свино́е са́ло.

larder n кладова́я sb.

large adj большо́й; n: at ~ (free) на свобо́де; **by and** ~ вообще́ говоря́. **largely** adj в значи́тельной сте́пени.

largesse n ще́дрость.

lark¹ n (bird) жа́воронок.

lark² n прока́за; vi (~ about) резви́ться impf.

larva n личи́нка.

laryngitis n ларинги́т. **larynx** n горта́нь.

lascivious adj похотли́вый.

laser n ла́зер.

lash n (blow) уда́р пле́тью; (eyelash) ресни́ца; vt (beat) хлеста́ть impf, хлестну́ть pf; (tie) привя́зывать impf, привяза́ть pf (to к+dat).

last¹ n (cobbler's) коло́дка.

last² adj (final) после́дний; (most recent) прошлый; **the year** (etc.) **before** ~ позапрошлый год (и т.д.); ~ **but one** предпосле́дний; ~ **night** вчера́ ве́чером; **at** ~ наконе́ц; adv (after all others) по́сле всех; (on the last occasion) в после́дний раз; (lastly) наконе́ц.

last³ vi (go on) продолжа́ться impf, продо́лжиться pf; дли́ться impf, про~ pf; (be preserved) сохраня́ться impf, сохрани́ться pf; (suffice) хвата́ть impf, хвати́ть pf. **lasting** adj (permanent) постоя́нный; (durable) про́чный.

lastly adv в заключе́ние; наконе́ц.

latch n щеко́лда.

late adj по́здний; (recent) неда́вний; (dead) поко́йный; **be** ~ **for** опа́здывать impf, опозда́ть pf на+acc; adv по́здно; n: of ~ за после́днее вре́мя.

lately adv за после́днее вре́мя.

latent adj скры́тый.

lateral adj боково́й.

lath n ре́йка, дра́нка (also collect).

lathe n тока́рный стано́к.

lather n (мы́льная) пе́на; vt & i мы́лить(ся) impf, на~ pf.

Latin adj лати́нский; n лати́нский язы́к; ~**-American** латиноамерика́нский.

latitude n свобо́да; (geog) широта́.

latter adj после́дний; ~**-day** совреме́нный. **latterly** adv за после́днее вре́мя.

lattice n решётка.

Latvia n Ла́твия. **Latvian** n латви́ец, -и́йка; латы́ш, ~ка; adj латви́йский, латы́шский.

laud vt хвали́ть impf, по~ pf. **laudable** adj похва́льный.

laugh n смех; vi смея́ться impf (at над+instr); ~ **it off** отшу́чиваться impf, отшути́ться pf; ~**ing-stock** посме́шище. **laughable** adj смешно́й. **laughter** n смех.

launch[1] vt (ship) спуска́ть impf, спусти́ть pf на́ воду; (rocket) запуска́ть impf, запусти́ть pf; (undertake) начина́ть impf, нача́ть pf; n спуск на́ воду; за́пуск. **launcher** n (for rocket) пускова́я устано́вка. **launching pad** n пускова́я площа́дка.

launch[2] n (naut) ка́тер.

launder vt стира́ть impf, вы́~ pf. **laund(e)rette** n пра́чечная sb самообслу́живания. **laundry** n (place) пра́чечная sb; (articles) бельё.

laurel n ла́вр(овое де́рево).

lava n ла́ва.

lavatory n убо́рная sb.

lavender n лава́нда.

lavish adj ще́дрый; (abundant) оби́льный; vt расточа́ть impf (upon +dat).

law n зако́н; (system) пра́во; ~ **and order** правопоря́док. **law-court** n суд. **lawful** adj зако́нный. **lawless** adj беззако́нный.

lawn n газо́н; ~**-mower** газонокоси́лка.

lawsuit n проце́сс.

lawyer n адвока́т, юри́ст.

lax adj сла́бый. **laxative** n слаби́тельное sb. **laxity** n сла́бость.

lay[1] adj (non-clerical) све́тский.

lay[2] vt (place) класть impf, положи́ть pf; (cable, pipes) прокла́дывать impf, проложи́ть pf; (carpet) стлать impf, по~ pf; (trap etc.) устра́ивать impf, устро́ить pf; (eggs) класть impf, положи́ть pf; v abs (lay eggs) нести́сь impf, с~ pf; ~ **aside** откла́дывать impf, отложи́ть pf; ~ **bare** раскрыва́ть impf, раскры́ть pf; ~ **a bet** держа́ть impf пари́ (**on** на+acc); ~ **down** (relinquish) отка́зываться impf, отказа́ться pf от +gen; (rule etc.) устана́вливать impf, установи́ть pf; ~ **off** (workmen) увольня́ть impf, уво́лить pf; ~ **out** (spread) выкла́дывать impf, вы́ложить pf; (garden) разбива́ть impf, разби́ть pf; ~ **the table** накрыва́ть impf, накры́ть pf стол (**for** (meal) к+dat); ~ **up** запаса́ть impf, запасти́ pf +acc, +gen; **be laid up** быть прико́ванным к посте́ли. **layabout** n безде́льник.

layer n слой, пласт.

layman n миря́нин; (non-expert) неспециали́ст.

laze vi безде́льничать impf. **laziness** n лень. **lazy** adj лени́вый; ~**-bones** лентя́й, ~ка.

lead[1] n (example) приме́р; (leadership) руково́дство; (position) пе́рвое ме́сто; (theat) гла́вная роль; (electr) про́вод; (dog's) поводо́к; vt води́ть indet, вести́ det; (be in charge of) руководи́ть impf +instr; (induce) побужда́ть impf, побуди́ть pf; vt & i (cards) ходи́ть impf (c+gen); vi (sport) занима́ть impf, заня́ть pf пе́рвое ме́сто; ~ **away** уводи́ть impf, увести́ pf; ~ **to** (result in) приводи́ть impf, привести́ pf к+dat.

lead[2] n (metal) свине́ц. **leaden** adj свинцо́вый.

leader n руководи́тель m, ~ница, ли́дер; (mus) пе́рвая скри́пка; (editorial) передова́я статья́. **leadership** n руково́дство.

leading adj веду́щий, выдаю́щийся; ~ **article** передова́я статья́.

leaf n лист; (of table) откидна́я доска́; vi: ~ **through** перели́стывать impf, перелиста́ть pf. **leaflet** n листо́вка.

league n ли́га; **in** ~ **with** в сою́зе с +instr.

leak n течь, уте́чка; vi (escape) течь impf; (allow water to ~) пропуска́ть *impf* во́ду; ~ **out** проса́чиваться *impf*, просочи́ться *pf*.

lean¹ *adj* (*thin*) худо́й; (*meat*) по́стный.

lean² *vt & i* прислоня́ть(ся) *impf*, прислони́ть(ся) *pf* (**against** к+*dat*); *vi* (~ **on**, **rely on**) опира́ться *impf*, опере́ться *pf* (**on** на+*acc*); (*be inclined*) быть скло́нным (**to**(**wards**) к+*dat*); ~ **back** отки́дываться *impf*, отки́нуться *pf*; ~ **out of** высо́вываться *impf*, вы́сунуться *pf* в +*acc*. **leaning** *n* скло́нность.

leap *n* прыжо́к, скачо́к; *vi* пры́гать *impf*, пры́гнуть *pf*; скака́ть *impf*; ~ **year** високо́сный год.

learn *vt* учи́ться *impf*, об~ *pf* +*dat*; (*find out*) узнава́ть *impf*, узна́ть *pf*. **learned** *adj* учёный. **learner** *n* учени́к, -и́ца. **learning** *n* (*studies*) уче́ние; (*erudition*) учёность.

lease *n* аре́нда; *vt* (*of owner*) сдава́ть *impf*, сдать *pf* в аре́нду; (*of tenant*) брать *impf*, взять *pf* в аре́нду. **leaseholder** *n* аренда́тор.

leash *n* при́вязь.

least *adj* наиме́ньший, мале́йший; *adv* ме́нее всего́; **at** ~ по кра́йней ме́ре; **not in the** ~ ничу́ть.

leather *n* ко́жа; *attrib* ко́жаный.

leave¹ *n* (*permission*) разреше́ние; (*holiday*) о́тпуск; **on** ~ в о́тпуске; **take** (**one's**) ~ проща́ться *impf*, прости́ться *pf* (**of** с+*instr*).

leave² *vt & i* оставля́ть *impf*, оста́вить *pf*; (*abandon*) покида́ть *impf*, поки́нуть *pf*; (*go away*) уходи́ть *impf*, уйти́ *pf* (**from** от+*gen*); уезжа́ть *impf*, уе́хать *pf* (**from** от+*gen*); (*go out of*) выходи́ть *impf*, вы́йти *pf* из+*gen*; (*entrust*) предоставля́ть *impf*, предоста́вить *pf* (**to** +*dat*); ~ **out** пропуска́ть *impf*, пропусти́ть *pf*.

lecherous *adj* развра́тный.

lectern *n* анало́й; (*in lecture room*) пюпи́тр.

lecture *n* (*discourse*) ле́кция; (*reproof*) нота́ция; *vi* (*deliver* ~(*s*)) чита́ть *impf*, про~ *pf* ле́кцию (-ии) (**on** по+*dat*); *vt* (*admonish*) чита́ть *impf*, про~ нота́цию+*dat*; ~ **room** аудито́рия. **lecturer** *n* ле́ктор; (*univ*) преподава́тель *m*, ~ница.

ledge *n* вы́ступ; (*shelf*) по́лочка.

ledger *n* гла́вная кни́га.

lee *n* защи́та; *adj* подве́тренный.

leech *n* (*worm*) пия́вка.

leek *n* лук-поре́й.

leer *vi* криви́ться *impf*, с~ *pf*.

leeward *n* подве́тренная сторона́; *adj* подве́тренный.

leeway *n* (*fig*) свобо́да де́йствий.

left *n* ле́вая сторона́; (**the L**~; *polit*) ле́вые *sb pl*; *adj* ле́вый; *adv* нале́во, сле́ва (**of** от+*gen*); ~**hander** левша́ *m & f*; ~**wing** ле́вый.

left-luggage office *n* ка́мера хране́ния.

leftovers *n pl* оста́тки *m pl*; (*food*) объе́дки (-ков) *pl*.

leg *n* нога́; (*of furniture etc.*) но́жка; (*of journey etc.*) эта́п.

legacy *n* насле́дство.

legal *adj* (*of the law*) правово́й; (*lawful*) лега́льный. **legality** *n* лега́льность. **legalize** *vt* легализи́ровать *impf & pf*.

legend *n* леге́нда. **legendary** *adj* легенда́рный.

leggings *n pl* вя́заные рейту́зы (-з) *pl*.

legible *adj* разбо́рчивый.

legion *n* легио́н.

legislate *vi* издава́ть *impf*, изда́ть *pf* зако́ны. **legislation** *n* законода́тельство. **legislative** *adj* законода́тельный. **legislator** *n* законода́тель *m*. **legislature** *n* законода́тельные учрежде́ния *neut pl*.

legitimacy *n* зако́нность; (*of child*) законнорождённость. **legitimate** *adj* зако́нный; (*child*) законнорождённый. **legitimize** *vt* узако́нивать *impf*, узако́нить *pf*.

leisure *n* свобо́дное вре́мя, досу́г; **at** ~ на досу́ге. **leisurely** *adj* нетороплвый.

lemon *n* лимо́н. **lemonade** *n* лимона́д.

lend *vt* дава́ть *impf*, дать *pf* взаймы́ (**to** +*dat*); ода́лживать *impf*, одолжи́ть *pf* (**to** +*dat*).

length *n* длина́; (*of time*) продолжи́тельность; (*of cloth*) отре́з; **at** ~ подро́бно. **lengthen** *vt & i* удлиня́ть(ся) *impf*, удлини́ть(ся) *pf*. **lengthways** *adv* в длину́, вдоль. **lengthy** *adj* дли́нный.

leniency *n* снисходи́тельность. **lenient** *adj* снисходи́тельный.

lens n ли́нза; (*phot*) объекти́в; (*anat*) хруста́лик.

Lent n вели́кий пост.

lentil n чечеви́ца.

Leo n Лев.

leopard n леопа́рд.

leotard n трико́ *neut indecl*.

leper n прокажённый *sb*. **leprosy** n прока́за.

lesbian n лесбия́нка; *adj* лесби́йский.

lesion n поврежде́ние.

less *adj* ме́ньший; *adv* ме́ньше, ме́нее; *prep* за вы́четом +*gen*.

lessee n аренда́тор.

lessen *vt* & *i* уменьша́ть(ся) *impf*, уме́ньшить(ся) *pf*.

lesser *adj* ме́ньший.

lesson n уро́к.

lest *conj* (*in order that not*) чтобы не; (*that*) как бы не.

let n (*lease*) сда́ча в наём; *vt* (*allow*) позволя́ть *impf*, позво́лить *pf* +*dat*; разреша́ть *impf*, разреши́ть *pf* +*dat*; (*rent out*) сдава́ть *impf*, сдать *pf* внаём (**to** +*dat*); *v aux* (*imperative*) (*1st person*) дава́й(те); (*3rd person*) пусть; ~ **alone** не говоря́ уже́ о+*prep*; ~ **down** (*lower*) опуска́ть *impf*, опусти́ть *pf*; (*fail*) подводи́ть *impf*, подвести́ *pf*; (*disappoint*) разочаро́вывать *impf*, разочарова́ть *pf*; ~ **go** выпуска́ть *impf*, вы́пустить *pf*; ~'**s go** пойдёмте!; пошли́!; пое́хали!; ~ **in(to)** (*admit*) впуска́ть *impf*, впусти́ть *pf* в+*acc*; (*into secret*) посвяща́ть *impf*, посвяти́ть *pf* в+*acc*; ~ **know** дава́ть *impf*, дать *pf* знать +*dat*; ~ **off** (*gun*) вы́стрелить *pf* из+*gen*; (*not punish*) отпуска́ть *impf*, отпусти́ть *pf* без наказа́ния; ~ **out** (*release, loosen*) выпуска́ть *impf*, вы́пустить *pf*; ~ **through** пропуска́ть *impf*, пропусти́ть *pf*; ~ **up** затиха́ть *impf*, зати́хнуть *pf*.

lethal *adj* (*fatal*) смерте́льный; (*weapon*) смертоно́сный.

lethargic *adj* летарги́ческий. **lethargy** n летарги́я.

letter n письмо́; (*symbol*) бу́ква; (*printing*) ли́тера; ~-**box** почто́вый я́щик. **lettering** n шрифт.

lettuce n сала́т.

leukaemia n лейкеми́я.

level n у́ровень; *adj* ро́вный; ~ **crossing** (железнодоро́жный) перее́зд; ~-**headed** уравнове́шенный; *vt* (**make** ~) выра́внивать *impf*, вы́ровнять *pf*; (*sport*) сра́внивать *impf*, сравня́ть *pf*; (*gun*) наводи́ть *impf*, навести́ *pf* (**at** в, на, +*acc*); (*criticism*) направля́ть *impf*, напра́вить *pf* (**at** про́тив+*gen*).

lever n рыча́г. **leverage** n де́йствие рычага́; (*influence*) влия́ние.

levity n легкомы́слие.

levy n (*tax*) сбор; *vt* (*tax*) взима́ть *impf* (**from** с+*gen*).

lewd *adj* (*lascivious*) похотли́вый; (*indecent*) са́льный.

lexicon n словарь *m*.

liability n (*responsibility*) отве́тственность (**for** за+*acc*); (*burden*) обу́за.

liable *adj* отве́тственный (**for** за+*acc*); (*susceptible*) подве́рженный (**to** +*dat*).

liaise *vi* подде́рживать *impf* связь (**c**+*instr*). **liaison** n связь; (*affair*) любо́вная связь.

liar n лгун, ~ья.

libel n клевета́; *vt* клевета́ть *impf*, на~ *pf* на+*acc*. **libellous** *adj* клеветни́ческий.

liberal n либера́л; *adj* либера́льный; (*generous*) ще́дрый.

liberate *vt* освобожда́ть *impf*, освободи́ть *pf*. **liberation** n освобожде́ние. **liberator** n освободи́тель *m*.

libertine n распу́тник.

liberty n свобо́да; **at** ~ на свобо́де.

Libra n Весы́ (-со́в) *pl*.

librarian n библиоте́карь *m*. **library** n библиоте́ка.

libretto n либре́тто *neut indecl*.

licence[1] n (*permission, permit*) разреше́ние, лице́нзия; (*liberty*) изли́шняя во́льность. **license, -ce**[2] *vt* (*allow*) разреша́ть *impf*, разреши́ть *pf* +*dat*; дава́ть *impf*, дать *pf* пра́во +*dat*.

licentious *adj* распу́щенный.

lichen n лиша́йник.

lick n лиза́ние; *vt* лиза́ть *impf*, лизну́ть *pf*.

lid n кры́шка; (*eyelid*) ве́ко.

lie[1] n (*untruth*) ложь; *vi* лгать *impf*, со~ *pf*.

lie[2] n: ~ **of the land** (*fig*) положе́ние веще́й; *vi* лежа́ть *impf*; (*be situated*) находи́ться *impf*; ~ **down** ложи́ться *impf*, лечь *pf*; ~ **in** остава́ться *impf* в посте́ли.

lieu *n*: **in** ~ **of** вме́сто+*gen*.

lieutenant *n* лейтена́нт.

life *n* жизнь; (*way of* ~) о́браз жи́зни; (*energy*) жи́вость. **lifebelt** *n* спаса́тельный по́яс. **lifeboat** *n* спаса́тельная ло́дка. **lifebuoy** *n* спаса́тельный круг. **lifeguard** *n* спаса́тель *m*, -ница. **life-jacket** *n* спаса́тельный жиле́т. **lifeless** *adj* безжи́зненный. **lifelike** *adj* реалисти́чный. **lifeline** *n* спаса́тельный коне́ц. **lifelong** *adj* пожи́зненный. **life-size(d)** *adj* в натура́льную величину́. **lifetime** *n* жизнь.

lift *n* (*machine*) лифт, подъёмник; (*force*) подъёмная си́ла; **give s.o. a** ~ подвози́ть *impf*, подвезти́ *pf*; *vt & i* поднима́ть(ся) *impf*, подня́ть(ся) *pf*.

ligament *n* свя́зка.

light[1] *n* свет, освеще́ние; (*source of* ~) ого́нь *m*, ла́мпа, фона́рь *m*; *pl* (*traffic* ~) светофо́р; **can I have a** ~? мо́жно прикури́ть?; ~**bulb** ла́мпочка; *adj* (*bright*) све́тлый; (*pale*) бле́дный; *vt & i* (*ignite*) зажига́ть(ся) *impf*, заже́чь(ся) *pf*; *vt* (*illuminate*) освеща́ть *impf*, освети́ть *pf*; ~ **up** освеща́ть(ся) *impf*, освети́ть(ся) *pf*; (*begin to smoke*) закури́ть *pf*.

light[2] *adj* (*not heavy*) лёгкий; ~**hearted** беззабо́тный.

lighten[1] *vt* (*make lighter*) облегча́ть *impf*, облегчи́ть *pf*; (*mitigate*) смягча́ть *impf*, смягчи́ть *pf*.

lighten[2] *vt* (*illuminate*) освеща́ть *impf*, освети́ть *pf*; *vi* (*grow bright*) светле́ть *impf*, по~ *pf*.

lighter *n* зажига́лка.

lighthouse *n* мая́к.

lighting *n* освеще́ние.

lightning *n* мо́лния.

lightweight *n* (*sport*) легкове́с; *adj* легкове́сный.

like[1] *adj* (*similar*) похо́жий (на+*acc*); **what is he** ~? что он за челове́к?

like[2] *vt* нра́виться *impf*, по~ *pf impers*+*dat*: **I** ~ **him** он мне нра́вится; люби́ть *impf*; *vi* (*wish*) хоте́ть *impf*; **if you** ~ е́сли хоти́те; **I should** ~ я хоте́л бы; мне хоте́лось

бы. **likeable** *adj* симпати́чный.

likelihood *n* вероя́тность. **likely** *adj* (*probable*) вероя́тный; (*suitable*) подходя́щий.

liken *vt* уподобля́ть *impf*, уподо́бить *pf* (**to** +*dat*).

likeness *n* (*resemblance*) схо́дство; (*portrait*) портре́т.

likewise *adv* (*similarly*) подо́бно; (*also*) то́же, та́кже.

liking *n* вкус (**for** к+*dat*).

lilac *n* сире́нь; *adj* сире́невый.

lily *n* ли́лия; ~ **of the valley** ла́ндыш.

limb *n* член.

limber *vi*: ~ **up** размина́ться *impf*, размя́ться *pf*.

limbo *n* (*fig*) состоя́ние неопределённости.

lime[1] *n* (*mineralogy*) и́звесть. **limelight** *n*: **in the** ~ (*fig*) в це́нтре внима́ния. **limestone** *n* известня́к.

lime[2] *n* (*fruit*) лайм.

lime[3] *n* (~-*tree*) ли́па.

limit *n* грани́ца, преде́л; *vt* ограни́чивать *impf*, ограни́чить *pf*. **limitation** *n* ограниче́ние. **limitless** *adj* безграни́чный.

limousine *n* лимузи́н.

limp[1] *n* хромота́; *vi* хрома́ть *impf*.

limp[2] *adj* мя́гкий; (*fig*) вя́лый.

limpid *adj* прозра́чный.

linchpin *n* чека́.

line[1] *n* (*long mark*) ли́ния, черта́; (*transport, tel*) ли́ния; (*cord*) верёвка; (*wrinkle*) морщи́на; (*limit*) грани́ца; (*row*) ряд; (*of words*) строка́; (*of verse*) стих; *vt* (*paper*) линова́ть *impf*, раз~ *pf*; *vt & i* (~ **up**) выстра́ивать(ся) *impf*, вы́строить(ся) *pf* в ряд.

line[2] *vt* (*clothes*) класть *impf*, положи́ть *pf* на подкла́дку.

lineage *n* происхожде́ние.

linear *adj* лине́йный.

lined[1] *adj* (*paper*) линованный; (*face*) морщи́нистый.

lined[2] *adj* (*garment*) на подкла́дке.

linen *n* полотно́; *collect* бельё.

liner *n* ла́йнер.

linesman *n* боково́й судья́ *m*.

linger *vi* заде́рживаться *impf*, задержа́ться *pf*.

lingerie *n* да́мское бельё.

lingering *adj* (*illness*) затяжно́й.

lingo *n* жарго́н.

linguist *n* лингви́ст. **linguistic** *adj* лингвисти́ческий. **linguistics** *n* лингви́стика.

lining *n* (*clothing etc.*) подкла́дка; (*tech*) облицо́вка.

link *n* (*of chain*) звено́; (*connection*) связь; *vt* соединя́ть *impf*, соедини́ть *pf*; свя́зывать *impf*, связа́ть *pf*.

lino(leum) *n* лино́леум.

lintel *n* перемы́чка.

lion *n* лев. **lioness** *n* льви́ца.

lip *n* губа́; (*of vessel*) край. **lipstick** *n* губна́я пома́да.

liquefy *vt & i* превраща́ть(ся) *impf*, преврати́ть(ся) *pf* в жи́дкое состоя́ние.

liqueur *n* ликёр.

liquid *n* жи́дкость; *adj* жи́дкий.

liquidate *vt* ликвиди́ровать *impf & pf*. **liquidation** *n* ликвида́ция; **go into** ~ ликвиди́роваться *impf & pf*.

liquor *n* (спиртно́й) напи́ток.

liquorice *n* лакри́ца.

list¹ *n* спи́сок; *vt* составля́ть *impf*, соста́вить *pf* спи́сок +*gen*; (*enumerate*) перечисля́ть *impf*, перечи́слить *pf*.

list² *vi* (*naut*) накреня́ться *impf*, крени́ться *impf*, накрени́ться *pf*.

listen *vi* слу́шать *impf*, по~ *pf* (**to** +*acc*). **listener** *n* слу́шатель *m*.

listless *adj* апати́чный.

litany *n* лита́ния.

literacy *n* гра́мотность.

literal *adj* буква́льный.

literary *adj* литерату́рный.

literate *adj* гра́мотный.

literature *n* литерату́ра.

lithe *adj* ги́бкий.

lithograph *n* литогра́фия.

Lithuania *n* Литва́. **Lithuanian** *n* лито́вец, -вка; *adj* лито́вский.

litigation *n* тя́жба.

litre *n* литр.

litter *n* (*rubbish*) сор; (*brood*) помёт; *vt* (*make untidy*) сори́ть *impf*, на~ *pf* (**with** +*instr*).

little *n* немно́гое; ~ **by** ~ ма́ло-пома́лу; **a** ~ немно́го +*gen*; *adj* ма́ленький, небольшо́й; (*in height*) небольшо́го ро́ста; (*in distance, time*) коро́ткий; *adv* ма́ло, немно́го.

liturgy *n* литурги́я.

live¹ *adj* живо́й; (*coals*) горя́щий; (*mil*) боево́й; (*electr*) под напряже́нием; (*broadcast*) прямо́й.

live² *vi* жить *impf*; ~ **down** загла́живать *impf*, загла́дить *pf*; ~ **on** (*feed on*) пита́ться *impf* +*instr*; ~ **through** пережива́ть *impf*, пережи́ть *pf*; ~ **until, to see** дожива́ть *impf*, дожи́ть *pf* до+*gen*; ~ **up to** жить *impf* согла́сно +*dat*.

livelihood *n* сре́дства *neut pl* к жи́зни.

lively *adj* живо́й.

liven (up) *vt & i* оживля́ть(ся) *impf*, оживи́ть(ся) *pf*.

liver *n* пе́чень; (*cul*) печёнка.

livery *n* ливре́я.

livestock *n* скот.

livid *adj* (*angry*) взбешённый.

living *n* сре́дства *neut pl* к жи́зни; **earn a** ~ зараба́тывать *impf*, зараба́тать *pf* на жизнь; *adj* живо́й; ~**room** гости́ная *sb*.

lizard *n* я́щерица.

load *n* груз; (*also fig*) бре́мя *neut*; (*electr*) нагру́зка; *pl* (*lots*) ку́ча; *vt* (*goods*) грузи́ть *impf*, по~ *pf*; (*vehicle*) грузи́ть *impf*, на~ *pf*; (*fig*) обременя́ть *impf*, обремени́ть *pf*; (*gun, camera*) заряжа́ть *impf*, заряди́ть *pf*.

loaf¹ *n* буха́нка.

loaf² *vi* безде́льничать *impf*. **loafer** *n* безде́льник.

loan *n* заём; *vt* дава́ть *impf*, дать *pf* взаймы́.

loath, loth *predic*: **be** ~ **to** не хоте́ть *impf* +*inf*.

loathe *vt* ненави́деть *impf*. **loathing** *n* отвраще́ние. **loathsome** *adj* отврати́тельный.

lob *vt* высоко́ подбра́сывать *impf*, подбро́сить *pf*.

lobby *n* вестибю́ль *m*; (*parl*) кулуа́ры (-ров) *pl*.

lobe *n* (*of ear*) мо́чка.

lobster *n* ома́р.

local *adj* ме́стный.

locality *n* ме́стность.

localized *adj* локализо́ванный.

locate *vt* (*place*) помеща́ть *impf*, помести́ть *pf*; (*find*) находи́ть *impf*, найти́ *pf*; **be** ~**d** находи́ться *impf*.

location *n* (*position*) местонахожде́ние; **on** ~ (*cin*) на нату́ре.

locative *adj* (*n*) ме́стный (паде́ж).

lock¹ *n* (*of hair*) ло́кон; *pl* во́лосы (-о́с, -оса́м) *pl*.

lock² *n* замóк; (*canal*) шлюз; *vt & i* запирáть(ся) *impf*, заперéть(ся) *pf*; ~ **out** не впускáть *impf*; ~ **up** (*imprison*) сажáть *impf*, посадúть *pf*; (*close*) закрывáть(ся) *impf*, закрúть(ся) *pf*.

locker *n* шкáфчик.

locket *n* медальóн.

locksmith *n* слéсарь *m*.

locomotion *n* передвижéние. **locomotive** *n* локомотúв.

lodge *n* (*hunting*) (охóтничий) дóмик; (*porter's*) сторóжка; (*Masonic*) лóжа; *vt* (*accommodate*) помещáть *impf*, помéстúть *pf*; (*complaint*) подавáть *impf*, подáть *pf*; *vi* (*reside*) жить *impf* (**with** y+*gen*); (*stick*) засáживать *impf*, засéсть *pf*. **lodger** *n* жилéц, жилúца. **lodging** *n* (*also pl*) квартúра, (снимáемая) кóмната.

loft *n* (*attic*) чердáк.

lofty *adj* óчень высóкий; (*elevated*) возвышенный.

log *n* бревнó; (*for fire*) полéно; ~**book** (*naut*) вáхтенный журнáл.

logarithm *n* логарúфм.

loggerhead *n*: be at ~s быть в ссóре.

logic *n* лóгика. **logical** *adj* (*of logic*) логúческий; (*consistent*) логúчный.

logistics *n pl* материáльно-технúческое обеспéчение; (*fig*) проблéмы *f pl* организáции.

logo *n* эмблéма.

loin *n* (*pl*) пояснúца; (*cul*) филéйная часть.

loiter *vi* слоняться *impf*.

lone, lonely *adj* одинóкий. **loneliness** *n* одинóчество.

long¹ *vi* (*want*) стрáстно желáть *impf*, по~ *pf* (**for** +*gen*); (*miss*) тосковáть *impf* (**for** по+*dat*).

long² *adj* (*space*) длúнный; (*time*) дóлгий; (*in measurements*) длинóй в+*acc*; **in the** ~ **run** в конéчном счéте; ~**-sighted** дальнозóркий; ~**-suffering** долготерпелúвый; ~**-term** долгосрóчный; ~**-winded** многоречúвый; *adv* дóлго; ~ **ago** (*ужé*) давнó; **as** ~ **as** покá; ~ **before** задóлго до+*gen*.

longevity *n* долговéчность.

longing *n* стрáстное желáние (**for** +*gen*); тоскá (**for** по+*dat*); *adj* тоскýющий.

longitude *n* долготá.

longways *adv* в длинý.

look *n* (*glance*) взгляд; (*appearance*) вид; (*expression*) выражéние; *vi* смотрéть *impf*, по~ *pf* (**at** на, в, +*acc*); (*appear*) выглядеть *impf* +*instr*; (*face*) выходúть *impf* (**towards, onto** на+*acc*); ~ **about** осмáтриваться *impf*, осмотрéться *pf*; ~ **after** (*attend to*) присмáтривать *impf*, присмотрéть *pf* за+*instr*; ~ **down on** презирáть *impf*; ~ **for** искáть *impf* +*acc*, +*gen*; ~ **forward to** предвкушáть *impf*, предвкусúть *pf*; ~ **in** он заглядывать *impf*, заглянýть *pf* к+*dat*; ~ **into** (*investigate*) рассмáтривать *impf*, рассмотрéть *pf*; ~ **like** быть похóжим на+*acc*; **it** ~**s like rain** похóже на (то, что бýдет) дождь; ~ **on** (*regard*) считáть *impf*, счесть *pf* (**as** +*instr*, за+*instr*); ~ **out** выглядывать *impf*, выглянуть *pf* (в окнó); быть насторожé; *imper* осторóжно!; ~ **over, through** просмáтривать *impf*, просмотрéть *pf*; ~ **round** (*inspect*) осмáтривать *impf*, осмотрéть *pf*; ~ **up** (*raise eyes*) поднимáть *impf*, поднять *pf* глазá; (*in dictionary etc.*) искáть *impf*; (*improve*) улучшáться *impf*, улýчшиться *pf*; ~ **up to** уважáть *impf*.

loom¹ *n* ткáцкий станóк.

loom² *vi* вырисóвываться *impf*, вырисовáться *pf*; (*fig*) надвигáться *impf*.

loop *n* петля; *vi* образóвывать *impf*, образовáть *pf* петлю; (*fasten with loop*) закреплять *impf*, закрепúть *pf* петлёй; (*wind*) обмáтывать *impf*, обмотáть *pf* (**around** вокрýг+*gen*).

loophole *n* бойнúца; (*fig*) лазéйка.

loose *adj* (*free; not tight*) свобóдный; (*not fixed*) неприкреплённый; (*connection, screw*) слáбый; (*lax*) распýщенный; **at a** ~ **end** без дéла.

loosen *vt & i* ослаблять(ся) *impf*, ослáбить(ся) *pf*.

loot *n* добы́ча; *vt* грáбить *impf*, о~ *pf*.

lop *vt* (*tree*) подрезáть *impf*, подрéзать *pf*; (~ **off**) отрубáть *impf*, отрубúть *pf*.

lope *vi* бéгать *indet*, бежáть *det* вприпры́жку.

lopsided *adj* кривобóкий.

loquacious *adj* болтлúвый.

lord *n* (*master*) господи́н; (*eccl*) Госпо́дь; (*peer; title*) лорд; *vt*: ~ it over помыка́ть *impf* +*instr*. **lordship** *n* (*title*) све́тлость.

lore *n* зна́ния *neut pl*.

lorry *n* грузови́к.

lose *vt* теря́ть *impf*, по~ *pf*; *vt & i* (*game etc.*) прои́грывать *impf*, проигра́ть *pf*; *vi* (*clock*) отстава́ть *impf*, отста́ть *pf*. **loss** *n* поте́ря; (*monetary*) убы́ток; (*in game*) про́игрыш.

lot *n* жре́бий; (*destiny*) у́часть; (*of goods*) па́ртия; a ~, ~s мно́го; the ~ всё, все *pl*.

loth *see* **loath**

lotion *n* лосьо́н.

lottery *n* лотере́я.

loud *adj* (*sound*) гро́мкий; (*noisy*) шу́мный; (*colour*) крича́щий; out ~ вслух. **loudspeaker** *n* громкоговори́тель *m*.

lounge *n* гости́ная *sb*; *vi* сиде́ть *impf* развали́сь; (*idle*) безде́льничать *impf*.

louse *n* вошь. **lousy** *adj* (*coll*) парши́вый.

lout *n* балбе́с, у́валень *m*.

lovable *adj* ми́лый. **love** *n* любо́вь (of, for к+*dat*); in ~ with влюблённый в+*acc*; *vt* люби́ть *impf*. **lovely** *adj* прекра́сный; (*delightful*) преле́стный. **lover** *n* любо́вник, -ица.

low *adj* ни́зкий, невысо́кий; (*quiet*) ти́хий.

lower[1] *vt* опуска́ть *impf*, опусти́ть *pf*; (*price, voice, standard*) понижа́ть *impf*, пони́зить *pf*.

lower[2] *adj* ни́жний.

lowland *n* ни́зменность.

lowly *adj* скро́мный.

loyal *adj* ве́рный. **loyalty** *n* ве́рность.

LP *abbr* (of **long-playing record**) долгоигра́ющая пласти́нка.

Ltd. *abbr* (of **Limited**) с ограни́ченной отве́тственностью.

lubricant *n* сма́зка. **lubricate** *vt* сма́зывать *impf*, сма́зать *pf*. **lubrication** *n* сма́зка.

lucid *adj* я́сный. **lucidity** *n* я́сность.

luck *n* (*chance*) слу́чай; (*good* ~) сча́стье, уда́ча; (*bad* ~) неуда́ча. **luckily** *adv* к сча́стью. **lucky** *adj* счастли́вый; be ~ везти́ *imp*, по~ *pf impers* +*dat*: I was ~ мне повезло́.

lucrative *adj* при́быльный.

ludicrous *adj* смехотво́рный.

lug *vt* (*drag*) таска́ть *indet*, тащи́ть *det*.

luggage *n* бага́ж.

lugubrious *adj* печа́льный.

lukewarm *adj* теплова́тый; (*fig*) прохла́дный.

lull *n* (*in storm*) зати́шье; (*interval*) переры́в; *vt* (*to sleep*) убаю́кивать *impf*, убаю́кать *pf*; (*suspicions*) усыпля́ть *impf*, усыпи́ть *pf*.

lullaby *n* колыбе́льная пе́сня.

lumbar *adj* поясни́чный.

lumber[1] *vi* (*move*) брести́ *impf*.

lumber[2] *n* (*domestic*) ру́хлядь; *vt* обременя́ть *impf*, обремени́ть *pf*. **lumberjack** *n* лесору́б.

luminary *n* свети́ло.

luminous *adj* светя́щийся.

lump *n* ком; (*swelling*) о́пухоль; *vt*: ~ together сме́шивать *impf*, смеша́ть *pf* (в одно́).

lunacy *n* безу́мие.

lunar *adj* лу́нный.

lunatic *adj* (*n*) сумасше́дший (*sb*).

lunch *n* обе́д; ~-hour, ~-time обе́денный переры́в; *vi* обе́дать *impf*, по~ *pf*.

lung *n* лёгкое *sb*.

lunge *vi* де́лать *impf*, с~ *pf* вы́пад (at про́тив+*gen*).

lurch[1] *n*: leave in the ~ покида́ть *impf*, поки́нуть *pf* в беде́.

lurch[2] *vi* (*stagger*) ходи́ть *indet*, идти́ *det* шата́ясь.

lure *n* прима́нка; *vt* прима́нивать *impf*, примани́ть *pf*.

lurid *adj* (*gaudy*) крича́щий; (*details*) жу́ткий.

lurk *vi* зата́иваться *impf*, затаи́ться *pf*.

luscious *adj* со́чный.

lush *adj* пы́шный, со́чный.

lust *n* по́хоть (of, for к+*dat*); *vi* стра́стно жела́ть *impf*, по~ *pf* (for +*gen*). **lustful** *adj* похотли́вый.

lustre *n* гля́нец. **lustrous** *adj* глянцеви́тый.

lusty *adj* (*healthy*) здоро́вый; (*lively*) живо́й.

lute *n* (*mus*) лю́тня.

luxuriant *adj* пы́шный.

luxuriate *vi* наслажда́ться *impf*, наслади́ться *pf* (in +*instr*).

luxurious *adj* роско́шный. **luxury** *n* ро́скошь.

lymph *attrib* лимфати́ческий.

lynch *vt* линчева́ть *impf* & *pf*.

lyric *n* ли́рика; *pl* слова́ *neut pl* пе́сни. **lyrical** *adj* лири́ческий.

M

MA *abbr* (*of Master of Arts*) маги́стр гуманита́рных нау́к.

macabre *adj* жу́ткий.

macaroni *n* макаро́ны (-н) *pl*.

mace *n* (*of office*) жезл.

machination *n* махина́ция.

machine *n* маши́на; (*state ~*) аппара́т; *attrib* маши́нный; **~-gun** пулемёт; **~ tool** стано́к; *vt* обраба́тывать *impf*, обрабо́тать *pf* на станке́; (*sew*) шить *impf*, с~ *pf* (на маши́не). **machinery** *n* (*machines*) маши́ны *f pl*; (*of state*) аппара́т. **machinist** *n* машини́ст; (*sewing*) шве́йник, -и́ца, швея́.

mackerel *n* ску́мбрия, макре́ль.

mackintosh *n* плащ.

mad *adj* сумасше́дший. **madden** *vt* беси́ть *impf*, вз~ *pf*. **madhouse** *n* сумасше́дший дом. **madly** *adv* безу́мно. **madman** *n* сумасше́дший *sb*. **madness** *n* сумасше́ствие. **madwoman** *n* сумасше́дшая *sb*.

madrigal *n* мадрига́л.

maestro *n* ма́эстро *m indecl*.

Mafia *n* ма́фия.

magazine *n* журна́л; (*of gun*) магази́н.

maggot *n* личи́нка.

magic *n* ма́гия, волшебство́; *adj* (*also* **magical**) волше́бный. **magician** *n* волше́бник; (*conjurer*) фо́кусник.

magisterial *adj* авторите́тный.

magistrate *n* судья́ *m*.

magnanimity *n* великоду́шие. **magnanimous** *adj* великоду́шный.

magnate *n* магна́т.

magnesium *n* ма́гний.

magnet *n* магни́т. **magnetic** *adj* магни́тный; (*attractive*) притяга́тельный. **magnetism** *n* магнети́зм; притяга́тельность. **magnetize** *vt* намагни́чивать *impf*, намагни́тить *pf*.

magnification *n* увеличе́ние.

magnificence *n* великоле́пие. **magnificent** *adj* великоле́пный.

magnify *vt* увели́чивать *impf*, увели́чить *pf*; (*exaggerate*) преувели́чивать *impf*, преувели́чить *pf*. **magnifying glass** *n* увеличи́тельное стекло́.

magnitude *n* величина́; (*importance*) ва́жность.

magpie *n* соро́ка.

mahogany *n* кра́сное де́рево.

maid *n* прислу́га. **maiden** *adj* (*aunt etc.*) незаму́жняя; (*first*) пе́рвый; **~ name** де́вичья фами́лия.

mail *n* (*letters*) по́чта; **~ order** почто́вый зака́з; *vt* посыла́ть *impf*, посла́ть *pf* по по́чте.

maim *vt* кале́чить *impf*, ис~ *pf*.

main *n* (*gas ~*; *pl*) магистра́ль; **in the ~** в основно́м; *adj* основно́й, гла́вный; (*road*) магистра́льный. **mainland** *n* матери́к. **mainly** *adv* в основно́м. **mainstay** *n* (*fig*) гла́вная опо́ра.

maintain *vt* (*keep up*) подде́рживать *impf*, поддержа́ть *pf*; (*family*) содержа́ть *impf*; (*machine*) обслу́живать *impf*, обслужи́ть *pf*; (*assert*) утвержда́ть *impf*. **maintenance** *n* подде́ржка; содержа́ние; обслу́живание.

maize *n* кукуру́за.

majestic *adj* вели́чественный. **majesty** *n* вели́чественность; (*title*) вели́чество.

major[1] *n* (*mil*) майо́р.

major[2] *adj* (*greater*) бо́льший; (*more important*) бо́лее ва́жный; (*main*) гла́вный; (*mus*) мажо́рный; *n* (*mus*) мажо́р. **majority** *n* большинство́; (*full age*) совершенноле́тие.

make *vt* де́лать *impf*, с~ *pf*; (*produce*) производи́ть *impf*, произвести́ *pf*; (*prepare*) гото́вить *impf*, при~ *pf*; (*amount to*) равня́ться *impf* +*dat*; (*earn*) зараба́тывать *impf*, зарабо́тать *pf*; (*compel*) заставля́ть *impf*, заста́вить *pf*; (*reach*) добира́ться *impf*, добра́ться *pf* до+*gen*; (*be in time for*) успева́ть *impf*, успе́ть *pf* на+*acc*; **be made of** состоя́ть *impf* из+*gen*; **~ as if**, **though** де́лать *impf*, с~ *pf* вид, что; **~ a bed** стели́ть *impf*, по~ *pf* посте́ль; **~ believe** притворя́ться *impf*, притвори́ться *pf*; **~-believe** притво́рство; **~ do with** дово́льство-

ваться *impf*, y~ *pf* +*instr*; ~ **off**
удира́ть *impf*, удра́ть *pf*; ~ **out**
(*cheque*) выпи́сывать *impf*, вы́писать *pf*; (*assert*) утвержда́ть *impf*,
утверди́ть *pf*; (*understand*) разбира́ть *impf*, разобра́ть *pf*; ~ **over**
передава́ть *impf*, переда́ть *pf*; ~ **up**
(*form*, *compose*, *complete*) составля́ть *impf*, соста́вить *pf*; (*invent*)
выду́мывать *impf*, вы́думать *pf*;
(*theat*) гримирова́ть(ся) *impf*, за~
pf; ~-**up** (*theat*) грим; (*cosmetics*)
косме́тика; (*composition*) соста́в; ~
it up мири́ться *impf*, по~ *pf* (with
c+*instr*); ~ **up for** возмеща́ть *impf*,
возмести́ть *pf*; ~ **up one's mind**
реша́ться *impf*, реши́ться *pf*. **make**
n ма́рка. **makeshift** *adj* вре́менный.
malady *n* боле́знь.
malaise *n* (*fig*) беспоко́йство.
malaria *n* маляри́я.
male *n* (*animal*) саме́ц; (*person*)
мужчи́на *m*; *adj* мужско́й.
malevolence *n* недоброжела́тельность. **malevolent** *adj* недоброжела́тельный.
malice *n* зло́ба. **malicious** *adj* зло́бный.
malign *vt* клевета́ть *impf*, на~ *pf*
на+*acc*. **malignant** *adj* (*harmful*)
зловре́дный; (*malicious*) зло́бный;
(*med*) злока́чественный.
malinger *vi* притворя́ться *impf*, притвори́ться *pf* больны́м. **malingerer**
n симуля́нт.
mallard *n* кря́ква.
malleable *adj* ко́вкий; (*fig*) пода́тливый.
mallet *n* (*деревя́нный*) молото́к.
malnutrition *n* недоеда́ние.
malpractice *n* престу́пная небре́жность.
malt *n* со́лод.
maltreat *vt* пло́хо обраща́ться *impf*
c+*instr*.
mammal *n* млекопита́ющее *sb*.
mammoth *adj* грома́дный.
man *n* (*human*, *person*) челове́к;
(*human race*) челове́чество; (*male*)
мужчи́на *m*; (*labourer*) рабо́чий *sb*;
pl (*soldiers*) солда́ты *m pl*; *vt* (*furnish with men*) укомплекто́вывать
impf, укомплектова́ть *pf* ли́чным
соста́вом; ста́вить *impf*, по~ *pf*
люде́й к+*dat*; (*stall etc.*) обслужи-

вать *impf*, обслужи́ть *pf*; (*gate*,
checkpoint) стоя́ть *impf* на+*prep*.
manacle *n* нару́чник; *vt* надева́ть
impf, наде́ть *pf* нару́чники на+*acc*.
manage *vt* (*control*) управля́ть *impf*
+*instr*; *vi*(&*t*) (*cope*) справля́ться
impf, спра́виться *pf* (c+*instr*); (*succeed*) суме́ть *pf*. **management** *n*
управле́ние (*of* +*instr*); (*the* ~) администра́ция. **manager** *n* управля́ющий *sb* (*of* +*instr*); ме́неджер.
managerial *adj* администрати́вный.
managing director *n* дире́ктор-распоряди́тель *m*.
mandarin *n* мандари́н.
mandate *n* манда́т. **mandated** *adj*
подманда́тный. **mandatory** *adj* обяза́тельный.
mane *n* гри́ва.
manful *adj* му́жественный.
manganese *n* ма́рганец.
manger *n* я́сли (-лей) *pl*; **dog in the
~** соба́ка на се́не.
mangle *vt* (*mutilate*) кале́чить *impf*,
ис~ *pf*.
mango *n* ма́нго *neut indecl*.
manhandle *vt* гру́бо обраща́ться
impf c+*instr*.
manhole *n* смотрово́й коло́дец.
manhood *n* возмужа́лость.
mania *n* ма́ния. **maniac** *n* манья́к,
-я́чка. **manic** *adj* маниака́льный.
manicure *n* маникю́р; *vt* де́лать
impf, c~ *pf* маникю́р +*dat*. **manicurist** *n* маникю́рша.
manifest *adj* очеви́дный; *vt* (*display*)
проявля́ть *impf*, прояви́ть *pf*; *n*
манифе́ст. **manifestation** *n* проявле́ние. **manifesto** *n* манифе́ст.
manifold *adj* разнообра́зный.
manipulate *vt* манипули́ровать *impf*
+*instr*. **manipulation** *n* манипуля́ция.
manly *adj* му́жественный.
mankind *n* челове́чество.
manner *n* (*way*) о́браз; (*behaviour*)
мане́ра; *pl* мане́ры *f pl*. **mannerism**
n мане́ра.
mannish *adj* мужеподо́бный.
manoeuvrable *adj* мане́вренный.
manoeuvre *n* мане́вр; *vt & i* маневри́ровать *impf*.
manor *n* поме́стье; (*house*) поме́щичий дом.
manpower *n* челове́ческие ресу́рсы
m pl.

manservant n слуга́ m.

mansion n особня́к.

manslaughter n непредумы́шленное уби́йство.

mantelpiece n ками́нная доска́.

manual adj ручно́й; n руково́дство. **manually** adv вручну́ю.

manufacture n произво́дство; vt производи́ть impf, произвести́ pf. **manufacturer** n фабрика́нт.

manure n наво́з.

manuscript n ру́копись.

many adj & n мно́го +gen, мно́гие pl; **how ~** ско́лько +gen.

map n ка́рта; (of town) план; vt: ~ **out** намеча́ть impf, наме́тить pf.

maple n клён.

mar vt по́ртить impf, ис~ pf.

marathon n марафо́н.

marauder n мароде́р. **marauding** adj мароде́рский.

marble n мра́мор; (toy) ша́рик; attrib мра́морный.

March n март; adj ма́ртовский.

march vi марширова́ть impf, про~ pf; n марш.

mare n кобы́ла.

margarine n маргари́н.

margin n (on page) по́ле; (edge) край; **profit ~** при́быль; **safety ~** запа́с про́чности.

marigold n ноготки́ (-ко́в) pl.

marijuana n марихуа́на.

marina n мари́на.

marinade n марина́д; vt маринова́ть impf, за~ pf.

marine adj морско́й; n (soldier) солда́т морско́й пехо́ты; pl морска́я пехо́та. **mariner** n моря́к.

marionette n марионе́тка.

marital adj супру́жеский, бра́чный.

maritime adj морско́й; (near sea) примо́рский.

mark[1] n (coin) ма́рка.

mark[2] n (for distinguishing) ме́тка; (sign) знак; (school) отме́тка; (trace) след; **on your ~s** на старт!; vt (indicate; celebrate) отмеча́ть impf, отме́тить pf; (school etc.) проверя́ть impf, прове́рить pf; (stain) па́чкать impf, за~ pf; (sport) закрыва́ть impf, закры́ть pf; **~ my words** попо́мни(те) мои́ слова́!; **~ out** размеча́ть impf, разме́тить pf. **marker** n знак; (in book) закла́дка.

market n ры́нок; **~ garden** огоро́д; **~-place** база́рная пло́щадь; vt продава́ть impf, прода́ть pf.

marksman n стрело́к.

marmalade n апельси́новый джем.

maroon[1] adj (n) (colour) тёмнобордо́вый (цвет).

maroon[2] vt (put ashore) выса́живать impf, вы́садить pf (на необита́емом о́строве); (cut off) отреза́ть impf, отре́зать pf.

marquee n тэнт.

marquis n марки́з.

marriage n брак; (wedding) сва́дьба; attrib бра́чный. **marriageable** adj: ~ **age** бра́чный во́зраст. **married** adj (man) жена́тый; (woman) заму́жняя, за́мужем; (to each other) жена́ты; (of ~ persons) супру́жеский.

marrow n ко́стный мозг; (vegetable) кабачо́к.

marry vt (of man) жени́ться impf & pf на +prep; (of woman) выходи́ть impf, вы́йти pf за́муж за +acc; vi (of couple) пожени́ться pf.

marsh n боло́то. **marshy** adj боло́тистый.

marshal n ма́ршал; vt выстра́ивать impf, вы́строить pf; (fig) собира́ть impf, собра́ть pf.

marsupial n су́мчатое живо́тное sb.

martial adj вое́нный; ~ **law** вое́нное положе́ние.

martyr n му́ченик, -ица; vt му́чить impf, за~ pf. **martyrdom** n му́ченичество.

marvel n чу́до; vi изумля́ться impf, изуми́ться pf. **marvellous** adj чуде́сный.

Marxist n маркси́ст; adj маркси́стский. **Marxism** n маркси́зм.

marzipan n марципа́н.

mascara n тушь.

mascot n талисма́н.

masculine adj мужско́й; (gram) мужско́го ро́да; (of woman) муже-подо́бный.

mash n карто́фельное пюре́ neut indecl; vt размина́ть impf, размя́ть pf.

mask n ма́ска; vt маскирова́ть impf, за~ pf.

masochism n мазохи́зм. **masochist** n мазохи́ст. **masochistic** adj мазохи́стский.

mason n ка́менщик; (**M~**) масо́н.
Masonic adj масо́нский. **masonry** n ка́менная кла́дка.

masquerade n маскара́д; vi: ~ **as** выдава́ть impf, вы́дать pf себя́ за +acc.

Mass n (eccl) ме́сса.

mass n ма́сса; (majority) большинство́; attrib ма́ссовый; ~ **media** сре́дства neut pl ма́ссовой информа́ции; ~-**produced** ма́ссового произво́дства; ~ **production** ма́ссовое произво́дство; vt масси́ровать impf & pf.

massacre n резня́; vt выреза́ть impf, вы́резать pf.

massage n масса́ж; vt масси́ровать impf & pf. **masseur, -euse** n массажи́ст, ~ка.

massive adj масси́вный.

mast n ма́чта.

master n (owner) хозя́ин; (of ship) капита́н; (teacher) учи́тель m; (**M~**, univ) маги́стр; (workman; artist) ма́стер; (original) по́длинник, оригина́л; be ~ **of** владе́ть impf +instr; ~-**key** отмы́чка; vt (overcome) преодолева́ть impf, преодоле́ть pf; справля́ться impf, спра́виться pf c+instr; (a subject) овладева́ть impf, овладе́ть pf +instr. **masterful** adj вла́стный. **masterly** adj мастерско́й. **masterpiece** n шеде́вр. **mastery** n (of a subject) владе́ние (of +instr).

masturbate vi мастурби́ровать impf.

mat n ко́врик, (at door) полови́к; (on table) подста́вка.

match[1] n спи́чка. **matchbox** n спи́чечная коро́бка.

match[2] n (equal) ро́вня m & f; (contest) матч, состяза́ние; (marriage) па́ртия; vi & t (go well (with)) гармони́ровать impf (c+instr); подходи́ть impf, подойти́ pf (к+dat).

mate[1] n (chess) мат.

mate[2] n (one of pair) саме́ц, са́мка; (fellow worker) това́рищ; (naut) помо́щник капита́на; vi (of animals) спа́риваться impf, спа́риться pf.

material n материа́л; (cloth) мате́рия; pl (necessary articles) принадле́жности f pl. **materialism** n материали́зм. **materialistic** adj материалисти́ческий. **materialize** vi осущест-

вля́ться impf, осуществи́ться pf.

maternal adj матери́нский; ~ **grandfather** де́душка с матери́нской стороны́. **maternity** n матери́нство; ~ **leave** декре́тный о́тпуск; ~ **ward** роди́льное отделе́ние.

mathematical adj математи́ческий. **mathematician** n матема́тик. **mathematics, maths** n матема́тика.

matinée n дневно́й спекта́кль m.

matriarchal adj матриарха́льный. **matriarchy** n матриарха́т.

matriculate vi быть при́нятым в вуз. **matriculation** n зачисле́ние в вуз.

matrimonial adj супру́жеский. **matrimony** n брак.

matrix n ма́трица.

matron n (hospital) ста́ршая сестра́.

matt adj ма́товый.

matted adj спу́танный.

matter n (affair) де́ло; (question) вопро́с; (substance) вещество́; (philos, med) мате́рия; (printed) материа́л; **a ~ of life and death** вопро́с жи́зни и сме́рти; **a ~ of opinion** спо́рное де́ло; **a ~ of taste** де́ло вку́са; **as a ~ of fact** факти́чески; со́бственно говоря́; **what's the ~?** в чём де́ло?; **what's the ~ with him?** что с ним?; ~-**of-fact** проза́ичный; vi име́ть impf значе́ние; **it doesn't ~** э́то не име́ет значе́ния; **it ~s a lot to me** для меня́ э́то о́чень ва́жно.

matting n рого́жа.

mattress n матра́с.

mature adj зре́лый; vi зреть impf, со~ pf. **maturity** n зре́лость.

maul vt терза́ть impf.

mausoleum n мавзоле́й.

mauve adj (n) розова́то-лило́вый (цвет).

maxim n сенте́нция.

maximum n ма́ксимум; adj максима́льный.

may v aux (possibility, permission) мочь impf, с~ pf; (possibility) возмо́жно, что +indicative; (wish) пусть +indicative.

May n (month) май; adj ма́йский ~ **Day** Пе́рвое sb ма́я.

maybe adv мо́жет быть.

mayonnaise n майоне́з.

mayor n мэр. **mayoress** n жена́ мэ́ра; же́нщина-мэр.

maze n лабири́нт.

meadow *n* луг.

meagre *adj* ску́дный.

meal[1] *n* еда́; **at ~times** во вре́мя еды́.

meal[2] *n* (*grain*) мука́. **mealy** *adj*: **~mouthed** сладкоречи́вый.

mean[1] *adj* (*average*) сре́дний; *n* (*middle point*) середи́на; *pl* (*method*) сре́дство, спо́соб; *pl* (*resources*) сре́дства *neut pl*; **by all ~s** коне́чно, пожа́луйста; **by ~s of** при по́мощи +*gen*, посре́дством +*gen*; **by no ~s** совсе́м не; **~s test** прове́рка нужда́емости.

mean[2] *adj* (*ignoble*) по́длый; (*miserly*) скупо́й; (*poor*) убо́гий.

mean[3] *vt* (*have in mind*) име́ть *impf* в виду́; (*intend*) намерева́ться *impf* +*inf*; (*signify*) зна́чить *impf*.

meander *vi* (*stream*) извива́ться *impf*; (*person*) броди́ть *impf*. **meandering** *adj* изви́листый.

meaning *n* значе́ние. **meaningful** *adj* (мно́го)значи́тельный. **meaningless** *adj* бессмы́сленный.

meantime, meanwhile *adv* ме́жду тем.

measles *n* корь. **measly** *adj* ничто́жный.

measurable *adj* измери́мый. **measure** *n* ме́ра; **made to ~** сши́тый по ме́рке; сде́ланный на зака́з; *vt* измеря́ть *impf*, изме́рить *pf*; (*for clothes*) снима́ть *impf*, снять *pf* ме́рку с+*gen*; *vi* име́ть *impf* +*acc*: **the room ~s 30 feet in length** ко́мната име́ет три́дцать фу́тов в длину́; **~ off, out** отмеря́ть *impf*, отме́рить *pf*; **~ up to** соотве́тствовать *impf* +*dat*. **measured** *adj* (*rhythmical*) ме́рный. **measurement** *n* (*action*) измере́ние; *pl* (*dimensions*) разме́ры *m pl*.

meat *n* мя́со. **meatball** *n* котле́та. **meaty** *adj* мяси́стый; (*fig*) содержа́тельный.

mechanic *n* меха́ник. **mechanical** *adj* механи́ческий; (*fig; automatic*) маши́нальный; **~ engineer** инжене́р-меха́ник; **~ engineering** машиностроéние. **mechanics** *n* меха́ника. **mechanism** *n* механи́зм. **mechanization** *n* механиза́ция. **mechanize** *vt* механизи́ровать *impf & pf*.

medal *n* меда́ль. **medallion** *n* меда́льо́н. **medallist** *n* медали́ст.

meddle *vi* вме́шиваться *impf*, вме-

ша́ться *pf* (**in, with** в+*acc*).

media *pl of* **medium**

mediate *vi* посре́дничать *impf*. **mediation** *n* посре́дничество. **mediator** *n* посре́дник.

medical *adj* медици́нский; **~ student** ме́дик, -и́чка. **medicated** *adj* (*impregnated*) пропи́танный лека́рством. **medicinal** *adj* (*of medicine*) лека́рственный; (*healing*) целе́бный. **medicine** *n* медици́на; (*substance*) лека́рство.

medieval *adj* средневеко́вый.

mediocre *adj* посре́дственный. **mediocrity** *n* посре́дственность.

meditate *vi* размышля́ть *impf*. **meditation** *n* размышле́ние. **meditative** *adj* заду́мчивый.

Mediterranean *adj* средиземномо́рский; *n* Средизе́мное мо́ре.

medium *n* (*means*) сре́дство; (*phys*) среда́; (*person*) ме́диум; *pl* (*mass media*) сре́дства *neut pl* ма́ссовой информа́ции; *adj* сре́дний; **happy ~** золота́я середи́на.

medley *n* смесь; (*mus*) попурри́ *neut indecl*.

meek *adj* кро́ткий.

meet *vt & i* встреча́ть(ся) *impf*, встре́тить(ся) *pf*; *vt* (*make acquaintance*) знако́миться *impf*, по~ *pf* с+*instr*; *vi* (*assemble*) собира́ться *impf*, собра́ться *pf*. **meeting** *n* встре́ча; (*of committee*) заседа́ние, ми́тинг.

megalomania *n* мегалома́ния.

megaphone *n* мегафо́н.

melancholic *adj* меланхоли́ческий. **melancholy** *n* грусть; *adj* уны́лый, гру́стный.

mellow *adj* (*colour, sound*) со́чный; (*person*) добро́душный; *vi* смягча́ться *impf*, смягчи́ться *pf*.

melodic *adj* мелоди́ческий. **melodious** *adj* мелоди́чный. **melody** *n* мело́дия.

melodrama *n* мелодра́ма. **melodramatic** *adj* мелодрамати́ческий.

melon *n* ды́ня; (*water-~*) арбу́з.

melt *vt & i* распла́вливать(ся) *impf*, растопи́ть(ся) *pf*; (*smelt*) пла́вить(ся) *impf*, рас~ *pf*; (*dissolve*) растворя́ть(ся) *impf*, раствори́ть(ся) *pf*; *vi* (*thaw*) та́ять *impf*, рас~ *pf*; **~ing point** то́чка плавле́ния.

member *n* член. **membership** *n* чле́нство; (*number of* ~) коли́чество чле́нов; *attrib* чле́нский.

membrane *n* перепо́нка.

memento *n* сувени́р. **memoir** *n pl* мемуа́ры (-ров) *pl*; воспомина́ния *neut pl*. **memorable** *adj* достопа́мятный. **memorandum** *n* запи́ска. **memorial** *adj* мемориа́льный; *n* па́мятник. **memorize** *vt* запомина́ть *impf*, запо́мнить *pf*. **memory** *n* па́мять; (*recollection*) воспомина́ние.

menace *n* угро́за; *vt* угрожа́ть *impf* +*dat*. **menacing** *adj* угрожа́ющий.

menagerie *n* звери́нец.

mend *vt* чини́ть *impf*, по~ *pf*; (*clothes*) што́пать *impf*, за~ *pf*; ~ **one's ways** исправля́ться *impf*, испра́виться *pf*.

menial *adj* ни́зкий, чёрный.

meningitis *n* менинги́т.

menopause *n* кли́макс.

menstrual *adj* менструа́льный. **menstruation** *n* менструа́ция.

mental *adj* у́мственный; (*of ~ illness*) психи́ческий; ~ **arithmetic** счёт в уме́. **mentality** *n* ум; (*character*) склад ума́.

mention *vt* упомина́ть *impf*, упомяну́ть *pf*; **don't ~ it** не́ за что!; **not to ~** не говоря́ уже́ о+*prep*.

menu *n* меню́ *neut indecl*.

mercantile *adj* торго́вый.

mercenary *adj* коры́стный; (*hired*) наёмный; *n* наёмник.

merchandise *n* това́ры *m pl*. **merchant** *n* купе́ц; торго́вец; ~ **navy** торго́вый флот.

merciful *adj* милосе́рдный. **mercifully** *adv* к сча́стью. **merciless** *adj* беспоща́дный.

mercurial *adj* (*person*) изме́нчивый. **mercury** *n* ртуть.

mercy *n* милосе́рдие; **at the ~ of** во вла́сти +*gen*.

mere *adj* просто́й; **a ~ £40** всего́ лишь со́рок фу́нтов. **merely** *adv* то́лько, про́сто.

merge *vt & i* слива́ть(ся) *impf*, сли́ть(ся) *pf*. **merger** *n* объедине́ние.

meridian *n* меридиа́н.

meringue *n* мере́нга.

merit *n* заслу́га, досто́инство; *vt* за-

слу́живать *impf*, заслужи́ть *pf* +*gen*.

mermaid *n* руса́лка.

merrily *adv* ве́село. **merriment** *n* весе́лье. **merry** *adj* весёлый; ~-**go-round** карусе́ль; ~-**making** весе́лье.

mesh *n* сеть; *vi* сцепля́ться *impf*, сцепи́ться *pf*.

mesmerize *vt* гипнотизи́ровать *impf*, за~ *pf*.

mess *n* (*disorder*) беспоря́док; (*trouble*) беда́; (*eating-place*) столо́вая *sb*; *vi*: ~ **about** вози́ться *impf*; ~ **up** по́ртить *impf*, ис~ *pf*.

message *n* сообще́ние. **messenger** *n* курье́р.

Messiah *n* месси́я *m*. **Messianic** *adj* мессиа́нский.

Messrs *abbr* господа́ (*gen* -д) *m pl*.

messy *adj* (*untidy*) беспоря́дочный; (*dirty*) гря́зный.

metabolism *n* обме́н веще́ств.

metal *n* мета́лл; *adj* металли́ческий. **metallic** *adj* металли́ческий. **metallurgy** *n* металлу́рги́я.

metamorphosis *n* метаморфо́за.

metaphor *n* мета́фора. **metaphorical** *adj* метафори́ческий.

metaphysical *adj* метафизи́ческий. **metaphysics** *n* метафи́зика.

meteor *n* метео́р. **meteoric** *adj* метеори́ческий. **meteorite** *n* метеори́т. **meteorological** *adj* метеорологи́ческий. **meteorology** *n* метеороло́гия.

meter *n* счётчик; *vt* измеря́ть *impf*, изме́рить *pf*.

methane *n* мета́н.

method *n* ме́тод. **methodical** *adj* методи́чный.

Methodist *n* методи́ст; *adj* методи́стский.

methodology *n* методоло́гия.

methylated *adj*: ~ **spirit(s)** денату́рат.

meticulous *adj* тща́тельный.

metre *n* метр. **metric(al)** *adj* метри́ческий.

metronome *n* метроно́м.

metropolis *n* столи́ца. **metropolitan** *adj* столи́чный; *n* (*eccl*) митрополи́т.

mettle *n* хара́ктер.

Mexican *adj* мексика́нский; *n* мексика́нец, -а́нка. **Mexico** *n* Ме́ксика.

mezzanine *n* антресо́ли *f pl*.

miaow *int* мя́у; *n* мяу́канье; *vi* мяу́кать *impf*, мяу́кнуть *pf*.
mica *n* слюда́.
microbe *n* микро́б. **microchip** *n* чип, микросхе́ма. **microcomputer** *n* микрокомпью́тер. **microcosm** *n* микроко́см. **microfilm** *n* микрофи́льм. **micro-organism** *n* микроорганизм. **microphone** *n* микрофо́н. **microscope** *n* микроско́п. **microscopic** *adj* микроскопи́ческий. **microwave** *n* микроволна́; ~ **oven** микроволно́вая печь.
mid *adj*: ~ **May** середи́на ма́я. **midday** *n* по́лдень *m*; *attrib* полу́денный. **middle** *n* середи́на; *adj* сре́дний; ~-**aged** сре́дних лет; **M~ Ages** сре́дние века́ *n pl*; ~-**class** буржуа́зный; ~**man** посре́дник; ~-**sized** сре́днего разме́ра. **middleweight** *n* сре́дний вес.
midge *n* мо́шка.
midget *n* ка́рлик, -ица.
midnight *n* по́лночь; *attrib* полуно́чный. **midriff** *n* диафра́гма. **midst** *n* середи́на. **midsummer** *n* середи́на ле́та. **midway** *adv* на полпути́. **midweek** *n* середи́на неде́ли. **midwinter** *n* середи́на зимы́.
midwife *n* акуше́рка. **midwifery** *n* акуше́рство.
might *n* мощь; **with all one's** ~ изо всех сил. **mighty** *adj* мо́щный.
migraine *n* мигре́нь.
migrant *adj* кочу́ющий; (*bird*) перелётный; *n* (*person*) пересе́ленец; (*bird*) перелётная пти́ца. **migrate** *vi* мигри́ровать *impf & pf*. **migration** *n* мигра́ция. **migratory** *adj* кочу́ющий; (*bird*) перелётный.
mike *n* микрофо́н.
mild *adj* мя́гкий.
mildew *n* пле́сень.
mile *n* ми́ля. **mileage** *n* расстоя́ние в ми́лях; (*of car*) пробе́г. **milestone** *n* верстово́й столб; (*fig*) ве́ха.
militancy *n* войнственность. **militant** *adj* войнствующий; *n* активи́ст. **military** *adj* вое́нный; *n* вое́нные *sb pl*. **militate** *vi*: ~ **against** говори́ть *impf* про́тив+*gen*. **militia** *n* мили́ция. **militiaman** *n* милиционе́р.
milk *n* молоко́; *attrib* моло́чный; *vt* дои́ть *impf*, по~ *pf*. **milkman** *n* продаве́ц молока́. **milky** *adj* моло́чный;

M~ Way Мле́чный Путь *m*.
mill *n* ме́льница; (*factory*) фа́брика; *vt* (*grain etc.*) моло́ть *impf*, с~ *pf*; (*metal*) фрезерова́ть *impf*, от~ *pf*; (*coin*) гурти́ть *impf*; *vi*: ~ **around** толпи́ться *impf*. **miller** *n* ме́льник.
millennium *n* тысячеле́тие.
millet *n* (*plant*) про́со; (*grain*) пшено́.
milligram(me) *n* миллигра́мм. **millimetre** *n* миллиме́тр.
million *n* миллио́н. **millionaire** *n* миллионе́р. **millionth** *adj* миллио́нный.
millstone *n* жёрнов; (*fig*) ка́мень *m* на ше́е.
mime *n* мим; (*dumb-show*) пантоми́ма; *vt* изобража́ть *impf*, изобрази́ть *pf* мими́чески. **mimic** *n* ми́мист; *vt* передра́знивать *impf*, передразни́ть *pf*. **mimicry** *n* имита́ция.
minaret *n* минаре́т.
mince *n* (*meat*) фарш; *vt* руби́ть *impf*; (*in machine*) пропуска́ть *impf*, пропусти́ть *pf* че́рез мясору́бку; *vi* (*walk*) семени́ть *impf*; **not** ~ **matters** говори́ть *impf* без обиняко́в. **mincemeat** *n* начи́нка из изю́ма, минда́ля и т.п.
mind *n* ум; **bear in** ~ име́ть *impf* в виду́; **change one's** ~ переду́мывать *impf*, переду́мать *pf*; **make up one's** ~ реша́ться *impf*, реши́ться *pf*; **you're out of your** ~ вы с ума́ сошли́; *vt* (*give heed to*) обраща́ть *impf*, обрати́ть *pf* внима́ние на+*acc*; (*look after*) присма́тривать *impf*, присмотре́ть *pf* за+*instr*; **I don't** ~ ничего́ не име́ю про́тив; **don't** ~ **me** не обраща́й(те) внима́ния на меня́!; ~ **you don't forget** смотри́ не забу́дь!; ~ **your own business** не вме́шивайтесь в чужи́е дела́!; **never** ~ ничего́! **mindful** *adj* по́мнящий. **mindless** *adj* бессмы́сленный.
mine[1] *poss pron* мой; свой.
mine[2] *n* ша́хта, рудни́к; (*fig*) исто́чник; (*mil*) ми́на; *vt* (*obtain from* ~) добыва́ть *impf*, добы́ть *pf*; (*mil*) мини́ровать *impf & pf*. **minefield** *n* ми́нное по́ле. **miner** *n* шахтёр.
mineral *n* минера́л; *adj* минера́льный; ~ **water** минера́льная вода́. **mineralogy** *n* минерало́гия.
mingle *vt & i* сме́шивать(ся) *impf*, смеша́ть(ся) *pf*.

miniature n миниатю́ра; adj миниатю́рный.

minibus n микроавто́бус.

minim n (mus) полови́нная но́та. **minimal** adj минима́льный. **minimize** vt (reduce) доводи́ть impf, довести́ pf до ми́нимума. **minimum** n ми́нимум; adj минима́льный.

mining n го́рное де́ло.

minister n мини́стр; (eccl) свяще́нник. **ministerial** adj министе́рский. **ministration** n по́мощь. **ministry** n (polit) министе́рство; (eccl) духове́нство.

mink n но́рка; attrib но́рковый.

minor adj (unimportant) незначи́тельный; (less important) второстепе́нный; (mus) мино́рный; n (person under age) несовершенноле́тний n; (mus) мино́р. **minority** n меньшинство́; (age) несовершенноле́тие.

minstrel n менестре́ль m.

mint¹ n (plant) мя́та; (peppermint) пе́речная мя́та.

mint² n (econ) моне́тный двор; in ~ **condition** но́венький; vt чека́нить impf, от~, вы́~ pf.

minuet n менуэ́т.

minus prep ми́нус+acc; без+gen; n ми́нус.

minuscule adj малю́сенький.

minute¹ n мину́та; pl протоко́л.

minute² adj ме́лкий. **minutiae** n pl ме́лочи (-че́й) f pl.

miracle n чу́до. **miraculous** adj чуде́сный.

mirage n мира́ж.

mire n (mud) грязь; (swamp) боло́то.

mirror n зе́ркало; vt отража́ть impf, отрази́ть pf.

mirth n весе́лье.

misadventure n несча́стный слу́чай.

misapprehension n недопонима́ние.

misappropriate vt незако́нно присва́ивать impf, присво́ить pf. **misbehave** vi ду́рно вести́ impf себя́. **misbehaviour** n дурно́е поведе́ние.

miscalculate vt непра́вильно рассчи́тывать impf, рассчита́ть pf; (fig, abs) просчи́тываться impf, просчита́ться pf. **miscalculation** n просчёт. **miscarriage** n (med) вы́кидыш; ~ **of justice** суде́бная оши́бка. **miscarry** vi (med) име́ть impf вы́кидыш.

miscellaneous adj ра́зный, разнообра́зный. **miscellany** n смесь.

mischief n (harm) вред; (naughtiness) озорство́. **mischievous** adj озорно́й. **misconception** n непра́вильное представле́ние. **misconduct** n дурно́е поведе́ние. **misconstrue** vt непра́вильно истолко́вывать impf, истолкова́ть pf.

misdeed, misdemeanour n просту́пок. **misdirect** vt непра́вильно направля́ть impf, напра́вить pf; (letter) непра́вильно адресова́ть impf & pf.

miser n скупе́ц. **miserable** adj (unhappy, wretched) несча́стный, жа́лкий; (weather) скве́рный. **miserly** adj скупо́й. **misery** n страда́ние.

misfire vi дава́ть impf, дать pf осе́чку. **misfit** n (person) неуда́чник. **misfortune** n несча́стье. **misgiving** n опасе́ние. **misguided** adj обма́нутый.

mishap n неприя́тность. **misinform** vt непра́вильно информи́ровать impf & pf. **misinterpret** vt неве́рно истолко́вывать impf, истолкова́ть pf. **misjudge** vt неве́рно оце́нивать impf, оцени́ть pf. **misjudgement** n неве́рная оце́нка. **mislay** vt затеря́ть pf. **mislead** vt вводи́ть impf, ввести́ pf в заблужде́ние. **mismanage** vt пло́хо управля́ть impf +instr. **mismanagement** n плохо́е управле́ние. **misnomer** n непра́вильное назва́ние.

misogynist n женоненави́стник. **misogyny** n женоненави́стничество.

misplaced adj неуме́стный. **misprint** n опеча́тка. **misquote** vt непра́вильно цити́ровать impf, про~ pf. **misread** vt (fig) непра́вильно истолко́вывать impf, истолкова́ть pf. **misrepresent** vt искажа́ть impf, искази́ть pf. **misrepresentation** n искаже́ние.

Miss n (title) мисс.

miss n про́мах; vi прома́хиваться impf, промахну́ться pf; vt (fail to hit, see, hear) пропуска́ть impf, пропусти́ть pf; (train) опа́здывать impf, опозда́ть pf на+acc; (regret absence of) скуча́ть impf по+dat; ~ **out** пропуска́ть impf, пропусти́ть pf; ~ **the point** не понима́ть impf, поня́ть pf су́ти.

misshapen *adj* уро́дливый.

missile *n* снаря́д, раке́та.

missing *adj* отсу́тствующий, недоста́ющий; (*person*) пропа́вший без ве́сти.

mission *n* ми́ссия; командиро́вка. **missionary** *n* миссионе́р. **missive** *n* посла́ние.

misspell *vt* непра́вильно писа́ть *impf*, на~ *pf*. **misspelling** *n* непра́вильное написа́ние.

mist *n* тума́н; *vt & i* затума́нивать(ся) *impf*, затума́нить(ся) *pf*.

mistake *vt* непра́вильно понима́ть *impf*, поня́ть *pf*; ~ **for** принима́ть *impf*, приня́ть *pf* за+*acc*; *n* оши́бка; **make a** ~ ошиба́ться *impf*, ошиби́ться *pf*. **mistaken** *adj* оши́бочный; **be** ~ ошиба́ться *impf*, ошиби́ться *pf*.

mister *n* ми́стер, господи́н.

mistletoe *n* оме́ла.

mistress *n* хозя́йка; (*teacher*) учи́тельница; (*lover*) любо́вница.

mistrust *vt* не доверя́ть *impf* +*dat*; *n* недове́рие. **mistrustful** *adj* недове́рчивый.

misty *adj* тума́нный.

misunderstand *vt* непра́вильно понима́ть *impf*, поня́ть *pf*. **misunderstanding** *n* недоразуме́ние.

misuse *vt* непра́вильно употребля́ть *impf*, употреби́ть *pf*; (*ill treat*) ду́рно обраща́ться *impf* с+*instr*; *n* непра́вильное употребле́ние.

mite *n* (*insect*) клещ; (*child*) кро́шка; **widow's** ~ ле́пта вдови́цы; **not a** ~ ничу́ть.

mitigate *vt* смягча́ть *impf*, смягчи́ть *pf*. **mitigation** *n* смягче́ние.

mitre *n* ми́тра.

mitten *n* рукави́ца.

mix *vt* меша́ть *impf*, с~ *pf*; *vi* сме́шиваться *impf*, смеша́ться *pf*; (*associate*) обща́ться *impf*; ~ **up** (*confuse*) пу́тать *impf*, с~ *pf*; **get ~ed up in** заме́шиваться *impf*, замеша́ться *pf* в+*acc*; *n* смесь. **mixer** *n* смеси́тель *m*; (*cul*) ми́ксер. **mixture** *n* смесь; (*medicine*) миксту́ра.

moan *n* стон; *vi* стона́ть *impf*, про~ *pf*.

moat *n* (крепостно́й) ров.

mob *n* толпа́; *vt* (*attack*) напада́ть *impf*, напа́сть *pf* толпо́й на+*acc*.

mobster *n* банди́т.

mobile *adj* подвижно́й, передвижно́й. **mobility** *n* подви́жность. **mobilization** *n* мобилиза́ция. **mobilize** *vt & i* мобилизова́ть(ся) *impf & pf*.

moccasin *n* мокаси́н (*gen pl* -н).

mock *vt & i* издева́ться *impf* над +*instr*; *adj* (*sham*) подде́льный; (*pretended*) мни́мый; ~**-up** *n* маке́т. **mockery** *n* издева́тельство; (*travesty*) паро́дия.

mode *n* (*manner*) о́браз; (*method*) ме́тод.

model *n* (*representation*) моде́ль; (*pattern, ideal*) образе́ц; (*artist's*) нату́рщик, -ица; (*fashion*) манеке́нщик, -ица; (*make*) моде́ль; *adj* образцо́вый; *vt* лепи́ть *impf*, вы́~, с~ *pf*; (*clothes*) демонстри́ровать *impf & pf*; *vi* (*act as* ~) быть нату́рщиком, -ицей; быть манеке́нщиком, -ицей; ~ **after, on** создава́ть *impf*, созда́ть *pf* по образцу́ +*gen*.

moderate *adj* (*various senses*; *polit*) уме́ренный; (*medium*) сре́дний; *vt* умеря́ть *impf*, уме́рить *pf*; *vi* стиха́ть *impf*, сти́хнуть *pf*. **moderation** *n* уме́ренность; **in** ~ уме́ренно.

modern *adj* совреме́нный; (*language, history*) но́вый. **modernization** *n* модерниза́ция. **modernize** *vt* модернизи́ровать *impf & pf*.

modest *adj* скро́мный. **modesty** *n* скро́мность.

modification *n* модифика́ция. **modify** *vt* модифици́ровать *impf & pf*.

modish *adj* мо́дный.

modular *adj* мо́дульный. **modulate** *vt* модули́ровать *impf*. **modulation** *n* модуля́ция. **module** *n* мо́дуль *m*.

mohair *n* мохе́р.

moist *adj* вла́жный. **moisten** *vt & i* увлажня́ть(ся) *impf*, увлажни́ть(ся) *pf*. **moisture** *n* вла́га.

molar *n* (*tooth*) коренно́й зуб.

mole[1] *n* (*on skin*) ро́динка.

mole[2] *n* (*animal*; *agent*) крот.

molecular *adj* молекуля́рный. **molecule** *n* моле́кула.

molest *vt* пристава́ть *impf*, приста́ть *pf* к+*dat*.

mollify *vt* смягча́ть *impf*, смягчи́ть *pf*.

mollusc *n* моллю́ск.

molten *adj* распла́вленный.

moment *n* моме́нт, миг; **at the** ~

сейча́с; **at the last ~** в после́днюю
мину́ту; **just a ~** сейча́с! **moment-
arily** adv на мгнове́ние. **momentary**
adj мгнове́нный. **momentous** adj
ва́жный. **momentum** n коли́чество
движе́ния; (impetus) дви́жущая
си́ла; **gather ~** набира́ть impf,
набра́ть pf ско́рость.

monarch n мона́рх. **monarchy** n мо-
на́рхия.

monastery n монасты́рь m. **monas-
tic** adj мона́шеский.

Monday n понеде́льник.

monetary adj де́нежный. **money** n
де́ньги (-нег, -ньга́м) pl; **~-lender**
ростовщи́к.

mongrel n дворня́жка.

monitor n (naut; TV) монито́р; vt
проверя́ть impf, прове́рить pf.

monk n мона́х.

monkey n обезья́на.

mono n мо́но neut indecl. **monochrome** adj одноцве́тный. **monog-
amous** adj единобра́чный. **monogamy** n единобра́чие. **monogram** n
моногра́мма. **monograph** n моно-
гра́фия. **monolith** n моноли́т.
monolithic adj моноли́тный. **monologue** n моноло́г. **monopolize** vt
монополизи́ровать impf & pf. **monopoly** n монопо́лия. **monosyllabic**
adj односло́жный. **monosyllable** n
односло́жное сло́во. **monotone** n
моното́нность; **in a ~** моното́нно.
monotonous adj моното́нный. **monotony** n моното́нность.

monsoon n (wind) муссо́н; (rainy
season) дождли́вый сезо́н.

monster n чудо́вище. **monstrosity** n
чудо́вище. **monstrous** adj чудо́вищ-
ный; (huge) грома́дный.

montage n монта́ж.

month n ме́сяц. **monthly** adj ме́сяч-
ный; n ежеме́сячник; adv ежеме́-
сячно.

monument n па́мятник. **monumental** adj монумента́льный.

moo vi мыча́ть impf.

mood¹ n (gram) наклоне́ние.

mood² n настрое́ние. **moody** adj ка-
при́зный.

moon n луна́. **moonlight** n лу́нный
свет; vi халту́рить impf. **moonlit** adj
лу́нный.

moor¹ n ме́стность, поро́сшая ве́ре-

ском. **moorland** n ве́ресковая пу́-
стошь.

moor² vt & i швартова́ть(ся) impf,
при~ pf. **mooring** n (place) прича́л;
pl (cables) швартó́вы m pl.

Moorish adj маврита́нский.

moose n америка́нский лось m.

moot adj спо́рный.

mop n шва́бра; vt протира́ть impf,
протере́ть pf (шва́брой); **~ one's
brow** вытира́ть impf, вы́тереть pf
лоб; **~ up** вытира́ть impf, вы́тереть
pf.

mope vi хандри́ть impf.

moped n мопе́д.

moraine n море́на.

moral adj мора́льный; n мора́ль; pl
нра́вы m pl. **morale** n мора́льное
состоя́ние. **morality** n нра́вствен-
ность, мора́ль. **moralize** vi морали-
зи́ровать impf.

morass n боло́то.

moratorium n морато́рий.

morbid adj боле́зненный.

more adj (greater quantity) бо́льше
+gen; (additional) ещё; adv бо́льше;
(forming comp) бо́лее; **and what is
~** и бо́льше того́; **~ or less** бо́лее
и́ли ме́нее; **once ~** ещё раз. **moreover** adv сверх того́; кро́ме того́.

morgue n морг.

moribund adj умира́ющий.

morning n у́тро; **in the ~** у́тром; **in
the ~s** по утра́м; attrib у́тренний.

moron n слабоу́мный sb.

morose adj угрю́мый.

morphine n мо́рфий.

Morse (code) n а́збука Мо́рзе.

morsel n кусо́чек.

mortal adj сме́ртный; (fatal) смер-
те́льный; n сме́ртный sb. **mortality**
n сме́ртность.

mortar n (vessel) сту́п(к)а; (cannon)
миномёт; (cement) (известко́вый)
раство́р.

mortgage n ссу́да на поку́пку до́ма;
vt закла́дывать impf, заложи́ть pf.

mortify vt унижа́ть impf, уни́зить pf.

mortuary n морг.

mosaic n моза́ика; adj моза́ичный.

mosque n мече́ть.

mosquito n кома́р.

moss n мох. **mossy** adj мши́стый.

most adj наибо́льший; n наибо́ль-
шее коли́чество; adj & n (majority)

большинство́ +gen; бо́льшая часть +gen; adv бо́льше всего́, наибо́лее; (forming superl) са́мый. **mostly** adv гла́вным о́бразом.

MOT (test) n техосмо́тр.

motel n моте́ль m.

moth n мотылёк; (clothes-~) моль.

mother n мать; vt относи́ться impf по-матери́нски к +dat; ~-**in-law** (wife's ~) тёща; (husband's ~) свекро́вь; ~-**of-pearl** перламу́тр; adj перламу́тровый; ~ **tongue** родно́й язы́к. **motherhood** n матери́нство. **motherland** n ро́дина. **motherly** adj матери́нский.

motif n моти́в.

motion n движе́ние; (gesture) жест; (proposal) предложе́ние; vt пока́зывать impf, показа́ть pf +dat же́стом, что́бы +past. **motionless** adj неподви́жный. **motivate** vt побужда́ть impf, побуди́ть pf. **motivation** n побужде́ние. **motive** n моти́в; adj дви́жущий.

motley adj пёстрый.

motor n дви́гатель m, мото́р; ~ **bike** мотоци́кл; ~ **boat** мото́рная ло́дка; ~ **car** автомоби́ль m; ~ **cycle** мотоци́кл; ~**cyclist** мотоцикли́ст; ~ **racing** автомоби́льные го́нки f pl; ~ **scooter** моторо́ллер; ~ **vehicle** автомаши́на. **motoring** n автомобили́зм. **motorist** n автомобили́ст, ~ка. **motorize** vt моторизова́ть impf & pf. **motorway** n автостра́да.

mottled adj кра́пчатый.

motto n деви́з.

mould[1] n (shape) фо́рма, фо́рмочка; vt формова́ть impf, с~ pf. **moulding** n (archit) лепно́е украше́ние.

mould[2] n (fungi) пле́сень. **mouldy** adj заплесневе́лый.

moulder vi разлага́ться impf, разложи́ться pf.

moult vi линя́ть impf, вы́~ pf.

mound n холм; (heap) на́сыпь.

Mount n (in names) гора́.

mount vt (ascend) поднима́ться impf, подня́ться pf на+acc; (~ a horse etc.) сади́ться impf, сесть pf на+acc; (picture) накле́ивать impf, накле́ить pf на карто́н; (gun) устана́вливать impf, установи́ть pf; ~ **up** (accumulate) нака́пливаться impf, накопи́ться pf; n (for picture) карто́н;

(horse) верхова́я ло́шадь.

mountain n гора́; attrib го́рный. **mountaineer** n альпини́ст, ~ка. **mountaineering** n альпини́зм. **mountainous** adj гори́стый.

mourn vt опла́кивать impf, опла́кать pf; vi скорбе́ть impf (**over** o+prep). **mournful** adj ско́рбный. **mourning** n тра́ур.

mouse n мышь.

mousse n мусс.

moustache n усы́ (усо́в) pl.

mousy adj мыши́ный; (timid) ро́бкий.

mouth n рот; (poetical) уста́ (-т) pl; (entrance) вход; (of river) у́стье; vt говори́ть impf, сказа́ть pf одни́ми губа́ми. **mouthful** n глото́к. **mouth-organ** n губна́я гармо́ника. **mouthpiece** n мундшту́к; (person) ру́пор.

movable adj подви́жной.

move n (in game) ход; (change of residence) переёзд; (movement) движе́ние; (step) шаг; vt & i дви́гать(ся) impf, дви́нуться pf; vt (affect) тро́гать impf, тро́нуть pf; (propose) вноси́ть impf, внести́ pf; vi (develop) развива́ться impf, разви́ться pf; (~ house) переезжа́ть impf, перее́хать pf; ~ **away** (vt & i) удаля́ть(ся) impf, удали́ть(ся) pf; (vi) уезжа́ть impf, уе́хать pf; ~ **in** въезжа́ть impf, въе́хать pf; ~ **on** идти́ impf, пойти́ pf да́льше; ~ **out** съезжа́ть impf, съе́хать pf (**of** c+gen). **movement** n движе́ние; (mus) moving n дви́жущийся; (touching) тро́гательный.

mow vt (also ~ **down**) коси́ть impf, с~ pf. **mower** n коси́лка.

MP abbr (of Member of Parliament) член парла́мента.

Mr abbr ми́стер, господи́н. **Mrs** abbr ми́ссис f indecl, госпожа́.

Ms n миз, госпожа́.

much adj & n мно́го +gen; мно́гое sb; adv о́чень (with comp adj) гора́здо.

muck n (dung) наво́з; (dirt) грязь; ~ **about** вози́ться impf; ~ **out** чи́стить impf, вы́~ pf; ~ **up** изга́живать impf, изга́дить pf.

mucous adj сли́зистый. **mucus** n слизь.

mud n грязь. **mudguard** n крыло́.

muddle vt пу́тать *impf*, с~ *pf*; vi: ~ **through** кое-ка́к справля́ться *impf*, спра́виться *pf*; n беспоря́док.

muddy adj гря́зный; vt обры́згивать *impf*, обры́згать *pf* гря́зью.

muff n му́фта.

muffle vt (*for warmth*) заку́тывать *impf*, заку́тать *pf*; (*sound*) глуши́ть *impf*, за~ *pf*.

mug n (*vessel*) кру́жка; (*face*) мо́рда.

muggy adj сыро́й и тёплый.

mulch n му́льча; vt мульчи́ровать *impf* & *pf*.

mule n мул.

mull vt: ~ **over** обду́мывать *impf*, обду́мать *pf*. **mulled** adj: ~ **wine** глинтве́йн.

mullet n (*grey* ~) кефа́ль; (*red* ~) бараба́лька.

multicoloured adj многокра́сочный.

multifarious adj разнообра́зный.

multilateral adj многосторо́нний.

multimillionaire n мультимиллионе́р. **multinational** adj многонациона́льный.

multiple adj составно́й; (*numerous*) многочи́сленный; ~ **sclerosis** рассе́янный склеро́з; n кра́тное число́; **least common** ~ о́бщее наиме́ньшее кра́тное *sb*. **multiplication** n умноже́ние. **multiplicity** n многочи́сленность. **multiply** vt (*math*) умножа́ть *impf*, умно́жить *pf*; vi размножа́ться *impf*, размно́житься *pf*.

multi-storey adj многоэта́жный.

multitude n мно́жество; (*crowd*) толпа́.

mum[1] adj: **keep** ~ молча́ть *impf*.

mum[2] n (*mother*) ма́ма.

mumble vt & i бормота́ть *impf*, про~ *pf*.

mummy[1] n (*archaeol*) му́мия.

mummy[2] n (*mother*) ма́ма, ма́мочка.

mumps n сви́нка.

munch vt жева́ть *impf*.

mundane adj земно́й.

municipal adj муниципа́льный. **municipality** n муниципалите́т.

munitions n pl вое́нное иму́щество.

mural n стенна́я ро́спись.

murder n уби́йство; vt убива́ть *impf*, уби́ть *pf*; (*language*) коверка́ть *impf*, ис~ *pf*. **murderer, murderess** n уби́йца *m* & *f*. **murderous** adj уби́йственный.

murky adj тёмный, мра́чный.

murmur n шёпот; vt & i шепта́ть *impf*, шепну́ть *pf*.

muscle n му́скул. **muscular** adj мы́шечный; (*person*) мускули́стый.

Muscovite n москви́ч, ~ка.

muse vi размышля́ть *impf*.

museum n музе́й.

mush n ка́ша.

mushroom n гриб.

music n му́зыка; (*sheet* ~) но́ты *f pl*; ~-**hall** мю́зик-хо́лл; ~ **stand** пюпи́тр. **musical** adj музыка́льный; n опере́тта. **musician** n музыка́нт.

musk n му́скус.

musket n мушке́т.

Muslim n мусульма́нин, -а́нка; adj мусульма́нский.

muslin n мусли́н.

mussel n ми́дия.

must v aux (*obligation*) до́лжен (-жна́) predic+inf; на́до impers+dat & inf; (*necessity*) ну́жно impers+dat & inf; ~ **not** (*prohibition*) нельзя́ impers +dat & inf.

mustard n горчи́ца.

muster vt собира́ть *impf*, собра́ть *pf*; (*courage etc.*) собира́ться *impf*, собра́ться *pf* с+instr.

musty adj за́тхлый.

mutation n мута́ция.

mute adj немо́й; n немо́й *sb*; (*mus*) сурди́нка. **muted** adj приглушённый.

mutilate vt уве́чить *impf*, из~ *pf*. **mutilation** n уве́чье.

mutineer n мяте́жник. **mutinous** adj мяте́жный. **mutiny** n мяте́ж; vi бунтова́ть *impf*, взбунтова́ться *pf*.

mutter vi бормота́ть *impf*; *impf*; n бормота́ние.

mutton n бара́нина.

mutual adj взаи́мный; (*common*) о́бщий.

muzzle n (*animal's*) мо́рда; (*on animal*) намо́рдник; (*of gun*) ду́ло; vt надева́ть *impf*, наде́ть *pf* намо́рдник на+acc; (*fig*) заставля́ть *impf*, заста́вить *pf* молча́ть.

my poss pron мой; свой.

myopia n близору́кость. **myopic** adj близору́кий.

myriad n мириа́ды (-д) *pl*; adj бесчи́сленный.

myrtle n мирт; *attrib* ми́ртовый.

myself *pron* (*emph*) (я) сам, сама; (*refl*) себя; -ся (*suffixed to vt*).
mysterious *adj* таинственный. **mystery** *n* тайна.
mystic(al) *adj* мистический; *n* мистик. **mysticism** *n* мистицизм. **mystification** *n* озадаченность. **mystify** *vt* озадачивать *impf*, озадачить *pf*.
myth *n* миф. **mythical** *adj* мифический. **mythological** *adj* мифологический. **mythology** *n* мифология.

N

nag¹ *n* (*horse*) лошадь.
nag² *vt* (*also* ~ *at*) пилить *impf* +*acc*; *vi* (*of pain*) ныть *impf*.
nail *n* (*finger-, toe-*~) ноготь *m*; (*metal spike*) гвоздь *m*; ~ **varnish** лак для ногтей; *vt* прибивать *impf*, прибить *pf* (гвоздями).
naive *adj* наивный. **naivety** *n* наивность.
naked *adj* голый; ~ **eye** невооружённый глаз. **nakedness** *n* нагота.
name *n* название; (*forename*) имя *neut*; (*surname*) фамилия; (*reputation*) репутация; **what is his** ~? как его зовут?; ~**plate** дощечка с фамилией; ~**sake** тёзка *m* & *f*; *vt* называть *impf*, назвать *pf*; (*appoint*) назначать *impf*, назначить *pf*. **nameless** *adj* безымянный. **namely** *adv* (а) именно; то есть.
nanny *n* няня.
nap *n* короткий сон; *vi* вздремнуть *pf*.
nape *n* загривок.
napkin *n* салфетка.
nappy *n* пелёнка.
narcissus *n* нарцисс.
narcotic *adj* наркотический; *n* наркотик.
narrate *vt* рассказывать *impf*, рассказать *pf*. **narration** *n* рассказ. **narrative** *n* рассказ; *adj* повествовательный. **narrator** *n* рассказчик.
narrow *adj* узкий; *vt* & *i* суживать(ся) *impf*, сузить(ся) *pf*. **narrowly** *adv* (*hardly*) чуть, еле-еле; **he** ~ **escaped drowning** он чуть не утонул. **narrow-minded** *adj* ограниченный. **narrowness** *n* узость.
nasal *adj* носовой; (*voice*) гнусавый.

nasturtium *n* настурция.
nasty *adj* неприятный, противный; (*person*) злой.
nation *n* (*people*) народ; (*country*) страна. **national** *adj* национальный, народный; (*of the state*) государственный; *n* подданный *sb*. **nationalism** *n* национализм. **nationalist** *n* националист, ~ка. **nationalistic** *adj* националистический. **nationality** *n* национальность; (*citizenship*) гражданство, подданство. **nationalization** *n* национализация. **nationalize** *vt* национализировать *impf* & *pf*.
native *n* (~ *of*) уроженец, -нка (+*gen*); (*aborigine*) туземец, -мка; *adj* (*innate*) природный; (*of one's birth*) родной; (*indigenous*) туземный; ~ **land** родина; ~ **language** родной язык; ~ **speaker** носитель *m* языка.
nativity *n* Рождество (Христово).
natter *vi* болтать *impf*.
natural *adj* естественный, природный; ~ **resources** природные богатства *neut pl*; ~ **selection** естественный отбор; *n* (*mus*) бекар. **naturalism** *n* натурализм. **naturalist** *n* натуралист. **naturalistic** *adj* натуралистический. **naturalization** *n* натурализация. **naturalize** *vt* натурализировать *impf* & *pf*. **naturally** *adv* естественно. **nature** *n* природа; (*character*) характер; **by** ~ по природе.
naught *n*: **come to** ~ сводиться *impf*, свестись *pf* к нулю.
naughty *adj* шаловливый.
nausea *n* тошнота. **nauseate** *vt* тошнить *impf impers* от +*gen*. **nauseating** *adj* тошнотворный. **nauseous** *adj*: **I feel** ~ меня тошнит.
nautical *n* морской.
naval *adj* (военно-)морской.
nave *n* неф.
navel *n* пупок.
navigable *adj* судоходный. **navigate** *vt* (*ship*) вести *impf*; (*sea*) плавать *impf* по+*dat*. **navigation** *n* навигация. **navigator** *n* штурман.
navvy *n* землекоп.
navy *n* военно-морской флот; ~ **blue** тёмно-синий.
Nazi *n* нацист, ~ка; *adj* нацистский. **Nazism** *n* нацизм.

NB *abbr* нотабе́не.

near *adv* бли́зко; ~ **at hand** под руко́й; ~ **by** ря́дом; *prep* во́зле+*gen*, о́коло+*gen*, у+*gen*; *adj* бли́зкий; ~**sighted** близору́кий; *vt & i* приближа́ться *impf*, прибли́зиться *pf* к +*dat*. **nearly** *adv* почти́.

neat *adj* (*tidy*) опря́тный, аккура́тный; (*clear*) чёткий; (*undiluted*) неразба́вленный.

nebulous *adj* нея́сный.

necessarily *adv* обяза́тельно. **necessary** *adj* необходи́мый; (*inevitable*) неизбе́жный. **necessitate** *vt* де́лать *impf*, с~ *pf* необходи́мым.

necessity *n* необходи́мость; неизбе́жность; (*object*) предме́т пе́рвой необходи́мости.

neck *n* ше́я; (*of garment*) вы́рез; ~ **and** ~ голова́ в го́лову. **necklace** *n* ожере́лье. **neckline** *n* вы́рез.

nectar *n* некта́р.

née adj урождённая.

need *n* нужда́; *vt* нужда́ться *impf* в+*prep*; **I** (*etc.*) ~ мне (*dat*) ну́жен (-жна́, -жно, -жны́) +*nom*; **I** ~ **five roubles** мне ну́жно пять рубле́й.

needle *n* игла́, иго́лка; (*knitting*) спи́ца; (*pointer*) стре́лка; *vt* придира́ться *impf*, придра́ться *pf* к+*dat*.

needless *adj* нену́жный; ~ **to say** разуме́ется. **needy** *adj* нужда́ющийся.

negation *n* отрица́ние. **negative** *adj* отрица́тельный; *n* отрица́ние; (*phot*) негати́в.

neglect *vt* пренебрега́ть *impf*, пренебре́чь *pf* +*instr*; не забо́титься *impf* о+*prep*; *n* пренебреже́ние; (*condition*) забро́шенность. **neglectful** *adj* небре́жный, невнима́тельный (**of** к+*dat*). **negligence** *n* небре́жность. **negligent** *adj* небре́жный. **negligible** *adj* незначи́тельный.

negotiate *vi* вести́ *impf* перегово́ры; *vt* (*arrange*) заключа́ть *impf*, заключи́ть *pf*; (*overcome*) преодолева́ть *impf*, преодоле́ть *pf*. **negotiation** *n* (*discussion*) перегово́ры *m pl*.

Negro *n* негр; *adj* негритя́нский.

neigh *n* ржа́ние; *vi* ржать *impf*.

neighbour *n* сосе́д, ~ка. **neighbourhood** *n* ме́стность; **in the** ~ **of** о́коло+*gen*. **neighbouring** *adj* сосе́дний. **neighbourly** *adj* доброссосе́дский.

neither *adv* та́кже не, то́же не; *pron* ни тот, ни друго́й; ~ ... **nor** ни... ни.

neon *n* нео́н; *attrib* нео́новый.

nephew *n* племя́нник.

nepotism *n* кумовство́.

nerve *n* нерв; (*courage*) сме́лость; (*impudence*) на́глость; **get on the** ~**s of** де́йствовать *impf*, по~ *pf* +*dat* на не́рвы. **nervous** *adj* не́рвный; ~ **breakdown** не́рвное расстро́йство. **nervy** *adj* нерво́зный.

nest *n* гнездо́; ~ **egg** сбереже́ния *neut pl*; *vi* гнезди́ться *impf*. **nestle** *vi* льнуть *impf*, при~ *pf*.

net[1] *n* сеть, се́тка; *vt* (*catch*) лови́ть *impf*, пойма́ть *pf* сетя́ми.

net[2], **nett** *adj* чи́стый; *vt* получа́ть *impf*, получи́ть *pf* ... чи́стого дохо́да.

Netherlands *n* Нидерла́нды (-ов) *pl*.

nettle *n* крапи́ва.

network *n* сеть.

neurologist *n* невро́лог. **neurology** *n* невроло́гия. **neurosis** *n* невро́з. **neurotic** *adj* невроти́ческий.

neuter *adj* сре́дний, сре́днего ро́да; *n* сре́дний род; *vt* кастри́ровать *impf & pf*. **neutral** *adj* нейтра́льный; *n* (*gear*) нейтра́льная ско́рость. **neutrality** *n* нейтралите́т. **neutralize** *vt* нейтрализова́ть *impf & pf*. **neutron** *n* нейтро́н.

never *adv* никогда́; ~ **again** никогда́ бо́льше; ~ **mind** ничего́!; всё равно́!; ~ **once** ни ра́зу. **nevertheless** *conj*, *adv* тем не ме́нее.

new *adj* но́вый; (*moon, potatoes*) молодо́й. **new-born** *adj* новорождённый. **newcomer** *n* прише́лец. **newfangled** *adj* новомо́дный. **newly** *adv* то́лько что, неда́вно. **newness** *n* новизна́.

news *n* но́вость, -ти *pl*, изве́стие, -ия *pl*. **newsagent** *n* продаве́ц газе́т. **newsletter** *n* информацио́нный бюллете́нь *m*. **newspaper** *n* газе́та. **newsprint** *n* газе́тная бума́га. **newsreel** *n* кинохро́ника.

newt *n* трито́н.

New Zealand *n* Но́вая Зела́ндия; *adj* новозела́ндский.

next *adj* сле́дующий, бу́дущий; *adv*

(~ *time*) в сле́дующий раз; (*then*) пото́м, зате́м; ~ **door** (*house*) в сосе́днем до́ме; (*flat*) в сосе́дней кварти́ре; ~ **of kin** ближа́йший ро́дственник; ~ **to** ря́дом с+*instr*; (*fig*) почти́. **next-door** *adj* сосе́дний; ~ **neighbour** ближа́йший сосе́д.

nib *n* перо́.

nibble *vt* & *i* грызть *impf*; *vt* обгрыза́ть *impf*, обгры́зть *pf*; (*grass*) щипа́ть *impf*; (*fish*) клева́ть *impf*.

nice *adj* (*pleasant*) прия́тный, хоро́ший; (*person*) ми́лый. **nicety** *n* то́нкость.

niche *n* ни́ша; (*fig*) своё ме́сто.

nick *n* (*scratch*) цара́пина; (*notch*) зару́бка; **in the ~ of time** в са́мый после́дний моме́нт; *vt* (*scratch*) цара́пать *impf*, о~ *pf*; (*steal*) сти́брить *pf*.

nickel *n* ни́кель *m*.

nickname *n* про́звище; *vt* прозыва́ть *impf*, прозва́ть *pf*.

nicotine *n* никоти́н.

niece *n* племя́нница.

niggardly *adj* скупо́й.

niggling *adj* ме́лочный.

night *n* ночь; (*evening*) ве́чер; **at ~** но́чью; **last ~** вчера́ ве́чером; *attrib* ночно́й; **~-club** ночно́й клуб. **nightcap** *n* ночно́й колпа́к; (*drink*) стака́нчик спиртно́го на́ ночь. **nightdress** *n* ночна́я руба́шка. **nightfall** *n* наступле́ние но́чи. **nightingale** *n* солове́й. **nightly** *adj* ежено́щный; *adv* ежено́щно. **nightmare** *n* кошма́р. **nightmarish** *adj* кошма́рный.

nil *n* нуль *m*.

nimble *adj* прово́рный.

nine *adj* & *n* де́вять; (*number 9*) девя́тка. **nineteen** *adj* & *n* девятна́дцать. **nineteenth** *adj* & *n* девятна́дцатый. **ninetieth** *adj* & *n* девяно́стый. **ninety** *adj* & *n* девяно́сто; *pl* (*decade*) девяно́стые го́ды (-до́в) *m pl*. **ninth** *adj* & *n* девя́тый.

nip *vt* (*pinch*) щипа́ть *impf*, щипну́ть *pf*; (*bite*) куса́ть *impf*, укуси́ть *pf*; ~ **in the bud** пресека́ть *impf*, пресе́чь *pf* в заро́дыше; *n* щипо́к; уку́с; **there's a ~ in the air** во́здух па́хнет моро́зцем.

nipple *n* сосо́к.

nirvana *n* нирва́на.

nit *n* гни́да.

nitrate *n* нитра́т. **nitrogen** *n* азо́т.

no *adj* (*not any*) никако́й, не оди́н; (*not a* (*fool etc.*)) (совсе́м) не; *adv* нет; (*ни́сколько*) не+*comp*; *n* отрица́ние, отка́з; (*in vote*) го́лос „про́тив"; ~ **doubt** несомне́нно; ~ **longer** уже́ не, бо́льше не; **no one** никто́; ~ **wonder** не удиви́тельно.

Noah's ark *n* Но́ев ковче́г.

nobility *n* (*class*) дворя́нство; (*quality*) благоро́дство. **noble** *adj* дворя́нский; благоро́дный. **nobleman** *n* дворяни́н.

nobody *pron* никто́; *n* ничто́жество.

nocturnal *adj* ночно́й.

nod *vi* кива́ть *impf*, кивну́ть *pf* голово́й; *n* киво́к.

nodule *n* узело́к.

noise *n* шум. **noiseless** *adj* бесшу́мный. **noisy** *adj* шу́мный.

nomad *n* коче́вник. **nomadic** *adj* кочево́й.

nomenclature *n* номенклату́ра. **nominal** *adj* номина́льный. **nominate** *vt* (*propose*) выдвига́ть *impf*, вы́двинуть *pf*; (*appoint*) назнача́ть *impf*, назна́чить *pf*. **nomination** *n* выдвиже́ние; назначе́ние. **nominative** *adj* (*n*) имени́тельный (паде́ж). **nominee** *n* кандида́т.

non-alcoholic *adj* безалкого́льный. **non-aligned** *adj* неприсоедини́вшийся.

nonchalance *n* беззабо́тность. **nonchalant** *n* беззабо́тный.

non-commissioned *adj*: ~ **officer** у́нтер-офице́р. **non-committal** *adj* укло́нчивый.

non-conformist *n* нонконформи́ст; *adj* нонконформи́стский.

nondescript *adj* неопределённый.

none *pron* (*no one*) никто́; (*nothing*) ничто́; (*not one*) не оди́н; *adv* ни́сколько не; ~ **the less** тем не ме́нее.

nonentity *n* ничто́жество.

non-existent *adj* несуществу́ющий. **non-fiction** *adj* документа́льный. **non-intervention** *n* невмеша́тельство. **non-party** *adj* беспарти́йный. **non-payment** *n* неплатёж.

nonplus *vt* ста́вить *impf*, по~ *pf* в тупи́к.

non-productive *adj* непроизводи́тельный. **non-resident** *adj* не проживающий (где-нибудь).

nonsense *n* ерунда́. **nonsensical** *adj* бессмы́сленный.

non-smoker *n* (*person*) некуря́щий *sb*; (*compartment*) купе́ *neut indecl*, для некуря́щих. **non-stop** *adj* безостано́вочный; (*flight*) беспоса́дочный; *adv* без остано́вок; без поса́док. **non-violent** *adj* ненаси́льственный.

noodles *n pl* лапша́.

nook *n* уголо́к.

noon *n* по́лдень *m*.

no one *see* **no**

noose *n* пе́тля.

nor *conj* и не; то́же; **neither ... ~** ни... ни.

norm *n* но́рма. **normal** *adj* норма́льный. **normality** *n* норма́льность. **normalize** *vt* нормализова́ть *impf* & *pf*.

north *n* се́вер; (*naut*) норд; *adj* се́верный; *adv* к се́веру, на се́вер; **~-east** се́веро-восто́к; **~-easterly, -eastern** се́веро-восто́чный; **~-west** се́веро-за́пад; **~-westerly, -western** се́веро-за́падный. **northerly** *adj* се́верный. **northern** *adj* се́верный. **northerner** *n* северя́нин, -я́нка. **northward(s)** *adv* на се́вер, к се́веру.

Norway *n* Норве́гия. **Norwegian** *adj* норве́жский; *n* норве́жец, -жка.

nose *n* нос; *vt*: **~ about, out** разню́хивать *impf*, разню́хать *pf*. **nosebleed** *n* кровотече́ние и́з носу. **nosedive** *n* пике́ *neut indecl*.

nostalgia *n* ностальги́я. **nostalgic** *adj* ностальги́ческий.

nostril *n* ноздря́.

not *adv* не; нет; ни; **~ at all** ниско́лько, ничу́ть; (*reply to thanks*) не сто́ит (благода́рности); **~ once** ни ра́зу; **~ that** не то, что́бы; **~ too** дово́льно +*neg*; **~ to say** что́бы не сказа́ть; **~ to speak of** не говоря́ уже́ о+*prep*.

notable *adj* заме́тный; (*remarkable*) замеча́тельный. **notably** *adv* (*especially*) осо́бенно; (*perceptibly*) заме́тно.

notary (public) *n* нота́риус.

notation *n* нота́ция; (*mus*) но́тное письмо́.

notch *n* зару́бка; *vt*: **~ up** вы́игрывать *impf*, вы́играть *pf*.

note *n* (*record*) заме́тка, за́пись; (*annotation*) примеча́ние; (*letter*) запи́ска; (*banknote*) банкно́т; (*mus*) но́та; (*tone*) тон; (*attention*) внима́ние; *vt* отмеча́ть *impf*, отме́тить *pf*; **~ down** запи́сывать *impf*, записа́ть *pf*. **notebook** *n* записна́я кни́жка. **noted** *adj* знамени́тый; изве́стный (**for** +*instr*). **notepaper** *n* почто́вая бума́га. **noteworthy** *adj* досто́йный внима́ния.

nothing *n* ничто́, ничего́; **~ but** ничего́ кро́ме+*gen*, то́лько; **~ of the kind** ничего́ подо́бного; **come to ~** конча́ться *impf*, ко́нчиться *pf* ниче́м; **for ~** (*free*) да́ром; (*in vain*) зря, напра́сно; **have ~ to do with** не име́ть *impf* никако́го отноше́ния к+*dat*; **there is (was) ~ for it (but to)** ничего́ друго́го не остаётся (остава́лось) (как); **to say ~ of** не говоря́ уже́ о+*prep*.

notice *n* (*sign*) объявле́ние; (*warning*) предупрежде́ние; (*attention*) внима́ние; (*review*) о́тзыв; **give (in) one's ~** подава́ть *impf*, пода́ть *pf* заявле́ние об ухо́де с рабо́ты; **give s.o. ~** предупрежда́ть *impf*, предупреди́ть *pf* об увольне́нии; **take ~ of** обраща́ть *impf*, обрати́ть *pf* внима́ния на+*acc*; **~-board** доска́ для объявле́ний; *vt* замеча́ть *impf*, заме́тить *pf*. **noticeable** *adj* заме́тный. **notification** *n* извеще́ние. **notify** *vt* извеща́ть *impf*, извести́ть *pf* (**of** о+*prep*).

notion *n* поня́тие.

notoriety *n* дурна́я сла́ва. **notorious** *adj* пресловутый.

notwithstanding *prep* несмотря́ на+*acc*; *adv* тём не ме́нее.

nought *n* (*nothing*) *see* **naught**; (*zero*) нуль *m*; (*figure 0*) ноль *m*.

noun *n* (и́мя *neut*) существи́тельное *sb*.

nourish *vt* пита́ть *impf*, на- *pf*. **nourishing** *adj* пита́тельный. **nourishment** *n* пита́ние.

novel *adj* но́вый; (*unusual*) необыкнове́нный; *n* рома́н. **novelist** *n* романи́ст. **novelty** *n* (*newness*) новизна́; (*new thing*) нови́нка.

November *n* ноя́брь *m*; *adj* ноя́брьский.

novice n (*eccl*) послушник, -ица; (*beginner*) новичóк.

now adv тепéрь, сейчáс; (*immediately*) тóтчас же; (*next*) тогдá; *conj*: ~ **(that)** раз, когдá; **(every)** ~ **and again, then** врéмя от врéмени; **by** ~ ужé; **from** ~ **on** впредь. **nowadays** adv в нáше врéмя.

nowhere adv (*place*) нигдé; (*direction*) никудá; *pron*: **I have** ~ **to go** мне нéкуда пойти.

noxious adj врéдный.

nozzle n сóпло.

nuance n нюáнс.

nuclear adj я́дерный. **nucleus** n ядрó.

nude adj обнажённый, нагóй; n обнажённая фигýра.

nudge vt подтáлкивать *impf*, подтолкнýть *pf* лóктем; n толчóк лóктем.

nudity n наготá.

nugget n самородóк.

nuisance n досáда; (*person*) раздражáющий человéк.

null adj: ~ **and void** недействительный. **nullify** vt аннулировать *impf* & *pf*. **nullity** n недействительность.

numb adj онемéлый; (*from cold*) окоченéлый; **go** ~ онемéть *pf*; (*from cold*) окоченéть *pf*.

number n (*total*) колѝчество; (*total*; *symbol*; *math*; *gram*) числó; (*identifying numeral*; *item*) нóмер; ~**plate** номернáя дощéчка; vt (*assign* ~ *to*) нумеровáть *impf*, за~, про~ *pf*; (*contain*) насчитывать *impf*; ~ **among** причислять *impf*, причислить *pf* к+*dat*; **his days are** ~**ed** егó дни сочтены.

numeral n цифра; (*gram*) (и́мя *neut*) числительное *sb*. **numerical** adj числовóй. **numerous** adj многочисленный; (*many*) мнóго +*gen pl*.

nun n монáхиня. **nunnery** n (жéнский) монастырь *m*.

nuptial adj свáдебный; n: *pl* свáдьба.

nurse n (*child's*) ня́ня; (*medical*) медсестрá; vt (*suckle*) кормить *impf*, на~, по~ *pf*; (*tend sick*) ухáживать *impf* за+*instr*; **nursing home** санатóрий; дом престарéлых. **nursery** n (*room*) дéтская *sb*; (*day* ~) я́сли (-лей) *pl*; (*for plants*) питóмник; ~ **rhyme** дéтские прибаýтки *f pl*; ~ **school** дéтский сад.

nut n орéх; (*for bolt etc.*) гáйка. **nutshell** n: **in a** ~ в двух словáх.

nutmeg n мускáтный орéх.

nutrient n питáтельное веществó. **nutrition** n питáние. **nutritious** adj питáтельный.

nylon n нейлóн; *pl* нейлóновые чулки (-лóк) *pl*.

nymph n нѝмфа.

O

O int о!; ах!

oaf n неуклю́жий человéк.

oak n дуб; *attrib* дубóвый.

oar n веслó. **oarsman** n гребéц.

oasis n оáзис.

oath n прися́га; (*expletive*) ругáтельство.

oatmeal n овся́нка. **oats** n *pl* овёс (овсá) *collect*.

obdurate adj упря́мый.

obedience n послушáние. **obedient** adj послýшный.

obese adj тýчный. **obesity** n тýчность.

obey vt слýшаться *impf*, по~ *pf* +*gen*; (*law, order*) подчиня́ться *impf*, подчини́ться *pf* +*dat*.

obituary n некролóг.

object n (*thing*) предмéт; (*aim*) цель; (*gram*) дополнéние; vi возражáть *impf*, возразить *pf* (**to** прóтив+*gen*); **I don't** ~ я не прóтив. **objection** n возражéние; **I have no** ~ я не возражáю. **objectionable** adj неприя́тный. **objective** adj объективный; n цель. **objectivity** n объективность. **objector** n возражáющий *sb*.

obligation n обязáтельство; **I am under an** ~ я обя́зан(а). **obligatory** adj обязáтельный. **oblige** vt обя́зывать *impf*, обязáть *pf*; **be** ~**d to** (*grateful*) быть обя́занным+*dat*. **obliging** adj услýжливый.

oblique adj косóй; (*fig*; *gram*) кóсвенный.

obliterate vt (*efface*) стирáть *impf*, стерéть *pf*; (*destroy*) уничтожáть *impf*, уничтóжить *pf*. **obliteration** n стирáние; уничтожéние.

oblivion n забвéние. **oblivious** adj (*forgetful*) забы́вчивый; **to be** ~ **of** не замечáть *impf* +*gen*.

oblong adj продолговáтый.

obnoxious adj проти́вный.

oboe n гобо́й.

obscene adj непристо́йный. **obscenity** n непристо́йность.

obscure adj (unclear) нея́сный; (little known) малоизве́стный; vt затемня́ть impf, затемни́ть pf; де́лать impf, с~ pf нея́сным. **obscurity** n нея́сность; неизве́стность.

obsequious adj подобостра́стный.

observance n соблюде́ние; (rite) обря́д. **observant** adj наблюда́тельный. **observation** n наблюде́ние; (remark) замеча́ние. **observatory** n обсервато́рия. **observe** vt (law etc.) соблюда́ть impf, соблюсти́ pf; (watch) наблюда́ть impf; (remark) замеча́ть impf, заме́тить pf. **observer** n наблюда́тель m.

obsess vt пресле́довать impf; **obsessed by** одержи́мый +instr. **obsession** n одержи́мость; (idea) навя́зчивая иде́я. **obsessive** adj навя́зчивый.

obsolete adj устаре́лый, вы́шедший из употребле́ния.

obstacle n препя́тствие.

obstetrician n акуше́р. **obstetrics** n акуше́рство.

obstinacy n упря́мство. **obstinate** adj упря́мый.

obstreperous adj бу́йный.

obstruct vt загражда́ть impf, загради́ть pf; (hinder) препя́тствовать impf, вос~ pf +dat. **obstruction** n загражде́ние; (obstacle) препя́тствие.

obstructive adj загражда́ющий; препя́тствующий.

obtain vt получа́ть impf, получи́ть pf; достава́ть impf, доста́ть pf.

obtrusive adj навя́зчивый; (thing) броса́ющийся в глаза́.

obtuse adj тупо́й.

obviate vt устраня́ть impf, устрани́ть pf.

obvious adj очеви́дный.

occasion n слу́чай; (cause) по́вод; (occurrence) собы́тие; vt причиня́ть impf, причини́ть pf. **occasional** adj ре́дкий. **occasionally** adv иногда́, вре́мя от вре́мени.

occult adj окку́льтный; n: the ~ окку́льт.

occupancy n заня́тие. **occupant** n жи́тель m, ~ница. **occupation** n заня́тие; (military ~) оккупа́ция; (profession) профе́ссия. **occupational** adj профессиона́льный; ~ **therapy** трудотерапи́я. **occupy** vt занима́ть impf, заня́ть pf; (mil) оккупи́ровать impf & pf.

occur vi (happen) случа́ться impf, случи́ться pf; (be found) встреча́ться impf; ~ **to** приходи́ть impf, прийти́ pf в го́лову+dat. **occurrence** n слу́чай, происше́ствие.

ocean n океа́н. **oceanic** adj океа́нский.

o'clock adv: (at) six ~ (в) шесть часо́в.

octagonal adj восьмиуго́льный.

octave n (mus) окта́ва.

October n октя́брь m; adj октя́брьский.

octopus n осьмино́г.

odd adj (strange) стра́нный; (not in a set) разро́зненный; (number) нечётный; (not paired) непа́рный; (casual) случа́йный; **five hundred ~** пятьсо́т с ли́шним; ~ **job** случа́йная рабо́та. **oddity** n стра́нность; (person) чуда́к, -а́чка. **oddly** adv стра́нно; ~ **enough** как э́то ни стра́нно. **oddment** n оста́ток. **odds** n pl ша́нсы m pl; **be at ~ with** (person) не ла́дить c+instr; (things) не соотве́тствовать impf +dat; **long (short) ~** нера́вные (почти́ ра́вные) ша́нсы m pl; **the ~ are that** вероя́тнее всего́, что; ~ **and ends** обры́вки m pl.

ode n о́да.

odious adj ненави́стный.

odour n за́пах.

oesophagus n пищево́д.

of prep expressing **1.** origin: из+gen: **he comes ~ a working-class family** он из рабо́чей семьи́; **2.** cause: от +gen: **he died ~ hunger** он у́мер от го́лода; **3.** authorship: gen: **the works ~ Pushkin** сочине́ния Пу́шкина; **4.** material: из+gen: **made ~ wood** сде́ланный из де́рева; **5.** reference: о+prep: **he talked ~ Lenin** он говори́л о Ле́нине; **6.** partition: gen (often in -у(-ю)): **a glass ~ milk, tea** стака́н молока́, ча́ю; из+gen: **one ~ them** оди́н из них; **7.** belonging: gen: **the capital ~ England** столи́ца А́нглии.

off *adv: in phrasal vv, see v, e.g.* **clear ~** убира́ться; *prep (from surface of)* c+*gen; (away from)* от+*gen;* **~ and on** вре́мя от вре́мени; **~-white** не совсе́м бе́лый.

offal *n* требуха́.

offence *n (insult)* оби́да; *(against law)* просту́пок, преступле́ние; **take ~** обижа́ться *impf,* оби́деться *pf* (**at** на+*acc*). **offend** *vt* обижа́ть *impf,* оби́деть *pf;* **~ against** наруша́ть *impf,* нару́шить *pf.* **offender** *n* правонаруши́тель *m,* ~ница. **offensive** *adj (attacking)* наступа́тельный; *(insulting)* оскорби́тельный; *(repulsive)* проти́вный; *n* нападе́ние.

offer *vt* предлага́ть *impf,* предложи́ть *pf; n* предложе́ние; **on ~** в прода́же.

offhand *adj* бесцеремо́нный.

office *n (position)* до́лжность; *(place, room etc.)* бюро́ *neut indecl,* конто́ра, канцеля́рия. **officer** *n* должностно́е лицо́; *(mil)* офице́р. **official** *adj* служе́бный; *(authorized)* официа́льный; *n* должностно́е лицо́. **officiate** *vi (eccl)* соверша́ть *impf,* соверши́ть *pf* богослуже́ние. **officious** *adj (intrusive)* навя́зчивый.

offing *n:* **be in the ~** предстоя́ть *impf.*

off-licence *n* ви́нный магази́н. **offload** *vt* разгружа́ть *impf,* разгрузи́ть *pf.* **off-putting** *adj* отта́лкивающий. **offset** *vt* возмеща́ть *impf,* возмести́ть *pf.* **offshoot** *n* о́тпрыск. **offshore** *adj* прибре́жный. **offside** *adv* вне игры́. **offspring** *n* пото́мок; *(collect)* пото́мки *m pl.*

often *adv* ча́сто.

ogle *vt & i* смотре́ть *impf* с вожделе́нием на+*acc.*

ogre *n* велика́н-людое́д.

oh *int* о!; ах!

ohm *n* ом.

oil *n* ма́сло; *(petroleum)* нефть; *(paint)* ма́сло, ма́сляные кра́ски *f pl; vt* сма́зывать *impf,* сма́зать *pf;* **~-painting** карти́на, напи́санная ма́сляными кра́сками; **~ rig** нефтяна́я вы́шка; **~-tanker** та́нкер; **~ well** нефтяна́я сква́жина. **oilfield** *n* месторожде́ние нефти. **oilskin** *n* клеёнка; *pl* непромока́емый костю́м.

oily *adj* масляни́стый.

ointment *n* мазь.

OK *adv & adj* хорошо́, норма́льно; *int* ла́дно!; *vt* одобря́ть *impf,* одо́брить *pf.*

old *adj* ста́рый; *(ancient; of long standing)* стари́нный; *(former)* бы́вший; **how ~ are you?** ско́лько тебе́, вам, *(dat)* лет?; **~ age** ста́рость; **~-age pension** пе́нсия по ста́рости; **old-fashioned** старомо́дный; **~ maid** ста́рая де́ва; **~ man** *(also father, husband)* стари́к; **~-time** стари́нный; **~ woman** стару́ха; *(coll)* стару́шка.

olive *n (fruit)* оли́вка; *(colour)* оли́вковый цвет; *adj* оли́вковый; **~ oil** оли́вковое ма́сло.

Olympic *adj* олимпи́йский; **~ games** Олимпи́йские и́гры *f pl.*

omelette *n* омле́т.

omen *n* предзнаменова́ние. **ominous** *adj* злове́щий.

omission *n* про́пуск; *(neglect)* упуще́ние. **omit** *vt (leave out)* пропуска́ть *impf,* пропусти́ть *pf; (neglect)* упуска́ть *impf,* упусти́ть *pf.*

omnibus *n (bus)* авто́бус; *(collection)* колле́кция.

omnipotence *n* всемогу́щество. **omnipotent** *adj* всемогу́щий. **omnipresent** *adj* вездесу́щий. **omniscient** *adj* всеве́дущий.

on *prep (position)* на+*prep; (direction)* на+*acc; (time)* в+*acc;* **~ the next day** на сле́дующий день; **~ Mondays** *(repeated action)* по поне́дельникам *(dat pl);* **~ the first of June** пе́рвого ию́ня *(gen); (concerning)* по+*prep,* о+*prep,* на+*acc; adv* да́льше, вперёд; *in phrasal vv, see vv, e.g.* **move ~** идти́ да́льше; **and so ~** и так да́лее, и т.д.; **be ~** *(film etc.)* идти́ *impf;* **further ~** да́льше; **later ~** по́зже.

once *adv (one)* раз; *(on past occasion)* одна́жды; *(formerly)* не́когда; **all at ~** неожи́данно; **at ~** сра́зу, неме́дленно; *(if, when)* как то́лько; **~ again, more** ещё раз; **~ and for all** раз и навсегда́; **~ or twice** не́сколько раз; **~ upon a time there lived ...** жил-был... .

oncoming *adj:* **~ traffic** встре́чное движе́ние.

one *adj* оди́н (одна́, -но́); *(only, sin-*

gle) еди́нственный; *n* оди́н; *pron: not usu translated; v translated in 2nd pers sg or by impers construction:* ~ **never knows** никогда́ не зна́ешь; **where can** ~ **buy this book?** где мо́жно купи́ть э́ту кни́гу?; ~ **after another** оди́н за други́м; ~ **and all** все до одного́; все как оди́н; ~ **and only** еди́нственный; ~ **and the same** оди́н и тот же; ~ **another** друг дру́га (*dat* -гу, *etc.*); ~ **fine day** в оди́н прекра́сный день; ~ **o'clock** час; ~ **parent family** семья́ с одни́м роди́телем; ~**-sided, -track, -way** односторо́нний; ~**-time** бы́вший; ~**way street** у́лица односторо́ннего движе́ния.

onerous *adj* тя́гостный.

oneself *pron* себя́; -ся (*suffixed to vt*).

onion *n* (*plant; pl collect*) лук; (*single* ~) лу́ковица.

onlooker *n* наблюда́тель *m*.

only *adj* еди́нственный; *adv* то́лько; **if** ~ е́сли бы то́лько; ~ **just** то́лько что; *conj* но.

onset *n* нача́ло.

onslaught *n* на́тиск.

onus *n* отве́тственность.

onward(s) *adv* вперёд.

ooze *vt & i* сочи́ться *impf*.

opal *n* опа́л.

opaque *adj* непрозра́чный.

open *adj* откры́тый; (*frank*) открове́нный; **in the** ~ **air** на откры́том во́здухе; ~**-minded** *adj* непредупреждённый; *vt & i* открыва́ть(ся) *impf*, откры́ть(ся) *pf; vi* (*begin*) начина́ться *impf*, нача́ться *pf*; (*flowers*) распуска́ться *impf*, распусти́ться *pf*. **opening** *n* откры́тие; (*aperture*) отве́рстие; (*beginning*) нача́ло; *adj* нача́льный, пе́рвый; (*introductory*) вступи́тельный.

opera *n* о́пера; *attrib* о́перный; ~**house** о́перный теа́тр.

operate *vi* де́йствовать *impf* (**upon** на+*acc*); (*med*) опери́ровать *impf & pf* (**on** +*acc*); *vt* управля́ть *impf* +*instr*.

operatic *adj* о́перный.

operating-theatre *n* операцио́нная *sb*. **operation** *n* де́йствие; (*med; mil*) опера́ция. **operational** *adj* (*in use*) де́йствующий; (*mil*) операти́вный. **operative** *adj* де́йствующий. **oper-**

ator *n* опера́тор; (*telephone* ~) телефони́ст, ~ка.

operetta *n* опере́тта.

ophthalmic *adj* глазно́й.

opinion *n* мне́ние; **in my** ~ по-мо́ему; ~ **poll** опро́с обще́ственного мне́ния. **opinionated** *adj* догмати́чный.

opium *n* о́пиум.

opponent *n* проти́вник.

opportune *adj* своевре́менный. **opportunism** *n* оппортуни́зм. **opportunist** *n* оппортуни́ст. **opportunistic** *n* оппортунисти́ческий. **opportunity** *n* слу́чай, возмо́жность.

oppose *vt* (*resist*) проти́виться *impf*, вос~ *pf* +*dat*; (*speak etc. against*) выступа́ть *impf*, вы́ступить *pf* про́тив+*gen*. **opposed** *adj* про́тив (**to** +*gen*); **as** ~ **to** в противополо́жность+*dat*. **opposing** *adj* проти́вный; (*opposite*) противополо́жный. **opposite** *adj* противополо́жный; (*reverse*) обра́тный; *n* противополо́жность; **just the** ~ как раз наоборо́т; *adv* напро́тив; *prep* (на)про́тив+*gen*. **opposition** *n* (*resistance*) сопротивле́ние; (*polit*) оппози́ция.

oppress *vt* угнета́ть *impf*. **oppression** *n* угнете́ние. **oppressive** *adj* угнета́ющий. **oppressor** *n* угнета́тель *m*.

opt *vi* выбира́ть *impf*, вы́брать *pf* (**for** +*acc*); ~ **out** не принима́ть *impf* уча́стия (**of** в+*prep*).

optic *adj* зри́тельный. **optical** *adj* опти́ческий. **optician** *n* о́птик. **optics** *n* о́птика.

optimism *n* оптими́зм. **optimist** *n* оптими́ст. **optimistic** *adj* оптимисти́ческий. **optimum** *adj* оптима́льный.

option *n* вы́бор. **optional** *adj* необяза́тельный.

opulence *n* бога́тство. **opulent** *adj* бога́тый.

opus *n* о́пус.

or *conj* и́ли; ~ **else** ина́че; ~ **so** прибли́зи́тельно.

oracle *n* ора́кул.

oral *adj* у́стный; *n* у́стный экза́мен.

orange *n* (*fruit*) апельси́н; (*colour*) ора́нжевый цвет; *attrib* апельси́новый; *adj* ора́нжевый.

oration n речь. **orator** n ора́тор.

oratorio n орато́рия.

oratory n (speech) красноре́чие.

orbit n орби́та; vt враща́ться impf по орби́те вокру́г+gen. **orbital** adj орбита́льный.

orchard n фрукто́вый сад.

orchestra n орке́стр. **orchestral** adj орке́стровый. **orchestrate** vt оркестрова́ть impf & pf. **orchestration** n орестро́вка.

orchid n орхиде́я.

ordain vt предпи́сывать impf, предписа́ть pf; (eccl) посвяща́ть impf, посвяти́ть pf (в духо́вный сан).

ordeal n тяжёлое испыта́ние.

order n поря́док; (command) прика́з; (for goods) зака́з; (insignia, medal; fraternity) о́рден; (archit) о́рдер; pl (holy ~) духо́вный сан; **in ~ to** (для того́) что́бы +inf; vt (command) прика́зывать impf, приказа́ть pf +dat; (goods etc.) зака́зывать impf, заказа́ть pf. **orderly** adj аккура́тный; (quiet) ти́хий; n (med) санита́р; (mil) ордина́рец.

ordinance n декре́т.

ordinary adj обыкнове́нный, обы́чный.

ordination n посвяще́ние.

ore n руда́.

organ n о́рган; (mus) орга́н. **organic** adj органи́ческий. **organism** n органи́зм. **organist** n органи́ст. **organization** n организа́ция. **organize** vt организо́вывать impf (pres not used), организова́ть impf (in pres) & pf; устра́ивать impf, устро́ить pf. **organizer** n организа́тор.

orgy n о́ргия.

Orient n Восто́к. **oriental** adj восто́чный.

orient, orientate vt ориенти́ровать impf &pf (o.s. -ся). **orientation** n ориента́ция.

orifice n отве́рстие.

origin n происхожде́ние, нача́ло. **original** adj оригина́льный; (initial) первонача́льный; (genuine) по́длинный; n оригина́л. **originality** n оригина́льность. **originate** vt порожда́ть impf, породи́ть pf; vi брать impf, взять pf нача́ло (from, in в+prep, от+gen); (arise) возника́ть impf, возни́кнуть pf. **originator** n

а́втор, инициа́тор.

ornament n украше́ние; vt украша́ть impf, укра́сить pf. **ornamental** adj декорати́вный.

ornate adj витиева́тый.

ornithologist n орнито́лог. **ornithology** n орнитоло́гия.

orphan n сирота́ m & f; vt: **be ~ed** сироте́ть impf, о~ pf. **orphanage** n сиро́тский дом. **orphaned** adj осироте́лый.

orthodox adj ортодокса́льный; (eccl, O~) правосла́вный. **orthodoxy** n ортодо́ксия; (O~) правосла́вие.

orthopaedic adj ортопеди́ческий.

oscillate vi колеба́ться impf, по~ pf. **oscillation** n колеба́ние.

osmosis n о́смос.

ostensible adj мни́мый. **ostensibly** adv я́кобы.

ostentation n выставле́ние напока́з. **ostentatious** adj показно́й.

osteopath n остеопа́т. **osteopathy** n остеопа́тия.

ostracize vt подверга́ть impf, подве́ргнуть pf остраки́зму.

ostrich n стра́ус.

other adj друго́й, ино́й; тот; **every ~** ка́ждый второ́й; **every ~ day** че́рез день; **on the ~ hand** с друго́й стороны́; **on the ~ side** на той стороне́, по ту сто́рону; **one or the ~** тот и́ли ино́й; **the ~ day** на дня́х, неда́вно; **the ~ way round** наоборо́т; **the ~s** остальны́е sb pl. **otherwise** adv & conj и́наче, а то.

otter n вы́дра.

ouch int ой!, ай!

ought v aux до́лжен (-жна́) (бы) +inf.

ounce n у́нция.

our, ours poss pron наш; свой. **ourselves** pron (emph) са́ми; (refl) себя́; -ся (suffixed to vb).

oust vt вытесня́ть impf, вы́теснить pf.

out adv **1.** in phrasal vv often rendered by pref вы-; **2.:** to be ~ in various senses: **he is ~** (not at home) его́ нет до́ма; (not in office etc.) он вы́шел; (sport) выходи́ть impf, вы́йти pf из игры́; (of fashion) вы́йти pf из мо́ды; (be published) вы́йти pf из печа́ти; (of candle etc.) поту́хнуть pf; (of flower) распусти́ться pf; (be unconscious) потеря́ть pf созна́ние; **3.:** ~**-and-~** отъя́вленный; **4.:** ~ **of** из+*gen*, вне+*gen*; ~ **of date** устаре́лый, старомо́дный; ~ **of doors** на откры́том во́здухе; ~ **of work** безрабо́тный.

outbid *vt* предлага́ть *impf*, предложи́ть *pf* бо́лее высо́кую це́ну, чем+*nom*. **outboard** *adj:* ~ **motor** подвесно́й мото́р *m*. **outbreak** n (*of anger, disease*) вспы́шка; (*of war*) нача́ло. **outbuilding** *n* надво́рная постро́йка. **outburst** *n* взрыв. **outcast** *n* изгна́нник. **outcome** *n* результа́т. **outcry** *n* (шу́мные) проте́сты *m pl*. **outdated** *adj* устаре́лый. **outdo** *vt* превосходи́ть *impf*, превзойти́ *pf*.

outdoor *adj*, **outdoors** *adv* на откры́том во́здухе, на у́лице.

outer *adj* (*external*) вне́шний, нару́жный; (*far from centre*) да́льний. **outermost** *adj* са́мый да́льний.

outfit *n* (*equipment*) снаряже́ние; (*set of things*) набо́р; (*clothes*) наря́д. **outgoing** *adj* уходя́щий; (*sociable*) общи́тельный. **outgoings** *n pl* изде́ржки *f pl*. **outgrow** *vt* выраста́ть *impf*, вы́расти *pf* из+*gen*. **outhouse** *n* надво́рная постро́йка.

outing *n* прогу́лка, экску́рсия.

outlandish *adj* дико́винный. **outlaw** *n* лицо́ вне зако́на; банди́т; *vt* объявля́ть *impf*, объяви́ть *pf* вне зако́на. **outlay** *n* изде́ржки *f pl*. **outlet** *n* выходно́е отве́рстие; (*fig*) (*market*) ры́нок; (*shop*) торго́вая то́чка. **outline** *n* очерта́ние, ко́нтур; (*sketch, summary*) набро́сок; *vt* оче́рчивать *impf*, очерти́ть *pf*; (*plans etc.*) набра́сывать *impf*, наброса́ть *pf*. **outlive** *vt* пережи́ть *pf*. **outlook** *n* перспекти́вы *f pl*; (*attitude*) кругозо́р. **outlying** *adj* перифери́йный. **outmoded** *adj* старомо́дный. **outnumber** *vt* чи́сленно превосходи́ть *impf*, превзойти́ *pf*. **out-patient** *n* амбулато́рный больно́й *sb*. **outpost** *n* форпо́ст. **output** *n* вы́пуск, проду́кция.

outrage *n* безобра́зие; (*indignation*) возмуще́ние; *vt* оскорбля́ть *impf*, оскорби́ть *pf*. **outrageous** *adj* возмути́тельный.

outright *adv* (*entirely*) вполне́; (*once for all*) раз (и) навсегда́; (*openly*)

откры́то; *adj* прямо́й. **outset** *n* нача́ло; **at the** ~ внача́ле; **from the** ~ с са́мого нача́ла.

outside *n* нару́жная сторона́; **at the** ~ са́мое бо́льшее; **from the** ~ извне́; **on the** ~ снару́жи; *adj* нару́жный, вне́шний; (*sport*) кра́йний; *adv* (on *the* ~) снару́жи; (*to the* ~) нару́жу; (*out of doors*) на откры́том во́здухе, на у́лице; *prep* вне+*gen*; за преде́лами+*gen*. **outsider** *n* посторо́нний *sb*; (*sport*) аутса́йдер.

outsize *adj* бо́льше станда́ртного разме́ра. **outskirts** *n pl* окра́ина. **outspoken** *adj* прямо́й. **outstanding** *adj* (*remarkable*) выдаю́щийся; (*unpaid*) неупла́ченный. **outstay** *vt:* ~ **one's welcome** заси́живаться *impf*, засиде́ться *pf*. **outstretched** *adj* распростёртый. **outstrip** *vt* обгоня́ть *impf*, обогна́ть *pf*.

outward *adj* (*external*) вне́шний, нару́жный; **outwardly** *adv* вне́шне, на вид. **outwards** *adv* нару́жу.

outweigh *vt* переве́шивать *impf*, переве́сить *pf*. **outwit** *vt* перехитри́ть *pf*.

oval *adj* ова́льный; *n* ова́л.

ovary *n* яи́чник.

ovation *n* ова́ция.

oven *n* (*industrial*) печь; (*domestic*) духо́вка.

over *adv & prep with vv: see vv; prep* (*above*) над+*instr*; (*through; covering*) по+*dat*; (*concerning*) о+*prep*; (*across*) че́рез+*acc*; (*on the other side of*) по ту сто́рону+*gen*; (*more than*) свы́ше+*gen*; бо́лее+*gen*; (*with age*) за+*acc*; **all** ~ (*finished*) всё ко́нчено; (*everywhere*) повсю́ду; **all** ~ **the country** по всей стране́; ~ **again** ещё раз; ~ **against** по сравне́нию с+*instr*; ~ **and above** не говоря́ уже́ о+*prep*; ~ **the telephone** по телефо́ну; ~ **there** вон там.

overall *n* хала́т; *pl* комбинезо́н; *adj* о́бщий. **overawe** *vt* внуша́ть *impf*, внуши́ть *pf* благогове́йный страх +*dat*. **overbalance** *vi* теря́ть *impf*, по~ *pf* равнове́сие. **overbearing** *adj* вла́стный. **overboard** *adv* (*motion*) за́ борт; (*position*) за бо́ртом. **overcast** *adj* о́блачный. **overcoat** *n* пальто́ *neut indecl*. **overcome** *vt* преодолева́ть *impf*, преодоле́ть *pf*;

adj охва́ченный. **overcrowded** *adj* перепо́лненный. **overcrowding** *n* переполне́ние. **overdo** *vt* (*cook*) пережа́ривать *impf*, пережа́рить *pf*; ~ **it, things** (*work too hard*) переутомля́ться *impf*, переутоми́ться *pf*; (*go too far*) переба́рщивать *impf*, переборщи́ть *pf*.

overdose *n* чрезме́рная до́за. **overdraft** *n* превыше́ние креди́та; (*amount*) долг ба́нку. **overdraw** *vi* превыша́ть *impf*, превы́сить *pf* креди́т (в ба́нке). **overdue** *adj* просро́ченный; **be** ~ (*late*) запа́здывать *impf*, запозда́ть *pf*. **overestimate** *vt* переоце́нивать *impf*, переоцени́ть *pf*. **overflow** *vi* перелива́ться *impf*, перели́ться *pf*; (*river etc.*) разлива́ться *impf*, разли́ться *pf*; (*outlet*) перели́в. **overgrown** *adj* заро́сший. **overhang** *vt & i* выступа́ть *impf* над+*instr*; *n* свес, вы́ступ.

overhaul *vt* ремонти́ровать *impf & pf*; *n:* ремо́нт. **overhead** *adv* наверху́, над голово́й; *adj* возду́шный, подвесно́й; *n:* накладны́е расхо́ды *m pl*. **overhear** *vt* неча́янно слы́шать *impf*, у~ *pf*. **overheat** *vt & i* перегрева́ть(ся) *impf*, перегре́ть(ся) *pf*. **overjoyed** *adj* в восто́рге (**at** от+*gen*). **overland** *adj* сухопу́тный; *adv* по су́ше. **overlap** *vt* части́чно покрыва́ть *impf*, покры́ть *pf*; *vi* части́чно совпада́ть *impf*, совпа́сть *pf*.

overleaf *adv* на оборо́те. **overload** *vt* перегружа́ть *impf*, перегрузи́ть *pf*. **overlook** *vt* (*look down on*) смотре́ть *impf* све́рху на+*acc*; (*of window*) выходи́ть *impf* на, в, +*acc*; (*not notice*) не замеча́ть *impf*, заме́тить *pf* +*gen*; (~ *offence etc.*) проща́ть *impf*, прости́ть *pf*.

overly *adv* сли́шком.

overnight *adv* (*during the night*) за ночь; (*suddenly*) неожи́данно; **stay** ~ ночева́ть *impf*, пере~ *pf*; *adj* ночно́й. **overpay** *vt* перепла́чивать *impf*, переплати́ть *pf*.

over-populated *adj* перенаселённый. **over-population** *n* перенаселё́нность. **overpower** *vt* одолева́ть *impf*, одоле́ть *pf*. **overpriced** *adj* завы́шенный в цене́. **over-production** *n* перепроизво́дство. **overrate**

vt переоце́нивать *impf*, переоцени́ть *pf*. **override** *vt* (*fig*) отверга́ть *impf*, отве́ргнуть *pf*. **overriding** *adj* гла́вный, реша́ющий. **overrule** *vt* отверга́ть *impf*, отве́ргнуть *pf*. **overrun** *vt* (*conquer*) завоёвывать *impf*, завоева́ть *pf*; **be** ~ **with** кише́ть *impf* +*instr*.

overseas *adv* за мо́рем, че́рез мо́ре; *adj* замо́рский. **oversee** *vt* надзира́ть *impf* за+*instr*. **overseer** *n* надзира́тель *m*, ~ница. **overshadow** *vt* затмева́ть *impf*, затми́ть *pf*. **overshoot** *vi* переходи́ть *impf*, перейти́ *pf* грани́цу. **oversight** *n* случа́йный недосмо́тр. **oversleep** *vi* просыпа́ть *impf*, проспа́ть *pf*. **overspend** *vi* тра́тить *impf* сли́шком мно́го. **overstate** *vt* преувели́чивать *impf*, преувели́чить *pf*. **overstep** *vt* переступа́ть *impf*, переступи́ть *pf* +*acc*, че́рез+*acc*.

overt *adj* я́вный, откры́тый.

overtake *vt* обгоня́ть *impf*, обогна́ть *pf*. **overthrow** *vt* сверга́ть *impf*, све́ргнуть *pf*. **overtime** *n* (*work*) сверхуро́чная рабо́та; (*payment*) сверхуро́чное *sb*; *adv* сверхуро́чно.

overtone *n* скры́тый намёк. **overture** *n* предложе́ние; (*mus*) увертю́ра.

overturn *vt & i* опроки́дывать(ся) *impf*, опроки́нуть(ся) *pf*. **overwhelm** *vt* подавля́ть *impf*, подави́ть *pf*. **overwhelming** *adj* подавля́ющий. **overwork** *vt & i* переутомля́ть(ся) *impf*, переутоми́ть(ся) *pf*; *n* переутомле́ние.

owe *vt* (~ *money*) быть до́лжным +*acc & dat*; (*be indebted*) быть обя́занным +*instr & dat*; **he, she, ~s me three roubles** он до́лжен, она́ должна́, мне три рубля́; **she ~s him her life** она́ обя́зана ему́ жи́знью.

owing *adj:* **be** ~ причита́ться *impf* (**to** +*dat*); ~ **to** из-за+*gen*, по причи́не+*gen*.

owl *n* сова́.

own *adj* свой; (свой) со́бственный; **on one's** ~ самостоя́тельно; (*alone*) оди́н; *vt* (*possess*) владе́ть *impf* +*instr*; (*admit*) признава́ть *impf*, призна́ть *pf*; ~ **up** признава́ться *impf*, призна́ться *pf*. **owner** *n* владе́лец. **ownership** *n* владе́ние

(of +*instr*), со́бственность.
ox *n* вол.
oxidation *n* окисле́ние. **oxide** *n* о́кись.
oxidize *vt* & *i* окисля́ть(ся) *impf*, окисли́ть(ся) *pf*. **oxygen** *n* кислоро́д.
oyster *n* у́стрица.
ozone *n* озо́н.

P

pace *n* шаг; (*fig*) темп; **keep ~ with** идти́ *impf* в но́гу с+*instr*; **set the ~** задава́ть *impf*, зада́ть *pf* темп; *vi*: **~ up and down** ходи́ть *indet* взад и вперёд. **pacemaker** *n* (*med*) электро́нный стимуля́тор.
pacifism *n* пацифи́зм. **pacifist** *n* пацифи́ст. **pacify** *vt* усмиря́ть *impf*, усмири́ть *pf*.
pack *n* у́зел, вьюк; (*soldier's*) ра́нец; (*hounds*) сво́ра; (*wolves*) ста́я; (*cards*) коло́да; *vt* (& *i*) упако́вывать(ся) *impf*, упакова́ть(ся) *pf*; (*cram*) набива́ть *impf*, наби́ть *pf*. **package** *n* посы́лка, паке́т; **~ holiday** организо́ванная тури́стическая пое́здка. **packaging** *n* упако́вка. **packet** *n* паке́т; па́чка; (*large sum of money*) ку́ча де́нег. **packing-case** *n* я́щик.
pact *n* пакт.
pad *n* (*cushion*) поду́шечка; (*shin ~ etc.*) щито́к; (*of paper*) блокно́т; *vt* подбива́ть *impf*, подби́ть *pf*. **padding** *n* наби́вка.
paddle[1] *n* (*oar*) весло́; *vi* (*row*) грести́ *impf*.
paddle[2] *vi* (*wade*) ходи́ть *indet*, идти́ *det*, пойти́ *pf* босико́м по воде́.
paddock *n* вы́гон.
padlock *n* вися́чий замо́к; *vt* запира́ть *impf*, запере́ть *pf* на вися́чий замо́к.
paediatric *adj* педиатри́ческий. **paediatrician** *n* педиа́тор.
pagan *n* язы́чник, -ица; *adj* язы́ческий. **paganism** *n* язы́чество.
page[1] *n* (*~-boy*) паж; *vt* (*summon*) вызыва́ть *impf*, вы́звать *pf*.
page[2] *n* (*of book*) страни́ца.
pageant *n* пы́шная проце́ссия. **pageantry** *n* пы́шность.
pail *n* ведро́.
pain *n* боль; *pl* (*efforts*) уси́лия *neut*

pl; **~-killer** болеутоля́ющее сре́дство; *vt* (*fig*) огорча́ть *impf*, огорчи́ть *pf*. **painful** *adj* боле́зненный; **be ~** (*part of body*) боле́ть *impf*. **painless** *adj* безболе́зненный. **painstaking** *adj* стара́тельный.
paint *n* кра́ска; *vt* кра́сить *impf*, по~ *pf*; (*portray*) писа́ть *impf*, на~ *pf* кра́сками. **paintbrush** *n* кисть. **painter** *n* (*artist*) худо́жник, -ица; (*decorator*) маля́р. **painting** *n* (*art*) жи́вопись; (*picture*) карти́на.
pair *n* па́ра; *often not translated with nn denoting a single object, e.g.* **a ~ of scissors** но́жницы (-ц) *pl*; **a ~ of trousers** па́ра брюк; *vt* спа́ривать *impf*, спа́рить *pf*; **~ off** разделя́ться *impf*, раздели́ться *pf* по па́рам.
Pakistan *n* Пакиста́н. **Pakistani** *n* пакиста́нец, -а́нка; *adj* пакиста́нский.
pal *n* прия́тель *m*, **~ница**.
palace *n* дворе́ц.
palatable *adj* вку́сный; (*fig*) прия́тный. **palate** *n* нёбо; (*fig*) вкус.
palatial *adj* великоле́пный.
palaver *n* (*trouble*) беспоко́йство; (*nonsense*) чепуха́.
pale[1] *n* (*stake*) кол; **beyond the ~** невообрази́мый.
pale[2] *adj* бле́дный; *vi* бледне́ть *impf*, по~ *pf*.
palette *n* пали́тра.
pall[1] *n* покро́в.
pall[2] *vi*: **~ on** надоеда́ть *impf*, надое́сть *pf* +*dat*.
palliative *adj* паллиати́вный; *n* паллиати́в.
pallid *adj* бле́дный. **pallor** *n* бле́дность.
palm[1] *n* (*tree*) па́льма; **P~ Sunday** Ве́рбное воскресе́нье.
palm[2] *n* (*of hand*) ладо́нь; *vt*: **~ off** всу́чивать *impf*, всучи́ть *pf* (**on** +*dat*).
palpable *adj* осяза́емый.
palpitations *n pl* сердцебие́ние.
paltry *adj* ничто́жный.
pamper *vt* балова́ть *impf*, из~ *pf*.
pamphlet *n* брошю́ра.
pan[1] *n* (*saucepan*) кастрю́ля; (*frying-~*) сковорода́; (*of scales*) ча́шка; *vt*: **~ out** промыва́ть *impf*, промы́ть *pf*; (*fig*) выходи́ть *impf*, вы́йти *pf*.
pan[2] *vi* (*cin*) панорами́ровать *impf* & *pf*.

panacea *n* панацéя.

panache *n* рисóвка.

pancake *n* блин.

pancreas *n* поджелýдочная железá.

panda *n* пáнда.

pandemonium *n* гвалт.

pander *vi*: ~ **to** потвóрствовать *impf* +*dat.*

pane *n* окóнное стеклó.

panel *n* панéль; (*control-*~) щит управлéния; (*of experts*) грýппа специалúстов; (*of judges*) жюри *neut indecl.* **panelling** *n* панéльная обшúвка.

pang *n pl* мýки (-к) *pl.*

panic *n* пáника; ~-**stricken** охвáченный пáникой; *vi* впадáть *impf,* впасть *pf* в пáнику. **panicky** *adj* панúческий.

pannier *n* корзúнка.

panorama *n* панорáма. **panoramic** *adj* панорáмный.

pansy *n* анютины глáзки (-зок) *pl.*

pant *vi* дышáть *impf* с одышкой.

panther *n* пантéра.

panties *n pl* трýсики (-ков) *pl.*

pantomime *n* рождéственское представлéние; (*dumb show*) пантомúма.

pantry *n* кладовáя *sb.*

pants *n pl* трусы (-сóв) *pl*; (*trousers*) брюки (-к) *pl.*

papal *adj* пáпский.

paper *n* бумáга; *pl* докумéнты *m pl*; (*newspaper*) газéта; (*wallpaper*) обóи (-óев) *pl*; (*treatise*) докла́д; *adj* бумáжный; *vt* оклéивать *impf,* оклéить *pf* обóями. **paperback** *n* кнúга в бумáжной облóжке. **paperclip** *n* скрéпка. **paperwork** *n* канцелярская рабóта.

par *n*: **feel below** ~ чýвствовать *impf* себя невáжно; **on a** ~ **with** наравнé с+*instr.*

parable *n* прúтча.

parabola *n* парáбола.

parachute *n* парашют; *vi* спускáться *impf,* спустúться *pf* с парашютом. **parachutist** *n* парашютúст.

parade *n* парáд; *vi* шествовать *impf*; *vt* (*show off*) выставля́ть *impf,* выставить *pf* напокáз.

paradigm *n* парадúгма.

paradise *n* рай.

paradox *n* парадóкс. **paradoxical** *adj*

парадоксáльный.

paraffin *n* (~ *oil*) керосúн.

paragon *n* образéц.

paragraph *n* абзáц.

parallel *adj* параллéльный; *n* параллéль; *vt* соотвéтствовать *impf* +*dat.*

paralyse *vt* парализовáть *impf & pf.* **paralysis** *n* паралúч.

parameter *n* парáметр.

paramilitary *adj* полувоéнный.

paramount *adj* первостепéнный.

paranoia *n* паранóйя. **paranoid** *adj*: **he is** ~ он паранóик.

parapet *n* (*mil*) брýствер.

paraphernalia *n* принадлéжности *f pl.*

paraphrase *n* перескáз; *vt* перескáзывать *impf,* пересказáть *pf.*

parasite *n* паразúт. **parasitic** *adj* паразитúческий.

parasol *n* зóнтик.

paratrooper *n* парашютúст-десáнтник.

parcel *n* пакéт, посылка.

parch *vt* иссушáть *impf,* иссушúть *pf*; **become** ~**ed** пересыхáть *impf,* пересóхнуть *pf.*

parchment *n* пергáмент.

pardon *n* прощéние; (*law*) помúлование; *vt* прощáть *impf,* простúть *pf*; (*law*) помúловать *pf.*

pare *vt* (*fruit*) чúстить *impf,* о~ *pf*; ~ **away, down** урéзывать *impf,* урéзать *pf.*

parent *n* родúтель *m,* ~ница. **parentage** *n* происхождéние. **parental** *adj* родúтельский.

parentheses *n pl* (*brackets*) скóбки *f pl.*

parish *n* прихóд. **parishioner** *n* прихожáнин, -áнка.

parity *n* рáвенство.

park *n* парк; (*for cars etc.*) стоя́нка; *vt & abs* стáвить *impf,* по~ *pf* (машúну). **parking** *n* стоя́нка.

parliament *n* парлáмент. **parliamentarian** *n* парламентáрий. **parliamentary** *adj* парлáментский.

parlour *n* гостúная *sb.*

parochial *adj* прихóдский; (*fig*) огранúченный. **parochialism** *n* огранúченность.

parody *n* парóдия; *vt* пародúровать *impf & pf.*

parole *n* чéстное слóво; **on** ~ освобождённый под чéстное слóво.

paroxysm n парокси́зм.

parquet n парке́т; *attrib* парке́тный.

parrot n попуга́й.

parry vt пари́ровать *impf & pf*, от~ *pf*.

parsimonious adj скупо́й.

parsley n петру́шка.

parsnip n пастерна́к.

parson n свяще́нник.

part n часть; (*in play*) роль; (*mus*) па́ртия; **for the most ~** бо́льшей ча́стью; **in ~** ча́стью; **for my ~** что каса́ется меня́; **take ~ in** уча́ствовать *impf* в+*prep*; **~-time** (за́нятый) непо́лный рабо́чий день; vt & i (*divide*) разделя́ть(ся) *impf*, раздели́ть(ся) *pf*; vi (*leave*) расстава́ться *impf*, расста́ться *pf* (**from, with** с+*instr*); **~ one's hair** де́лать *impf*, с~ *pf* себе́ пробо́р.

partake vi принима́ть *impf*, приня́ть *pf* уча́стие (**in, of** в+*prep*); (*eat*) есть *impf*, съ~ *pf* (**of** +*acc*).

partial adj части́чный; (*biased*) пристра́стный; **~ to** неравноду́шный к+*dat*. **partiality** n (*bias*) пристра́стность. **partially** adv части́чно.

participant n уча́стник, -ица (**in** +*gen*). **participate** vi уча́ствовать *impf* (**in** в+*prep*). **participation** n уча́стие.

participle n прича́стие.

particle n части́ца.

particular adj осо́бый, осо́бенный; (*fussy*) разбо́рчивый; n подро́бность; **in ~** в ча́стности.

parting n (*leave-taking*) проща́ние; (*of hair*) пробо́р.

partisan n (*adherent*) сторо́нник; (*mil*) партиза́н; *attrib* (*biased*) пристра́стный; партиза́нский.

partition n (*wall*) перегоро́дка; (*polit*) разде́л; vt разделя́ть *impf*, раздели́ть *pf*; **~ off** отгора́живать *impf*, отгороди́ть *pf*.

partly adv части́чно.

partner n (*in business*) компаньо́н; (*in dance, game*) партнёр, ~ша.

partnership n това́рищество.

partridge n куропа́тка.

party n (*polit*) па́ртия; (*group*) гру́ппа; (*social gathering*) вечери́нка; (*law*) сторона́; **be a ~ to** принима́ть *impf*, приня́ть *pf* уча́стие в+*prep*; *attrib* парти́йный; **~ line** (*polit*)

ли́ния па́ртии; (*telephone*) о́бщий телефо́нный про́вод; **~ wall** о́бщая стена́.

pass vt & i (*go past*; *of time*) проходи́ть *impf*, пройти́ *pf* (**by** ми́мо +*gen*); (*travel past*) проезжа́ть *impf*, прое́хать *pf* (**by** ми́мо+*gen*); (**~** *examination*) сдава́ть *impf*, сдать *pf* (экза́мен); vt (*sport*) пасова́ть *impf*, пасну́ть *pf*; (*overtake*) обгоня́ть *impf*, обогна́ть *pf*; (*time*) проводи́ть *impf*, провести́ *pf*; (*hand on*) передава́ть *impf*, переда́ть *pf*; (*law, resolution*) утвержда́ть *impf*, утверди́ть *pf*; (*sentence*) выноси́ть *impf*, вы́нести *pf* (**upon** +*dat*); **~ as, for** слыть *impf*, про~ *pf* +*instr*, за+*acc*; **~ away** (*die*) скончáться *pf*; **~ o.s. off as** выдава́ть *impf*, вы́дать *pf* себя́ за+*acc*; **~ out** теря́ть *impf*, по~ *pf* созна́ние; **~ over** (*in silence*) обходи́ть *impf*, обойти́ *pf* молча́нием; **~ round** передава́ть *impf*, переда́ть *pf*; **~ up** подава́ть *impf*, пода́ть *pf*; (*miss*) пропуска́ть *impf*, пропусти́ть *pf*, n (*permit*) про́пуск; (*sport*) пас; (*geog*) перева́л; **come to ~** случа́ться *impf*, случи́ться *pf*; **make a ~ at** пристава́ть *impf*, приста́ть *pf* к+*dat*.

passable adj проходи́мый, прое́зжий; (*not bad*) неплохо́й.

passage n прохо́д; (*of time*) тече́ние; (*sea trip*) рейс; (*in house*) коридо́р; (*in book*) отры́вок; (*mus*) пасса́ж.

passenger n пассажи́р.

passer-by n прохо́жий *sb*.

passing adj (*transient*) мимолётный; n: **in ~** мимохо́дом.

passion n страсть (**for** к+*dat*). **passionate** adj стра́стный.

passive adj пасси́вный; (*gram*) страда́тельный; n страда́тельный зало́г. **passivity** n пасси́вность.

Passover n евре́йская Па́сха.

passport n па́спорт.

password n паро́ль *m*.

past adj про́шлый; (*gram*) проше́дший; n про́шлое *sb*; (*gram*) проше́дшее вре́мя *neut*; *prep* ми́мо +*gen*; (*beyond*) за+*instr*; *adv* ми́мо.

pasta n макаро́нные изде́лия *neut pl*.

paste n (*of flour*) те́сто; (*creamy mixture*) па́ста; (*glue*) клей; (*jewellery*) страз; *vt* накле́ивать *impf*, накле́ить *pf*.

pastel *n* (*crayon*) пасте́ль; (*drawing*) рису́нок пасте́лью; *attrib* пасте́льный.

pasteurize *vt* пастеризова́ть *impf* & *pf*.

pastime *n* времяпрепровожде́ние.

pastor *n* па́стор. **pastoral** *adj* (*bucolic*) пастора́льный; (*of pastor*) па́сторский.

pastry *n* (*dough*) те́сто; (*cake*) пиро́жное *sb*.

pasture *n* (*land*) па́стбище.

pasty[1] *n* пирожо́к.

pasty[2] *adj* (~-*faced*) бле́дный.

pat *n* шлепо́к; (*of butter etc.*) кусо́к; *vt* хлопа́ть *impf*, по~ *pf*.

patch *n* запла́та; (*over eye*) повя́зка (на глазу́); (*spot*) пятно́; (*of land*) уча́сток земли́; *vt* ста́вить *impf*, по~ *pf* запла́ту на+*acc*; ~ **up** (*fig*) ула́живать *impf*, ула́дить *pf*. **patchwork** *n* лоску́тная рабо́та; *attrib* лоску́тный. **patchy** *adj* неро́вный.

pâté *n* паште́т.

patent *adj* я́вный; ~ **leather** лакиро́ванная ко́жа; *n* пате́нт; *vt* патентова́ть *impf*, за~ *pf*.

paternal *adj* отцо́вский. **paternity** *n* отцо́вство.

path *n* тропи́нка, тропа́; (*way*) путь *m*.

pathetic *adj* жа́лкий.

pathological *adj* патологи́ческий. **pathologist** *n* пато́лог.

pathos *n* па́фос.

pathway *n* тропи́нка, тропа́.

patience *n* терпе́ние; (*cards*) пасья́нс. **patient** *adj* терпели́вый; *n* больно́й *sb*, пацие́нт, ~ка.

patio *n* терра́са.

patriarch *n* патриа́рх. **patriarchal** *adj* патриарха́льный.

patriot *n* патрио́т, ~ка. **patriotic** *adj* патриоти́ческий. **patriotism** *n* патриоти́зм.

patrol *n* патру́ль *m*; **on** ~ на дозо́ре; *vt* & *i* патрули́ровать *impf*.

patron *n* покрови́тель *m*; (*of shop*) клие́нт. **patronage** *n* покрови́тельство. **patroness** *n* покрови́тельница. **patronize** *vt* (*treat condescendingly*) снисходи́тельно относи́ться *impf*, к+*dat*. **patronizing** *adj* покро-

ви́тельственный.

patronymic *n* о́тчество.

patter[1] *vi* (*sound*) бараба́нить *impf*; *n* постуки́вание.

patter[2] *n* (*speech*) скорогово́рка.

pattern *n* (*design*) узо́р; (*model*) образе́ц; (*sewing*) вы́кройка.

paunch *n* брюшко́.

pauper *n* бедня́к.

pause *n* па́уза, переры́в; (*mus*) ферма́та; *vi* остана́вливаться *impf*, останови́ться *pf*.

pave *vt* мости́ть *impf*, вы́~ *pf*; ~ **the way** подготовля́ть *impf*, подгото́вить *pf* по́чву (**for** для+*gen*). **pavement** *n* тротуа́р.

pavilion *n* павильо́н.

paw *n* ла́па; *vt* тро́гать *impf* ла́пой; (*horse*) бить *impf* копы́том.

pawn[1] *n* (*chess*) пе́шка.

pawn[2] *n*: **in** ~ в закла́де; *vt* закла́дывать *impf*, заложи́ть *pf*. **pawnbroker** *n* ростовщи́к. **pawnshop** *n* ломба́рд.

pay *vt* плати́ть *impf*, за~, у~ *pf* (**for** за+*acc*); (*bill etc.*) опла́чивать *impf*, оплати́ть *pf*; *vi* (*be profitable*) окупа́ться *impf*, окупи́ться *pf*; *n* жа́лованье, зарпла́та; ~ **packet** полу́чка; ~-**roll** платёжная ве́домость. **payable** *adj* подлежа́щий упла́те. **payee** *n* получа́тель *m*. **payload** *n* поле́зная нагру́зка. **payment** *n* упла́та, платёж.

pea *n* (*also pl, collect*) горо́х.

peace *n* мир; **in** ~ в поко́е; ~ **and quiet** мир и тишина́. **peaceable**, **peaceful** *adj* ми́рный.

peach *n* пе́рсик.

peacock *n* павли́н.

peak *n* (*of cap*) козырёк; (*summit*, *fig*) верши́на; ~ **hour** часы́ *m pl* пик.

peal *n* (*sound*) звон, трезво́н; (*of laughter*) взрыв.

peanut *n* ара́хис.

pear *n* гру́ша.

pearl *n* (*also fig*) жемчу́жина; *pl* (*collect*) же́мчуг.

peasant *n* крестья́нин, -я́нка; *attrib* крестья́нский.

peat *n* торф.

pebble *n* га́лька.

peck *vt* & *i* клева́ть *impf*, клю́нуть *pf*; *n* клево́к.

pectoral *adj* грудно́й.

peculiar adj (distinctive) своеобра́зный; (strange) стра́нный; ~ **to** сво́йственный +dat. **peculiarity** n осо́бенность; стра́нность.

pecuniary adj де́нежный.

pedagogical adj педагоги́ческий.

pedal n педа́ль; vi нажима́ть impf, нажа́ть pf педа́ль; (ride bicycle) е́хать impf, по~ pf на велосипе́де.

pedant n педа́нт. **pedantic** adj педанти́чный.

peddle vt торгова́ть impf вразно́с +instr.

pedestal n пьедеста́л.

pedestrian adj пешехо́дный; (prosaic) прозаи́ческий; n пешехо́д; ~ **crossing** перехо́д.

pedigree n родосло́вная sb; adj поро́дистый.

pedlar n разно́счик.

pee n пи-пи́ neut indecl; vi мочи́ться impf, по~ pf.

peek vi (~ **in**) загля́дывать impf, загляну́ть pf; (~ **out**) выгля́дывать impf, вы́глянуть pf.

peel n кожура́; vt очища́ть impf, очи́стить pf; vi (skin) шелуши́ться impf; (paint, ~ **off**) сходи́ть impf, сойти́ pf. **peelings** n pl очи́стки (-ков) pl.

peep vi (~ **in**) загля́дывать impf, загляну́ть pf; (~ **out**) выгля́дывать impf, вы́глянуть pf; n (glance) бы́стрый взгляд; ~**hole** глазо́к.

peer[1] vi всма́триваться impf, всмотре́ться pf (**at** в+acc).

peer[2] n (noble) пэр; (person one's age) све́рстник.

peeved adj раздражённый. **peevish** adj раздражи́тельный.

peg n ко́лышек; (clothes ~) крючо́к; (for hat etc.) ве́шалка; **off the** ~ гото́вый; vt прикрепля́ть impf, прикрепи́ть pf ко́лышком, -ками.

pejorative adj уничижи́тельный.

pelican n пелика́н.

pellet n ша́рик; (shot) дроби́на.

pelt[1] n (skin) шку́ра.

pelt[2] vt забра́сывать impf, заброса́ть pf; vi (rain) бараба́нить impf.

pelvis n таз.

pen[1] n (for writing) ру́чка; ~**friend** друг по перепи́ске.

pen[2] n (enclosure) заго́н.

penal adj уголо́вный. **penalize** vt

штрафова́ть impf, о~ pf. **penalty** n наказа́ние; (sport) штраф; ~ **area** штрафна́я площа́дка; ~ **kick** штрафно́й уда́р. **penance** n епитимья́.

penchant n скло́нность (**for** к+dat).

pencil n каранда́ш; ~**sharpener** точи́лка.

pendant n подве́ска.

pending adj (awaiting decision) ожида́ющий реше́ния; prep (until) в ожида́нии +gen, до+gen.

pendulum n ма́ятник.

penetrate vt проника́ть impf, прони́кнуть pf в+acc. **penetrating** adj проница́тельный; (sound) пронзи́тельный. **penetration** n проникнове́ние; (insight) проница́тельность.

penguin n пингви́н.

penicillin n пеницилли́н.

peninsula n полуо́стров.

penis n пе́нис.

penitence n раска́яние. **penitent** adj раска́ивающийся; n ка́ющийся гре́шник.

penknife n перочи́нный нож.

pennant n вы́мпел.

penniless adj без гроша́.

penny n пе́нни neut indecl, пенс.

pension n пе́нсия; vt: ~ **off** увольня́ть impf, уво́лить pf на пе́нсию. **pensionable** adj (age) пенсио́нный. **pensioner** n пенсионе́р, ~ка.

pensive adj заду́мчивый.

pentagon n пятиуго́льник; **the P~** Пентаго́н.

Pentecost n Пятидеся́тница.

penthouse n шика́рная кварти́ра на ве́рхнем этаже́.

pent-up adj (anger etc.) сде́рживаемый.

penultimate adj предпосле́дний.

penury n нужда́.

peony n пио́н.

people n pl (persons) лю́ди pl; sg (nation) наро́д; vt населя́ть impf, насели́ть pf.

pepper n пе́рец; vt пе́рчить impf, на~, по~ pf. **peppercorn** n перчи́нка.

peppermint n пе́речная мя́та; (sweet) мя́тная конфе́та.

per prep (for each) (person) на+acc; **as** ~ согла́сно+dat; ~ **annum** в год; ~ **capita** на челове́ка; ~ **hour** в час; ~ **se** сам по себе́.

perceive vt воспринима́ть impf, восприня́ть pf.

per cent adv & n проце́нт. **percentage** n проце́нт; (part) часть.

perceptible adj заме́тный. **perception** n восприя́тие; (quality) понима́ние. **perceptive** adj то́нкий.

perch¹ n (fish) о́кунь m.

perch² n (roost) насе́ст; vi сади́ться impf, сесть pf. **perched** adj высоко́ сидя́щий, располо́женный.

percussion n (~ instruments) уда́рные инструме́нты m pl.

peremptory adj повели́тельный.

perennial adj (enduring) ве́чный; n (bot) многоле́тнее расте́ние.

perestroika n перестро́йка.

perfect adj соверше́нный; (gram) перфе́ктный; n перфе́кт; vt соверше́нствовать impf, y~ pf. **perfection** n соверше́нство. **perfective** adj (n) соверше́нный (вид).

perforate vt перфори́ровать impf & pf. **perforation** n перфора́ция.

perform vt (carry out) исполня́ть impf, испо́лнить pf; (theat, mus) игра́ть impf, сыгра́ть pf; vi выступа́ть impf, вы́ступить pf; (function) рабо́тать impf. **performance** n исполне́ние; (of person, device) де́йствие; (of play etc.) представле́ние, спекта́кль m; (of engine etc.) эксплуатацио́нные ка́чества neut pl. **performer** n исполни́тель m.

perfume n духи́ (-хо́в) pl; (smell) арома́т.

perfunctory adj пове́рхностный.

perhaps adv мо́жет быть.

peril n опа́сность, риск. **perilous** adj опа́сный, риско́ванный.

perimeter n вне́шняя грани́ца; (geom) пери́метр.

period n пери́од; (epoch) эпо́ха. **periodic** adj периоди́ческий. **periodical** adj периоди́ческий; n периоди́ческое изда́ние.

peripheral adj перифери́йный. **periphery** n перифери́я.

periscope n периско́п.

perish vi погиба́ть impf, поги́бнуть pf; (spoil) по́ртиться impf, ис~ pf. **perishable** adj скоропо́ртящийся.

perjure v: ~ o.s. наруша́ть impf, нару́шить pf кля́тву. **perjury** n лжесвиде́тельство.

perk¹ n льго́та.

perk² vi: ~ up оживля́ться impf, оживи́ться pf. **perky** adj бо́йкий.

perm n пермане́нт. **permanence** n постоя́нство. **permanent** adj постоя́нный.

permeable adj проница́емый. **permeate** vt проника́ть impf, прони́кнуть pf в+acc.

permissible adj допусти́мый. **permission** n разреше́ние. **permissive** adj (сли́шком) либера́льный; ~ society о́бщество вседозво́ленности. **permissiveness** n вседозво́ленность. **permit** vt разреша́ть impf, разреши́ть pf +dat; n про́пуск.

permutation n перестано́вка.

pernicious adj па́губный.

perpendicular adj перпендикуля́рный; n перпендикуля́р.

perpetrate vt соверша́ть impf, соверши́ть pf. **perpetrator** n винова́тый.

perpetual adj ве́чный. **perpetuate** vt увекове́чивать impf, увекове́чить pf. **perpetuity** n ве́чность; in ~ навсегда́, наве́чно.

perplex vt озада́чивать impf, озада́чить pf. **perplexity** n озада́ченность.

persecute vt пресле́довать impf. **persecution** n пресле́дование.

perseverance n насто́йчивость. **persevere** vi насто́йчиво, продолжа́ть impf (in, at etc. +acc, inf).

Persian n перс, ~ия́нка; adj перси́дский.

persist vi упо́рствовать impf (in в+prep); насто́йчиво продолжа́ть impf (in +acc, inf). **persistence** n упо́рство. **persistent** adj упо́рный.

person n челове́к; (in play; gram) лицо́; in ~ ли́чно. **personable** adj привлека́тельный. **personage** n ли́чность. **personal** adj ли́чный. **personality** n ли́чность. **personally** adv ли́чно. **personification** n олицетворе́ние. **personify** vt олицетворя́ть impf, олицетвори́ть pf.

personnel n ка́дры (-ров) pl, персона́л; ~ department отде́л ка́дров.

perspective n перспекти́ва.

perspiration n пот. **perspire** vi поте́ть impf, вс~ pf.

persuade vt (convince) убежда́ть impf, убеди́ть pf (of в+prep); (induce) угова́ривать *impf*, уговори́ть *pf*. **persuasion** *n* убежде́ние. **persuasive** *adj* убеди́тельный.

pertain *vi*: ~ to (*relate*) относи́ться *impf* отнести́сь *pf* к+*dat*.

pertinent *adj* уме́стный.

perturb *vt* трево́жить *impf*, вс~ *pf*.

peruse *vt* (*read*) внима́тельно чита́ть *impf*, про~ *pf*; (*fig*) рассма́тривать *impf*, рассмотре́ть *pf*.

pervade *vt* наполня́ть *impf*. **pervasive** *adj* распространённый.

perverse *adj* капри́зный. **perversion** *n* извраще́ние. **pervert** *vt* извраща́ть *impf*, изврати́ть *pf*; *n* извращённый челове́к.

pessimism *n* пессими́зм. **pessimist** *n* пессими́ст. **pessimistic** *adj* пессимисти́ческий.

pest *n* вреди́тель *m*; (*fig*) зану́да. **pester** *vt* пристава́ть *impf*, приста́ть *pf* к+*dat*. **pesticide** *n* пестици́д.

pet *n* (*animal*) дома́шнее живо́тное *sb*; (*favourite*) люби́мец, -мица; ~ **shop** зоомагази́н; *vt* ласка́ть *impf*.

petal *n* лепесто́к.

peter *vi*: ~ out (*road*) исчеза́ть *impf*, исче́знуть *pf*; (*stream*; *enthusiasm*) иссяка́ть *impf*, исся́кнуть *pf*.

petite *adj* ма́ленькая.

petition *n* пети́ция; *vt* подава́ть *impf*, пода́ть *pf* проше́ние +*dat*. **petitioner** *n* проси́тель *m*.

petrified *adj* окамене́лый; be ~ (*fig*) оцепене́ть *pf* (with от+*gen*).

petrol *n* бензи́н; ~ **pump** бензоколо́нка; ~ **station** бензозапра́вочная ста́нция; ~ **tank** бензоба́к. **petroleum** *n* нефть.

petticoat *n* ни́жняя ю́бка.

petty *adj* ме́лкий; ~ **cash** де́ньги (де́нег, -ньга́м) *pl* на ме́лкие расхо́ды.

petulant *adj* раздражи́тельный.

pew *n* (церко́вная) скамья́.

phallic *adj* фалли́ческий. **phallus** *n* фа́ллос.

phantom *n* фанто́м.

pharmaceutical *adj* фармацевти́ческий. **pharmacist** *n* фармаце́вт. **pharmacy** *n* фарма́ция; (*shop*) апте́ка.

phase *n* фа́за; *vt*: ~ in, out посте́пенно вводи́ть *impf*, упраздня́ть *impf*.

Ph.D. *abbr* (*of* **Doctor of Philosophy**)

кандида́т нау́к.

pheasant *n* фаза́н.

phenomenal *adj* феномена́льный. **phenomenon** *n* фено́мен.

phial *n* пузырёк.

philanderer *n* волоки́та *m*.

philanthropic *adj* филантропи́ческий. **philanthropist** *n* филантро́п. **philanthropy** *n* филантро́пия.

philately *n* филатели́я.

philharmonic *adj* филармони́ческий. **Philistine** *n* (*fig*) фили́стер.

philosopher *n* фило́соф. **philosophical** *adj* филосо́фский. **philosophize** *vi* филосо́фствовать *impf*. **philosophy** *n* филосо́фия.

phlegm *n* мокрота́. **phlegmatic** *adj* флегмати́ческий.

phobia *n* фо́бия.

phone *n* телефо́н; *vt* & *i* звони́ть *impf*, по~ *pf* +*dat*. See also **telephone**

phonetic *adj* фонети́ческий. **phonetics** *n* фоне́тика.

phoney *n* подде́льный.

phosphorus *n* фо́сфор.

photo *n* фо́то *neut indecl*. **photocopier** *n* копирова́льная маши́на. **photocopy** *n* фотоко́пия; *vt* де́лать *impf*, с~ *pf* фотоко́пию +*gen*. **photogenic** *adj* фотогени́чный. **photograph** *n* фотогра́фия; *vt* фотографи́ровать *impf*, с~ *pf*. **photographer** *n* фото́граф. **photographic** *adj* фотографи́ческий. **photography** *n* фотогра́фия.

phrase *n* фра́за; *vt* формули́ровать *impf*, с~ *pf*.

physical *adj* физи́ческий; ~ **education** физкульту́ра; ~ **exercises** заря́дка. **physician** *n* врач. **physicist** *n* фи́зик. **physics** *n* фи́зика.

physiological *n* физиологи́ческий. **physiologist** *n* физио́лог. **physiology** *n* физиоло́гия. **physiotherapist** *n* физиотерапе́вт. **physiotherapy** *n* физиотерапи́я.

physique *n* телосложе́ние.

pianist *n* пиани́ст, ~ка. **piano** *n* фортепья́но *neut indecl*; (*grand*) роя́ль *m*; (*upright*) пиани́но *neut indecl*.

pick[1] *vt* (*flower*) срыва́ть *impf*, сорва́ть *pf*; (*gather*) собира́ть *impf*, собра́ть *pf*; (*select*) выбира́ть *impf*, вы́брать *pf*; ~ one's nose, teeth ковыря́ть *impf*, ковырну́ть *pf* в носу́, в зуба́х; ~ **a quarrel** иска́ть *impf* ссо́ры (**with** c+*instr*); ~ **one's way** выбира́ть *impf*, вы́брать *pf* доро́гу; ~ **on** (*nag*) придира́ться *impf* к+*dat*; ~ **out** отбира́ть *impf*, отобра́ть *pf*; ~ **up** (*lift*) поднима́ть *impf*, подня́ть *pf*; (*acquire*) приобрета́ть *impf*, приобрести́ *pf*; (*fetch*) (*on foot*) заходи́ть *impf*, зайти́ *pf* за+*instr*; (*in vehicle*) заезжа́ть *impf*, заёхать *pf* за+*instr*; (*a cold; a girl*) подцепля́ть *impf*, подцепи́ть *pf*; ~ **o.s. up** поднима́ться *impf*, подня́ться *pf*; ~**up** (*truck*) пика́п; (*electron*) звукоснима́тель *m*.

pick² *n* вы́бор; (*best part*) лу́чшая часть; **take your** ~ выбира́й(те)!

pick³, **pickaxe** *n* кирка́.

picket *n* (*person*) пике́тчик, -и́ца; (*collect*) пике́т; *vt* пикети́ровать *impf*.

pickle *n* соле́нье; *vt* соли́ть *impf*, по~ *pf*. **pickled** *adj* солёный.

pickpocket *n* карма́нник.

picnic *n* пикни́к.

pictorial *adj* изобрази́тельный; (*illustrated*) иллюстри́рованный. **picture** *n* карти́на; (*of health etc.*) воплоще́ние; (*film*) фильм; **the** ~**s** кино́ *neut indecl*; (*to o.s.*) предста́вля́ть *impf*, предста́вить *pf* себе́. **picturesque** *adj* живопи́сный.

pie *n* пиро́г.

piece *n* кусо́к, часть; (*one of set*) шту́ка; (*of paper*) листо́к; (*mus, literature*) произведе́ние; (*chess*) фигу́ра; (*coin*) моне́та; **take to** ~**s** разбира́ть *impf*, разобра́ть *pf* (на ча́сти); ~ **of advice** сове́т; ~ **of information** све́дение; ~ **of news** но́вость; ~**work** сде́льщина; ~**worker** сде́льщик; *vt*: ~ **together** воссоздава́ть *impf*, воссозда́ть *pf* карти́ну +*gen*. **piecemeal** *adv* по частя́м.

pier *n* (*mole*) мол; (*projecting into sea*) пирс; (*of bridge*) бык; (*between windows etc.*) просте́нок.

pierce *vt* пронза́ть *impf*, пронзи́ть *pf*; (*ears*) прока́лывать *impf*, проколо́ть *pf*. **piercing** *adj* пронзи́тельный.

piety *n* на́божность.

pig *n* свинья́. **pigheaded** *adj* упря́мый. **piglet** *n* поросёнок. **pigsty** *n* свина́рник. **pigtail** *n* коси́чка.

pigeon *n* го́лубь; ~**hole** отделе́ние для бума́г.

pigment *n* пигме́нт. **pigmentation** *n* пигмента́ция.

pike *n* (*fish*) щу́ка.

pilchard *n* сарди́н(к)а.

pile¹ *n* (*heap*) ку́ча, ки́па; *vt*: ~ **up** сва́ливать *impf*, свали́ть *pf* в ку́чу; (*load*) нагружа́ть *impf*, нагрузи́ть *pf* (**with** +*instr*); *vi*: ~ **in(to), on** забира́ться *impf*, забра́ться *pf* в+*acc*; ~ **up** накопля́ться, нака́пливаться *impf*, накопи́ться *pf*.

pile² *n* (*on cloth etc.*) ворс.

piles *n pl* геморро́й *collect*.

pilfer *vt* ворова́ть *impf*.

pilgrim *n* пилигри́м. **pilgrimage** *n* пало́мничество.

pill *n* пилю́ля; **the** ~ противозача́точная пилю́ля.

pillage *vt* гра́бить *impf*, о~ *pf*; *v abs* мародёрствовать *impf*.

pillar *n* столб; ~**box** стоя́чий почто́вый я́щик.

pillion *n* за́днее сиде́нье (мотоци́кла).

pillory *n* позо́рный столб; *vt* (*fig*) пригвожда́ть *impf*, пригвозди́ть *pf* к позо́рному столбу́.

pillow *n* поду́шка. **pillowcase** *n* на́волочка.

pilot *n* (*naut*) ло́цман; (*aeron*) пило́т; *adj* о́пытный, про́бный; *vt* пилоти́ровать *impf*.

pimp *n* сво́дник.

pimple *n* прыщ.

pin *n* була́вка; (*peg*) па́лец; ~**point** то́чно определя́ть *impf*, определи́ть *pf*; ~**stripe** то́нкая полоска; прика́лывать *impf*, приколо́ть *pf*; (*press*) прижима́ть *impf*, прижа́ть *pf* (**against** к+*dat*).

pinafore *n* пере́дник.

pincers *n pl* (*tool*) кле́щи (-ще́й) *pl*, пинце́т; (*claw*) клешни́ *f pl*.

pinch *vt* щипа́ть *impf*, (у)щипну́ть *pf*; (*finger in door etc.*) прищемля́ть *impf*, прищеми́ть *pf*; (*of shoe*) жать *impf*; (*steal*) стяну́ть *pf*; *n* щипо́к; (*of salt*) щепо́тка; **at a** ~ в кра́йнем слу́чае.

pine¹ *vi* томи́ться *impf*; ~ **for** тоскова́ть *impf* по+*dat*, *prep*.

pine² *n* (*tree*) сосна́.

pineapple *n* анана́с.

ping-pong *n* пинг-по́нг.

pink *n* (*colour*) ро́зовый цвет; *adj* ро́зовый.

pinnacle *n* верши́на.

pint *n* пи́нта.

pioneer *n* пионе́р, ~ка; *vt* прокла́-дывать *impf*, проложи́ть *pf* путь к+*dat*.

pious *adj* на́божный.

pip¹ *n* (*seed*) зёрнышко.

pip² *n* (*sound*) бип.

pipe *n* труба́; (*mus*) ду́дка; (*for smoking*) тру́бка; ~-dream пуста́я мечта́; *vt* пуска́ть *impf*, пусти́ть *pf* по труба́м; *vi* ~ down затиха́ть *impf*, зати́хнуть *pf*. **pipeline** *n* трубопро-во́д; (*oil* ~) нефтепрово́д. **piper** *n* волы́нщик. **piping** *adj*: ~ hot с пы́лу.

piquant *adj* пика́нтный.

pique *n*: in a fit of ~ в поры́ве раз-дражéния.

pirate *n* пира́т.

pirouette *n* пируэ́т; *vi* де́лать *impf*, с~ *pf* пируэ́т(ы).

Pisces *n* Ры́бы *f pl*.

pistol *n* пистоле́т.

piston *n* по́ршень *m*.

pit *n* я́ма; (*mine*) ша́хта; (*orchestra* ~) орке́стр; (*motor-racing*) запра́вочно-ремо́нтный пункт; *vt*: ~ against вы-ставля́ть *impf*, вы́ставить *pf* про́тив +*gen*.

pitch¹ *n* (*resin*) смола́; ~-black чёр-ный как смоль; ~-dark о́чень тём-ный.

pitch² *vt* (*camp, tent*) разбива́ть *impf*, разби́ть *pf*; (*throw*) броса́ть *impf*, бро́сить *pf*; *vi* (*fall*) па́дать *impf*, (у)па́сть *pf*; (*ship*) кача́ть *impf*, *n* (*football* ~ *etc.*) площа́дка; (*degree*) у́ровень *m*; (*mus*) высота́; (*slope*) укло́н.

pitcher *n* (*vessel*) кувши́н.

pitchfork *n* ви́лы (-л) *pl*.

piteous *adj* жа́лкий.

pitfall *n* запа́дня.

pith *n* сердцеви́на; (*essence*) суть. **pithy** *adj* (*fig*) содержа́тельный.

pitiful *adj* жа́лкий. **pitiless** *adj* без-жа́лостный.

pittance *n* жа́лкие гроши́ (-ше́й) *pl*.

pity *n* жа́лость; it's a ~ жа́лко, жаль; take ~ on сжа́литься *pf* над+*instr*; what a ~ как жа́лко!; *vt* жале́ть *impf*, по~ *pf*; I ~ you мне жаль тебя́.

pivot *n* сте́ржень *m*; (*fig*) центр; *vi* враща́ться *impf*.

pixie *n* эльф.

pizza *n* пи́цца.

placard *n* афи́ша, плака́т.

placate *vt* умиротворя́ть *impf*, уми-ротвори́ть *pf*.

place *n* ме́сто; in ~ of вме́сто+*gen*; in the first, second, ~ во-пе́рвых, во-вторы́х; out of ~ не на ме́сте; (*unsuitable*) неуме́стный; take ~ случа́ться *impf*, случи́ться *pf*; (*pre-arranged event*) состоя́ться *pf*; take the ~ of заменя́ть *impf*, замени́ть *pf*; *vt* (*stand*) ста́вить *impf*, по~ *pf*; (*lay*) класть *impf*, положи́ть *pf*; (*an order etc.*) помеща́ть *impf*, поме-сти́ть *pf*.

placenta *n* плаце́нта.

placid *adj* споко́йный.

plagiarism *n* плагиа́т. **plagiarize** *vt* заи́мствовать *impf* & *pf*.

plague *n* чума́; *vt* му́чить *impf*, за~, из~ *pf*.

plaice *n* ка́мбала.

plain *n* равни́на; *adj* (*clear*) я́сный; (*simple*) просто́й; (*ugly*) некраси́-вый; ~-clothes policeman переоде́-тый полице́йский *sb*.

plaintiff *n* исте́ц, исти́ца.

plaintive *adj* жа́лобный.

plait *n* коса́; *vt* плести́ *impf*, с~ *pf*.

plan *n* план; *vt* плани́ровать *impf*, за~, с~ *pf*; (*intend*) намерева́ться *impf* +*inf*.

plane¹ *n* (*tree*) плата́н.

plane² *n* (*tool*) руба́нок; *vt* строга́ть *impf*, вы́~ *pf*.

plane³ *n* (*surface*) пло́скость; (*level*) у́ровень *m*; (*aeroplane*) самолёт.

planet *n* плане́та.

plank *n* доска́.

plant *n* расте́ние; (*factory*) заво́д; *vt* сажа́ть *impf*, посади́ть *pf*; (*fix firmly*) про́чно ста́вить *impf*, по~ *pf*; (*garden etc.*) заса́живать *impf*, засади́ть *pf* (with +*instr*).

plantation *n* (*of trees*) (лесо)насаж-де́ние; (*of cotton etc.*) планта́ция.

plaque *n* доще́чка.

plasma *n* пла́зма.

plaster *n* пла́стырь *m*; (*for walls etc.*) штукату́рка; (*of Paris*) гипс; *vt* (*wall*) штукату́рить *impf*, от~, о~ *pf*; (*cover*) облепля́ть *impf*, облепи́ть *pf.* **plasterboard** *n* сухáя штукатýрка. **plasterer** *n* штукатýр.

plastic *n* пластмáсса; *adj* (*malleable*) пласти́чный; (*made of* ~) пластмáссовый; ~ **surgery** пласти́ческая хирурги́я.

plate *n* тарéлка; (*metal sheet*) лист; (*in book*) (вкладнáя) иллюстрáция; (*name* ~ *etc.*) дощéчка.

plateau *n* платó *neut indecl.*

platform *n* платфóрма; (*rly*) перрóн.

platinum *n* плáтина.

platitude *n* банáльность.

platoon *n* взвод.

plausible *adj* правдоподóбный.

play *vt & i* игрáть *impf*, сыгрáть *pf* (*game*) в+*acc*, (*instrument*) на+*prep*, (*record*) стáвить *impf*, по~ *pf*; ~ **down** преуменьшáть *impf*, преумéньшить *pf*; ~ **a joke, trick, on** подшýчивать *impf*, подшути́ть *pf* над +*instr*; ~ **off** игрáть *impf*, сыгрáть *pf* реша́ющую пáртию; ~**off** реша́ющая встрéча; ~ **safe** дéйствовать *impf* навернякá; *n* игрá; (*theat*) пьéса. **player** *n* игрóк; (*actor*) актёр, актри́са; (*musician*) музыкáнт. **playful** *adj* игри́вый. **playground** *n* площáдка для игр. **playgroup, playschool** *n* дéтский сад. **playing** *n*: ~**-card** игрáльная кáрта; ~**-field** игровáя площáдка. **playmate** *n* друг дéтства. **plaything** *n* игрýшка. **playwright** *n* драматýрг.

plea *n* (*entreaty*) мольбá; (*law*) заявлéние. **plead** *vi* умоля́ть *impf* (**with** +*acc*; **for** o+*prep*); *vt* (*offer as excuse*) ссылáться *impf*, сослáться *pf* на+*acc*; ~ (**not**) **guilty** (не) признавáть *impf*, признáть *pf* себя́ вино́вным.

pleasant *adj* прия́тный. **pleasantry** *n* любéзность. **please** *vt* нрáвиться *impf*, по~ *pf* +*dat*; *imper* пожáлуйста; бýдьте добры́. **pleased** *adj* довóльный; *predic* рад. **pleasing, pleasurable** *adj* прия́тный. **pleasure** *n* удовóльствие.

pleat *n* склáдка; *vt* плиссировáть *impf*.

plebiscite *n* плебисци́т.

plectrum *n* плéктр.

pledge *n* (*security*) залóг; (*promise*) зарóк, обещáние; *vt* отдавáть *impf*, отдáть *pf* в залóг; ~ **o.s.** обя́зываться *impf*, обязáться *pf*; ~ **one's**

word давáть *impf*, дать *pf* слóво.

plentiful *adj* оби́льный. **plenty** *n* изоби́лие; ~ **of** мнóго+*gen*.

plethora *n* (*fig*) изоби́лие.

pleurisy *n* плеври́т.

pliable *adj* ги́бкий.

pliers *n pl* плоскогýбцы (-цев) *pl*.

plight *n* незави́дное положéние.

plimsolls *n pl* спорти́вные тáпочки *f pl.*

plinth *n* пли́нтус.

plod *vi* тащи́ться *impf*.

plonk *vt* плю́хнуть *pf*.

plot *n* (*of land*) учáсток; (*of book etc.*) фáбула; (*conspiracy*) зáговор; *vt* (*on graph, map, etc.*) наноси́ть *impf*, нанести́ на грáфик, на кáрту; *v abs* (*conspire*) составля́ть *impf*, состáвить *pf* зáговор.

plough *n* плуг; *vt* пахáть *impf*, вс~ *pf*; *vi*: ~ **through** пробивáться *impf*, проби́ться *pf* сквозь+*acc*.

ploy *n* улóвка.

pluck *n* (*courage*) смéлость; *vt* (*chicken*) щипáть *impf*, об~ *pf*; (*mus*) щипáть *impf*; (*flower*) срывáть *impf*, сорвáть *pf*; ~ **up courage** собирáться *impf*, собрáться *pf* с дýхом; *vi*: ~ **at** дёргать *impf*, дёрнуть *pf*. **plucky** *adj* смéлый.

plug *n* (*stopper*) прóбка; (*electr*) ви́лка; (*electr socket*) розéтка; *vt* (~ *up*) затыкáть *impf*, заткнýть *pf*; ~ **in** включáть *impf*, включи́ть *pf*.

plum *n* сли́ва.

plumage *n* оперéние.

plumb *n* лот; *adv* вертикáльно; (*fig*) тóчно; *vt* измеря́ть *impf*, измéрить *pf* глубинý+*gen*; (*fig*) проникáть *impf*, прони́кнуть *pf* в+*acc*; ~ **in** подключáть *impf*, подключи́ть *pf*. **plumber** *n* водопровóдчик. **plumbing** *n* водопровóд.

plume *n* (*feather*) перó; (*on hat etc.*) султáн.

plummet *vi* пáдать *impf*, (у)пáсть *pf*.

plump[1] *adj* пýхлый.

plump[2] *vi*: ~ **for** выбирáть *impf*, вы́брать *pf*.

plunder *vt* грáбить *impf*, о~ *pf*; *n* добы́ча.

plunge *vt & i* (*immerse*) погружáть(ся) *impf*, погрузи́ть(ся) *pf* (**into** в+*acc*); *vi* (*dive*) ныря́ть *impf*, нырнýть *pf*; (*rush*) бросáться *impf*, брóситься *pf.* **plunger** *n* плу́нжер.

pluperfect *n* давнопроше́дшее вре́мя *neut.*

plural *n* мно́жественное число́. **pluralism** *n* плюрали́зм. **pluralistic** *adj* плюралисти́ческий.

plus *prep* плюс+*acc*; *n* (знак) плюс.

plushy *adj* шика́рный.

plutonium *n* плуто́ний.

ply *vt* (*tool*) рабо́тать *impf* +*instr*; (*task*) занима́ться *impf* +*instr*; (*keep supplied*) по́тчевать *impf* (**with** +*instr*); ~ **with questions** засыпа́ть *impf*, засы́пать *pf* вопро́сами.

plywood *n* фане́ра.

p.m. *adv* по́сле полу́дня.

pneumatic *adj* пневмати́ческий; ~ **drill** отбо́йный молото́к.

pneumonia *n* воспале́ние лёгких.

poach[1] *vt* (*cook*) вари́ть *impf*; ~**ed egg** яйцо́-пашо́т.

poach[2] *vi* браконье́рствовать *impf*. **poacher** *n* браконье́р.

pocket *n* карма́н; **out of** ~ в убы́тке; ~ **money** карма́нные де́ньги (-нег, -ньга́м) *pl*; *vt* класть *impf*, положи́ть *pf*. в карма́н.

pock-marked *adj* рябо́й.

pod *n* стручо́к.

podgy *adj* то́лстенький.

podium *n* трибу́на; (*conductor's*) пульт.

poem *n* стихотворе́ние; (*longer* ~) поэ́ма. **poet** *n* поэ́т. **poetess** *n* поэте́сса. **poetic(al)** *adj* поэти́ческий. **poetry** *n* поэ́зия, стихи́ *m pl*.

pogrom *n* погро́м.

poignancy *n* острота́. **poignant** *adj* о́стрый.

point[1] *n* то́чка; (*place*; *in list*) пункт; (*in score*) очко́; (*in time*) моме́нт; (*in space*) ме́сто; (*essence*) суть; (*sense*) смысл; (*sharp* ~) остриё; (*tip*) ко́нчик; (*power* ~) ште́псель *m*; *pl* (*rly*) стре́лка; **be on the** ~ **of** (*doing*) собира́ться *impf*, собра́ться *pf* +*inf*; **beside, off, the** ~ некста́ти; **that is the** ~ в э́том и де́ло; **the** ~ **is that** де́ло в том, что; **there is no** ~ (*in doing*) нет смы́сла (+*inf*); **to the** ~ кста́ти; ~**blank** прямо́й; ~ **of view** то́чка зре́ния.

point[2] *vt* (*wall*) расшива́ть *impf*, расши́ть *pf* швы+*gen*; (*gun etc.*) наводи́ть *impf*, навести́ *pf* (**at** на+*acc*);

vi по-, у-, ка́зывать *impf*, по-, у-, каза́ть *pf* (**at, to** impf); **pointed** *adj* (*sharp*) о́стрый. **pointer** *n* указа́тель *m*, стре́лка. **pointless** *adj* бессмы́сленный.

poise *n* уравнове́шенность. **poised** *adj* (*composed*) уравнове́шенный; (*ready*) гото́вый (**to** к+*dat*).

poison *n* яд; *vt* отравля́ть *impf*, отрави́ть *pf*. **poisonous** *adj* ядови́тый.

poke *vt* (*prod*) ты́кать *impf*, ткнуть *pf*; ~ **fun at** подшу́чивать *impf*, подшути́ть *pf* над+*instr*; (*thrust*) сова́ть *impf*, су́нуть *pf*; ~ **the fire** меша́ть *impf*, по~ *pf* у́гли в ками́не; *n* тычо́к. **poker**[1] *n* (*rod*) кочерга́.

poker[2] *n* (*cards*) по́кер.

poky *adj* те́сный.

Poland *n* По́льша.

polar *adj* поля́рный; ~ **bear** бе́лый медве́дь *m.* **polarity** *n* поля́рность. **polarize** *vt* поляризова́ть *impf & pf.*

pole[1] *n* (*geog*; *phys*) по́люс; ~**-star** Поля́рная звезда́.

pole[2] *n* (*rod*) столб, шест; ~**-vaulting** прыжо́к с шесто́м.

Pole *n* поля́к, по́лька.

polecat *n* хорёк.

polemic *adj* полеми́ческий; *n* поле́мика.

police *n* поли́ция; (*as pl*) полице́йские *sb*; (*in Russia*) мили́ция; ~ **station** полице́йский уча́сток. **policeman** *n* полице́йский *sb*, полисме́н; (*in Russia*) милиционе́р. **policewoman** *n* же́нщина-полице́йский *sb*; (*in Russia*) же́нщина-милиционе́р.

policy[1] *n* поли́тика.

policy[2] *n* (*insurance*) по́лис.

polio *n* полиомиели́т.

Polish *adj* по́льский.

polish *n* (*gloss, process*) полиро́вка; (*substance*) политу́ра; (*fig*) лоск; *vt* полирова́ть *impf*, от~ *pf*; ~ **off** расправля́ться *impf*, распра́виться *pf* с+*instr*. **polished** *adj* отто́ченный.

polite *adj* ве́жливый. **politeness** *n* ве́жливость.

politic *adj* полити́чный. **political** *adj* полити́ческий; ~ **economy** полит-эконо́мика; ~ **prisoner** политзаключённый *sb.* **politician** *n* поли́тик. **politics** *n* поли́тика.

poll *n* (*voting*) голосова́ние; (*opinion* ~) опро́с; **go to the** ~**s** голосова́ть *impf*, про~ *pf*; *vt* получа́ть *impf*, получи́ть *pf*.

pollen *n* пыльца́. **pollinate** *vt* опыля́ть *impf*, опыли́ть *pf*.

polling *attrib*: ~ **booth** каби́на для голосова́ния; ~ **station** избира́тельный уча́сток.

pollutant *n* загрязни́тель *m*. **pollute** *vt* загрязня́ть *impf*, загрязни́ть *pf*. **pollution** *n* загрязне́ние.

polo *n* по́ло *neut indecl*; ~-**neck sweater** водола́зка.

polyester *n* полиэфи́р. **polyethylene** *n* полиэтиле́н. **polyglot** *n* полигло́т; *adj* многоязы́чный. **polygon** *n* многоуго́льник. **polymer** *n* полиме́р. **polystyrene** *n* полистиро́л. **polytechnic** *n* техни́ческий вуз. **polythene** *n* полиэтиле́н. **polyunsaturated** *adj*: ~ **fats** полиненасы́щенные жиры́ *n pl*. **polyurethane** *n* полиурета́н.

pomp *n* пы́шность. **pomposity** *n* напы́щенность. **pompous** *adj* напы́щенный.

pond *n* пруд.

ponder *vt* обду́мывать *impf*, обду́мать *pf*; *vi* размышля́ть *impf*, размы́слить *pf*.

ponderous *adj* тяжелове́сный.

pony *n* по́ни *m indecl*.

poodle *n* пу́дель *m*.

pool[1] *n* (*of water*) прудо́к; (*puddle*) лу́жа; (*swimming* ~) бассе́йн.

pool[2] *n* (*collective stakes*) совоку́пность ста́вок; (*common fund*) о́бщий фонд; *vt* объединя́ть *impf*, объедини́ть *pf*.

poor *adj* бе́дный; (*bad*) плохо́й; *n*: **the** ~ бедня́к *m pl*. **poorly** *predic* нездоро́в.

pop[1] *vi* хло́пать *impf*, хло́пнуть *pf*; *vt* (*put*) бы́стро всу́нуть *pf* (**into** в+*acc*); ~ **in on** забега́ть *impf*, забежа́ть *pf* к+*dat*; *n* хлопо́к.

pop[2] *adj* поп-; ~ **concert** поп-конце́рт; ~ **music** поп-му́зыка.

pope *n* Па́па *m*.

poplar *n* то́поль *m*.

poppy *n* мак.

populace *n* просто́й наро́д. **popular** *adj* наро́дный; (*liked*) популя́рный. **popularity** *n* популя́рность. **popularize** *vt* популяризи́ровать *impf* & *pf*. **populate** *vt* населя́ть *impf*, насе-

ли́ть *pf*. **population** *n* населе́ние.

populous *adj* (мно́го)лю́дный.

porcelain *n* фарфо́р.

porch *n* крыльцо́.

porcupine *n* дикобра́з.

pore[1] *n* по́ра.

pore[2] *vi*: ~ **over** погружа́ться *impf*, погрузи́ться *pf* в+*acc*.

pork *n* свини́на.

pornographic *adj* порнографи́ческий. **pornography** *n* порногра́фия.

porous *adj* по́ристый.

porpoise *n* морска́я свинья́.

porridge *n* овся́ная ка́ша.

port[1] *n* (*harbour*) порт; (*town*) порто́вый го́род.

port[2] *n* (*naut*) ле́вый борт.

port[3] *n* (*wine*) портве́йн.

portable *adj* портати́вный.

portend *vt* предвеща́ть *impf*. **portent** *n* предзнаменова́ние. **portentous** *adj* злове́щий.

porter[1] *n* (*at door*) швейца́р.

porter[2] *n* (*carrier*) носи́льщик.

portfolio *n* портфе́ль *m*; (*artist's*) па́пка.

porthole *n* иллюмина́тор.

portion *n* часть, до́ля; (*of food*) по́рция.

portly *adj* доро́дный.

portrait *n* портре́т. **portray** *vt* изобража́ть *impf*, изобрази́ть *pf*. **portrayal** *n* изображе́ние.

Portugal *n* Португа́лия. **Portuguese** *n* португа́лец, -лка; *adj* португа́льский.

pose *n* по́за; *vt* (*question*) ста́вить *impf*, по~ *pf*; (*a problem*) представля́ть *impf*, предста́вить *pf*; *vi* пози́ровать *impf*; ~ **as** выдава́ть *impf*, вы́дать *pf* себя́ за+*acc*.

posh *adj* шика́рный.

posit *vt* постули́ровать *impf* & *pf*.

position *n* положе́ние, пози́ция; **in a ~ to** в состоя́нии +*inf*; *vt* ста́вить *impf*, по~ *pf*.

positive *adj* положи́тельный; (*convinced*) уве́ренный; (*proof*) несомне́нный; *n* (*phot*) позити́в.

possess *vt* облада́ть *impf* +*instr*; владе́ть *impf* +*instr*; (*of feeling etc.*) овладева́ть *impf*, овладе́ть *pf* +*instr*. **possessed** *adj* одержи́мый. **possession** *n* владе́ние (**of** +*instr*); *pl* со́бственность. **possessive** *adj* со́бственнический. **possessor** n обладáтель m.

possibility n возмóжность. **possible** adj возмóжный; **as much as ~** скóлько возмóжно; **as soon as ~** как мóжно скорéе. **possibly** adv возмóжно, мóжет (быть).

post¹ n (pole) столб; vt (~ up) вывéшивать impf, вы́весить pf.

post² n (station) пост; (job) дóлжность; vt (station) расставля́ть impf, расстáвить pf; (appoint) назначáть impf, назнáчить pf.

post³ n (letters, ~ office) пóчта; **by ~** пóчтой, attrib почтóвый; **~-box** почтóвый я́щик; **~-code** почтóвый и́ндекс; **~ office** пóчта; vt (send by ~) отправля́ть impf, отпрáвить pf по пóчте; (put in ~-box) опускáть impf, опусти́ть pf в почтóвый я́щик.

postage n почтóвый сбор, почтóвые расхóды m pl; **~ stamp** почтóвая мáрка. **postal** adj почтóвый; **~-order** почтóвый перевóд. **postcard** n откры́тка.

poster n афи́ша, плакáт.

poste restante n до вострéбования.

posterior adj зáдний; n зад.

posterity n потóмство.

post-graduate n аспирáнт.

posthumous adj посмéртный.

postman n почтальóн. **postmark** n почтóвый штéмпель m.

post-mortem n вскры́тие трýпа.

postpone vt отсрóчивать impf, отсрóчить pf. **postponement** n отсрóчка.

postscript n постскри́птум.

postulate vt постули́ровать impf & pf.

posture n пóза, положéние.

post-war adj послевоéнный.

posy n букéтик.

pot n горшóк; (cooking ~) кастрю́ля; **~-shot** вы́стрел наугáд; vt (food) консерви́ровать impf, за~ pf; (plant) сажáть impf, посади́ть pf в горшóк; (billiards) загоня́ть impf, загнáть pf в лýзу.

potash n потáш. **potassium** n кáлий.

potato n (also collect) картóшка; (plant; also collect) картóфель m (no pl).

potency n си́ла. **potent** adj си́льный.

potential adj потенциáльный; n потенциáл. **potentiality** n потенциáльность.

pot-hole n (in road) вы́боина.

potion n зéлье.

potter¹ vi: **~ about** вози́ться impf.

potter² n гончáр. **pottery** n (goods) гончáрные издéлия neut pl; (place) гончáрная sb.

potty¹ adj (crazy) помéшанный (about на+prep).

potty² n ночнóй горшóк.

pouch n сýмка.

poultry n домáшняя пти́ца.

pounce vi: **~ (up)on** набрáсываться impf, набрóситься pf на+acc.

pound¹ n (measure) фунт; **~ sterling** фунт стéрлингов.

pound² vt (strike) колоти́ть impf, по~ pf по+dat, в+acc; vi (heart) колоти́ться impf; **~ along** (run) мчáться impf с грóхотом.

pour vt лить impf; **~ out** наливáть impf, нали́ть pf; vi ли́ться impf; **it is ~ing (with rain)** дождь льёт как из ведрá.

pout vi дýть(ся) impf, на~ pf.

poverty n бéдность; **~-stricken** убóгий.

POW abbr военноплéнный sb.

powder n порошóк; (cosmetic) пýдра; vt пýдрить impf, на~ pf. **powdery** adj порошкообрáзный.

power n (vigour) си́ла; (might) могýщество; (ability) спосóбность; (control) власть; (authorization) полномóчие; (State) держáва; **~ cut** перерыв электропитáния; **~ point** розéтка; **~ station** электростáнция.

powerful adj си́льный. **powerless** adj бесси́льный.

practicable adj осуществи́мый.

practical adj практи́ческий. **practically** adv практи́чески. **practice** n прáктика; (custom) обы́чай; (mus) заня́тия neut pl; **in ~** на прáктике; **put into ~** осуществля́ть impf, осуществи́ть pf. **practise** vt (also abs of doctor etc.) практиковáть impf, упражня́ться impf в+prep; (mus) занимáться impf, заня́ться pf на +prep. **practised** adj óпытный.

practitioner n (doctor) практикýющий врач; **general ~** врач óбщей прáктики.

pragmatic adj прагмати́ческий. **pragmatism** n прагмати́зм. **pragmatist** n прагмáтик.

prairie *n* пре́рия.
praise *vt* хвали́ть *impf*, по~ *pf*; *n* похвала́. **praiseworthy** *adj* похва́льный.
pram *n* де́тская коля́ска.
prance *vi* (*horse*) гарцева́ть *impf*; (*fig*) задава́ться *impf*.
prank *n* вы́ходка.
prattle *vi* лепета́ть; *n* ле́пет.
prawn *n* креве́тка.
pray *vi* моли́ться *impf*, по~ *pf* (**to** +*dat*; **for** о+*prep*). **prayer** *n* моли́тва.
preach *vt & i* пропове́дывать *impf*. **preacher** *n* пропове́дник.
preamble *n* преа́мбула.
pre-arrange *vt* зара́нее организо́вывать *impf*, организова́ть *pf*.
precarious *adj* ненадёжный; опа́сный.
precaution *n* предосторо́жность. **precautionary** *adj*: ~ **measures** ме́ры предосторо́жности.
precede *vt* предше́ствовать *impf* +*dat*. **precedence** *n* предпочте́ние. **precedent** *n* прецеде́нт. **preceding** *adj* предыду́щий.
precept *n* наставле́ние.
precinct *n* двор; *pl* окре́стности *f pl*. **pedestrian** ~ уча́сток для пешехо́дов; **shopping** ~ торго́вый пасса́ж.
precious *adj* драгоце́нный; (*style*) мане́рный; *adv* о́чень.
precipice *n* обры́в. **precipitate** *adj* (*person*) опроме́тчивый; *vt* (*throw down*) низверга́ть *impf*, низве́ргнуть *pf*; (*hurry*) ускоря́ть *impf*, ускоря́ть *pf*. **precipitation** *n* (*meteorol*) оса́дки *m pl*. **precipitous** *adj* обры́вистый.
précis *n* конспе́кт.
precise *adj* то́чный. **precisely** *adv* то́чно; (*in answer*) и́менно. **precision** *n* то́чность.
preclude *vt* предотвраща́ть *impf*, предотврати́ть *pf*.
precocious *adj* ра́но разви́вшийся.
preconceived *adj* предвзя́тый. **preconception** *n* предвзя́тое мне́ние.
pre-condition *n* предпосы́лка.
precursor *n* предше́ственник.
predator *n* хи́щник. **predatory** *adj* хи́щный.
predecessor *n* предше́ственник.
predestination *n* предопределе́ние.

predetermine *vt* предреша́ть *impf*, предреши́ть *pf*.
predicament *n* затрудни́тельное положе́ние.
predicate *n* (*gram*) сказу́емое *sb*. **predicative** *adj* предикати́вный.
predict *vt* предска́зывать *impf*, предсказа́ть *pf*. **predictable** *adj* предсказу́емый. **prediction** *n* предсказа́ние.
predilection *n* пристра́стие (**for** к +*dat*).
predispose *vt* предрасполага́ть *impf*, предрасположи́ть *pf* (**to** к+*dat*). **predisposition** *n* предрасположе́ние (**to** к+*dat*).
predominance *n* преоблада́ние. **predominant** *adj* преоблада́ющий. **predominate** *vi* преоблада́ть *impf*.
pre-eminence *n* превосхо́дство. **pre-eminent** *adj* выдаю́щийся.
pre-empt *vt* (*fig*) завладева́ть *impf*, завладе́ть *pf* +*instr* пре́жде други́х. **pre-emptive** *adj* (*mil*) упрежда́ющий.
preen *vt* (*of bird*) чи́стить *impf*, по~ *pf* клю́вом; ~ **o.s.** (*be proud*) горди́ться *impf* собо́й.
pre-fab *n* сбо́рный дом. **pre-fabricated** *adj* сбо́рный.
preface *n* предисло́вие.
prefect *n* префе́кт; (*school*) ста́роста *m*.
prefer *vt* предпочита́ть *impf*, предпоче́сть *pf*. **preferable** *adj* предпочти́тельный. **preference** *n* предпочте́ние. **preferential** *adj* предпочти́тельный.
prefix *n* приста́вка.
pregnancy *n* бере́менность. **pregnant** *adj* бере́менная.
prehistoric *adj* доистори́ческий.
prejudice *n* предубежде́ние; (*detriment*) уще́рб; *vt* наноси́ть *impf*, нанести́ *pf* уще́рб+*dat*; ~ **against** предубежда́ть *impf*, предубеди́ть *pf* про́тив+*gen*; **be ~d against** име́ть *impf* предубежде́ние про́тив +*gen*.
preliminary *adj* предвари́тельный.
prelude *n* прелю́дия.
premarital *adj* добра́чный.
premature *adj* преждевре́менный.
premeditated *adj* преднаме́ренный.
premier *adj* пе́рвый; *n* премье́р-мини́стр. **première** *n* премье́ра.

premise, premiss n (*logic*) (пред)-
посы́лка. **premises** n pl помеще́-
ние.
premium n пре́мия.
premonition n предчу́вствие.
preoccupation n озабо́ченность;
(*absorbing subject*) забо́та. **preoccupied** adj озабо́ченный. **preoc-
cupy** vt поглоща́ть impf, поглоти́ть
pf.
preparation n приготовле́ние; pl
подгото́вка (**for** к+dat); (*substance*)
препара́т. **preparatory** adj подго-
тови́тельный. **prepare** vt & i при-,
под-, гота́вливать(ся) impf, при-,
под-, гото́вить(ся) pf (**for** к+dat).
prepared adj гото́вый.
preponderance n переве́с.
preposition n предло́г.
prepossessing adj привлека́тель-
ный.
preposterous adj неле́пый.
prerequisite n предпосы́лка.
prerogative n прерогати́ва.
presage vt предвеща́ть impf.
Presbyterian n пресвитериа́нин,
-а́нка; adj пресвитериа́нский.
prescribe vt предпи́сывать impf,
предписа́ть pf; (*med*) пропи́сывать
impf, прописа́ть pf. **prescription** n
(*med*) реце́пт.
presence n прису́тствие; ~ **of mind**
прису́тствие ду́ха. **present** adj при-
су́тствующий; (*being dealt with*)
да́нный; (*existing now*) ны́нешний;
(*also gram*) настоя́щий; *predic* на-
лицо́; **be** ~ прису́тствовать impf (**at**
на+prep); ~**day** ны́нешний; n: the
~ настоя́щее sb; (*gram*) настоя́щее
вре́мя neut; (*gift*) пода́рок; **at** ~ в
настоя́щее вре́мя neut; **for the** ~
пока́; vt (*introduce*) представля́ть
impf, предста́вить pf (**to** +dat);
(*award*) вруча́ть impf, вручи́ть
pf; (*a play*) ста́вить impf, по~ pf;
(*a gift*) преподноси́ть impf, препод-
нести́ pf +dat (**with** +acc); ~ **o.s.**
явля́ться impf, яви́ться pf. **present-
able** adj прили́чный. **presentation**
n (*introducing*) представле́ние;
(*awarding*) подноше́ние.
presentiment n предчу́вствие.
presently adv вско́ре.
preservation n сохране́ние. **preservative** n консерва́нт. **preserve** vt

(*keep safe*) сохраня́ть impf, со-
храни́ть pf; (*maintain*) храни́ть
impf; (*food*) консерви́ровать impf,
за~ pf; n (*for game etc*) запове́дник;
(*jam*) варе́нье.
preside vi председа́тельствовать
impf (**at** на+prep). **presidency** n
президе́нтство. **president** n прези-
де́нт. **presidential** adj президе́нт-
ский. **presidium** n прези́диум.
press n (*machine*) пресс; (*printing
firm*) типогра́фия; (*publishing house*)
изда́тельство; (*the* ~) пре́сса, пе-
ча́ть; ~ **conference** пресс-конфе-
ре́нция; vt (*button etc*) нажима́ть
impf, нажа́ть pf; (*clasp*) прижима́ть
impf, прижа́ть pf (**to** к+dat); (*iron*)
гла́дить impf, вы́~ pf; (*insist on*)
наста́ивать impf, настоя́ть pf на
+prep; (*urge*) угова́ривать impf; ~
on (*make haste*) потора́пливаться
impf.
pressing adj неотло́жный. **pressure**
n давле́ние; ~**cooker** скорова́рка;
~ **group** инициати́вная гру́ппа.
pressurize vt (*fig*) ока́зывать impf,
оказа́ть pf давле́ние на+acc. **pres-
surized** adj гермети́ческий.
prestige n прести́ж. **prestigious** adj
прести́жный.
presumably adv предположи́тельно.
presume vt полага́ть impf; (*venture*)
позволя́ть impf, позво́лить pf себе́.
presumption n предположе́ние;
(*arrogance*) самонаде́янность. **presumptuous** adj самонаде́янный.
presuppose vt предполага́ть impf.
pretence n притво́рство. **pretend** vt
притворя́ться impf, притвори́ться
pf (**to be** +instr); де́лать impf, с~ pf
вид (что); vi: ~ **to** претендова́ть
impf на+acc. **pretender** n претен-
де́нт. **pretension** n прете́нзия. **pre-
tentious** adj претенцио́зный.
pretext n предло́г.
prettiness n милови́дность. **pretty**
adj хоро́шенький; adv дово́льно.
prevail vi (*predominate*) преобла-
да́ть impf; ~ (**up**)**on** угова́ривать
impf, уговори́ть pf. **prevalence** n
распростране́ние. **prevalent** adj
распространённый.
prevaricate vi уви́ливать impf увиль-
ну́ть pf.
prevent vt (*stop from happening*)

предупрежда́ть *impf*, предупреди́ть *pf*; (*stop from doing*) меша́ть *impf*, по~ *pf* +*dat*. **prevention** *n* предупрежде́ние. **preventive** *adj* предупреди́тельный.

preview *n* предвари́тельный просмо́тр.

previous *adj* предыду́щий; *adv*: ~ **to** до+*gen*; пре́жде чем +*inf*. **previously** *adv* ра́ньше.

pre-war *adj* довое́нный.

prey *n* (*animal*) добы́ча; (*victim*) же́ртва (**to** +*gen*); **bird of** ~ хи́щная пти́ца; *vi*: ~ (**up**)**on** (*emotion etc.*) му́чить *impf*.

price *n* цена́; ~**-list** прейскура́нт; *vt* назнача́ть *impf*, назна́чить *pf* це́ну +*gen*. **priceless** *adj* бесце́нный.

prick *vt* коло́ть *impf*, у~ *pf*; (*conscience*) му́чить *impf*; ~ **up one's ears** навостри́ть *pf* у́ши; *n* уко́л.

prickle *n* (*thorn*) колю́чка; (*spine*) игла́. **prickly** *adj* колю́чий.

pride *n* го́рдость; ~ **o.s. on** горди́ться *impf* +*instr*.

priest *n* свяще́нник; (*non-Christian*) жрец.

prig *n* педа́нт.

prim *adj* чо́порный.

primarily *adv* первонача́льно; (*above all*) пре́жде всего́. **primary** *adj* основно́й; ~ **school** нача́льная шко́ла. **prime** *n*: **in one's** ~ в расцве́те сил; *adj* (*chief*) гла́вный; ~ **minister** премье́р-мини́стр; *vt* (*engine*) заправля́ть *impf*, запра́вить *pf*; (*bomb*) активизи́ровать *impf* & *pf*; (*with facts*) инструкти́ровать *impf* & *pf*; (*with paint etc.*) грунтова́ть *impf*, за~ *pf*. **primer** *n* (*paint etc.*) грунт. **prim(a)eval** *adj* первобы́тный. **primitive** *adj* первобы́тный; (*crude*) примити́вный. **primordial** *adj* исконный.

primrose *n* первоцве́т; (*colour*) бле́дно-жёлтый цвет.

prince *n* принц; (*in Russia*) князь. **princely** *adj* кня́жеский; (*sum*) огро́мный. **princess** *n* принце́сса; (*wife*) княги́ня; (*daughter*) княжна́.

principal *n* гла́вный; *n* дире́ктор. **principality** *n* кня́жество. **principally** *adv* гла́вным о́бразом.

principle *n* при́нцип; **in** ~ в при́нципе; **on** ~ принципиа́льно. **prin-**

cipled *adj* принципиа́льный.

print *n* (*mark*) след; (*also phot*) отпеча́ток; (*printing*) печа́ть; (*picture*) о́ттиск; **in** ~ в прода́же; **out of** ~ распро́данный; *vt* (*impress*) запечатлева́ть *impf*, запечатле́ть *pf*; (*book etc.*) печа́тать *impf*, на~ *pf*; (*write*) писа́ть *impf*, на~ *pf* печа́тными бу́квами; (*phot*; ~ **out**, **off**) отпеча́тывать *impf*, отпеча́тать *pf*; ~ **out** (*of computer etc.*) распеча́тывать *impf*, распеча́тать *pf*; ~**-out** распеча́тка. **printer** *n* (*person*) печа́тник, типо́граф; (*of computer*) при́нтер. **printing** *n* печа́тание; ~**-press** печа́тный стано́к.

prior *adj* пре́жний; *adv*: ~ **to** до+*gen*. **priority** *n* приорите́т. **priory** *n* монасты́рь *m*.

prise *vt*: ~ **open** взла́мывать *impf*, взлома́ть *pf*.

prism *n* при́зма.

prison *n* тюрьма́; *attrib* тюре́мный; ~ **camp** ла́герь *m*. **prisoner** *n* заключённый *sb*; (~ **of war**) (вое́нно)пле́нный *sb*.

pristine *adj* нетро́нутый.

privacy *n* уедине́ние; (*private life*) ча́стная жизнь. **private** *adj* (*personal*) ча́стный, ли́чный; (*confidential*) конфиденциа́льный; **in** ~ наедине́; в ча́стной жи́зни; *n* рядово́й *sb*.

privation *n* лише́ние.

privilege *n* привиле́гия. **privileged** *adj* привелигиро́ванный.

privy *adj*: ~ **to** посвящённый в+*acc*.

prize *n* пре́мия, приз; ~**-winner** призёр; *vt* высоко́ цени́ть *impf*.

pro[1] *n*: ~**s and cons** до́воды *m pl* за и про́тив.

pro[2] *n* (*professional*) профессиона́л.

probability *n* вероя́тность. **probable** *adj* вероя́тный. **probably** *adv* вероя́тно.

probate *n* утвержде́ние завеща́ния.

probation *n* испыта́тельный срок; (*law*) усло́вный пригово́р; **got two years** ~ получи́л два го́да усло́вно. **probationary** *adj* испыта́тельный.

probe *n* (*med*) зонд; (*fig*) рассле́дование; *vt* зонди́ровать *impf*; (*fig*) рассле́довать *impf* & *pf*.

probity *n* че́стность.

problem *n* пробле́ма, вопро́с; (*math*)

зада́ча. **problematic** *adj* проблема-
ти́чный.

procedural *adj* процеду́рный. **procedure** *n* процеду́ра. **proceed** *vi* (*go
further*) идти́ *impf*, пойти́ *pf* да́ль-
ше; (*act*) поступа́ть *impf*, поступи́ть
pf; (*abs*, ~ *to say*; *continue*) про-
должа́ть *impf*, продо́лжить *pf*; (*of
action*) продолжа́ться *impf*, продол-
жи́ться *pf*; ~ **from** исходи́ть *impf*
из, от+*gen*; ~ **to** (*begin to*) при-
нима́ться *impf*, приня́ться *pf* +*inf*.
proceedings *n pl* (*activity*) де́ятель-
ность; (*legal* ~) судопроизво́дство;
(*published report*) труды́ *m pl*,
запи́ски *f pl*. **proceeds** *n pl* вы́руч-
ка. **process** *n* проце́сс; *vt* обраба́-
тывать *impf*, обрабо́тать *pf*. **procession** *n* проце́ссия, ше́ствие.

proclaim *vt* провозглаша́ть *impf*,
провозгласи́ть *pf*. **proclamation** *n*
провозглаше́ние.

procure *vt* достава́ть *impf*, доста́ть *pf*.
prod *vt* ты́кать *impf*, ткнуть *pf*; *n*
тычо́к.

prodigal *adj* расточи́тельный.

prodigious *adj* огро́мный. **prodigy**
n: **child** ~ вундерки́нд.

produce *vt* (*evidence etc.*) представ-
ля́ть *impf*, предста́вить *pf*; (*ticket
etc.*) предъявля́ть *impf*, предъяви́ть
pf; (*play etc.*) ста́вить *impf*, по~ *pf*;
(*manufacture; cause*) производи́ть
impf, произвести́ *pf*; *n* (*collect*)
проду́кты *m pl*. **producer** *n* (*econ*)
производи́тель *m*; (*of play etc.*) режиссёр. **product** *n* проду́кт; (*result*)
результа́т. **production** *n* произво́д-
ство; (*of play etc.*) постано́вка. **productive** *adj* продукти́вный; (*fruitful*) плодотво́рный. **productivity** *n*
производи́тельность.

profane *adj* све́тский; (*blasphemous*)
богоху́льный. **profanity** *n* бого-
ху́льство.

profess *vt* (*pretend*) притворя́ться
impf, притвори́ться *pf* (**to be** +*instr*);
(*declare*) заявля́ть *impf*, заяви́ть *pf*;
(*faith*) испове́довать *impf*. **profession** *n* (*job*) профе́ссия. **professional**
adj профессиона́льный; *n* профес-
сиона́л. **professor** *n* профе́ссор.

proffer *vt* предлага́ть *impf*, пред-
ложи́ть *pf*.

proficiency *n* уме́ние. **proficient** *adj*
уме́лый.

profile *n* про́филь *m*.

profit *n* (*benefit*) по́льза; (*monetary*)
при́быль; *vt* приноси́ть *impf*, при-
нести́ *pf* по́льзу +*dat*; *vi*: ~ **from**
по́льзоваться *impf*, вос~ *pf* +*instr*;
(*financially*) получа́ть *impf*, полу-
чи́ть *pf* при́быль на+*prep*. **profitable** *adj* (*lucrative*) при́быльный;
(*beneficial*) поле́зный. **profiteering**
n спекуля́ция.

profligate *adj* распу́тный.

profound *adj* глубо́кий.

profuse *adj* оби́льный. **profusion** *n*
изоби́лие.

progeny *n* пото́мство.

prognosis *n* прогно́з.

program(m)e *n* програ́мма; *vt* про-
грамми́ровать *impf*, за~ *pf*. **pro-
grammer** *n* программи́ст.

progress *n* прогре́сс; (*success*) успе́-
хи *m pl*; **make** ~ де́лать *impf*, с~ *pf*
успе́хи; *vi* продвига́ться *impf*, про-
дви́нуться *pf* вперёд. **progression**
n продвиже́ние. **progressive** *adj*
прогресси́вный.

prohibit *vt* запреща́ть *impf*, запре-
ти́ть *pf*. **prohibition** *n* запреще́ние;
(*on alcohol*) сухо́й зако́н. **prohibi-
tive** *adj* запрети́тельный; (*price*) не-
досту́пный.

project *vt* (*plan*) проекти́ровать
impf, с~ *pf*; (*a film*) демонстри́-
ровать *impf*, про~ *pf*; *vi* (*jut out*)
выступа́ть *impf*, *n* прое́кт. **projectile** *n* снаря́д. **projection** *n* (*cin*)
прое́кция; (*protrusion*) вы́ступ; (*forecast*) прогно́з. **projector** *n* прое́к-
тор.

proletarian *adj* пролета́рский. **proletariat** *n* пролетариа́т.

proliferate *vi* распространя́ться
impf, распространи́ться *pf*. **prolif-
eration** *n* распростране́ние.

prolific *adj* плодови́тый.

prologue *n* проло́г.

prolong *vt* продлева́ть *impf*, про-
дли́ть *pf*.

promenade *n* ме́сто для гуля́нья; (*at
seaside*) на́бережная *sb*; *vi* прогу́-
ливаться *impf*, прогуля́ться *pf*.

prominence *n* изве́стность. **prominent** *adj* выступа́ющий; (*distinguished*) выдаю́щийся.

promiscuity *n* лёгкое поведе́ние.

promiscuous *adj* лёгкого поведе́ния.

promise *n* обеща́ние; *vt* обеща́ть *impf & pf*. **promising** *adj* многообеща́ющий.

promontory *n* мыс.

promote *vt* (*in rank*) продвига́ть *impf*, продви́нуть *pf*; (*assist*) спосо́бствовать *impf & pf* +*dat*; (*publicize*) реклами́ровать *impf*. **promoter** *n* (*of event etc.*) аге́нт. **promotion** *n* (*in rank*) продвиже́ние; (*comm*) рекла́ма.

prompt *adj* бы́стрый, неме́дленный; *adv* ро́вно; *vt* (*incite*) побужда́ть *impf*, побуди́ть *pf* (**to** к+*dat*; +*inf*); (*speaker; also fig*) подска́зывать *impf*, подсказа́ть *pf* +*dat*; (*theat*) суфли́ровать *impf* +*dat*; *n* подска́зка. **prompter** *n* суфлёр.

prone *adj* (лежа́щий) ничко́м; *predic*: ~ **to** скло́нен (-онна́, -о́нно) к+*dat*.

prong *n* зубе́ц.

pronoun *n* местоиме́ние.

pronounce *vt* (*declare*) объявля́ть *impf*, объяви́ть *pf*; (*articulate*) произноси́ть *impf*, произнести́ *pf*. **pronounced** *adj* я́вный; заме́тный. **pronouncement** *n* заявле́ние. **pronunciation** *n* произноше́ние.

proof *n* доказа́тельство; (*printing*) корректу́ра; ~-**reader** корре́ктор; *adj* (*impenetrable*) непроница́емый (**against** для+*gen*); (*not yielding*) неподдаю́щийся (**against** +*dat*).

prop[1] *n* (*support*) подпо́рка; (*fig*) опо́ра; *vt* (~ **open, up**) подпира́ть *impf*, подпере́ть *pf*; (*fig*) подде́рживать *impf*, поддержа́ть *pf*.

prop[2] *n* (*theat*) *see* **props**

propaganda *n* пропага́нда.

propagate *vt & i* размножа́ть(ся) *impf*, размно́жить(ся) *pf*; (*disseminate*) распространя́ть(ся) *impf*, распространи́ть(ся) *pf*. **propagation** *n* размноже́ние; распростране́ние.

propel *vt* приводи́ть *impf*, привести́ *pf* в движе́ние. **propeller** *n* винт.

propensity *n* накло́нность (**to** к+*dat*; +*inf*).

proper *adj* (*correct*) пра́вильный; (*suitable*) подходя́щий; (*decent*) присто́йный; ~ **noun** и́мя со́бственное.

properly *adv* как сле́дует.

property *n* (*possessions*) со́бственность, иму́щество; (*attribute*) сво́йство; *pl* (*theat*) реквизи́т.

prophecy *n* проро́чество. **prophesy** *vt* проро́чить *impf*, на~ *pf*. **prophet** *n* проро́к. **prophetic** *adj* проро́ческий.

propitious *adj* благоприя́тный.

proponent *n* сторо́нник.

proportion *n* пропо́рция; (*due relation*) соразме́рность; *pl* разме́ры *m pl*. **proportional** *adj* пропорциона́льный. **proportionate** *adj* соразме́рный (**to** +*dat*; c+*instr*).

proposal *n* предложе́ние. **propose** *vt* предлага́ть *impf*, предложи́ть *pf*; (*intend*) предполага́ть *impf*; *vi* (~ *marriage*) де́лать *impf*, с~ *pf* предложе́ние (**to** +*dat*). **proposition** *n* предложе́ние.

propound *vt* предлага́ть *impf*, предложи́ть *pf* на обсужде́ние.

proprietor *n* со́бственник, хозя́ин.

propriety *n* прили́чие.

props *n pl* (*theat*) реквизи́т.

propulsion *n* движе́ние вперёд.

prosaic *adj* прозаи́ческий.

proscribe *vt* (*forbid*) запреща́ть *impf*, запрети́ть *pf*.

prose *n* про́за.

prosecute *vt* пресле́довать *impf*. **prosecution** *n* суде́бное пресле́дование; (*prosecuting party*) обвине́ние. **prosecutor** *n* обвини́тель *m*.

prospect *n* вид; (*fig*) перспекти́ва; *vi*: ~ **for** иска́ть *impf*. **prospective** *adj* бу́дущий. **prospector** *n* разве́дчик. **prospectus** *n* проспе́кт.

prosper *vi* процвета́ть *impf*. **prosperity** *n* процвета́ние. **prosperous** *adj* процвета́ющий; (*wealthy*) зажи́точный.

prostate (gland) *n* проста́та.

prostitute *n* проститу́тка. **prostitution** *n* проститу́ция.

prostrate *adj* распростёртый, (лежа́щий) ничко́м; (*exhausted*) обесси́ленный; (*with grief*) уби́тый (**with** +*instr*).

protagonist *n* гла́вный геро́й; (*in contest*) протагони́ст.

protect *vt* защища́ть *impf*, защити́ть. **protection** *n* защи́та. **protective** *adj* защи́тный. **protector** *n* защи́тник.

protégé(e) n протеже́ m & f indecl.

protein n бело́к.

protest n проте́ст; vi протестова́ть impf & pf; vt (affirm) утвержда́ть impf.

Protestant n протеста́нт, ~ка; adj протеста́нтский.

protestation n (торже́ственное) заявле́ние (о+prep; что); (protest) проте́ст.

protocol n протоко́л.

proton n прото́н.

prototype n прототи́п.

protract vt тяну́ть impf. **protracted** adj дли́тельный.

protrude vi выдава́ться impf, вы́даться pf.

proud adj го́рдый; **be ~ of** горди́ться impf +instr.

prove vt дока́зывать impf, доказа́ть pf; vi ока́зываться impf, оказа́ться pf (**to be** +instr). **proven** adj дока́занный.

provenance n происхожде́ние.

proverb n посло́вица. **proverbial** adj воше́дший в погово́рку; (well-known) общеизве́стный.

provide vt (supply person) снабжа́ть impf, снабди́ть pf (**with** +instr); (supply thing) предоставля́ть impf, предоста́вить pf (**to, for** +dat); дава́ть impf, дать pf (**to, for** +dat); vi: ~ **for** предусма́тривать impf, предусмотре́ть pf +acc; (~ for family etc.) содержа́ть impf +acc. **provided (that)** conj при усло́вии, что; е́сли то́лько.

providence n провиде́ние; (foresight) предусмотри́тельность.

provident adj предусмотри́тельный. **providential** adj счастли́вый.

providing see **provided (that)**

province n о́бласть; pl (the ~) прови́нция. **provincial** adj провинциа́льный.

provision n снабже́ние; pl (food) прови́зия; (in agreement etc.) положе́ние; **make ~ against** принима́ть impf, приня́ть pf ме́ры про́тив+gen. **provisional** adj вре́менный. **proviso** n усло́вие.

provocation n провока́ция. **provocative** adj провокацио́нный. **provoke** vt провоци́ровать impf, с~ pf; (call forth, cause) вызыва́ть impf, вы́звать pf.

prow n нос.

prowess n уме́ние.

prowl vi ры́скать impf.

proximity n бли́зость.

proxy n полномо́чие; (person) уполномо́ченный sb, замести́тель m; **by ~** по дове́ренности; **stand ~ for** быть impf замести́телем +gen.

prudence n благоразу́мие. **prudent** adj благоразу́мный.

prudery n притво́рная стыдли́вость. **prudish** adj ни в ме́ру стыдли́вый.

prune[1] n (plum) черносли́в.

prune[2] vt (trim) об-, под-, реза́ть impf, об-, под-, ре́зать pf.

pry vi сова́ть impf нос (**into** в+acc).

PS abbr (of **postscript**) постскри́птум.

psalm n псало́м.

pseudonym n псевдони́м.

psyche n пси́хика. **psychiatric** adj психиатри́ческий. **psychiatrist** n психиа́тр. **psychiatry** n психиатри́я. **psychic** adj ясновидя́щий. **psychoanalysis** n психоана́лиз. **psychoanalyst** n психоанали́тик. **psychoanalytic(al)** adj психоаналити́ческий. **psychological** adj психологи́ческий. **psychologist** n психо́лог. **psychology** n психоло́гия. **psychopath** n психопа́т. **psychopathic** adj психопати́ческий. **psychosis** n психо́з. **psychotherapy** n психотерапи́я.

PTO abbr (of **please turn over**) см. на об., смотри́ на оборо́те.

pub n пивна́я sb.

puberty n полова́я зре́лость.

public adj обще́ственный; (open) публи́чный, откры́тый; ~ **school** ча́стная сре́дняя шко́ла; n пу́блика, обще́ственность; **in ~** откры́то, публи́чно. **publication** n изда́ние.

publicity n рекла́ма. **publicize** vt реклами́ровать impf & pf. **publicly** adv публи́чно, откры́то. **publish** vt публикова́ть impf, о~ pf; (book) издава́ть impf, изда́ть pf. **publisher** n изда́тель m. **publishing** n (business) изда́тельское де́ло; ~ **house** изда́тельство.

pucker vt & i мо́рщить(ся) impf, с~ pf.

pudding n пу́динг, запека́нка; (dessert) сла́дкое sb.

puddle n лу́жа.

puff n (of wind) поры́в; (of smoke) дымо́к; ~ **pastry** слоёное те́сто; vi пыхте́ть impf, ~ **at** (pipe etc.) попы́хивать impf +instr; vt: ~ **up, out** (inflate) надува́ть impf, наду́ть pf.

pugnacious adj драчли́вый.

puke vi рвать impf, вы́~ pf impers +acc.

pull vt тяну́ть impf, по~ pf; таска́ть indet, тащи́ть det, по~ pf; (a muscle) растя́гивать impf, растяну́ть pf; vt & i дёргать impf, дёрнуть pf (at (за)+acc); ~ **s.o's leg** разы́грывать impf, разыгра́ть pf; ~ **the trigger** спуска́ть impf, спусти́ть pf куро́к; ~ **apart, to pieces** разрыва́ть impf, разорва́ть pf; (fig) раскритикова́ть pf; ~ **down** (demolish) сноси́ть impf, снести́ pf; ~ **in** (of train) прибыва́ть impf, прибы́ть pf; (of vehicle) подъезжа́ть impf, подъе́хать pf к обо́чине (доро́ги); ~ **off** (garment) стя́гивать impf, стяну́ть pf; (achieve) успе́шно заверша́ть impf, заверши́ть pf; ~ **on** (garment) натя́гивать impf, натяну́ть pf; ~ **out** (vt) (remove) выта́скивать impf, вы́тащить pf; (vi) (withdraw) отка́зываться impf, отказа́ться pf от уча́стия (of в+prep); (of vehicle) отъезжа́ть impf, отъе́хать pf от обо́чины (доро́ги); (of train) отходи́ть impf, отойти́ pf (от ста́нции); ~ **through** выжива́ть impf, вы́жить pf; ~ **o.s. together** брать impf, взять pf себя́ в ру́ки; ~ **up** (vt) подтя́гивать impf, подтяну́ть pf; (vt & i) (stop) остана́вливать(ся) impf, останови́ть(ся) pf; n тя́га; (fig) блат.

pulley n блок.

pullover n пуло́вер.

pulp n пу́льпа.

pulpit n ка́федра.

pulsate vi пульси́ровать impf. **pulse** n пульс.

pulses n pl (food) бобо́вые sb.

pulverize vt размельча́ть impf, размельчи́ть pf.

pummel vt колоти́ть impf, по~ pf.

pump n насо́с; vt кача́ть impf; ~ **in(to)** вка́чивать impf, вкача́ть pf; ~ **out** выка́чивать impf, вы́качать pf; ~ **up** нака́чивать impf, накача́ть pf.

pumpkin n ты́ква.

pun n каламбу́р.

punch[1] vt (with fist) ударя́ть impf, уда́рить pf кулако́м; (hole) пробива́ть impf, проби́ть pf; (a ticket) компости́ровать impf, про~ pf; ~ **up** дра́ка; n (blow) уда́р кулако́м; (for tickets) компо́стер; (for piercing) перфора́тор.

punch[2] n (drink) пунш.

punctilious adj щепети́льный.

punctual adj пунктуа́льный. **punctuality** n пунктуа́льность.

punctuate vt ста́вить impf, по~ pf зна́ки препина́ния в+acc; (fig) прерыва́ть impf, прерва́ть pf. **punctuation** n пунктуа́ция; ~ **marks** зна́ки m pl препина́ния.

puncture n проко́л; vt прока́лывать impf, проколо́ть pf.

pundit n (fig) знато́к.

pungent adj е́дкий.

punish vt нака́зывать impf, наказа́ть pf. **punishable** adj наказу́емый. **punishment** n наказа́ние.

punitive adj кара́тельный.

punter n (gambler) игро́к; (client) клие́нт.

puny adj хи́лый.

pupil n учени́к, -и́ца; (of eye) зрачо́к.

puppet n марионе́тка, ку́кла.

puppy n щено́к.

purchase n поку́пка; (leverage) то́чка опо́ры; vt покупа́ть impf, купи́ть pf. **purchaser** n покупа́тель m.

pure adj чи́стый.

purée n пюре́ neut indecl.

purely adv чи́сто.

purgatory n чисти́лище; (fig) ад. **purge** vt очища́ть impf, очи́стить pf; n очище́ние; (polit) чи́стка.

purification n очи́стка. **purify** vt очища́ть impf, очи́стить pf.

purist n пури́ст.

puritan, P., n пурита́нин, -а́нка. **puritanical** adj пурита́нский.

purity n чистота́.

purple adj (n) пурпу́рный, фиоле́товый (цвет).

purport vt претендова́ть impf.

purpose n цель, наме́рение; **on** ~ наро́чно; **to no** ~ напра́сно. **purposeful** adj целеустремлённый. **purposeless** adj бесце́льный. **purposely** adv наро́чно.

purr *vi* мурлы́кать *impf*.

purse *n* кошелёк; *vt* поджима́ть *impf*, поджа́ть *pf*.

pursue *vt* пресле́довать *impf*. **pursuit** *n* пресле́дование; (*pastime*) заня́тие.

purveyor *n* поставщи́к.

pus *n* гной.

push *vt* толка́ть *impf*, толкну́ть *pf*; (*press*) нажима́ть *impf*, нажа́ть *pf*; (*urge*) подта́лкивать *impf*, подтолкну́ть *pf*; *vi* толка́ться *impf*; **be ~ed for** име́ть *impf* ма́ло+*gen*; **he is ~ing fifty** ему́ ско́ро сту́кнет пятьдеся́т; **~ one's way** проти́скиваться *impf*, проти́снуться *pf*; **~ around** (*person*) помыка́ть *impf* +*instr*; **~ aside** (*also fig*) отстраня́ть *impf*, отстрани́ть *pf*; **~ away** отта́лкивать *impf*, оттолкну́ть *pf*; **~ off** (*vi*) (*in boat*) отта́лкиваться *impf*, оттолкну́ться *pf* (от бе́рега); (*go away*) убира́ться *impf*, убра́ться *pf*; **~ on** (*vi*) продолжа́ть *impf* путь; *n* толчо́к; (*energy*) эне́ргия. **pushchair** *n* коля́ска. **pusher** *n* (*drugs*) продаве́ц нарко́тиков. **pushy** *adj* напо́ристый.

puss, pussy(-cat) *n* ки́ска.

put *vt* класть *impf*, положи́ть *pf*; (*upright*) ста́вить *impf*, по~ *pf*; помеща́ть *impf*, помести́ть *pf*; (*into specified state*) приводи́ть *impf*, привести́ *pf*; (*express*) выража́ть *impf*, вы́разить *pf*; (*a question*) задава́ть *impf*, зада́ть *pf*; **~ an end, a stop, to** класть *impf*, положи́ть *pf* коне́ц +*dat*; **~ o.s. in another's place** ста́вить *impf*, по~ *pf* себя́ на ме́сто +*gen*; **~ about** (*rumour etc.*) распространя́ть *impf*, распространи́ть *pf*; **~ away** (*tidy*) убира́ть *impf*, убра́ть *pf*; (*save*) откла́дывать *impf*, отложи́ть *pf*; **~ back** (*in place*) ста́вить *impf*, по~ *pf* на ме́сто; (*clock*) переводи́ть *impf*, перевести́ *pf* наза́д; **~ by** (*money*) откла́дывать *impf*, отложи́ть *pf*; **~ down** класть *impf*, положи́ть *pf*; (*suppress*) подавля́ть *impf*, подави́ть *pf*; (*write down*) запи́сывать *impf*, записа́ть *pf*; (*passengers*) выса́живать *impf*, вы́садить *pf*; (*attribute*) припи́сывать *impf*, приписа́ть *pf* (**to** +*dat*); **~ forward** (*proposal*) предлага́ть *impf*, предложи́ть *pf*; (*clock*) переводи́ть

impf, перевести́ *pf* вперёд; **~ in** (*install*) устана́вливать *impf*, установи́ть *pf*; (*a claim*) предъявля́ть *impf*, предъяви́ть *pf*; (*interpose*) вставля́ть *impf*, вста́вить *pf*; **~ in an appearance** появля́ться *impf*, появи́ться *pf*; **~ off** (*postpone*) откла́дывать *impf*, отложи́ть *pf*; (*repel*) отта́лкивать *impf*, оттолкну́ть *pf*; (*dissuade*) отгова́ривать *impf*, отговори́ть *pf* от+*gen*, +*inf*; **~ on** (*clothes*) надева́ть *impf*, наде́ть *pf*; (*kettle, a record, a play*) ста́вить *impf*, по~ *pf*; (*turn on*) включа́ть *impf*, включи́ть *pf*; (*add to*) прибавля́ть *impf*, приба́вить *pf*; **~ on airs** ва́жничать *impf*; **~ on weight** толсте́ть *impf*, по~ *pf*; **~ out** (*vex*) обижа́ть *impf*, оби́деть *pf*; (*inconvenience*) затрудня́ть *impf*, затрудни́ть *pf*; (*a fire etc.*) туши́ть *impf*, по~ *pf*; **~ through** (*tel*) соединя́ть *impf*, соедини́ть *pf* по телефо́ну; **~ up** (*building*) стро́ить *impf*, по~ *pf*; (*hang up*) ве́шать *impf*, пове́сить *pf*; (*price*) повыша́ть *impf*, повы́сить *pf*; (*a guest*) дава́ть *impf*, дать *pf* ночле́г +*dat*; (*as guest*) ночева́ть *impf*, пере~ *pf*; **~ up to** (*instigate*) подбива́ть *impf*, подби́ть *pf* на+*acc*; **~ up with** терпе́ть *impf*.

putative *adj* предполага́емый.

putrefy *vi* гнить *impf*, с~ *pf*. **putrid** *adj* гнило́й.

putty *n* зама́зка.

puzzle *n* (*enigma*) зага́дка; (*toy etc.*) головоло́мка; (*jigsaw*) моза́ика; *vt* озада́чивать *impf*, озада́чить *pf*; **~ out** разга́дывать *impf*, разга́дать *pf*; *vi*: **~ over** лома́ть *impf* себе́ го́лову над+*instr*.

pygmy *n* пигме́й.

pyjamas *n pl* пижа́ма.

pylon *n* пило́н.

pyramid *n* пирами́да.

pyre *n* погреба́льный костёр.

python *n* пито́н.

Q

quack[1] *n* (*sound*) кря́канье; *vi* кря́кать *impf*, кря́кнуть *pf*.

quack[2] *n* шарлата́н.

quad *n* (*court*) четырёхуго́льный двор; *pl* (*quadruplets*) че́тверо близнецо́в. **quadrangle** *n* (*figure*) четырёхуго́льник; (*court*) четырёхуго́льный двор. **quadrant** *n* квадра́нт.

quadruped *n* четвероно́гое живо́тное *sb*. **quadruple** *adj* четверно́й; *vt & i* учетверя́ть(ся) *impf*, учетвери́ть(ся) *pf*. **quadruplets** *n pl* четверо близнецо́в.

quagmire *n* боло́то.

quail *n* (*bird*) пе́репел.

quaint *adj* причу́дливый.

quake *vi* дрожа́ть *impf* (**with** от +*gen*). **Quaker** *n* ква́кер, ∼ка.

qualification *n* (*for post etc.*) квалифика́ция; (*reservation*) огово́рка. **qualified** *adj* компете́нтный; (*limited*) ограни́ченный. **qualify** *vt & i* (*prepare for job*) гото́вить(ся) *impf* (**for** к+*dat*; +*inf*); *vt* (*render fit*) де́лать *impf*, с∼ *pf* приго́дным; (*entitle*) дава́ть *impf*, дать *pf* пра́во +*dat* (**to** на+*acc*); (*limit*): ∼ **what one says** сде́лать *pf* огово́рку; *vi* получа́ть *impf*, получи́ть *pf* дипло́м; ∼ **for** (*be entitled to*) име́ть *impf* пра́во на+*acc*.

qualitative *adj* ка́чественный. **quality** *n* ка́чество.

qualm *n* сомне́ние; (*of conscience*) угрызе́ние со́вести.

quandary *n* затрудни́тельное положе́ние.

quantify *vt* определя́ть *impf*, определи́ть *pf* коли́чество +*gen*. **quantitative** *adj* коли́чественный. **quantity** *n* коли́чество.

quarantine *n* каранти́н.

quarrel *n* ссо́ра; *vi* ссо́риться *impf*, по∼ *pf* (**with** с+*instr*; **about, for** из-за+*gen*). **quarrelsome** *adj* вздо́рный.

quarry[1] *n* (*for stone etc.*) каменоло́ммня; *vt* добыва́ть *impf*, добы́ть *pf*.

quarry[2] *n* (*prey*) добы́ча.

quart *n* ква́рта. **quarter** *n* че́тверть; (*of year*; *of town*) кварта́л; *pl* кварти́ры *f pl*; **a** ∼ **to one** без че́тверти час; ∼**-final** че́тверть-фина́л; *vt* (*divide*) дели́ть *impf*, раз∼ *pf* на четы́ре ча́сти; (*lodge*) расквартиро́вывать *impf*, расквартирова́ть *pf*. **quarterly** *adj* кварта́льный; *adv* раз в кварта́л. **quartet** *n* кварте́т.

quartz *n* кварц.

quash *vt* (*annul*) аннули́ровать *impf & pf*; (*crush*) подавля́ть *impf*, подави́ть *pf*.

quasi- *in comb* квази-.

quaver *vi* дрожа́ть *impf*; *n* (*mus*) восьма́я *sb* но́ты.

quay *n* на́бережная *sb*.

queasy *adj*: **I feel** ∼ меня́ тошни́т.

queen *n* короле́ва; (*cards*) да́ма; (*chess*) ферзь *m*.

queer *adj* стра́нный.

quell *vt* подавля́ть *impf*, подави́ть *pf*.

quench *vt* (*thirst*) утоля́ть *impf*, утоли́ть *pf*; (*fire, desire*) туши́ть *impf*, по∼ *pf*.

query *n* вопро́с; *vt* (*express doubt*) выража́ть *impf* сомне́ние в+*prep*. **quest** *n* по́иски *m pl*; **in** ∼ **of** в по́исках+*gen*. **question** *n* вопро́с; **beyond** ∼ вне сомне́ния; **it is a** ∼ **of** э́то вопро́с+*gen*; **it is out of the** ∼ об э́том не мо́жет быть и ре́чи; **the person in** ∼ челове́к, о кото́ром идёт речь; **the** ∼ **is this** де́ло в э́том; ∼ **mark** вопроси́тельный знак; *vt* расспра́шивать *impf*, распроси́ть *pf*; (*interrogate*) допра́шивать *impf* допроси́ть *pf*; (*doubt*) сомнева́ться *impf* в+*prep*. **questionable** *adj* сомни́тельный. **questionnaire** *n* вопро́сник.

queue *n* о́чередь; *vi* стоя́ть *impf* в о́череди.

quibble *n* софи́зм; (*minor criticism*) приди́рка; *vi* придира́ться *impf*; (*argue*) спо́рить *impf*.

quick *adj* ско́рый, бы́стрый; ∼**-tempered** вспы́льчивый; ∼**-witted** нахо́дчивый; *n*: **to the** ∼ за живо́е; *adv* ско́ро, бы́стро; *as imper* скоре́е! **quicken** *vt & i* ускоря́ть(ся) *impf*, ускори́ть(ся) *pf*. **quickness** *n* быстрота́. **quicksand** *n* зыбу́чий песо́к. **quicksilver** *n* ртуть.

quid *n* фунт.

quiet *n* (*silence*) тишина́; (*calm*) споко́йствие; *adj* ти́хий; споко́йный; *int* ти́ше!; *vt & i* успока́ивать(ся) *impf*, успоко́ить(ся) *pf*.

quill *n* перо́; (*spine*) игла́.

quilt *n* (стёганое) одея́ло; *vt* стега́ть *impf*, вы́∼ *pf*. **quilted** *adj* стёганый.

quintessential *adj* наибо́лее суще́ственный.

quintet *n* квинте́т. **quins, quintuplets**

quip 417 raisin

n pl пять близнецо́в.

quip *n* острота́; остри́ть *impf*, c~ *pf*.

quirk *n* причу́да. **quirky** *adj* с причу́дами.

quit *vt* (*leave*) покида́ть *impf*, поки́нуть *pf*; (*stop*) перестава́ть *impf*, переста́ть *pf*; (*give up*) броса́ть *impf*, бро́сить *pf*; (*resign*) уходи́ть *impf*, уйти́ *pf* c+*gen*.

quite *adv* (*wholly*) совсе́м; (*rather*) дово́льно; ~ **a few** дово́льно мно́го.

quits *predic*: **we are** ~ мы с тобо́й кви́ты; **I am** ~ **with him** я расквита́лся (*past*) с ним.

quiver *vi* (*tremble*) трепета́ть *impf*; *n* тре́пет.

quiz *n* викторина. **quizzical** *adj* насме́шливый.

quorum *n* кво́рум.

quota *n* но́рма.

quotation *n* цита́та; (*of price*) цена́; ~ **marks** кавы́чки (-чек) *pl*. **quote** *vt* цити́ровать *impf*, про~ *pf*; ссыла́ться *impf*, сосла́ться *pf* на+*acc*; (*price*) назнача́ть *impf*, назна́чить *pf*.

R

rabbi *n* равви́н.

rabbit *n* кро́лик.

rabble *n* сброд.

rabid *adj* бе́шеный. **rabies** *n* бе́шенство.

race[1] *n* (*ethnic* ~) ра́са; род.

race[2] *n* (*contest*) (*on foot*) бег; (*of cars etc.; fig*) го́нка, го́нки *f pl*; (*of horses*) ска́чки *f pl*; ~**track** трек; (*for horse* ~) скакова́я доро́жка; *vi* (*compete*) состяза́ться *impf* в ско́рости; (*rush*) мча́ться *impf*; *vt* бежа́ть *impf* наперегонки́ c+*instr*. **racecourse** *n* ипподро́м. **racehorse** *n* скакова́я ло́шадь.

racial *adj* ра́совый. **rac(ial)ism** *n* раси́зм. **rac(ial)ist** *n* раси́ст, ~ка; *adj* раси́стский.

racing *n* (*horses*) ска́чки *f pl*; (*cars*) го́нки *f pl*; ~ **car** го́ночный автомоби́ль *m*; ~ **driver** го́нщик.

rack *n* (*for hats etc.*) ве́шалка; (*for plates etc.*) стелла́ж; (*in train etc.*) се́тка; *vt*: ~ **one's brains** лома́ть *impf* себе́ го́лову.

racket[1] *n* (*bat*) раке́тка.

racket[2] *n* (*uproar*) шум; (*illegal activity*) рэ́кет. **racketeer** *n* рэкети́р.

racy *adj* колори́тный.

radar *n* (*system*) радиолока́ция; (*apparatus*) радиолока́тор, рада́р; *attrib* рада́рный.

radiance *n* сия́ние. **radiant** *adj* сия́ющий. **radiate** *vt* & *i* излуча́ть(ся) *impf*, излучи́ться *pf*. **radiation** *n* излуче́ние. **radiator** *n* батаре́я; (*in car*) радиа́тор.

radical *adj* радика́льный; *n* радика́л.

radio *n* ра́дио *neut indecl*; *vt* ради́ровать *impf* & *pf* +*dat*.

radioactive *adj* радиоакти́вный. **radioactivity** *n* радиоакти́вность. **radiographer** *n* рентгено́лог. **radiologist** *n* радио́лог; рентгено́лог. **radiotherapy** *n* радиотерапи́я.

radish *n* реди́ска.

radius *n* ра́диус.

raffle *n* лотере́я; *vt* разы́грывать *impf*, разыгра́ть *pf* в лотере́е.

raft *n* плот.

rafter *n* (*beam*) стропи́ло.

rag *n* тря́пка; *pl* (*clothes*) лохмо́тья (-ьев) *pl*.

rage *n* я́рость; **all the** ~ после́дний крик мо́ды; *vi* беси́ться *impf*; (*storm etc.*) бушева́ть *impf*.

ragged *adj* (*jagged*) зазу́бренный; (*of clothes*) рва́ный.

raid *n* налёт; (*by police*) обла́ва; *vt* де́лать *impf*, c~ *pf* налёт на+*acc*.

rail *n* пери́ла (-л) *pl*; (*rly*) рельс; **by** ~ по́ездом. **railing** *n* пери́ла (-л) *pl*. **railway** *n* желе́зная доро́га; *attrib* железнодоро́жный. **railwayman** *n* железнодоро́жник.

rain *n* дождь *m*; *v impers*: **it is** (**was**) ~**ing** идёт (шёл) дождь; *vt* осыпа́ть *impf*, осы́пать *pf* +*instr* (**upon** +*acc*); *vi* осыпа́ться *impf*, осы́паться *pf*. **rainbow** *n* ра́дуга. **raincoat** *n* плащ. **raindrop** *n* дождева́я ка́пля. **rainfall** *n* (*amount of rain*) коли́чество оса́дков. **rainy** *adj* дождли́вый; ~ **day** чёрный день *m*.

raise *vt* (*lift*) поднима́ть *impf*, подня́ть *pf*; (*heighten*) повыша́ть *impf*, повы́сить *pf*; (*provoke*) вызыва́ть *impf*, вы́звать *pf*; (*money*) собира́ть *impf*, собра́ть *pf*; (*children*) расти́ть *impf*.

raisin *n* изю́минка; *pl* (*collect*) изю́м.

rake n (tool) гра́бли (-бель & -блей) pl; vt грести́ impf; (~ together, up) сгреба́ть impf, сгрести́ pf.

rally vt & i спла́чивать(ся) impf, сплоти́ть(ся) pf; vi (after illness etc.) оправля́ться impf, опра́виться pf; n (meeting) слёт; ми́тинг; (motoring ~) (авто)ра́лли neut indecl; (tennis) обме́н уда́рами.

ram n (sheep) бара́н; vt (beat down) трамбова́ть impf, у~ pf; (drive in) вбива́ть impf, вбить pf.

ramble vi (walk) прогу́ливаться impf, прогуля́ться pf; (speak) бубни́ть impf; n прогу́лка. **rambling** adj (incoherent) бессвя́зный.

ramification n (fig) после́дствие.

ramp n скат.

rampage vi бу́йствовать impf.

rampant adj (plant) бу́йный; (unchecked) безу́держный.

rampart n вал.

ramshackle adj ве́тхий.

ranch n ра́нчо neut indecl.

rancid adj прого́рклый.

rancour n зло́ба.

random adj случа́йный; at ~ науда́чу.

range n (of mountains) цепь; (artillery ~) полиго́н; (of voice) диапазо́н; (scope) круг, преде́лы m pl; (operating distance) да́льность; vi (vary) колеба́ться impf, по~ pf; (wander) броди́ть impf; ~ over (include) охва́тывать impf, охвати́ть pf.

rank[1] n (row) ряд; (taxi ~) стоя́нка такси́; (grade) зва́ние, чин, ранг; vt (classify) классифици́ровать impf & pf; (consider) счита́ть impf (as +instr); vi: ~ with быть в числе́+gen.

rank[2] adj (luxuriant) бу́йный; (in smell) злово́нный; (gross) я́вный.

rankle vi боле́ть impf.

ransack vt (search) обша́ривать impf, обша́рить pf; (plunder) гра́бить impf, о~ pf.

ransom n вы́куп; vt выкупа́ть impf, вы́купить pf.

rant vi вопи́ть impf.

rap n стук; vt (резко) ударя́ть impf, уда́рить pf; vi стуча́ть impf, сту́кнуть pf.

rape[1] vt наси́ловать impf, из~ pf; n изнаси́лование.

rape[2] n (plant) рапс.

rapid adj бы́стрый; n: pl поро́г, быстрина́. **rapidity** n быстрота́.

rapt adj восхищённый; (absorbed) поглощённый. **rapture** n восто́рг. **rapturous** adj восто́рженный.

rare[1] adj (of meat) недожа́ренный.

rare[2] adj ре́дкий. **rarity** n ре́дкость.

rascal n плут.

rash[1] n сыпь.

rash[2] adj опроме́тчивый.

rasher n ло́мтик (беко́на).

rasp n (file) ра́шпиль m; (sound) скре́жет; vt: ~ out га́ркнуть pf.

raspberry n мали́на (no pl; usu collect).

rasping adj (sound) скрипу́чий.

rat n кры́са; ~ race го́нка за успе́хом.

ratchet n храпови́к.

rate n но́рма, ста́вка; (speed) ско́рость; pl ме́стные нало́ги m pl; at any ~ во вся́ком слу́чае; vt оце́нивать impf, оцени́ть pf; (consider) счита́ть impf; vi счита́ться impf (as +instr).

rather adv скоре́е; (somewhat) дово́льно; he (she) had (would) ~ он (она́) предпочёл (-чла́) бы+inf.

ratification n ратифика́ция. **ratify** vt ратифици́ровать impf & pf.

rating n оце́нка.

ratio n пропо́рция.

ration n паёк, рацио́н; vt норми́ровать impf & pf; be ~ed выдава́ться impf, вы́даться pf по ка́рточкам.

rational adj разу́мный. **rationalism** n рационали́зм. **rationality** n разу́мность. **rationalize** vt обосно́вывать impf, обоснова́ть pf; (industry etc.) рационализи́ровать impf & pf.

rattle vi & t (sound) греме́ть impf (+instr); ~ along (move) грохота́ть impf; ~ off (utter) отбараба́нить pf; n (sound) треск, гро́хот; (toy) погрему́шка. **rattlesnake** n грему́чая змея́.

raucous adj ре́зкий.

ravage vt опустоша́ть impf, опустоши́ть pf; n: pl разруши́тельное де́йствие.

rave vi бре́дить impf; ~ about быть в восто́рге от+gen.

raven n во́рон.

ravenous adj голо́дный как волк.

ravine n уще́лье.

ravishing *adj* восхити́тельный.

raw *adj* сыро́й; (*inexperienced*) нео́пытный; ~ **material(s)** сырьё (*no pl*).

ray *n* луч.

raze *vt*: ~ **to the ground** ровня́ть *impf*, с~ *pf* с землёй.

razor *n* бри́тва; ~**-blade** ле́звие.

reach *vt* (*attain, extend to, arrive at*) достига́ть *impf*, дости́чь & дости́гнуть *pf* +gen, до+gen; доходи́ть *impf*, дойти́ *pf* до+gen; (*with hand*) дотя́гиваться *impf*, дотяну́ться *pf* до+gen; *vi* (*extend*) простира́ться *impf*; *n* досяга́емость; (*pl, of river*) тече́ние.

react *vi* реаги́ровать *impf* & *pf* (**to** на+*acc*). **reaction** *n* реа́кция. **reactionary** *adj* реакцио́нный; *n* реакционе́р. **reactor** *n* реа́ктор.

read *vt* чита́ть *impf*, про~, прочéсть *pf*; (*mus*) разбира́ть *impf*, разобра́ть *pf*; (~ *a meter etc.*) снима́ть *impf*, снять *pf* показа́ния +gen; (*univ*) изуча́ть *impf*; (*interpret*) толкова́ть *impf*. **readable** *adj* интере́сный. **reader** *n* чита́тель *m*, ~ница; (*book*) хрестома́тия.

readily *adv* (*willingly*) охо́тно; (*easily*) легко́. **readiness** *n* гото́вность.

reading *n* чте́ние; (*on meter*) показа́ние.

ready *adj* гото́вый (**for** к+*dat*, на+*acc*); **get** ~ гото́виться *impf*; ~**-made** гото́вый; ~ **money** нали́чные де́ньги (-нег, -ньга́м) *pl*.

real *adj* настоя́щий, реа́льный; ~ **estate** недви́жимость. **realism** *n* реали́зм. **realist** *n* реали́ст. **realistic** *adj* реалисти́чный, -и́ческий. **reality** *n* действи́тельность; **in** ~ действи́тельно. **realization** *n* (*of plan etc.*) осуществле́ние; (*of assets*) реализа́ция; (*understanding*) осозна́ние. **realize** *vt* (*plan etc.*) осуществля́ть *impf*, осуществи́ть *pf*; (*assets*) реализова́ть *impf* & *pf*; (*apprehend*) осознава́ть *impf*, осозна́ть *pf*. **really** *adv* действи́тельно, в са́мом де́ле.

realm *n* (*kingdom*) короле́вство; (*sphere*) о́бласть.

reap *vt* жать *impf*, сжать *pf*; (*fig*) пожина́ть *impf*, пожа́ть *pf*.

rear[1] *vt* (*lift*) поднима́ть *impf*, подня́ть *pf*; (*children*) воспи́тывать *impf*, воспита́ть *pf*; *vi* (*of horse*) станови́ться *impf*, стать *pf* на дыбы́.

rear[2] *n* за́дняя часть; (*mil*) тыл; **bring up the** ~ замыка́ть *impf*, замкну́ть *pf* ше́ствие; *adj* за́дний; (*also mil*) ты́льный. **rearguard** *n* арьерга́рд; ~ **action** арьерга́рдный бой.

rearmament *n* перевооруже́ние.

rearrange *vt* меня́ть *impf*.

reason *n* (*cause*) причи́на, основа́ние; (*intellect*) ра́зум, рассу́док; *vi* рассужда́ть *impf*; ~ **with** (*person*) угова́ривать *impf* +*acc*. **reasonable** *adj* разу́мный; (*inexpensive*) недорого́й.

reassurance *n* успока́ивание. **reassure** *vt* успока́ивать *impf*, успоко́ить *pf*.

rebate *n* ски́дка.

rebel *n* повста́нец; *vi* восстава́ть *impf*, восста́ть *pf*. **rebellion** *n* восста́ние. **rebellious** *adj* мяте́жный.

rebound *vi* отска́кивать *impf*, отскочи́ть *pf*; *n* рикоше́т.

rebuff *n* отпо́р; *vt* дава́ть *impf*, дать *pf* +*dat* отпо́р.

rebuild *vt* перестра́ивать *impf*, перестро́ить *pf*.

rebuke *vt* упрека́ть *impf*, упрекну́ть *pf*; *n* упрёк.

rebuttal *n* опроверже́ние.

recalcitrant *adj* непоко́рный.

recall *vt* (*an official*) отзыва́ть *impf*, отозва́ть *pf*; (*remember*) вспомина́ть *impf*, вспо́мнить *pf*; *n* о́тзыв; (*memory*) па́мять.

recant *vi* отрека́ться *impf*, отре́чься *pf*.

recapitulate *vt* резюми́ровать *impf* & *pf*.

recast *vt* переде́лывать *impf*, переде́лать *pf*.

recede *vi* отходи́ть *impf*, отойти́ *pf*.

receipt *n* (*receiving*) получе́ние; *pl* (*amount*) вы́ручка; (*written* ~) квита́нция. **receive** *vt* (*admit, entertain*) принима́ть *impf*, приня́ть *pf*; (*get, be given*) получа́ть *impf*, получи́ть *pf*. **receiver** *n* (*radio, television*) приёмник; (*tel*) тру́бка.

recent *adj* неда́вний; (*new*) но́вый. **recently** *adv* неда́вно.

receptacle *n* вмести́лище. **reception** *n* приём; ~ **room** приёмная *sb*. **receptionist** *n* секрета́рь *m*, -рша, в

приёмной. **receptive** *adj* воспри-
имчивый.

recess *n* (*parl*) кани́кулы (-л) *pl*;
(*niche*) ни́ша. **recession** *n* спад.

recipe *n* реце́пт.

recipient *n* получа́тель *m*.

reciprocal *adj* взаи́мный. **recipro-
cate** *vt* отвеча́ть *impf* (взаи́мно-
стью) на+*acc*.

recital *n* (со́льный) конце́рт. **recitation** *n* публи́чное чте́ние. **recite** *vt*
деклами́ровать *impf*, про~ *pf*; (*list*)
перечисля́ть *impf*, перечи́слить *pf*.

reckless *adj* (*rash*) опроме́тчивый;
(*careless*) неосторо́жный.

reckon *vt* подсчи́тывать *impf*, под-
счита́ть *pf*; (*also regard as*) счита́ть
impf, счесть *pf* (**to be** +*instr*); *vi*: ~
on рассчи́тывать *impf*, рассчита́ть
pf на+*acc*; ~ **with** счита́ться *impf*
с+*instr*. **reckoning** *n* счёт; **day of** ~
час распла́ты.

reclaim *vt* тре́бовать *impf*, по~ *pf*
обра́тно; (*land*) осва́ивать *impf*,
осво́ить *pf*.

recline *vi* полулежа́ть *impf*.

recluse *n* затво́рник.

recognition *n* узнава́ние; (*acknowledgement*) призна́ние. **recognize** *vt*
узнава́ть *impf*, узна́ть *pf*; (*acknowledge*) признава́ть *impf*, призна́ть *pf*.

recoil *vi* отпря́дывать *impf*, отпря́-
нуть *pf*.

recollect *vt* вспомина́ть *impf*, вспо́м-
нить *pf*. **recollection** *n* воспомина́-
ние.

recommend *vt* рекомендова́ть *impf*
& *pf*. **recommendation** *n* рекомен-
да́ция.

recompense *n* вознагражде́ние; *vt*
вознагражда́ть *impf*, вознагради́ть
pf.

reconcile *vt* примиря́ть *impf*, прими-
ри́ть *pf*; ~ **o.s.** примиря́ться *impf*,
примири́ться *pf* (**to** с+*instr*). **recon-
ciliation** *n* примире́ние.

reconnaissance *n* разве́дка. **reconnoitre** *vt* разве́дывать *impf*, разве́-
дать *pf*.

reconstruct *vt* перестра́ивать *impf*,
перестро́ить *pf*. **reconstruction** *n*
перестро́йка.

record *vt* запи́сывать *impf*, записа́ть
pf; *n* за́пись; (*minutes*) протоко́л;
(*gramophone* ~) грампласти́нка;

(*sport etc.*) реко́рд; **off the** ~ не-
официа́льно; *adj* реко́рдный; ~-
breaker, -holder рекордсме́н, ~ка;
~-**player** прои́грыватель *m*. **recorder** *n* (*mus*) блок-фле́йта. **recording** *n* за́пись.

recount[1] *vt* (*narrate*) переска́зывать
impf, пересказа́ть *pf*.

re-count[2] *vt* (*count again*) пересчи́-
тывать *impf*, пересчита́ть *pf*; *n*
пересчёт.

recoup *vt* возвраща́ть *impf*, верну́ть
pf (**losses** поте́рянное).

recourse *n*: **have** ~ **to** прибега́ть
impf, прибе́гнуть *pf* к+*dat*.

recover *vt* (*regain possession*) полу-
ча́ть *impf*, получи́ть *pf* обра́тно;
возвраща́ть *impf*, верну́ть *pf*; *vi* (~
health) поправля́ться *impf*, попра́-
виться *pf* (**from** по́сле+*gen*). **recovery** *n* возвраще́ние; выздоровле́-
ние.

recreate *vt* воссоздава́ть *impf*, вос-
созда́ть *pf*.

recreation *n* развлече́ние, о́тдых.

recrimination *n* взаи́мное обвине́-
ние.

recruit *n* новобра́нец; *vt* вербова́ть
impf, за~ *pf*. **recruitment** *n* вер-
бо́вка.

rectangle *n* прямоуго́льник. **rectangular** *adj* прямоуго́льный.

rectify *vt* исправля́ть *impf*, испра́-
вить *pf*.

rector *n* (*priest*) прихо́дский свяще́н-
ник; (*univ*) ре́ктор. **rectory** *n* дом
прихо́дского свяще́нника.

rectum *n* прямáя кишка́.

recuperate *vi* поправля́ться *impf*,
попра́виться *pf*. **recuperation** *n*
выздоровле́ние.

recur *vi* повторя́ться *impf*, повто-
ри́ться *pf*. **recurrence** *n* повторе́-
ние. **recurrent** *adj* повторя́ющийся.

recycle *vt* перераба́тывать *impf*,
перерабо́тать *pf*.

red *adj* кра́сный; (*of hair*) ры́жий; *n*
кра́сный цвет; (*polit*) кра́сный *sb*;
in the ~ в долгу́; ~-**handed** с по-
ли́чным; ~ **herring** ло́жный след;
~-**hot** раскалённый докрасна́; **R**~
Indian инде́ец, индиа́нка; ~ **tape**
волоки́та. **redcurrant** *n* кра́сная
сморо́дина (*no pl*; *usu collect*). **redden** *vt* окра́шивать *impf*, окра́сить

pf в кра́сный цвет; *vi* красне́ть *impf*, по~ *pf*. **reddish** *adj* красноватый; (*hair*) рыжева́тый.

redecorate *vt* отде́лывать *impf*, отде́лать *pf*.

redeem *vt* (*buy back*) выкупа́ть *impf*, вы́купить *pf*; (*from sin*) искупа́ть *impf*, искупи́ть *pf*. **redeemer** *n* искупи́тель *m*. **redemption** *n* вы́куп; искупле́ние.

redeploy *vt* передислоци́ровать *impf* & *pf*.

redo *vt* переде́лывать *impf*, переде́лать *pf*.

redouble *vt* удва́ивать *impf*, удвои́ть *pf*.

redress *vt* исправля́ть *impf*, испра́вить *pf*; ~ **the balance** восстана́вливать *impf*, восстанови́ть *pf* равнове́сие; *n* возмеще́ние.

reduce *vt* (*decrease*) уменьша́ть *impf*, уме́ньшить *pf*; (*lower*) снижа́ть *impf*, сни́зить *pf*; (*shorten*) сокраща́ть *impf*, сократи́ть *pf*; (*bring to*) доводи́ть *impf*, довести́ *pf* (**to** в+*acc*). **reduction** *n* уменьше́ние, сниже́ние, сокраще́ние; (*discount*) ски́дка.

redundancy *n* (*dismissal*) увольне́ние. **redundant** *adj* изли́шний; **make** ~ увольня́ть *impf*, уво́лить *pf*.

reed *n* (*plant*) тростни́к; (*in oboe etc.*) язычо́к.

reef *n* риф.

reek *n* вонь; *vi*: ~ (**of**) воня́ть *impf* (+*instr*).

reel[1] *n* кату́шка; *vt*: ~ **off** (*story etc.*) отбараба́нить *pf*.

reel[2] *vi* (*stagger*) поша́тываться *impf*, пошатну́ться *pf*.

refectory *n* (*monastery*) тра́пезная *sb*; (*univ*) столо́вая *sb*.

refer *vt* (*direct*) отсыла́ть *impf*, отосла́ть *pf* (**to** к+*dat*); *vi*: ~ **to** (*cite*) ссыла́ться *impf*, сосла́ться *pf* на +*acc*; (*mention*) упомина́ть *impf*, упомяну́ть *pf* +*acc*. **referee** *n* судья́ *m*; *vt* суди́ть *impf*. **reference** *n* (*to book etc.*) ссы́лка; (*mention*) упомина́ние; (*testimonial*) характери́стика; ~ **book** спра́вочник. **referendum** *n* рефере́ндум.

refine *vt* очища́ть *impf*, очи́стить *pf*. **refined** *adj* (*in style etc.*) утончённый; (*in manners*) культу́рный. **re-**

finement *n* утончённость. **refinery** *n* (*oil* ~) нефтеочисти́тельный заво́д.

refit *vt* переобору́довать *impf* & *pf*.

reflect *vt* отража́ть *impf*, отрази́ть *pf*; *vi* размышля́ть *impf*, размы́слить *pf* (**on** о+*prep*). **reflection** *n* отраже́ние; размышле́ние; **on** ~ поду́мав. **reflective** *adj* (*thoughtful*) серьёзный. **reflector** *n* рефле́ктор.

reflex *n* рефле́кс; *adj* рефле́кторный. **reflexive** *adj* (*gram*) возвра́тный.

reform *vt* реформи́ровать *impf* & *pf*; *vt* & *i* (*of people*) исправля́ть(ся) *impf*, испра́вить(ся) *pf*; *n* рефо́рма; исправле́ние. **Reformation** *n* Реформа́ция.

refract *vt* преломля́ть *impf*, преломи́ть *pf*.

refrain[1] *n* припе́в.

refrain[2] *vi* возде́рживаться *impf*, воздержа́ться *pf* (**from** от+*gen*).

refresh *vt* освежа́ть *impf*, освежи́ть *pf*. **refreshments** *n pl* напи́тки *m pl*.

refrigerate *vt* охлажда́ть *impf*, охлади́ть *pf*. **refrigeration** *n* охлажде́ние. **refrigerator** *n* холоди́льник.

refuge *n* убе́жище; **take** ~ находи́ть *impf*, найти́ *pf* убе́жище. **refugee** *n* бе́женец, -нка.

refund *vt* возвраща́ть *impf*, возврати́ть *pf*; (*expenses*) возмеща́ть *impf*, возмести́ть *pf*; *n* возвраще́ние (де́нег); возмеще́ние.

refusal *n* отка́з. **refuse**[1] *vt* отка́зывать *impf*, отказа́ть *pf*.

refuse[2] *n* му́сор.

refute *vt* опроверга́ть *impf*, опрове́ргнуть *pf*.

regain *vt* возвраща́ть *impf*, верну́ть *pf*.

regal *adj* короле́вский.

regale *vt* угоща́ть *impf*, угости́ть *pf* (**with** +*instr*).

regalia *n pl* рега́лии *f pl*.

regard *vt* смотре́ть *impf*, по~ *pf* на+*acc*; (*take into account*) счита́ться *impf* с+*instr*; ~ **as** счита́ть *impf* +*instr*, за+*instr*; **as** ~**s** что каса́ется+*gen*; *n* (*esteem*) уваже́ние; (*attention*) внима́ние; *pl* приве́т. **regarding** *prep* относи́тельно+*gen*. **regardless** *adv* не обраща́я внима́ния; ~ **of** не счита́ясь с+*instr*.

regatta *n* рега́та.
regenerate *vt* перерожда́ть *impf*, перероди́ть *pf*. **regeneration** *n* перерожде́ние.
regent *n* ре́гент.
régime *n* режи́м.
regiment *n* полк. **regimental** *adj* полково́й. **regimentation** *n* регламента́ция.
region *n* регио́н. **regional** *adj* региона́льный.
register *n* рее́стр; (*also mus*) реги́стр; *vt* регистри́ровать *impf*, за~ *pf*; (*a letter*) отправля́ть *impf*, отпра́вить *pf* заказны́м. **registered** *adj* (*letter*) заказно́й. **registrar** *n* регистра́тор. **registration** *n* регистра́ция; ~ **number** но́мер маши́ны. **registry** *n* регистрату́ра; ~ **office** загс.
regression *n* регре́сс. **regressive** *adj* регресси́вный.
regret *vt* сожале́ть *impf* о+*prep*; *n* сожале́ние. **regretful** *adj* по́лный сожале́ния. **regrettable** *adj* приско́рбный. **regrettably** *adv* к сожале́нию.
regular *adj* регуля́рный; (*also gram*) пра́вильный; *n* (*coll*) завсегда́тай. **regularity** *n* регуля́рность. **regulate** *vt* регули́ровать *impf*, у~ *pf*. **regulation** *n* регули́рование; *pl* пра́вила *neut pl*.
rehabilitate *vt* реабилити́ровать *impf* & *pf*. **rehabilitation** *n* реабилита́ция.
rehearsal *n* репети́ция. **rehearse** *vt* репети́ровать *impf*, от~ *pf*.
reign *n* ца́рствование; *vi* ца́рствовать *impf*; (*fig*) цари́ть *impf*.
reimburse *vt* возмеща́ть *impf*, возмести́ть *pf* (+*dat of person*). **reimbursement** *n* возмеще́ние.
rein *n* по́вод.
reincarnation *n* перевоплоще́ние.
reindeer *n* се́верный оле́нь *m*.
reinforce *vt* подкрепля́ть *impf*, подкрепи́ть *pf*. **reinforcement** *n* (*also pl*) подкрепле́ние.
reinstate *vt* восстана́вливать *impf*, восстанови́ть *pf*. **reinstatement** *n* восстановле́ние.
reiterate *vt* повторя́ть *impf*, повтори́ть *pf*.
reject *vt* отверга́ть *impf*, отве́ргнуть

pf; (*as defective*) бракова́ть *impf*, за~ *pf*; *n* брак. **rejection** *n* отка́з (*of* от+*gen*).
rejoice *vi* ра́доваться *impf*, об~ *pf* (*in, at* +*dat*). **rejoicing** *n* ра́дость.
rejoin *vt* (*вновь*) присоединя́ться *impf*, присоедини́ться *pf* к+*dat*.
rejuvenate *vt* омола́живать *impf*, омолоди́ть *pf*.
relapse *n* рециди́в; *vi* сно́ва впада́ть *impf*, впасть *pf* (*into* в+*acc*); (*into illness*) сно́ва заболева́ть *impf*, заболе́ть *pf*.
relate *vt* (*tell*) расска́зывать *impf*, рассказа́ть *pf*; (*connect*) свя́зывать *impf*, связа́ть *pf*; *vi* относи́ться *impf* (*to* к+*dat*). **related** *adj* ро́дственный.
relation *n* отноше́ние; (*person*) ро́дственник, -ица. **relationship** *n* (*connection; liaison*) связь; (*kinship*) родство́. **relative** *adj* относи́тельный; *n* ро́дственник, -ица. **relativity** *n* относи́тельность.
relax *vt* ослабля́ть *impf*, осла́бить *pf*; *vi* (*rest*) расслабля́ться *impf*, рассла́биться *pf*. **relaxation** *n* ослабле́ние; (*rest*) о́тдых.
relay *n* (*shift*) сме́на; (*sport*) эстафе́та; (*electr*) реле́ *neut indecl*; *vt* передава́ть *impf*, переда́ть *pf*.
release *vt* (*set free*) освобожда́ть *impf*, освободи́ть *pf*; (*unfasten, let go*) отпуска́ть *impf*, отпусти́ть *pf*; (*film etc.*) выпуска́ть *impf*, вы́пустить *pf*; *n* освобожде́ние; вы́пуск.
relegate *vt* переводи́ть *impf*, перевести́ *pf* (в ни́зшую гру́ппу). **relegation** *n* перево́д (в ни́зшую гру́ппу).
relent *vi* смягча́ться *impf*, смягчи́ться *pf*. **relentless** *adj* непреста́нный.
relevance *n* уме́стность. **relevant** *adj* относя́щийся к де́лу; уме́стный.
reliability *n* надёжность. **reliable** *adj* надёжный. **reliance** *n* дове́рие. **reliant** *adj*: be ~ upon зави́сеть *impf* от+*gen*.
relic *n* оста́ток, рели́квия.
relief[1] *n* (*art, geol*) релье́ф.
relief[2] *n* (*alleviation*) облегче́ние; (*assistance*) по́мощь; (*in duty*) сме́на. **relieve** *vt* (*alleviate*) облегча́ть *impf*, облегчи́ть *pf*; (*replace*) сменя́ть *impf*, смени́ть *pf*; (*unburden*) освобожда́ть *impf*, освободи́ть *pf* (*of* от+*gen*).

religion n рели́гия. **religious** adj религио́зный.

relinquish vt оставля́ть impf, оста́вить pf; (right etc.) отка́зываться impf, отказа́ться pf от+gen.

relish n (enjoyment) смак; (cul) припра́ва; vt смакова́ть impf.

relocate vt & i перемеща́ть(ся) impf, перемести́ть(ся) pf.

reluctance n неохо́та. **reluctant** adj неохо́тный; **be ~ to** не жела́ть impf +inf.

rely vi полага́ться impf, положи́ться pf (**on** на+acc).

remain vi остава́ться impf, оста́ться pf. **remainder** n оста́ток. **remains** n pl оста́тки m pl; (human ~) оста́нки (-ков) pl.

remand vt содержа́ть impf под стра́жей; **be on ~** содержа́ться impf под стра́жей.

remark vt замеча́ть impf, заме́тить pf; n замеча́ние. **remarkable** adj замеча́тельный.

remarry vi вступа́ть impf, вступи́ть pf в но́вый брак.

remedial adj лече́бный. **remedy** n сре́дство (**for** от, про́тив+gen); vt исправля́ть impf, испра́вить pf.

remember vt по́мнить impf, вспомина́ть impf, вспо́мнить pf; (greet) передава́ть impf, переда́ть pf приве́т от+gen (**to** +dat). **remembrance** n па́мять.

remind vt напомина́ть impf, напо́мнить pf +dat (**of** +acc, о+prep). **reminder** n напомина́ние.

reminiscence n воспомина́ние. **reminiscent** adj напомина́ющий.

remiss predic небре́жный. **remission** n (pardon) отпуще́ние; (med) реми́ссия. **remit** vt пересыла́ть impf, пересла́ть pf. **remittance** n перево́д де́нег; (money) де́нежный перево́д.

remnant n оста́ток.

remonstrate vi: **~ with** увещева́ть impf +acc.

remorse n угрызе́ния neut pl со́вести. **remorseful** adj по́лный раска́яния. **remorseless** adj безжа́лостный.

remote adj отдалённый; **~ control** дистанцио́нное управле́ние.

removal n (taking away) удале́ние; (of obstacles) устране́ние. **remove** vt (take away) убира́ть impf, убра́ть pf; (get rid of) устраня́ть impf, устрани́ть pf.

remuneration n вознагражде́ние. **remunerative** adj вы́годный.

renaissance n возрожде́ние; **the R~** Возрожде́ние.

render vt воздава́ть impf, возда́ть pf; (help etc.) ока́зывать impf, оказа́ть pf; (role etc.) исполня́ть impf, испо́лнить pf; (stone) штукату́рить impf, о~, от~ pf. **rendering** n исполне́ние.

rendezvous n (meeting) свида́ние.

renegade n ренега́т, ~ка.

renew vt (extend; continue) возобновля́ть impf, возобнови́ть pf; (replace) обновля́ть impf, обнови́ть pf. **renewal** n (воз)обновле́ние.

renounce vt отверга́ть impf, отве́ргнуть pf; (claim) отка́зываться impf, отказа́ться pf от+gen.

renovate vt ремонти́ровать impf, от~ pf. **renovation** n ремо́нт.

renown n сла́ва. **renowned** adj изве́стный; **be ~ for** сла́виться impf +instr.

rent n (for home) квартпла́та; (for premises) (аре́ндная) пла́та; vt (of tenant) арендова́ть impf & pf; (of owner) сдава́ть impf, сдать pf.

renunciation n (repudiation) отрица́ние; (of claim) отка́з.

rep n (comm) аге́нт.

repair vt ремонти́ровать impf, от~ pf; n (also pl) ремо́нт (only sg); почи́нка; **in good/bad ~** в хоро́шем/плохо́м состоя́нии.

reparations n pl репара́ции f pl.

repatriate vt репатрии́ровать impf & pf. **repatriation** n репатриа́ция.

repay vt отпла́чивать impf, отплати́ть pf (person +dat). **repayment** n отпла́та.

repeal vt отменя́ть impf, отмени́ть pf; n отме́на.

repeat vt & i повторя́ть(ся) impf, повтори́ть(ся) pf; n повторе́ние. **repeatedly** adv неоднокра́тно.

repel vt отта́лкивать impf, оттолкну́ть pf; (enemy) отража́ть impf, отрази́ть pf.

repent vi раска́иваться impf, раска́яться pf. **repentance** n раска́яние.

repentant *adj* раскаивающийся.

repercussion *n* последствие.

repertoire *n* репертуар. **repertory** *n* (*store*) запас; (*repertoire*) репертуар; ~ **company** постоянная труппа.

repetition *n* повторение. **repetitious, repetitive** *adj* повторяющийся.

replace *vt* (*put back*) класть *impf*, положить *pf* обратно; (*substitute*) заменять *impf*, заменить *pf* (**by** +*instr*). **replacement** *n* замена.

replay *n* переигровка.

replenish *vt* пополнять *impf*, пополнить *pf*.

replete *adj* насыщенный; (*sated*) сытый.

replica *n* копия.

reply *vt & i* отвечать *impf*, ответить *pf* (**to** на+*acc*); *n* ответ.

report *vt* сообщать *impf*, сообщить *pf*; *vi* докладывать *impf*, доложить *pf*; (*present o.s.*) являться *impf*, явиться *pf*; *n* сообщение; доклад; (*school*) табель *m*; (*sound*) звук взрыва, выстрела. **reporter** *n* корреспондент.

repose *n* (*rest*) отдых; (*peace*) покой.

repository *n* хранилище.

repossess *vt* изымать *impf*, изъять *pf* за неплатёж.

reprehensible *adj* предосудительный.

represent *vt* представлять *impf*, (*portray*) изображать *impf*, изобразить *pf*. **representation** *n* (*being represented*) представительство; (*statement of case*) представление; (*portrayal*) изображение. **representative** *adj* изображающий (**of** +*acc*); (*typical*) типичный; *n* представитель *m*.

repress *vt* подавлять *impf*, подавить *pf*. **repression** *n* подавление, репрессия. **repressive** *adj* репрессивный.

reprieve *vt* отсрочивать *impf*, отсрочить *pf* +*dat* приведение в исполнение (смертного) приговора; *n* отсрочка приведения в исполнение (смертного) приговора; (*fig*) передышка.

reprimand *n* выговор; *vt* делать *impf*, с~ *pf* выговор +*dat*.

reprint *vt* переиздавать *impf*, переиздать *pf*; *n* переиздание.

reprisal *n* ответная мера.

reproach *vt* упрекать *impf*, упрекнуть *pf* (**with** в+*prep*). **reproachful** *adj* укоризненный.

reproduce *vt* воспроизводить *impf*, воспроизвести *pf*; *vi* размножаться *impf*, размножиться *pf*. **reproduction** *n* (*action*) воспроизведение; (*object*) репродукция; (*of offspring*) размножение. **reproductive** *adj* воспроизводительный.

reproof *n* выговор. **reprove** *vt* делать *impf* с~ *pf* выговор +*dat*.

reptile *n* пресмыкающееся *sb*.

republic *n* республика. **republican** *adj* республиканский; *n* республиканец, -нка.

repudiate *vt* (*renounce*) отказываться *impf*, отказаться *pf* от+*gen*; (*reject*) отвергать *impf*, отвергнуть *pf*. **repudiation** *n* отказ (**of** от+*gen*).

repugnance *n* отвращение. **repugnant** *adj* противный.

repulse *vt* отражать *impf*, отразить *pf*. **repulsion** *n* отвращение. **repulsive** *adj* отвратительный.

reputable *adj* пользующийся хорошей репутацией. **reputation, repute** *n* репутация. **reputed** *adj* предполагаемый. **reputedly** *adv* по общему мнению.

request *n* просьба; **by, on,** ~ по просьбе; *vt* просить *impf*, по~ *pf* +*acc*, +*gen* (*person* +*acc*).

requiem *n* реквием.

require *vt* (*demand*; *need*) требовать *impf*, по~ *pf* +*gen*; (*need*) нуждаться *impf* в+*prep*. **requirement** *n* требование; (*necessity*) потребность. **requisite** *adj* необходимый; *n* необходимая вещь. **requisition** *n* реквизиция; *vt* реквизировать *impf & pf*.

resale *n* перепродажа.

rescind *vt* отменять *impf*, отменить *pf*.

rescue *vt* спасать *impf*, спасти *pf*; *n* спасение. **rescuer** *n* спаситель *m*.

research *n* исследование (+*gen*); (*occupation*) исследовательская работа; *vi*: ~ **into** исследовать *impf & pf* +*acc*. **researcher** *n* исследователь *m*.

resemblance *n* сходство. **resemble**

vt походи́ть *impf* на+*acc*.

resent *vt* возмуща́ться *impf*, возмути́ться *pf*. **resentful** *adj* возмущённый. **resentment** *n* возмуще́ние.

reservation *n* (*doubt*) огово́рка; (*booking*) предвари́тельный зака́з; (*land*) резерва́ция. **reserve** *vt* (*keep*) резерви́ровать *impf* & *pf*; (*book*) зака́зывать *impf*, заказа́ть *pf*; *n* (*stock*; *mil*) запа́с, резе́рв; (*sport*) запасно́й игро́к; (*nature* ~ *etc*.) запове́дник; (*proviso*) огово́рка; (*self-restraint*) сде́ржанность; *attrib* запасно́й. **reserved** *adj* (*person*) сде́ржанный. **reservist** *n* резерви́ст.

reservoir *n* (*for water*) водохрани́лище; (*for other fluids*) резервуа́р.

resettle *vt* переселя́ть *impf*, пересели́ть *pf*. **resettlement** *n* переселе́ние.

reshape *vt* видоизменя́ть *impf*, видоизмени́ть *pf*.

reshuffle *n* перестано́вка.

reside *vi* прожива́ть *impf*. **residence** *n* (*residing*) прожива́ние; (*abode*) местожи́тельство; (*official* ~ *etc*.) резиде́нция. **resident** *n* (*постоя́нный*) жи́тель *m*, ~ница; *adj* прожива́ющий; (*population*) постоя́нный. **residential** *adj* жило́й.

residual *adj* оста́точный. **residue** *n* оста́ток.

resign *vt* отка́зываться *impf*, отказа́ться *pf* от+*gen*; *vi* уходи́ть *impf*, уйти́ *pf* в отста́вку; ~ **o.s. to** покоря́ться *impf*, покори́ться *pf* +*dat*. **resignation** *n* отста́вка, заявле́ние об отста́вке; (*being resigned*) поко́рность. **resigned** *adj* поко́рный.

resilient *adj* выно́сливый.

resin *n* смола́.

resist *vt* сопротивля́ться *impf* +*dat*; (*temptation*) устоя́ть *pf* пе́ред+*instr*. **resistance** *n* сопротивле́ние. **resistant** *adj* сто́йкий.

resolute *adj* реши́тельный. **resolution** *n* (*character*) реши́тельность; (*vow*) заро́к; (*at meeting etc.*) резолю́ция; (*of problem*) разреше́ние. **resolve** *vt* (*decide*) реша́ть *impf*, реши́ть *pf*; (*settle*) разреша́ть *impf*, разреши́ть *pf*; *n* реши́тельность; (*decision*) реше́ние.

resonance *n* резона́нс. **resonant** *adj*

зву́чный.

resort *vi*: ~ **to** прибега́ть *impf*, прибе́гнуть *pf* к+*dat*; *n* (*place*) куро́рт; **in the last** ~ в кра́йнем слу́чае.

resound *vi* (*of sound etc.*) раздава́ться *impf*, разда́ться *pf*; (*of place*) оглаша́ться *impf*, огласи́ться *pf* (**with** +*instr*).

resource *n* (*usu pl*) ресу́рс. **resourceful** *adj* нахо́дчивый.

respect *n* (*relation*) отноше́ние; (*esteem*) уваже́ние; **with** ~ **to** что каса́ется+*gen*; *vt* уважа́ть *impf*. **respectability** *n* респекта́бельность. **respectable** *adj* прили́чный. **respectful** *adj* почти́тельный. **respective** *adj* свой. **respectively** *adv* соотве́тственно.

respiration *n* дыха́ние. **respirator** *n* респира́тор. **respiratory** *adj* дыха́тельный.

respite *n* переды́шка.

resplendent *adj* блиста́тельный.

respond *vi*: ~ **to** отвеча́ть *impf*, отве́тить *pf* на+*acc*; (*react*) реаги́ровать *impf*, про~, от~ *pf* на+*acc*. **response** *n* (*ответ*); (*reaction*) о́тклик. **responsibility** *n* отве́тственность; (*duty*) обя́занность. **responsible** *adj* отве́тственный (**to** пе́ред +*instr*; **for** за+*acc*); (*reliable*) надёжный. **responsive** *adj* отзы́вчивый.

rest[1] *vi* отдыха́ть *impf*, отдохну́ть *pf*; *vt* (*place*) класть *impf*, положи́ть *pf*; (*allow to* ~) дава́ть *impf*, дать *pf* о́тдых+*dat*; *n* (*repose*) о́тдых; (*peace*) поко́й; (*mus*) па́уза; (*support*) опо́ра.

rest[2] *n* (*remainder*) оста́ток; (*the others*) остальны́е *sb pl*.

restaurant *n* рестора́н.

restful *adj* успока́ивающий.

restitution *n* возвраще́ние.

restive *adj* беспоко́йный.

restless *adj* беспоко́йный.

restoration *n* реставра́ция; (*return*) восстановле́ние. **restore** *vt* реставри́ровать *impf* & *pf*; (*return*) восстана́вливать *impf*, восстанови́ть *pf*.

restrain *vt* уде́рживать *impf*, удержа́ть *pf* (**from** от+*gen*). **restraint** *n* сде́ржанность.

restrict *vt* ограни́чивать *impf*, ограни́чить *pf*. **restriction** *n* ограниче́ние. **restrictive** *adj* ограничи́тельный.

result vi следовать impf; происходить impf (from из+gen); ~ in кончаться impf, кончиться pf +instr; n результат; as a ~ в результате (of +gen).

resume vt & i возобновлять(ся) impf, возобновить(ся) pf. **résumé** n резюме neut indecl. **resumption** n возобновление.

resurrect vt (fig) воскрешать impf, воскресить pf. **resurrection** n (of the dead) воскресение; (fig) воскрешение.

resuscitate vt приводить impf, привести pf в сознание.

retail n розничная продажа; attrib розничный; adv в розницу; vt продавать impf, продать pf в розницу; vi продаваться impf в розницу. **retailer** n розничный торговец.

retain vt удерживать impf, удержать pf.

retaliate vi отплачивать impf, отплатить pf тем же. **retaliation** n отплата, возмездие.

retard vt замедлять impf, замедлить pf. **retarded** adj отсталый.

retention n удержание. **retentive** adj (memory) хороший.

reticence n сдержанность. **reticent** adj сдержанный.

retina n сетчатка.

retinue n свита.

retire vi (withdraw) удаляться impf, удалиться pf; (from office etc.) уходить impf, уйти pf в отставку. **retired** adj в отставке. **retirement** n отставка. **retiring** adj скромный.

retort[1] vt отвечать impf, ответить pf резко; n возражение.

retort[2] n (vessel) реторта.

retrace vt: ~ one's steps возвращаться impf, возвратиться pf.

retract vt (draw in) втягивать impf, втянуть pf; (take back) брать impf, взять pf назад.

retreat vi отступать impf, отступить pf; n отступление; (withdrawal) уединение; (place) убежище.

retrenchment n сокращение расходов.

retrial n повторное слушание дела.

retribution n возмездие.

retrieval n возвращение; (comput) поиск (информации); vt брать impf,

взять pf обратно.

retrograde adj (fig) реакционный.

retrospect n: in ~ ретроспективно.

retrospective adj (law) имеющий обратную силу.

return vt & i (give back; come back) возвращать(ся) impf, возвратить(ся) impf, вернуть(ся) pf; vt (elect) избирать impf, избрать pf; n возвращение; возврат; (profit) прибыль; by ~ обратной почтой; in ~ взамен (for +gen); many happy ~s! с днём рождения!; ~ match ответный матч; ~ ticket обратный билет.

reunion n встреча (друзей и т. п.); family ~ сбор всей семьи. **reunite** vt воссоединять impf, воссоединить pf.

reuse vt снова использовать impf & pf.

rev n оборот; vt & i.: ~ up рвануть(ся) pf.

reveal vt обнаруживать impf, обнаружить pf. **revealing** adj показательный.

revel vi пировать impf; ~ in наслаждаться impf +instr.

revelation n откровение.

revenge vt: ~ o.s. мстить impf, ото~ pf (for за+acc; on +dat); n месть.

revenue n доход.

reverberate vi отражаться impf. **reverberation** n отражение; (fig) отзвук.

revere vt почитать impf. **reverence** n почтение. **Reverend** adj (in title) (его) преподобие. **reverent(ial)** adj почтительный.

reverie n мечтание.

reversal n (change) изменение; (of decision) отмена. **reverse** adj обратный; ~ gear задний ход; vt (change) изменять impf, изменить pf; (decision) отменять impf, отменить pf; vi давать impf, дать pf задний ход; n (the ~) обратное sb, противоположное sb; (~ gear) задний ход; (~ side) обратная сторона. **reversible** adj обратимый; (cloth) двусторонний. **reversion** n возвращение. **revert** vi возвращаться impf (to в+acc, к+dat); (law) переходить impf, перейти pf (to к+dat).

review n (re-examination) пересмотр; (mil) парад; (survey) обзор;

(*criticism*) реце́нзия; *vt* (*re-examine*) пересма́тривать *impf*, пересмотре́ть *pf*; (*survey*) обозрева́ть *impf*, обозре́ть *pf*; (*troops etc.*) принима́ть *impf*, приня́ть *pf* пара́д+*gen*; (*book etc.*) рецензи́ровать *impf*, про~ *pf*. **reviewer** *n* рецензе́нт.

revise *vt* пересма́тривать *impf*, пересмотре́ть *pf*; исправля́ть *impf*, испра́вить *pf*; *vi* (*for exam*) гото́виться *impf* (**for** к+*dat*). **revision** *n* пересмо́тр, исправле́ние.

revival *n* возрожде́ние; (*to life etc.*) оживле́ние. **revive** *vt* возрожда́ть *impf*, возроди́ть *pf*; (*resuscitate*) оживля́ть *impf*, оживи́ть *pf*; *vi* ожива́ть *impf*, ожи́ть *pf*.

revoke *vt* отменя́ть *impf*, отмени́ть *pf*.

revolt *n* бунт; *vt* вызыва́ть *impf*, вы́звать *pf* отвраще́ние у+*gen*; *vi* бунтова́ть *impf*, взбунтова́ться *pf*. **revolting** *adj* отврати́тельный.

revolution *n* (*single turn*) оборо́т; (*polit*) револю́ция. **revolutionary** *adj* революцио́нный = *n* революционе́р. **revolutionize** *vt* революциони́ровать *impf* & *pf*. **revolve** *vt* & *i* враща́ть(ся) *impf*. **revolver** *n* револьве́р.

revue *n* ревю́ *neut indecl*.

revulsion *n* отвраще́ние.

reward *n* вознагражде́ние; *vt* (воз)награжда́ть *impf*, (воз)награди́ть *pf*.

rewrite *vt* перепи́сывать *impf*, переписа́ть *pf*; (*recast*) переде́лывать *impf*, переде́лать *pf*.

rhapsody *n* рапсо́дия.

rhetoric *n* рито́рика. **rhetorical** *adj* ритори́ческий.

rheumatic *adj* ревмати́ческий. **rheumatism** *n* ревмати́зм.

rhinoceros *n* носоро́г.

rhododendron *n* рододе́ндрон.

rhubarb *n* реве́нь *m*.

rhyme *n* ри́фма; *pl* (*verse*) стихи́ *m pl*; *vt* & *i* рифмова́ть(ся) *impf*.

rhythm *n* ритм. **rhythmic(al)** *adj* ритми́ческий, -чный.

rib *n* ребро́.

ribald *adj* непристо́йный.

ribbon *n* ле́нта.

rice *n* рис.

rich *adj* бога́тый; (*soil*) ту́чный;

(*food*) жи́рный. **riches** *n pl* бога́тство. **richly** *adv* (*fully*) вполне́.

rickety *adj* (*shaky*) расша́танный.

ricochet *vi* рикошети́ровать *impf* & *pf*.

rid *vt* освобожда́ть *impf*, освободи́ть *pf* (**of** от+*gen*); **get ~ of** избавля́ться *impf*, изба́виться *pf* от+*gen*. **riddance** *n*: **good ~!** ска́тертью доро́га!

riddle *n* (*enigma*) зага́дка.

riddled *adj*: **~ with** изрешечённый; (*fig*) прони́занный.

ride *vi* е́здить *indet*, е́хать *det*, по~ *pf* (**on horseback** верхо́м); *vt* е́здить *indet*, е́хать *det*, по~ *pf* в, на+*prep*; *n* пое́здка, езда́. **rider** *n* вса́дник, -ица; (*clause*) дополне́ние.

ridge *n* хребе́т; (**on cloth**) ру́бчик; (**of roof**) конёк.

ridicule *n* насме́шка; *vt* осме́ивать *impf*, осмея́ть *pf*. **ridiculous** *adj* смешно́й.

riding *n* (**horse-~**) (верхова́я) езда́.

rife *predic* распространённый.

riff-raff *n* подо́нки (-ков) *pl*.

rifle *n* винто́вка; *vt* (*search*) обы́скивать *impf*, обыска́ть *pf*.

rift *n* тре́щина (*also fig*).

rig *vt* оснаща́ть *impf*, оснасти́ть *pf*; **~ out** наряжа́ть *impf*, наряди́ть *pf*; **~ up** скола́чивать *impf*, сколоти́ть *pf*; *n* бурова́я устано́вка. **rigging** *n* такела́ж.

right *adj* (*position*; *justified*; *polit*) пра́вый; (*correct*) пра́вильный; (*the one wanted*) тот; (*suitable*) подходя́щий; **~ angle** прямо́й у́гол; *vt* исправля́ть *impf*, испра́вить *pf*; *n* пра́во; (*what is just*) справедли́вость; (**~ side**) пра́вая сторона́; (**the R~**; *polit*) пра́вые *sb pl*; **be in the ~** быть пра́вым; **by ~** по пра́ву; **~ of way** пра́во прохо́да, прое́зда; *adv* (*straight*) пря́мо; (*exactly*) то́чно, как раз; (*to the full*) соверше́нно; (*correctly*) пра́вильно; как сле́дует; (**on the ~**) спра́во (**of** от+*gen*); (**to the ~**) напра́во; **~ away** сейча́с.

righteous *adj* (*person*) пра́ведный; (*action*) справедли́вый.

rightful *adj* зако́нный.

rigid *adj* жёсткий; (*strict*) стро́гий. **rigidity** *n* жёсткость; стро́гость.

rigmarole *n* каните́ль.

rigorous adj стро́гий. **rigour** n стро́гость.

rim n (of wheel) о́бод; (spectacles) опра́ва. **rimless** adj без опра́вы.

rind n кожура́.

ring[1] n кольцо́; (circle) круг; (boxing) ринг; (circus) (циркова́я) аре́на; ~ **road** кольцева́я доро́га; vt (encircle) окружа́ть impf, окружи́ть pf.

ring[2] vi (sound) звони́ть impf, по~ pf; (ring out, of shot etc.) раздава́ться impf, разда́ться pf; (of place) оглаша́ться impf, огласи́ться pf (with +instr); vt звони́ть impf, по~ pf в+acc; ~ **back** перезва́нивать impf, перезвони́ть pf; ~ **off** пове́сить pf тру́бку; ~ **up** звони́ть impf, по~ pf +dat; звони́ть, звоно́к.

ringleader n глава́рь m.

rink n като́к.

rinse vt полоска́ть impf, вы́~ pf; n полоска́ние.

riot n бунт; **run** ~ бу́йствовать impf; (of plants) бу́йно разраста́ться impf, разрасти́сь pf; vi бунтова́ть impf, взбунтова́ться pf. **riotous** adj бу́йный.

rip vt & i рва́ть(ся) impf; разо~ pf; ~ **up** разрыва́ть impf, разорва́ть pf; n проре́ха, разре́з.

ripe adj зре́лый, спе́лый. **ripen** vt де́лать impf, с~ pf зре́лым; vi созрева́ть impf, созре́ть pf. **ripeness** n зре́лость.

ripple n рябь; vt & i покрыва́ть(ся) impf, покры́ть(ся) pf ря́бью.

rise vi поднима́ться impf, подня́ться pf; повыша́ться impf, повы́ситься pf; (get up) встава́ть impf, встать pf; (rebel) восстава́ть impf, восста́ть pf; (sun etc.) в(о)сходи́ть impf, взойти́; n подъём, возвыше́ние; (in pay) приба́вка; (of sun etc.) восхо́д. riser n: he is an early ~: он ра́но встаёт. **rising** n (revolt) восста́ние.

risk n риск; vt рискова́ть impf, рискну́ть pf +instr. **risky** adj риско́ванный.

risqué adj непристо́йный.

rite n обря́д. **ritual** n ритуа́л; adj ритуа́льный.

rival n сопе́рник, -ица; adj сопе́рничающий; vt сопе́рничать impf c+instr. **rivalry** n сопе́рничество.

river n река́. **riverside** attrib прибре́жный.

rivet n заклёпка; vt заклёпывать impf, заклепа́ть pf; (fig) прико́вывать impf, прикова́ть pf (on к+dat).

road n доро́га; (street) у́лица; ~**block** загражде́ние на доро́ге; ~**map** (доро́жная) ка́рта; ~ **sign** доро́жный знак. **roadside** n обо́чина; attrib придоро́жный. **roadway** n мостова́я sb.

roam vt & i броди́ть impf (по+dat).

roar n (animal's) рёв; vi реве́ть impf.

roast vt & i жа́рить(ся) impf, за~, из~ pf; adj жа́реный; ~ **beef** ро́стбиф; n жарко́е sb.

rob vt гра́бить impf, о~ pf; красть impf, у~ pf у+gen (of +acc); (deprive) лиша́ть impf, лиши́ть pf (of +gen). **robber** n граби́тель m. **robbery** n грабёж.

robe n (also pl) ма́нтия.

robin n мали́новка.

robot n ро́бот.

robust adj кре́пкий.

rock[1] n (geol) (го́рная) поро́да; (cliff etc.) скала́; (large stone) большо́й ка́мень m; on the ~s (in difficulty) на мели́; (drink) со льдом.

rock[2] vt & i кача́ть(ся) impf, качну́ть(ся) pf; n (mus) рок; ~**ing-chair** кача́лка; ~ **and roll** рок-н-ро́лл.

rockery n альпина́рий.

rocket n раке́та; vi подска́кивать impf, подскочи́ть pf.

rocky adj скали́стый; (shaky) ша́ткий.

rod n (stick) прут; (bar) сте́ржень m; (fishing-~) у́дочка.

rodent n грызу́н.

roe[1] n икра́; (soft) моло́ки (-о́к) pl.

roe[2] (-deer) n косу́ля.

rogue n плут.

role n роль.

roll[1] n (cylinder) руло́н; (register) реéстр; (bread) бу́лочка; ~-**call** перекли́чка.

roll[2] vt & i ката́ть(ся) indet, кати́ть(ся) det, по~ pf; (~ up) свёртывать(ся) impf, сверну́ть(ся) pf; vt (~ out) (dough) раска́тывать impf, раската́ть pf; vi (sound) греме́ть impf; ~ **over** перевора́чиваться impf, переверну́ться pf; n (of drums) бараба́нная дробь; (of thunder) раска́т.

roller n (small) ро́лик; (large) като́к;

(*for hair*) бигуди́ *neut indecl*; ~-**skates** коньки́ *m pl* на ро́ликах.

rolling *adj* (*of land*) холми́стый; ~-**pin** ска́лка. ~-**stock** подвижно́й соста́в.

Roman *n* ри́млянин, -я́нка; *adj* ри́мский; ~ **Catholic** (*n*) като́лик, -и́чка; (*adj*) ри́мско-католи́ческий.

romance *n* (*tale*; *love affair*) рома́н; (*quality*) рома́нтика; (*mus*) рома́нс.

Romanesque *adj* рома́нский.

Romania *n* Румы́ния. **Romanian** *n* румы́н, ~ка; *adj* румы́нский.

romantic *adj* романти́чный, -ческий. **romanticism** *n* романти́зм.

romp *vi* вози́ться *impf*.

roof *n* кры́ша; ~ **of the mouth** нёбо; *vt* крыть *impf*, покры́ть *pf*.

rook[1] *n* (*chess*) ладья́.

rook[2] *n* (*bird*) грач.

room *n* ко́мната; (*space*) ме́сто. **roomy** *adj* просто́рный.

roost *n* насе́ст.

root[1] *n* ко́рень *m*; **take** ~ укореня́ться *impf*, укорени́ться *pf*; *vi* пуска́ть *impf*, пусти́ть *pf* ко́рни; ~ **out** вырыва́ть *impf*, вы́рвать *pf* с ко́рнем; **rooted to the spot** прико́ванный к ме́сту.

root[2] *vi* (*rummage*) ры́ться *impf*; ~ **for** боле́ть *impf* за +*acc*.

rope *n* верёвка; ~-**ladder** верёвочная ле́стница; *vt*: ~ **in** (*enlist*) втя́гивать *impf*, втяну́ть *pf*; ~ **off** о(т)гора́живать *impf*, о(т)городи́ть *pf* верёвкой.

rosary *n* чётки (-ток) *pl*.

rose *n* ро́за; (*nozzle*) се́тка.

rosemary *n* розмари́н.

rosette *n* розе́тка.

rosewood *n* розовое де́рево.

roster *n* расписа́ние дежу́рств.

rostrum *n* трибу́на.

rosy *adj* ро́зовый; (*cheeks*) румя́ный.

rot *n* гниль; (*nonsense*) вздор; *vi* гнить *impf*, с~ *pf*; *vt* гнои́ть *impf*, с~ *pf*.

rota *n* расписа́ние дежу́рств. **rotary** *adj* враща́тельный, ротацио́нный. **rotate** *vt* & *i* враща́ть(ся) *impf*. **rotation** *n* враще́ние; **in** ~ по о́череди.

rote *n*: **by** ~ наизу́сть.

rotten *adj* гнило́й; (*fig*) отврати́тельный.

rotund *adj* (*round*) кру́глый; (*plump*)

по́лный.

rouble *n* рубль *m*.

rough *adj* (*uneven*) неро́вный; (*coarse*) гру́бый; (*sea*) бу́рный; (*approximate*) приблизи́тельный; ~ **copy** чернови́к; *n*: **the** ~ тру́дности *f pl*; *vt*: ~ **it** жить *impf* без удо́бств. **roughage** *n* гру́бая пи́ща. **roughly** *adv* гру́бо; (*approximately*) приблизи́тельно.

roulette *n* руле́тка.

round *adj* кру́глый; ~-**shouldered** суту́лый; *n* (~ *object*) круг; (*circuit*; *also pl*) обхо́д; (*sport*) тур, ра́унд; (*series*) ряд; (*ammunition*) патро́н; (*of applause*) взрыв; *adv* вокру́г; (*in a circle*) по кру́гу; **all** ~ круго́м; **all the year** ~ кру́глый год; *prep* вокру́г+*gen*; круго́м+*gen*; по+*dat*; ~ **the corner** (*motion*) за́ угол, (*position*) за угло́м; *vt* (*go* ~) огиба́ть *impf*, обогну́ть *pf*; ~ **off** (*complete*) заверша́ть *impf*, заверши́ть *pf*; ~ **up** сгоня́ть *impf*, согна́ть *pf*; ~-**up** заго́н; (*raid*) обла́ва. **roundabout** *n* (*merry-go-round*) карусе́ль; (*road junction*) кольцева́я тра́нспортная развя́зка; *adj* око́льный.

rouse *vt* буди́ть *impf*, раз~ *pf*; (*to action etc.*) побужда́ть *impf*, побуди́ть *pf* (**to** к+*dat*). **rousing** *adj* восто́рженный.

rout *n* (*defeat*) разгро́м.

route *n* маршру́т, путь *m*.

routine *n* заведённый поря́док, режи́м; *adj* устано́вленный; очередно́й.

rove *vi* скита́ться *impf*.

row[1] *n* (*line*) ряд.

row[2] *vi* (*in boat*) грести́ *impf*.

row[3] *n* (*dispute*) ссо́ра; (*noise*) шум; *vi* ссо́риться *impf*, по~ *pf*.

rowdy *adj* бу́йный.

royal *adj* короле́вский; (*majestic*) великоле́пный. **royalist** *n* роялист; *adj* роялистский. **royalty** *n* член, чле́ны *pl*, короле́вской семьи́; (*fee*) а́вторский гонора́р.

rub *vt* & *i* тере́ть(ся) *impf*; *vt* (*polish*; *chafe*) натира́ть *impf*, натере́ть *pf*; (~ *dry*) вытира́ть *impf*, вы́тереть *pf*; ~ **in, on** втира́ть *impf*, втере́ть *pf*; ~ **out** стира́ть *impf*, стере́ть *pf*; ~ **it in** растравля́ть *impf*, растрави́ть *pf* ра́ну.

rubber *n* резина; (*eraser, also ~ band*) резинка; *attrib* резиновый; **~ stamp** (*fig*) штамповать *impf*.

rubbish *n* мусор; (*nonsense*) чепуха.

rubble *n* щебень *m*.

rubella *n* краснуха.

ruby *n* рубин.

ruck *vt* (*~ up*) мять *impf*, из~, с~ *pf*.

rucksack *n* рюкзак.

rudder *n* руль *m*.

ruddy *adj* (*face*) румяный; (*damned*) проклятый.

rude *adj* грубый. **rudeness** *n* грубость.

rudimentary *adj* рудиментарный. **rudiments** *n pl* основы *f pl*.

rueful *adj* печальный.

ruff *n* (*frill*) брыжи (-жей) *pl*; (*of feathers, hair*) кольцо (перьев, шерсти) вокруг шеи.

ruffian *n* хулиган.

ruffle *n* оборка; *vt* (*hair*) ерошить *impf*, взъ~ *pf*; (*water*) рябить *impf*; (*person*) смущать *impf*, смутить *pf*.

rug *n* (*mat*) ковёр; (*wrap*) плед.

rugby *n* регби *neut indecl*.

rugged *adj* (*rocky*) скалистый.

ruin *n* (*downfall*) гибель *f*; (*building, ruins*) развалины *f pl*, руины *f pl*; *vt* губить *impf*, по~ *pf*. **ruinous** *adj* губительный.

rule *n* правило; (*for measuring*) линейка; (*government*) правление; **as a ~** как правило; *vt & i* править *impf* (+*instr*); (*decree*) постановлять *impf*, постановить *pf*; **~ out** исключать *impf*, исключить *pf*. **ruled** *adj* линованный. **ruler** *n* (*person*) правитель *m*, ~ница; (*object*) линейка. **ruling** *n* (*of court etc.*) постановление.

rum *n* (*drink*) ром.

Rumania(n) *see* **Romania(n)**

rumble *vi* громыхать *impf*; *n* громыхание.

ruminant *n* жвачное (животное) *sb*. **ruminate** *vi* (*fig*) размышлять *impf* (*over*, о+*prep*).

rummage *vi* рыться *impf*.

rumour *n* слух; *vt*: **it is ~ed that** ходят слухи (*pl*), что.

rump *n* крестец; **~ steak** ромштекс.

rumple *vt* мять *impf*, из~, с~ *pf*; (*hair*) ерошить *impf*, взъ~ *pf*.

run *vi* бегать *indet*, бежать *det*, по~ *pf*; (*work, of machines*) работать *impf*; (*ply, of bus etc.*) ходить *indet*, идти *det*; (*seek election*) выставлять *impf*, выставить *pf* свою кандидатуру; (*of play etc.*) идти *impf*; (*ink, dye*) расплываться *impf*, расплыться *pf*; (*flow*) течь *impf*; (*of document*) гласить *impf*; *vt* (*manage, operate*) управлять *impf* +*instr*; (*a business etc.*) вести *impf*; **~ dry, low** иссякать *impf*, иссякнуть *pf*; **~ risks** рисковать *impf*; **~ across, into** (*meet*) встречаться *impf*, встретиться *pf* c+*instr*; **~ away** (*flee*) убегать *impf*, убежать *pf*; **~ down** (*knock down*) задавить *impf* (*disparage*) принижать *impf*, принизить *pf*; **be ~ down** (*of person*) переутомиться *pf* (*in past tense*); **~-down** (*decayed*) запущенный; **~ in** (*engine*) обкатывать *impf*, обкатать *pf*; **~ into** *see* **~ across**; **~ out** кончаться *impf*, кончиться *pf*; **~ out of** истощать *impf*, истощить *pf* свой запас +*gen*; **~ over** (*glance over*) бегло просматривать *impf*, просмотреть *pf*; (*injure*) задавить *impf*, задавить *pf*; **~ through** (*pierce*) прокалывать *impf*, проколоть *pf*; (*money*) проматывать *impf*, промотать *pf*; (*review*) повторять *impf*, повторить *pf*; **~ to** (*reach*) (*of money*) хватать *impf*, хватить *pf* impers+*gen* на+*acc*; **the money won't ~ to a car** этих денег не хватит на машину; **~ up against** наталкиваться *impf*, натолкнуться *pf* на +*acc*; *n* бег; (*sport*) перебежка; (*journey*) поездка; (*period*) полоса; **at a ~** бегом; **on the ~** в бегах; **~ on** большой спрос на+*acc*; **in the long ~** в конце концов.

rung *n* ступенька.

runner *n* (*also tech*) бегун; (*of sledge*) полоз; (*bot*) побег; **~ bean** фасоль; **~-up** участник, занявший второе место. **running** *n* бег; (*management*) управление (*of* +*instr*); **be in the ~** иметь *impf* шансы; *adj* бегущий; (*of ~*) беговой; (*after pl n, in succession*) подряд; **~ commentary** репортаж; **~ water** водопровод. **runway** *n* взлётно-посадочная полоса.

rupee *n* рупия.

rupture *n* разрыв; *vt & i* проры-

ва́ть(ся) *impf*, прорва́ть(ся) *pf*.
rural *adj* се́льский.
ruse *n* уло́вка.
rush[1] *n* (*bot*) тростни́к.
rush[2] *vt & i* (*hurry*) торопи́ть(ся) *impf*, по~ *pf*; *vi* (*dash*) броса́ться *impf*, бро́ситься *pf*; (*of water*) нести́сь *impf*; по~ *pf*; *vt* (*to hospital etc.*) умча́ть *pf*; *n* (*of blood etc.*) прили́в; (*hurry*) спе́шка; **be in a** ~ торопи́ться *impf*; ~-**hour(s)** часы́ *m pl* пик.
Russia *n* Росси́я. **Russian** *n* ру́сский *sb*; *adj* (*of ~ nationality, culture*) ру́сский; (*of ~ State*) росси́йский.
rust *n* ржа́вчина; *vi* ржаве́ть *impf*, за~, по~ *pf*.
rustic *adj* дереве́нский.
rustle *n* ше́лест, шо́рох, шурша́ние; *vi & t* шелесте́ть *impf* (+*instr*); ~ **up** раздобыва́ть *impf*; раздобы́ть *pf*.
rusty *adj* ржа́вый.
rut *n* колея́.
ruthless *adj* безжа́лостный.
rye *n* рожь; *attrib* ржано́й.

S

Sabbath *n* (*Jewish*) суббо́та; (*Christian*) воскресе́нье. **sabbatical** *n* годи́чный о́тпуск.
sable *n* со́боль.
sabotage *n* диве́рсия; *vt* саботи́ровать *impf & pf*. **saboteur** *n* диверса́нт.
sabre *n* са́бля.
sachet *n* упако́вка.
sack[1] *vt* (*plunder*) разгра́бить *pf*.
sack[2] *n* мешо́к; (*dismissal*): **get the** ~ быть уво́ленным; *vt* увольня́ть *impf*, уво́лить *pf*. **sacking** *n* (*hessian*) мешкови́на.
sacrament *n* та́инство; (*Eucharist*) прича́стие. **sacred** *adj* свяще́нный, свято́й. **sacrifice** *n* же́ртва; *vt* же́ртвовать *impf*, по~ *pf* +*instr*. **sacrilege** *n* святота́тство. **sacrosanct** *adj* свяще́нный.
sad *adj* печа́льный, гру́стный. **sadden** *vt* печа́лить *impf*, о~ *pf*.
saddle *n* седло́; *vt* седла́ть *impf*, о~ *pf*; (*burden*) обременя́ть *impf*, обремени́ть *pf* (**with** +*instr*).
sadism *n* сади́зм. **sadist** *n* сади́ст.

sadistic *adj* сади́стский.
sadness *n* печа́ль, грусть.
safe *n* сейф; *adj* (*unharmed*) невреди́мый; (*out of danger*) в безопа́сности; (*secure*) безопа́сный; (*reliable*) надёжный; ~ **and sound** цел и невреди́м. **safeguard** *n* предохрани́тельная ме́ра; *vt* предохраня́ть *impf*, предохрани́ть *pf*. **safety** *n* безопа́сность; ~-**belt** реме́нь *m* безопа́сности; ~ **pin** англи́йская була́вка; ~-**valve** предохрани́тельный кла́пан.
sag *vi* (*of rope, curtain*) провиса́ть *impf*, прови́снуть *pf*; (*of ceiling*) прогиба́ться *impf*, прогну́ться *pf*.
saga *n* са́га.
sage[1] *n* (*herb*) шалфе́й.
sage[2] *n* (*person*) мудре́ц; *adj* му́дрый.
Sagittarius *n* Стреле́ц.
sail *n* па́рус; *vt* (*a ship*) управля́ть *impf* +*instr*; *vi* пла́вать *indet*, плыть *det*; (*depart*) отплыва́ть *impf*, отплы́ть *pf*. **sailing** *n* (*sport*) па́русный спорт; ~-**ship** па́русное су́дно. **sailor** *n* матро́с, моря́к.
saint *n* свято́й *sb*. **saintly** *adj* свято́й.
sake *n*: **for the** ~ **of** ра́ди+*gen*.
salad *n* сала́т; ~-**dressing** припра́ва к сала́ту.
salami *n* саля́ми *f indecl*.
salary *n* жа́лованье.
sale *n* прода́жа; (*also amount sold*) сбыт (*no pl*); (*with reduced prices*) распрода́жа; **be for** ~ продава́ться *impf*. **saleable** *adj* хо́дкий. **salesman** *n* продаве́ц. **saleswoman** *n* продавщи́ца.
salient *adj* основно́й.
saliva *n* слюна́.
sallow *adj* желтова́тый.
salmon *n* лосо́сь *m*.
salon *n* сало́н. **saloon** *n* (*on ship*) сало́н; (*car*) седа́н; (*bar*) бар.
salt *n* соль; ~-**cellar** соло́нка; ~ **water** морска́я вода́; ~-**water** морско́й; *adj* солёный; *vt* соли́ть *impf*, по~ *pf*. **salty** *adj* солёный.
salutary *adj* благотво́рный. **salute** *n* отда́ча че́сти; (*with guns*) салю́т; *vt & i* отдава́ть *impf*, отда́ть *pf* честь (+*dat*).
salvage *n* спасе́ние; *vt* спаса́ть *impf*, спасти́ *pf*.

salvation *n* спасе́ние; S~ **Army** А́рмия спасе́ния.

salve *n* мазь; *vt*: ~ **one's conscience** успока́ивать *impf*, успоко́ить *pf* со́весть.

salvo *n* залп.

same *adj*: **the** ~ тот же (са́мый); (*applying to both or all*) оди́н; (*identical*) одина́ковый; *pron*: **the** ~ одно́ и то́ же, то же са́мое; *adv*: **the** ~ таки́м же о́бразом, так же; **all the** ~ всё-таки, тем не ме́нее. **sameness** *n* однообра́зие.

samovar *n* самова́р.

sample *n* образе́ц; *vt* про́бовать *impf*, по~ *pf*.

sanatorium *n* санато́рий.

sanctify *vt* освяща́ть *impf*, освяти́ть *pf*. **sanctimonious** *adj* ха́нжеский. **sanction** *n* са́нкция; *vt* санкциони́ровать *impf* & *pf*. **sanctity** *n* (*holiness*) свя́тость; (*sacredness*) свяще́нность. **sanctuary** *n* святи́лище; (*refuge*) убе́жище; (*for wild life*) запове́дник.

sand *n* песо́к; *vt* (~ *down*) шку́рить *impf*, по~ *pf*; ~-**dune** дюна.

sandal *n* санда́лия.

sandalwood *n* санда́ловое де́рево.

sandbank *n* о́тмель.

sandpaper *n* шку́рка; *vt* шлифова́ть *impf*, от~ *pf* шку́ркой.

sandstone *n* песча́ник.

sandwich *n* бутербро́д; *vt*: ~ **between** вти́скивать *impf*, всти́снуть *pf* ме́жду+*instr*.

sandy *adj* (*of sand*) песча́ный; (*like sand*) песо́чный; (*hair*) рыжева́тый.

sane *adj* норма́льный; (*sensible*) разу́мный.

sang-froid *n* самооблада́ние.

sanguine *adj* оптимисти́ческий.

sanitary *adj* санита́рный; гигиени́ческий; ~ **towel** гигиени́ческая поду́шка. **sanitation** *n* (*conditions*) санита́рные усло́вия *neut pl*; (*system*) водопрово́д и канализа́ция. **sanity** *n* психи́ческое здоро́вье; (*good sense*) здра́вый смысл.

sap *n* (*bot*) сок; *vt* (*exhaust*) истоща́ть *impf*, истощи́ть *pf*.

sapling *n* са́женец.

sapphire *n* сапфи́р.

sarcasm *n* сарка́зм. **sarcastic** *adj* сарка́сти́ческий.

sardine *n* сарди́на.

sardonic *adj* сардони́ческий.

sash[1] *n* (*scarf*) куша́к.

sash[2] *n* (*frame*) скользя́щая ра́ма; ~-**window** подъёмное окно́.

satanic *adj* сатани́нский.

satchel *n* ра́нец, су́мка.

satellite *n* спу́тник, сателли́т (*also fig*); ~ **dish** параболи́ческая анте́нна; таре́лка (*coll*); ~ **TV** спу́тниковое телеви́дение.

satiate *vt* насыща́ть *impf*, насы́тить *pf*.

satin *n* атла́с.

satire *n* сати́ра. **satirical** *adj* сатири́ческий. **satirist** *n* сати́рик. **satirize** *vt* высме́ивать *impf*, вы́смеять *pf*.

satisfaction *n* удовлетворе́ние. **satisfactory** *adj* удовлетвори́тельный. **satisfy** *vt* удовлетворя́ть *impf*, удовлетвори́ть *pf*; (*hunger, curiosity*) утоля́ть *impf*, утоли́ть *pf*.

saturate *vt* насыща́ть *impf*, насы́тить *pf*; **I got** ~**d** (*by rain*) я промо́к до ни́тки. **saturation** *n* насыще́ние.

Saturday *n* суббо́та.

sauce *n* со́ус; (*cheek*) на́глость. **saucepan** *n* кастрю́ля. **saucer** *n* блю́дце. **saucy** *adj* на́глый.

Saudi *n* сау́довец, -вка; *adj* сау́довский. **Saudi Arabia** *n* Сау́довская Ара́вия.

sauna *n* фи́нская ба́ня.

saunter *vi* прогу́ливаться *impf*.

sausage *n* соси́ска; (*salami-type*) колбаса́.

savage *adj* ди́кий; (*fierce*) свире́пый; (*cruel*) жесто́кий; *n* дика́рь *m*; *vt* искуса́ть *pf*. **savagery** *n* ди́кость; жесто́кость.

save *vt* (*rescue*) спаса́ть *impf*, спасти́ *pf*; (*money*) копи́ть *impf*, на~ *pf*; (*put aside, keep*) бере́чь *impf*; (*avoid using*) эконо́мить *impf*, с~ *pf*; *vi*: ~ **up** копи́ть *impf*, на~ *pf* де́ньги. **savings** *n pl* сбереже́ния *neut pl*; ~ **bank** сберега́тельная ка́сса. **saviour** *n* спаси́тель *m*.

savour *vt* смакова́ть *impf*.

savoury *adj* пика́нтный; (*fig*) поря́дочный.

saw *n* пила́; *vt* пили́ть *impf*; ~ **up** распи́ливать *impf*, распили́ть *pf*. **sawdust** *n* опи́лки (-лок) *pl*.

saxophone *n* саксофо́н.

say vt говори́ть impf, сказа́ть pf; **to ~ nothing of** не говоря́ уже́ о+prep; **that is to ~** то есть; (let us) ~ ска́жем; **it is said (that)** говоря́т (что); n (opinion) мне́ние; (influence) влия́ние; **have one's ~** вы́сказаться pf. **saying** n погово́рка.

scab n (on wound) струп; (polit) штрейкбре́хер.

scabbard n но́жны (gen -жен) pl.

scaffold n эшафо́т. **scaffolding** n леса́ (-со́в) pl.

scald vt обва́ривать impf, обвари́ть pf.

scale n (ratio) масшта́б; (grading) шкала́; (mus) га́мма; vt (climb) взбира́ться impf, взобра́ться pf на+acc; ~ **down** понижа́ть impf, пони́зить pf.

scales[1] n pl (of fish) чешуя́ (collect).

scales[2] n pl весы́ (-со́в) pl.

scallop n гребешо́к; (decoration) фесто́н.

scalp n ко́жа головы́.

scalpel n ска́льпель m.

scaly adj чешу́йчатый; (of boiler etc.) покры́тый на́кипью.

scamper vi бы́стро бе́гать impf; (frolic) резви́ться impf.

scan vt & i (verse) сканди́ровать(ся) impf; vt (intently) рассма́тривать impf; (quickly) просма́тривать impf, просмотре́ть pf; (med) просве́чивать impf, просвети́ть pf; n просве́чивание.

scandal n сканда́л; (gossip) спле́тни (-тен) pl. **scandalize** vt шоки́ровать impf & pf. **scandalous** adj сканда́льный.

Scandinavia n Скандина́вия. **Scandinavian** adj скандина́вский.

scanty adj ску́дный.

scapegoat n козёл отпуще́ния.

scar n шрам; vt оставля́ть impf, оста́вить pf шрам на+prep.

scarce adj дефици́тный; (rare) ре́дкий. **scarcely** adv едва́. **scarcity** n дефици́т; ре́дкость.

scare vt пуга́ть impf, ис~, на~ pf; ~ **away, off** отпу́гивать impf, отпугну́ть pf; n па́ника. **scarecrow** n пу́гало.

scarf n шарф.

scarlet adj (n) а́лый (цвет).

scathing adj уничтожа́ющий.

scatter vt & i рассыпа́ть(ся) impf, рассы́пать(ся) pf; (disperse) рассе́ивать(ся) impf, рассе́ять(ся) pf; **brained** ве́треный. **scattered** adj разбро́санный; (sporadic) отде́льный.

scavenge vi ры́ться impf в отбро́сах. **scavenger** n (person) му́сорщик; (animal) живо́тное sb, пита́ющееся па́далью.

scenario n сцена́рий. **scene** n (place of disaster etc.) ме́сто; (place of action) ме́сто де́йствия; (view) вид, пейза́ж; (picture) карти́на; (theat) сце́на, явле́ние; (incident) сце́на; **behind the ~s** за кули́сами; **make a ~** устра́ивать impf, устро́ить pf сце́ну. **scenery** n (theat) декора́ция; (landscape) пейза́ж. **scenic** adj живопи́сный.

scent n (smell) арома́т; (perfume) духи́ (-хо́в) pl; (trail) след. **scented** adj души́стый.

sceptic n ске́птик. **sceptical** adj скепти́ческий. **scepticism** n скепти́цизм.

schedule n (timetable) расписа́ние; vt составля́ть impf, соста́вить pf расписа́ние +gen.

schematic adj схемати́ческий. **scheme** n (plan) прое́кт; (intrigue) махина́ция; vi интригова́ть impf.

schism n раско́л.

schizophrenia n шизофрени́я. **schizophrenic** adj шизофрени́ческий; n шизофре́ник.

scholar n учёный sb: **scholarly** adj учёный. **scholarship** n учёность; (payment) стипе́ндия.

school n шко́ла; attrib шко́льный; vt (train) приуча́ть impf, приучи́ть pf (to к+dat, +inf). **school-book** n уче́бник. **schoolboy** n шко́льник. **schoolgirl** n шко́льница. **schooling** n обуче́ние. **school-leaver** n выпускни́к, -и́ца. **school teacher** n учи́тель m, ~ница.

schooner n шху́на.

sciatica n и́шиас.

science n нау́ка; ~ **fiction** нау́чная фанта́стика. **scientific** adj нау́чный. **scientist** n учёный sb.

scintillating adj блиста́тельный.

scissors n pl но́жницы (-ц) pl.

scoff vi (mock) смея́ться impf (at над+instr).

scold vt брани́ть impf, вы́~ pf.

scoop n (large) черпа́к; (ice-cream ~) ло́жка для моро́женого; vt (~ out, up) вычёрпывать impf, вы́черпать pf.

scooter n (motor ~) моторо́ллер.

scope n (range) преде́лы m pl; (chance) возмо́жность.

scorch vt (fingers) обжига́ть impf, обжёчь pf; (clothes) сжига́ть impf, сжечь pf.

score n (of points etc.) счёт; (mus) партиту́ра; pl (great numbers) мно́жество; vt (notch) де́лать impf, с~ pf зару́бки на+prep; (points etc.) получа́ть impf, получи́ть pf; (mus) оркестрова́ть impf & pf; vi (keep ~) вести́ impf, с~ pf счёт. **scorer** n счётчик.

scorn n презре́ние; vt презира́ть impf презре́ть pf. **scornful** adj презри́тельный.

Scorpio n Скорпио́н.

scorpion n скорпио́н.

Scot n шотла́ндец, -дка. **Scotch** n (whisky) шотла́ндское ви́ски neut indecl. **Scotland** n Шотла́ндия. **Scots, Scottish** adj шотла́ндский.

scoundrel n подле́ц.

scour[1] vt (cleanse) отчища́ть impf, отчи́стить pf.

scour[2] vt & i (rove) ры́скать impf (по+dat).

scourge n бич.

scout n разве́дчик; (S~) бойска́ут; vi: ~ about разы́скивать impf (for +acc).

scowl vi хму́риться impf, на~ pf; n хму́рый взгляд.

scrabble vi: ~ about ры́ться impf.

scramble vi кара́бкаться impf, вс~ pf; (struggle) дра́ться impf (for за +acc); ~d eggs яи́чница-болту́нья.

scrap[1] n (fragment etc.) кусо́чек; pl оста́тки m pl; pl (of food) объе́дки (-ков) pl; ~ metal металлоло́м; vt сдава́ть impf, сдать pf в утиль.

scrap[2] n (fight) дра́ка; vi дра́ться impf.

scrape vt скрести́ impf; (graze) цара́пать impf, о~ pf; ~ off отскреба́ть impf, отскрести́ pf; ~ through (exam) с трудо́м выде́рживать impf, вы́держать pf; ~ together наскреба́ть impf, наскрести́ pf.

scratch vt цара́пать impf, о~ pf; vt & i (when itching) чеса́ть(ся) impf, по~ pf; n цара́пина.

scrawl n кара́кули f pl; vt писа́ть impf, на~ pf кара́кулями.

scrawny adj сухопа́рый.

scream n крик; vi крича́ть impf, кри́кнуть pf.

screech n визг; vi визжа́ть impf.

screen n ши́рма; (cin, TV) экра́н; ~play сцена́рий; vt (protect) защища́ть impf, защити́ть pf; (hide) укрыва́ть impf, укры́ть pf; (show film etc.) демонстри́ровать impf & pf; (check on) проверя́ть impf, прове́рить pf; ~ off отгора́живать impf, отгороди́ть pf ши́рмой.

screw n винт; vt (~ on) приви́нчивать impf, привинти́ть pf; (~ up) зави́нчивать impf, завинти́ть pf; (crumple) ко́мкать impf, с~ pf; ~ up one's eyes щу́риться impf, со~ pf. **screwdriver** n отвёртка.

scribble vt строчи́ть impf, на~ pf; n кара́кули f pl.

script n (of film etc.) сцена́рий; (of speech etc.) текст; (writing system) письмо́; ~-writer сценари́ст.

Scripture n свяще́нное писа́ние.

scroll n сви́ток; (design) завито́к.

scrounge vt (cadge) стреля́ть impf, стрельну́ть pf; vi попроша́йничать impf.

scrub[1] n (brushwood) куста́рник; (area) за́росли f pl.

scrub[2] vt мыть impf, вы́~ pf щёткой.

scruff n: by the ~ of the neck за ши́ворот.

scruffy adj обо́дранный.

scrum n схва́тка вокру́г мяча́.

scruple n (also pl) колеба́ния neut pl; угрызе́ния neut pl со́вести. **scrupulous** adj скрупулёзный.

scrutinize vt рассма́тривать impf. **scrutiny** n рассмотре́ние.

scuffed adj поцара́панный.

scuffle n потасо́вка.

sculpt vt вая́ть impf, из~ pf. **sculptor** n ску́льптор. **sculpture** n скульпту́ра.

scum n на́кипь.

scurrilous adj непристо́йный.

scurry vi поспе́шно бе́гать indet, бежа́ть det.

scuttle[1] n (coal ~) ведёрко для угля.
scuttle[2] vi (run away) удирать impf, удрать pf.
scythe n коса.
sea n море; attrib морской; ~ **front** набережная sb; ~**gull** чайка; ~**level** уровень m моря; ~**lion** морской лев; ~**shore** побережье. **seaboard** n побережье. **seafood** n продукты m pl моря.
seal[1] n (on document etc.) печать; vt скреплять impf, скрепить pf печатью; (close) запечатывать impf, запечатать pf; ~ **up** заделывать impf, заделать pf.
seal[2] n (zool) тюлень m; (fur-~) котик.
seam n шов; (geol) пласт.
seaman n моряк, матрос.
seamless adj без шва.
seamstress n швея.
seance n спиритический сеанс.
seaplane n гидросамолёт.
searing adj палящий.
search vt обыскивать impf, обыскать pf; vi искать impf (for +acc); n поиски m pl; обыск; ~**party** поисковая группа. **searching** adj (look) испытующий. **searchlight** n прожектор.
seasick adj: I was ~ меня укачало. **seaside** n берег моря.
season n сезон; (one of four) время neut года; ~ **ticket** сезонный билет; vt (flavour) приправлять impf, приправить pf. **seasonable** adj по сезону; (timely) своевременный. **seasonal** adj сезонный. **seasoning** n приправа.
seat n (place) место; (of chair) сиденье; (chair) стул; (bench) скамейка; (of trousers) зад; ~ **belt** привязной ремень m; vt сажать impf, посадить pf; (of room etc.) вмещать impf, вместить pf; be ~ed садиться impf, сесть pf.
seaweed n морская водоросль.
secateurs n pl секатор.
secede vi откалываться impf, отколоться pf. **secession** n откол.
secluded adj укромный. **seclusion** n укромность.
second[1] adj второй; ~**class** второклассный; ~**hand** подержанный; (of information) из вторых рук; ~

rate второразрядный; ~ **sight** ясновидение; on ~ **thoughts** взвесив всё ещё раз; have ~ **thoughts** передумывать impf, передумать pf (about +acc); n второй sb; (date) второе (число); (time) секунда; pl (comm) товар второго сорта; ~**hand** (of clock) секундная стрелка; vt (support) поддерживать impf, поддержать pf; (transfer) откомандировывать impf откомандировать pf. **secondary** adj вторичный, второстепенный; (education) средний.
secondly adv во-вторых.
secrecy n секретность. **secret** n тайна, секрет; adj тайный, секретный; (hidden) потайной.
secretarial adj секретарский. **secretariat** n секретариат. **secretary** n секретарь m, -рша; (minister) министр.
secrete vt (conceal) укрывать impf, укрыть pf; (med) выделять impf, выделить pf. **secretion** n укрывание; (med) выделение.
secretive adj скрытный.
sect n секта. **sectarian** adj сектантский.
section n секция; (of book) раздел; (geom) сечение. **sector** n сектор.
secular adj светский. **secularization** n секуляризация.
secure adj (safe) безопасный; (firm) надёжный; (emotionally) уверенный; vt (fasten) закреплять impf, закрепить pf; (guarantee) обеспечивать impf, обеспечить pf; (obtain) доставать impf, достать pf. **security** n безопасность; (guarantee) залог; pl ценные бумаги f pl.
sedate adj степенный.
sedation n успокоение. **sedative** n успокаивающее средство.
sedentary adj сидячий.
sediment n осадок.
seduce vt соблазнять impf, соблазнить pf. **seduction** n обольщение. **seductive** adj соблазнительный.
see vt & i видеть impf, у~ pf; vt (watch, look) смотреть impf, по~ pf; (find out) узнавать impf, узнать pf; (understand) понимать impf, понять pf; (meet) видеться impf, у~ pf с+instr; (imagine) представлять impf, представить pf себе; (escort,

~ **off**) провожа́ть *impf*, проводи́ть *pf*; ~ **about** (*attend to*) забо́титься *impf*, по~ *pf* o+*prep*; ~ **through** (*fig*) ви́деть *impf*, наскво́зь+*acc*.

seed *n* се́мя *neut*. **seedling** *n* се́янец; *pl* расса́да. **seedy** *adj* (*shabby*) потрёпанный.

seeing (that) *conj* ввиду́ того́, что.

seek *vt* иска́ть *impf* +*acc, gen*.

seem *vi* каза́ться *impf*, по~ *pf* (+*instr*). **seemingly** *adv* по-ви́димому.

seemly *adj* прили́чный.

seep *vi* проса́чиваться *impf*, просочи́ться *pf*.

seethe *vi* кипе́ть *impf*, вс~ *pf*.

segment *n* отре́зок; (*of orange etc.*) до́лька; (*geom*) сегме́нт.

segregate *vt* отделя́ть *impf*, отдели́ть *pf*. **segregation** *n* сегрега́ция.

seismic *adj* сейсми́ческий.

seize *vt* хвата́ть *impf*, схвати́ть *pf*; *vi*: ~ **up** заеда́ть *impf*, зае́сть *pf* *impers*+*acc*; ~ **upon** ухва́тываться *impf*, ухвати́ться *pf* за+*acc*. **seizure** *n* захва́т; (*med*) припа́док.

seldom *adv* ре́дко.

select *adj* и́збранный; *vt* отбира́ть *impf*, отобра́ть *pf*. **selection** *n* (*choice*) вы́бор. **selective** *adj* разбо́рчивый.

self *n* со́бственное «я» *neut indecl*.

self- *in comb* само-; ~**-absorbed** эгоцентри́чный; ~**-assured** самоуве́ренный; ~**-catering** (*accommodation*) жильё с ку́хней; ~**-centred** эгоцентри́чный; ~**-confessed** открове́нный; ~**-confidence** самоуве́ренность; ~**-confident** самоуве́ренный; ~**-conscious** засте́нчивый; ~**-contained** (*person*) незави́симый; (*flat etc.*) отде́льный; ~**-control** самооблада́ние; ~**-defence** самозащи́та; ~**-denial** самоотрече́ние; ~**-determination** самоопределе́ние; ~**-effacing** скро́мный; ~**-employed person** незави́симый предпринима́тель *m*; ~**-esteem** самоуваже́ние; ~**-evident** очеви́дный; ~**-governing** самоуправля́ющий; ~**-help** самопо́мощь; ~**-importance** самомне́ние; ~**-imposed** доброво́льный; ~**-indulgent** изба́лованный; ~**-interest** со́бственный интере́с; ~**-pity** жа́лость к себе́; ~**-portrait** автопортре́т; ~**-preservation** самосохране́ние; ~**-reliance** само-

стоя́тельность; ~**-respect** самоуваже́ние; ~**-righteous** *adj* ха́нжеский; ~**-sacrifice** самопоже́ртвование; ~**-satisfied** самодово́льный; ~**-service** самообслу́живание (*attrib: in gen after n*); ~**-styled** самозва́нный; ~**-sufficient** самостоя́тельный.

selfish *adj* эгоисти́чный. **selfless** *adj* самоотве́рженный.

sell *vt & i* продава́ть(ся) *impf*, прода́ть(ся) *pf*; *vt* (*deal in*) торгова́ть *impf* +*instr*; ~ **out** распродава́ть *impf*, распрода́ть *pf*. **seller** *n* продаве́ц. **selling** *n* прода́жа. **sell-out** *n*: **the play was a** ~ пье́са прошла́ с аншла́гом.

Sellotape *n* (*propr*) ли́пкая ле́нта.

semantic *adj* семанти́ческий. **semantics** *n* сема́нтика.

semblance *n* ви́димость.

semen *n* се́мя *neut*.

semi- *in comb* полу-; ~**-detached house** дом, разделённый о́бщей стено́й. **semibreve** *n* це́лая но́та. **semicircle** *n* полукру́г. **semicircular** *adj* полукру́глый. **semicolon** *n* то́чка с запято́й. **semiconductor** *n* полупроводни́к. **semifinal** *n* полуфина́л.

seminar *n* семина́р. **seminary** *n* семина́рия.

semiquaver *n* шестна́дцатая но́та.

semitone *n* полуто́н.

senate *n* сена́т; (*univ*) сове́т. **senator** *n* сена́тор.

send *vt* посыла́ть *impf*, посла́ть *pf* (**for** за+*instr*); ~ **off** отправля́ть *impf*, отпра́вить *pf*; ~**-off** про́воды (-дов) *pl*. **sender** *n* отправи́тель *m*.

senile *adj* ста́рческий. **senility** *n* ста́рческое слабоу́мие.

senior *adj* (*n*) ста́рший (*sb*); ~ **citizen** стари́к, стару́ха. **seniority** *n* старшинство́.

sensation *n* сенса́ция; (*feeling*) ощуще́ние. **sensational** *adj* сенсацио́нный.

sense *n* чу́вство; (*good* ~) здра́вый смысл; (*meaning*) смысл; *pl* (*sanity*) ум; *vt* чу́вствовать *impf*. **senseless** *adj* бессмы́сленный.

sensibility *n* чувстви́тельность; *pl* самолю́бие. **sensible** *adj* благоразу́мный. **sensitive** *adj* чувстви́тельный; (*touchy*) оби́дчивый. **sensitiv-**

ity *n* чувстви́тельность.
sensory *adj* чувстви́тельный.
sensual, sensuous *adj* чу́вствен-
ный.
sentence *n* (*gram*) предложе́ние;
(*law*) пригово́р; *vt* пригова́ривать
impf, приговори́ть *pf* (**to** к+*dat*).
sentiment *n* (*feeling*) чу́вство; (*opinion*) мне́ние. **sentimental** *adj* сенти-
мента́льный. **sentimentality** *n* сен-
тимента́льность.
sentry *n* часово́й *sb*.
separable *adj* отдели́мый. **separate**
adj отде́льный; *vt & i* отделя́ть(ся)
impf, отдели́ть(ся) *pf*. **separation** *n*
отделе́ние. **separatism** *n* сепара-
ти́зм. **separatist** *n* сепарати́ст.
September *n* сентя́брь *m*; *adj* сен-
тя́брьский.
septic *adj* септи́ческий.
sepulchre *n* моги́ла.
sequel *n* (*result*) после́дствие; (*continuation*) продолже́ние. **sequence**
n после́довательность; ~ **of events**
ход собы́тий.
sequester *vt* секвестрова́ть *impf &
pf*.
sequin *n* блёстка.
Serb(ian) *adj* се́рбский; *n* серб, ~ка.
Serbia *n* Се́рбия. **Serbo-Croat(ian)**
adj сербскохорва́тский.
serenade *n* серена́да.
serene *adj* споко́йный. **serenity** *n*
споко́йствие.
serf *n* крепостно́й *sb*. **serfdom** *n*
крепостно́е пра́во.
sergeant *n* сержа́нт.
serial *adj*: ~ **number** сери́йный но́-
мер; *n* (*story*) рома́н с продолже́-
нием; (*broadcast*) сери́йная поста-
но́вка. **serialize** *vt* ста́вить *impf*,
по~ *pf* в не́скольких частя́х. **series** *n* (*succession*) ряд (*broadcast*)
се́рия переда́ч.
serious *adj* серьёзный. **seriousness**
n серьёзность.
sermon *n* про́поведь.
serpent *n* змея́.
serrated *adj* зазу́бренный.
serum *n* сы́воротка.
servant *n* слуга́ *m*, служа́нка. **serve**
vt служи́ть *impf*, по~ *pf* +*dat* (**as,
for** +*instr*); (*attend to*) обслу́живать
impf, обслужи́ть *pf*; (*food; ball*) по-
дава́ть *impf*, пода́ть *pf*; (*sentence*)

отбыва́ть *impf*, отбы́ть *pf*; (*writ
etc.*) вруча́ть *impf*, вручи́ть *pf*; (*on
+dat*); *vi* (*be suitable*) годи́ться (**for**
на+*acc*, для+*gen*); (*sport*) подава́ть
impf, пода́ть *pf* мяч; **it** ~**s him right**
поде́лом ему́ (*dat*). **service** *n* (*act
of serving; branch of public work*)
eccl слу́жба; (*quality of* ~) обслу́-
живание; (*of car etc.*) техобслу́-
живание; (*set of dishes*) серви́з; (*sport*)
пода́ча; (*transport*) сообще́ние; **at
your** ~ к ва́шим услу́гам; *vt* (*car*)
проводи́ть *impf*, провести́ *pf* тех-
обслу́живание +*gen*; ~ **charge** пла́-
та за обслу́живание; ~ **station** ста́н-
ция обслу́живания. **serviceable** *n*
(*useful*) поле́зный; (*durable*) про́ч-
ный. **serviceman** *n* военнослу́жа-
щий *sb*.
serviette *n* салфе́тка.
servile *adj* рабо́лепный.
session *n* заседа́ние, се́ссия.
set[1] *vt* (*put*; ~ *clock, trap*) ста́вить
impf, по- *pf*; (*table*) накрыва́ть *impf*,
накры́ть *pf*; (*bone*) вправля́ть *impf*,
впра́вить *pf*; (*hair*) укла́дывать
impf, уложи́ть *pf*; (*gem*) оправля́ть
impf, опра́вить *pf*; (*bring into state*)
приводи́ть *impf*, привести́ *pf* (**in, to**
в+*acc*); (*example*) подава́ть *impf*,
пода́ть *pf*; (*task*) задава́ть *impf*,
зада́ть *pf*; *vi* (*solidify*) тверде́ть
impf, за~ *pf*; застыва́ть *impf*,
засты́(ну)ть *pf*; (*sun etc.*) заходи́ть
impf, зайти́ *pf*; сади́ться *impf*, сесть
pf; ~ **about** (*begin*) начина́ть *impf*,
нача́ть *pf*; (*attack*) напада́ть *impf*,
напа́сть *pf* на+*acc*; ~ **back** (*impede*)
препя́тствовать *impf*, вос~ *pf* +*dat*;
~-**back** неуда́ча; ~ **in** наступа́ть
impf, наступи́ть *pf*; ~ **off** (*on journey*) отправля́ться *impf*, отпра́вить-
ся *pf*; (*enhance*) оттеня́ть *impf*,
оттени́ть *pf*; ~ **out** (*state*) излага́ть
impf, изложи́ть *pf*; (*on journey*) *see*
~ **off**; ~ **up** (*business*) осно́вывать
impf, основа́ть *pf*.
set[2] *n* набо́р, компле́кт; (*of dishes*)
серви́з; (*radio*) приёмник; (*television*) телеви́зор; (*tennis*) сет; (*theat*)
декора́ция; (*cin*) съёмочная пло-
ща́дка.
set[3] *adj* (*established*) устано́влен-
ный.
settee *n* дива́н.

setting n (frame) опра́ва; (surroundings) обстано́вка; (of mechanism etc.) устано́вка; (of sun etc.) захо́д.

settle vt (decide) реша́ть impf, реши́ть pf; (reconcile) ула́живать impf, ула́дить pf; (a bill etc.) опла́чивать impf, оплати́ть pf; (calm) успока́ивать impf, успоко́ить pf; vi поселя́ться impf, посели́ться pf; (subside) оседа́ть impf, осе́сть pf; ~ **down** уса́живаться impf, усе́сться pf (to за+acc). **settlement** n поселе́ние; (agreement) соглаше́ние; (payment) упла́та. **settler** n поселе́нец.

seven adj & n семь; (number 7) семёрка. **seventeen** adj & n семна́дцать. **seventeenth** adj & n семна́дцатый. **seventh** adj & n седьмо́й; (fraction) седьма́я sb. **seventieth** adj & n семидеся́тый. **seventy** adj & n се́мьдесят; pl (decade) семидеся́тые го́ды (-до́в) m pl.

sever vt (cut off) отреза́ть impf, отре́зать pf; (relations) разрыва́ть impf, разорва́ть pf.

several pron (adj) не́сколько (+gen).

severance n разры́в; ~ **pay** выходно́е посо́бие.

severe adj стро́гий, суро́вый; (pain, frost) си́льный; (illness) тяжёлый. **severity** n стро́гость, суро́вость.

sew vt шить impf, с~ pf; ~ **on** пришива́ть impf, приши́ть pf; ~ **up** зашива́ть impf, заши́ть pf.

sewage n сто́чные во́ды f pl; ~-**farm** поля́ neut pl ороше́ния. **sewer** n сто́чная труба́. **sewerage** n канализа́ция.

sewing n шитьё; ~-**machine** швейная маши́на.

sex n (gender) пол; (sexual activity) секс; **have** ~ име́ть impf сноше́ние. **sexual** adj полово́й, сексуа́льный; ~ **intercourse** полово́е сноше́ние. **sexuality** n сексуа́льность. **sexy** adj эроти́ческий.

sh int ти́ше!; тсс!

shabby adj ве́тхий.

shack n лачу́га.

shackles n pl око́вы (-в) pl.

shade n тень; (of colour, meaning) отте́нок; (lamp-~) абажу́р; **a** ~ чуть-чу́ть; vt затеня́ть impf, затени́ть pf; (eyes etc.) заслоня́ть impf, заслони́ть pf; (drawing) тушева́ть

impf, за~ pf. **shadow** n тень; vt (follow) та́йно следи́ть impf за+instr. **shadowy** adj тёмный. **shady** adj тени́стый; (suspicious) подозри́тельный.

shaft n (of spear) дре́вко; (arrow; fig) стрела́; (of light) луч; (of cart) огло́бля; (axle) вал; (mine, lift) ша́хта.

shaggy adj лохма́тый.

shake vt & i трясти́(сь) impf; vi (tremble) дрожа́ть impf; vt (weaken) колеба́ть impf, по~ pf; (shock) потряса́ть impf потрясти́ pf; ~ **hands** пожима́ть impf, пожа́ть pf ру́ку (with +dat); ~ **one's head** покача́ть pf голово́й; ~ **off** стря́хивать impf, стряхну́ть pf; (fig) избавля́ться impf, изба́виться pf от+gen. **shaky** adj ша́ткий.

shallow adj ме́лкий; (fig) пове́рхностный.

sham vt & i притворя́ться impf, притвори́ться pf +instr; n притво́рство; (person) притво́рщик, -ица; adj притво́рный.

shambles n xaóc.

shame n (guilt) стыд; (disgrace) позо́р; **what a** ~! как жаль!; vt стыди́ть impf, при~ pf. **shameful** adj позо́рный. **shameless** adj бессты́дный.

shampoo n шампу́нь m.

shanty[1] n (hut) хиба́рка; ~ **town** трущо́ба.

shanty[2] n (song) матро́сская пе́сня.

shape n фо́рма; vt придава́ть impf, прида́ть pf фо́рму+dat; vi: ~ **up** скла́дываться impf, сложи́ться pf. **shapeless** adj бесфо́рменный. **shapely** adj стро́йный.

share n до́ля; (econ) а́кция; vt дели́ть impf, по~ pf; (opinion etc.; ~ **out**) разделя́ть impf, раздели́ть pf. **shareholder** n акционе́р.

shark n аку́ла.

sharp adj о́стрый; (steep) круто́й; (sudden; harsh) ре́зкий; n (mus) дие́з; adv (with time) ро́вно; (of angle) кру́то. **sharpen** vt точи́ть impf, на~ pf.

shatter vt & i разбива́ть(ся) impf, разби́ть(ся) pf вдре́безги; vt (hopes etc.) разруша́ть impf, разру́шить pf.

shave vt & i брить(ся) impf, по~ pf; n бритьё. **shaver** n электри́ческая бри́тва.

shawl *n* шаль.

she *pron* она́.

sheaf *n* сноп; (*of papers*) свя́зка.

shear *vt* стричь *impf*, о~ *pf.* **shears** *n pl* но́жницы (-ц) *pl.*

sheath *n* но́жны (*gen* -жен) *pl.*

shed[1] *n* сара́й.

shed[2] *vt* (*tears, blood, light*) пролива́ть *impf*, проли́ть *pf*; (*skin, clothes*) сбра́сывать *impf*, сбро́сить *pf.*

sheen *n* блеск.

sheep *n* овца́. **sheepish** *adj* сконфу́женный. **sheepskin** *n* овчи́на; ~ **coat** дублёнка.

sheer *adj* (*utter*) су́щий; (*textile*) прозра́чный; (*rock etc.*) отве́сный.

sheet *n* (*on bed*) простыня́; (*of glass, paper, etc.*) лист.

sheikh *n* шейх.

shelf *n* по́лка.

shell *n* (*of mollusc etc.*) ра́ковина; (*of tortoise*) щит; (*of egg, nut*) скорлупа́; (*of building etc.*) о́стов; (*explosive* ~) снаря́д; *vt* (*peas etc.*) лущи́ть *impf*, об~ *pf*; (*bombard*) обстре́ливать *impf*, обстреля́ть *pf.* **shellfish** *n* (*mollusc*) моллю́ск; (*crustacean*) ракообра́зное *sb.*

shelter *n* убе́жище; *vt* (*provide with refuge*) приюти́ть *pf*; *vt & i* укрыва́ть(ся) *impf*, укры́ть(ся) *pf.*

shelve[1] *vt* (*defer*) откла́дывать *impf*, отложи́ть *pf.*

shelve[2] *vi* (*slope*) отло́го спуска́ться *impf.*

shelving *n* (*shelves*) стелла́ж.

shepherd *n* пасту́х; *vt* проводи́ть *impf*, провести́ *pf.*

sherry *n* хе́рес.

shield *n* щит; *vt* защища́ть *impf*, защити́ть *pf.*

shift *vt & i* (*change position*) перемеща́ть(ся) *impf*, перемести́ть(ся) *pf*; (*change*) меня́ть(ся) *impf*; *n* переме́щение; переме́на; (*of workers*) сме́на; ~ **work** сме́нная рабо́та. **shifty** *adj* ско́льзкий.

shimmer *vi* мерца́ть *impf*; *n* мерца́ние.

shin *n* го́лень.

shine *vi* свети́ть(ся) *impf*; (*glitter*) блесте́ть *impf*; (*excel*) блиста́ть *impf*; (*sun, eyes*) сия́ть *impf*; *vt* (*a light*) освеща́ть *impf*, освети́ть *pf*

фонарём (**on** +*acc*); *n* гля́нец.

shingle *n* (*pebbles*) га́лька.

shingles *n* опоя́сывающий лиша́й.

shiny *adj* блестя́щий.

ship *n* кора́бль *m*; су́дно; *vt* (*transport*) перевози́ть *impf*, перевезти́ *pf*; (*dispatch*) отправля́ть *impf*, отпра́вить *pf.* **shipbuilding** *n* судостро́ительство. **shipment** *n* (*dispatch*) отпра́вка; (*goods*) па́ртия. **shipping** *n* суда́ (-до́в) *pl.* **shipshape** *adv* в по́лном поря́дке. **shipwreck** *n* кораблекруше́ние; **be** ~**ed** терпе́ть *impf*, по~ *pf* кораблекруше́ние. **shipyard** *n* верфь.

shirk *vt* уви́ливать *impf*, увильну́ть *pf* от+*gen*.

shirt *n* руба́шка.

shit (*vulg*) *n* говно́; *vi* срать *impf*, по~ *pf.*

shiver *vi* (*tremble*) дрожа́ть *impf*; *n* дрожь.

shoal *n* (*of fish*) ста́я.

shock *n* (*emotional*) потрясе́ние; (*impact*) уда́р, толчо́к; (*electr*) уда́р то́ком; (*med*) шок; *vt* шоки́ровать *impf.* **shocking** *adj* (*outrageous*) сканда́льный; (*awful*) ужа́сный.

shoddy *adj* халту́рный.

shoe *n* ту́фля; *vt* подко́вывать *impf*, подкова́ть *pf.* **shoe-lace** *n* шнуро́к. **shoemaker** *n* сапо́жник. **shoe-string** *n*: **on a** ~ с небольши́ми сре́дствами.

shoo *int* кш!; *vt* прогоня́ть *impf*, прогна́ть *pf.*

shoot *vt & i* (*discharge*) стреля́ть *impf* (*a gun* из+*gen*; **at** в+*acc*, по +*dat*); (*arrow*) пуска́ть *impf*, пусти́ть *pf*; (*kill*) застре́ливать *impf*, застрели́ть *pf*; (*execute*) расстре́ливать *impf*, расстреля́ть *pf*; (*hunt*) охо́титься *impf* на+*acc*; (*football*) бить *impf* (по воро́там); (*cin*) снима́ть *impf*, снять *pf* (фильм); *vi* (*go swiftly*) проноси́ться *impf*, пронести́сь *pf*; ~ **down** (*aircraft*) сбива́ть *impf*, сбить *pf*; ~ **up** (*grow*) бы́стро расти́ *impf*, по~ *pf*; (*prices*) подска́кивать *impf*, подскочи́ть *pf*; *n* (*branch*) росто́к, побе́г; (*hunt*) охо́та. **shooting** *n* стрельба́; (*hunting*) охо́та; ~**-gallery** тир.

shop *n* магази́н; (*workshop*) мастерска́я *sb*, цех; ~ **assistant** продаве́ц,

-вщи́ца; **~-lifter** магази́нный вор; **~-lifting** воровство́ в магази́нах; **~ steward** цехово́й ста́роста *m*; **~-window** витри́на; *vi* де́лать *impf*, с~ *pf* поку́пки (*f pl*). **shopkeeper** *n* ла́вочник. **shopper** *n* покупа́тель *m*, ~ница. **shopping** *n* поку́пки *f pl*; **go, do one's ~** де́лать *impf*, с~ *pf* поку́пки; **~-centre** торго́вый центр.

shore¹ *n* бе́рег.

shore² *vi*: **~ up** подпира́ть *impf*, подпере́ть *pf*.

short *adj* коро́ткий; (*not tall*) ни́зкого ро́ста; (*deficient*) недоста́точный; **be ~ of** испы́тывать *impf*, испыта́ть *pf* недоста́ток в+*prep*; (*curt*) ре́зкий; **in ~** одни́м сло́вом; **~-change** обсчи́тывать *impf*, обсчита́ть *pf*; **~ circuit** коро́ткое замыка́ние; **~ cut** коро́ткий путь *m*; **~-list** оконча́тельный спи́сок; **~-list** включа́ть *impf*, включи́ть *pf* в оконча́тельный спи́сок; **~-lived** недолгове́чный; **~-sighted** близору́кий; (*fig*) недальнови́дный; **~ story** расска́з; **in ~ supply** дефици́тный; **~-tempered** вспы́льчивый; **~-term** краткосро́чный; **~-wave** коротковолно́вый. **shortage** *n* недоста́ток. **shortcoming** *n* недоста́ток. **shorten** *vt & i* укора́чивать(ся) *impf*, укороти́ть(ся) *pf*. **shortfall** *n* дефици́т. **shorthand** *n* стеногра́фия; **~ typist** машини́стка-стенографи́стка. **shortly** *adv*: **~ after** вско́ре (по́сле +*gen*); **~ before** незадо́лго (до+*gen*). **shorts** *n pl* шо́рты (-т) *pl*.

shot *n* (*discharge of gun*) вы́стрел; (*pellets*) дробь; (*person*) стрело́к; (*attempt*) попы́тка; (*phot*) сни́мок; (*cin*) кадр; (*sport*) (*stroke*) уда́р; (*throw*) бросо́к; **like a ~** неме́дленно; **~-gun** дробови́к.

should *v aux* (*ought*) до́лжен (бы) +*inf*: **you ~ know that** вы должны́ э́то знать; **he ~ be here soon** он до́лжен бы быть тут ско́ро; (*conditional*) бы +*past*: **I ~ say** я бы сказа́л(а); **I ~ like** я бы хоте́л(а).

shoulder *n* плечо́; **~-blade** лопа́тка; **~-strap** брете́лька; взва́ливать *impf*, взвали́ть *pf* на пле́чи; (*fig*) брать *impf*, взять *pf* на себя́.

shout *n* крик; *vi* крича́ть *impf*, кри́кнуть *pf*; **~ down** перекри́кивать *impf*, перекрича́ть *pf*.

shove *n* толчо́к; *vt & i* толка́ть(ся) *impf*, толкну́ть *pf*; **~ off** (*coll*) убира́ться *impf*, убра́ться *pf*.

shovel *n* лопа́та; *vt* (**~ up**) сгреба́ть *impf*, сгрести́ *pf*.

show *vt* пока́зывать *impf*, показа́ть *pf*; (*exhibit*) выставля́ть *impf*, вы́ставить *pf*; (*film etc.*) демонстри́ровать *impf*, про~ *pf*; *vi* (*also ~ up*) быть ви́дным, заме́тным; **~ off** (*vi*) привлека́ть *impf*; привле́чь *pf* к себе́ внима́ние; **~ up see vi**; (*appear*) появля́ться *impf*, появи́ться *pf*; *n* (*exhibition*) вы́ставка; (*theat*) спекта́кль *m*; (*effect*) ви́димость; **~ of hands** голосова́ние подня́тием руки́; **~-case** витри́на; **~-jumping** соревнова́ние по ска́чкам; **~-room** сало́н. **showdown** *n* развя́зка.

shower *n* (*rain*) до́ждик; (*hail*; *fig*) град; (**~-bath**) душ; *vt* осыпа́ть *impf*, осы́пать *pf* +*instr* (**on** +*acc*); *vi* принима́ть *impf*, приня́ть *pf* душ. **showery** *adj* дождли́вый.

showpiece *n* образе́ц. **showy** *adj* показно́й.

shrapnel *n* шрапне́ль.

shred *n* клочо́к; **not a ~** ни ка́пли; *vt* мельчи́ть *impf*, из~ *pf*.

shrewd *adj* проница́тельный.

shriek *vi* визжа́ть *impf*; взви́гнуть *pf*.

shrill *adj* пронзи́тельный.

shrimp *n* креве́тка.

shrine *n* святы́ня.

shrink *vi* сади́ться *impf*, сесть *pf*; (*recoil*) отпря́нуть *pf*; *vt* вызыва́ть *impf*, вы́звать *pf* уса́дку у+*gen*; **~ from** избега́ть *impf* +*gen*. **shrinkage** *n* уса́дка.

shrivel *vi* смо́рщиваться *impf*, смо́рщиться *pf*.

shroud *n* са́ван; *vt* (*fig*) оку́тывать *impf*, оку́тать *pf* (**in** +*instr*).

Shrove Tuesday вто́рник на ма́сленой неде́ле.

shrub *n* куст. **shrubbery** *n* куста́рник.

shrug *vt & i* пожима́ть *impf*, пожа́ть *pf* (плеча́ми).

shudder *n* содрога́ние; *vi* содрога́ться *impf*, содрогну́ться *pf*.

shuffle *vt & i* (*one's feet*) ша́ркать *impf* (нога́ми); *vt* (*cards*) тасова́ть *impf*, с~ *pf*; *n* тасо́вка.

shun *vt* избегать *impf* +*gen*.

shunt *vi* (*rly*) маневрировать *impf*, c~ *pf*; *vt* (*rly*) переводить *impf*, перевести *pf* на запасной путь.

shut *vt* & *i* (*also* ~ *down*) закрывать(ся) *impf*, закрыть(ся) *pf*; ~ **out** (*exclude*) исключать *impf*, исключить *pf*; (*fence off*) загораживать *impf*, загородить *pf*; (*keep out*) не пускать *impf*, пустить *pf*; ~ **up** (*vi*) замолчать *pf*; (*imper*) заткнись!

shutter *n* ставень *m*; (*phot*) затвор.

shuttle *n* челнок.

shy[1] *adj* застенчивый.

shy[2] *vi* (*in alarm*) отпрядывать *impf*, отпрянуть *pf*.

Siberia *n* Сибирь. **Siberian** *adj* сибирский; *n* сибиряк, -ячка.

sick *adj* больной; **be** ~ (*vomit*) рвать *impf*, вы~ *pf impers* +*acc*: **he was** ~ его вырвало; **feel** ~ тошнить *impf impers* +*acc*; **be** ~ **of** надоедать *impf*, надоесть *pf* +*nom* (*object*) & *dat* (*subject*): **I'm** ~ **of her** она мне надоела; ~**-leave** отпуск по болезни. **sicken** *vt* вызывать *impf*, вызвать *pf* тошноту, (*disgust*) отвращение, у+*gen*; *vi* заболевать *impf*, заболеть *pf*. **sickening** *adj* отвратительный.

sickle *n* серп.

sickly *adj* болезненный; (*nauseating*) тошнотворный. **sickness** *n* болезнь; (*vomiting*) тошнота.

side *n* сторона; (*of body*) бок; ~ **by** ~ рядом (**with** c+*instr*); **on the** ~ на стороне; *vi*: ~ **with** вставать *impf*, встать *pf* на сторону+*gen*; ~**-effect** побочное действие; ~**-step** (*fig*) уклоняться *impf*, уклониться *pf* от+*gen*; ~**-track** (*distract*) отвлекать *impf*, отвлечь *pf*. **sideboard** *n* буфет; *pl* баки (-к) *pl*. **sidelight** *n* боковой фонарь *m*. **sideline** *n* (*work*) побочная работа.

sidelong *adj* (*glance*) косой.

sideways *adv* боком.

siding *n* запасной путь *m*.

sidle *vi*: ~ **up to** подходить *impf*, подойти *pf* к (+*dat*) бочком.

siege *n* осада; **lay** ~ **to** осаждать *impf*, осадить *pf*; **raise the** ~ **of** снимать *impf*, снять *pf* осаду c+*gen*.

sieve *n* сито; *vt* просеивать *impf*, просеять *pf*.

sift *vt* просеивать *impf*, просеять *pf*; (*fig*) тщательно рассматривать *impf*, рассмотреть *pf*.

sigh *vi* вздыхать *impf*, вздохнуть *pf*; *n* вздох.

sight *n* (*faculty*) зрение; (*view*) вид; (*spectacle*) зрелище; *pl* достопримечательности *f pl*; (*on gun*) прицел; **at first** ~ с первого взгляда; **catch** ~ **of** увидеть *pf*; **know by** ~ знать *impf* в лицо; **lose** ~ **of** терять *impf*, по~ *pf* из виду; (*fig*) упускать *impf*, упустить *pf* из виду.

sign *n* знак; (*indication*) признак; (~*board*) вывеска; *vt* & *abs* подписывать(ся) *impf*, подписать(ся) *pf*; *vt* (*give* ~) подавать *impf*, подать *pf* знак; ~ **on** (*as unemployed*) записываться *impf*, записаться *pf* в списки безработных; (~ *up*) наниматься *impf*, наняться *pf*.

signal *n* сигнал; *vt* & *i* сигнализировать *impf* & *pf*. **signal-box** *n* сигнальная будка. **signalman** *n* сигнальщик.

signatory *n* подписавший *sb*; (*of treaty*) сторона, подписавшая договор.

signature *n* подпись.

significance *n* значение. **significant** *adj* значительный. **signify** *vt* означать *impf*.

signpost *n* указательный столб.

silage *n* силос.

silence *n* молчание, тишина; *vt* заставить *pf* замолчать. **silencer** *n* глушитель *m*. **silent** *adj* (*not speaking*) безмолвный; (*of film*) немой; (*without noise*) тихий; **be** ~ молчать *impf*.

silhouette *n* силуэт; *vt*: **be** ~**d** вырисовываться *impf*, вырисоваться *pf* (**against** на фоне+*gen*).

silicon *n* кремний. **silicone** *n* силикон.

silk *n* шёлк; *attrib* шёлковый. **silky** *adj* шелковистый.

sill *n* подоконник.

silly *adj* глупый.

silo *n* силос.

silt *n* ил.

silver *n* серебро; (*cutlery*) столовое серебро; *adj* (*of* ~) серебряный; (*silvery*) серебристый; ~**-plated** посеребрённый. **silversmith** *n* серебряных дел мастер. **silverware** *n*

столо́вое серебро́. **silvery** *adj* сере́-
бри́стый.

similar *adj* подо́бный (**to** +*dat*). **similarity** *n* схо́дство. **similarly** *adv* по-
до́бным о́бразом.

simile *n* сравне́ние.

simmer *vt* кипяти́ть *impf* на ме́д-
ленном огне́; *vi* кипе́ть *impf* на
ме́дленном огне́; ~ **down** успока́-
иваться *impf*, успоко́иться *pf*.

simper *vi* жема́нно улыба́ться *impf*,
улыбну́ться *pf*.

simple *adj* просто́й; ~**-minded** тупо-
ва́тый. **simplicity** *n* простота́. **sim-
plify** *vt* упроща́ть *impf*, упрости́ть
pf. **simply** *adv* про́сто.

simulate *vt* притворя́ться *impf*, при-
твори́ться *pf* +*instr*; (*conditions etc.*)
модели́ровать *impf & pf*. **simulated**
adj (*pearls etc.*) иску́сственный.

simultaneous *adj* одновреме́нный.

sin *n* грех; *vi* греши́ть *impf*, со~ *pf*.

since *adv* с тех пор; *prep* с+*gen*; *conj*
с тех пор как; (*reason*) так как.

sincere *adj* и́скренний. **sincerely**
adv и́скренне; **yours** ~ и́скренне
Ваш. **sincerity** *n* и́скренность.

sinew *n* сухожи́лие.

sinful *adj* гре́шный.

sing *vt & i* петь *impf*, про~, с~ *pf*.

singe *vt* пали́ть *impf*, о~ *pf*.

singer *n* певе́ц, -ви́ца.

single *adj* оди́н; (*unmarried*) (*of man*)
нежена́тый; (*of woman*) незаму́ж-
няя; (*bed*) односпа́льный; ~**-handed**
без посторо́нней по́мощи; ~**-minded**
целеустремлённый, ~ **parent** мать/
оте́ц-одино́чка; ~ **room** ко́мната на
одного́; *n* (*ticket*) биле́т в оди́н ко-
не́ц; *pl* (*tennis etc.*) одино́чная игра́
vt: ~ **out** выделя́ть *impf*, вы́делить
pf. **singly** *adv* по-одному́.

singular *n* еди́нственное число́; *adj*
еди́нственный; (*unusual*) необы-
ча́йный. **singularly** *adv* необыча́йно.

sinister *adj* злове́щий.

sink *vi* (*descend slowly*) опуска́ться
impf, опусти́ться *pf*; (*in mud etc.*)
погружа́ться *impf*, погрузи́ться *pf*;
(*in water*) тону́ть *impf*, по~ *pf*; *vt*
(*ship*) топи́ть *impf*, по~ *pf*; (*pipe,
post*) вка́пывать *impf*, вкопа́ть *pf*;
n ра́ковина.

sinner *n* гре́шник, -ица.

sinus *n* па́зуха.

sip *vt* пить *impf*, ма́ленькими глот-
ка́ми; *n* ма́ленький глото́к.

siphon *n* сифо́н; ~ **off** (*also fig*)
перека́чивать *impf*, перекача́ть *pf*.

sir *n* сэр.

siren *n* сире́на.

sister *n* сестра́; ~**-in-law** (*husband's
sister*) золо́вка; (*wife's sister*) своя́-
ченица; (*brother's wife*) неве́стка.

sit *vi* (*be sitting*) сиде́ть *impf*; (~
down) сади́ться *impf*, сесть *pf*; (*parl,
law*) заседа́ть *impf*; *vt* уса́живать
impf, усади́ть *pf*; (*exam*) сдава́ть
impf; ~ **back** отки́дываться *impf*,
отки́нуться *pf*; ~ **down** сади́ться
impf, сесть *pf*; ~ **up** приподнима́ть-
ся *impf*, приподня́ться *pf*; (*not go
to bed*) не ложи́ться *impf* спать.

site *n* (*where a thing takes place*) ме́-
сто; (*where a thing is*) местополо-
же́ние.

sitting *n* (*parl etc.*) заседа́ние; (*for
meal*) сме́на; ~**-room** гости́ная *sb*.

situated *adj*: **be** ~ находи́ться *impf*.

situation *n* местоположе́ние; (*circumstances*) положе́ние; (*job*) ме́сто.

six *adj & n* шесть; (*number 6*) шестёрка. **sixteen** *adj & n* шестна́дцать.
sixteenth *adj & n* шестна́дцатый.
sixth *adj & n* шесто́й; (*fraction*) ше-
ста́я *sb*. **sixtieth** *adj & n* шести-
деся́тый. **sixty** *adj & n* шестьдеся́т;
pl (*decade*) шестидеся́тые го́ды
(-до́в) *m pl*.

size *n* разме́р; *vt*: ~ **up** оце́нивать
impf, оцени́ть *pf*. **sizeable** *adj* зна-
чи́тельный.

sizzle *vi* шипе́ть *impf*.

skate[1] *n* (*fish*) скат.

skate[2] *n* (*ice-*~) конёк; (*roller-*~)
конёк на ро́ликах; *vi* ката́ться *impf*
на конька́х; **skating-rink** като́к.

skeleton *n* скеле́т.

sketch *n* зарисо́вка; (*theat*) скетч; *vt
& i* зарисо́вывать *impf*, зарисова́ть
pf. **sketchy** *adj* схемати́ческий;
(*superficial*) пове́рхностный.

skew *adj* косо́й; **on the** ~ ко́со.

skewer *n* ве́ртел.

ski *n* лы́жа; ~**-jump** трампли́н; *vi* хо-
ди́ть *impf* на лы́жах.

skid *n* зано́с; *vi* заноси́ть *impf*, за-
нести́ *pf impers*+*acc*.

skier *n* лы́жник. **skiing** *n* лы́жный
спорт.

skilful adj иску́сный. **skill** n мастерство́; (countable) поле́зный на́вык. **skilled** adj иску́сный; (trained) квалифици́рованный.

skim vt снима́ть impf, снять pf (cream сли́вки pl, scum на́кипь) c+gen; vi скользи́ть impf (over, along по+dat); ~ **through** бе́гло просма́тривать impf, просмотре́ть pf; adj: ~ **milk** снято́е молоко́.

skimp vt & i скупи́ться impf (на+acc). **skimpy** adj ску́дный.

skin n ко́жа; (hide) шку́ра; (of fruit etc.) кожура́; (on milk) пёнка; vt сдира́ть impf, содра́ть pf ко́жу, шку́ру, c+gen; (fruit) снима́ть impf, снять pf кожуру́ c+gen. **skinny** adj то́щий.

skip[1] vi скака́ть impf; (with rope) пры́гать impf че́рез скака́лку; vt (omit) пропуска́ть impf, пропусти́ть pf.

skip[2] n (container) скип.

skipper n (naut) шки́пер.

skirmish n схва́тка.

skirt n ю́бка; vt обходи́ть impf, обойти́ pf стороно́й; ~**ing-board** пли́нтус.

skittle n ке́гля; pl ке́гли f pl.

skulk vi (hide) скрыва́ться impf; (creep) кра́сться impf.

skull n че́реп.

skunk n скунс.

sky n не́бо. **skylark** n жа́воронок. **skylight** n окно́ в кры́ше. **skyline** n горизо́нт. **skyscraper** n небоскрёб.

slab n плита́; (of cake etc.) кусо́к.

slack adj (loose) сла́бый; (sluggish) вя́лый; (negligent) небре́жный; n (of rope) слабина́; pl брю́ки (-к) pl.

slacken vt ослабля́ть impf, осла́бить pf; vt & i (slow down) замедля́ть(ся) impf, заме́длить(ся) pf; vi ослабева́ть impf, ослабе́ть pf.

slag n шлак.

slam vt & i захло́пывать(ся) impf, захло́пнуть(ся) pf.

slander n клевета́; vt клевета́ть impf, на~ pf на+acc. **slanderous** adj клеветни́ческий.

slang n жарго́н. **slangy** adj жарго́нный.

slant vt & i наклоня́ть(ся) impf, наклони́ть(ся) pf; n укло́н. **slanting** adj косо́й.

slap vt шлёпать impf, шлёпнуть pf; n шлепо́к; adv пря́мо. **slapdash** adj небре́жный. **slapstick** n фарс.

slash vt (cut) поро́ть impf, рас~ pf; (fig) уре́зывать impf, уре́зать pf; n разре́з; (sign) дробь.

slat n пла́нка.

slate[1] n сла́нец; (for roofing) (кро́вельная) пли́тка.

slate[2] vt (criticize) разноси́ть impf, разнести́ pf.

slaughter n (of animals) убо́й; (massacre) резня́; vt (animals) ре́зать impf, за~ pf; (people) убива́ть impf, уби́ть pf. **slaughterhouse** n бо́йня.

Slav n славяни́н, -я́нка; adj славя́нский.

slave n раб, рабы́ня; vi рабо́тать impf как раб. **slavery** n ра́бство.

Slavic adj славя́нский.

slavish adj ра́бский.

Slavonic adj славя́нский.

slay vt убива́ть impf, уби́ть pf.

sleazy adj убо́гий.

sledge n са́ни (-не́й) pl.

sledge-hammer n кува́лда.

sleek adj гла́дкий.

sleep n сон; **go to** ~ засыпа́ть impf, засну́ть pf; vi спать impf; (spend the night) ночева́ть impf, пере~ pf. **sleeper** n спя́щий sb; (on track) шпа́ла; (sleeping-car) спа́льный ваго́н. **sleeping** adj спя́щий; ~**bag** спа́льный мешо́к; ~**car** спа́льный ваго́н; ~**pill** снотво́рная табле́тка. **sleepless** adj бессо́нный. **sleepy** adj со́нный.

sleet n мо́крый снег.

sleeve n рука́в; (of record) конве́рт.

sleigh n са́ни (-не́й) pl.

sleight-of-hand n ло́вкость рук.

slender adj (slim) то́нкий; (meagre) ску́дный; (of hope etc.) сла́бый.

sleuth n сы́щик.

slice n кусо́к; vt (~ up) нареза́ть impf, наре́зать pf.

slick adj (dextrous) ло́вкий; (crafty) хи́трый; n нефтяна́я плёнка.

slide vi скользи́ть impf; vt (drawer etc.) задвига́ть impf, задви́нуть pf; n (children's ~) го́рка; (microscope ~) предме́тное стекло́; (phot) диапозити́в, слайд; (for hair) зако́лка.

sliding adj (door) задвижно́й.

slight[1] adj (slender) то́нкий; (inconsiderable) небольшо́й; (light) лёгкий; **not the ~est** ни мале́йшего, -шей (gen); **not in the ~est** ничу́ть.

slight[2] vt пренебрега́ть impf, пренебре́чь pf +instr; n оби́да.

slightly adv слегка́, немно́го.

slim adj то́нкий; (chance etc.) сла́бый; vi худе́ть impf, по~ pf.

slime n слизь. **slimy** adj сли́зистый; (person) ско́льзкий.

sling vt (throw) швыря́ть impf, швырну́ть pf; (suspend) подве́шивать impf, подве́сить pf; n (med) пе́ревязь.

slink vi кра́сться impf.

slip n (mistake) оши́бка; (garment) комбина́ция; (pillowcase) на́волочка; (paper) листо́чек; **~ of the tongue** обмо́лвка; **give the ~** ускользну́ть pf от+gen; vi скользи́ть impf, скользну́ть pf; (fall over) поскользну́ться pf; (from hands etc.) выска́льзывать impf, вы́скользнуть pf; vt (insert) сова́ть impf, су́нуть pf; **~ off** (depart) ускольза́ть impf, ускользну́ть pf; **~ up** (make mistake) ошиба́ться impf, ошиби́ться pf. **slipper** n та́пка. **slippery** adj ско́льзкий.

slit vt разреза́ть impf, разре́зать pf; (throat) перере́зать pf; n щель; (cut) разре́з.

slither vi скользи́ть impf.

sliver n ще́пка.

slob n неря́ха m & f.

slobber vi пуска́ть impf, пусти́ть pf слю́ни.

slog vt (hit) си́льно ударя́ть impf, уда́рить pf; (work) упо́рно рабо́тать impf.

slogan n ло́зунг.

slop n: pl помо́и (-о́ев) pl; vt & i выплёскивать(ся) impf, вы́плескать(ся) pf.

slope n (artificial) накло́н; (geog) склон; vi име́ть impf накло́н. **sloping** adj накло́нный.

sloppy adj (work) неря́шливый; (sentimental) сентимента́льный.

slot n отве́рстие; **~-machine** автома́т; vt: **~ in** вставля́ть impf, вста́вить pf.

sloth n лень.

slouch vi (stoop) суту́литься impf.

slovenly adj неря́шливый.

slow adj ме́дленный; (tardy) медли́тельный; (stupid) тупо́й; (business) вя́лый; **be ~** (clock) отстава́ть impf, отста́ть pf; adv ме́дленно; vt & i (~ down, up) замедля́ть(ся) impf, заме́длить(ся) pf.

sludge n (mud) грязь; (sediment) отсто́й.

slug n (zool) слизня́к.

sluggish adj вя́лый.

sluice n шлюз.

slum n трущо́ба.

slumber n сон; vi спать impf.

slump n спад; vi ре́зко па́дать impf, (у)па́сть pf; (of person) сва́ливаться impf, свали́ться pf.

slur vt говори́ть impf невня́тно; (stigma) пятно́.

slush n сля́коть.

slut n (sloven) неря́ха; (trollop) потаску́ха.

sly adj хи́трый; **on the ~** тайко́м.

smack[1] vi: **~ of** па́хнуть impf +instr.

smack[2] n (slap) шлепо́к; vt шлёпать impf, шлёпнуть pf.

small adj ма́ленький, небольшо́й, ма́лый; (of agent, particles; petty) ме́лкий; **~ change** ме́лочь; **~-scale** мелкомасшта́бный; **~ talk** све́тская бесе́да.

smart[1] vi са́днить impf impers.

smart[2] adj элега́нтный; (brisk) бы́стрый; (cunning) ло́вкий; (sharp) смека́листый (coll).

smash vt & i разбива́ть(ся) impf, разби́ть(ся) pf; vi: **~ into** вреза́ться impf, вре́заться pf в+acc; n (crash) гро́хот; (collision) столкнове́ние; (blow) си́льный уда́р.

smattering n пове́рхностное зна́ние.

smear vt сма́зывать impf, сма́зать pf; (dirty) па́чкать impf, за~, ис~ pf; (discredit) поро́чить impf, о~ pf; n (spot) пятно́; (slander) клевета́; (med) мазо́к.

smell n (sense) обоня́ние; (odour) за́пах; vt чу́вствовать impf за́пах+gen; (sniff) ню́хать impf, по~ pf; vi: **~ of** па́хнуть impf +instr. **smelly** adj воню́чий.

smelt vt (ore) пла́вить impf; (metal) выплавля́ть impf, вы́плавить pf.

smile vi улыба́ться impf, улыбну́ться pf; n улы́бка.

smirk *vi* ухмыля́ться *impf*, ухмыль-ну́ться *pf*; *n* ухмы́лка.

smith *n* кузне́ц.

smithereens *n*: (in)to ~ вдре́безги.

smithy *n* ку́зница.

smock *n* блу́за.

smog *n* тума́н (с ды́мом).

smoke *n* дым; **~-screen** дымова́я заве́са; *vt & i* (*cigarette etc.*) кури́ть *impf*, по~ *pf*; *vt* (*cure; colour*) копти́ть *impf*, за~ *pf*; *vi* (*abnormally*) дыми́ть *impf*; (*of fire*) дыми́ться *impf*. **smoker** *n* кури́льщик, -ица, куря́щий *sb*. **smoky** *adj* ды́мный.

smooth *adj* (*surface etc.*) гла́дкий; (*movement etc.*) пла́вный; *vt* пригла́живать *impf*, пригла́дить *pf*; ~ **over** сгла́живать *impf*, сгла́дить *pf*.

smother *vt* (*stifle, also fig*) души́ть *impf*, за~ *pf*; (*cover*) покрыва́ть *impf*, покры́ть *pf*.

smoulder *vi* тлеть *impf*.

smudge *n* пятно́; *vt* сма́зывать *impf*, сма́зать *pf*.

smug *adj* самодово́льный.

smuggle *vt* провози́ть *impf*, провезти́ *pf* контраба́ндой; (*convey secretly*) проноси́ть *impf*, пронести́ *pf*. **smuggler** *n* контрабанди́ст. **smuggling** *n* контраба́нда.

smut *n* са́жа; (*indecency*) непристо́йность. **smutty** *adj* гря́зный; непристо́йный.

snack *n* заку́ска; ~ **bar** заку́сочная *sb*, (*within institution*) буфе́т.

snag *n* (*fig*) загво́здка; *vt* зацепля́ть *impf*, зацепи́ть *pf*.

snail *n* ули́тка.

snake *n* змея́.

snap *vi* (*of dog or person*) огрыза́ться *impf*, огрызну́ться *pf* (**at** на+*acc*); *vt & i* (*break*) обрыва́ть(ся) *impf*, оборва́ть(ся) *pf*; *vt* (*make sound*) щёлкать *impf*, щёлкнуть *pf* +*instr*; ~ **up** (*buy*) расхва́тывать *impf*, расхвата́ть *pf*; *n* (*sound*) щёлк; (*photo*) сни́мок; *adj* (*decision*) скоропали́тельный. **snappy** *adj* (*brisk*) живо́й; (*stylish*) шика́рный. **snapshot** *n* сни́мок.

snare *n* лову́шка.

snarl *vi* рыча́ть *impf*, за~ *pf*; *n* рыча́ние.

snatch *vt* хвата́ть *impf*, (с)хвати́ть *pf*; *vi*: ~ **at** хвата́ться *impf*, (с)хва-

ти́ться *pf* за+*acc*; *n* (*fragment*) обры́вок.

sneak *vi* (*slink*) кра́сться *impf*; *vt* (*steal*) стащи́ть *pf*; *n* я́бедник, -ица (*coll*). **sneaking** *adj* та́йный. **sneaky** *adj* лука́вый.

sneer *vi* насмеха́ться *impf* (**at** над +*instr*).

sneeze *vi* чиха́ть *impf*, чихну́ть *pf*; *n* чиха́нье.

snide *adj* ехи́дный.

sniff *vi* шмы́гать *impf*, шмыгну́ть *pf* но́сом; *vt* ню́хать *impf*, по~ *pf*.

snigger *vi* хихи́кать *impf*, хихи́кнуть *pf*; *n* хихи́канье.

snip *vt* ре́зать *impf* (но́жницами); ~ **off** среза́ть *impf*, сре́зать *pf*.

snipe *vi* стреля́ть *impf* из укры́тия (**at** в+*acc*); (*fig*) напада́ть *impf*, напа́сть *pf* на+*acc*. **sniper** *n* сна́йпер.

snippet *n* отре́зок; *pl* (*of news etc.*) обры́вки *m pl*.

snivel *vi* (*run at nose*) распуска́ть *impf*, распусти́ть *pf* со́пли; (*whimper*) хны́кать *impf*.

snob *n* сноб. **snobbery** *n* сноби́зм. **snobbish** *adj* сноби́стский.

snoop *vi* шпио́нить *impf*; ~ **about** разню́хивать *impf*, разню́хать *pf*.

snooty *adj* чва́нный.

snooze *vi* вздремну́ть *pf*; *n* коро́ткий сон.

snore *vi* храпе́ть *impf*.

snorkel *n* шно́ркель *m*.

snort *vi* фы́ркать *impf*, фы́ркнуть *pf*.

snot *n* со́пли (-ле́й) *pl*.

snout *n* ры́ло, мо́рда.

snow *n* снег; **~-white** белосне́жный; *vi*: **it is ~ing, it snows** идёт снег; **~ed under** зава́ленный рабо́той; **we were ~ed up, in** нас занесло́ сне́гом. **snowball** *n* снежо́к. **snowdrop** *n* подсне́жник. **snowflake** *n* снежи́нка. **snowman** *n* сне́жная ба́ба. **snowstorm** *n* мете́ль. **snowy** *adj* сне́жный; (*snow-white*) белосне́жный.

snub *vt* игнори́ровать *impf & pf*.

snuff[1] *n* (*tobacco*) ню́хательный таба́к.

snuff[2] *vt*: ~ **out** туши́ть *impf*, по~ *pf*.

snuffle *vi* сопе́ть *impf*.

snug *adj* ую́тный.

snuggle *vi*: ~ **up to** прижима́ться *impf*, прижа́ться *pf* к+*dat*.

so *adv* так; (*in this way*) так, таким образом; (*thus, at beginning of sentence*) итак; (*also*) также, тоже; *conj* (*therefore*) поэтому; **and ~ on** и так далее; **if ~** в таком случае; **~ ... as** так(ой)... как; **~ as to** с тем чтобы; **~-called** так называемый; **(in) ~ far as** настолько; **~ long!** пока!; **~ long as** поскольку; **~ much** настолько; **~ much ~** до такой степени; **much the better** тем лучше; **~ that** чтобы; **~... that** так... что; **~ to say, speak** так сказать; **~ what?** ну и что?

soak *vt* мочить *impf*, на~ *pf*; (*drench*) промачивать *impf*, промочить *impf*; **~ up** впитывать *impf*, впитать *pf*; *vi*: **~ through** просачиваться *impf*, просочиться *pf*; **get ~ed** промокать *impf*, промокнуть *pf*.

soap *n* мыло; *vt* мылить *impf*, на~ *pf*; **~ opera** многосерийная передача; **~ powder** стиральный порошок. **soapy** *adj* мыльный.

soar *vi* парить *impf*; (*prices*) подскакивать *impf*, подскочить *pf*.

sob *vi* рыдать *impf*; *n* рыдание.

sober *adj* трезвый; *vt & i*: **~ up** отрезвлять(ся) *impf*, отрезвить(ся) *pf*. **sobriety** *n* трезвость.

soccer *n* футбол.

sociable *adj* общительный. **social** *adj* общественный, социальный; **S~ Democrat** социал-демократ; **~ sciences** общественные науки *f pl*; **~ security** социальное обеспечение. **socialism** *n* социализм. **socialist** *n* социалист; *adj* социалистический. **socialize** *vt* общаться *impf*. **society** *n* общество. **sociological** *adj* социологический. **sociologist** *n* социолог. **sociology** *n* социология.

sock *n* носок.

socket *n* (*eye*) впадина; (*electr*) штепсель *m*; (*for bulb*) патрон.

soda *n* сода; **~-water** содовая вода.

sodden *adj* промокший.

sodium *n* натрий.

sodomy *n* педерастия.

sofa *n* диван.

soft *adj* мягкий; (*sound*) тихий; (*colour*) неяркий; (*malleable*) ковкий; (*tender*) нежный; **~ drink** безалкогольный напиток. **soften** *vt & i*

смягчать(ся) *impf*, смягчить(ся) *pf*. **softness** *n* мягкость. **software** *n* программное обеспечение.

soggy *adj* сырой.

soil¹ *n* почва.

soil² *vt* пачкать *impf*, за~, ис~ *pf*.

solace *n* утешение.

solar *adj* солнечный.

solder *n* припой; *vt* паять *impf*; (*~ together*) спаивать *impf*, спаять *pf*. **soldering iron** *n* паяльник.

soldier *n* солдат.

sole¹ *n* (*of foot, shoe*) подошва.

sole² *n* (*fish*) морской язык.

sole³ *adj* единственный.

solemn *adj* торжественный. **solemnity** *n* торжественность.

solicit *vt* просить *impf*, по~ *pf* +*acc, gen*, о+*prep*; *vi* (*of prostitute*) приставать *impf* к мужчинам. **solicitor** *n* адвокат. **solicitous** *adj* заботливый.

solid *adj* (*not liquid*) твёрдый; (*not hollow; continuous*) сплошной; (*firm*) прочный; (*pure*) чистый; *n* твёрдое тело; *pl* твёрдая пища. **solidarity** *n* солидарность. **solidify** *vi* затвердевать *impf*, затвердеть *pf*. **solidity** *n* твёрдость; прочность.

soliloquy *n* монолог.

solitary *adj* одинокий, уединённый; **~ confinement** одиночное заключение. **solitude** *n* одиночество, уединение.

solo *n* соло *neut indecl*; *adj* сольный; *adv* соло. **soloist** *n* солист, ~ка.

solstice *n* солнцестояние.

soluble *adj* растворимый. **solution** *n* раствор; (*of puzzle etc.*) решение. **solve** *vt* решать *impf*, решить *pf*. **solvent** *adj* растворяющий; (*financially*) платёжеспособный; *n* растворитель *m*.

sombre *adj* мрачный.

some *adj & pron* (*any*) какой-нибудь; (*a certain*) какой-то; (*a certain amount or number of*) некоторый, *or often expressed by noun in* (*partitive*) *gen*; (*several*) несколько+*gen*; (**~ people, things**) некоторые *pl*; **~ day** когда-нибудь; **~ more** ещё; **~ ... others** одни... другие. **somebody, someone** *n, pron* (*def*) кто-то; (*indef*) кто-нибудь. **somehow** *adv* как-то; как-нибудь; (*for* *some reason*) почему́-то; ~ **or other** так и́ли ина́че.

somersault *n* са́льто *neut indecl*; *vi* кувырка́ться *impf*, кувыр(к)ну́ться *pf*.

something *n & pron* (*def*) что́-то; (*indef*) что́-нибудь; ~ **like** (*approximately*) приблизи́тельно; (*a thing like*) что́-то вро́де+*gen*. **sometime** *adv* не́когда; *adj* бы́вший. **sometimes** *adv* иногда́. **somewhat** *adv* не́сколько, дово́льно. **somewhere** *adv* (*position*) (*def*) где́-то; (*indef*) где́-нибудь; (*motion*) куда́-то; куда́-нибудь.

son *n* сын; ~-**in-law** зять *m*.

sonata *n* сона́та.

song *n* пе́сня.

sonic *adj* звуково́й.

sonnet *n* соне́т.

soon *adv* ско́ро; (*early*) ра́но; **as ~ as** как то́лько; **as ~ as possible** как мо́жно скоре́е; ~**er or later** ра́но и́ли по́здно; **the ~er the better** чем ра́ньше, тем лу́чше.

soot *n* са́жа, ко́поть.

soothe *vt* успока́ивать *impf*, успоко́ить *pf*; (*pain*) облегча́ть *impf*, облегчи́ть *pf*.

sophisticated *adj* (*person*) искушённый; (*equipment*) сло́жный.

soporific *adj* снотво́рный.

soprano *n* сопра́но (*voice*) *neut* & (*person*) *f indecl*.

sorcerer *n* колду́н. **sorcery** *n* колдовство́.

sordid *adj* гря́зный.

sore *n* боля́чка; *adj* больно́й; **my throat is ~** у меня́ боли́т го́рло.

sorrow *n* печа́ль. **sorrowful** *adj* печа́льный. **sorry** *adj* жа́лкий; *predic*: **be ~** жале́ть *impf* (**about** о+*prep*); жаль *impers*+*dat* (**for** +*gen*); ~! извини́(те)!

sort *n* род, вид, сорт; *vt* (*also* ~ **out**) сортирова́ть *impf*; (*also fig*) разбира́ть *impf*, разобра́ть *pf*.

sortie *n* вы́лазка.

SOS *n* (ра́дио)сигна́л бе́дствия.

soul *n* душа́.

sound[1] *adj* (*healthy, thorough*) здоро́вый; (*in good condition*) испра́вный; (*logical*) здра́вый, разу́мный; (*of sleep*) кре́пкий.

sound[2] *n* (*noise*) звук, шум; *attrib*

звуково́й; ~ **effects** звуковы́е эффе́кты *m pl*; *vi* звуча́ть *impf*, про~ *pf*.

sound[3] *vt* (*naut*) измеря́ть *impf*, изме́рить *pf* глубину́ +*gen*; ~ **out** (*fig*) зонди́ровать *impf*, по~ *pf*; *n* зонд.

sound[4] *n* (*strait*) проли́в.

soup *n* суп; *vt*: ~**ed up** форси́рованный.

sour *adj* ки́слый; ~ **cream** смета́на; *vt & i* (*fig*) озлобля́ть(ся) *impf*, озло́бить(ся) *pf*.

source *n* исто́чник; (*of river*) исто́к.

south *n* юг; (*naut*) зюйд; *adj* ю́жный; *adv* к ю́гу, на юг; ~-**east** ю́го-восто́к; ~-**west** ю́го-за́пад. **southerly** *adj* ю́жный. **southern** *adj* ю́жный. **southerner** *n* южа́нин, -а́нка. **southward(s)** *adv* на юг, к ю́гу.

souvenir *n* сувени́р.

sovereign *adj* сувере́нный; *n* мона́рх. **sovereignty** *n* суверените́т.

soviet *n* сове́т; **S~ Union** Сове́тский Сою́з; *adj* (**S~**) сове́тский.

sow[1] *n* свинья́.

sow[2] *vt* (*seed*) се́ять *impf*, по~ *pf*; (*field*) засе́ивать *impf*, засе́ять *pf*.

soya *n*: ~ **bean** со́евый боб.

spa *n* куро́рт.

space *n* (*place, room*) ме́сто; (*expanse*) простра́нство; (*interval*) промежу́ток; (*outer ~*) ко́смос; *attrib* косми́ческий; *vt* расставля́ть *impf*, расста́вить *pf* с промежу́тками. **spacecraft, -ship** *n* косми́ческий кора́бль *m*. **spacious** *adj* просто́рный.

spade *n* (*tool*) лопа́та; *pl* (*cards*) пи́ки (пик) *pl*.

spaghetti *n* спаге́тти *neut indecl*.

Spain *n* Испа́ния.

span *n* (*of bridge*) пролёт; (*aeron*) разма́х; *vt* (*of bridge*) соединя́ть *impf*, соедини́ть *pf* сто́роны +*gen*; (*river*) берега́ +*gen*; (*fig*) охва́тывать *impf*, охвати́ть *pf*.

Spaniard *n* испа́нец, -нка. **Spanish** *adj* испа́нский.

spank *vt* шлёпать *impf*, шлёпнуть *pf*.

spanner *n* га́ечный ключ.

spar[1] *n* (*aeron*) лонжеро́н.

spar[2] *vi* бокси́ровать *impf*; (*fig*) препира́ться *impf*.

spare *adj* (*in reserve*) запасно́й; (*extra, to ~*) ли́шний; (*of seat, time*)

свобо́дный; ~ **parts** запасны́е ча́сти
f pl; ~ **room** ко́мната для госте́й; *n*:
pl запча́сти *f pl*; *vt* (*grudge*) жале́ть
impf, по~ *pf* +*acc, gen*; **he** ~**d no
pains** он не жале́л трудо́в; (*do without*) обходи́ться *impf*, обойти́сь *pf*
без+*gen*; (*time*) уделя́ть *impf*, уде-
ли́ть *pf*; (*show mercy towards*) ща-
ди́ть *impf*, по~ *pf*; (*save from*) изба-
вля́ть *impf*, изба́вить *pf* от+*gen*: ~
me the details изба́вьте меня́ от
подро́бностей.

spark *n* и́скра; ~**-plug** запа́льная
свеча́; *vt* (~ *off*) вызыва́ть *impf*,
вы́звать *pf*.

sparkle *vi* сверка́ть *impf*.

sparrow *n* воробе́й.

sparse *adj* ре́дкий.

Spartan *adj* спарта́нский.

spasm *n* спазм. **spasmodic** *adj* спаз-
моди́ческий.

spastic *n* парали́тик.

spate *n* разли́в; (*fig*) пото́к.

spatial *adj* простра́нственный.

spatter, splatter *vt* (*liquid*) бры́згать
impf +*instr*; (*person etc.*) забры́зги-
вать *impf*, забры́згать *pf* (**with**
+*instr*); *vi* плеска́ть(ся) *impf*, плес-
ну́ть *pf*.

spatula *n* шпа́тель *m*.

spawn *vt & i* мета́ть *impf* (икру́); *vt*
(*fig*) порожда́ть *impf*, породи́ть *pf*.

speak *vt & i* говори́ть *impf*, сказа́ть
pf; *vi* (*make speech*) выступа́ть *impf*,
вы́ступить *pf* (с ре́чью); (~ *out*)
выска́зываться *impf*, вы́сказаться
pf (**for** за+*acc*; **against** про́тив+*gen*).

speaker *n* говоря́щий *sb*; (*giving
speech*) выступа́ющий *sb*; (*orator*)
ора́тор; (**S**~, *parl*) спи́кер; (*loud-*~)
громкоговори́тель *m*.

spear *n* копьё; *vt* пронза́ть *impf*,
пронзи́ть *pf* копьём. **spearhead** *vt*
возглавля́ть *impf*, возгла́вить *pf*.

special *adj* осо́бый, специа́льный.
specialist *n* специали́ст, ~ка. **speciality** *n* специа́льность **specialization** *n* специализа́ция. **specialize** *vt
& i* специализи́ровать(ся) *impf &
pf*. **specially** *adv* осо́бенно.

species *n* вид.

specific *adj* осо́бенный. **speci-
fication(s)** *n* специфика́ция. **specify**
vt уточня́ть *impf*, уточни́ть *pf*.

specimen *n* образе́ц, экземпля́р.

speck *n* кра́пинка, пя́тнышко.
speckled *adj* кра́пчатый.

spectacle *n* зре́лище; *pl* очки́ (-ко́в)
pl.

spectacular *adj* эффе́ктный; (*amazing*) потряса́ющий.

spectator *n* зри́тель *m*.

spectre *n* при́зрак.

spectrum *n* спектр.

speculate *vi* (*meditate*) размышля́ть
impf, размы́слить *pf* (**on** о+*prep*);
(*conjecture*) гада́ть *impf*; (*comm*)
спекули́ровать *impf*. **speculation** *n*
(*conjecture*) дога́дка; (*comm*) спеку-
ля́ция. **speculative** *adj* гипотети́че-
ский; спекуляти́вный. **speculator** *n*
спекуля́нт.

speech *n* речь. **speechless** *adj* (*fig*)
онеме́вший.

speed *n* ско́рость; *vi* мча́ться *impf*,
про~ *pf*; (*illegally*) превыша́ть *impf*,
превы́сить *pf* ско́рость; *vt*: ~ **up**
ускоря́ть *impf*, уско́рить *pf*. **speed-
boat** *n* быстрохо́дный ка́тер. **speed-
ometer** *n* спидо́метр. **speedy** *adj*
бы́стрый, ско́рый.

spell[1] *n* (*charm*) загово́р.

spell[2] *vt* (*say*) произноси́ть *impf*,
произнести́ *pf* по бу́квам; (*write*)
пра́вильно писа́ть *impf*, на~ *pf*; **how
do you** ~ **that word?** как пи́шется
э́то сло́во?

spell[3] *n* (*period*) пери́од.

spellbound *adj* зачаро́ванный.

spelling *n* правописа́ние.

spend *vt* (*money; effort*) тра́тить
impf, ис~, по~ *pf*; (*time*) проводи́ть
impf, провести́ *pf*.

sperm *n* спе́рма.

sphere *n* сфе́ра; (*ball*) шар. **spherical** *adj* сфери́ческий.

spice *n* пря́ность; *vt* приправля́ть
impf, припра́вить *pf*. **spicy** *adj* пря́-
ный; (*fig*) пика́нтный.

spider *n* пау́к.

spike *n* (*point*) остриё; (*on fence*)
зубе́ц; (*on shoes*) шип.

spill *vt & i* (*liquid*) пролива́ть(ся)
impf, проли́ть(ся) *pf*; (*dry substance*)
рассыпа́ть(ся) *impf*, рассы́пать(ся)
pf.

spin *vt* (*thread etc.*) прясть *impf*, с~
pf; (*coin*) подбра́сывать *impf*, подб-
ро́сить *pf*; *vt & i* (*turn*) кружи́ть-
(ся) *impf*; ~ **out** (*prolong*) затяги́-

вать *impf*, затянуть *pf*.
spinach *n* шпинат.
spinal *adj* спинной; ~ **column** спинной хребет; ~ **cord** спинной мозг.
spindle *n* ось *m*. **spindly** *adj* длинный и тонкий.
spine *n* (*anat*) позвоночник, хребет; (*prickle*) игла; (*of book*) корешок.
spineless *adj* (*fig*) бесхарактерный.
spinning *n* прядение; ~**-wheel** прялка.
spinster *n* незамужняя женщина.
spiral *adj* спиральный; (*staircase*) винтовой; *n* спираль; *vi* (*rise sharply*) резко возрастать *impf*, возрасти *pf*.
spire *n* шпиль *m*.
spirit *n* дух, душа; *pl* (*mood*) настроение; *pl* (*drinks*) спиртное *sb*; ~ **level** ватерпас; *vt*: ~ **away** тайно уносить *impf*, унести *pf*. **spirited** *adj* живой. **spiritual** *adj* духовный. **spiritualism** *n* спиритизм. **spiritualist** *n* спирит.
spit[1] *n* (*skewer*) вертел.
spit[2] *vi* плевать *impf*, плюнуть *pf*; (*of rain*) моросить *impf*; (*of fire*) разбрызгивать *impf*, разбрызгать *pf* искры; (*sizzle*) шипеть *impf*; *vt*: ~ **out** выплёвывать *impf*, выплюнуть *pf*; ~**ing image** точная копия; *n* слюна.
spite *n* злоба; **in** ~ **of** несмотря на +*acc*. **spiteful** *adj* злобный.
spittle *n* слюна.
splash *vt* (*person*) забрызгивать *impf*, забрызгать *pf* (*with* +*instr*); (~ *liquid*) брызгать *impf* +*instr*; *vi* плескать(ся) *impf*, плеснуть *pf*; (*move*) шлёпать *impf*, шлёпнуть *pf* (*through* по+*dat*); *n* (*act, sound*) плеск; (*mark made*) пятно.
splatter *see* spatter
spleen *n* селезёнка.
splendid *adj* великолепный. **splendour** *n* великолепие.
splice *vt* (*ropes etc.*) сращивать *impf*, срастить *pf*; (*film, tape*) склеивать *impf*, склеить *pf* концы+*gen*.
splint *n* шина.
splinter *n* осколок; (*in skin*) заноза; *vt & i* расщеплять(ся) *impf*, расщепить(ся) *pf*.
split *n* расщелина, расщеп; (*schism*) раскол; *pl* шпагат; *vt & i* расщеплять(ся) *impf*, расщепить(ся) *pf*;

раскалывать(ся) *impf*, расколоть(ся) *pf*; *vt* (*divide*) делить *impf*, раз~ *pf*; ~ **second** мгновение ока; ~ **up** (*part company*) расходиться *impf*, разойтись *pf*.
splutter *vi* брызгать *impf* слюной; *vt* (*utter*) говорить *impf* захлёбываясь.
spoil *n* (*booty*) добыча; *vt & i* (*damage, decay*) портить(ся) *impf*, ис~ *pf*; *vt* (*indulge*) баловать *impf*, из~ *pf*.
spoke *n* спица.
spokesman, **-woman** *n* представитель *m*, ~ница.
sponge *n* губка; ~ **cake** бисквит; *vt* (*wash*) мыть *impf*, вы~, по~ *pf* губкой; *vi*: ~ **on** жить *impf* на счёт+*gen*.
sponger *n* приживальщик. **spongy** *adj* губчатый.
sponsor *n* спонсор; *vt* финансировать *impf & pf*.
spontaneity *n* спонтанность. **spontaneous** *adj* спонтанный.
spoof *n* пародия.
spooky *adj* жуткий.
spool *n* катушка.
spoon *n* ложка; *vt* черпать *impf*, черпнуть *pf* ложкой. **spoonful** *n* ложка.
sporadic *adj* спорадический.
sport *n* спорт; ~**s car** спортивный автомобиль *m*; *vt* щеголять *impf*, щегольнуть *pf* +*instr*. **sportsman** *n* спортсмен. **sporty** *adj* спортивный.
spot *n* (*place*) место; (*mark*) пятно; (*pimple*) прыщик; **on the** ~ на месте; (*at once*) сразу; ~ **check** выборочная проверка; *vt* (*notice*) замечать *impf*, заметить *pf*. **spotless** *adj* абсолютно чистый. **spotlight** *n* прожектор; (*fig*) внимание. **spotty** *adj* прыщеватый.
spouse *n* супруг, ~а.
spout *vi* бить *impf* струёй; хлынуть *pf*; (*pontificate*) ораторствовать *impf*; *vt* извергать *impf*, извергнуть *pf*; (*verses etc.*) декламировать *impf*, про~ *pf*; *n* (*tube*) носик; (*jet*) струя.
sprain *vt* растягивать *impf*, растянуть *pf*; *n* растяжение.
sprawl *vi* (*of person*) разваливаться *impf*, развалиться *pf*; (*of town*) раскидываться *impf*, раскинуться *pf*.

spray[1] *n* (*flowers*) вет(оч)ка.

spray[2] *n* брызги (-г) *pl*; (*atomizer*) пульверизатор; *vt* опрыскивать *impf*, опрыскать *pf* (**with** +*instr*); (*cause to scatter*) распылять *impf*, распылить *pf*.

spread *vt* & *i* (*news, disease, etc.*) распространять(ся) *impf*, распространить(ся) *pf*; *vt* (~ **out**) расстилать *impf*, разостлать *pf*; (*unfurl, unroll*) развёртывать *impf*, развернуть *pf*; (*bread etc.* +*acc*; *butter etc.* +*instr*) намазывать *impf*, намазать *pf*; *n* (*expansion*) распространение; (*span*) размах; (*feast*) пир; (*paste*) паста.

spree *n* кутёж; **go on a ~** кутить *impf*, кутнуть *pf*.

sprig *n* веточка.

sprightly *adj* бодрый.

spring *vi* (*jump*) прыгать *impf*, прыгнуть *pf*; *vt* (*tell unexpectedly*) неожиданно сообщать *impf*, сообщить *pf* (**on** +*dat*); ~ **a leak** давать *impf*, дать *pf* течь; ~ **from** (*originate*) происходить *impf*, произойти *pf* из+*gen*; *n* (*jump*) прыжок; (*season*) весна, *attrib* весенний; (*water*) источник; (*elasticity*) упругость; (*coil*) пружина; ~**-clean** генеральная уборка. **springboard** *n* трамплин.

sprinkle *vt* (*with liquid*) опрыскивать *impf*, опрыскать *pf* (**with** +*instr*); (*with solid*) посыпать *impf*, посыпать *pf* (**with** +*instr*). **sprinkler** *n* разбрызгиватель *m*.

sprint *vi* бежать *impf* на короткую дистанцию; (*rush*) рвануться *pf*; *n* спринт. **sprinter** *n* спринтер.

sprout *vi* пускать *impf*, пустить *pf* ростки; *n* росток; *pl* брюссельская капуста.

spruce[1] *adj* нарядный, элегантный; *vt*: ~ **o.s. up** приводить *impf*, привести *pf* себя в порядок.

spruce[2] *n* ель.

spur *n* шпора; (*fig*) стимул; **on the ~ of the moment** под влиянием минуты; *vt*: ~ **on** подхлёстывать *impf*, подхлестнуть *pf*.

spurious *adj* поддельный.

spurn *vt* отвергать *impf*, отвергнуть *pf*.

spurt *n* (*jet*) струя; (*effort*) рывок; *vi* бить *impf* струёй; (*make an effort*) делать *impf*, с~ *pf* рывок.

spy *n* шпион; *vi* шпионить *impf* (**on** за+*instr*). **spying** *n* шпионаж.

squabble *n* перебранка; *vi* вздорить *impf*, по~ *pf*.

squad *n* команда, группа.

squadron *n* (*mil*) эскадрон; (*naut*) эскадра; (*aeron*) эскадрилья.

squalid *adj* убогий.

squall *n* шквал.

squalor *n* убожество.

squander *vt* растрачивать *impf*, растратить *pf*.

square *n* (*shape*) квадрат; (*in town*) площадь; (*on paper, material*) клетка; (*instrument*) наугольник; *adj* квадратный; (*meal*) плотный; ~ **root** квадратный корень *m*; *vt* (*accounts*) сводить *impf*, свести *pf*; (*math*) возводить *impf*, возвести *pf* в квадрат; *vi* (*correspond*) соответствовать *impf* (**with** +*dat*).

squash *n* (*crowd*) толкучка; (*drink*) сок; *vt* раздавливать *impf*, раздавить *pf*; (*suppress*) подавлять *impf*, подавить *pf*; *vi* втискиваться *impf*, втиснуться *pf*.

squat *adj* приземистый; *vi* сидеть *impf* на корточках; ~ **down** садиться *impf*, сесть *pf* на корточки.

squatter *n* незаконный жилец.

squawk *n* клёкот; *vi* клекотать *impf*.

squeak *n* писк; (*of object*) скрип; пищать *impf*, пискнуть *pf*; (*of object*) скрипеть *impf*, скрипнуть *pf*. **squeaky** *adj* писклявый, скрипучий.

squeal *n* визг; *vi* визжать *impf*, визгнуть *pf*.

squeamish *adj* брезгливый.

squeeze *n* (*crush*) давка; (*pressure*) сжатие; (*hand*) пожатие; *vt* давить *impf*, сжимать *impf*, сжать *pf*; ~ **in** впихивать(ся) *impf*, впихнуть(ся) *pf*; втискивать(ся) *impf*, втиснуть(ся) *pf*; ~ **out** выжимать *impf*, выжать *pf*; ~ **through** протискивать(ся) *impf*, протиснуть(ся) *pf*.

squelch *vi* хлюпать *impf*, хлюпнуть *pf*.

squid *n* кальмар.

squint *n* косоглазие; *vi* косить *impf*; (*screw up eyes*) щуриться *impf*.

squire *n* сквайр, помещик.

squirm *vi* (*wriggle*) извиваться *impf*, извиться *pf*.

squirrel *n* бе́лка.

squirt *n* струя́; *vi* бить *impf* струёй; *vt* пуска́ть *impf*, пусти́ть *pf* струю́ (*substance* +*gen*; **at** на+*acc*).

St. *abbr* (*of* **Street**) ул., у́лица; (*of* **Saint**) св., Свято́й, -а́я.

stab *n* уда́р (ножо́м *etc.*); (*pain*) вне-за́пная о́страя боль; *vt* наноси́ть *impf*, нанести́ *pf* уда́р (ножо́м *etc.*) (*person* +*dat*).

stability *n* усто́йчивость, стаби́ль-ность. **stabilize** *vt* стабилизи́ровать *impf* & *pf*.

stable *adj* усто́йчивый, стаби́льный; (*psych*) уравнове́шенный; *n* коню́ш-ня.

staccato *n* стакка́то *neut indecl*; *adv* стакка́то; *adj* отры́вистый.

stack *n* ку́ча; *vt* скла́дывать *impf*, сложи́ть *pf* в ку́чу.

stadium *n* стадио́н.

staff *n* (*personnel*) штат, сотру́дники *m pl*; (*stick*) посо́х, жезл; *adj* штат-ный; (*mil*) штабно́й.

stag *n* саме́ц-оле́нь *m*.

stage *n* (*theat*) сце́на; (*period*) ста́-дия; *vt* (*theat*) ста́вить *impf*, по~ *pf*; (*organize*) организова́ть *impf* & *pf*; ~**manager** режиссёр.

stagger *vi* шата́ться *impf*, шатну́ть-ся *pf*; *vt* (*hours of work etc.*) рас-пределя́ть *impf*, распредели́ть *pf*. **be staggered** *vi* поража́ться *impf*, порази́ться *pf*. **staggering** *adj* по-тряса́ющий.

stagnant *adj* (*water*) стоя́чий; (*fig*) засто́йный. **stagnate** *vi* заста́ивать-ся *impf*, застоя́ться *pf*; (*fig*) косне́ть *impf*, за~ *pf*.

staid *adj* степе́нный.

stain *n* пятно́; (*dye*) кра́ска; *vt* па́ч-кать *impf*, за~, ис~ *pf*; (*dye*) окра́-шивать *impf*, окра́сить *pf*; ~**ed glass** цветно́е стекло́. **stainless** *adj*: ~ **steel** нержаве́ющая сталь.

stair *n* ступе́нька. **staircase, stairs** *n pl* ле́стница.

stake *n* (*stick*) кол; (*bet*) ста́вка; (*comm*) до́ля; **be at** ~ быть поста́в-ленным на ка́рту; *vt* (*mark out*) огора́живать *impf*, огороди́ть *pf* ко́льями; (*support*) укрепля́ть *impf*, укрепи́ть *pf* коло́м; (*risk*) ста́вить *impf*, по~ *pf* на ка́рту.

stale *adj* несве́жий; (*musty, damp*)

за́тхлый; (*hackneyed*) изби́тый.

stalemate *n* пат; (*fig*) тупи́к.

stalk *n* сте́бель *m*; *vt* высле́живать *impf*; *vi* (& *t*) (*stride*) ше́ствовать *impf* (по+*dat*).

stall *n* сто́йло; (*booth*) ларёк; *pl* (*theat*) парте́р; *vi* (*of engine*) гло́х-нуть *impf*, за~ *pf*; (*play for time*) отта́гивать *impf*, оття́нуть *pf* вре́-мя; *vt* (*engine*) нечая́нно заглуша́ть *impf*, заглуши́ть *pf*.

stallion *n* жеребе́ц.

stalwart *adj* сто́йкий; *n* сто́йкий при-ве́рженец.

stamina *n* выно́сливость.

stammer *vi* заика́ться *impf*; *n* заика́-ние.

stamp *n* печа́ть; (*postage*) (почто́-вая) ма́рка; *vt* штампова́ть *impf*; *vi* то́пать *impf*, то́пнуть *pf* (нога́ми); ~ **out** поборо́ть *pf*.

stampede *n* пани́ческое бе́гство; *vi* обраща́ться *impf* в пани́ческое бе́г-ство.

stance *n* пози́ция.

stand *n* (*hat, coat*) ве́шалка; (*music*) пюпи́тр; (*umbrella, support*) под-ста́вка; (*booth*) ларёк; (*taxi*) сто-я́нка; (*at stadium*) трибу́на; (*pos-ition*) пози́ция; (*resistance*) сопро-тивле́ние; *vi* стоя́ть *impf*; (~ **up**) вста-ва́ть *impf*, встать *pf*; (*remain in force*) остава́ться *impf*, оста́ться в си́ле; *vt* (*put*) ста́вить *impf*, по~ *pf*; (*endure*) терпе́ть *impf*, по~ *pf*; ~ **back** отходи́ть *impf*, отойти́ *pf* (**from** от+*gen*); (*not go forward*) держа́ть-ся *impf* позади́; ~ **by** (*vi*) (*not inter-fere*) не вме́шиваться *impf*, вме-ша́ться *pf*; (*be ready*) быть *impf* на гото́ве; (*vt*) (*support*) подде́рживать *impf*, поддержа́ть *pf*; (*stick to*) приде́рживаться *impf* +*gen*; ~ **down** (*resign*) уходи́ть *impf*, уйти́ *pf* с по́ста (**as** +*gen*); ~ **for** (*signify*) озна-ча́ть *impf*; (*tolerate*) **I shall not** ~ **for it** я не потерплю́; ~**in** замести́-тель *m*; ~ **in** (*for*) замеща́ть *impf*, замести́ть *pf*; ~ **out** выделя́ться *impf*, вы́делиться *pf*; ~ **up** встава́ть *impf*, встать *pf*; ~ **up for** (*defend*) отста́ивать *impf*, отстоя́ть *pf*; ~ **up to** (*endure*) выде́рживать *impf*, вы́-держать *pf*; (*not give in to*) проти-востоя́ть *impf* +*dat*.

standard n (*norm*) станда́рт, норм; (*flag*) зна́мя *neut*; ~ **of living** жи́зненный у́ровень m; *adj* норма́льный, станда́ртный. **standardization** n нормализа́ция, стандартиза́ция. **standardize** vt стандартизи́ровать *impf* & *pf*; нормализова́ть *impf* & *pf*.

standing n положе́ние; *adj* (*upright*) стоя́чий; (*permanent*) постоя́нный.

standpoint n то́чка зре́ния.

standstill n остано́вка, засто́й, па́уза; **be at a** ~ стоя́ть *impf* на мёртвой то́чке; **bring (come) to a** ~ остана́вливать(ся) *impf*, останови́ть(ся) *pf*.

stanza n строфа́.

staple[1] n (*metal bar*) скоба́; (*for paper*) скре́пка; vt скрепля́ть *impf*, скрепи́ть *pf*.

staple[2] n (*product*) гла́вный проду́кт; *adj* основно́й.

star n звезда́; (*asterisk*) звёздочка; vi игра́ть *impf*, сыгра́ть *pf* гла́вную роль. **starfish** n морска́я звезда́.

starboard n пра́вый борт.

starch n крахма́л; vt крахма́лить *impf*, на~ *pf*. **starchy** adj крахма́листый; (*prim*) чо́порный.

stare n при́стальный взгляд; vi при́стально смотре́ть *impf* (**at** на+*acc*).

stark adj (*bare*) го́лый; (*desolate*) пусты́нный; (*sharp*) ре́зкий; adv соверше́нно.

starling n скворе́ц.

starry adj звёздный.

start n нача́ло; (*sport*) старт; vi начина́ться *impf*, нача́ться *pf*; (*engine*) заводи́ться *impf*, завести́сь *pf*; (*set out*) отправля́ться *impf*, отпра́виться *pf*; (*shudder*) вздра́гивать *impf*, вздро́гнуть *pf*; (*sport*) старто́вать *impf* & *pf*; vt начина́ть *impf*, нача́ть *pf* (*gerund, inf, +inf by +gerund* с того́, что...; **with** +*instr*, с +*gen*); (*car, engine*) заводи́ть *impf*, завести́ *pf*; (*fire, rumour*) пуска́ть *impf*, пусти́ть *pf*; (*found*) осно́вывать *impf*, основа́ть *pf*. **starter** n (*tech*) ста́ртёр; (*cul*) заку́ска. **starting-point** n отправно́й пункт.

startle vt испуга́ть *pf*.

starvation n го́лод. **starve** vi голода́ть *impf*; (*to death*) умира́ть *impf*, умере́ть с го́лоду; vt мори́ть *impf*,

по~, у~ *pf* го́лодом. **starving** adj голода́ющий; (*hungry*) о́чень голо́дный.

state n (*condition*) состоя́ние; (*polit*) госуда́рство, штат; *adj* (*ceremonial*) торже́ственный; пара́дный; (*polit*) госуда́рственный; vt (*announce*) заявля́ть *impf*, заяви́ть *pf*; (*expound*) излага́ть *impf*, изложи́ть *pf*. **stateless** adj не име́ющий гражда́нства. **stately** adj величе́ственный. **statement** n заявле́ние; (*comm*) отчёт. **statesman** n госуда́рственный де́ятель m.

static adj неподви́жный.

station n (*rly*) вокза́л, ста́нция; (*social*) обще́ственное положе́ние; (*meteorological, hydro-electric power, radio etc.*) ста́нция; (*post*) пост; vt размеща́ть *impf*, размести́ть *pf*.

stationary adj неподви́жный.

stationery n канцеля́рские принадле́жности f pl; (*writing-paper*) почто́вая бума́га; ~ **shop** канцеля́рский магази́н.

statistic n статисти́ческое да́нное. **statistical** adj статисти́ческий. **statistician** n стати́стик. **statistics** n стати́стика.

statue n ста́туя. **statuette** n статуэ́тка.

stature n рост; (*merit*) кали́бр.

status n ста́тус. **status quo** n ста́тус-кво́ neut indecl.

statute n стату́т. **statutory** adj устано́вленный зако́ном.

staunch adj ве́рный.

stave vt: ~ **off** предотвраща́ть *impf*, предотврати́ть *pf*.

stay n (*time spent*) пребыва́ние; vi (*remain*) остава́ться *impf*, оста́ться *pf* (**to dinner** обе́дать); (*put up*) остана́вливаться *impf*, останови́ться *pf* (**at** (*place*) в+*prep*; **at** (*friends' etc.*) у+*gen*); (*live*) жить; ~ **behind** остава́ться *impf*, оста́ться *pf*; ~ **in** остава́ться *impf*, оста́ться *pf* до́ма; ~ **up** не ложи́ться *impf* спать; (*trousers*) держа́ться *impf*. **staying-power** n выно́сливость.

stead n: **stand s.o. in good** ~ ока́зываться *impf*, оказа́ться *pf* поле́зным кому́-л.

steadfast adj сто́йкий, непоколеби́мый.

steady adj (firm) усто́йчивый; (continuous) непреры́вный; (wind, temperature) ро́вный; (speed) постоя́нный; (unshakeable) непоколеби́мый; vt приводи́ть impf, привести́ pf в равнове́сие.

steak n бифште́кс.

steal vt & abs ворова́ть impf, с~ pf; красть impf, у~ pf; vi (creep) кра́сться impf, подкра́дываться impf, подкра́сться pf. **stealth** n: by ~ укра́дкой. **stealthy** adj ворова́тый, та́йный, скры́тый.

steam n пар; **at full** ~ на всех пара́х; **let off** ~ (fig) дава́ть impf, дать pf вы́ход свои́м чу́вствам; vt па́рить impf; vi па́риться impf, по~ pf; (vessel) ходи́ть indet, идти́ det на пара́х; ~ **up** (mist over) запотева́ть impf, запоте́ть pf; потеть impf, за~, от~ pf; ~ **engine** парова́я маши́на. **steamer**, **steamship** n парохо́д. **steamy** adj напо́лненный па́ром; (passionate) горя́чий.

steed n конь m.

steel n сталь; adj стально́й; vt: ~ **o.s.** ожесточа́ться impf, ожесточи́ться pf; ~ **works** сталелите́йный заво́д. **steely** adj стально́й.

steep[1] adj круто́й; (excessive) чрезме́рный.

steep[2] vt (immerse) погружа́ть impf, погрузи́ть pf (in в+acc); (saturate) пропи́тывать impf, пропита́ть pf (in +instr).

steeple n шпиль m. **steeplechase** n ска́чки f pl с препя́тствиями.

steer vt управля́ть impf, пра́вить impf +instr; v abs рули́ть impf; ~ **clear of** избега́ть impf, избежа́ть pf +gen. **steering-wheel** n руль m.

stem[1] n сте́бель m; (of wine-glass) но́жка; (ling) осно́ва; vi: ~ **from** происходи́ть impf, произойти́ pf от+gen.

stem[2] vt (stop) остана́вливать impf, останови́ть pf.

stench n злово́ние.

stencil n трафаре́т; (tech) шабло́н; vt наноси́ть impf, нанести́ pf по трафаре́ту. **stencilled** adj трафаре́тный.

step n (pace, action) шаг; (dance) па neut indecl; (of stairs, ladder) ступе́нь; ~ **by** ~ шаг за ша́гом; **in** ~ в но́гу; **out of** ~ не в но́гу; **take** ~s

принима́ть impf, приня́ть pf ме́ры vi шага́ть impf, шагну́ть pf; ступа́ть impf, ступи́ть pf; ~ **aside** сторони́ться impf, по~ pf; ~ **back** отступа́ть impf, отступи́ть pf; ~ **down** (resign) уходи́ть impf, уйти́ pf в отста́вку; ~ **forward** выступа́ть impf, вы́ступить pf; ~ **in** (intervene) вме́шиваться impf, вмеша́ться pf; ~ **on** наступа́ть impf, наступи́ть pf на +acc (s.o.'s foot кому́-л. на́ ногу); ~ **over** переша́гивать impf, перешагну́ть pf +acc, че́рез+acc; ~ **up** (increase) повыша́ть impf, повы́сить pf. **step-ladder** n стремя́нка. **stepping-stone** n ка́мень m для перехо́да; (fig) сре́дство. **steps** n pl ле́стница.

stepbrother n сво́дный брат. **stepdaughter** n па́дчерица. **stepfather** n о́тчим. **stepmother** n ма́чеха. **stepsister** n сво́дная сестра́. **stepson** n па́сынок.

steppe n степь.

stereo n (system) стереофони́ческая систе́ма; (stereophony) стереофо́ния; adj (recorded in ~) сте́рео indecl. **stereophonic** adj стереофони́ческий. **stereotype** n стереоти́п. **stereotyped** adj стереоти́пный.

sterile adj стери́льный. **sterility** n стери́льность. **sterilization** n стерилиза́ция. **sterilize** vt стерилизова́ть impf & pf.

sterling n сте́рлинг; **pound** ~ фунт сте́рлингов; adj сте́рлинговый.

stern[1] n корма́.

stern[2] adj суро́вый, стро́гий.

stethoscope n стетоско́п.

stew n (cul) мя́со тушёное вме́сте с овоща́ми; vt & i (cul) туши́ть(ся) impf, с~ pf; (fig) томи́ть(ся) impf.

steward n бортпроводни́к. **stewardess** n стюарде́сса.

stick[1] n па́лка; (of chalk etc.) па́лочка; (hockey) клю́шка.

stick[2] vt (spear) зака́лывать impf, заколо́ть pf; (make adhere) прикле́ивать impf, прикле́ить pf (to к+dat); (coll) (put) ста́вить impf, по~ pf; (lay) класть impf, положи́ть pf; (endure) терпе́ть impf, вы́~ pf; vi (adhere) ли́пнуть impf (to к+dat); прилипа́ть impf, прили́пнуть pf (to к+dat); ~ **in** (thrust in) втыка́ть *impf*, воткну́ть *pf*; (*into opening*) всо́вывать *impf*, всу́нуть *pf*; ~ **on** (*glue on*) накле́ивать *impf*, накле́ить *pf*; ~ **out** (*thrust out*) высо́вывать *impf*, вы́сунуть *pf* (*from* из+*gen*); (*project*) торча́ть *impf*; ~ **to** (*keep to*) приде́рживаться *impf*, придержа́ться *pf* +*gen*; (*remain at*) не отвлека́ться *impf* от+*gen*; ~ to**gether** держа́ться *impf* вме́сте; ~ **up for** защища́ть *impf*, защити́ть *pf*; **be, get, stuck** застрева́ть *impf*, застря́ть *pf*. **sticker** *n* накле́йка.

sticky *adj* ли́пкий.

stiff *adj* жёсткий, неги́бкий; (*prim*) чо́порный; (*difficult*) тру́дный; (*penalty*) суро́вый; **be** ~ (*ache*) боле́ть *impf*. **stiffen** *vt* де́лать *impf*, с~ *pf* жёстким; *vi* станови́ться *impf*, стать *pf* жёстким. **stiffness** *n* жёсткость; (*primness*) чо́порность.

stifle *vt* души́ть *impf*, за~ *pf*; (*suppress*) подавля́ть *impf*, подави́ть *pf*; (*sound*) заглуша́ть *impf*, заглуши́ть *pf*; *vi* задыха́ться *impf*, задохну́ться *pf*. **stifling** *adj* уду́шливый.

stigma *n* клеймо́.

stile *n* перела́з (*coll*).

stilettos *n pl* ту́фли *f pl* на шпи́льках.

still *adv* (всё) ещё; (*nevertheless*) тем не ме́нее; (*motionless*) неподви́жно; **stand** ~ не дви́гаться *impf*, дви́нуться *pf*; *n* (*quiet*) тишина́; *adj* ти́хий; (*immobile*) неподви́жный. **still-born** *adj* мертворождённый. **still life** *n* натюрмо́рт. **stillness** *n* тишина́.

stilted *adj* ходу́льный.

stimulant *n* возбужда́ющее сре́дство. **stimulate** *vt* возбужда́ть *impf*, возбуди́ть *pf*. **stimulating** *adj* возбуди́тельный. **stimulation** *n* возбужде́ние. **stimulus** *n* сти́мул.

sting *n* (*wound*) уку́с; (*stinger; fig*) жа́ло; *vt* жа́лить *impf*, у~ *pf*; *vi* (*burn*) жечь *impf*. **stinging** *adj* (*caustic*) язви́тельный.

stingy *adj* скупо́й.

stink *n* вонь; *vi* воня́ть *impf* (*of* +*instr*). **stinking** *adj* воню́чий.

stint *n* срок; *vi*: ~**on** скупи́ться *impf*, по~ *pf* на+*acc*.

stipend *n* (*salary*) жа́лование; (*grant*) стипе́ндия.

stipulate *vt* обусло́вливать *impf*, обусло́вить *pf*. **stipulation** *n* усло́вие.

stir *n* (*commotion*) шум; *vt* (*mix*) меша́ть *impf*, по~ *pf*; (*excite*) возбужда́ть *impf*, вз~ *pf*; *vi* (*move*) шевели́ться *impf*, шевельну́ться *pf*; ~ **up** возбужда́ть *impf*, возбуди́ть *pf*. **stirring** *adj* волну́ющий.

stirrup *n* стре́мя *neut*.

stitch *n* стежо́к; (*knitting*) пе́тля; (*med*) шов; (*pain*) ко́лики *f pl*; *vt* (*embroider, make line of* ~es) строчи́ть *impf*, про~ *pf*; (*join by sewing, make, suture*) сшива́ть *impf*, сшить *pf*; ~ **up** зашива́ть *impf*, заши́ть *pf*. **stitching** *n* (*stitches*) стро́чка.

stoat *n* горноста́й.

stock *n* (*store*) запа́с; (*of shop*) ассортиме́нт; (*live*~) скот; (*cul*) бульо́н; (*lineage*) семья́; (*fin*) а́кции *f pl*; **in** ~ в нали́чии; **out of** ~ распро́дан; **take** ~ **of** крити́чески оце́нивать *impf*, оцени́ть *pf*; *adj* станда́ртный; **и** име́ть в нали́чии; ~ **up** запаса́ться *impf*, запасти́сь *pf* (**with** +*instr*). **stockbroker** *n* биржево́й ма́клер. **stock-exchange** *n* би́ржа. **stockpile** *n* запа́с; *vt* накапливать *impf*, накопи́ть *pf*. **stock-taking** *n* переучёт.

stocking *n* чуло́к.

stocky *adj* призе́мистый.

stodgy *adj* тяжёлый.

stoic(al) *adj* сто́ический. **stoicism** *n* стоици́зм.

stoke *vt* топи́ть *impf*.

stolid *adj* флегмати́чный.

stomach *n* желу́док, (*also surface of body*) живо́т; *vt* терпе́ть *impf*, по~ *pf*. **stomach ache** *n* боль в животе́.

stone *n* ка́мень *m*; (*of fruit*) ко́сточка; *adj* ка́менный; *vt* побива́ть *impf*, поби́ть *pf* камня́ми; (*fruit*) вынима́ть *impf*, вы́нуть *pf* ко́сточки из+*gen*. **Stone Age** *n* ка́менный век. **stone-deaf** *adj* соверше́нно глухо́й. **stone-mason** *n* ка́менщик. **stonily** *adv* с ка́менным выраже́нием, хо́лодно. **stony** *adj* камени́стый; (*fig*) ка́менный.

stool *n* табуре́т, табуре́тка.

stoop *n* суту́лость; *vt & i* суту́лить(ся) *impf*, с~ *pf*; (*bend* (*down*)) наклоня́ть(ся) *impf*, наклони́ть(ся) *pf;* ~ **to** (*abase o.s.*) унижа́ться *impf,* уни́зиться *pf* до+*gen;* (*condescend*) снисходи́ть *impf,* снизойти́ *pf* до +*gen.* **stooped, stooping** *adj* суту́лый.

stop *n* остано́вка; **put a** ~ **to** положи́ть *pf* коне́ц +*dat; vt* остана́вливать *impf,* останови́ть *pf;* (*discontinue*) прекраща́ть *impf,* прекрати́ть *pf;* (*restrain*) уде́рживать *impf,* удержа́ть *pf* (**from** от+*gen*); *vi* остана́вливаться *impf,* останови́ться *pf;* (*discontinue*) прекраща́ться *impf,* прекрати́ться *pf;* (*cease*) переставaть *impf,* переста́ть *pf* (+*inf*); ~ **up** *vt* затыка́ть *impf,* заткну́ть *pf.* **stoppage** *n* остано́вка; (*strike*) забасто́вка. **stopper** *n* про́бка. **stop-press** *n* э́кстренное сообще́ние в газе́те. **stop-watch** *n* секундоме́р.

storage *n* хране́ние. **store** *n* запа́с; (*storehouse*) склад; (*shop*) магази́н; **set** ~ **by** цени́ть *impf;* **what is in** ~ **for me?** что ждёт меня́ впереди́?; *vt* запаса́ть *impf,* запасти́ *pf;* (*put into storage*) сдава́ть *impf,* сдать *pf* на хране́ние. **storehouse** *n* склад. **store-room** кладова́я *sb.*

storey *n* эта́ж.

stork *n* а́ист.

storm *n* бу́ря, (*thunder* ~) гроза́; *vt* (*mil*) штурмова́ть *impf; vi* бушева́ть *impf.* **stormy** *adj* бу́рный.

story *n* расска́з, по́весть; (*anecdote*) анекдо́т; (*plot*) фа́була; ~**-teller** расска́зчик.

stout *adj* (*strong*) кре́пкий; (*staunch*) сто́йкий; (*portly*) доро́дный.

stove *n* (*with fire inside*) печь; (*cooker*) плита́.

stow *vt* укла́дывать *impf,* уложи́ть *pf.* **stowaway** *n* безбиле́тный пассажи́р.

straddle *vt* (*sit astride*) сиде́ть *impf* верхо́м на+*prep;* (*stand astride*) стоя́ть *impf,* расста́вив но́ги над+*instr.*

straggle *vi* отстава́ть *impf,* отста́ть *pf.* **straggler** *n* отста́вший *sb.* **straggling** *adj* разбро́санный. **straggly** *adj* растрёпанный.

straight *adj* прямо́й; (*undiluted*) неразба́вленный; *predic* (*in order*) в поря́дке; *adv* пря́мо; ~ **away** сра́зу. **straighten** *vt* & *i* выпрямля́ть(ся) *impf,* вы́прямить(ся) *pf; vt* (*put in*

order) поправля́ть *impf,* попра́вить *pf.* **straightforward** *adj* прямо́й; (*simple*) просто́й.

strain[1] *n* (*tension*) натяже́ние; (*sprain*) растяже́ние; (*effort, exertion*) напряже́ние; (*tendency*) скло́нность; (*sound*) звук; *vt* (*stretch*) натя́гивать *impf,* натяну́ть *pf;* (*sprain*) растя́гивать *impf,* растяну́ть *pf;* (*exert*) напряга́ть *impf,* напря́чь *pf;* (*filter*) проце́живать *impf,* процеди́ть *pf; vi* (*also exert o.s.*) напряга́ться *impf,* напря́чься *pf.* **strained** *adj* натя́нутый. **strainer** *n* (*tea* ~) си́течко; (*sieve*) си́то.

strain[2] *n* (*breed*) поро́да.

strait(s) *n* (*geog*) проли́в. **straitjacket** *n* смири́тельная руба́шка. **straits** *n pl* (*difficulties*) затрудни́тельное положе́ние.

strand[1] *n* (*hair, rope*) прядь; (*thread, also fig*) нить.

strand[2] *vt* сажа́ть *impf,* посади́ть *pf* на мель. **stranded** *adj* на мели́.

strange *adj* стра́нный; (*unfamiliar*) незнако́мый; (*alien*) чужо́й. **strangely** *adv* стра́нно. **strangeness** *n* стра́нность. **stranger** *n* незнако́мец.

strangle *vt* души́ть *impf,* за~ *pf.* **stranglehold** *n* мёртвая хва́тка. **strangulation** *n* удуше́ние.

strap *n* реме́нь *m; vt* (*tie up*) стя́гивать *impf,* стяну́ть *pf* ремнём. **strapping** *adj* ро́слый.

stratagem *n* хи́трость. **strategic** *adj* стратеги́ческий. **strategist** *n* страте́г. **strategy** *n* страте́гия.

stratum *n* слой.

straw *n* соло́ма; (*drinking*) соло́минка; **the last** ~ после́дняя ка́пля; *adj* соло́менный.

strawberry *n* клубни́ка (*no pl; usu collect*); (*wild* ~) земляни́ка (*no pl; usu collect*).

stray *vi* сбива́ться *impf,* сби́ться *pf;* (*digress*) отклоня́ться *impf,* отклони́ться *pf; adj* (*lost*) заблуди́вшийся; (*homeless*) бездо́мный; *n* (*from flock*) отби́вшееся от ста́да живо́тное *sb;* ~ **bullet** шальна́я пу́ля.

streak *n* полоса́ (**of luck** везе́ния); (*tendency*) жи́лка; *vi* (*rush*) проноси́ться *impf,* пронести́сь *pf.* **streaked** *adj* с полоса́ми (**with**

+*gen*). **streaky** *adj* полоса́тый; (*meat*) с просло́йками жи́ра.

stream *n* (*brook*, *tears*) ручей; (*brook*, *flood*, *tears*, *people etc.*) пото́к; (*current*) тече́ние; **up/down** ~ вверх/вниз по тече́нию; *vi* течь *impf*; струи́ться *impf*; (*rush*) проноси́ться *impf*, пронести́сь *pf*; (*blow*) развева́ться *impf*. **streamer** *n* вы́мпел. **stream-lined** *adj* обтека́емый; (*fig*) хорошо́ нала́женный.

street *n* у́лица; *adj* у́личный; ~ **lamp** у́личный фона́рь *m*.

strength *n* си́ла; (*numbers*) чи́сленность; **on the** ~ **of** в си́лу+*gen*. **strengthen** *vt* уси́ливать *impf*, уси́лить *pf*.

strenuous *adj* (*work*) тру́дный; (*effort*) напряжённый.

stress *n* напряже́ние; (*mental*) стресс; (*emphasis*) ударе́ние; *vt* (*accent*) ста́вить *impf*, по~ *pf* ударе́ние на+*acc*; (*emphasize*) подчёркивать *impf* подчеркну́ть *pf*. **stressful** *adj* стре́ссовый.

stretch *n* (*expanse*) отре́зок; **at a** ~ (*in succession*) подря́д; *vt & i* (*widen*, *spread out*) растя́гивать(ся) *impf*, растяну́ть(ся) *pf*; (*in length*, ~ *out limbs*) вытя́гивать(ся) *impf*, вы́тянуть(ся) *pf*; (*tauten*) натя́гивать(ся) *impf*, натяну́ть(ся) *pf*; (*extend, e.g. rope*, ~ *forth limbs*) протя́гивать(ся) *impf*, протяну́ть(ся) *pf*; *vi* (*material*, *land*) тяну́ться *impf*; ~ **one's legs** (*coll*) размина́ть *impf*, размя́ть *pf* но́ги. **stretcher** *n* носи́лки (-лок) *pl*.

strew *vt* разбра́сывать *impf*, разброса́ть *pf*; ~ **with** посыпа́ть *impf*, посы́пать *pf* +*instr*.

stricken *adj* поражённый.

strict *adj* стро́гий. **stricture(s)** *n* (стро́гая) кри́тика.

stride *n* (большо́й) шаг; *pl* (*fig*) успе́хи *m pl*; **to take sth in one's** ~ преодолева́ть *impf*, преодоле́ть *pf* что-л. без уси́лий; *vi* шага́ть *impf*.

strident *adj* ре́зкий.

strife *n* раздо́р.

strike *n* (*refusal to work*) забасто́вка; (*mil*) уда́р; *vi* (*be on* ~) бастова́ть *impf*; (*go on* ~) забастова́ть *pf*; (*attack*) ударя́ть *impf*, уда́рить *pf*; (*the hour*) бить *impf*, про~ *pf*; *vt* (*hit*)

ударя́ть *impf*, уда́рить *pf*; (*impress*) поража́ть *impf*, порази́ть *pf*; (*discover*) открыва́ть *impf*, откры́ть *pf*; (*match*) зажига́ть *impf*, заже́чь *pf*; (*the hour*) бить *impf*, про~ *pf*; (*occur to*) приходи́ть *impf*, прийти́ *pf* в го́лову+*dat*; ~ **off** вычёркивать *impf*, вы́черкнуть *pf*; ~ **up** начина́ть *impf*, нача́ть *pf*. **striker** *n* забасто́вщик. **striking** *adj* порази́тельный.

string *n* бечёвка; (*mus*) струна́; (*series*) ряд; *pl* (*mus*) стру́нные инструме́нты *m pl*; ~ **bag**, ~ **vest** се́тка; *vt* (*thread*) низа́ть *impf*, на~ *pf*; ~ **along** (*coll*) води́ть *impf* за нос; ~ **out** (*prolong*) растя́гивать *impf*, растяну́ть *pf*; **strung up** (*tense*) напряжённый. **stringed** *adj* стру́нный. **stringy** *adj* (*fibrous*) волокни́стый; (*meat*) жи́листый.

stringent *adj* стро́гий.

strip[1] *n* полоса́, поло́ска.

strip[2] *vt* (*undress*) раздева́ть *impf*, разде́ть *pf*; (*deprive*) лиша́ть *impf*, лиши́ть *pf* (**of** +*gen*); ~ **off** (*tear off*) сдира́ть *impf*, содра́ть *pf*; *vi* раздева́ться *impf*, разде́ться *pf*. **strip-tease** *n* стрипти́з.

stripe *n* полоса́. **striped** *adj* полоса́тый.

strive *vi* (*endeavour*) стреми́ться *impf* (**for** к+*dat*); (*struggle*) боро́ться *impf* (**for** за+*acc*; **against** про́тив +*gen*).

stroke *n* (*blow*, *med*) уда́р; (*of oar*) взмах; (*swimming*) стиль *m*; (*of pen etc.*) штрих; (*piston*) ход; *vt* гла́дить *impf*, по~ *pf*.

stroll *n* прогу́лка; *vi* прогу́ливаться *impf*, прогуля́ться *pf*.

strong *adj* си́льный; (*stout*, *of drinks*) кре́пкий; (*healthy*) здоро́вый; (*opinion etc.*) твёрдый. **stronghold** *n* кре́пость. **strong-minded, strong-willed** *adj* реши́тельный.

structural *adj* структу́рный. **structure** *n* структу́ра; (*building*) сооруже́ние; *vt* организова́ть *impf & pf*.

struggle *n* борьба́; *vi* боро́ться *impf* (**for** за+*acc*; **against** про́тив+*gen*); (*writhe*, ~ *with* (*fig*)) би́ться (**with** над+*instr*).

strum *vi* бренча́ть *impf* (**on** на +*prep*).

strut[1] *n* (*vertical*) сто́йка; (*horizontal*) распо́рка.

strut[2] *vi* ходи́ть *indet*, идти́ *det* го́голем.

stub *n* огры́зок; (*cigarette*) оку́рок; (*counterfoil*) корешо́к; *vt*: ~ one's toe ударя́ться *impf*, уда́риться *pf* ного́й (on на+*acc*); ~ out гаси́ть *impf*, по~ *pf*.

stubble *n* жнивьё; (*hair*) щети́на.

stubborn *adj* упря́мый. **stubbornness** *n* упря́мство.

stucco *n* штукату́рка.

stud[1] *n* (*collar, cuff*) за́понка; (*nail*) гвоздь *m* с большо́й шля́пкой; *vt* (*bestrew*) усе́ивать *impf*, усе́ять *pf* (with +*instr*).

stud[2] *n* (*horses*) ко́нный заво́д.

student *n* студе́нт, ~ка.

studied *adj* напускно́й.

studio *n* сту́дия.

studious *adj* лю́бящий нау́ку; (*diligent*) стара́тельный.

study *n* изуче́ние; *pl* заня́тия *neut pl*; (*investigation*) иссле́дование; (*art, mus*) этю́д; (*room*) кабине́т; *vt* изуча́ть *impf*, изучи́ть *pf*; учи́ться *impf*, об~ *pf* +*dat*; (*scrutinize*) рассма́тривать *impf*, рассмотре́ть *pf*; *vi* (*take lessons*) учи́ться *impf*, об~ *pf*; (*do one's studies*) занима́ться *impf*.

stuff *n* (*material*) материа́л; (*things*) ве́щи *f pl*; *vt* набива́ть *impf*, наби́ть *pf*; (*cul*) начиня́ть *impf*, начини́ть *pf*; (*cram into*) запи́хивать *impf*, запиха́ть *pf* (into в+*acc*); (*shove into*) сова́ть *impf*, су́нуть *pf* (into в+*acc*); *vi* (*overeat*) объеда́ться *pf*. **stuffiness** *n* духота́. **stuffing** *n* наби́вка; (*cul*) начи́нка. **stuffy** *adj* ду́шный.

stumble *vi* (*also fig*) спотыка́ться *impf*, споткну́ться *pf* (over о+*acc*); ~ upon натыка́ться *impf*, наткну́ться *pf* на+*acc*. **stumbling-block** *n* ка́мень *m* преткнове́ния.

stump *n* (*tree*) пень *m*; (*pencil*) огры́зок; (*limb*) культя́; *vt* (*perplex*) ста́вить *impf*, по~ *pf* в тупи́к.

stun *vt* (*also fig*) оглуша́ть *impf*, оглуши́ть *pf*. **stunning** *adj* потряса́ющий.

stunt[1] *n* трюк.

stunt[2] *vt* заде́рживать *impf*, заде́ржать *pf* рост+*gen*. **stunted** *adj* низ-

коро́слый.

stupefy *vt* оглуша́ть *impf*, оглуши́ть *pf*. **stupendous** *adj* колосса́льный. **stupid** *adj* глу́пый. **stupidity** *n* глу́пость. **stupor** *n* оцепене́ние.

sturdy *adj* кре́пкий.

stutter *n* заика́ние; *vi* заика́ться *impf*.

sty[1] *n* (*pig~*) свина́рник.

sty[2] *n* (*on eye*) ячме́нь *m*.

style *n* стиль *m*; (*taste*) вкус; (*fashion*) мо́да; (*sort*) род; (*of hair*) причёска. **stylish** *adj* мо́дный. **stylist** *n* (*of hair*) парикма́хер. **stylistic** *adj* стилисти́ческий. **stylize** *vt* стилизова́ть *impf & pf*.

stylus *n* игла́ звукоснима́теля.

suave *adj* обходи́тельный.

subconscious *adj* подсозна́тельный; *n* подсозна́ние. **subcontract** *vt* дава́ть *impf*, дать *pf* подря́дчику. **subcontractor** *n* подря́дчик. **subdivide** *vt* подразделя́ть *impf*, подраздели́ть *pf*. **subdivision** *n* подразделе́ние. **subdue** *vt* покоря́ть *impf*, покори́ть *pf*. **subdued** *adj* (*suppressed, dispirited*) пода́вленный; (*soft*) мя́гкий; (*indistinct*) приглушённый. **sub-editor** *n* помо́щник реда́ктора.

subject *n* (*theme*) те́ма; (*discipline, theme*) предме́т; (*question*) вопро́с; (*thing on to which action is directed*) объе́кт; (*gram*) подлежа́щее *sb*; (*national*) по́дданный *sb*; *adj*: ~ to (*susceptible to*) подве́рженный+*dat*; (*on condition that*) при усло́вии, что...; е́сли; be ~ to (*change etc.*) подлежа́ть *impf* +*dat*; *vt*: ~ to подверга́ть *impf*, подве́ргнуть *pf* +*dat*. **subjection** *n* подчине́ние. **subjective** *adj* субъекти́вный. **subjectivity** *n* субъекти́вность. **subject-matter** *n* (*of book, lecture*) содержа́ние, те́ма; (*of discussion*) предме́т.

subjugate *vt* покоря́ть *impf*, покори́ть *pf*. **subjugation** *n* покоре́ние.

subjunctive (mood) *n* сослага́тельное наклоне́ние.

sublet *vt* передава́ть *impf*, переда́ть *pf* в субаре́нду.

sublimate *vt* сублими́ровать *impf & pf*. **sublimation** *n* сублима́ция. **sublime** *adj* возвы́шенный.

subliminal *adj* подсозна́тельный.

sub-machine-gun *n* автома́т. **submarine** *n* подво́дная ло́дка. **submerge** *vt* погружа́ть *impf*, погрузи́ть *pf*. **submission** *n* подчине́ние; (*for inspection*) представле́ние. **submissive** *adj* поко́рный. **submit** *vi* подчиня́ться *impf*, подчини́ться *pf* (**to** +*dat*); *vt* представля́ть *impf*, предста́вить *pf*. **subordinate** *n* подчинённый *sb*; *adj* подчинённый; (*secondary*) второстепе́нный; (*gram*) прида́точный; *vt* подчиня́ть *impf*, подчини́ть *pf*. **subscribe** *vi* подпи́сываться *impf*, подписа́ться *pf* (**to** на+*acc*); ~ **to** (*opinion*) присоединя́ться *impf*, присоедини́ться *pf* к+*dat*. **subscriber** *n* подпи́счик; абоне́нт. **subscription** *n* подпи́ска, абонеме́нт; (*fee*) взнос. **subsection** *n* подразде́л. **subsequent** *adj* после́дующий. **subsequently** *adv* впосле́дствии. **subservient** *adj* рабо́лепный. **subside** *vi* убыва́ть *impf*, убы́ть *pf*; (*soil*) оседа́ть *impf*, осе́сть *pf*. **subsidence** *n* (*soil*) оседа́ние. **subsidiary** *adj* вспомога́тельный; (*secondary*) второстепе́нный; *n* филиа́л. **subsidize** *vt* субсиди́ровать *impf* & *pf*. **subsidy** *n* субси́дия. **subsist** *vi* (*live*) жить *impf* (**on** +*instr*). **substance** *n* вещество́; (*essence*) су́щность, суть; (*content*) содержа́ние. **substantial** *adj* (*durable*) про́чный; (*considerable*) значи́тельный; (*food*) пло́тный. **substantially** *adv* (*basically*) в основно́м; (*considerably*) значи́тельно. **substantiate** *vt* обосно́вывать *impf*, обоснова́ть *pf*. **substitute** *n* (*person*) замести́тель *m*; (*thing*) заме́на; *vt* заменя́ть *impf*, замени́ть *pf* +*instr* (**for** +*acc*); I ~ **water for milk** заменя́ю молоко́ водо́й. **substitution** *n* заме́на. **subsume** *vt* относи́ть *impf*, отнести́ *pf* к како́й-л. катего́рии. **subterfuge** *n* уве́ртка. **subterranean** *adj* подзе́мный. **subtitle** *n* подзаголо́вок; (*cin*) субти́тр. **subtle** *adj* то́нкий. **subtlety** *n* то́нкость.

subtract *vt* вычита́ть *impf*, вы́честь *pf*. **subtraction** *n* вычита́ние. **suburb** *n* при́город. **suburban** *adj* при́городный. **subversion** *n* подрывна́я де́ятельность. **subversive** *adj* подрывно́й. **subway** *n* подзе́мный перехо́д.

succeed *vi* удава́ться *impf*, уда́ться *pf*; **the plan will** ~ план уда́стся; **he** ~**ed in buying the book** ему́ удало́сь купи́ть кни́гу; (*be successful*) преуспева́ть *impf*, преуспе́ть *pf* (**in** в+*prep*); (*follow*) сменя́ть *impf*, смени́ть *pf*; (*be heir*) насле́довать *impf* & *pf* (**to** +*dat*). **succeeding** *adj* после́дующий. **success** *n* успе́х. **successful** *adj* успе́шный. **succession** *n* (*series*) ряд; (*to throne*) престолонасле́дие; **right of** ~ пра́во насле́дования; **in** ~ подря́д, оди́н за други́м. **successive** *adj* (*consecutive*) после́довательный. **successor** *n* прее́мник.

succinct *adj* сжа́тый.

succulent *adj* со́чный.

succumb *vi* (*to pressure*) уступа́ть *impf*, уступи́ть *pf* (**to** +*dat*); (*to temptation*) поддава́ться *impf*, подда́ться *pf* (**to** +*dat*).

such *adj* тако́й; ~ **people** таки́е лю́ди; ~ **as** (*for example*) так наприме́р; (*of a kind as*) тако́й как; ~ **beauty as yours** така́я красота́ как ва́ша; (*that which*) тот, кото́рый; **I shall read** ~ **books as I like** я бу́ду чита́ть те кни́ги, кото́рые мне нра́вятся; ~ **as to** тако́й, что́бы; **his illness was not** ~ **as to cause anxiety** его́ боле́знь была́ не тако́й (серьёзной), что́бы вы́звать беспоко́йство; ~ **and** ~ тако́й-то; *pron* тако́в; ~ **was his character** тако́в был его́ хара́ктер; **as** ~ сам по себе́; ~ **is not the case** э́то не так. **suchlike** *pron* (*inanimate*) тому́ подо́бное; (*people*) таки́е лю́ди *pl*.

suck *vt* соса́ть *impf*; ~ **in** вса́сывать *impf*, всоса́ть *pf*; (*engulf*) заса́сывать *impf*, засоса́ть *pf*; ~ **out** выса́сывать *impf*, вы́сосать *pf*; ~ **up** **to** (*coll*) подли́зываться *impf*, подлиза́ться *pf* к+*dat*. **sucker** *n* (*biol, rubber device*) присо́ска; (*bot*) корнево́й побе́г. **suckle** *vt* корми́ть *impf*, на~ *pf* гру́дью. **suction** *n* вса́сывание.

sudden *adj* внеза́пный. **suddenly** *adv* вдруг. **suddenness** *n* внеза́пность.

sue *vt* & *i* подава́ть *impf*, пода́ть *pf*

в суд (на+*acc*); ~ **s.o. for damages** предъявля́ть *impf*, предъяви́ть *pf* (к) кому́-л. иск о возмеще́нии уще́рба.

suede *n* за́мша; *adj* за́мшевый.

suet *n* нутряно́е са́ло.

suffer *vt* страда́ть *impf*, по~ *pf* +*instr*, от+*gen*; (*loss, defeat*) терпе́ть *impf*, по~ *pf*; (*tolerate*) терпе́ть *impf*; *vi* страда́ть *impf*, по~ *pf* (from +*instr*, от+*gen*). **sufferance** *n*: he is here on ~ его́ здесь те́рпят. **suffering** *n* страда́ние.

suffice *vi* & *t* быть доста́точним (для+*gen*); хвата́ть *impf*, хвати́ть *pf impers*+*gen* (+*dat*). **sufficient** *adj* доста́точный.

suffix *n* су́ффикс.

suffocate *vt* удуша́ть *impf*, удуши́ть *pf*; *vi* задыха́ться *impf*, задохну́ться *pf*. **suffocating** *adj* уду́шливый. **suffocation** *n* удуше́ние.

suffrage *n* избира́тельное пра́во.

suffuse *vt* залива́ть *impf*, зали́ть *pf* (with +*instr*).

sugar *n* са́хар; *adj* са́харный; *vt* подсла́щивать *impf*, подсласти́ть *pf*; ~ **basin** са́харница; ~ **beet** са́харная свёкла; ~ **cane** са́харный тро́стник. **sugary** *adj* са́харный; (*fig*) слаща́вый.

suggest *vt* предлага́ть *impf*, предложи́ть *pf*; (*evoke*) напомина́ть *impf*, напо́мнить *pf*; (*imply*) намека́ть *impf*, намекну́ть *pf* на+*acc*; (*indicate*) говори́ть *impf* о+*prep*. **suggestion** *n* предложе́ние; (*psych*) внуше́ние. **suggestive** *adj* вызыва́ющий мы́сли (of о+*prep*); (*indecent*) соблазни́тельный.

suicidal *adj* самоуби́йственный; (*fig*) губи́тельный. **suicide** *n* самоуби́йство; **commit** ~ соверша́ть *impf*, соверши́ть *pf* самоуби́йство.

suit *n* (*clothing*) костю́м; (*law*) иск; (*cards*) масть; **follow** ~ (*fig*) сле́довать *impf*, по~ *pf* приме́ру; *vt* (*be convenient for*) устра́ивать *impf*, устро́ить *pf*; (*adapt*) приспоса́бливать *impf*, приспосо́бить *pf*; (*be ~able for, match*) подходи́ть *impf*, подойти́ *pf* (+*dat*); (*look attractive on*) идти́ *impf* +*dat*. **suitability** *n* приго́дность. **suitable** *adj* (*fitting*) подходя́щий; (*convenient*) удо́бный.

suitably *adv* соотве́тственно. **suitcase** *n* чемода́н.

suite *n* (*retinue*) сви́та; (*furniture*) гарниту́р; (*rooms*) апарта́менты *m pl*; (*mus*) сюи́та.

suitor *n* покло́нник.

sulk *vi* ду́ться *impf*. **sulky** *adj* наду́тый.

sullen *adj* угрю́мый.

sully *vt* пятна́ть *impf*, за~ *pf*.

sulphur *n* се́ра. **sulphuric** *adj*: ~ **acid** се́рная кислота́.

sultana *n* (*raisin*) изю́минка; *pl* кишми́ш (*collect*).

sultry *adj* зно́йный.

sum *n* су́мма; (*arithmetical problem*) арифмети́ческая зада́ча; *pl* арифме́тика; *v*: ~ **up** *vi* & *t* (*summarize*) подводи́ть *impf*, подвести́ *pf* ито́ги (+*gen*); *vt* (*appraise*) оце́нивать *impf*, оцени́ть *pf*.

summarize *vt* сумми́ровать *impf* & *pf*. **summary** *n* резюме́ *neut indecl*, сво́дка; *adj* сумма́рный; (*dismissal*) бесцеремо́нный.

summer *n* ле́то; *attrib* ле́тний. **summer-house** *n* бесе́дка.

summit *n* верши́на; ~ **meeting** встре́ча на верха́х.

summon *vt* вызыва́ть *impf*, вы́звать *pf*; ~ **up one's courage** собира́ться *impf*, собра́ться *pf* с ду́хом. **summons** *n* вы́зов; (*law*) пове́стка в суд; *vt* вызыва́ть *impf*, вы́звать *pf* в суд.

sumptuous *adj* роско́шный.

sun *n* со́лнце; **in the** ~ на со́лнце. **sunbathe** *vi* загора́ть *impf*. **sunbeam** *n* со́лнечный луч. **sunburn** *n* зага́р; (*inflammation*) со́лнечный ожо́г. **sunburnt** *adj* загоре́лый; **become** ~ загора́ть *impf*, загоре́ть *pf*. **Sunday** *n* воскресе́нье.

sundry *adj* ра́зный; **all and** ~ всё и вся.

sunflower *n* подсо́лнечник. **sunglasses** *n pl* очки́ (-ко́в) *pl* от со́лнца.

sunken *adj* (*cheeks, eyes*) впа́лый; (*submerged*) погружённый; (*ship*) зато́пленный; (*below certain level*) ни́же (како́го-л. у́ровня).

sunlight *n* со́лнечный свет. **sunny** *adj* со́лнечный. **sunrise** *n* восхо́д со́лнца. **sunset** *n* зака́т. **sunshade**

n (*parasol*) зо́нтик; (*awning*) наве́с. **sunshine** *n* со́лнечный свет. **sunstroke** *n* со́лнечный уда́р. **suntan** *n* зага́р. **sun-tanned** *adj* загоре́лый. **super** *adj* замеча́тельный. **superb** *adj* превосхо́дный. **supercilious** *adj* высокоме́рный. **superficial** *adj* пове́рхностный. **superficiality** *n* пове́рхностность. **superfluous** *adj* ли́шний. **superhuman** *adj* сверхчелове́ческий. **superintendent** *n* заве́дующий *sb* (*of* +*instr*); (*police*) ста́рший полице́йский офице́р. **superior** *n* ста́рший *sb*; *adj* (*better*) превосхо́дный; (*in rank*) ста́рший; (*haughty*) высокоме́рный. **superiority** *n* превосхо́дство. **superlative** *adj* превосхо́дный; *n* (*gram*) превосхо́дная сте́пень. **superman** *n* сверхчелове́к. **supermarket** *n* универса́м. **supernatural** *adj* сверхъесте́ственный. **superpower** *n* сверхдержа́ва. **supersede** *vt* заменя́ть *impf*, замени́ть *pf*. **supersonic** *adj* сверхзвуково́й. **superstition** *n* суеве́рие. **superstitious** *adj* суеве́рный. **superstructure** *n* надстро́йка. **supervise** *vt* наблюда́ть *impf* за+*instr*. **supervision** *n* надзо́р. **supervisor** *n* нача́льник; (*of studies*) руководи́тель *m*.

supper *n* у́жин; **have ~** у́жинать *impf*, по~ *pf*.

supple *adj* ги́бкий. **suppleness** *n* ги́бкость.

supplement *n* (*to book*) дополне́ние; (*to periodical*) приложе́ние; *vt* дополня́ть *impf*, допо́лнить *pf*. **supplementary** *adj* дополни́тельный.

supplier *n* поставщи́к. **supply** *n* (*stock*) запа́с; (*econ*) предложе́ние; *pl* (*mil*) припа́сы (-ов) *pl*, *vt* снабжа́ть *impf*, снабди́ть *pf* (*with* +*instr*). **support** *n* подде́ржка, опо́ра; *vt* подде́рживать *impf*, поддержа́ть *pf*, (*family*) содержа́ть *impf*. **supporter** *n* сторо́нник. **supportive** *adj* уча́стливый.

suppose *vt* (*think*) полага́ть *impf*; (*presuppose*) предполага́ть *impf*, предположи́ть *pf*; (*assume*) допуска́ть *impf*, допусти́ть *pf*. **supposed** *adj* (*assumed*) предполога́емый. **supposition** *n* предположе́ние.

suppress *vt* подавля́ть *impf*, пода-

ви́ть *pf*. **suppression** *n* подавле́ние.
supremacy *n* госпо́дство. **supreme** *adj* верхо́вный.

surcharge *n* наце́нка.

sure *adj* уве́ренный (*of* в+*prep*; *that* что); (*reliable*) ве́рный; **~ enough** действи́тельно; **he is ~ to come** он обяза́тельно придёт; **make ~ of** (*convince o.s.*) убежда́ться *impf*, убеди́ться *pf* в+*prep*; **make ~ that** (*check up*) проверя́ть *impf*, прове́рить *pf* что. **surely** *adv* наверняка́. **surety** *n* пору́ка; **stand ~ for** руча́ться *impf*, поручи́ться *pf* за+*acc*.

surf *n* прибо́й; *vi* занима́ться *impf*, заня́ться *pf* сёрфингом.

surface *n* пове́рхность; (*exterior*) вне́шность; **on the ~** (*fig*) вне́шне; **under the ~** (*fig*) по существу́; *adj* пове́рхностный; *vi* всплыва́ть *impf*, всплыть *pf*.

surfeit *n* (*surplus*) изли́шек.

surge *n* волна́; *vi* (*rise, heave*) вздыма́ться *impf*; (*emotions*) нахлы́нуть *pf*; **~ forward** ри́нуться *pf* вперёд.

surgeon *n* хиру́рг. **surgery** *n* (*treatment*) хирурги́я; (*place*) кабине́т; (*~ hours*) приёмные часы́ *m pl* (врача́). **surgical** *adj* хирурги́ческий.

surly *adj* (*morose*) угрю́мый; (*rude*) гру́бый.

surmise *vt & i* предполага́ть *impf*, предположи́ть *pf*.

surmount *vt* преодолева́ть *impf*, преодоле́ть *pf*.

surname *n* фами́лия.

surpass *vt* превосходи́ть *impf*, превзойти́ *pf*.

surplus *n* изли́шек; *adj* изли́шний.

surprise *n* (*astonishment*) удивле́ние; (*surprising thing*) сюрпри́з; *vt* удивля́ть *impf*, удиви́ть *pf*; (*come upon suddenly*) застава́ть *impf*, заста́ть *pf* враспло́х; **be ~d** (*at*) удивля́ться *impf*, удиви́ться *pf* (+*dat*). **surprising** *adj* удиви́тельный.

surreal *adj* сюрреалисти́ческий. **surrealism** *n* сюрреали́зм. **surrealist** *n* сюрреали́ст; *adj* сюрреалисти́ческий.

surrender *n* сда́ча; (*renunciation*) отка́з; *vt* сдава́ть *impf*, сдать *pf*; (*give up*) отка́зываться *impf*, отказа́ться *pf* от+*gen*; *vi* сдава́ться *impf*, сда́ться *pf*; **~ o.s. to** предава́ться *impf*, преда́ться *pf* +*dat*.

surreptitious *adj* та́йный.

surrogate *n* замени́тель *m*.

surround *vt* окружа́ть *impf*, окружи́ть *pf* (**with** +*instr*). **surrounding** *adj* окружа́ющий. **surroundings** *n* (*environs*) окре́стности *f pl*; (*milieu*) среда́.

surveillance *n* надзо́р.

survey *n* (*review*) обзо́р; (*inspection*) инспе́кция; (*poll*) опро́с; *vt* (*review*) обозрева́ть *impf*, обозре́ть *pf*; (*inspect*) инспекти́ровать *impf*, про~ *pf*; (*poll*) опра́шивать *impf*, опроси́ть *pf*. **surveyor** *n* инспе́ктор.

survival *n* (*surviving*) выжива́ние; (*relic*) пережи́ток. **survive** *vt* пережива́ть *impf*, пережи́ть *pf*; *vi* выжива́ть *impf*, вы́жить *pf*. **survivor** *n* уцеле́вший *sb*; (*fig*) боре́ц.

susceptible *adj* подве́рженный (**to** влия́нию +*gen*); (*sensitive*) чувстви́тельный (**to** к+*dat*); (*impressionable*) впечатли́тельный.

suspect *n* подозрева́емый *sb*; *adj* подозри́тельный; *vt* подозрева́ть *impf* (**of** в+*prep*); (*assume*) полага́ть *impf* (**that** что).

suspend *vt* (*hang up*) подве́шивать *impf*, подве́сить *pf*; (*interrupt*) приостана́вливать *impf*, приостанови́ть *pf*; (*debar temporarily*) вре́менно отстраня́ть *impf*, отстрани́ть *pf*; ~**ed sentence** усло́вный пригово́р. **suspender** *n* (*stocking*) подвя́зка. **suspense** *n* неизве́стность. **suspension** *n* (*halt*) приостано́вка; (*of car*) рессо́ры *f pl*; ~ **bridge** вися́чий мост.

suspicion *n* подозре́ние; **on** ~ по подозре́нию (**of** в+*loc*); (*trace*) отте́нок. **suspicious** *adj* подозри́тельный.

sustain *vt* (*support*) подде́рживать *impf*, поддержа́ть *pf*; (*suffer*) потерпе́ть *pf*. **sustained** *adj* (*uninterrupted*) непреры́вный. **sustenance** *n* пи́ща.

swab *n* (*mop*) шва́бра; (*med*) тампо́н; (*specimen*) мазо́к.

swagger *vi* расха́живать *impf* с ва́жным ви́дом.

swallow[1] *n* глото́к; *vt* прогла́тывать *impf*, проглоти́ть *pf*; ~ **up** поглоща́ть *impf*, поглоти́ть *pf*.

swallow[2] *n* (*bird*) ла́сточка.

swamp *n* боло́та; *vt* залива́ть *impf*, зали́ть *pf*; (*fig*) зава́ливать *impf*, завали́ть *pf* (**with** +*instr*). **swampy** *adj* боло́тистый.

swan *n* ле́бедь *m*.

swap *n* обме́н; *vt* (*for different thing*) меня́ть *impf*, об~, по~ *pf* (**for** на +*acc*); (*for similar thing*) обме́ниваться *impf*, обменя́ться *pf* +*instr*.

swarm *n* рой; (*crowd*) толпа́; *vi* рои́ться *impf*; толпи́ться *impf*; (*teem*) кише́ть *impf* (**with** +*instr*).

swarthy *adj* сму́глый.

swastika *n* сва́стика.

swat *vt* прихло́пывать *impf*, прихло́пнуть *pf*.

swathe *n* (*expanse*) простра́нство; *vt* (*wrap*) заку́тывать *impf*, заку́тать *pf*.

sway *n* (*influence*) влия́ние; (*power*) власть *vt* & *i* кача́ть(ся) *impf*, качну́ть(ся) *pf*; *vt* (*influence*) име́ть *impf* влия́ние на+*acc*.

swear *vi* (*vow*) кля́сться *impf*, по~ *pf*; (*curse*) руга́ться *impf*, ругну́ться *pf*; ~**word** руга́тельство.

sweat *n* пот; *vi* поте́ть *impf*, вс~ *pf*. **sweater** *n* сви́тер. **sweaty** *adj* по́тный.

swede *n* брю́ква.

Swede *n* швед, ~дка. **Sweden** *n* Шве́ция. **Swedish** *adj* шве́дский.

sweep *n* (*span*) разма́х; (*chimney-*~) трубочи́ст; *vt* подмета́ть *impf*, подмести́ *pf*; *vi* (*go majestically*) ходи́ть *indet*, идти́ *det*, пойти́ *pf* велича́во; (*move swiftly*) мча́ться *impf*; ~ **away** смета́ть *impf*, смести́ *pf*. **sweeping** *adj* (*changes*) радика́льный; (*statement*) огу́льный.

sweet *n* (*sweetmeat*) конфе́та; (*dessert*) сла́дкое *sb*; *adj* сла́дкий; (*fragrant*) души́стый; (*dear*) ми́лый. **sweeten** *vt* подсла́щивать *impf*, подсласти́ть *pf*. **sweetheart** *n* возлю́бленный, -нная *sb*. **sweetness** *n* сла́дость.

swell *vi* (*up*) опуха́ть *impf*, опу́хнуть *pf*; *vt* & *i* (*a sail*) надува́ть(ся) *impf*, наду́ть(ся) *pf*; *vt* (*increase*) увели́чивать *impf*, увели́чить *pf*; *n* (*of sea*) зыбь. **swelling** *n* о́пухоль.

swelter *vi* изнемога́ть *impf* от жары́. **sweltering** *adj* зно́йный.

swerve *vi* ре́зко свёртывать, свора́чивать *impf*, сверну́ть *pf*.

swift adj быстрый.
swig n глоток; vt хлебать impf.
swill n пойло; vt (rinse) полоскать impf, вы~ pf.
swim vi плавать indet, плыть det; vt (across) переплывать impf, переплыть pf +acc, через+acc. **swimmer** n пловец, пловчиха. **swimming** n плавание. **swimming-pool** n бассейн для плавания. **swim-suit** n купальный костюм.
swindle vt обманывать impf, обмануть pf; n обман. **swindler** n мошенник.
swine n свинья.
swing vi качаться impf, качнуться pf; vt качать impf, качнуть pf +acc, instr; (arms) размахивать impf +instr; n качание; (shift) крен; (seat) качели (-лей) pl; **in full** ~ в полном разгаре.
swingeing adj (huge) громадный; (forcible) сильный.
swipe n сильный удар; vt с силой ударять impf, ударить pf.
swirl vi крутиться impf; n (of snow) вихрь m.
swish vi (cut the air) рассекать impf, рассечь pf воздух со свистом; (rustle) шелестеть impf; vt (tail) взмахивать impf, взмахнуть pf +instr; (brandish) размахивать impf +instr; n (of whip) свист; (rustle) шелест.
Swiss n швейцарец, -царка; adj швейцарский.
switch n (electr) выключатель m; (change) изменение; vt & i (also ~ over) переключать(ся) impf, переключить(ся) pf; vt (swap) меняться impf, об~, по~ pf +instr; ~ **off** выключать impf, выключить pf; ~ **on** включать impf, включить pf. **switchboard** n коммутатор.
Switzerland n Швейцария.
swivel vt & i вращать(ся) impf.
swollen adj вздутый.
swoon n обморок; vi падать impf, упасть pf в обморок.
swoop vi: ~ **down** налетать impf, налететь pf (on на+acc); n налёт; **at one fell** ~ одним ударом.
sword n меч.
sycophantic adj льстивый.
syllable n слог.
syllabus n программа.

symbol n символ. **symbolic(al)** adj символический. **symbolism** n символизм. **symbolize** vt символизировать impf.
symmetrical adj симметрический. **symmetry** n симметрия.
sympathetic adj сочувственный. **sympathize** vi сочувствовать impf (with +dat). **sympathizer** n сторонник. **sympathy** n сочувствие.
symphony n симфония.
symposium n симпозиум.
symptom n симптом. **symptomatic** adj симтоматичный.
synagogue n синагога.
synchronization n синхронизация. **synchronize** vt синхронизировать impf & pf.
syndicate n синдикат.
syndrome n синдром.
synonym n синоним. **synonymous** adj синонимический.
synopsis n конспект.
syntax n синтаксис.
synthesis n синтез. **synthetic** adj синтетический.
syphilis n сифилис.
Syria n Сирия. **Syrian** n сириец, сирийка; adj сирийский.
syringe n шприц; vt спринцевать impf.
syrup n сироп; (treacle) патока.
system n система; (network) сеть; (organism) организм. **systematic** adj систематический. **systematize** vt систематизировать impf & pf.

T

tab n (loop) петелька; (on uniform) петлица; (of boot) ушко; **keep ~s on** следить impf за+instr.
table n стол; (chart) таблица; ~**cloth** скатерть, ~**spoon** столовая ложка; ~ **tennis** настольный теннис; vt (for discussion) предлагать impf, предложить pf на обсуждение.
tableau n живая картина.
tablet n (pill) таблетка; (of stone) плита; (memorial ~) мемориальная доска; (name plate) дощечка.
tabloid n (newspaper) малоформатная газета; (derog) бульварная газета.

taboo *n* табу́ *neut indecl*; *adj* за-
прещённый.

tacit *adj* молчали́вый. **taciturn** *adj*
неразгово́рчивый.

tack[1] *n* (*nail*) гво́здик; (*stitch*) намёт-
ка; (*naut*) галс; (*fig*) курс; *vt* (*fasten*) прикрепля́ть *impf*, прикрепи́ть
pf гвоздика́ми; (*stitch*) смётывать
impf, смета́ть *pf* на живу́ю ни́тку;
(*fig*) добавля́ть *impf*, доба́вить *pf*
((on)to +*dat*); *vi* (*naut*, *fig*) лави́-
ровать *impf*.

tack[2] *n* (*riding*) сбру́я (*collect*).

tackle *n* (*requisites*) снасть (*collect*);
(*sport*) блокиро́вка; *vt* (*problem*)
бра́ться *impf*, взя́ться *pf* за+*acc*;
(*sport*) блоки́ровать *impf* & *pf*.

tacky *adj* ли́пкий.

tact *n* такт(и́чность). **tactful** *adj* так-
ти́чный.

tactical *adj* такти́ческий. **tactics** *n*
pl та́ктика.

tactless *adj* беста́ктный.

tadpole *n* голова́стик.

Tadzhikistan *n* Таджикиста́н.

tag *n* (*label*) ярлы́к; (*of lace*) нако-
не́чник; *vt* (*label*) прикрепля́ть
impf, прикрепи́ть *pf* ярлы́к на+*acc*;
vi: ~ **along** (*follow*) тащи́ться *impf*
сзади́; **may I** ~ **along?** мо́жно с
ва́ми?

tail *n* хвост; (*of shirt*) ни́жний коне́ц;
(*of coat*) фа́лда; (*of coin*) обра́тная
сторона́ моне́ты; **heads or** ~**s**
орёл и́ли ре́шка?; *pl* (*coat*) фрак;
vt (*shadow*) выслёживать *impf*; *vi*:
~ **away**, **off** постепе́нно умень-
ша́ться *impf*, (*grow silent*, *abate*)
затиха́ть *impf*. **tailback** *n* хвост.

tailcoat *n* фрак.

tailor *n* портно́й *sb*; ~-**made** сши́тый
на зака́з; (*fig*) сде́ланный индиви-
дуа́льно.

taint *vt* по́ртить *impf*, ис~ *pf*.

Taiwan *n* Тайва́нь *m*.

take *vt* (*various senses*) брать *impf*,
взять *pf*; (*also seize*, *capture*) за-
хва́тывать *impf*, захвати́ть *pf*; (*receive*, *accept*; ~ *breakfast*; ~ *medicine*; ~ *steps*) принима́ть *impf*, при-
ня́ть *pf*; (*convey*, *escort*) провожа́ть
impf, проводи́ть *pf*; (*public transport*) е́здить *indet*, е́хать *det*, по~
pf +*instr*, на+*prep*; (*photograph*)
снима́ть *impf*, снять *pf*; (*occupy*; ~

time) занима́ть *impf*, заня́ть *pf*;
(*impers*) **how long does it** ~?
ско́лько вре́мени ну́жно?; (*size in
clothing*) носи́ть *impf*; (*exam*) сда-
ва́ть *impf*; *vi* (*be successful*) име́ть
impf успе́х (*of injection*) прививи-
ва́ться *impf*, приви́ться *pf*; ~ **after**
походи́ть *impf* на+*acc*; ~ **away** (*remove*) убира́ть *impf*, убра́ть *pf*;
(*subtract*) вычита́ть *impf*, вы́честь
pf; ~-**away** магази́н, где продаю́т на
вы́нос; ~ **back** (*return*) возвраща́ть
impf, возврати́ть *pf*; (*retrieve*, *retract*) брать *impf*, взять *pf* наза́д; ~
down (*in writing*) запи́сывать *impf*,
записа́ть *pf*; (*remove*) снима́ть *impf*,
снять *pf*; ~ **s.o.**, **sth for**, **to be**
принима́ть *impf*, приня́ть *pf* за+*acc*;
~ **from** отнима́ть *impf*, отня́ть *pf* у,
от+*gen*; ~ **in** (*carry in*) вноси́ть
impf, внести́ *pf*; (*lodgers*; *work*)
брать *impf*, взять *pf*; (*clothing*)
ушива́ть *impf*, уши́ть *pf*; (*understand*) понима́ть *impf*, поня́ть *pf*;
(*deceive*) обма́нывать *impf*, обма-
ну́ть *pf*; ~ **off** (*clothing*) снима́ть
impf, снять *pf*; (*mimic*) передра́з-
нивать *impf*, передразни́ть *pf*;
(*aeroplane*) взлета́ть *impf*, взлете́ть
pf; ~-**off** (*imitation*) подража́ние;
(*aeron*) взлёт; ~ **on** (*undertake*; *hire*)
брать *impf*, взять *pf* на себя́; (*acquire*) приобрета́ть *impf*, приобре-
сти́ *pf*; (*at game*) сража́ться *impf*,
срази́ться *pf* с+*instr* (**at** +*acc*); ~
out вынима́ть *impf*, вы́нуть *pf*;
(*dog*) выводи́ть *impf*, вы́вести *pf*
(**for a walk** на прогу́лку); (*to theatre*,
restaurant etc.) приглаша́ть *impf*,
пригласи́ть *pf* (**to** в+*acc*); **we took
them out every night** мы при-
глаша́ли их куда́-нибудь ка́ждый
ве́чер; ~ **it out on** срыва́ть *impf*,
сорва́ть *pf* всё на+*prep*; ~ **over** при-
нима́ть *impf*, приня́ть *pf* руково́д-
ство +*instr*; ~ **to** (*thing*) пристра-
сти́ться *pf* к+*dat*; (*person*) привя́-
зываться *impf*, привяза́ться *pf* к
+*dat*; (*begin*) станови́ться *impf*,
стать *pf* +*inf*; ~ **up** (*interest oneself
in*) занима́ться *impf*, заня́ться *pf*;
(*with an official etc.*) обраща́ться
impf, обрати́ться *pf* с+*instr*, к+*dat*;
(*challenge*) принима́ть *impf*, при-
ня́ть *pf*; (*time*, *space*) занима́ть *impf*,

заня́ть *pf*; ~ **up with** (*person*) свя́-
зываться *impf*, связа́ться *pf* с+*instr*;
n (*cin*) дубль *m*.

taking *adj* привлека́тельный.

takings *n pl* сбор.

talcum powder *n* тальк.

tale *n* расска́з.

talent *n* тала́нт. **talented** *adj* тала́нт-
ливый.

talk *vi* разгова́ривать *impf* (**to, with**
с+*instr*); (*gossip*) спле́тничать *impf*,
на~ *pf*; *vt & i* говори́ть *impf*, по~
pf; ~ **down to** говори́ть свы-
сока́ с+*instr*; ~ **into** угова́ривать
impf, уговори́ть *pf* +*inf*; ~ **out of**
отгова́ривать *impf*, отговори́ть *pf*
+*inf*, от+*gen*; ~ **over** (*discuss*) об-
сужда́ть *impf*, обсуди́ть *pf*; ~ **round**
(*persuade*) переубежда́ть *impf*, пе-
реубеди́ть *pf*; *n* (*conversation*) раз-
гово́р; (*lecture*) бесе́да; *pl* перего-
во́ры (-ров) *pl*. **talkative** *adj* раз-
гово́рчивый; (*derog*) болтли́вый.

talker *n* говоря́щий *sb*; (*chatterer*)
болту́н (*coll*); (*orator*) ора́тор. **talk-
ing-to** *n* (*coll*) вы́говор.

tall *adj* высо́кий; (*in measurements*)
ро́стом в+*acc*.

tally *n* (*score*) счёт; *vi* соотве́тство-
вать (**with** +*dat*).

talon *n* ко́готь *m*.

tambourine *n* бу́бен.

tame *adj* ручно́й; (*insipid*) пре́сный;
vt прируча́ть *impf*, приручи́ть *pf*.
tamer *n* укроти́тель *m*.

tamper *vi*: ~ **with** (*meddle*) тро́гать
impf, тро́нуть *pf*; (*forge*) подде́лы-
вать *impf*, подде́лать *pf*.

tampon *n* тампо́н.

tan *n* (*sun~*) зага́р; *adj* желтова́то-
кори́чневый; *vt* (*hide*) дуби́ть *impf*,
вы́~ *pf*; (*beat*) (*coll*) выбдаси́ть *impf*,
от~ *pf*; *vi* загора́ть *impf*, загоре́ть
pf; (*of sun*): **tanned** загоре́лый.

tang *n* (*taste*) ре́зкий при́вкус;
(*smell*) о́стрый за́пах.

tangent *n* (*math*) каса́тельная *sb*;
(*trigonometry*) та́нгенс; **go off at a**
~ отклоня́ться *impf*, отклони́ться
pf от те́мы.

tangerine *n* мандари́н.

tangible *adj* осяза́емый.

tangle *vt & i* запу́тывать(ся) *impf*,
запу́таться *pf*; *n* пу́таница.

tango *n* та́нго *neut indecl*.

tangy *adj* о́стрый; ре́зкий.

tank *n* бак; (*mil*) танк.

tankard *n* кру́жка.

tanker *n* (*sea*) та́нкер; (*road*) авто-
цисте́рна.

tantalize *vt* дразни́ть *impf*.

tantamount *predic* равноси́лен (-льна)
(**to** +*dat*).

tantrum *n* при́ступ раздраже́ния.

tap[1] *n* кран; *vt* (*resources*) испо́ль-
зовать *impf & pf*; (*telephone conversation*) подслу́шивать *impf*.

tap[2] *n* (*knock*) стук; *vt* стуча́ть *impf*,
по~ *pf* в+*acc*, по+*dat*; ~**-dance** (*vi*)
отбива́ть *impf*, отби́ть *pf* чечётку;
(*n*) чечётка; ~**-dancer** чечёточник,
-ица.

tape *n* (*cotton strip*) тесьма́; (*adhesive, magnetic, measuring, etc.*) ле́н-
та; ~**-measure** руле́тка; ~ **recorder**
магнитофо́н; ~ **recording** за́пись; *vt*
(*seal*) закле́ивать *impf*, закле́ить *pf*;
(*record*) запи́сывать *impf*, записа́ть
pf на ле́нту.

taper *vt & i* су́живать(ся) *impf*, су́-
зить(ся) *pf*.

tapestry *n* гобеле́н.

tar *n* дёготь *m*.

tardy *adj* (*slow*) медли́тельный; (*late*)
запозда́лый.

target *n* мише́нь, цель.

tariff *n* тари́ф.

tarmac *n* (*material*) гудро́н; (*road*)
гудрони́рованное шоссе́ *neut indecl*;
(*runway*) бетони́рованная площа́д-
ка; *vt* гудрони́ровать *impf & pf*.

tarnish *vt* де́лать *impf*, с~ *pf* ту́ск-
лым; (*fig*) пятна́ть *impf*, за~ *pf*; *vi*
тускне́ть *impf*, по~ *pf*.

tarpaulin *n* брезе́нт.

tarragon *n* эстраго́н.

tart[1] *adj* (*taste*) ки́слый; (*fig*) ко́лкий.

tart[2] *n* (*pie*) сла́дкий пиро́г.

tart[3] *n* (*prostitute*) шлю́ха.

tartan *n* шотла́ндка.

tartar *n* ви́нный ка́мень *m*.

task *n* зада́ча; **take to** ~ де́лать *impf*,
с~ *pf* вы́говор+*dat*; ~ **force** опера-
ти́вная гру́ппа.

Tass *abbr* ТАСС, Телегра́фное
аге́нтство Сове́тского Сою́за.

tassel *n* ки́сточка.

taste *n* (*also fig*) вкус; **take a** ~ **of**
про́бовать *impf*, по~ *pf*; *vt* чу́вст-
вовать *impf*, по~ *pf* вкус+*gen*;

(*sample*) про́бовать *impf*, по~ *pf*; (*fig*) вкуша́ть *impf*, вкуси́ть *pf*; (*wine etc.*) дегусти́ровать *impf & pf*; *vi* име́ть *impf* вкус, при́вкус (*of* +*gen*). **tasteful** *adj* (сде́ланный) со вку́сом. **tasteless** *adj* безвку́сный. **tasting** *n* дегуста́ция. **tasty** *adj* вку́сный.

tatter *n pl* лохмо́тья (-ьев) *pl*. **tattered** *adj* обо́рванный.

tattoo *n* (*design*) татуиро́вка; *vt* татуи́ровать *impf & pf*.

taunt *n* насме́шка; *vt* насмеха́ться *impf* над+*instr*.

Taurus *n* Теле́ц.

taut *adj* ту́го натя́нутый; тугой.

tavern *n* таве́рна.

tawdry *adj* мишу́рный.

tawny *adj* рыжева́то-кори́чневый.

tax *n* нало́г; ~-**free** освобождённый от нало́га; *vt* облага́ть *impf*, обложи́ть *pf* нало́гом; (*strain*) напряга́ть *impf*, напря́чь *pf*; (*patience*) испы́тывать *impf*, испыта́ть *pf*. **taxable** *adj* подлежа́щий обложе́нию нало́гом. **taxation** *n* обложе́ние нало́гом. **taxing** *adj* утоми́тельный. **taxpayer** *n* налогоплате́льщик.

taxi *n* такси́ *neut indecl*; ~-**driver** води́тель *m* такси́; ~-**rank** стоя́нка такси́; *vi* (*aeron*) рули́ть *impf*.

tea *n* чай; ~ **bag** паке́тик с сухи́м ча́ем; ~ **cloth**, ~ **towel** полоте́нце для посу́ды; ~ **cosy** чехо́льчик (для ча́йника); ~-**cup** ча́йная ча́шка; ~-**leaf** ча́йный лист; ~-**pot** ча́йник; ~**spoon** ча́йная ло́жка; ~ **strainer** ча́йное си́течко.

teach *vt* учи́ть *impf*, на~ *pf* (*person* +*acc*; *subject* +*dat, inf*); преподава́ть *impf* (*subject* +*acc*); (*coll*) проучи́вать *impf*, проучи́ть *pf*. **teacher** *n* учи́тель *m*, ~ница; преподава́тель *m*, ~ница; ~-**training college** педагоги́ческий институ́т. **teaching** *n* (*instruction*) обуче́ние; (*doctrine*) уче́ние.

teak *n* тик; *attrib* ти́ковый.

team *n* (*sport*) кома́нда; (*of people*) брига́да; (*of horses etc.*) упря́жка; ~-**mate** член той же кома́нды; ~**work** сотру́дничество; *vi* (~ **up**) объединя́ться *impf*, объедини́ться *pf*.

tear[1] *n* (*rent*) проре́ха; *vt* (*also* ~ **up**) рвать *impf*; (*also* ~ **up**) разрыва́ть

impf, разорва́ть *pf*; *vi* рва́ться *impf*; (*rush*) мча́ться *impf*; ~ **down, off** срыва́ть *impf*, сорва́ть *pf*; ~ **out** вырыва́ть *impf*, вы́рвать *pf*.

tear[2] *n* (~-*drop*) слеза́; ~-**gas** слезоточи́вый газ. **tearful** *adj* слезли́вый.

tease *vt* дразни́ть *impf*.

teat *n* сосо́к.

technical *adj* техни́ческий; ~ **college** техни́ческое учи́лище. **technicality** *n* форма́льность. **technically** *adv* (*strictly*) форма́льно. **technician** *n* те́хник. **technique** *n* те́хника; (*method*) ме́тод. **technology** *n* техноло́гия, те́хника. **technological** *adj* технологи́ческий. **technologist** *n* техно́лог.

teddy-bear *n* медвежо́нок.

tedious *adj* ску́чный. **tedium** *n* ску́ка.

teem[1] *vi* (*swarm*) кише́ть *impf* (**with** +*instr*).

teem[2] *vi*: **it is** ~**ing** (**with rain**) дождь льёт как из ведра́.

teenage *adj* ю́ношеский. **teenager** *n* подро́сток. **teens** *n pl* во́зраст от трина́дцати до девятна́дцати лет.

teeter *vi* кача́ться *impf*, качну́ться *pf*.

teethe *vi*: **the child is teething** у ребёнка проре́зываются зу́бы; **teething troubles** (*fig*) нача́льные пробле́мы *f pl*.

teetotal *adj* тре́звый. **teetotaller** *n* тре́звенник.

telecommunication(s) *n* да́льняя связь. **telegram** *n* телегра́мма. **telegraph** *n* телегра́ф; ~ **pole** телегра́фный столб. **telepathic** *adj* телепати́ческий. **telepathy** *n* телепа́тия. **telephone** *n* телефо́н; *vt* (*message*) телефони́ровать *impf & pf* +*acc*, о+*prep*; (*person*) звони́ть *impf*, по~ *pf* (по телефо́ну) +*dat*; ~ **box** телефо́нная бу́дка; ~ **directory** телефо́нная кни́га; ~ **exchange** телефо́нная ста́нция; ~ **number** но́мер телефо́на. **telephonist** *n* телефони́ст, ~ка. **telephoto lens** *n* телеобъекти́в. **telescope** *n* телеско́п. **telescopic** *adj* телескопи́ческий. **televise** *vt* пока́зывать *impf*, показа́ть *pf* по телеви́дению. **television** *n* телеви́дение; (*set*) телеви́зор; *attrib* телевизио́нный. **telex** *n* те́лекс.

tell *vt & i* (*relate*) расска́зывать *impf*,

рассказа́ть *pf* (*thing told* +*acc,* o*+prep; person told* +*dat*); *vt* (*utter, inform*) говори́ть *impf,* сказа́ть *pf* (*thing uttered* +*acc; thing informed about* o*+prep; person informed* +*dat*); (*order*) веле́ть *impf* & *pf* +*dat;* ~ **one thing from another** отлича́ть *impf,* отличи́ть *pf* +*acc* от+*gen; vi* (*have an effect*) ска́зываться *impf,* сказа́ться *pf* (**on** на+*prep*); ~ **off** отчи́тывать *impf,* отчита́ть *pf;* ~ **on,** ~ **tales about** я́бедничать *impf,* на~ *pf* на+*acc.* **teller** *n* (*of story*) расска́зчик; (*of votes*) счётчик; (*in bank*) касси́р. **telling** *adj* (*effective*) эффекти́вный; (*significant*) многозначи́тельный. **telltale** *n* спле́тник; *adj* преда́тельский.

temerity *n* дёрзость.

temp *n* рабо́тающий *sb* вре́менно; *vi* рабо́тать *impf* вре́менно.

temper *n* (*character*) нрав; (*mood*) настрое́ние; (*anger*) гнев; **lose one's** ~ выходи́ть *impf,* вы́йти *pf* из себя́; *vt* (*fig*) смягча́ть *impf,* смягчи́ть *pf.*

temperament *n* темпера́мент. **temperamental** *adj* темпера́ментный.

temperance *n* (*moderation*) уме́ренность; (*sobriety*) тре́звенность. **temperate** *adj* уме́ренный.

temperature *n* температу́ра; (*high* ~) повы́шенная температу́ра; **take s.o.'s** ~ измеря́ть *impf,* изме́рить *pf* температу́ру +*dat.*

tempest *n* бу́ря. **tempestuous** *adj* бу́рный.

template *n* шаблон.

temple[1] *n* (*religion*) храм.

temple[2] *n* (*anat*) висо́к.

tempo *n* темп.

temporal *adj* (*of time*) временно́й; (*secular*) мирско́й.

temporary *adj* вре́менный.

tempt *vt* соблазня́ть *impf,* соблазни́ть *pf;* ~ **fate** испы́тывать *impf,* испыта́ть *pf* судьбу́. **temptation** *n* собла́зн. **tempting** *adj* соблазни́тельный.

ten *adj* & *n* де́сять; (*number 10*) деся́тка. **tenth** *adj* & *n* деся́тый.

tenable *adj* (*logical*) разу́мный.

tenacious *adj* це́пкий. **tenacity** *n* це́пкость.

tenancy *n* (*renting*) наём помеще́ния; (*period*) срок аре́нды. **tenant**

n аренда́тор.

tend[1] *vi* (*be apt*) име́ть скло́нность (**to** к+*dat,* +*inf*).

tend[2] *vt* (*look after*) уха́живать *impf* за+*instr.*

tendency *n* тенде́нция. **tendentious** *adj* тенденцио́зный.

tender[1] *vt* (*offer*) предлага́ть *impf,* предложи́ть *pf; vi* (*make* ~ **for**) подава́ть *impf,* пода́ть *pf* зая́вку (на торга́х); *n* предложе́ние; **legal** ~ зако́нное платёжное сре́дство.

tender[2] *adj* (*delicate, affectionate*) не́жный. **tenderness** *n* не́жность.

tendon *n* сухожи́лие.

tendril *n* у́сик.

tenement *n* (*dwelling-house*) жило́й дом; ~**house** многокварти́рный дом.

tenet *n* до́гмат, при́нцип.

tennis *n* те́ннис.

tenor *n* (*direction*) направле́ние; (*purport*) смысл; (*mus*) те́нор.

tense[1] *n* вре́мя *neut.*

tense[2] *vt* напряга́ть *impf,* напря́чь *pf; adj* напряжённый. **tension** *n* напряже́ние.

tent *n* пала́тка.

tentacle *n* щу́пальце.

tentative *adj* (*experimental*) про́бный; (*preliminary*) предвари́тельный.

tenterhooks *n pl:* **be on** ~ сиде́ть *impf* как на иго́лках.

tenth *see* **ten**

tenuous *adj* (*fig*) неубеди́тельный.

tenure *n* (*of property*) владе́ние; (*of office*) пребыва́ние в до́лжности; (*period*) срок; (*guaranteed employment*) несменя́емость.

tepid *adj* теплова́тый.

term *n* (*period*) срок; (*univ*) семе́стр; (*school*) че́тверть; (*technical word*) те́рмин; (*expression*) выраже́ние; *pl* (*conditions*) усло́вия *neut pl;* (*relations*) отноше́ния *neut pl;* **on good** ~**s** в хоро́ших отноше́ниях; **come to** ~**s with** (*resign o.s. to*) покоря́ться *impf,* покори́ться *pf* к+*dat; vt* называ́ть *impf,* назва́ть *pf.*

terminal *adj* коне́чный; (*med*) сме́ртельный; *n* (*electr*) зажи́м; (*computer, aeron*) термина́л; (*terminus*) коне́чная остано́вка.

terminate *vt* & *i* конча́ть(ся) *impf,* ко́нчить(ся) *pf* (**in** +*instr*). **termination** *n* прекраще́ние.

terminology *n* терминоло́гия.

terminus *n* коне́чная остано́вка.

termite *n* терми́т.

terrace *n* терра́са; (*houses*) ряд домо́в.

terracotta *n* террако́та.

terrain *n* ме́стность.

terrestrial *adj* земно́й.

terrible *adj* ужа́сный. **terribly** *adv* ужа́сно.

terrier *n* терье́р.

terrific *adj* (*huge*) огро́мный; (*splendid*) потряса́ющий. **terrify** *vt* ужаса́ть *impf*, ужасну́ть *pf*.

territorial *adj* территориа́льный. **territory** *n* террито́рия.

terror *n* у́жас; (*person; polit*) терро́р. **terrorism** *n* террори́зм. **terrorist** *n* террори́ст, ~ка. **terrorize** *vt* терроризи́ровать *impf* & *pf*.

terse *adj* кра́ткий.

tertiary *adj* трети́чный; (*education*) вы́сший.

test *n* испыта́ние, про́ба; (*exam*) экза́мен; контро́льная рабо́та; (*analysis*) ана́лиз; ~-tube проби́рка; *vt* (*try out*) испы́тывать *impf*, испыта́ть *pf*; (*check up on*) проверя́ть *impf*, прове́рить *pf*; (*give exam to*) экзаменова́ть *impf*, про~ *pf*.

testament *n* завеща́ние; **Old, New T~** Ве́тхий, Но́вый заве́т.

testicle *n* я́ичко.

testify *vi* свиде́тельствовать *impf* (**to** в по́льзу+*gen*; **against** про́тив+*gen*); *vt* (*declare*) заявля́ть *impf*, заяви́ть *pf*; (*be evidence of*) свиде́тельствовать о+*prep*.

testimonial *n* рекоменда́ция, характери́стика. **testimony** *n* свиде́тельство.

tetanus *n* столбня́к.

tetchy *adj* раздражи́тельный.

tête-à-tête *n* & *adv* тет-а-те́т.

tether *n*: **be at, come to the end of one's ~** дойти́ *pf* до то́чки; *vt* привя́зывать *impf*, привяза́ть *pf*.

text *n* текст. **textbook** *n* уче́бник.

textile *adj* тексти́льный; *n* ткань; *pl* тексти́ль *m* (*collect*).

textual *adj* текстово́й.

texture *n* тексту́ра.

than *conj* (*comparison*) чем; **other ~** (*except*) кро́ме+*gen*.

thank *vt* благодари́ть *impf*, по~ *pf* (**for** за+*acc*); **~ God** сла́ва Бо́гу; ~ **you** спаси́бо; благодарю́ вас; *n pl* благода́рность; **~s to** (*good result*) благодаря́ +*dat*; (*bad result*) из-за+*gen*. **thankful** *adj* благода́рный. **thankless** *adj* неблагода́рный. **thanksgiving** *n* благодаре́ние.

that *demonstrative adj & pron* тот; ~ **which** тот кото́рый; *rel pron* кото́рый; *conj* что; (*purpose*) что́бы; *adv* так, до тако́й сте́пени.

thatched *adj* соло́менный.

thaw *vt* раста́пливать *impf*, растопи́ть *pf*; *vi* та́ять *impf*, рас~ *pf*.

the *def article, not translated*; *adv* тем; **the ... the ...** чем...тем; **~ more ~ better** чем бо́льше, тем лу́чше.

theatre *n* теа́тр; (*lecture ~*) аудито́рия; (*operating ~*) операцио́нная *sb*; **~-goer** театра́л. **theatrical** *adj* театра́льный.

theft *n* кра́жа.

their, theirs *poss pron* их; свой.

theme *n* те́ма.

themselves *pron* (*emph*) (они́) са́ми; (*refl*) себя́; -ся (*suffixed to vt*).

then *adv* (*at that time*) тогда́; (*after that*) пото́м; **now and ~** вре́мя от вре́мени; *conj* в тако́м слу́чае, тогда́; *adj* тогда́шний; **by ~** к тому́ вре́мени; **since ~** с тех пор.

thence *adv* отту́да. **thenceforth, -forward** *adv* с того́/э́того вре́мени.

theologian *n* тео́лог. **theological** *adj* теологи́ческий. **theology** *n* теоло́гия.

theorem *n* теоре́ма. **theoretical** *adj* теорети́ческий. **theorize** *vi* теоретизи́ровать *impf*. **theory** *n* тео́рия.

therapeutic *adj* терапевти́ческий. **therapist** *n* (*psychotherapist*) психотерапе́вт. **therapy** *n* терапи́я.

there *adv* (*place*) там; (*direction*) туда́; *int* вот!; ну!; **~ is** есть, име́ется (-́ются); **~ you are** (*on giving sth*) пожа́луйста. **thereabouts** *adv* (*near*) побли́зости; (*approximately*) приблизи́тельно. **thereafter** *adv* по́сле э́того. **thereby** *adv* таки́м о́бразом. **therefore** *adv* поэ́тому. **therein** *adv* в э́том. **thereupon** *adv* зате́м.

thermal *adj* теплово́й, терми́ческий; (*underwear*) тёплый.

thermometer *n* термо́метр, гра́дусник. **thermos** *n* те́рмос. **thermostat**

n термоста́т.

thesis *n* (*proposition*) те́зис; (*dissertation*) диссерта́ция.

they *pron* они́.

thick *adj* то́лстый, (*in measurements*) толщино́й в+*acc*; (*dense*) густо́й; (*stupid*) тупо́й; ~-**skinned** толстоко́жий. **thicken** *vt* & *i* утолща́ть(ся) *impf*, утолсти́ть(ся) *pf*; (*make, become denser*) сгуща́ть(ся) *impf*, сгусти́ть(ся) *pf*; *vi* (*become more intricate*) усложня́ться *impf*, усложни́ться *pf*. **thicket** *n* ча́ща. **thickness** *n* (*also dimension*) толщина́; (*density*) густота́; (*layer*) слой. **thickset** *adj* корена́стый.

thief *n* вор. **thieve** *vi* ворова́ть *impf*. **thievery** *n* воровство́.

thigh *n* бедро́.

thimble *n* напёрсток.

thin *adj* (*slender*; *not thick*) то́нкий; (*lean*) худо́й; (*too liquid*) жи́дкий; (*sparse*) ре́дкий; *vt* & *i* де́лать(ся) *impf*, с~ *pf* то́нким, жи́дким; *vi*: (*also* ~ *out*) реде́ть *impf*, по~ *pf*; *vt*: ~ **out** проре́живать *impf*, прореди́ть *pf*.

thing *n* вещь; (*object*) предме́т; (*matter*) де́ло.

think *vt* & *i* ду́мать *impf*, по~ *pf* (**about, of** о+*prep*); (*consider*) счита́ть *impf*, счесть *pf* (**to be** +*instr*, за+*acc*; **that** что); *vi* (*reflect, reason*) мы́слить *impf*; (*intend*) намерева́ться *impf* (*of doing* +*inf*); ~ **out** проду́мывать *impf*, проду́мать *pf*; ~ **over** обду́мывать *impf*, обду́мать *pf*; ~ **up, of** приду́мывать *impf*, приду́мать *pf*. **thinker** *n* мысли́тель *m*. **thinking** *adj* мы́слящий; *n* (*reflection*) размышле́ние; **to my way of** ~ по моему́ мне́нию.

third *adj* & *n* тре́тий; (*fraction*) треть; **T~ World** стра́ны *f pl* тре́тьего ми́ра.

thirst *n* жа́жда (**for** +*gen* (*fig*)); (*fig*) жа́ждать *impf* (**for** +*gen*). **thirsty** *adj*: **be** ~ хоте́ть *impf* пить.

thirteen *adj* & *n* трина́дцать. **thirteenth** *adj* & *n* трина́дцатый.

thirtieth *adj* & *n* тридца́тый. **thirty** *adj* & *n* три́дцать; *pl* (*decade*) тридца́тые го́ды (-до́в) *m pl*.

this *demonstrative adj* & *pron* э́тот; **like** ~ вот так; ~ **morning** сего́дня у́тром.

thistle *n* чертополо́х.

thither *adv* туда́.

thorn *n* шип. **thorny** *adj* колю́чий; (*fig*) терни́стый.

thorough *adj* основа́тельный; (*complete*) соверше́нный. **thoroughbred** *adj* чистокро́вный. **thoroughfare** *n* прое́зд; (*walking*) прохо́д. **thoroughgoing** *adj* радика́льный. **thoroughly** *adv* (*completely*) соверше́нно. **thoroughness** *n* основа́тельность.

though *conj* хотя́; несмотря́ на то, что; **as** ~ как бу́дто; *adv* одна́ко.

thought *n* мысль; (*meditation*) размышле́ние; (*intention*) наме́рение; *pl* (*opinion*) мне́ние. **thoughtful** *adj* заду́мчивый; (*considerate*) внима́тельный. **thoughtless** *adj* необду́манный; (*inconsiderate*) невнима́тельный.

thousand *adj* & *n* ты́сяча. **thousandth** *adj* & *n* ты́сячный.

thrash *vt* бить *impf*, по~ *pf*; ~ **out** (*discuss*) обстоя́тельно обсужда́ть *impf*, обсуди́ть *pf*; *vi*: ~ **about** мета́ться *impf*. **thrashing** *n* (*beating*) взбу́чка (*coll*).

thread *n* ни́тка, нить (*also fig*); (*of screw etc.*) резьба́; *vt* (*needle*) продева́ть *impf*, проде́ть *pf* ни́тку в +*acc*; (*beads*) нани́зывать *impf*, наниза́ть *pf*; ~ **one's way** пробира́ться *impf*, пробра́ться *pf* (**through** че́рез+*acc*). **threadbare** *adj* потёртый.

threat *n* угро́за. **threaten** *vt* угрожа́ть *impf*, грози́ть *impf*, по~ *pf* (*person* +*dat*; **with** +*instr*; *to do* +*inf*).

three *adj* & *n* три; (*number 3*) тро́йка; ~-**dimensional** трёхме́рный; ~**quarters** три че́тверти. **threefold** *adj* тройно́й; *adv* втро́йне. **threesome** *n* тро́йка.

thresh *vt* молоти́ть *impf*.

threshold *n* поро́г.

thrice *adv* три́жды.

thrift *n* бережли́вость. **thrifty** *adj* бережли́вый.

thrill *n* тре́пет; *vt* восхища́ть *impf*, восхити́ть *pf*; **be thrilled** быть в восто́рге. **thriller** *n* приключе́нческий, детекти́вный (*novel*) рома́н, (*film*) фильм. **thrilling** *adj* захва́тывающий.

thrive *vi* процвета́ть *impf*.

throat *n* го́рло.

throb *vi* (*heart*) си́льно би́ться *impf*; пульси́ровать *impf*; *n* бие́ние; пульса́ция.

throes *n pl*: in the ~ в мучи́тельных попы́тках.

thrombosis *n* тромбо́з.

throne *n* трон, престо́л; come to the ~ вступа́ть *impf*, вступи́ть *pf* на престо́л.

throng *n* толпа́; *vi* толпи́ться *impf*; *vt* заполня́ть *impf*, запо́лнить *pf*.

throttle *n* (*tech*) дро́ссель *m*; *vt* (*strangle*) души́ть *impf*, за~ *pf*; (*tech*) дроссели́ровать *impf* & *pf*; ~ **down** сбавля́ть *impf*, сба́вить *pf* газ.

through *prep* (*across, via, ~ opening*) че́рез+*acc*; (*esp ~ thick of*) сквозь+*acc*; (*air, streets etc.*) по+*dat*; (*agency*) посре́дством+*gen*; (*reason*) из-за+*gen*; *adv* наскво́зь; (*from beginning to end*) до конца́; be ~ with (*sth*) ока́нчивать *impf*, око́нчить *pf* (*s.o.*) порыва́ть *impf*, порва́ть *pf* с+*instr*; put ~ (*on telephone*) соединя́ть *impf*, соедини́ть *pf*; ~ and ~ совершённо; *adj* (*train*) прямо́й; (*traffic*) сквозно́й. **throughout** *adv* повсю́ду, во всех отноше́ниях; *prep* по всему́ (всей, всему)+*dat*; *pl* всем)+*dat*; (*from beginning to end*) с нача́ла до конца́+*gen*.

throw *n* бросо́к; *vt* броса́ть *impf*, бро́сить *pf*; (*confuse*) смуща́ть *impf*, смути́ть *pf*; (*rider*) сбра́сывать *impf*, сбро́сить *pf*; (*party*) устра́ивать *impf*, устро́ить *pf*; ~ o.s. into броса́ться *impf*, бро́ситься *pf* в+*acc*; ~ **away, out** выбра́сывать *impf*, вы́бросить *pf*; ~ **down** сбра́сывать *impf*, сбро́сить *pf*; ~ **in** (*add*) добавля́ть *impf*, доба́вить *pf*; (*sport*) вбра́сывать *impf*, вбро́сить *pf*; ~ **in** вбра́сывание мяча́; ~ **off** сбра́сывать *impf*, сбро́сить *pf*; ~ **open** распа́хивать *impf*, распахну́ть *pf*; ~ **out** (*see also* ~ *away*) (*expel*) выгоня́ть *impf*, вы́гнать *pf*; (*reject*) отверга́ть *impf*, отве́ргнуть *pf*; ~ **over, up** (*abandon*) броса́ть *impf*, бро́сить *pf*; ~ **up** подбра́сывать *impf*, подбро́сить *pf*; (*vomit*) рвать *impf*, вы́~ *pf impers*; he threw up его́ вы́рвало.

thrush *n* (*bird*) дрозд.

thrust *n* (*shove*) толчо́к; (*tech*) тя́га; *vt* (*shove*) толка́ть *impf*, толкну́ть *pf*; (~ *into, out of*; *give quickly, carelessly*) сова́ть *impf*, су́нуть *pf*.

thud *n* глухо́й звук; *vi* па́дать *impf*, *pf* с глухи́м сту́ком.

thug *n* головоре́з (*coll*).

thumb *n* большо́й па́лец; **under the** ~ **of** под башмако́м у+*gen*; *vt*: ~ **through** перели́стывать *impf*, перелиста́ть *pf*; ~ **a lift** голосова́ть *impf*, про~ *pf*.

thump *n* (*blow*) тяжёлый уда́р; (*thud*) глухо́й звук, стук; *vt* колоти́ть *impf*, по~ *pf* в+*acc*, по+*dat*; *vi* колоти́ться *impf*.

thunder *n* гром; *vi* греме́ть *impf*; **it thunders** гром греми́т. **thunderbolt** *n* уда́р мо́лнии. **thunderous** *adj* громово́й. **thunderstorm** *n* гроза́. **thundery** *adj* грозово́й.

Thursday *n* четве́рг.

thus *adv* так, таки́м о́бразом.

thwart *vt* меша́ть *impf*, по~ *pf* +*dat*; (*plans*) расстра́ивать *impf*, расстро́ить *pf*.

thyme *n* тимья́н.

thyroid *n* (~ *gland*) щитови́дная железа́.

tiara *n* тиа́ра.

tick *n* (*noise*) ти́канье; (*mark*) пти́чка; *vi* ти́кать *impf*, ти́кнуть *pf*; *vt* отмеча́ть *impf*, отме́тить *pf* пти́чкой; ~ **off** (*scold*) отде́лывать *impf*, отде́лать *pf*.

ticket *n* биле́т; (*label*) ярлы́к; (*season* ~) ка́рточка; (*cloakroom* ~) номеро́к; (*receipt*) квита́нция; ~ **collector** контролёр; ~ **office** (биле́тная) ка́сса.

tickle *n* щеко́тка; *vt* щекота́ть *impf*, по~ *pf*; (*amuse*) весели́ть *impf*, по~, раз~ *pf*; *vi* щекота́ть *impf*, по~ *pf impers*; **my throat ~s** у меня́ щеко́чет в го́рле. **ticklish** *adj* (*fig*) щекотли́вый; **to be** ~ боя́ться *impf* щеко́тки.

tidal *adj* прили́во-отли́вный; ~ **wave** прили́вная волна́.

tide *n* прили́в и отли́в; **high** ~ прили́в; **low** ~ отли́в; (*current, tendency*) тече́ние; **the** ~ **turns** (*fig*) собы́тия принима́ют друго́й оборо́т; *vt*: ~ **over** помога́ть *impf*, помо́чь *pf* +*dat of person* спра́виться (*difficulty* c+*instr*); **will this money ~ you over?** вы протя́нете с э́тими деньга́ми?

tidiness *n* аккура́тность. **tidy** *adj* аккура́тный; (*considerable*) поря́дочный; *vt* убира́ть *impf*, убра́ть *pf*; приводи́ть *impf*, привести́ *pf* в поря́док.

tie *n* (*garment*) га́лстук; (*cord*) завя́зка; (*link*; *tech*) связь; (*equal points etc.*) ра́вный счёт; **end in a ~** зака́нчиваться *impf*, зако́нчиться *pf* вничью́; (*burden*) обу́за; *pl* (*bonds*) у́зы (уз) *pl*; *vt* свя́зывать *impf*, связа́ть *pf* (*also fig*); (**~ up**) завя́зывать *impf*, завяза́ть *pf*; (*restrict*) ограни́чивать *impf*, ограни́чить *pf*; **~ down** (*fasten*) привя́зывать *impf*, привяза́ть *pf*; **~ up** (*tether*) привя́зывать *impf*, привяза́ть *pf*; (*parcel*) перевя́зывать *impf*, перевяза́ть *pf*; *vi* (*be ~d*) завя́зываться *impf*, завяза́ть *pf*; (*sport*) сыгра́ть *pf* вничью́; **~ in, up, with** совпада́ть *impf*, совпа́сть *pf* c+*instr*.

tier *n* ряд, я́рус.

tiff *n* размо́лвка.

tiger *n* тигр.

tight *adj* (*cramped*) те́сный; у́зкий; (*strict*) стро́гий; (*taut*) туго́й; **~ corner** (*fig*) тру́дное положе́ние. **tighten** *vt & i* натя́гиваться *impf*, натяну́ться *pf*; (*clench, contract*) сжима́ть(ся) *impf*, сжа́ть(ся) *pf*; **~ one's belt** поту́же затя́гивать *impf*, затяну́ть *pf* по́яс (*also fig*); **~ up** (*discipline etc.*) подтя́гивать *impf*, подтяну́ть *pf* (*coll*). **tightly** *adv* (*strongly*) про́чно; (*closely, cramped*) те́сно.

tightrope *n* натя́нутый кана́т. **tights** *n pl* колго́тки (-ток) *pl.*

tile *n* (*roof*) черепи́ца (*also collect*); (*decorative*) ка́фель *m* (*also collect*); *vt* крыть *impf*, по~ *pf* черепи́цей, ка́фелем. **tiled** *adj* (*roof*) черепи́чный; (*floor*) ка́фельный.

till[1] *prep* до+*gen*; **not ~** то́лько (**Friday** в пя́тницу; **the next day** на сле́дующий день); *conj* пока́ не; **not ~ только когда́.**

till[2] *n* ка́сса.

till[3] *vt* возде́лывать *impf*, возде́лать *pf.*

tiller *n* (*naut*) ру́мпель *m.*

tilt *n* накло́н; **at full ~** по́лным хо́дом;

vt & i наклоня́ть(ся) *impf*, наклони́ть(ся) *pf*; (*heel* (*over*)) крени́ть(ся) *impf*, на~ *pf.*

timber *n* лесоматериа́л.

time *n* вре́мя *neut*; (*occasion*) раз; (*mus*) такт; (*sport*) тайм; *pl* (*period*) времена́ *pl*; (*in comparison*) раз; **five ~s as big** в пять раз бо́льше; (*multiplication*) **four ~s** four четы́режды четы́ре; **~ and ~ again, ~ after ~** не раз, ты́сячу раз; **at a ~** ра́зом, одновреме́нно; **at the ~** в э́то вре́мя; **at ~s** времена́ми; **at the same ~** в то же вре́мя; **before my ~** до меня́; **for a long ~** до́лго; (*up to now*) давно́; **for the ~ being** пока́; **from ~ to ~** вре́мя от вре́мени; **in ~** (*early enough*) во́-время; (*with ~*) со вре́менем; **in good ~** заблаговре́менно; **in ~ with** в такт +*dat*; **in no ~** момента́льно; **on ~** во́-время; **one at a ~** по одному́; **be in ~** успева́ть *impf*, успе́ть *pf* (**for** к+*dat*; на+*acc*); **have ~ to** (*manage*) успева́ть *impf*, успе́ть *pf* +*inf*; **have a good ~** хорошо́ проводи́ть *impf*, провести́ *pf* вре́мя; **it is ~** пора́ (**to** +*inf*); **what is the ~?** кото́рый час?; **~ bomb** бо́мба заме́дленного де́йствия; **~-consuming** отнима́ющий мно́го вре́мени; **~ difference** ра́зница во вре́мени; **~-lag** отстава́ние во вре́мени; **~ zone** часово́й по́яс; *vt* (*choose ~*) выбира́ть *impf*, вы́брать *pf* вре́мя +*gen*; (*ascertain ~ of*) измеря́ть *impf*, изме́рить *pf* вре́мя +*gen*. **~less** *adj* ве́чный. **timely** *adj* своевре́менный. **timetable** *n* расписа́ние; гра́фик.

timid *adj* ро́бкий.

tin *n* (*metal*) о́лово; (*container*) ба́нка; (*cake-~*) фо́рма; (*baking ~*) про́тивень *m*; **~ foil** оловя́нная фольга́; **~-opener** консе́рвный нож; **~ned food** консе́рвы (-вов) *pl.*

tinge *n* отте́нок; *vt* (*also fig*) слегка́ окра́шивать *impf*, окра́сить *pf.*

tingle *vi* (*sting*) коло́ть *impf impers*; **my fingers ~** у меня́ ко́лет па́льцы; **his nose ~d with the cold** моро́з пощи́пывал ему́ нос; (*burn*) горе́ть *impf.*

tinker *vi*: **~ with** вози́ться *impf* c+*instr.*

tinkle *n* звон, звя́канье; *vi* (*& t*) звене́ть *impf* (+*instr*).

tinsel *n* мишура.

tint *n* оттéнок; *vt* подкрáшивать *impf*, подкрáсить *pf*.

tiny *adj* крóшечный.

tip[1] *n* (*end*) кóнчик.

tip[2] *n* (*money*) чаевы́е (-ы́х) *pl*; (*advice*) совéт; (*dump*) свáлка; *vt & i* (*tilt*) наклоня́ть(ся) *impf*, наклони́ть(ся) *pf*; (*give* ~) давáть *impf*, дать *pf* (*person +dat*; *money* дéньги на чай, *information* чáстную информáцию); ~ **out** вывáливать *impf*, вы́валить *pf*; ~ **over**, **up** (*vt & i*) опроки́дывать(ся) *impf*, опроки́нуть(ся) *pf*.

Tippex *n* (*propr*) бели́ла.

tipple *n* напи́ток.

tipsy *adj* подвы́пивший.

tiptoe *n*: **on** ~ на цы́почках.

tip-top *adj* превосхóдный.

tirade *n* тирáда.

tire *vt* (*weary*) утомля́ть *impf*, утоми́ть *pf*; *vi* утомля́ться *impf*, утоми́ться *pf*. **tired** *adj* устáлый; **be** ~ **of**: **I am** ~ **of him** он мне надоéл; **I am** ~ **of playing** мне надоéло игрáть; ~ **out** изму́ченный. **tiredness** *n* устáлость. **tireless** *adj* неутоми́мый. **tiresome** *adj* надоéдливый. **tiring** *adj* утоми́тельный.

tissue *n* ткань; (*handkerchief*) бумáжная салфéтка. **tissue-paper** *n* папирóсная бумáга.

tit[1] *n* (*bird*) сини́ца.

tit[2] *n*: ~ **for tat** зуб за́ зуб.

titbit *n* лáкомый кусóк; (*news*) пикáнтная нóвость.

titillate *vt* щекотáть *impf*, по~ *pf*.

title *n* (*of book etc.*) заглáвие; (*rank*) звáние; (*sport*) звáние чемпиóна; ~**holder** чемпиóн; ~**page** ти́тульный лист; ~ **role** заглáвная роль. **titled** *adj* титулóванный.

titter *n* хихи́канье; *vi* хихи́кать *impf*, хихи́кнуть *pf*.

to *prep* (*town, a country, theatre, school, etc.*) в+*acc*; (*the sea, the moon, the ground, post-office, meeting, concert, north, etc.*) на+*acc*; (*the doctor; towards; up* ~; *one's surprise etc.*) к+*dat*; (*with accompaniment of*) под+*acc*; (*in toast*) за+*acc*; (*time*) **ten minutes** ~ **three** без десяти́ три; (*compared with*) в сравнéнии с+*instr*; **it is ten** ~ **one that** дéвять из десяти́ за то, что; ~ **the left (right)** налéво (напрáво); (*in order to*) чтóбы+*inf*; *adv*: **shut the door** ~ закрóйте дверь; **come** ~ приходи́ть *impf*, прийти́ *pf* в сознáние; ~ **and fro** взад и вперёд.

toad *n* жáба. **toadstool** *n* погáнка.

toast *n* (*bread*) поджáренный хлеб; (*drink*) тост; *vt* (*bread*) поджáривать *impf*, поджáрить *pf*; (*drink*) пить *impf*, вы́~ *pf* за здорóвье +*gen*. **toaster** *n* тóстер.

tobacco *n* табáк. **tobacconist's** *n* (*shop*) табáчный магази́н.

toboggan *n* сáни (-нéй) *pl*; *vi* катáться *impf* на санáх.

today *adv* сегóдня; (*nowadays*) в нáши дни; *n* сегóдняшний день *m*; ~**'s newspaper** сегóдняшняя газéта.

toddler *n* малы́ш.

toe *n* пáлец ноги́; (*of sock etc.*) носóк; *vt*: ~ **the line** (*fig*) ходи́ть *indet* по стру́нке.

toffee *n* (*substance*) ири́с; (*a single* ~) ири́ска.

together *adv* вмéсте; (*simultaneously*) одноврéменно.

toil *n* тяжёлый труд; *vi* труди́ться *impf*.

toilet *n* туалéт; ~ **paper** туалéтная бумáга. **toiletries** *n pl* туалéтные принадлéжности *f pl*.

token *n* (*sign*) знак; (*coin substitute*) жетóн; **as a** ~ **of** в знак +*gen*; *attrib* символи́ческий.

tolerable *adj* терпи́мый; (*satisfactory*) удовлетвори́тельный. **tolerance** *n* терпи́мость. **tolerant** *adj* терпи́мый. **tolerate** *vt* терпéть *impf*, по~ *pf*; (*allow*) допускáть *impf*, допусти́ть *pf*. **toleration** *n* терпи́мость.

toll[1] *n* (*duty*) пóшлина; **take its** ~ скáзываться *impf*, сказáться *pf* (**on** на+*prep*).

toll[2] *vi* звони́ть *impf*, по~ *pf*.

tom(-cat) *n* кот.

tomato *n* помидóр; *attrib* томáтный.

tomb *n* моги́ла. **tombstone** *n* надгрóбный кáмень *m*.

tomboy *n* сорванéц.

tome *n* том.

tomorrow *adv* зáвтра; *n* зáвтрашний день *m*; ~ **morning** зáвтра у́тром; **the day after** ~ послезáвтра; **see you**

~ до за́втра.

ton *n* то́нна; (*pl, lots*) ма́сса.

tone *n* тон; *vt*: ~ **down** смягча́ть *impf*, смягчи́ть *pf*; ~ **up** тонизи́ровать *impf* & *pf*.

tongs *n* щипцы́ (-цо́в) *pl*.

tongue *n* язы́к; ~-**in-cheek** с насме́шкой, ирони́чески; ~-**tied** косноязы́чный; ~-**twister** скорогово́рка.

tonic *n* (*med*) тонизи́рующее сре́дство; (*mus*) то́ника; (*drink*) напи́ток «то́ник».

tonight *adv* сего́дня ве́чером.

tonnage *n* тонна́ж.

tonsil *n* минда́лина. **tonsillitis** *n* тонзилли́т.

too *adv* сли́шком; (*also*) та́кже, то́же; (*very*) о́чень; (*moreover*) к тому́ же; **none** ~ не сли́шком.

tool *n* инструме́нт; (*fig*) ору́дие.

toot *n* гудо́к; *vi* гуде́ть *impf*.

tooth *n* зуб; (*tech*) зубе́ц; *attrib* зубно́й; ~-**brush** зубна́я щётка. **toothache** *n* зубна́я боль. **toothless** *adj* беззу́бый. **toothpaste** *n* зубна́я па́ста. **toothpick** *n* зубочи́стка. **toothy** *adj* зуба́стый (*coll*).

top[1] *n* (*toy*) волчо́к.

top[2] *n* (*of object; fig*) верх; (*of hill etc.*) верши́на; (*of tree*) верху́шка; (*of head*) маку́шка; (*lid*) кры́шка; (*upper part*) ве́рхняя часть; ~ **hat** цили́ндр; ~-**heavy** переве́шивающий в свое́й ве́рхней ча́сти; ~-**secret** соверше́нно секре́тный; **on** ~ **of** (*position*) на+*prep*, сверх+*gen*; (*on to*) на+*acc*; **on** ~ **of everything** сверх всего́; **from** ~ **to bottom** све́рху до́низу; **at the** ~ **of one's voice** во весь го́лос; **at** ~ **speed** во весь опо́р; *adj* ве́рхний, вы́сший, са́мый высо́кий; (*foremost*) пе́рвый; *vt* (*cover*) покрыва́ть *impf*, покры́ть *pf*; (*exceed*) превосходи́ть *impf*, превзойти́ *pf*; (*cut* ~ *off*) обреза́ть *impf*, обре́зать *pf* верху́шку +*gen*; ~ **up** (*with liquid*) долива́ть *impf*, доли́ть *pf*.

topic *n* те́ма, предме́т. **topical** *adj* актуа́льный.

topless *adj* с обнажённой гру́дью.

topmost *adj* са́мый ве́рхний; са́мый ва́жный.

topographical *adj* топографи́ческий. **topography** *n* топогра́фия.

topple *vt* & *i* опроки́дывать(ся) *impf*, опроки́нуть(ся) *pf*.

topsy-turvy *adj* повёрнутый вверх дном; (*disorderly*) беспоря́дочный; *adv* вверх дном.

torch *n* электри́ческий фона́рь *m*; (*flaming*) фа́кел.

torment *n* муче́ние, му́ка; *vt* му́чить *impf*, за~, из~ *pf*.

tornado *n* торна́до *neut indecl*.

torpedo *n* торпе́да; *vt* торпеди́ровать *impf* & *pf*.

torrent *n* пото́к. **torrential** *adj* (*rain*) проливно́й.

torso *n* ту́ловище; (*art*) торс.

tortoise *n* черепа́ха. **tortoise-shell** *n* черепа́ха.

tortuous *adj* изви́листый.

torture *n* пы́тка; (*fig*) му́ка; *vt* пыта́ть *impf*; (*torment*) му́чить *impf*, за~, из~ *pf*.

toss *n* бросо́к; **win (lose) the** ~ (не) выпада́ть *impf*, вы́пасть *pf* жре́бий *impers* (**I won the** ~ мне вы́пал жре́бий); *vt* броса́ть *impf*, бро́сить *pf*; (*coin*) подбра́сывать *impf*, подбро́сить *pf*; (*head*) вски́дывать *impf*, вски́нуть *pf*; (*salad*) переме́шивать *impf*, перемеша́ть *pf*; *vi* (*in bed*) мета́ться *impf*; ~ **aside, away** отбра́сывать *impf*, отбро́сить *pf*; ~ **up** броса́ть *impf*, бро́сить *pf* жре́бий.

tot[1] *n* (*child*) малы́ш; (*of liquor*) глото́к.

tot[2]: ~ **up** (*vt*) скла́дывать *impf*, сложи́ть *pf*; (*vi*) равня́ться *impf* (**to** +*dat*).

total *n* ито́г, су́мма; *adj* о́бщий; (*complete*) по́лный; **in** ~ в це́лом, вме́сте; *vt* подсчи́тывать *impf*, подсчита́ть *pf*; *vi* равня́ться *impf* +*dat*.

totalitarian *adj* тоталита́рный. **totality** *n* вся су́мма целико́м; **the** ~ **of** весь. **totally** *adv* соверше́нно.

totter *vi* шата́ться *impf*.

touch *n* прикоснове́ние; (*sense*) осяза́ние; (*shade*) отте́нок; (*taste*) при́вкус; (*small amount*) чу́точка; (*of illness*) лёгкий при́ступ; **get in** ~ **with** свя́зываться *impf*, связа́ться *pf* с+*instr*; **keep in (lose)** ~ **with** подде́рживать *impf*, поддержа́ть *pf* (теря́ть *impf*, по~ *pf*) связь, конта́кт с+*instr*; **put the finishing**

~es to отде́лывать *impf*, отде́лать *pf*; *vt* (*lightly*) прикаса́ться *impf*, прикосну́ться *pf* к+*dat*; каса́ться *impf*, косну́ться *pf* +*gen*; (*also disturb*; *affect*) тро́гать *impf*, тро́нуть *pf*; (*be comparable with*) идти́ *impf* в сравне́нии с+*instr*; *vi* (*be contiguous*; *come into contact*) соприкаса́ться *impf*, соприкосну́ться *pf*; **~ down** приземля́ться *impf*, приземли́ться *pf*; **~down** поса́дка; **~ (up)on** (*fig*) каса́ться *impf*, косну́ться *pf* +*gen*; **~ up** поправля́ть *impf*, попра́вить *pf*. **touched** *adj* тро́нутый. **touchiness** *n* оби́дчивость. **touching** *adj* тро́гательный. **touchstone** *n* про́бный ка́мень *m*. **touchy** *adj* оби́дчивый.

tough *adj* жёсткий; (*durable*) про́чный; (*difficult*) тру́дный; (*hardy*) выно́сливый. **toughen** *vt & i* де́лать(ся) *impf*, с~ *pf* жёстким.

tour *n* (*journey*) путеше́ствие, пое́здка; (*excursion*) экску́рсия; (*of artistes*) гастро́ли *f pl*; (*of duty*) объе́зд; *vi* (*& t*) путеше́ствовать *impf* (по+*dat*); (*theat*) гастроли́ровать *impf*. **tourism** *n* тури́зм. **tourist** *n* тури́ст, ~ка.

tournament *n* турни́р.

tousle *vt* взъеро́шивать *impf*, взъеро́шить *pf* (*coll*).

tout *n* зазыва́ла *m*; (*ticket ~*) жучо́к.

tow *vt* букси́ровать *impf*; *n*: **on ~** на букси́ре.

towards *prep* к+*dat*.

towel *n* полоте́нце.

tower *n* ба́шня; *vi* вы́ситься *impf*, возвыша́ться *impf* (**above** над+*instr*).

town *n* го́род; *attrib* городско́й; **~ hall** ра́туша. **townsman** *n* горожа́нин.

toxic *adj* токси́ческий.

toy *n* игру́шка; *vi*: **~ with** (*sth in hands*) верте́ть *impf* в рука́х; (*trifle with*) игра́ть *impf* (с)+*instr*.

trace *n* след; *vt* (*track* (*down*)) высле́живать *impf*, вы́следить *pf*; (*copy*) кальки́ровать *impf*, с~ *pf*; **~ out** (*plan*) набра́сывать *impf*, наброса́ть *pf*; (*map*, *diagram*) черти́ть *impf*, на~ *pf*.

tracing-paper *n* ка́лька.

track *n* (*path*) доро́жка; (*mark*) след; (*rly*) путь *m*, (*sport*, *on tape*) доро́ж-

ка; (*on record*) за́пись; **~ suit** трениро́вочный костю́м; **off the beaten ~** в глуши́; **go off the ~** (*fig*) отклоня́ться *impf*, отклони́ться *pf* от те́мы; **keep ~ of** следи́ть *impf* за +*instr*; **lose ~ of** теря́ть *impf*, по~ *pf* след+*gen*; *vt* просле́живать *impf*, проследи́ть *pf*; **~ down** высле́живать *impf*, вы́следить *pf*.

tract[1] *n* (*land*) простра́нство.

tract[2] *n* (*pamphlet*) брошю́ра.

tractor *n* тра́ктор.

trade *n* торго́вля; (*occupation*) профе́ссия, ремесло́; **~ mark** фабри́чная ма́рка; **~ union** профсою́з; **~unionist** член профсою́за; *vi* торгова́ть *impf* (**in** +*instr*); *vt* (*swap like things*) обме́ниваться *impf*, обменя́ться *pf* +*instr*; (**~ for sth different**) обме́нивать *impf*, обменя́ть *pf* (**for** на+*acc*); **~ in** сдава́ть *impf*, сдать *pf* в счёт поку́пки но́вого. **trader, tradesman** *n* торго́вец. **trading** *n* торго́вля.

tradition *n* тради́ция. **traditional** *adj* традицио́нный. **traditionally** *adv* по тради́ции.

traffic *n* движе́ние; (*trade*) торго́вля; **~ jam** про́бка; *vi* торгова́ть *impf* (**in** +*instr*). **trafficker** *n* торго́вец (**in** +*instr*). **traffic-lights** *n pl* светофо́р.

tragedy *n* траге́дия. **tragic** *adj* траги́ческий.

trail *n* (*trace*, *track*) след; (*path*) тропи́нка; *vt* (*track*) высле́живать *impf*, вы́следить *pf*; *vt & i* (*drag*) таска́ть(ся) *indet*, тащи́ть(ся) *det*. **trailer** *n* (*on vehicle*) прице́п; (*cin*) (кино)ро́лик.

train *n* по́езд; (*of dress*) шлейф; *vt* (*instruct*) обуча́ть *impf*, обучи́ть *pf* (**in** +*dat*); (*prepare*) гото́вить *impf* (**for** к+*dat*); (*sport*) трениро́вать *impf*, на~ *pf*; (*animals*) дрессирова́ть *impf*, вы́~ *pf*; (*aim*) наводи́ть *impf*, навести́ *pf*; (*plant*) направля́ть *impf*, напра́вить *pf* рост+*gen*; *vi* приготовля́ться *impf*, пригото́виться *pf* (**for** к+*dat*); (*sport*) трениро́ваться *impf*, на~ *pf*. **trainee** *n* стажёр, практика́нт. **trainer** *n* (*sport*) тре́нер; (*of animals*) дрессиро́вщик; (*shoe*) кроссо́вка. **training** *n* обуче́ние; (*sport*) трениро́вка; (*of animals*) дрессиро́вка; **~-college** (*teachers'*) педагоги́ческий институ́т.

traipse *vi* таска́ться *indet*, тащи́ться *det*.

trait *n* черта́.

traitor *n* преда́тель *m*, ~ница.

trajectory *n* траекто́рия.

tram *n* трамва́й.

tramp *n* (*vagrant*) бродя́га *m*; *vi* (*walk heavily*) то́пать *impf*. **trample** *vt* топта́ть *impf*, по~, ис~ *pf*; ~ **down** выта́птывать *impf*, вы́топтать *pf*; ~ **on** (*fig*) попира́ть *impf*, попра́ть *pf*.

trampoline *n* бату́т.

trance *n* транс.

tranquil *adj* споко́йный. **tranquillity** *n* споко́йствие. **tranquillize** *vt* успока́ивать *impf*, успоко́ить *pf*. **tranquillizer** *n* транквилиза́тор.

transact *vt* (*business*) вести́ *impf*; (*a deal*) заключа́ть *impf*, заключи́ть *pf*. **transaction** *n* де́ло, сде́лка; *pl* (*publications*) труды́ *m pl*.

transatlantic *adj* трансатланти́ческий.

transcend *vt* превосходи́ть *impf*, превзойти́ *pf*. **transcendental** *adj* (*philos*.) трансцендента́льный.

transcribe *vt* (*copy out*) перепи́сывать *impf*, переписа́ть *pf*. **transcript** *n* ко́пия. **transcription** *n* (*copy*) ко́пия.

transfer *n* (*of objects*) перено́с, перемеще́ние; (*of money*; *of people*) перево́д; (*of property*) переда́ча; (*design*) переводна́я карти́нка; *vt* (*objects*) переноси́ть *impf*, перенести́ *pf*; перемеща́ть *impf*, перемести́ть *pf*; (*money*; *people*; *design*) переводи́ть *impf*, перевести́ *pf*; (*property*) передава́ть *impf*, переда́ть *pf*; *vi* (*to different job*) переходи́ть *impf*, перейти́ *pf*; (*change trains etc.*) переса́живаться *impf*, пересе́сть *pf*. **transferable** *adj* допуска́ющий переда́чу.

transfix *vt* (*fig*) прико́вывать *impf*, прикова́ть *pf* к ме́сту.

transform *vt* & *i* преобразо́вывать(ся) *impf*, преобразова́ть(ся) *pf*; ~ **into** (*i*) превраща́ть(ся) *impf*, преврати́ть(ся) *pf* в+*acc*. **transformation** *n* преобразова́ние; превраще́ние. **transformer** *n* трансформа́тор.

transfusion *n* перелива́ние (кро́ви).

transgress *vt* наруша́ть *impf*, нару́шить *pf*; *vi* (*sin*) греши́ть *impf*, за~ *pf*. **transgression** *n* наруше́ние; (*sin*) грех.

transience *n* мимолётность. **transient** *adj* мимолётный.

transistor *n* транзи́стор; ~ **radio** транзи́сторный приёмник.

transit *n* транзи́т; **in** ~ (*goods*) при перево́зке; (*person*) по пути́; ~ **camp** транзи́тный ла́герь *m*. **transition** *n* перехо́д. **transitional** *adj* перехо́дный. **transitive** *adj* перехо́дный. **transitory** *adj* мимолётный.

translate *vt* переводи́ть *impf*, перевести́ *pf*. **translation** *n* перево́д. **translator** *n* перево́дчик.

translucent *adj* полупрозра́чный.

transmission *n* переда́ча. **transmit** *vt* передава́ть *impf*, переда́ть *pf*. **transmitter** *n* (*радио*)переда́тчик.

transparency *n* (*phot*) диапозити́в. **transparent** *adj* прозра́чный.

transpire *vi* (*become known*) обнару́живаться *impf*, обнару́житься *pf*; (*occur*) случа́ться *impf*, случи́ться *pf*.

transplant *vt* переса́живать *impf*, пересади́ть *pf*; (*med*) де́лать *impf*, с~ *pf* переса́дку+*gen*; *n* (*med*) переса́дка.

transport *n* (*various senses*) тра́нспорт; (*conveyance*) перево́зка; *attrib* тра́нспортный; *vt* перевози́ть *impf*, перевезти́ *pf*. **transportation** *n* тра́нспорт, перево́зка.

transpose *vt* переставля́ть *impf*, переста́вить *pf*; (*mus*) транспони́ровать *impf* & *pf*. **transposition** *n* перестано́вка; (*mus*) транспониро́вка.

transverse *adj* попере́чный.

transvestite *n* трансвести́т.

trap *n* лову́шка (*also fig*), западня́; *vt* (*catch*) лови́ть *impf*, пойма́ть *pf* (в лову́шку); (*jam*) защемля́ть *impf*, защеми́ть *pf*. **trapdoor** *n* люк.

trapeze *n* трапе́ция.

trapper *n* звероло́в.

trappings *n pl* (*fig*) (*exterior attributes*) вне́шние атрибу́ты *m pl*; (*adornments*) украше́ния *neut pl*.

trash *n* дрянь (*coll*). **trashy** *adj* дрянно́й.

trauma n тра́вма. **traumatic** adj травмати́ческий.

travel n путеше́ствие; ~ **agency** бюро́ neut indecl путеше́ствий; ~ **sick: be** ~**-sick** ука́чивать impf; укача́ть pf impers +acc; **I am** ~**-sick in cars** меня́ в маши́не ука́чивает; vi путеше́ствовать impf, vt объезжа́ть impf, объе́хать pf. **traveller** n путеше́ственник; (salesman) коммивояжёр; ~**'s cheque** тури́стский чек.

traverse vt пересека́ть impf, пересе́чь pf.

travesty n паро́дия.

trawler n тра́улер.

tray n подно́с; **in-** (**out-**)~ корзи́нка для входя́щих (исходя́щих) бума́г.

treacherous adj преда́тельский; (unsafe) ненадёжный. **treachery** n преда́тельство.

treacle n па́тока.

tread n похо́дка; (stair) ступе́нька; (of tyre) проте́ктор; vi ступа́ть impf, ступи́ть pf; ~ **on** наступа́ть impf, наступи́ть pf на+acc; vt топта́ть impf.

treason n изме́на.

treasure n сокро́вище; vt высоко́ цени́ть impf. **treasurer** n казначе́й. **treasury** n (also fig) сокро́вищница; **the T~** госуда́рственное казначе́йство.

treat n (pleasure) удово́льствие; (entertainment) угоще́ние; vt (have as guest) угоща́ть impf, угости́ть pf (**to** +instr); (med) лечи́ть impf (**for** от +gen; **with** +instr); (behave towards) обраща́ться impf c+instr; (process) обраба́тывать impf, обрабо́тать pf (**with** +instr); (discuss) трактова́ть impf о+prep; (regard) относи́ться impf, отнести́сь pf к+dat (**as** как к+dat). **treatise** n тракта́т. **treatment** n (behaviour) обраще́ние; (med) лече́ние; (processing) обрабо́тка; (discussion) тракто́вка. **treaty** n догово́р.

treble adj тройно́й; (trebled) утро́енный; adv втро́е; n (mus) дискант; vt & i утра́ивать(ся) impf, утро́ить(ся) pf.

tree n де́рево.

trek n (migration) переселе́ние; (journey) путеше́ствие; vi (migrate) пересели́ться impf, переселя́ться pf;

(journey) путеше́ствовать impf.

trellis n шпале́ра; (for creepers) решётка.

tremble vi дрожа́ть impf (**with** от +gen). **trembling** n дрожь; **in fear and** ~ трепеща́.

tremendous adj (huge) огро́мный; (excellent) потряса́ющий.

tremor n дрожь; (earthquake) толчо́к. **tremulous** adj дрожа́щий.

trench n кана́ва, ров; (mil) око́п.

trend n направле́ние, тенде́нция. **trendy** adj мо́дный.

trepidation n тре́пет.

trespass n (on property) наруше́ние грани́ц; vi наруша́ть impf, нару́шить pf грани́цу (**on** +gen); (fig) вторга́ться impf, вто́ргнуться pf (**on** в+acc). **trespasser** n наруши́тель m.

trestle n ко́злы (-зел, -злам) pl; ~ **table** стол на ко́злах.

trial n (test) испыта́ние (also ordeal), про́ба; (law) проце́сс, суд; (sport) попы́тка; **on** ~ (probation) на испыта́нии; (of objects) взя́тый на про́бу; (law) под судо́м; ~ **and error** ме́тод проб и оши́бок.

triangle n треуго́льник. **triangular** adj треуго́льный.

tribal adj племенно́й. **tribe** n пле́мя neut.

tribulation n го́ре, несча́стье.

tribunal n трибуна́л.

tributary n прито́к. **tribute** n дань; **pay** ~ (fig) отдава́ть impf, отда́ть pf дань (уваже́ния) (**to** +dat).

trice n: **in a** ~ мгнове́нно.

trick n (ruse) хи́трость; (deception) обма́н; (conjuring ~) фо́кус; (stunt) трюк; (joke) шу́тка; (habit) привы́чка; (cards) взя́тка; **play a** ~ **on** игра́ть impf, сыгра́ть pf шу́тку с +instr; vt обма́нывать impf, обману́ть pf. **trickery** n обма́н.

trickle vi сочи́ться impf.

trickster n обма́нщик. **tricky** adj сло́жный.

tricycle n трёхколёсный велосипе́д.

trifle n пустя́к; **a** ~ (adv) немно́го +gen; vi шути́ть impf, по~ pf (**with** c+instr). **trifling** adj пустяко́вый.

trigger n (of gun) куро́к; vt: ~ **off** вызыва́ть impf, вы́звать pf.

trill n трель.

trilogy n трило́гия.

trim n поря́док, гото́вность; **in fighting** ~ в боево́й гото́вности; **in good** ~ (sport) в хоро́шей фо́рме; (haircut) подстри́жка; adj опря́тный; vt (cut, clip, cut off) подреза́ть impf, подреза́ть pf; (hair) подстрига́ть impf, подстри́чь pf; (a dress etc.) отде́лывать impf, отде́лать pf. **trimming** n (on dress) отде́лка; (to food) гарни́р.

Trinity n Тро́ица.

trinket n безделу́шка.

trio n т́рио neut indecl; (of people) тро́йка.

trip n поéздка, путеше́ствие, экску́рсия; (business ~) командиро́вка; vi (stumble) спотыка́ться impf, споткну́ться pf (over o+acc); vt (also ~ up) подставля́ть impf, подста́вить pf но́жку +dat (also fig); (confuse) запу́тывать impf, запу́тать pf.

triple adj тройно́й; (tripled) утро́енный; vt & i утра́ивать(ся) impf, утро́ить(ся) pf. **triplet** n (mus) трио́ль; (one of ~s) близне́ц (из тро́йни); pl тро́йня.

tripod n трено́жник.

trite adj бана́льный.

triumph n торжество́, побе́да; vi торжествова́ть impf, вос~ pf (over над+instr). **triumphal** adj триумфа́льный. **triumphant** adj (exultant) торжеству́ющий; (victorious) победоно́сный.

trivia n pl ме́лочи (-че́й) pl. **trivial** adj незначи́тельный. **triviality** n тривиа́льность. **trivialize** vt опошля́ть impf, опо́шлить pf.

trolley n теле́жка; (table on wheels) сто́лик на колёсиках. **trolley-bus** n тролле́йбус.

trombone n тромбо́н.

troop n гру́ппа, отря́д; pl (mil) войска́ neut pl; vi идти́ impf, по~ pf стро́ем.

trophy n трофе́й; (prize) приз.

tropic n тро́пик. **tropical** adj тропи́ческий.

trot n рысь; vi рыси́ть impf; (rider) éздить indet, éхать det, по~ pf ры́сью; (horse) ходи́ть indet, идти́ det, пойти́ pf ры́сью.

trouble n (worry) беспоко́йство, трево́га; (misfortune) беда́; (unpleasantness) неприя́тности f pl; (effort, pains) труд; (care) забо́та; (disrepair) неиспра́вность (with в+prep); (illness) боле́знь; **heart** ~ больно́е се́рдце; **~-maker** нарушитель m, ~ница споко́йствия; **ask for** ~ напра́шиваться impf, напроси́ться pf на неприя́тности; **be in** ~ име́ть impf неприя́тности; **get into** ~ попа́сть pf в беду́; **take** ~ стара́ться impf, по~ pf; **take the** ~ труди́ться impf, по~ pf (to +inf); **the** ~ **is (that)** беда́ в том, что; vt (make anxious, disturb, give pain) беспоко́ить impf, по~ pf; **may I** ~ **you for ...?** мо́жно попроси́ть у вас +acc?; vi (take the ~) труди́ться impf. **troubled** adj беспоко́йный. **troublesome** adj (restless, fidgety) беспоко́йный; (capricious) капри́зный; (difficult) тру́дный.

trough n (for food) корму́шка.

trounce vt (beat) поро́ть impf, вы~ pf; (defeat) разбива́ть impf, разби́ть pf.

troupe n тру́ппа.

trouser-leg n штани́на (coll). **trousers** n pl брю́ки (-к) pl, штаны́ (-но́в) pl.

trout n форе́ль.

trowel n (for building) мастеро́к; (garden ~) садо́вый сово́к.

truancy n прогу́л. **truant** n прогу́льщик; **play** ~ прогу́ливать impf, прогуля́ть pf.

truce n переми́рие.

truck[1] n: **have no** ~ **with** не име́ть impf никаки́х дел с+instr.

truck[2] n (lorry) грузови́к; (rly) ваго́н-платфо́рма.

truculent adj свире́пый.

trudge vi уста́ло тащи́ться impf.

true adj (faithful, correct) ве́рный; (correct) пра́вильный; (story) правди́вый; (real) настоя́щий; **come** ~ сбыва́ться impf, сбы́ться pf.

truism n трюи́зм. **truly** adv (sincerely) и́скренне; (really, indeed) действи́тельно; **yours** ~ пре́данный Вам.

trump n ко́зырь m; vt бить impf, по~ pf ко́зырем; ~ **up** фабрикова́ть impf, с~ pf.

trumpet n труба́; vt (proclaim) труби́ть impf о+prep. **trumpeter** n труба́ч.

truncate vt усека́ть impf, усе́чь pf.

truncheon n дуби́нка.

trundle vt & i ката́ть(ся) indet, кати́ть(ся) det, по~ pf.

trunk n (stem) ствол; (anat) ту́ловище; (elephant's) хо́бот; (box) сунду́к; pl (swimming) пла́вки (-вок) pl; (boxing etc.) трусы́ (-со́в) pl; ~ **call** вы́зов по междугоро́дному телефо́ну; ~ **road** магистра́льная доро́га.

truss n (girder) фе́рма; (med) грыжево́й банда́ж; vt (tie (up), bird) свя́зывать impf, связа́ть pf; (reinforce) укрепля́ть impf, укрепи́ть pf.

trust n дове́рие; (body of trustees) опе́ка; (property held in ~) дове́рительная со́бственность; (econ) трест; **take on** ~ принима́ть, приня́ть pf на ве́ру; vt доверя́ть impf, дове́рить pf +dat (with +acc) **to** +inf); vi (hope) наде́яться impf, по~ pf. **trustee** n опеку́н. **trustful, trusting** adj дове́рчивый. **trustworthy, trusty** adj надёжный, ве́рный.

truth n пра́вда; **tell the** ~ говори́ть impf, сказа́ть pf пра́вду; **to tell you the** ~ по пра́вде говоря́. **truthful** adj правди́вый.

try n (attempt) попы́тка; (test, trial) испыта́ние, про́ба; vt (taste; sample) про́бовать impf, по~ pf; (patience) испы́тывать impf, испыта́ть pf; (law) суди́ть impf (**for** за+acc); vi (endeavour) стара́ться impf, по~ pf; ~ **on** (clothes) примеря́ть impf, приме́рить pf. **trying** adj тру́дный.

tsar n царь m. **tsarina** n цари́ца.

tub n ка́дка; (bath) ва́нна; (of margarine etc.) упако́вка.

tubby adj то́лстенький.

tube n тру́бка, труба́; (toothpaste etc.) тю́бик; (underground) метро́ neut indecl.

tuber n клу́бень m. **tuberculosis** n туберкулёз.

tubing n тру́бы m pl. **tubular** adj тру́бчатый.

tuck n (in garment) скла́дка; vt (thrust into, ~ away) засо́вывать impf, засу́нуть pf; (hide away) пря́тать impf, с~ pf; ~ **in** (shirt etc.) заправля́ть impf, запра́вить pf; ~ **in, up** (blanket, skirt) подтыка́ть impf, подоткну́ть pf; ~ **up** (sleeves) засу́чивать impf, засучи́ть pf; (in bed) укрыва́ть impf, укры́ть pf.

Tuesday n вто́рник.

tuft n пучо́к.

tug vt тяну́ть impf, по~ pf; vi (sharply) дёргать impf, дёрнуть pf (**at** за+acc); n рыво́к; (tugboat) букси́р.

tuition n обуче́ние (**in** +dat).

tulip n тюльпа́н.

tumble vi (fall) па́дать impf, (у)па́сть pf; n паде́ние. **tumbledown** adj полуразру́шенный. **tumbler** n стака́н.

tumour n о́пухоль.

tumult n (uproar) суматóха; (agitation) волне́ние. **tumultuous** adj шу́мный.

tuna n туне́ц.

tundra n ту́ндра.

tune n мело́дия; **in** ~ в тон, (of instrument) настро́енный; **out of** ~ не в тон, фальши́вый, (of instrument) расстро́енный; **change one's** ~ (пере)меня́ть impf, перемени́ть pf тон; vt (instrument; radio) настра́ивать impf, настро́ить pf; (engine etc.) регули́ровать impf, от~ pf; ~ **in** настра́ивать impf, настро́ить pf (radio) ра́дио (**to** на+acc); vi: ~ **up** настра́ивать impf, настро́ить pf инструме́нт(ы). **tuneful** adj мелоди́чный. **tuner** n (mus) настро́йщик; (receiver) приёмник.

tunic n туни́ка; (of uniform) ки́тель m.

tuning n настро́йка; (of engine) регулиро́вка; ~-**fork** камерто́н.

tunnel n тунне́ль m; vi прокла́дывать impf, проложи́ть pf тунне́ль m.

turban n тюрба́н.

turbine n турби́на.

turbulence n бу́рность; (aeron) турбуле́нтность. **turbulent** adj бу́рный.

tureen n су́пник.

turf n дёрн.

turgid adj (pompous) напы́щенный.

Turk n ту́рок, турча́нка. **Turkey** n Ту́рция.

turkey n индю́к, f инде́йка; (dish) индю́шка.

Turkish adj туре́цкий. **Turkmenistan** n Туркмениста́н.

turmoil n (disorder) беспоря́док; (uproar) суматóха.

turn n (change of direction) поворо́т;

(*revolution*) оборо́т; (*service*) услу́-
га; (*change*) измене́ние; (*one's ~ to
do sth*) о́чередь; (*theat*) но́мер; ~ **of
phrase** оборо́т ре́чи; **at every ~** на
ка́ждом шагу́; **by, in turn(s)** по
о́череди; *vt* (*handle, key, car around,
etc.*) повора́чивать *impf*, поверну́ть
pf; (*revolve, rotate*) враща́ть *impf*;
(*page; on its face*) перевёртывать
impf, переверну́ть *pf*; (*direct*) на-
правля́ть *impf*, напра́вить *pf*; (*cause
to become*) де́лать *impf*, с~ *pf +instr*;
(*on lathe*) точи́ть *impf*, вы́точить *pf*; *vi* (*change
direction*) повора́чивать *impf*, повер-
ну́ть *pf*; (*rotate*) враща́ться *impf*; (*~
round*) повора́чиваться *impf*, повер-
ну́ться *pf*; (*become*) станови́ться
impf, стать *pf +instr*; ~ **against**
ополча́ться *impf*, ополчи́ться *pf* на
+*acc*, про́тив+*gen*; ~ **around** *see* ~
round; ~ **away** (*vt & i*) отвора́чи-
вать(ся) *impf*, отверну́ть(ся) *pf*;
(*refuse admittance*) прогоня́ть *impf*,
прогна́ть *pf*; ~ **back** (*vi*) повора́-
чивать *impf*, поверну́ть *pf* наза́д;
(*vt*) (*bend back*) отгиба́ть *impf*, ото-
гну́ть *pf*; ~ **down** (*refuse*) отклоня́ть
impf, отклони́ть *pf*; (*collar*) отгиба́ть
impf, отогну́ть *pf*; (*make quieter*)
де́лать *impf*, с~ *pf* ти́ше; ~ **grey** (*vi*)
седе́ть *impf*, по~ *pf*; ~ **in** (*so as to
face inwards*) повора́чивать *impf*,
поверну́ть *pf* вовну́трь; ~ **inside out**
выора́чивать *impf*, вы́вернуть *pf*
наизна́нку; ~ **into** (*change into*) (*vt
& i*) превраща́ть(ся) *impf*, пре-
врати́ть(ся) *pf* в+*acc*; (*street*)
свора́чивать *impf*, сверну́ть *pf* в
+*acc*; ~ **off** (*light, radio etc.*) вы-
ключа́ть *impf*, вы́ключить *pf*; (*tap*)
закрыва́ть *impf*, закры́ть *pf*; (*vi*)
(*branch off*) свора́чивать *impf*,
сверну́ть *pf*; ~ **on** (*light, radio etc.*)
включа́ть *impf*, включи́ть *pf*; (*tap*)
открыва́ть *impf*, откры́ть *pf*; (*attack*) напада́ть *impf*, напа́сть *pf* на
+*acc*; ~ **out** (*light etc.*): *see* ~ **off;**
(*prove to be*) ока́зываться *impf*,
оказа́ться *pf* (**to be** +*instr*); (*drive
out*) выгоня́ть *impf*, вы́гнать *pf*;
(*pockets*) вывёртывать *impf*, вы́-
вернуть *pf*; (*be present*) приходи́ть
impf, прийти́ *pf*; (*product*) выпу-
ска́ть *impf*, вы́пустить *pf*; ~ **over**
(*page, on its face, roll over*) (*vt & i*)

перевёртывать(ся) *impf*, переверну́ть(ся) *pf*; (*hand over*) передава́ть
impf, переда́ть *pf*; (*think about*)
обду́мывать *impf*, обду́мать *pf*;
(*overturn*) (*vt & i*) опроки́дывать-
(ся) *impf*, опроки́нуть(ся) *pf*; ~ **pale**
бледне́ть *impf*, по~ *pf*; ~ **red**
красне́ть *impf*, по~ *pf*; ~ **round** (*vi*)
(*rotate*) ~ *one's back*; ~ *to face sth*)
повёртываться *impf*, поверну́ться
pf; (~ *to face*) обора́чиваться *impf*,
оберну́ться *pf*; (*vt*) повёртывать
impf, поверну́ть *pf*; ~ **sour** скиса́ть
impf, ски́снуть *pf*; ~ **to** обраща́ться
impf, обрати́ться *pf* к+*dat* (**for** за
+*instr*); ~ **up** (*appear*) появля́ться
impf, появи́ться *pf*; (*be found*) на-
ходи́ть *impf*, найти́сь *pf*; (*shorten
garment*) подшива́ть *impf*, подши́ть
pf; (*crop up*) подвёртываться *impf*,
подверну́ться *pf*; (*bend up; stick up*)
(*vt & i*) загиба́ть(ся) *impf*, загну́ть-
(ся) *pf*; (*make louder*) де́лать *impf*,
с~ *pf* гро́мче; ~ **up one's nose** во-
роти́ть *impf* нос (**at** от+*gen*) (*coll*);
~ **upside down** перевора́чивать
impf, переверну́ть *pf* вверх дном.
turn-out *n* коли́чество приходя́щих.
turn-up *n* (*on trousers*) обшла́г.
turner *n* то́карь *m*.
turning *n* (*road*) поворо́т. **turning-
point** *n* поворо́тный пункт.
turnip *n* ре́па.
turnover *n* (*econ*) оборо́т; (*of staff*)
теку́честь рабо́чей си́лы.
turnpike *n* доро́жная заста́ва.
turnstile *n* турнике́т.
turntable *n* (*rly*) поворо́тный круг;
(*gramophone*) диск.
turpentine *n* скипида́р.
turquoise *n* (*material, stone*) бирюза́;
adj бирюзо́вый.
turret *n* ба́шенка.
turtle *n* черепа́ха.
turtle-dove *n* го́рлица.
tusk *n* би́вень *m*, клык.
tussle *n* дра́ка; *vi* дра́ться *impf* (**for**
за+*acc*).
tutor *n* (*private teacher*) ча́стный до-
ма́шний учи́тель *m*, ~ница; (*univ*)
преподава́тель *m*, ~ница; (*primer*)
уче́бник; *vt* (*instruct*) обуча́ть *impf*,
обучи́ть *pf* (**in** +*dat*); (*give lessons
to*) дава́ть *impf*, дать *pf* уро́ки+*dat*;
(*guide*) руководи́ть *impf* +*instr*.

tutorial n консультация.

tutu n (ballet) пачка.

TV abbr (of **television**) ТВ, телевидение; (set) телевизор.

twang n (of string) резкий звук (натянутой струны); (voice) гнусавый голос.

tweak n щипок; vt щипать impf, (у)щипнуть pf.

tweed n твид.

tweezers n pl пинцет.

twelfth adj & n двенадцатый. **twelve** adj & n двенадцать.

twentieth adj & n двадцатый. **twenty** adj & n двадцать; pl (decade) двадцатые годы (-дов) m pl.

twice adv дважды; ~ **as** вдвое, в два раза +comp.

twiddle vt (turn) вертеть impf +acc, instr; (toy with) играть impf +instr; ~ **one's thumbs** (fig) бездельничать impf.

twig n веточка, прут.

twilight n сумерки (-рек) pl.

twin n близнец; pl (Gemini) Близнецы m pl; ~ **beds** пара односпальных кроватей; ~ **brother** брат-близнец; ~ **town** город-побратим.

twine n бечёвка, шпагат; vt (twist, weave) вить impf, с~ pf; vt & i (~ round) обвивать(ся) impf, обвить(ся) pf.

twinge n приступ (боли); (of conscience) угрызение.

twinkle n мерцание; (of eyes) огонёк; vi мерцать impf, сверкать impf. **twinkling** n мерцание; in the ~ **of an eye** в мгновение ока.

twirl vt & i (twist, turn) вертеть(ся) impf; (whirl, spin) кружить(ся) impf.

twist n (bend) изгиб, поворот; (~ing) кручение; (in story) поворот фабулы; vt скручивать impf, крутить impf, с~ pf; (distort) искажать impf, исказить pf; (sprain) подвёртывать impf, подвернуть pf; vi (climb, meander, twine) виться impf. **twisted** adj искривлённый (also fig).

twit n дурак.

twitch n подёргивание; vt & i дёргать(ся) impf, дёрнуть(ся) pf (at за +acc).

twitter n щебет; vi щебетать impf, чирикать impf.

two adj & n два, две (f); (collect; 2 pairs) двое; (number 2) двойка; in ~ (in half) надвое, пополам; ~-**seater** двухместный (автомобиль); ~-**way** двусторонний. **twofold** adj двойной; adv вдвойне. **twosome** n пара.

tycoon n магнат.

type n тип, род; (printing) шрифт; vt писать impf, на~ pf на машинке. **typescript** n машинопись. **typewriter** n пишущая машинка. **typewritten** adj машинописный.

typhoid n брюшной тиф.

typical adj типичный. **typify** vt служить impf, по~ pf типичным примером +gen.

typist n машинистка.

typography n книгопечатание; (style) оформление.

tyrannical adj тиранический. **tyrant** n тиран.

tyre n шина.

U

ubiquitous adj вездесущий.

udder n вымя neut.

UFO abbr (of **unidentified flying object**) НЛО, неопознанный летающий объект.

ugh int тьфу!

ugliness n уродство. **ugly** adj некрасивый, уродливый; (unpleasant) неприятный.

UK abbr (of **United Kingdom**) Соединённое Королевство.

Ukraine n Украина. **Ukrainian** n украинец, -нка; adj украинский.

ulcer n язва.

ulterior adj скрытый.

ultimate adj (final) последний, окончательный; (purpose) конечный. **ultimately** adv в конечном счёте, в конце концов. **ultimatum** n ультиматум.

ultrasound n ультразвук. **ultra-violet** adj ультрафиолетовый.

umbilical adj: ~ **cord** пуповина.

umbrella n зонтик, зонт.

umpire n судья m; vt & i судить impf.

umpteenth adj: for the ~ **time** в который раз.

unabashed adj без всякого смущения. **unabated** adj неослабленный.

unable *adj*: be ~ to не мочь *impf*, с~ *pf*; быть не в состоя́нии; (*not know how to*) не уме́ть *impf*, с~ *pf*.
unabridged *adj* несокращённый.
unaccompanied *adj* без сопровожде́ния; (*mus*) без аккомпанеме́нта. **unaccountable** *adj* необъясни́мый. **unaccustomed** *adj* (*not accustomed*) непривы́кший (**to** к+*dat*); (*unusual*) непривы́чный. **unadulterated** *adj* настоя́щий; (*utter*) чисте́йший. **unaffected** *adj* непринуждённый. **unaided** *adj* без по́мощи, самостоя́тельный. **unambiguous** *adj* недвусмы́сленный. **unanimity** *n* единоду́шие. **unanimous** *adj* единоду́шный. **unanswerable** *adj* (*irrefutable*) неопровержи́мый. **unarmed** *adj* невооружённый. **unashamed** *adj* бессо́вестный. **unassailable** *adj* непристу́пный; (*irrefutable*) неопровержи́мый. **unassuming** *adj* скро́мный. **unattainable** *adj* недосяга́емый. **unattended** *adj* без присмо́тра. **unattractive** *adj* непривлека́тельный. **unauthorized** *adj* неразрешённый. **unavailable** *adj* не име́ющийся в нали́чии, недосту́пный. **unavoidable** *adj* неизбе́жный. **unaware** *predic*: be ~ of не сознава́ть *impf* +*acc*; не знать *impf* o+*prep*. **unawares** *adv* врасплóх.
unbalanced *adj* (*psych*) неуравнове́шенный. **unbearable** *adj* невыноси́мый. **unbeatable** *adj* (*unsurpassable*) не могу́щий быть превзойдённым; (*invincible*) непобеди́мый. **unbeaten** *adj* (*undefeated*) непокорённый; (*unsurpassed*) непревзойдённый. **unbelief** *n* неве́рие. **unbelievable** *adj* невероя́тный. **unbeliever** *n* неве́рующий *sb*. **unbiased** *adj* беспристра́стный. **unblemished** *adj* незапя́тнанный. **unblock** *vt* прочища́ть *impf*, прочи́стить *pf*. **unbolt** *vt* отпира́ть *impf*, отпере́ть *pf*. **unborn** *adj* ещё не рождённый. **unbounded** *adj* неограни́ченный. **unbreakable** *adj* небью́щийся. **unbridled** *adj* разну́зданный. **unbroken** *adj* (*intact*) неразби́тый, це́лый; (*continuous*) непреры́вный; (*unsurpassed*) непоби́тый; (*horse*) необъе́зженный. **unbuckle** *vt* расстёгивать *impf*, расстегну́ть *pf*. **unburden** *vt*:

~ o.s. отводи́ть *impf*, отвести́ *pf* ду́шу. **unbutton** *vt* расстёгивать *impf*, расстегну́ть *pf*.
uncalled-for *adj* неуме́стный. **uncanny** *adj* жу́ткий, сверхъесте́ственный. **unceasing** *adj* непреры́вный. **unceremonious** *adj* бесцеремо́нный. **uncertain** *adj* (*not sure, hesitating*) неуве́ренный; (*indeterminate*) неопределённый, нея́сный; be ~ (*not know for certain*) тóчно не знать *impf*; **in no ~ terms** недвусмы́сленно. **uncertainty** *n* неизве́стность; неопределённость. **unchallenged** *adj* не вызыва́ющий возраже́ний. **unchanged** *adj* неизмени́вшийся. **unchanging** *adj* неизменя́ющийся. **uncharacteristic** *adj* нетипи́чный. **uncharitable** *adj* немилосе́рдный, жесто́кий. **uncharted** *adj* неиссле́дованный. **unchecked** *adj* (*unrestrained*) необу́зданный. **uncivilized** *adj* нецивилизо́ванный. **unclaimed** *adj* невостре́бованный.
uncle *n* дя́дя *m*.
unclean *adj* нечи́стый. **unclear** *adj* нея́сный. **uncomfortable** *adj* неудо́бный. **uncommon** *adj* необыкнове́нный; (*rare*) ре́дкий. **uncommunicative** *adj* неразгово́рчивый, сде́ржанный. **uncomplaining** *adj* безро́потный. **uncomplicated** *adj* несло́жный. **uncompromising** *adj* бескомпроми́ссный. **unconcealed** *adj* нескрыва́емый. **unconcerned** *adj* (*unworried*) беззабо́тный; (*indifferent*) равноду́шный. **unconditional** *adj* безогово́рочный, безусло́вный. **unconfirmed** *adj* неподтверждённый. **unconnected** *adj* ~ **with** не свя́занный с+*instr*. **unconscious** *adj* (*also unintentional*) бессозна́тельный; (*predic*) без созна́ния; be ~ of не сознава́ть *impf* +*gen*; *n* подсозна́тельное *sb*. **unconsciousness** *n* бессозна́тельное состоя́ние. **unconstitutional** *adj* неконституцио́нный. **uncontrollable** *adj* неудержи́мый. **uncontrolled** *adj* бесконтро́льный. **unconventional** *adj* необы́чный; оригина́льный. **unconvincing** *adj* неубеди́тельный. **uncooked** *adj* сыро́й. **uncooperative** *adj* неотзы́вчивый. **uncouth** *adj* грубый. **uncover** *vt* раскрыва́-

impf, раскры́ть *pf*. **uncritical** *adj* некрити́чный.

unctuous *adj* еле́йный.

uncut *adj* неразре́занный; (*unabridged*) несокращённый.

undamaged *adj* неповреждённый.

undaunted *adj* бесстра́шный. **undecided** *adj* (*not settled*) нерешённый; (*irresolute*) нереши́тельный. **undefeated** *adj* непокорённый. **undemanding** *adj* нетре́бовательный. **undemocratic** *adj* недемократи́ческий. **undeniable** *adj* неоспори́мый.

under *prep* (*position*) под+*instr*; (*direction*) под+*acc*; (*fig*) под +*instr*; (*less than*) ме́ньше+*gen*; (*in view of, in the reign, time of*) при+*prep*; ~**age** несовершенноле́тний; ~ **way** на ходу́; *adv* (*position*) внизу́; (*direction*) вниз; (*less*) ме́ньше.

undercarriage *n* шасси́ *neut indecl*. **underclothes** *n pl* ни́жнее бельё. **undercoat** *n* (*of paint*) грунто́вка. **undercover** *adj* та́йный. **undercurrent** *n* подво́дное тече́ние; (*fig*) скры́тая тенде́нция. **undercut** *vt* (*price*) назнача́ть *impf*, назна́чить *pf* бо́лее ни́зкую це́ну чем+*nom*. **underdeveloped** *adj* слаборазви́тый. **underdog** *n* неуда́чник.

underdone *adj* недожа́ренный. **underemployment** *n* непо́лная за́нятость. **underestimate** *vt* недооце́нивать *impf*, недооцени́ть *pf*; *n* недооце́нка. **underfoot** *adv* под нога́ми.

undergo *vt* подверга́ться *impf*, подве́ргнуться *pf* +*dat*; (*endure*) переноси́ть *impf*, перенести́ *pf*. **undergraduate** *n* студе́нт, ~ка. **underground** *n* (*rly*) метро́ *neut indecl*; (*fig*) подпо́лье; *adj* подзе́мный; (*fig*) подпо́льный; *adv* под землёй; (*fig*) подпо́льно. **undergrowth** *n* подле́сок. **underhand** *adj* закули́сный. **underlie** *vt* (*fig*) лежа́ть *impf* в осно́ве +*gen*. **underline** *vt* подчёркивать *impf*, подчеркну́ть *pf*. **underlying** *adj* лежа́щий в осно́ве. **underling** *n* подчинённый *sb*.

undermine *vt* (*authority*) подрыва́ть *impf*, подорва́ть *pf*; (*health*) разруша́ть *impf*, разру́шить *pf*.

underneath *adv* (*position*) внизу́; (*direction*) вниз; *prep* (*position*) под

+*instr*; (*direction*) под+*acc*; *n* ни́жняя часть; *adj* ни́жний.

undernourished *adj* исхуда́лый; **be** ~ недоеда́ть *impf*.

underpaid *adj* низкоопла́чиваемый. **underpants** *n pl* трусы́ (-со́в) *pl*. **underpass** *n* прое́зд под полотно́м доро́ги; тонне́ль *m*. **underpin** *vt* подводи́ть *impf*, подвести́ *pf* фунда́мент под+*acc*; (*fig*) подде́рживать *impf*, поддержа́ть *pf*. **underprivileged** *adj* обделённый; (*poor*) бе́дный. **underrate** *vt* недооце́нивать *impf*, недооцени́ть *pf*.

underscore *vt* подчёркивать *impf*, подчеркну́ть *pf*. **under-secretary** *n* замести́тель *m* мини́стра. **underside** *n* ни́жняя сторона́, низ. **undersized** *adj* малоро́слый. **understaffed** *adj* неукомплекто́ванный.

understand *vt* понима́ть *impf*, поня́ть *pf*; (*have heard say*) слы́шать *impf*. **understandable** *adj* поня́тный. **understanding** *n* понима́ние; (*agreement*) соглаше́ние; *adj* (*sympathetic*) отзы́вчивый.

understate *vt* преуменьша́ть *impf*, преуме́ньшить *pf*. **understatement** *n* преуменьше́ние.

understudy *n* дублёр.

undertake *vt* (*enter upon*) предпринима́ть *impf*, предприня́ть *pf*; (*responsibility*) брать *impf*, взять *pf* на себя́; (+*inf*) обя́зываться *impf*, обяза́ться *pf*. **undertaker** *n* гробовщи́к. **undertaking** *n* предприя́тие; (*pledge*) гара́нтия.

undertone *n* (*fig*) подте́кст; **in an** ~ вполго́лоса. **underwater** *adj* подво́дный. **underwear** *n* ни́жнее бельё. **underweight** *adj* исхуда́лый. **underworld** *n* (*mythology*) преиспо́дняя *sb*; (*criminals*) престу́пный мир. **underwrite** *vt* (*guarantee*) гаранти́ровать *impf* & *pf*. **underwriter** *n* страхо́вщик.

undeserved *adj* незаслу́женный. **undesirable** *adj* нежела́тельный; *n* нежела́тельное лицо́. **undeveloped** *adj* нера́звитый; (*land*) незастро́енный. **undignified** *adj* недосто́йный. **undiluted** *adj* неразба́вленный. **undisciplined** *adj* недисципли́ни́рованный. **undiscovered** *adj* неоткры́тый. **undisguised** *adj* я́вный.

undisputed adj бесспо́рный. **undistinguished** adj заура́дный. **undisturbed** adj (untouched) нетро́нутый; (peaceful) споко́йный. **undivided** adj: ~ **attention** по́лное внима́ние **undo** vt (open) открыва́ть impf, откры́ть pf; (untie) развя́зывать impf, развяза́ть pf; (unbutton, unhook, unbuckle) расстёгивать impf, расстегну́ть pf; (destroy, cancel) уничтожа́ть impf, уничто́жить pf. **undoubted** adj несомне́нный. **undoubtedly** adv несомне́нно. **undress** vt & i раздева́ть(ся) impf, разде́ть(ся) pf. **undue** adj чрезме́рный. **unduly** adv чрезме́рно.

undulating adj волни́стый; (landscape) холми́стый.

undying adj (eternal) ве́чный.

unearth vt (dig up) выка́пывать impf, вы́копать pf из земли́; (fig) раска́пывать impf, раскопа́ть pf. **uneasiness** n (anxiety) беспоко́йство; (awkwardness) нело́вкость. **uneasy** adj беспоко́йный; нело́вкий. **uneconomic** adj нерента́бельный. **uneconomical** adj (car etc.) неэкономи́чный; (person) неэконо́мный. **uneducated** adj необразо́ванный. **unemployed** adj безрабо́тный. **unemployment** n безрабо́тица; ~ **benefit** посо́бие по безрабо́тице. **unending** adj бесконе́чный. **unenviable** adj незави́дный. **unequal** adj нера́вный. **unequalled** adj непревзойдённый. **unequivocal** adj недвусмы́сленный. **unerring** adj безоши́бочный.

uneven adj неро́вный. **uneventful** adj непримеча́тельный. **unexceptional** adj обы́чный. **unexpected** adj неожи́данный. **unexplored** adj неиссле́дованный.

unfailing adj неизме́нный; (inexhaustible) неисчерпа́емый. **unfair** adj несправедли́вый. **unfaithful** adj неве́рный. **unfamiliar** adj незнако́мый; (unknown) неве́домый. **unfashionable** adj немо́дный. **unfasten** vt (detach, untie) открепля́ть impf, открепи́ть pf; (undo, unbutton, unhook) расстёгивать impf, расстегну́ть pf; (open) открыва́ть impf, откры́ть pf. **unfavourable** adj неблагоприя́тный. **unfeeling** adj

бесчу́вственный. **unfinished** adj незако́нченный. **unfit** adj него́дный; (unhealthy) нездоро́вый. **unflagging** adj неослабева́ющий. **unflattering** adj неле́стный. **unflinching** adj непоколеби́мый. **unfold** vt & i развёртывать(ся) impf, разверну́ть(ся) pf; vi (fig) раскрыва́ться impf, раскры́ться pf. **unforeseen** adj непредви́денный. **unforgettable** adj незабыва́емый. **unforgivable** adj непрости́тельный. **unforgiving** adj непроща́ющий. **unfortunate** adj несча́стный; (regrettable) неуда́чный; n неуда́чник. **unfortunately** adv к сожале́нию. **unfounded** adj необосно́ванный. **unfriendly** adj недружелю́бный. **unfulfilled** adj (hopes etc.) неосуществлённый; (person) неудовлетворённый. **unfurl** vt & i развёртывать(ся) impf, разверну́ть(ся) pf. **unfurnished** adj немеблиро́ванный.

ungainly adj неуклю́жий. **ungovernable** adj неуправля́емый. **ungracious** adj нелюбе́зный. **ungrateful** adj неблагода́рный. **unguarded** adj (incautious) неосторо́жный.

unhappiness n несча́стье. **unhappy** adj несчастли́вый. **unharmed** adj невреди́мый. **unhealthy** adj нездоро́вый; (harmful) вре́дный. **unheard-of** adj неслы́ханный. **unheeded** adj незаме́ченный. **unheeding** adj невнима́тельный. **unhelpful** adj бесполе́зный; (person) неотзы́вчивый. **unhesitating** adj реши́тельный. **unhesitatingly** adv без колеба́ния. **unhindered** adj беспрепя́тственный. **unhinge** vt (fig) расстра́ивать impf, расстро́ить pf. **unholy** adj (impious) нечести́вый; (awful) ужа́сный. **unhook** vt (undo hooks of) расстёгивать impf, расстегну́ть pf; (uncouple) расцепля́ть impf, расцепи́ть pf. **unhurt** adj невреди́мый.

unicorn n единоро́г.

unification n объедине́ние.

uniform n фо́рма; adj единообра́зный; (unchanging) постоя́нный. **uniformity** n единообра́зие.

unify vt объединя́ть impf, объедини́ть pf.

unilateral adj односторо́нний.

unimaginable *adj* невообрази́мый. **unimaginative** *adj* лишённый воображе́ния, прозаи́чный. **unimportant** *adj* нева́жный. **uninformed** *adj* (*ignorant*) несве́дущий (**about** в +*prep*); (*ill-informed*) неосведомлённый. **uninhabited** *adj* необита́емый. **uninhibited** *adj* нестеснённый. **uninspired** *adj* бана́льный. **unintelligible** *adj* непоня́тный. **unintentional** *adj* неча́янный. **unintentionally** *adv* неча́янно. **uninterested** *adj* незаинтересо́ванный. **uninteresting** *adj* неинтере́сный. **uninterrupted** *adj* непреры́вный.

union *n* (*alliance*) сою́з; (*joining together, alliance*) объедине́ние; (*trade* ~) профсою́з. **unionist** *n* член профсою́за; (*polit*) унио́нист.

unique *adj* уника́льный.

unison *n*: **in** ~ (*mus*) в унисо́н; (*fig*) в согла́сии.

unit *n* едини́ца; (*mil*) часть.

unite *vt & i* соединя́ть(ся) *impf*, соедини́ть(ся) *pf*; объединя́ть(ся) *impf*, объедини́ть(ся) *pf*. **united** *adj* соединённый, объединённый; **U~ Kingdom** Соединённое Короле́вство; **U~ Nations** Организа́ция Объединённых На́ций; **U~ States** Соединённые Шта́ты *m pl* Аме́рики. **unity** *n* еди́нство.

universal *adj* всео́бщий; (*many-sided*) универса́льный. **universe** *n* вселе́нная *sb*; (*world*) мир.

university *n* университе́т; *attrib* университе́тский.

unjust *adj* несправедли́вый. **unjustifiable** *adj* непрости́тельный. **unjustified** *adj* неопра́вданный.

unkempt *adj* нечёсаный. **unkind** *adj* недо́брый, злой. **unknown** *adj* неизве́стный.

unlawful *adj* незако́нный. **unleaded** *adj* неэтили́рованный. **unleash** *vt* (*also fig*) развя́зывать *impf*, развяза́ть *pf*.

unless *conj* е́сли… не.

unlike *adj* непохо́жий (на+*acc*); (*in contradistinction to*) в отли́чие от +*gen*. **unlikely** *adj* маловероя́тный; **it is** ~ **that** вряд ли. **unlimited** *adj* неограни́ченный. **unlit** *adj* неосвещённый. **unload** *vt* (*vehicle etc.*) разгружа́ть *impf*, разгрузи́ть *pf*; (*goods etc.*) выгружа́ть *impf*, вы́грузить *pf*. **unlock** *vt* отпира́ть *impf*, отпере́ть *pf*; открыва́ть *impf*, откры́ть *pf*. **unlucky** *adj* (*number etc.*) несчастли́вый; (*unsuccessful*) неуда́чный.

unmanageable *adj* тру́дный, непоко́рный. **unmanned** *adj* автомати́ческий. **unmarried** *adj* холосто́й; (*of man*) нежена́тый; (*of woman*) незаму́жняя. **unmask** *vt* (*fig*) разоблача́ть *impf*, разоблачи́ть *pf*. **unmentionable** *adj* неупомина́емый. **unmistakable** *adj* несомне́нный, я́сный. **unmitigated** *adj* (*thorough*) отъя́вленный. **unmoved** *adj*: **be** ~ остава́ться *impf*, оста́ться *pf* равноду́шен, -шна.

unnatural *adj* неесте́ственный. **unnecessary** *adj* нену́жный. **unnerve** *vt* лиша́ть *impf*, лиши́ть *pf* му́жества; (*upset*) расстра́ивать *impf*, расстро́ить *pf*. **unnoticed** *adj* незаме́ченный.

unobserved *adj* незаме́ченный. **unobtainable** *adj* недосту́пный. **unobtrusive** *adj* скро́мный, ненавя́зчивый. **unoccupied** *adj* неза́нятый, свобо́дный; (*house*) пусто́й. **unofficial** *adj* неофициа́льный. **unopposed** *adj* не встре́тивший сопротивле́ния. **unorthodox** *adj* неортодокса́льный.

unpack *vt* распако́вывать *impf*, распакова́ть *pf*. **unpaid** *adj* (*bill*) неупла́ченный; (*person*) не получа́ющий пла́ты; (*work*) беспла́тный. **unpalatable** *adj* невку́сный; (*unpleasant*) неприя́тный. **unparalleled** *adj* несравни́мый. **unpleasant** *adj* неприя́тный. **unpleasantness** *n* неприя́тность. **unpopular** *adj* непопуля́рный. **unprecedented** *adj* беспрецеде́нтный. **unpredictable** *adj* непредсказу́емый. **unprejudiced** *adj* беспристра́стный. **unprepared** *adj* неподгото́вленный, негото́вый. **unprepossessing** *adj* непривлека́тельный. **unpretentious** *adj* просто́й, без прете́нзий. **unprincipled** *adj* беспри́нципный. **unproductive** *adj* непродукти́вный. **unprofitable** *adj* невы́годный. **unpromising** *adj* малообеща́ющий. **unprotected** *adj* незащищённый. **unproven** *adj* недока́занный. **unprovoked** adj непрово-ци́рованный. **unpublished** adj не-опублико́ванный, неи́зданный. **un-punished** adj безнака́занный.

unqualified adj неквалифици́рован-ный; (unconditional) безогово́роч-ный. **unquestionable** adj несомне́н-ный, неоспори́мый. **unquestion-ably** adv несомне́нно, бесспо́рно.

unravel vt & i распу́тывать(ся) impf, распу́тать(ся) pf; vt (solve) разга́-дывать impf, разгада́ть pf. **unread** adj (book etc.) непрочи́танный. **un-readable** adj (illegible) неразбо́рчи-вый; (boring) неудобочита́емый. **unreal** adj нереа́льный. **unrealistic** adj нереа́льный. **unreasonable** adj (person) неразу́мный; (behaviour, demand, price) необосно́ванный. **unrecognizable** adj неузнава́емый. **unrecognized** adj непри́знанный. **unrefined** adj неочи́щенный; (man-ners etc.) гру́бый. **unrelated** adj не име́ющий отноше́ния (to к+dat), несвя́занный (to с+instr); we are ~ мы не ро́дственники. **unrelenting** adj (ruthless) безжа́лостный; (unre-mitting) неосла́бный. **unreliable** adj ненадёжный. **unremarkable** adj не-выдаю́щийся. **unremitting** adj не-осла́бный; (incessant) беспреста́н-ный. **unrepentant** adj нераска́яв-шийся. **unrepresentative** adj нети-пи́чный. **unrequited** adj: ~ love не-разделённая любо́вь. **unreserved** adj (full) по́лный; (open) открове́нный; (unconditional) безогово́рочный; (seat) незаброни́рованный. **unre-solved** adj нерешённый. **unrest** n беспоко́йство; (polit) волне́ния neut pl. **unrestrained** adj несде́ржанный. **unrestricted** adj неограни́ченный. **unripe** adj незре́лый. **unrivalled** adj бесподо́бный. **unroll** vt & i развёр-тывать(ся) impf, разверну́ть(ся) pf. **unruffled** adj (smooth) гла́дкий; (calm) споко́йный. **unruly** adj непо-ко́рный.

unsafe adj опа́сный; (insecure) нена-дёжный. **unsaid** adj: leave ~ мол-ча́ть impf o+prep. **unsaleable** adj нехо́дкий. **unsalted** adj несолё-ный. **unsatisfactory** adj неудовлет-вори́тельный. **unsatisfied** adj не-удовлетворённый. **unsavoury** adj

(unpleasant) неприя́тный; (disreput-able) сомни́тельный. **unscathed** adj невреди́мый; (predic) цел и невре-ди́м. **unscheduled** adj (transport) внеочередно́й; (event) незаплани́-рованный. **unscientific** adj ненау́ч-ный. **unscrew** vt & i отви́нчивать-(ся) impf, отвинти́ть(ся) pf. **unscru-pulous** adj беспринци́пный. **unseat** vt (of horse) сбра́сывать impf, сбро́-сить pf с седла́; (parl) лиша́ть impf, лиши́ть pf парла́ментского ман-да́та.

unseemly adj неподоба́ющий. **un-seen** adj неви́данный. **unselfcon-scious** adj непосре́дственный. **un-selfish** adj бескоры́стный. **unsettle** vt выбива́ть impf, вы́бить pf из ко-ле́й; (upset) расстра́ивать impf, рас-стро́ить pf. **unsettled** adj (weather) неусто́йчивый; (unresolved) нере-шённый. **unsettling** adj волну́ю-щий. **unshakeable** adj непоколеби́-мый. **unshaven** adj небри́тый. **un-sightly** adj непригля́дный, уро́дли-вый. **unsigned** adj неподпи́санный. **unskilful** adj неуме́лый. **unskilled** adj неквалифици́рованный. **unso-ciable** adj необщи́тельный. **unsold** adj непро́данный. **unsolicited** adj непро́шеный. **unsolved** adj нере-шённый. **unsophisticated** adj про-сто́й. **unsound** adj (unhealthy, un-wholesome) нездоро́вый; (not solid) непро́чный; (unfounded) необосно́-ванный; of ~ mind душевнобольно́й. **unspeakable** adj (inexpressible) невы-рази́мый; (very bad) отврати́тель-ный. **unspecified** adj то́чно не ука́-занный, неопределённый. **unspoilt** adj неиспо́рченный. **unspoken** adj невы́сказанный. **unstable** adj не-усто́йчивый; (mentally) неуравно-ве́шенный. **unsteady** adj неусто́й-чивый. **unstuck** adj: come ~ откле́-иваться impf, откле́иться pf; (fig) прова́ливаться impf, провали́ться pf. **unsuccessful** adj неуда́чный, безуспе́шный. **unsuitable** adj непод-ходя́щий. **unsuited** adj неприго́д-ный. **unsung** adj невоспе́тый. **un-supported** adj неподде́ржанный. **unsure** adj неуве́ренный (of o.s. в себе́). **unsurpassed** adj непревзой-дённый. **unsurprising** adj неудиви́-

тельный. **unsuspected** adj (unforeseen) непредвиденный. **unsuspecting** adj неподозревающий. **unsweetened** adj неподслащённый. **unswerving** adj непоколебимый. **unsympathetic** adj несочувствующий. **unsystematic** adj несистематичный.

untainted adj неиспорченный. **untangle** vt распутывать impf, распутать pf. **untapped** adj: ~ **resources** неиспользованные ресурсы m pl. **untenable** adj несостоятельный. **untested** adj неиспытанный. **unthinkable** adj невообразимый. **unthinking** adj бездумный. **untidiness** n неопрятность; (disorder) беспорядок. **untidy** adj неопрятный; (in disorder) в беспорядке. **untie** vt развязывать impf, развязать pf; (set free) освобождать impf, освободить pf. **until** prep до+gen; not ~ не раньше +gen; ~ **then** до тех пор; conj пока, пока... не; **not** ~ только когда.

untimely adj (premature) безвременный; (inappropriate) неуместный. **untiring** adj неутомимый. **untold** adj (incalculable) бессчётный, несметный; (inexpressible) невыразимый. **untouched** adj нетронутый. **untoward** adj неблагоприятный. **untrained** adj необученный. **untried** adj неиспытанный. **untroubled** adj спокойный. **untrue** adj неверный. **untrustworthy** adj ненадёжный. **untruth** n неправда, ложь. **untruthful** adj лживый.

unusable adj непригодный. **unused** adj неиспользованный; (unaccustomed) непривыкший (**to** к+dat); **I am** ~ **to this** я к этому не привык. **unusual** adj необыкновенный, необычный. **unusually** adv необыкновенно. **unutterable** adj невыразимый.

unveil vt (statue) торжественно открывать impf, открыть pf; (disclose) обнародовать impf & pf.

unwanted adj нежеланный. **unwarranted** adj неоправданный. **unwary** adj неосторожный. **unwavering** adj непоколебимый. **unwelcome** adj нежелательный; (unpleasant) неприятный. **unwell** adj нездоровый. **unwieldy** adj громоздкий. **unwilling**

adj несклонный; **be** ~ не хотеть impf, за~ pf (**to** +inf). **unwillingly** adv неохотно. **unwillingness** n неохота. **unwind** vt & i разматывать(ся) impf, размотать(ся) pf; (rest) отдыхать impf, отдохнуть pf. **unwise** adj не(благо)разумный. **unwitting** adj невольный. **unwittingly** adv невольно. **unworkable** adj неприменимый. **unworldly** adj не от мира сего. **unworthy** adj недостойный. **unwrap** vt развёртывать impf, развернуть pf. **unwritten** adj: ~ **law** неписаный закон.

unyielding adj упорный, неподатливый.

unzip vt расстёгивать impf, расстегнуть pf (молнию+gen).

up adv (motion) наверх, вверх; (position) наверху, вверху; ~ **and down** вверх и вниз; (back and forth) взад и вперёд; ~ **to** (towards) к+dat; (as far as, until) до+gen; ~ **to now** до сих пор; **be** ~ **against** иметь impf дело с+instr; **it is** ~ **to you**+inf, это вам+inf, вы должны+inf; **what's** ~? что случилось?; в чём дело?; **your time is** ~ ваше время истекло; ~ **and about** на ногах; **he isn't** ~ **yet** он ещё не встал; **he isn't** ~ **to this job** он не годится для этой работы; prep вверх по+dat; (along) (вдоль) по+dat; vt повышать impf, повысить; vi (leap up) взять; adj: ~-**to-date** современный; (fashionable) модный; ~-**and-coming** многообещающий; n: ~**s and downs** (fig) превратности f pl судьбы.

upbringing n воспитание.

update vt модернизировать impf & pf; (a book etc.) дополнять impf, дополнить pf.

upgrade vt повышать impf, повысить pf (по службе).

upheaval n потрясение.

uphill adj (fig) тяжёлый; adv в гору.

uphold vt поддерживать impf, поддержать pf.

upholster vt обивать impf, обить pf. **upholsterer** n обойщик. **upholstery** n обивка.

upkeep n содержание.

upland n гористая часть страны; adj нагорный.

uplift vt поднимать impf, поднять pf.

up-market *adj* дорого́й.

upon *prep* (*position*) на+*prep*, (*motion*) на+*acc*; *see* **on**

upper *adj* ве́рхний; (*socially, in rank*) вы́сший; **gain the ~ hand** оде́рживать *impf*, одержа́ть *pf* верх (**over** над+*instr*); *n* передо́к. **uppermost** *adj* са́мый ве́рхний, вы́сший; **be ~ in person's mind** бо́льше всего́ занима́ть *impf*, заня́ть *pf* мы́сли кого́-л.

upright *n* сто́йка; *adj* вертика́льный; (*honest*) че́стный; **~ piano** пиани́но *neut indecl.*

uprising *n* восста́ние.

uproar *n* шум, гам.

uproot *vt* вырыва́ть *impf*, вы́рвать *pf* с ко́рнем; (*people*) выселя́ть *impf*, вы́селить *pf.*

upset *n* расстро́йство; *vt* расстра́ивать *impf*, расстро́ить *pf*; (*overturn*) опроки́дывать *impf*, опроки́нуть *pf*; *adj* (*miserable*) расстро́енный; **~ stomach** расстро́йство желу́дка.

upshot *n* развя́зка, результа́т.

upside-down *adj* переве́рнутый вверх дном; *adv* вверх дном; (*in disorder*) в беспоря́дке.

upstairs *adv* (*position*) наверху́; (*motion*) наве́рх; *n* ве́рхний эта́ж; *adj* находя́щийся в ве́рхнем этаже́.

upstart *n* вы́скочка *m & f.*

upstream *adv* про́тив тече́ния; (*situation*) вверх по тече́нию.

upsurge *n* подъём, волна́.

uptake *n*: **be quick on the ~** бы́стро сообража́ть *impf*, сообрази́ть *pf.*

upturn *n* (*fig*) улучше́ние. **upturned** *adj* (*face etc.*) по́днятый кве́рху; (*inverted*) переве́рнутый.

upward *adj* напра́вленный вверх. **upwards** *adv* вверх; **~ of** свы́ше +*gen.*

uranium *n* ура́н.

urban *adj* городско́й.

urbane *adj* ве́жливый.

urchin *n* мальчи́шка *m.*

urge *n* (*incitement*) побужде́ние; (*desire*) жела́ние; *vt* (*impel*, **~ on**) подгоня́ть *impf*, подогна́ть *pf*; (*warn*) предупрежда́ть *impf*, предупреди́ть *pf*; (*try to persuade*) убежда́ть *impf*. **urgency** *n* сро́чность, ва́жность; **a matter of great ~** сро́чное де́ло. **urgent** *adj* сро́чный; (*insistent*) настоя́тельный. **urgently** *adv* сро́чно.

urinate *vi* мочи́ться *impf*, по~ *pf.* **urine** *n* моча́.

urn *n* у́рна.

US(A) *abbr* (*of* United States of America) США, Соединённые Шта́ты Аме́рики.

usable *adj* го́дный к употребле́нию. **usage** *n* употребле́ние; (*treatment*) обраще́ние. **use** *n* (*utilization*) употребле́ние, по́льзование; (*benefit*) по́льза; (*application*) примене́ние; **is no ~ (-ing)** бесполе́зно (+*inf*); **make ~ of** испо́льзовать *impf & pf*; по́льзоваться *impf* +*instr*; *vt* употребля́ть *impf*, употреби́ть *pf*; по́льзоваться *impf* +*instr*; (*apply*) применя́ть *impf*, примени́ть *pf*; (*treat*) обраща́ться *impf* c+*instr*; **I ~d to see him often** я ча́сто его́ встреча́л; **be, get ~d to** привыка́ть *impf*, привы́кнуть *pf* к+*dat*; **~ up** расхо́довать *impf*, из~ *pf.* **used** *adj* (*second-hand*) ста́рый. **useful** *adj* поле́зный; **come in ~, prove ~** пригоди́ться *pf* (**to** +*dat*). **useless** *adj* бесполе́зный. **user** *n* потреби́тель *m.*

usher *n* (*theat*) билетёр; *vt* (*lead in*) вводи́ть *impf*, ввести́ *pf*; (*proclaim*, **~ in**) возвеща́ть *impf*, возвести́ть *pf.* **usherette** *n* билетёрша.

USSR *abbr* (*of* Union of Soviet Socialist Republics) СССР, Сою́з Сове́тских Социалисти́ческих Респу́блик.

usual *adj* обыкнове́нный, обы́чный; **as ~** как обы́чно. **usually** *adv* обыкнове́нно, обы́чно.

usurp *vt* узурпи́ровать *impf & pf.* **usurper** *n* узурпа́тор.

usury *n* ростовщи́чество.

utensil *n* инструме́нт; *pl* у́тварь, посу́да.

uterus *n* ма́тка.

utilitarian *adj* утилита́рный. **utilitarianism** *n* утилитари́зм. **utility** *n* поле́зность; *pl*: **public utilities** коммуна́льные услу́ги *f pl.* **utilize** *vt* испо́льзовать *impf & pf.*

utmost *adj* (*extreme*) кра́йний; **this is of the ~ importance to me** э́то для меня́ кра́йне ва́жно; *n*: **do one's ~** де́лать *impf*, с~ *pf* всё возмо́жное.

Utopia *n* уто́пия. **utopian** *adj* утопи́ческий.

utter *attrib* по́лный, абсолю́тный; (*out-and-out*) отъя́вленный (*coll*); *vt* произноси́ть *impf*, произнести́ *pf*; (*let out*) издава́ть *impf*, изда́ть *pf*. **utterance** *n* (*uttering*) произнесе́ние; (*pronouncement*) выска́зывание. **utterly** *adv* соверше́нно.

Uzbek *n* узбе́к, -е́чка. **Uzbekistan** *n* Узбекиста́н.

V

vacancy *n* (*for job*) вака́нсия, свобо́дное ме́сто; (*at hotel*) свобо́дный но́мер. **vacant** *adj* (*post*) вака́нтный; (*post; not engaged, free*) свобо́дный; (*empty*) пусто́й; (*look*) отсу́тствующий. **vacate** *vt* освобожда́ть *impf*, освободи́ть *pf*. **vacation** *n* кани́кулы (-л) *pl*; (*leave*) о́тпуск.

vaccinate *vt* вакцини́ровать *impf* & *pf*. **vaccination** *n* приви́вка (**against** от, про́тив+*gen*). **vaccine** *n* вакци́на.

vacillate *vi* колеба́ться *impf*. **vacillation** *n* колеба́ние.

vacuous *adj* пусто́й. **vacuum** *n* ва́куум; (*fig*) пустота́; ~-**clean** чи́стить *impf*, вы́~, по~ *pf* пылесо́сом; ~ **cleaner** пылесо́с; ~ **flask** те́рмос.

vagabond *n* бродя́га *m*.

vagary *n* капри́з.

vagina *n* влага́лище.

vagrant *n* бродя́га *m*.

vague *adj* (*indeterminate, uncertain*) неопределённый; (*unclear*) нея́сный; (*dim*) сму́тный; (*absent-minded*) рассе́янный. **vagueness** *n* неопределённость, нея́сность; (*absent-mindedness*) рассе́янность.

vain *adj* (*futile*) тще́тный, напра́сный; (*empty*) пусто́й; (*conceited*) тщесла́вный; **in** ~ напра́сно.

vale *n* дол, доли́на.

valentine *n* (*card*) поздрави́тельная ка́рточка с днём свято́го Валенти́на.

valet *n* камерди́нер.

valiant *adj* хра́брый.

valid *adj* действи́тельный; (*weighty*) ве́ский. **validate** *vt* (*ratify*) утвержда́ть *impf*, утверди́ть *pf*. **validity** *n* действи́тельность; (*weightiness*)

ве́скость.

valley *n* доли́на.

valour *n* до́блесть.

valuable *adj* це́нный; *n pl* це́нности *f pl*. **valuation** *n* оце́нка. **value** *n* це́нность; (*math*) величина́; *pl* це́нности *f pl*; ~-**added tax** нало́г на доба́вленную сто́имость; ~ **judgement** субъекти́вная оце́нка; *vt* (*estimate*) оце́нивать *impf*, оцени́ть *pf*; (*hold dear*) цени́ть *impf*.

valve *n* (*tech, med, mus*) кла́пан; (*tech*) ве́нтиль *m*; (*radio*) электро́нная ла́мпа.

vampire *n* вампи́р.

van *n* фурго́н.

vandal *n*ванда́л. **vandalism** *n* вандали́зм. **vandalize** *vt* разруша́ть *impf*, разру́шить *pf*.

vanguard *n* аванга́рд.

vanilla *n* вани́ль.

vanish *vi* исчеза́ть *impf*, исче́знуть *pf*.

vanity *n* (*futility*) тщета́; (*conceit*) тщесла́вие.

vanquish *vt* побежда́ть *impf*, победи́ть *pf*.

vantage-point *n* (*mil*) наблюда́тельный пункт; (*fig*) вы́годная пози́ция.

vapour *n* пар.

variable *adj* изме́нчивый; (*weather*) неусто́йчивый, переме́нный; *n* (*math*) переме́нная (величина́). **variance** *n*: **be at** ~ **with** (*contradict*) противоре́чить *impf*+*dat*; (*disagree*) расходи́ться *impf*, разойти́сь *pf* во мне́ниях с+*instr*. **variant** *n* вариа́нт. **variation** *n* (*varying*) измене́ние; (*variant*) вариа́нт; (*variety*) разнови́дность; (*mus*) вариа́ция.

varicose *adj*: ~ **veins** расшире́ние вен.

varied *adj* разнообра́зный. **variegated** *adj* разноцве́тный. **variety** *n* разнообра́зие; (*sort*) разнови́дность; (*a number*) ряд; ~ **show** варьете́ *neut indecl*. **various** *adj* ра́зный.

varnish *n* лак; *vt* лакирова́ть *impf*, от~ *pf*.

vary *vt* разнообра́зить *impf*, меня́ть *impf*; *vi* (*change*) меня́ться *impf*; (*differ*) ра́зниться *impf*.

vase *n* ва́за.

Vaseline *n* (*propr*) вазели́н.

vast adj громадный. **vastly** adv значительно.

VAT abbr (of **value-added tax**) налог на добавленную стоимость.

vat n чан, бак.

vaudeville n водевиль m.

vault[1] n (leap) прыжок; vi перепрыгивать impf, перепрыгнуть pf; vi прыгать impf, прыгнуть pf.

vault[2] n (arch, covering) свод; (cellar) погреб; (tomb) склеп. **vaulted** adj сводчатый.

VDU abbr (of **visual display unit**) монитор.

veal n телятина.

vector n (math) вектор.

veer vi (change direction) изменять impf, изменить pf направление; (turn) поворачивать impf, повернуть pf.

vegetable n овощ; adj овощной. **vegetarian** n вегетарианец, -нка; attrib вегетарианский. **vegetate** vi (fig) прозябать impf. **vegetation** n растительность.

vehemence n (force) сила; (passion) страстность. **vehement** adj (forceful) сильный; (passionate) страстный.

vehicle n транспортное средство; (motor ~) автомобиль m; (medium) средство.

veil n вуаль; (fig) завеса. **veiled** adj скрытый.

vein n вена; (of leaf, streak) жилка; **in the same** ~ в том же духе.

velocity n скорость.

velvet n бархат; adj бархатный. **velvety** adj бархатистый.

vending-machine n торговый автомат. **vendor** n продавец, -вщица.

vendetta n вендетта.

veneer n фанера; (fig) лоск.

venerable adj почтенный. **venerate** vt благоговеть impf перед+instr. **veneration** n благоговение.

venereal adj венерический.

venetian blind n жалюзи neut indecl.

vengeance n месть; **take** ~ мстить impf, ото~ pf (**on** +dat; **for** за+acc); **with a** ~ вовсю. **vengeful** adj мстительный.

venison n оленина.

venom n яд. **venomous** adj ядовитый.

vent[1] n (opening) выход (also fig), отверстие; vt (feelings) давать impf, дать pf выход+dat; изливать impf, излить pf (**on** на+acc).

vent[2] n (slit) разрез.

ventilate vt проветривать impf, проветрить pf. **ventilation** n вентиляция. **ventilator** n вентилятор.

ventriloquist n чревовещатель m.

venture n предприятие; vi (dare) осмеливаться impf, осмелиться pf; vt (risk) рисковать impf +instr.

venue n место.

veranda n веранда.

verb n глагол. **verbal** adj (oral) устный; (relating to words) словесный; (gram) отглагольный. **verbatim** adj дословный; adv дословно. **verbose** adj многословный.

verdict n приговор.

verge n (also fig) край; (of road) обочина; (fig) грань; **on the** ~ **of** на грани+gen; **he was on the** ~ **of telling all** он чуть не рассказал всё; vi: ~ **on** граничить impf с+instr.

verification n проверка; (confirmation) подтверждение. **verify** vt проверять impf, проверить pf; (confirm) подтверждать impf, подтвердить pf.

vermin n вредители m pl.

vernacular n родной язык; местный диалект; (homely language) разговорный язык.

versatile adj многосторонний.

verse n (also bibl) стих; (stanza) строфа; (poetry) стихи m pl. **versed** adj опытный, сведущий (**in** в+prep).

version n (variant) вариант; (interpretation) версия; (text) текст.

versus prep против+gen.

vertebra n позвонок; pl позвоночник. **vertebrate** n позвоночное животное sb.

vertical adj вертикальный; n вертикаль.

vertigo n головокружение.

verve n живость, энтузиазм.

very adj (that ~ same) тот самый; (this ~ same) этот самый; **at that** ~ **moment** в тот самый момент; (precisely) как раз; **you are the** ~ **person I was looking for** как раз вас я искал; **the** ~ (even the) даже, один; **the** ~ **thought frightens me** одна,

да́же, мысль об э́том меня́ пуга́ет;
(*the extreme*) са́мый; **at the ~ end** в
са́мом конце́; *adv* о́чень; **~ much**
о́чень; **~ much** +*comp* гора́здо
+*comp*; **~**+*superl*, *superl*; **~ first**
са́мый пе́рвый; **~ well** (*agreement*)
хорошо́, ла́дно; **not ~** не о́чень,
дово́льно +*neg*.

vessel *n* сосу́д; (*ship*) су́дно.

vest[1] *n* ма́йка; (*waistcoat*) жиле́т.

vest[2] *vt* (*with power*) облека́ть *impf*,
обле́чь *pf* (**with** +*instr*). **vested** *adj*:
~ interest ли́чная заинтересо́ван-
ность; **~ interests** (*entrepreneurs*)
кру́пные предпринима́тели *m pl*.

vestibule *n* вестибю́ль *m*.

vestige *n* (*trace*) след; (*sign*) при́знак.

vestments *n pl* (*eccl*) облаче́ние.
vestry *n* ри́зница.

vet *n* ветерина́р; *vt* (*fig*) проверя́ть
impf, прове́рить *pf*.

veteran *n* ветера́н; *adj* ста́рый.

veterinary *adj* ветерина́рный; *n* ве-
терина́р.

veto *n* ве́то *neut indecl*; *vt* налага́ть
impf, наложи́ть *pf* ве́то на+*acc*.

vex *vt* досажда́ть *impf*, досади́ть *pf*
+*dat*. **vexation** *n* доса́да. **vexed** *adj*
(*annoyed*) серди́тый; (*question*) спо́р-
ный. **vexatious, vexing** *adj* доса́д-
ный.

via *prep* че́рез+*acc*.

viable *adj* (*able to survive*) жизне-
спосо́бный; (*feasible*) осуществи́мый.

viaduct *n* виаду́к.

vibrant *adj* (*lively*) живо́й. **vibrate** *vi*
вибри́ровать *impf*; *vt* (*make ~*) за-
ставля́ть *impf*, заста́вить *pf* вибри́-
ровать. **vibration** *n* вибра́ция. **vi-
brato** *n* вибра́то *neut indecl*.

vicar *n* прихо́дский свяще́нник. **vic-
arage** *n* дом свяще́нника.

vicarious *adj* чужо́й.

vice[1] *n* (*evil*) поро́к.

vice[2] *n* (*tech*) тиски́ (-ко́в) *pl*.

vice- *in comb* вице-, замести́тель *m*;
~-chairman замести́тель *m* председа-
да́теля; **~-chancellor** (*univ*) проре́к-
тор; **~-president** вице-президе́нт.

viceroy *n* вице-коро́ль *m*.

vice versa *adv* наоборо́т.

vicinity *n* окре́стность; **in the ~** по-
бли́зости (**of** от+*gen*).

vicious *adj* зло́бный; **~ circle** поро́ч-
ный круг.

vicissitude *n* превра́тность.

victim *n* же́ртва; (*of accident*) по-
страда́вший *sb*. **victimization** *n* пре-
сле́дование. **victimize** *vt* пресле́до-
вать *impf*.

victor *n* победи́тель *m*, **~ница**.

Victorian *adj* викториа́нский.

victorious *adj* победоно́сный. **victory** *n* побе́да.

video *n* (**~ recorder, ~ cassette, ~
film**) ви́део *neut indecl*; **~ camera**
видеока́мера; **~ cassette** видеокас-
се́та; **~ (cassette) recorder** видео-
магнитофо́н; *vt* **~ game** видеоигра́; *vt*
запи́сывать *impf*, записа́ть *pf* на
ви́део.

vie *vi* сопе́рничать *impf* (**with** с+*instr*;
for в+*prep*).

Vietnam *n* Вьетна́м. **Vietnamese** *n*
вьетна́мец, -мка; *adj* вьетна́мский.

view *n* (*prospect*, *picture*) вид; (*opinion*) взгляд; (*viewing*) просмо́тр;
(*inspection*) осмо́тр; **in ~ of** ввиду́
+*gen*; **on ~** вы́ставленный для обо-
зре́ния; **with a ~ to** с це́лью+*gen*,
+*inf*; *vt* (*pictures etc.*) рассма́тривать
impf; (*inspect*) осма́тривать *impf*,
осмотре́ть *pf*; (*mentally*) смотре́ть
impf на+*acc*. **viewer** *n* зри́тель *m*,
~ница. **viewfinder** *n* видоиска́тель
m. **viewpoint** *n* то́чка зре́ния.

vigil *n* бо́дрствование; **keep ~** бо́др-
ствовать *impf*, дежу́рить *impf*. **vigilance** *n* бди́тельность. **vigilant** *adj*
бди́тельный. **vigilante** *n* дружи́нник.

vigorous *adj* си́льный, энерги́чный.
vigour *n* си́ла, эне́ргия.

vile *adj* гну́сный. **vilify** *vt* черни́ть
impf, о~ *pf*.

villa *n* ви́лла.

village *n* дере́вня; *attrib* дереве́н-
ский. **villager** *n* жи́тель *m* дере́вни.

villain *n* злоде́й.

vinaigrette *n* припра́ва из у́ксуса и
оли́вкового ма́сла.

vindicate *vt* опра́вдывать *impf*, оп-
равда́ть *pf*. **vindication** *n* оправда́-
да́ние.

vindictive *adj* мсти́тельный.

vine *n* виногра́дная лоза́.

vinegar *n* у́ксус.

vineyard *n* виногра́дник.

vintage *n* (*year*) год; (*fig*) вы́пуск;
attrib (*wine*) ма́рочный; (*car*) архаи́-
ческий.

viola n (*mus*) альт.

violate vt (*treaty, privacy*) наруша́ть *impf*, нару́шить *pf*; (*grave*) оскверня́ть *impf*, оскверни́ть *pf*. **violation** n наруше́ние; оскверне́ние.

violence n (*physical coercion, force*) наси́лие; (*strength, force*) си́ла. **violent** adj (*person, storm, argument*) свире́пый; (*pain*) си́льный; (*death*) наси́льственный. **violently** adv си́льно, о́чень.

violet n (*bot*) фиа́лка; (*colour*) фиоле́товый цвет; adj фиоле́товый.

violin n скри́пка. **violinist** n скрипа́ч, ~ка.

VIP abbr (*of* **very important person**) о́чень ва́жное лицо́.

viper n гадю́ка.

virgin n де́вственница, (*male*) де́вственник; **V~ Mary** де́ва Мари́я. **virginal** adj де́вственный. **virginity** n де́вственность. **Virgo** n Де́ва.

virile adj му́жественный. **virility** n му́жество.

virtual adj факти́ческий. **virtually** adv факти́чески. **virtue** n (*excellence*) доброде́тель; (*merit*) досто́инство; **by ~ of** на основа́нии+*gen*. **virtuosity** n виртуо́зность. **virtuoso** n виртуо́з. **virtuous** adj доброде́тельный.

virulent adj (*med*) вируле́нтный; (*fig*) зло́бный.

virus n ви́рус.

visa n ви́за.

vis-à-vis prep (*with regard to*) по отноше́нию к+*dat*.

viscount n вико́нт. **viscountess** n виконте́сса.

viscous adj вя́зкий.

visibility n ви́димость. **visible** adj ви́димый. **visibly** adv я́вно, заме́тно.

vision n (*sense*) зре́ние; (*apparition*) виде́ние; (*dream*) мечта́; (*insight*) проница́тельность. **visionary** adj (*unreal*) при́зрачный; (*impracticable*) неосуществи́мый; (*insightful*) проница́тельный; n (*dreamer*) мечта́тель m.

visit n посеще́ние, визи́т; vt посеща́ть *impf*, посети́ть *pf*; (*call on*) заходи́ть *impf*, зайти́ *pf* к+*dat*. **visitation** n официа́льное посеще́ние. **visitor** n гость m, посети́тель m. **visor** n (*of cap*) козырёк; (*in car*)

солнцезащи́тный щито́к; (*of helmet*) забра́ло.

vista n перспекти́ва, вид.

visual adj (*of vision*) зри́тельный; (*graphic*) нагля́дный; ~ **aids** нагля́дные посо́бия neut pl. **visualize** vt представля́ть *impf*, предста́вить *pf* себе́.

vital adj абсолю́тно необходи́мый (**to, for** для+*gen*); (*essential to life*) жи́зненный; **of ~ importance** первостепе́нной ва́жности. **vitality** n (*liveliness*) эне́ргия. **vitally** adv жи́зненно.

vitamin n витами́н.

vitreous adj стекля́нный.

vitriolic adj (*fig*) е́дкий.

vivacious adj живо́й. **vivacity** n жи́вость.

viva (voce) n у́стный экза́мен.

vivid adj (*bright*) я́ркий; (*lively*) живо́й. **vividness** n я́ркость; жи́вость.

vivisection n вивисе́кция.

vixen n лиси́ца-са́мка.

viz. adv то есть, а и́менно.

vocabulary n (*range, list, of words*) словарь m; (*range of words*) запа́с слов; (*of a language*) слова́рный соста́в.

vocal adj голосово́й; (*mus*) вока́льный; (*noisy*) шу́мный; ~ **chord** голосова́я свя́зка. **vocalist** n певе́ц, -ви́ца.

vocation n призва́ние. **vocational** adj профессиона́льный.

vociferous adj шу́мный.

vodka n во́дка.

vogue n мо́да; **in ~** в мо́де.

voice n го́лос; vt выража́ть *impf*, вы́разить *pf*.

void n пустота́; adj пусто́й; (*invalid*) недействи́тельный; ~ **of** лишённый +*gen*.

volatile adj (*chem*) летю́чий; (*person*) непостоя́нный, неусто́йчивый.

volcanic adj вулкани́ческий. **volcano** n вулка́н.

vole n (*zool*) полёвка.

volition n во́ля; **by one's own ~** по свое́й во́ле.

volley n (*missiles*) залп; (*fig*) град; (*sport*) уда́р с лёта; vt (*sport*) уда́рять *impf*, уда́рить *pf* с лёта. **volleyball** n волейбо́л.

volt n вольт. **voltage** n напряже́ние.

voluble *adj* говорли́вый.

volume *n* (*book*) том; (*capacity, size*) объём; (*loudness*) гро́мкость. **voluminous** *adj* обши́рный.

voluntary *adj* доброво́льный. **volunteer** *n* доброво́лец; *vt* предлага́ть *impf*, предложи́ть *pf*; *vi* (*offer*) вызыва́ться *impf*, вы́зваться *pf* (*inf*, +*inf*; **for** в+*acc*); (*mil*) идти́ *impf*, пойти́ *pf* доброво́льцем.

voluptuous *adj* сластолюби́вый.

vomit *n* рво́та; *vt* (& *i*) рвать *impf*, вы́рвать *pf impers* (+*instr*); **he was ~ing blood** его́ рва́ло кро́вью.

voracious *adj* прожо́рливый; (*fig*) ненасы́тный.

vortex *n* (*also fig*) водоворо́т, вихрь *m*.

vote *n* (*poll*) голосова́ние; (*individual* ~) го́лос; **the ~** (*suffrage*) пра́во го́лоса; (*resolution*) во́тум *no pl*; ~ **of no confidence** во́тум недове́рия (**in** +*dat*); ~ **of thanks** выраже́ние благода́рности; *vi* голосова́ть *impf*, про~ *pf* (**for** за+*acc*; **against** про́тив+*gen*); *vt* (*allocate by* ~) ассигнова́ть *impf* & *pf*; (*deem*) признава́ть *impf*, призна́ть *pf*; **the film was ~d a failure** фильм был при́знан неуда́чным; ~ **in** избра́ть *impf*, избра́ть *pf* голосова́нием. **voter** *n* избира́тель *m*.

vouch *vi*: ~ **for** руча́ться *impf*, поручи́ться *pf* за+*acc*. **voucher** *n* (*receipt*) распи́ска; (*coupon*) тало́н.

vow *n* обе́т; *vt* кля́сться *impf*, по~ *pf* в+*prep*.

vowel *n* гла́сный *sb*.

voyage *n* путеше́ствие.

vulgar *adj* вульга́рный, гру́бый, по́шлый. **vulgarity** *n* вульга́рность, по́шлость.

vulnerable *adj* уязви́мый.

vulture *n* гриф; (*fig*) хи́щник.

W

wad *n* комо́к; (*bundle*) па́чка. **wadding** *n* (*padding*) наби́вка.

waddle *vi* ходи́ть *indet*, идти́ *det*, пойти́ *pf* вперева́лку (*coll*).

wade *vt* & *i* (*river*) переходи́ть *impf*, перейти́ *pf* вброд; *vi*: ~ **through** (*mud etc.*) пробира́ться *impf*, про-

бра́ться *pf* по+*dat*; (*sth boring etc.*) одолева́ть *impf*, одоле́ть *pf*.

wafer *n* ва́фля.

waffle[1] *n* (*dish*) ва́фля.

waffle[2] *vi* трепа́ться *impf*.

waft *vt* & *i* нести́(сь) *impf*, по~ *pf*.

wag *vt* & *i* (*tail*) виля́ть *impf*, вильну́ть *pf* (+*instr*); *vt* (*finger*) грози́ть *impf*, по~ *pf* +*instr*.

wage[1] *n* (*pay*) *see* **wages**

wage[2] *vt*: ~ **war** вести́ *impf*, про~ *pf* войну́.

wager *n* пари́ *neut indecl*; *vi* держа́ть *impf* пари́ (**that** что); *vt* ста́вить *impf* по~ *pf*.

wages *n pl* за́работная пла́та.

waggle *vt* & *i* пома́хивать *impf*, помаха́ть *pf* (+*instr*).

wag(g)on *n* (*carriage*) пово́зка; (*cart*) теле́га; (*rly*) ваго́н-платфо́рма.

wail *n* вопль *m*; *vi* вопи́ть *impf*.

waist *n* та́лия; (*level of* ~) по́яс; ~-**deep, high** (*adv*) по по́яс. **waistband** *n* по́яс. **waistcoat** *n* жиле́т. **waistline** *n* та́лия.

wait *n* ожида́ние; **lie in** ~ (**for**) подстерега́ть *impf*; подстере́чь *pf*; *vi* (& *t*) (*also* ~ **for**) ждать *impf* (+*gen*); *vi* (*be a waiter, waitress*) быть официа́нтом, -ткой; ~ **on** обслу́живать *impf*, обслужи́ть *pf*. **waiter** *n* официа́нт. **waiting** *n*: ~-**list** спи́сок; ~-**room** приёмная *sb*; (*rly*) зал ожида́ния. **waitress** *n* официа́нтка.

waive *vt* отка́зываться *impf*, отказа́ться *pf* от+*gen*.

wake[1] *n* (*at funeral*) поми́нки (-нок) *pl*.

wake[2] *n* (*naut*) кильва́тер; **in the** ~ **of** по сле́ду +*gen*, за+*instr*.

wake[3] *vt* (*also* ~ **up**) буди́ть *impf*, раз~ *pf*; *vi* (*also* ~ **up**) просыпа́ться *impf*, просну́ться *pf*.

Wales *n* Уэ́льс.

walk *n* (*walking*) ходьба́; (*gait*) похо́дка; (*stroll*) прогу́лка; (*path*) тропа́; ~-**out** (*strike*) забасто́вка; (*as protest*) демонстрати́вный ухо́д; ~-**over** лёгкая побе́да; **ten minutes'** ~ **from here** де́сять мину́т ходьбы́ отсю́да; **go for a** ~ идти́ *impf*, пойти́ *pf* гуля́ть; **from all** ~**s of life** всех слоёв о́бщества; *vi* ходи́ть *indet*, идти́ *det*, пойти́ *pf*; гуля́ть *impf*, по~ *pf*; ~ **away, off** уходи́ть *impf*, уйти́

pf; ~ **in** входи́ть *impf*, войти́ *pf*; ~
out выходи́ть *impf*, вы́йти *pf*; ~ **out**
on броса́ть *impf*, бро́сить *pf*; *vt*
(*traverse*) обходи́ть *impf*, обойти́ *pf*;
(*take for* ~) выводи́ть *impf*, вы́-
вести *pf* гуля́ть. **walker** *n* ходо́к.
walkie-talkie *n* ра́ция. **walking** *n*
ходьба́; ~**-stick** трость.
Walkman *n* (*propr*) во́кмен.
wall *n* стена́; *vt* обноси́ть *impf*, об-
нести́ *pf* стено́й; ~ **up** (*door, win-*
dow) заде́лывать *impf*, заде́лать *pf*;
(*brick up*) замуро́вывать *impf*, за-
мурова́ть *pf*.
wallet *n* бума́жник.
wallflower *n* желтофио́ль.
wallop *vt* си́льно уда́р; *vt* си́льно
ударя́ть *impf*, уда́рить *pf*.
wallow *vi* валя́ться *impf*; ~ **in** (*give*
o.s. up to) погружа́ться *impf*, погру-
зи́ться *pf* в+*acc*.
wallpaper *n* обо́и (обо́ев) *pl*.
walnut *n* гре́цкий оре́х; (*wood, tree*)
оре́ховое де́рево, оре́х.
walrus *n* морж.
waltz *n* вальс; *vi* вальси́ровать *impf*.
wan *adj* бле́дный.
wand *n* па́лочка.
wander *vi* броди́ть *impf*; (*also of*
thoughts etc.) блужда́ть *impf*; ~ **from**
the point отклоня́ться *impf*, откло-
ни́ться *pf* от те́мы. **wanderer** *n* стра́н-
ник.
wane *n*: **be on the** ~ убыва́ть *impf*;
vi убыва́ть *impf*, убы́ть *pf*; (*weaken*)
ослабева́ть *impf*, ослабе́ть *pf*.
wangle *vt* заполуча́ть *impf*, заполу-
чи́ть *pf*.
want *n* (*lack*) недоста́ток; (*require-*
ment) потре́бность; (*desire*) жела́-
ние; **for** ~ **of** за недоста́тком +*gen*;
vt хоте́ть *impf*, за~ *pf* +*gen, acc*;
(*need*) нужда́ться *impf* в+*prep*; **I** ~
you to come at six я хочу́, что́бы
ты пришёл в шесть. **wanting** *adj*:
be ~ недостава́ть *impf* (*impers*
+*gen*); **experience is** ~ недостаёт
о́пыта.
wanton *adj* (*licentious*) распу́тный;
(*senseless*) бессмы́сленный.
war *n* война́; (*attrib*) вое́нный; **at** ~
в состоя́нии войны́; ~ **memorial**
па́мятник па́вшим в войне́.
ward *n* (*hospital*) пала́та; (*child etc.*)
подопе́чный *sb*; (*district*) райо́н; *vt*:

~ **off** отража́ть *impf*, отрази́ть *pf*.
warden *n* (*prison*) нача́льник; (*col-*
lege) ре́ктор; (*hostel*) коменда́нт.
warder *n* тюре́мщик.
wardrobe *n* гардеро́б.
warehouse *n* склад. **wares** *n pl*
изде́лия *neut pl*, това́ры *m pl*.
warfare *n* война́.
warhead *n* боева́я голо́вка.
warily *adv* осторо́жно.
warlike *adj* вои́нственный.
warm *n* тепло́; *adj* (*also fig*) тёплый;
~**-hearted** серде́чный; *vt & i* греть-
(ся) *impf*; согрева́ть(ся) *impf*, со-
гре́ть(ся) *pf*; ~ **up** (*food etc.*) подо-
грева́ть(ся) *impf*, подогре́ть(ся) *pf*;
(*liven up*) оживля́ть(ся) *impf*, ожи-
ви́ть(ся) *pf*; (*sport*) размина́ться
impf, размя́ться *pf*; (*mus*) разы́-
грываться *impf*, разыгра́ться *pf*.
warmth *n* тепло́; (*cordiality*) сер-
де́чность.
warn *vt* предупрежда́ть *impf*, пре-
дупреди́ть *pf* (**about** о+*prep*). **warn-**
ing *n* предупрежде́ние.
warp *vt & i* (*wood*) коро́бить(ся)
impf, по~, с~ *pf*; *vt* (*pervert*) из-
враща́ть *impf*, изврати́ть *pf*.
warrant *n* (*for arrest etc.*) о́рдер; *vt*
(*justify*) опра́вдывать *impf*, оправ-
да́ть *pf*; (*guarantee*) гаранти́ровать
impf & pf. **warranty** *n* гара́нтия.
warrior *n* во́ин.
warship *n* вое́нный кора́бль *m*.
wart *n* борода́вка.
wartime *n*: **in** ~ во вре́мя войны́.
wary *adj* осторо́жный.
wash *n* мытьё; (*thin layer*) то́нкий
слой; (*lotion*) примо́чка; (*surf*) при-
бо́й; (*backwash*) попу́тная волна́; **at**
the ~ в сти́рке; **have a** ~ мы́ться
impf, по~ *pf*; ~**-basin** умыва́льник;
~**-out** (*fiasco*) прова́л; ~**-room** умы-
ва́льная *sb*; *vt & i* мы́ть(ся) *impf*,
вы́~, по~ *pf*; *vt* (*clothes*) стира́ть
impf, вы́~ *pf*; (*of sea*) омыва́ть
impf; ~ **away, off, out** смыва́ть(ся)
impf, смы́ть(ся) *pf*; (*carry away*)
сноси́ть *impf*, снести́ *pf*; ~ **up** (*rinse*)
спола́скивать *impf*, сполосну́ть *pf*;
~ **up** (*dishes*) мыть *impf*, вы́~, по~
pf (посу́ду); ~ **one's hands (of it)**
умыва́ть *impf*, умы́ть *pf* ру́ки.
washed-out *adj* (*exhausted*) утомлённый. **washer** *n* (*tech*) ша́йба.

washing n (*of clothes*) стирка; (*clothes*) бельё; **~-machine** стиральная машина; **~-powder** стиральный порошок; **~-up** (*action*) мытьё посуды; (*dishes*) грязная посуда; **~-up liquid** жидкое мыло для мытья посуды.

wasp n оса.

wastage n утечка. **waste** n (*desert*) пустыня; (*refuse*) отбросы m pl; (*of time, money, etc.*) растрата; **go to ~** пропадать *impf*, пропасть *pf* даром; *adj* (*desert*) пустынный; (*superfluous*) ненужный; (*uncultivated*) невозделанный; **lay ~** опустошать *impf*, опустошить *pf*; **~land** пустырь m; **~ paper** ненужная бумаги f pl; (*for recycling*) макулатура; **~ products** отходы (-дов) pl; **~ paper basket** корзина для бумаги; *vt* тратить *impf*, ис~ *pf*; (*time*) терять *impf*, по~ *pf*; *vi*: **~ away** чахнуть *impf*, за~ *pf*. **wasteful** adj расточительный.

watch n (*timepiece*) часы (-сов) pl; (*duty*) дежурство; (*naut*) вахта; **keep ~ over** наблюдать *impf* за+*instr*; **~dog** сторожевой пёс; **~-tower** сторожевая башня; *vt* (*observe*) наблюдать *impf*; (*keep an eye on*) следить *impf* за+*instr*; (*look after*) смотреть *impf*, по~ *pf* за+*instr*; **~ television, a film** смотреть *impf*, по~ *pf* телевизор, фильм; *vi* смотреть *impf*; **~ out** (*be careful*) беречься *impf* (**for** +*gen*); **~ out for** ждать *impf* +*gen*; **~ out!** осторожно! **watchful** adj бдительный. **watchman** n (ночной) сторож. **watchword** n лозунг.

water n вода; **~-colour** акварель; **~-heater** кипятильник; **~-main** водопроводная магистраль; **~-melon** арбуз; **~-pipe** водопроводная труба; **~-ski** (n) водная лыжа; **~-skiing** водолыжный спорт; **~-supply** водоснабжение; **~-way** водный путь m; *vt* (*flowers etc.*) поливать *impf*, полить *pf*; (*animals*) поить *impf*, на~ *pf*; (*irrigate*) орошать *impf*, оросить *pf*; *vi* (*eyes*) слезиться *impf*; (*mouth*): **my mouth ~s** у меня слюнки текут; **~ down** разбавлять *impf*, разбавить *pf*. **watercourse** n русло. **watercress** n кресс водяной.

waterfall n водопад. **waterfront** n часть города примыкающая к берегу. **watering-can** n лейка. **waterlogged** adj заболоченный. **watermark** n водяной знак. **waterproof** adj непромокаемый; n непромокаемый плащ. **watershed** n водораздел. **waterside** n берег. **watertight** adj водонепроницаемый; (*fig*) неопровержимый. **waterworks** n pl водопроводные сооружения neut pl. **watery** adj водянистый.

watt n ватт.

wave vt (*hand etc.*) махать *impf*, махнуть *pf* +*instr*; (*flag*) размахивать *impf* +*instr*; vi (**~ hand**) махать *impf*, по~ *pf* (**at** +*dat*); (*flutter*) развеваться *impf*; **~ aside** отмахиваться *impf*, отмахнуться *pf* от+*gen*; **~ down** останавливать *impf*, остановить *pf*; n (*in various senses*) волна; (*of hand*) взмах; (*in hair*) завивка. **wavelength** n длина волны. **waver** vi колебаться *impf*. **wavy** adj волнистый.

wax n (*in ear*) сера; vt вощить *impf*, на~ *pf*. **waxwork** n восковая фигура; pl музей восковых фигур.

way n (*road, path, route; fig*) дорога, путь m; (*direction*) сторона; (*manner*) образ; (*method*) способ; (*respect*) отношение; (*habit*) привычка; **by the ~** (*fig*) кстати, между прочим; **on the ~** по дороге, по пути; **this ~** (*direction*) сюда; (*in this ~*) таким образом; **the other ~ round** наоборот; **under ~** на ходу; **be in the ~** мешать *impf*; **get out of the ~** уходить *impf*, уйти *pf* с дороги; **give ~** (*yield*) поддаваться *impf*, поддаться *pf* (**to** +*dat*); (*collapse*) обрушиваться *impf*, обрушиться *pf*; **go out of one's ~ to** стараться *impf*, по~ *pf* изо всех сил +*inf*; **get, have, one's own ~** добиваться *impf*, добиться *pf* своего; **make ~** уступать *impf*, уступить *pf* дорогу (**for** +*dat*). **waylay** vt (*lie in wait for*) подстерегать *impf*, подстеречь *pf*; (*stop*) перехватывать *impf*, перехватить *pf* по пути. **wayside** adj придорожный; n: **fall by the ~** выбывать *impf*, выбыть *pf* из строя.

wayward adj своенравый.

WC abbr (of water-closet) убо́рная sb.
we pron мы.

weak adj сла́бый. **weaken** vt ослабля́ть impf, осла́бить pf; vi слабе́ть impf, о~ pf. **weakling** n (person) сла́бый челове́к; (plant) сла́бое расте́ние. **weakness** n сла́бость.

weal n (mark) рубе́ц.

wealth n бога́тство; (abundance) изоби́лие. **wealthy** adj бога́тый.

wean vt отнима́ть impf, отня́ть pf от груди́; (fig) отуча́ть impf, отучи́ть pf (of, from от+gen).

weapon n ору́жие. **weaponry** n вооруже́ние.

wear n (wearing) но́ска; (clothing) оде́жда; (~ and tear) изно́с; vt носи́ть impf; быть в+prep; **what shall I ~?** что мне наде́ть?; vi носи́ться impf; ~ **off** (pain, novelty) проходи́ть impf, пройти́ pf; (cease to have effect) перестава́ть impf, переста́ть pf де́йствовать; ~ **out** (clothes) изна́шивать(ся) impf, износи́ть(ся) pf; (exhaust) изму́чивать impf, изму́чить pf.

weariness n уста́лость. **wearing, wearisome** adj утоми́тельный. **weary** adj уста́лый; vt & i утомля́ть(ся) impf, утоми́ть(ся) pf.

weasel n ла́ска.

weather n пого́да; **be under the ~** нева́жно себя́ чу́вствовать impf; ~-**beaten** обве́тренный; ~ **forecast** прогно́з пого́ды; vt (storm etc.) выде́рживать impf, вы́держать pf; (expose to atmosphere) подверга́ть impf, подве́ргнуть pf атмосфе́рным влия́ниям. **weather-cock, weathervane** n флю́гер. **weatherman** n метеоро́лог.

weave[1] vt & i (fabric) ткать impf, co~ pf; vt (fig; also wreath etc.) плести́ impf, c~ pf. **weaver** n ткач, ~и́ха.

weave[2] vi (wind) ви́ться impf.

web n (cobweb; fig) паути́на; (fig) сплете́ние. **webbed** adj перепо́нчатый. **webbing** n тка́ная ле́нта.

wed vt (of man) жени́ться impf & pf на+prep; (of woman) выходи́ть impf, вы́йти pf за́муж за+acc; (unite) сочета́ть impf & pf; vi пожени́ться pf. **wedded** adj супру́жеский; ~ **to** (fig) пре́данный +dat. **wedding** n сва́дьба,

бракосочета́ние; ~-**cake** сва́дебный торт; ~-**day** день m сва́дьбы; ~-**dress** подвене́чное пла́тье; ~-**ring** обруча́льное кольцо́.

wedge n клин; vt (~ open) закли́нивать impf, закли́нить pf; vt & i: ~ **in(to)** вкли́нивать(ся) impf, вкли́нить(ся) pf (в+acc).

wedlock n брак; **born out of** ~ рождённый вне бра́ка, внебра́чный.

Wednesday n среда́.

weed n сорня́к; ~-**killer** гербици́д; vt поло́ть impf, вы́~ pf; ~ **out** удаля́ть impf, удали́ть pf. **weedy** adj (person) то́щий.

week n неде́ля; ~-**end** суббо́та и воскре́сенье, выходны́е sb pl. **weekday** n бу́дний день m. **weekly** adj еженеде́льный; (wage) неде́льный; adv еженеде́льно; n еженеде́льник.

weep vi пла́кать impf. **weeping willow** n плаку́чая и́ва.

weigh vt (also fig) взве́шивать impf, взве́сить pf; (consider) обду́мывать impf, обду́мать pf; vt & i (so much) ве́сить impf; ~ **down** отягоща́ть impf, отяготи́ть pf; ~ **on** тяготи́ть impf; ~ **out** отве́шивать impf, отве́сить pf; ~ **up** (appraise) оце́нивать impf, оцени́ть pf. **weight** n (also authority) вес; (load, also fig) тя́жесть; (sport) шта́нга; (influence) влия́ние; **lose** ~ худе́ть impf, по~ pf; **put on** ~ толсте́ть impf, по~ pf; ~-**lifter** штанги́ст; ~-**lifting** подня́тие тя́жостей; vt (make heavier) утяжеля́ть impf, утяжели́ть pf. **weightless** adj невесо́мый. **weighty** adj ве́ский.

weir n плоти́на.

weird adj (strange) стра́нный.

welcome n приём; adj жела́нный; (pleasant) прия́тный; **you are** ~ (don't mention it) пожа́луйста; **you are** ~ **to use my bicycle** мой велосипе́д к ва́шим услу́гам; **you are** ~ **to stay the night** вы мо́жете переночева́ть у меня́/нас; vt приве́тствовать impf (& pf in past tense); int добро́ пожа́ловать!

weld vt сва́ривать impf, свари́ть pf. **welder** n сва́рщик.

welfare n благосостоя́ние; **W~ State** госуда́рство всео́бщего благосостоя́ния.

well[1] n коло́дец; (for stairs) ле́стничная клетка.

well² *vi:* ~ **up** (*anger etc.*) вскипать *impf*, вскипеть *pf*; **tears** ~ed **up** глаза наполнились слезами.

well³ *adj* (*healthy*) здоровый; **feel** ~ чувствовать *impf*, по~ *pf* себя хорошо, здоровым; **get** ~ поправляться *impf*, поправиться *pf*; **look** ~ хорошо выглядеть *impf*; **all is** ~ всё в порядке; *int* ну(!); *adv* хорошо; (*very much*) очень; **as** ~ тоже; **as** ~ **as** (*in addition to*) кроме+*gen*; **it may** ~ **be true** вполне возможно, что это так; **very** ~! хорошо!; ~ **done!** молодец!; ~-**balanced** уравновешенный; ~-**behaved** (благо)воспитанный; ~-**being** благополучие; ~-**bred** благовоспитанный; ~-**built** крепкий; ~-**defined** чёткий; ~-**disposed** благосклонный; ~ **done** (*cooked*) (хорошо) прожаренный; ~-**fed** откормленный; ~-**founded** обоснованный; ~-**groomed** (*person*) холёный; ~-**heeled** состоятельный; ~-**informed** (хорошо) осведомлённый (**about** в+*prep*); ~-**known** известный; ~-**meaning** действующий из лучших побуждений; ~-**nigh** почти; ~-**off** состоятельный; ~-**paid** хорошо оплачиваемый; ~-**preserved** хорошо сохранившийся; ~-**to-do** состоятельный; ~-**wisher** доброжелатель *m*.

wellington (boot) *n* резиновый сапог. **Welsh** *adj* уэльский. **Welshman** *n* валлиец. **Welshwoman** *n* валлийка.

welter *n* путаница.

wend *vt:* ~ **one's way** держать *impf* путь.

west *n* запад; (*naut*) вест; *adj* западный; *adv* на запад, к западу. **westerly** *adj* западный. **western** *adj* западный; *n* (*film*) вестерн. **westward(s)** *adv* на запад, к западу.

wet *adj* мокрый; (*paint*) непросохший; (*rainy*) дождливый; ~ **through** промокший до нитки; *n* (*dampness*) влажность; (*rain*) дождь *m*; *vt* мочить *impf*, на~ *pf*.

whack *n* (*blow*) удар; *vt* колотить *impf*, по~ *pf*. **whacked** *adj* разбитый.

whale *n* кит.

wharf *n* пристань.

what *pron* (*interrog, int*) что; (*how much*) сколько; (*rel*) (то,) что; ~ (...)

for зачем; ~ **if** а что если; ~ **is your name** как вас зовут?; *adj* (*interrog, int*) какой; ~ **kind of** какой. **whatever, whatsoever** *pron* что бы ни +*past* (~ **you think** что бы вы ни думали); всё, что (**take** ~ **you want** возьмите всё, что хотите); *adj* какой бы ни+*past* (~ **books he read(s)** какие бы книги он ни прочитал); (*at all*): **there is no chance** ~ нет никакой возможности; **is there any chance** ~? есть ли хоть какая-нибудь возможность?

wheat *n* пшеница.

wheedle *vt* (*coax into doing*) уговаривать *impf*, уговорить *pf* с помощью лести; (~ *out of*) выманивать *impf*, выманить *pf* y+*gen*.

wheel *n* колесо; (*steering* ~, *helm*) руль *m*; (*potter's*) гончарный круг; *vt* (*push*) катать *indet*, катить *det*, по~ *pf*; *vt* & *i* (*turn*) повёртывать(ся) *impf*, повернуть(ся) *pf*; *vi* (*circle*) кружиться *impf*. **wheelbarrow** *n* тачка. **wheelchair** *n* инвалидное кресло.

wheeze *vi* сопеть *impf*.

when *adv* когда; *conj* когда, в то время как; (*whereas*) тогда как; (*if*) если; (*although*) хотя. **whence** *adv* откуда. **whenever** *adv* когда же; *conj* (*every time*) всякий раз когда; (*at any time*) когда бы ни; (*no matter when*) когда бы ни+*past*; **we shall have dinner** ~ **you arrive** во сколько бы вы ни приехали, мы пообедаем.

where *adv* & *conj* (*place*) где; (*whither*) куда; **from** ~ откуда. **whereabouts** *adv* где; *n* местонахождение. **whereas** *conj* тогда как; хотя. **whereby** *adv* & *conj* посредством чего. **wherein** *adv* & *conj* в чём. **wherever** *adv* & *conj* (*place*) где бы ни+*past*; (*whither*) куда бы ни+*past*; ~ **he goes** куда бы он ни пошёл; ~ **you like** где/куда хотите. **wherewithal** *n* средства *neut pl*.

whet *vt* точить *impf*, на~ *pf*; (*fig*) возбуждать *impf*, возбудить *pf*.

whether *conj* ли; **I don't know** ~ **he will come** я не знаю, придёт ли он; ~ **he comes or not** придёт (ли) он или нет.

which *adj* (*interrog, rel*) какой; *pron* (*interrog*) какой; (*person*) кто; (*rel*) кото́рый; (*rel to whole statement*) что; ~ **is** ~? (*persons*) кто из них кто?; (*things*) что-что? **whichever** *adj & pron* како́й бы ни+*past* (~ **book you choose** каку́ю бы кни́гу ты ни вы́брал); любо́й (**take** ~ **book you want** возьми́те любу́ю кни́гу).

whiff *n* за́пах.

while *n* вре́мя *neut*; **a little** ~ недо́лго; **a long** ~ до́лго; **for a long** ~ (*up to now*) давно́; **for a** ~ на вре́мя; **in a little** ~ ско́ро; **it is worth** ~ сто́ит э́то сде́лать; *vt*: ~ **away** проводи́ть *impf*, провести́ *pf*; *conj* пока́; в то вре́мя как; (*although*) хотя́; (*contrast*) а; **we went to the cinema** ~ **they went to the theatre** мы ходи́ли в кино́, а они́ в теа́тр. **whilst** *see* **while**

whim *n* при́хоть, капри́з.

whimper *vi* хны́кать *impf*; (*dog*) скули́ть *impf*.

whimsical *adj* капри́зный; (*odd*) причу́дливый.

whine *n* (*wail*) вой; (*whimper*) хны́канье; *vi* (*dog*) скули́ть *impf*; (*wail*) выть; (*whimper*) хны́кать *impf*.

whinny *vi* ти́хо ржать *impf*.

whip *n* кнут, хлыст, *vt* (*lash*) хлеста́ть *impf*, хлестну́ть *pf*; (*cream*) сбива́ть *impf*, сбить *pf*; ~ **off** ски́дывать *impf*, ски́нуть *pf*; ~ **out** выхва́тывать *impf*, вы́хватить *pf*; ~ **round** бы́стро поверну́ться *impf*, поверну́ться *pf*; ~-**round** сбор де́нег; ~ **up** (*stir up*) разжига́ть *impf*, разже́чь *pf*.

whirl *n* круже́ние; (*of dust, fig*) вихрь *m*; (*turmoil*) сумато́ха; *vt & i* кружи́ть(ся) *impf*, за~ *pf*. **whirlpool** *n* водоворо́т. **whirlwind** *n* вихрь *m*.

whirr *vi* жужжа́ть *impf*.

whisk *n* (*of twigs etc.*) ве́ничек; (*utensil*) муто́вка; (*movement*) пома́хивание; *vt* (*cream etc.*) сбива́ть *impf*, сбить *pf*; ~ **away, off** (*brush off*) сма́хивать *impf*, смахну́ть *pf*; (*take away*) бы́стро уноси́ть *impf*, унести́ *pf*.

whisker *n* (*human*) во́лос на лице́; (*animal*) ус; *pl* (*human*) бакенба́рды *f pl*.

whisky *n* ви́ски *neut indecl*.

whisper *n* шёпот; *vt & i* шепта́ть *impf*, шепну́ть *pf*.

whistle *n* (*sound*) свист; (*instrument*) свисто́к; *vi* свисте́ть *impf*, свист-

нуть *pf*; *vt* насви́стывать *impf*.

white *adj* бе́лый; (*hair*) седо́й; (*pale*) бле́дный; (*with milk*) с молоко́м; **paint** ~ кра́сить *impf*, по~ *pf* в бе́лый свет; ~-**collar worker** слу́жащий *sb*; ~ **lie** неви́нная ложь; *n* (*colour*) бе́лый цвет; (*egg, eye*) бело́к; (~ *person*) бе́лый *sb*. **whiten** *vt* бели́ть *impf*, на~, по~, вы́~ *pf*; *vi* беле́ть *impf*, по~ *pf*. **whiteness** *n* белизна́.

whitewash *n* побе́лка; *vt* бели́ть *impf*, по~ *pf*; (*fig*) обеля́ть *impf*, обели́ть *pf*.

whither *adv & conj* куда́.

Whitsun *n* Тро́ица.

whittle *vt*: ~ **down** уменьша́ть *impf*, уме́ньшить *pf*.

whiz(z) *vi*: ~ **past** просвисте́ть *pf*.

who *pron* (*interrog*) кто; (*rel*) кото́рый.

whoever *pron* кто бы ни+*past*; (*he who*) тот, кто.

whole *adj* (*entire*) весь, це́лый; (*intact, of number*) це́лый; *n* (*thing complete*) це́лое *sb*; (*all there is*) весь *sb*; (*sum*) су́мма; **on the** ~ в о́бщем. **wholehearted** *adj* беззаве́тный. **whole-heartedly** *adv* от всего́ се́рдца. **wholemeal** *adj* из непросе́янной муки́. **wholesale** *adj* опто́вый; (*fig*) ма́ссовый; *adv* о́птом. **wholesaler** *n* опто́вый торго́вец. **wholesome** *adj* здоро́вый. **wholly** *adv* по́лностью.

whom *pron* (*interrog*) кого́ *etc.*; (*rel*) кото́рого *etc.*

whoop *n* крик; *vi* крича́ть *impf*, кри́кнуть *pf*; ~ **it up** бу́рно весели́ться *impf*; ~**ing cough** коклю́ш.

whore *n* проститу́тка.

whose *pron* (*interrog, rel*) чей; (*rel*) кото́рого.

why *adv* почему́; *int* да ведь!

wick *n* фити́ль *m*.

wicked *adj* ди́кий. **wickedness** *n* ди́кость.

wicker *attrib* плетёный.

wicket *n* (*cricket*) воро́тца.

wide *adj* широ́кий; (*extensive*) обши́рный; (*in measurements*) в+*acc* ширино́й; ~ **awake** по́лный внима́ния; ~ **open** широко́ откры́тый; *adv* (*off target*) ми́мо це́ли. **widely** *adv* широко́. **widen** *vt & i* расширя́ть(ся) *impf*, расши́рить(ся) *pf*. **widespread** *adj* распространённый.

widow *n* вдова́. **widowed** *adj* овдовéвший. **widower** n вдовéц.

width n ширинá; (*fig*) широтá; (*of cloth*) полóтнище.

wield vt (*brandish*) размáхивать impf +instr; (*power*) пóльзоваться impf +instr.

wife n женá.

wig n парúк.

wiggle vt & i (*move*) шевелúть(ся) impf, по~, шевельнýть(ся) pf (+instr).

wigwam n вигвáм.

wild adj дúкий; (*flower*) полевóй; (*uncultivated*) невоздéланный; (*tempestuous*) бýйный; (*furious*) нейстóвый; (*ill-considered*) необдýманный; be ~ **about** быть без умá от+gen; ~-**goose chase** сумасбрóдная затéя; n: pl дéбри (-рей) pl. **wildcat** adj (*unofficial*) неофициáльный. **wilderness** n пустыня. **wildfire** n: **spread like** ~ распространяться impf, распространúться pf с молниенóсной быстротóй. **wildlife** n живáя прирóда. **wildness** n дúкость.

wile n хúтрость.

wilful adj (*obstinate*) упрямый; (*deliberate*) преднамéренный.

will n вóля; (~-*power*) сúла вóли; (*at death*) завещáние; **against one's** ~ прóтив вóли; **of one's own free** ~ доброврóльно; **with a** ~ с энтузиáзмом; **good** ~ дóбрая вóля; **make one's** ~ писáть impf, на~ pf завещáние; vt (*want*) хотéть impf, за~ pf +gen, acc; v aux: **he** ~ **be president** он бýдет президéнтом; **he** ~ **return tomorrow** он вернётся зáвтра; ~ **you open the window?** открóйте окнó, пожáлуйста. **willing** adj готóвый; (*eager*) старáтельный. **willingly** adv охóтно. **willingness** n готóвность. **willow** n úва.

willy-nilly adv вóлей-невóлей.

wilt vi поникáть impf, понúкнуть pf.

wily adj хúтрый.

win n побéда; vt & i выúгрывать impf, выиграть pf; vt (*obtain*) добивáться impf, добúться pf +gen; ~ **over** уговáривать impf, уговорúть pf; (*charm*) располагáть impf, расположúть pf к себé.

wince vi вздрáгивать impf, вздрóгнуть pf.

winch n лебёдка; поднимáть impf, поднять pf с пóмощью лебёдки.

wind[1] n (*air*) вéтер; (*breath*) дыхáние; (*flatulence*) вéтры m pl; ~ **instrument** духовóй инструмéнт; ~-**swept** открытый ветрáм; **get** ~ **of** пронюхивать impf, пронюхать pf; vt (*make gasp*) заставлять impf, застáвить pf задохнýться.

wind[2] vi (*meander*) вúться impf; извивáться impf; vt (*coil*) намáтывать impf, намотáть pf; (*watch*) заводúть impf, завестú pf; (*wrap*) укýтывать impf, укýтать pf; ~ **up** (vt) (*reel*) смáтывать impf, смотáть pf; (*watch*) see **wind**[2]; (vt & i) (*end*) кончáть(ся) impf, кóнчить(ся) pf. **winding** adj (*meandering*) извúлистый; (*staircase*) винтовóй.

windfall n пáдалица; (*fig*) золотóй дождь.

windmill n ветряная мéльница.

window n окнó; (*of shop*) витрúна; ~-**box** нарýжный ящик для цветóв; ~-**cleaner** мóйщик óкон; ~-**dressing** оформлéние витрúн; (*fig*) показýха; ~-**frame** окóнная рáма; ~-**ledge** подокóнник; ~-**pane** окóнное стеклó; ~-**shopping** рассмáтривание витрúн; ~-**sill** подокóнник.

windpipe n дыхáтельное гóрло. **windscreen** n ветровóе стеклó; ~ **wiper** двóрник. **windsurfer** n виндсёрфингúст. **windsurfing** n виндсёрфинг. **windward** adj навéтренный. **windy** adj вéтреный.

wine n винó; ~ **bar** вúнный погребóк; ~ **bottle** вúнная бутылка; ~ **list** кáрта вин; ~-**tasting** дегустáция вин. **wineglass** n рюмка. **winery** n вúнный завóд. **winy** adj вúнный.

wing n (*also polit*) крылó; (*archit*) флúгель m; (*sport*) фланг; pl (*theat*) кулúсы f pl. **winged** adj крылáтый.

wink n (*blink*) моргáние; (*as sign*) подмúгивание; vi мигáть impf, мигнýть pf; подмúгивать impf, подмигнýть pf +dat; (*fig*) смотрéть impf, по~ pf сквозь пáльцы на+acc.

winkle vt: ~ **out** выковыривать impf, выковырять pf.

winner n победúтель m, ~ница. **winning** adj (*victorious*) выигравший; (*shot etc.*) решáющий; (*charming*) обаятельный; n: pl выигрыш; ~-**post** фúнишный столб.

winter n зимá; attrib зúмний. **wintry**

adj зи́мний; (*cold*) холо́дный.

wipe *vt* (*also ~ out inside of*) вытира́ть *impf*, вы́тереть *pf*; **~ away**, **off** стира́ть *impf*, стере́ть *pf*; **~ out** (*exterminate*) уничтожа́ть *impf*, уничто́жить *pf*; (*cancel*) смыва́ть *impf*, смыть *pf*.

wire *n* про́волока; (*carrying current*) про́вод; **~ netting** про́волочная се́тка. **wireless** *n* ра́дио *neut indecl*. **wiring** *n* электропрово́дка. **wiry** *adj* жи́листый.

wisdom *n* му́дрость; **~ tooth** зуб му́дрости. **wise** *adj* му́дрый; (*prudent*) благоразу́мный.

wish *n* жела́ние; **with best ~es** всего́ хоро́шего, с наилу́чшими пожела́ниями; *vt* хоте́ть *impf*, за~ *pf* (**I ~ I could see him** мне хоте́лось бы его́ ви́деть; **I ~ to go** я хочу́ пойти́; **I ~ you to come early** я хочу́, что́бы вы ра́но пришли́; **I ~ the day were over** хорошо́ бы день уже́ ко́нчился); жела́ть *impf* +*gen* (**I ~ you luck** жела́ю вам уда́чи); (*congratulate on*) поздравля́ть *impf*, поздра́вить *pf* (**I ~ you a happy birthday** поздравля́ю тебя́ с днём рожде́ния); *vi*: **~ for** жела́ть *impf* +*gen*; мечта́ть *impf* о+*prep*. **wishful** *adj*: **~ thinking** самообольще́ние; приня́тие жела́емого за действи́тельное.

wisp *n* (*of straw*) пучо́к; (*hair*) кло́чок; (*smoke*) стру́йка.

wisteria *n* глици́ния.

wistful *adj* тоскли́вый.

wit *n* (*mind*) ум; (*wittiness*) остроу́мие; (*person*) остря́к; **be at one's ~'s end** не знать *impf* что де́лать.

witch *n* ве́дьма; **~-hunt** охо́та за ве́дьмами. **witchcraft** *n* колдовство́.

with *prep* (*in company of, together ~*) (*вме́сте*) с+*instr*; (*as a result of*) от+*gen*; (*at house of, in keeping of*) у+*gen*; (*by means of*) +*instr*; (*in spite of*) несмотря́ на+*acc*; (*including*) включа́я+*acc*; **~ each/one another** друг с дру́гом.

withdraw *vt* (*retract*) брать *impf*, взять *pf* наза́д; (*hand*) отдёргивать *impf*, отдёрнуть *pf*; (*cancel*) снима́ть *impf*, снять *pf*; (*mil*) выводи́ть *impf*, вы́вести *pf*; (*money from circulation*) изыма́ть *impf*, изъя́ть из обраще́ния; (*diplomat etc.*) отзы-

ва́ть *impf*, отозва́ть *pf*; (*from bank*) брать *impf*, взять *pf*; *vi* удаля́ться *impf*, удали́ться *pf*; (*drop out*) выбыва́ть *impf*, вы́быть *pf*; (*mil*) отходи́ть *impf*, отойти́ *pf*. **withdrawal** *n* (*retraction*) взя́тие наза́д; (*cancellation*) сня́тие; (*mil*) отхо́д; (*money from circulation*) изъя́тие; (*departure*) ухо́д. **withdrawn** *adj* за́мкнутый.

wither *vi* вя́нуть *impf*, за~ *pf*. **withering** *adj* (*fig*) уничтожа́ющий.

withhold *vt* (*refuse to grant*) не дава́ть *impf*, дать *pf* +*gen*; (*payment*) уде́рживать *impf*, удержа́ть *pf*; (*information*) ута́ивать *impf*, утаи́ть *pf*.

within *prep* (*inside*) внутри́+*gen*, в+*prep*; (**~ the limits of**) в преде́лах +*gen*; (*time*) в тече́ние +*gen*; *adv* внутри́; **from ~** изнутри́.

without *prep* без+*gen*; **~ saying goodbye** не проща́ясь; **do ~** обходи́ться *impf*, обойти́сь *pf* без+*gen*.

withstand *vt* выде́рживать *impf*, вы́держать *pf*.

witness *n* (*person*) свиде́тель *m*; (*eye~*) очеви́дец; (*to signature etc.*) завери́тель *m*; **bear ~ to** свиде́тельствовать *impf*, за~ *pf*; **~-box** ме́сто для свиде́тельских показа́ний; *vt* быть свиде́телем+*gen*; (*document etc.*) заверя́ть *impf*, заве́рить *pf*.

witticism *n* остро́та. **witty** *adj* остроу́мный.

wizard *n* волше́бник, колду́н.

wizened *adj* морщи́нистый.

wobble *vt & i* шата́ть(ся) *impf*, шатну́ть(ся) *pf*; *vi* (*voice*) дрожа́ть *impf*. **wobbly** *adj* ша́ткий.

woe *n* го́ре; **~ is me!** го́ре мне! **woeful** *adj* жа́лкий.

wolf *n* волк; *vt* пожира́ть *impf*, пожра́ть *pf*.

woman *n* же́нщина. **womanizer** *n* воло́кита. **womanly** *adj* же́нственный.

womb *n* ма́тка.

wonder *n* чу́до; (*amazement*) изумле́ние; (**it's) no ~** неудиви́тельно; *vt* интересова́ться *impf* (**I ~ who will come** интере́сно, кто придёт); *vi*: **I shouldn't ~ if** неудиви́тельно бу́дет, е́сли; **I ~ if you could help me** не могли́ бы вы мне помо́чь?; **~ at** удивля́ться *impf*, удиви́ться *pf* +*dat*. **wonderful, wondrous** *adj* замеча́тельный.

wont *n*: **as is his** ~ по своему обыкновению; *predic*: **be** ~ **to** иметь привычку+*inf*.

woo *vt* ухаживать *impf* за+*instr*.

wood *n* (*forest*) лес; (*material*) дерево; (*firewood*) дрова *pl*. **woodcut** *n* гравюра на дереве. **wooded** *adj* лесистый. **wooden** *adj* (*also fig*) деревянный. **woodland** *n* лесистая местность; *attrib* лесной. **woodpecker** *n* дятел. **woodwind** *n* деревянные духовые инструменты *m pl*. **woodwork** *n* столярная работа; (*wooden parts*) деревянные части (-тей) *pl*. **woodworm** *n* жучок. **woody** *adj* (*plant etc.*) деревянистый; (*wooded*) лесистый.

wool *n* шерсть. **woollen** *adj* шерстяной. **woolly** *adj* шерстистый; (*indistinct*) неясный.

word *n* слово; (*news*) известие; **by** ~ **of mouth** устно; **have a** ~ **with** поговорить *pf* с+*instr*; **in a** ~ одним словом; **in other** ~**s** другими словами; ~ **for** ~ слово в слово; ~ **processor** компьютер(-издатель) *m*; *vt* выражать *impf*, выразить *pf*; формулировать *impf*, с~ *pf*. **wording** *n* формулировка.

work *n* работа; (*labour; toil; scholarly* ~) труд; (*occupation*) занятие; (*studies*) занятия *neut pl*; (*of art*) произведение; (*book*) сочинение; *pl* (*factory*) завод; (*mechanism*) механизм; **at** ~ (*doing* ~) за работой; (*at place of* ~) на работе; **out of** ~ безработный; ~**-force** рабочая сила; ~**-load** нагрузка; *vi* (*also function*) работать *impf* (**at, on** над+*instr*); (*study*) заниматься *impf*, заняться *pf*; (*also toil, labour*) трудиться *impf*; (*have effect, function*) действовать *impf*; (*succeed*) удаваться *impf*, удаться *pf*; *vt* (*operate*) управлять *impf* +*instr*; обращаться *impf* с+*instr*; (*wonders*) творить *impf*, со~ *pf*; (*soil*) обрабатывать *impf*, обработать *pf*; (*compel to* ~) заставлять *impf*, заставить *pf* работать; ~ **in** вставлять *impf*, вставить *pf*; ~ **off** (*debt*) отрабатывать *impf*, отработать *pf*; (*weight*) сгонять *impf*, согнать *pf*; (*energy*) давать *impf*, дать *pf* выход +*dat*; ~ **out** (*solve*) находить *impf*, найти *pf* решение +*gen*; (*plans etc.*)

разрабатывать *impf*, разработать *pf*; (*sport*) тренироваться *impf*; **everything** ~**ed out well** всё кончилось хорошо; ~ **out at** (*amount to*) составлять *impf*, составить *pf*; ~ **up** (*perfect*) вырабатывать *impf*, выработать *pf*; (*excite*) возбуждать *impf*, возбудить *pf*; (*appetite*) нагуливать *impf*, нагулять *pf*. **workable** *adj* осуществимый, реальный. **workaday** *adj* будничный. **workaholic** *n* труженик. **worker** *n* работник; (*manual*) рабочий *sb*. **working** *adj*: ~ **class** рабочий класс; ~ **hours** рабочее время *neut*; ~ **party** комиссия. **workman** *n* работник. **workmanlike** *adj* искусный. **workmanship** *n* искусство, мастерство. **workshop** *n* мастерская *sb*.

world *n* мир, свет; *attrib* мировой; ~**-famous** всемирно известный; ~ **war** мировая война; ~**-wide** всемирный. **worldly** *adj* мирской; (*person*) опытный.

worm *n* червь *m*; (*intestinal*) глист; *vt*: ~ **o.s. into** вкрадываться *impf*, вкрасться *pf* в+*acc*; ~ **out** выведывать *impf*, выведать *pf* (**of** у+*gen*); ~ **one's way** пробираться *impf*, пробраться *pf*.

worry *n* (*anxiety*) беспокойство; (*care*) забота; *vt* беспокоить *impf*, о~ *pf*; *vi* беспокоиться *impf*, о~ *pf* (**about** о+*prep*).

worse *adj* худший; *adv* хуже; *n*: **from bad to** ~ всё хуже и хуже. **worsen** *vt* & *i* ухудшать(ся) *impf*, ухудшить(ся) *pf*.

worship *n* поклонение (**of** +*dat*); (*service*) богослужение; *vt* поклоняться *impf* +*dat*; (*adore*) обожать *impf*. **worshipper** *n* поклонник, -ица.

worst *adj* наихудший, самый плохой; *adv* хуже всего; *n* самое плохое.

worth *n* (*value*) цена, ценность; (*merit*) достоинство; **give me a pound's** ~ **of petrol** дайте мне бензина на фунт; *adj*: **be** ~ (*of equal value to*) стоить *impf* (**what is it** ~? сколько это стоит?); (*deserve*) стоить *impf* +*gen* (**is this film** ~ **seeing?** стоит посмотреть этот фильм?). **worthless** *adj* ничего не стоящий; (*useless*) бесполезный. **worthwhile** *adj* стоящий. **worthy** *adj* достойный.

would *v aux* (*conditional*): he ~ be angry if he found out он бы рассерди́лся, е́сли бы узна́л; (*expressing wish*) she ~ like to know она́ бы хоте́ла знать; I ~ rather я бы предпочёл; (*expressing indirect speech*): he said he ~ be late он сказа́л, что придёт по́здно.

would-be *adj*: ~ actor челове́к мечта́ющий стать актёром.

wound *n* ра́на; *vt* ра́нить *impf & pf*. **wounded** *adj* ра́неный.

wrangle *n* препира́ние; *vi* препира́ться *impf*.

wrap *n* (*shawl*) шаль; *vt* (*also ~ up*) завёртывать *impf*, заверну́ть *pf*; ~ up (*in wraps*) заку́тывать(ся) *impf*, заку́тать(ся) *pf*; ~ped up in (*fig*) поглощённый +*instr*. **wrapper** *n* обёртка. **wrapping** *n* обёртка; ~ paper обёрточная бума́га.

wrath *n* гнев.

wreak *vt*: ~ havoc on разоря́ть *impf*, разори́ть *pf*.

wreath *n* вено́к.

wreck *n* (*ship*) оста́нки (-ов) корабля́; (*vehicle, person, building, etc.*) разва́лина; *vt* (*destroy, also fig*) разруша́ть *impf*, разру́шить *pf*; be ~ed терпе́ть *impf*, по~ *pf* круше́ние; (*of plans etc.*) ру́хнуть *pf*. **wreckage** *n* обло́мки *m pl* круше́ния.

wren *n* крапи́вник.

wrench *n* (*jerk*) дёрганье; (*tech*) га́ечный ключ; (*fig*) боль; *vt* (*snatch, pull out*) вырыва́ть *impf*, вы́рвать *pf* (from y+*gen*); ~ open взла́мывать *impf*, взлома́ть *pf*.

wrest *vt* (*wrench*) вырыва́ть *impf*, вы́рвать *pf* (from y+*gen*).

wrestle *vi* боро́ться *impf*. **wrestler** *n* боре́ц. **wrestling** *n* борьба́.

wretch *n* несча́стный *sb*; (*scoundrel*) негодя́й. **wretched** *adj* жа́лкий; (*unpleasant*) скве́рный.

wriggle *vi* извива́ться *impf*, изви́ться *pf*; (*fidget*) ёрзать *impf*; ~ out of уви́ливать *impf*, увильну́ть от+*gen*.

wring *vt* (*also ~ out*) выжима́ть *impf*, вы́жать *pf*; (*extort*) исторга́ть *impf*, исто́ргнуть *pf* (from y+*gen*); (*neck*) свёртывать *impf*, сверну́ть *pf* (of +*dat*); ~ one's hands лома́ть *impf*, с~ *pf* ру́ки.

wrinkle *n* морщи́на; *vt & i* мо́рщить-

(ся) *impf*, с~ *pf*.

wrist *n* запя́стье; ~-watch нару́чные часы́ (-со́в) *pl*.

writ *n* пове́стка.

write *vt & i* писа́ть *impf*, на~ *pf*; ~ down запи́сывать *impf*, записа́ть *pf*; ~ off (*cancel*) спи́сывать *impf*, списа́ть *pf*; the car was a ~-off маши́на была́ соверше́нно испо́рчена; ~ out выпи́сывать *impf*, вы́писать *pf* (in full по́лностью); ~ up (*account of*) подро́бно опи́сывать *impf*, описа́ть *pf*; (*notes*) перепи́сывать *impf*, переписа́ть *pf*; ~-up (*report*) отчёт. **writer** *n* писа́тель *m*, ~ница.

writhe *vi* ко́рчиться *impf*, с~ *pf*.

writing *n* (*handwriting*) по́черк; (*work*) произведе́ние; in ~ в пи́сьменной фо́рме; ~-paper почто́вая бума́га.

wrong *adj* (*incorrect*) непра́вильный, неве́рный; (*the wrong …*) не тот (I have bought the ~ book я купи́л не ту кни́гу; you've got the ~ number (*tel*) вы не туда́ попа́ли); (*mistaken*) непра́вый (you are ~ ты непра́в); (*unjust*) несправедли́вый; (*sinful*) дурно́й; (*out of order*) нела́дный; (*side of cloth*) ле́вый; ~ side out наизна́нку; ~ way round наоборо́т; *n* зло; (*injustice*) несправедли́вость; be in the ~ быть непра́вым; do ~ греши́ть *impf*, со~ *pf*; *adv* непра́вильно, неве́рно; go ~ не получа́ться *impf*, получи́ться *pf*; *vt* обижа́ть *impf*, оби́деть *pf*; (be unjust to) быть несправедли́вым к+*dat*. **wrongdoer** *n* престу́пник, гре́шник, -ица. **wrongful** *adj* несправедли́вый. **wrongly** *adv* непра́вильно; (*unjustly*) несправедли́во.

wrought *adj*: ~ iron сва́рочное желе́зо.

wry *adj* (*smile*) криво́й; (*humour*) сухо́й, ирони́ческий.

X

xenophobia *n* ксенофо́бия.

X-ray *n* (*picture*) рентге́н(овский сни́мок); *pl* (*radiation*) рентге́новы лучи́ *m pl*; *vt* (*photograph*) де́лать *impf*, с~ *pf* рентге́н +*gen*.

Y

yacht *n* я́хта. **yachting** *n* па́русный спорт. **yachtsman** *n* яхтсме́н.

yank *vt* рвану́ть *pf*.

yap *vi* тя́вкать *impf*, тя́вкнуть *pf*.

yard[1] *n* (*piece of ground*) двор.

yard[2] *n* (*measure*) ярд. **yardstick** *n* (*fig*) мери́ло.

yarn *n* пря́жа; (*story*) расска́з.

yawn *n* зево́к; *vi* зева́ть *impf*, зевну́ть *pf*; (*chasm etc.*) зия́ть *impf*.

year *n* год; ~ **in**, ~ **out** из го́да в год. **yearbook** *n* ежего́дник. **yearly** *adj* ежего́дный, годово́й; *adv* ежего́дно.

yearn *vi* тоскова́ть *impf* (**for** по+*dat*). **yearning** *n* тоска́ (**for** по+*dat*).

yeast *n* дро́жжи (-же́й) *pl*.

yell *n* крик; *vi* крича́ть *impf*, кри́кнуть *pf*.

yellow *adj* жёлтый; *n* жёлтый цвет. **yellowish** *adj* желтова́тый.

yelp *n* визг; *vi* визжа́ть *impf*, ви́згнуть *pf*.

yes *adv* да; *n* утвержде́ние, согла́сие; (*in vote*) го́лос «за».

yesterday *adv* вчера́; *n* вчера́шний день *m*; ~ **morning** вчера́ у́тром; **the day before** ~ позавчера́; ~**'s newspaper** вчера́шняя газе́та.

yet *adv* (*still*) ещё; (*so far*) до сих пор; (*in questions*) уже́; (*nevertheless*) тем не ме́нее; **as** ~ пока́, до сих пор; **not** ~ ещё не; *conj* одна́ко, но.

yew *n* тис.

Yiddish *n* и́диш.

yield *n* (*harvest*) урожа́й; (*econ*) дохо́д; *vt* (*fruit, revenue, etc.*) приноси́ть *impf*, принести́ *pf*; дава́ть *impf*, дать *pf*; (*give up*) сдава́ть *impf*, сдать *pf*; *vi* (*give in*) (*to enemy etc.*) уступа́ть *impf*, уступи́ть *pf* (**to** +*dat*); (*give way*) поддава́ться *impf*, подда́ться *pf* (**to** +*dat*).

yoga *n* йо́га.

yoghurt *n* кефи́р.

yoke *n* (*also fig*) ярмо́; (*fig*) и́го; (*of dress*) коке́тка; *vt* впряга́ть *impf*, впрячь *pf* в ярмо́.

yolk *n* желто́к.

yonder *adv* вон там; *adj* вон тот.

you *pron* (*familiar sg*) ты; (*familiar pl, polite sg & pl*) вы; (*one*) *not usu*

translated; *v translated in 2nd pers sg or by impers construction*: ~ **never know** никогда́ не зна́ешь.

young *adj* молодо́й; **the** ~ молодёжь; *n* (*collect*) детёныши *m pl*. **youngster** *n* ма́льчик, де́вочка.

your(s) *poss pron* (*familiar sg; also in letter*) твой; (*familiar pl, polite sg & pl; also in letter*) ваш; свой. **yourself** *pron* (*emph*) (*familiar sg*) (ты) сам (*m*), сама́ (*f*); (*familiar pl, polite sg & pl*) (вы) са́ми; (*refl*) себя́; -ся (*suffixed to vt*); **by** ~ (*independently*) самостоя́тельно, сам; (*alone*) оди́н.

youth *n* (*age*) мо́лодость; (*young man*) ю́ноша *m*; (*collect, as pl*) молодёжь; ~ **club** молодёжный клуб; ~ **hostel** молодёжная турба́за. **youthful** *adj* ю́ношеский.

Yugoslavia *n* Югосла́вия.

Z

zany *adj* смешно́й.

zeal *n* рве́ние, усе́рдие. **zealot** *n* фана́тик. **zealous** *adj* ре́вностный, усе́рдный.

zebra *n* зе́бра.

zenith *n* зени́т.

zero *n* нуль *m*, ноль *m*.

zest *n* (*piquancy*) пика́нтность; (*ardour*) энтузиа́зм; ~ **for life** жизнера́достность.

zigzag *n* зигза́г; *adj* зигзагообра́зный; *vi* де́лать *impf*, с~ *pf* зигза́ги; идти́ де́т зигза́гами.

zinc *n* цинк.

Zionism *n* сиони́зм. **Zionist** *n* сиони́ст.

zip *n* (~ *fastener*) (застёжка-)мо́лния; *vt & i*: ~ **up** застёгивать(ся) *impf*, застегну́ть(ся) *pf* на мо́лнию.

zodiac *n* зодиа́к; **sign of the** ~ знак зодиа́ка.

zombie *n* челове́к спя́щий на ходу́.

zone *n* зо́на; (*geog*) по́яс.

zoo *n* зоопа́рк. **zoological** *adj* зоологи́ческий; ~ **garden(s)** зоологи́ческий сад. **zoologist** *n* зоо́лог. **zoology** *n* зооло́гия.

zoom *vi* (*rush*) мча́ться *impf*; ~ **in** (*phot*) де́лать *impf*, с~ *pf* наплы́в; ~ **lens** объекти́в с переме́нным фо́кусным расстоя́нием.

Zulu *adj* зулу́сский; *n* зулу́с, ~ка.

Appendix I **Spelling Rules**

It is assumed that the user is acquainted with the following spelling rules which affect Russian declension and conjugation.

1. **ы, ю,** and **я** do not follow **г, к, х, ж, ч, ш,** and **щ;** instead, **и, у,** and **а** are used, e.g. **ма́льчики, кричу́, лежа́т, нача́ми;** similarly, **ю** and **я** do not follow **ц;** instead, **у** or **а** are used.

2. Unstressed **о** does not follow **ж, ц, ч, ш,** or **щ;** instead, **е** is used, e.g. **му́жем, ме́сяцев, хоро́шее.**

Appendix II **Declension of Russian Nouns**

The following patterns are regarded as regular and are not shown in the dictionary entries. Forms marked * should be particularly noted.

1 *Masculine*

Singular	nom	acc	gen	dat	instr	prep
	обе́д	~	~а	~у	~ом	~е
	слу́ча|й	~й	~я	~ю	~ем	~е
	марш	~	~а	~у	~ем	~е
	каранда́ш	~	~а́	~у́	~о́м*	~е́
	сцена́ри|й	~й	~я	~ю	~ем	~и*
	портфе́л|ь	~ь	~я	~ю	~ем	~е

Plural	nom	acc	gen	dat	instr	prep
	обе́д|ы	~ы	~ов	~ам	~ами	~ах
	слу́ча|и	~и	~ев	~ям	~ями	~ях
	ма́рш|и	~и	~ей*	~ам	~ами	~ах
	карандаш|и́	~и́	~е́й*	~а́м	~а́ми	~а́х
	сцена́ри|и	~и	~ев*	~ям	~ями	~ях
	портфе́л|и	~и	~ей*	~ям	~ями	~ях

2 *Feminine*

Singular	nom	acc	gen	dat	instr	prep
	газе́т|а	~у	~ы	~е	~ой	~е
	ба́н|я	~ю	~и	~е	~ей	~е
	ли́ни|я	~ю	~и	~и*	~ей	~и*
	ста́ту|я	~ю	~и	~е*	~ей	~е*
	бол|ь	~ь	~и	~и*	~ью*	~и*

Plural	nom	acc	gen	dat	instr	prep
газе́т|ы		~ы	~	~ам	~ами	~ах
ба́н|и		~и	~ь*	~ям	~ями	~ях
ли́ни|и		~и	~й*	~ям	~ями	~ях
ста́ту|и		~и	~й*	~ям	~ями	~ях
бо́л|и		~и	~ей*	~ям	~ями	~ях

3 *Neuter*

Singular	nom	acc	gen	dat	instr	prep
чу́вств|о		~о	~а	~у	~ом	~е
учи́лищ|е		~е	~а	~у	~ем	~е
зда́ни|е		~е	~я	~ю	~ем	~и*
ущел|ье		~ье	~ья	~ью	~ьем	~ье

Plural	nom	acc	gen	dat	instr	prep
чу́вств|а		~а	~	~ам	~ами	~ах
учи́лищ|а		~а	~	~ам	~ами	~ах
зда́ни|я		~я	~й*	~ям	~ями	~ях
ущел|ья		~ья	~ий*	~ьям	~ьями	~ьях

Appendix III **Declension of Russian Adjectives**

The following patterns are regarded as regular and are not shown in the dictionary entries.

Singular	nom	acc	gen	dat	instr	prep
Masculine	тёпл|ый	~ый	~ого	~ому	~ым	~ом
Feminine	тёпл|ая	~ую	~ой	~ой	~ой	~ой
Neuter	тёпл|ое	~ое	~ого	~ому	~ым	~ом

Plural	nom	acc	gen	dat	instr	prep
Masculine	тёпл|ые	~ые	~ых	~ым	~ыми	~ых
Feminine	тёпл|ые	~ые	~ых	~ым	~ыми	~ых
Neuter	тёпл|ые	~ые	~ых	~ым	~ыми	~ых

Appendix IV Conjugation of Russian Verbs

The following patterns are regarded as regular and are not shown in the dictionary entries.

1. **-е-** conjugation

(a) **чита́|ть**	~ю	~ешь	~ет	~ем	~ете	~ют
(b) **сия́|ть**	~ю	~ешь	~ет	~ем	~ете	~ют
(c) **про́б|овать**	~ую	~уешь	~ует	~уем	~уете	~уют
(d) **рис|ова́ть**	~у́ю	~у́ешь	~у́ет	~у́ем	~у́ете	~у́ют

2. **-и-** conjugation

(a) **говор|и́ть**	~ю	~и́шь	~и́т	~и́м	~и́те	~я́т
(b) **стро́|ить**	~ю	~ишь	~ит	~им	~ите	~ят

Notes

1. Also belonging to the **-е-** conjugation are:

i)   most other verbs in **-ать** (but see Note 2(v) below), e.g. **жа́ждать** (жа́жду, -ждешь); **пря́тать** (пря́чу, -чешь), **колеба́ть** (коле́блю, -блешь).

ii) verbs in **-еть** for which the 1st pers sing **-ею** is given, e.g. **жале́ть**.

iii) verbs in **-нуть** for which the 1st pers sing **-ну** is given (e.g. **вя́нуть**), **ю** becoming **у** in the 1st pers sing and 3rd pers pl.

iv) verbs in **-ять** which drop the **я** in conjugation, e.g. **ла́ять** (ла́ю, ла́ешь); **се́ять** (се́ю, се́ешь).

2. Also belonging to the **-и-** conjugation are:

i)   verbs in consonant + **-ить** which change the consonant in the first person singular, e.g. **досади́ть** (-ажу́, -ади́шь), or insert an **-л-**, e.g. **доба́-вить** (доба́влю, -вишь).

ii) other verbs in vowel + **-ить**, e.g. **затаи́ть, кле́ить** (as 2b above).

iii) verbs in **-еть** for which the 1st pers sing is given as consonant + **ю** or **у**, e.g. **звене́ть** (-ню́, -ни́шь), **ви́деть** (ви́жу, ви́дишь).

iv) two verbs in **-ять** (**стоя́ть, боя́ться**).

v)   verbs in **-ать** whose stem ends in **ч, ж, щ,** or **ш,** not changing between the infinitive and conjugation, e.g. **крича́ть** (-чу́, -чи́шь). Cf. Note 1(i).

Key to the Russian Alphabet

Capital	*Lower-case*	*Approximate English Sound*
А	а	a
Б	б	b
В	в	v
Г	г	g
Д	д	d
Е	е	ye
Ё	ё	yo
Ж	ж	zh (as in measure)
З	з	z
И	и	i
Й	й	y
К	к	k
Л	л	l
М	м	m
Н	н	n
О	о	o
П	п	p
Р	р	r
С	с	s
Т	т	t
У	у	oo
Ф	ф	f
Х	х	kh (as in lo*ch*)
Ц	ц	ts
Ч	ч	ch
Ш	ш	sh
Щ	щ	shch
Ъ	ъ	˝ ('hard sign'; not pronounced as separate sound)
Ы	ы	y
Ь	ь	´ ('soft sign'; not pronounced as separate sound)
Э	э	e
Ю	ю	yu
Я	я	ya